curity Analysis and Portfolio Management

Security Analysis and Portfolio Management

Cheng F. Lee
Rutgers University, New Brunswick

Joseph E. Finnerty
University of Illinois, Urbana

Donald H. Wort
University of California, Hayward

SCOTT, FORESMAN/LITTLE, BROWN HIGHER EDUCATION
A Division of Scott, Foresman and Company
Glenview, Illinois   London, England

To my wife, Schwinne, and our fantastic children, John and Alice
CHENG F. LEE

To Sandy, Matt, and Dan. You light up my life
JOSEPH E. FINNERTY

To my wife, Karen
DONALD H. WORT

Acknowledgments for materials not credited on the page where they appear are listed in the Acknowledgments section at the back of the book. This section is to be considered a legal extension of the copyright page.

Library of Congress Cataloging-in-Publication Data

Lee, Cheng F.
Security analysis and portfolio management / Cheng F. Lee, Joseph E. Finnerty, Donald Wort.
p. cm.
Includes bibliographical references.
ISBN 0-673-38635-X
1. Investment analysis. 2. Portfolio management. I. Finnerty, Joseph E. II. Wort, Donald. III. Title.
HG4529.L44 1990
332.6—dc20
89-24395
CIP

1 2 3 4 5 6—KPF—94 93 92 91 90 89

Preface

Security Analysis and Portfolio Management integrates the many topics of modern investment analysis. It provides a balanced presentation of theories, institutions, markets, academic research, and practical applications, and presents both basic concepts and advanced principles. Topic coverage is especially broad: in analyzing securities, we look at stocks and bonds, options and futures, foreign exchange, and international securities. The discussion of options and futures includes a detailed analysis of hedging strategies. A unique chapter on market indexes teaches students the basics of index formation, calculation, and usage, and illustrates the important role that these indexes play in model formation, performance evaluation, investment strategy, and hedging techniques. In addition, complete sections on program trading, portfolio insurance, duration and bond immunization, performance measurements, and the timing of stock selection provide real-world applications of investment theory.

Security Analysis and Portfolio Management first discusses how finance theory and statistical and mathematical tools can be used effectively to analyze and determine the market value of bonds, stocks, options, futures, and options on futures. Second, based on this information, the text investigates issues related to equity portfolios, bond portfolios, and international portfolios. For equity-portfolio selection, the text discusses Markowitz's full-information methods, Sharpe's index methods, and the performance measure method. Finally, the efficient-market hypothesis, mutual-fund timing and selectivity, and portfolio insurance are also explored in detail.

The chapters in this book fall into five groups. The material in Chapters 2–7 review and extend the concepts and methods that students have learned from basic corporate-finance and investment courses. Chapters 8–11 present both the theoretical and empirical issues concerning the use of the market model, the CAPM, the APT, and risk diversification in security analysis and portfolio management. Chapters 12–15 use the theories and methods presented in the first eleven chapters to investigate futures and options. Chapters 16–21 cover applications of portfolio theories and models developed in

the preceding chapters. Finally, Chapter 22 is meant only for advanced students who require an in-depth derivation of the Black–Scholes option-pricing model in terms of the stochastic differential equations. It can be skipped over without loss of continuity.

Accounting information is essential for business decision making because it describes both the financial assets and the real assets of a firm. Historical accounting information has been used extensively by security analysts and portfolio managers, while proponents of the semi-strong form of the efficient-market hypothesis regard such information as valueless. In Chapter 2, ratio analysis, regression analysis, and earnings-per-share estimation are considered. The use of financial information in security analysis is emphasized. The role of the investment advisor in evaluating and rating the financial instruments of various companies is employed as an example of the ways that accounting information can be used to make valuation recommendations.

Chapter 3 deals with the measurement and the growth determination of rates of return on security investments. In addition to defining the holding-period return and the holding-period yield, three alternative methods for calculating average rates of return are discussed. These estimates can be used either to determine historical investment performance or to forecast future performance. It is shown that a weighted unbiased estimator can be used to reduce or eliminate the bias in forecasting rates of return.

Alternative methods of estimating growth rates are also discussed in Chapter 3. The relative advantages of these alternative methods are explored both theoretically and empirically. Possible applications of growth-rate estimation in security analysis and portfolio management are discussed.

Chapter 4 reviews both pre-Modigliani and Miller and M and M valuation theories in detail. The basic concepts of the CAPM and the option-pricing model are also explored in order to construct a rectangular theoretical framework of valuation. This chapter reviews basic theories that students have learned from a first course on either financial management or investment. Topics in this chapter can be used as review or as major theoretical background for understanding later chapters of this text.

Chapter 5 extends the valuation analysis to the specific case of the debt instruments of corporations. Issues related to the yield curve, and the term structure of interest rates and bond ratings, are carefully analyzed. Chapter 6 discusses the computation of alternative market indexes and examines the possible biases associated with using these indexes in investment analysis. The historical behavior of market indexes and index forecasting are also explored. The Wilshire 5000 index is discussed in detail.

In Chapter 7, sources of risk and basic portfolio analysis are investigated and used as a framework for further analysis of the CAPM and the market model. Chapter 8 discusses utility theory and Markowitz's full-information model of portfolio selection in detail. In Chapter 9 the market model and the

CAPM are evaluated both theoretically and empirically. The applications of the market model to risk decomposition are analyzed using both fixed-coefficient and random-coefficient regression models. Methods of forecasting beta coefficients are explored, using both accounting and market information.

Chapter 10 addresses how Markowitz's full-information portfolio-selection process can be simplified through the use of index models. In Chapter 11 multi-index models and the APT are discussed from both a theoretical and an empirical basis.

Chapter 12 discusses the basic issues of futures markets and futures contracts. In addition, two alternative hedging methods are investigated in detail. Chapter 13 explores the use of commodity futures, financial futures, and stock-index futures. The valuation of these futures and their use in hedging are investigated. Chapters 14 and 15 outline the basic concepts of put and call options, and the option-pricing model is derived using a binomial-model approach. Alternative applications of the OPT in the making of investment decisions are explored in detail.

Chapter 16 deals with the concept of an efficient market and the empirical evidence that supports or refutes this hypothesis. The implications of market efficiency for security analysts and portfolio managers are also stressed. Chapter 17 discusses timing and selectivity of stocks and mutual funds from both a fundamental-analysis and a technical-analysis perspective. Some forecasting models are examined, and Fama's breakdown of overall investment performance into several specific components is also covered.

Chapter 18 illustrates how the Sharpe and Treynor performance measures can be used to simplify the portfolio-selection procedure. In Chapter 19, issues relating to international diversification, exchange-rate risk, the international CAPM, and international portfolio-selection methods are investigated in detail. Chapter 20 presents a discussion of the issues involved in the management of a fixed-income portfolio. Both duration and bond immunization are carefully analyzed in this chapter. Chapter 21 examines the use of hedging and portfolio-insurance strategies for equity and bond portfolios.

This book is suitable for a second investment course at both the undergraduate and the graduate level. However, because *Security Analysis and Portfolio Management* addresses both the theoretical and the empirical sides of issues, and because it discusses both basic concepts and more advanced topics, it is suitable for a more quantitatively oriented first course in investment.

In the development of this book we have benefited from the reviews and comments of many individuals, including colleagues and students from the University of Illinois at Urbana-Champaign and other universities. We especially want to acknowledge the insightful comments and corrections of Louis Scott, University of Georgia; Steve Sears, Texas Tech; Cheryl Frohlich-Plumber, University of North Florida; Kent Zumwalt, Colorado

State University; Henry R. Oppenheimer, Rhode Island University; A. G. Malliaris, Loyola University; Charles Corrado, Loyola University; Ron Moy, Rutgers University; John C. Lee, Laventhol and Horwath; C. C. Yang, National Taiwan University; and Raymond Altimix, First of America Bank.

Cheng F. Lee
Joseph E. Finnerty
Donald H. Wort

Contents in Brief

Contents

Chapter 3

Common Stock: Return, Growth, and Risk *38*

Chapter 6

The Uses and Calculation of Market Indexes *150*

Chapter 7

Sources of Risk and Their Determination *179*

Chapter 8

Markowitz Portfolio-Selection Model *210*

Chapter 9

Capital Asset Pricing Model and Beta Forecasting 255

Chapter 12

Futures Valuation and Hedging *354*

Chapter 13

Commodity Futures, Financial Futures, and Stock-Index Futures *392*

Chapter 14

Options and Option Strategies *444*

Chapter 15

Option Valuation and Hedging *486*

Chapter 16

The Efficient-Market Hypothesis and Security Valuation *541*

Chapter 17

Timing and Selectivity of Stocks and Mutual Funds *570*

Chapter 18

Performance-Measure Approaches for Selecting Optimum Portfolios *621*

Chapter 19

International Diversification *643*

Chapter 20

Bond Portfolios: Management and Strategy *672*

Chapter 21

Portfolio Insurance and Synthetic Options *705*

Chapter 22

Itô's Calculus: Derivation of the Black–Scholes Option-Pricing Model *737*

Appendix Tables *765*

Acknowledgments *771*

Author Index *775*

Subject Index *780*

1 Introduction to Security Analysis and Portfolio Management

The growth in the number of financial instruments, and in the volume of trade in these instruments, today offers both a challenge and an opportunity to the student of finance. The challenge? To master the descriptive characteristics and uses of financial instruments. The opportunity? A highly rewarding investment career.

Such a challenge is timely, crucial, and apropos to current market activities. Figure 1–1 and Table 1–1 show that the volume in U.S. capital markets of new issues of traditional financial instruments (bonds, stocks, and preferreds) has more than tripled between 1980 and 1988. Most growth has occurred in debt securities, probably in response to the large decline in interest rates between 1980 and 1988; and common stock has likewise experienced an increase during this period. Moreover, the volume of Eurobond issues in the international capital market, which is relatively free of interference, has increased even more (as can be seen in Table 1–2). Although the international market has recently witnessed a flurry of issues of international equity, all increases in the international market have been in the form of debt instruments (loans, notes, and bonds). These increases are also a function of the dramatic decline in interest rates during the 1980s.

Increases in new issues of primary-market securities reflect an increase in demand for capital by business units. The primary market for corporate offerings involves the sale of securities by the issuing firm. The proceeds of the sale of these securities are received by the firm in the form of new capital to be used either for new investments or for refinancing maturing debt obligations.

Secondary markets involve already existing issues that are traded among investors. In this case, the instruments are traded between the current investors and the potential investors in a corporation. The proceeds of the

sale do not go to the firm but to the current owners of the security. Secondary markets serve two major roles. First, they provide liquidity to investors who acquire securities in the primary market. The amount of trading in the secondary market has experienced growth, as shown in Table 1-3. Second, these markets provide a continuous mechanism for price determination from which firms have an idea about the amount of capital they could raise and the terms they need to offer in order to induce potential investors to purchase new issues of securities.

Another dimension of the growth of financial markets is the increase in the types of financial instrument being issued in both the primary and secondary markets. Table 1-4 (page 5) is a partial list of the exchanges and the types of futures contracts and options currently traded around the world.

The 1980s have been marked by far-reaching changes in international capital markets. In particular, the financial markets have been characterized by increasing liberalization of regulation and innovation as well as intense competition. Barriers to diversification through portfolio investment in transnational security markets are being lowered, and financial risks are being repackaged and redistributed into different portfolios. The emergence of swaps, which permit borrowers (and investors) to separate the choice of markets (and credits) from the choice of currency and/or interest-rate risk, has been an important development in the international portfolio-management scene. It is estimated that the market for interest-rate swaps exceeded $150 billion during 1987.

FIGURE 1-1   Volume of New Issues Sold in the United States, 1980–1988
($ billions)

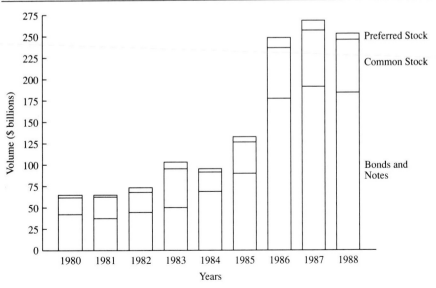

Source: *Economic Report of the President*, 1989.

TABLE 1-1 Volume of New Issues Sold in the United States ($ billions)

Year	Common	Preferred	Bonds
1980	19.4	3.5	42.4
1981	25.5	1.7	37.7
1982	23.7	4.9	44.7
1983	45.3	7.9	50.1
1984	22.5	4.3	68.7
1985	36.7	7.0	89.7
1986	59.0	12.2	177.5
1987	65.8	11.6	191.3
1988	62.0	7.3	184.2

Source: Economic Report of the President, 1989.

TABLE 1-2 Eurobond Issues by Currency of Issue, 1980–1987 ($ millions)

Currency	1980	1981	1982	1983
U.S. dollar	16,427 (68.5%)	26,830 (84.9%)	43,959 (85.1%)	38,406 (79.2%)
Deutsche mark	3,607 (15.0)	1,277 (4.0)	2,588 (5.0)	3,776 (7.8)
Canadian dollar	279 (1.2)	634 (2.0)	1,201 (2.3)	1,039 (2.1)
Dutch guilder	1,043 (4.4)	529 (1.7)	645 (1.2)	735 (1.5)
French franc	986 (4.1)	533 (1.7)	4 (0.0)	(0.0)
Japanese yen	304 (1.3)	368 (1.2)	374 (0.7)	212 (0.4)
Pound sterling	974 (4.1)	501 (1.6)	748 (1.4)	1,915 (3.9)
ECU	65 (0.3)	309 (1.0)	1,980 (3.8)	2,095 (4.3)
Other	285 (1.2)	635 (2.0)	146 (0.3)	305 (0.6)
Total	23,970 (100%)	31,616 (100%)	51,645 (100%)	48,483 (100%)

Currency	1984	1985	1986	1987
U.S. dollar	65,334 (80.2%)	96,822 (70.9%)	118,096 (62.9%)	56,727 (40.4%)
Deutsche mark	4,324 (5.3)	9,612 (7.0)	17,127 (9.1)	15,518 (11.0)
Canadian dollar	2,147 (2.6)	2,912 (2.1)	5,067 (2.7)	5,891 (4.2)
Dutch guilder	689 (0.8)	649 (0.5)	973 (0.5)	1,237 (0.9)
French franc		1,123 (0.8)	3,523 (1.9)	1,899 (1.4)
Japanese yen	1,190 (1.5)	6,615 (4.8)	18,516 (9.9)	23,116 (16.5)
Pound sterling	3,965 (4.9)	6,130 (4.5)	10,585 (5.6)	14,997 (10.7)
ECU	2,938 (3.6)	6,903 (5.1)	7,057 (3.8)	7,423 (5.3)
Other	834 (1.0)	5,777 (4.2)	6,804 (3.6)	13,673 (9.7)
Total	81,420 (100%)	136,543 (100%)	187,747 (100%)	140,481 (100%)

Source: David K. Eiteman and Arthur I. Stonehill, *Multinational Business Finance* (Addison-Wesley, 1989). Data from OECD.

TABLE 1-3   Average Daily Share Volume (millions of shares)

Year	NYSE	AMEX
1980	45	6
1981	47	5
1982	65	5
1983	85	8
1984	91	6
1985	109	8
1986	141	12
1987	189	14
1988	161	10

Source: NYSE Fact Book, 1989, courtesy New York Stock Exchange, Inc., and *AMEX Fact Book*, 1988, reprinted with the permission of the American Stock Exchange, Inc.

The opportunity in investment careers can either be in security analysis or portfolio management for both domestic and international firms. A more rapid increase in international capital markets also enhances the opportunity for investment careers.

With this innovative and growing environment serving as a backdrop, this study of security analysis and portfolio management begins with an explanation of the objectives of each of these areas.

OBJECTIVE OF SECURITY ANALYSIS

The ultimate objective of security analysis is to develop theoretical models that can be used to determine the value of financial instruments such as stocks, preferred, bonds, options, futures, and options on futures so that a comparison can be made of these values with the prices at which these instruments are currently trading in securities markets. Such a comparison aids investors and security analysts wishing to make investment decisions. Security analysts are continually looking for undervalued or overvalued situations. Undervalued situations, where the theoretical value is higher than the present market value, offer the opportunity to invest in instruments that are expected to have above-average returns; overvalued situations, where the theoretical value is below the current market value, offer the opportunity to sell instruments whose prices are expected to fall. An even more aggressive investor can short sell the overvalued instruments for above-average returns.

There are many factors to be considered in security analysis, and many general approaches that can be taken. A selection of those considered most useful to security analysts are covered in detail in the first and final sections of this book.

TABLE 1-4 Options and Futures Exchanges

American Stock Exchange	*COMEX*	*New York Mercantile Exchange*

American Stock Exchange

Major Market Index Option

Chicago Board of Trade

T-Bond
T-Bond Option
10-Year T-Note
10-Year T-Note Option
Major Market Index
Maxi Stock Index
Municipal Bond Index
NASDAQ 100 Index

Chicago Mercantile Exchange

British Pound
Canadian Dollar
Deutsch mark
Japanese Yen
Swiss Franc
European Currency Unit
British Pound Option
Canadian Dollar Option
Deutschemark Option
Japanese Yen Option
Swiss Franc Option
S&P 500 Index
S&P 250 OTC Index
S&P 500 Option
Eurodollaɪ
T-Bill
Eurodollar Option
T-Bill Option

Chicago Board Options Exchange

S&P 100 Option
S&P 500 Option
British Pound Option
Canadian Dollar Option
Deutschemark Option
French Franc
Japanese Yen Option
Swiss Franc Option
T-Bond Option
5-Year T-Note Option

COMEX

Gold
Silver
Gold Option
Silver Option

FINEX

U.S. Dollar Index
European Currency Unit

Hong Kong Futures Exchange

Hong Kong Stock Index

International Petroleum Exchange

Gas Oil

Kansas City Board of Trade

Value Line Average Index

LIFFE

Eurodollar
Pound Sterling
Sterling Currency
Long Gilt
FTSE 100 Index
U.S. Treasury Bond
Pound/Dollar Option

Montreal Stock Exchange

T-Bill Option
Canadian Bond Option

New York Futures Exchange

NYSE Composite Index
NYSE Composite Index
  Option
CRS Index

New York Stock Exchange

Composite Index Option
Double Index Option
Beta Index Option

New York Mercantile Exchange

No. 2 Heating Oil
Crude Oil
Leaded Gasoline
Unleaded Gasoline

Pacific Stock Exchange

Technology Index Option

MATIF PARIS

French 7-10 Year Government
  Note
French 90-Day T-Bill

Philadelphia Stock Exchange

British Pound Option
Canadian Dollar Option
Deutschemark Option
Japanese Yen Option
Swiss Franc Option
European Currency Unit Option
Value Line Average Index
  Option

SIMEX

Deutschemark
Japanese Yen
Eurodollar

Sydney Futures Exchange

All Ordinaries Stock Index
90-Day Bank Bill
U.S. Dollar
Australian 10-Year T-Bond

Tokyo Stock Exchange

Yen Bond

Toronto Futures Exchange

TSE 300 Index

Toronto Stock Exchange

TSE 300 Index Option

Source: Adapted from *Future's Magazine's* 1989 Reference Guide to Futures-Options Markets, pp. 112–127.

OBJECTIVE OF PORTFOLIO MANAGEMENT

Portfolio management seeks to combine securities so that the overall return of the portfolio is enhanced and the risk to the portfolio is reduced. Thus, determination of superior performance is made for the entire portfolio or combination of securities, rather than separately for each individual security.

BASIC APPROACHES TO SECURITY ANALYSIS AND PORTFOLIO MANAGEMENT

There are many approaches to security analysis. The most traditional categorization has been to divide security analysis into **fundamental analysis** and **technical analysis.** Fundamental analysis rests on the belief that at any point in time, there is a basic intrinsic value for the stock market, for industries, and for individual securities. These values depend on the relationship between information and the theoretical determinants of value. The fundamental-analysis approach requires both a correct theoretical model of valuation and access to relevant information.

Technical analysis is based on the idea that prices of financial instruments move in trends that persist through time and also recur over time. It is based on the belief that as random information comes to the financial markets, it is not immediately reflected in security prices. Rather, as knowledge of the information spreads among the market participants, they react to it by buying and selling financial instruments. This spreading of the information indicates that the changes in market prices move in trends over a period of time. Technical analysis stems from the premise that investors can identify the movements or trends in the movement of prices and use this information to generate above-average returns.

The last two decades have seen the development of the **efficient-market hypothesis (EMH).** This explanation for the behavior of prices in financial markets is based on the concept of a "fair game" model. This model requires that the price-determination process use all of the relevant information that is available at any point in time to determine the value or price of a financial instrument. For ease of the empirical testing of the EMH, there have evolved three forms of the hypothesis: (1) the weak form, (2) the semistrong form, and (3) the strong form. The weak form states that current stock prices fully reflect all historical information including the historical sequence of prices, price changes, trading volume, and so on. Hence knowledge of past events or the use of a trading rule based on past events will not consistently generate above-average investment performance. The semistrong form states that stock prices (in addition to historic information of the weak form) fully reflect all public information such as corporate earnings, dividends, economic or political news, and so forth. This implies that inves-

tors who purchase securities based on information that is public will pay a price for a security that has already been adjusted for the value of the information. The strong form states that security prices fully reflect all information, both public and private. Hence it implies that no group of investors or market participants can outperform the market even though they have monopolistic access to information. In Chapter 16 extensive discussions of the empirical evidence and the implications of the EMH for portfolio management and security analysis are presented.

In terms of basic philosophy about portfolio management and security analysis, it is our belief that an investor with superior training, intellect, and judgment can turn in a superior performance. One of the roles of security analysis is to keep the market relatively efficient. There are two extreme views currently circulating about the stock market:

1. Institutional investors dominate the market, and it is impossible for the individual investor to outperform the professional portfolio manager.
2. The professional portfolio manager cannot consistently outperform the market; therefore, even the naivest individual investor has a chance to turn in a superior performance because of blind luck.

The philosophy of this text falls somewhere between the two opposing views. Professional investment management should be able to provide superior performance vis à vis private individuals; but some knowledgeable individuals will be able to outperform the professionals in certain special circumstances. The question of how to evaluate the various aspects of the performance of security analysts and portfolio managers is discussed in Chapters 17 and 18.

A final dimension of the performance issue that needs special emphasis is time. Studies by Summers (1986) and Fama and French (1988) indicate that given a longer time horizon, the financial markets may not be as efficient as was once generally believed. Either because of the econometric problems with previous research methodology (as pointed out by Summers) or because of the long-run negative serial correlation of security returns (found by Fama and French) there is some doubt about the evidence that supports the EMH.

GENERAL AREAS OF COVERAGE

Theory

The primary theoretical approaches presented in order to determine the value and risk of security instruments include:

1. Classical theory (Gordon dividend model)
2. Modigliani and Miller (M and M) theories
3. Capital asset pricing theory (CAPM)

4. Option-pricing theory (OPT)

5. Arbitrage pricing theory (APT)

In Chapter 4 a rectangular framework of finance theory is used to review the first four theories; arbitrage pricing theory (APT) is explored in Chapter 11. An integration of these alternative theoretical approaches provides a useful frame of reference for the security analyst and the portfolio manager to do fundamental analysis.

Methods

Throughout this text a basic knowledge of certain statistical and mathematical procedures and techniques is assumed. Nevertheless, the emphasis is on how these techniques can help produce better investment decisions or help clarify the underlying factors of security analysis and portfolio management, rather than on a mere discussion of the techniques as an end in themselves.

Statistical Distributions.   *Risk* is defined as the probability of success (a positive outcome) or failure (a negative outcome). In order to quantify risk, ways to measure it and to express its different levels are needed. Statistical distributions are a good tool for both requirements. Of particular interest are the normal and log normal distributions, as shown in Figure 1–2.

In thinking about the range over which rates of return can occur, losses (negative returns) or gains (positive returns) can be envisioned, and the normal distribution can be used to represent these outcomes of gains and losses. Quite frequently in the study of security analysis and portfolio management, it is convenient to make the assumptions of normality for the sake of mathematical simplicity.

However, in considering the values or prices of financial instruments, it must be realized that none can ever take on a negative price so that the minimum value of a financial instrument is zero (i.e., it is worthless). In this case, when discussing price or value, the log normal distribution is more

FIGURE 1–2   Statistical Distribution

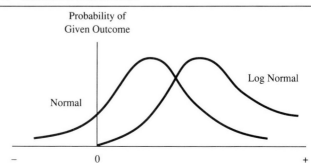

appropriate (as can be seen in Figure 1–2) because it has zero as its minimum value. This corresponds nicely to the distribution of prices or values of financial instruments. Furthermore, the log normal distribution is not symmetric, so that in addition to mean and variance the skewness of the distribution is of interest.

Investors with no knowledge about the shape of the distribution of expected outcomes, either returns or prices, are said to be *faced with uncertainty.* Dealing with both risk (knowledge of the distribution) and uncertainty (no knowledge of the distribution) is one of the major objectives of portfolio management and security analysis, so various kinds of statistical distributions must be dealt with.

Regression Technique. *Simple linear regression* is a statistical technique that fits a straight line to a set of data points, thus providing an expression for a relationship between two variables. One of the more widely used regression techniques is the method of least squares, discussed in Kohler (1985, 531–82). If x_i is the independent variable and y_i is the dependent variable, the linear equation

$$y_i = \alpha + \beta x_i + e_i \tag{1.1}$$

can be solved, where

α = intercept,
β = slope of the least-squares line, and
e_i = error term.

The values α and β for n observations of x and y can be estimated as

$$\hat{\alpha} = \frac{(\Sigma y)(\Sigma x^2) - (\Sigma x)(\Sigma xy)}{n(\Sigma x^2) - (\Sigma x)^2} = \bar{y} - \hat{\beta}\bar{x} \tag{1.2}$$

$$\hat{\beta} = \frac{n(\Sigma xy) - (\Sigma x)(\Sigma y)}{n(\Sigma x^2) - (\Sigma x)^2} = \frac{\text{Cov}(x,y)}{\text{Var}(x)} \tag{1.3}$$

in which Cov (x,y) stands for the covariance—that is,

$$\sum_{i=1}^{n} \frac{(y_i - \bar{y})(x_i - \bar{x})}{n}$$

and Var (x) stands for

$$\sum_{i=1}^{n} \frac{(x_i - \bar{x})^2}{n}$$

Substituting $\hat{\alpha}$ and $\hat{\beta}$ into Equation (1.1), the estimated least-squares regression line is obtained

$$\hat{y}_i = \hat{\alpha} + \hat{\beta} x_i \tag{1.4}$$

In Figure 1–3, $\hat{e}_i = y_i - \hat{y}_i$ represents the difference between actual data of dependent variable (y_i) and estimated y_i $(\hat{y}_i)$. Equation (1.4) is ob-

FIGURE 1-3   Least-Squares Regression

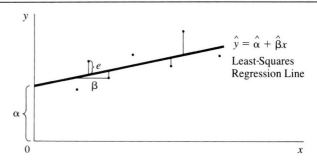

tained by minimizing the sum of the squares of all e_i. This method thus is called the **least-squares method.** It is illustrated in Sample Problem 1.1.

Sample Problem 1.1

If $\bar{y} = 7, \bar{x} = 8$, Cov $(y_i, x_i) = 4$ and Var $(x_i) = 16$, then from Equations (1.2) and (1.3) $\hat{\beta} = \cdots = 0.25$, $\hat{\alpha} = 7 - (0.25)(8) = 5$. Substituting the estimated $\hat{\beta}$ and $\hat{\alpha}$ into Equation (1.4), the estimated least-squares regression line can be expressed as

$$\hat{y}_i = 5 + 0.25\, x_i$$ ●

The least-squares method of linear regression can be used as a forecasting technique or as a technique for identifying the underlying pattern or relationship between two variables. In the course of the text many applications of the regression technique will be seen.

In Equation (1.2) **beta** (β), the slope coefficient of the regression equation, is equal to the covariance divided by the variance. The phenomena represented by the covariance term measure how x and y move in relation to each other. In our study of portfolio analysis and management it is this relative movement or covariance term that is of paramount importance. The relative or systematic risk of a portfolio is of interest, not just its variability or variance term. (This concept is especially important in the latter half of the text.)

A final word of caution about what the regression technique cannot do: linear regression can be useful in making estimates, but regression and similar statistical techniques must be used with caution. A straight line can be fitted to any data. Even if the fundamental relationship between the two variables is not linear, it may seem by using the regression technique that there is a linear relationship. This problem is shown in Figure 1-4.

Equation (1.1) is a simple linear regression as there is only one independent variable (x_i) in this regression. If there is more than one independent

FIGURE 1-4 Nonlinear Relationship

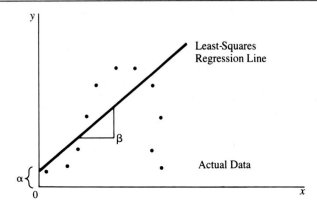

variable in the linear regression, then Equation (1.1) can be generalized as

$$y_i = a_0 + a_1 x_{1i} + a_2 x_{2i} + \cdots + a_n x_{ni} \qquad \textbf{(1.5)}$$

where a_0 is the intercept and $a_i (i = 1, 2, \ldots, n)$ is the slope associated with $x_{ji} (j = 1, 2, \ldots, n)$. The estimation procedure of this multiple linear regression can be found in Kohler (1985, 583–639). Applications of the multiple linear regression are discussed in detail in Chapter 11.

Some additional statistical techniques are useful in seeing how well the regression line actually describes the relationship between the two variables. Of interest, then, is not only the relationship between two variables but also the accuracy of the estimate of the linear relationship. In spite of its limitations, linear regression is a useful technique in supporting intuitive beliefs or investigating relationships in security analysis and portfolio management.

Maximization Procedures. A **linear-optimization model** is a method of maximizing or minimizing an objective function that is subject to a number of linear constraints. The general form of the problem can be written as

$$\text{Max} \quad (\alpha_1 x_1 + \alpha_2 x_2) \qquad \textbf{(1.6)}$$

Subject to

$$-x_1 + 4x_2 \geq 0 \qquad \textbf{(1.7)}$$

$$x_1 + x_2 = 1 \qquad \textbf{(1.8)}$$

$$x_1, x_2 \geq 0 \qquad \textbf{(1.9)}$$

where α_1, α_2 are the percentages of a portfolio invested in securities 1 and 2, respectively. x_1 and x_2 are average rates of return for securities 1 and 2, respectively.

The problem is to maximize the return on the portfolio. As shown by the objective function, with the restrictions stated in Equation (1.7), the invest-

ment in security 2 should be at least 20 percent ($-x_1 + 4x_2 \geq 0$); and, as stated in Equation (1.8), the funds of the portfolio should be 100 percent invested ($x_1 + x_2 = 1$).[1] Further, the nonnegativity conditions ($x_1, x_2 \geq 0$) preclude the short selling of either security 1 or 2. The procedure for solving this kind of optimization problem is tedious; it is discussed in detail in Appendix 10A at the end of Chapter 10.

In the section of the book concerning portfolio-selection models and asset-pricing theories, this maximization framework is used in discussing the compositions of portfolios and the valuations of assets in a market setting.

Applications

In the next chapter the evaluation (*security analysis*) of Abbott Laboratories is presented as an overview to security analysis and portfolio management. Thereafter, throughout the text a topic is introduced and discussed from both theoretical and practical (actual usage) perspectives. Various types of portfolios are evaluated in the context of modern portfolio theory—equity portfolios, bond portfolios, mixed portfolios, and even internationally diversified portfolios. Study is made of various institutional frameworks for portfolio management, including mutual funds, pension funds, banks, and insurance companies.

SUMMARY

The expansion taking place in the financial markets around the world requires a firm foundation in the relevant theories of valuation.

This chapter has identified the objectives of portfolio management and security analysis and has laid out the general framework of our approach in the study of this subject: (1) learn the relevant theory, (2) be familiar with quantitative techniques and methodology, and (3) look at real-world examples or applications. Each chapter contains this basic structure.

QUESTIONS AND PROBLEMS

1. Discuss the total trading volume of pricing and secondary markets for bonds, stocks, and other securities for the last decade.
2. What are security analysis and portfolio management? Is there any relationship between these two topics?

---

[1] An alternative way of stating these constraints is $x_1 \leq 0.8$, $x_2 \geq 0.2$.

3. Define a simple regression model. What is the basic principle used to estimate the parameters of this model?

4. Discuss the linear-optimization model.

REFERENCES

Brealey, Richard A. *An Introduction to Risk and Return from Common Stock*, 2nd ed. MIT Press, 1981.

Darst, David M. *The Handbook of the Bond and Money Markets*. McGraw-Hill, 1981.

Fama, Eugene F., and Merton H. Miller. *The Theory of Finance*. Holt, Rinehart and Winston, 1972.

———, and Kenneth R. French. "Permanent and Temporary Components of Stock Prices." *Journal of Political Economy*, v. 96 (April 1988), pp. 246–73.

Graham, Ben, D. Dodd, and S. Cottle. *Security Analysis: Principles and Techniques*, 4th ed. McGraw-Hill, 1962.

Kohler, Heinz. *Statistics for Business and Economics*. Scott, Foresman and Company, 1985.

Lee, C. F., and J. E. Finnerty. *Corporate Finance: Theory, Methods and Applications*. Harcourt Brace Jovanovich, 1990.

Malkiel, Burton A. *A Random Walk Down Wall Street*, 4th ed. W. W. Norton, 1985.

Summers, Lawrence H. "Do We Really Know that Financial Markets are Efficient?" Discussion Paper No. 1237, Harvard Institute of Economic Research, 1986.

West, Richard R. "The Teaching of Investment: Is Witchcraft Still Appropriate?" *Journal of Financial and Quantitative Analysis*, v. 9 (November 1974), pp. 789–93.

2 Information and Security Valuations

The purpose of a texbook on security analysis and portfolio management is to illustrate how relevant information can be transformed and analyzed in order that:

1. The security analyst can recommend buy, hold, or sell strategies, depending on the divergence between the theoretical value of a security and its current market value.
2. The portfolio manager can assemble various types of securities of different companies to achieve a desired level of return given limitations on the amount of acceptable risk.

This chapter briefly describes some of the major sources of information needed to achieve these objectives. Information about Abbott Laboratories is used to illustrate how the security analyst can make a determination of the market value or investment worth of a firm. In later chapters these sources of information are used to provide input to the portfolio manager wishing to evaluate the suitability of individual securities for inclusion in the optimal portfolio.

SOURCES OF INFORMATION

Four levels of information are necessary for the security analyst and portfolio manager:

1. Economy-wide information
2. Financial market information
3. Industry information
4. Individual company information

The Economy

The condition of the U.S. and world economies has an important impact on the activities and performance of financial market participants. Table 2–1 lists some of the sources of information about the U.S. and world economies.

TABLE 2–1   Sources of Information about the U.S. and World Economies

GOVERNMENT SOURCES

Statistical Abstracts of the United States	Prepared by the Bureau of the Census, this contains extensive statistics on social, political, and economic information about the U.S. economy.
Survey of Current Business	A monthly publication of the Department of Commerce. Twice a year the *Business Statistics* supplement is published; this contains more than 2,500 time series of monthly, quarterly, and yearly data about the U.S. economy. A detailed description of each series is provided.
Federal Reserve Bulletin	A monthly publication of the Board and Governors of the Federal Reserve System, its major emphasis is on the monetary statistics and other financial statistics of the U.S. economy.
Business Conditions Digest	The Department of Commerce publishes a monthly series of data and charts of leading economic indicators, coincident indicators, and lagging indicators of the U.S. economy.
Economic Report of the President	The President sends a report of the state of the U.S. economy to Congress at the beginning of each year. Each report contains a summary of the past year's economic events and the major problems the economy will be facing the next year. Additionally there are statistical series of economic variables for the U.S. economy.
International Finance Statistics and U.N. Statistical Notebook	Good sources of data on worldwide economics and finance.

GENERAL FINANCIAL PRESS

The Wall Street Journal	A daily newspaper covering the economy and the financial markets. It offers extensive price data for securities.
Business Week	A weekly focusing on topics about business and the economy.
Fortune	A biweekly featuring articles about business and the economy.
Economist	A weekly filled with articles and reports relating to the world economy.

TABLE 2-2   Sources of Information about the Financial Markets

GENERAL FINANCIAL PRESS

The New York Times	Either local or national editions are available daily throughout the country featuring articles and price information on the major financial markets.
Commercial and Financial Chronicle	A weekly offering price information on equity securities.
Barron's	A weekly magazine featuring articles and price information on most financial markets, domestic as well as international.
Finance	A monthly magazine providing articles about financial markets.
Euromoney	A monthly magazine with articles and data on international capital and money markets.
Institutional Investor	A monthly featuring articles aimed at the managers of large institutional portfolios.
Financial Analysts Journal	A bimonthly featuring articles of interest to financial analysts.
Journal of Portfolio Management	A quarterly publishing articles of interest to portfolio managers.

GOVERNMENT SOURCES

Statistical Bulletin	A monthly publication of the Securities and Exchange Commission (SEC) emphasizing equity securities.
Annual Report of the SEC	A yearly report of the SEC highlighting major events in the financial markets.

PRIVATE SOURCES

New York Stock Exchange (NYSE) Fact Book	Annual published by the NYSE; contains extensive data on the trading on the NYSE.
AMEX Statistical Review	An annual of the AMEX; contains data on the trading on the AMEX.
Dow Jones Investor's Handbook	A yearly publication of the earnings, dividends, and prices of the Dow Jones Averages; published since 1939.
Standard & Poor's Trading and Security Statistics	Published yearly, featuring historical data on all of the S&P indexes.

Financial Markets

Data on the prices and trading volume of various financial instruments provide input to various valuation models used by the security analyst and portfolio manager to determine investment value. Table 2–2 lists some of the various sources of information about the financial markets.

TABLE 2-3   Sources of Information about Industries

TRADE ASSOCIATIONS AND INDUSTRY PUBLICATIONS

Iron and Steel Age	*Computers*
Institute of Life Insurance	*Chemical Week*
American Bankers Association	*Aviation Week*
Machine Tool Association	*Automotive News*

PRIVATE SOURCES

Dun and Bradstreet Key Business Ratios	Lists financial ratios for 125 industries.
Robert Morris Associates	Lists financial ratios for medium- and small-sized firms in various industries.
Standard & Poor's Investment Advisory Service, Industry Surveys, and Outlook	Provides information and data on major events in various industries.
Moody's Manuals	Provide information and financial data on various industries.

GOVERNMENT

U.S. Industrial Outlook	An annual analysis of 200 industries.
Reports on specific industries	Census of Mineral Industries
	Census of Selected Service Industries
	Census of Construction Industry
	Census of Transportation
	Census of Retail Trade
	Census of Wholesale Trade
	Annual Survey of Manufactures
	Financial Census for Manufacturing Corporations

Industry Information

The majority of information about individual industries is provided by the various trade associations of each specific industry. In Table 2–3 the sources of industry information are shown.

Corporate Information

The most obvious source of information about a specific company is the company itself. Either because of disclosure regulations or voluntary disclosure, a large amount of information about each publicly traded company becomes available each day. Table 2–4 lists the major sources of information about individual companies.

Given the large amount of information that is available, it is the job of security analysts and portfolio managers to analyze this information in order

TABLE 2-4 Sources of Information about Individual Companies

CORPORATE

Annual Reports	All firms whose securities are publicly held and traded are required to disseminate to their security holders an annual report of operations and financial position. Basic financial statements such as an income statement, balance sheet, sources and uses of funds, and changes in retained earnings are included in all annual reports.
Security Prospectus	If a firm is issuing new securities, financial information about the firm must be released to the public before the new securities can be issued.

GOVERNMENT

Required Report	Form 10K: Form 10K is a very detailed annual report that publicly traded firms must submit to the SEC. These reports will be furnished to the public upon request to the firm. Information is also submitted quarterly in the form of a 10Q report.

PRIVATE

Standard & Poor's Corporation Record	Provides annual financial data on individual companies.
Moody's Manuals	Provide annual historical and financial data on individual firms.
Value Line Investment Service	Offers historical and financial information on 1,700 companies as well as quality recommendations as to the investment value of specific firms.
Brokerage Firms' Reports	Usually offer specific recommendations about the investment worth of individual firms' securities—for example, buy, sell, hold.

PRIVATE COMPUTERIZED DATABASES

Compustat	S&P computerized database has approximately 3,500 companies covering twenty years of financial and market-price data.
University of Chicago Stock Price Tapes	The Center for Research on Security Prices (CRSP) offers monthly and daily price data from various exchanges.

to make knowledgeable investment decisions. The following case example, which focuses on Abbott Laboratories, illustrates how the information presented above can be gathered and utilized in such an analysis.

THE DETERMINATION OF THE INVESTMENT WORTH OF ABBOTT LABORATORIES

The purpose of this section is to explain and illustrate some of the techniques and analyses used in modern security analysis. After a brief description of Abbott Laboratories and the business environment in which it operates, this section demonstrates how accounting information can be used to generate an analysis of key financial ratios and a forecast of future ratios.

Abbott Laboratories is primarily in the business of developing, manufacturing, and marketing a diversified line of human health-care products. The company markets its products internationally, with about 36 percent of its sales outside the United States. A breakdown of 1985 sales by general product category is shown in Table 2–5.

While the worldwide growing demand for high-quality health care should provide substantial growth potential, two factors threaten to adversely affect the firm's future sales and earnings—escalating health-care costs and currency-exchange fluctuations. The efforts to alleviate the impact of inflation on health-care costs through government regulation and voluntary industry programs are uncertain in terms of their effect on companies such as Abbott, and such efforts must be watched closely. Currency-exchange fluctuations will also continue to affect Abbott Laboratories significantly because of Abbott's relatively heavy involvement in foreign operations.

Both factors can have a substantial impact on the investment performance of Abbott's securities. Nevertheless, they are mostly exogenous and subject to rapid changes that are difficult to predict; thus the remainder of this chapter concentrates on more tangible considerations.

Accounting Information and Abbott's Financial Position

Financial-Ratio Analysis. The financial position of Abbott Labs is first considered by performing a ratio analysis for the company and its industry.

TABLE 2–5 Abbott Laboratories 1985 Sales

Product Type	Volume of Sales ($ millions)	Percent of Sales	Percent of Earnings
Hospital and laboratory	973.9	42	61
Pharmaceutical and nutritional	1,181.9	50	33
Other	186.7	8	6
Total	2,342.5	100	100

Source: Moody's Industrial Manual, 1986.

FIGURE 2-1   Liquidity Ratios for Abbott Laboratories and the Medical Hospital Supply Industry (CR = current ratio, QR = quick ratio)

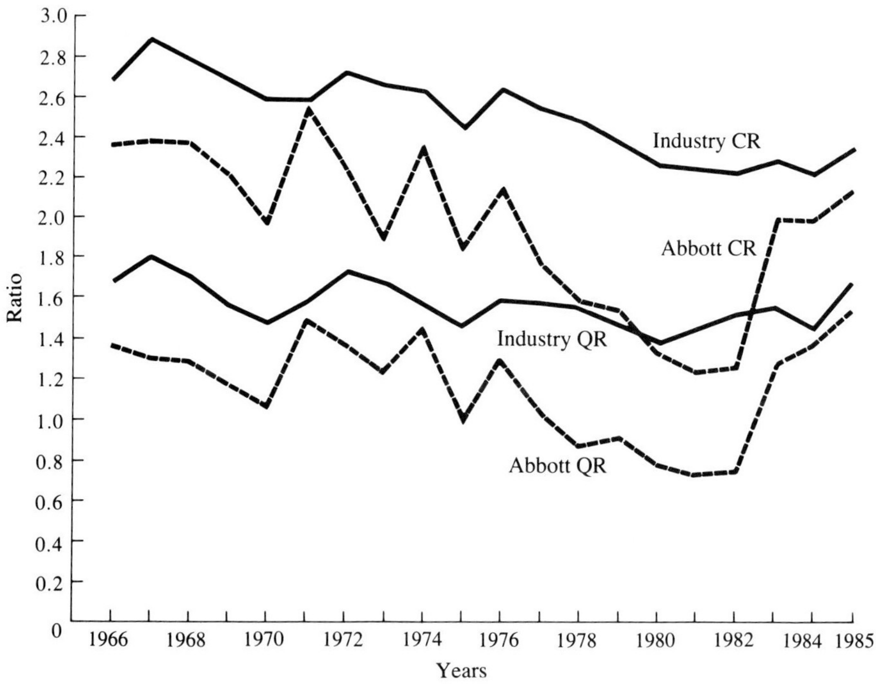

Source: Data from *Moody's Industrial Manual,* 1986.

Figures 2-1 through 2-6 illustrate different performance indicators and their trends for both Abbott and the drug industry in general over a twenty-year period, 1966-1985. The ratios used are classified into four types: (1) liquidity, (2) leverage, (3) activity, and (4) profitability.

Liquidity Ratios.   **Liquidity ratios** measure the firm's ability to meet its maturing short-term obligations. Two such ratios are the current ratio and the quick ratio. The current ratio (current assets/current liabilities) is the most common measure of short-term solvency. Figure 2-1 shows the current ratio for Abbott Labs to be consistently below the industry average over the twenty-year period.

The quick ratio [(current assets − inventories)/current liabilities] measures the firm's ability to pay off short-term obligations without relying on inventories, which are the least liquid of the current assets. Figure 2-1 shows that the quick ratio for Abbott also has been consistently lower than the industry average.

Overall, these ratios indicate that Abbott Labs is not in a very good position to meet its current liabilities. Both ratios are substantially below the averages for the industry.

FIGURE 2-2   Leverage Ratios for Abbott Laboratories and the Medical Hospital Supply Industry: Total Debt/Total Assets

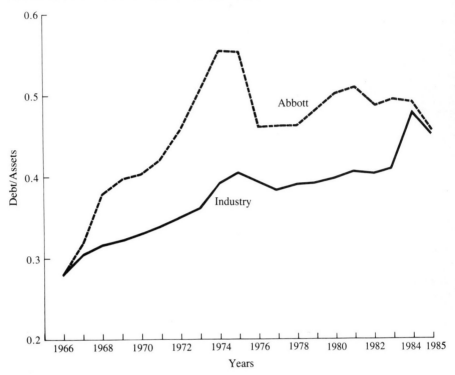

Source: Data from *Moody's Industrial Manual,* 1986.

Leverage Ratios.   Leverage ratios measure the importance of debt in the firm's financing. Two leverage ratios are analyzed: the total-debt-to-total-assets ratio and the times-interest-earned ratio. The ratio of total debt to total assets measures the percentage of total funds provided by creditors. Creditors prefer moderate debt ratios, while owners may prefer a higher amount of leverage. If the owners have provided only a small amount of the financing, the creditors bear most of the risk of the company. Owners also gain if a large amount of debt is used, as they maintain control of the firm with a lower level of investment. Also, if the firm earns more on the borrowed funds than it pays in interest, the owners gain a higher return. Abbott Labs' total-debt-to-total-assets ratio is a little higher than that of the industry, and this small difference, as shown in Figure 2-2, has been maintained for the past two years.

The times-interest-earned ratio (earnings before interest and taxes/interest charges) measures the company's ability to meet interest costs. For Abbott Labs this has been consistently below the industry average, as shown in Figure 2-3.

FIGURE 2–3   Leverage Ratios for Abbott Laboratories and the Medical Hospital
Supply Industry: Times-Interest-Earned Ratios

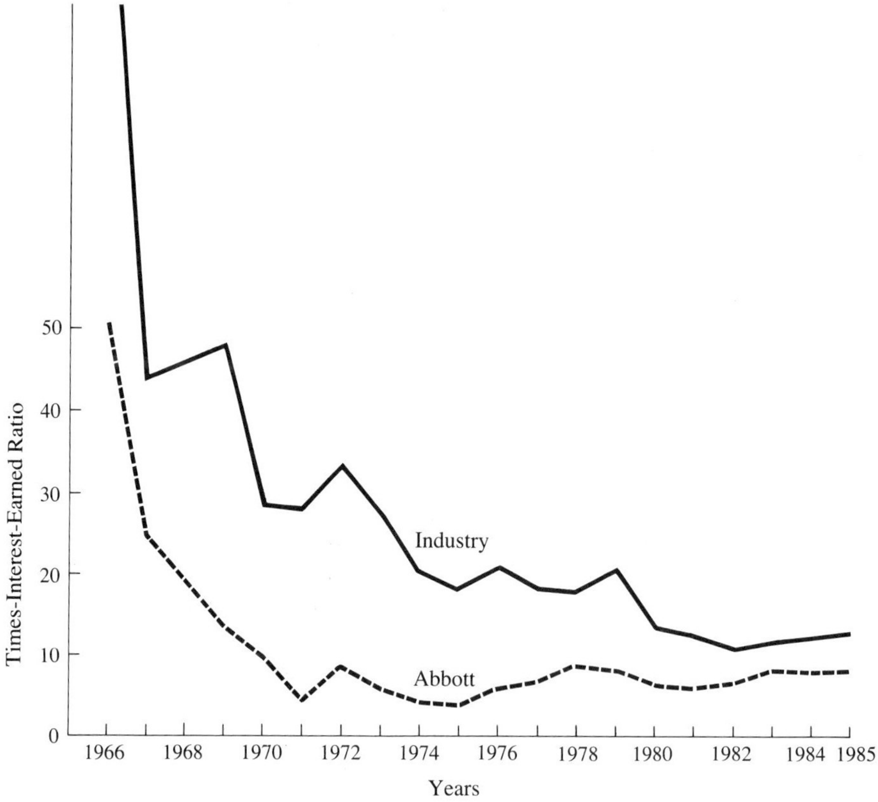

Source: Data from *Moody's Industrial Manual*, 1986.

These two leverage ratios indicate that Abbott utilizes more debt than the industry, on average, and that it may not be able to cover its fixed charges as well as others in the industry. Thus Abbott Labs may be somewhat limited in its ability to add significant levels of additional debt at this time.

Activity Ratios.   **Activity ratios** measure how well a firm is using its resources. Four activity ratios are analyzed: (1) inventory turnover, (2) average collection period, (3) fixed-asset turnover, and (4) total asset turnover. Inventory turnover (sales/inventory) for Abbott has been increasing since 1974, reaching a high of 7.2 in 1985. This compares favorably with the industry, as shown in Figure 2–4A. In 1985 the industry value was 6.4; Abbott has consistently been above the industry average.

The average collection period (receivables/sales per day) measures the accounts-receivable turnover. As shown in Figure 2–4B, the average collection period for Abbott Labs has been falling since 1974, reaching a low of 56

FIGURE 2–4A   Activity Ratios for Abbott Laboratories and the Medical Hospital Supply Industry: Inventory-Turnover Ratios

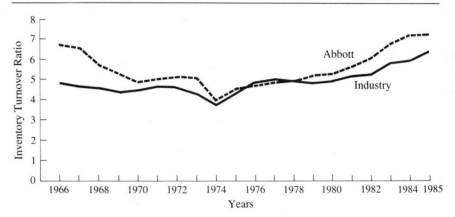

Source: Data from *Moody's Industrial Manual,* 1986.

FIGURE 2–4B   Activity Ratios for Abbott Laboratories and the Medical Hospital Supply Industry: Average Collection Period

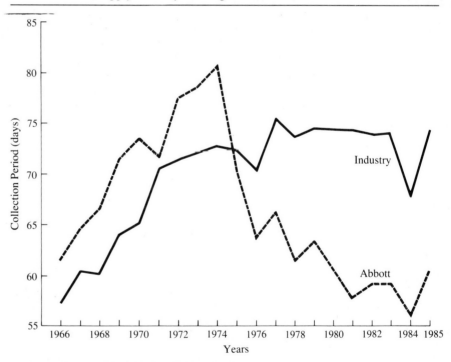

Source: Data from *Moody's Industrial Manual,* 1986.

days in 1984, but increasing to 60 days in 1985. Since 1975, the collection period for Abbott Labs has been lower than that of the industry, a favorable comparison, as shown in Figure 2–4B.

FIGURE 2–5A   Activity Ratios for Abbott Laboratories and the Medical Hospital Supply Industry: Fixed-Asset Utilization

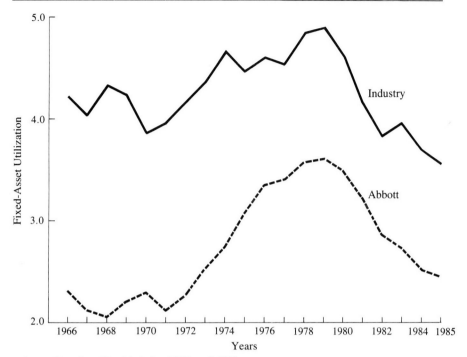

Source: Data from *Moody's Industrial Manual*, 1986.

The fixed-asset turnover (sales to net fixed assets) measures the turnover of plant and equipment—a measure of capacity utilization. In 1979, the fixed-asset turnover for Abbott Labs was 3.6, which subsequently dropped to 2.4 in 1985. Figure 2–5A shows that Abbott has been consistently below the industry for the entire period, although the gap between them has been declining. In 1985, the industry figure was 3.5. This indicates that Abbott is not using its fixed assets to the extent that other firms in the industry are. The decline in fixed-asset turnover for Abbott Labs over the past six years is not a favorable sign, but it seems to reflect the movement occurring in the industry.

Total-asset turnover (sales/total assets) for Abbott has been fairly steady over the entire period. As shown in Figure 2–5B, the ratio is below the industry average, indicating that Abbott is not generating a sufficient volume of business for the level of investments made.

Overall, analysis of the activity ratios gives conflicting signs about Abbott Labs' utilization of its resources. The inventory-turnover ratio and average collection period for this firm compare quite favorably to the industry, but the total-asset turnover for Abbott Labs is well below the industry average. The fixed-asset turnover, while lower for this company, is not very different from that of the industry.

FIGURE 2–5B   Activity Ratios for Abbott Laboratories and the Medical Hospital Supply Industry: Total-Asset Utilization

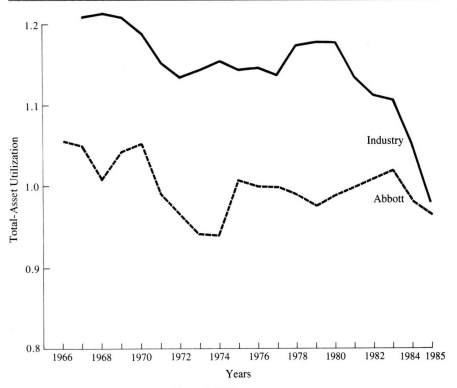

Source: Data from *Moody's Industrial Manual*, 1986.

Profitability Ratios.   **Profitability ratios** measure how well the firm is being managed. Three profitability ratios are analyzed: (1) net profit margin, (2) return on total assets, and (3) return on equity. Net profit margin (net income/sales) gives the profit per dollar of sales. Figure 2–6A indicates that the net profit margin for Abbott has been generally increasing over the entire period. It is above the net profit margin for the industry and much less volatile.

The return on total assets (net income/total assets) measures the return on total investment in the firm. In 1980 this ratio was 10.39 percent for Abbott, and it increased to 13.50 percent in 1985. As shown in Figure 2–6B, the return on total assets for Abbott Labs has been above the industry average since 1982.

The return on equity (net income/equity) measures the rate of return on the stockholder's investment. For Abbott Labs, this ratio, as shown in Figure 2–6C on page 28, has been rising steadily since 1976. In 1985 the value was 24 percent and, except for 1979 and 1984, the value has always been

FIGURE 2-6A   Profitability Ratios for Abbott Laboratories and the Medical Hospital Supply Industry: Profit Margin

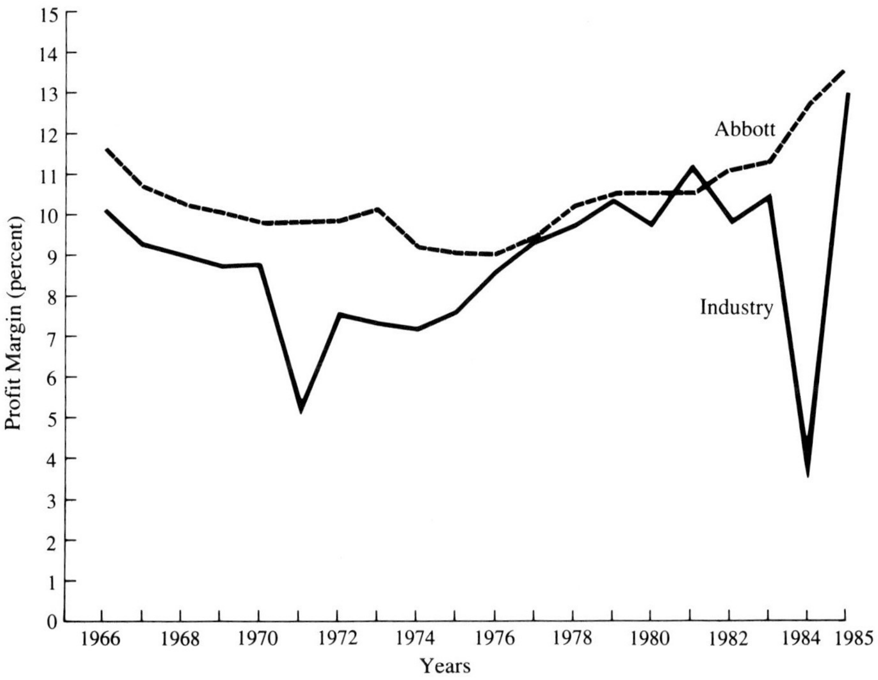

Source: Data from *Moody's Industrial Manual*, 1986.

above the industry average.[1] While the industry ratio has been increasing, it has not been doing so as quickly as Abbott's has.

In sum, the profitability ratios look somewhat favorable for Abbott relative to the industry. In all three areas of profitability, the ratios for Abbott in recent years are higher than those for the industry. This speaks well of the management of the firm.

Summary of Ratio Use.   An analysis of the four sets of ratios used to compare Abbott Labs with the medical and hospital supply industry at large shows that the profitability ratios present a favorable picture of Abbott, as all three ratios are above the industry average. These measures of return are high even though the activity ratios for Abbott Labs overall are below the industry average. Thus, if Abbott could use its resources as effectively as

---

[1] With Abbott's greater use of debt, this is not unexpected. This tradeoff between higher financial risk and higher return on equity would have to be judged in the context of investor's risk-aversion characteristics.

FIGURE 2–6B   Profitability Ratios for Abbott Laboratories and the Medical Hospital Supply Industry: Return on Total Assets

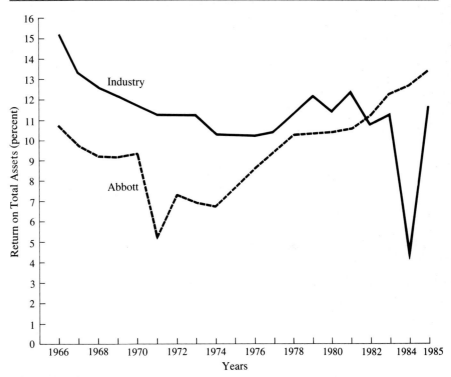

Source: Data from *Moody's Industrial Manual,* 1986.

the industry, then its profitability would be at an even higher level. Nevertheless, the other two groups of ratios indicate that Abbott Labs may not be able to maintain these high profit margins. Abbott has a higher percentage of debt than the industry average and covers its interest expense at a lower level than the industry. Thus, in the future it may face borrowing constraints that could adversely affect its profit. In addition, the low liquidity ratios indicate that the higher risk associated with investment in this firm is a factor to be considered as an offset to its higher profitability.

Dynamic Adjustment of Financial Ratios

To investigate whether firms periodically adjust their financial ratios to predetermined targets based on industry-wide averages, Lev (1969) and Lee and Finnerty (1989) suggest some time-series relationships for financial ratios:

$$X_{jt} = X_{jt-1} + \delta_j (I_{jt-1}) \qquad (j = 1, 2, \ldots, K,$$
$$t = 1, 2, \ldots, T) \qquad \textbf{(2.1)}$$

FIGURE 2-6C   Profitability Ratios for Abbott Laboratories and the Medical Hospital Supply Industry: Return on Total Equity

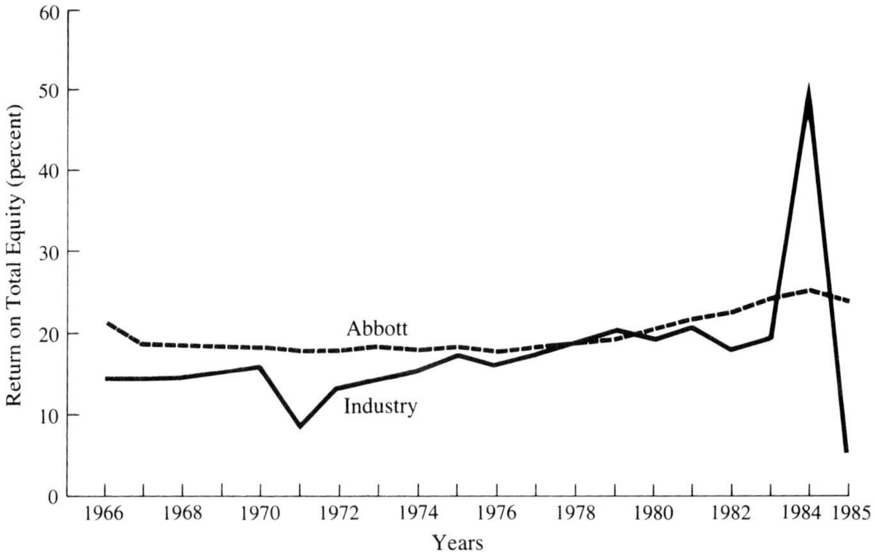

Source: Data from *Moody's Industrial Manual*, 1986.

where

$$X_{jt} = \text{individual firm's } j\text{th financial ratio at time } t;$$
$$X_{jt-1} = \text{individual firm's } j\text{th financial ratio at time } t-1;$$
$$I_{jt-1} = \text{industry average } j\text{th financial ratio at time } t-1; \text{ and}$$
$$\delta_j = \text{partial adjustment coefficient for } j\text{th ratio.}$$

This ratio-adjustment process implies that the current magnitude of a financial ratio is equal to last period's magnitude of this financial ratio plus an adjustment term. This adjustment term is equal to the difference between I_{jt-1} and X_{jt-1} times the partial adjustment coefficient δ_j. δ_j can be estimated through use of a regression technique and then can be employed to analyze the evolution of a firm's financial ratios over time. Sample Problem 2.1 provides further illustration.

Sample Problem 2.1

To determine whether Abbott Labs adjusts its financial ratios according to this partial adjustment model, annual values of five of Abbott's financial ratios and their corresponding industry averages from 1966 to 1985 are used to estimate Equation 2.1 for all five ratios. The ratios considered are current ratio (CR); net profit margin (NPM); total-asset turnover (TAT); times-interest-earned ratio (TIE); and debt-to-equity ratio (DTE). Results of the regressions are summarized as follows.

Current Ratio:

$$CR_t - CR_{t-1} = 0.4547 \, (CR^I_{t-1} - CR_{t-1}) - 0.2785$$
$$(t = 1.8201) \qquad\qquad (\overline{R}^2 = 0.0497)$$

where CR^I_{t-1} is the industry average of CR in period $t-1$.

Net Profit Margin:

$$NPM_t - NPM_{t-1} = 0.0397 \, (NPM^I_{t-1} - NPM_{t-1}) + 0.0022$$
$$(t = -0.3824) \qquad\qquad (\overline{R}^2 = 0.0497)$$

where NPM^I_{t-1} is the industry average of NPM in period $t-1$.

Total-Asset Turnover:

$$TAT_t - TAT_{t-1} = 0.2732 \, (TAT^I_{t-1} - TAT_{t-1}) - 0.0488$$
$$(t = 0.8658) \qquad\qquad (\overline{R}^2 = 0.1211)$$

where TAT^I_{t-1} is the industry average of TAT in period $t - 1$.

Times-Interest-Earned Ratio:

$$TIE_t - TIE_{t-1} = -0.2991 \, (TIE^I_{t-1} - TIE_{t-1}) + 3.0569$$
$$(t = 6.5036) \qquad\qquad (\overline{R}^2 = 0.7133)$$

where TIE is the industry average of TIE in period $t - 1$.

Debt-to-Equity Ratio:

$$DTE_t - DTE_{t-1} = 0.3006 \, (DTE^I_{t-1} - DTE_{t-1}) + 0.1065$$
$$(t = 2.3109) \qquad\qquad (\overline{R} = 0.9928)$$

where DTE^I_{t-1} is the industry average of DTE in period $t - 1$.

The t-statistic test results show that only the regression slopes for TIE and DTE are significantly different from zero at a 95 percent significance level. These results indicate that Abbott Labs adjusts its leverage to the industry mean, thus providing assistance in the prediction of its future debt policy given industry norms.

In addition, the partial adjustment coefficients (δ_j) associated with times-interest-earned and debt-to-equity ratios are respectively -0.2991 and 0.3006●

Forecasts of Sales, Earnings, and Dividends

In this section, several methods are used to forecast 1986 sales, earnings, and dividends for Abbott Laboratories. Table 2–6 shows the sales, earnings per share (EPS), dividends per share (DPS), and the dividend payout ratio for the past twenty years.

Sales Forecast. One method that can be used to forecast sales is to compute the growth rate of sales and apply this rate to the 1985 figure. The following exponential growth relationship is used to find the growth rate. Define sales

TABLE 2-6   Abbott Laboratories Sales, EPS, DPS, and Payout Ratio

Year	Sales ($ millions)	EPS	DPS	Payout Ratio
1966	265.8	0.1269	0.0625	0.49
1967	303.3	0.1313	0.0625	0.48
1968	351.0	0.1469	0.0625	0.43
1969	403.9	0.1481	0.0672	0.45
1970	457.5	0.1825	0.0688	0.38
1971	458.1	0.1069	0.0688	0.64
1972	521.8	0.1800	0.0688	0.38
1973	620.4	0.2094	0.0734	0.35
1974	765.4	0.2500	0.0806	0.32
1975	940.6	0.3213	0.0906	0.28
1976	1084.8	0.4075	0.1075	0.26
1977	1244.9	0.4950	0.1375	0.28
1978	1445.0	0.6200	0.1800	0.29
1979	1683.2	0.7425	0.2400	0.32
1980	2038.2	0.8650	0.2875	0.33
1981	2342.5	1.0050	0.3450	0.34
1982	2602.4	1.1850	0.4050	0.34
1983	2927.8	1.4300	0.4800	0.34
1984	3103.9	1.6700	0.5750	0.34
1985	3360.3	1.9400	0.6750	0.34

Source: Moody's Industrial Manual, 1986.

in the base year, or year zero, as sales 0. Here 1966 is the year zero, and sales 0 are $265.8 million. Let g be the continuous growth rate per annum in sales. Then sales in the nth year after year zero in sales$_n$ are

$$\text{Sales}_n = (\text{Sales}_0) \, e^{g \cdot n} \qquad (2.2)$$

where e is the natural constant approximately equal to 2.71828.

Taking the natural log of the quantities on both sides of Equation (2.2) gives

$$\ln_c (\text{Sales}_n) = \ln_c (\text{Sales}_0) + g \cdot n \qquad (2.3)$$

$$\ln_c (\text{Sales}_n) = a_0 + a_1 \cdot n + \epsilon_n \qquad (2.4)$$

where ln means natural logarithm.

Equation (2.4) can be used to estimate the growth rate g for the sales of Abbott Labs. For this, the historical data on sales from Table 2-6 are used to estimate the values of a_0 and a_1; given these two values the sales can be forecasted in any year in the future. Using historic time-series data of earnings, sales, dividends, and so on, a simple regression can be run to obtain an estimate of g as shown by Equation (2.4). (A complete discussion of this technique is presented in Chapter 3.)

The estimate of a_1 is the growth rate. For Abbott Labs, the obtained estimates are:

$$\ln \text{Sales}_n = 5.3959 + 0.14226n \qquad (R^2 = 0.9928)$$
$$(t = 51.026)$$

This indicates that the growth rate is 14.2 percent, and the resulting 1986 sales forecast is $3,837.4 million.

Another method used to estimate sales is to use a nonlinear time-trend analysis—that is, regressing historical data against n and n^2:

$$\text{Sales}_n = 335.45 - 36.055n + 9.6808\,n^2 \qquad (R^2 = 0.9959)$$
$$(t = 3.3467)\,(t = 19.4271)$$

Substituting 21 for n gives a 1986 sales estimate of $3,847.5 million.

Earnings Forecast.   The earnings per share can be forecast by finding the growth rate of EPS and applying it to the 1985 EPS. The growth rate is estimated by regressing ln EPS against time. The estimated equation is:

$$\ln \text{EPS}_n = -2.5925 + 0.1589n \qquad (\overline{R}^2 = 0.9505)$$
$$(t = 19.1265)$$

This indicates that the growth rate is 15.9 percent; applying this growth rate to 1985 EPS yields a 1986 forecast of $2.25 per share.

Another forecast of EPS can be obtained via a nonlinear time-trend analysis. The following equation is obtained:

$$\text{EPS}_n = 0.2678 - 0.0697n \quad + \quad 0.0075n^2 \qquad (\overline{R}^2 = 0.9941)$$
$$(t = 9.8252) \qquad (t = 22.7677)$$

Substituting 21 for n, the resulting 1986 EPS forecast is $2.11.

To conclude, forecasts of EPS for Abbott Labs range from $2.11 to $2.25. A compromise estimate for 1986 EPS is $2.20.

Dividend Forecast.   Dividends per share for 1986 can be found by calculating the growth rate of dividends and applying this to 1985 DPS. The growth rate is found by regressing ln DPS_n against time:

$$\ln \text{DPS}_n = -3.3821 + 0.1372n \qquad (\overline{R}^2 = 0.9037)$$
$$(t = 13.389)$$

Thus the growth rate in DPS is 13.7 percent, and the resulting forecast for 1986 DPS is $0.77.

Another method to forecast DPS is to use the historical payout ratio (see Table 2–6) and apply it to the estimate of EPS obtained for 1986. For Abbott Laboratories, the dividend payout ratio has been steady for the last five years. The average payout ratio for the last five years is 0.34. Therefore, (0.34) × (forecast of 1986 EPS) yields an estimate of DPS for 1986. As the forecasts for EPS ranged from $2.11 to $2.25, the resulting forecasts for DPS range from $0.71 to $0.76, with $0.75 the best estimate.

Using the historical information about Abbott Labs, the following estimates for 1986 have been made:

Sales	$3,837 to $3,847 million
EPS	$2.11 to $2.25
DPS	$0.71 to $0.76

The purpose of presenting the extensive analysis of Abbott Labs is twofold: (1) to demonstrate the linkage between total information available and the information that is useful for security analysis; and (2) to illustrate that investment analysis requires familiarity with accounting, corporate finance, and statistics.

SUMMARY

This chapter has discussed alternative sources of information needed for doing security analysis and portfolio management. Information about Abbott Laboratories has been used to illustrate how financial-accounting ratios can be employed to analyze a firm's book value and accounting. In this analysis the regression technique discussed in Chapter 1 has been utilized to complete the related analysis.

The remaining chapters of this text discuss in detail the various kinds of analyses that can be used in the evaluation of a firm's securities, with emphasis on why the information is useful to security analysts and portfolio managers.

QUESTIONS AND PROBLEMS

1. What is accounting information? List two sources for obtaining accounting information about a firm.
2. What is the value of accounting information in the process of security analysis?
3. What are the limits of accounting information?
4. Explain why security analysts use financial ratios rather than absolute numbers in their analyses.
5. You know that Widget Company earned 10 percent on their equity last year. Does this number provide you with any information regarding Widget's management? Is there any other information that you need? What is it and how will you use it?
6. What are internal liquidity ratios? List two.
7. What is the significance of the dynamic adjustment process of ratios?

8. How are target ratios obtained?
9. In the table that follows, you are given information about Abbott Laboratories' sales and their total assets. Calculate total-asset turnover for these years.

Year	Sales ($ millions)	Total Assets ($ millions)	Year	Sales ($ millions)	Total Assets ($ millions)
1968	351.0	345.4	1978	1445.0	1467.6
1969	403.9	387.6	1979	1683.2	1754.4
1970	457.5	434.1	1980	2038.2	2062.8
1971	458.1	464.6	1981	2342.5	2355.6
1972	521.8	539.1	1982	2602.4	2566.9
1973	620.4	666.4	1983	2927.9	2821.6
1974	765.4	817.3	1984	3104.0	3170.4
1975	940.6	925.5	1985	3360.3	3468.4
1976	1084.8	1076.2	1986	3870.7	3865.6
1977	1244.9	1253.7	1987	4387.9	4385.7

Source: Moody's Industrial Manual, 1986.

10. What is the importance of forecasting sales, earnings, and dividends in security analysis and portfolio management? What methods are used to forecast these variables?
11. Use the sales figures given in Problem 9 to forecast sales and total assets for Abbott Laboratories in 1988.

APPENDIX 2A: REGRESSION ANALYSIS

In economics and finance, researchers are often interested in the specification of a functional relationship between two variables, such as $y = f(x)$. We refer to y as the dependent variable and x as the independent variable. Because we cannot expect a perfect relationship between y and x, we write the relationship as $y = f(x) + e$, where e is a random error term. The error occurs because of measurement errors in y or misspecification in the function $f(x)$.

Often we choose to specify a linear functional relationship, such as:

$$y_n = a_0 + a_1 x_n + \epsilon_n$$

where

y_n = dependent variable in time period n;
x_n = independent variable in time period n;
a_0 = intercept term;
a_1 = slope of our regression line; and
ϵ_n = random error term.

For example, a marketing manager might be interested in the relationship between advertising and sales. The following regression model could then be estimated:

$$\text{Sales}_n = a_0 + a_1 \text{ Advertising}_n + \epsilon_n$$

where

$$\text{Sales}_n = \text{sales in month } n$$
$$\text{Advertising}_n = \text{advertising budget in month } n$$

The slope a_1 would measure the relationship between sales and advertising.

In other words, regression analysis is a technique that mathematically fits a line to a series of points on a scatter diagram, as indicated in Figure 2A–1. Fitting a line through these points can be done in several ways. One method would involve fitting a line by "eyeballing" the data. Clearly, this method will lead to arbitrarily drawn lines. A more sophisticated technique, known as the method of least squares, allows us to determine the best line.

The method of least squares is a technique that fits a line by minimizing the sum of the squared error terms. The error terms (ϵ_1, ϵ_2, ϵ_3, and ϵ_4) are the difference between the actual observations and the regression line, as indicated in Figure 2A–2.

Forecasting and Regression Analysis

One method that can be used to forecast financial data is known as *trend analysis*. In trend analysis a regression line is fitted to the financial variable over time. For example, to forecast sales for 1988, the data on sales for Abbott Labs given in Table 2–6 could be plotted. A trend line would then be

FIGURE 2A–1   Scatter Diagram

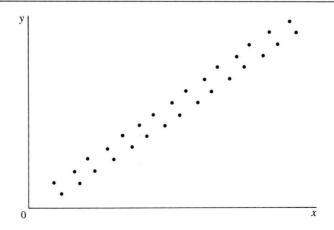

FIGURE 2A-2   Regression Line and Error Terms

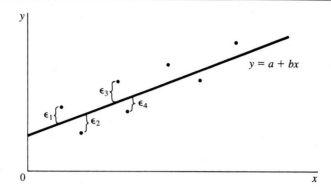

fitted using the method of least squares. This trend line could then be used to forecast next year's sales. Formally, the following sales model would be estimated:

$$\text{Sales}_n = a_0 + a_1 n + \epsilon_n$$

where

Sales_n = sales in year n;
   n = year;
   ϵ_n = error term; and
a_0, a_1 = constants to be estimated.

The results of the regression are written

$$\text{Sales}_n = -566.66 + 188.08n \qquad (\bar{R}^2 = 0.9144)$$
$$(t = 14.61)$$

From the scatter diagram for sales, it is apparent that sales are growing at an accelerating rate. In this case, fitting a simple trend line may not produce adequate forecasts of future sales. In cases such as this, nonlinear time-trend analysis may be employed—that is, regress historical data against n and n^2. The results of this regression are written:

$$\text{Sales}_n = 353.92 - 42.07n + 10.01n^2$$
$$(t = 4.21) \quad (t = 23.75)$$

A plot of the regression lines using a linear time trend (Figure 2A-3) and a nonlinear time trend (Figure 2A-4) indicate that the nonlinear time trend is more appropriate for estimating sales.

   To produce a forecast for sales in 1988, simply plug into the regression equation:

Forecast using linear trend = $3,759.18 million
Forecast using nonlinear trend = $4,681.60 million

FIGURE 2A-3 Linear Trend Sales Forecast

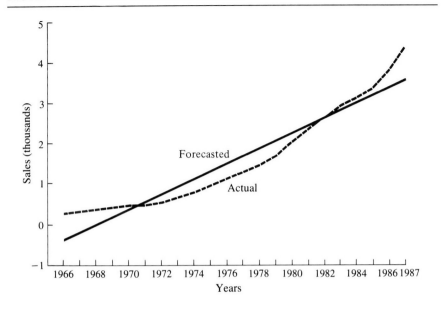

FIGURE 2A-4 Nonlinear Trend Sales Forecast

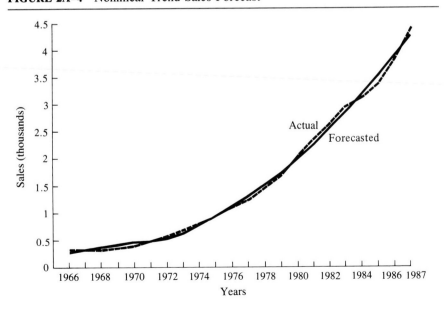

REFERENCES

Business Statistics. Superintendent of Documents, U.S. Government Printing Office, Washington, D.C., 1988.

Economic Report of the President. Superintendent of Documents, U.S. Government Printing Office, Washington, D.C., 1988.

Federal Reserve Bulletin. Board of Governors of the Federal Reserve System, Washington, D.C., 1988.

Financial Dynamics. Standard & Poor's Compustat Services, Inc., 1988.

Industry Norms and Key Business Ratios. Dun and Bradstreet Corporation, 1976–1988.

Lee, C. F., and J. E. Finnerty. *Corporate Finance: Theory, Methods and Applications*. Harcourt Brace Jovanovich, 1990.

Lev, Baruch. "Industry Averages as Targets for Financial Ratios." *Journal of Accounting Research,* v. 7 (Autumn 1969), pp. 290–99.

Moody's Industrial Manual. Moody's Investors Services, Inc., 1988.

Robert Morris Associates Statement Studies. Robert Morris Associates, 1988.

Standard & Poor's Stock Report—NYSE. Standard & Poor's Corporation, January 1988.

The Value Line Investment Survey. Value Line, Inc., 1988.

3

Common Stock: Return, Growth, and Risk

Investors in financial assets are compensated for the assumption of risk by earning an appropriate rate of return. This rate of return is composed of a percentage change in the market value of the assets and the yield of interest or dividends. The concept of return is crucial to the study of security analysis and portfolio management; therefore, accurate measurement of the rate of return is of vital concern. In the first part of this chapter, the concepts of holding-period return, holding-period yield, arithmetic mean, and geometric mean are defined and examined. This is followed by a discussion of a mixture of the arithmetic mean and geometric mean, as well as various ways of determining growth. The final section of the chapter presents different kinds of risks and the analytical measures commonly used to quantify risk.

In security analysis and portfolio management, growth-rate estimates of earnings, dividends, and price per share are important factors in determining the value of an investment. A regression method was demonstrated in Chapter 2, and in the latter part of this chapter both the compound-sum and the regression methods are developed in detail. Data from Pennzoil Oil Company for 1974–1986 are used to show how alternative growth-rate estimation methods can be useful in security analysis.

HOLDING-PERIOD RETURN

To measure the relative ending wealth, the **holding-period return (HPR)** is proposed by the financial profession to do the analysis. The HPR is the ratio of the terminal value of the investment (plus all cash distributions—that is,

interest or dividend payments—received during the holding period) to the initial value of the investment. Mathematically, this can be expressed as:

$$\text{HPR}_t = (1 + r_t) = \frac{P_t + C_t}{P_{t-1}} \tag{3.1}$$

where:

P_t and P_{t-1} = the market value of the investment in period t and period $t-1$, respectively; and

C_t = the cash distributions paid during the holding period.

Sample Problem 3.1 illustrates the calculation of the holding-period return.

Sample Problem 3.1

The table lists Pennzoil Company stock price and dividend data for thirteen years. In order to calculate the HPR for 1986, add the terminal value of the stock ($66.00) to the dividend received during 1986 ($2.20) and divide the sum by the initial value of the stock for 1986 ($64.00).

Pennzoil Company HPR and HPY

Year	Closing Price ($)	Annual Dividend ($)	Annual HPR	Annual HPY (percent)
1974	16.07	1.05	—	—
1975	12.92	1.20	.879	−12.1
1976	22.17	1.31	1.809	80.9
1977	19.58	1.70	0.960	−4.0
1978	20.50	2.00	1.149	14.9
1979	44.125	1.50	2.226	122.60
1980	50.375	2.00	1.187	18.70
1981	48.00	2.20	0.997	−0.30
1982	35.125	2.20	0.778	−22.20
1983	34.00	2.20	1.031	3.10
1984	44.50	2.20	1.374	37.40
1985	64.00	2.20	0.726	−27.40
1986	66.00	2.20	1.065	6.50

Source: Moody's Industrial Manual, 1987.

Solution

$$\text{HPR(1986)} = \frac{\$66.00 + \$2.20}{\$64.00} = \frac{\$68.20}{\$64.00} = 1.065$$

HOLDING-PERIOD YIELD

Holding-period yield (HPY) is a measurement of investment performance related to HPR. The HPY is the ratio of the change in the market value of the investment plus cash distributions received during the period divided by the original value of the investment. This is represented by:

$$\text{HPY}_t = (r_t) = \frac{(P_t - P_{t-1}) + C_t}{P_{t-1}} = \frac{P_t + C_t}{P_{t-1}} - 1 \qquad (3.2)$$

From this expression it is easy to see that HPY is equal to HPR − 1. Thus, the 1986 HPY for Pennzoil, as indicated in the fifth column of the table in Sample Problem 3.1, is expressed as:

$$\text{HPY}(1986) = \frac{(\$66.00 - \$64.00) + \$2.20}{\$64.00} = 0.065, \text{ or } 6.5\%$$

The HPY defined in Equation (3.2) is a discrete type of HPY. It assumes that the cash flows and investments occur at specific points in time. In this case, $64.00 is invested at the beginning of the year, and $2.20 is assumed to be received at year end, when the price is $66.00. The HPR and HPY of Pennzoil Company during 1975–1986, as indicated in the table in Sample Problem 3.1, reflect the investment performance during this period.

The time-series distribution of the HPR is important in the analysis of security investments and the management of security portfolios. As shall be seen at the end of this chapter, when the riskiness of an investment is considered, the variability of the HPR or the HPY is one of its measures. The two most important types of probability distributions used in investment analysis are the normal and the log normal distributions. If the HPR is normally distributed, the mean and the standard deviation are sufficient to describe the shape of the HPR distribution adequately. If some skewness to the distribution exists, the log normal distribution will be more appropriate in describing the distribution of returns.

In this study of portfolio theory we assume that investors make their portfolio decisions on the basis of mean and standard deviation of rate of return. Since the normal distribution is fully represented by the mean and standard deviation, it is important to know whether the distribution being used in portfolio analysis is indeed normal. The distribution of stock returns has been shown by Fama (1965) to be abnormal. Additionally, Elton and Gruber (1974), using the concept of limited liability for investors, argue that normality and limited liability are inconsistent. The most an investor can lose is 100 percent, whereas the potential gain from an investment is limitless in theory; hence, the distribution of returns cannot be normal where infinitely large gains have a nonzero probability.

Figure 3–1 shows the log normal and normal probability distributions for the holding-period return $(1 + r)$ and holding-period yield (r).

FIGURE 3-1 Normal and Log Normal Distributions

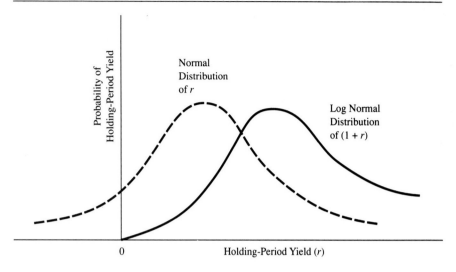

Assuming that returns are log normally distributed (which more correctly reflects the true state of the world) does not negate the use of the mean and standard deviation in portfolio analysis. Further issues related to log normal distributions are covered in the portfolio theory section of the text.

The table in Sample Problem 3.1 uses a one-period or discrete model for calculating the HPR and HPY, assuming that the cash flow occurs at the end of the period. It is usually more realistic to deal with many periods and compounded returns when evaluating real-world investments.

The frequency of compounding influences the HPR and HPY calculations in the following way:

$$\text{HPY}_t^c = \ln\left(\frac{P_t + C_t}{P_{t-1}}\right) \tag{3.3}$$

where HPY_t^c is the holding-period rate of return with continuous compounding, and ln is the natural logarithm.

If $P_t = \$66$, $P_{t-1} = \$64$, and $C_t = \$2.20$, then

$$\text{HPY}_t^c = \ln\left(\frac{\$66 + \$2.20}{\$64}\right) = 0.0635$$

More generally, the rate of return with continuous compounding for a given period is expressed by:

$$\text{HPR}_t^d = 1 + \text{HPY}^d = \exp(\text{HPY}^c) \tag{3.4}$$

where HPY_t^d is the discrete holding-period rate of return and exp (e) is 2.718, the base of natural logarithms. By taking the natural log of both sides of Equation (3.4):

$$\ln(1 + \text{HPY}^d) = \text{HPY}^c \tag{3.5}$$

For example, if $1,000 invested for one year produces an ending cash flow of $1,271, the HPR^d is 1.271, for a HPY^d of 27.1 percent. The continuously compounded rate implicit in this investment is calculated by using Equation (3.5):

$$\ln (1 + 0.271) = 0.24$$

for a HPY^c of 24 percent. In every case except HPY^d = 0, the continuously compounded return is always less than the discrete return.

On the other hand, given a continuous return, the discrete return can be calculated using Equation (3.6):

$$HPY^d = \exp (HPY^c) - 1 \tag{3.6}$$

For example, if the HPY^c is 18.5 percent, the HPY^d is $e^{0.185} - 1$, or 20.3 percent.

Arithmetic Mean

The **arithmetic mean** of HPY is one of the measures used to evaluate the performance of an investment. The arithmetic mean is the sum of the values of the data points divided by the number of such data points. In computational form, this can be expressed:

$$\overline{X} = \frac{\sum_{t=1}^{n} X_t}{n} \tag{3.7}$$

where:

$\overline{X}$ = the arithmetic mean of HPY; and
X_t = the HPY in tth year.

From the table in Sample Problem 3.1, the arithmetic mean of Pennzoil stock HPYs over a twelve-year period, 1975–1986, can be calculated:

$$\overline{X} = \frac{2.181}{12} = 0.182$$

This implies that, on average, the investment has increased in value by 18.2 percent per year. Is this really a meaningful number? Probably not.

There are some complications to be aware of when employing the arithmetic mean. First, the arithmetic mean is quite sensitive to extreme values. For example, suppose that over a five-year period, a stock returned 5 percent in four years and 50 percent in one year. The arithmetic mean would be 0.70/5 = 0.14, or 14 percent. With only the arithmetic mean as a guide, the returns might be expected to be scattered about 14 percent. Upon inspection, however, it is found that the stock returned only 5 percent most of the time. The implication is that the arithmetic mean has an upward bias that increases directly with the variability of the data. Another disadvantage of using the arithmetic mean relating to variability is of particular concern to

security analysts. This problem can best be described by the following. Consider a stock whose price rises from $10 to $15 one year and drops back to $10 the next. The annual HPY would be 50 percent in the first year and -33 percent in the second year. While the annual arithmetic mean return would be 8.5 percent, it is clear that the return equals zero, as the value of the investment is still $10. Another measure of the mean return is necessary.

Geometric Mean

An alternative average measure for evaluating the investment performance is the **geometric mean.** The geometric mean is the nth root of the product of the n values of the data points:

$$\overline{g} = \sqrt[n]{X_1 \cdot X_2 \cdot \ \cdots \ \cdot X_n} \tag{3.8}$$

Holding-period returns rather than holding-period yields are used in calculating the geometric mean of rates of return because negative or zero yields will result in meaningless answers, a consequence of necessarily taking the nth root of negative numbers. The nth roots of negative numbers are imaginary numbers. There is no economic interpretation of an imaginary number.

To see how the geometric mean deals with the problems encountered with the arithmetic mean, it is useful to return to the examples of the previous section. The geometric average annual rate of return ($\overline{g}$) for a stock yielding 5 percent for four years and 50 percent for one year would be calculated as:

$$\overline{g} = \sqrt[5]{1.05 \times 1.05 \times 1.05 \times 1.05 \times 1.50}$$
$$= \sqrt[5]{1.823}$$
$$= 1.128$$

Subtracting 1.0 from the HPR, the HPY is 0.128, or 12.8%. This is less than the 14 percent arithmetic mean. In dealing with the other arithmetic-mean problems—that is, computing an average return when the actual return is zero—the geometric mean provides a suitable solution.

$$\overline{g} = \sqrt{1.50 \times 0.667}$$
$$= \sqrt{1.0} = 1.0$$

Subtracting 1.0 from the HPR, the HPY is 0.0, or 0 percent.

The geometric mean HPR of Pennzoil stock for the twelve-year period noted above is expressed as:

$$\overline{g} = \sqrt[12]{3.9373} = 1.1210$$

The geometric-mean return (HPY) is 12.1 percent, considerably different from the arithmetic-mean estimate of 18.2 percent. Comparison of the terminal wealth that would be accumulated using the geometric- and arithmetic-mean return estimates with the actual terminal wealth will help determine which is more accurate.

The original price of Pennzoil stock was $16.07. Cash dividends amounting to $23.96 were distributed over the twelve-year period, and the terminal price of the stock was $66.00. Thus, the actual terminal wealth, assuming no reinvestment of the intermediate cash flow, was $89.96. Since application of 18.2 percent growth rate to the initial price of $16.07 over twelve years yields a terminal wealth position of $119.52, use of the arithmetic mean overstates the terminal wealth by $29.56. Use of the geometric mean of 12.1 percent, on the other hand, yields the result of $63.27, where the difference between the actual terminal wealth and the estimated terminal wealth is $26.69. This is an underestimated value instead of an overestimated value.

The best estimate of a future value for a given distribution is still the arithmetic average because it represents the expected value of the distribution. The arithmetic mean is most useful for determining the central tendency of a distribution *at a point in time* (that is, for cross-sectional analysis). However, the geometric mean is best suited for measuring a stock's compound rate of return *over time* (that is, time-series analysis). Hence, the geometric average or compound return should always be used when dealing with the returns of securities over time.

The rationale for this particular observation revolves around the biases involved in the calculations of the arithmetic and geometric means. The arithmetic mean tends to be biased toward extreme observations, whereas the geometric mean penalizes extreme observations. That is, the geometric mean provides more of a smoothing process.

In analyzing past time-series data the geometric mean is usually more representative of actual data (as in the Pennzoil example).

In order to simplify the computations involved in calculating the geometric mean, logarithms can be used to calculate the nth root.[1]

$$\bar{g} = \sqrt[n]{X_1 \cdot X_2 \cdot \cdots \cdot X_n} \tag{3.9}$$

$$\ln(\bar{g}) = \frac{1}{n}(\ln X_1 + \ln X_2 + \cdots + \ln X_n)$$

$$\text{antilog}[\log(\bar{g})] = \text{antilog}\left(\frac{1}{n}\sum_{t=1}^{n}\log X_t\right)$$

$$\bar{g} = \text{antilog}\left(\frac{1}{n}\sum_{t=1}^{n}\log X_t\right) \tag{3.10}$$

For a three-year period example, in which the holding periods were $X_1 = 1.10$, $X_2 = 1.15$, and $X_3 = X_n = 0.98$, the use of Equation (3.9) would give the following results:

$$\bar{g} = \sqrt[3]{1.10 \times 1.15 \times 0.98}$$
$$= \sqrt[3]{1.2397}$$
$$= 1.074$$

---

[1] In this application, the use of base 10 or ordinary logarithms will yield the same results.

Using Equation (3.10) as follows, the same result can be obtained:

$$\begin{aligned}
\overline{g} &= \text{antilog} \left[\tfrac{1}{3} \left(\log 1.10 + \log 1.15 + \log 0.98 \right) \right] \\
&= \text{antilog} \left[\tfrac{1}{3} \left(0.0414 + 0.0607 - 0.0088 \right) \right] \\
&= \text{antilog} \left[\tfrac{1}{3} \left(0.0933 \right) \right] \\
&= \text{antilog } 0.0311 \\
&= 1.074
\end{aligned}$$

Weighted Unbiased Mean

When consideration is given to the types of applications for average rates of return to (1) determine the historical profit rate of an investment and (2) to assess the long-run expected rate of return of some investment instruments, the importance of accuracy and a lack of bias is apparent. For example, an executive who is enrolled in a company's pension plan would certainly try to assess the magnitude of his or her retirement fund when determining a current schedule of personal savings. As another example, an actuary calculating premiums for a life-insurance policy would need to make some assumption about long-run expected rates of return and would typically base assessments of future rates of return upon past experience. Blume (1974) has investigated the possible bias in using either arithmetic average ($\overline{x}$) or geometric average ($\overline{g}$) to forecast such expected rates of return and has proposed four alternative unbiased estimators: (1) simple unbiased, (2) overlapped unbiased, (3) weighted unbiased, and (4) adjusted unbiased. Since Blume has also mathematically and empirically shown that the weighted unbiased estimator is the most efficient estimator and is the most robust for nonnormal and nonstationary data, only this estimator is discussed here. The definition of the **weighted unbiased estimator, $M(W)$,** is

$$M(W) = \left(\frac{T - n}{T - 1} \right) \overline{X} + \left(\frac{n - 1}{T - 1} \right) \overline{g} \qquad \textbf{(3.11)}$$

where

$T =$ the number of HPRs used to estimate the historical average returns; and

$n =$ the number of investment-horizon periods for which a particular investment is to be held.

For example, to estimate the average holding-period return for a five-year horizon using the Pennzoil Company data, it can be seen that $T = 13$, $n = 5$, and

$$\begin{aligned}
M(W) &= \frac{13 - 5}{13 - 1} (1.182) + \frac{5 - 1}{13 - 1} (1.121) \\[2mm]
&= \frac{8}{12} (1.182) + \frac{4}{12} (1.121) \\[2mm]
&= 0.788 + 0.374 \\[2mm]
&= 1.162
\end{aligned}$$

Therefore, application of the weighted unbiased estimator approach would lead to an estimated average holding-period return of 16.2 percent, if the holding period is expected to be five years. A shorter holding-period assumption would result in a higher estimated HPR (that is, closer to $\overline{X}$), and a longer holding-period assumption would result in a lower estimated HPR (that is, closer to $\overline{g}$). These results are consistent with investors' intuitive inclination to be more conservative with longer-term estimates of return.

COMMON-STOCK VALUATION APPROACHES

Arithmetic, geometric, and weighted unbiased means are three alternative averages useful in evaluating the historical performance of an investment. Nevertheless, while it is important to be aware of an investment's past performance, it is crucial to understand the ingredients for determining the market value of common stock in future investment performance evaluation. There are four logically equivalent approaches for estimating the market value of common stock.

1. The stream of dividends approach
2. The current earnings plus future investment opportunities approach
3. The discounted cash-flow approach
4. The stream of earnings approach

These four methods are explored in more detail in Chapter 4. For now, the derivation and implications of the stream of dividends approach is presented. In general, there are three ways to express this approach, as indicated in Equations (3.12), (3.13), and (3.14):

$$P_0 = \sum_{t=1}^{n} \frac{d_t}{(1 + k)^t} \qquad (3.12)$$

$$P_0 = \frac{d_1}{k - g} \qquad (3.13)$$

$$P_0 = \frac{d_1}{k} \qquad (3.14)$$

where:

P_0 = current price per share;
d_t = expected dividends per share in period t;
k = capitalization rate;
n = terminal time period; and
g = the growth rate of dividends per share.

Both Equations (3.13) and (3.14) can be derived from Equation (3.12). If n approaches infinity, k is larger than g, and dividends grow at a constant rate so that $d_t = d_0(1 + g)^t$, it can be shown that Equation (3.12) reduces to

Equation (3.13), commonly called the *Gordon dividend model.*[2] If the growth rate of dividends is zero, Equation (3.13) reduces to Equation (3.14). These three valuation expressions are important for security analysis and portfolio management because they can be used to calculate the theoretical value of common stock, and variations on them can be used to calculate the value of bonds and other investment instruments. To use these models, estimates of the appropriate capitalization rate (k) and the growth rate (g) for dividends are required. In the following section, alternative methods for estimating the growth rate are explored in accordance with the concepts of the compounding process and linear regression.

GROWTH-RATE ESTIMATION AND ITS APPLICATION

The purpose of this section is to show how growth rates can be mathematically estimated. The application of these estimated growth rates is briefly discussed.

Compound-Sum Method

One method of estimating the growth rate uses the **compounding process.** Both discrete and continuous compounding are basic concepts in financial management and investment analysis. These concepts are expressed mathematically in Equations (3.15) and (3.16):

$$P_n = P_0 (1 + i)^n \qquad (3.15)$$
$$P_n = P_0 e^{in} \qquad (3.16)$$

where

P_0 = the price at time zero;
P_n = the price at time n;
i = the compound interest rate; and
e = a constant equal to 2.718.

Equation (3.15) describes a discrete compounding process and Equation (3.16) describes a continuous compounding process.

The relationship between Equations (3.15) and (3.16) can be illustrated by using an intermediate expression such as:

$$P_n = P_0\left(1 + \frac{i}{m}\right)^{mn} \qquad (3.17)$$

---

[2] Substituting $d_i = d_0(1 + g)^t$ into Equation (3.12) and letting $k > g$ and n approach infinity:

$$P_0 = d_0\left[\left(\frac{1 + g}{1 + k}\right) + \left(\frac{1 + g}{1 + k}\right)^2 + \cdots + \left(\frac{1 + g}{1 + k}\right)^\infty\right]$$
$$= d_0\left(\frac{1 + g}{1 + k}\right)\left[\frac{1}{1 - \left(\frac{1 + g}{1 + k}\right)}\right] = \frac{d_0(1 + g)}{k - g} = \frac{d_1}{k - g}$$

where m is the frequency of compounding in each year. If $m = 4$, Equation (3.17) describes a quarterly compounding process; if $m = 365$, it describes a daily process; and if m approaches infinity, it describes a continuous compounding process. Thus Equation (3.16) can be derived from Equation (3.17) in the following manner. Based upon the definition

$$\lim_{m \to \infty} \left(1 + \frac{1}{m}\right)^m = e = 2.718 \tag{3.18}$$

Equation (3.17) can be rewritten:

$$\lim_{m \to \infty} P_n = \lim P_0 \left(1 + \frac{1}{m/i}\right)^{m/i(in)} = P_0 e^{in} \tag{3.19}$$

The growth rate of earnings or dividends can be estimated either mathematically or statistically. Mathematically, the growth rate can be estimated by using either Equation (3.15) or (3.16). Rewriting Equation (3.15) using the symbol for growth rate, g, in place of i:

$$P_n = P_0 (1 + g)^n \tag{3.20}$$

From Equation (3.20), it is clear that:

$$(1 + g)^n = \frac{P_n}{P_0} \tag{3.21}$$

Given values for P_0, P_n, and n, and using a compound sum table, the value of g can easily be obtained. This approach is called the **compound-sum method** for estimating growth rates. While the advantage of this method is its simplicity, it ignores other information points between the first and last period.

Suppose there are two firms whose dividend payments patterns are as shown in Table 3–1. Using the compound-sum method the growth rate of firm ABC can be calculated:

$$(1 + g)^m = \frac{P_m}{P_0} = \frac{1.77}{1.00}$$

TABLE 3–1   Dividend Behavior of Firms ABC and XYZ in Dividends per Share (DPS, dollars)

Year	ABC	XYZ
1980	1.00	1.00
1981	1.00	1.10
1982	1.00	1.21
1983	1.00	1.33
1984	1.00	1.46
1985	1.00	1.61
1986	1.77	1.77

Using a compound-sum table where $n = 6$ and interest factor $= 1.77$, $g = 10$ percent. The compound-sum method also yields a growth rate of 10 percent for firm XYZ. Yet it becomes clear that the dividend behavior of these firms is distinctly different when looking at the dividends per share in Table 3–1.

Regression Method

To use all the information available to the security analysts, two regression equations can be employed. These equations can be derived from Equations (3.15) and (3.16) by letting $i = g$ and taking the logarithm (ln):

$$\ln P_n = \ln P_0 + n \ln (1 + g) \qquad \textbf{(3.22)}$$
$$\ln P_n = \ln P_0 + gn \qquad \textbf{(3.23)}$$

Both Equations (3.22) and (3.23) indicate that P_n is linearly related to n. Using the data in Table 3–1 for companies ABC and XYZ we can estimate the growth rates for their respective dividend streams. Graphs of the regression equations for ABC and XYZ are shown in Figure 3–2. The slope of the regression using Equation (3.23) for ABC shows an estimated value for

FIGURE 3–2   Regression Models for ABC and XYZ

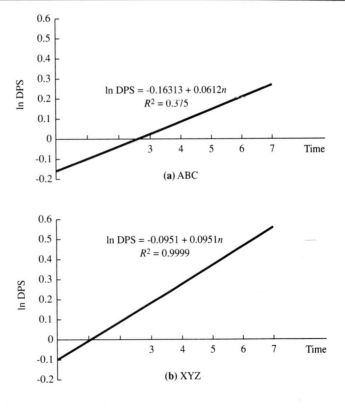

(a) ABC

(b) XYZ

growth of about 6 percent. The estimate for XYZ is 9.5 percent. If Equation (3.22) had been used to estimate the growth, then the antilog of the regression slope estimate would equal the growth rate.

One-Period Growth Model

Another method of estimating the growth rate involves the use of percentage change in some variable such as earnings per share, dividend per share, or price per share in a **one-period growth model.** The one-period growth model is the model in which the same growth will continue forever. If b stands for the fraction of earnings retained within the firm, r stands for the rate of return the firm will earn on all new investments, and I_t stands for investment at t, a very simple expression for growth is obtained. Growth in earnings arises from the return on new investments. Therefore, earnings can be written:

$$E_t = E_{t-1} + rI_{t-1} \qquad (3.24)$$

where:

$$E_t = \text{earnings in period } t; \text{ and}$$
$$E_{t-1} = \text{earnings in period } t-1.$$

If the firm's retention rate is constant, then:

$$E_t = E_{t-1} + rbE_{t-1} = E_{t-1}(1 + rb) \qquad (3.25)$$

Growth in earnings is the percentage change in earnings, or:

$$g = \frac{E_t - E_{t-1}}{E_{t-1}} = \frac{E_{t-1}(1 + rb) - E_{t-1}}{E_{t-1}} \qquad (3.26)$$
$$= rb$$

Since a constant proportion of earnings is assumed to be paid out each year, the growth in earnings equals the growth in dividends, or:

$$g_E = g_D = rb$$

If firm M has a retention rate of 50 percent and an average return on investment of 20 percent, then the expected growth in dividends on earnings can be expressed as:

$$g_E = g_0 = rb = (0.20)(0.50) = 0.1, \text{ or } 10\%$$

Using this expression for growth, Equation (3.13) can be rewritten:

$$P = \frac{D_1}{k - rb} \qquad (3.27)$$

Alternatively, this model can be stated in terms of the capitalization rate:

$$k = \frac{D_1}{P_0} + rb \qquad (3.28)$$

It is worthwhile to examine the implications of this model for the growth in stock prices over time. The growth in stock price is

$$g_p = \frac{P_{t+1} - P_t}{P_t} \qquad (3.29)$$

Recognizing that P_t and P_{t+1} can be defined by Equation (3.27), with the exception that D_{t+1} must be replaced by $D(1 + br)$:

$$g_p = br$$

Thus, under the assumption of a constant retention rate, for a one-period model, dividends, earnings, and prices are all expected to grow at the same rate.

Investors may use a one-period model in selecting stocks, but future profitability of investment opportunities plays an important role in determining the value of the firm and its EPS and DPS. The rate of return on new investments can be expressed as a fraction, c (perhaps larger than one), of the rate of return security holders require, or:

$$r = ck$$

Substituting this into Equation (3.28) and rearranging:

$$k = \frac{(1 - b)E}{(1 - cb)P_0} \qquad (3.30)$$

If a firm has no extraordinary investment opportunities ($r = k$), then $c = 1$ and the rate of return that security holders require is simply the inverse of the stock's price/earnings ratio. On the other hand, if the firm has investment opportunities that are expected to offer a return above that required by the firm's stockholders ($c > 1$), the earnings/price ratio at which the firm sells will be below the rate of return required by investors.

An investor could predict next year's dividends, the firm's long-term growth rate, and the rate of return stockholders require for holding the stock. Equation (3.13) could then be solved for the theoretical price of the stock that could be compared with its present price. Stocks that have theoretical prices above actual price are candidates for purchase; those with theoretical prices below their actual price are candidates for sale or for short sale. Sample Problem 3.2 provides further illustration of the one-period growth model.

Sample Problem 3.2

The use of the one-period model can be illustrated with a simple example using the Pennzoil data from the following table.

Selected Financial Data for Pennzoil Oil Company

Year	Time X_1	EPS X_2	DPS Price X_3	Price per Share X_4
1974	1	$3.47	$1.05	$16.07
1975	2	3.04	1.20	12.92
1976	3	4.32	1.31	22.17
1977	4	3.34	1.70	19.58
1978	5	3.74	2.00	20.50
1979	6	4.69	1.50	44.125
1980	7	5.90	2.00	50.375
1981	8	4.23	2.20	48.00
1982	9	3.60	2.20	35.125
1983	10	3.03	2.20	34.00
1984	11	2.23	2.20	44.50
1985	12	2.25	2.20	64.00
1986	13	2.08	2.20	66.00
Mean		$3.53	$1.843	$36.720
Standard Deviation		1.044	0.418	17.101
Coefficient of Variation		0.4657	0.295	0.227

Source: Moody's Industrial Manual, 1987.

Solution
At the end of 1986, Pennzoil's stock was selling for $66.00 a share. The capitalization rate can be calculated using Equation (3.28):

$$k = \frac{d_1}{P_0} + rb, \quad \text{or} \quad k = \frac{d_1}{P_0} + g$$

The current dividend yield is expressed:

$$\frac{d_1}{P_0} = \frac{\$2.20}{\$66.00} = 0.0333, \text{ or } 3.33\%$$

If Pennzoil's dividend is expected to grow at 10 percent per year:

$$k = 3.33 + 10.00$$
$$k = 13.33$$

Thus, the required rate of return as estimated is 13.33 percent.

Alternatively, Equation (3.27) could be used to estimate the theoretical value of Pennzoil Stock. If the dividend is expected to stay at $2.20, and $K = 13.33$, then estimates for the retention rate and the expected return for investments are required. For the sake of example, it is assumed that a retention rate of 50 percent and an expected return from investment of 18 percent yields a value of 9 percent for b times r. This gives an estimated value for the stock of:

$$P = \frac{d_1}{k - br} = \frac{2.20}{0.1333 - (0.5)(0.18)} = \$50.80$$

While Pennzoil stock would seem to be overvalued selling at $66.00 a share, notice the sensitivity of this valuation equation to both the estimate of the appropriate discount rate (required rate of return) and the estimate of the long-term growth rate. For example, if Pennzoil's required rate of return had been 12.33 percent rather than 13.33 percent, its theoretical price would have been $66.00●

It seems logical to assume that firms that have grown at a very high rate will not continue to do so into the infinite future. Likewise, firms with very poor growth might improve in the future. Although a single growth rate could be found, it is difficult to estimate this single number. In order to give greater flexibility to this technique many analysts have turned to multiple-period (two or three periods) growth-rate models. Each period has a specific growth rate associated with the firm's prospects in the short run and also the long run.

Two-Period Growth Model

The simplest extension of the one-period model is to assume that a period of extraordinary growth will continue for a certain number of years, after which growth will change to a level at which it is expected to continue indefinitely. This kind of model is called the **two-period growth model.**

If it is assumed that the length of the first period is n years, that the growth rate in the first period is g_1, and that P_n is the price at the end of period n, the value of the stock can be written:

$$P = \frac{d_1}{1 + k} + \frac{d_1(1 + g_1)}{(1 + k)^2} + \frac{d_1(1 + g_1)^2}{(1 + k)^3} + \cdots + \frac{d_1(1 + g_1)^{n-1}}{(1 + k)^n} + \frac{P_n}{(1 + k)^n}$$

where:

d_1 = the current dividend per share; and

g_i = the growth rate during period i.

Using the formula for the sum of geometric progression as defined as the

sum first term $[1 - $ (common ratio)$^n]/(1 - $ common ratio), where n is the number of terms summed over, the value of the stock can be written:

$$P_0 = d_1 \left(\frac{1 - \left(\frac{1 + g_1}{1 + k} \right)^n}{k - g_1} \right) + \frac{P_n}{(1 + k)^n} \qquad \textbf{(3.31)}$$

After n periods, it is assumed that the firm exhibits a constant growth forever. If g_2 is the growth in the second period and d_{n+1} is the dividend in the $n + 1$ period:

$$P_n = \frac{d_{n+1}}{k - g_2}$$

The dividend in the $n + 1$ period can be expressed in terms of the dividend in the first period:

$$d_{n+1} = d_1(1 + g_1)^n (1 + g_2)$$

Making substitutions for P_n and d_{n+1} the two-period model becomes:

$$P_0 = d_1 \left(\frac{1 - \left(\frac{(1 + g_1)^n}{(1 + k)^n} \right)}{k - g_1} \right) + \frac{d_1}{(k - g_2)} \left(\frac{1 + g_1}{1 + k} \right)^n (1 + g_2) \qquad \textbf{(3.32)}$$

This formula can easily be solved for the theoretical price of any stock. For example, Firm OPQ pays a dividend of $1.00 per share which is expected to grow at 10 percent for five years and 5 percent thereafter. The investors in OPQ require a rate of return of 15 percent. The current price of OPQ stocks using Equation (3.32) should be

$$P = 1.00 \left(\frac{1 - \frac{(1 + 0.10)^5}{(1.15)^5}}{0.15 - 0.10} \right) + \frac{1.00}{0.15 - 0.05} \left(\frac{1 + 0.10}{1 + 0.15} \right)^5 (1 + 0.05)$$

$$= 3.985 + 8.405$$

$$= \$12.39$$

Three-Period Growth Model

A logical extension of the two-period model is the **three-period growth model.** The three-period growth model implies that there exist three different growth rates for the whole growth valuation process. The resultant model would assume that in the first period growth is expected to be constant at some level. A forecast must be made of both the level of growth and the duration of period one. During period two the growth changes from its value in period one to a different level. Both the duration and the pattern of change of growth in period two must be forecast. The third and final period is the period of steady-state growth.

Look at Firm OPQ again. If, instead of forecasting a growth rate of 5 percent during the second period, the three-period model is used to forecast

at a 7 percent growth rate during the sixth through tenth years and at a 5 percent growth rate from the eleventh year thereafter, the price of OPQ stock can be calculated using Equation (3.32).

$$P = d_1 \left(\frac{1 - \dfrac{(1 + g_1)^n}{(1 + k)^n}}{k - g_1} \right) + d_1 (1 + g_1)^n (1 + g_2) \left(\frac{1 - \dfrac{(1 + g_2)^{M-n}}{(1 + k)^{M-n}}}{k - g_2} \right)$$

$$+ \frac{D(1 + g_1)^n (1 + g_2)^{M-n} (1 + g_3)}{(1 + k)^M (k - g_3)} \quad \text{(3.32A)}$$

where M is the end of the second period and other terms are defined as before.

$$P = 1.00 \left(\frac{1 - \dfrac{(1.10)^5}{(1.15)^5}}{0.15 - 0.10} \right) + 1.00(1.10)^5(1.07) \left(\frac{1 - \dfrac{(1.07)^5}{(1.15)^5}}{0.15 - 0.07} \right)$$

$$+ \frac{1.00(1.1)^5 (1.07)^5 (1.05)}{(1.15)^{10} (0.15 - 0.05)}$$

$$= 3.985 + 6.520 + 5.862$$

$$= \$16.05$$

The additional information about the three periods of OPQ's growth yields a different answer for the theoretical market price of the shares. Since the firm experiences five years of growth at 7 percent during the second period, which is larger than the 5 percent growth assumed in the two-period model, the market price per share is $3.66 per share higher when we use the three-period model.

In Sample Problem 3.3, a set of actual data is employed to show how these concepts can be used to help security analysts and portfolio managers analyze the expected value of a firm.

Sample Problem 3.3

To demonstrate how the concepts of growth rate and stock-valuation model discussed in the previous sections can be used to analyze securities, the per-share values for price, earnings, and dividends of Pennzoil Oil Company during 1974–1986 are used. (See the table in Sample Problem 3.2.) The mean and the standard deviations of the EPS are higher than the mean and standard deviation of the DPS. As expected, on average Pennzoil earns more per share in earnings than they pay out in dividends; nevertheless, the variability of the earning stream is greater than the variability of the dividend stream. In comparing the dispersion of two different series there generally is a problem with simply comparing the magnitude of the respective standard deviations. The standard deviation is an absolute measure of dispersion and as such is influenced by the size of the numbers in the series. To compare the dispersion of two series, the **coefficient of variation (CV),** is usually employed. The CV is defined as the standard deviation (SD) divided by the

TABLE 3–2A   Covariance Matrix

Variable		Time 1	EPS 2	DPS 3	PPS 4	ln EPS 5	ln DPS 6	ln PPS 7
Time	1	14.00	−0.5348	1.4250	49.148	−0.2402	0.8635	1.5744
EPS	2		1.0903	−0.0212	7.291	0.3066	−0.0032	0.2031
DPS	3			0.1752	4.722	−0.0127	0.1069	0.1535
PPS	4				292.4578	1.5915	2.9146	8.7230
ln EPS	5					0.0888	−0.0050	0.0403
ln DPS	6						0.0658	0.0949
ln PPS	7							0.2667

expected return (ER). The larger the CV, the greater the dispersion relative to the mean. In this case the EPS still has a greater dispersion than the dividend series.

The expected value per share for Pennzoil Oil is determined using the Gordon model as expressed in Equation (3.13). To use this valuation approach, it is necessary to estimate the dividends per share in the next period, the capitalization rate, and the growth rate of dividends per share. The capitalization rate can be estimated by the earnings yield method, the weighted cost of capital method, or the capital asset pricing model (CAPM) method (discussed in Chapter 9). The following numerical example uses a required return of 16 percent for Pennzoil and the compound-sum method of computing dividends per share growth rate. (Use of Equation (3.21) yields a growth rate of 13 percent.) Substituting these values into Equation (3.13) yields:

$$P_0 = \frac{2.20}{0.16 - 0.13} = \$73.33$$

This theoretical value is a higher value than the average price for the period (\$36.72) and the current price (\$66.00). The primary problems associated with this stock-valuation approach involve the adequacy of using averages of past data to estimate the future and using the compound-sum method to estimate the growth rate. In this example, the compound-sum growth method ignores the fact that the dividends per share remained constant for six of the thirteen years●

The data from the table in Sample Problem 3.2 can be used to show how the growth rates of dividends and earnings per share can be estimated by the regression method. To estimate the related regression parameters and to provide a base for discussion of other implications, covariances and correlation coefficients for time, EPS, DPS, PPS, ln EPS, ln DPS, and ln PPS are presented in Tables 3–2A and 3–2B. The covariance matrix in Table 3–2A

TABLE 3-2B   Correlation Matrix

Variable		Time 1	EPS 2	DPS 3	PPS 4	ln EPS 5	ln DPS 6	ln PPS 7
Time	1	1.0000	−0.1369	0.9099	0.7681	−0.2154	0.8997	0.8148
EPS	2		1.0000	−0.0487	0.4083	0.9858	−0.0122	0.3766
DPS	3			1.0000	0.6597	−0.1022	0.9960	0.7103
PPS	4				1.0000	0.3123	0.6644	0.9877
ln EPS	5					1.0000	−0.0657	0.2902
ln DPS	6						1.0000	0.7168
ln PPS	7							1.0000

presents variances (elements on the diagonal) and covariances (elements off the diagonal). The correlation matrix in Table 3-2B presents correlation coefficients.

Conceptually, both the covariance and the correlation coefficient can be used to measure the extent to which two variables move together. The correlation coefficient is most commonly used because it is a standardized unit-free measure. Correlation coefficients range from −1.0 (perfect negative correlation) to +1.0 (perfect positive correlation). The concepts introduced here will be useful in understanding the diversification process discussed later in this book.

Some implications can be drawn from the sign and the magnitude of the correlation coefficients in Table 3-2B. The correlation coefficient between time and price per share (row 1, column 4) is 0.7681, indicating that the price has increased over time. The coefficient between time and dividends per share (row 1, column 3) is 0.9099, implying that dividends were generally increasing over time. The coefficient of correlation between time and earnings per share (row 1, column 2), −0.1369, is so close to zero that it essentially implies random fluctuations in earnings over time.

Following the format of Equations (3.22) and (3.23), the models for regressing X_5 and X_6 on X_1 can be defined:

$$X_5 = a_0 + a_1 X_1 + e_5 \tag{3.33}$$
$$X_6 = b_0 + b_1 X_1 + e_6 \tag{3.34}$$

where:

a_0, a_1 and b_0, b_1 = regression parameters; and
e_5 and e_6 = error terms.

The formulas necessary to estimate the slopes a_1 and b_1 are represented by:

$$a_1 = \text{Cov}\,(X_1, X_5)/\text{Var}(X_1) \tag{3.35}$$
$$b_1 = \text{Cov}\,(X_1, X_6)/\text{Var}(X_1) \tag{3.36}$$

Based on the information listed in Table 3–2A, the estimated slopes are

$$a_1 = \frac{-0.2402}{14.00} = -0.0171 \qquad (t = 0.6616)$$

$$b_1 = \frac{0.8635}{14.00} = 0.0617 \qquad (t = 6.1839)$$

The estimated Student's t-statistic, shown in parentheses, is used to show whether the regression estimate is significantly different from zero. Given values of the regression estimate and the degrees of freedom, we see that a_1 is not significantly different from zero and that b_1 is statistically significant. This verifies the aforementioned implications, which were drawn from the correlation matrix—that is, the growth rate of earnings per share as estimated by a_1 is essentially zero (-1.71 percent) and the growth rate of dividends per share as estimated by b_1 is positive at 6.17 percent.

Use of the regression-generated growth rate for dividends per share of 6.17 percent in the valuation equation yields:

$$P_0 = \frac{\$2.20}{0.16 - 0.0617} = \$22.38$$

which is closer to the average price for the period ($36.72) than the 1986 price of $66.00 per share. Thus, use of the regression method in this case is not as useful as the compound-sum method in valuing the shares of Pennzoil.

RISK

Up to this point the discussion has centered only on various measures of return. Whenever return is considered, risk must be considered as well. In this section various types of risk are defined and the various quantitative measures of risk are presented.

Definitions of Risk

In general, **risk** can be defined as the probability of success or failure. More specifically, any investment that has more than one possible return for a given holding period is defined as risky. As long as expectation of return cannot be guaranteed, the investor is facing risk. By this definition every asset possesses some degree of risk; even Treasury bills (T-bills) involve some risk with respect to the real rate of return. Unless the nominal rate of discount on the T-bill is exactly equal to the normal expected return of investors, investors in T-bills are facing risk. This is so because realized inflation may be different from expected inflation.

All investments involve some degree of risk, and there are large differences between the risks of various financial instruments. For example,

T-bills have a different degree of risk than stocks or options. In order to discuss the relative as well as the absolute degree of the risk of various financial instruments, quantitative measures of risk are needed. Consistent with the definition of risk, such measures should provide a summary of the degree to which realized return is different from expected return. That is to say, such measures give an indication of the dispersion of the possible returns.

If the distribution of returns is symmetrical, two meaningful measures of dispersion are available: the **variance** and the **standard deviation.** The variance is equal to the average of the squared deviations from the mean of the distribution. It is generally denoted by the symbol σ^2 and is defined:

$$\sigma^2 = \sum_i^n (\overline{X} - X_i)^2 P_r(x_i) \tag{3.37}$$

or

$$= E(X^2) - [E(X)]^2$$

where:

$$\overline{X} = \text{the mean of the distribution and } \overline{X} = E(X);$$
$$X_i = \text{the } i\text{th observation of return;}$$
$$P_r(x_i) = \text{the probability that } x_i \text{ will be realized;}$$
$$E(X^2) = \text{the expectation of the return squared; and}$$
$$[E(X)]^2 = \text{the square of the mean return.}$$

To obtain the standard deviation, σ, merely take the square root of the variance. So long as the distribution of returns is symmetrical with a finite variance and an investor's risk aversion can be approximated by an appropriate utility function, the variance or the standard deviation is a useful measure of risk.

The calculations of variance and standard deviation of returns for Company A and Company B are illustrated in Table 3-3. As shown in Table 3-3, security B is riskier than security A because the dispersion of possible outcomes for B is larger than for A. When the variance or standard deviations are employed to measure risk for individual securities, it is assumed that the securities are not being held in a portfolio.

Sources of Risk

Sources of risk are important for understanding the degree of fluctuation for an investment over time. Sources of risk can be from firm-specific factors or market and economic factors.

Firm-Specific Factors.   The total risk of a firm's security can be divided into two categories: (1) those that relate to the issuer of the security and (2) those that relate to all securities. The types of risk that are issuer specific are called **business risk** and **financial risk.** Business risk relates to the fluctua-

TABLE 3-3 Calculation of Variance and Standard Deviation of Returns

Returns x_i	Probability of x_i	$(x_i - \bar{x})^2$	$(x_i - \bar{x})^2 P_r x_i$
Company A			
0.10	0.10	0.0004	0.00004
0.11	0.20	0.0001	0.00002
0.12	0.40	0.0	0.0
0.13	0.20	0.0001	0.00002
0.14	0.10	0.0004	0.00004
			$\sigma^2 = 0.00012$
$\overline{X}_A = 12\%$			$\sigma = 0.0109$
Company B			
-0.10	0.20	0.0264	0.052812
0.05	0.30	0.00016	0.000048
0.10	0.30	0.0014	0.000421
0.20	0.20	0.0189	0.003781
			$\sigma^2 = 0.057062$
$\overline{X}_B = 6.5\%$			$\sigma = 0.2388$

tions in the growth of the operating cash flows of the issuers. Financial risk is related to the mix of debt and equity in the capital structure of the issuer.

For a corporate issuer of securities, business risk is determined by the fluctuations of prices of its products, demand for its products, the costs of production, and technological change and managerial efficiency. Securities of firms in different industries have different dispersions of returns because of these factors; for example, a utility has quite constant returns while an automobile firm has more variable returns.

The second factor that affects the variability of return from investment in corporate securities is the financial structure of the issuer. The assets of a firm can be financed by either debt or equity. The use of debt promises the investor a fixed return, and the equity holder's return is leveraged or the fluctuation of return magnified. For investors in both debt and equity, the greater the amount of debt in the firm's capital structure, the greater is the variance of returns.

Market and Economic Factors.   As has been noted, the return on investment is made up of the cash flow from interest or dividends and the future price of the security. The price that is realized when the security matures or is sold may be fixed or variable. Additionally, if the security is sold before it matures, the future price is uncertain. Hence the variance of return (risk) is significantly related to the degree of price volatility over time. Prices of

financial instruments vary as the general rates of interest change. There is an inverse relationship between interest rates and the price of securities—that is, when interest rates go up the price of a security falls. Decreases in interest rates, on the other hand, cause the price to rise.

The impact of the changes in interest rates on the rate of return of government bonds is a good example of how interest rates can affect the return of investors. Government bonds are not subject to business or financial risk, but the rate of return realized by investors depends upon the movements in interest rates. As will be shown in Chapter 5, the relationship between movements in the interest rate and the prices of securities depends upon such factors as the maturity of the security, the timing and size of the cash flows, and the rate of reinvestment available to the investor.

Actual rates of inflation are rarely equal to the rates of inflation expected by investors. The difference adds another element of uncertainty to the variability of returns. Investors in a bond expect to receive a stream of promised nominal cash flows in the future. If the level of prices changes differently from what investors expect, then their realized real rate of return will differ from what they expected at the time of investment. If the price level increases to a greater degree than what investors expect, their realized return will be smaller; and if prices don't increase as rapidly as investors expect, their realized return will be greater than they anticipated. For investors in equities, as the level of inflation increases the amount of uncertainty with respect to how inflation will help or harm the economy, industries, companies, and financial markets increases; and this increase in uncertainty has an adverse affect on the rates of return realized by investors. Hence, not only does inflation affect risk but the level of inflation is an important variable as well. High levels of inflation present an opportunity for greater variability and uncertainty, therefore adversely affecting security returns; while low levels of inflation reduce uncertainty about future price-level changes, thus favorably affecting security prices.

COVARIANCE AND CORRELATION

The **covariance** is a measure of how returns on assets move together. If the time series of returns are moving in the same direction, the covariance is positive. If one series is increasing and the other is decreasing, the covariance is negative. If series move in an unrelated fashion relative to one another, the covariance is a small number or zero.

If we divide the covariance between the return series of two assets by the product of the standard deviations of the two series, we have the correlation coefficient between the two series. Basically it is similar to a covariance that has been standardized by the variability of each series. Its range of values

falls between $+1$ (perfectly positively correlated) and -1 (perfectly negatively correlated).

The formulas for the covariance and the correlation coefficient are shown in Equations (3.38) and (3.39).

$$\text{Cov } (XY) = \sigma_X \sigma_Y \, \rho_{XY} = \frac{\sum_{i=1}^{n} (X_i - \overline{X}_i)(Y_i - \overline{Y}_i)}{n} \qquad (3.38)$$

where:

ρ_{XY} = the correlation coefficient between series X and Y; and
$\overline{X}_i$ and $\overline{Y}_i$ = the means of the X and Y series, respectively.

Based upon the definition of covariance, ρ_{XY} can be defined:

$$\rho_{XY} = \frac{\text{Cov } (XY)}{\sigma_X \sigma_Y} \qquad (3.39)$$

In Table 3–4 the covariance and the correlation of security returns are calculated. From Table 3–4 we can see that the returns of securities A and B are slightly negatively correlated, and the covariance of X and Y is a small negative number. As will be seen in Chapter 7, these may be good securities to hold together in a portfolio because of the lack of correlation between their returns.

TABLE 3–4 Covariance and Correlation of Security Returns

Company X		Company Y						
Time Period	Return	Time Period	Return	$(X - \overline{X})$	$(Y - \overline{Y})$	$(X - \overline{X})(Y - \overline{Y})$	$(X - \overline{X})^2$	$(Y - \overline{Y})^2$
1	0.10	1	−0.10	0.05	−0.09	−0.0045	0.0025	0.0081
2	−0.05	2	0.05	−0.1	0.06	−0.006	0.01	0.0036
3	0.15	3	0.0	0.1	0.01	0.001	0.01	0.0001
4	0.05	4	−0.10	0.00	−0.09	0.0	0.0	0.0081
5	0.0	5	0.10	−0.05	−0.04	0.002	0.0025	0.0016
Mean =	0.05	Mean =	−0.01			−0.0075	0.0250	0.0215

$\sigma_x^2 = 0.025/5 \quad = \quad 0.005$

$N = 5$ $\qquad\qquad\qquad\qquad\qquad \sigma_x = 0.0707$

$\sigma_y^2 = 0.0215/5 \quad = \quad 0.0043$

$\sigma_y = 0.0656$

$$\text{Cov } (XY) = \frac{-0.0075}{5} = -0.0015 \qquad \text{Correlation coefficient } \rho_{XY} = \frac{-0.0015}{(0.0707)(0.0656)} = -0.3234$$

SYSTEMATIC AND UNSYSTEMATIC RISK
AND THE MARKET MODEL

In the discussion of the sources of risk, we identified sources of risk that originated from the issuer of the security and sources of risk that affected securities in general. In these sections this distinction is developed further in the context of the market model. The issuer-specific risk is called **unsystematic risk,** because it is unique to each issuer of securities and does not affect all financial securities. The market-related risk affecting all securities is called the **systematic risk.**

In order to analyze or measure the degree of systematic and unsystematic risk that a security contains, a model of the return-generating process must be identified. A widely accepted model to achieve this is called the **market model** and is shown by Equation (3.40):

$$\tilde{R}_{it} = \alpha_i + \beta_i \tilde{R}_{mt} + \tilde{e}_{it} \tag{3.40}$$

where:

$\tilde{R}_{it}$ = return on the ith security during time t;
α_i = the intercept of the regression model;
β_i = a measure of systematic risk of the ith security;
$\tilde{R}_m$ = the random return on the market index in period t; and
$\tilde{e}_{it}$ = the measure of unsystematic risk of security i.

In general Equation (3.40) identifies a linear relationship between the return on the market (R_m) and the return on an individual security (R_i). (A more complete discussion of the market model is presented later in this text.)

In addition to the return on a security, investors are also interested in its risk or variability. Using Equation (3.40), the market model, it is possible to identify the components of risk for an individual stock in terms of the variance of return for the stock i. This is shown in Equation (3.41):

$$\sigma^2(\tilde{R}_i) = \beta_i \sigma^2(\tilde{R}_m) + \sigma^2(\tilde{e}_i) \tag{3.41}$$

where:

$\sigma^2(\tilde{R}_m)$ = the degree of systematic risk; and
$\sigma^2(\tilde{e}_i)$ = the degree of unsystematic risk contained in the total risk of security i, $\sigma^2(\tilde{R}_i)$.

The size of β_i in general depends on how closely the movements of the individual security returns are correlated with the movements of the market index. Using the definitions of the slope coefficient of a regression equation as discussed in Chapter 1:

$$\beta_i = \frac{\text{Cov}(\tilde{R}_i, \tilde{R}_m)}{\sigma^2(\tilde{R}_m)} = \frac{E(\tilde{R}_i, \tilde{R}_m) - E(\tilde{R}_i)E(\tilde{R}_m)}{\sigma^2(\tilde{R}_m)} \tag{3.42}$$

As has been seen before, the covariance between two variables is equal to the respective standard deviations times the correlation coefficient, the β_i in Equation (3.42) can therefore be restated in terms of the correlation coefficient, as shown in Equation (3.43):

$$\beta_i = \frac{\sigma(\tilde{R}_i)\sigma(\tilde{R}_m)\ \rho_{im}}{\sigma^2(\tilde{R}_m)} = \sigma(\tilde{R}_i)\ \frac{\rho_{im}}{\sigma(\tilde{R}_m)} \tag{3.43}$$

In general, the measure of systematic risk of a security is a function of the variability of return of both the security and the market, $\sigma(R_i)$ and $\sigma(R_m)$, and the correlation between the movement of returns of the security and the market ρ_{im}.

The systematic risks of various securities differ due to their relationships with the market; hence, ranking securities by their correlation coefficient is equivalent to ranking them by their systematic risks. Securities with large βs are high-risk securities. Securities with β equal to one imply that the risk characteristics of these securities are identical with that market. Securities with low betas are defensive securities, and their returns are less volatile than the market.

A firm's beta can be estimated by regression analysis. This approach assumes that the past relationship between a stock's return and market return will continue into the future. Ordinary least-squares regression is used to identify the historical relationship.

The use of regression analysis to determine the firm's beta requires the selection of an appropriate index of market returns. In Chapter 6 a discussion of the various indexes will be presented; as will be seen, the theory of portfolio construction and capital asset pricing requires that the appropriate market index be a value weighted portfolio of all the risky assets. It is difficult to find such an index, so various proxies are often used, such as the Dow Jones Industrial Average (DJIA), Standard and Poor's 500 (S&P 500), the New York Stock Exchange Composite, the Fisher Index, and so on. Once a suitable index has been selected, the next decision involves the time period over which the returns data should be collected.

The basic problem centers around the tradeoff of using a large volume of data for long periods versus using only current relevant data. For statistical reasons, the greater the number of observations the better the forecasting properties. However, the more current the data, the more relevant it is to the future because conditions may have changed in the market, making data from the distant past relatively useless. As a general rule, five years of monthly data seems to be used quite frequently as a balance between relevance and having a large enough number of observations.

The next step is to calculate the rate of return for the individual security and the market index. In general, it is best to use the holding-period yield as calculated by Equation (3.3).

$$\text{HPY} = \ln\left(\frac{P_t + C_t}{P_{t-1}}\right) \tag{3.3}$$

After the index, time-period, and holding-period yields have been calculated, the next step is to run the ordinary least-squares regression of

$$\ln\left(\frac{P_t + C_t}{P_{t-1}}\right) = \alpha + \beta \ln\left(\frac{I_t + C_t}{I_{t-1}}\right) \tag{3.44}$$

in which I_t is the index value and the other variables are as previously defined.

A final variable of interest is the R^2 or coefficient of determination. This variable measures the fraction of variability of the dependent variable that is explained by the influence of the independent variable. The closer the R^2 is to 1.0, the higher the percentage of the variability in the security's return than is explained by movements in the return on the market portfolio. The R^2 provides a measure of a stock's unsystematic risk. Stocks with a large R^2 have low unsystematic risk, while if the R^2 is close to zero, the unsystematic risk of the security is large. Sample Problem 3.4 provides further illustration.

Sample Problem 3.4

Using a Lotus program the market model is run on returns for Abbott Labs, IBM, and the Fisher Index. The data and results of this analysis are shown in the table on page 66.

The table that follows shows the estimates of systematic risk (β) and R^2 (adjusted coefficient of determination) for Abbott Labs and IBM.

Abbott	IBM
β = 0.91	β = 0.76
R^2 = 0.322	R^2 = 0.317

The security returns of Abbott move very closely with the market while IBM is somewhat less. About 68 percent of the total risk of both Abbott and IBM is embodied in unsystematic risk. This can be seen by looking at the R^2 statistic. Since both regressions have R^2 of approximately 0.32, systematic risk makes up about 32 percent of the total risk. The remaining risk, $1 - R^2$, is the unsystematic risk●

There are differences in the methods of calculating returns—using different indexes; using different holding periods (daily, weekly, monthly); and using different time periods. This causes estimates of systematic and unsystematic risk to vary from one analyst to another for a given security; hence, care should be taken in using the beta estimate for forecasting security returns. A good knowledge of the various variables used is necessary in order to ensure a reasonable forecast.

The Market Model for Sample Problem 3.4: $\ln(1 + R_i) = \ln(1 + R_m) + e_i$

Date	Fisher Market Index	Abbott Labs	IBM	Date	Fisher Market Index	Abbott Labs	IBM
810130	−0.0434	−0.0212	−0.0516	830729	−0.0301	0.0156	0.0010
810227	0.0182	0.0886	0.0114	830831	0.0117	−0.0334	0.0006
810331	0.0437	0.0021	−0.0292	830930	0.0191	0.0293	0.0617
810430	−0.0142	−0.0315	−0.0601	831031	−0.0179	0.0517	−0.0010
810529	0.0104	−0.0346	0.0168	831130	0.0257	−0.1136	−0.0665
810630	−0.0099	0.1300	−0.0149	831230	−0.0060	0.0084	0.0394
810731	0.0008	−0.1133	−0.0302	840131	−0.0074	−0.0304	−0.0646
810831	−0.0553	−0.0586	−0.0025	840229	−0.0362	−0.0315	−0.0256
810930	−0.0578	−0.0048	−0.0181	840330	0.0184	−0.0266	0.0340
811030	0.0580	0.0887	−0.0485	840430	0.0045	0.0833	−0.0022
811130	0.0455	0.0533	0.0750	840531	−0.0534	−0.1073	−0.0444
811231	−0.0274	−0.0886	0.0436	840629	0.0220	0.1044	−0.0186
820129	−0.0213	0.0807	0.1187	840731	−0.0184	0.0040	0.0473
820226	−0.0509	−0.0086	−0.0140	840831	0.1119	0.0862	0.1273
820331	−0.0097	0.0087	−0.0343	840928	0.0026	−0.1191	0.0040
820430	0.0425	0.0590	0.0753	841031	0.0017	−0.0048	0.0119
820528	−0.0287	−0.0533	−0.0294	841130	−0.0104	0.0030	−0.0231
820630	−0.0204	−0.0087	−0.0142	841231	0.0243	0.0121	0.0113
820730	−0.0211	0.0597	0.0825	850131	0.0788	0.1389	0.1076
820831	0.1237	0.1618	0.0874	850228	0.0150	0.0132	−0.0094
820930	0.0119	−0.0036	0.0408	850329	0.0023	0.1071	−0.0522
821029	0.1148	0.0741	0.0886	850430	−0.0029	−0.0311	−0.0039
821130	0.0490	0.0269	0.0937	850531	0.0558	0.0613	0.0255
821231	0.0167	0.0131	0.1127	850628	0.0178	0.0601	−0.0379
830131	0.0345	0.0474	0.0273	850731	−0.0020	−0.0266	0.0616
830228	0.0274	−0.0062	0.0100	850830	−0.0035	0.0428	−0.0278
830331	0.0345	0.0717	0.0278	850930	−0.0357	−0.0194	−0.0217
830429	0.0727	0.0872	0.1499	851031	0.0461	0.0326	0.0484
830531	0.0041	−0.0672	−0.0410	851129	0.0685	0.0687	0.0845
830630	0.0394	0.1095	0.0809	851231	0.0455	0.0984	0.1127

Abbott Regression Output		*IBM Regression Output*	
Constant	0.007812	Constant	0.009546
Standard error of Y estimate	0.054103	Standard error of Y estimate	0.045821
R^2	0.322663	R^2	0.317598
Number of observations	60	Number of observations	60
Degrees of freedom	58	Degrees of freedom	58
X coefficient(s)	0.912546	X coefficient(s)	0.763906
Standard error of coefficient	0.173607	Standard error of coefficient	0.147030

Source: Data from *Moody's Industrial Manual*, 1987.

SUMMARY

This chapter has examined return, growth, and risk for common-stock variation. First discussed were three alternative means—arithmetic, geometric, and weighted unbiased means—used to calculate the holding-period return and holding-period yield. An analysis was then presented of two alternative methods—compound-sum and regression methods—used to calculate the growth rate of EPS and DPS. Finally, sources of risk were qualitatively identified and quantitatively analyzed. An understanding of these concepts is crucial, for this information and these techniques are essential to accurate security analysis and successful portfolio management.

QUESTIONS AND PROBLEMS

1. What is the relationship between HPR and HPY?
2. Suppose you purchased XYZ Corporation's stock last year at a price of $100, and you sold it this year for $107 after receiving a $5 dividend. Calculate your holding-period return and your holding-period yield.
3. Use the data given in Sample Problem 3.1 to calculate the HPR and HPY if you purchased Pennzoil stock in 1980 and sold it in 1986.
4. How does the normal distribution differ from the log normal distribution? Is there any reason why one distribution is preferred?
5. What is the relationship between discrete HPY and the continuous HPY?
6. What is the arithmetic mean? What is the geometric mean? What are the advantages and disadvantages of each?
7. What is the weighted unbiased mean? When does it approach the arithmetic mean? the geometric mean?
8. Use the data given in Sample Problem 3.1 to calculate the weighted unbiased mean for Pennzoil's holding-period return. Assume the number of investment horizon periods is six and that you will be using the HPR for 1980–86 in your estimate.
9. What is risk? How is it measured? What are the components of risk?
10. What is systematic risk? What is unsystematic risk? What is the significance of these two types of risk?
11. You are given the security-return information about two companies as shown in the table at the top of page 68.
    (a) Find the covariance and correlation between the returns for companies A and B.
    (b) Explain why correlation and covariance are important in portfolio management.

Time Period	Return A	Return B
1	0.10	0.09
2	0.08	0.10
3	0.07	0.09
4	0.05	0.12

12. Evaluate the following statement: "Because investors dislike risk (as measured by the standard deviation) they require a higher rate of return for holding stocks that have a higher standard deviation of their returns."

13. What is the market model? What is beta? Why is beta important to portfolio management? How can we estimate beta?

14. What is regression analysis? Why is it an important tool for portfolio managers?

15. Use the data given in Problem 9 of Chapter 2 to forecast sales using regression analysis. Use a nonlinear trend model and a sales growth model.

16. You are given the following information about XYZ Company's stock.

Return on XYZ's Stock (percent)

1980	8.0
1981	10.0
1982	−4.0
1983	5.3
1984	12.2
1985	14.3
1986	−10.2
1987	19.3
1988	16.4

(a) Calculate the arithmetic mean for the company's returns.
(b) Calculate the geometric mean for the company's returns.
(c) Why do the answers in (a) and (b) differ?

APPENDIX 3A: LOGARITHMS AND THEIR PROPERTIES

Logarithms were originally developed to simplify computations. Today calculators and computers make this use of logarithms obsolete; nevertheless, they still have useful properties for application in rate of return estimation.

If *M* and *N* are positive numbers and *b* is a positive number that is a base, then:

$$M = b^x \qquad N = b^y, \quad \text{and} \quad MN = b^{x+y}$$

From these relations we have:

$$\log_b M = x \qquad \log_b N = y, \quad \text{and} \quad \log_b MN = x + y$$

Using these relations, some useful properties can be discussed.

1. The logarithm of a product is the sum of the logarithms of the components:

$$\log_b (MN) = \log_b M + \log_b N$$

2. Since

$$\frac{M}{N} = \frac{b^x}{b^y} = b^{x-y}$$

$$\log_b (M/N) = x - y$$
$$= \log_b M - \log_b n$$

The logarithm of a quotient is the logarithm of the numerator minus the logarithm of the denominator.

3. Since

$$M^r = b^{xr}$$
$$\log_b M^r = xr$$
$$= r \log_b M$$

The logarithm of a number raised to a power equals the power times the logarithm of the number.

The natural logarithm is in terms of the base e, where e is a number equal to 2.71828. As it turns out, the limit of $(1 + 1/n)^n = e$ as n approaches infinity. This is important in finance because the compounding term used is of the form in the parentheses. The symbol ln is used to represent natural logarithms instead of $\log_e$.

APPENDIX 3B: ln X_2, ln X_3, AND ln X_4 AND THEIR ESTIMATES

Information listed in the tables on page 70 can be used to calculate (1) total variance, (2) explained variance, and (3) unexplained variance and coefficient of determination. Explicit definitions of these formulas can be found in Chapter 3.

ln X_2 t	Actual	Estimated	Residual
1	2.7770	2.7609	0.0161
2	2.5588	2.8794	−0.3206
3	3.0987	1.3501	0.1131
4	1.2060	1.3333	−0.1273
5	1.3191	1.3166	0.0025
6	1.5454	1.2998	0.2456
7	1.7749	1.2831	0.4198
8	1.4422	1.2664	0.1758
9	1.2809	1.2496	0.3133
10	1.1806	1.2328	−0.1242
11	0.8020	1.2161	−0.4141

ln X_3 t	Actual	Estimated	Residual
1	0.0488	0.1709	−0.1221
2	0.1823	0.2454	−0.0631
3	0.2700	0.3199	−0.0499
4	0.5306	0.3944	0.1362
5	0.6931	0.4689	0.2242
6	0.4055	0.5434	−0.1379
7	0.6391	0.6178	0.0753
8	0.7885	0.6924	0.0961
9	0.7885	0.7669	0.0216
10	0.7885	0.8414	−0.0529
11	0.7885	0.9158	−0.1273

ln X_4 t	Actual	Estimated	Residual
1	2.7770	2.7609	0.0161
2	2.5588	2.8794	−0.3206
3	3.0987	2.9779	0.1008
4	2.9745	3.1164	−0.1419
5	3.0204	3.2349	−0.2145
6	3.7870	3.3534	0.4336
7	3.9194	3.4719	0.4475
8	3.8712	3.5905	0.2807
9	3.5589	3.7090	−0.1501
10	3.5264	3.8274	−0.3011
11	3.7955	3.9460	−0.1505

REFERENCES

Blume, Marshall E. "Unbiased Estimators of Long-Run Expected Rates of Return." *Journal of the American Statistical Association,* v. 69 (September 1974), pp. 634–38.

―――――, and I. Friend. "Risk, Investment Strategy and the Long-Run Rates of Return." *The Review of Economics and Statistics,* v. 56 (August 1974), pp. 259–69.

Cheng, P. L., and M. K. Deets. "Statistical Biases and Security Rates of Return." *Journal of Financial and Quantitative Analysis,* v. 6 (June 1971), pp. 977–94.

Elton, Edwain J., and Martin J. Gruber. "Portfolio Theory When Investment Relatives Are Lognormally Distributed." *Journal of Finance,* v. 29 (September 1974), pp. 1265–73.

Fama, Eugene F. "The Behavior of Stock Market Prices." *Journal of Business,* v. 38 (January 1965), pp. 34–105.

Latane, Henry A., Donald L. Tuttle, and Charles P. Jones. *Security Analysis and Portfolio Management,* 2nd ed. Ronald Press, 1975.

Lee, Cheng F. *Financial Analysis and Planning: Theory and Application.* Addison-Wesley Publishing Company, 1985.

Levy, Robert. "Measurement of Investment Performance." *Journal of Financial and Quantitative Analysis,* v. 3 (March 1968), pp. 35–57.

Long, Susan W. "Risk-Premium Curve vs. Capital Market Line: Differences Explained." *Financial Management* (Spring 1978), pp. 60–64.

Pratt, Shannon R. "Relationship Between Variability of Past Return and Levels of Future Returns for Common Stocks, 1920-60." In E. Bruce Frederickson, *Frontiers of Investment Analysis,* 2nd ed. International Textbook Co., 1971, pp. 338–53.

Reilly, Frank K. *Investment Analysis and Portfolio Management,* 2nd ed. The Dryden Press, 1985.

Rogalski, R. J., and S. M. Tinic. "Risk-Premium Curve vs. Capital Market Line: A Re-Examination." *Financial Management* (Spring 1978), pp. 73–84.

Rothstein, Marvin. "On Geometric and Arithmetic Portfolio Performance Indexes." *Journal of Financial and Quantitative Analysis,* v. 7 (September 1972), pp. 1983–92.

Soldofsky, R. M., and R. L. Miller. "Risk-Premium Curve vs. Capital Market Line: A Further Word." *Financial Management,* v. 7 (Spring 1978), pp. 65–72.

Young, W. E., and R. H. Trent. "Geometric Mean Approximations of Individual Security and Portfolio Performance." *Journal of Financial and Quantitative Analysis,* v. 4 (June 1969), pp. 179–99.

4 Introduction to Valuation Theories

Value determination of financial instruments is important in security analysis and portfolio management. Valuation theories are the basic tools for determining the intrinsic value of alternative financial instruments. This chapter provides a general review of the financial theory that most students of finance would have already received in basic corporate finance and investment classes. Synthesis and integration of the valuation theories are necessary for the student of investments in order to have a proper perspective of security analysis and portfolio management.

The basic policy areas involved in the management of a company are (1) investment policy, (2) financial policy, (3) dividend policy, and (4) production policy. Since the determination of the market value of a firm is affected by the way management sets and implements these policies, they are of critical importance to the security analyst. The security analyst must evaluate management decisions in each of these areas and convert information about company policy into price estimates of the firm's securities. This chapter examines these policies within a financial theory framework, dealing with valuation models.

There are four alternative but interrelated valuation models of financial theory that might be useful for the analysis of securities and the management of portfolios:

1. Discounted cash-flow valuation theory (classical financial theory)
2. M and M valuation theory
3. Capital asset pricing model (CAPM)
4. Option-pricing theory (OPT)

The discounted cash-flow valuation and M and M theories are discussed in the typical required corporate-finance survey course for both bachelor's and master's programs in business. The main purpose of this chapter is to review these theories and discuss their interrelationships. The discounted cash-flow model is first reviewed by extending some of the basic valuation

concepts that were introduced in Chapter 3. In the second section, the four alternative evaluation methods developed by M and M in their 1961 article are discussed. Their three propositions and their revision with taxes are explored, including possible applications of their theories in security analysis. Miller's inclusion of personal taxes is discussed. The third section includes a brief overview of CAPM concepts, which is covered in more detail in Chapter 9; and the fourth section introduces option-pricing theory, which is discussed in Chapter 14.

DISCOUNTED CASH-FLOW VALUATION THEORY

Discounted cash-flow valuation theory is the basic tool for determining the theoretical price of a corporate security. The price of a corporate security is equal to the present value of future benefits of ownership. For example, for common stock, these benefits include dividends received while the stock is owned plus capital gains earned during the ownership period. If we assume a one-period investment and a world of certain cash flows, the price paid for a share of stock, P_0, will equal the sum of the present value of a certain dividend per share, d_1 (assumed to be paid as a single flow at year end), and the selling price per share P_1:

$$P_0 = \frac{d_1 + P_1}{1 + k} \tag{4.1}$$

in which k is the rate of discount assuming certainty. P_1 can be similarly expressed in terms of d_2 and P_2:

$$P_1 = \frac{d_2 + P_2}{1 + k} \tag{4.2}$$

If P_1 in Equation (4.1) is substituted into Equation (4.2), a two-period expression is derived:

$$P_0 = \frac{d_1}{(1+k)} + \frac{d_2}{(1+k)^2} + \frac{P_2}{(1+k)^2} \tag{4.3}$$

It can be seen, then, that an infinite time-horizon model can be developed in which no selling point need be indicated and P_0 can be expressed as the sum of the present value of all future dividends:

$$P_0 = \sum_{t=1}^{\infty} \frac{d_t}{(1 + k)^t} \tag{4.4}$$

Equation (4.4) is identical to Equation (3.12) of the last chapter.

Since the total market value of the firms' equity is equal to the market price per share multiplied by the number of shares outstanding, Equation (4.4) may be re-expressed in terms of total market value MV_0:

$$MV_0 = \sum_{t=1}^{\infty} \frac{D_t}{(1 + k)^t} \tag{4.5}$$

in which D_t = total dollars of dividends paid during year t.

Using this basic valuation approach as a means of expressing the appropriate objective of the firm's management, the valuation of a firm's securities can be analyzed in a world of certainty.

Sample Problem 4.1

XYZ Company will pay dividends of $3 and $4 in years one and two, respectively. In addition, the market price per share is predicted to be $30 at the end of the second year, and the discount rate is 12 percent. Substituting this information into Equation (4.3) the current theoretical price per share can be calculated.

Solution

$$P_0 = \frac{\$3}{(1 + 0.12)} + \frac{\$4 + \$30}{(1 + 0.12)^2}$$

$$= \$29.78$$

BOND VALUATION

Bond valuation is a relatively easy process, as the income stream the bondholder will receive is known with a high degree of certainty. Barring a firm's default, the income stream consists of the periodic coupon payments and the repayments of the principal at maturity. These cash flows must be discounted to the present using the required rate of return for the bond.

The basic principles of bond valuation are represented in the equation:

$$PV = \sum_{t=1}^{n} \frac{CF_t}{(1 + k_b)^t} \tag{4.6}$$

where:

PV = present value of the bond;
n = the number of periods to maturity;
CF_t = the cash flow (interest and principal) received in period t;
k_b = the required rate of return of the bondholders (equal to risk-free rate i plus a risk premium).

Perpetuity

The first (and most extreme) case of bond valuation involves a **perpetuity**, a bond with no maturity date and perpetual interest payments. Such bonds do exist. In 1814, the English government floated a large bond issue to consolidate the various small issues they had used to pay for the Napoleonic Wars. Such bonds are called *consols,* and the owners are entitled to a fixed amount of interest income annually in perpetuity. In this case, Equation (4.6) collapses into:

$$PV = \frac{CF}{k_b} \tag{4.7}$$

Thus, the valuation depends directly on the periodic interest payment and the required rate of return for the bond. It can be seen that required rates of return, necessitated by a higher rate of inflation or an increase in the perceived risk of the bond, lower the present value, decreasing the bond's market value. For example, if the stated annual interest payment on the perpetuity bond is $50 and the required rate of return in the market is 10 percent, the price of the security is stated:

$$PV = \$50/0.10 = \$500$$

If its issuing price had been $1,000, it can be seen that the required rate of return would have been only 5 percent (k_b = CF/PV = $50/$1000 = 0.05, or 5%).

Term Bonds

Most bonds are **term bonds,** which mature at some definite point in time. Thus, Equation (4.6) should be respecified to take this fact into account:

$$PV = \sum_{t=1}^{n} \frac{I_t}{(1 + k_b)^t} + \frac{P_n}{(1 + k_b)^n} \tag{4.8}$$

where:

I_t = the annual coupon interest payment;
P_n = the principal amount (face value) of the bond; and
n = the number of periods to maturity.

Sample Problem 4.2

If a corporate bond issued by XYZ Company has the following characteristics:

$$
\begin{aligned}
\text{Annual coupon payment} &= \$90 \\
\text{Face value} &= \$1{,}000 \\
\text{Number of years till bond matures} &= 5 \\
\text{Return required by bondholders} &= 12 \text{ percent}
\end{aligned}
$$

Then Equation (4.8) can be used to calculate the theoretical value of this bond.

$$
\begin{aligned}
\text{PV} &= \frac{\$90}{(1 + 0.12)} + \frac{\$90}{(1 + 0.12)^2} + \frac{\$90}{(1 + 0.12)^3} \\
&\quad + \frac{\$90}{(1 + 0.12)^4} + \frac{\$90}{(1 + 0.12)^5} + \frac{\$1{,}000}{(1 + 0.12)^5} \\
&= \$891.83
\end{aligned}
$$

Again, it should be noted that the market price, PV, of a bond is affected by changes in the rate of inflation. If inflation increases, the discount rate must also increase to compensate the investor for the resultant decreases in the value of the debt repayment. The present value of each period's interest payment thus decreases, and the price of the bond falls. The bondholder is always exposed to interest-rate risk, the variance of bond prices resulting from fluctuations in the level of interest rates. Interest-rate risk, or price volatility of a bond caused by changes in interest-rate levels, is directly related to the term to maturity. There are two types of risk premiums associated with interest-rate risk as it applies to corporate bonds. The **bond maturity premium** refers to the net return from investing in long-term government bonds rather than the short-term bills. Since corporate bonds generally possess default risk, another of the components of corporate bond rates of return is **default premium.** The bond default premium is the net increase in return from investing in long-term corporate bonds rather than in long-term government bonds.

Additional features of a bond can affect its valuation. **Convertible bonds,** those with a provision for conversion into shares of common stock, are generally more valuable than a firm's straight bonds for several reasons. First, the investor receives the potential of positive gains from conversion, should the market price of a firm's common stock rise above the conversion price. If the stock price is greater than conversion price, the convertible bond generally sells at or above its conversion value. Second, the bondholder also receives the protection of fixed income payment, regardless of the current price of the stock—assuring the investor that the price of the bond will be at least equal to that of a straight bond, should stock prices fail to increase sufficiently. Third, for any given firm the coupon rate of return from its bonds is generally greater than the dividend rate of return (dividend yield) from their common stock—thus causing a measure of superiority for a convertible bond over its conversion into common stock until stock dividends rise above the bond's coupon rate. Even then, the convertible bond may be preferred by investors because of the higher degree of certainty of

interest payments as compared to dividends that would decline should earnings fall.

A **sinking fund provision** may also increase the value of a bond, at least at its time of issue. A sinking-fund agreement specifies a schedule by which the sinking-fund will retire the bond issue gradually over its life. By providing cash to the sinking-fund for use in redeeming the bonds, this provision ensures the investor some potential demand for the bond, thus increasing slightly the liquidity of the investment.

Finally, the possibility that the bond may be called will generally lower the value relative to a noncallable bond. A call provision stipulates that the bond may be retired by the issuer at a certain price, usually above par or face value. Therefore, in periods of large downward interest movements, a company may be able to retire a high coupon bond and issue new bonds with a lower interest payment requirement. A call feature increases the risk to an investor in that his expected high interest payments may be called away from him, if overall interest rate levels decline.

COMMON-STOCK VALUATION

Common-stock valuation is complicated by an uncertainty of cash flows to the investor, necessarily greater than that for bond valuation.[1]

Not only might the dividends voted to shareholders each period change in response to management's assessment concerning the current level of earnings stability, future earnings prospects, or other factors, but the price of the stock may also either rise or fall—resulting in either capital gains or losses, if the shares are sold. Thus the valuation process requires the forecasting of both capital gains and the stream of expected dividends. Both must also be discounted at the required rate of return of the common stockholders.

$$P_0 = \frac{d_1}{1 + k} + \frac{d_2}{(1 + k)^2} + \cdots + \frac{P_n}{(1 + k)^n} \qquad (4.9)$$

where:

P_0 = the present value, or price, of the common stock per share;
d = the dividend payment per share;
k = the required rate of return of the common stockholders; and
P_n = the price of the stock in period n when sold.

However, P_n can also be expressed as the sum of all discounted dividends to be received from period n forward into the future. Thus, the value at the

---

[1] This is true because foregoing interest payments puts the firm into default, while missing dividend payments does not.

present time can be expressed as an infinite series of discounted dividend payments:

$$P_0 = \sum_{t=1}^{\infty} \frac{d_t}{(1 + k)^t} \qquad (4.4)$$

in which d_t is the dividend payment in period t.

Several possibilities exist regarding the growth of dividend payments over time. First, dividends may be assumed to be a constant amount, and the formula for the stock's valuation is simply Equation (4.7), where CF is the constant dividend and k is the required rate of return of the common stockholder.

Second, dividends may be expected to grow at some constant rate, g. In such a case, a dividend at time t is simply the compound value of the present dividend (i.e., $P_t = (1 + g)^t d_0$). Under this assumption, as in Chapter 3, if $g < k$, the valuation equation can be simplified to:

$$P_0 = \frac{d_1}{(k - g)} \qquad (4.10)$$

This equation represents the **Gordon growth model,** which is identical to Equation (3.13) of the last chapter. Note that a critical condition for this model is that the constant growth of dividends must be less than the constant required rate of return. The zero growth situation is a special case of this model, in which:

$$P_0 = \frac{d_1}{k} \qquad (4.11)$$

This is Equation (3.14) of the previous chapter.

Finally, dividends can exhibit a period of supernormal growth (i.e., g is greater than k) before declining to the normal growth situation assumed in the Gordon model (g is less than k). Supernormal growth often occurs during the "takeoff" phase in a firm's life cycle. That is, a firm may experience a life cycle analogous to that of a product: first, a low-profit introductory phase, then a takeoff phase of high growth and high profits, leveling off at a plateau during its mature stage, perhaps followed by a period of declining earnings. Computer and electronics manufacturers experienced a period of supernormal growth during the 1960s, as did semiconductor firms during the 1970s. Bioengineering firms appear to be the supergrowth firms of the 1980s.

Sample Problem 4.3

LBO, Inc., has just paid a dividend of $6 per share. In addition, dividends are expected to grow at a constant rate of 3 percent per year. If shareholders require a 7 percent annual rate of return, what should be the current theoretical price of LBO's stock?

Equation (4.10) can be used to calculate the current theoretical price. However, Equation (4.10) uses the dividend expected to be received next year, while the current information relates to the dividend received this year. Because dividends are expected to grow at a constant rate, next year's dividend should just be the future value of this year's dividend compounded at the growth rate of dividends.

Solution

$$d_1 = d_0(1 + g)$$
$$= \$6(1 + 0.03)$$
$$= \$6.18$$

Substituting into Equation (4.10) gives the current theoretical price of LBO's stock.

$$P_0 = \frac{\$6.18}{0.07 - 0.03}$$
$$= \$154.50$$

The valuation of a supernormal growth stock requires some estimate of the length of the supernormal growth period. The current price of the stock will then consist of two components: (1) the present value of the stock during the supernormal growth period, and (2) the present value of the stock price at the end of the supernormal growth period:

$$P_0 = \sum_{t=1}^{n} \frac{d_0(1 + g_s)^t}{(1 + k)^t} + \frac{\dfrac{d_{n+1}}{k - g_n}}{(1 + k)^n} \tag{4.12}$$

where:

g_s = supernormal growth rate;
n = the number of periods before the growth drops from supernormal to normal;
k = the required rate of return of the stockholders; and
g_n = the normal growth rate of dividends (assumed to be constant thereafter).

Equation (4.12) is similar to Equation (3.31) of the last chapter.

As we can see from our development of the discounted cash-flow financial theory, the primary determinant of value for securities is the cash flow received by the investors. Anything that affects the cash flow, such as the dividend policy, investment policy, financing policy, and production policy of the firm, needs to be evaluated in order to determine a market price.

Some shortcomings of this approach include the overemphasis on the evaluation of the individual firm to the exclusion of portfolio concepts and the interrelationship with the overall market indexes. Most of the classical models are also static in nature, overlooking the concept of dynamic growth.

Nevertheless, a fundamental approach to security valuation—the stream of dividends approach—has evolved from this theory.

M AND M VALUATION THEORY

Modigliani and Miller (M and M, 1961) have proposed four alternative valuation methods to determine the theoretical value of common stocks. This section discusses these valuation approaches in some detail. M and M's four more or less distinct approaches to the valuation of common stock are:

1. The discounted cash-flow approach
2. The current earnings plus future investment opportunities approach
3. The stream of dividends approach
4. The stream of earnings approach

Working from a valuation expression referred to by M and M as the "fundamental principle of valuation":

$$P_0 = \frac{1}{1 + k} (d_1 + P_1) \tag{4.13}$$

M and M further developed a valuation formula to serve as a point of reference and comparison among the four valuation approaches:

$$V_0 = \sum_{t=0}^{\infty} \frac{1}{(1 + k)^{t+1}} (X_t - I_t) \tag{4.14}$$

where:

V_0 = the current market value of the firm;
X_t = net operating earnings in period t; and
I_t = new investment during period t.

In this context, the discounted cash-flow approach can be expressed:

$$V_0 = \sum_{t=0}^{\infty} \frac{1}{(1 + k)^{t+1}} (R_t - O_t) \tag{4.15}$$

in which R_t is the stream of cash receipts by the firm and O_t is the stream of cash outlays of the firm. This fundamental principle is based on the assumption of "perfect markets," "rational behavior," and "perfect certainty" as defined by M and M. Since X_t differs from R_t and I_t differs from O_t only by the cost of goods sold and depreciation expense, if $(R_t - O_t)$ equals $(X_t - I_t)$, then (4.15) is equivalent to (4.14) and the discounted cash-flow approach is an extension of Equation (4.13), the fundamental valuation principle. Hence, the security analyst must be well versed in generally

accepted accounting principles in order to evaluate the worth of accounting earnings or $(X_t - I_t)$.

The **investment-opportunities approach** seems in some ways the most natural approach from the standpoint of an investor. This approach takes into account the ability of the firm's management to issue securities at "normal" market rates of return and invest in the opportunities, providing a rate higher than the normal rate of return. M and M develop from this framework the following expression, which they show can also be derived from Equation (4.14):

$$V_0 = \frac{X_0}{k} + \sum_{t=0}^{\infty} \frac{I_t (k_t^* - k)}{(1 + k)^{t+1}} \tag{4.16}$$

in which X_0 is the perpetual net operating earning and k_t^* is the "higher than normal" rate of return on new investment I_t.

From the expression it can be seen that if a firm cannot generate a rate of return on its new investments higher than the normal rate, k, the price/earnings ratio applied to the firm's earnings will be equal to $1/k$, thus implying simple expansion rather than growth over time. An important variable for security analysis is a firm's P/E ratio (or earnings multiple), defined as:

$$\text{P/E ratio} = \frac{\text{Market price}}{\text{Earnings per share}}$$

Conceptually the P/E ratio is determined by three factors: (1) the investor's required rate of return (K), (2) the retention ratio of the firm's earning, b, where b is equal to 1 minus the dividend payout ratio, and (3) the firm's expected return on investment (r). Using the constant-growth model (Equation 4.10):

$$P_0 = \frac{d_1}{k - g}$$

$$P_0 = \frac{E_1(1 - b)}{k - (br)}$$

$$\frac{P_0}{E_1} = \frac{1 - b}{k - (br)} \tag{4.17}$$

in which b is the retention rate and E_1 is the next period's expected profit.

The P_0/E ratio is theoretically equal to the payout ratio of a firm, divided by the difference between the investor's required return and the firm's growth rates. In the above relationship a direct relationship has been identified between price/earnings ratio and discount cash-flow valuation model.

The **stream-of-dividends approach** has been by far the most popular in the literature of valuation; it was developed in the pre M and M period. Assuming an infinite time horizon, this approach defines the current market price of

a share of common stock as equal to the discounted present value of all future dividends:

$$P_0 = \sum_{t=0}^{\infty} \frac{1}{(1 + k)^{t+1}} (d_t) \tag{4.18}$$

Restating in terms of total market value:

$$V_0 = \sum_{t=0}^{\infty} \frac{1}{(1 + k)^{t+1}} (D_t) \tag{4.19}$$

With no outside financing, it can be seen that $D_t = X_t - I_t$ and:

$$V_0 = \sum_{t=0}^{\infty} \frac{1}{(1 + k)^{t+1}} (X_t - I_t)$$

which is Equation (4.14). With outside financing through the issuance of shares of new common stock, it can be shown that:

$$V_0 = \sum_{t=0}^{\infty} \frac{1}{(1 + k)^{t+1}} (D_t + V_{t+1} - m_{t+1} {}^*P_{t+1}) \tag{4.20}$$

in which m_{t+1} is the number of new shares issued at price P_{t+1}. For the infinite horizon, the value of the firm is equal to the investments it makes and the new capital it raises, or:

$$V_{t+1} - (m_{t+1})(P_{t+1}) = I_t - (X_t - D_t)$$

Thus, Equation (4.20) can also be written:

$$V_0 = \sum_{t=0}^{\infty} \frac{1}{(1 + k)^{t+1}} (X_t - I_t) \tag{4.14}$$

Given the M and M ideal assumptions, the above result implies irrelevance of dividends because the market value of the dividends provided to the new stockholders must always be precisely the same as the increase in current dividends. This is in direct disagreement with the findings of the discounted cash-flow model, where dividends are a major determinant of value. In this case, dividends have no impact on value, and the firm's investment policy is the most important determinant of value. Security analysis should concern itself with the future investment opportunities of the firm and forget about dividends.

M and M also developed the **stream-of-earnings approach,** which takes account of the fact that additional capital must be acquired at some cost in order to maintain the stream of future earnings at its current level. The capital to be raised is I_t and its cost is K percent per period thereafter; thus, the current value of the firm under this approach can be stated:

$$V_0 = \sum_{t=0}^{\infty} \frac{1}{(1 + k)^{t+1}} (X_t - I_t)$$

which, again, is Equation (4.14).

Because under none of these four theoretical approaches does the term D_t remain in the final valuation expression and because X_t, I_t, and k are assumed to be independent of D_t, M and M conclude that the current value of a firm is independent of its current and future dividend decisions. The amount gained by stockholders is offset exactly by the decline in the market value of their stock. In the short run, this effect is observed when a stock goes ex-dividend—that is, if the market price of the stock falls by the amount of the dividend on the last day, the old shareholders are entitled to receive a dividend payment. The stock's value is then dependent only upon the expected future earnings stream of the firm. Security analysts spend much time and effort forecasting a firm's expected earnings.

While the above analysis ignores the case in which external financing is obtained through the issuance of debt, in such a situation M and M's *position* then rests upon their indifference proposition with respect to leverage (M and M, 1958), discussed elsewhere in this chapter. Since that analysis shows that under a set of assumptions consistent with their "fundamental principal of valuation" the real cost of debt in a world of no taxation is equal to the real cost of equity financing, M and M conclude that the means of external financing used to offset the payment of dividends does not affect their hypothesis that dividends are irrelevant.

Prior to Miller and Modigliani's 1961 article, the classical view held that dividend policy was a major determinant of the value of the corporation and that firms should seek their "optimal payout ratios" to maximize their value. M and M's conclusions about the irrelevance of dividend policy, given investment policy, collided head-on with the existing classical view. The view that the value of the firm is independent of dividend policy also extends into a world with corporate taxes but without personal taxes.

Review and Extension of M and M Proposition I

The existence of optimal capital structure has become one of the important issues for academicians and practitioners in finance. While classical finance theorists argue that there is an optimal capital structure for a firm, the new classical financial theory developed by M and M (1958, 1963) has cast doubt upon the existence of such an optimal structure. The specific assumptions that they made, consistent with the dividend irrelevance analysis previously outlined, include:

1. Capital markets are perfect (frictionless).
2. Both individuals and firms can borrow and lend at the risk-free rate.
3. Firms use risk-free debt and risky equity.
4. There are only corporate taxes (that is, there are no wealth taxes or personal income taxes).
5. All cash flow streams are perpetuities (that is, no growth).

Developing the additional concepts of risk class and homemade leverage,

M and M derived their well-known **Proposition I,** both with and without corporate taxes.[2]

If all firms are in the same risk class, then their expected risky future net operating cash flow $(\tilde{X})$ varies only by a scale factor. Under this circumstance, the correlation between two firms' net operating income (NOI) within a risk class should be equal to 1.0. This implies that the rates of return will be equal for all firms in the same risk class, that is:

$$R_{it} = \frac{\tilde{X}_{it} - \tilde{X}_{it-1}}{X_{it-1}} \tag{4.21}$$

and because $\tilde{X}_{it} = C\tilde{X}_{jt}$ where C is the scale factor:

$$R_{jt} = \frac{C\tilde{X}_{jt} - C\tilde{X}_{jt}}{C\tilde{X}_{jt-1}} = R_{it} \tag{4.22}$$

in which R_{it} and R_{jt} are rates of return for the ith and jth firms, respectively. Therefore, if two streams of cash flow differ by only a scale factor, they will have the same distributions of returns and the same risk, and they will require the same expected return.

The concept of **homemade leverage** is used to refer to the leverage created by individual investors who sell their own debt while **corporate leverage** is used to refer to the debt floated by the corporation. Using the assumption that the cost of homemade leverage is equal to the cost of corporate leverage, M and M (1958) derived their Proposition I both with and without taxes. However, the Proposition I with taxes was not correct, and they subsequently corrected this result in their 1963 paper. Mathematically, M and M's Proposition I can be defined:

$$V_j = (S_j + B_j) = X_j/\rho_k \tag{4.23}$$

and Proposition I with taxes can be defined as

$$V_j^L = \frac{(1 - \tau_j)X_j}{\rho_k^\tau} + \frac{\tau I_j}{r} = V_j^U + \tau B_j \tag{4.24}$$

In Equation (4.23), B_j, S_j, and V_j are, respectively, the market value of debt, common shares, and the firm. X_j is the expected profit before deduction of interest, ρ_k the required rate of return or the cost of capital in risk class k. In Equation (4.24), ρ_k^τ is the required rate of return used to capitalize the expected returns net of tax for the unlevered firm with long-run average earnings before tax and interest of (X_j) in risk class k. τ_j is the corporate tax rate for the jth firm, I_j is the total interest expense for the jth firm, and r is the market interest rate used to capitalize the certain cash inflows generated by

---

[2] In 1985 Franco Modigliani won the Nobel Prize for his work on the life cycle of savings and his contribution to what has become known as the M and M theory, discussed in this section.

risk-free debt. B_j is total risk-free debt floated by the jth firm, and V^L and V^U are the market values of the leveraged and unleveraged firms, respectively.

By comparing these two equations, we find that the advantages of a firm with leverage will increase that firm's value by $\tau_j B_j$—that is, the corporate tax rate times the total debt floated by that firm. One of the important implications of this proposition is that there is no optimal capital structure for the firm unless there are bankruptcy costs associated with its debt flotation. If there are bankruptcy costs, then a firm will issue debt until its tax benefit is equal to the bankruptcy cost, thus providing, in such a case, an optimal capital structure for the firm. In addition to the bankruptcy costs, information signalling [see Leland and Pyle (1977) and Ross (1977)] and differential expectations between shareholders and bondholders can be used to justify the possible existence of an optimal structure of a firm. The existence of optimal capital structure is an important issue for security analysts to investigate because it affects the value of the firm and the value of the firm's securities. Is a firm with a high level of debt more valuable than a similar firm with very little debt? M and M say either it doesn't matter or that the highly leveraged firm is more valuable.

The important assumptions used to prove the M and M Proposition I with taxes are that (1) there are no transaction costs; (2) homemade leverage is equal to corporate leverage; (3) corporate debt is riskless; and (4) there is no bankruptcy cost. Overall, M and M's Proposition I implies that there is no optimal capital structure. If there is a tax structure that systematically provides a lower after-tax real cost of debt relative to the after-tax real cost of equity, the corporation will maximize the proportion of debt in their capital structure and will issue as much debt as possible to maximize the tax shield associated with the deductibility of interest.

Stiglitz (1969) extends M and M's proposition using a general equilibrium state preference framework. He is able to show that M and M's results do not depend on risk classes, competitive capital markets, or agreement by investors. The only two fundamental assumptions are that there is no bankruptcy and individuals can borrow at the same rate as firms. Stiglitz (1974) develops the argument that there may exist a determinate debt-equity ratio for the economy as a whole, but not for the individual firm.

Miller's Proposition on Debt and Taxes

Miller (1977) argues that although there is no optimal capital structure for an individual firm, in the aggregate case there may be an optimal structure. In balancing bankruptcy cost against tax shelter, an optimal capital structure is derived, just as the classical view has always maintained.

The Tax Reform Act of 1986 taxes dividends and long-term capital gains at the same top rate of 28 percent. This is a major change from the old 50 percent rate on dividends and 20 percent rate on long-term capital gains. The

new tax bill has also shifted the major tax burden to corporations and away from individuals. Even though the maximum corporate tax rate will decrease to 34 percent from the current top rate of 46 percent, corporations will be paying more taxes because of the loss of the Investment Tax Credits and the Accelerated Cost Recovery System depreciation allowances.

These changes in the tax code will shift the emphasis of corporate management from retaining earnings in order to generate price appreciation and capital gains to the payout of corporate funds in the form of dividends.

In his presidential address at the Annual Meeting of the American Finance Association, Merton Miller (1977) incorporates personal taxes into the Modigliani and Miller (1958, 1963) argument for the relationship between the firm's leverage and cost of capital.

M and M's Proposition I shows that the value of the leveraged firm equals the value of the unleveraged firm plus the tax shield associated with interest payments, as shown by Equation (4.24):

$$V^L = V^U + t_c B \qquad\qquad (4.24)$$

where:

V^L = the value of the leveraged firm;
V^U = the value of the unleveraged firm;
t_c = the corporate tax rate; and
B = the value of the firm's debt.

Miller generalizes the M and M relationship shown in Equation (4.24) to include personal taxes on dividends and capital gains as well as taxes on interest income, to yield:

$$V^L = V^U + \left[1 - \frac{(1 - t_c)(1 - t_{ps})}{(1 - t_{pB})} \right] B \qquad (4.25)$$

in which t_{ps} is the personal tax rate on income from stock and t_{pB} is the personal tax rate on income from bonds.

Using Equation (4.25) and the assumption of market equilibrium, and the fact that individual investors can defer income on stocks indefinitely (or that there exists a group of investors who are tax exempt, namely $t_{ps} = 0$), Miller argues that for the economy as a whole there is an optimal amount of debt, but for individual firms there is no optimal capital structure. Using Equation (4.25) the impact on firm value caused by the tax code changes embodied in the Tax Reform Act of 1986 was examined.

In general, by using the 1963 M and M relationship and the 1977 Miller relationship for tax shields we can identify an upper and lower bound for the change in value associated with interest tax shields. These upper and lower bounds are shown in Figure 4–1.

The upper bound is defined by the M and M arguments as $t_c B$—or, as discussed by Miller, the case where equity and debt income are taxed at the same rate. The lower bound is zero, which can occur under four circum-

FIGURE 4–1   Upper and Lower Bounds on the Value of Interest Tax Shelter

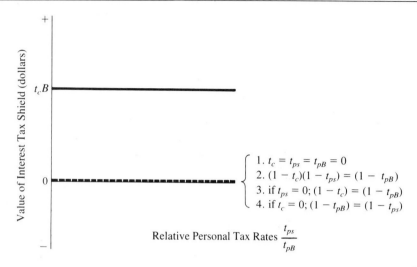

$$1.\ t_c = t_{ps} = t_{pB} = 0$$
$$2.\ (1 - t_c)(1 - t_{ps}) = (1 - t_{pB})$$
$$3.\ \text{if } t_{ps} = 0;\ (1 - t_c) = (1 - t_{pB})$$
$$4.\ \text{if } t_c = 0;\ (1 - t_{pB}) = (1 - t_{ps})$$

Relative Personal Tax Rates $\dfrac{t_{ps}}{t_{pB}}$

stances, labeled 1 through 4 in Figure 4–1. If there is no corporate or personal tax then there is no tax shield from interest deductibility. Case 2 shows that if the product of the after-tax factors for corporate and personal tax on equity equals the after-tax factor for debt, then the term

$$\frac{(1 - t_c)(1 - t_{ps})}{1 - t_{pB}}$$

equals one and the tax shield has zero value. This means that the after-tax cost of equity is equal to the after-tax cost of debt; it is highly unlikely that this could occur and so it is only shown as a feasible reason for a zero value of the tax shield. Cases 3 and 4 are of more practical interest: although not addressed directly in Miller's article, they serve as the limiting case to discuss the relationship between personal tax on equity and bond income and the size of the interest tax shield. Case 3 can be generalized to $t_{ps} < t_{pB}$ (the tax on equity income is less than the tax on bond income), and case 4 to $t_{pB} < t_{ps}$ (the tax on bond income is less than the tax on equity income).

In Figure 4–1 the x- (horizontal) axis is defined as the relative personal tax rate, that is, the ratio of t_{ps} to t_{pB}. Three situations for the value of t_{ps}/t_{pB} are considered: it may be (1) less than one, (2) equal to one, or (3) greater than one. These three cases are shown in Figure 4–2 by the letters A, B, and C. *Case A.* In this situation, if $t_{pB} > t_{ps}$, the tax rate on debt income will be higher than the tax rate on stock income, which was quite feasible under the old tax system where capital gains received preferential tax treatment. The value of the tax shield could be almost as high as the upper bound. To the other extreme, the tax shield could be zero or even negative if t_{ps} was very large and t_{pB} was close to zero. Clearly, if the tax shield became negative,

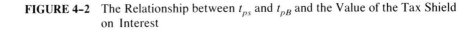

FIGURE 4-2 The Relationship between t_{ps} and t_{pB} and the Value of the Tax Shield on Interest

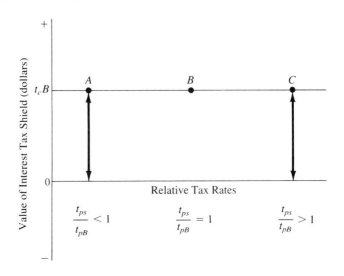

corporations would cease issuing debt securities—so zero is actually the lower bound of this case.

Case B. If the taxation on bond income is the same as the taxation of stock income, the value of the tax shield under Miller's approach will equal the original M and M value of $t_c B$, as shown by case B in Figure 4-2.

Case C. Finally, if the personal tax on stock income is higher than the personal tax on bond income, a range of values for the tax shield on interest is possible, as shown by C in Figure 4-2. The lower end of the range approaches zero for small values of t_{pB} and large values of t_{ps}. If the tax rate on equity is very high and the tax rate on bonds is very low, the value of the tax shield will approach zero. At the upper end of the range, if the tax rate on equity income is only slightly larger than the tax rate on debt income, the value of the interest tax shield will approach $t_c B$.

THE TAX REFORM ACT OF 1986 AND ITS IMPACT ON FIRM VALUE

Before the Tax Reform Act of 1986 the situation was generally similar to Case A. The tax rate on equity income was less than the tax rate on debt income. This can be shown to be true for two reasons: (1) the capital-gains portion of equity income was taxed at relatively low rates (that is, 20 percent maximum), and (2) the equity investors could defer the realization of capital gains indefinitely (that is, they were taxed at a zero rate). In either case, the tax rate on equity income was lower than the tax rate on debt income. One of

the provisions of the Tax Reform Act was to abolish the preferential treatment for capital-gains income. By itself this would cause t_{ps} to move toward equality with t_{pB}, and the situation would be approaching that of Case B.

Another aspect of the Tax Reform Act was to lower the marginal corporate tax rate. By itself this would tend to lower the upper bound or reduce the value of the tax shield on interest. However, this reduction in the corporate tax rate was offset by a reduction in many of the tax credits that were formerly available to corporations. Therefore, it would appear that even though the benefit derived from the tax shield on interest is being reduced, the number and value of other tax shields are also being reduced or eliminated; this would in general cause the interest tax shield to be more highly valued because of the scarcity of other tax shields. The increase in the interest tax-shield value can be accomplished by the corporation issuing more bonds, thereby increasing the value of B in the relationship $t_c B$. Even though t_c is going down, the decrease can be offset by an increase in B. The actual change in the value of the tax shield of interest is an empirical question, but it appears that because of risk considerations, the decrease in t_c will have a greater impact than the possible offsetting increase in B. Therefore, the upper bound on the value of the interest tax shield will undoubtedly shift downward.

Considering these changes in the tax code—reduction of personal rates, equaling of personal tax rate on bond and equity income, and the reduction in the corporate tax rate—we envision the following scenario. Figure 4–3 illustrates the general position of the value of the interest tax shield up to the end of 1986. The upper bound is the value of the tax shield of $t_c B$, and the situation is as in Case A. The reduction in the tax rate on corporations will reduce the upper bound of the tax shield to $t_c' B'$. The elimination of the

FIGURE 4–3   The Impact of the Tax Reform Act of 1986 on the Value of the Interest Tax Shield

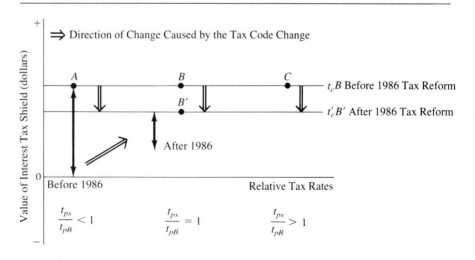

preferential treatment of capital gains will lead from a case A situation to a case B situation. However, the fact that investors can still defer capital gains will prevent t_{ps} from equaling t_{pB} exactly, so a case B situation will not be totally achieved.

CORPORATE RESPONSE TO THE TAX REFORM ACT OF 1986

The Tax Reform Act of 1986 raises the after-tax cost to borrow and invest for both individuals and businesses. Hence the new tax law will cause investors to place more importance on dividends, at the same time reducing the amount of investment of firms, thereby allowing them to increase dividends.

But dividends will still remain inferior to capital gains from the perspective of certain taxpayers because of the double taxation problem. Dividends are paid out of corporate profits on an after-tax basis, and then the dividend income is taxed a second time for certain recipients. In contrast, if a firm reinvests the cash flows and causes the firm to gain in price, the investor will receive a capital gain because of price appreciation. The tax on the capital gain can be deferred by the investor until some future time, which is an advantage.

Firms faced with substantial capital investments in the near future will be placed in a precarious position. As the tax benefits of income tax credit (ITC) and accelerated cost recovery system (ACRS) are eliminated or reduced, the remaining tax shields will become more valuable, even though the reduction in tax rates will reduce the marginal value of the tax shield. Thus a greater reliance on financing corporate needs through the issuance of debt is the predicted trend.

Both of these changes, the dividend effect and the debt increase, will noticeably impact the economy and the financial markets. Additionally, the level of uncertainty for the decision maker concerning tax policy has increased. For example, the ITC has been eliminated twice before since its introduction in 1962, and in both cases it was restored within a year and a half.

Taggart (1980) introduces uncertainty into the bond's cost (recall that previous work assumed bonds to be risk free). Since costs might stem from several sources, undergoing or attempting to avoid the bankruptcy process may consume real resources; conflicts of interest between shareholders and bondholders could lead to suboptimal decisions from the firm's standpoint, and negotiation and enforcement of debt contracts might be costly. Taggart extends Miller's analysis of the relationship between tax considerations and corporate capital structures to conditions of incomplete capital markets and special costs associated with corporate debt. Unlike Miller's model, however, the capital structure of any one firm is not found to be a matter of indifference to all shareholders at a market equilibrium. This is attributable in part to the costs of debt, which dictate a tendency for more debt to be

issued by those firms with lower costs. With the introduction of uncertainty, corporate shares and tax-exempt bonds are no longer perfect substitutes. Therefore, two distinct clienteles emerge, one demanding that firms have as much debt as possible, and one demanding firms have as little debt as possible. Firms in a given risk class would move to one or the other extreme in proportion to the relative demands from the two clienteles. In the presence of debt costs the high-leverage firms will be those with the lowest debt costs.

DeAngelo and Masulis (1980) extend Miller's (1977) analysis to include other tax shields, such as depreciation and investment tax credit. They find that a constant marginal personal tax on debt versus declining marginal corporate tax savings from leverage leads to an optimum degree of leverage, which equates the marginal personal tax cost and the marginal corporate tax benefit. The marginal corporate tax benefit declines as more debt is added to the capital structure, because of the probability of at least partial loss of the debt tax shield in the presence of corporate tax shield substitutes for debt and existing debt tax shield, since there is a ceiling on the total use of tax shields. This optimum degree of leverage is a unique interior solution in market equilibrium.

Shelton (1981) contests the M and M assumption that homemade leverage is equal to corporate leverage. He calls this "equal access" and points out that, in reality, corporations have better access to the debt markets than individuals. Individuals must pay a premium in the market as a result of the information asymmetry about their capacity and willingness to repay. This unequal access, in combination with the fact that individuals in differing tax brackets benefit in varying ways from the corporate leverage, complicates M and M's analysis. The implication is that individuals cannot recreate the same position by buying the unleveraged firm and issuing their own debt as they could obtain by buying the stock of a leveraged firm. Since M and M's assumptions generally do not hold, it can be shown that there is an optimum debt for a corporation. Barnea, Haugen, and Senbet (1985) use market imperfections and agency costs to show that an optimal structure consistent with the classical financial theory does exist. Hence, the choice of an optimal amount of debt is an important issue in security analysis and portfolio management.

For the no-tax version, it appears that M and M are ignoring the fact that within prudent ranges of usage, debt is a low-cost source of funds. Nevertheless, M and M's argument here is that the increase in perceived financial risk with an increase of debt in the capital structure will cause an increase in required rate of return for the equity holders of the firm that will just offset the use of more low-cost debt capital. When corporate taxes are assumed, however, the tax deductibility of interest payments leads to the implication within their model that the firm should use as much debt as possible (see Equation 4.24). The reason for this apparently extreme result is their original assumption of no bankruptcy costs. Since in reality bankruptcy costs are quite large, use of imprudent levels of debt would be so costly that an optimal capital structure is still implied.

The important implications of this section for security analysts are that dividend policy and leverage policy may not be as significant in the determination of the market value of the firm as originally assumed, and that primary emphasis should be put on the investment policy of the firm. The impact of dividend policy seems to be closely involved with the information content included in the dividend decisions of management, as the same valuation can be determined using approaches that do not specifically include dividends. The impact of debt leverage is heavily dependent upon the tax laws concerning the deductibility of interest payments. The degree of financial leverage observed empirically varies substantially from industry to industry and even between firms in the same industry, depending largely upon the coexistent degree of operating leverage and the level of sales volatility. Firms with relatively low business risk are able to support a high percentage of debt in their capital structure, and firms with relatively high business risk cannot.

CAPITAL ASSET PRICING MODEL (CAPM)

At about the same time as M and M were developing their work, developments in portfolio theory were leading to a model describing the formation of capital asset prices in a world of uncertainty: the **capital asset pricing model (CAPM).**

The CAPM is a generalized version of M and M theory in which M and M theory is provided with a link to the market:

$$E(R_j) = R_f + \beta_j [E(R_m) - R_f] \qquad (4.26)$$

where:

R_j = the rate of return for security j;

β_j = a volatility measure relating the rate of return on security j with that of the market over time;

R_m = the rate of return for the overall market (typically measured by the rate of return reflected by a market index, such as the S&P 500); and

R_f = the risk-free rate available in the market (usually the rate of return on U.S. Treasury bills is used as a proxy).

In the CAPM framework, the valuation of a company's securities is dependent not only upon their cash flows but also upon those of other securities available for investment. It is assumed that much of the total risk, as measured by standard deviation of return, can be diversified away by combining the stock of a firm being analyzed with those of other companies. Unless the cash flows from these securities are perfectly positively correlated, smoothing or diversification will take place. Thus, the security return can be divided into two components: a systematic component that is per-

fectly correlated with the overall market return and an unsystematic component that is independent of the market return:

$$\text{Security return} = \text{Systematic return} + \text{Unsystematic return} \quad \textbf{(4.27)}$$

Since the security return is perfectly correlated with the market return, it can be expressed as a constant, **beta,** multiplied by the market return (R_m). The beta is a volatility index, measuring the sensitivity of the security return to changes in the market return. The unsystematic return is a residual of the relationship of R_j with R_m.

As has been previously noted, the standard deviation of the probability distribution of a security's rate of return is considered to be an appropriate measure of the total risk of that security. This total risk can be broken down into systematic and unsystematic components, just as noted above for security return:

$$\text{Total security risk} = \text{Systematic risk} + \text{Unsystematic risk} \quad \textbf{(4.28)}$$

Diversification is achieved only when securities that are not perfectly correlated with one other are combined. The unsystematic risk components tend to cancel each other since they are all residuals from the relationship of security returns with the overall market return. In the process, the portfolio risk measure declines without any corresponding lowering of portfolio return (see Figure 4–4). It is assumed in this illustration that the selection of additional securities as the portfolio size is increased is performed in some random manner, although any selection process other than intentionally choosing perfectly correlated securities will suffice. Unsystematic risk is shown to be gradually eliminated until the portfolio risk is completely market related. While for an actual portfolio the systematic risk will not

FIGURE 4–4   Diversification Process

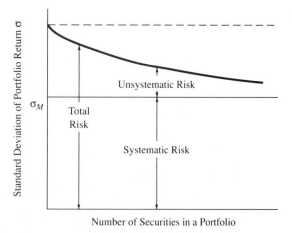

Number of Securities in a Portfolio

remain constant as securities are added, the intent is to show that the unsystematic-risk portion can be diversified away, leaving the market-related systematic portion as the only relevant measure of risk. Empirical studies have shown that a portfolio of about twenty securities not highly correlated with one another will provide a high degree of diversification. Although capital-market theory assumes that all investors will hold the market portfolio, it is neither necessary nor realistic to assume that all investors will be satisfied with the market level of risk. There are basically two ways that investors can adjust their risk level within the CAPM theoretical framework. First, funds for investment can be divided between the market portfolio and risk-free securities. The capital-market line (CML) is derived assuming such a tradeoff function.

This is illustrated in Figure 4–5, in which point M is the market portfolio and points on the CML below and above M imply lending and borrowing at the risk-free rate. The second way of adjusting the portfolio risk level is by investing in a fully diversified portfolio of securities (that is, the correlation coefficient of the portfolio with the market, r_{pm}, is equal to 1.0) that has a weighted average beta equal to the systematic-risk level desired:

$$\beta_p = \sum_{j=1}^{n} W_j \beta_j \tag{4.29}$$

in which W_j is the proportion of total funds invested in security j. Since in the CAPM systematic risk as measured by beta is the only risk that need be undertaken, it follows that no risk premium should be expected for the bearing of unsystematic risk. With that in mind, the relationship between expected return and risk can be better defined through the illustration of the security-market line (SML) in Figure 4–6 in which R_m and β_m are the expected return and risk level of the market portfolio. In equilibrium, all securities and combinations of securities are expected to lie along this line. In contrast, only fully diversified portfolios would be expected to fall along the CML, because only with full diversification is total risk equal to systematic risk alone. Sample Problem 4.4 provides further illustration, and a much

FIGURE 4–5   Capital-Market Line

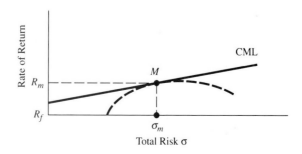

FIGURE 4-6   Security-Market Line

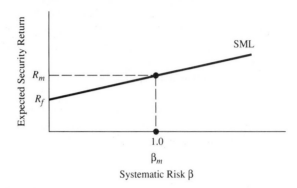

more detailed description of the use of CAPM in making investment decisions is included in later chapters of this book.

Sample Problem 4.4

The following is known about the market and LBO, Inc.:

$$
\begin{aligned}
\text{Three-month T-bill rate} &= 8 \text{ percent} \\
\text{Expected return on the S\&P 500} &= 11 \text{ percent} \\
\text{Estimated beta for LBO's stock} &= 1.5
\end{aligned}
$$

Substituting into Equation (4.26) solves for the expected return on LBO's stock.

Solution

$$
\begin{aligned}
E(R_{\text{LBO}}) &= 8\% + 1.5 \, (11\% - 8\%) \\
&= 12.5\%
\end{aligned}
$$

OPTION VALUATION

Option contracts give their holders the right to buy and sell a specific asset at some specified price on or before a specified date. Since these contracts can be valued in relation to common stock, the basic concepts involved have a number of applications to financial theory and to the valuation of other financial instruments. (A more theoretical discussion of option-pricing theory is included in Chapters 14 and 15.)

While there are a variety of option contracts—for example, call options, put options, combinations of calls and puts, convertible securities, and

warrants—this chapter's discussion is limited to **call options.** A call option gives the holder the right to buy a share of stock at a specified price, known as the exercise price, and the basic American option can be exercised at any time through the expiration date. The value of the option at expiration is the difference between the market price of the underlying stock and its exercise price (with a minimum value of zero, of course).

While several factors affect the value of an option, the most important factor is the price volatility of the stock—the greater the volatility, the greater the value of the option, other things remaining the same. We will also note that the longer the time left before expiration and the higher the level of interest rates in the market, the greater the option value, all other things held the same.

The theoretical value of a call option at expiration is the difference between the market price of the underlying common stock, P_s, and the exercise price of the option, E, or zero, whichever is greater:

$$C = \text{Max} \, (P_s - E, 0) \tag{4.30}$$

When the price of the stock is greater than the exercise price, the option has a positive theoretical value which will increase dollar for dollar with the price of the stock. When the market price of the stock is equal to or less than the exercise price, the option has a theoretical value of zero, as shown in Figure 4–7. Nevertheless, as long as some time remains before expiration, the actual market price of the option (referred to as the option premium at the time of issue) is likely to be greater than its theoretical value. This increment above the theoretical value is called the *time value* or *speculative value* of the option, and its size will depend primarily on the perceived likelihood of a profitable move in the price of the stock before expiration of the option. Sample Problem 4.5 provides further illustration.

Sample Problem 4.5

A call option written on LBO, Inc.'s, stock has an exercise price of $95. Calculate the value of the call option when the option expires if the price of the stock at expiration is (a) $106, (b) $92.

Solution
According to Equation (4.30), the call option can take on only two values. If the call option expires "in the money," its value will be the difference between the stock price and the exercise price. If the call option expires "out of the money," its value will be equal to zero because the option holder does not have to exercise this option.

(a) Call expires "in the money":

$$C = \$106 - \$95$$
$$= \$11$$

FIGURE 4-7   Theoretical and Actual Values of a Call Option

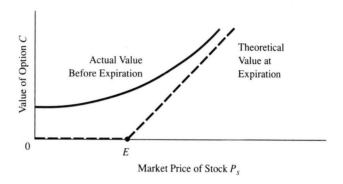

(b) Call expires "out of the money," so option will not be exercised:

$$C = \$0$$

The full range of possible values for the market price of the option is from the theoretical value on the low side to the market price of the stock itself on the high side. For the option price to be equal to the stock price, an infinite time to expiration would be implied. For the option price to be equal to the theoretical value only, imminent expiration would be implied. For virtually all options for which the value would be determined, however, the option price would fall somewhere between these two extremes. Because an option costs less than its underlying stock, the percentage change in option price is greater than the percentage change in stock price, given some increase in the market price of the stock. Thus, a leveraged rate of return can be earned by investment in the option rather than the stock. As stock price continues to increase, the difference between the percentage change in option price and the percentage change in stock price will tend to converge.

Thus far it has been shown that the value of an option will be a function of the underlying stock price, the exercise price of the option, and the time to maturity. Yet there is still another factor that is probably the single most important variable affecting the speculative value of the option. That is the **price volatility** of the underlying stock. The greater the probability of significant change in the price of the stock, the more likely it is that the option can be exercised at a profit before expiration. Sample Problem 4.6 provides further illustration.

Sample Problem 4.6

At the beginning of some time period, investment may be considered in options on stock A and stock B, both of which have an exercise price of $48. If the probabilities of stock price at the end of the period are as indicated in

the table, the theoretical values of option A and option B can also be determined using Equation (4.29). While the expected value of the stock prices for A and B is the same, $50, the expected theoretical values are $3.40 for option A and $7.40 for option B.

Stock Price and Option Price

Probability	*0.1*	*0.2*	*0.4*	*0.2*	*0.1*
Price of stock A	$40	$45	$50	$55	$60
Theoretical value of option A	0	0	$ 2	$ 7	$12
Price of stock B	$30	$40	$50	$60	$70
Theoretical value of option B	0	0	$ 2	$12	$22

Exercise price of option A = Exercise price of option B = $48.

$$\text{Option A} = (0)\,(0.1) + (0)\,(0.2) + (2)\,(0.4) + (7)\,(0.2) + (12)\,(0.1)$$
$$= \$3.40$$

$$\text{Option B} = (0)\,(0.1) + (0.2) + (2)\,(0.4) + (12)\,(0.2) + (22)\,(0.1)$$
$$= \$7.40$$

The greater expected value of the option with greater stock-price volatility that is shown, therefore, results from the fact that the value of an option cannot be less than zero. Consequently, the value of an option is not a function of the expected value of the stock price at a point in time but a function of the volatility of stock price.

There is another factor affecting the speculative premium for options. This is the level of interest rates in the market—specifically for option analysis, the *call money* rate charged by brokers for the use of margin in common-stock accounts. As this concept is discussed later, it is sufficient here to point out that the leverage achieved through option investment is similar to that achieved through direct margin purchase of the underlying common stock, but without the explicit interest cost involved in the latter. Thus, the higher the call money rate, the greater the savings from the use of options and the greater the speculative value of the option.

To summarize, there are five variables necessary to determine the value of an American call option (ignoring dividends on the common stock, the effect of which is discussed in Chapter 14):

1. and 2. *Stock price–Exercise price:* The relationship between these two prices determines whether the option has a positive theoretical value.
3. *Time to maturity:* The longer the time to maturity, the greater the speculative value of the option because the chances for a profitable movement in the price of the stock are increased.

4. *Volatility of stock price:* There is a positive relationship between the volatility of the underlying stock price and the speculative value of the option because with greater volatility, there is greater potential for gain on the upside and greater benefit from the downside protection involved with the option.

5. *Interest rate:* The higher the call money rate for direct margin purchase of common stock, the greater the relative value of being able to achieve equal amounts of leverage through the alternative of option purchase.

The factors that affect the value of an option can be written in a functional form:

$$C = f(S, X, \sigma^2, T, r_f) \qquad \textbf{(4.31)}$$

where:

C = value of the option;
S = stock price;
X = exercise price;
σ^2 = variance of the stock;
T = time to expiration; and
r_f = risk-free rate.

The value of the option increases as a function of the value of the stock for a given exercise price and maturity date. The lower the exercise price, the greater the value of the option. The longer the time to maturity, the higher the value of the option. The holder of an option will prefer more variance in the price of the stock to less. The greater the variance (price volatility) the greater the probability that the stock price will exceed the exercise price and thus benefit the holder.

Considering two related financial securities—common stock and the option on the common stock—it is possible to illustrate how a risk-free hedged position can be developed. In this way, unprofitable price movements in one of the securities will be offset by profitable price movements in the other. The hedge ratio determines the portion of stock held long in relation to the options in the short position (or vice-versa). With a complete hedge, the value of the hedged position can be shown to be the same regardless of the stock-price outcome. In efficient financial markets, the rate of return earned on perfectly hedged positions will be the risk-free rate. Consequently, it is then possible to determine the appropriate option price at the beginning of the period. If the actual market price is above or below this value, arbitrage would then drive the option price toward its correct level. In Chapter 14, this process and the development of the Black-Scholes (1973) continuous type of option-pricing model and Cox and Rubinstein's (1979) discrete type of binomial option-pricing model will be analyzed in some detail. Option-pricing models and their applications are discussed (in great detail) in Chapters 14, 15, and 21.

SUMMARY

This chapter has reviewed and summarized four alternative valuation theories—discounted cash flow, M and M, CAPM, and OPT—which are basic to introductory courses in financial management or investments. These theories can directly and indirectly become guidelines for further study of security analysis and portfolio management. Derivations and applications of CAPM and OPT to security analysis and portfolio management are studied in detail in later chapters.

QUESTIONS AND PROBLEMS

1. What is arbitrage? Why is it such an important concept in security analysis and portfolio management?
2. Calculate the value of a security that will pay $10/year in perpetuity, if investors require an 8 percent return.
3. Calculate the value of a bond that has an annual coupon rate of 9 percent and a maturity value of $1,000. Assume the bond matures in five years and that bondholders require an 11 percent return.
4. What is a callable bond? Other things being equal, which bond will have greater value, a callable bond or a noncallable bond?
5. Evaluate the following statement: "Because investors purchase a security for its expected cash flow, the dividend policy of a firm will affect the value of the firm's stock."
6. You are given the following information:

   Return on three-month T-bills = 6%
   Expected return on S&P 500   = 9%

   (a) Draw the security-market line.
   (b) Calculate the expected rate of return on a stock with a beta equal to 1.5.
7. Define the following terms:
   (a) call option
   (b) put option
   (c) exercise price
8. What are the advantages of purchasing a call option on IBM stock rather than purchasing the stock itself? Are there any disadvantages?
9. Evaluate the following statement: "Because most individuals dislike risk, the higher the variance of IBM's stock price, the lower the value of put and call options written on IBM's stock."
10. What is the call money rate? Carefully explain the relationship between the call money rate and the value of an option.

11. What is a perpetuity? What would a bond that pays $110 per year in perpetuity be worth if bondholders required a 12 percent return?

12. Briefly explain Modigliani and Miller's Proposition I and its importance to modern financial theory.

REFERENCES

Barnea, A., R. A. Haugen, and L. W. Senbet. "Market Imperfections, Agency Problems, and Capital Structure: A Review." *Financial Management,* v. 10 (Summer 1981), pp. 7–22.

Beranek, W. "Research Directions in Finance." *Quarterly Journal of Economics and Business,* v. 21 (Spring 1981), pp. 6–24.

Brealey, R., and S. Myers. *Principles of Corporate Finance.* McGraw-Hill Book Company, 1988.

Brigham, E. F. *Financial Management: Theory and Practice,* 4th ed. Dryden Press, 1988.

Copeland, T. E., and J. F. Weston. *Financial Theory and Corporate Policy,* 3rd ed. Addison-Wesley Publishing Company, 1988.

DeAngelo, Harry, and Ronald W. Masulis. "Optimal Capital Structure Under Corporate and Personal Taxation." *Journal of Financial Economics,* v. 8 (March 1980), pp. 3–29.

Fama, E. F., and M. H. Miller. *Theory of Finance.* Holt, Rinehart and Winston, 1972.

Galai, D., and R. W. Masulis. "The Option Pricing Model and the Risk Factor of Stock." *Journal of Financial Economics,* v. 3 (March 1976), pp. 53–81.

Haley, C. W., and L. D. Schall. *Theory of Financial Decision,* 2nd ed. McGraw-Hill Book Company, 1979.

Hsia, C. C. "Coherence of the Modern Theories of Finance." *The Financial Review,* v. 16 (Winter 1981), pp. 27–42.

Jensen, M. C., and W. H. Meckling. "Can the Corporation Survive?" *Financial Analysts Journal,* v. 34 (January/February 1978), pp. 31–37.

Lee, Cheng F. *Financial Analysis and Planning: Theory and Application. A Book of Readings.* Addison-Wesley Publishing Company, 1983.

————. *Financial Analysis and Planning: Theory and Applications.* Addison-Wesley Publishing Company, 1985.

————, and Joseph E. Finnerty. *Corporate Finance: Theory, Method, and Applications.* Harcourt Brace Jovanovich, 1990.

————, and J. C. Junkus. "Financial Analysis and Planning: An Overview." *Journal of Economics and Business,* v. 34 (August 1983), pp. 257–83.

Leland, H., and D. Pyle. "Informational Asymmetrics, Financial Structure and Financial Intermediation." *Journal of Finance,* v. 28 (September 1973), pp. 911–22.

Mao, J. C. F. *Quantitative Analysis of Financial Decisions.* The Macmillan Company, 1969.

Miller, Merton H. "The Modigliani-Miller Proposition After 30 Years." *Journal of Economic Perspectives,* v. 2 (Fall 1988), pp. 99–120.

————. "Debt and Taxes." *Journal of Finance,* v. 32 (May 1977), pp. 101–75.

————, and F. Modigliani. "Dividend Policy Growth and the Valuation of Shares." *Journal of Business,* v. 34 (1961), pp. 411–33.

Modigliani, F., and M. Miller. "The Cost of Capital, Corporation Finance and the Theory of Investment." *American Economic Review,* v. 48 (June 1958), pp. 261–97.

————. "Corporate Income Taxes and the Cost of Capital: A Correction." *American Economic Review,* v. 53 (June 1963), pp. 433–43.

Pogue, G. A., and K. Lull. "Corporate Finance: An Overview." *Sloan Management Review,* v. 15 (Spring 1974), pp. 19–38.

Reilly, Frank K. *Investment Analysis and Portfolio Management,* 2nd ed. Dryden Press, 1985.

Ross, S. A. "The Determination of Financial Structure: The Incentive Signalling Approach." *Bell Journal of Economics* (Spring, 1977), pp. 23–40.

Stiglitz, Joseph E. "On the Irrelevance of Corporate Financial Policy." *The American Economic Review,* v. 54 (December 1974), pp. 851–66.

————. "A Re-Examination of the Modigliani-Miller Theorem." *The American Economic Review,* v. 54 (December 1969), pp. 784–93.

Taggart, Robert A., Jr. "Taxes and Corporate Capital Structure in an Incomplete Market." *Journal of Finance,* v. 35 (June 1980).

Van Horne, J. C. *Financial Management and Policy,* 6th ed. Prentice-Hall, 1985.

Weston, J. F. "Developments in Finance Theory." *Financial Management,* v. 10 (Tenth Anniversary Issue, 1981), pp. 5–22.

————, and Thomas E. Copeland. *Managerial Finance,* 8th ed. Dryden Press, 1986.

5 Bond Valuation and Analysis

Of the many investment vehicles available to individuals and portfolio managers, the **bond** is one of the best known and most widely used. While in general a bond can be defined as a long-term fixed obligation of an issuer, there are many types of bonds that can be purchased. For example, bonds can vary by the type of issuer: U.S. Treasury, federal agencies, municipalities, and corporations. Bonds available in the market also vary according to their maturity, coupon rate, callability, and sinking-fund provisions. These bond fundamentals are discussed in the first section.

The second section focuses on the basic model, which states that an investor's required rate of return on any bond is equal to the risk-free rate plus a risk premium. This risk premium can be quantified using the capital asset pricing model (CAPM) approach. Through the use of market return and beta of the CAPM, we explore the computation and use of bond betas.

In the third section, bond-rating procedures are examined and related to the systematic risk of bonds—that is, the bond beta. Theory and estimation for the term structure of interest rates are the topics of the next section; emphasis is placed on the use of this analysis in making better investment decisions. The fundamentals of convertible-bond investment are included in the final section.

BOND FUNDAMENTALS

Types of issuer and bond provisions are two fundamental factors to consider in analyzing bond valuation.

Type of Issuer

Bonds issued by different agencies represent different return and risk. Therefore, it is important to understand the classification of a bond issuer.

U.S. Treasury. As almost everyone is aware, the U.S. government is a large issuer of debt securities. While much of this debt is in the form of short maturity **Treasury bills (T-bills),** which are short-term debt obligations of the U.S. government, there are also many T-note or T-bond issues available for purchase. Both **T-notes** and **T-bonds** are long-term, government debt instruments. T-notes have initial maturities of ten years or less and T- bonds have maturities longer than ten years. The primary distinguishing factor of federal debt is its virtually nonexistent default risk. At the time of issue, their maturity is ten years or more; and they carry a coupon rate, which means that a specified amount of interest is paid semiannually over the life of the issue in addition to the face-value repayment at maturity. The Treasury usually has included a five-year-before-maturity call provision, in which the Treasury can call back the bonds from the investors by repaying the principal and any accumulated interest, but the most recent issues have eliminated this provision. By convention, the callable bonds are priced in the market using the first call date as the effective maturity and by using fractions of a 365-day year to compute accumulated interest.

T-bonds are sold on an auction basis through the Federal Reserve banks and their branch offices. They can be on either a registered or bearer basis. While in the case of registered T-bonds the owners' names are recorded in the Treasury's books, thus lowering the risk from theft, bearer bonds are simpler to transfer and have attached coupons, which can be "clipped" and submitted to any bank for collection of the semiannual interest payments as they become due.

In addition to T-bonds, the Treasury also issues short- and intermediate-term marketable securities via T-bills and T-notes. The notes differ from the bonds in terms of initial maturity only. They are limited by law to an original maturity of one to ten years, while T-bonds can have any maturity longer than ten years. Both tend to be issued for a minimum denomination of $1000 and pay interest semiannually.

Treasury bills are highly liquid and free of default risk. They are sold weekly through a competitive-bidding process conducted by the Federal Reserve System. Currently there are three maturity categories: (1) thirteen weeks, (2) twenty-six weeks, and (3) fifty-two weeks. Bills are sold in minimum denominations of $10,000 and in multiples of $5,000 thereafter. Furthermore, they are issued only in book-entry form. Purchases are evidenced by printed receipts.

The **Treasury yield curve** is a widely used tool for investors and traders. Figure 5-1 presents the data necessary to determine the yield curve. The yield to maturity is defined as the interest rate that equates the current price of a bond or a bill with the present value of the future cash flows that will occur over the life of the bond or bill.

Figure 5-1 lists the important information for each government bond issue: the coupon rate, the maturity, the bid and ask prices, and the yield to maturity.

FIGURE 5-1 Treasury Bonds, Notes, and Bills

TREASURY BONDS, NOTES & BILLS

Wednesday, March 22, 1989

Representative Over-the-Counter quotations based on transactions of $1 million or more as of 4 p.m. Eastern time.

Hyphens in bid-and-asked and bid changes represent 32nds; 101-01 means 101 1/32. a-Plus 1/64. b-Yield to call date. d-Minus 1/64. k-Nonresident aliens exempt from withholding taxes. n-Treasury notes. p-Treasury note; nonresident aliens exempt from withholding taxes.

Source: Bloomberg Financial Markets

TREASURY BONDS AND NOTES

Rate	Mat. Date		Bid	Asked	Bid Chg.	Yld.
11¼	1989	Mar p	99-31	100-02	-01	7.97
6⅜	1989	Mar p	99-28	99-31	....	7.57
7⅛	1989	Apr p	99-21	99-24	....	9.27
14⅜	1989	Apr n	100-05	100-08	....	9.78
6⅞	1989	May p	99-18	99-21	+01	9.03
9¼	1989	May n	99-27	99-31	....	9.17
8	1989	May p	99-20	99-23	....	9.28
11¾	1989	May n	100-07	100-10	+01	9.20
7⅜	1989	Jun p	99-12	99-15	+01	9.21
9⅝	1989	Jun p	99-30	100-01	+01	9.30
7⅝	1989	Jul p	99-08	99-11	+02	9.41
14½	1989	Jul n	101-12	101-15	....	9.44
7¾	1989	Aug p	99-04	99-07	+03	9.56
6⅝	1989	Aug p	98-24	98-28	+02	9.48
13⅞	1989	Aug n	101-16	101-20	-01	9.53
8½	1989	Sep k	99-08	99-12	+02	9.75
9⅜	1989	Sep p	99-21	99-25	+01	9.81
11⅞	1989	Oct n	100-28	100-31	-02	10.03
7⅞	1989	Oct p	98-23	98-27	-01	9.86
6⅜	1989	Nov p	97-23	97-27	+01	9.87
10¾	1989	Nov n	100-12	100-16	-01	9.89
12¾	1989	Nov p	101-19	101-23	-03	9.89
7¾	1989	Nov p	98-17	98-21	+03	9.78
7⅞	1989	Dec p	98-11	98-15	+02	9.95
8⅜	1989	Dec p	98-23	98-27	+01	9.93
7⅜	1990	Jan k	97-27	97-31	+03	9.88
10½	1990	Jan n	100-07	100-11	-01	10.01
3½	1990	Feb	94-15	95-01	-10	9.37
6½	1990	Feb k	97-01	97-05	+03	9.86
7⅛	1990	Feb k	97-15	97-19	+03	9.86
11	1990	Feb p	100-25	100-29	+02	9.90
7¼	1990	Mar p	97-11	97-15	+04	9.91
7⅜	1990	Mar p	97-14	97-18	+03	9.94
10½	1990	Apr n	100-13	100-17	+03	9.95
7⅝	1990	Apr p	97-17	97-21	+03	9.90
7⅞	1990	May k	97-22	97-26	+03	9.92
8¼	1990	May	98-03	98-09	-01	9.85
8⅛	1990	May p	97-29	98-01	+03	9.90
11⅜	1990	May p	101-10	101-14	+01	9.99
7¼	1990	Jun p	96-24	96-28	+04	9.90
8	1990	Jun p	97-19	97-23	+04	9.93
10¾	1990	Jul n	100-25	100-29	+03	9.97
8⅜	1990	Jul p	97-30	98-02	+01	9.92
7⅞	1990	Aug k	97-08	97-12	+04	9.92
9⅞	1990	Aug p	99-27	99-31	+03	9.88
10¾	1990	Aug n	100-31	101-03	+02	9.88
8⅝	1990	Aug	98-06	98-10	+04	9.90
6¾	1990	Sep p	95-16	95-20	+05	9.91
8½	1990	Sep p	97-29	98-01	+03	9.92
11½	1990	Oct n	102-01	102-05	....	9.97
8¼	1990	Oct p	97-14	97-18	+02	9.92
8	1990	Nov p	97-02	97-06	+03	9.88
9⅝	1990	Nov k	99-16	99-20	+03	9.86
13	1990	Nov n	104-16	104-20	+05	9.87
8⅞	1990	Nov p	98-11	98-15	+04	9.86
6⅝	1990	Dec p	94-25	94-29	+06	9.81
9⅛	1990	Dec p	98-25	98-29	+05	9.80
9	1991	Jan p	98-16	98-20	+06	9.81
11¾	1991	Jan n	102-30	103-02	+04	9.85
7⅛	1991	Feb p	95-22	95-26	+06	9.84
9⅛	1991	Feb k	98-23	98-27	+06	9.80
9⅜	1991	Feb p	99-06	99-10	+05	9.77
6¾	1991	Mar p	94-12	94-16	+06	9.81
12⅜	1991	Apr n	104-15	104-19	+05	9.85
8⅛	1991	May p	96-20	96-24	+06	9.83
14½	1991	May n	109-26	109-30	+05	9.27
7⅞	1991	Jun n	96	96-04	+07	9.81
13¾	1991	Jul n	107-21	107-25	+04	9.89
7½	1991	Aug p	94-31	95-03	+05	9.84
8¾	1991	Aug p	97-18	97-22	+05	9.85
14⅞	1991	Aug n	111	111-04	+03	9.57
9⅛	1991	Sep k	98-10	98-14	+04	9.84
12¼	1991	Oct p	105-06	105-10	+08	9.85
6½	1991	Nov p	92-06	92-10	+07	9.86
8½	1991	Nov p	96-28	97	+06	9.81
14¼	1991	Nov n	110-27	110-31	+08	9.45
8¼	1991	Dec k	96-04	96-08	+08	9.82
11⅝	1992	Jan p	104-02	104-06	+07	9.87
6⅝	1992	Feb p	91-31	92-03	+08	9.82
9⅛	1992	Feb p	98-10	98-14	+07	9.75
14⅝	1992	Feb n	112-03	112-07	-01	9.68
7⅞	1992	Mar p	94-29	95-01	+07	9.81
11¾	1992	Apr	104-23	104-27	+04	9.87
6⅝	1992	May k	91-11	91-15	+09	9.84
13¾	1992	May n	110-01	110-05	+02	9.90
8¼	1992	Jun p	95-18	95-22	+09	9.81
10⅜	1992	Jul p	101-11	101-15	+05	9.83
4¼	1987-92	Aug	94-09	94-27	+20	5.95
7¼	1992	Aug	92-28	93	+11	9.71
8¼	1992	Aug p	95-16	95-20	+10	9.79
8¾	1992	Sep p	96-28	97	+09	9.78
9¾	1992	Oct p	99-26	99-30	+11	9.77
8⅜	1992	Nov p	95-18	95-22	+08	9.80
10½	1992	Nov n	101-30	102-02	+10	9.80
9⅛	1992	Dec p	98-01	98-05	+09	9.71
8¾	1993	Jan p	96-22	96-26	+10	9.76
4	1988-93	Feb	94-12	94-26	+20	5.49
6¾	1993	Feb	90-01	90-19	+10	9.70
7⅞	1993	Feb	94-07	94-12	+10	9.63
8¼	1993	Feb p	95-01	95-05	+10	9.77
10⅞	1993	Feb n	103-12	103-16	+10	9.77
7⅜	1993	Apr p	92	92-04	+10	9.77
7⅜	1993	May	92-22	92-26	+09	9.77
10⅝	1993	May n	101-02	101-06	+10	9.76
7¼	1993	Jul p	91-08	91-12	+12	9.74
7½	1988-93	Aug	91-28	92	+14	9.78
8⅝	1993	Aug	96-12	96-20	+14	9.58
8¾	1993	Aug p	96-16	96-20	+12	9.71
11⅞	1993	Aug n	107-11	107-15	+14	9.74
7⅛	1993	Oct p	90-21	90-25	+14	9.67
8⅝	1993	Nov	96-04	96-10	+14	9.62
11¾	1993	Nov n	107-09	107-13	+14	9.72
9	1993	Nov p	97-17	97-21	+14	9.62
7	1994	Jan p	89-22	89-26	+12	9.69
9	1994	Feb	98-03	98-07	+14	9.46
8⅞	1994	Feb p	96-28	97	+13	9.64
7	1994	Apr p	89-16	89-20	+14	9.64
4⅛	1989-94	May	94-05	94-23	+24	5.31
13⅛	1994	May p	113-13	113-17	+13	9.71
9½	1994	May p	99-12	99-16	+13	9.61
8	1994	Jul n	93-04	93-08	+14	9.65
8¾	1994	Aug	96-24	97	+14	9.47
12⅝	1994	Aug p	111-29	112-01	+13	9.70
9½	1994	Oct p	99-10	99-14	+13	9.63
10⅛	1994	Nov	101-27	101-31	+11	9.66
11⅝	1994	Nov	108-07	108-11	+12	9.67
8⅝	1995	Jan p	95-13	95-17	+08	9.64
3	1995	Feb	94-10	94-28	+25	3.98
10½	1995	Feb	103-24	103-28	+12	9.62
11¼	1995	Feb p	106-28	107	+12	9.66
8⅜	1995	Apr p	94-08	94-12	+09	9.62
10⅜	1995	May	103-10	103-14	+14	9.62
11¼	1995	May p	107-05	107-09	+12	9.65
12⅝	1995	May	114-07	114-11	+15	9.49
8⅞	1995	Jul p	96-18	96-22	+13	9.58
10½	1995	Aug p	103-31	104-03	+13	9.62
8⅝	1995	Oct p	95-10	95-14	+13	9.58
9½	1995	Nov p	99-16	99-20	+12	9.57
11½	1995	Nov	109-08	109-12	+15	9.56
9¼	1996	Jan	98-16	98-20	+13	9.52
8⅞	1996	Feb p	96-15	96-19	+13	9.56
7⅜	1996	May p	88-22	88-26	+12	9.57
7¼	1996	Nov p	87-17	87-21	+14	9.56
8⅝	1997	Aug k	94-25	94-29	+14	9.52
8½	1997	May k	94-06	94-10	+15	9.52
8⅞	1997	Nov p	96-06	96-10	+13	9.51
8⅛	1998	Feb p	91-23	91-27	+13	9.50
9	1998	May p	97-06	97-10	+16	9.44
9¼	1998	Aug p	98-19	98-23	+16	9.46
7	1993-98	May	84-28	85	+16	9.49
3½	1998	Nov	93-31	94-17	+26	4.19
8⅞	1998	Nov p	96-06	96-10	+15	9.46
8⅞	1999	Feb p	96-12	96-16	+16	9.42
8½	1994-99	May	93-08	93-12	+16	9.53
7⅞	1995-00	Feb	89-01	89-05	+16	9.49
8⅜	1995-00	Aug	92-05	92-09	+16	9.50
11¾	2001	Feb	116-07	116-13	+16	9.42
13⅛	2001	May	126-11	126-17	+20	9.41
8	1996-01	Aug	90-04	90-10	+20	9.33
13⅜	2001	Aug	128-12	128-18	+20	9.42
15¾	2001	Nov	148-05	148-11	+20	9.38
14¼	2002	Feb	135-28	136-02	+13	9.37
11⅝	2002	Nov	116-10	116-16	+17	9.45
10¾	2003	Feb	109-29	110-03	+20	9.43
10¾	2003	May	109-31	110-05	+17	9.43
11⅛	2003	Aug	113-01	113-07	+16	9.43
11⅞	2003	Nov	119	119-06	+14	9.43
12⅜	2004	May	123-09	123-15	+19	9.43
13¾	2004	Aug	134-20	134-26	+18	9.42
11⅝	2004	Nov k	117-20	117-26	+17	9.42
8¼	2000-05	May	90-09	90-15	+15	9.41
12	2005	May k	121-06	121-12	+18	9.40
10¾	2005	Aug k	110-31	111-05	+18	9.40
9⅜	2006	Feb k	100-04	100-10	+17	9.34
7⅝	2002-07	Feb	85-02	85-08	+17	9.33
7⅞	2002-07	Nov	86-29	87-03	+17	9.35
8⅜	2003-08	Aug	91-02	91-08	+18	9.36
8¾	2003-08	Nov	94-09	94-15	+17	9.37
9⅛	2004-09	May	97-13	97-19	+18	9.39
10⅜	2004-09	Nov	107-03	107-09	+17	9.47
11¾	2005-10	Feb	118-09	118-15	+20	9.48
10	2005-10	May	104-09	104-15	+21	9.45
12¾	2005-10	Nov	127	127-06	+22	9.47
13⅞	2006-11	May	136-19	136-25	+23	9.49
14	2006-11	Nov	138-04	138-10	+25	9.48
10⅜	2007-12	Nov	107-25	107-31	+16	9.45
12	2008-13	Aug	122	122-06	+24	9.48
13¼	2009-14	May	133-14	133-20	+25	9.48
12½	2009-14	Aug k	127	127-06	+25	9.46
11¾	2009-14	Nov k	120-23	120-29	+25	9.43
11¼	2015	Feb k	118-18	118-24	+23	9.32
10⅝	2015	Aug k	112-22	112-28	+19	9.31
9⅞	2015	Nov k	105-12	105-18	+20	9.30
9¼	2016	Feb k	99-13	99-19	+20	9.29
7¼	2016	May k	79-31	80-03	+17	9.27
7½	2016	Nov k	82-12	82-16	+19	9.26
8¾	2017	May k	94-23	94-27	+20	9.27
8⅞	2017	Aug k	95-31	96-03	+19	9.27
9⅛	2018	May k	98-19	98-23	+20	9.25
9	2018	Nov k	97-15	97-19	+19	9.24
8⅞	2019	Feb k	96-09	96-13	+19	9.23

U.S. TREASURY BILLS

Mat. date	Bid	Asked	Yield	Mat. date	Bid	Asked	Yield
	Discount				Discount		
-1989-				7-13	8.96	8.92	9.30
3-23	9.16	9.04	9.17	7-20	8.96	8.92	9.32
3-30	8.06	7.99	8.11	7-27	8.99	8.95	9.37
4- 6	8.61	8.54	8.69	8- 3	9.06	9.02	9.46
4-13	8.81	8.69	8.86	8-10	9.00	8.96	9.41
4-20	9.16	9.09	9.28	8-17	8.96	8.92	9.39
4-27	9.20	9.16	9.37	8-24	9.00	8.96	9.45
5- 4	9.06	9.02	9.24	8-31	9.00	8.96	9.46
5-11	9.12	9.06	9.30	9- 7	8.98	8.94	9.46
5-18	8.96	8.92	9.17	9-14	9.00	8.96	9.50
5-25	8.96	8.92	9.19	9-21	9.00	8.97	9.53
6- 1	8.96	8.92	9.20	9-28	9.03	8.99	9.55
6- 8	9.02	8.98	9.28	10-26	9.02	8.98	9.55
6-15	8.98	8.95	9.27	11-24	9.00	8.96	9.56
6-22	9.01	8.98	9.32	12-21	8.97	8.93	9.56
6-29	8.96	8.92	9.27	-1990-			
7- 6	9.01	8.97	9.34	1-18	8.95	8.91	9.58
				2-15	8.97	8.93	9.65
				3-15	8.95	8.91	9.68

Source: The Wall Street Journal, March 22, 1989.

The **bid and ask prices** represent the prices at which dealers in government bonds are willing to buy and sell the various Treasury bonds and notes. For T-bills the bid and ask prices are quoted in terms of discount from par. Suppose, for instance, a bill has thirty days to maturity and it is currently quoted at a discount of 5.8 percent. Its price can be determined by using Equation (5.1):

$$d = \frac{360}{n} \frac{100 - P}{100} \qquad \text{(5.1)}$$

where:

    d = the discount rate;
    n = the number of days until maturity; and
    P = the price per $100 of face value of the bill.

$$0.058 = \frac{360}{30} \frac{100 - P}{100}$$
$$P = \$99.517 \text{ per } \$100 \text{ of face value}$$

In general, a **bid and ask spread** (the difference at which the market maker or dealer is willing to buy or sell a security) is the price of liquidity service provided by the dealer who bridges the gap between buying and selling in the marketplace. The size of the bid and ask spread is a function of the frequency of trading of the security. More actively traded securities have narrow bid and ask spreads while less actively traded securities have much wider spreads.

Using the data listed in Figure 5–1 the yield curve can be constructed; moreover, both the freehand and regression methods can be used to construct the yield curve. These results are discussed in the section on term structure of interest later in this chapter. Figure 5–2 presents the yield curve in terms of the freehand method on December 31, 1976. In Figure 5–2 the vertical axis represents yield to maturity and the horizontal axis represents the time to maturity.

Most of the time the yield curve is positive, as shown in Figure 5–2, with long-term issues yielding more than short-term issues. The higher yield for a twenty-three-year bond compared with a three-month bill, for example, would compensate a bond investor for the greater risk of price declines and the uncertainty about the long-term economic outlook.

Investors can use yield curves in several ways. First, although yield curves may not be highly reliable and accurate indicators of future interest rates, they form a consensus of how the market participants think interest rates will move in the future. An upward-sloping yield curve indicates that rates are expected to rise, and a downward-sloping yield curve indicates that rates are expected to fall. Second, the investor can use the yield curve to help select the maturity of his investments. For example, if an investor plans to invest a sum of money for five years, there are many alternative ways to reach this objective—buy a five-year bond and hold it until it

FIGURE 5-2   U.S. Government Bond Yield Curve as of December 31, 1976

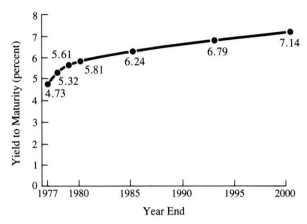

Source: U.S. Treasury Bulletin (January 1977).

matures; buy a one-year bond and, when it matures, buy another one-year bond, and so forth until the desired maturity date is reached; buy a longer-term bond, say, ten years, and sell it after five years have passed. These are three of the many alternative ways that the investor can obtain his or her objective. Analysis of the yield curve can aid the investor in evaluating the profit potential of various strategies.

A third and final use of the yield curve is in identifying individual issues that are either greatly overpriced or underpriced relative to the current yield curve. (For example, if you found a twenty-year U.S. government bond yielding 9 percent, when the yield curve shown in Figure 5-2 shows similar maturity bonds yielding 6½ to 7 percent, you undoubtedly would be interested in finding out why this individual bond was priced differently.)

Federal Agencies.   Federal agencies such as the Government National Mortgage Association (GNMA or "Ginny Mae") and government-sponsored enterprises such as the Small Business Administration (SBA) also issue bonds.

Neither type of **agency bond** is a direct obligation of the Treasury even though some agencies are government sponsored or guaranteed. The net effect is that agency bonds are considered almost default-risk free (if not legally so in all cases) and, therefore, are typically priced to provide only a slightly higher yield than their corresponding T-bond counterparts.

Municipalities.   "Municipality" is a general term commonly used to include all nonfederal government entities. Therefore, **municipal bonds** include those issued by states, counties, cities, and state and local government-established authorities (nonfederal agencies).

There are basically only two types of municipal bonds—general-obligation bonds and revenue bonds. **General-obligation bonds (GOs)** are backed by the "full faith and credit" of the issuing governmental unit, which basically means that the unit may tax its constituents to the legal limit, if necessary, to pay the principal and interest on the bonds.

On the other hand, **revenue bonds** are backed only by the revenues generated by the project being financed. The issuing governmental unit is not directly responsible for any debt service on such bonds beyond that which is self-generated. Of course, since it is a market reality that municipalities with outstanding revenue issues in default will be severely handicapped in securing any future revenue bond financing, investors tend to expect the sponsoring units to cover project revenue shortages. The degree of this expectation varies from municipality to municipality, but to the extent it exists the yields on revenue bonds will be only slightly higher than those on GOs.

In recent years, large variability in interest rates has hampered commercial and economic development in the United States, particularly at the local level. As a result, creative financing plans for such projects as new shopping centers, downtown business redevelopment, and even hotels have included the cooperation of local municipalities, most often city governments. This cooperation has taken the form of city issuances of tax-free industrial revenue and economic development bonds. Buyers of these issues tend not to look to the cities for ultimate payment, because the municipalities are not likely to accept the same level of responsibility that they would for city-originated projects. Therefore, the marketability and yields of these bonds are more directly related to the financial strength of the business entity involved. Congress has tightened regulations, and in some cases eliminated certain types of issues, in order to limit the volume of industrial revenue and economic development bonds because of perceived abuses in which many municipalities have been considered too lax.

The primary distinguishing feature of municipal bonds is the federal income-tax exemption. This exemption is in effect a federal subsidy to state and local governments to assist them in financing their needs.

For many investors the exemption provides an attractive vehicle for investment. Since tax-free municipal bonds are priced in the market according to the average marginal tax rate of their buyers, those investors at the high end of the tax-rate spectrum stand to benefit the most. The equation most commonly used for determining the equivalent taxable yield (ETY) of a tax-exempt issue is:

$$\text{ETY} = \frac{\text{Tax-exempt coupon rate}}{(1 - \tau)} \qquad (5.2)$$

where τ = the marginal tax rate of the investor. So an investor in the 30-percent tax bracket would consider a 9-percent municipal bond to be equivalent to a 13-percent taxable bond $[9/(1 - 0.3) = 13]$.

However, this equation is only applicable to bonds that are selling at par value because capital gains and their different rate of taxation are ignored. For issues not selling at par, the yield portions from interest and capital gains must be estimated and evaluated at their appropriately different rates of taxation in order to get a true after-tax comparison.[1] In general for municipal bonds, the interest payments are tax exempt and any capital gains are taxed as normal income.

Corporations.   Corporations issue a variety of long-term debt securities. They differ mainly in the type of collateral supporting the bonds. These range from mortgage bonds secured by real assets to debentures secured simply by the general credit of the issuing firm.

While public utilities dominate the corporate bond sector, corporates are also issued by industrial, transportation, financial, and other types of firms. Corporate bonds are attractive to many investors because of their high yields relative to government debt and their low risk compared to corporate equity issues.

Bond Provisions

Bond provisions such as maturity classes, debentures, coupon, maturity, callability, and sinking funds are discussed in this section.

Maturity Classes.   Bonds are usually grouped by their maturity classes. **Short-term bonds** are any bonds maturing within five years. **Medium-term bonds** mature in five to about ten years. **Long-term bonds** may run twenty years or more. Short-term bonds may be secured or unsecured and are common in industrial financing. Real-estate or equipment mortgages or other securities usually attempt to secure medium-term bonds, as do railroads and utilities. Capital-intensive industries such as airlines and utilities with long expectations of equipment life and associated costs are heavy users of long-term bonds.

Mortgage Bond.   A **mortgage bond** is an issue secured with a lien on real property or buildings. A *blanket mortgage* is an issue secured with a lien on all assets of a firm. The mortgage bond may be open-end, limited open-end, or closed-end, or it may contain an after-acquired property clause. An open-end mortgage allows more bonds to be issued on the same mortgage contract. There are usually limitations on the amount of additional borrowing. Normally, the open-end mortgage contains an after-acquired property clause, which provides that all property acquired after the first mortgage was

---

[1] For more precise measures, see M. L. Leibowitz, *Total After-Tax Bond Performance and Yield Measures*, Salomon Brothers, 1974.

issued be added to the property already pledged as security by the contract. A limited open-end mortgage allows the firm to use additional borrowings up to a specified maximum amount; a closed-end mortgage prohibits additional borrowing on that property. The type of mortgage and the provisions that are behind the mortgage bond determine its risk and return.

Debentures. **Debentures** are unsecured bonds. They are issued with no liens against specific property, although a claim against earnings exists. All assets not specifically pledged, or any balance remaining after payment of secured debts from previously pledged assets, are available to pay the legal claims of general creditors. *Subordinate debentures* are debentures that are specifically made subordinate to all other general creditors holding claims on assets.

Coupons. A **bond coupon** is the stated amount of interest that the firm (or government) promises to pay each year of the bond's life. In practice it is most often paid semiannually, and it is frequently expressed as a percentage of the par value of the bond. The par value is the stated amount of principal that will be paid at the termination of the bond. (For corporate bonds, the par value is almost always $1,000 and will be assumed to be so in our examples unless otherwise stated.) While the coupon rate is one of the determinants of a bond's investment yield, coupon rates are only equal among bonds selling at the par value.

Maturity. Another important factor affecting the investment return of bonds is their maturity, or time remaining to repayment of principal. In fact, the most popular yield measure for bonds is **yield to maturity (YTM),** or promised yield. The YTM is defined as the discount rate that will equate the present value of all remaining cash flows to the bond investor (periodic interest payment and par value at maturity) to the current price in the market. (It is identical to the market rate of discount used in Chapter 4 in discussing bond valuation.)

Callability. The **call provision** allows the issuing firm to terminate the bond issue before maturity. This provision may include a deferral clause that prevents the firm from exercising this right for a number of years. Such a clause is more valued by investors during periods in which coupons are historically high. In any case, this provision, as well as any other provision perceived to be an advantage to either the issuer or the buyer, has an impact on the pricing of the issue.

Since the call provision is clearly an advantage to the issuer, the effective yield that must be provided to new-issue buyers is higher for callable bonds. Callability is also used with increasing frequency in issues of preferred stock and is probably most important to the issuer of convertible bonds. This latter point is discussed in more detail later in the chapter.

The call provision has an impact on bond investment yields in another important way. To the extent that a bond issue is expected to be called, the call provision shortens the bond's expected maturity. Investors allow for this by relying on computed estimates of **yield to call (YTC)** rather than YTM. The computational procedure is similar to that for YTM, in that the YTC is the discount rate that equates the present value of all the cash flows expected through the point of call—that is, the interest payments and the call price. The only differences are fewer interest payments and the substitution of the call price at the call date for the face-value payment at the stated maturity date. Thus, the key distinguishing feature is the effective maturity.

The **call price** is the sum of the face value and the call premium, both of which are set in the bond indenture at the time of original issue. It should also be noted that the YTC is a more uncertain rate than the YTM. This is so because the call date is often difficult to estimate, while the maturity date is fixed. As a result, there may be more variability in bond prices for bonds that can be called.

The linkage of bonds and put options has occurred in recent years. A putable debenture is a bond that carries a put option providing that the investor can sell the bond back to the issuer at a specified exercise price prior to the maturity date of the bond. A putable bond can be viewed as a regular debt instrument that has a bundle of put options written by the issuer of the bond to the investors who own the bond. These options grant valuable sale rights to investors and impose purchase obligations on the issuer. Investors pay for these valuable rights by accepting a coupon rate on the bond that is lower than that normally associated with a similar bond without the put provision. A very common example of a putable bond is a U.S. Savings Bond. Each bond specifies a redemption schedule of increasing prices at which the investor can sell the bond back to the Treasury at a specific date in the future. An investor can choose to sell the bond back to the Treasury or hold the bond until it matures.

Sinking Funds.   The effective maturity of a bond is also impacted by the sinking-fund provision. The typical **sinking fund** involves a partial liquidation of the total issue each year as specified in the indenture. Therefore, the average maturity of the individual bonds making up the issue is reduced. While this process will impact the investment yield in a less drastic way than an expected call, the relatively small number of bonds being retired each year has not led to the calculation of a special yield similar to the YTC.

Theoretically, sinking-fund bonds are priced on the basis of a weighted-average maturity. The **yield to weighted-average maturity (YTWAM)** could be computed as the discount rate that would equate all of the cash inflows, including the sinking-fund early retirements, to the current price of the bond. The payoff inflows would have to be estimated as either the call price, if the bonds are expected to be selling at prices that are higher than the call price, or at an estimated market price, if they are expected to be selling at less than

the call price. Again it is clear that uncertainty is injected into the pricing process.

BOND VALUATION, BOND INDEX, AND BOND BETA

Bond valuation, bond index, bond beta, and other related issues are the subjects of this section.

Bond Valuation

The valuation or price determination of bonds was stated in Chapter 4 to be accomplished by computing the present value of all future cash flows to be received by the security holder. That is,

$$P_0 = \sum_{t=1}^{n} \frac{C_t}{(1 + k_b)^t} + \frac{P_n}{(1 + k_b)^n} \qquad (5.3)$$

where:

P_0 = the price of the bond at the time zero;
C_t = coupon interest payment in period t;
P_n = face value of bond to be paid at period n;
k_b = required rate of return of bondholders; and
n = number of periods to maturity.

Sample Problem 5.1 provides further illustration.

Sample Problem 5.1

In 1988 the IBM 9-percent bonds maturing in 2003, when the required rate of return of bondholders is 10 percent, should be selling for $922.785.

$$P_0 = \sum_{t=1}^{30} \frac{\$45}{(1 + 0.05)^t} + \frac{\$1,000}{(1.05)^{30}}$$

$$= \$45(15,373) + \$1,000 (0.231)$$

$$= \$691.785 + \$231$$

$$= \$922.785$$

It should be noted that since corporate bonds pay interest semiannually, Equation (5.3) must be adjusted to reflect these semiannual payments. This can be done by dividing the annual interest payment of $90 per year by two, thereby increasing the number of periods til maturity from fifteen years to 30 six-month intervals, and dividing the required rate of return by two.

In this chapter the same process indicated in Equation (5.3) is used to determine the investors' yield, given the existence of the current bond price. The bond yields most used by investors and analysts are: (1) current yield (CY), (2) yield to maturity (YTM, also called promised yield), (3) yield to call (YTC), and (4) realized yield (RY).

Current yield is computed by dividing the coupon interest payment by the current market price of the bond.

$$\text{CY} = \frac{C}{P_0} \tag{5.4}$$

Sample Problem 5.2 provides further illustration.

Sample Problem 5.2

For the IBM bond of Sample Problem 5.1, the current yield is 9.75 percent. This can be calculated in terms of Equation (5.4) as:

$$\text{CY} = \frac{\$90}{\$922.785} = 0.0975$$

This is a measure that reflects the rate of return on actual investment, but it is not a complete measure of a bond investor's rate of return. It is used by some analysts to compare with dividend yields on alternative investments in common stocks●

A more complete measure of bond return is the yield to maturity, because it takes into account all of the cash flows to be received over the entire life of the bond. It is commonly considered the appropriate discount rate [k_b in Equation (5.3)] and can be computed on a trial-and-error basis (most investors use special-function calculators or bond-yield tables) given the values of P_0, C_t, P_n, and n. There is also an approximation method based on a return on investment approach:

$$\text{AYTM} = \frac{C + \dfrac{P_n - P_0}{n}}{\dfrac{P_n + P_0}{2}} \tag{5.5}$$

where:

$$C = \text{annual coupon interest payment;}$$
$$P_n - P_0 = \text{amount of discount at which bond is selling; and}$$
$$\frac{P_n + P_0}{2} = \text{the average investment over the period to maturity.}$$

Sample Problem 5.3 provides further illustration.

Sample Problem 5.3

If an AT&T 2001 bond with a coupon of 7 percent was selling for $790 in 1988, its AYTM could be calculated by using Equation (5.5).

$$\text{AYTM} = \frac{70 + \dfrac{1000 - 790}{13}}{\dfrac{1000 + 790}{2}}$$

$$= 9.6\%$$

In fact, the actual yield to maturity for this bond, given this information, is 9.78 percent⬤

When it seems likely that a bond will be called before maturity, the time to the expected call date is a more appropriate measure of the maturity of the issue. In this case, analysts will try to estimate the most likely call date and compute the yield to call. Both Equations (5.3) and (5.5) can be adjusted to allow for this. For clarity of exposition, the approximation Equation (5.5) is adjusted:

$$\text{AYTC} = \frac{C + \dfrac{P_c - P_0}{n_c}}{\dfrac{P_c + P_0}{2}} \tag{5.6}$$

where:

P_c = estimated market price at the call date; and
n_c = time to estimated call date.

Often, the first possible call date is used by analysts as the estimated call date, particularly when the coupon rate is high and the bond seems likely to be called. Sample Problem 5.4 illustrates this concept.

Sample Problem 5.4

If the AT&T 2001 bond of Sample Problem 5.3 is callable in 1995 at $1,010, the approximate yield to call can be calculated by using Equation (5.6).

$$\text{AYTC} = \frac{70 + \dfrac{1010 - 790}{7}}{\dfrac{1010 + 790}{2}}$$

$$= 11.26\%$$

This is higher than the yield to maturity for two reasons: (1) $1,010 is earned at call instead of $1,000 at maturity, and (2) the capital gain is earned over a shorter period of time—seven instead of thirteen years⬤

A realized yield can be computed as the ex-post rate of return earned over a past period, or it can be more usefully referred to as an expected yield to be realized over a holding period shorter than the time to maturity. Using the approximation format:

$$\text{ARY} = \frac{C + \dfrac{P_{hp} - P_0}{n_{hp}}}{\dfrac{P_{hp} + P_0}{2}} \tag{5.7}$$

where:

P_{hp} = estimated market price at the end of the holding period; and
n_{hp} = time to the end of the estimated holding period.

As shown in the example for calculating the price of a bond using Equation (5.3), an adjustment for semiannual compounding must be made. The general rule for this adjustment is to multiply n by 2 and to divide C and K by 2. The results of these adjustments for the examples of this section are shown in Table 5-1.

Bond Indexes

The Salomon Brothers High-Grade, Long-Term Bond Index and the Lehman Brothers–Kuhn, Loeb Bond Index are the best known and most widely quoted bond indexes available today. Before specifying their content and makeup, it is useful to consider some of the general problems involved in trying to accurately index the overall bond market. Published yield data cover only a relatively few of the total number of issues. Most bonds are not listed on the major exchanges but trade in the over-the-counter market (OTC). There is no central location or source of transaction prices for bonds. Another problem is that many issues, even those listed on major exchanges, are not actively traded, thus leading to inefficient pricing. As interest rates change over time, "old" price quotes become totally inaccurate. In addition, even for listed bonds, the larger institutional sales and purchases will often take place off the exchanges at prices that can be significantly different from the odd-lot type transactions taking place on the exchanges.

TABLE 5–1 Semiannual Adjustments

AT&T	2001 (percent)	Adjustment for Semiannual Interest (percent)
AYTM	9.6	4.81 semiannual = 9.62 annualized
AYTC	11.26	5.63 semiannual = 11.26 annualized

To avoid the problems mentioned above, bond traders at Salomon Brothers individually price all publicly offered issues rated AA or better and make up a package of indexes over various spans of time—for example, the latest month, the last three months, the calendar year to date, the past twelve months, and the past four quarters. Their monthly report includes several useful subcategories of the overall market data, but the basic measure is the total rate-of-return index, using a market value weighted approach.

Lehman Brothers–Kuhn, Loeb (LBKL) take a completely different approach to resolving the pricing problems of corporate bonds. They compute theoretical prices by programming in factors such as bond ratings, maturities, coupon rates, sinking-fund provisions, call and call-protection provisions, and dollar amounts outstanding. Yield-curve and yield-spread factors are programmed in on a monthly basis in order to stay as up to date as possible with market conditions. Verification with market quotations is made for those issues that have current active data available, and actual quotations are used for U.S. Treasury and agency bonds. The LBKL group also produces a package of bond indexes, including the Bond Index, the Long-Term Corporate Bond Indexes, and the U.S. Government/Agency Bond Index. Several thousand corporate bonds of BBB grade or better, and several hundred government and agency issues, are included in the indexes at any given time. The LBKL group also subcategorizes its index information in ways useful to bond analysts and investors.

Bond Beta

The **bond beta** is computed similarly to its counterpart, the **stock beta.** The bond beta is a ratio of the covariance of bond return with the market to the variance in the market. As a useful risk measure, of course, the bond beta should be related to the risk of default and the price-level risk associated with interest-rate changes. Since bond ratings have been used for many years to relate a firm's operating and financial characteristics to the likelihood of default, it was logical to expect these ratings to be inversely related to bond betas.

Prior studies by Beaver, Kettler, and Scholes (1970) and others have shown that there is a significant relationship between stock betas and internal corporate variables. In addition, Pinches and Mingo (1973) and others have found that internal corporate variables have a significant relationship with bond ratings. Following from such leads, Reilly and Joehnk (1976) and Weinstein (1981, 1983) have studied the relationship of bond betas with bond ratings and interest-rate risk.

Before looking further into the results of these interesting empirical studies, it is essential to define the bond beta. In the following linear regression model:

$$\tilde{R}_{bt} = \alpha + \beta \tilde{R}_{mt} + \tilde{\epsilon}_{bt} \tag{5.8}$$

where:

$\tilde{R}_{bt}$ = the estimated holding-period return on bond b at time t;
$\tilde{R}_{mt}$ = the estimated holding-period return on some market index at time t;
$\tilde{\epsilon}_{bt}$ = the residual random-error term (assumed to have a mean of zero);
α = the regression intercept; and
β = the bond beta.

An important question involving this regression is what to use as the market index. Is an index like the S&P 500, commonly used to compute stock betas, appropriate for bond betas? Would an index totally consisting of bonds provide superior results? Reilly and Joehnk (1976) use five different market indexes.

1. Moody's Average Corporate Bond Yield Index
2. Moody's Lagged Corporate Bond Yield Index
3. Moody's Segregated Group-Rating Bond Yield Index
4. S&P 500 Composite Stock Price Index
5. Moody's Average Corporate Bond Index converted to a price basis

Weinstein (1981) estimates bond beta using these different market indexes:

1. The CRSP value-weighted NYSE index (including dividends),[2]
2. A bond index developed by Ibbotson (1978), and
3. A combined index with a 0.7 weight on the CRSP index and 0.3 on the Ibbotson index.

This third index is used again by Weinstein (1983) because the earlier study seems to show that this is the best market-portfolio measure of the three used in that study.

Weinstein computes correlation coefficients between βs calculated from each market index for each year of his study (1962–1975). The results indicate a very high degree of correlation between the stock index and the combined index (mostly 0.89 or higher), a moderately high correlation between the bond index and the combined index (0.3 to 0.8); but mixed results for the correlation between the stock index and the bond index (negative in the early years and positive in the later years). In general, his estimations of bond betas using the three different market indexes show that the choice of index is quite important. He concludes that the combined index provides the most reliable results.

---

[2] CRSP is the Center for Research on Security Prices; the CRSP index contains every stock listed on the New York Stock Exchange. Each security is weighted in the index by its market value as a percentage of the total value of the New York Stock Exchange. Hence large, high-value firms such as IBM would have a greater weight than smaller-value firms.

As will be shown, the market model illustrated by Equation (5.8) requires a market index that, in theory, is representative of all risky assets. Hence Weinstein's results are supportive of the theory. When measuring a security's systematic risk (β), the more representative the index, the better the measure.

Reilly and Joehnk (1976) find that among the three bond-yield series used to measure market return, the Average Corporate Bond Yield Index (measure number 1 in the list above) and the Segregated Group-Rating Bond Yield Index (measure number 3) are both clearly superior to the Lagged Corporate Bond Yield Index (measure number 2). This "superiority" as measured by Reilly and Joehnk is in terms of lower unsystematic risk or standard error of the estimate (SEE). A perfect market-portfolio measure would have no unsystematic risk.

Reilly and Joehnk (1976) also compare market measures 4 and 5, the S&P 500 Composite Stock Price Index and the Average Corporate Bond Index converted to a price basis. While the former is better in terms of lower autocorrelation results, the bond-price index is clearly superior in terms of lower unsystematic risk (SEE).

To summarize, both the Weinstein and the Reilly–Joehnk studies show:

1. The choice of a market index has a significant effect on the bond betas determined therefrom.
2. Indexes made up of only common stocks are inferior to those including at least some bonds determining bond beta.
3. Bonds have a low level of systematic risk as measured by bond beta.

The next topic we examine is the relationship between this risk measure and the rating assigned to bonds by agencies such as Moody's and Standard and Poor's.

It would be expected, if beta is a useful measure of the risk inherent in bond investment, that this measure is inversely related to the bond ratings assigned to the issuing firms. However, the results from the Reilly–Joehnk study (1976) do not consistently support this hypothesis. The authors conjecture that this may be true because bond ratings are assigned by the agencies on the likelihood of default, while the market risk measure (beta) depends upon the relationship between the changes in market yields (prices). The major short-run determinants of bond yields are overall macroeconomic factors, which will tend to have a similar effect on all risk classes of bonds. Therefore, the risk measured by beta would not necessarily be closely related to bond ratings that concentrate on the probability of default. The chance of default generally involves not only macroeconomic but also individual firm factors.

Weinstein (1981) finds similar results over the first four classes, AAA to BAA, that is, there is no consistent relationship between bond betas and bond ratings. Nevertheless, he does find a significant relationship in the inverse direction, as would be predicted, when the lower-class bonds (BA,

B, and below) are considered. This is likely because the probability of default is so low for high-rated bonds and only becomes a factor in beta measurements for the low-rated bonds. In any case, Weinstein (1981) and Reilly–Joehnk (1976) find that the systematic risk (beta) of corporate bonds is an important factor to be considered by security analysts and portfolio managers.

BOND-RATING PROCEDURES

Bond ratings obviously are of interest to the academic community as evidenced by the number of bond-rating studies published in recent years. Ratings are even more important to the issuers and purchasers of the securities. From the investor's viewpoint, the ratings are an indication of the quality or safety of the issue; while from the issuers' viewpoint, the ratings have a direct impact on the cost of their funds.

Bonds are classified according to credit risk by three bond-rating companies: (1) Moody's Investor Services, (2) Standard & Poor's, and (3) Fitch Investor Services. The purpose of their ratings is to provide investors a measure of default risk that would be difficult and costly to obtain on their own.

The rating categories for the two best-known services, Moody's and Standard & Poor's, are described in Table 5–2. The services tend to emphasize that their ratings are based upon a mixture of qualitative and quantitative factors that cannot be simulated by models that rely entirely on performance ratios or other quantitative measurements. A number of researchers have attempted in various ways to develop models that will predict either the ratings themselves or the occurrence of rating changes. Probably the best known of these studies is one conducted by Pinches and Mingo (PM, 1973) in which they develop and test a factor analysis/multiple-discriminant analysis (MDA) model for predicting bond ratings. Using the factor analysis as a screen, thirty-five firm- or issue-related variables believed to influence the rating of a bond issue are reduced to seven factors or dimensions that explain 63 percent of the variation in the data.[3] These seven factors include:

1. Size
2. Financial leverage
3. Long-term capital intensiveness
4. Return on investment

---

[3] Some variables were standardized and a log transformation was applied to others to improve normality and reduce heteroskedasticity.

TABLE 5–2   Moody's and Standard & Poor's Rating Categories for Bonds

Moody's Rating	Description	Standard & Poor's Rating	Description
Aaa	Bonds of highest quality.	AAA	Bonds of highest quality.
Aa	Bonds of high quality.	AA	High-quality debt obligations.
A	Bonds whose security of principal and interest is considered adequate but may be impaired in the future.	A	Bonds that have a strong capacity to pay interest and principal but may be susceptible to adverse effects.
Baa	Bonds of medium grade that are neither highly protected nor poorly secured.	BBB	Bonds that have an adequate capacity to pay interest and principal, but are more vulnerable to adverse economic conditions or changing circumstances.
Ba	Bonds of speculative quality whose future cannot be considered well assured.	BB	Bonds of lower medium grade with few desirable investment characteristics.
B	Bonds that lack characteristics of a desirable investment.		
Caa	Bonds in poor standing that may be defaulted.	B & CCC	Primarily speculative bonds with great uncertainties and major risk if exposed to adverse conditions.
Ca	Speculative bonds that are often in default.	C	Income bonds on which no interest is being paid.
C	Bonds with little probability of any investment value (lowest rating).	D	Bonds in default.

5. Short-term capital intensiveness
6. Earnings stability
7. Debt and debt-coverage stability

One variable from each factor is entered into a MDA procedure in order to determine which variables best describe the differences between the ratings groups. The MDA model performing best includes the following variables.

1. Subordination
2. Years of consecutive dividends
3. Issue size
4. The five-year mean of (net income + interest)/interest
5. The five-year mean of long-term debt/total assets
6. Net income/total assets

Linear classification procedures are then used to determine that 70 percent of the original sample, 65 percent of a holdout sample, and 56 percent of a new sample are correctly classified, respectively.[4] The Baa group, which

---

[4] The holdout sample consisted of bonds in the same year as the original sample, while the new sample consisted of bonds issued in the first six months of the following year.

includes both subordinated and nonsubordinated bonds, is the most difficult to classify. Only four of twenty-five Baa-rated bonds are correctly classified in the holdout and new samples. Pinches and Mingo's conclusion about this result is that the Baa class is difficult to predict because of the subordination feature. All sample bonds rated below Baa are subordinated, while all but two sample bonds rated above Baa are nonsubordinated.[5] Thirteen of the bonds rated Baa are subordinated and twelve are nonsubordinated.

In their 1975 follow-up study, PM conclude that quadratic rather than linear classification rules are superior. Two alternative models are presented. The first approach uses the quadratic procedure and determines that 65 percent of the bonds are correctly classified. Pinches and Mingo's second approach is completed in two steps. The bonds are first divided into two groups, subordinated and nonsubordinated, and one discriminate model is then developed for each group. When the classification results are combined, more than 75 percent of the bonds are correctly classified.

In a study using the 132-bond data base of the PM studies, Zumwalt and Wort (ZW, 1980) develop MDA models for all adjacent groups of two classifications (Aa-A, A-Baa, Ba-B), as well as for the PM five-group model. First looking at the ZW results for the five-group model, 84 of the 132 bonds (63.6 percent) are correctly classified, and, as in the case of the PM study, those bonds rated Baa are the most difficult to classify. Only six of twenty-five, or 24 percent of the Baa, are correctly classified. In order to examine the problem more closely, group overlap statistics are computed. While group means for the variables may be significantly different, classification can still be quite difficult, if the groups exhibit a substantial amount of overlap among the individual variables for each bond. In fact, the results do show a substantial amount of overlap of the A-, Baa-, and Ba-rated bonds, with less overlap between Aa and A, and Ba and B. These results help explain the difficulty encountered in classifying the Baa-rated bonds.

The adjacent group classifications are quite good overall, with 87.5 percent of the Aa-A groups, 68.6 percent of the A-Baa groups, 71.0 percent of the Baa-Ba groups, and 88.1 percent of the Ba-B groups correctly classified. Even the percentage of correct Baa classifications is an improvement, 52 percent when paired with A-rated bonds and 44 percent when paired with Ba-rated bonds—an average of 48 percent.

Zumwalt and Wort also find some interesting results when comparing the percent of total discriminating power among the five variables. While the five-group model identifies years of consecutive dividends and issue size as the two most important variables in the overall model, the two-group analysis allows more specific insights. For example, years of consecutive dividends is the most important variable for the two lowest ratings comparisons (Baa-Ba and Ba-B) and the second most important for the highest rating

---

[5] In PM's follow-up study (1975), they eliminate the two A-rated subordinated bonds in order to more directly compare the results of several models and to focus on the subordination feature.

comparison (Aa-A). Issue size is the most important variable for the two highest rating comparisons (Aa-A and A-Baa) and is third and fifth, respectively, in importance for the Baa-Ba and Ba-B comparisons. In examining the rationale for these results it must be understood that these variables are really proxies for more basic investment attributes, such as creditworthiness and probability of default. For example, issue size is likely to be directly correlated with creditworthiness. While it is common for firms issuing Aa- and A-rated bonds to have paid dividends for many years consecutively (thus rendering this variable comparatively useless as a distinguishing factor), relative creditworthiness can be judged on the basis of issue size as indicated in the linkage described above. For firms issuing the lower-rated bonds, the size range of bond issues may be limited somewhat by the lack of creditworthiness as indicated more directly by continuing ability to make dividend payments to the firm's common stockholders.

The use of quantitative models to predict bond ratings or the changes in bond ratings may be just an academic exercise. Several empirical studies have shown that the investment market adjusts bond prices in response to new information items much more efficiently than the bond-ratings services. That is, by the time a bond rating has been changed upward or downward by the services, the information that caused the rating to change has already been reflected in the bond price. Hence what investors need is a better understanding of what types of information affect the pricing of bonds.

Hettenhouse and Sartoris (1980) and Weinstein (1977) show that the ratings changes themselves have very little informational value to analysts and investors. While the bond market has generally been found to be less efficient than the stock market, it is apparently efficient enough to be able to price bonds independently of the information supplied by the rating agencies. While this is true, the continuing existence of rating services indicates that some segments of the market consider bond ratings useful information in the assessment of relative risk. Hence, it is important to understand the procedures and information used to evaluate the bonds by the bond-rating agencies, as discussed in this section. The next section focuses on an important concept—term structure of interest for bond valuation.

TERM STRUCTURE OF INTEREST

The theory of term structure and its estimators is investigated in this section. In addition, applications of term structure are discussed.

Theory

Market interest rates influence the rate of return on bond investments as well as the variability of that rate of return. It is important, therefore, to examine the development and impact of term or maturity structure on the market interest rates.

FIGURE 5–3   Yield-Curve Patterns

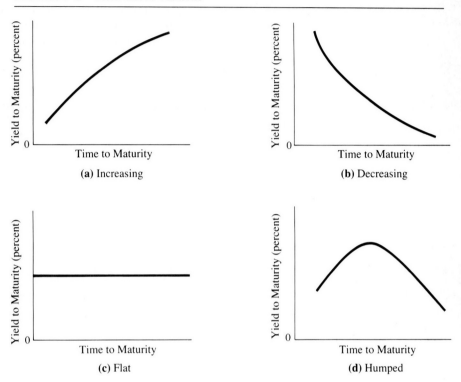

The **term structure of interest rates** is typically described by the yield curve, a static representation of the relationship between term to maturity and yield to maturity (YTM) that exists at a given point in time, within a given risk class of bonds. All other bond features, such as coupon, callability, and market sector, should also remain constant in this cross-sectional comparison. Khoury (1983) points out that term structure and yield curves are only equivalent for pure discount bonds, that is, for bonds that have no interim coupon payments, only a simple payment at the maturity of the issue.[6] This is so because the YTM of coupon issues is more properly a function of a weighted average term to maturity. This problem is again addressed in Chapter 20 in connection with the concept of bond duration.

Yield curves, measured at a point in time, show the market yield/maturity expectations at the time of measurement only. These expectations can and do change over time, sometimes abruptly. In general, the yield curve approximates four patterns or shapes, as shown in Figure 5–3.

---

[6] Pure discount bonds are also called zero-coupon bonds. Some investment dealers in the bond market have recently begun to manufacture zero-coupon bonds from regular U.S. Treasury issues by "stripping" the coupon payments away from the overall bond-payment structure and marketing them separately as single-payment investments. Early in 1985, the U.S. Treasury began making this process easier by separating the registration of coupon payments and maturity payments upon issuance.

Historically, the increasing yield curve has been most common. It has an added intuitive appeal to investors because of the implication that farther distant cash flows should require a higher risk premium, other things remaining the same. The decreasing curve for the most part has not been common in the past, although it occurred frequently in the late 1970s and early 1980s as interest rates reached historically high levels. The humped curve tends to occur during transition periods from high to low levels and reflects this transition through higher intermediate-term rates. Flat curves occur rarely for any significant period of time. There are theories that have been developed to explain the yield-curve patterns. The most common of these are: (1) the expectations hypothesis, (2) the liquidity-preference hypothesis, (3) the market-segmentation hypothesis, and (4) preferred habitat.

Most economists agree that the expectations hypothesis is the best single description of this theoretical foundation of term structure. According to this demand-based theory, the expectations of market participants concerning the likely course of future interest-rate movements determine the market demand for each bond maturity class. Given a set of appropriate assumptions, it can be shown through this approach that the interest rate for any long-term issue can be measured as the geometric mean of the series of expected single-period interest rates leading up to the maturity period of the issue being examined; or more simply, that long-term rates are the geometric mean of expected short-term rates. The expectations hypothesis implies that investors, as a group, are indifferent to the specific maturities held and that on average, bonds of all maturities are perfect substitutes for one another:

$$(1 + R_n) = \left[\prod_{t=1}^{n} (1 + r_t) \right]^{1/n} \tag{5.9}$$

where:

R_n = YTM for a bond with n years to maturity; and
r_t = one-year forward rate that is expected to occur in year t.

Sample Problem 5.5 provides further illustration.

Sample Problem 5.5

As indicated in the figure, the forward rate r_t takes on the values 5 percent, 6 percent, and 4 percent for t = 1, 2, and 3, respectively. Each of these is a forward rate occurring at some future time. Equation (5.9) can be used to calculate the yield-to-maturity rate R_n where n = 2.

$$
\begin{aligned}
1 + R_2 &= \sqrt{(1 + r_1)(1 + r_2)} \\
&= \sqrt{(1 + 0.05)(1 + 0.06)} \\
&= 1.055 - 1 \\
&= 0.055
\end{aligned}
$$

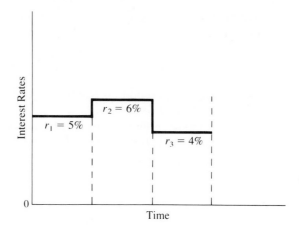

In using the expectations hypothesis to evaluate long-term bonds, investors are not likely to try to estimate each period's expected forward rate to the point of maturity. However, they can use rates available on existing issues of varying maturities to estimate implied one-year yields. To do so, Equation (5.9) can be rewritten:

$$(1 + r_n) = \frac{(1 + R_n)^n}{(1 + R_{n-1})^{n-1}} \tag{5.10}$$

Sample Problem 5.6 provides further illustration.

Sample Problem 5.6

If six-year Treasury bonds have a current YTM of 9 percent and five-year Treasury bonds have a current YTM of 8 percent, the implied one-year forward rate expected in year six would be

$$(1 + r_6) = \frac{(1.09)^6}{(1.08)^5} = \frac{1.68}{1.47}$$
$$= 1.14$$

and r_6 is expected to be 14 percent. Note that the implied one-year forward rate beginning in the sixth year is greater than either the current five- or six-year YTMs. This is the result of an upward-sloping yield curve and the time value of money●

While the pure version of the expectations theory assumes investors' risk neutrality at the margin, the liquidity-preference theory can be considered to be another version of the expectations theory with investors' risk aversion

assumed at the margin. That is, investors are assumed to view long-term maturities as inherently riskier than short-term maturities.

$$(1 + R_n) = \left[\prod_{t=1}^{n} (1 + r_t + L_t) \right]^{1/n} \tag{5.11}$$

in which L_t is the liquidity premium demanded by investors and increases as t increases from 1 to n.

With liquidity premiums built into the yield curve, the implied forward rates that can be extracted from the interest-rate term structures are higher than the future rates otherwise expected by investors—that is, they are upward-biased estimates. This upward bias means that the yield curves will always have relatively higher slopes than under the pure expectations hypothesis, which produces unbiased estimates. An implication is that investors will no longer view bonds of different maturity as perfect substitutes for one another. With liquidity premiums included YTMs on coupon bonds will not be fully realized, even if all the expected future rates are realized, because the investor is paying a higher price the longer the maturity of the bond. This higher price will reduce the yield that the investor actually receives.

In terms of substitutability, the third theory, the market-segmentation hypothesis, assumes that bonds of different maturities are not adequate substitutes for one another. Under this hypothesis the maturity requirements of investors are so strong that they will tend to restrict their investments to specific segments of the term structure. For example, insurance companies will invest in intermediate-term maturities, while commercial banks will invest in shorter maturities. While many institutional investors will try to match asset and liability maturities, it is not clear that such preferences will cause the term structure to primarily reflect supply and demand within maturity subcategories rather than the investor's expectations and liquidity premiums.

The consensus of empirical evidence concerning term-structure hypotheses seems to favor a combination of the expectations theory and the liquidity-preference theory (see Kessel, 1971). There has been little support for the market-segmentation hypothesis. While it has adherents among practitioners, it has been generally ignored by academicians as a viable supporting hypothesis. Modigliani and Swatch (MS, 1967) do attempt to blend all three hypotheses into what they call the preferred-habitat theory, which states that investors who ordinarily invest only in a given maturity range could be induced into other maturities by a sufficient risk premium. Their theory is characterized by a multiple-horizon market and a willingness on the part of investors to acquire instruments within a range called a habitat. Risk for an investor will increase as the maturity of an investment exceeds the investor's horizon, and with risk increasing a similar increasing return will be required. However, the market will not be willing to pay these ever-increasing returns. Borrowers will eventually find investors with risk pro-

files dictated by the longer horizon needed by the borrower, within an acceptable interest-rate range for both parties.

Any yield-curve shape can be explained by the expectations theory. A descending curve stems from the belief that future short-term rates will be less than current short-term rates. An ascending curve results from investor forecasts of higher short-term rates. The humped yield curve can be explained by saying rates are expected to rise in the near term before they decline in the distant future.

Any yield-curve shape explained by the expectations theory can be explained by the liquidity-preference theory. However, the observed market yield curve is higher than that predicted by the expectations theory by the amount of the liquidity premium. The liquidity-preference theory helps explain why upward-sloping curves are considered the norm.

Both the segmentation theory and the preferred-habitat theory explain the yield-curve shape through supply and demand forces within the various maturity horizons of the curve. MS were not able to conclusively verify their hybrid theory empirically, but many economists do believe that term structure can be best understood only with proper attention being allotted to expectations, liquidity premiums, and supply/demand factors.

Estimation

There are two methods that can be used to estimate yield curves: (1) the **freehand method** and (2) the **regression method.**

To construct a yield curve using the freehand method, a graph is plotted of the yield to maturity and time to maturity for government bonds. Figure 5–1 illustrates this. Figure 5–1 presents the yields for Treasury bonds, notes, and bills from *The Wall Street Journal* for Wednesday, March 22, 1989. To plot a yield curve, the first step is to convert the date the bond matures into years. This is done by first looking at bonds that mature on April 30, 1989. To convert this maturity date into years, the number of days until the bond matures is divided by 365. In this case, the bond matures in thirty-nine days, or 0.1068 years (39/365). This process is continued until all the maturity dates have been converted into years. Table 5A–1 in the appendix at the end of this chapter presents the yield to maturity and time to maturity for the Treasury bonds and notes of Figure 5–1. Column 1 lists the yield to maturity while column 2 lists the time to maturity. To plot the yield curve using the freehand method, simply plot the time to maturity on the x-axis and the yield to maturity on the y-axis. Figure 5–4 gives a scatter plot of time to maturity and yield to maturity for Treasury bonds and notes on March 22, 1989.

The freehand method for estimating the yield curve simply involves drawing a curve through the scatter plot of Figure 5–4. It is clear that where the curve is drawn is somewhat arbitrary.

In Figure 5–4 notice that the yield curve is humped—that is, as time to maturity increases, the yields on Treasury securities rise and then begin to

FIGURE 5–4   Yield Curve for U.S. Treasury Bonds and Notes as of March 22, 1989

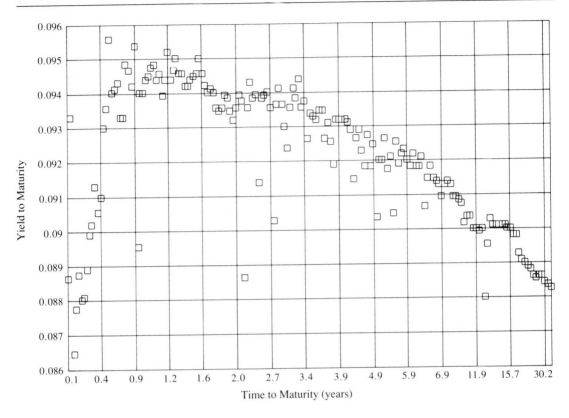

fall. Why does the yield curve have such a strange shape? One possible explanation concerns where the economy is in the business cycle. Following a long economic expansion, the Federal Reserve may begin to worry about inflation. It may then increase short-term interest rates to combat inflation. However, because the market does not expect higher interest rates to persist, the yield on long-term bonds will be lower than the yield on short-term bonds.

One criticism of the freehand method is that it cannot be relied upon by investors to be reproducible. Where the curve will be drawn is arbitrary. In addition, the yield curve uses securities that are not fully homogeneous. For example, the bonds, notes, and bills used to plot the Treasury yield curve have differences in coupons and callability.

Ecols and Elliott (EE, 1976) develop a revised construction approach in order ". . . to present a reproducible analytical structure for extracting yield curves from market data." Basically, they use regression techniques to fit the curve, rather than the Treasury's freehand approach, and they specifi-

cally include the impact of coupon on the shape of the yield curve. Starting from Equation (5.9), they derive a regression equation which can be used to estimate the yield curve.

$$(1 + R_n) = \left[\prod_{t=1}^{n} (1 + r_t)\right]^{1/n} \tag{5.9}$$

This can be rewritten as:

$$(1 + R_n) = (1 + R_1)^{1/n}\left[\prod_{t=2}^{n}(1 + r_t)\right]^{1/n} \tag{5.12}$$

Taking the logs of both sides yields:

$$\ln (1 + R_n) = \frac{1}{n} \ln (1 + R_1) + \frac{1}{n}\sum_{t=2}^{n} \ln (1 + r_t) \tag{5.13}$$

If the forward rate structures are an exponential progression, it can be shown that:

$$\frac{1}{n}\sum_{t=2}^{n-1} \ln (1 + r_t) = \ln k_1 - \frac{k_2}{2} - \frac{\ln k_1}{n} + \frac{k_2}{2}n \tag{5.14}$$

where k_1 and k_2 are constants and t is the maturity of a given bond. Substituting this expression into Equation (5.13):

$$\ln (1 + R_t) = \frac{1}{t} [\ln (1 + R_1) - \ln k_1] + t(k_2/2) + \ln k_1 - \frac{k_2}{2} \tag{5.15}$$

or, in regression form:

$$\ln (1 + R_t) = a(1/t) + b(t) + c + e_t \tag{5.16}$$

where a, b, and c are estimated regression coefficients.

Assigning various values to a and b, the various shapes of the yield curve can be depicted as indicated in Figure 5–5. This regression model provides a framework that can be used to measure yield curves that are rising, humped, decreasing, or flat by using the estimated values of the regression coefficients a and b.

The model shown by Equation (5.16) can be modified to incorporate the effect of coupon values on the term structure by adding an additional variable for the coupon values of the bonds being used to estimate the yield curve:

$$\ln (1+R_t) = a(1/t) + b(t) + c + d(x) + e_t \tag{5.17}$$

where x is the coupon rate of the bond. Sample Problem 5.7 provides further illustration.

FIGURE 5-5   Regression Coefficients and Yield-Curve Shape

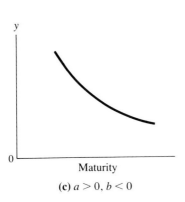

(a) $a < 0, b < 0$

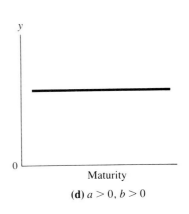

(b) $a < 0, b > 0$

(c) $a > 0, b < 0$

(d) $a > 0, b > 0$

Sample Problem 5.7

Using the data on Treasury bonds, notes, and bills shown in Table 5A–1 (pages 145–146), the regression shown in Equation (5.17) was run yielding estimates of a, b, c, and d.

Figure 5–6 shows a plot of the yield curve based on the regression results presented in Table 5–3. Figure 5–7 (page 132) shows a plot of the yield curve based on results that incorporate coupons into the regression: these results are presented in Table 5–4 (page 132). These curves were drawn by simply substituting the values of t, $1/t$, and x into the regression equations presented in the tables. Notice that yield curves based on the regression method provide three advantages: (1) it is easier to see the relationship between the yield to maturity and time to maturity, (2) the regression method, unlike the freehand method, is not arbitrarily drawn, and (3) by using the regression

FIGURE 5-6   First Yield-Curve Plot for Sample Problem 5.7

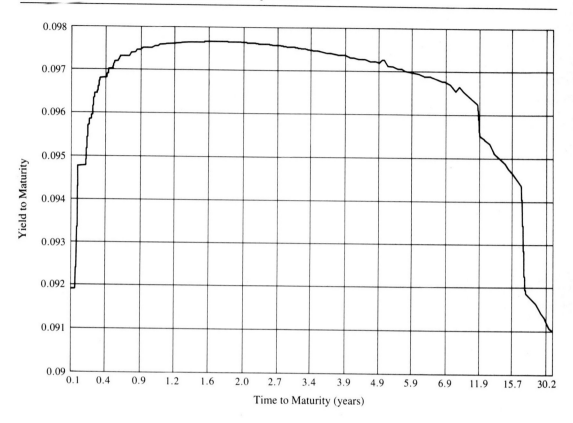

TABLE 5-3   Regression Results for Sample Problem 5.7

Regression output: $\ln(1+R_t) = a(1/t) + b(t) + c + et$

Constant		0.093929
Standard error of Y estimate		0.001379
R^2		0.551916
Number of observations		171
Degrees of freedom		168
	a	b
X coefficient(s)	-0.00063	-0.00022
Standard error of coefficients	0.000084	0.000015

FIGURE 5-7   Second Yield-Curve Plot for Sample Problem 5.7, Incorporating Coupons

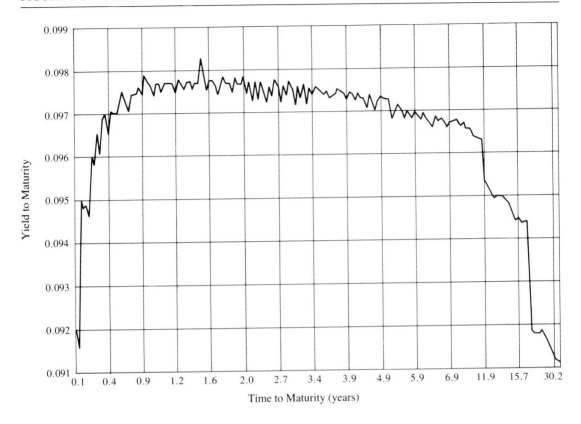

TABLE 5-4   Regression Results for Sample Problem 5.7, Incorporating Coupons

Regression output: $\ln(1+R_t) = a(1/t) + b(t) + d(x) + c + et$			
Constant			0.094528
Standard error of Y estimate			0.001375
R^2			0.557047
Number of observations			171
Degrees of freedom			167
	a	b	d
X coefficient(s)	-0.00063	-0.00021	-0.00006
Standard error of coefficients	0.000084	0.000015	0.000046

method it is possible to account for the nonhomogeneity of securities, such as different coupons.

The correct calculations of forward market rates of interest involve only yields on fully discounted notes. In the regression model used for estimating the yield curve, a correction for the coupon effect has been incorporated. The use of the model to estimate an implied forward rate insures that a correction for variations in the coupon effect over time is taken into consideration.

In capital-market theory, the risk-free rate is a concept with considerable theoretical significance. The yield to maturity on a coupon-bearing risk-free government bond depends upon the rate at which the future interest cash inflows can be reinvested. Because this future reinvestment is uncertain, a coupon-bearing risk-free government bond is not truly risk free even though it has no default risk. The only strictly risk-free yield is the rate on a zero-coupon government bond.

In the sample of government bond yields shown in Figure 5–1, there are no zero-coupon bonds; the range of coupons is from a coupon rate of 3½ percent to 15¾ percent. Equation (5.17) can be used to extrapolate an estimate of a new coupon bond for a given maturity. For example, a two-year Treasury note with a 12-percent coupon could be expected to yield 9.65 percent based on the March 23, 1989, term structure as indicated in Table 5–5 below.

As with any extrapolation, there may be a problem with extrapolating outside of the sample range. Hence, caution should be exercised in using the risk-free yield estimate obtained from this technique●

Sample Problem 5.7 examines a case in which the yield curve is inverted. Sample Problem 5.8 examines a more commonly observed yield curve, based on data from February 11, 1987.

TABLE 5–5   Estimated Yield of a Two-Year, 12-Percent Coupon Note

$$\ln (1 + R_t) = -0.00063 \, (1/2) - 0.00021 \, (2) - 0.00006 \, (12)$$
$$+ \ 0.094528$$
$$= 0.092128$$

To transform $\ln (1 + R_t)$ into the yield to maturity, take the exponential of both sides of the equation:

$$1 + R_t = \exp [0.092128]$$
$$= 1.0965$$
$$R_t = 1.0965 - 1$$
$$= 0.0965 \text{ or } 9.65\%$$

FIGURE 5-8 Yield-Curve Plot for U.S. Treasury Notes and Bonds as of February 11, 1987, for Sample Problem 5.8

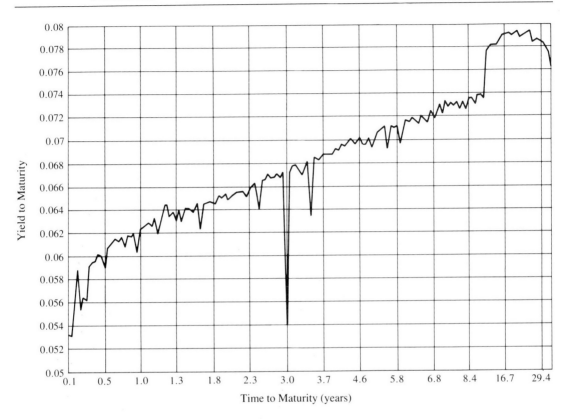

Sample Problem 5.8

Table 5A-2 in the appendix to this chapter (pages 146–147) presents data on yields and time to maturity for Treasury bonds and notes on February 11, 1987. Figure 5-8 presents a scatter plot of the data from this period. Figures 5-9 and 5-10 (next page and page 136) present estimates of the yield curve based on the regression results of Table 5-6 (page 137). Notice that the yield curve presented here has the more commonly observed positive slope. Generally, yield curves are positively sloped because investors require a premium for holding less liquid long-term bonds. Table 5-7 (page 137) presents a forecast for a two-year note with a 12-percent coupon. It predicts a yield of 8.05 percent

FIGURE 5–9 Regression Yield Curve for Sample Problem 5.8:

$$\ln (1 + R_t) = a\left(\frac{1}{t}\right) + b(t) + c + et$$

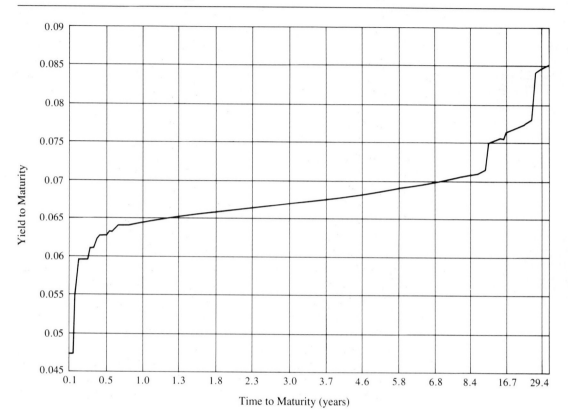

Time to Maturity (years)

CONVERTIBLE BONDS AND THEIR VALUATION

Convertible bonds are long-term debt securities that can be converted into a specified number of shares of common stock at the option of the bond-holder. The ratio of exchange can be expressed either in terms of a conversion ratio (CR), which is simply the number of shares into which one bond is convertible—for example, twenty shares per bond—or in terms of a conversion price (CP), which is equal to the bond's face value (FV) divided by the conversion ratio.

$$CP = \frac{FV}{CR} \tag{5.18}$$

FIGURE 5–10   Regression Yield Curve for Sample Problem 5.8:

$$\ln\,(1\,+\,R_t)\,=\,a\!\left(\frac{1}{t}\right)\,+\,b(t)\,+\,d(x)\,+\,c\,+\,e_t$$

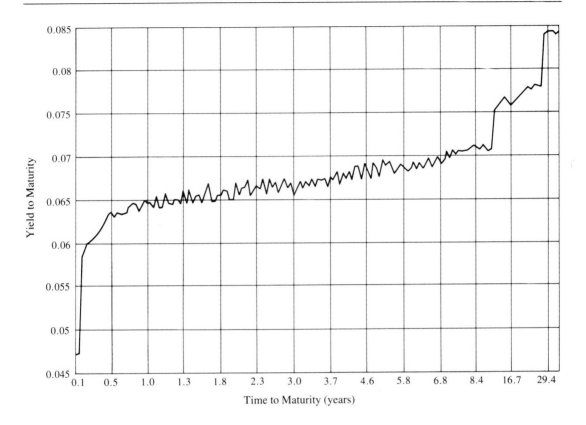

With a face value of $1,000 and a conversion ratio of 20, the conversion price is $1,000/20 or $50.

Often these basic conversion terms change over the life of the convertible-bond issue. For example, the conversion price may increase in discrete stages—that is, $50 for the first five years, $55 for the next five years, and so on. The reason the issuer might employ such a strategy is to shorten the time before conversion if the common-stock price increased enough to make conversion otherwise likely.

The conversion price should not be confused with the bond's conversion value (CV), the total market value of the bond in terms of the stock into

TABLE 5-6   Regression Results for Sample Problem 5.8

Regression output: $\ln(1+R_t) = a(1/t) + b(t) + c + et$

Constant		0.063436
Standard error of Y estimate		0.002595
R^2		0.802753
Number of observations		160
Degrees of freedom		157
	a	*b*
X coefficient(s)	−0.00143	0.000607
Standard error of coefficients	0.000140	0.000032

Regression output: $\ln(1+R_t) = a(1/t) + b(t) + d(x) + c + et$

Constant		0.061174	
Standard error of Y estimate		0.002541	
R^2		0.812113	
Number of observations		160	
Degrees of freedom		156	
	a	*b*	*d*
X coefficient(s)	−0.00146	0.000596	0.000230
Standard error of coefficients	0.000137	0.000032	0.000082

which it is convertible. The conversion value can be computed by multiplying the conversion ratio by the price of the firm's common stock, P_s:

$$CV = (CR)(P_s) \qquad (5.19)$$

For the current example, if the price of the stock is \$40 per share, the conversion value would be $(20)(\$40) = \$800$. Because it would otherwise cause arbitrage opportunities, the convertible bond will not sell in the market for less than its conversion value.

TABLE 5-7   Estimated Yield of a Two-Year, 12-percent Coupon Note

$$\ln(1 + R_t) = -0.00146\,(1/2) + 0.00596\,(2) - 0.00023\,(12)$$
$$+ 0.063436$$
$$= 0.077386$$

To transform $\ln(1 + R_t)$ into the yield to maturity, take the exponential of both sides of the equation:

$$1 + R_t = \exp[0.077386]$$
$$= 1.08046$$
$$R_t = 1.08046 - 1$$
$$= 0.08046 \text{ or } 8.05\%$$

The convertible bond also provides the investor with a fixed return in the form of its coupon payments. The present value of these periodic coupons (usually paid semiannually, as for regular nonconvertible bonds) plus the present value of the face value to be paid at maturity will equal what is called the investment value (IV) of the convertible bond:

$$\text{IV} = \sum_{t=1}^{n} \frac{I}{(1 + k)^t} + \frac{\text{FV}}{(1 + k)^n} \qquad (5.20)$$

where:

FV = the face value of the bond;
 I = the periodic coupon payments;
 k = the investor's required rate of return; and
 n = the number of periods until the maturity of the issue.

Because a convertible bond is effectively a hybrid security with some of the features of bonds and some of common stock, its value both as a bond and as common stock must be considered in order to value it. When the conversion value exceeds the investment value, the convertible-bond price (P_{cv}) is related primarily to the conversion value; and when the conversion value is less than the investment value, P_{cv} is related primarily to the investment value. Figure 5–11 provides further illustration.

A convertible bond will ordinarily sell at a premium over the investment value, primarily because of the conversion option, and will sell at a premium above the conversion value because of the floor established by its investment value. This investment-value floor is not constant over time, but will actually vary with interest-rate movements and perceived changes in the financial risk of the issuing company. For example, if interest rates increase or the firm's financial risk increases (possibly accompanied by a lower bond rating) the floor can decrease, thus providing less protection to the convertible bondholder. If the face value of the convertible is higher than the investment value (as it ordinarily would be at the time of issue because of the bond's conversion potential), the investment value will increase over time, other things held constant. This is true because the ultimate price is always the face value at maturity. The size of the premiums reflected in the convertible bond's price would be larger the more volatile the underlying stock price if the bond had a significant conversion potential.

As indicated above, the convertible bond actually has two types of premiums, the premium over investment value, IV, and the premium over conversion value, CV. At relatively high common-stock prices, the value of the investment floor becomes negligible and the IP becomes insignificant: the bond is selling at a price very close to its conversion value. Another factor causing P_{CV} to closely approximate CV at high stock prices is that if the conversion value exceeded the call price of the bond, the firm could exercise its call option and effectively force conversion. Upon conversion, of course, the convertible bond would be worth only its conversion value. If, on the other hand, the convertible-bond price were close to the investment

FIGURE 5-11   Investment Value, Conversion Value, and the Price of a Convertible Bond

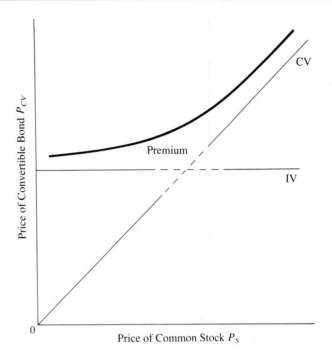

value, it would be an indication that the conversion potential of the bond is negligible.

The main reason for convertible-bond premiums is the hybrid nature of the security. It offers downside protection against stock-price declines at the same time that it provides upside price-appreciation potential similar to straight common-stock investment. However, other factors also influence the size of the premiums to some extent. For example, transaction costs charged for convertible-bond purchases are ordinarily lower than for common-stock purchases. This should increase the convertible-bond premiums, other things held constant. Another factor that might have an upward influence is the fact that certain regulated financial institutions are more restricted in their common-stock investment than in their purchase of convertible bonds (see Brigham, 1966). An additional factor taken into account by convertible-bond investors is the comparison of the common-stock dividend yield (d/P_s) and the current yield (I/P_{cv}) of the convertible bond. The greater the common stock's dividend yield is relative to the convertible bond's interest yield, the less attractive the convertible and the lower the premiums on it.

With the definitions of investment value, conversion value, and the premiums associated with them in hand, it is possible to take a more rigorous

approach to the valuation of convertible bonds. Using the simplifying assumptions of a single-period investment horizon and a constant term structure of interest rates over that horizon, convertible bonds can be separated into two categories: (1) those for which IV > CV and (2) those for which CV > IV.

For convertible bonds in which IV > CV, investors set prices for these securities primarily for their bond value and only secondarily because of their conversion potential. The single-period cash flows could be expressed as the sum of the face value (FV), the coupon payment (I), and the expected gain upon conversion. This last flow is a function of the stock price per share in state i at period 1 (P_{si1}). For all values of P_{si1} greater than the corresponding values of IV/CR:

$$\text{Expected conversion profit} = \sum_{i=1}^{m} [(P_{si1})(\text{CR}) - \text{IV}_{i1}][\Pi_{i1}] \quad \textbf{(5.21)}$$

where:

$$(P_{si1})(\text{CR}) = \text{CV}_1$$
$$\Pi_{i1} = \text{the probability of occurrence for } P_s \text{ values at time } i.$$

Therefore:

$$\text{Expected CV} = \text{FV}_1 + I_1 + \sum_{i=1}^{m} [(P_{si1})(\text{CR}) - \text{IV}_{i1}][\Pi_{i1}] \quad \textbf{(5.22)}$$

Using the k_d, the required rate of return for straight debt investments, and k_s, the required rate of return for straight common-stock investments, the value of the debt-dominated convertible bond (IV > CV) can be expressed:

$$P_{CVD} = \frac{\text{FV}_1 + I_1}{(1 + k_d)} + \frac{\sum_{i=1}^{m} [P_{si1})(\text{CR}) - \text{IV}_{i1}][\Pi_{i1}]}{(1 + k_s)} \quad \textbf{(5.23)}$$

Since $\text{FV}_1 + I_1/(1 + k_d)$ is equal to IV_0 Equation (5.24) can be written:

$$P_{CVD} = \text{IV}_0 + \frac{\sum_{i=1}^{m} [(P_{si1})(\text{CR}) - \text{IV}_1][\Pi_{i1}]}{(1 + k_s)} \quad \textbf{(5.24)}$$

The price of a convertible bond with IV > CV is equal to the sum of its current investment value and the present value of the expected conversion profit. Since $P_{CVD} - \text{IV}$ is equal to the current premium over investment value, IP,

$$\text{IP} = \frac{\sum_{i=1}^{m} [(P_{si1})(\text{CR}) - \text{IV}_{i1}][\Pi_{i,1}]}{(1 + k_s)} \quad \textbf{(5.25)}$$

That is, IP is equal to the present value of the expected conversion profit.

For convertible bonds in which CV > IV, investors set prices for these securities primarily for their conversion potential and secondarily for their

investment-value floor protection. This floor protection is also a function of the common-stock price probability distribution. For all values of P_{si1} less than or equal to the corresponding values of IV_1/CR:

$$\text{Expected floor protection} = \sum_{i=1}^{m} [IV_{i1} - (P_{si1})(CR)][\Pi_{i1}] \quad (5.26)$$

Therefore:

$$\text{Expected CV}_1 = (CR)[E(P_{si1})] + I_1 + \sum_{i=1}^{m} [IV_{i1} - (P_{si1})(CR)][\Pi_{i1}] \quad (5.27)$$

Discounting at the appropriate rates, the value of the stock-dominated convertible bond (CV > IV) can be expressed:

$$P_{CVS} = \frac{(CR)[E(P_{si1})] + \sum_{i=1}^{m} [IV_{i1} - (P_{si1})(CR)][\Pi_{i1}]}{(1 + k_s)} + \frac{I}{(1 + k_d)} \quad (5.28)$$

Since the current price of common stock P_{s0} can be written in terms of the present value of the sum of the expected period-1 price P_1 and the expected period-1 dividends d:

$$P_0 = \frac{E(P_1) + E(d_1)}{(1 + k_s)} \quad (5.29)$$

it can also be shown that

$$\frac{(CR)[E(P_{si1})]}{(1 + k_s)} = (CR)(P_0) - \frac{(CR)[E(d_1)]}{(1 + k_s)} \quad (5.30)$$

Substituting into Equation (5.28):

$$P_{CVS} = (CR)(P_0) + \frac{I}{(1 + k_d)} - \frac{E(d_1)(CR)}{(1 + k_s)} + \frac{\sum_{i=1}^{m} IV_1 - [(CR)(P_{si1})][\Pi_{i1}]}{(1 + k_s)} \quad (5.31)$$

Thus, with $(CR)(P_0) = CV_0$:

$$P_{CVS} = CV_0 + \left\{ \frac{I_1}{(1 + k_d)} - \frac{E(d_1)(CR)}{(1 + k_s)} \right\} + \frac{\sum_{i=1}^{m} IV_{i1} - (CR)(P_{si1})[\Pi_{i1}]}{(1 + k_s)} \quad (5.32)$$

The price of a convertible bond with CV > IV is then equal to the sum of its current conversion value, the present value of the difference between the coupon interest payments on the bond and the expected dividend that would be paid upon conversion, and the present value of the expected floor protection.

Since $P_{CVS} - CV$ is equal to the current premium over investment value CP:

$$CP = \left\{ \frac{I_1}{(1 + k_d)} - \frac{E(d_1)(R)}{(1 + k_s)} \right\}^t + \frac{\sum_{i=1}^{m} IV_{i1} - [(CR)(P_{si1})][\Pi_{i1}]}{(1 + k_s)} \quad (5.33)$$

That is, CP is equal to the present value of the income-stream differential between the bond and an equivalent amount of common stock, and the present value of the floor protection.

Even though the preceding analysis of convertible-bond valuation was made under simplifying assumptions, the removal of each of them could be shown to uphold the basic logic and results that were found. Empirical testing by Walter and Que (WQ, 1973) and West and Largay (WL, 1972) essentially shows that the relationships developed here seem to hold up in the markets for convertible bonds. For example, WQ notes that for bonds with CV > IV, premiums decline at a decreasing rate as the difference between CV and IV increases. They also note that the premiums are positively correlated with the difference between bond coupons and stock dividends. For bonds with IV > CV, WQ finds that the premium declines at a decreasing rate as the CV/IV ratio declines, that is, as the probability of profitable conversion decreases. The WL study's results basically agree with those of WQ. However, neither study finds conclusive results concerning the impact of systematic risk on bond premiums. An alternative way of viewing convertible bonds is presented by Brennen and Schwartz (1977, 1980). In their view, a convertible bond is a combination of a regular bond and a call option. Chapters 14 and 15 discuss option theory and apply option theory to valuing convertibles.

SUMMARY

This chapter has considered how security analysts and portfolio managers deal with some of the complex problems associated with the analysis and valuation of bonds. A study was made of the types of bonds available and the basic fundamentals relating to their valuation. The impact of systematic risk on the valuation models was analyzed and some of the available empirical evidence was reviewed. From the evidence, it seems clear that the choice of a market index is quite important and that the inclusion of bonds in the market index is helpful in explaining the relationship between return and risk.

Bond ratings were examined and prediction models were developed to help identify the factors that need to be considered by investors. The ratings themselves seem to be impounded efficiently into bond prices, so that their informational content to investors is suspect. Considerable emphasis was placed on the theories of the term structure of interest rates and the resulting yield curves. It appears that properly constructed yield curves can be useful to investors in the forecasting of interest rates, to help identify mispriced bonds, to help investors manage their bond portfolios, and to provide an analytical base for investment strategies, such as riding the yield curve.

In the final section, convertible bonds were separated for further analysis because their hybrid nature (an investment mixture of debt and stock) causes special problems for analysts trying to value them in the market. It was demonstrated that the valuation process is more manageable with some simplifying assumptions and the categorization of convertible bonds according to the relative sizes of their investment value and their conversion value. It was shown that the premium over the investment value is equal to the sum of the present value of the difference between bond coupons and expected stock dividends and the present value of the bond's floor protection.

Bond valuation and analysis can be used in security analysis and portfolio management to determine fair value of bond prices and the potential risk-related interest-rate fluctuations of liquidity conditions. Consequently, both security analysts and portfolio managers need command of the concepts, theory, and techniques discussed in this chapter.

QUESTIONS AND PROBLEMS

1. Define the following terms.
   (a) par value
   (b) yield to maturity
   (c) zero-coupon bond
   (d) yield curve
   (e) coupon interest rate

2. You notice that the yield curve for Treasury securities has the shape shown in the figure.
   (a) Discuss in detail some of the theories that might explain the shape of the yield curve.

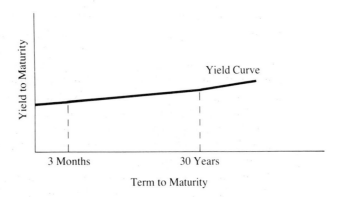

(b) If you were buying these bonds, would you buy long-term or short-term bonds?

3. You are given the following information about ABC Corporation's bonds.

Years until bond matures	3 years
Coupon rate	12 percent
Maturity value	$1,000
Current market price	$1,050

If you assume that interest payments are made annually and that you require a 10 percent rate of return, would you purchase this bond?

4. Calculate the yield to maturity for a bond that matures in five years and has a coupon rate of 9 percent, a par value of $1,000, and a current market price of $953. Assume that interest payments are made semiannually.

5. You are considering two bonds for investment purposes:

   Bond A: A $10,000 par-value zero-coupon bond with a term to maturity of five years and a market yield of 9 percent.

   Bond B: A $10,000 par-value coupon bond with a 9-percent coupon rate, a term to maturity of five years, and a market yield of 9 percent.

   (a) Calculate the initial price of both bonds at a market yield of 9 percent, assuming semiannual compounding.

   (b) Calculate the percentage change in the price of the bonds if the market yields rise by three percentage points (300 basis points).

6. What is call risk? What effect does call risk have on the promised yield to maturities?

7. Compare the following two bonds:

   Bond A: A tax-free municipal bond selling at par with a coupon rate of 6 percent, a maturity value of $10,000, and a term to maturity of four years.

   Bond B: A corporate bond selling at par with a coupon rate of 9 percent, a maturity value of $10,000, and a term to maturity of four years.

   If you assume that both bonds have the same default risk and that your marginal tax rate is 28 percent, which bond would you purchase?

8. What are revenue bonds? What are general-obligation bonds? If New York City issues both revenue and general-obligation bonds, which type of bond would be expected to have the greater risk? Which type of bond would have the greater yield to maturity?

9. Briefly explain the relationship between bond prices and the market rate of interest.

10. A bond that matures in twenty years has a call date five years from today. If the coupon rate is 9 percent, the maturity value is $10,000, and the current market price is $11,000, calculate the appropriate yield.

APPENDIX 5A: WORKSHEETS FOR YIELD CURVES

TABLE 5A-1   Worksheet for Estimating Yield Curves for Sample Problem 5.7

(1) R_t	(2) t	(3) x	(1) R_t	(2) t	(3) x	(1) R_t	(2) t	(3) x
0.0927	0.1068	7.125	0.0985	1.1918	8.250	0.0957	2.4441	14.880
0.0978	0.1068	14.375	0.0990	1.1918	8.125	0.0984	2.5247	9.130
0.0903	0.1918	6.875	0.0999	1.1918	11.375	0.0985	2.6107	12.250
0.0917	0.1918	9.250	0.0990	1.2740	7.250	0.0986	2.6913	6.500
0.0928	0.1918	8.000	0.0993	1.2740	8.000	0.0981	2.6913	8.500
0.0920	0.1918	11.750	0.0997	1.3589	10.750	0.0945	2.6913	14.250
0.0921	0.2740	7.375	0.0992	1.3589	8.375	0.0982	2.7774	8.250
0.0930	0.2740	9.625	0.0992	1.4438	7.875	0.0987	2.8607	11.630
0.0941	0.3589	7.625	0.0988	1.4438	10.750	0.0982	2.9358	6.630
0.0944	0.3589	14.500	0.0988	1.4438	8.625	0.0975	2.9358	9.130
0.0956	0.4438	7.750	0.0990	1.4438	8.625	0.0968	2.9358	14.630
0.0948	0.4438	6.625	0.0991	1.5247	0.675	0.0981	3.0274	7.880
0.0953	0.4438	13.875	0.0992	1.5247	8.500	0.0987	3.1080	11.750
0.0975	0.5260	8.500	0.0997	1.6107	11.500	0.0984	3.1941	6.630
0.0981	0.5260	9.375	0.0992	1.6107	8.250	0.0990	3.1941	13.750
0.1003	0.6110	11.875	0.0988	1.6913	8.000	0.0981	3.2747	8.250
0.0986	0.6110	7.875	0.0986	1.6913	9.630	0.0983	3.3607	10.380
0.0987	0.6932	6.375	0.0987	1.6913	13.000	0.0971	3.4441	7.250
0.0989	0.6932	10.750	0.0986	1.6913	8.880	0.0979	3.4441	8.250
0.0978	0.6932	12.750	0.0981	1.7774	6.630	0.0978	3.5247	8.750
0.0978	0.6932	7.750	0.0980	1.7774	9.130	0.0977	3.6107	9.750
0.0995	0.7781	7.875	0.0981	1.8607	9.000	0.0980	3.6913	8.380
0.0993	0.7781	8.375	0.0985	1.8607	11.750	0.0980	3.6913	10.500
0.0988	0.8630	7.375	0.0984	1.9358	7.380	0.0971	3.7774	9.130
0.1001	0.8630	10.500	0.0980	1.9358	9.130	0.0976	3.8607	8.750
0.0937	0.9397	3.500	0.0977	1.9358	9.380	0.0970	3.9358	6.750
0.0986	0.9397	6.500	0.0981	2.0174	6.750	0.0963	3.9358	7.880
0.0986	0.9397	7.125	0.0985	2.1080	12.380	0.0977	3.9358	8.250
0.0990	0.9397	11.000	0.0983	2.1941	8.130	0.0977	3.9358	10.880
0.0991	1.0247	7.250	0.0927	2.1941	14.500	0.0977	4.1080	7.380
0.0994	1.0247	7.375	0.0981	2.2747	7.880	0.0977	4.1941	7.630
0.0995	1.1068	10.500	0.0989	2.3603	13.750	0.0976	4.1941	10.130
0.0990	1.1068	7.625	0.0984	2.4441	7.500	0.0974	4.3607	7.250
0.0992	1.1918	7.875	0.0985	2.4441	8.750	0.0958	4.4441	8.630

TABLE 5A-1 *(continued)*

(1) R_t	(2) t	(3) x	(1) R_t	(2) t	(3) x	(1) R_t	(2) t	(3) x
0.0971	4.4441	8.750	0.0965	6.1941	11.250	0.0937	12.9358	14.250
0.0974	4.4441	11.880	0.0949	6.1941	12.630	0.0945	13.6913	11.630
0.0967	4.6107	7.130	0.0958	6.3607	8.880	0.0943	13.9358	10.750
0.0962	4.6913	8.630	0.0962	6.4441	10.500	0.0943	14.1941	10.750
0.0972	4.6913	11.750	0.0958	6.6107	8.630	0.0943	14.4441	11.130
0.0962	4.6913	9.000	0.0957	6.6913	9.500	0.0943	14.6913	11.880
0.0969	4.8607	7.000	0.0956	6.6913	11.500	0.0943	15.1941	12.380
0.0946	4.3958	9.000	0.0952	6.8607	9.250	0.0942	15.4441	13.750
0.0964	4.3958	8.880	0.0956	6.9358	8.880	0.0942	15.6913	11.630
0.0964	5.1080	7.000	0.0957	7.1941	7.380	0.0940	16.1941	12.000
0.0971	5.1941	13.130	0.0956	7.6913	7.250	0.0940	16.4441	10.750
0.0961	5.1941	9.500	0.0952	7.4441	8.630	0.0934	16.9358	9.380
0.0965	5.3607	8.000	0.0952	7.1941	8.500	0.0932	26.9358	11.250
0.0947	5.4441	8.750	0.0951	7.6913	8.880	0.0931	27.4441	10.630
0.0970	5.4441	12.630	0.0950	7.9358	8.130	0.0930	27.6913	9.880
0.0963	5.6107	9.500	0.0944	8.1941	9.000	0.0929	27.9358	9.250
0.0966	5.6913	10.130	0.0946	8.4441	9.250	0.0927	28.1941	7.250
0.0967	5.6913	11.630	0.0946	8.6913	8.880	0.0926	28.6913	7.500
0.0964	5.8607	8.630	0.0942	8.9358	8.880	0.0927	29.1941	8.750
0.0962	5.9358	10.500	0.0942	11.9358	11.750	0.0927	29.4441	8.880
0.0966	5.9358	11.250	0.0941	12.1941	13.130	0.0925	30.1941	9.130
0.0962	6.1080	8.380	0.0942	12.4441	13.380	0.0924	30.6913	9.000
0.0962	6.1941	10.380	0.0920	12.6913	15.750	0.0923	30.9358	8.880

TABLE 5A-2 Yields and Time to Maturity for Treasury Bonds and Notes as of February 11, 1987

(1) R_t	(2) t	(3) x	(1) R_t	(2) t	(3) x	(1) R_t	(2) t	(3) x
0.0532	0.0833	10.25	0.0616	0.7500	7.62	0.0644	1.2500	7.12
0.0531	0.0833	10.75	0.0613	0.7500	8.50	0.0644	1.2500	9.88
0.0567	0.1667	9.75	0.0617	0.7500	11.00	0.0634	1.2500	10.00
0.0588	0.2500	9.12	0.0608	0.7500	12.60	0.0638	1.3333	7.00
0.0553	0.2500	12.00	0.0618	0.8333	11.25	0.0630	1.3333	13.62
0.0564	0.2500	12.50	0.0617	0.8333	7.88	0.0640	1.4167	6.62
0.0561	0.2500	14.00	0.0619	0.9167	8.12	0.0630	1.4167	14.00
0.0591	0.3333	8.50	0.0604	0.9167	12.37	0.0641	1.5000	6.12
0.0595	0.3333	10.50	0.0622	1.0000	10.12	0.0641	1.5000	9.50
0.0595	0.4167	8.88	0.0624	1.0000	10.37	0.0639	1.5000	10.50
0.0602	0.5000	8.88	0.0627	1.0000	8.00	0.0638	1.5833	6.37
0.0601	0.5000	12.37	0.0629	1.0833	12.00	0.0645	1.5833	11.37
0.0592	0.5000	13.75	0.0625	1.0833	7.12	0.0623	1.6667	15.37
0.0607	0.5833	9.00	0.0633	1.1667	6.62	0.0645	1.6667	6.37
0.0608	0.5833	11.12	0.0619	1.1667	13.25	0.0647	1.7500	6.25
0.0614	0.6667	8.88	0.0630	1.2500	8.25	0.0647	1.7500	8.75

TABLE 5A–2 *(continued)*

(1) R_t	(2) t	(3) x	(1) R_t	(2) t	(3) x	(1) R_t	(2) t	(3) x
0.0645	1.7500	8.62	0.0687	3.7500	13.00	0.0733	7.4167	12.62
0.0645	1.7500	11.75	0.0687	3.8333	6.62	0.0728	7.6667	10.12
0.0652	1.8333	10.62	0.0693	3.9167	11.75	0.0732	7.6667	11.62
0.0650	1.8333	6.25	0.0691	4.0000	9.12	0.0730	7.9167	10.50
0.0654	1.9167	6.12	0.0697	4.0833	12.37	0.0732	7.9167	11.25
0.0648	1.9167	14.62	0.0695	4.1667	8.12	0.0726	8.1667	10.37
0.0652	2.0000	8.00	0.0698	4.1667	14.25	0.0733	8.1667	11.25
0.0652	2.0000	11.37	0.0701	4.3333	13.75	0.0726	8.1667	12.62
0.0655	2.0833	11.25	0.0696	4.4167	7.50	0.0735	8.4167	10.50
0.0655	2.1667	14.37	0.0698	4.4167	14.88	0.0736	8.6667	9.50
0.0656	2.2500	6.88	0.0703	4.5833	12.25	0.0731	8.6667	11.50
0.0651	2.2500	9.25	0.0696	4.6667	6.50	0.0739	8.9167	8.88
0.0658	2.2500	11.75	0.0697	4.6667	14.25	0.0739	9.1667	7.37
0.0660	2.3333	9.62	0.0702	4.8333	11.62	0.0735	9.6667	7.25
0.0663	2.4167	14.50	0.0693	4.9167	6.62	0.0776	14.6667	11.75
0.0640	2.5000	6.62	0.0702	4.9167	14.62	0.0781	14.9167	13.12
0.0665	2.5000	13.88	0.0707	5.0833	11.75	0.0782	15.1667	13.37
0.0665	2.5833	9.37	0.0710	5.1667	13.75	0.0781	15.4167	15.75
0.0671	2.6667	11.88	0.0711	5.3333	10.37	0.0785	15.6667	14.25
0.0667	2.7500	6.37	0.0692	5.4167	7.25	0.0790	15.5833	11.62
0.0668	2.7500	10.75	0.0712	5.5833	9.75	0.0791	16.6667	10.75
0.0671	2.7500	12.75	0.0710	5.6667	10.50	0.0792	16.9167	10.75
0.0668	2.8333	8.37	0.0712	5.8333	8.75	0.0790	17.1667	11.12
0.0673	2.9167	10.50	0.0696	5.9167	6.75	0.0792	17.4167	11.88
0.0519	3.0000	3.50	0.0712	5.9167	7.88	0.0794	17.9167	12.37
0.0672	3.0000	6.50	0.0717	5.9167	10.88	0.0789	18.0000	13.75
0.0678	3.0000	11.00	0.0715	6.0833	7.37	0.0791	18.4167	11.62
0.0678	3.0833	7.25	0.0719	6.1667	10.12	0.0793	18.9167	12.00
0.0674	3.1667	10.50	0.0717	6.3333	7.25	0.0794	19.1667	10.75
0.0669	3.2500	8.25	0.0714	6.4167	8.62	0.0784	19.6667	9.37
0.0680	3.2500	11.37	0.0721	6.4167	11.88	0.0787	28.6667	11.25
0.0682	3.3333	7.25	0.0719	6.5833	7.12	0.0785	29.1667	10.62
0.0635	3.4167	10.75	0.0715	6.6667	8.62	0.0785	29.4167	9.88
0.0685	3.5000	9.88	0.0725	6.6667	11.75	0.0780	29.6667	9.25
0.0683	3.5000	10.75	0.0718	6.8333	7.00	0.0778	29.9167	7.25
0.0683	3.5833	6.75	0.0720	6.9167	9.00	0.0763	30.4166	7.50
0.0688	3.6667	11.50	0.0731	7.1667	13.12			
0.0688	3.7500	9.62	0.0722	7.4167	8.75			

REFERENCES

Beaver, W. H., P. Kettler, and M. Scholes. "The Association Between Market Determined and Accounting Determined Risk Measures." *Accounting Review,* v. 45 (1970), pp. 654–82.

Brennan, M. J., and E. Schwartz. "Analyzing Convertible Bonds." *Journal of Financial and Quantitative Analysis,* v. 15 (November 1980), pp. 907–29.

_____. "Convertible Bonds: Valuation and Optimal Strategies for Call and Conversion." *Journal of Finance,* v. 32 (December 1977), pp. 1699–1715.

Brigham, E. F. "An Analysis of Convertible Debentures: Theory and Some Empirical Evidence." *Journal of Finance,* v. 21 (1966), pp. 35–54.

Ecols, E., and John W. Elliot. "A Quantitative Yield Curve Model of Estimating the Term Structure of Interest Rates." *Journal of Financial and Quantitative Analysis,* v. 11 (March 1976), pp. 80–90.

Fisher, L., and R. L. Weil. "Coping With the Risk of Interest Rate Fluctuations: Returns to Bond Holders from Naive and Optimal Strategies." *Journal of Business,* October 1971, pp. 408–31.

Folger, H. Russell. "Managing Bond Portfolios." Chapter 9 in *Investment Managers Handbook,* ed. by Summer Levine. Dow Jones-Irwin, 1980, pp. 316–17.

Gushee, C. H. "How to Hedge a Bond Investment." *Financial Analysts Journal,* v. 37 (March/April, 1981), pp. 44–51.

Hettenhouse, George W., and William L. Sartoris. "An Analysis of the Informational Value of Bond-Rating Changes." *Quarterly Review of Economics and Business,* v. 16 (Summer 1976), pp. 68–78.

Homer, Sidney, and Martin L. Leibowitz. *Inside the Yield Book.* Prentice-Hall, Inc., and New York Institute of Finance, 1972.

Hopewell, M. H., and G. G. Kaufman. "Bond Price Volatility and Term to Maturity: A Generalized Respecification." *American Economic Review,* September 1973, pp. 749–53.

Ibbotson, Roger G., and Rex A. Singuefield. *Stocks, Bonds, Bills, and Inflation: Historical Returns (1926–1981).* Financial Analysts Researchers Foundation Charlottesville, Virginia, 1982.

Kessel, Reuben A. "Inflation-Caused Wealth Redistribution: A Test of a Hypothesis." *American Economic Review,* v. 46, pp. 128–41.

Khoury, Sarkis J. *Investments.* Macmillan Publishing Company, 1983.

Leibowitz, M. L. *Total After-Tax Bond Performance and Yield Measures.* Salomon Brothers, 1974.

McCulloch, Houston J. "An Estimation of the Liquidity Premium." *Journal of Political Economy,* v. 83 (January/February 1975), pp. 95–119.

Modigliani, Franco, and R. Swatch. "Debt Management and the Term Structure of Interest Rates: An Empirical Analysis of Recent Experience." *Journal of Political Economy,* v. 75 (Supplement, August 1967), pp. 569–89.

Pinches, George E., and Kent A. Mingo. "A Multivariate Analysis of Industrial Bond Ratings." *Journal of Finance,* v. 28 (March 1973), pp. 1–18.

_____. "The Role of Subordination and Industrial Bond Ratings." *Journal of Finance,* v. 30 (March 1975), pp. 201–206.

Reilly, Frank K., and Michael D. Joehnk. "The Association between Market-Determined Risk Measures for Bonds and Bond Ratings." *Journal of Finance,* v. 31 (December 1976), pp. 1387–1403.

Walter, J. E., and Augustine V. Que. "The Valuation of Convertible Bonds." *Journal of Finance,* v. 28 (July 1973), pp. 713–32.

Weinstein, Mark I. "The Systematic Risk of Corporate Bonds." *Journal of Financial and Quantitative Analysis,* v. 38 (December 1983), 1515–29.

_____. "Bond Systematic Risk and the Option Pricing Model." *Journal of Finance,* v. 38 (December 1983), pp. 1415–30.

_____. "The Effect of Rating Change Announcement on Bond Price." *Journal of Financial Economics,* v. 5 (December 1977), pp. 329–50.

West, Richard R. "Bond Ratings, Bond Yields and Financial Regulations." *Journal of Law and Economics,* v. 1 (April 1973), pp. 159–68.

_____, and James A. Largay III. "Premium on Convertible Bonds: Comment." *Journal of Finance,* v. 27 (December 1972), pp. 1156–62.

Zumwalt, J. Kent, and Don Wort. "An Examination of Factors Influencing Bond Rating." *Akron Business and Economics Review* (Fall 1980), pp. 31–35.

6 The Uses and Calculation of Market Indexes

The topic of market indexes has always been of great importance in the world of security analysis and portfolio management because the indexes are commonly used by investors to reflect the level and performance of the market. These market measures can be used as a standard of investment performance as well as a critical factor in the determination of required rates of return for individual securities and portfolios. For example, the determination of the required rate of return for a security investment through the use of the capital asset pricing model (CAPM) necessitates an estimate of the current level of return on the market portfolio—usually proxied by a broadly based market index. Market-index values have also been commonly used to provide insights into such economic variables as the growth of economic output and corporate returns. Recent years, however, have seen an explosion in the potential value of market-index information because of new options and futures contracts, in addition to the development of market-index mutual funds that have made these indexes directly tradable investment opportunities. The full set of implications for security analysts and portfolio managers, as well as for the individual investor, has not yet been fully developed in the literature of finance. Some of these implications are explored in later sections of this chapter.

This chapter discusses five main topics. The first section discusses alternative methods for compiling stock and price indexes, while the second section describes alternative market indexes. This is followed by a discussion of the uses of market indexes. The fourth section investigates both the historical behavior of market indexes and the implications of their use for forecasting; and the fifth section focuses on market-index proxy errors and their impact on beta estimates and efficient-market hypothesis (EMH) tests.

ALTERNATIVE METHODS FOR COMPILATION OF STOCK AND PRICE INDEXES

Many different indexes are computed and compiled for the use of investors. While some indexes have been developed using an equal weighting approach (equal dollar amounts assumed to be invested in each component), the primary types utilized are either price weighted or value weighted. Both these methods are employed in the compilation of stock consumer-price (cost) indexes. Stock indexes are directly used in security analysis and portfolio management, and consumer-price (cost) indexes are used in measuring the change of purchasing power. It should be noted that consumer-price (cost) information is also useful in security analysis and portfolio management.

Price-Weighted and Quantity-Weighted Indexes

In a **price-weighted index** the basic approach is to sum the prices of the component securities used in the index and divide this sum by the number of components; in other words, to compute a simple arithmetic average. The Dow-Jones Industrial Average (DJIA) is the most familiar index of this type. To allow for the impact of stock splits and stock dividends, which could destroy the consistency and comparability of price-weighted index data over time, an adjustment of either the reported price data or the divisor itself is required. As will be seen below, the DJIA has used a divisor adjustment for some time now.

A price-weighted index such as the DJIA is not strictly speaking an index at all—it is an average. The concept of indexing involves the comparison of currently computed averages with some base value. For example, the current levels of the Standard & Poor's 500 index (S&P 500) are compared with the average level for the base period of 1941–1943. The S&P 500 is also the most widely used example of a **value-weighted stock index.** In such an index the weight of each component stock is equal to its market value in relation to that of all the stocks included. The use of market value (price per share multiplied by the number of shares outstanding) obviates the necessity of adjusting for stock splits or stock dividends.

Two classical forms of indexes are the Paasche index and the Laspeyres index. Both of these are used as methods for determining the consumer price index. They measure price inflation because quantity is held constant.

$$\text{Paasche price index} = \frac{\Sigma P_{jt}\, Q_{jt}}{\Sigma P_{j0}Q_{jt}} \qquad (6.1)$$

$$\text{Laspeyres price index} = \frac{\Sigma P_{jt}Q_{j0}}{\Sigma P_{j0}Q_{j0}} \qquad (6.2)$$

where:

P_{jt} = price per unit for jth commodity in period t;
P_{j0} = price per unit for jth commodity in period 0;
Q_{jt} = the quantity of jth commodity in period t; and
Q_{j0} = the quantity of jth commodity in period 0.

Equations (6.1) and (6.2) can be used to construct Fisher's ideal price index:

$$\text{Fisher's ideal price index} = \sqrt{\left(\frac{\Sigma P_{jt}\ Q_{jt}}{\Sigma P_{j0}\ Q_{jt}}\right)\left(\frac{\Sigma P_{jt}\ Q_{j0}}{\Sigma P_{j0}\ Q_{j0}}\right)} \tag{6.3}$$

Similarly, **quantity-weighted indexes** can be defined:

$$\text{Laspeyres quantity index} = \frac{\Sigma Q_{jt}\ P_{j0}}{\Sigma Q_{j0}\ P_{j0}} \tag{6.4}$$

$$\text{Paasche quantity index} = \frac{\Sigma Q_{jt}\ P_{jt}}{\Sigma Q_{j0}\ P_{jt}} \tag{6.5}$$

$$\text{Fisher's ideal quantity index} = \sqrt{\left(\frac{\Sigma Q_{jt}\ P_{j0}}{\Sigma Q_{j0}\ P_{j0}}\right) \times \left(\frac{\Sigma Q_{jt}\ P_{jt}}{\Sigma Q_{j0}\ P_{jt}}\right)} \tag{6.6}$$

Sample Problem 6.1 provides further illlustration.

Sample Problem 6.1

To show how the indexes mentioned above can be used to analyze real-world issues Newbold (1984, 662–68) uses weekly price and volume data shown in the first two tables (opposite page) to compile the weighted aggregate price indexes and quantity indexes as listed in the third and fourth tables (page 154 and page 155), respectively.[1]

To demonstrate how the price index is compiled, the Laspeyres price index for the second week is calculated as follows. The data of the first two tables indicate that the total cost of purchasing the quantities shown (in hundreds of thousands of shares) in the first week, which will be used as base period, was

$(8.2)\ (20\frac{1}{4}) + (4.3)\ (4\frac{1}{8}) + (14.4)\ (5\frac{1}{4}) + (27.1)\ (46\frac{1}{8}) = \$150.9$ million

At the prices prevailing in the second week the total cost of purchasing the same shares would have been

$(8.2)\ (19\frac{7}{8}) + (4.3)\ (4\frac{1}{8}) + (14.4)\ (6) + (27.1)\ (45\frac{1}{4}) = \$149.3$ million

---

[1] From Paul Newbold, *Statistics for Business and Economics,* second edition, © 1988, pp. 656, 657, 657–61, and 662–64. Adapted by permission of Prentice Hall, Inc., Englewood Cliffs, New Jersey.

Prices of Stock in Four Automobile Corporations for the First Twelve Weeks of 1981, with the Unweighted Aggregate Index of Prices

Week	Ford	American Motors	Chrysler	General Motors	Average	Index of Average
1	20²⁄₈	4⅛	5²⁄₈	46⅛	18.93750	100.0
2	19⅞	4⅛	6	45²⁄₈	18.81250	99.3
3	19	4⅛	5⅛	45²⁄₈	18.46875	97.5
4	19⁶⁄₈	4⅛	5⅝	46	18.87500	99.7
5	20²⁄₈	3⅞	6	48²⁄₈	19.59375	103.5
6	19⅞	3⅞	5⅜	48⅝	19.43750	102.6
7	19⅜	4	5⅜	47⁶⁄₈	19.12500	101.0
8	19⅝	4	5⅜	50⅛	19.78125	104.5
9	21⅛	4⅛	5⁶⁄₈	51⅛	20.62500	108.9
10	22³⁄₈	4⅜	5⅜	51	20.78125	109.7
11	25	4⁶⁄₈	7²⁄₈	54	22.75000	120.1
12	23	4⅜	6⅝	52⁶⁄₈	21.68750	114.5

Source: Newbold, P. *Statistics for Business and Economics,* Prentice-Hall, Inc., 1984, p. 656.

Volume of Transactions in Shares of Four Automobile Corporations for the First Twelve Weeks of 1981 (hundreds of thousands)

Week	Ford	American Motors	Chrysler	General Motors
1	8.2	4.3	14.4	27.1
2	6.3	1.5	16.0	12.9
3	6.7	1.3	6.9	12.1
4	4.5	1.9	4.4	13.6
5	4.3	2.7	5.0	21.9
6	5.4	1.5	3.8	17.3
7	3.8	1.7	3.1	11.7
8	4.3	1.5	3.8	23.8
9	5.4	1.8	4.9	17.0
10	9.5	3.5	4.1	21.4
11	13.7	4.4	18.1	25.0
12	8.3	2.6	11.3	20.5

Source: Newbold (1984), p. 657.

Substituting these numbers into Equation (6.2), the Laspeyres price index for the second week is obtained:

$$100 \left(\frac{1.493}{1.509} \right) = 98.9$$

Weighted Aggregate Price Indexes for First Twelve Weeks of 1981

Week	Laspeyres Price Index	Paasche Price Index	Fisher's Price Ideal Index
1	100.0	100.0	100.0
2	98.9	99.8	99.3
3	98.0	97.7	97.8
4	99.9	99.7	99.8
5	104.5	104.4	104.4
6	104.4	104.4	104.4
7	102.6	102.5	102.5
8	107.0	107.7	107.3
9	110.6	110.6	110.6
10	110.1	110.4	110.2
11	118.8	119.5	119.1
12	114.8	114.8	114.8

Source: Newbold (1984), pp. 657–661.

Value-Weighted Indexes

So far, indexes of quantity as well as price have been defined. It would seem appropriate to measure total cost of the consumer's purchases in terms of cost index as:

$$\text{Cost index} = \frac{\Sigma P_{jt}\, Q_{jt}}{\Sigma P_{j0}\, Q_{j0}} \qquad (6.7)$$

The cost index is the basic form used for compiling the **value-weighted stock index.**

The Paasche index tends to underestimate the inflation rate while the Laspeyres index tends to overestimate the true inflationary impact over time. Stock indexes are intended to be a measure of value growth. The standard form of value-weighted stock indexes is expressed:

$$\text{Stock index} = \frac{\Sigma P_{jt}\, \Sigma Q_{jt}}{\Sigma P_{j0}\, \Sigma Q_{j0}} \qquad (6.8)$$

Therefore, changes in the index level could be the result of either price changes or volume changes. The price effect can be separated out by using one of the constant-quantity approaches as defined in Equations (6.1), (6.2), or (6.8). From a security analyst's point of view, it might even be useful to divide indexes such as the S&P 500 into subgroups that are either inflation favorable or inflation unfavorable. The quantity effect is also not really an exogenous factor. It can be separated out by using one of the constant-price approaches as defined in Equations (6.4), (6.5), or (6.6). There are at least three ways in which the concept of quantity is important in index construction and interpretation. First, there is the number of shares outstanding,

Weighted Aggregate Quantity Indexes for First Twelve Weeks of 1981

Week	Laspeyres Price Index	Paasche Price Index	Fisher's Price Ideal Index
1	100.0	100.0	100.0
2	53.9	54.3	54.1
3	48.7	48.6	48.6
4	49.7	49.6	49.6
5	75.2	75.1	75.1
6	61.9	61.9	61.9
7	42.4	42.4	42.4
8	80.3	80.8	80.5
9	61.4	61.4	61.4
10	80.5	80.7	80.6
11	102.3	102.9	102.6
12	78.4	78.4	78.4

Source: Newbold (1984), pp. 662–664.

which is used to determine a firm's market value. Experienced analysts know that this quantity is an understatement of the true number of shares implied in price determination in the market. Even the accounting profession has taken steps to force companies to include "share equivalents" when computing earnings-per-share figures that will be reported to their stock-holders. To the extent that share equivalents change over time, the rate of change in value-weighted stock indexes will be misstated, as will the level of the indexes. A second quantity-effect concept deals with market-volume figures—the number of shares traded in the market per unit of time. The implications of this technical concept are not well understood and are not taken account of in the stock indexes. A stock-velocity measure might be useful to financial analysts, similar to the money-velocity measurements used by economists. A third quantity-effect concept is related to supply-and-demand relationships, in which the amount of securities issued depends positively on the securities' selling price. Thus, stock quantity will increase relatively (because of new issues) during periods in which prices are perceived to be high and will decline relatively (because of repurchases) during periods in which prices are perceived to be low. More will be said about this quantity effect in later chapters dealing with market efficiency and the capital asset pricing model.

ALTERNATIVE MARKET INDEXES

In this section the seven important stock indexes mentioned earlier are discussed. Following each discussion an illustration is provided.

Dow Jones Industrial Average

The **Dow Jones Industrial Average (DJIA)** is probably the best known and most widely quoted of all the market indexes. Its latest value is broadcast many times a day, even on the least news-oriented top-40 radio stations. The Financial News Cable Network reports it every ninety seconds during a trading day. It is also probably the most criticized representation of the overall market among the available major stock indexes. The DJIA is a price-weighted arithmetic average of thirty large, well-known industrial stocks, all of which are listed on the New York Stock Exchange. The computation involves summing the current prices of the thirty stocks and then dividing by a divisor that is adjusted to allow for any stock splits or large stock dividends.

$$\text{DJIA} = \sum_{i=t}^{30} \frac{P_{it}}{DV_t} \qquad (6.9)$$

where:

P_{it} = the closing price of stock i on day t; and
DV_t = the adjusted divisor on day t.

As can be seen in Table 6–1, the adjustment process is designed to keep the index value the same as it would have been if the split had not occurred. Similar adjustments have been made when it has been found necessary to replace one of the component stocks with the stock of another company. The consistency and comparability of index values at different points in time are thus protected. Nevertheless, the adjustment process used for the DJIA has not been accepted without criticism. Since price weighting itself causes

TABLE 6–1   Adjustment of DJIA Divisor to Allow for a Stock Split

Stock	Price before Split	Price after 2-for-1 Stock Split by Stock A
A	60	30
B	30	30
C	20	20
D	10	90
	120	

$$\text{Average} = \frac{120}{4} = 30 \qquad \text{Adjustment of divisor} = \frac{90}{30} = 3$$

$$\text{Average} = \frac{90}{3} = 30$$

$$\text{Divisor before Split} = 4 \qquad \text{Divisor after Split} = 3$$

high-priced stocks to dominate the series, this same effect can cause a shift in this balance when fast-growing firms split their stock. For example, a 20-percent increase in the price of Stock A from Table 6–1 would in itself have caused a 10-percent increase in the value of the sample index before the split, while a 20-percent increase in Stock B would have caused only a 5-percent increase in the index value. After the two-for-one split of Stock A, a 20-percent increase in either Stock A or Stock B would produce the same effect on the index value (a 6.7-percent increase), illustrating a downward shift in the importance of Stock A relative to the other stocks in the sample. This type of an effect could lead to the fastest-growing stocks having the least importance in determining the index values.

Other criticisms of the DJIA center around its emphasis on using only large, mature, "blue-chip" firms (and a small number of them at that) that do not seem to be similar to most companies in the market. The attitude of the multitudes that watch its daily movement seems to be "as the DJIA goes, so goes the economy." Since studies measuring the correlation of daily price changes of the DJIA with other broader indexes of NYSE stocks have found correlation coefficients ranging from 0.89 to 0.92, this attitude may be justified in the short run.[2]

Standard & Poor's Composite 500 Index

The second most popular market index, **Standard & Poor's Composite 500 Index (S&P 500),** is a value-weighted index of four hundred industrial stocks, forty utility stocks, twenty transportation stocks, and forty financial stocks. It is computed as follows:

$$\text{S\&P}_t = \frac{\Sigma P_{it}\, Q_{it}}{\Sigma P_{i0}\, Q_{i0}} \times 10 \qquad \textbf{(6.10)}$$

where:

P_{it} = price of stock i in period t;
Q_{it} = number of shares outstanding for stock i in period t;
P_{i0} = price of stock i in the base period 0; and
Q_{i0} = number of shares outstanding for stock i in base period 0;

and the base period is 1941–1943.

Since 1976, when the makeup of the S&P 500 was changed to include financial stocks, the index has for the first time included stocks from the **over-the-counter (OTC) market.** ("Over the counter" recalls the trading practices of the 1800s, when buyers and sellers of unlisted stocks traded their stocks over the bank counter.) This was necessary because many of the stocks of major financial institutions are traded on the OTC market.

---

[2] See Reilly, F. K., *Investments,* Dryden Press, 1985.

While the S&P 500 is much more comprehensive in makeup—thus more representative of the overall market—than the DJIA, its total number of components is still small compared to the theoretically available market portfolio of all investment opportunities. The value-weighting computational approach is also subject to the criticism that firms with the largest market values have the most influence on the computed level. While this is certainly true, it is also true of the market portfolio itself, and should not be a problem except to the extent that the S&P 500 sample does not sufficiently reflect the makeup of the market portfolio. This cannot be properly evaluated empirically because of the impossibility of specifying the market portfolio accurately. In any case, the S&P 500 has gained added significance recently because of the development of options, futures contracts, and options on futures contracts for this index.[3] This has created a new opportunity for portfolio managers by providing a new means to adjust the risk and return of a portfolio to desired levels. By adjusting the proportion of the futures position to the valuation of the portfolio, the portfolio manager can theoretically attain any risk–return combination desired. These opportunities are discussed in further detail in later chapters.

New York Stock Exchange Composite Index

Another commonly used value-weighted index is the **New York Stock Exchange (NYSE) Composite Index,** inaugurated in 1966 and consisting of the market values of all of the common stocks listed on the New York Stock Exchange. While it includes many more stocks than the S&P 500 (about 1,700), this index can still be criticized as a proxy for the market portfolio because it contains none of the companies that cannot be listed, or choose not to be listed, on the NYSE.

Value Line Composite Index

The **Value Line (VL) Composite Index** is an equal-weighted geometric average of stock prices computed as a ratio with a base date of June 30, 1961 (set at 100). A recent breakdown of stocks in the index included 1,502 industrials, 177 utilities, and 14 rails, making a total of 1,693 stocks. Each market day the closing price of each stock is divided by the closing price of the preceding day, with the preceding day set at 100. The resulting indexes of change for that day are then geometrically averaged—the nth root of n items. The geometric average change for that day is then multiplied by the value of the average on the preceding day to get the latest value. The preceding day's prices are first adjusted for any stock splits or dividends.

---

[3] Other indexes for which options and futures contracts have been developed include the NYSE Composite Index, the Value Line Stock Index, and a subset of the S&P 500, the S&P 100.

A problem associated with the VL index is that the geometric average understates the central tendency of cross-sectional data (see Chapter 3). The arithmetic mean is superior for this purpose. Lawrence Fisher (1966) suggests that the least bias will result from the use of a mixed mean, in which a weighted combination of the arithmetic and geometric mean would be used to prepare the index. This index is available on the CRSP (Center for Research on Security Prices) tapes generated at the University of Chicago. It has been used frequently by academicians and practitioners in their work when a market index is required.

Wilshire 5000 Equity Index

The **Wilshire 5000 Equity Index,** prepared by Wilshire Associates of Santa Monica, California, is a value-weighted and equal-weighted index that is increasing in usage because it contains most equity securities available for investment, including all NYSE and AMEX issues plus the most active stocks on the OTC market.

The following formula is used to compute the index:

$$I_t = I_{t-1} \left(\frac{\sum_{j=1}^{n} (S_{jt}) P_{jt}}{\sum_{j=1}^{n} (S_{jt-1}) P_{jt-1}} \right) \tag{6.11}$$

where:

I_t = index value for the tth period;
n = number of stocks in index;
P_{jt} = price of the jth security for the tth period; and
S_{jt} = shares outstanding of the jth security for the tth period.

In the event that P_{jt} is not available for a given security, that security is dropped from the summations. If P_{jt-1} is not available but P_{jt} is—that is, a security has just resumed trading—the last available price is substituted for P_{jt-1}.

The Major Market Index

The **Major Market Index (MMI)** is a price-weighted index of twenty blue-chip stocks. It was first constructed as the basis for an index option that was introduced in September of 1983 by the American Stock Exchange. The index is constructed by adding up the prices of the twenty component stocks and dividing the sum by a number reflecting stock splits, deletions, and additions. Fifteen of the twenty stocks of the MMI are also in the Dow Jones Industrial Average. This index is particularly suitable for stock and futures arbitrage. Because the index is so narrow (only twenty stocks), arbitrageurs can easily and cheaply construct the cash market positions of the underlying stocks.

Standard & Poor's Composite 100 Index

Very recently a subset of the S&P 500 called the **S&P 100** was developed for use in the futures and options markets. While it may seem strange in the context of the increasing development of broader indexes that this more narrowly based index would be formed, it will become clear that the basis for its popularity is related to margin requirements in the options market. Sample Problem 6.2 provides further illustration.

Sample Problem 6.2

To illustrate the seven indexes just discussed, daily quotations from *The Wall Street Journal* for January 10 to January 25, 1989, are presented in the table on page 161●

THE USERS AND USES OF MARKET INDEXES

People from many walks of life use and are affected by market indexes. Economists and statisticians use stock-market indexes to study long-term growth patterns in the economy, to analyze and forecast business-cycle patterns, and to relate stock indexes to other time-series measures of economic activity. Investors, both individual and institutional, use the market index as a benchmark against which to evaluate the performance of their own or institutional portfolios. The answer to the question, ''Did you beat the market?'' has important ramifications for all types of investors. Market technicians in many cases base their decisions to buy and sell on the patterns that appear in the time series of the market indexes. The final use of the market index is in portfolio analysis. In discussions of the market model and systematic risk earlier in this chapter it became evident that the relevant riskiness of a security is determined by the relationship between that security's return and the return on the market.

Among economists and statisticians one of the major uses of stock-market indexes is as a leading economic indicator. Judging by how long they have been employed, leading indicators of economic activity must be considered a forecasting success. Unlike econometric modeling, the leading economic indicator approach to forecasting does not require assumptions about what causes economic behavior. Instead, it relies on statistically detecting patterns among economic variables that can be used to forecast turning points in economic activity. Table 6–2 presents a list of the time series currently being used by the U.S. Department of Commerce as leading economic indicators.

A recent development in the financial market is the growth of futures and options on stock-market indexes. Index options have been by far the most important of the numerous new financial instruments introduced during the

Major Stock Indexes for January 10, 1989–January 25, 1989

Indexes	1/10	1/11	1/12	1/13	1/16	1/17	1/18	1/19	1/20	1/23	1/24	1/25
Dow-Jones Industrial Average (DJIA)	2193.21	2206.43	2222.32	2226.07	2224.64	2214.64	2238.75	2239.11	2235.3	2218.39	2256.43	2265.89
S&P 500	280.38	282.01	283.17	283.87	284.14	283.55	286.53	286.90	286.6	284.50	288.49	289.14
NYSE	157.85	158.65	159.26	159.58	159.78	159.48	161.01	161.25	161.1	160.13	161.99	162.33
Value Line	235.89	236.45	237.10	237.32	237.49	236.96	238.90	239.58	239.7	238.44	239.86	240.14
Wilshire 5000	2768.12	2780.39	2790.59	2795.82	2798.06	2792.76	2819.10	2824.94	2824.8	2807.98	2837.91	2843.98
Major Market Index (MMI)	428.43	430.57	434.07	435.47	435.82	434.86	439.67	439.05	438.3	435.91	443.56	444.78
S&P 100	265.67	267.44	268.90	269.35	269.61	269.01	272.23	272.42	271.6	269.92	274.16	274.72

Source: The Wall Street Journal, January 10–January 25, 1989, p. C2.

TABLE 6–2   The Index of Leading Indicators (includes twelve data series)

BEA Series Number	Description of Series	Weight
1	Average workweek of production workers, manufacturing	0.984
3	Layoff rate, manufacturing (inverted)	1.025
8	New orders, consumer goods and materials, 1972 dollars	1.065
12	Index of net business formation	0.984
19	Index of stock prices (Standard and Poor)	1.079
20	Contracts and orders, plant and equipment, 1972 dollars	0.971
29	Building permits, private housing	1.025
32	Vendor performance	0.930
36	Change in inventories on hand and on order, 1972 dollars	0.957
92	Percent change in sensitive prices (smoothed)	0.971
104	Percent change in total liquid assets (smoothed)	1.011
105	Money supply (M1), 1972 dollars	1.065

Source: Handbook of Cyclical Indicators (May 1977), U.S. Department of Commerce.

1980s. The development of the index options has made it possible for institutional investors to deal with the entire market rather than individual stocks, and thus to open up new kinds of investment strategies. As will be shown, the potential for options and futures strategies to reduce risk and change return patterns is almost limitless.

Besides the seven indexes discussed in the last section, Merrill Lynch and Wilshire Associates have compiled an index called the **Merrill Lynch–Wilshire Capital Markets Index (CMI).** The CMI is a market-value weighted index created to measure the total return performance of the combined domestic taxable fixed-income and equity market. This unique new investment tool currently tracks more than 10,000 bonds and stocks. The CMI has been used in (1) asset-allocation decisions, (2) performance measurement, (3) sector-investment analysis, and (4) portfolio structuring. The composition of CMI is presented in Figure 6–1.

HISTORICAL BEHAVIOR OF MARKET INDEXES AND THE IMPLICATIONS OF THEIR USE FOR FORECASTING

It is useful at this point to observe how some of the market indexes have behaved historically and to study the implications of their use in forecasting.

Historical Behavior

Tables 6–3 and 6–4 on page 164 compare annualized rates of return computed over one-year through ten-year holding periods for pairs of the most widely used market indexes. These rates of return are computed using March 31, 1984, as the closing date of each holding period.

FIGURE 6-1   The Merrill Lynch–Wilshire Capital-Markets Index

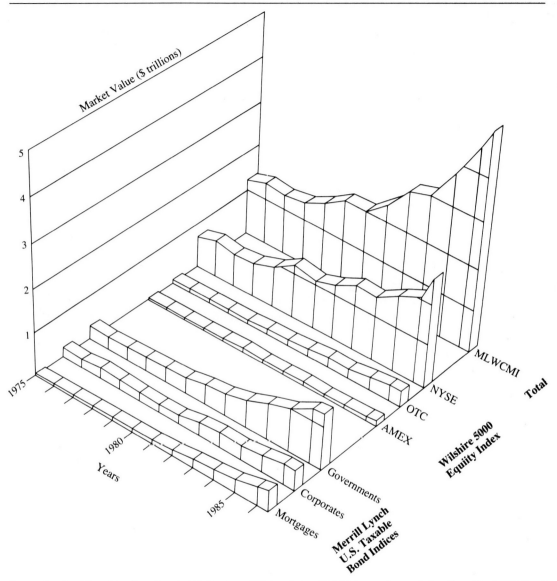

Source: Reprinted from The Merrill Lynch–Wilshire Capital Markets Index, Fall, 1987 issue, by permission. Copyright © 1987 **Merrill Lynch**, Pierce, Fenner & Smith Incorporated.

As can be seen in Table 6–3, there are some differences, notably in rates of return for any given year, but the relative year-to-year movement is very similar. The correlation coefficient between rates of return computed from these two indexes over this time period is 0.97398, giving a coefficient of determination of 0.94222. This means that 94.22 percent of the movement in the returns on the DJIA can be considered to be related to the concurrent movement in returns on the S&P 500. So even though there are substantial

TABLE 6-3   Annualized Rates of Return: DJIA vs. S&P 500 (dividends included)

Holding Period (years)	DJIA	S&P 500
1	8.0	8.7
2	25.4	25.3
3	11.1	10.8
4	16.8	17.4
5	12.5	15.1
6	13.9	15.9
7	9.6	12.7
8	7.8	11.0
9	10.6	12.8
10	9.0	10.7

differences in the way these indexes are computed, there is a high correlation in the way they behave. Figure 6-2 presents the historical graph of the S&P 500 during the period 1961–1988.

Table 6-4 compares annualized rates of return for two commonly used indexes that include a much larger number of stocks, the NYSE composite and the Value Line composite. While the sample sizes are somewhat comparable, the VL indicator is an equal-weighted geometric index, while the NYSE is a value-weighted arithmetic index. As Cootner (1966) points out: "As long as there is any variability among its components, any geometric index will grow more slowly or decline more swiftly than the corresponding arithmetic index." (See Chapter 3 for further discussion of the differences between arithmetic and geometric means.) While comparison of the rates of return of the two indexes shows that, except for the one-year holding period,

TABLE 6-4   Annualized Rates of Return: NYSE vs. VL (dividends not included)

Holding Period (years)	NYSE	VL
1	4.1	1.6
2	19.2	20.6
3	5.4	5.7
4	12.3	14.5
5	9.9	10.7
6	10.7	11.5
7	8.0	10.5
8	6.6	9.5
9	8.4	11.6
10	6.2	8.8

FIGURE 6-2 The S&P 500, 1961–1988 (monthly averages; 1941–1943 = 10; shaded areas indicate recessions)

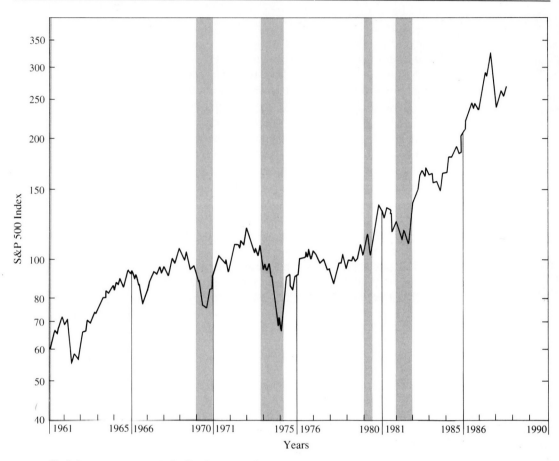

Shaded areas represent periods of business recessions.

Source: Analyst's Outlook. Standard & Poor's, 1988 p. 186.

the geometric VL index has outperformed the arithmetic NYSE index, it can be proved mathematically that with an identical sample of stocks the aforementioned relationship between the two indexes will hold true. The correlation coefficient between the returns computed from these two indexes over this time period is 0.94412, giving a coefficient of determination of 0.87777. This means that 87.777 percent of the returns on the NYSE can be considered to be related to the movement in returns on the VL. Again there is a high correlation between returns computed with alternative market return proxies. This conclusion generally conforms with past analyses by Fisher and Lorie (1970), Reilly (1985), and others.

Implications

What are the implications for security analysts and portfolio managers who might be using such indexes as proxies for the return on the market portfolio? The results seem to imply that differences among the available indexes, while occasionally significant over short time periods, are not very great over longer time periods. In his study using daily price changes, Reilly (1985) finds that even on a short-run basis the DJIA is highly correlated with other indexes that are based primarily on stocks listed on the New York Stock Exchange. In fact, the concensus of stock-index research seems to indicate that the main cause of lower correlated return is the use of relatively higher-risk samples, such as samples made up primarily of American Stock Exchange or over-the-counter stocks [see Reilly (1985)]. It would therefore seem appropriate for forecasters of market return to use market-index proxies that are broadly based in nature and that basically reflect the average risk across all investment opportunities. Roll's (1978) research, in which use of different indexes was shown to give conflicting portfolio-performance decisions in marginal situations, has clearly demonstrated that this can be important and has probably led to the increased use in recent years of indexes such as the Wilshire 5000. (The Wilshire 5000 Equity Index is graphed in Figure 6–3. Monthly returns for the Wilshire 5000 Equity Indexes are listed in Appendix 6A, pages 171–177.)

MARKET-INDEX PROXY ERRORS AND THEIR IMPACT ON BETA ESTIMATES AND EFFICIENT-MARKET-HYPOTHESIS TESTS

This section concerns how the stock index can be used to calculate the market rates of return. The issue related to proxy error in estimating the market model (see Chapter 4) is also studied.

Market indexes are used as proxy variables to calculate the return on the market portfolio R_m in the "market model."

$$R_{jt} = \alpha_j + \beta_j R_{mt} + e_{jt} \qquad (6.12)$$

where:

R_{jt} = the return in the jth security in period $t;$
α_j = the intercept of a market model for the jth security;
β_j = the systematic risk measure of security $j;$
R_{mt} = the return on the market index in period $t;$ and
e_{jt} = a random error term.

Estimations of β_j (beta) can be made empirically by regressing R_{it} on R_{mt}, where R_m is proxied by using a rate of return based on a market index, such as the S&P 500. For example:

FIGURE 6–3   The Wilshire 5000 Equity Index

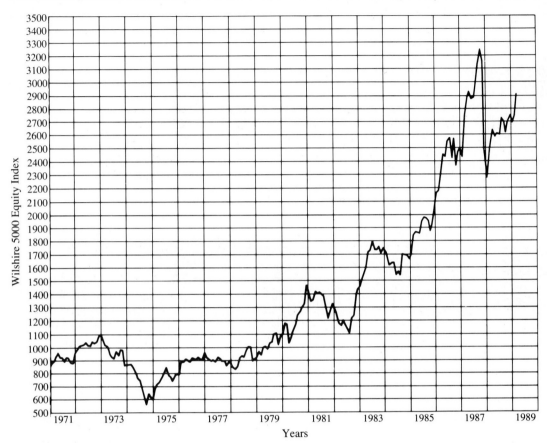

Source: Wilshire Associates.

$$R_{mt} = \frac{I_t - I_{t-1} + d_t}{I_{t-1}} \qquad (6.13)$$

where I_{t-1} and I_t are the S&P 500 index levels at the beginning and end of period t, respectively, and d_t is the dividends paid on the index stocks during period t.

It should be noted that the estimated R_{mt} can be subject to measurement error (Roll 1978; Lee 1976). Globally, the market rate of return should include not only the equity return but also bonds, gold, and so on. Even within the various equity indexes there are different levels of measurement error. The reason for this is inherent in the differences among the indexes—for example, index composition and weighting scheme. This kind of index-proxy error is not only a concern for academicians but should be a concern for industry practitioners and security analysts as well, especially since the

development of market-index investment vehicles such as index options and index futures. (These instruments are discussed in detail in Chapters 12 through 16.)

INDEX-PROXY ERROR, PERFORMANCE MEASURE, AND THE EMH TEST

A potentially serious problem is involved in the use of a market index to represent the market portfolio. Strictly speaking, the market portfolio consists of all available investment opportunities, weighted according to their proportion of the total market value. While an index such as the S&P 500 is also value weighted and includes many more component firms than a narrowly based index such as the DJIA, it includes only common-stock investments, and only a small proportion of the total available. Because of this, many financial analysts are beginning to use broader indexes, such as the Wilshire 5000. Nevertheless, while this index is value weighted and includes all stocks for which daily prices are available, it still does not include "all available investment opportunities." Richard Roll (1977) questions the adequacy of using a market index as a market-portfolio proxy. He points out that the linear relationship between beta and the required rate of return for a security follows from the efficiency of the market portfolio, and that this linearity is not independently testable. A proxy such as the S&P 500 may be mean-variance efficient while the market portfolio is not, and it might be mean-variance inefficient when the market portfolio is efficient. Roll thinks that the CAPM and the market portfolio are therefore untestable without accurate specification of the "true" market portfolio. Since the latter is impossible, therefore, so is the former. Roll (1978) strengthens his argument by showing that different indexes used as proxies for the market portfolio can cause different portfolio-performance rankings.

This is quite a serious matter, indeed, because many financial analysts and portfolio managers are evaluated using CAPM-based performance-measurement models—for example, the Jensen model, in which "alpha" values are measured to determine whether a portfolio is performing well. The alpha is the intercept value of an ex-post regression of the risk premiums achieved over time by an individual portfolio analyzed on the market-risk premium over the same time period. Since

$$R_{pt} - R_{ft} = \alpha_p + \beta_p(R_{mt} - R_{ft}) + e_{pt} \qquad \textbf{(6.14)}$$

where:

R_{pt} = rate of return for a portfolio in period t;
R_{ft} = riskless rate in period t;
R_{mt} = market rate of return in period t;
β_p = systematic risk for a portfolio; and
e_{pt} = an error term.

FIGURE 6–4   Risk-Premium Characteristic Lines

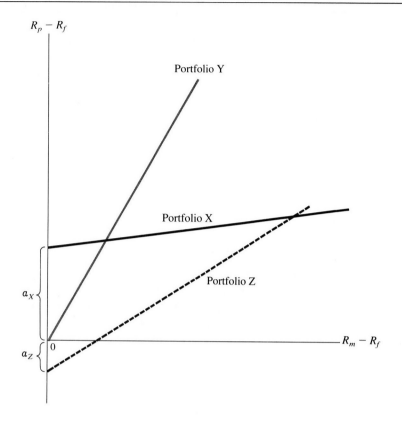

it follows that Jensen's performance measurement can be computed:

$$\alpha_p = [\bar{R}_p - R_f] - \beta_p [\bar{R}_m - R_f] \qquad \textbf{(6.15)}$$

$\bar{R}_p$ and $\bar{R}_m$ represent averaged rates of return for a portfolio and market rates of return, respectively.

A plot of risk-premium characteristic lines for three portfolios is shown in Figure 6–4. It can be said that Portfolio X has shown superior performance over the time period analyzed because its alpha is significantly positive. This is true because the CAPM model leads to the conclusion that, under equilibrium conditions, the alpha intercept should be equal to zero. Figure 6–4 also suggests that Portfolio Z has shown inferior performance because of the significantly negative alpha, and Portfolio Y has performed as would be predicted by the CAPM. (Other models, such as those developed by Sharpe and Treynor, are studied in more detail in later chapters of this book.) The point being made here is that beta-estimation problems can have important and far-reaching implications. These empirical problems, as well as problems dealing with the fundamental assumptions of the theory, have led other researchers such as Stephen Ross (1976) to seek alternative models,

among them the arbitrage pricing theory (APT) discussed in Chapter 11. As will be seen in later chapters, these alternative models have empirical and theoretical problems of their own.

Market-index proxy errors, through their impact on beta estimation, also impact heavily upon tests of the efficient-market hypothesis (EMH). This is true because a test of market efficiency (security prices fully reflect all available information) must be based on a model of market equilibrium (for example, the CAPM), and any test is therefore simultaneously a test of efficiency and a test of the assumed equilibrium model. (EMH is discussed in Chapter 16.)

SUMMARY

This chapter has described basic market-index information needed to do security analysis and portfolio management, as well as methods of compiling stock-market and price indexes and historical behavior of stock indexes. Moreover, the impact of proxy errors associated with market rates of return on beta estimates and EMH tests has been discussed. The concepts and information discussed in this chapter underscore the importance of alternative stock indexes for both individual and institutional investors.

QUESTIONS AND PROBLEMS

1. What is a market index? What are some of the uses of market indexes for security analysis?
2. Give two different methods used to weight indexes.
3. Compare the Paasche and Laspeyres price indexes. What are the benefits and disadvantages of each index?
4. What is the DJIA? How many stocks are included in the index? What method is used to weight the stocks?
5. What stocks make up the S&P 500? What method is used to weight the stocks? Why do some people consider this index to be a better measure of market performance than the DJIA?
6. Carefully explain the differences between calculating an index using a geometric average versus an arithmetic average.
7. Briefly explain Roll's criticism of market indexes as proxies of the market portfolio.
8. Briefly compare the advantages and disadvantages of using a narrowly focused index such as the DJIA with that of a broad-based index like the Wilshire 5000.
9. Using Section C of *The Wall Street Journal,* define the major indexes and discuss their usefulness.

APPENDIX 6A: MONTHLY RETURNS FOR THE WILSHIRE 5000 EQUITY INDEXES

TABLE 6A-1   Monthly Returns for the Wilshire 5000 Equity Indexes, 1/29/71–12/31/84

Month Ending	Value-Weighted Index			Equal-Weighted Index		
	Price Appreciation* (percent)	Dividends Yield (percent)	Total Return (percent)	Price Appreciation (percent)	Dividends Yield (percent)	Total Return (percent)
1/29/71	5.184	0.127	5.311	14.528	0.114	14.642
2/26/71	1.381	0.418	1.799	4.982	0.216	5.198
3/31/71	4.266	0.209	4.475	5.702	0.199	5.901
4/30/71	3.479	0.104	3.583	3.857	0.100	3.957
5/28/71	−3.707	0.401	−3.306	−4.692	0.217	−4.475
6/30/71	0.226	0.166	0.392	−1.534	0.182	−1.352
7/30/71	−3.688	0.103	−3.585	−4.822	0.100	−4.722
8/31/71	3.524	0.450	3.974	3.870	0.241	4.111
9/30/71	−0.540	0.163	−0.377	−0.346	0.180	−0.166
10/29/71	−4.035	0.179	−3.856	−5.471	0.123	−5.348
11/30/71	−0.704	0.416	−0.288	−3.481	0.253	−3.228
12/31/71	8.966	0.177	9.143	11.667	0.200	11.867
1/31/72	2.895	0.120	3.015	10.110	0.109	10.219
2/29/72	2.976	0.395	3.371	4.606	0.209	4.815
3/30/72	0.726	0.202	0.928	0.524	0.168	0.692
4/28/72	0.629	0.106	0.735	0.896	0.102	0.998
5/31/72	1.363	0.416	1.779	−1.782	0.221	−1.561
6/30/72	−2.228	0.149	−2.079	−3.400	0.178	−3.222
7/31/72	−0.381	0.105	−0.276	−2.747	0.111	−2.636
8/31/72	3.120	0.386	3.506	1.070	0.221	1.291
9/29/72	−0.938	0.164	−0.774	−2.794	0.166	−2.628
10/31/72	0.762	0.138	0.900	−1.241	0.135	−1.106
11/30/72	4.273	0.418	4.691	4.017	0.257	4.274
12/29/72	0.928	0.136	1.064	−1.513	0.188	−1.325
1/31/73	−2.801	0.115	−2.686	−2.973	0.090	−2.883
2/28/73	−4.688	0.357	−4.331	−7.707	0.190	−7.517
3/30/73	−0.842	0.154	−0.688	−2.921	0.194	−2.727
4/30/73	−5.066	0.127	−4.939	−7.340	0.135	−7.205
5/31/73	−2.830	0.453	−2.377	−8.621	0.262	−8.359
6/29/73	−0.986	0.170	−0.816	−4.213	0.201	−4.012
7/31/73	5.483	0.140	5.623	11.303	0.135	11.438
8/31/73	−3.472	0.431	−3.041	−4.686	0.261	−4.425
9/28/73	5.101	0.156	5.257	7.770	0.174	7.944

* Represents monthly percentage change in Wilshire 5000 Equity Index.

TABLE 6A-1 *(continued)*

Month Ending	Value-Weighted Index			Equal-Weighted Index		
	Price Appreciation* (percent)	*Dividends Yield (percent)*	*Total Return (percent)*	*Price Appreciation (percent)*	*Dividends Yield (percent)*	*Total Return (percent)*
10/31/73	− 0.029	0.173	0.144	0.125	0.149	0.274
11/30/73	− 12.684	0.474	− 12.210	− 18.335	0.274	− 18.061
12/31/73	0.833	0.200	1.033	− 4.521	0.285	− 4.236
1/31/74	0.214	0.158	0.372	13.350	0.165	13.515
2/28/74	− 0.175	0.467	0.292	0.513	0.279	0.792
3/29/74	− 2.682	0.199	− 2.483	0.682	0.246	0.928
4/30/74	− 4.691	0.180	− 4.511	− 5.788	0.173	− 5.615
5/31/74	− 4.944	0.556	− 4.388	− 7.562	0.322	− 7.240
6/28/74	− 2.702	0.238	− 2.464	− 3.620	0.287	− 3.333
7/31/74	− 7.192	0.180	− 7.012	− 5.687	0.192	− 5.495
8/30/74	− 9.659	0.670	− 8.989	− 9.071	0.369	− 8.702
9/30/74	− 11.289	0.296	− 10.993	− 8.507	0.319	− 8.188
10/31/74	16.250	0.313	16.563	9.238	0.252	9.490
11/29/74	− 4.934	0.714	− 4.220	− 5.554	0.408	− 5.146
12/31/74	− 2.883	0.297	− 2.586	− 8.634	0.417	− 8.217
1/31/75	14.431	0.194	14.625	31.170	0.241	31.411
2/28/75	5.525	0.672	6.197	5.510	0.351	5.861
3/31/75	2.444	0.281	2.725	8.283	0.346	8.629
4/30/75	4.615	0.212	4.827	3.092	0.190	3.282
5/30/75	5.015	0.614	5.629	7.483	0.352	7.835
6/30/75	4.720	0.240	4.960	7.321	0.298	7.619
7/31/75	− 6.321	0.188	− 6.133	− 1.078	0.187	− 0.891
8/29/75	− 2.644	0.532	− 2.112	− 5.116	0.316	− 4.800
9/30/75	− 4.129	0.286	− 3.843	− 4.324	0.356	− 3.968
10/31/75	5.332	0.252	5.584	1.418	0.217	1.635
11/28/75	2.618	0.544	3.162	1.688	0.326	2.014
12/31/75	− 1.247	0.255	− 0.992	− 0.396	0.381	− 0.015
1/30/76	12.283	0.204	12.487	19.963	0.180	20.143
2/27/76	0.161	0.511	0.672	10.993	0.279	11.272
3/31/76	2.448	0.249	2.697	2.346	0.289	2.635
4/30/76	− 1.088	0.132	− 0.956	− 0.453	0.237	− 0.216
5/28/76	− 1.580	0.624	− 0.956	− 2.003	0.306	− 1.697
6/30/76	4.011	0.224	4.235	2.938	0.172	3.110
7/30/76	− 0.762	0.142	− 0.620	0.446	0.162	0.608
8/31/76	− 0.761	0.589	− 0.172	− 1.725	0.348	− 1.377
9/30/76	2.199	0.227	2.426	1.490	0.287	1.777

* Represents monthly percentage change in Wilshire 5000 Equity Index.

TABLE 6A–1 *(continued)*

	Value-Weighted Index			Equal-Weighted Index		
Month Ending	Price Appreciation* (percent)	Dividends Yield (percent)	Total Return (percent)	Price Appreciation (percent)	Dividends Yield (percent)	Total Return (percent)
10/29/76	−2.262	0.184	−2.078	−2.539	0.185	−2.354
11/30/76	−0.072	0.693	0.621	2.530	0.388	2.918
12/31/76	6.108	0.213	6.321	10.683	0.341	11.024
1/31/77	−3.702	0.161	−3.541	3.324	0.175	3.499
2/28/77	−2.056	0.589	−1.467	0.143	0.306	0.449
3/31/77	−1.240	0.246	−0.994	1.150	0.289	1.439
4/29/77	0.520	0.143	0.663	1.576	0.092	1.668
5/31/77	−1.260	0.129	−1.131	2.302	0.249	2.551
6/30/77	4.196	0.912	5.108	5.182	0.298	5.480
7/29/77	−1.471	0.131	−1.340	4.165	0.172	4.337
8/31/77	−1.991	0.697	−1.294	−0.605	0.340	−0.265
9/30/77	−0.021	0.283	0.262	1.036	0.268	1.304
10/31/77	−4.040	0.212	−3.828	−2.208	0.215	−1.993
11/30/77	3.616	0.835	4.451	7.258	0.372	7.630
12/30/77	0.589	0.258	0.847	1.602	0.348	1.950
1/31/78	−5.724	0.191	−5.533	−1.132	0.176	−0.956
2/28/78	−1.734	0.730	−1.004	2.291	0.374	2.665
3/31/78	3.106	0.341	3.447	6.560	0.332	6.892
4/28/78	8.092	0.179	8.271	8.538	0.171	8.709
5/31/78	1.553	0.822	2.375	6.640	0.367	7.007
6/30/78	−1.362	0.273	−1.089	0.525	0.299	0.824
7/31/78	5.579	0.183	5.762	5.241	0.169	5.410
8/31/78	3.608	0.671	4.279	9.303	0.331	9.634
9/29/78	−0.802	0.286	−0.516	0.085	0.258	0.343
10/31/78	−10.961	0.251	−10.710	−18.607	0.201	−18.406
11/30/78	2.415	0.812	3.227	3.949	0.412	4.361
12/29/78	1.589	0.288	1.877	1.050	0.371	1.421
1/31/79	4.564	0.235	4.799	9.601	0.222	9.823
2/28/79	−3.009	0.688	−2.321	−2.253	0.349	−1.904
3/30/79	6.601	0.285	6.886	8.463	0.326	8.789
4/30/79	0.710	0.238	0.948	2.573	0.216	2.789
5/31/79	−2.344	0.845	−1.499	−0.916	0.359	−0.557
6/29/79	4.798	0.272	5.070	5.153	0.321	5.474
7/31/79	0.966	0.224	1.190	1.886	0.211	2.097
8/31/79	5.746	0.797	6.543	7.507	0.386	7.893
9/28/79	0.365	0.267	0.632	−0.528	0.240	−0.288

* Represents monthly percentage change in Wilshire 5000 Equity Index.

TABLE 6A–1 *(continued)*

Month Ending	Value-Weighted Index Price Appreciation* (percent)	Dividends Yield (percent)	Total Return (percent)	Equal-Weighted Index Price Appreciation (percent)	Dividends Yield (percent)	Total Return (percent)
10/31/79	−7.422	0.294	−7.128	−10.276	0.229	−10.047
11/30/79	5.427	0.774	6.201	6.253	0.405	6.658
12/31/79	2.354	0.295	2.649	4.735	0.357	5.092
1/31/80	6.930	0.242	7.172	9.144	0.231	9.375
2/29/80	−0.454	0.679	0.225	−2.590	0.338	−2.252
3/31/80	−12.429	0.284	−12.145	−16.146	0.319	−15.827
4/30/80	4.516	0.226	4.742	5.061	0.222	5.283
5/30/80	5.108	0.781	5.889	6.819	0.412	7.231
6/30/80	3.371	0.333	3.704	3.892	0.385	4.277
7/31/80	6.646	0.245	6.891	9.722	0.207	9.929
8/29/80	2.006	0.559	2.565	5.548	0.327	5.875
9/30/80	2.635	0.283	2.918	3.068	0.281	3.349
10/31/80	2.257	0.274	2.531	2.958	0.224	3.182
11/28/80	10.252	0.595	10.847	5.230	0.274	5.504
12/31/80	−4.230	0.265	−3.965	−3.813	0.288	−3.525
1/30/81	−4.445	0.171	−4.274	−0.195	0.166	−0.029
2/27/81	0.691	0.595	1.286	−0.205	0.288	0.083
3/31/81	4.706	0.306	5.012	7.561	0.293	7.854
4/30/81	−0.986	0.227	−0.759	2.820	0.227	3.047
5/29/81	0.705	0.634	1.339	4.220	0.276	4.496
6/30/81	−1.387	0.636	−0.751	−1.274	0.267	−1.007
7/31/81	−0.655	0.177	−0.478	−2.009	0.149	−1.860
8/31/81	−6.155	0.638	−5.517	−7.317	0.240	−7.077
9/30/81	−6.843	0.286	−6.557	−9.007	0.222	−8.785
10/30/81	5.711	0.327	6.038	8.065	0.215	8.280
11/30/81	3.818	0.684	4.502	2.573	0.267	2.840
12/31/81	−3.015	0.286	−2.729	−1.155	0.246	−0.909
1/29/82	−3.023	0.144	−2.879	−1.679	0.118	−1.561
2/26/82	−6.172	0.645	−5.527	−4.759	0.233	−4.526
3/31/82	−1.424	0.398	−1.026	−0.409	0.274	−0.135
4/30/82	4.139	0.183	4.322	5.772	0.214	5.986
5/28/82	−3.629	0.815	−2.814	−2.402	0.269	−2.133
6/30/82	−2.825	0.345	−2.480	−3.410	0.255	−3.155
7/30/82	−2.261	0.166	−2.095	−0.546	0.121	−0.425
8/31/82	10.934	0.997	11.931	7.799	0.318	8.117
9/30/82	1.300	0.290	1.590	3.905	0.219	4.124

* Represents monthly percentage change in Wilshire 5000 Equity Index.

TABLE 6A-1   *(concluded)*

	Value-Weighted Index			Equal-Weighted Index		
Month Ending	*Price Appreciation* (percent)*	*Dividends Yield (percent)*	*Total Return (percent)*	*Price Appreciation (percent)*	*Dividends Yield (percent)*	*Total Return (percent)*
10/29/82	11.453	0.246	11.699	13.863	0.174	14.037
11/30/82	4.214	0.676	4.890	9.551	0.243	9.794
12/31/82	1.130	0.233	1.363	3.254	0.214	3.468
1/31/83	3.953	0.206	4.159	12.194	0.141	12.335
2/28/83	2.594	0.613	3.207	5.266	0.241	5.507
3/31/83	3.365	0.298	3.653	6.182	0.215	6.397
4/29/83	7.302	0.130	7.432	8.207	0.110	8.317
5/31/83	0.758	0.533	1.291	10.085	0.214	10.299
6/30/83	3.572	0.300	3.872	4.785	0.186	4.971
7/29/83	−3.251	0.126	−3.125	−1.396	0.103	−1.293
8/31/83	0.040	0.545	0.585	−2.505	0.200	−2.305
9/30/83	1.368	0.293	1.661	0.448	0.161	0.609
10/31/83	−2.867	0.175	−2.692	−5.417	0.121	−5.296
11/30/83	2.331	0.503	2.834	4.127	0.190	4.317
12/30/83	−1.352	0.244	−1.108	−1.563	0.185	−1.378
1/31/84	−1.797	0.191	−1.606	0.738	0.162	0.900
2/29/84	−4.472	0.494	−3.978	−5.108	0.179	−4.929
3/30/84	1.054	0.343	1.397	1.188	0.198	1.386
4/30/84	0.089	0.174	0.263	−1.674	0.118	−1.556
5/31/84	−5.831	0.519	−5.312	−4.530	0.180	−4.350
6/29/84	2.029	0.390	2.419	1.873	0.207	2.080
7/31/84	−2.191	0.203	−1.988	−4.293	0.125	−4.168
8/31/84	10.749	0.591	11.340	10.609	0.207	10.816
9/28/84	−0.238	0.297	0.059	0.518	0.154	0.672
10/31/84	−0.306	0.293	−0.013	−1.563	0.148	−1.415
11/30/84	−1.533	0.454	−1.079	−2.358	0.170	−2.188
12/31/84	2.105	0.329	2.434	1.388	0.191	1.579

* Represents monthly percentage change in Wilshire 5000 Equity Index.

Source: Wilshire Associates.

TABLE 6A–2   Monthly Returns for Wilshire 5000 Equity Indexes, 1/31/85–1/31/89

Month Ending	Value-Weighted Index			Equal-Weighted Index		
	Price Appreciation* (percent)	Dividends Yield (percent)	Total Return (percent)	Price Appreciation (percent)	Dividends Yield (percent)	Total Return (percent)
1/31/85	8.415	0.237	8.652	13.453	0.163	13.616
2/28/85	1.249	0.448	1.697	5.711	0.174	5.885
3/29/85	−0.456	0.322	−0.134	−0.087	0.185	0.098
4/30/85	−0.377	0.178	−0.199	0.028	0.121	0.149
5/31/85	5.154	0.583	5.737	3.346	0.187	3.533
6/28/85	1.519	0.326	1.845	0.913	0.153	1.066
7/31/85	−0.246	0.226	−0.020	−3.231	0.098	3.329
8/30/85	−1.007	0.652	−0.355	0.514	0.251	0.765
9/30/85	−4.192	0.282	−3.910	−5.128	0.152	−4.976
10/31/85	4.208	0.243	4.451	3.324	0.118	3.442
11/29/85	6.501	0.432	6.933	6.505	0.158	6.663
12/31/85	4.236	0.305	4.541	4.359	0.152	4.511
1/31/86	0.897	0.177	1.074	5.399	0.103	5.502
2/28/86	6.952	0.450	7.402	6.647	0.144	6.791
3/31/86	5.107	0.257	5.364	5.642	0.154	5.796
4/30/86	−0.858	0.174	−0.684	2.602	0.100	2.702
5/30/86	4.713	0.378	5.091	4.540	0.125	4.665
6/30/86	1.128	0.241	1.369	1.744	0.138	1.882
7/31/86	−6.142	0.172	−5.970	−6.760	0.119	−6.641
8/29/86	6.263	0.358	6.621	3.434	0.141	3.575
9/30/86	−8.183	0.220	−7.963	−4.870	0.179	−4.691
10/31/86	4.869	0.172	5.041	3.818	0.090	3.908
11/28/86	1.139	0.360	1.499	0.357	0.115	0.472
12/31/86	−2.742	0.262	−2.480	−2.195	0.153	−2.042
1/30/87	12.651	0.153	12.804	13.557	0.098	13.655
2/27/87	4.550	0.348	4.898	8.979	0.126	9.105
3/31/87	2.157	0.242	2.399	5.461	0.139	5.600
4/30/87	−1.902	0.235	−1.667	−0.546	0.097	−0.449
5/29/87	0.319	0.210	0.529	1.187	0.111	1.298
6/30/87	4.225	0.251	4.476	3.550	0.130	3.680
7/31/87	4.314	0.135	4.449	4.800	0.092	4.892
8/31/87	3.550	0.334	3.884	2.348	0.116	2.464
9/30/87	−2.306	0.195	−2.111	−1.476	0.143	−1.333
10/30/87	−22.948	0.169	−22.779	−25.555	0.068	−25.487
11/30/87	−7.525	0.395	−7.130	−5.429	0.180	−5.249
12/31/87	6.979	0.315	7.294	6.612	0.210	6.822

* Represents monthly percentage change in Wilshire 5000 Equity Index.

TABLE 6A-2 *(concluded)*

Month Ending	Value-Weighted Index			Equal-Weighted Index		
	Price Appreciation* (percent)	*Dividends Yield (percent)*	*Total Return (percent)*	*Price Appreciation (percent)*	*Dividends Yield (percent)*	*Total Return (percent)*
1/29/88	4.166	0.174	4.340	10.303	0.118	10.421
2/29/88	4.684	0.597	5.281	8.278	0.206	8.484
3/31/88	−1.965	0.290	−1.675	5.960	0.168	6.128
4/29/88	0.951	0.172	1.123	1.482	0.096	1.578
5/31/88	−0.227	0.431	0.204	−0.547	0.168	−0.379
6/30/88	4.881	0.271	5.152	5.555	0.204	5.759
7/29/88	−1.004	0.285	−0.719	−0.054	0.157	0.103
8/31/88	−3.285	0.465	−2.820	−2.324	0.160	−2.164
9/30/88	3.567	0.250	3.817	2.011	0.204	2.215
10/31/88	1.631	0.303	1.934	−1.043	0.120	−0.923
11/30/88	−2.210	0.466	−1.744	−3.820	0.194	−3.626
12/30/88	1.799	0.356	2.155	2.312	0.235	2.547
1/31/89	6.531	0.281	6.812	6.173	0.151	6.324

* Represents monthly percentage change in Wilshire 5000 Equity Index.

Source: Wilshire Associates.

REFERENCES

Cootner, Paul. "Stock Market Indexes—Fallacies and Illusions." *Commercial and Financial Chronicle,* September 29, 1966, p. 18.

Eubank, Arthur A. "Risk–Return Contrasts: NYSE, AMEX and OTC." *Journal of Portfolio Management,* v. 3 (Summer 1977), pp. 25–30.

Fisher, Lawrence. "Some New Stock Market Indexes." *Journal of Business,* v. 39 (January 1966), pp. 191–225.

———, and James Lorie. "Some Studies of Variability of Returns on Investments in Common Stock." *Journal of Business,* v. 43 (April 1970), pp. 99–134.

Latane, Henry A., Donald L. Tuttle, and William E. Young. "Market Indexes and Their Implications for Portfolio Management." *Financial Analysts Journal,* v. 27 (September/October 1971), pp. 75–85.

Lee, C. F. "Investment Horizon and the Functional Form of the CAPM." *Review of Economics and Statistics,* v. 58 (August 1976), pp. 356–63.

Newbold, P. *Statistics for Business and Economics,* 1st ed. Prentice-Hall, Inc., 1984.

Reilly, Frank K. *Investment Analysis and Portfolio Management,* 2nd ed. Dryden Press, 1985.

Roll, Richard. "A Critique of the Asset Pricing Theory's Tests." *Journal of Financial Economics,* v. 4 (March 1977), pp. 129–76.

———. "Ambiguity When Performance Is Measured by the Securities Market Line." *Journal of Finance,* v. 33 (September 1978), pp. 1051–69.

———. "Performance Evaluations and Benchmark Error I and II." *Journal of Portfolio Management,* v. 6 and 7 (Summer 1980 and Winter 1981), pp. 5–12, 17–22.

Ross, Stephen A. "The Arbitrage Theory of Capital Asset Pricing." *Journal of Economic Theory,* v. 13 (December 1976), pp. 341–60.

Rudd, Andrew T. "The Revised Dow-Jones Industrial Average: New Wine in Old Bottles?" *Financial Analysts Journal,* v. 35 (October/November 1979), pp. 57–61, 63.

7 Sources of Risk and Their Determination

This chapter focuses on the various types of risk. An understanding of sources of risk and their determination is very useful for doing meaningful security analysis and portfolio management; thus, discussing risk prior to an exploration of portfolio-selection models is essential. In this chapter methods of measuring risk are defined by using basic statistical methods, and both the concepts and applications of the dominance principle and portfolio theory are discussed in some detail.

A discussion of the different types of risk and their classification is followed by a review of the concepts and applications of portfolio analysis. The dominance principle as well as the necessity of using performance measures as a means to compare performance among different portfolios are treated. The determination of the commercial lending rate in accordance with risk and return concepts is then analyzed, and the final section of this chapter concerns calculations of the market rate of return and the market risk premium.

RISK CLASSIFICATION AND MEASUREMENT

Chapter 3 discussed the rates of returns on financial assets and the total, systematic, and unsystematic risks associated with these returns. **Risk** is defined as the probability of success or failure. To be able to measure risk, it is necessary to define the range of outcomes and the probability that these outcomes will occur. A probability distribution may be determined either subjectively or objectively; a subjective determination is made by the individual about the likelihood of various future outcomes, while an objective determination involves measuring past data that are associated with the frequency of certain types of outcomes.

In either case, a subjective or objective determination requires a quantitative measure of risk. The measure most commonly used is the standard deviation or the variance of the possible returns. In considering two securities, A and B, it is possible to use a subjective approach, an objective approach, or a combination of the two approaches to indicate the expected range of outcomes and the probability that each outcome will occur. Figure 7–1 illustrates the distribution of return possibilities for these two securities.

While the standard deviation is stated in rates of return, the variance is stated in terms of the rate of return squared. Since it is more natural to discuss rates of return rather than rates of return squared, risk is usually measured with the standard deviation of returns. Nevertheless, for statistical purposes it is usually more convenient to use the variance rather than the standard deviation. Either risk measure is appropriate because the standard deviation is merely a simple mathematical transformation of the variance.

It is the job of the security analyst to provide estimates of a financial asset's risk. Supplying estimates of a security variance or standard deviation is one method of estimating the total risk of a security.

Why do securities have differing levels of total risk? What factors cause the returns of securities to vary? Table 7–1 defines various types of risk and in so doing offers answers to these questions, and in analyzing the risks defined in Table 7–1 the following paragraphs provide further illustration.

At any point a security or a portfolio could be subject to a number of these risks. In general, the various risks are not mutually exclusive, nor are they additive. By mutually exclusive is meant that the fact that a portfolio contains a certain kind of risk does not mean that it also contains other types of risk. By additive is meant that if a portfolio contains a number of different types of risk, the total risk of the portfolio is simply the sum of the individual risks. Additionally, some of the risks defined in Table 7–1 are easily quantified or measured—for example, using beta to measure systematic risk—while other types of risk may not have well-defined quantitative risk measures such as management risk or political risk. Finally, it should be noted that the types of risk listed in Table 7–1 are mutually exclusive.

Call Risk

An investor who purchases a security, whether it is a debt instrument or equity, usually has a pretty good idea of his or her investment horizon—that is, how long he or she intends to hold the security. If the issuer calls the bond or repurchases the stock at a point in time prior to the end of the investor's investment horizon, the return earned by the investor may be less than expected. The investor is facing **call risk** (see Table 7–1 for a detailed definition).

Generally all corporate bonds and preferred stocks are callable at some point during the life of the security. Investors do not like this call feature, because bonds are most often called after interest rates have fallen, so that

FIGURE 7-1   Probability Distributions Between Securities A and B

Security A

i	r	P_{ri}
1	-0.30	0.04
2	-0.20	0.06
3	-0.10	0.10
4	0.00	0.30
5	0.10	0.30
6	0.20	0.10
7	0.30	0.06
8	0.40	0.04

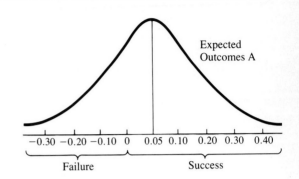

Expected return A

$$E(R) = -0.3(0.04) - 0.2(0.06) - 0.1(0.1)$$
$$+ 0(0.3) + 0.1(0.3) + 0.2(0.1)$$
$$+ 0.3(0.06) + 0.4(0.04)$$
$$= 0.05$$

Variance A

$$\sigma_A^2 = (-0.3 - 0.05)^2(0.04)$$
$$+ (-0.2 - 0.05)^2(0.06)$$
$$+ (-0.01 - 0.05)^2(0.1)$$
$$+ (0 - 0.05)^2(0.3)$$
$$+ (0.1 - 0.05)^2(0.3)$$
$$+ (0.2 - 0.05)^2(0.1)$$
$$+ (0.3 - 0.05)^2(0.06)$$
$$+ (0.4 - 0.05)^2(0.04)$$
$$= 0.001812$$

Security B

i	r	P_{ri}
1	-0.10	0.10
2	0.00	0.40
3	0.10	0.40
4	0.20	0.10

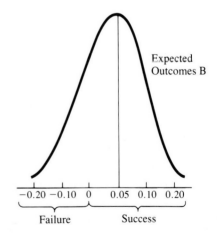

Expected return B

$$E(R) = -0.1(0.1) + 0(0.4) + 0.1(0.4)$$
$$+ 0.2(0.1)$$
$$= 0.05$$

Variance B

$$\sigma_B^2 = (-0.1 - 0.05)^2(0.1)$$
$$+ (0 - 0.05)^2(0.4)$$
$$+ (0.1 - 0.05)^2(0.4)$$
$$+ (0.2 - 0.05)^2(0.1)$$
$$= 0.00149$$

TABLE 7–1   Types of Risk

Risk Type	*Description*
Call risk	The variability of return caused by the repurchase of the security before its stated maturity.
Convertible risk	The variability of return caused when one type of security is converted into another type of security.
Default risk	The probability of a return of zero when the issuer of the security is unable to make interest and principal payments—or for equities, the probability that the market price of the stock will go to zero when the firm goes bankrupt.
Interest-rate risk	The variability of return caused by the movement of interest rates.
Management risk	The variability of return caused by bad management decisions; this is usually a part of the unsystematic risk of a stock, although it can affect the amount of systematic risk.
Marketability risk	The variability of return caused by the commissions and price concessions associated with selling an illiquid asset.
Political risk	The variability of return caused by changes in laws, taxes, or other government actions.
Purchasing-power risk	The variability of return caused by inflation, which erodes the real value of the return.
Systematic risk	The variability of a single security's return caused by the general rise or fall of the entire market.
Unsystematic risk	The variability of return caused by factors unique to the individual security.

the issuer can replace them with a new issue of bonds at a lower interest rate. When a bond is called, instead of receiving the expected interest flows for the remainder of his or her investment horizon the investor must reinvest the proceeds received from the issuer at a lower rate of interest. It is this reinvestment at a new lower rate of interest that causes the yield or return of the bond to be different than what the investor expected.

For this reason, in periods of high interest rates, when interest rates are expected to drop to lower levels in the future, bonds that are call protected for a certain number of years usually sell at a higher price than callable bonds. Thus a deferred call feature can cause an interest spread or differential to develop vis-à-vis a similar issue with no call feature or an issue that is immediately callable. The size of the interest differential varies with the investor's expectations about the future movement of interest rates.

Whether a bond is callable immediately after it is issued or after a deferred period, the actual call of the bond involves the payment of a premium over the par value of the bond by the issuer.

Convertible Risk

If a bond or a preferred stock is convertible into a stated number of shares of common stock of the corporation issuing the original security, the rate of return of the investment may vary because the value of the underlying common stock has increased or decreased. This kind of investment is facing **convertible risk,** as described in Table 7–1. A convertible security normally has a lower coupon rate, or stated dividend (in the case of preferred stocks), because investors are willing to accept a lower contractual return from the company in order to be able to share in any rise in the price of the firm's common stock. The size of the yield spread between straight and convertible securities is dependent on the future prospects of the individual firm and the general level of interest rates.

The difference between the value paid for the conversion right and the actual returns experienced over the life of the security increases the variability of returns associated with the investment.

Default Risk

The quality of the issue or the chances of bankruptcy for the issuer have a significant impact on the rate of return of a security. A lower-quality issue will sell at a lower price and thus offer a higher yield than a similar security issued by a higher-quality issuer. This is true in all segments of the securities markets. Hence, most investors hold diversified portfolios in order to reduce their exposure to any one security going into default or the issuer going bankrupt. The risk relating to default or bankruptcy is called **default risk,** as described in Table 7–1.

Interest-Rate Risk

As the general level of interest rates changes, the value of an individual security also changes. As interest rates rise, the value of existing securities falls, and vice versa. Additionally, longer-term securities are more affected by a given change in the general level of interest rates than are shorter-term securities. The fluctuation of security returns caused by the movement of interest rates is called **interest-rate risk,** as described in Table 7–1.

For example, Bond A has a coupon of 7 percent and a maturity of ten years, and Bond B has a coupon of 7 percent and a maturity of five years. If interest rates go from 7 percent to 8 percent, the price of A will fall $6.75 for each $100 of par value, whereas the price of B will fall only $4.00 for each $100 of par value.

Another factor that affects the amount of price change for a given interest-rate change is the size of the coupon. The lower the coupon rate of an issue, the more widely its price will change for a given change in interest rates. For example, Bond C is a twenty-year bond with a 4 percent coupon and a market value of $68 when the general level of interest rates are 7 percent. Bond D is a twenty-year bond with a 7 percent coupon, so its market value is par $100. If interest rates go from 7 percent to 8 percent, the value of Bond C will fall to $60.38, a decrease in value of 11.3 percent based on its market price [(60.38 − 68)/68], whereas Bond D's value will fall by 9.8 percent [(90.2 − 100)/100].

In general, a shorter-maturity, higher-coupon security is subject to less interest-rate risk than a long-term, low coupon security.

Management Risk

Management risk, as indicated in Table 7–1, is caused by errors of a firm's managers when they make business and financing decisions. **Business risk** refers to the degree of fluctuation of net income associated with different types of business operations. This kind of risk is related to different types of business and operating strategies. **Financial risk** refers to the variability of returns associated with leverage decisions. How much of the firm should be financed with equity and how much should be financed with debt?

It should be noted that both business risk and financial risk are not necessarily constant over time. Both risks can be affected by the fluctuations of the business cycle or by changes in government policy.

Jensen and Meckling have presented a theory, called **agency theory,** that deals with the problem of management errors and their impact on security owners. An agent–principal relationship exists when decision-making authority is delegated. The modern corporation is a good example of this phenomenon. The owners or shareholders of the firm delegate the decision-making authority to the firm's managers, who are in reality employees or agents of the owners. Other things being equal, the managers make decisions that satisfy the needs of the managers rather than the desires of the owners unless the firm's owners can protect themselves from management decisions. Some have argued that it is the function of financial arrangements using bond covenants, options, and so on, to narrow the divergence of goals between a firm's owners and its managers. In any case, it is the possibility of management error or divergent goals that is one of the causes of variability of return for securities.

Marketability (Liquidity) Risk

The **marketability risk** (or **liquidity risk**) of a security (see the description in Table 7–1) affects the rate of return received by its owner. Marketability is made up of two components: (1) the volume of securities that can be bought or sold in a short period of time without adversely affecting the price, and (2)

the amount of time necessary to complete the sale of a given number of securities. Other things being equal, the less marketable a security, the lower its price or the higher its yield. A highly liquid security—for example, IBM shares traded on the New York Stock Exchange (NYSE)—can be purchased or sold in large quantities in a very short time. Millions of shares of IBM are traded every day on the NYSE. The stock of a small firm traded over the counter (OTC) may trade only a few hundred shares a week and is said to be illiquid.

One good measure of the marketability of a security is the spread between the bid and ask prices. The **bid price** is the current price at which the security can be sold and the **ask price** is the current price at which the security can be bought. The bid price is always lower than the ask price. The bid–ask spread is the cost of selling the asset quickly. That is to say, it is the amount of margin required by the market maker to stand ready to buy or sell reasonable amounts of the security quickly. The more illiquid the security the wider the bid–ask spread.

Political Risk

International **political risk** (as described in Table 7–1) stems from the political climate and conditions of a foreign country. For instance, if a government is unstable, as is the case in some South American countries, there may be wild fluctuations in interest rates due to a lack of confidence by the population and the business community. There may even be some chance of sabotage of plant and equipment or other acts of terrorism. Contracts may not be upheld or enforceable. These are all factors that may cause the rate of return on certain securities to vary.

Domestic political risk takes the form of laws, taxes, and government regulations. As the government changes the tax law, the returns of securities can be greatly affected. For example, the Tax Reform Act of 1986 probably had a very important role in the bull market of January to August 1987, when the Dow-Jones Industrial Average went from below 1900 to above 2700.

Purchasing-Power Risk

Purchasing-power risk, as described in Table 7–1, is related to the possible shrinkage in the real value of a security even though its nominal value is increasing. For example, if the nominal value of a security goes from $100 to $200, the owner of this security is pleased because the investment has doubled in value. But suppose that, concurrent with the value increase of 100 percent, the rate of inflation is 200 percent—that is, a basket of goods costing $100 when the security was purchased now costs $300. The investor has a "money illusion" of being better off in nominal terms. The investment did increase from $100 to $200; nevertheless, in real terms, whereas the $100 at time zero could purchase a complete basket of goods, after the inflation

only 2/3 of a basket can now be purchased. Hence, the investor has suffered a loss of value.

Systematic and Unsystematic Risk

In Chapter 3 **total risk** was defined as the sum of **systematic** and **unsystematic risk** (see Table 7–1). Total risk is also equal to the sum of all of the risk components just discussed. However, the importance and the contribution to total risk depends on the type of security under consideration. The total risk of bonds contains a much larger fraction of interest-rate risk than the total risk of a stock. Each of the types of risk discussed may contain a systematic component that cannot be diversified away and an unsystematic component that can be reduced or eliminated, if the securities are held in a portfolio.

It is assumed throughout this text that rational investors are averse to risk, whatever its source; hence a knowledge of various risk-management techniques is essential. Toward that end this chapter now focuses on the management of risk through diversification.

PORTFOLIO ANALYSIS AND APPLICATION

Essential to adequate diversification is a knowledge of the primary concepts of portfolio analysis and their application. This section focuses on basic analysis and applications; more advanced portfolio theory and methods will be discussed in Chapters 8, 10, and 18.

A portfolio can be defined as any combination of assets or investments. **Portfolio analysis** is used to determine the return and risk for these combinations of assets. Portfolio concepts and methods are employed here to formally develop the idea of the dominance principle and some other measures of portfolio performance.

Expected Return on a Portfolio

The **rate of return on a portfolio** is simply the weighted average of the returns of individual securities in the portfolio. For example, 40 percent of the portfolio is invested in a security with a 10 percent expected return (security A); 30 percent is invested in security B with a 5 percent expected return; and 30 percent is invested in security C with a 12 percent expected return. The expected rate of return on this portfolio can be expressed:

$$\overline{R}_p = W_a\overline{R}_a + W_b\overline{R}_b + W_c\overline{R}_c$$
$$= (0.4)(0.1) + (0.3)(0.5) + (0.3)(0.12)$$
$$= 0.091$$

in which W_a, W_b, and W_c are the percentages of the portfolio invested in securities A, B, and C, respectively. The summation of these weights is equal to one. R_p represents the expected rate of return for the portfolio and is the weighted average of the securities' expected rate of return. In general, the expected return on an n-asset portfolio is defined by Equation (7.1):

$$\overline{R}_p = \sum_{i=1}^{n} \overline{R}_i W_i \qquad (7.1)$$

where:

$$\sum_{i=1}^{n} W_i = 1$$

W_i = the proportion of the individual's investment allocated to security i; and

R_i = the expected rate of return for security i.

Variance and Standard Deviation of a Portfolio

The riskiness of a portfolio is measured by the **standard deviation** (or **variance**) of the portfolio. To calculate the standard deviation of a portfolio, we should first identify the covariance among the securities within the portfolio. The covariance between two securities used to formulate a portfolio can be defined as:

$$\begin{aligned} \text{Cov } (W_1 R_1, W_2 R_2) &= \sum_{t=1}^{N} \frac{(W_1 R_{1t} - W_1 \overline{R}_1)(W_2 R_{2t} - W_2 \overline{R}_2)}{N - 1} \\ &= W_1 W_2 \sum_{t=1}^{N} \frac{(R_{1t} - \overline{R}_1)(R_{2t} - \overline{R}_2)}{N - 1} \\ &= W_1 W_2 \text{ Cov } (R_1, R_2) \end{aligned} \qquad (7.2)$$

where:

R_{1t} = the rate of return for the first security in period t;

R_{2t} = the rate of return for the second security in period t;

$\overline{R}_1$ and $\overline{R}_2$ = average rates of return for the first security and the second security, respectively; and

Cov (R_1, R_2) = the covariance between R_1 and R_2.

The covariance as indicated in Equation (7.2) can be used to measure the covariability between two securities (or assets) when they are used to formulate a portfolio. With this measure the variance for a portfolio with two securities can be derived:

$$\text{Var } (W_1 R_{1t} + W_2 R_{2t}) = \sum_{t=1}^{N} \frac{[(W_1 R_{1t} + W_2 R_{2t}) - (W_1 \overline{R}_1 + W_2 \overline{R}_2)]^2}{N - 1}$$

Sample Problem 7.1 provides further illustration.

Sample Problem 7.1

If you have two securities, you can use Equation (7.2) to calculate the portfolio variance as follows:

$$\text{Security } 1 \qquad\qquad \text{Security } 2$$

$$
\begin{array}{llll}
W_1 = 40\% & & W_2 = 60\% & \\
t = 1 & \overline{R}_{1t} = 10\% & t = 1 & \overline{R}_{2t} = 5\% \\
2 & 15\% & 2 & 10\% \\
3 & 20\% & 3 & 15\% \\
\overline{R}_1 = 15\% & & \overline{R}_2 = 10\% &
\end{array}
$$

$$
\begin{aligned}
\text{Var}(W_1 R_{1t} + W_2 R_{2t}) &= \sum_{t=1}^{N} \frac{[(W_1 R_{1t} + W_2 R_{2t}) - (W_1 \overline{R}_1 + W_2 \overline{R}_2)]^2}{N-1} \\
&= [(0.4)(0.1) + (0.6)(0.05) - (0.4)(0.15) + (0.6)(0.1)]^2/2 \\
&\quad + [(0.4)(0.15) + (0.6)(0.1) - (0.4)(0.15) + (0.6)(0.1)]^2/2 \\
&\quad + [(0.4)(0.2) + (0.6)(0.15) - (0.4)(0.15) + (0.6)(0.1)]^2/2 \\
&= \frac{(0.07 - 0.12)^2}{2} + \frac{(0.12 - 0.12)^2}{2} + \frac{(0.17 - 0.12)^2}{2}
\end{aligned}
$$

Var portfolio = 0.0025

The riskiness of a portfolio can be measured by the standard deviation of returns, as indicated in Equation (7.3):

$$
\sigma_p = \sqrt{\frac{\sum_{t=1}^{N}(\overline{R}_{pt} - \overline{R}_p)^2}{N-1}} \tag{7.3}
$$

where σ_p is the standard deviation of the portfolio's return and $\overline{R}_p$ is the expected return of the n possible returns. Figure 7–2 illustrates possible distributions for two portfolios, assuming the same expected return but different levels of risk. Since portfolio B's variability is greater than that of portfolio A, investors regard portfolio B as riskier than portfolio A.

The Two-Asset Case

To explain the fundamental aspect of the risk-diversification process in a portfolio, consider the **two-asset case.** Following Equation (7.3):

$$
\begin{aligned}
\sigma_p &= \sqrt{\frac{\sum_{t=1}^{N}(R_{pt} - \overline{R}_p)^2}{N-1}} \\
&= \sqrt{\frac{\sum_{t=1}^{N}[W_1^2(R_{1t} - \overline{R}_1)^2 + W_2^2(R_{2t} - \overline{R}_2)^2 + 2W_1 W_2(R_{1t} - \overline{R}_1)(R_{2t} - \overline{R}_2)]}{N-1}} \\
&= \sqrt{W_1^2 \text{Var}(R_{1t}) + W_2^2 \text{Var}(R_{2t}) + 2W_1 W_2 \text{Cov}(R_1, R_2)} \tag{7.4}
\end{aligned}
$$

FIGURE 7-2   Probability Distributions of Returns for Two Portfolios

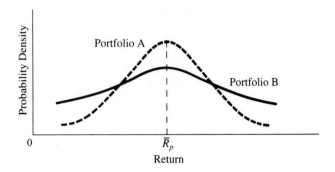

where $W_1 + W_2 = 1$. By the definition of correlation coefficients between R_1 and R_2 (ρ_{12}), the Cov (R_1, R_2) can be rewritten:

$$\text{Cov } (R_1, R_2) = \rho_{12}\sigma_1\sigma_2 \tag{7.5}$$

where σ_1 and σ_2 are the standard deviations of the first and second security, respectively. From Equations (7.4) and (7.5), the standard deviation of a two-security portfolio can be defined:

$$\begin{aligned}\sigma_p &= \sqrt{\text{Var } (W_1R_{1t} + W_2R_{2t})} \\ &= \sqrt{W_1^2\sigma_1^2 + (1 - W_1)^2\sigma_2^2 + 2W_1(1 - W_1)\rho_{12}\sigma_1\sigma_2}\end{aligned} \tag{7.6}$$

Sample Problem 7.2 provides further illustration.

Sample Problem 7.2

For securities 1 and 2 used in the previous example, applying Equation (7.6) should give the same results for portfolio variance.

	Security 1	*Security 2*
	$\sigma_1^2 = 0.0025$	$\sigma_2^2 = 0.0025$
	$W_1 = 0.4$	$W_2 = 0.6$
	$\rho_{12} = +1$	

$$\begin{aligned}\sigma_p &= \sqrt{(0.4)^2(0.0025) + (0.6)^2(0.0025) + 2(0.4)(0.6)(1)(0.05)(0.05)} \\ &= \sqrt{0.0025}\end{aligned}$$

$\sigma_p = 0.05$ or Var portfolio $= 0.0025$, the same answer as for Sample Problem 7.1●

If $\rho_{12} = 1.0$ Equation (7.6) can be simplified to the linear expression:

$$\sigma_p = W_1\sigma_1 + W_2\sigma_2$$

where $W_2 = (1 - W_1)$. Since Equation (7.6) is a quadratic equation, some value of W_1 minimizes σ_p. To obtain this value, differentiate Equation (7.6) with respect to W_1 and set this derivative equal to zero. Solving for W_1:

$$W_1 = \frac{\sigma_2(\sigma_2 - \rho_{12}\sigma_1)}{\sigma_1^2 + \sigma_2^2 - 2\rho_{12}\sigma_1\sigma_2} \tag{7.7}$$

A condition needed for Equation (7.7) is that $W_1 \leq 1$; that is, no more than 100 percent of the portfolio can be in any single security, and negative positions (short positions) can be maintained on any security.

If $\rho_{12} = 1$, Equation (7.7) reduces from:

$$\frac{\partial \sigma_p}{\partial W_1} = [W_1^2\sigma_1^2 + (1 - W_1)^2\sigma_2^2 + 2W_1(1 - W_1)\rho_{12}\sigma_1\sigma_2]^{-1/2}$$

$$\times [2W_1\sigma_1^2 - 2(1 - W_1)\sigma_2^2 + 2(1 - 2W_1)\rho_{12}\sigma_1\sigma_2]$$

$$= \frac{W_1[\sigma_1^2\sigma_2^2 - 2\int_{12}\sigma_1\sigma_2] - [\sigma_2^2 - \rho_{12}\sigma_1\sigma_2]}{[W_1^2\sigma_1^2 + (1 - W_1)^2\sigma_2^2 + 2W_1(1 - W_1)\rho_{12}\sigma_1\sigma_2]}$$

to:

$$W_1 = \frac{\sigma_2(\sigma_2 - \sigma_1)}{(\sigma_2 - \sigma_1)(\sigma_2 - \sigma_1)} \tag{7.7A}$$

$$= \frac{\sigma_2}{\sigma_2 - \sigma_1}$$

Returning to the sample problems for securities 1 and 2, since the standard deviations are equal and the securities are perfectly positively correlated, Equation (7.7A) indicates that there is no value for W_1 that will minimize the portfolio variance. The weight from W_1 that gives the minimum-variance portfolio is $0.05/(0.05 - 0.05)$ or $0.05/0$, which is undefined.

If $\rho_{12} = -1$, Equation (7.7) reduces to:

$$W_1 = \frac{\sigma_2(\sigma_2 + \sigma_1)}{(\sigma_1 + \sigma_2)(\sigma_1 + \sigma_2)} \tag{7.7B}$$

$$= \frac{\sigma_2}{\sigma_2 + \sigma_1}$$

However, if the correlation coefficient between 1 and 2 is -1, then the minimum-variance portfolio must be divided equally between security 1 and security 2—that is:

$$W_1 = \frac{0.05}{0.05 + 0.05}$$

$$= 0.5$$

As an expanded form of Equation (7.6), a portfolio can be written:

$$\sigma_p = \left[\sum_{i=1}^{n} W_i^2 \sigma_i^2 + 2 \sum_{i=1}^{n-1} \sum_{j=i+1}^{n} W_i W_j \rho_{ij} \sigma_i \sigma_j \right]^{1/2}$$

$$= \left[\sum_{j=1}^{n} \sum_{i=1}^{n} W_i W_j \, \text{Cov} \, (R_{it}, R_{jt}) \right]^{1/2}$$

(7.8)

where:

W_i and W_j = the investor's investment allocated to security i and security j, respectively;

ρ_{ij} = the correlation coefficient between security i and security j; and

n = the number of securities included in the portfolio.

Since Equation (7.8) has n securities, there are n variance terms (that is, $W_i^2 \sigma_i^2$) and $(n^2 - n)$ covariance terms (that is, $W_i W_j \rho_{12} \sigma_i \sigma_j$). If $n = 200$, Equation (7.8) will have 200 variance terms and 39,800 covariance terms, and any practical application will require a great amount of information as well as many computations. This issue will be discussed in more detail in Chapter 8; in the meanwhile, Sample Problem 7.3 provides further illustration.

Sample Problem 7.3

Consider two stocks, A and B: $\overline{R}_A = 10, \overline{R}_B = 15, \sigma_A = 4$, and $\sigma_B = 6$. (1) If a riskless portfolio could be formed from A and B, what would be the expected return of R_p? (2) What would the expected return be if $\rho_{AB} = 0$?

Solution

1. $\sigma_p = (W_A^2 \sigma_A^2 + (1 - W_A)^2 \sigma_B^2 + 2W_A(1 - W_A)\rho_{AB}\sigma_A \sigma_B)^{1/2}$

If we let $\rho_{AB} = -1$

$$\sigma_P = [W_A \sigma_A - (1 - W_A)\sigma_B]$$
$$\sigma_P = 0 = 4W_A - 6(1 - W_A)$$
$$W_A = 3/5$$

So

$$\overline{R}_P = W_A \overline{R}_A + (1 - W_A)R_B$$
$$= \left(\frac{3}{5}\right)(10) + \left(\frac{2}{5}\right)(15)$$
$$= 12\%$$

2. If we let $\rho_{AB} = 0$

$$\sigma_p = [W_A^2\sigma_A^2 + (1 - W_A)^2\sigma_B^2]^{1/2}$$

$$\frac{\partial\sigma_P}{\partial W_A} = \frac{1}{2}[2W_A\sigma_A^2 + 2(1 - W_A)\sigma_B^2(-1)][W_A^2\sigma_A^2 + (1 - W_A)^2\sigma_B^2]^{-1/2}$$

$$= 0$$

$$W_A\sigma_A^2 - (1 - W_A)\sigma_B^2 = 0$$
$$W_A = \sigma_B^2/(\sigma_A^2 + \sigma_B^2)$$
$$= \sigma_B^2/(4^2 + 6^2)$$
$$= 9/13$$
$$\overline{R}_p = \frac{9}{13}(10) + \frac{4}{13}(15)$$
$$= \frac{150}{13}$$
$$= 11.54\%$$

THE EFFICIENT PORTFOLIO AND RISK DIVERSIFICATION

Utilizing the definitions of standard deviation of expected return of a portfolio discussed previously, this section discusses the concepts of the **efficient portfolio** and **risk diversification.**

The Efficient Portfolio

By definition, a portfolio is efficient, if there exists no other portfolio having the same expected return at a lower variance of returns. Moreover, a portfolio is efficient if no other portfolio has a higher expected return at the same risk of returns.

This suggests that given two investments, A and B, investment A will be preferred to B if:

$$E(A) > E(B) \quad \text{and} \quad \text{Var (A)} = \text{Var (B)}$$

or

$$E(A) = E(B) \quad \text{and} \quad \text{Var (A)} < \text{Var (B)}$$

where:

$E(A)$ and $E(B)$ = the expected returns of A and B; and
Var (A) and Var (B) = their respective variances or risk.

The mean returns and variance of every investment opportunity can be calculated and plotted as a single point on a mean–standard deviation diagram, as shown in Figure 7–3.

FIGURE 7–3 The Efficient Frontier in Portfolio Analysis

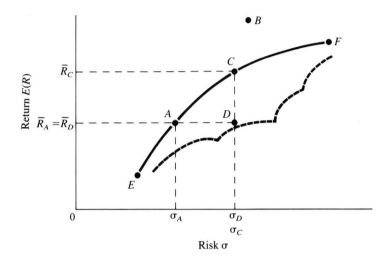

All points below curve *EF* represent portfolio combinations that are possible. Point *D* represents a portfolio of investments with a return R_D and risk σ_D. All points above *EF* are combinations of risk and returns that do not exist. Point *B* would therefore represent risk and return that cannot be obtained with any combination of investments.

The *EF* curve is also called the **efficient frontier** because all points below the curve are dominated by a point found on the curve. For instance, suppose a firm is willing to assume a maximum level of risk σ_D. It can obtain a return of R_D with portfolio D or move to point *C* on the frontier and receive a higher return R_C with that portfolio. Therefore, *C* dominates *D* because it would be preferred to *D*. For the same level of risk, it has a higher return.

A similar argument could be made in terms of risk. If the firm wants to achieve a return of R_A, it will select portfolio A over D, because A represents the same return at a smaller level of risk or standard deviation: $\sigma_A < \sigma_B$. Therefore, point *D* is not efficient but points *A* and *C* are. A decision maker could, therefore, select any point on the frontier and feel secure in knowing that a better portfolio is not available. Sample Problem 7.4 further illustrates this concept.

Sample Problem 7.4

To show how the portfolio concepts and methods discussed in this section can be used to do practical analysis, monthly rates of return for January, 1980 to December, 1984 for Pennzoil and Coca Cola are used as examples.

The basic statistical estimates for these two firms are average monthly rates of return and the variance–covariance matrix. The average monthly rates of return for Pennzoil (PZ) and Coca Cola (CK) are 0.0093 and 0.0306, respectively. The variances and covariances are listed in the following table.

Variance–Covariance Matrix

	PZ	CK
Pennzoil	0.0107391	−0.000290
Coke	−0.000290	0.0495952

From Equation (7.7), we have:

$$W_1 = \frac{0.0495952 + 0.000290}{0.0107391 + 0.0495952 + 0.00058}$$
$$= \frac{0.0498852}{0.069143}$$
$$= 0.8189$$
$$W_2 = 1.0 - 0.8189 = 0.1811$$

Using the weight estimates and Equations (7.2) and (7.3):

$$E(\overline{R}_p) = (0.8189)(0.0093) + (0.1811)(0.0306)$$
$$= 0.01316$$
$$\sigma_p^2 = (0.8189)^2 (0.0107391) + (0.1811)^2 (0.0495952)$$
$$+ 2(0.8189)(0.1811)(-0.000290)$$
$$= 0.0088$$
$$\sigma_p = 0.0940$$

When ρ_{12} is less than 1.00 it indicates that the combination of the two securities will result in a total risk less than their added respective risks. This is the diversification effect. If ρ_{12} were equal to 1.00, this would mean that the combination of the two securities has no diversification effect at all.

The correlation coefficient of $\rho_{12} = -0.0125659$ indicates that a portfolio combining Pennzoil and Coca Cola would show a diversification effect and a reduction in risk.

Corporate Application of Diversification

The effect of diversification is not necessarily limited to securities but may have wider applications at the corporate level. Frequently, managers will justify undertaking many product lines because of the effects of diversification. Instead of "putting all of the eggs in one basket," the investment risks are spread out among many lines of services or products in hope of reducing the overall risks involved and maximizing returns. To what degree this diversification takes place in other types of corporate decisions depends on

the decision maker's preference for risk and return. The overall goal is to reduce business risk fluctuations of net income. However, it should be noted that investors can do their own homemade diversification, which generally reduces the need of corporate diversification.

This type of corporate diversification can be taken to the multinational level. For example, General Motors has overseas divisions throughout the world. Although these divisions all produce the same product, autos and auto parts, GM's status as a multinational corporation allows it to take advantage of the diversifying effects of different exchange rates and political and economic climates. This issue will be explored in detail in Chapter 19.

The Dominance Principle

The **dominance principle** has been developed as a means of conceptually understanding the risk/return tradeoff. As with the efficient-frontier analysis, we must assume an investor prefers returns and dislikes risks. For example, as depicted in Figure 7–4, if an individual is prepared to experience risk associated with σ_A, he or she can obtain a higher expected return with portfolio A (R_A) than with portfolio B (R_B). Thus A dominates B and would be preferred. Similarly, if an individual were satisfied with a return of $\overline{R}_B$, he or she would select portfolio B over C because the risks associated with B are less ($\sigma_B < \sigma_C$). Therefore using the dominance principle reinforces the choice of an efficient portfolio and is also a method in determining it.

Figure 7–4 makes clear that points *A* and *B* are directly comparable because they have a common standard deviation, σ_A. Points *B* and *C* are directly comparable because of a common return, $\overline{R}_B$. Now consider portfolio D. How does its risk versus return compare with the other portfolios shown in Figure 7–4? It is difficult to say because the risk and return are not directly comparable using the dominance principle. This is the basic limita-

FIGURE 7–4   The Dominance Principle in Portfolio Analysis

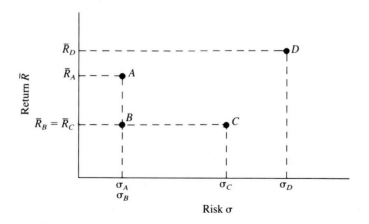

tion of the dominance principle—that portfolios without a common risk or return factor are not directly comparable.

Three Performance Measures

For such a situation it becomes necessary to use some other performance measure. There are basically three important portfolio performance measures taught in investment courses: (1) the Sharpe, (2) the Treynor, and (3) the Jensen measures.

The **Sharpe measure (SP)** [Sharpe (1966)] is of immediate concern. Given two of the portfolios depicted in Figure 7–4, portfolios B and D, their relative risk–return tradeoff performance can be compared using the equations:

$$\mathrm{SP}_D = \frac{\overline{R}_D - R_f}{\sigma_D} \quad \text{and} \quad \mathrm{SP}_B = \frac{\overline{R}_B - R_f}{\sigma_B}$$

where:

$\mathrm{SP}_D,\ \mathrm{SP}_B$ = Sharpe performance measures;
$\overline{R}_D,\ \overline{R}_B$ = the average return of each portfolio;
R_f = risk-free rate; and
$\sigma_D,\ \sigma_B$ = the respective standard deviation on risk of each portfolio.

Because the numerator is the average return reduced by the risk-free rate, it represents the average risk premium of each portfolio. Dividing the risk premium by the total risk per portfolio results in a measure of the return (premium) per unit of risk for each portfolio. The Sharpe performance measure equation will therefore allow a direct comparison of any portfolio, given its risk and returns.

Consider Figure 7–5; portfolio A is being compared to portfolio B. If a riskless rate exists, then all investors would prefer A to B because combinations of A and the riskless asset give higher returns for the same level of risk than combinations of the riskless asset and B. The preferred portfolio lies on the ray passing through R_f that is furthest in the counterclockwise direction (the ray that has the greatest slope). Sample Problem 7.5 further illustrates this concept.

Sample Problem 7.5

An insurance firm is trying to decide between two investment funds. From past performance they were able to calculate the average returns and standard deviations for these funds. (See the table in the middle of page 197.) The current T-bill rate is 9.5 percent and the firm will use this as a measure of the risk-free rate.

FIGURE 7-5   Combinations of Portfolio and the Risk-Free Investment

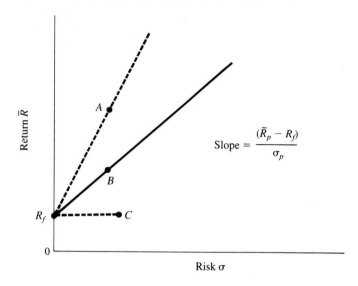

$$\text{Slope} = \frac{(\bar{R}_p - R_f)}{\sigma_p}$$

	Smyth Fund	Jones Fund
Average return R (percent)	18	16
Standard deviation σ (percent)	20	15

Risk-free rate = R_f (percent) = 9.5

Using the Sharpe performance measure, the risk–return measurements for these two firms are:

$$SP_{Smyth} = \frac{0.18 - 0.095}{0.20} = 0.425$$

$$SP_{Jones} = \frac{0.16 - 0.095}{0.15} = 0.433$$

It is clear that the Jones fund has a slightly better performance and would be the better alternative of the two.

The Sharpe measure looks at the risk–return decision from the point of view of an investor choosing a portfolio to represent the majority of his or her investment. An investor choosing a portfolio to represent a large part of his or her wealth would likely be concerned with the full risk of the portfolio, and the standard deviation is a measure of that risk.

On the other hand, if the risk level of the portfolio is already determined by the investor and what is important is to evaluate the performance of the portfolio over and above the total market performance, perhaps the proper risk measure would be the relationship between the return on the portfolio and the return on the market, or beta. All combinations of a riskless asset and a risky portfolio lie on a straight line connecting them. The slope of the line connecting the risky asset A and the risk-free rate is $(\overline{R}_A - R_f)/\sigma_A$. Here, as in the Sharpe measure, an investor would prefer the portfolio on the most counterclockwise ray emanating from the riskless asset. This measure, called the **Treynor measure (TP),** developed by Treynor in 1965, examines differential return when beta is the risk measure. Sample Problem 7.6 provides further illustration.

Sample Problem 7.6

Rank the portfolios shown in the table based on the Sharpe measure. Assume R_f = 8 percent. If R_f = 5 percent, how does the order change?

Portfolio	Return (percent)	Risk (percent)
A	50	50
B	19	15
C	12	9
D	9	5
E	8.5	1

Solution

Sharpe measure

$$SP_M = \frac{\overline{R}_M - R_f}{\sigma}$$

$$SP_A = 0.84$$
$$SP_B = 0.73$$
$$SP_C = 0.44$$
$$SP_D = 0.20$$
$$SP_E = 0.50$$

Ranked by the Sharpe measure, A > B > E > C > D. The Sharpe measure indicates that portfolio A is the most desirable: it has the highest return per unit of risk.

For R_f = 5 percent

$$SP_A = 0.90$$
$$SP_B = 0.933$$
$$SP_C = 0.77$$
$$SP_D = 0.80$$

$$SP_E = 3.5$$

The order changes to E > B > A > D > C. E is now the best portfolio as it has the highest return per unit of risk●

The Treynor measure can be expressed by the following:

$$TP = \frac{\overline{R}_j - R_f}{\beta_j}$$

where:

$\overline{R}_j$ = average return of jth portfolio;
R_f = risk-free rate; and
β_j = beta coefficient for jth portfolio.

The Treynor performance measure uses the beta coefficient (systematic risk) instead of total risk for the jth portfolio (σ_j) as a risk measure. Applications of the TP are similar to the SP as discussed previously.[1]

Jensen (1968, 1969) has proposed a measure referred to as the *Jensen differential performance index* (**Jensen's measure**). The differential return can be viewed as the difference in return earned by the portfolio compared to the return that the capital asset pricing line implies should be earned.

Consider the line connecting the riskless rate and the market portfolio. A manager could obtain any point along this line by investing in the market portfolio and mixing this with the riskless asset to obtain the desired risk level. If the constructed portfolio is actively managed, then one measure of performance is the difference in return earned by actively managing the portfolio, compared with what would have been earned if the portfolio had been passively constructed of the market portfolio and the riskless asset to achieve the same risk level. The slope of the line connecting the riskless asset and the market portfolio is $(\overline{R}_M - R_f)/\beta_M$, and the intercept must be the riskless rate. The beta on the market portfolio is one; therefore, the CAPM equation results in:

$$\overline{R}_p = R_f + (\overline{R}_M - R_f)\beta_p.$$

Jensen's measure (JM) is the differential return of the managed portfolio's actual return less the return on the portfolio of identical beta that lies on the line connecting the riskless asset and the market portfolio. Algebraically, Jensen's measure is expressed:

$$JM = \overline{R}_p - [R_f + (\overline{R}_M - R_f)\beta_p]$$

Figure 7-6 depicts portfolio rankings for the Jensen measure, and Sample Problem 7.7 provides further illustration.

---

[1] Discussion of the Treynor measure adapted from J. Treynor, "How to Rate Management of Investment Funds," *Harvard Business Review*, volume 43 (January/February 1965), pp. 63–75. Adapted by permission.

FIGURE 7-6   Jensen's Measure for Portfolio Rankings

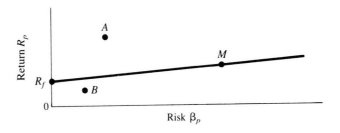

Sample Problem 7.7

Rank the portfolios in the table according to Jensen's measure:

1. Assuming R_M = 10 percent and R_f = 8 percent
2. Assuming R_M = 12 percent and R_f = 8 percent
3. Assuming $R_M = R_f$ = 8 percent
4. Assuming R_M = 12 percent and R_f = 4 percent

Portfolio	R_i (percent)	σ (percent)	β_i
A	50	50	2.5
B	19	15	2.0
C	12	9	1.5
D	9	5	1.0
E	8.5	1	0.25

Solution

$$R_i = R_f + \beta_i(R_M - R_f) \qquad JM = (R_i - R_f) - \beta_i(R_M - R_f)$$

1.
$$JM_A = \ 37 \text{ percent}$$
$$JM_B = \ \ 7 \text{ percent}$$
$$JM_C = \ \ 1 \text{ percent}$$
$$JM_D = \ -2 \text{ percent}$$
$$JM_E = \ \ 0 \text{ percent}$$
Ranked by the Jensen measure A > B > C > E > D.

2.
$$JM_A = \ \ \ 32 \text{ percent}$$
$$JM_B = \ \ \ \ 3 \text{ percent}$$
$$JM_C = \ \ -2 \text{ percent}$$
$$JM_D = \ \ -3 \text{ percent}$$
$$JM_E = \ -0.5 \text{ percent}$$
The rank changes to A > B > E > C > D.

3.

$$JM_A = \quad 42 \text{ percent}$$
$$JM_B = \quad 11 \text{ percent}$$
$$JM_C = \quad 4 \text{ percent}$$
$$JM_D = \quad 1 \text{ percent}$$
$$JM_E = \quad 0.5 \text{ percent}$$

The rank is A > B > C > D > E.

4.

$$JM_A = \quad 26 \text{ percent}$$
$$JM_B = \quad -1 \text{ percent}$$
$$JM_C = \quad -4 \text{ percent}$$
$$JM_D = \quad -3 \text{ percent}$$
$$JM_E = \quad 2.5 \text{ percent}$$

The rank now is A > E > B > D > C●

Interrelationship among Three Performance Measures. It should be noted that all three performance measures are interrelated. For instance, if $\rho_{pm} = \sigma_{pm}/\sigma_p\sigma_m = 1$, then the Jensen measure divided by σ_p becomes equivalent to the Sharpe measure. Since

$$\beta_p = \sigma_{pm}/\sigma_m^2 \quad \text{and} \quad \rho_{pm} = \sigma_{pm}/\sigma_p\sigma_m$$

the Jensen measure JM must be multiplied by $1/\sigma_p$ in order to derive the equivalent Sharpe measure:

$$\frac{JM}{\sigma_p} = \frac{[\overline{R}_p - R_F]}{\sigma_p} - \frac{[\overline{R}_M - R_F]}{\sigma_m}\frac{(\sigma_{pm})}{\sigma_m\sigma_p}$$
$$= \frac{[\overline{R}_p - R_F]}{\sigma_p} - \frac{[\overline{R}_M - R_F]}{\sigma_m}$$
$$= SP_p - SP_m \quad \text{(common constant)}$$

If the Jensen measure JM is divided by β_p, it is equivalent to the Treynor measure TM plus some constant common to all portfolios:

$$\frac{JM}{\beta_p} = \frac{[\overline{R}_p - R_F]}{\beta_p} - \frac{[\overline{R}_M - R_F]\beta_p}{\beta_p}$$
$$= TM_p - [\overline{R}_M - R_F]$$
$$= TM_p - \text{common constant}$$

Sample Problem 7.8 provides further illustration.

Sample Problem 7.8

Continuing with the example used for the Sharpe performance measure in Sample Problem 7.5, assume that in addition to the information already provided the market return is 10 percent, the beta of the Smyth Fund is 0.8, and the Jones Fund beta is 1.1. Then, according to the capital asset pricing line, the implied return earned should be:

$$\overline{R}_{Smyth} = 0.095 + (0.10 - 0.095)(0.8) = 0.099$$
$$\overline{R}_{Jones} = 0.095 + (0.10 - 0.095)(1.1) = 0.1005$$

Using the Jensen measure, the risk–return measurements for these two firms are:

$$JM_{Smyth} = 0.18 - 0.099 = 0.081$$
$$JM_{Jones} = 0.16 - 0.1005 = 0.0595$$

From these calculations, it is clear that the Smyth Fund has a better performance and would be the better alternative of the two. Note that this is the opposite of the results determined from the Sharpe performance measure in Sample Problem 7.5. Computing the Treynor measure would reinforce the Jensen results. More analysis of these performance measures will be undertaken in detail in Chapter 18●

DETERMINATION OF COMMERCIAL LENDING RATE

This section concerns a process for estimating the lending rate a financial institution would extend to a firm or the borrowing rate a firm would feel is reasonable based on economic, industry, and firm-specific factors.

As shown previously, part of the rate of return is based on the risk-free rate. The risk-free rate R_f must first be forecasted for three types of economic conditions—boom, normal, and poor.

The second component of the lending rate is the risk premium (R_p). This can be calculated individually for each firm by examining the change in earnings before interest and taxes (EBIT) under the three types of economic conditions. The EBIT is used by the lender as an indicator of the ability of the potential borrower to repay borrowed funds.

Table 7–2 has been constructed based on the methods discussed previously. In total there are nine possible lending rates under the three different

TABLE 7–2   Possible Lending Rates

Economic Conditions	R_f (percent)	Probability	EBIT ($ millions)	Probability	R_p (percent)
Boom	12.0	0.25	2.5	0.40	3
			1.5	0.30	5
			0.5	0.30	8
Normal	10.0	0.50	2.5	0.40	3
			1.5	0.30	5
			0.5	0.30	8
Poor	8.0	0.25	2.5	0.40	3
			1.5	0.30	5
			0.5	0.30	8

TABLE 7–3   Construction of Actual Lending Rates

Economic Conditions	(A) R_f (percent)	(B) Probability	(C) R_f (percent)	(D) Probability	(B × D) Joint Probability of Occurrence	(A + C) Lending Rate (percent)
Boom	12	0.25	3.0	0.40	0.100	15
			5.0	0.30	0.075	17
			8.0	0.30	0.075	20
Normal	10	0.50	3.0	0.40	0.200	13
			5.0	0.30	0.150	15
			8.0	0.30	0.150	18
Poor	8	0.25	3.0	0.40	0.100	11
			5.0	0.30	0.075	13
			8.0	0.30	0.075	16

economic conditions. The construction of these lending rates is shown in Table 7–3. This table shows that during a boom the risk-free rate is set at 12-percent, but the risk premium can take on different values. There is a 40-percent chance that it will be 3.0 percent, a 30-percent chance it will be 5.0 percent, and a 30-percent chance it will be 8.0 percent. The products of the R_p probabilities and the R_f probability are the joint probabilities of occurrence for the lending rates computed from these parameters. Therefore, there is a 10-percent chance that a firm will be faced with a 15-percent lending rate during a boom, a 7.5-percent chance of a 17-percent rate, and a 7.5-percent chance of an 18-percent rate. This process applies for the other conditions, normal and poor, as well.

Based upon the mean and variance equations (7.1) and (7.2) it is possible to calculate the expected lending rate and its variance. Using the information provided in Table 7–3, the weighted average can be calculated:

$$
\begin{aligned}
R = &\ (0.100)(15\%) + (0.075)(17\%) + (0.075)(20\%) + (0.200)(13\%) \\
&+ (0.150)(15\%) + (0.150)(18\%) + (0.100)(11\%) + (0.075)(13\%) \\
&+ (0.075)(16\%) \\
= &\ 15.1\%
\end{aligned}
$$

with a standard deviation of:

$$
\begin{aligned}
\sigma = &\ [(0.100)(15 - 15.1)^2 + (0.075)(17 - 15.1)^2 + (0.075)(20 - 15.1)^2 \\
&+ (0.200)(13 - 15.1)^2 + (0.150)(15 - 15.1)^2 + (0.150)(18 - 15.1)^2 \\
&+ (0.100)(11 - 15.1)^2 + (0.075)(13 - 15.1)^2 \\
&+ (0.075)(16 - 15.1)^2]^{1/2} \\
= &\ (0.001 + 0.271 + 1.801 + 0.882 + 0.0015 + 1.2615 + 1.681 \\
&+ 0.331 + 0.061) \\
= &\ 2.51\%
\end{aligned}
$$

If this distribution is indeed approximately normal, the mean and standard deviation can be employed to make some statistical inferences. Figure 7–7

FIGURE 7–7   Probability of X_i in the Intervals $\pm 1\sigma$, $\pm 2\sigma$, $\pm 3\sigma$

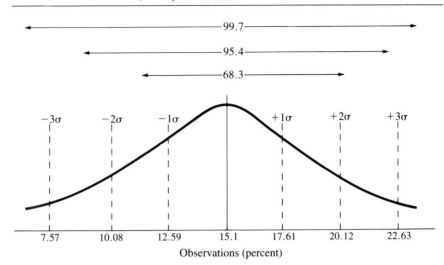

Observations (percent)

makes it clear that 68.3 percent of the observations of a standard normal distribution are within one standard deviation of the mean, 95.4 percent are within two standard deviations, and 99.7 percent within three.

Since the average lending rate is assumed to be normally distributed with a mean of 15.1 percent and a standard deviation of 2.51 percent, it is clear that almost all (99.7 percent) of the lending rates will lie in the range from 7.57 percent to 22.63 percent, because 7.57 percent is three standard deviations below 15.1 percent and 22.63 percent is three standard deviations above the mean. It is also clear that 68.3 percent of the rates will lie in the range of 12.59 percent to 17.61 percent.

THE MARKET RATE OF RETURN AND MARKET RISK PREMIUM

The **market rate of return** is the return that can be expected from the market portfolio. This portfolio consists of all risky assets—that is, stocks, bonds, real estate, coins, and so on. Because *all* risky assets are included, the market portfolio is a completely diversified portfolio. All unsystematic risks related to each individual asset would, therefore, be diversified away. The remaining risk is systematic risk, that which influences all risky assets.

The market rate of return can be calculated using one of several types of market indicator series, such as the Dow-Jones Industrial Average, the Standard and Poor (S&P) 500, or the New York Stock Exchange Index, using the following equation:

$$\frac{I_t - I_{t-1}}{I_{t-1}} = R_{mt} \tag{7.9}$$

where:

R_{mt} = market rate of return at time t;
I_t = market index at t; and
I_{t-1} = market index at $t - 1$.

This equation calculates the percent change in the market index during period t and the previous period $t - 1$. This change is the rate of return an investor would expect to receive in t had he or she invested in $t - 1$.

A **risk-free investment** is one in which the investor is sure about the timing and amount of income streams arising from that investment. However, for most types of investments, investors are uncertain about the timing and amount of income of their investments. The types of risks involved in investments can be quite broad, from the relatively riskless T-bills to highly risky speculative stocks.

The reasonable investor dislikes risks and uncertainty and would, therefore, require an additional return on his investment to compensate for this uncertainty. This return, called the **risk premium,** is added to the nominal risk-free rate. The risk premium is derived from several major sources of uncertainty or risk, as was discussed at the beginning of this chapter.

Table 7–4 illustrates this concept. In this table the market rate of return using the S&P 500 was calculated using Equation (7.9) to devise average quarterly returns. Quarterly T-bill rates are listed in the fourth column. The T-bill rate was deducted from the market return rate ($R_m - R_f$) to devise the risk premium. In most of 1981 and the first two quarters of 1982 the market was in decline, with low returns resulting in each quarter. This allowed the T-bill investors to obtain a higher return than the market return and resulted in negative risk premiums.

The second half of 1982 demonstrated an increasing market level and higher market returns. The fourth quarter of 1982 saw a 16.79-percent return, the highest in the past eight quarters. This allowed market rates to leap beyond the riskless T-bill rate, and the result was a positive risk premium. The first half of 1983 also revealed a positive market risk premium. However, the market-risk premiums from the third quarter of 1983 to the first quarter of 1985 were all negative. Negative risk premiums also occurred through 1986 and 1987 during the period of fluctuation in the level of stock market prices. The fourth quarter of 1987 reflects the October, 1987 stock-market crash, which resulted in a loss of almost 25 percent in the S&P average.

Theoretically it is not possible for a risk premium required by investors to be negative. Taking on risk involves some positive cost. Nevertheless, using short-run estimators as in Table 7–4 may result in negative figures because they reflect the fluctuations of the market. The basic problem with using actual market data to assess risk premiums has to do with the difference

TABLE 7–4 Market Returns and T-Bill Rates by Quarters

Quarter	S&P 500	(A) Market Return (percent)	(B) T-Bill Rate (percent)	(A) − (B) Risk Premium (percent)
1980				
IV	135.76			
1981				
I	136.00	+ 0.18	13.36	− 13.18
II	131.21	− 3.52	14.73	− 18.25
III	116.18	− 12.94	14.70	− 27.64
IV	122.55	+ 5.48	10.85	− 5.37
1982				
I	111.96	− 8.64	12.68	− 21.32
II	110.61	− 1.21	12.47	− 13.68
III	120.42	+ 8.87	7.92	+ 0.95
IV	140.64	+ 16.79	7.94	+ 8.85
1983				
I	152.96	+ 8.76	8.35	0.41
II	168.11	+ 9.90	8.79	1.11
III	166.07	− 1.22	9.00	− 10.22
IV	164.93	− 0.69	9.00	− 9.69
1984				
I	159.18	− 3.49	9.52	− 13.01
II	153.18	− 3.77	9.87	− 13.64
III	166.10	+ 8.43	10.37	− 1.94
IV	167.24	+ 0.68	8.06	− 7.37
1985				
I	180.66	+ 8.02	8.52	− 0.50
II	188.89	+ 4.55	6.95	− 2.4
III	184.06	− 2.62	7.10	− 9.72
IV	207.26	+ 12.60	7.07	+ 5.53
1986				
I	232.33	+ 12.09	6.56	+ 5.53
II	245.30	+ 5.58	6.21	− 0.63
III	238.27	− 2.86	5.21	− 8.07
IV	248.61	+ 4.33	5.43	− 1.10
1987				
I	292.47	+ 17.64	5.59	+ 12.05
II	301.36	+ 3.03	5.69	− 2.66
III	318.66	+ 5.74	6.40	+ 0.05
IV	240.96	− 24.38	5.77	− 30.10

between expected returns (which are always positive) and realized returns (which may be positive or negative). It becomes evident that investors' expectations will not always be realized.

SUMMARY

This chapter has defined the basic concepts of risk and risk measurement. The efficient-portfolio concept and its implementation was demonstrated using the relationships of risk and return. The dominance principle and performance measures were also discussed and illustrated. Finally, the interest rate and market rate of return were used as measurements to show how the commercial lending rate and the market risk premium can be calculated.

Overall, this chapter has introduced uncertainty analysis assuming previous exposure to certainty concepts. Further application of the concepts discussed in this chapter as related to security analysis and portfolio management are explored in later chapters.

QUESTIONS AND PROBLEMS

1. What is risk? What are some of the ways to measure risk?
2. Define the following terms:
   - (a) call risk
   - (b) convertible risk
   - (c) default risk
   - (d) interest-rate risk
   - (e) management risk
   - (f) marketability risk
   - (g) purchasing-power risk
   - (h) systematic risk
   - (i) unsystematic risk
   - (j) efficient portfolio
3. Calculate the expected return and variance for a portfolio consisting of two stocks, A and B.

$$E(R_A) = 12\% \qquad E(R_B) = 16\%$$
$$W_A = 0.3 \qquad \text{Var}(R_B) = 3\%$$
$$\text{Var}(R_A) = 2\% \qquad \text{Cov}(R_A, R_B) = 1\%$$

4. If a portfolio consists of twenty-five stocks, how many variance terms will there be? How many different covariance terms will there be?
5. You are given the information in the table about three stocks under different economic conditions.

Economic Conditions	R_A (percent)	R_B (percent)	R_C (percent)	P_i (percent)
Recession	10	9	20	20
Normal growth	11	8	10	30
Inflation	12	6	20	50

(a) Calculate the expected return and variance for each security.

(b) Calculate the covariance and correlation coefficient for each pair of assets.

(c) Find the expected return for a portfolio consisting of equal amounts of stocks A, B, and C.

6. Carefully explain the dominance principle and its importance to portfolio theory.

7. Compare the Sharpe measure of portfolio performance with the Treynor measure. Under what conditions will they be equivalent?

8. Rank the portfolios A through F in the table using both the Sharpe and Treynor measures. Assume that the risk-free rate is 5 percent.

Portfolios	$E(R)$ (percent)	σ (percent)	β
A	10	4	2
B	8	12	3
C	11	9	2.4
D	13	20	1.5
E	9	6	1.7
F	7	2	0.3

9. Compare the Jensen measure of portfolio performance to the Treynor measure.

REFERENCES

Ben-Horin, M., and H. Levy. "Total Risk, Diversifiable Risk and Non-Diversifiable Risk: A Pedagogic Note." *Journal of Financial and Quantitative Analysis,* v. 15 (June 1980), pp. 289–95.

Bowman, R. G. "The Theoretical Relationship Between Systematic Risk and Financial (Accounting) Variables." *Journal of Finance,* v. 34 (June 1979), pp. 617–30.

Elton, E. J., and M. J. Gruber. *Modern Portfolio Theory and Investment Analysis.* John Wiley and Sons, Inc., 1984.

Evans, J. L., and S. H. Archer. "Diversification and the Reduction of Dispersion: An Empirical Analysis." *Journal of Finance,* v. 23 (December 1968), pp. 761–67.

Francis, J. C., and S. H. Archer. *Portfolio Analysis.* Prentice-Hall, Inc., 1979.

Ibbotson, R. G., and R. A. Sinquefield. "Stocks, Bonds, Bills, and Inflation: Simulations of the Future (1976–2000)." *Journal of Business,* v. 49 (July 1976), pp. 313–38.

Jensen, Michael C. "The Performance of Mutual Funds in the Period 1945–1964." *Journal of Finance,* v. 23 (May 1968), pp. 389–416.

————. "Risk, the Pricing of Capital Assets, and the Evaluation of Investment Portfolios." *Journal of Business,* v. 42 (April 1969), pp. 167–85.

Markowitz, H. M. *Portfolio Selection: Efficient Diversification of Investments.* John Wiley and Sons, Inc., 1959.

Modigliani, F., and G. A. Pogue. "An Introduction to Risk and Return." *Financial Analysis Journal,* v. 30 (May–June 1974), pp. 69–86.

Robicheck, A. A., and R. A. Cohn. "The Economic Determinants of Systematic Risk." *Journal of Finance,* v. 29 (May 1974), pp. 439–47.

Schall, L. D. "Asset Valuation, Firm Investment, and Firm Diversification." *Journal of Business,* v. 45 (January 1972), pp. 11–28.

Sharpe, W. F. "Mutual Fund Performance." *Journal of Business,* v. 39 (January 1966), pp. 119–38.

Thompson, D. J. "Sources of Systematic Risk in Common Stocks." *Journal of Business,* v. 49 (April 1976), pp. 173–88.

Tobin, J. "Liquidity Preference as Behavior Toward Risk." *Review of Economic Studies,* v. 25 (February 1958), pp. 65–86.

Treynor, J. "How to Rate Management of Investment Funds." *Harvard Business Review,* v. 43, (January/February 1965), pp. 63–75.

8 Markowitz Portfolio-Selection Model

In this chapter basic portfolio analysis concepts and techniques discussed in Chapter 7 are used to discuss the Markowitz portfolio-selection model and other related issues in portfolio analysis. Before Harry Markowitz (1952, 1959) developed his portfolio-selection technique into what came to be called modern portfolio theory (MPT), security-selection models focused primarily on the returns generated by investment opportunities. The Markowitz theory retained the emphasis on return; but it elevated risk to a coequal level of importance, and the concept of portfolio risk was born. Whereas risk has been considered an important factor and variance an accepted way of measuring risk, Markowitz was the first to clearly and rigorously show how the variance of a portfolio can be reduced through the impact of diversification. He demonstrated that by combining securities that are not perfectly positively correlated into a portfolio, the portfolio variance can be reduced.

The **Markowitz model** is based on several assumptions concerning the behavior of investors:

1. A probability distribution of possible returns over some holding period can be estimated by investors.
2. Investors have single-period utility functions in which they maximize utility within the framework of diminishing marginal utility of wealth.
3. Variability about the possible values of return is used by investors to measure risk.
4. Investors use only expected return and risk to make investment decisions.
5. Expected return and risk as used by investors are measured by the first two moments of the probability distribution of returns—expected value and variance.
6. Return is desirable; risk is to be avoided.

It follows, then, that a security or portfolio is considered efficient if there exists no other investment opportunity with a higher level of return at a given level of risk and no other opportunity with a lower level of risk at a given level of return.

MEASUREMENT OF RETURN AND RISK

This section focuses on the return and risk measurements utilized in applying the Markowitz model to efficient portfolio selection.

Return

Using the probability distribution of expected returns for a portfolio, investors are assumed to measure the level of return by computing the **expected value** of the distribution.

$$E(R_p) = \sum_{i=1}^{n} W_i E(R_i) \tag{8.1}$$

where:

$$\sum_{i=1}^{n} W_i = 1.0;$$
n = the number of securities;
W_i = the proportion of the funds invested in security i;
R_i, R_p = the return on the ith security and portfolio p; and
$E(\ )$ = the expectation of the variable in the parentheses.

Thus the return computation is nothing more than finding the weighted average return of the securities included in the portfolio. The risk measurement to be discussed in the next section is not quite so simple, however. For only in the case of perfect positive correlation among all its components is the standard deviation of the portfolio equal to the weighted average standard deviation of its component securities.

Risk

Risk is assumed to be measurable by the variability around the expected value of the probability distribution of returns. The most accepted measures of this variability are the **variance** and **standard deviation.** The variance of a single security is the expected value of the sum of the squared deviations from the mean, and the standard deviation is the square root of the variance. The variance of a portfolio combination of securities is equal to the weighted average **covariance** of the returns on its individual securities:

$$\text{Var}(R_p) = \sum_{i=1}^{n} \sum_{j=1}^{n} W_i W_j \text{Cov}(R_i, R_j) \tag{8.2}$$

Covariance can also be expressed in terms of the correlation coefficient as follows:

$$\text{Cov } (R_i, R_j) = r_{ij}\sigma_i\sigma_j = \sigma_{ij} \tag{8.3}$$

Where r_{ij} = correlation coefficient between the rates of return on security i, R_i, and the rates of return on security j, R_j, and σ_i and σ_j represent standard deviations of R_i and R_j, respectively. Therefore:

$$\text{Var } (R_p) = \sum_{i=1}^{n}\sum_{j=1}^{n} W_i W_j r_{ij}\sigma_i\sigma_j \tag{8.4}$$

For a portfolio with two securities, A and B, the following expression can be developed:

$$
\begin{aligned}
\text{Var } (R_p) &= \sum_{i=A}^{B}\sum_{j=A}^{B} W_i W_j r_{ij}\sigma_i\sigma_j \\
&= W_A W_A r_{AA}\sigma_A\sigma_A + W_A W_B r_{AB}\sigma_A\sigma_B \\
&\quad + W_B W_A r_{BA}\sigma_B\sigma_A + W_B W_B r_{BB}\sigma_B\sigma_B
\end{aligned}
$$

Since r_{AA} and $r_{BB} = 1.0$ by definition, terms can be simplified and rearranged, yielding:

$$\text{Var } (R_p) = W_A^2 \sigma_A^2 + W_B^2 \sigma_B^2 + 2W_A W_B r_{AB}\sigma_A\sigma_B \tag{8.5}$$

For a three-security portfolio, the variance of portfolio can be defined:

$$
\begin{aligned}
\text{Var } (R_p) &= \sum_{i=A}^{C}\sum_{j=A}^{C} W_i W_j r_{ij}\sigma_i\sigma_j \\
&= W_A W_A r_{AA}\sigma_A\sigma_A + W_A W_B r_{AB}\sigma_A\sigma_B + W_A W_C r_{AC}\sigma_A\sigma_C \\
&\quad + W_B W_A r_{AB}\sigma_B\sigma_A + W_B W_B r_{BB}\sigma_B\sigma_B + W_B W_C r_{BC}\sigma_B\sigma_C \\
&\quad + W_C W_A r_{CA}\sigma_C\sigma_A + W_C W_B r_{CB}\sigma_C\sigma_B + W_C W_C r_{CC}\sigma_C\sigma_C
\end{aligned}
$$

Again simplifying and rearranging yields:

$$
\begin{aligned}
\text{Var } (R_p) = {} & W_A^2 \sigma_A^2 + W_B^2 \sigma_B^2 + W_C^2 \sigma_C^2 + 2(W_A W_B r_{AB}\sigma_A\sigma_B \\
& + W_A W_C r_{AC}\sigma_A\sigma_C + W_B W_C r_{BC}\sigma_B\sigma_C) \tag{8.6}
\end{aligned}
$$

Thus, as the number of securities increases from two to three, there is one more variance term, and two more covariance terms. The general formula for determining the number of terms that must be computed (NTC) to determine the variance of a portfolio with N securities is

$$\text{NTC} = N \text{ variances} + \frac{N^2 - N}{2} \text{ covariances}$$

For the two-security example two variances were involved, σ_A^2 and σ_B^2, and $(2^2 - 2)/2 = (4 - 2)/2 = 1$ covariance, σ_{AB}, or three computations. For the three-security case, three variances and $(3^2 - 3)/2 = (9 - 3)/2 = 3$ covariances were needed, σ_{AB}, σ_{AC}, and σ_{BC}, or six computations. With four securities, the total number would be $4 + (4^2 - 4)/2 = 4 + (16 - 4)/2 = 4 + 6 = 10$ computations. As can be seen from these examples, the

TABLE 8-1 Portfolio Size and Variance Computations

Number of Securities	Number of Var and Cov Terms
2	3
3	6
4	10
5	15
10	55
15	120
20	210
25	325
50	1,275
75	2,850
100	5,050
250	31,375
500	125,250

number of covariance terms increases by $N - 1$, and the number of variance terms increases by one, as N increases by 1 unit.

If $r_{AB} = r_{AC} = r_{BC} = 1$, then the securities are perfectly positively correlated with each other, and Equation (8.6) reduces to:

$$\text{Var} (R_p) = (W_A \, \sigma_A + W_B \, \sigma_B + W_C \, \sigma_C)^2 \qquad \textbf{(8.6')}$$

This implies that the standard deviation of the portfolio is equal to the weighted average standard deviation of its component securities. In other words:

$$\text{Standard deviation of } R_p = W_A \, \sigma_A + W_B \, \sigma_B + W_C \, \sigma_C$$

Table 8-1 clearly illustrates the tremendous estimation and computational load that exists using the Markowitz diversification approach. Chapter 10 illustrates how this problem can be alleviated.

UTILITY THEORY, UTILITY FUNCTIONS, AND INDIFFERENCE CURVES

In this section utility theory and functions, which are needed for portfolio analyses (Chapters 8, 10, and 18), and capital asset models (Chapters 9 and 11) are discussed in some detail.

Utility theory is the foundation for the theory of choice under uncertainty. Following Henderson and Quandt (1980), cardinal and ordinal theories are the two major alternatives used by economists to determine how people and

FIGURE 8-1   Utility Functions

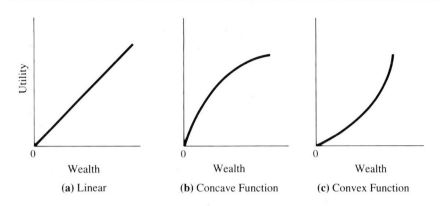

(a) Linear   (b) Concave Function   (c) Convex Function

societies choose to allocate scarce resources and to distribute wealth among one another over time.[1]

Utility Functions

Economists define the relationships between psychological satisfaction and wealth as "utility." An upward-sloping relationship, as shown in Figure 8–1, identifies the phenomena of increasing wealth and increasing satisfaction as being directly related. These relationships can be classified into linear, concave, and convex utility functions.

In Figure 8–1(a), for each unit change in wealth, there is a linear utility function, an equal increase in satisfaction or utility. A doubling of wealth will double satisfaction, and so on. This is probably not very realistic: a dollar increase in wealth from $1 to $2 is probably more important than an increase from $1 million to $2 million, because the marginal utility diminishes with increased wealth.

In Figure 8–1(b) the concave utility function shows the relationship of an increase in wealth and a less than proportional increase in utility. In other words, the marginal utility of wealth decreases as wealth increases. As mentioned above, the $1 increase from $1 to $2 of wealth is more important to the individual than the increase from $1 million to $1,000,001. Each successive increase in wealth adds less satisfaction as the level of wealth rises.

---

[1] A *cardinal utility* implies that a consumer is capable of assigning to every commodity or combination of commodities a number representing the amount or degree of utility associated with it. An *ordinal utility* implies that a consumer needs not be able to assign numbers that represent (in arbitrary unit) the degree or amount of utility associated with commodity or combination of commodity. The consumer can only rank and order the amount or degree of utility associated with commodity.

Finally, Figure 8–1(c) is a convex utility function, which denotes a more than proportional increase in satisfaction for each increase in wealth. Behaviorally, the richer you are the more satisfaction you receive in getting an additional dollar of wealth.

The utility theory primarily used in finance is that developed by Von Newmann and Morgenstern (VNM, 1947). VNM define investor utility as a function of rates of return or wealth. Mao (1969) points out that the VNM utility theory is really somewhere between the cardinal and ordinal utility theories. The function associated with the VNM's utility theory in terms of wealth can be defined:

$$U = f(\mu_w, \sigma_w)$$

where μ_w indicates expected future wealth and σ_w represents the predicted standard deviation of the possible divergence of actual future wealth from μ_w.

Investors are expected to prefer a higher expected future wealth to a lower value. Moreover, they are generally risk averse as well. That is, they prefer a lower value of σ_w to a higher value, given the level of μ_w.[2] These assumptions imply that the **indifference curves** relating μ_w and σ_w will be upward sloping, as indicated in Figure 8–2. In Figure 8–2, each indifference curve is an expected utility isoquant showing all the various combinations of risk and return that provide an equal amount of expected utility for the investor.

FIGURE 8–2   Indifference Curves of Utility Functions

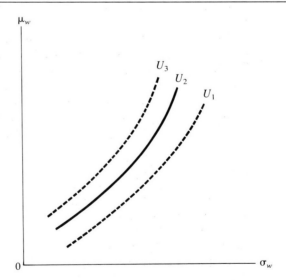

---

[2] Technically, these conditions can be represented mathematically by $\partial U/\partial \mu_w > 0$ and $\partial U/\partial \sigma_w < 0$.

In explaining how investment decisions or portfolio choices are made, utility theory is used here not to imply that individuals actually make decisions using a utility curve, but rather as an expository vehicle that helps explain how investors presumably act. In general, humans behave as if more is better than less (the utility curve is upward sloping) and marginal utility is decreasing (the utility curve is concave).

In an uncertain environment it becomes necessary to ascertain how different individuals will react to risky situations. The risk is defined as the probability of success or failure. Alternatively, risk could be described as variability of outcomes, payoffs, or returns. This implies that there is a distribution of outcomes associated with each investment decision. What is needed is a linkage between utility or expected utility and risk. Expected utility has been defined as the numerical value assigned to the probability distribution associated with a particular portfolio's return. This numerical value is calculated by taking a weighted average of the utilities of the various possible returns. The weights are the probabilities of occurrence associated with each of the possible returns. It is calculated by the following formula:

$$E(U) = \sum_{i}^{n} U(w_i)P_i \qquad (8.7)$$

where:

$E(U)$ = expected utility;
$U(w_i)$ = the utility of the ith outcome w_i; and
P_i = the Probability of the ith outcome.

Sample Problem 8.1 provides further illustration.

Sample Problem 8.1

Given investments A and B as shown in the table, determine the utilities of A and B for the given utility functions.

A		B	
Outcome w_i	Probability	Outcome w_i	Probability
10	2/5	9	2/3
5	2/5	3	1/3
1	1/5		

1. $U(w) = w$
2. $U(w) = w^2$
3. $U(w) = w^2 - w$

Solution

1. For $U(w) = w$

$$\text{Utility A} = \tfrac{2}{5}(10) + \tfrac{2}{5}(5) + \tfrac{1}{5}(1) = 6\tfrac{1}{5}$$
$$\text{Utility B} = \tfrac{2}{3}(9) + \tfrac{1}{3}(3) = 7$$

2. For $U(w) = w^2$

$$\text{Utility A} = \tfrac{2}{5}(100) + \tfrac{2}{5}(25) + \tfrac{1}{5}(1) = 50\tfrac{1}{5}$$
$$\text{Utility B} = \tfrac{2}{3}(81) + \tfrac{1}{3}(9) = 57$$

3. For $U(w) = w - w$ (use results from 1 and 2)

$$\text{Utility A} = 50\tfrac{1}{5} - 6\tfrac{1}{5} = 44$$
$$\text{Utility B} = 57 - 7 = 50$$

In all three cases, B has the higher degree of utility because it has a higher expected value as well as a smaller dispersion than A●

Linear Utility Function and Risk.   It is useful now to consider how the shape of an individual's utility function affects his or her reaction to risk. Assume that an individual who has $5,000 and whose behavior is a linear utility function [Figure 8–1(a)] is offered a chance to gain $10,000 with a probability of 1/2 or to lose $10,000 with a probability of 1/2. What should he or she pay for such an opportunity? The answer is nothing, for as can be seen in Figure 8–3, this individual would be no better or worse off accepting or rejecting this opportunity. If he rejected the offer, his wealth would be $5,000 with utility U_1; if he paid nothing for the opportunity, his wealth would remain at $5,000 with Utility U_1. Any payment for this chance would reduce his wealth and therefore be undesirable. This is so because the expected value of the fair game is zero:

$$\tfrac{1}{2}(10,000) + \tfrac{1}{2}(-10,000) = 0$$

Figure 8–3 illustrates this concept.

Concave Utility Function and Risk.   Now consider an individual whose behavior is a concave utility function. If this individual participates and wins, her utility is shown by point U_W in Figure 8–4. But if she loses, her position is shown by U_L. The expected value of this fair game, having a 50-percent chance of winning and a 50-percent chance of losing, is shown by point A.[3] The utility of the fair game is U_F. A comparison of U_F with her initial position, U_i, shows that the investor should not accept this fair game.

---

[3] Following Fama (1970) and Alexander and Francis (1986: 177) a fair game means that the expected returns, given information set θ, equal the expected returns without the information set. Note that this does not mean the expected returns are zero or positive—they could be negative.

FIGURE 8-3   Risk-Neutral Investors and Fair Games

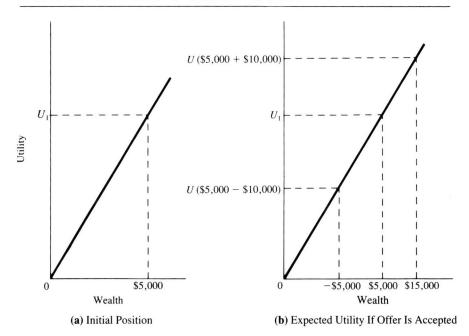

(a) Initial Position

(b) Expected Utility If Offer Is Accepted

As shown in Figure 8-4 the utility of winning $(U_W - U_i)$ is less than the utility of losing $(U_i - U_L)$. Therefore, the utility of doing nothing is greater than the expected utility of accepting the fair game. In fact, the individual should be willing to pay up to the difference between the utility of winning and the utility of losing $(U_i - U_L) - (U_W - U_i)$ to avoid being involved in this situation. Alexander and Francis (1986) theoretically analyze this issue in more detail. Hence investors with concave utility functions are said to be risk averse. That is, they would reject a fair game because the utility derived from winning is less than the utility lost should they lose the game. In other words, the expected utility of participating in a fair game is negative. Sample Problem 8.2 provides further illustration.

Sample Problem 8.2

Given the following utility functions for four investors, what can you conclude about their reaction towards a fair game?

1. $w^3 - 4w^2$
2. w^4
3. e^{-2w} and
4. $e^{2w} - 4w^2$

FIGURE 8-4   Risk-Averse Investors and Fair Games

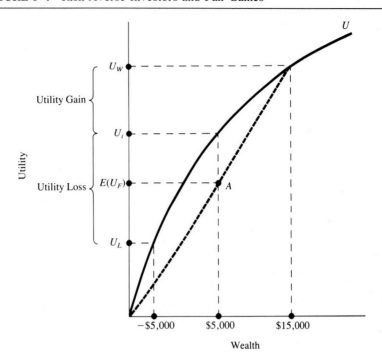

Evaluate the second derivative of the utility functions according to the following rules.

$$w''(0) < 0 \text{ implies risk averse}$$
$$w''(0) = 0 \text{ implies risk neutral}$$
$$w''(0) > 0 \text{ implies risk seeker}$$

Solution

1.
$$u(w) = w^3 - 4w^2$$
$$u'(w) = 3w^2 - 8w$$
$$u''(w) = 6w - 8$$
$$u''(0) = -8 < 0$$

This implies the investor is risk averse and would reject a fair gamble.

2.
$$u(w) = w^4$$
$$u'(w) = 4w^3$$
$$u''(w) = 12w^2$$
$$u''(0) = 0$$

This implies risk neutrality, hence indifference to a fair gamble.

3.
$$u(w) = e^{-2w}$$
$$u'(w) = -2e^{-2w}$$
$$u''(w) = 4e^{-2w}$$
$$u''(0) = 4 > 0$$

This implies risk preference; the investor would seek a fair gamble.

4.
$$u(w) = e^{2w} - 4w^2$$
$$u'(w) = 2e^{2w} - 8w$$
$$u''(w) = 4e^{2w} - 8$$
$$u''(0) = -4 < 0$$

This implies risk aversity; the investor would reject a fair gamble ●

The convex utility function is not realistic in real-world decisions; therefore, it is not further explored at this point. The following section discusses the implications of alternative utility functions in terms of indifference curves.

Indifference Curves

Indifference (utility-function) curves are abstract theoretical concepts. They cannot as a practical matter be used to actually measure how individuals make investment decisions—or any other decisions, for that matter. They are, however, useful tools for building models that illustrate the relationship between risk and return. An investor's utility function can be utilized conceptually to derive an indifference curve, which shows individual preference for risk and return.[4] An indifference curve can be plotted in the risk–return space such that the investor's utility is equal all along its length. The investor is indifferent to various combinations of risk and return, hence the name indifference curve. The slope of the indifference curve is a function of the investor's particular preference for a lower but safer return versus a larger but riskier return. Various types of investor's indifference curves are shown in Figure 8–5.

The risk-averse investor demands a large amount of additional return for a small increase in risk, hence the almost vertical indifference curve. The level of satisfaction derived from each combination of risk and return is shown by U_1, U_2, U_3, and U_4. The higher the subscript, the higher the level of utility; hence, U_4 has the highest level of utility. The risk-averse investor not only demands a high level of return for additional risk but also derives a higher level of utility for lower risk. Each of the individuals shown in Figure 8–5 demonstrates a different preference for risk and return.

---

[4] By definition, an indifference curve shows all combinations of products (investments) A and B that will yield same level of satisfaction or utility to consume. This kind of analysis is based upon ordinal rather than cardinal utility theory.

FIGURE 8–5   Indifference Curves for Various Types of Individuals

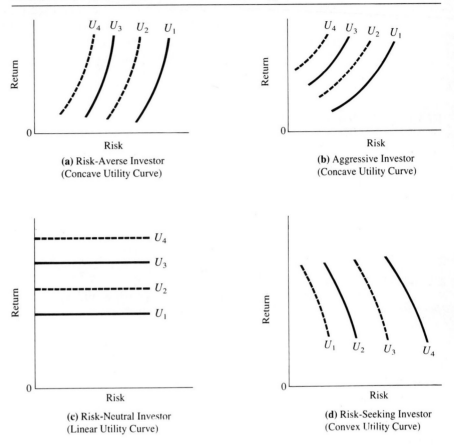

(a) Risk-Averse Investor
(Concave Utility Curve)

(b) Aggressive Investor
(Concave Utility Curve)

(c) Risk-Neutral Investor
(Linear Utility Curve)

(d) Risk-Seeking Investor
(Convex Utility Curve)

Later in this chapter different levels of risk and return are evaluated for securities and portfolios when a decision must be made concerning which security or portfolio is better than another. It is at that point in the analysis that indifference curves of hypothetical individuals are employed to help determine which securities or portfolios are desirable and which ones are not. Basically, values for return and risk will be plotted for a number of portfolios as well as indifference curves for different types of investors. The investor's optimal portfolio will then be the one identified with the highest level of utility for the various indifference curves.

Investors generally hold more than one type of investment asset in their portfolio. Besides securities an investor may hold real estate, gold, art, and so on. Thus, given the measures of risk and return for individual securities developed, the measures of risk and return may be used for portfolios of risky assets. Risk-averse investors hold portfolios rather than individual securities as a means of eliminating unsystematic risk; hence the examina-

tion of risk and return will continue in terms of portfolios rather than individual securities. Indifference curves can be used to indicate investors' *willingness* to trade risk for return; now investors' ability to trade risk for return needs to be represented in terms of indifference curves and efficient portfolios, as discussed in the next section.

EFFICIENT PORTFOLIOS

Efficient portfolios may contain any number of asset combinations. Two examples are shown, a two-asset combination and a three-asset portfolio; both are studied from graphical and mathematical solution perspectives.

The degree to which a two-security portfolio reduces variance of returns depends on the degree of correlation between the returns of the securities. This can be best illustrated by expressing the variability in terms of standard deviation (the square root of the variance):

$$\sigma_p = \sqrt{W_A^2 \sigma_A^2 + W_B^2 \sigma_B^2 + 2W_A W_B r_{AB} \sigma_A \sigma_B} \qquad (8.8)$$

First, assume that $r_{AB} = 1.0$, which would mean that Securities A and B are perfectly positively correlated. Then:

$$\sigma_p = \sqrt{W_A^2 \sigma_A^2 + W_B^2 \sigma_B^2 + 2W_A W_B \sigma_A \sigma_B}$$

or:

$$\sigma_p = \sqrt{(W_A \sigma_A + W_B \sigma_B)^2}$$

so:

$$\sigma_p = W_A \sigma_A + W_A \sigma_B \qquad (8.9)$$

With the securities perfectly positively correlated, the standard deviation of the portfolio combination is equal to the weighted average of the standard deviation of the component securities. Since the correlation coefficient cannot be greater than 1.0, the weighted average represents the highest possible values of the portfolio standard deviation as discussed previously in this chapter. In this case, there is no diversification taking place. With any correlation coefficient less than 1.0, there will be a diversification effect, and this effect will be larger the lower the value of the correlation coefficient.

The ultimate diversification impact occurs if $r_{AB} = -1.0$, perfect negative correlation.

$$\sigma_p = \sqrt{W_A^2 \sigma_A^2 + W_B^2 \sigma_B^2 - 2W_A W_B \sigma_4 \sigma_B}$$

This can be reduced to:

$$\sigma_p = \sqrt{(W_A \sigma_A - W_B \sigma_B)^2} \qquad (8.10)$$
$$= W_A \sigma_A - W_B \sigma_B$$

Sample Problem 8.3 provides further illustration.

Sample Problem 8.3

Two-Security Portfolio Diversification. Assume that $R_A = 10$ percent, $R_B = 8$ percent, $\sigma_A = 4$ percent, and $\sigma_B = 3$ percent. Since the values for both R_A and σ_A are greater than those for R_B and σ_B, respectively, there is no dominant choice between the two securities. Higher return is associated with higher risk. Additionally, assume that $r_{AB} = 1.0$ and that the securities are equally weighted in the portfolio. It follows then that:

$$
\begin{aligned}
\sigma_p &= \sqrt{(0.5)^2\,(4)^2 + (0.5)^2(3)^2 + (2)(0.5)(0.5)(1.0)(4)(3)} \\
&= \sqrt{(0.25)(16) + (0.25)(9) + (2)(0.25)(12)} \\
&= \sqrt{4 + 2.25 + 6} \\
&= \sqrt{12.25} \\
&= 3.5
\end{aligned}
$$

Notice that this is the same result that would have been achieved using Equation (8.9), $\sigma_p = (0.5)(4) + (0.5)(3) = 2 + 1.5 = 3.5$ percent. If $r_{AB} = 0.5$ there still is positive correlation, but as it is not perfect positive correlation, there is a diversification effect.

$$
\begin{aligned}
\sigma_p &= \sqrt{(0.5)^2\,(4)^2 + (0.5)^2\,(3)^2 + (2)(0.5)(0.5)(0.5)(4)(3)} \\
&= \sqrt{4 + 2.25 + 3} \\
&= \sqrt{9.25} \\
&= 3.04
\end{aligned}
$$

This reduction of σ_p from 3.50 to 3.04 is the effect of diversification. Notice that the first two terms under the square root radical were unaffected and that the third term was only half the size it was with no diversification. The diversification impact from a lower correlation coefficient occurs in the covariance term only. If security A and B were independent of one another, that is, $r_{AB} = 0$, it is clear that the covariance term would equal zero.

$$
\begin{aligned}
\sigma_p &= \sqrt{4 + 2.25 + (2)(0.5)(0.5)(0)(4)(3)} \\
&= \sqrt{4 + 2.25 + 0} \\
&= \sqrt{6.25} \\
&= 2.5
\end{aligned}
$$

and the diversification impact reduces σ_{AB} to 2.50.

If security A and B were perfectly and negatively correlated, that is, $\rho_{AB} = -1$, substituting the numbers from the example, first into Equation (8.8), gives

$$
\begin{aligned}
\sigma_p &= \sqrt{4 + 2.25 + (2)(0.5)(0.5)(-1.0)(4)(3)} \\
&= \sqrt{6.25 - 6} \\
&= \sqrt{0.25} \\
&= 0.5
\end{aligned}
$$

and into Equation (8.10):

$$\sigma_p = (0.5)(4) - (0.5)(3) = 2 - 1.5 = 0.5$$

With the appropriate weighting factors, the σ_p may be reduced to zero if there is negative correlation. For example, if $W_A = 3/7$ and $W_B = 4/7$ in this problem:

$$\sigma_p = (3/7)(4) - (4/7)(3)$$
$$= 0$$

Portfolio Combinations

Assume that the actual correlation coefficient is 0.50. By varying the weights of the two securities and plotting the combinations in the risk–return space, it is possible to derive a set of portfolios (see Table 8–2) that form an elliptical curve (see Figure 8–6). The amount of curvature in the ellipse varies with the degree of correlation between the two securities. If there were perfect positive correlation, all of the combinations would lie on a straight line between points A and B. If the combinations were plotted with the assumption of perfect negative correlation, the curvature would be more pronounced and one of the points ($W_A = 0.43$, $W_B = 0.57$) would actually be on the vertical axis (a risk of zero).

This process could be repeated for all combinations of investments; the result is graphed in Figure 8–7. In Figure 8–7 the area within curve $XVYZ$ is the feasible opportunity set representing all possible portfolio combinations. The curve YV represents all possible efficient portfolios and is the **efficient frontier**. The line segment VX is on the feasible opportunity set, but not on the efficient frontier; all points on VX represent inefficient portfolios.

The portfolios and securities that lie on the frontier VX in Figure 8–7 would not be likely candidates for investors to hold. This is so because they do not meet the criteria of maximizing expected return for a given level of

TABLE 8-2 Possible Risk–Return Combination ($R_A = 0.10$, $R_B = 0.08$, $\sigma_A = 0.04$, $\sigma_B = 0.03$, $\rho_{AB} = 0.5$)

Portfolio	W_A	W_B	R_p (percent)	σ_p (percent)
1	1.00	0.00	10.0	4.00
2	0.75	0.25	9.5	3.44
3	0.50	0.50	9.0	3.04
4	0.25	0.75	8.5	2.88
5	0.00	1.00	8.0	3.00

FIGURE 8–6   The Relationship between Correlation and Portfolio Risk

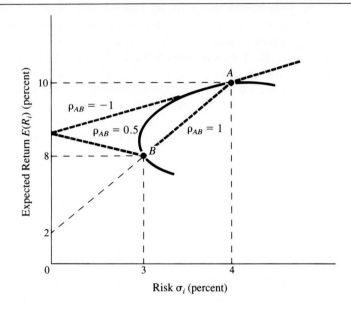

FIGURE 8–7   The Minimum-Variance Set

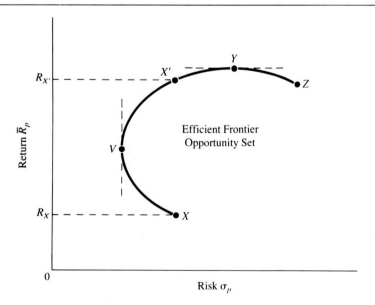

risk or minimizing risk for a given level of return. This is easily seen by comparing the portfolio represented by points X and X'. Since investors always prefer more expected return than less for a given level of risk, X' is always better than X. Using similar reasoning, investors would always prefer V to X because it has both a higher return and a lower level of risk. In fact, the portfolio at point V is identified as the **minimum-variance portfolio**, since no other portfolio exists that has a lower variance.

For each of the combinations of individual securities and inefficient portfolios in Figure 8–7 there is a corresponding portfolio along the efficient frontier that either has a higher return given the same risk or a lower risk given the same return. However, points on the efficient frontier do not dominate one another. While point Y has considerably higher return than point V, it also has considerably higher risk. The optimal portfolio along the efficient frontier is not unique with this model and depends upon the risk/return tradeoff utility function of each investor. Portfolio selection, then, is determined by plotting investors' utility functions together with the efficient-frontier set of available investment opportunities. No two investors will select the same portfolio except by chance or if their utility curves are identical. In Figure 8–8, two sets of indifference curves labeled U and U' are shown together with the efficient frontier. The U curves have a higher slope, indicating a greater level of risk aversion. The investor is indifferent to any combination of R_P and σ_p along a given curve, for example, U_1, U_2, or U_3. The U' curve would be appropriate for a less risk-averse investor—that is,

FIGURE 8–8 Indifference Curves and the Minimum-Variance Set

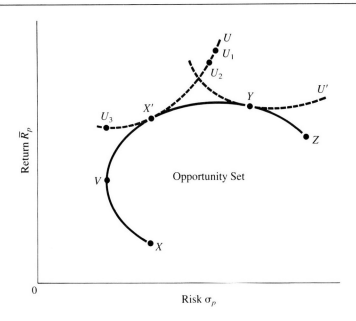

one who would be willing to accept relatively higher risk to obtain higher levels of return. The optimal portfolio would be the one that provides the highest utility—a point in the northwest direction (higher return and lower risk). This point will be at the tangent of a utility curve and the efficient frontier. The tangency point for the risk-averse investor in Figure 8-8 is point X'; for the less risk-averse investor it is point Y. Each investor is logically selecting the optimal portfolio given his or her risk–return preference, and neither is more correct than the other.

Individual investors sometimes find it necessary to restrict their portfolios to include a relatively small number of securities. Mutual-fund portfolios, on the other hand, often contain securities from more than five hundred different companies. To give some idea of the number of securities that is necessary to achieve a high level of diversification, Levy and Sarnat (1971) considered a naive strategy of equally weighted portfolios—that is, of dividing the total investment into equal proportions among component securities. Plotting the variance of the portfolios developed in this manner against the number of securities making up the portfolios will result in a function similar to that illustrated in Figure 8-9. As can be seen, the additional reduction in portfolio variance rapidly levels off as the number of securities is increased beyond five. An earlier study by Evans and Archer (1968) shows that the percentage of diversification that can be achieved with randomly selected, equally weighted portfolios levels off rapidly beyond a portfolio size of about fifteen.

Short Selling

Short selling (or "going short") is a very regulated type of market transaction. It involves selling shares of a stock that are borrowed in expectation of a fall in the security's price. When and if the price declines, the investor

FIGURE 8-9   Naive Diversification Reduces Risk to the Systematic Level in a Randomly Selected Portfolio

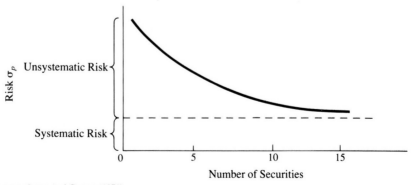

Source: Levy and Sarnat (1971).

buys an equivalent number of shares of the same stock at the new lower price and returns to the lender the stock that was borrowed. The Federal Reserve Board requires short selling customers to deposit 50 percent of the net proceeds of such short sales with the brokerage firm carrying out the transaction. Another key requirement of a short sale, set by the Securities and Exchange Act of 1934, is that the short sale must occur at a price higher than the preceding sale—or at the same price as the preceding sale, if that took place at a higher price than a preceding price. This is the so-called uptick or zero-tick rule. It prevents the price of a security from successively falling because of continued short selling.

Relaxing the assumption of no short selling in this development of the efficient frontier involves a modification of the analysis of the previous section. The efficient frontier analyzed in the previous sections was bounded on both ends by Y and the minimum variance portfolio V, respectively, as shown in Figure 8–7. Point Y is called the **maximum-return portfolio,** since there is no other portfolio with a higher return. This point is normally an efficient security or portfolio with the greatest level of risk and return. It could also be a portfolio of securities, all having the same highest levels of risk and return. Point Z is normally a single security with the lowest level of return, although it could be a portfolio of securities, all having the same low level of return.

The Black (1972) model is identical to the Markowitz model except that it allows for short selling.[5] That is, the nonnegativity constraint on the amount that can be invested in each security is relaxed, $W_A \gtrless 0$. A negative value for the weight invested in a security is allowed, tantamount to allowing a short sale of the security. The new efficient frontier that can be derived with short selling is shown in Figure 8–10A.

The major difference between the frontier in Figure 8–10A (short selling) and Figure 8–10B (no short selling) is the disappearance of the end points Y and Z. An investor could sell the lowest-return security short (X) and take the proceeds and invest them in the highest-return security (Y). If the number of short sales is unrestricted, then by a continuous short selling of X and reinvesting in Y the investor could generate an infinite expected return. Hence the upper bound of the highest-return portfolio would no longer be Y but infinity (shown by the arrow on the top of the efficient frontier). Likewise the investor could short sell the highest-return security Y and reinvest the proceeds into the lowest-yield security X, thereby generating a return less than the return on the lowest-return security. Given no restriction on the amount of short selling, an infinitely negative return can be achieved, thereby removing the lower bound of X on the efficient frontier. But rational investors will not short sell a high-return stock and buy a low-return stock.

---

[5] Most texts do not identify the Markowitz model with restrictions on short sales. Markowitz (1952), in fact, excluded short sales.

FIGURE 8–10A   The Efficient Frontier with Short Selling

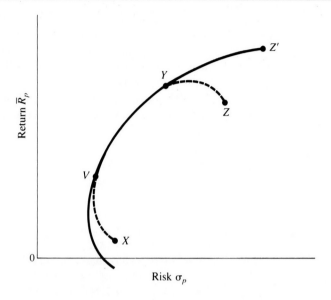

FIGURE 8–10B   Efficient Frontiers With and Without Short Selling and Margin Requirements

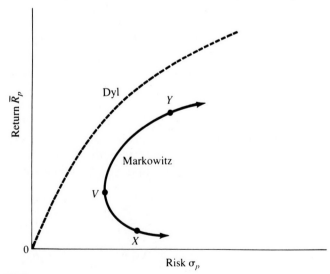

Source: Dyl (1975).

The portfolios on VZ' always dominate those of VX, as shown in Figure 8–10A.

Whether an investor engages in any of this short-selling activity depends on the investor's own unique set of indifference curves. Hence, short selling generally will increase the range of alternative investments from the minimum-variance portfolio to plus or minus infinity. However, in the Black model with short selling, no provision was made for the SEC margin requirement. Dyl (1975) imposed the margin requirement on short selling and added it to the Markowitz development of the efficient frontier.

The Dyl Model.   Dyl introduced short selling with margin requirements by creating a new set of risky securities, the ones sold short, which are negatively correlated with the existing set of risky securities. These new securities greatly enhance the diversification effect when they are placed in portfolios. The **Dyl model** affects the efficient frontier in two ways: (1) If the investor were to combine in equal weight any long position in a security or portfolio with a short position in a security or a portfolio, the resulting portfolio would yield zero return and zero variance and (2) any combination of unequal weighted long or short positions would yield portfolios with higher returns and lower risk levels. Overall, these two effects will yield an efficient frontier that dominates the Markowitz efficient frontier. Figure 8–10B compares the Dyl and Markowitz efficient frontiers.

Even though the inclusion of short selling changes the location and boundaries of the efficient frontier, the concavity of the curve is still intact. This is important in that it preserves the efficient frontier as the locus of optimal portfolios for risk-averse investors. As long as the efficient frontier remains concave, by using indifference curves it will be possible to locate the optimal portfolio for each investor.

Techniques for Calculating the Efficient Frontier with Short Selling.   Since there are thousands of securities from which the investor can choose for portfolio formation, it can be very costly and time consuming to calculate the efficient frontier set. One way of determining the optimal investment proportions in a portfolio is to hold the return constant and solve for the weighting factors ($W_1 \ldots , W_n$ for n securities) that minimize the variance, given the constraint that all weights sum to one and that the constant return equals the expected return developed from the portfolio. The optimal weights can then be obtained by minimizing the Lagrange function C for portfolio variance.

$$C = \sum_{i=1}^{n} \sum_{j=1}^{n} W_i \, W_j \, r_{ij} \, \sigma_i \, \sigma_j + \lambda_1 \left(1 - \sum_{i=1}^{n} W_i \right)$$
$$+ \lambda_2 \left[E^* - \sum_{i=1}^{n} W_i \, E(R_i) \right]$$

(8.11)

in which λ_1 and λ_2 are the Lagrange multipliers, E^* and $E(R_i)$ are targeted rate of return and expected rate of return for security i, respectively, r_{ij} is the correlation coefficient between i and j, and other variables are as previously defined.

Function C has $n + 2$ unknowns: $W_1, \ldots, W_n$, λ_1, and λ_2. By differentiating C with respect to W_i, λ_1, and λ_2 and equating the first derivatives to zero, $n + 2$ equations can be derived to solve for $n + 2$ unknowns. As shown in the empirical example later in this chapter, matrix algebra is best suited to this solution process. By using this approach the minimum variance can be computed for any given level of expected portfolio return (subject to the other constraint that the weights sum to one). In practice it is best to use a computer because of the explosive increase in the number of calculations as the number of securities considered grows. The efficient set that is generated by the aforementioned approach [Equation (8.11)] is sometimes called the **minimum-variance set** because of the minimizing nature of the Lagrangian solution.

Thus far no specific distribution for measuring returns has been assumed. In most cases specific distribution of returns will be needed when applying the portfolio model. The normal and log normal are two of the most commonly used distributions.

The Normal Distribution. As you undoubtedly are aware, the **normal (probability) distribution** is a bell-shaped curve centered on the mean of a given population or sample distribution. The area under the curve is an accumulation of probabilities that sum to one. With half of the area lying to the left and half to the right of the mean, probability statements may be made about the underlying sample that makes up the distribution.

Within the scope of the Markowitz model, the normal distribution may be applied because of the use of the mean-variance assumptions. The formation of probability statements from the underlying sample is a result of the standard deviation (square root of the variance) quantifying the spread of the distribution. If the sample is normally distributed, approximately 68 percent of the observations will lie within one standard deviation on either side of the mean, approximately 95 percent will lie within two standard deviations, and approximately 99 percent will lie within three standard deviations. This ability to ascertain intervals of confidence for the observations allows the utilization of the normal distribution to predict ranges within which the portfolio returns will lie.

Utilizing the standard normal distribution (mean of zero, standard deviation of one), any set of mean-variance data can be standardized to develop probability statements about returns on a given portfolio. Standardization is an algebraic operation in which the mean is subtracted from a given return and this difference is divided by the standard deviation. The resultant metric is then standard normal and can be compared with the tabulated values to calculate probabilistic quantities of occurrence. Within this framework, any

hypothesized level of return can be assigned a probability of occurrence given a probabilistic value of occurrence that is based upon the nature of the sample.

For expository purposes, suppose the mean return on a particular investment is 10 percent for a given period, and that historically these returns have a variance of 0.16 percent. It is of interest to know what the probabilities are of obtaining a 15 percent or greater return, or a return less than or equal to 8 percent. These probabilities may be evaluated by using the normal distribution, as stated in notation below:

$$P(X \geq 0.15 \mid R_P = 0.1, \sigma_P^2 = 0.0016)$$
$$P(X \leq 0.08 \mid R_P = 0.1, \sigma_P^2 = 0.0016)$$

by standardizing the probability statements to z values:

$$P\left(z \geq \frac{0.15 - 0.1}{0.04} = 1.25\right)$$
$$P\left(z \leq \frac{0.08 - 0.1}{0.04} = -0.5\right)$$

(8.12)

These standardized values can then be compared with the tabulated z values found in tables of the standardized normal distribution, such as the one at the end of this book (Table V). For $z \geq 1.2$ the probability is 0.1151, and for $z = 0.05$ the probability is 0.3085. Therefore this investment has an 11.51 percent chance of obtaining a 15 percent or more return, and a 30.85 percent chance of obtaining 8 percent or less.

It is extremely difficult to make probabilistic statements when using the normal distribution. Given that the return data utilized are ex post, the predictive ability of the normal distribution based on historical data is limited. The past does not always predict the future; hence, this problem is somewhat alleviated by an assumption that the security under consideration is in a static state. Nevertheless, as shown by research and common sense, this assumption is rather bold, and the use of the normal distribution should be limited to comparisons of various past portfolio returns.

Another difficulty with the normal distribution is that if the distribution of the sample is skewed in any way, the standard deviation will not properly reflect the equivalent areas under the curve on either side of the mean. This problem will be discussed and solved in the next section through the application of the **log normal distribution.** A variable is log normally distributed if a logarithm of this variable is normally distributed.

The Log Normal Distribution. The log normal distribution discussed in Chapter 3 is explored further in this section. The approach outlined in the last section for delineating the efficient frontier assumes that the security-return data are normally distributed. In reality, most financial researchers would agree that security-return data tend to be positively skewed. This skewness can be a serious problem in accurately developing the efficient frontier with the Markowitz model because of the assumption that only the first two moments of the return distribution, mean and variance, are important.

One reason for returns being positively skewed is the inability of the investor to lose more than 100 percent of his or her investment, effectively creating a lower bound to portfolio returns. This is called the limited-liability constraint. But since capital gains and dividends could conceivably be infinite, the upper tail of the distribution of returns has no upper bounds. The range of probable returns is spread towards the positive side and therefore contains a potential bias when it is utilized in developing statistical estimates.

If the return distributions are significantly skewed, the efficient frontier can be more accurately determined with the use of logarithmically transformed holding-period returns. That is, each holding-period return for security i with holding period T $(1 + R_{iT})$ is transformed by computing its natural logarithm, $\ln (1 + R_{iT})$. The logarithmic transformation converts a data set of discretely compounded returns into continuously compounded returns. The distribution of discrete time returns will be more positively skewed the larger the differencing interval used to measure the returns; that is, if skewness exists in the return distribution, annual data will be more positively skewed than monthly data, which will be more skewed than weekly data.

The continuous compounding implied in the logarithmically transformed data will virtually eliminate any positive skewness existing in the raw return data when rates of return are log normally distributed. It is practically possible to directly derive the efficient frontier using means and variances of logarithmically transformed data. Under this circumstance, assume that utility functions use continuous returns and variances, and then use the $\ln (1 + R_p)$ transformation on discrete data. To deal with the untransformed log normally distributed data, Elton and Gruber (1976) use the mean and variance of log normal distributed as defined in Equations (8.13) and (8.14) to derive the efficient frontier. In other words, they first delineate the efficient frontier by using the means and variances of the untransformed data and then use Equations (8.13) and (8.14) to determine the subset of the $[E(1 + R_p), \sigma(1 + R_p)]$ efficient frontier in terms of log-transformed data, $\ln (1 + R_p)$.

$$E(1 + R_P) = e^{E(r_p) + 1/2\sigma^2} \tag{8.13}$$

where $r_p = \ln (1 + R_p)$ and σ is the standard deviation of r_p.

$$\sigma^2(1 + R_p) = (e^{2E(r_p) + \sigma^2}) (e^{\sigma^2} - 1) \tag{8.14}$$

where $r_p = \ln (1 + R_p)$ and $\sigma^2 = \text{Var} (r_p)$. Use of the logarithmic transformation can also be shown to eliminate less desirable portfolios in the lowest-return segment of the efficient frontier computer using the raw data.[6] Before moving on to an example, however, it will be useful to briefly summarize the portfolio-selection process.

---

[6] See W. Baumol, "An Expected Gain—Confidence Limits Criterion for Portfolio Selection," *Management Science*, October 1963.

Again, the Markowitz model of portfolio selection is a mathematical approach for deriving optimal portfolios; that is, portfolios that satisfy the following conditions.

1. The least risk for a given level of expected return (minimum-variance portfolios)
2. The greatest expected return for a given level of risk (efficient portfolios)

How does a portfolio manager apply these techniques in the real world?

The process would normally begin with a universe of securities available to the fund manager. These securities would be determined by the goals and objectives of the mutual fund. For example, a portfolio manager who runs a mutual fund specializing in health-care stocks would be required to select securities from the universe of health-care stocks. This would greatly reduce the analysis of the fund manager by limiting the number of securities available.

The next step in the process would be to determine the proportions of each security to be included in the portfolio. To do this, the fund manager would begin by setting a target rate of return for the portfolio. After determining the target rate of return, the fund manager can determine the different proportions of each security that will allow the portfolio to reach this target rate of return.

The final step in the process would be for the fund manager to find the portfolio with the lowest variance given the target rate of return. The next section uses a graphical approach to derive the optimal portfolios for the case of three securities.

Three-Security Empirical Solution

To faciliate a realistic example, actual data have been taken from a set of monthly returns generated by the Dow-Jones 30 Industrials. This example focuses on the returns and risk of the first three industrial companies—ALD (Allied Corporation), AA (Aluminum Company of America), and AMB (American Brands)—for the period January, 1980–December, 1984. The data used are tabulated in Table 8–3. Both graphical and mathematical analyses are employed to obtain an empirical solution.

Graphical Analysis. To begin to develop the efficient frontier graphically, it is necessary to move from the three dimensions necessitated by the three-security portfolio to a two-dimensional problem by transforming the third security into an implicit solution from the other two.[7] To do this it must be

---

[7] The process of finding the efficient frontier graphically described in this section was originally developed by Markowitz (1952). Francis and Archer (1979) have discussed this subject in detail.

TABLE 8-3   Data for Three Securities

Company	$E(r_i)$	σ_i^2	Cov (R_i, R_j)
Allied Corporation	0.0084	0.0066	$\sigma_{12} = 0.0022$
Aluminum Company of America	0.0127	0.0077	$\sigma_{23} = 0.0002$
American Brands	0.0187	0.0032	$\sigma_{13} = 0.0005$

noted that since the summation of the weights of the three securities is equal to unity, then implicitly:

$$W_3 = 1 - W_1 - W_2 \tag{8.15}$$

Additionally, the above relation may be substituted into Equation (8.1):

$$
\begin{aligned}
E(R_p) &= W_1 E(R_1) + W_2 E(R_2) + W_3 E(R_3) \\
&= W_1 E(R_1) + W_2 E(R_2) + (1 - W_1 - W_2) E(R_3) \\
&= W_1 E(R_1) + W_2 E(R_2) + E(R_3) - W_1 E(R_3) - W_2 E(R_3) \\
&= [E(R_1) - E(R_3)] W_1 + [E(R_2) - E(R_3)] W_2 + E(R_3)
\end{aligned}
\tag{8.16}
$$

Finally, inserting the values for the first and second securities yields:

$$
\begin{aligned}
E(R_p) &= (0.0084 - 0.0187) W_1 + (0.0127 - 0.0187) W_2 + 0.0187 \\
&= -0.0103 W_1 - 0.006 W_2 + 0.0187
\end{aligned}
\tag{8.17}
$$

As can be seen, Equation (8.17) is a linear function in two variables and as such is readily graphable. Since given a certain level of portfolio return the function will solve jointly for the weights of securities 1 and 2, it solves indirectly for the weight of security 3.

The variance formula shown in Equation (8.2) is converted in a similar manner by substituting in Equation (8.15) as follows:

$$\sigma_p^2 = \sum_{i=1}^{3} \sum_{j=1}^{3} W_i W_j \, \text{Cov} \, (R_i, R_j) = \text{Var} \, (R_p) \tag{8.18}$$

$$
\begin{aligned}
&= W_1^2 \sigma_{11} + W_2^2 \sigma_{22} + W_3^2 \sigma_{33} + 2W_1 W_2 \sigma_{12} + 2W_1 W_3 \sigma_{13} \\
&\quad + 2W_2 W_3 \sigma_{23} \\
&= W_1^2 \sigma_{11} + W_2^2 \sigma_{22} + (1 - W_1 - W_2)^2 \sigma_{33} + 2W_1 W_2 \sigma_{12} \\
&\quad + 2W_1 (1 - W_1 - W_2) \sigma_{13} + 2W_2 (1 - W_1 - W_2) \sigma_{23} \\
&= (\sigma_{11} + \sigma_{33} - 2\sigma_{13}) W_1^2 + (2\sigma_{33} + 2\sigma_{12} - 2\sigma_{13} - 2\sigma_{23}) W_1 W_2 \\
&\quad + (\sigma_{22} + \sigma_{33} - 2\sigma_{23}) W_2^2 + (-2\sigma_{33} + 2\sigma_{13}) W_1 \\
&\quad + (-2\sigma_{33} + 2\sigma_{23}) W_2 + \sigma_{33}
\end{aligned}
$$

Inserting the covariances and variances of the three securities from Table 8-3:

$$
\begin{aligned}
\sigma_p^2 &= [0.0066 + 0.0032 - 2(0.00050)]W_1^2 + [2(0.0032) + 2(0.0022) \\
&\quad - 2(0.0005) - 2(0.0002)]W_1W_2 + [0.0077 + 0.0032 \\
&\quad - 2(0.0002)]W_2^2 + [-2(0.0032) + 2(0.0005)]W_1 \\
&\quad + [-2(0.0032) + 2(0.0002)]W_2 + 0.0032 \\
&= 0.0088W_1^2 + 0.0094W_1W_2 + 0.0105W_2^2 - 0.0054W_1 \\
&\quad - 0.006W_2 + 0.0032
\end{aligned}
\tag{8.19}
$$

Minimum-Risk Portfolio. Part of the graphical solution is the determination of the minimum-risk portfolio. Standard partial derivatives are taken of Equation (8.18) with respect to the directly solved weight factors as follows:

$$
\begin{aligned}
\frac{\partial \sigma_p^2}{\partial W_1} &= 2(\sigma_{11} + \sigma_{33} - 2\sigma_{13})W_1 + (2\sigma_{33} + 2\sigma_{12} - 2\sigma_{13} - 2\sigma_{23})W_2 \\
&\quad + (-2\sigma_{33} + 2\sigma_{13}) = 0 \\
\frac{\partial \sigma_p^2}{\partial W_2} &= (2\sigma_{33} + 2\sigma_{12} - 2\sigma_{13} - 2\sigma_{23})W_1 + 2(\sigma_{22} + \sigma_{33} - 2\sigma_{23})W_2 \\
&\quad + (2\sigma_{23} - 2\sigma_{33}) = 0
\end{aligned}
\tag{8.20}
$$

When these two partial derivatives are set equal to zero and the unknown weight factors are solved for, the minimum risk portfolio is derived. Using the numeric values from Table 8–3:

$$
\begin{aligned}
\frac{\partial \sigma_p^2}{\partial W_1} &= 2[0.0066 + 0.0032 - 2(0.005)]W_1 + [2(0.0032) + 2(0.0022) \\
&\quad - 2(0.005) - 2(0.0002)]W_2 + [-2(0.0032) + 2(0.005)] \\
&= 0.0176W_1 + 0.0094W_2 - 0.0054 = 0 \\
\frac{\partial \sigma_p^2}{\partial W_2} &= [2(0.0032) + 2(0.0022) - 2(0.0005) - 2(0.0002)]W_1 + 2[0.0077 \\
&\quad + 0.0032 - 2(0.0002)]W_2 + [2(0.0002) - 2(0.0032)] \\
&= 0.0094W_1 + 0.021W_2 - 0.006 = 0
\end{aligned}
\tag{8.21}
$$

By solving these two equations simultaneously the weights of the minimum-risk portfolio are derived. This variance represents the lowest possible portfolio-variance level achievable, given variance and covariance data for these stocks. This can be represented by the point V of Figure 8–8. This solution is an algebraic exercise that yields $W_1 = 0.195$ and $W_2 = 0.203$ and therefore, through Equation (8.15), $W_3 = 0.602$.

The Iso-Expected Return Line. The variance and return equations have been derived and it is now time to complete the graphing procedure. To begin the graphing, the iso-expected return function lines must be delineated given various levels of expected return. The **iso-expected return line** is a line that has the same expected return on every point of the line. Utilizing Equation (8.17), three arbitrary returns are specified: 0.0167, 0.025, 0.029 (these correspond to 20-percent, 30-percent, and 35-percent annual returns). These three monthly returns are then set equal to Equation (8.17), and graphing is now possible by setting W_2 equal to zero or other values to solve for W_1. For example, if $W_2 = 0$ and $E(R_p) = 0.0167$, then W_1 can be solved as follows. (See Table 8–4 for final results.)

TABLE 8-4   Iso-Return Lines

	Target Return		
	0.0167	*0.025*	*0.029*
W_2	W_1	W_1	W_1
−1.0	0.776674	−0.02915	−0.4175
−0.5	0.485424	−0.32040	−0.70875
0.0	0.194174	−0.61165	−1
0.5	−0.09707	−0.90290	−1.29125
1.0	−0.38832	−1.19415	−1.5825

$$0.0167 = -0.0103W_1 - 0.006(0) + 0.0187$$
$$-0.0103W_1 = 0.0167 - 0.0187 = -0.0020$$
$$W_1 = 0.1942$$
$$0.0167 = -0.0103(0) - 0.006W_2 + 0.0187$$

In a similar fashion, other points are calculated and are listed in Table 8–4. A line may be drawn between the points to develop the various iso-expected return function lines. There are a multitude of possible return functions, but only these three lines (IR_1, IR_2 and IR_3) in terms of the data listed in Table 8–4 are shown in Figure 8–11. In Figure 8–11 vertical axis and horizontal axis represent W_1 and W_2, respectively. Each point on the iso-expected

FIGURE 8-11   Iso-Return Lines

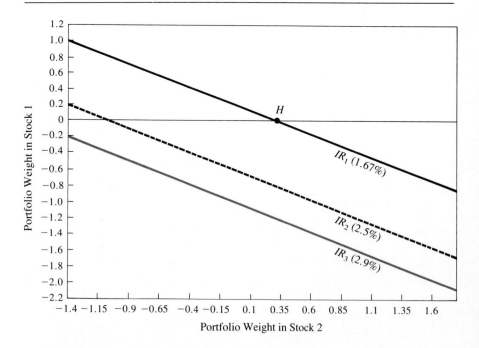

return line of Figure 8–11 represents a different combination of weights placed in the three securities. The issue now is to determine the portfolio that lies on the iso-expected return line with the lowest variance. Table 8–5 shows the portfolio variances as we move along the iso-expected return line. For example, moving along the iso-expected return line associated with an expected return of 1.67 percent, note that the minimum variance portfolio is associated with weights of 0.189 in security 2 and 0.084 in security 1.

Iso-Variance Ellipses. As is seen from Table 8–5 the minimum-variance portfolio can be found by moving along the iso-expected return line until the minimum-variance portfolio is reached. To better visualize this, examine the variance of a portfolio as the proportions in security 1 and security 2 are changed. A plot of these points will allow the family of iso-variance ellipses to be traced. The **iso-variance ellipses** are the ellipses that have the same variance on every point of this ellipse curve. It should be noted that an ellipse is an egg-shaped circle of points with a common center and orientation. The minimum-risk portfolio variance is the center of all possible ellipses as it has the least risk. It will be desirable, then, to find this minimum-risk value, as no other weighting scheme of these three securities will develop a lesser risk. The solutions of Equation (8.21) have determined that the weights associated with the minimum-risk portfolio are $W_1 = 0.195$, $W_2 = 0.203$, and $W_3 = 0.602$. Substituting this information listed in Table 8–3 into Equation (8.2), the variance of the minimum-risk portfolio is:

TABLE 8–5   Portfolio Variance along the Iso-Return Line

	0.0167		0.025		0.029	
W_2	W_1	Var	W_1	Var	W_1	Var
−1.000	0.776674	0.013513	−0.02915	0.020138	−0.41750	0.02741
−0.750	0.631049	0.009254	−0.17477	0.016051	−0.56313	0.02341
−0.500	0.485424	0.005995	−0.32040	0.012964	−0.70875	0.02040
−0.250	0.339799	0.003738	−0.46602	0.010879	−0.85438	0.01840
0.000	0.194174	0.002483	−0.61165	0.009795	−1.00000	0.01740
0.125	0.121362	0.002230	−0.68446	0.009628	−1.07281	0.01727*
0.146	0.109129	0.002213	−0.69669	0.009625*	−1.08505	0.01728
0.189	0.084082	0.002198*	−0.72174	0.009640	−1.11009	0.01731
0.250	0.048549	0.002228	−0.75727	0.009712	−1.14563	0.01740
0.500	−0.09707	0.002975	−0.90290	0.010631	−1.29125	0.01840
0.750	−0.24270	0.004724	−1.04852	0.012550	−1.43688	0.02040
1.000	−0.38832	0.007473	−1.19415	0.015472	−1.58250	0.02341

* Note: Underlined variances indicate minimum variance portfolios.

$$\text{Var}\,(R_p) = \sum_{i=1}^{n}\sum_{j=1}^{n}\; W_i W_j \, \text{Cov}(R_i,R_j)$$

$$= W_1^2\,\sigma_{11} + W_2^2\,\sigma_{22} + W_3^2\,\sigma_{33} + 2W_1\,W_2\,\sigma_{12} + 2W_2\,W_3\,\sigma_{23}$$
$$+ 2W_1\,W_3\,\sigma_{13}$$
$$= (0.195)^2\,(0.0066) + (0.203)^2\,(0.0077) + (0.602)^2\,(0.0032)$$
$$+ 2(0.195)(0.203)(0.0022) + 2(0.203)(0.602)(0.0002)$$
$$+ 2(0.195)(0.602)(0.005)$$
$$= 0.0021$$

Note that the variance of the minimum-risk portfolio can be used as a base for graphing the iso-variance ellipses. It can be completed by taking Equation (8.18) and holding one of the weights, say W_2 portfolio variance Var (R_p), constant. Bring the Var (R_p) to the right-hand side of the equation, and notice that the equation is of a quadratic form and can be solved using the quadratic formula:

$$W_1 = \frac{-b \pm \sqrt{b^2 - 4ac}}{2a} \tag{8.22}$$

where

$a\;=\;$ all coefficients of W_1^2;
$b\;=\;$ all coefficients of W_1; and
$c\;=\;$ all coefficients that are not multiplied by W_1 or W_1^2; or
$a\;=\;\sigma_{11} + \sigma_{33} - 2\sigma_{13}$;
$b\;=\;(2\sigma_{33} + 2\sigma_{12} - 2\sigma_{13} - 2\sigma_{23})W_2 - 2\sigma_{33} + 2\sigma_{13}$; and
$c\;=\;(\sigma_{22} + \sigma_{33} - 2\sigma_{23})W_2^2 + (-2\sigma_{33} + 2\sigma_{23})W_2 + \sigma_{33} - \text{Var}\,(R_p)$.

Substituting the numbers from the data of Table 8–3 into Equation (8.18) yields:

$$\text{Var}\,(R_P) = 0.0088W_1^2 + 0.0094W_1W_2 + 0.0105W_2^2 - 0.0054W_1$$
$$- 0.006W_2 + 0.0032$$
$$0 = 0.0088W_1^2 + 0.0094W_1W_2 + 0.0105\,W_2^2 - 0.0054W_1$$
$$- 0.006W_2 + 0.0032 - \text{Var}\,(R_P)$$

where

$a\;=\;0.0088$;
$b\;=\;0.0094W_2 - 0.0054$; and
$c\;=\;0.0105W_2^2 - 0.006W_2 + 0.0032 - \text{Var}\,(R_P)$.

When these expressions are plugged into the quadratic formula:

$$W_1 = \frac{-(0.0094W_2 - 0.0054) \pm \sqrt{b^2 - 4ac}}{2(0.0088)} \tag{8.23}$$

where

$$b^2 = (0.0094W_2 - 0.0054)^2$$
$$4ac = 4\{(0.0088)[0.0105W_2^2 - 0.006W_2 + 0.0032 - \text{Var }(R_p)]\}$$

This is a solution for the two points of W_1 (W_{11} and W_{12}) for a given portfolio variance and weight of the second security (W_2). When selecting the level of Var (R_p) *it is best to choose a value that is slightly larger than the minimum-risk value. This assures the calculation of a possible portfolio, since no portfolio of these three securities may have less risk. Additionally, an initial selection of a value for W_2* close to the minimum-risk portfolio W_2 will be desirable.

In sum, Equation (8.23) can be used to construct the iso-variance ellipse for given Var (R_p) in terms of arbitrary W_2. By jointly considering iso-expected return lines and iso-variance ellipses, efficient portfolios can be identified that are defined as the portfolios with the minimum variance given the expected rate of return. This task can be done by computer, as mentioned in the last section. To obtain the weights of an efficient portfolio, the following set of instructions must be entered into the computer.

1. Find the portfolio weights that minimize portfolio variance, subject to the target expected rate-of-return constraint. For this case, target rates of return are 1.67, 2.50, or 2.90 percent. The sum of the portfolio weights for all stocks in the portfolio must be equal to one. Mathematically, this instruction is defined in Equation (8.15).
2. The expected return and variance for a three-security portfolio is defined in Equations (8.16) and (8.18), respectively.
3. The estimated expected return, variance, and covariance as defined in Table 8–3 should be entered into the computer for estimation.

Using $E(R_p) = 1.67$ percent as an example, at point H in Figure 8–11, $W_1 = 0$ and $W_2 = 0.30$. From the relationship $W_3 = 1 - W_1 - W_2 = 1 - 0 - 0.30 = 0.70$. In other words, the point H represents three portfolio weights for the three stocks. The computer substitutes weights, variances, and covariances (listed in Table 8–3) into Equation (8.18) to obtain portfolio variance. The portfolio variance consistent with the weights of point H is computed. The computer now moves by some predetermined distance either northwest or southeast along the 1.67-percent iso-expected return line. From this kind of search, the minimum variance associated with this 1.67-percent iso-expected return line is identified to be 0.0022, as indicated in Table 8–5. By a similar procedure, the minimum variances associated with 2.5 percent and 2.9 percent iso-expected return lines are identified to be 0.0096 and 0.0173, respectively. When minimum variances associated with predefined iso-expected return are identified, the optimal weights associated with expected returns equal to 2.5 and 2.9 percent in terms of data indicated in Table 8–3 are also calculated. These results are indicated in Table 8–5.

Using the minimum variances associated with iso-expected returns (1.67,

2.5, and 2.9 percent), three iso-variance ellipses can be drawn as IV_1, IV_2, and IV_3.

When Var $(R_p) = 0.0022$ and $W_2 = 0.25$, the quadratic formula from Equation (8.23) above yields two roots.

$$W_{11} = \frac{-(-0.00305) + \sqrt{(-0.00305)^2 - 0.0000055}}{2(0.0088)}$$

$$= 0.284090$$

$$W_{12} = \frac{-(-0.00305) - \sqrt{(-0.00305)^2 - 0.0000055}}{2(0.0088)}$$

$$= 0.062500$$

To solve for W_{11} and W_{12} we need $b^2 > 4ac$. Solving for the variance:

$$7.989\ W_2^2 - 3.1159\ W_2 + 2.372 < -1,000\ \text{Var}\ (R_p)$$

If W_2 and Var (r_p) are not selected so that $b^2 > 4ac$, Equation (8.23) will require taking the square root of a negative number, and mathematically the solution will be an imaginary number. Solving W_2 in terms of an imaginary number is not meaningful; therefore we only consider the case when $b^2 > 4ac$.

The variance chosen was the minimum variance of the portfolio associated with $E(R_P) = 0.0167$. Actually, any variance might have realistically been chosen as long as it exceeded the minimum-risk portfolio variance. Table 8-6 lists various W_{11} and W_{12} values for given levels of W_2 and Var (R_p). In addition, Table 8-6 presents the value of b^2 and $4ac$ to check

TABLE 8-6   Various W_1 given W_2 and Var (R_p)

W_2	Var (R_p)	b	b^2	c	$4ac$	W_{11}	W_{12}
0.10	0.0022	−0.00446	0.000019	0.000505	0.000017	0.336051	0.170766
0.15	0.0022	−0.00399	0.000015	0.000336	0.000011	0.341529	0.111879
0.20	0.0022	−0.00352	0.000012	0.000022	0.000007	0.322474	0.077525
0.25	0.0022	−0.00305	0.000009	0.000156	0.000005	0.284090	0.062500
0.30	0.0022	−0.00258	0.000006	0.000145	0.000005	0.217383	0.075798
−0.75	0.0096	−0.01245	0.000155	0.004006	0.000141	0.919847	0.494925
0.00	0.0096	−0.0054	0.000029	−0.0064	−0.00022	1.213134	−0.59949
0.30	0.0096	−0.00258	0.000006	−0.00725	−0.00025	1.066330	−0.77314
0.50	0.0096	−0.007	0.000000	−0.00677	−0.00023	0.918105	−0.83855
1.15	0.0096	0.00541	0.000029	0.000586	0.000020	−0.14045	−0.47432
−1.15	0.0173	−0.01621	0.000262	0.006686	0.000235	1.218481	0.623563
−0.50	0.0173	−0.0101	0.000102	−0.00847	−0.00029	1.710695	−0.56296
0.00	0.0173	−0.0054	0.000029	−0.0141	−0.00049	1.609281	−0.99564
0.75	0.0173	0.00165	0.000002	−0.01269	−0.00044	1.110932	−1.29843
1.50	0.0173	0.0087	0.000075	0.000525	0.000018	−0.06456	−0.92407

FIGURE 8–12   Iso-Variance Ellipses

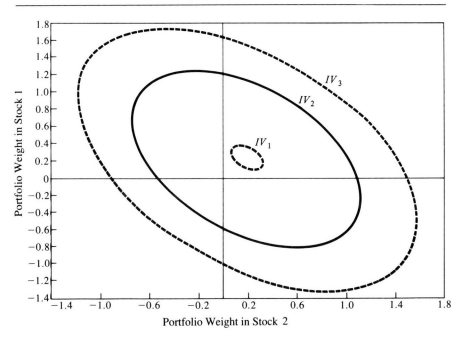

whether or not the root is a real number. It should be noticed that all possible variances are higher than the minimum-risk portfolio variance. Data from Table 8–6 are used to draw three iso-variance ellipses, as indicated in Figures 8–12 and 8–13.

The Critical Line and Efficient Frontier. After the iso-expected return functions and iso-variance ellipses have been plotted, it is an easy task to delineate the efficient frontier. By definition, the efficient portfolio is the portfolio with the highest return for any given risk. In Figure 8–13, the efficient portfolios are those where a given iso-expected return line is just tangent to the variance ellipse. *MRPABC* is denoted as the **critical line;** all portfolios that lie between points *MRP* and *C* are said to be efficient, and the weights of these portfolios may be read directly from the graph. From the graph, portfolio weights for the portfolios that minimize variances, given a 1.67-, 2.50-, or 2.90-percent expected rate of return are listed in Table 8–5. It is possible, given these various weights, to calculate the $E(R_P)$ and the variances of these portfolios, as indicated in Table 8–7. The efficient frontier is then developed by plotting each risk–return combination, as shown in Figure 8–14.

In this section a step-wise graphical approach has been employed to obtain optimal weights for a three-security portfolio. In the next section a mathematical optimization approach is used to calculate the optimal weight for a three-security portfolio.

FIGURE 8-13   Iso-Variance Ellipses and Iso-Return Lines

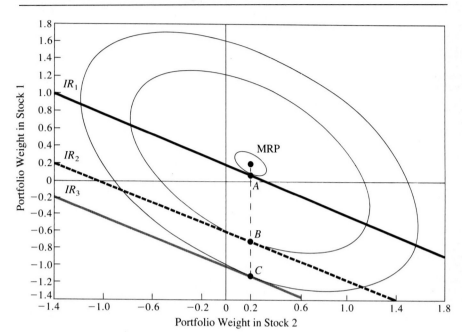

Mathematical Analysis.   The same efficient frontier can be obtained mathematically through the use of the Lagrangian multipliers. The Lagrangian method allows the minimization or maximization of an objective function when the objective function is subject to some constraints.

One of the goals of portfolio analysis is minimizing the risk or variance of the portfolio, subject to the portfolio's attaining some target expected rate of return, and also subject to the portfolio weights' summing to one. The problem can be stated mathematically:

$$\text{Min } \sigma_p^2 = \sum_{i=1}^{n} \sum_{j=1}^{n} W_i \, W_j \, \sigma_{ij}$$

TABLE 8-7   Weights, $\overline{R}_p$, and σ_p for Efficient Points

Portfolio*	W_1	W_2	W_3	$E(R_p)$	Var (R_p)	$\sigma(R_p)$
A	0.084	0.189	0.727	0.0167	0.0022	0.047
B	− .696	0.146	1.550	0.0250	0.0096	0.098
C	− 1.073	0.125	1.948	0.0290	0.0173	0.132

* Portfolios A, B, and C represent expected returns of 1.67, 2.5, and 2.9 percent, respectively.

FIGURE 8-14 The Efficient Frontier for the Data of Table 8-7

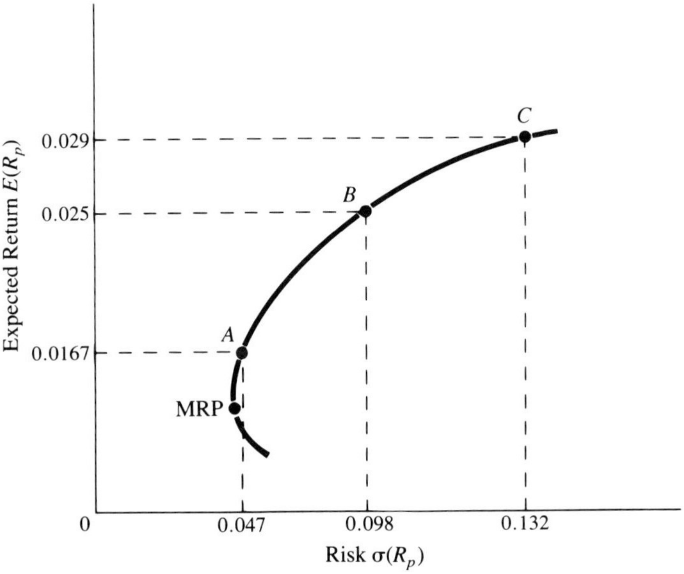

Subject to

(i)
$$\sum_{i=1}^{n} W_i \, E(R_i) = E^*$$

where E^* is the target expected return and

(ii)
$$\sum_{i=1}^{n} W_i = 1.0$$

The first constraint simply says that the expected return on the portfolio should equal the target return determined by the portfolio manager. The second constraint says that the weights of the securities invested in the portfolio must sum to one.

The Lagrangian objective function can be written:

$$C = \sum_{i=1}^{n} \sum_{j=1}^{n} W_i \, W_j \, \mathrm{Cov}\,(R_i, R_j) + \lambda_1 \left(1 - \sum_{i=1}^{n} W_i\right) + \lambda_2 \left[E^* - \sum_{i=1}^{n} W_i \, E(R_i)\right] \tag{8.11}$$

Taking the partial derivatives of this equation with respect to each of the variables, $W_1 \, W_2, \, W_3, \, \lambda_1, \, \lambda_2$, and setting the resulting five equations equal to zero yields the minimization of risk subject to the Lagrangian constraints. This system of five equations and five unknowns can be solved by the use of matrix algebra. Briefly, the Jacobian matrix of these equations is

$$\begin{bmatrix} 2\sigma_{11} & 2\sigma_{12} & 2\sigma_{13} & 1 & E(R_1) \\ 2\sigma_{21} & 2\sigma_{22} & 2\sigma_{23} & 1 & E(R_2) \\ 2\sigma_{31} & 2\sigma_{32} & 2\sigma_{33} & 1 & E(R_3) \\ 1 & 1 & 1 & 0 & 0 \\ E(R_1) & E(R_2) & E(R_3) & 0 & 0 \end{bmatrix} \times \begin{bmatrix} W_1 \\ W_2 \\ W_3 \\ \lambda_1 \\ \lambda_2 \end{bmatrix} = \begin{bmatrix} 0 \\ 0 \\ 0 \\ 1 \\ E^* \end{bmatrix} \quad \textbf{(8.24)}$$

Therefore, it is possible to premultiply both sides of the matrix equation of (8.24), AW = K, by the inverse of A (denoted A^{-1}) and solve for the W column. This is possible because all values in the A and K matrices are known or arbitrarily set.

The first problem is the inversion of the matrix of coefficients. First, derive the determinant of matrix A. Next, after developing the signed, inverted matrix of cofactors for A, divide the cofactors by the determinant, resulting in the inversion of the original matrix. Finally, premultiply the column vector for the investment weights.

Plugging the data listed in Table 8–3 and $E^* = 0.0167$ into the matrix above yields:

$$\begin{bmatrix} 0.0132 & 0.0044 & 0.001 & 1 & 0.0084 \\ 0.0044 & 0.0154 & 0.0004 & 1 & 0.0127 \\ 0.001 & 0.0004 & 0.0064 & 1 & 0.0187 \\ 1 & 1 & 1 & 0 & 0 \\ 0.0084 & 0.0127 & 0.0187 & 0 & 0 \end{bmatrix} \times \begin{bmatrix} W_1 \\ W_2 \\ W_3 \\ \lambda_1 \\ \lambda_2 \end{bmatrix} = \begin{bmatrix} 0 \\ 0 \\ 0 \\ 1 \\ 0.0167 \end{bmatrix} \quad \textbf{(8.25)}$$

When matrix A is properly inverted and postmultiplied by K, the solution vector $A^{-1}K$ is derived:

$$\begin{matrix} W & & A^{-1}K \\ \begin{bmatrix} W_1 \\ W_2 \\ W_3 \\ \lambda_1 \\ \lambda_2 \end{bmatrix} & = & \begin{bmatrix} 0.0844 \\ 0.1885 \\ 0.7271 \\ -0.2080 \\ -0.0009 \end{bmatrix} \end{matrix} \quad \textbf{(8.26)}$$

Using the matrix operation on the other two arbitrary returns yields the results shown in Table 8–7.

As can be seen in the composition of Portfolios B and C, the weights of security 1 are negative, implying that this security should be sold short in order to generate an efficient portfolio. It should be noted that the results of Table 8–7 are similar to those of Table 8–5. Therefore, both graphical and mathematical methods can be used to calculate the optimal weights.

With the knowledge of the efficient-portfolio weights given that $E(R_p)$ is equal to 0.0167, 0.0250, and 0.0290, the variances of the efficient portfolios may be derived from plugging the numbers into Equation (8.2). Taking the square root of the variances to derive the standard deviation, the various risk–return combinations can be plotted and the efficient frontier graphed, as shown in Figure 8–13 in the previous section. As can be seen from compar-

ing this figure to the graphical derivation of the efficient frontier derived graphically, the results are almost the same.

Portfolio Determination with Specific Adjustment for Short Selling

By using a definition of short sales developed by Lintner (1965) the computation procedure for the efficient frontier can be modified. Lintner defines short selling as putting up an amount of money equal to the value of the security sold short. Thus the short sale is a use rather than a source of funds to the short seller. The total funds the investor invests short, plus the funds invested long, must add up to the original investment. The proportion of funds invested short is $|X_i|$, since $X_i < 0$. The constraint in the minimization problem concerning the weights of the individual securities needs to be modified to incorporate this fact. Additionally, the final portfolio weight (output of the matrix inversion) must be rescaled so the sum of the absolute value of the weights equals one. By defining short sales in this manner, the efficient frontier does not extend to infinity (as shown in Figure 8–10A) but resembles the efficient frontier in Figure 8–10B.

Weekly rates of return (calculated from the weekly closing price listed in *The Wall Street Journal*) for IBM, Caterpillar, and Salomon Brothers are used to perform the analysis in this section. The sample period is from January to November, 1986. The Markowitz model determines optimal asset allocation by minimizing portfolio variance using a constrained optimization procedure:

$$\text{Min Var } (R_p) = \sum_{i=1}^{3} \sum_{j=1}^{3} W_i W_j \sigma_{ij} \tag{8.2}$$

Subject to:

(i)
$$\sum_{i=1}^{3} W_i E(R_i) = E^* \tag{8.1}$$

(ii)
$$\sum_{i=1}^{3} |W_i| = 1.0 \tag{8.1}$$

Where the E^* is the investors' desired rate of return, and where the absolute value of the weights $|W_i|$ allows for a given W_i to be negative (sold short) but maintains the requirement that all funds are invested or their sum equals one.

The Lagrangian function is

$$\text{Min } L = \sum_{i=1}^{n} \sum_{j=1}^{n} W_i W_j + \lambda_1 \sum_{i=1}^{n} [W_i E(R_i) - E^*] + \lambda_2 \left(\sum_{i=1}^{n} W_i - 1 \right)$$

Again, derivatives with respect to W_i's and λ's are found. Setting these equations equal to zero leaves the following system of equations in matrix form:

$$
\underset{C}{\begin{bmatrix}
2\sigma_{11} & 2\sigma_{12} & \cdots & 2\sigma_{1n} & E(R_1) & 1 \\
2\sigma_{21} & 2\sigma_{22} & \cdots & 2\sigma_{2n} & E(R_2) & 1 \\
\vdots & \vdots & & \vdots & \vdots & \vdots \\
2\sigma_{n1} & 2\sigma_{n2} & \cdots & 2\sigma_{nn} & E(R_n) & 1 \\
E(R_1) & E(R_2) & \cdots & E(R_n) & 0 & 0 \\
1 & 1 & \cdots & 1 & 0 & 0
\end{bmatrix}}
\times
\underset{X}{\begin{bmatrix}
W_1 \\ W_2 \\ \vdots \\ W_n \\ \lambda_1 \\ \lambda_2
\end{bmatrix}}
=
\underset{K}{\begin{bmatrix}
0 \\ 0 \\ \vdots \\ 0 \\ E^* \\ 1
\end{bmatrix}}
$$

To solve this matrix:

$$
\begin{aligned}
CX &= K \\
C^{-1}CX &= C^{-1}K \\
IX &= C^{-1}K \\
X &= C^{-1}K
\end{aligned}
$$

where

C^{-1} is the inverse of matrix C and
I is the identity matrix.

The solution to the above formula will give the weights in terms of E^*.

By using IBM, Caterpillar, and Salomon Brothers a three-security portfolio will be formed and optimal weights will be solved for.

Security	Monthly $E(R_i)$	σ_i^2	σ_{12}	σ_{13}	σ_{23}
Caterpillar	0.0010063	0.0068860	0.0017656		
IBM	0.018903	0.0029742		0.0037459	
Salomon Brothers	0.021642	0.0144070			0.0027304

Substituting these values into the matrix:

$$
\begin{bmatrix}
0.0138 & 0.0035 & 0.0075 & 0.0010 & 1 \\
0.0035 & 0.0059 & 0.0055 & 0.0189 & 1 \\
0.0075 & 0.0055 & 0.0288 & 0.0216 & 1 \\
0.0010 & 0.0189 & 0.0216 & 0 & 0 \\
1 & 1 & 1 & 0 & 0
\end{bmatrix}
\times
\begin{bmatrix}
W_1 \\ W_2 \\ W_3 \\ \lambda_1 \\ \lambda_2
\end{bmatrix}
=
\begin{bmatrix}
0 \\ 0 \\ 0 \\ E^* \\ 1
\end{bmatrix}
$$

$$E^* = 0.013$$

By solving using the identity-matrix technique the weights for the three securities can be obtained:

$$
\begin{aligned}
\text{Caterpillar} &= 0.322 \\
\text{IBM} &= 0.734 \\
\text{Salomon Brothers} &= -0.053
\end{aligned}
$$

By using the following relationship to rescale these weights so that the second constraint for the sum of the absolute values of the weights to equal one is satisfied:

$$W_{|A|} = \frac{|A|}{|A| + |B| + |C|} \qquad (8.27)$$

The rescaled absolute weights are:

$$W_{CP} = \frac{0.322}{0.322 + 0.734 + 0.053} = .0290$$

$$W_{IBM} = \frac{0.734}{0.322 + 0.734 + 0.053} = 0.661$$

$$W_{SB} = \frac{0.053}{0.322 + 0.734 + 0.053} = 0.048$$

The return on this portfolio is:

$$\overline{R}_p = (0.29)(0.0010063) + (0.661)(0.018903) + (-0.048)(0.021642)$$
$$= 1.17\%$$

The variance:

$$\sigma_p^2 = (0.29)^2 (0.0068860) + (0.661)^2 (0.0029742) + (-0.048)^2 (0.014407)$$
$$+ 2(0.29)(0.661)(0.0017656) + 2(0.28)(-0.048)(0.003749)$$
$$+ 2(0.661)(-0.048)(0.0027404)$$
$$= 0.00231$$

Portfolio Determination without Short Selling

The minimization problem under study can be modified to include the restriction of no short selling by adding a third constraint:

$$W_i \geq 0, \qquad i = 1, \ldots, N$$

The addition of this nonnegativity constraint precludes negative values for the weights (that is, no short selling). The problem now is a quadratic programming problem similar to the ones solved so far, except that the optimal portfolio may fall in an unfeasible region. In this circumstance the next best optimal portfolio is elected that meets all of the constraints. An example of this situation is shown in Figure 8–15.[8]

In Figure 8–15(a) the optimal portfolio is located in the region of positive values for weights W_i^*, and thereby satisfies the constraint $W_i^* \geq 0$. In Figure 8–15(b) the optimal portfolio shown by W_i^* falls in a region where W_i are negative, and so the constraint is not satisfied. The next best optimal portfolio is shown by B, and this is the solution of the problem that satisfies the nonnegativity constraint. Additional discussion of the problems is pre-

---

[8] In Figure 8–15(a) and (b) the vertical axis is defined as $(\overline{R}_p - R_f)/\sigma_p$, which is the Sharpe performance measure as defined in Chapter 7. $(\overline{R}_p - R_f)/\sigma_p$ is the objective function for portfolio optimization; it will be explored in Chapter 18.

FIGURE 8–15   Optimal Portfolio in Feasible and Unfeasible Regions

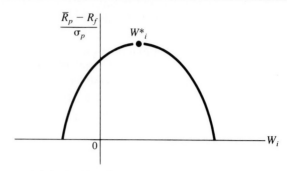

(a) Optimal Portfolio in Feasible Region ($W^*_i > 0$)

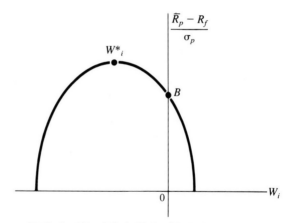

(b) Optimal Portfolio in Unfeasible Region ($W^*_i < 0$)

sented in Chapters 10 and 18. Most recently, Lewis (1988) has developed a simple algorithm for the portfolio-selection problem. His method is based on an interactive use of the Markowitz critical-line method for solving quadratic programs. In Figures 8–15(a) and (b) the vertical axis is defined as $(R_p - R_f)/\sigma_p$. This is a Sharpe performance mean, as defined in Chapter 7, and can be regarded as the objective function for a portfolio selection. (See Chapter 18 for the justification.)

SUMMARY

This chapter has focused on the foundations of Markowitz's model and on derivation of efficient frontier through the creation of efficient portfolios of varying risk and return. It has been shown that an investor can increase expected utility through portfolio diversification as long as there is no

perfect positive correlation among the component securities. The extent of the benefit increases as the correlation is lower, and also increases with the number of securities included.

The Markowitz model can be applied to develop the efficient frontier that delineates the optimal portfolios that match the greatest return with a given amount of risk. Also, this frontier shows the dominant portfolios as having the lowest risk given a stated return. This chapter has included methods of solving for the efficient frontier both graphically and through a combination of calculus and matrix algebra, with and without explicitly incorporating short selling.

Chapter 10 illustrates how the crushing computational load involved in implementing the Markowitz model can be alleviated through the use of the index portfolio, and how the tenets of the Markowitz efficient frontier are still met.

QUESTIONS AND PROBLEMS

1. Calculate the expected return of a portfolio 25 percent of which consists of stock A, with an expected return of 8 percent, and 75 percent of which is stock B, with an expected return of 12 percent.

2. Carefully explain why the variance of a portfolio is not represented by a weighted average of the variances of the individual securities which make up the portfolio.

3. Determine the risk preferences of investors with the following utility functions.
   (a) $U(w) = Ae^{Bw}$ $A, B > 0$
   (b) $U(w) = 5w + 2w^{-3}$
   (c) $U(w) = w^{-2/3}$
   (d) $U(w) = 3w - e^{-2w}$

4. What is a fair game? Will risk-averse investors enter into a fair game? risk-neutral investors? risk-preferring investors?

5. You are given the following information about two stocks.

State of Economy	Return A (percent)	Return B (percent)	Probability P_i
Recession	10	9	30
Normal Growth	11	7	20
Inflation	12	4	50

   (a) Calculate the risk and return for stock A and stock B.
   (b) Calculate the risk and return of a portfolio consisting 60 percent of stock A and 40 percent of stock B.

6. Define what is meant by an efficient portfolio and an inefficient portfolio. How can the dominance principle be used to define the concept of the efficient portfolio?

7. What is short selling? What is the efficient frontier? How does the efficient frontier change when short selling is not allowed?

8. Carefully explain how margin requirements on short sales effect the efficient frontier.

9. Draw the relationship between risk and return for a portfolio consisting of two stocks, A and B, when:
   (a) correlation between A and B is 0;
   (b) correlation between A and B is $+1$; and
   (c) correlation between A and B is -1.

10. You are given the following information about stocks A and B.

$$E(R_A) = 16\%$$
$$E(R_B) = 10\%$$
$$\sigma_A = 3\%$$
$$\sigma_B = 2\%$$
$$\rho_{A,B} = 0.8$$

You have $20,000 to invest.
   (a) Find the expected rate of return and variance on a portfolio consisting of the optimal weights for A and B.
   (b) Suppose you would like to invest an additional $5,000 in the portfolio consisting of A and B. If there is a risk-free asset that has a rate of return of 5 percent, explain how you would do this. What is the rate of return and variance on this investment?

11. You are the investment advisor for John Doe, a young hot-shot lawyer, and also for Jane Roe, an elderly widow. John can be considered a very aggressive investor, while Jane is a very conservative investor. Carefully explain how the portfolios you select for them would differ.

12. Discuss the procedure of using Markowitz's optimal portfolio-selection model to determine the optimal weights for a portfolio.

REFERENCES

Alexander, G. J., and J. C. Francis. *Portfolio Analysis*. Prentice-Hall, Inc., 1986.

Baumol, W. J. "An Expected Gain–Confidence Limit Criterion for Portfolio Selection." *Management Science* (October 1963), pp. 171–82.

Bertsekas, Dimitris. "Necessary and Sufficient Conditions for Existence of an Optimal Portfolio." *Journal of Economic Theory*, v. 8 (June 1974), pp. 235–47.

Black, Fischer. "Capital Market Equilibrium with Restricted Borrowing." *Journal of Business,* v. 45 (July 1972), pp. 444–55.

Blume, M. "Portfolio Theory: A Step Toward Its Practical Application." *Journal of Business,* v. 43 (April 1970), pp. 152–73.

Brealey, R. A., and S. D. Hodges. "Playing with Portfolios." *Journal of Finance,* v. 30 (March 1975), pp. 125–34.

Breen, William, and Richard Jackson. "An Efficient Algorithm for Solving Large-Scale Portfolio Problems." *Journal of Financial and Quantitative Analysis,* v. 6 (January 1971), pp. 627–37.

Brennan, M. J. "The Optimal Number of Securities in a Risky Asset Portfolio Where There Are Fixed Costs of Transaction: Theory and Some Empirical Results." *Journal of Financial and Quantitative Analysis,* v. 10 (September 1975), pp. 483–96.

Cohen, Kalman, and Jeffery Pogue. "An Empirical Evaluation of Alternative Portfolio-Selection Models." *Journal of Business,* v. 46 (April 1967), pp. 166–93.

Dyl, Edward A. "Negative Betas: The Attractions of Selling Short." *Journal of Portfolio Management,* v. 1 (Spring 1975), pp. 74–76.

Elton, E. J., and Martin Gruber. "Portfolio Theory When Investment Relatives Are Log Normally Distributed." *Journal of Finance,* v. 29 (September 1974), pp. 1265–73.

———, and M. E. Padberg. "Simple Criteria for Optimal Portfolio Selection." *Journal of Finance,* v. 11 (December 1976), pp. 1341–57.

———. "Simple Criteria for Optimal Portfolio Selection: Tracing Out the Efficient Frontier." *Journal of Finance,* v. 13 (March 1978), pp. 296–302.

Evans, J., and S. Archer. "Diversification and the Reduction of Dispersion: An Empirical Analysis." *Journal of Finance.* v. 3 (December 1968), pp. 761–67.

Fama, E. F. "Efficient Capital Markets: A Review of Theory and Empirical Work." *Journal of Finance,* v. 25 (May 1970), pp. 383–417.

Feller, W. *An Introduction to Probability Theory and Its Application,* v. 1. John Wiley and Sons, Inc., 1968.

Francis, J. C., and S. H. Archer. *Portfolio Analysis.* Prentice-Hall, Inc., 1979.

Gressis, N., George Philiippatos, and J. Hayya. "Multiperiod Portfolio Analysis and the Inefficiencies of the Market Portfolio." *Journal of Finance,* v. 31 (September 1976). pp.1115–26.

Henderson, J., and R. Quandt. *Microeconomic Theory: A Mathematical Approach,* 3d ed. McGraw-Hill, 1980.

Levy, H. and M. Sarnat. "A Note on Portfolio Selection and Investors' Wealth." *Journal of Financial and Quantitative Analysis,* v. 6 (January 1971), pp. 639–42.

Lewis, A. L. "A Simple Algorithm for the Portfolio Selection Problem." *Journal of Finance*, v. 43 (March 1988), pp. 71–82.

Lintner, John, "The Valuation of Risk Assets and the Selection of Risky Investments in Stock Portfolio and Capital Budgets," *Review of Economics and Statistics*, v. 47 (February 1965), pp. 13–27.

Mao, J. C. F. *Quantitative Analysis of Financial Decisions*. The Macmillan Company, 1968.

Markowitz, Harry M. *Portfolio Selection*. Cowles Foundation Monograph 16. John Wiley and Sons, Inc., 1959.

_____. "Portfolio Selection." *Journal of Finance*, v. 1 (December 1952), pp. 77–91.

_____. "Markowitz Revisited." *Financial Analysts Journal*, v. 32 (September/October 1976), pp. 47–52.

_____. *Mean-Variance Analysis in Portfolio Choice and Capital Markets*. Blackwell, 1987.

Martin, A. D., Jr. "Mathematical Programming of Portfolio Selections." *Management Science*, v. 1 (1955), pp. 152–66.

Merton, Robert. "An Analytical Derivation of Efficient Portfolio Frontier." *Journal of Financial and Quantitative Analysis*, v. 7 (September 1972), pp. 1851–72.

Mossin, Jan. "Optimal Multiperiod Portfolio Policies," *Journal of Business* (April 1968), pp. 215–29.

Ross, Stephen A. "On the General Validity of the Mean-Variance Approach in Large Markets," In *Financial Economics: Essays in Honor of Paul Cootner*, ed. by William F. Sharpe and Cathryn M. Cootner. Prentice-Hall, Inc., 1982, pp. 52–84.

Sharpe, W. F. *Portfolio Theory and Capital Markets*. McGraw-Hill, 1970.

Von Neumann, J., and O. Morgenstern. *Theory of Games and Economic Behavior*, 2nd ed. Princeton University Press, 1947.

9 Capital Asset Pricing Model and Beta Forecasting

One of the important financial theories is the **capital asset pricing model,** commonly referred to as **CAPM.** Briefly touched upon in Chapter 4, it constitutes the major topic of this chapter; in addition, alternative methods for forecasting beta (systematic risk) are discussed.

Using the concepts of basic portfolio analysis and the dominance principle discussed in the last two chapters, two alternative methods are employed to derive the CAPM. The discussion concerns how the market model can be used to decompose (that is, divide) risk into two components, systematic and unsystematic risk, as well as applications of the beta coefficient and procedures for forecasting a beta coefficient.

A graphical approach is first utilized to derive the CAPM, after which a mathematical approach to the derivation is developed that illustrates how the market model can be used to decompose total risk into two components. This is followed by a discussion of the importance of beta in security analysis and further exploration of the determination and forecasting of beta. The discussion closes with the applications and implications of the CAPM; and the appendix offers empirical evidence of the risk–return relationship.

A GRAPHICAL APPROACH TO THE DERIVATION OF THE CAPITAL ASSET PRICING MODEL

Following the risk–return tradeoff principle and the portfolio diversification process, Sharpe (1964), Lintner (1965), and Mossin (1966) have developed an asset pricing model that can determine both the market price of a portfolio and the price of an individual security. They focus upon the pricing determination of those parts of security risk that can be eliminated through diversification as well as those that cannot.

Systematic risk is that part of total risk that results from the common variability of stock prices and the subsequent tendency of stock prices to move together with the general market. The other portion of total risk is **unsystematic risk,** the result of variables peculiar to the firm or industry—for example, a labor strike or resource shortage.

Systematic risk, also referred to as *market risk,* reflects the swings of the general market. Some stocks and portfolios can be very sensitive to movements in the market, while others show more independence and stability. The universally accepted notion for the measure of a stock's or a portfolio's relative sensitivity to the market based upon its past record is the Greek letter **beta (β).** The estimation, application, and forecasting of beta are discussed in the following sections.

The Lending, Borrowing, and Market Portfolios

Chapter 7 assumed that the efficient frontier was constructed with risky assets only. If there existed both risk-free and risky assets, investors would then have the choice of investing in one or the other, or in some combination of the two.

The concept of the risk-free asset is generally proxied by a government security, such as the Treasury bill (T-bill). T-bills are backed by the Federal government and are default free, hence considered riskless. An investor's portfolio can be composed of different combinations of riskless and risky assets. Figure 9-1 is a graph of different sets of portfolio opportunities; it includes the risk-free asset with a return of R_f. Since the riskless asset has zero risk, it is represented by a point on the vertical axis.

With the additional alternative to invest in risk-free assets that yield a return of R_f, the investor is able to create new combinations of portfolios that combine the risk-free assets with the risky assets. The investor is thus able to achieve any combination of risk and return that lies along the line connecting R_f and a tangent point M_p, the market portfolio. All portfolios along the line $R_f M_p C$ are preferred to the risky portfolio opportunities on the curve AM_pB. Therefore, the points on the line $R_f M_p C$ represent the best attainable combinations of risk and return.

At point R_f an investor has all available funds invested in the riskless asset and expects to receive the return of R_f. The portfolios along the line $R_f M_p$ are lending portfolios and contain combinations of investments in the risk-free asset and investments in a portfolio of risky assets M_p. These are called *lending portfolios* because investors are, in effect, lending money to the government at the risk-free rate, when they invest in the risk-free asset.

At point M_p the investor wants only risky assets and has put his wealth into the risky-asset portfolio, which is called the **market portfolio.** The investor at this point is neither lending nor borrowing. An alternative view is that at this point the investor may be lending and borrowing equal amounts that just offset each other. At M_p, investors receive a rate of return R_m and undertake risk σ_m.

FIGURE 9-1   The Capital Market Line

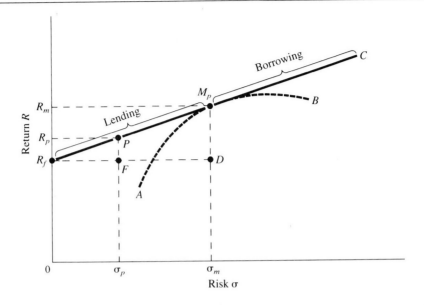

If it is assumed that the investor can borrow money at the risk-free rate R_f and invest this money in the risky portfolio M_p, he will be able to derive portfolios with higher rates of return but with higher risks along the line extending beyond M_pC. The portfolios along line M_pC are **borrowing portfolios.** They are so called because they contain a negative amount of the risk-free asset. The negative amount invested in the risk-free asset can be viewed as borrowing funds at the risk-free rate and investing in risky assets. The borrowing for investment is called *margin* and is controlled by the government. Therefore, the new efficient frontier becomes R_fM_pC and is referred to as the **capital market line (CML).** The capital market line describes the relationship between expected return and total risk.

The Capital Market Line

An illustration and explanation of the capital market line have already been provided; the equation for the CML is

$$E(R_p) = R_f + [E(R_m) - R_f]\frac{\sigma_p}{\sigma_m} \tag{9.1}$$

where:

$$R_f = \text{the risk-free rate;}$$
$$R_m = \text{return on market portfolio } M_p;$$
$$R_p = \text{return on the portfolio consisting of the risk-free asset and portfolio } M_p; \text{ and}$$
$$\sigma_p, \sigma_m = \text{the standard deviations of the portfolio and the market, respectively.}$$

The implementation of Equation (9.1) can be explained graphically. An investor has three choices in terms of investments. He may invest in the riskless asset R_f, in the market portfolio M_p, or in any other efficient portfolio along the capital market line, such as portfolio P of Figure 9–1.

If the investor puts his money into the riskless asset he can receive a certain return of R_f; if his investments are put into the market portfolio he can expect an average return of R_m and risk of σ_m; if he invests in portfolio P he can expect an average return of R_p with risk of σ_p. The difference between R_m and R_f ($R_m - R_f$) is called the **market risk premium.**

The investor of portfolio P only needs to take on risk of σ_p, so his risk premium is ($R_p - R_f$). This is less than the market risk premium because the investor is taking on a smaller amount of risk, $\sigma_p < \sigma_m$.

By geometric theory, triangles $R_f PF$ and $R_f M_p D$ are similar. Consequently, they are directly proportional. Thus:

$$E(R_p) - R_f = [E(R_m) - R_f] \frac{\sigma_p}{\sigma_m}$$

At equilibrium all investors will want to hold a combination of the risk-free asset and the tangency portfolio (M_p). Since the market is cleared at equilibrium—that is, prices are such that the demand for all marketable assets equals their supply—the tangency portfolio M_p must represent the market portfolio. An individual security's proportional makeup (X_i) in the market portfolio will be the ratio of its market value (its equilibrium price times the total number of shares outstanding) to the total market value of all securities in the market, or:

$$X_i = \frac{\text{Market value of individual asset}}{\text{Market value of all assets}} \qquad \textbf{(9.2)}$$

Thus at equilibrium prices are such that supply is equated to demand, and all securities in the market will be represented in the market portfolio according to their market value.

Given the capital market line (CML), assuming that investors are interested only in mean and variance of return, the CML will dominate all other attainable portfolios and securities because of the dominance principle, as discussed in Chapter 7. This implies that they will attempt to put some portion of their wealth into the market portfolio of risky assets, depending on their individual risk preference.

Since it has been established that the market portfolio is the only relevant portfolio of risky assets, the relevant risk measure of any individual security is its contribution to the risk of the market portfolio. The beta coefficient relates the covariance between security and market to the market's total variance, and it is the relevant market-risk measure. This will be explored in the next two sections. Notationally, beta is:

$$\beta_i = \frac{\sigma_{im}}{\sigma_m^2} = \frac{\text{Cov}(R_i, R_m)}{\text{Var}(R_m)}$$

Sample Problem 9.1 provides further illustration about risk/return tradeoffs.

Sample Problem 9.1

Describe the kinds of assets that could characterize the risk/return tradeoffs depicted by A, B, and C in the figure.

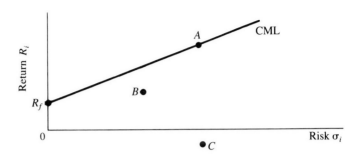

Solution

A is a correctly priced asset, perhaps a stock or a portfolio. B is an overpriced asset, perhaps a bond selling at too large a premium. C is an asset with expected negative return—for example, a lottery ticket. The price of the lottery ticket is too high to be justified by the expected value of winning the jackpot. Even though the jackpot may be large, the probability of winning it is very small, hence its expected value is small. Therefore, the cost of the ticket is greater than the expected value of winning, which yields a negative return

The Security Market Line—The Capital Asset Pricing Model

An asset's systematic risk with the market, β, is the only relevant risk measure of capital asset pricing for the individual asset and the portfolio. Consequently, a derivation of the relationship between systematic risk and return can be made where the expected linear relationship between these two variables is referred to as the **security market line (SML),** illustrated by Figure 9–2.

To derive the graphical picture of the SML it is necessary to list a few assumptions concerning the investors and the securities market.

1. Investors are risk averse.
2. The CAPM is a one-period model because it is assumed that investors maximize the utility of their end-of-period wealth.
3. All investors have the same efficient frontier—that is, they have homogeneous expectations concerning asset returns and risk.
4. Portfolios can be characterized by their means and variances.

FIGURE 9-2   The Capital Asset Pricing Model Showing the Security Market Line

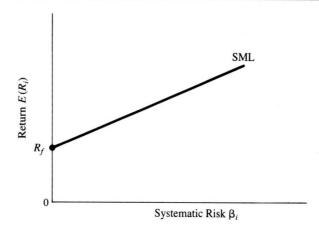

5. There exists a risk-free asset with a return R_f, the rate at which all investors borrow or lend. The borrowing rate is equal to the lending rate.
6. All assets are marketable and perfectly divisible, and their supplies are fixed.
7. There are no transaction costs.
8. Investors have all information available to them at no cost.
9. There are no taxes or regulations associated with trading.

All individual assets or portfolios will fall along the SML. The position of an asset will depend on its systematic risk or beta. The required risk premium for the market is $R_m - R_f$, and β_m is equal to one. Given the SML, the return on a risky asset is equal to:

$$E(R_i) = R_f + \beta_i\,[E(R_m) - R_f] \qquad (9.3)$$

where:

$$
\begin{aligned}
E(R_i) &= \text{the expected rate of return for asset } i; \\
R_f &= \text{the expected risk-free rate;} \\
\beta_i &= \text{the measure of normalized systematic risk (beta) of asset } i; \text{ and} \\
E(R_m) &= \text{the expected return on the market portfolio.}
\end{aligned}
$$

(Note: This security market line is also generally called the capital asset pricing model (CAPM). The mathematical derivation of this model will be shown in the next section.)

The relationship between the CML and the SML can be seen by rearranging the definition of the beta coefficient:

$$\beta_i = \frac{\text{Cov }(R_i, R_m)}{\text{Var }(R_m)} = \frac{\sigma_{im}}{\sigma_m^2} = \frac{\rho_{i,m}\sigma_i\sigma_m}{\sigma_m^2} = \frac{\rho_{i,m}\sigma_i}{\sigma_m} \qquad (9.4)$$

where:

σ_i = standard deviation of a security's rate of return;
σ_m = standard deviation of the market rate of return;
$\rho_{i,m}$ = the correlation coefficient of R_i and R_m; and

$$\rho_{im} = \frac{\sigma_{im}}{\sigma_i \sigma_m}.$$

If $\rho_{im} = 1$, then Equation (9.3) reduces to:

$$E(R_i) = R_f + \frac{\sigma_i}{\sigma_m} [E(R_m) - R_f] \qquad (9.3')$$

If $\rho_{i,m} = 1$, this implies that this portfolio is an efficient portfolio. If i is an individual security, it implies that the returns and risks associated with the asset are perfectly correlated with the market as a whole. There are several implications:

1. Equation (9.3) is a generalized case of Equation (9.3′).
2. The SML instead of the CML should be used to price an individual security or an inefficient portfolio.
3. The CML prices the risk premium in terms of total risk, and the SML prices the risk premium in terms of systematic risk.

Sample Problem 9.2 provides further illustration.

Sample Problem 9.2

Suppose the expected return on the market portfolio is 10% and that $R_f = 6$ percent. Further, suppose that you were confronted with an investment opportunity to buy a security with return expected to be 12 percent and with $\beta = 1.2$. Should you undertake this investment?

Solution

$$R_i = a + b\beta_i$$

for the market portfolio with $\beta = 1$ we have

$$0.10 = a + (b \times 1) = a + b$$

and for the risk-free rate with $\beta = 0$, we have

$$0.06 = a + (b \times 0) = a$$

Solving these equations for a and b yields:

$$a = 0.06$$
$$b = 0.04$$

For the security with $\beta = 1.2$ the expected return given the SML is

$$R_i = 0.06 + 0.04(1.2) = 0.108$$

Since 12% > 10.8%, the security is undervalued—that is, the security should be purchased since its return is above the equilibrium return of 10.8 percent for that level of risk●

MATHEMATICAL APPROACH TO THE DERIVATION OF THE CAPITAL ASSET PRICING MODEL

Using the assumptions about efficient and perfect markets stated earlier in the chapter, we can show how Sharpe derived the capital asset pricing model (CAPM).

Sharpe (1964) used a general risky asset that did not lie along the CML and dubbed it I. Risk and return for the possible combinations of security I with the market portfolio M are shown by Figure 9–3. The average return and standard deviation for any I–M combination can be approached in the Markowitz fashion for a two-asset case:

(i) $$E(R_p) = w_i E(R_i) + (1 - w_i) E(R_m)$$

(ii) $$\sigma(R_p) = (w_i^2\sigma_i^2 + (1 - w_i)^2\sigma_m^2 + 2(1 - w_i)w_i\sigma_{im})^{1/2}$$

(9.5)

in which w_i represents excess demand for I or demand greater than its equilibrium weight in portfolio M.

The changes in mean and standard deviation as the proportion w_i changes are represented by:

$$\frac{\partial E(R_p)}{\partial w_i} = E(R_i) - E(R_m)$$

$$\frac{\partial \sigma(R_p)}{\partial w_i} = \frac{1/2[(w_i^2\sigma_i^2 + (1 - w_i)^2\sigma_m^2 + 2w_i(1 - w_i)\sigma_{im})]^{-1/2}}{\times [(2w_i\sigma_i^2 - 2\sigma_m^2 + 2w_i\sigma_m^2 + 2\sigma_{im} - 4w_i\sigma_{im})]} \quad \textbf{(9.6)}$$

FIGURE 9–3   The Opportunity Set Provided by Combinations of Risky Asset *I* and the Market Portfolio *M*

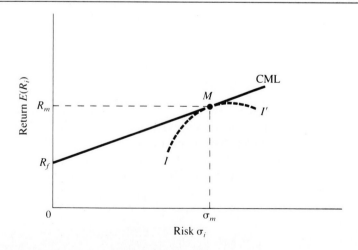

When $w_i = 0$, the ith security is held in proportion to its total market value, and there is no excess demand for security I. This is the key insight to Sharpe's argument, for when $w_i = 0$, it is possible to equate the slope of the curve IMI' with the capital market line, thus obtaining an expression for the return on any risky security I. At equilibrium when $w_i = 0$, the slope along the IMI' curve will be equal to

$$\frac{\partial E(R_f)}{\partial \sigma(R_p)} = \frac{\dfrac{\partial E(R_p)}{\partial w_i}}{\dfrac{\partial \sigma(R_p)}{\partial w_i}} = \frac{E(R_i) - E(R_m)}{\dfrac{\sigma_{im} - \sigma_{im}^2}{\sigma_m}} \tag{9.7}$$

The slope of the capital market line at point M is

$$\frac{E(R_m) - R_f}{\sigma_m} \tag{9.8}$$

Setting Equation (9.7) equal to Equation (9.8) and rearranging the terms to solve for $E(R_i)$ gives the equation for the security market line or CAPM:

$$E(R_i) = R_f + [E(R_m) - R_f]\frac{\sigma_{im}}{\sigma_m^2} \tag{9.9}$$

This represents the return on any risky asset I. At equilibrium, every risky asset will be priced so that it lies along the security market line. It should be noted that the term σ_{im}/σ_m^2 represents the beta coefficient for the regression of R_i vs. R_m, so that Equation (9.9) can be rewritten as

$$E(R_i) = R_f + [E(R_m) - R_f]\beta_i \tag{9.10}$$

which is the formula for the CAPM.

THE MARKET MODEL AND RISK DECOMPOSITION

To use the capital asset pricing model the market model must be employed to estimate the beta (systematic risk). In addition, the market model can be used to do risk decomposition. Both the market model and risk decomposition are discussed in this section.

The Market Model

As noted previously, the total risk of a portfolio or security can be conceived as the sum of its systematic and unsystematic risks. The equation that expresses these concepts states that the return on any asset at time t can be expressed as a linear function of the market return at time t plus a random-error component. Thus, the market model is expressed as:

$$R_{i,t} = \alpha_i + \beta_i R_{m,t} + e_{i,t} \tag{9.11}$$

where:

$R_{i,t}$ = the return of the ith security in time t;
α_i = the intercept of the regression;
β_i = the slope;
$R_{m,t}$ = the market return at time t; and
$e_{i,t}$ = random error term.

Risk Decomposition

The regression model of Equation (9.11), which describes the risky asset's characteristics relative to the market portfolio, is also called the *characteristic line*. Since beta is the slope coefficient for this regression (market model) it demonstrates how responsive returns for the individual earning assets are to the market portfolio. By using the market model, the total variance for security i (σ_i^2) can be represented by and decomposed into:

$$\sigma_i^2 = \beta_i^2 \sigma_m^2 + \sigma_{ei}^2 \qquad (9.12)$$

in which $\beta_i^2 \sigma_m^2$ is the systematic-risk component of total risk and σ_{ei}^2 is the unsystematic component.

The CAPM as developed here is expressed in terms of expected values. Since expected values are not directly measured, we must transform the CAPM into an expression that uses observable variables. Assuming that on average expected returns $E(R_{i,t})$ for a security equal realized returns, returns can be expressed as:

$$R_{i,t} = E(R_{i,t}) + \beta_i[R_{m,t} - E(R_{m,t})] + e_{i,t} \qquad (9.13)$$

in which $e_{i,t}$ is a random error term.

Assuming that the expected value of the error term is 0, that it is uncorrelated with the term $[R_{m,t} - E(R_{m,t})]$, and that Cov $(e_{i,t}, e_{i,t-1}) = 0$, the expression for $E(R_{i,t})$ can be substituted from the CAPM equation (9.10) into (9.13):

$$R_{i,t} = R_{f,t} + [E(R_{m,t}) - R_{f,t}]\beta_i + [R_{m,t} - E(R_{m,t})]\beta_i + e_{i,t}$$

Simplifying this equation:

$$R_{i,t} - R_{f,t} = \alpha_i + \beta_i(R_{m,t} - R_{f,t}) + e_{i,t} \qquad (9.14)$$

where α_i is the intercept. All variables of Equation (9.14) can be estimated from observed data. Equation (9.14) is called the **risk-premium version** of the market model. It is similar to the market model indicated in Equation (9.11), except that instead of using the total returns R_i and R_m, it uses the risk-premium portion of the returns, or $R_i - R_f$ and $R_m - R_f$. Sample Problem 9.3 provides further illustration.

Sample Problem 9.3

To show how Equations (9.11) and (9.12) can be used, we will use monthly return data from Pennzoil and Coca Cola. The time period covers January, 1980 to December, 1984. Their average return, beta coefficient, total variance, and residual variance are as indicated in the table below. We can see that Pennzoil with $\beta = 1.3825$ is more sensitive to the fluctuations of the market than Coca Cola with $\beta = 0.44978$.

	Return $\overline{R}_i$	Beta β_i	Residual Variance σ^2_{ei}	Total Variance σ^2_i
Pennzoil	0.010228	1.3825	0.007343	0.010791
Coca Cola	0.016460	0.44978	0.002868	0.003163

Both the magnitude of total variance and beta of Pennzoil were larger than for Coca Cola, although the average rates of return for Coca Cola were higher for Pennzoil. Hence Coca Cola was a more desirable security, if that was the only choice the investor had●

Why Beta Is Important for Security Analysis

Implications and applications of beta coefficients in security analysis will be discussed in this section. Beta is used as a measurement of risk: it gauges the sensitivity of a stock or portfolio relative to the market, as indicated in Equation (9.11). A beta of 1.0 is characteristic of a broad market index such as the NYSE index or the S&P 500. A beta of 2.0 indicates that the stock will swing twice as far in either direction than a fall or rise in the market average. If the market gains 15 percent, a security of beta $= 2$ is expected to gain 30 percent. Conversely, should the market fall 15 percent, the stock is expected to fall 30 percent.

A beta of 0.50 indicates that the stock is more stable than the market and will move only half as much as the market. For example, if the market loses 20 percent, a stock with beta $= 0.50$ will lose only 10 percent of the market; and if the market should gain 20 percent, the stock will gain only 10 percent. High-beta stocks have been classified as aggressive while low-beta stocks are referred to as defensive. From the table in Sample Problem 9.3 it is clear that Pennzoil is an offensive stock while Coca Cola is a defensive stock.

The CAPM has illustrated the concept that risks are associated with portfolios where the relevant (systematic) risk of an individual security is dependent upon the security's effect on portfolio risk. Therefore, the CAPM equation $E(R_i) = R_f + \beta_i [E(R_m) - R_f]$ represents a description of how rates

of return are established in the marketplace assuming investors behave according to the assumptions of the model. Thus a stock's beta measures its contributions to the risk of the portfolio and is therefore a measure of the stock's riskiness relative to the market.

In the previous section it was found that the rates of return of stock i are presumed to bear a linear relationship with the market rate of return as defined in Equation (9.11). Equation (9.11) is a fixed-coefficent market model. Following Fabozzi and Francis (1978), Sunder (1980), and Lee and Chen (1980), a random-coefficient market model can be defined as Equation (9.15A) or Equation (9.15B):

$$R_{it} = \alpha_i + \beta_{it} R_{mt} + e_{it} \tag{9.15A}$$
$$R_{it} - R_{ft} = \alpha_i' + \beta_{it}' (R_{mt} - R_{ft}) + e_{it} \tag{9.15B}$$

in which $\beta_{it} = \beta_i + \eta_{it}$. η_{it} represents the random fluctuation associated with the beta coefficient. Using the random-coefficient market model, the total risk can be decomposed into three components, as defined in Equation (9.16):

$$\sigma_i^2 = \beta_j^2 \sigma_m^2 + \sigma_{\epsilon i}^2 + \sigma_\eta^2 \sigma_m^2 \tag{9.16}$$

in which $\sigma_\eta^2 \sigma_m^2$ represents an interaction risk between the market and the random fluctuation of the β. Equation (9.16) is a generalized case of Equation (9.12). It contains systematic risk, unsystematic risk, and a risk term that reflects any interaction between the systematic and unsystematic risk.

Both fixed-coefficient and random-coefficient market models can be used to do security analysis and portfolio selection, discussed later in this text.

The relationship between total risk, market risk, and firm-specific risk can be shown as:

Total risk = Market risk + Firm-specific risk

Since firm-specific risk can be eliminated by diversification:

Relevant risk = Market risk

Beta is important for the investment manager because it can be used (1) to select individual stocks for investment; (2) to construct portfolios of financial assets with desired levels of risk and return; and (3) to evaluate the performance of portfolio managers. Details of the various uses of beta and the CAPM are provided later in this text. Sample Problem 9.4 provides further illustration.

Sample Problem 9.4

Given the SML $\overline{R}_i = 0.06 + 0.08\beta_i$, what should the expected return of a security be if it has a β twice as great as a similar security returning 18 percent?

Solution

$$\overline{R}_i = 0.06 + 0.08\beta = 0.18$$

Solving for β yields

$$\beta = 1.5$$

Therefore, the security's β is $2 \times 1.5 = 3.0$ and the required return is:

$$\overline{R}_i = 0.06 + 0.08(3.0)$$
$$= 0.30$$

A 30-percent return is required●

Determination of Systematic Risk

As mentioned above, systematic risk is nondiversifiable because it runs across industries and companies and affects all securities. Chapter 7 discussed many factors that determine risk. At this point we are interested only in those management decisions that can be related to the degree of systematic risk a firm exhibits—namely, the operating decisions and the financing decisions of management.

There are two dimensions of risk that affect a firm's systematic risk. The first is **financial risk,** the additional risk placed on the firm and its stockholders due to the firm's decision to be leveraged—that is, to take on additional debt. The second, **business risk,** is the riskiness involved with a firm's operations, if it takes on no debt.

A particular firm's capital structure affects the riskiness inherent in the company's common stock and thus affects its required rate of return and the price of the stock. A company's capital-structure policy requires choosing between risk and return. Taking on increasing levels of debt increases the riskiness of the firm's earning stream, but it usually also results in a higher expected rate of return. High levels of risk tend to lower a stock's price, but a high level of expected rates of return tends to raise it. Therefore, striking a balance with the optimal capital structure maximizes the price of the stock.

Business risk is the risk inherent in a firm's operations. It can also be defined as the uncertainty inherent in projection of future operating income or **earnings before interest and taxes (EBIT).** Fluctuations in EBIT can result from a number of factors. On the national level these can be economic factors such as inflationary or recessionary times. At the industry level some factors may be the level of competition between similar industries, natural or manmade catastrophes, labor strikes, price controls, and so on. There are a host of possibilities that affect EBIT by raising or lowering its level.

Uncertainty regarding future income flows is a function of the company's business risk. It may fluctuate among industries, among firms, and across time. The extent of business risk is dependent upon the firm and the industry. Cyclical industries such as steel production or automobile manufacture have especially high business risks because they are dependent upon the

strength of the economy. The retail food industry is considered to be quite stable because food is a necessary good that will be purchased regardless of the state of the economy.

Business risk is dependent upon several factors, the more important of which are listed here:

1. *Demand variability:* Stability in the levels of demand for the firm's product results in a reduction of business risk.

2. *Sales price variability:* Highly volatile prices result in high-risk, volatile markets; therefore, stability of prices results in reduction of business risk.

3. *Suppliers' price variability:* Firms whose input prices are highly variable are exposed to higher levels of risk.

4. *Output price flexibility relative to input prices:* As a result of inflation, a firm that is able to raise its output prices with increasing input costs minimizes its business risk.

When a firm uses debt or financial leverage, business risk and financial risk are concentrated on the stockholders. For example, if a firm is capitalized only with common equity, then the investors all share the business risk in proportion to their ownership of stock. If, however, a firm is 50 percent levered (50 percent of the corporation is financed by debt, the other half by common equity), the investors who put up the equity will then have to bear all business risk and some financial risk.

The effect of leverage upon return on assets (ROA) and return on equity (ROE) and its effect upon the stockholders can be generalized as follows:

1. The use of leverage or debt generally increases ROE.

2. The standard deviation of ROA (σ_{ROA}) is a measure of business risk while the standard deviation of ROE (σ_{ROE}) is a measure of the risk borne by stockholders. $\sigma_{ROA} = \sigma_{ROE}$ if the firm is not levered; otherwise with the use of debt $\sigma_{ROE} > \sigma_{ROA}$, an indication that business risk is being borne by stockholders.

3. The difference between σ_{ROE} and σ_{ROA} is the actual risk stockholders face and a measure of the increased risk resulting from financial leverage. Thus

$$\text{Risk of financial leverage} = \sigma_{ROE}^2 - \sigma_{ROA}^2$$

GROWTH RATES, ACCOUNTING BETAS, AND VARIANCE IN EBIT

Besides leverage, other financial variables associated with the firm can affect the beta coefficient. These are the growth rate, accounting beta, and variance in EBIT.

Growth Rates

The **growth rate** can be measured in terms of the growth in total assets or the growth in sales. It is determined by the percentage change between two periods.

$$\frac{\text{sales}_t - \text{sales}_{t-1}}{\text{sales}_{t-1}} \times 100\% \quad \text{or} \quad \frac{\text{total assets}_t - \text{total assets}_{t-1}}{\text{total assets}_{t-1}} \times 100\%$$

Another method to measure growth rates is presented by Higgins (1984). Growth and its management present special problems in financial planning. From a financial perspective growth is not always a blessing. Rapid growth can put considerable strain on a company's resources, and unless management is aware of this effect and takes active steps to control it, rapid growth can lead to bankruptcy. It becomes necessary, therefore, to define a company's sustainable growth rate:

$$\frac{\Delta S}{S} = g^* = \frac{P(1 - D)(1 + L)}{T - P(1 - D)(1 + L)} \tag{9.17}$$

where:

$P =$ the profit margin on all sales;
$D =$ the target dividend payout ratio;
$L =$ the target debt to equity ratio;
$T =$ the ratio of total assets to sales;
$S =$ annual sales; and
$\Delta S =$ the increase in sales during the year.

How is Equation (9.17) derived? Assuming a company is not raising new equity, the cash to finance growth must come from retained profits and new borrowings:

Retained profits = Profits − Dividends
= Profit margin × Total sales − Dividends
= $P(S + \Delta S)(1 - D)$

Further, because the company wants to maintain a target debt-to-equity ratio equal to L, each dollar added to the owners' equity enables it to increase its indebtedness by \$$L$. Since the owners' equity will rise by an amount equal to retained profits:

New borrowings = Retained profit × Target debt-to-equity ratio
= $P(S + \Delta S)(1 - D)L$

The use of cash represented by the increase in assets must equal the two sources of cash (retained profits and new borrowings):

$$\text{Uses of cash} = \text{Sources of cash}$$
$$\text{Increases in assets} = \text{Retained profits} + \text{New borrowings}$$
$$\Delta ST = P(S + \Delta S)(1 - D) + P(S + \Delta S)(1 - D)L$$
$$\Delta ST = P(1 - D)(1 + L)S + P(1 - D)(1 + L)\,\Delta S$$
$$\Delta S[T - P(1 - D)(1 + L)] = P(1 - D)(1 + L)S$$
$$\frac{\Delta S}{S} = \frac{P(1 - D)(1 + L)}{T - P(1 - D)(1 + L)}$$

In Equation (9.17) the $\Delta S/S$ or g^* is the firm's sustainable growth rate assuming no infusion of new equity. Therefore, a company's growth rate in sales must equal the indicated combination of four ratios, P, D, L, and T. In addition, if the company's growth rate differs from g^*, one or more of the ratios must change. For example, suppose a company grows at a rate in excess of g^*. Then it must either use its assets more efficiently or it must alter its financial policies. Efficiency is represented by the profit margin and asset-to-sales ratio. It therefore would need to increase its profit margin (P) or decrease its asset-to-sales ratio (T) in order to increase efficiency. Financial policies are represented by payout or leverage ratios. In this case, a decrease in its payout ratio (D) or an increase in its leverage (L) would be necessary to alter its financial policies to accommodate a different growth rate. It should be noted that increasing efficiency is not always possible and altering financial policies not always wise. [For other available methods to alter growth the reader is referred to Chapter 8 of Lee (1985).]

Accounting Beta

The **accounting beta** can be calculated from earnings-per-share data. Using EPS as an example, beta can be computed as follows:

$$\text{EPS}_{i,t} = \alpha_i + \beta_i \,\text{EPS}_{m,t} + e_{i,t}$$

where:

$\text{EPS}_{i,t}$ = earnings per share of firm i at time t;
$\text{EPS}_{m,t}$ = earnings per share of market average at time t; and
$e_{i,t}$ = error term.

The estimate of β_i is the EPS type of accounting beta.

Variance in EBIT

The **variance in EBIT** (X) can be defined as:

$$\frac{\sum_{t=1}^{n} (X_t - \overline{X})^2}{n - 1}$$

in which X_t = earnings before interest and taxes in period t, and $\overline{X}$ = average EBIT.

The total variance of EBIT can be used to measure the overall fluctuation of accounting earnings for a firm.

Capital–Labor Ratio

The **capital–labor ratio** has an impact upon the magnitude of the beta coefficient. In order to examine this impact it is necessary to examine the capital–labor ratio.

A production function is a function that can be seen as a function of labor and capital:

$$Q = f(K, L) \tag{9.18}$$

where K = capital and L = labor. K/L (the capital–labor ratio) is generally used to measure a firm's degree of capital intensity. Corporations often choose between increasing their capital intensity through installation of computers, use of robotics in place of labor, or increase in labor inputs. Small industries that specialize in hand-crafted or -tooled goods will have to increase their capital ratio in order to increase production. However, it has been the trend in recent years for many growth-oriented firms, whether manufacturers or other members of the business sector, to increase their efficiencies through increased investments in capital. Auto manufacturers are finding that robots are able to assemble cars of high and consistent quality at only a fraction of the cost of workers.

Capital intensity results in increased total risks and generally results in an increase in beta. Large investments are often needed to fully automate a plant or to computerize a bank completely. Taking on debt or issuing securities is normally how these capitalization increases are financed. If the capital–labor ratio is greater than one—that is, if K is greater than L—a firm is capital intensive. If the capital–labor ratio is less than one—that is, if K is less than L—then there is a reduction in capital intensity and a shift towards human-resource investment.

Fixed Costs and Variable Costs

Business risk is dependent upon the extent a firm builds **fixed costs** into its operations. If a large percentage of a firm's costs are fixed, costs cannot decline proportionally when demand falls off. If fixed costs are high, then a slight drop in sales can lead to large declines in EBIT. Therefore, the higher a firm's fixed costs are, the greater its business risk and, generally, the higher its beta.

A firm with a large amount of fixed costs is said to have a *large degree of operating leverage*. An example of these costs may be the highly skilled workers of an engineering firm. The firm cannot hire and fire experienced and highly skilled workers easily; therefore, the workers must be retained

and paid during a period of slack demand. Similarly, a firm that is highly leveraged will be characterized by the scenario that small changes in sales will result in large changes in operating income.

Variable costs have the opposite effect, because they are adjustable to the firm's needs. Should a drop in sales occur, variable costs can be lowered to meet the lowered output.

The extent to which firms can control their operating leverage is dependent upon their technological needs. Companies that require large investments in fixed assets—such as steel mills, auto manufacturers, and airlines—will have large fixed costs and operating leverages. Therefore, how much a company is willing to undertake operating leverages must come into play during capital-budgeting decisions. If the company is risk averse, it may opt for alternatives with smaller investments and fixed costs.

A company's having a larger percentage of fixed costs generally implies that they use more capital-intensive types of technology in production. For example, an auto manufacturer such as General Motors has a higher percentage of fixed costs than a food manufacturer such as General Foods. Therefore, GM's capital–labor ratio can be expected to be higher than that of General Foods. An implication of this phenomenon is that General Foods has a lower beta than General Motors.

Beta Forecasting

Analysts and investment managers who use the CAPM and beta are interested in whether the beta coefficient and the standard-deviation statistics for different securities and portfolios are stable through time or whether they change in a predictable fashion. If the beta coefficient and standard deviation are stable, then using a beta derived from current and historical price data is fine, because the beta today is the same as the beta in the future. However, if the beta coefficient and standard deviation are unstable or vary through time, the analyst or manager must forecast a beta's future value before employing it.

The available evidence on the stability of beta indicates that the beta on an individual security is generally not stable, while portfolios have stable betas. Hence we are faced with the problem of forecasting future betas in order to use the CAPM for individual securities. **Beta forecasting** refers to using the historical beta estimates or other historical financial information to forecast future betas.

Beaver, Kettler, and Scholes (1970) argue that if it is possible to find the underlying determinants of beta, such knowledge can be used to help forecast future betas. Beaver et al. use accounting information from the financial statements of firms to help in the estimation of beta. They conclude that using both price and accounting information shows promise for better beta estimates.

Rosenberg and Marathe (1975) use fifty-four factors in six categories to estimate betas. Their factors include historical price information, price/

earning ratios, financial ratios, and statistical measures associated with the market model. They support the notion that betas are determined by fundamental factors related to firms in addition to market pricing data.

Given that the most useful beta is one that can be forecasted correctly, and that the beta is related to the financial and business risk of the firm as well as the degree to which a firm's businesses co-vary with the total economy, it becomes necessary to determine the best way to forecast beta. The next section addresses this issue.

Market-Based versus Accounting-Based Beta Forecasting

Market-based beta forecasts are based upon market information alone. Historical betas of firms are used as a proxy for their future betas. This implies that the unadjusted sample beta, $\hat{\beta}_t$, is equal to the population value of future beta:

$$\beta_{t+1} = \hat{\beta}_t \qquad \text{(9.19A)}$$

Alternatively, there may be a systematic relationship between the estimated betas for the first period and those of the second period, as shown by Blume (1971):

$$\hat{\beta}_{i,t+1} = a_0 + a_1 \hat{\beta}_{i,t} \qquad \text{(9.19B)}$$

in which $\hat{\beta}_{i,t+1}$ and $\hat{\beta}_{i,t}$ estimated beta for the ith firm in period $t + 1$ and t respectively. Sample Problem 9.5 provides further illustration.

Sample Problem 9.5

If $\hat{a}_0 = 0.35$, $\hat{a}_1 = 0.80$, and $\hat{\beta}_{i,t} = 1.2$, then the future beta can be either

$$\beta_{t+1} = 1.2 \qquad \text{or}$$
$$\beta_{t+1} = 0.35 + (0.80)\,(1.2) = 1.31$$

It is worthwhile to note that Value Line uses Equation (9.19B) to estimate the future beta●

Accounting-based beta forecasts rely upon the relationships of accounting information such as the growth rate of the firm, EBIT, leverage, and the accounting beta as a basis for forecasting beta. To use accounting information in beta forecasts, the historical beta estimates are first cross-sectionally related to accounting information such as growth rate, variance of EBIT, leverage, accounting beta, and so on:

$$\beta_i = a_0 + a_1 X_{1i} + a_2 X_{2i} + a_j X_{ji} + \ldots + a_m X_{mi} \qquad \text{(9.20)}$$

where X_{ji} is the jth accounting variables for ith firm, and a_j is the regression coefficient.

Some researchers have found that the historically based beta is the best forecast, while others have found that the accounting-based beta is best. Lee, Newbold, Finnerty, and Chu (1986) use composite concepts to show that both accounting and market information are useful for beta forecasting. They find that neither beta forecasts based upon market information nor those based on accounting information are conditionally more efficient with respect to each other. It can be inferred, then, that each set of forecasts contains useful information for the prediction of systematic risk.

The statistical procedure used by Lee et al. (1986) is the ordinary least-squares method. Ordinary least squares is a statistical procedure for finding the best fitting straight line for a set of points; it seems in many respects a formalization of the procedure employed when fitting a line by eye. For instance, when visually fitting a line to a set of data, the ruler is moved until it appears that the deviations of the points from the prospective line have been minimized. If the predicted value of y_i (dependent variable) obtained from the fitted line is denoted as $\hat{y}_i$, the prediction equation becomes:

$$\hat{y}_i = \hat{\beta}_0 + \hat{\beta}_1 x_i,$$

where $\hat{\beta}_0$ and $\hat{\beta}_1$ represent estimates of the true β_0 and β_1; x_i is an independent variable.

Graphically, the vertical lines drawn from the prediction line to each point represent the deviations of the points from the predicted value of y. Thus the deviation of the ith point is $y_i - \hat{y}_i$, where:

$$\hat{y}_i = \hat{\beta}_0 + \hat{\beta}_1 x_i$$

In order to find the best fit it is necessary to minimize the deviations of the points. A criterion of best fit that is often employed is known as the *principle of least squares*. It may be stated as follows: Choose the best fitting line as the one that minimizes the sum of squares of the errors (SSE) of the observed values of y from those predicted. Expressed mathematically:

$$\text{SSE} = \sum_{i=1}^{n} (y_i - \hat{y}_i)^2$$

Further, the mean sum of squares of the error (MSSE) of the observed values of y could be minimized from the predicted mean. Expressed mathematically:

$$\text{MSSE} = \frac{\sum_{i=1}^{n} (y_i - \hat{y}_i)^2}{n}$$

Mincer and Zarnowitz (1969) suggest a decomposition of the mean squared error term into three components representing bias, inefficiency, and random error. Mathematically, this is represented:

$$\frac{\sum_{i=1}^{n} (y_i - \hat{y}_i)^2}{n} = (\bar{y} - \hat{y}_i)^2 + (S_y - \rho S_y)^2 + (1 - \rho^2)S_y^2$$

where $\bar{y}$, S_y, and ρ represent the mean, standard deviation, and correlation coefficient of y, respectively.

Using the ordinary least-squares method, Lee et al. (1986) show that it is possible to achieve better forecasts by combining two types of betas. Using an ordinary least-squares estimate of β_{OLS} and a Bayesian adjustment procedure of Vasicek (1973) as defined in Equation (9.21):

$$\beta_V = \frac{\dfrac{\bar{\beta}}{V(\hat{\beta})} + \dfrac{\hat{\beta}_{OLS}}{V(\hat{\beta}_{OLS})}}{\dfrac{1}{V(\hat{\beta})} + \dfrac{1}{V(\hat{\beta}_{OLS})}} \tag{9.21}$$

where:

$\hat{\beta}_{OLS}$ = the least-squares estimate of a first-period individual beta;

$V(\hat{\beta}_{OLS})$ = variance estimate of β_{OLS};

$\bar{\beta}$ = the cross-sectional mean value of estimated β_{OLS};

$V(\hat{\beta})$ = the cross-sectional variance of estimated β_{OLS}; and

β_V = the Bayesian adjusted beta.

Equation (9.21) indicates that the Vasicek type of Bayesian adjustment beta is a weighted average of $\bar{\beta}$ and β_{OLS}. The weights are

$$w_1 = \frac{\dfrac{1}{V(\hat{\beta})}}{\dfrac{1}{V(\hat{\beta})} + \dfrac{1}{V(\hat{\beta}_{OLS})}} \quad \text{and} \quad w_2 = \frac{\dfrac{1}{V(\hat{\beta}_{OLS})}}{\dfrac{1}{V(\hat{\beta})} + \dfrac{1}{V(\hat{\beta}_{OLS})}}$$

The authors first use first-period regressions projected forward to obtain forecasts of the second-period betas. The summary of the stepwise regression for the first-period data is given in Table 9–1. Table 9–2 summarizes the overall mean squared errors together with the mean squared error decomposition.

Lee et al. (1986) note that for forecasts developed without the Bayesian adjustment, the accounting-based forecast is better, in terms of overall mean squared error. This advantage results entirely from inefficiency in the Mincer–Zarnowitz sense of the market-based forecast. By contrast, the Bayesian-adjusted market-based forecasts suffer far less from this problem and, as a result, the mean squared prediction error for Bayesian-adjusted market-based forecasts are only marginally larger than the accounting-based forecasts—0.0667 compared to 0.0640.

Lee et al. (1986) tested a composite predictor for beta consisting of both a market beta and an accounting beta. Table 9–3 on page 276 shows the results of using this composite method to forecast beta for both the Bayesian-adjusted and nonadjusted model. In Table 9–3, $\hat{\beta}_{OLS}$ (2) represents the OLS estimated beta in the second period. $\hat{\beta}_{OLS}^A$ and $\hat{\beta}_V^A$ represent accounting-based beta without and with Bayesian adjustment, respectively. By comparing both MSE (market) of 0.893 and 0.0667 and MSE(accounting) of 0.0677

TABLE 9-1 Summary of Stepwise Regression Results for First-Period Data

Dependent Variable Adjusted R^2	$\hat{\beta}_{OLS}$ 0.245	$\hat{\beta}_V$ 0.236
Independent Variables	Coefficients (t-values)	
Intercept	0.911 (11.92)	1.037 (12.71)
Financial leverage	0.704 (5.31)	0.599 (5.81)
Dividend payout	−0.175 (−3.50)	−0.108 (−2.85)
Sales	0.030 (3.02)	0.018 (2.28)
Operating income	0.011 (2.18)	0.026 (2.28)
Assets	— —	−0.026 (−2.41)

Source: Lee, C. F., P. Newbold, J. E. Finnerty, and C. C. Chu. *The Financial Review,* v. 21 (February 1986), p. 59.

and 0.0640 with MSE(composite) of 0.0545 and 0.0530, respectively, it can be concluded that on the basis of mean squared error, the composite predictor outperforms either the market- or accounting-information predictor. Of the models used for the composite predictor, it appears that the Bayesian adjustment case is superior.

From research it appears, then, that accounting-based and market-based forecasts can be combined to produce a superior composite forecast of beta.

TABLE 9-2 Mean Squared Error Decompositions for Forecasts of Second-Period Betas

	Market-Based Forecasts		Accounting-Based Forecasts	
	Without Bayesian Adjustment	With Bayesian Adjustment	Without Bayesian Adjustment	With Bayesian Adjustment
Bias	0.0003	0.0000	0.0003	0.0000
Inefficiency	0.0309	0.0090	0.0015	0.0001
Random error	0.0581	0.0577	0.0659	0.0638
Total mean squared error	0.0893	0.0667	0.0677	0.0640

Source: Lee et al. *The Financial Review,* v. 21 (February 1986), p. 600.

TABLE 9–3 Results for the Estimation of Market- and Accounting-Based Composite With and Without Bayesian Adjustment

	Without Bayesian Adjustment $\hat{\beta}_{OLS}(2) = a + b_1 \hat{\beta}^A_{OLS} + b_2 \hat{\beta}_{OLS} + w$		
	Intercept	$\hat{\beta}^A_{OLS}$	$\hat{\beta}_{OLS}$
Coefficients	0.251	0.399	0.370
Standard errors	0.104	0.102	0.052
		MSE = 0.0545	

	With Bayesian Adjustment $\hat{\beta}_{OLS}(2) = a + b_1 \hat{\beta}^A_V + b_2 \hat{\beta}_V + w$		
	Intercept	$\hat{\beta}^A_V$	$\hat{\beta}_V$
Coefficients	−0.096	0.606	0.475
Standard errors	0.134	0.133	0.067
		MSE = 0.0530	

Source: Lee et al. *The Financial Review,* v. 21 (February 1986), p. 61.

SOME APPLICATIONS AND IMPLICATIONS OF THE CAPITAL ASSET PRICING MODEL

Since its development, the uses of the capital asset pricing model (CAPM) have extended into all areas of corporate finance and investments. The CAPM can be applied to two aspects of the capital-budgeting problem: (1) determining the cost of capital and (2) assessing the riskiness of a project under consideration. The CAPM can also be useful in a real-estate problem, deciding to lease or buy.

The use of the CAPM can be extended into valuation of the entire firm. Because of its impact upon firm valuation, the CAPM has been of great use in the merger-analysis area of financial analysis. The CAPM has also been used to test various financial theories. By including a dividend term and considering its effects, the CAPM can be used to test the effects of the firm's dividend policy. An area that has received a great deal of attention is the use of the CAPM in testing the efficient-market hypothesis.

An application of the CAPM to the capital-budgeting process concerns the valuation of risky projects. If accurate estimates can be made about the systematic risk of a project, then the CAPM can be used to determine the return necessary to compensate the firm for the project's risk. If the sum of the estimated cash flows discounted by the CAPM-calculated required rate of return is positive, then the firm should undertake the project.

Rubinstein (1973) demonstrates how the CAPM can be used to value securities and to calculate their risk-adjusted equilibrium price. First, the

CAPM must be converted to using price variables instead of expected return. It may be rewritten:

$$E(R_i) = \frac{P_1 - P_0}{P_0}$$

where:

R_i = the expected returns for the ith firms;
P_1 = the price of stock in time 1; and
P_0 = the price of stock in the previous period.

Thus, the CAPM is redefined:

$$\frac{E(P_1) - P_0}{P_0} = R_{f,t} + [E(R_m) - R_f]\frac{\sigma_{im}}{\sigma_m^2} \tag{9.22}$$

or, rearranging Equation (9.22):

$$P_0 = \frac{E(P_1)}{1 + R_f + [E(R_m) - R_f]\frac{\sigma_{im}}{\sigma_m^2}}$$

Thus the rate of return used to discount the expected end-of-period price contains a risk premium dependent upon the security's systematic risk.

CAPM has also been applied in the analysis of mergers. It has been shown that the risks of a portfolio can be substantially reduced with the inclusion of securities that are not perfectly correlated in terms of returns. This principle also applies with respect to the mergers between firms. The merging of two firms with different product lines, called a *conglomerate merger*, creates diversification, considered of great benefit. Suppose that one firm sells a product that is recession resistant; then a decrease in earnings of one division of the conglomerate will be offset by the steady earnings of another division. The overall result will be a relatively stable income stream despite shifting trends in the economy.

SUMMARY

This chapter has discussed the basic concepts of risk and diversification and how they pertain to the CAPM. The procedures for deriving the CAPM itself were presented, and the CAPM was shown to be an extension of the capital market line theory. The possible uses of the CAPM in financial management were also indicated.

The concept of beta and its importance to the financial manager was introduced. Beta represents the systematic risk of a firm and is a comparison measure between a particular firm's security or portfolio risk and the market average. Systematic risk was further discussed through an investigation of

the beta coefficient and the impact of other important financial variables on the magnitude of the beta coefficient.

The statistical method of least squares and its application were introduced, and beta forecasts based on the least-squares method were compared with those based on market information, accounting information, and a composite-predictor beta forecast composed of both accounting and market information. The composite predictor appears to yield a better forecast than either the market-information or accounting-information forecasts separately.

QUESTIONS AND PROBLEMS

1. What is the capital market line? What is the security market line? What are the differences between the two? What is their relationship?

2. You are the insurance commissioner in the state of California. BBB Insurance Company's stock has a rate of return of 9 percent. BBB's executives argue that this is too low and that they should be granted a rate increase. If the risk-free rate is 5 percent, the expected return on the NYSE is 9 percent and BBB's stock has a $\beta = 2$, would you grant the rate increase?

3. You are trying to decide whether to purchase the stock of ABC Company. To make this decision, you have the following information available to you:

$$\text{Current price} = \$100$$
$$\text{Expected price next year} = \$105$$
$$\text{Dividend paid next year} = \$10$$
$$R_f = 5\%$$
$$E(R_m) = 8\%$$
$$\beta_{ABC} = 1.5$$

Should you purchase ABC's stock?

4. You are given the following information about two correctly priced securities.

$$E(R_A) = 7\% \qquad \beta_A = 0.7$$
$$E(R_B) = 9\% \qquad \beta_B = 1.3$$

(a) Derive the equation for the security market line.
(b) Plot the security market line.
(c) If stock C has an expected return of 15 percent and a beta value of 2, is it correctly priced?

5. Define the market model. How can the parameters of a market model be estimated?

6. Explain how to derive the CAPM with the existence of borrowing and lending rates.

7. You are given the following equation for the standard CAPM.

$$E(R_j) = 0.07 + 0.12\beta_j$$

   (a) What is the risk-free rate?
   (b) What is the return on the market?
   (c) What is the market risk premium?

8. What is beta? Why is beta a better measure of risk than the standard deviation?

9. Briefly discuss some of Roll's (1977) criticisms regarding empirical tests of the CAPM. (See Appendix 9A.)

10. You are given the following information about Widget Company and the market.

$$\text{Cov}(R_W, R_m) = 0.003$$
$$\sigma_m = 2\%$$
$$E(R_m) = 9\%$$
$$R_f = 5\%$$

   Calculate the expected return on Widget Company's stock.

11. Economists have tested the empirical CAPM

$$R_i = R_f + \beta_i(R_m - R_f) + e_i$$

   by estimating the equation

$$\overline{R}_i = a_0 + a_1 b_i + e_i$$

   in which $\overline{R}_i = R_i - R_f$ and b_i = the estimate of β from the market model regression.

   (a) What parameter estimates a_0 and a_1 would be consistent with the CAPM?
   (b) Discuss briefly the results of some of these empirical tests.
   (c) What are some of the econometric problems associated with these tests?

12. You are given the following information about stock A and the market.

$$E(R_m) = 10\% \qquad\qquad \sigma_m = 6\%$$
$$\sigma_A = 3\% \qquad \text{Cov}(R_A R_m) = 0.0048$$

   Assume you can borrow or lend as much as you like at the risk-free rate of 5 percent. What is the systematic risk of stock A? Using the assumptions of the CAPM, find the expected return on A.

13. Discuss how the beta coefficient can be forecasted. How can accounting-based and composite-based models be used to forecast the beta coefficient?

APPENDIX 9A: EMPIRICAL EVIDENCE FOR THE RISK–RETURN RELATIONSHIP

The validity of the CAPM can be borne out partly through observations of actual portfolios held in the marketplace. As discussed in Chapters 7 and 8, there exist two primary relationships between risk and return. First, the rates of return of efficient portfolios are linear functions of their riskiness as measured by their standard deviation. This is illustrated by the capital market line (CML). Second, the rate of return of an individual asset is determined by its contribution of risk to the portfolio, and this is measured by beta, where beta has a linear relationship with the security's expected rate of return. This is illustrated by the security market line (SML).

The performance of mutual funds can be employed to test the explanatory powers of the linear relationship between risk and return of the CML. Mutual funds are professionally managed and therefore the most visible type of portfolio, easily used for comparison testing. One study was performed by Sharpe (1966) to test the performance of a fund and the relationship between its rate of return and risk over time. Sharpe computed average annual returns and the standard deviations of these returns for thirty-four mutual funds from 1954 to 1963. His model implies that portfolios with higher risks will receive higher returns. This Sharpe found to be true for all thirty-four funds. He calculated the correlation between average returns and their standard deviations to be 0.836, indicating that more than 80 percent of the difference in returns was due to differences in risk.

Sharpe also found that there was a linear relationship between returns and risks, except in the region of very high risks. Sharpe's study provides basic support to the contention that the CML explains the relationship between risk and return, both in portfolio theory and in the marketplace.

Another study was performed by Jensen (1969). He studied the correlation of beta coefficients (market sensitivity) and the expected return of mutual funds. On the basis of analysis of 115 mutual funds over a nine-year period he was able to conclude that high returns were associated with high volatility or high systematic risks. He also found evidence that beta coefficients are a valid and accurate measure of risk.

Both the Sharpe and Jensen studies on the risk and return of mutual funds show that an empirical risk–return relationship does exist among mutual funds. [However, Sharpe used the capital market line to perform his empirical tests while Jensen used the security market line, derived by Sharpe (1964).]

The second implication of the risk–return relationship is that the risk premium on individual assets depends on the contribution each makes to the riskiness of the entire portfolio.

The CAPM is a simple linear model expressed in terms of expected returns and expected risk. In its ex-ante form:

$$E(R_i) = R_f + [E(R_m) - R_f]\beta_i \qquad \textbf{(9A.1)}$$

Although many of the aforementioned extensions of the model support this simple linear form, others suggest that it may not be linear, that factors other than beta are needed to explain $E(R_i)$, or that the R_f is not the appropriate riskless rate.

The first step necessary to empirically test the theoretical CAPM is to transform it from expectations (ex-ante) form into a form that uses observed data. On average, the expected rate of return on an asset is equal to the realized rate of return. This can be written:

$$R_{it} = E(R_{it}) + \beta_i \delta_{mt} + e_{it}$$

where:

$$\delta_{mt} = R_{mt} - E(R_{mt});$$
$$E(\delta_{mt}) = 0;$$
$$e_{it} = \text{a random error term;}$$
$$\text{Cov } (e_{it}, \delta_{mt}) = 0;$$
$$\text{Cov } (e_{it}, e_{it-1}) = 0; \text{ and}$$
$$\beta_{it} = \text{Cov } (R_{it} R_{mt})/\text{Var } (R_{mt}).$$

When CAPM is empirically tested it is usually written in the following form:

$$R'_{pt} = \gamma_0 + \gamma_1 \beta_p + e_{pt} \qquad \textbf{(9A.2)}$$

where:

$$\gamma_1 = \overline{R}_{mt} - \overline{R}_{ft}$$
$$R'_{pt} = R_{pt} - R_{ft}$$

These relationships can be stated as follows.

1. The intercept term γ_0 should not be significantly different from zero.
2. Beta should be the only factor that explains the rate of return on a risky asset. If other terms, such as residual variance, dividend yields, price/earnings ratios, firm size, or beta squared are included in an attempt to explain return, they should have no explanatory power.
3. The relationship should be linear in beta.
4. The coefficient of beta, γ_1, should be equal to $\overline{R}_{mt} - \overline{R}_{ft}$.
5. When the equation is estimated over very long periods of time, the rate of return on the market portfolio should be greater than the risk-free rate.

The work of Jensen (1972) provides a comprehensive and unifying review of the theoretical developments and the empirical work done in the field until that year. In his paper he points out that

> the main result of the original papers in this area is the demonstration that one can derive the individual's demand function for assets, aggregate these demands to obtain equilibrium prices (or expected returns) solely as a function of potentially measurable market parameters. Thus the model becomes testable.

Let us now summarize the empirical work of Douglas (1969), Black, Jensen, and Scholes (1972), and Fama and MacBeth (1973). The first pub-

lished test of the CAPM was by Douglas (1969), who regressed the returns of a large cross-sectional sample of common stocks on their own variances and on their beta coefficients β_i, obtained by market models. His results are in variance with the Sharpe-Lintner-Mossin model, for he found that the return was positively related to the variance of the security but not the covariance with the index of returns.

Douglas also summarizes some of the work of Lintner (1965), who estimates beta from a typical market model. Douglas then adds a term for the standard deviation of error (proxy for unsystematic risk). He finds that the coefficient for the unsystematic risk is both positive and significant, the intercept term is higher than the appropriate risk-free rate, and the coefficient for the market risk premium is too low.

Black, Jensen, and Scholes observe that cross-sectional tests may not provide direct validation of the CAPM, and they proceed to construct a time-series test, which they consider more powerful. Their results lead them to assert that the usual form of the CAPM does not provide an accurate description of the structure of security returns. Their results indicate that βs are non-zero and are directly related to the risk level. Low-beta securities earn significantly more on average than predicted by the model, and high-risk securities earn significantly less on average than predicted by the model. They go on to argue for a two-factor model:

$$R_{it} = (1 - \beta_i)R_{zt} + \beta_i(R_{mt}) + e_{it} \qquad \textbf{(9A.3)}$$

If $E(R_z) = 0$ then the Sharpe-Lintner-Mossin CAPM would be consistent with this model. However, the cross-sectional term for the intercept is a constant and not equal to zero. They then proceed to look for a rationale of this finding in Black's zero-beta model.

Fama and MacBeth (1973) test (1) a linear relationship between return on the portfolio and the portfolio's beta and (2) whether unsystematic risk has an effect between portfolio return and a risk measure in addition to beta. Their basic estimation equation is:

$$\tilde{R}_{it} = \tilde{\gamma}_{0t} + \tilde{\gamma}_{1t}\,\overline{\beta}_i + \tilde{\gamma}_{2t}\,\overline{\beta}_i^2 + \gamma_{3t}\overline{\sigma}_i^2(\mu) + \tilde{e}_{it} \qquad \textbf{(9A.4)}$$

in which γ_{0t} is the intercept term, $\overline{\beta}_i$ is the average of the β_i for all individual securities in portfolio i, and $\overline{\sigma}_i(\mu)$ is the average of the residual standard deviations from all securities in portfolio j.

Although they find that there are variables in addition to the portfolio beta that systematically affect period-by-period returns (which are apparently related to the average squared beta of the portfolio and the risk factor other than beta), they dismiss the latter as "almost surely proxies," since "there is no rationale for their presence in our stochastic risk–return model." Their results seem to suggest that the Sharpe-Lintner-Mossin model does not hold. The intercept factor, γ_{0t}, is generally greater than R_F, and $\tilde{\gamma}_{1t}$ is substantially less than $\overline{R}_m - \overline{R}_f$. This seems to indicate that the zero-beta model is more consistent with the data.

Blume and Husick (1973) find empirical evidence to indicate that historical rates of return may sometimes foreshadow changes in future betas, and that stocks with higher transaction costs should yield somewhat higher gross expected returns. Their data indicate that beta is not stationary over time, that it does change over time as a function of price. Transaction-cost effects appear less important than the informational effects of price in explaining future returns or future betas. Therefore, the return-generating process may be more complex than what has been assumed.

Blume and Friend (1973) examine both theoretically and empirically the reasons why the CAPM does not adequately explain differential returns on financial assets. Empirically the risk–return tradeoffs implied by stocks on the New York Stock Exchange for three different periods after World War II cast doubt on the validity of the CAPM either in its S-L-M form or zero-beta form. However, they do confirm the linearity of the relationship for NYSE stocks.

Rosenberg and McKibben (1973) observe that predictions of the riskiness of returns on common stocks can be based on fundamental accounting data for the firm and also on the previous history of stock prices. This paper tries to combine both sources of information to provide efficient predictions. A stochastic model of the parameters is built and the mean squared error is used as a criterion for the evaluation of the forecasting performance of estimators. They conclude that the results "strongly confirm the usefulness of the specific risk predictions based on the accounting descriptors."

Merton (1980) is concerned with the estimation of the expected return on the market. He notes that the current practice for estimating the expected market return adds the historical average realized excess market returns to the current observed interest rate. However, while this model explicitly reflects the dependence of the market return on the interest rate, it fails to account for the effects of changes in the level of market risk. Three models of equilibrium expected market returns are elaborated, and estimation procedures that incorporate the prior restriction that equilibrium expected excess returns on the market must be positive are derived and applied to return data for the period 1926–1978. The following are the principal conclusions of the study.

1. The nonnegativity restriction above should be explicitly included as part of the specifications.

2. Estimators that use realized returns should be adjusted for heteroskedasticity.

Roll (1977) directs an attack on the empirical tests of the CAPM. While recognizing that the theory is testable in principle, he asserts that "no correct and unambiguous test to the theory [has] appeared in the literature and there is practically no possibility that such a test can be accomplished in the future." This conclusion is derived from the mathematical equivalence between the individual return beta linearity and the market portfolio's mean-

variance efficiency. Therefore, any valid test presupposes complete knowledge of the market portfolio's composition. The major results reported by Roll from his theoretical inquiry include:

1. The only testable hypothesis is that the market portfolio is mean-variance efficient.
2. All other so-called implications of the CAPM are not independently testable.
3. In any sample there will always be an infinite number of ex-post mean-variance efficient portfolios; betas calculated will satisfy the linearity relation exactly, whether or not the true market portfolio is mean-variance efficient.
4. The theory is not testable unless the exact composition of the true market portfolio is known and used in the tests.
5. Using a proxy for the market portfolio does not solve the problem, for the proxy itself might be mean-variance efficient even when the true market portfolio is not, and conversely.
6. Empirical tests that reject the S-L-M model have results fully compatible with the S-L-M model and a specification error in the measured market portfolio.
7. If the selected index is mean-variance efficient, then the betas of all assets are related to their mean returns by the same linear function (all assets and portfolios fall exactly on the SML).
8. For every ranking of performances obtained with a mean-variance inefficient index, there exists another non-efficient index that reverses the ranking.

Roll's critique is a broad indictment of most of the accepted empirical evidence concerning the CAPM theory.

Anomalies in the Semi-Strong Efficient-Market Hypothesis

Three anomalies in the semi-strong efficient-market hypothesis are noteworthy. Four authors—Basu, Banz, Reinganum, and Keim—deal with these three anomalies: (1) P/E ratios; (2) size effects; and (3) the January effect.

Basu (1977) empirically notes that a firm with a low P/E ratio, when adjusted for risk, has an excess return over firms that have a high P/E ratio. If this is true, then there are implications for the market's efficiency, the validity of the CAPM, or both. However, Basu found that the excess returns, when adjusted for transaction costs, taxes, and so forth, were so much smaller as to be insignificant. Therefore, CAPM and market efficiency were supported. In conjecturing why a difference in P/E ratios could affect the returns of the firm, we believe the relationship may involve the firm's ability to raise debt. A low P/E ratio may indicate more difficulty in raising capital than a high P/E ratio. This difficulty in raising capital could result in

different lending and borrowing rates for different firms. Therefore, a Brennan version of the standard CAPM pricing model may be more applicable. Or the APT model (see Chapter 11) may be more appropriate in pricing the assets where one of the factors involved captures the P/E effect.

Reinganum (1981) also empirically tests the P/E effect and finds the same results as Basu. In addition, Reinganum was concerned with the efficiency of the market. In order to see if the market was informationally efficient, Reinganum also looked at returns of firms with neither high nor low P/E ratios. He found these firms to be correctly priced. From these results he conjectures that the market was informationally efficient, but CAPM did not allow for the P/E effect on returns. Therefore an APT model with the P/E effect as one of its factors would be preferable to the CAPM model.

Banz (1981) empirically tests the effect of firm size, finding that small-company stock returns were higher than large-company stock returns. Banz argues that the P/E ratio serves as a proxy for the size of a firm and not vice versa. His conjecture about why this anomaly exists centers around informational distribution. A small firm's information distribution is somewhat limited, which causes investors to be wary of buying the stock and depresses the price. Banz suggests the APT valuation model may be more robust than the CAPM in that the APT would be able to capture the size effect by using a P/E ratio as a proxy for the size effect as a factor in the model. Since the distribution of information affects a firm's ability to raise capital (less information on a firm may cause a firm to pay a premium for capital) the premium would indicate that the lending and borrowing rates of different firms are not the same. A valuation model capturing different lending and borrowing rates was provided by Brennan (1971). The utilization of this model could be implemented where rates differed for large and small firms. If small firms do not borrow in the capital market, then Black's no-borrowing CAPM would be more suitable than the standard CAPM.

Keim (1983) empirically tests one of the most baffling anomalies, the January effect. He found that for stocks with excess returns, over 50 percent of these excess returns were realized in January. In addition, 50 percent of the January excess return occurs in the first week of January. This phenomenon of excess returns occurring in the month following the tax-year end has been found empirically in Great Britain also. Although Keim offers no rationale for this phenomenon, others have tried to find tax reasons for this anomaly. The selling of assets in January rather than December to postpone capital gains taxes to the next taxable year has been one suggested rationale. Unlike the P/E and size effects, this anomaly does not have a clear proxy that could be utilized as a factor in an APT model. CAPM does not capture the effect well, and without any theoretical or economical rationale for this effect, any valuation model would be hard pressed to account for it.

Many of the authors seem to conclude that the standard CAPM is not working well, and that alternative valuation models should be considered to capture these anomalies. This might imply that security analysis and portfolio management techniques can be used to beat the market.

REFERENCES

Banz, R. W. "The Relationship Between Return and Market Value of Common Stocks." *Journal of Financial Economics,* v. 9 (March 1981), pp. 3–18.

Basu, S. "Investment Performance of Common Stocks in Relation to Their Price-Earnings Ratios: A Test of the Efficient Markets Hypothesis." *Journal of Finance,* v. 32 (June 1977), pp. 663–82.

Beaver, W., P. Kettler, and M. Scholes. "The Association Between Market Determined and Accounting Determined Risk Measures." *Accounting Review,* v. 45 (October 1970), pp. 654–82.

Black, F., M. C. Jensen, and M. Scholes. "The Capital Asset Pricing Model: Some Empirical Tests." In *Studies in the Theory of Capital Markets,* ed. M. C. Jensen. Praeger, 1972, pp. 20–46.

Blume, M. E. "On the Assessment of Risk." *Journal of Finance,* v. 26 (March 1971), pp. 1–10.

———, and I. Friend. "A New Look at the Capital Asset Pricing Model." *Journal of Finance,* v. 28 (March 1973), pp. 19–34.

———, and F. Husick. "Price, Beta, and Exchange Listing." *Journal of Finance,* v. 28 (March 1973), pp. 19–34.

Brennan, M. J. "Capital Market Equilibrium with Divergent Borrowing and Lending Rate." *Journal of Financial and Quantitative Analysis,* v. 7 (December 1971), pp. 1197–1205.

Douglas, G. W. "Risk in the Equity Markets: An Empirical Appraisal of Market Efficiency." *Yale Economic Essays,* v. 9 (Spring 1969), pp. 3–45.

Fabozzi, F. J., and J. C. Francis. "Beta as a Random Coefficient." *Journal of Financial and Quantitative Analysis,* v. 13 (March 1978), pp. 101–16.

Fama, Eugene F. "Risk, Return and Equilibrium: Some Clarifying Comments." *Journal of Finance,* v. 23 (March 1968), pp. 29–40.

———, and J. MacBeth. "Risk, Return and Equilibrium: Empirical Tests." *Journal of Political Economy,* v. 31 (May–June 1973), pp. 607–36.

Francis, J. C. *Investments: Analysis and Management,* 4th ed. McGraw-Hill Book Company, 1986.

Higgins, R. C. "Growth, Dividend Policy and Cost of Capital in the Electric Utility Industry." *Journal of Finance,* v. 29 (December 1974), pp. 1189–1201.

———. *Analysis for Financial Management.* Richard D. Irwin, 1984.

Jensen, M. C. "Capital Markets: Theory and Evidence," *The Bell Journal of Economic and Management Science,* v. 3 (Autumn 1972), pp. 357–98.

———, "Risk, the Pricing of Capital Assets, and the Evaluation of Investment Portfolio." *Journal of Business,* v. 42 (April 1969), pp. 607–36.

Keim, D. B. "Size-Related Anomalies and Stock Return Seasonality: Fur-

ther Empirical Evidence." *Journal of Financial Economics,* v. 11 (June 1983), pp. 13–32.

Lee, C. F. *Financial Analysis and Planning: Theory and Application.* Addison-Wesley Publishing Company, 1985.

————, and S. N. Chen. "A Random Coefficient Model for Reexamining Risk Decomposition Method and Risk-Return Relationship Test." *Quarterly Review of Economics and Business,* v. 20 (March 1980), pp. 58–69.

————, P. Newbold, J. E. Finnerty, and C. C. Chu. "On Accounting-Based, Market-Based and Composite-Based Beta Predictions: Methods and Implications." *The Financial Review,* v. 21 (February 1986), pp. 51–68.

Lintner, J. "The Valuation of Risk Assets and the Selection of Risky Investments in Stock Portfolios and Capital Budgets." *Review of Economics and Statistics,* v. 47 (February 1965), pp. 13–37.

Merton, R. C. "On Estimating the Expected Return on the Market, An Exploratory Investigation." *Journal of Financial Economics,* v. 8 (December 1980), pp. 323–61.

Miller, M., and M. Scholes. "Rates of Return in Relation to Risk: A Reexamination of Some Recent Findings." *In Studies in Theory of Capital Markets,* ed. M. C. Jensen. Praeger, 1972, pp. 47–78.

Mincer, J., and V. Zarnowitz. "The Evaluation of Economic Forecasts." In *Economic Forecasts and Expectations,* ed. J. Mincer. National Bureau of Economic Research, 1969.

Mossin, J. "Equilibrium in a Capital Asset Market." *Econometria,* v. 34 (October 1966), pp. 768–873.

Reinganum, M. R. "Misspecification of Capital Asset Pricing: Empirical Anomalies Based on Earnings Yields and Market Values." *Journal of Financial Economics,* v. 8 (March 1981), pp. 19–46.

Roll, R. "A Critique of the Asset Pricing Theory's Tests—Part I: On Past and Potential Testability of the Theory." *Journal of Financial Economics,* v. 4 (March 1977), pp. 129–76.

————. "Ambiguity When Performance Is Measured by the Securities Market Line." *Journal of Finance,* v. 33 (September 1978), pp. 1051–69.

Rosenberg, B., and V. Marathe. "Tests of the Capital Asset Pricing Hypothesis." Working Paper No. 32 of the Research Program in France. Graduate School of Business and Public Administration, University of California, Berkeley, May 1975.

Rosenberg, B., and W. McKibben. "The Prediction of Systematic and Specific Risk in Common Stocks." *Journal of Finance and Quantitative Analysis,* v. 8 (March 1973), pp. 317–33.

Rubinstein, M. E. "A Mean-Variance Synthesis of Corporate Financial Theory." *Journal of Finance,* v. 28 (March 1973), pp. 167–68.

Sharpe, W. "Capital Asset Prices: A Theory of Market Equilibrium under

Conditions of Risk." *Journal of Finance,* v. 19 (September 1964), pp. 425–42.

———. "Mutual Fund Performance." *Journal of Business,* January 1966, pp. 119–38.

Sunder, S. "Stationarity of Market Risk: Random Coefficients Tests for Individual Stocks." *Journal of Finance,* v. 35 (September 1980), pp. 883–96.

Vasicek, O. A. "A Note on Using Cross-Sectional Information in Bayesian Estimation of Security Betas." *Journal of Finance,* v. 28 (December 1973), pp. 1233–39.

10 Index Models for Portfolio Selection

Chapter 8 presented and discussed the Markowitz model for delineating the efficient frontier. Numerous examples were shown that indicated the potentially crushing number of computations resulting from the calculations for even a three-security portfolio. This chapter offers some simplifying assumptions that reduce the overall number of calculations through the use of the Sharpe single-index and multiple-index models.

The essential difference between the single- and multiple-index models is the assumption that the single-index model explains the return of a security or a portfolio with only the market. The multiple-index model describes portfolio returns through the use of more than one index. The investor may quantify the return on a portfolio by seeking an index that is representative of the market together with indexes that are representative of the industries of which the component securities are members or exhibit some other common factor. More is said about the multiple-index model later in the chapter; for now the single-index model is the focus of discussion.

THE SINGLE-INDEX MODEL

The major simplifying assumption that yields the index model from Markowitz's portfolio theory is that covariances between individual securities contained in the portfolio are zero. This assumption greatly reduces the number of calculations needed to find the set of efficient portfolios. The use of the index model necessitates additional statistical estimates for the parameters of the index; nevertheless, these additions are minor in comparison to the reduction in the calculation load as a result of ignoring the covariance terms between securities.

Suggested by Markowitz (1959), the **single-index model** was fully developed by Sharpe (1970), who assumed that the covariances could be over-

looked. The return of an individual security was tied to two factors—a random effect and the performance of some underlying market index. Notationally:

$$R_{it} = a_i + b_i R_{It} + e_{it} \tag{10.1}$$

where:

a_i and b_i = regression parameters for the ith firm;
R_{It} = the tth return of some underlying market index;
R_{it} = the tth return on security i; and
e_{it} = the tth random effect for the ith security.

Equation (10.1) is the market model as discussed in the last chapter. This regression makes several assumptions about the random effect term.

1. The expected value of the tth random effect for security i is zero. More explicitly, $E(e_{it}) = 0$.
2. The variance of the error terms is constant. This amounts to the assumption that the errors are homoscedastic.
3. There is no relationship between the errors and the return on the market: Cov $(e_{it}, R_{It}) = 0$.
4. The random effects are not serially correlated: $E(e_{it}, e_{it + n}) = 0$.
5. The ith security's random effect is unrelated to any other random effects of any other security: $E(e_{it}, e_{jt}) = 0$.

The fifth assumption guarantees that the regression coefficients a_i and b_i are the best unbiased linear estimators of the true parameters.

An investigation of some of the results of the previous assumptions is in order. The expected value of the return on security i is equal to the sum of the intercept, the adjusted return on the index, and some random effect. This can be expressed:

$$\begin{aligned} E(R_i) &= E(a_i + b_i R_{It} + e_{it}) \\ &= E(a_i) + E(b_i R_{It}) + E(e_{it}) \end{aligned} \tag{10.2}$$

Because a_i and b_i are constants, and $E(e_{it})$ is equal to zero:

$$r_i = E(R_i) = a_i + b_i r_I \tag{10.3}$$

where r_I is equal to the mean of the returns on the market index.

If the mean of the returns on security i equals r_i, then the variance of security i is equal to the expected value of squared deviations from r_{it}. This translates to:

$$\begin{aligned} \sigma_i^2 &= E(R_{it} - r_i)^2 \\ &= E[(a_i + b_i R_{It} + e_{it}) - (a_i + b_i r_I)]^2 \\ &= E[b_i(R_{It} - r_I) + e_{it}]^2 \\ &= b_i^2 E(R_{It} - r_I)^2 + 2b_i E[e_{it}(R_{It} - r_I)] + E(e_{it})^2 \end{aligned} \tag{10.4}$$

By the third assumption the covariance of the random effect and the devia-

tion of the index return from its mean are zero; also, the expected value of the squared errors is equal to the variance of the random effect. Thus:

$$\begin{aligned}\sigma_i^2 &= b_i^2\, E(R_{It} - r_I)^2 + E(e_{it})^2 \\ &= b_i^2\, \sigma_I^2 + \sigma_{ei}^2\end{aligned} \tag{10.5}$$

This is equivalent to saying that the variance of the returns on a security is made up of some adjusted quantity of the variance of the market (usually referred to as systematic risk) plus the variance of the random effects exclusive to that particular security (unsystematic risk).

The last result to be investigated from these assumptions involves a minor step into abstraction in which the possibility of interaction between two securities and the market index is considered. It is suggested that because variations in the returns of two different securities are not interrelated but only connected to the market index, the covariance between the two securities can be derived from the twice-adjusted variance of the market index (once by the b coefficient of the first security with the market and again by the b coefficient of the second security with the market). The investigation starts with a statement about the covariance of the two securities:

$$\begin{aligned}\sigma_{ij} &= E[(R_{it} - r_i)(R_{jt} - r_j)] \\ &= E[((a_i + b_i\,R_{It} + e_{it}) - (a_i + b_i r_I)) \\ &\quad \times ((a_j + b_j\,R_{It} + e_{jt}) - (a_j + b_j\,r_I))] \\ &= E[(b_i(R_{It} - r_I) + e_{it}) \times (b_j(R_{It} - r_I) + e_{jt})] \\ &= b_i b_j\, E(R_{It} - r_I)^2 + b_i\, E(e_{jt}(R_{It} - r_I)) \\ &\quad + b_j E(e_{it}(R_{It} - r_I)) + E(e_{it}e_{jt})\end{aligned} \tag{10.6}$$

Since according to the third and fourth assumptions the last three terms of the last summation are equal to zero:

$$\sigma_{ij} = b_i b_j \sigma_I^2 \tag{10.7}$$

The number of calculations necessary to utilize the Markowitz model is $N + (N^2 - N)/2$, as shown in the last chapter. For a portfolio with a hundred securities, this translates to 5,050 calculations. With the Sharpe single-index model, only 100 estimates are needed for the various security-regression coefficients and only one variance calculation, the variance of the returns on the market. In addition, 100 estimates of the unsystematic risk σ_{ei}^2 are also needed for the single-index model. Hence, the single-index model has dramatically reduced the input information needed.[1]

Deriving the Single-Index Model

So far only the Sharpe single-index model has been utilized to study the returns of a single security i as determined by its relation to the returns on a market index.

---

[1] Discussion of the single-index model adapted in part from W. F. Sharpe, *Portfolio Theory and Capital Markets.* McGraw-Hill, 1970. Adapted by permission.

Expected Return of a Portfolio.   Now consider the return on a portfolio of n securities. The return of a portfolio of n securities is the weighted summation of the individual returns of the component securities. Notationally:

$$E(R_{pt}) = \sum_{i=1}^{n} x_i \, E(R_i)$$

Where R_{pt} is the rate of return for a portfolio in period t and x_i is the weight associated with the ith security.

$$R_{it} = a_i + b_i \, R_{It} + e_{it}$$

$$
\begin{aligned}
R_{pt} &= \sum_{i=1}^{n} x_i \, (a_i + b_i \, R_{It} + e_{it}) \\
&= \sum_{i=1}^{n} x_i \, (a_i + e_{it}) + \sum_{i=1}^{n} x_i \, (b_i R_{It}) \\
&= \sum_{i=1}^{n} x_i \, a_i + \sum_{i=1}^{n} (x_i b_i) \, (R_{It}) + \sum_{i=1}^{n} x_i e_{it}
\end{aligned}
\tag{10.8A}
$$

Thus,

$$E(R_{pt}) = \sum_{i=1}^{n} x_i a_i + \sum_{i=1}^{n} (x_i b_i) \, E(R_{It}) \tag{10.8B}$$

This equation indicates that the return of a portfolio may be decomposed into the summation of the weighted returns peculiar to the individual securities and the summation of the weighted adjusted return on the market index. Thus the portfolio may be viewed as a combination of n basic securities and a weighted adjusted return from an investment in the market index.

Variance of a Portfolio.   To derive the variance of the portfolio σ_p^2, consider first that the mean return of the portfolio is equal to the expected value of the return on the portfolio. Then, following the definition of σ_p^2 in Chapter 7 and Equations (10.5) and (10.7), we obtain:

$$
\begin{aligned}
\sigma_p^2 &= E[(R_{pt} - E(R_{pt}))^2] \\
&= \sum_{i=1}^{n} x_i^2 \sigma_{ei}^2 + \sum_{i=1}^{n} \sum_{j=1}^{n} x_i x_j b_i b_j \sigma_I^2 \\
&= \left[\sum_{i=1}^{n} x_i b_i \right]\left[\sum_{j=1}^{n} x_j b_j \right] \sigma_I^2 + \sum_{i=1}^{n} x_i^2 \sigma_{ei}^2
\end{aligned}
\tag{10.9}
$$

Because the weighted sum of the b_i coefficients is equal to the coefficient of the portfolio $\sum_{i=1}^{n} x_i b_i = b_p$, similarly $\sum_{j=1}^{n} x_j b_j = b_p$. Hence, the last equation reduces to:

$$\sigma_p^2 = b_p^2 \sigma_I^2 + \sum_{i=1}^{n} x_i^2 \sigma_{ei}^2 \tag{10.10}$$

It was shown in Chapter 8 that when the number of component securities in a portfolio approaches fifteen, the unique risk of the component securities is reduced through diversification. In Equation (10.10) the last term, the weighted sum of the random effect variances, approach zero as n increases. So, again, as the number of securities increases, the unsystematic risk is reduced and the remaining risk of the portfolio is the adjusted variance of the market index. Sample Problem 10.1 further illustrates this concept.

Sample Problem 10.1

Given the following information, what should the β of the portfolio (b_p) be?

$$\sigma_p^2 = 0.082, \qquad \sigma_I^2 = 0.041, \qquad \sum_{i=1}^{n} x_i^2 \sigma_{ei}^2 = 0$$

Solution
Substituting related information into Equation (10.10):

$$\begin{aligned} b_p^2 &= \frac{\sigma_I^2}{\sigma_p^2} \\ &= \frac{0.082}{0.041} \\ &= 2.0 \end{aligned}$$

Therefore, $b_p = 1.414$●

Equation (10.8B) implies that the portfolio can be viewed as an investment in n basic securities and a weighted adjusted return in the market, or

$$\sum_{i=1}^{n} (x_i b_i)\, E(R_{It})$$

The return on the market can be decomposed as a combination of the expected return plus some random effect. When this random effect is positive, the atmosphere is bullish and when it is negative, the atmosphere is bearish. Notationally:

$$\begin{aligned} R_{It} &= E(R_{It}) + e_{n+1,t} \\ &= a_{n+1} + e_{n+1,t} \end{aligned} \qquad \textbf{(10.11)}$$

This bit of algebraic maneuvering enables the weighted adjusted investment in the market to be viewed as an investment in an artificial security, the $(n+1)$th of an n-security portfolio. The weight for this $(n+1)$th security is the sum of the n weights multiplied by their respective related coefficients to the market index. Thus:

$$x_{n+1} = \sum_{i=1}^{n} x_i b_i \qquad \textbf{(10.12)}$$

The reason for this divergence in notation resulting in the definition of the $(n+1)$th security's return and weight is that Equation (10.8) can be simplified to yield a working model for portfolio analysis. Substituting the last results for x_{n+1} and R_{It} into Equation (10.8) yields:

$$
\begin{aligned}
R_{pt} &= \sum_{i=1}^{n} x_i(a_i + e_{it}) + x_{n+1}(a_{n+1} + e_{n+1,t}) \\
&= \sum_{i=1}^{n+1} x_i(a_i + e_{it})
\end{aligned}
\tag{10.13}
$$

Because the expected value of the random-effect terms is zero, the summation that results after the application of the expectations operator can be expressed:

$$
\begin{aligned}
E(R_{pt}) &= \sum_{i=1}^{n} x_i\, a_i + x_{n+1}\, E(R_{It}) \\
&= \sum_{i=1}^{n+1} x_i\, a_i
\end{aligned}
\tag{10.14}
$$

This yields a formula for the return of a portfolio that is easily applied to portfolio analysis. Before proceeding, however, it is necessary to simplify the variance formula so that it may be used as well.

Remembering that the variance of the portfolio is the expected value of the squared deviations from the expected market return, the last results concerning R_{pt} and $E(R_{pt})$ may be applied:

$$
\begin{aligned}
\text{Var}\,(R_{pt}) &= E\left\{\left[\sum_{i=1}^{n+1} x_i(a_i + e_{it})\right] - E\left[\sum_{i=1}^{n+1} x_i(a_i + e_{it})\right]\right\}^2 \\
&= E\left\{\left[\sum_{i=1}^{n+1} x_i(a_i + e_{it})\right] - \sum_{i=1}^{n+1} x_i[E(a_i) + E(e_{it})]\right\}^2 \\
&= E\left\{\left[\sum_{i=1}^{n+1} x_i(a_i + e_{it})\right] - \sum_{i=1}^{n+1} x_i E(a_i)\right\}^2 \\
&= E\left(\sum_{i=1}^{n+1} x_i e_{it}\right)^2 \\
&= \text{Var}\left(\sum_{i=1}^{n+1} x_i e_{it}\right)
\end{aligned}
\tag{10.15}
$$

This result follows from the assumption that the covariances are equal to zero. Additionally, each variance term is only a weighted sum of the errors around the market return. The direct usefulness of the last two conclusions will become apparent when solving for the security weights. Sample Problem 10.2 provides further illustration.

Sample Problem 10.2

Given R_{It}, R_{it}, and α_i as indicated in the table shown below and the fact that $\sum_{t=1}^{n} \beta_i R_{It} = 56$, using the relationship

$$\sum_{t=1}^{n} R_{it} = n\alpha_i + \sum_{t=1}^{n} \beta_i R_{It} + \sum_{t=1}^{n} e_{it}$$

find the values for α_i, β_i, and e_i.

Solution

$$\sum_{t=1}^{n} R_{It} = 28, \quad \text{so} \quad \beta_i = \frac{\sum_{t=1}^{n} \beta_i R_{It}}{\sum_{t=1}^{n} R_{It}}$$

$$= \frac{56}{28}$$

$$= 2$$

Substitute the values $\sum_{t=1}^{n} R_{it} = 64$, $\sum_{t=1}^{n} \beta_i R_{It} = 56$, $n = 4$ into the regression line

$$\sum_{t=1}^{n} R_{it} = n\alpha_i + \sum_{t=1}^{n} \beta_i R_{It} + \sum_{t=1}^{n} e_{it}$$

and solve for α_i.

R_{It}	R_{it}	α_i	$\beta_i R_{It}$	e_i
4	12	2	8	$12 - 2 - 8 = 2$
6	14	2	12	$14 - 2 - 12 = 0$
10	20	2	20	$20 - 2 - 20 = -2$
8	18	2	16	$18 - 2 - 16 = 0$
28	64	8	56	0

The $\beta_i R_{It}$ column in the table is filled by simply multiplying $\beta(=2)$ by the R_{It} column. The e_i's are the amounts such that $R_{it} = \alpha + \beta_i R_{mt} + e_{it}$ is an equality so $R_{it} = \alpha_i + \beta_i R_{It} + e_{it}$ is satisfied. From the last column of the table we know that $\sum_{i=1}^{n} e_{it} = 0$. Therefore

$$\alpha_i = \frac{64 - 56 + 0}{4} = 2$$

In this section, the expected return $E(R_{pt})$ and the variance of a portfolio Var (R_{pt}) in terms of the single-index model has been derived. In the following section, the optimal portfolio selection procedures discussed in Chapter 8 are used to explore the single-index optimum-portfolio selection model.

Portfolio Analysis and the Single-Index Model

Before beginning the portfolio analysis using the single-index model, it is necessary to explain a derivation of security weights through the use of the Lagrangian calculus maximization discussed in Chapter 8. The maximization procedure maximizes a linear combination of the following two equations:[2]

$$\text{Max} \quad \begin{aligned} E(R_p) &= \sum_{i=1}^{n+1} x_i\, E(R_i) \quad \text{or} \\ -\text{Var}\,(R_p) &= -\text{Var}\left(\sum_{i=1}^{n+1} x_i e_{it}\right) \end{aligned} \tag{10.16A}$$

subject to $\sum_{i=1}^{n+1} x_i = 1$ and

$$x_{n+1} = \sum_{i=1}^{n} x_i b_i \tag{10.16B}$$

The first constraint is equivalent to requiring that the sum of the weights of the component securities is equal to one. The second constraint requires that the weight of the market index within the portfolio returns is equal to the summation of the weighted adjustment factors of the component securities. This requirement is as described in Equation (10.16B).

Combining the above two objective functions with the two constraints yields a Lagrangian function:

$$\begin{aligned} P &= \Phi E(R_p) - \text{Var}\,(R_p) + \lambda_1\left(\sum_{i=1}^{n} x_i - 1\right) + \lambda_2\left(\sum_{i=1}^{n} x_i b_i - x_{n+1}\right) \\ &= \Phi \sum_{i=1}^{n+1} x_i a_i - \sum_{i=1}^{n+1} x_i^2\, \text{Var}\,(e_{it}) + \lambda_1\left(\sum_{i=1}^{n} x_i - 1\right) + \lambda_2\left(\sum_{i=1}^{n} x_i b_i - x_{n+1}\right) \end{aligned} \tag{10.16C}$$

The only difference between this maximization function and the minimization shown in Chapter 8, beyond intent, is that instead of fixing some arbitrary value of return needed (E^*), an attempt can be made to quantify the

---

[2] The maximization of the negative of the variance is equivalent to the minimization of the variance itself. This can be viewed as originating from the negative spectrum of the number line and maximizing towards zero.

level of risk aversion that the investors of the portfolio require, thereby placing the portfolio on the efficient frontier not by desired return but by level of utility, as discussed in Chapter 8. This indication of risk aversion is denoted by the Greek letter Φ (*phi*). When low values are exhibited, risk aversion is pronounced; when high values are in evidence, substantial risk taking is allowed. This notion of the level of risk aversion is best pictured in Figure 10–1. In Figure 10–1, A represents an investor's objective function to minimize the risk only—therefore, the aggressiveness to return is zero. C represents an investor's objective function to maximize returns only—therefore, the aggressiveness to return is infinite. At B an investor's attitude toward return and risk is between A and C.

Figure 10–2 provides further illustration of the approach being utilized. What is depicted is the variation of the objective function P as the parameter denoting risk is varied. Again, notice that the risk–return relation for a low Φ is lower than that for the more risk-taking, high value of Φ. Points A and C are as discussed for Figure 10–1. Lines BD and $B'D'$ represent the objective function when the risk-aversion parameter is equal to one. Note that BD instead of $B'D'$ represents the maximization of the objective function. In sum, different values of Φ generate different optimal objective functions.

Consider now the three-security portfolio. In this framework, the preceding objective function expands to:

$$P = \Phi x_1 a_1 + \Phi x_2 a_2 + \Phi x_3 a_3 + \Phi x_4 a_4 - x_1^2 \, \text{Var} \, (e_{1t})$$
$$- x_2^2 \, \text{Var} \, (e_{2t}) - x_3^2 \, \text{Var} \, (e_{3t}) - x_4^2 \, \text{Var} \, (e_{4t}) + \lambda_1 x_1 + \lambda_1 x_2 \quad \textbf{(10.17)}$$
$$+ \lambda_1 x_3 - \lambda_1 + \lambda_2 \, x_1 b_1 + \lambda_2 x_2 b_2 + \lambda_2 x_3 b_3 - \lambda_2 x_4$$

Take note of all terms in the preceding equation that contain a_4 and x_4. By utilizing the relations of the individual securities to the market, it has been possible to delete most of the calculations necessitated by the full Markowitz

FIGURE 10–1   Level of Risk Aversion and Investors' Investment Attitude

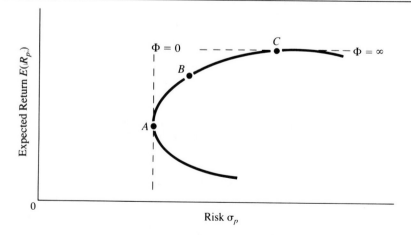

FIGURE 10–2 Level of Risk Aversion and Objective Function

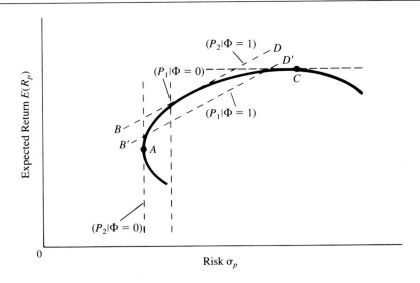

variance–covariance model. The return that will be generated from an optimal portfolio derived through this maximization rests on the estimation of the future expected return and variance of the index. This will lead to the availability of ranging analysis for these estimations, which will produce robust estimates for the security weights highlighted at the end of this section.

To proceed with the Lagrangian maximization it is necessary to notice that the above equation has six unknowns—the four weights and the two Lagrangian coefficients. All other values are expected to be known or estimated. To maximize, the partial derivative of the objective function is taken with respect to each of the six variables:

$$\frac{\partial P}{\partial x_1} = \Phi a_1 - 2x_1\sigma_1^2 + \lambda_1 + \lambda_2 b_1 = 0$$

$$\frac{\partial P}{\partial x_2} = \Phi a_2 - 2x_2\sigma_2^2 + \lambda_1 + \lambda_2 b_2 = 0$$

$$\frac{\partial P}{\partial x_3} = \Phi a_3 - 2x_3\sigma_3^2 + \lambda_1 + \lambda_2 b_3 = 0 \qquad \textbf{(10.18)}$$

$$\frac{\partial P}{\partial x_4} = \Phi a_4 - 2x_4\sigma_4^2 - \lambda_2 = 0$$

$$\frac{\partial P}{\partial \lambda_1} = x_1 + x_2 + x_3 - 1 = 0$$

$$\frac{\partial P}{\partial \lambda_2} = x_1 b_1 + x_2 b_2 + x_3 b_3 - x_4 = 0$$

where:

$$\sigma_1^2 = \text{Var} (e_{1t});$$
$$\sigma_2^2 = \text{Var} (e_{2t});$$
$$\sigma_3^2 = \text{Var} (e_{3t}); \text{ and}$$
$$\sigma_4^2 = \text{Var} (e_{4t}).$$

Equation (10.18) is a set of six equations in six unknowns when set equal to zero. These six equations can be rewritten in matrix format:

$$
\begin{matrix}
A & x & = & k
\end{matrix}
$$

$$
\begin{bmatrix}
-2\sigma_1^2 & 0 & 0 & 0 & 1 & b_1 \\
0 & -2\sigma_2^2 & 0 & 0 & 1 & b_2 \\
0 & 0 & -2\sigma_3^2 & 0 & 1 & b_3 \\
0 & 0 & 0 & -2\sigma_4^2 & 0 & -1 \\
1 & 1 & 1 & 0 & 0 & 0 \\
b_1 & b_2 & b_3 & -1 & 0 & 0
\end{bmatrix}
\begin{bmatrix}
x_1 \\ x_2 \\ x_3 \\ x_4 \\ \lambda_1 \\ \lambda_2
\end{bmatrix}
=
\begin{bmatrix}
-\Phi a_1 \\ -\Phi a_2 \\ -\Phi a_3 \\ -\Phi a_4 \\ 1 \\ 0
\end{bmatrix}
\quad \textbf{(10.19A)}
$$

Equation (10.19A) has related the individual securities to the index and has discarded the use of numerous covariance terms. The majority of the elements of the matrix indicated in the first matrix of Equation (10.19A) are zero.

As in Chapter 8, to solve for the x column vector of variables the P matrix is inverted and each side of the equation is premultiplied by A^{-1}. This yields the x column vector of variables on the left-hand side and A^{-1} multiplied by k, the solution column vector, on the right-hand side.

$$Ax = k$$
$$A^{-1} A x = A^{-1} k \qquad \textbf{(10.19B)}$$
$$Ix = A^{-1} k$$

where I is the identity matrix.

The procedure of solving Equations (10.19A) and (10.19B) was discussed in Chapter 8. A linear-programming approach to solve this kind of model is discussed in the first appendix of this chapter.

In order to estimate a single-index type of optimal portfolio the estimates of a market model are needed; a discussion of the market model and beta estimates is therefore needed as well.

The Market Model and Beta

Equation (10.1) defines the market model:

$$R_{it} = a_i + b_i R_{It} + e_{it} \qquad \textbf{(10.1)}$$

From this market model, a_i, b_i, Var (e_{it}) and Var (R_{It}) can be estimated: all are required for the single-index type of optimal portfolio.

So far the regression coefficient has been referred to as b_i when, in fact, it is a risk relationship of a security with the market. Quantified as the

covariance of security i with the market index divided by the variance of the return of the market, beta is a relational coefficient of the returns of security i as they vary with the returns of the market. Notationally:

$$b_i = \frac{\sigma_{i,I}}{\sigma_I^2} = \sum_{t=1}^{n} \frac{[(R_{it} - r_{it})(R_{It} - r_{It})]}{(R_{It} - r_{It})^2} \qquad (10.20)$$

Of course, due to the continuous nature of security returns, the result of the above calculation is an estimate and therefore subject to error. This error can be quantified by the use of standard error estimates, which provide the ability to make interval estimations for future predictions. The following discussion is related to the **beta estimate** and its forecasting as discussed in Chapter 9.

Because of the linkage between security returns and the firm's underlying fundamental nature, beta estimates will vary over time. It is the job of the security analyst to decide how to modify not only the beta estimate but also the period of time from which the sample of returns is to be drawn. Some popular security-evaluation techniques use a tiered growth model to correspond to the product life-cycle theory. Within the scope of this theory, beta estimates for the relation of that security to the market will vary with respect to the time period chosen for the sample of returns. It is obvious that the returns generated by a firm in its infancy have very little correlation with returns during the growth or maturity phase. It is up to the analyst to judge which phase a company may be in and to adjust the beta estimates accordingly.

Assume for expository purposes that all stocks move in perfect alignment with the market, and therefore the security returns all produce beta estimates of 1. It could then be said that any estimation of betas above 1 would indicate positive sampling error, and all estimates below 1 negative sampling error. Future periods would show returns that caused movement from either side of the estimate deviation back towards 1. Blume (1975) shows that the adjustment of a beta in one period could accurately predict the adjustment in subsequent periods. Utilizing regression analysis, Blume demonstrates that a historical beta could be adjusted successfully to predict future levels. Large brokerage houses have taken this theory a little further by applying weighted averages of historic and average betas in adjusting beta estimates. This has the advantage of being simple to calculate, but it has the ability nevertheless to adjust beta back towards an average level. (This kind of beta-adjustment process was discussed in the last chapter; the Value Line beta estimate is essentially based upon this process, as explored in Chapter 9.)

Historic beta estimates give the analyst a feeling for how the firm is generating returns to an investor but give very little guidance about the firm's underlying fundamental nature. It is held that a firm's balance-sheet ratios over time can indicate how risky the firm is relative to the market. Using seven financial quantities of a firm, Beaver, Kettler, and Scholes

(BKS, 1970) show that betas can be estimated by multiple regression relating the financial levels to the riskiness of the firm. Using

1. Dividend payout
2. Asset growth
3. Leverage
4. Liquidity
5. Asset size
6. Earnings volatility, and
7. Accounting beta (relation of earnings of the firm with the earnings of the economy as a whole)

BKS show not only that each of the variables carries a logical relation to the market but also that the multiple regression is significant. Other studies, most notably Rosenberg (1976), use many more fundamental factors in the regression for estimating betas.

Historic betas are of consequence because of their relation with market returns; nevertheless, the sampling period tends to crowd out the information contained in returns due to recent developments for the firm. Fundamental betas tend to recognize significant changes in the makeup of a firm—for example, a change in debt structure, or liquidity. The disadvantage related to fundamental betas is that they treat intercompany responsiveness as constant. It is patently obvious that a small firm taking on a large debt will be at much more risk than a Ford or GM doing the same.

Because of the advantages and disadvantages apparent in both types of beta estimates, it has been shown that a combination of the estimates is more suitable to risk classification. Rosenberg and McKibben (1973) found that intercompany responsiveness is substantial, so an analysis was undertaken to introduce these variations into the regression. Utilizing a set of dummy variables to capture the advantages of both types of betas, Rosenberg and Marathe (Berkeley Working Paper Series) have described a multiple regression for the beta estimate of a firm that include information such as variability, level of success, relative size, and growth potential. By using a very large and complex model they found that the forecasting ability of the regression analysis is substantial, but they were inconclusive as to whether the benefit of the analysis outweighs the computational cost.

Forecasting future beta levels holds its roots in the difficulty of forecasting the fundamental nature of the firm itself. This section has briefly looked over some of the available adjustment processes for beta estimation. While reasonable in its scope, this coverage of the adjustment process is by no means complete. Additional research material is cited at the end of this chapter for use in further study. It should be kept in mind during future readings that the more sophisticated an adjustment process is, the more likely it is that the computational costs will outweigh the improvement of the beta forecast.

MULTIPLE INDEXES AND THE MULTIPLE-INDEX MODEL

The previous section reviewed the possibilities of adjusting the beta estimate in the single-index model to capture some of the information concerning a firm not contained in the historic returns. The **multiple-index model (MIM)** pursues the same problem as beta adjustment, but approaches the problem from a different angle. The multiple-index model tackles the problem of relation of a security not only to the market by including a market index, but also to other indexes that quantify other movements. For example, U.S. Steel has returns on its securities that are related to the market, but due to the declining nature of the American steel industry there is also some relation to the steel industry itself. If an index could be developed that represented the movement of the U.S. steel industry, it could be utilized in the return analysis, and a more accurate estimate of possible security returns for U.S. Steel could be derived.

The assumption underlying the single-index model is that the returns of a security vary only with the market index. The expansion provided by the multiple-index model includes factors that affect a security's return beyond the effects of the market as a whole. Realistically any index might be used, but well-known, published indexes are usually incorporated. These may include general business indicators, industry-specific indicators, or even self-constructed indexes concerning the structure of the firm itself. The model to be addressed contains L indexes; nevertheless, a few examples of possible indexes of interest are offered. The multi-index model is related to the arbitrage pricing model developed by Ross (1976, 1977), which will be explored in detail in the next chapter.

The covariance of a security's return with other market influences can be added directly to the index model by quantifying the effects through the use of additional indexes. If the single-index model were expanded to take into account interest rates, factory orders, and several industry-related indexes, the model would change to:

$$R_i = a_i^* + b_{i1}^* I_1^* + b_{i2}^* I_2^* + \cdots + b_{iM}^* I_M^* + c_i \qquad (10.21)$$

In this depiction of the multiple-index model, I_j^* is the actual level of index j, while b_{ij}^* is the actual responsiveness of security i to index j. If the component of the security return is not related to any of the indexes then this index model can be divided into two parts: (1) a_i, the expected value of the unique return, and (2) c_i, which represents the distribution of the random effect. c_i has a mean effect of zero and a variance of σ_{ci}^2.

This model can be utilized with multiple regression techniques, but if the indexes are unrelated to each other the calculations would be made much simpler. This assumption reduces the number of calculations, as compared with the Markowitz full variance–covariance model, but is obviously more complex than the single-index model. To assure that the indexes are unre-

lated, the index variables can be orthogonalized (made uncorrelated) by completing inter-regressions on the indexes themselves.

Assume there is a hypothetical model that deals with two indexes:

$$R_i = a_i^* + b_{i1}^* I_1^* + b_{i2} I_2^* + c_i \tag{10.22}$$

Suppose the indexes are the market index and an index of wholesale prices. If these two indexes are correlated, the correlation may be removed from either index.

To remove the relation between I_1^* and I_2^*, the coefficients of the following equation can be derived by regression analysis:

$$I_2^* = e_0 + e_1 I_1^* + d_i$$

where:

e_0 and e_1 = the regression coefficients; and
$\quad\quad d_i$ = the random error term.

By the assumptions of regression analysis, d_i is uncorrelated with I_1. Therefore:

$$\hat{d}_i = I_2^* - (\hat{e}_0 + \hat{e}_1 I_1^*)$$

which is an index of the performance of the sector index without the effect of I_1 (the market removed). Defining:

$$I_2 = \hat{d}_i = I_2^* - \hat{e}_0 - \hat{e}_1 I_1^*$$

an index is obtained that is uncorrelated with the market. By solving for I_2^* and substituting into Equation (10.22):

$$R_i = a_i^* + b_{i1}^* I_1^* + b_{i2}^* I_2 - b_{i2}^* \hat{e}_0 - b_{i2}^* \hat{e}_1 I_1^* + c_i$$

Rearranging:

$$R_i = (a_i^* - b_{i2}^* \hat{e}_0) + (b_{i1}^* - b_{i2}^* \hat{e}_1) I_1^* + b_{i2}^* I_2 + c_i$$

If the first set of terms in the brackets are defined as a_i and the second set of terms are defined as b_{i1}, $b_{i2}^* = b_{i2}$, $I_1^* = I_1$, and $c_i = e_i$, the equation can be expressed:

$$R_i = a_i + b_{i1} I_1 + b_{i2} I_2 + e_i \tag{10.23}$$

in which I_1 and I_2 are totally uncorrelated: the goal has been achieved. As will be seen later, these simplifying calculations will make the job of determining variance and covariance much simpler.

The expected return can be expressed:

$$\begin{aligned}
E(R_{it}) &= E(a_i + b_{i1} I_{1t} + b_{i2} I_{2t} + e_{it}) \\
&= E(a_i) + E(b_{i1} I_{1t}) + E(b_{i2} I_{2t}) + E(e_{it}) \\
&= a_i + b_{i1} \bar{I}_1 + b_{i2} \bar{I}_2
\end{aligned} \tag{10.24}$$

Since a_i, b_{i1}, and b_{i2} are constants, $E(e_i) = 0$ by assumption, where $\bar{I}_1 = E(I_{1t})$ and $\bar{I}_2 = E(I_{2t})$.

Variance can be expressed:

$$
\begin{aligned}
\sigma^2 &= E(R_{it} - R_i)^2 \qquad \text{where } R_i = E(R_{it}) \\
&= E[(a_i + b_{i1}I_1 + b_{i2}I_2 + e_{it}) - (a_i + b_{i1}\bar{I}_1 + b_{i2}\bar{I}_2)]^2 \\
&= E[(a_1 - a_i) + b_{i1}(I_{1t} - \bar{I}_1) + b_{i1}(I_{2t} - \bar{I}_2) + e_i]^2 \\
&= E[b_{i1}(I_{1t} - \bar{I}_1)^2 + b_{i1}b_{i2}(I_{1t} - \bar{I}_1)(I_{2t} - \bar{I}_2) \\
&\qquad + b_{i2}^2(I_{2t} - \bar{I}_2)^2 + b_{i1}(I_{1t} - \bar{I}_1)e_{it} \\
&\qquad + b_{i2}(I_{2t} - \bar{I}_2)e_{it} + e_{it}^2] \\
&= b_{i1}^2 E(I_{1t} - \bar{I}_1)^2 + b_{i1}b_{i2}E[(I_{1t} - \bar{I}_1)(I_{2t} - \bar{I}_2)] \\
&\qquad + b_{i2}^2 E(I_{2t} - \bar{I}_2) + b_{i1}E[(I_{1t} - \bar{I}_1)e_i] \\
&\qquad + b_{i2}E[(I_{2t} - \bar{I}_2)e_i] + E(e_i^2)
\end{aligned}
$$

But by assumption:

$$
\begin{aligned}
E[(I_{1t} - \bar{I}_1)(I_{2t} - \bar{I}_2)] &= 0 \\
E[(I_{1t} - \bar{I}_1)e_i] &= 0 \\
E[(I_{2t} - \bar{I}_2)e_i] &= 0
\end{aligned}
$$

and

$$
\begin{aligned}
E(I_{1t} - \bar{I}_1)^2 &= \sigma_1^2 \\
E(I_{2t} - \bar{I}_2)^2 &= \sigma_2^2 \\
E(e_i^2) &= \sigma_{ei}^2;
\end{aligned}
$$

therefore,

$$
\sigma_i^2 = b_{i1}^2\,\sigma_1^2 + b_{i2}^2\,\sigma_2^2 + \sigma_{ei}^2 \tag{10.25}
$$

Covariance between security i and security j can be expressed

$$
\begin{aligned}
\sigma_{ij} &= E[(R_{it} - R_i)(R_{jt} - R_j)] \text{ [where } R_i = E(R_{it}) \text{ and } R_j = E(R_{jt}) \\
&= E\{[(a_i + b_{i1}I_1 + b_{i2}I_{2t} + e_{1t}) - (a_i + b_{i1}\bar{I}_1 + b_{i2}\bar{I}_2)] \\
&\qquad \times [(a_j + b_{j1}I_{1t} + b_{j2}I_{2t} + e_{jt}) - (a_j + \bar{b}_{j1}\bar{I}_1 + \bar{b}_{j2}\bar{I}_2)]\} \\
&= E\{[b_{i1}(I_{1t} - \bar{I}_1) + b_{i2}(I_{2t} - \bar{I}_2) + e_i] \times [b_{j1}(I_{1t} - \bar{I}_1) \\
&\qquad + (b_{j2}(I_{2t} - \bar{I}_2) + e_{jt}]\} \\
&= E[b_{i1}b_{j1}(I_{1t} - \bar{I}_1)^2 + b_{i2}b_{j2}(I_{2t} - \bar{I}_2)^2] \\
&= b_{j1}b_{j1}\sigma_1^2 + b_{i2}b_{j2}\sigma_2^2
\end{aligned} \tag{10.26}
$$

since all remaining expected values of the cross-product terms equal zero.

The extended results of expected return variance and covariance for a multi-index and more than two indexes can be found in the second appendix of this chapter.

One simplifying way of applying the multiple-index model is to start with the basic market model and add indexes to reflect industry-related effects. If the firm has 100 percent of its operations in one industry, Equation (10.23) can be used to represent a two-index model with market index and industry

index. In general this approach reduces the number of data inputs to $4N + 2I + 2$. These data inputs are: (1) the expected return and variance for each stock and market index; (2) the covariance between the individual security and the market index and the industry index; and (3) the mean and variance of each industry index. Although this is a larger number of data inputs than for the simple market model, the accuracy of the estimation of security return increases. So the tradeoff is one of more information (higher cost to use) versus greater accuracy of the forecasted security return.

Care must be taken in applying the multiple-index model. It is often the case that the additional information resulting from the application of a higher-complexity model is outweighed by the computational cost increase. In an attempt at making the model as parsimonious as possible, it is necessary to judge the increased information gained by utilizing the more complex model. This can be accomplished by examining the mean square error for the forecast of the actual historic values. Although not within the scope of this text, the ability to judge the accuracy of a forecast is essential and can be acquired from any good statistical forecasting text. Sample Problem 10.3 provides further illustration of the single-index model.

Sample Problem 10.3

During the discussion of the single-index model, a method was presented for determining optimal portfolio weights given different levels of risk aversion. In this section a three-security portfolio is examined in which the returns of the securities are related to a market index.

	$\overline{R}_i$	Var (R_i)	Cov (R_i, R_I)	b_i
Allied Corporation	0.0084	0.0066	0.0023	1.15
Aluminum Company of America	0.0127	0.0077	0.0018	0.90
American Brands	0.0187	0.0032	0.0011	0.55
Dow Jones 30	0.0125	0.0020	0.0020	1.00

The same securities are used as in Chapter 8 (Table 8–3); the Dow Jones 30 Industrials are included as the market index. The securities and the index have the following observed parameter estimates taken from actual monthly returns during the period 1980–1984 (see table). The table includes the calculation of the beta estimate for each security. Check these figures, remembering that beta is equal to the covariance of security i with the market divided by the variance of the market returns.

Going back to the calculus maximization derivation of optimal portfolio weights, recall that a linear combination of the following two factors is being maximized:

$$E(R_p) = \sum_{i=1}^{n+1} x_i \, E(R_i) \quad \text{or}$$

$$-\text{Var}\,(R_p) = -\,\text{Var}\left(\sum_{i=1}^{n+1} x_i e_{it}\right)$$

(10.16A)

subject to

$$\sum_{i=1}^{n+1} x_i = 1 \quad \text{and}$$

$$\sum_{i=1}^{n} x_i b_i = x_{n+1}$$

(10.16B)

$$P = \Phi E(R_p) - \text{Var}\,(R_p) + \lambda_1\left(\sum_{i=1}^{n} x_i - 1\right) + \lambda_2\left(\sum_{i=1}^{n} x_i b_i - x_{n+1}\right)$$

$$= \Phi \sum_{i=1}^{n+1} x_i a_i - \sum_{i=1}^{n+1} x_i^2 \,\text{Var}\,(R_i) + \lambda_1\left(\sum_{i=1}^{n} x_i - 1\right) + \lambda_2\left(\sum_{i=1}^{n} x_i b_i - x_{n+1}\right)$$

(10.16C)

The only difference between this maximization function and the minimization shown in Chapter 8, beyond intent, is that instead of fixing some arbitrary value of return needed (E^*), an attempt is made to quantify the level of risk aversion that the holders of the portfolio require, thereby placing the portfolio on the efficient frontier, not by desired return, but by level of utility. Consider again a three-security portfolio. In this framework, the preceding objective function expands to:

$$\begin{aligned}
P = {} & \Phi x_1 a_1 + \Phi x_2 a_2 + \Phi x_3 a_3 + \Phi x_4 a_4 - x_1^2 \,\text{Var}\,(R_1) \\
& - x_2^2 \,\text{Var}\,(R_2) - x_3^2 \,\text{Var}\,(R_3) - x_4^2 \,\text{Var}\,(R_4) + \lambda_1 x_1 + \lambda_1 x_2 \\
& + \lambda_1 x_3 - \lambda_1 + \lambda_2 x_1 b_1 + \lambda_2 x_2 b_2 + \lambda_2 x_3 b_3 - \lambda_2 x_4 \quad \textbf{(10.17)}
\end{aligned}$$

Take note of all terms in the preceding equation that contain a_4 and x_4. By utilizing the individual securities' relations to the market, it has been possible to delete most of the calculations necessitated by the Markowitz full variance–covariance model. The return that will be generated from an optimal portfolio derived through this maximization rests on the estimation of the future expected return and variance of the index.

By partially differentiating the above objective function with respect to each of the weights and the λ's, it is possible to develop the following six equations in six unknowns:

$$\frac{\partial P}{\partial x_1} = \Phi a_1 - 2x_1\sigma_1^2 + \lambda_1 + \lambda_2 b_1 = 0$$

$$\frac{\partial P}{\partial x_2} = \Phi a_2 - 2x_2\sigma_2^2 + \lambda_1 + \lambda_2 b_2 = 0$$

$$\frac{\partial P}{\partial x_3} = \Phi a_3 - 2x_3\sigma_3^2 + \lambda_1 + \lambda_2 b_3 = 0$$

(10.18)

$$\frac{\partial P}{\partial x_4} = \Phi a_4 - 2x_4\sigma_4^2 + \lambda_1 + \lambda_2 b_4 = 0$$

$$\frac{\partial P}{\partial \lambda_1} = x_1 + x_2 + x_3 - 1 = 0$$

$$\frac{\partial P}{\partial \lambda_2} = x_1 b_1 + x_2 b_2 + x_3 b_3 - x_4 = 0$$

As shown in Equation (10.19), these last six equations can be transformed into Jacobian Matrix notation. A matrix can be developed by utilizing the set of data in the first table of this problem and a Φ of 1.0 (denoting moderate risk aversion):

$$
\begin{array}{ccc}
 A & x & = & k
\end{array}
$$

$$
\begin{bmatrix}
-0.013 & 0 & 0 & 0 & 1 & 1.15 \\
0 & -0.015 & 0 & 0 & 1 & 0.90 \\
0 & 0 & -0.006 & 0 & 1 & 0.55 \\
0 & 0 & 0 & -0.004 & 0 & -1.0 \\
1.0 & 1.0 & 1.0 & 0 & 0 & 0 \\
1.15 & 0.90 & 0.55 & -1.0 & 0 & 0
\end{bmatrix}
\begin{bmatrix}
x_1 \\ x_2 \\ x_3 \\ x_4 \\ \lambda_1 \\ \lambda_2
\end{bmatrix}
=
\begin{bmatrix}
-0.0084 \\ -0.0127 \\ -0.0187 \\ -0.0125 \\ 1.0 \\ 0
\end{bmatrix}
$$

When the P matrix is inverted and premultiplies each side of the equation:

$$
\begin{array}{ccc}
x & = & A^{-1}k
\end{array}
$$

$$
\begin{bmatrix}
x_1 \\ x_2 \\ x_3 \\ x_4 \\ \lambda_1 \\ \lambda_2
\end{bmatrix}
\begin{bmatrix}
0.0304 \\ 0.1820 \\ 0.7876 \\ 0.6306 \\ 0.0163 \\ -0.0190
\end{bmatrix}
$$

This solution vector shows that investment should be divided 3.04 percent in Allied Corporation, 18.2 percent in Aluminum Company of America, and 78.76 percent in American Brands. Additionally, the weight of x_4 is the sum of the weighted adjustments as indicated in Equation (10–16B). The return on this portfolio is the weighted sum of the individual returns:

$$
\begin{aligned}
E(R_p) &= \sum_{i=1}^{n} x_i E(R_i) \\
&= [(0.0304 \times 0.0084) + (0.1820 \times 0.0127) + (0.7876 \times 0.0187)] \\
&= 0.01730
\end{aligned}
$$

The variance of the portfolio is the sum of the weighted variance and covariance terms:

$$
\text{Var}(R_p) = \sum_{i=1}^{n}\sum_{j=1}^{n} x_i x_j \sigma_{ij}
$$

Taking the covariance expressions:

$$Var (R_p) = [(0.0304^2 \times 0.0066) + (0.1820^2 \times 0.0077)$$
$$+ (0.7876^2 \times 0.0032) + (0.0304 \times 0.1820 \times 0.0022)$$
$$+ (0.1820 \times 0.7876 \times 0.002) + (0.0304 \times 0.7876 \times 0.0005)]$$
$$= 0.0022$$

A portfolio has been developed that is efficient within the realm of this model. Below in the table are listed the portfolios derived by varying the utility factor Φ from 0 (totally risk averse) to 2 (more aggressive risk posture). This last table offers the ability to develop an efficient frontier

Portfolio	Φ	x_1	x_2	x_3	R_p	Var (R_p)	σ_p
1	0.0	0.09	0.22	0.69	0.0165	0.0022	0.0467
2	0.5	0.06	0.20	0.74	0.0169	0.0023	0.0475
3	1.0	0.03	0.18	0.79	0.0173	0.0024	0.0487
4	1.5	0.00	0.16	0.84	0.0177	0.0025	0.0502
5	2.0	−0.03	0.14	0.89	0.0181	0.0027	0.0520

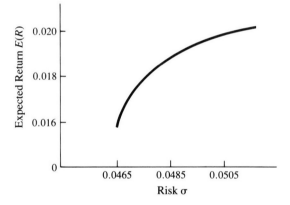

under the Sharpe single-index model. The figure shows that the portfolios start to trace out an efficient boundary. For a fuller graph, the analyst would continue the calculations with ever higher values of Φ stretching the efficient frontier●

SUMMARY

This chapter has discussed the essentials of single- and multiple-index models. The theoretical underpinnings of the theories have been explored and numerical examples have been provided. An efficient boundary has been derived under the guidelines of the model and the quantitative analysis of the

related parameters has been studied. It has been shown that both single-index and multi-index models can be used to simplify the Markowitz model for portfolio section; remember, however, that the multi-index model is much more complicated than the single-index model.

QUESTIONS AND PROBLEMS

1. You are given monthly return data for two stocks and the NYSE as shown in the table.

Month	D (percent)	E (percent)	NYSE (percent)
1	5.30	7.3	4.5
2	6.25	8.2	5.2
3	-2.12	-10.2	1.1
4	12.75	15.4	10.3
5	-3.4	-2.0	-1.3
6	8.6	9.5	10.5
7	9.2	8.2	7.6
8	-2.1	-1.0	0
9	-8.3	-10.2	-7.4
10	10.2	11.5	9.3
11	5.4	5.9	4.2
12	6.2	7.2	8.5

(a) Calculate the α (alpha) and β (beta) for each stock.
(b) Compute the variance of the residuals of each regression.
(c) Calculate the correlation between each stock and the market.
(d) Compute the mean return and variance of an optimal portfolio consisting of these two stocks in terms of the single-index model.

2. Assume that you have determined that a two-index model best describes the return process. The first index is a market index while the second is an industry index. Is it possible to remove the impact of the market from the industry?

3. Derive the formulas for the expected return, variance, and covariance of any stock given a two-index model in which the indexes are orthogonal.

4. Assume that returns are generated by an L-index model:

$$R_i = a_i + b_{i1} I_1 + b_{i2} I_2 + \cdots + b_{iL} I_L + e_i$$

(a) Interpret the coefficients $a_i, b_{i1}, \ldots, b_{iL}$.
(b) Derive the variance of this model.

5. Carefully explain the relationship between the single-index model and the Markowitz model of portfolio theory. How many different terms must be

calculated in a portfolio consisting of *n* securities using the Markowitz model? the single-index model?

APPENDIX 10A: A LINEAR-PROGRAMMING APPROACH TO PORTFOLIO-ANALYSIS MODELS

Sharpe (1967) developed a simplified portfolio-analysis model designed to be formulated as a linear-programming problem. Jacob (1974) developed a linear-programming model for small investors that delineates efficient portfolios composed of only a few securities. Both of these approaches have as their objectives: (1) a reduction in the amount of data required and (2) a reduction in the amount of computer capability required to solve the portfolio-selection problem.

Sharpe approaches the problem of capturing the essence of mean-variance portfolio selection in a linear-programming formulation by:

1. Making a diagonal transformation of the variables that will convert the problem into a diagonal form, and

2. Using a piecewise linear approximation for each of the terms for variance.

The LP that results from the use of market responsiveness as the risk measure and the imposition of an upper limit on investment in each security is

$$\text{Max } P = \lambda \left[\sum_{i=1}^{n} x_i E(R_i) \right] - (1 - \lambda) \left[\sum_{i=1}^{n} x_i \beta_i \right] \qquad \textbf{(10A.1)}$$

subject to:

$$\sum_{i=1}^{n} x_i = 1$$
$$0 \leq x_i \leq U$$

where:

x_i = the fraction of the portfolio invested in security *i*;

$E(R_i)$ = the expected returns of security *i*;

β_i = the beta coefficient of security *i*;

U = the maximum fraction of the portfolio that may be held in any one security; and

λ = a parameter reflecting the degree of risk aversion.

The λ is used in generating the efficient frontier. The value of λ corresponds to the rate of substitution of return for risk measured by the individual security β, while the U maximum percentage to be invested in any one security greatly reduces the number of securities that will be needed for diversification.

Building on this framework, Jacob derives a LP model that allows the small investor explicit control over the number of securities held. Jacob's LP model incorporates the effects of unsystematic risk as well as systematic risk, the beta in the Sharpe LP. Jacob's model is to minimize

Systematic risk   Unsystematic risk

$$\sigma^2(R_p) = \frac{1}{K}\left(\sum_{i=1}^{n} x_i\beta_i\right)^2 \sigma^2(R_m) + \left(\frac{1}{K}\right)^2 \sum_{i=1}^{n} x_i^2\sigma^2(e_i) \qquad \textbf{(10A.2)}$$

subject to:

$$\frac{1}{K}\sum_{i=1}^{n} x_i E(R_i) \leq E^*(R_p)$$

$$\sum_{i=1}^{n} x_i = K \qquad x_i = 0 \text{ or } 1$$

where:

x_i = the investment in security i—all, or nothing;

$E(R_i)$ = the expected return on security i equal to $\alpha_i + \beta_i R_m$;

K = the desired upper bound on the number of securities the investor is willing to consider, usually in the range of 15 to 20;

β_i = the measure of systematic risk;

$\sigma^2(e_i)$ = the measure of unsystematic risk; and

$E^*(R_p)$ = the lowest acceptable rate of return the investor is willing to earn on his or her portfolio.

An additional simplification is to turn the objective function of Equation (10A.2) into a linear relationship. Since the decision variables (x_i) are binary valued, the unsystematic-risk term of the objective function is already linear. Given that the portfolio beta $\left(\sum_{i=1}^{n} x_i\beta_i\right)/K$ is very close to unity, a reasonable linear approximation to the first term in the objective function is provided by:

$$\frac{1}{K}\left[\sum_{i=1}^{n} x_i\beta_i\sigma^2(R_m)\right] = \sigma^2(R_m)\left(\frac{1}{K}\sum_{i=1}^{n} x_i\beta_i\right)^2$$

After division by K and rearrangement of terms, the objective function can be restated:

$$Z = \sum_{i=1}^{n} x_i\left[\beta_i\sigma^2(R_m) + \frac{1}{K}\sigma^2(e_i)\right]$$

Letting $Z_i = \beta_i\sigma^2(R_m) + (1/K)\sigma^2(e_i)$, the problem can be cast as:

$$\text{Minimize } Z = \lambda\sum_{i=1}^{n} x_i Z_i - (1 - \lambda)\sum_{i=1}^{n} x_i E(R_i)$$

subject to:

$$\sum_{i=1}^{n} x_i = 1.0 \qquad 0 \le x_i \le 1/K \qquad i = 1, 2, \dots, N$$

in which λ is varied from zero to one. This problem can be solved by the linear-programming approach suggested by Sharpe (1967). An example of solving this problem can be found in Jacob (1974).

APPENDIX 10B: EXPECTED RETURN, VARIANCE, AND COVARIANCE FOR A MULTI-INDEX MODEL

Using the orthogonalization technique discussed in the text, the multi-index model (MIM) is transformed into:

$$R_i = a_i + b_{i1}I_1 + b_{i2}I_2 + \cdots + b_{iL} I_L + c_i \qquad \text{(10B.1)}$$

in which all I_j are uncorrelated with each other. To interpret the transformed indexes, notice that I_2 is now the difference between the actual level of the index and the level it would be, given the level of the other indexes. Also, b_{i2} is now the sensitivity of security i's return to a change in I_2, given that all other indexes are held constant.

It is also convenient, beyond making the indexes uncorrelated, to assume that the covariance of the residuals with the indexes is equal to zero. With this final assumption the MIM can be recapped as follows. Generalized equation:

$$R_i = a_i + b_{i1}I_1 + b_{i2}I_2 + \cdots + b_{iL}I_L + c_i$$

for all securities $i = 1$ to N, and:

1. $E(c_i) = 0$
2. $\text{Var}(c_i) = \sigma_{ci}^2$
3. $\text{Var}(I_j) = \sigma_{Ij}^2$
4. $\text{Cov}(I_j, I_k) = E[(I_j - \bar{I}_j)(I_k - \bar{I}_k)] = 0, \bar{I}_j = E(I_j), \bar{I}_{ci} = E(I_{ci})$
5. $\text{Cov}(c_i, I_j) = E[c_i(I_j - \bar{I}_j)] = 0$
6. $\text{Cov}(c_i, c_j) = E(c_i, c_j) = 0$ for all i, j, and k.

The last statement is equivalent to the residuals being unrelated, which is to say that the only reason for common comovement of returns is due to the movement of the indexes. Although this is like ignoring some of a model's shortcomings, it facilitates a usable model to obtain a quantified idea of future return patterns.

The expected value of the model with the multiple indexes is:

$$\begin{aligned} E(R_i) &= E(a_i + b_{i1}I_1 + b_{i2}I_2 + \cdots + b_{iL}I_L + c_i) \\ &= E(a_i) + E(b_{i1}I_1) + E(b_{i2}I_2) + \cdots + E(b_{iL}I_L) + E(c_i) \end{aligned}$$

because a and the b's are constants, and the expected value of the residuals is equal to zero:

$$r_i = a_i + b_{i1}\bar{I}_1 + b_{i2}\bar{I}_2 + \cdots + b_{iL}\bar{I}_L \qquad \text{(10B.2)}$$

where $\bar{I}_j$ is the expected value of index j.

The variance of the returns using multiple indexes is:

$$\sigma_i^2 = E(R_i - r_i)^2$$

where r_i is the expected value of the returns of security i. Substituting R_i and r_i from above:

$$\sigma_i^2 = E[(a_i + b_{i1}I_1 + b_{i2}I_2 + \cdots + b_{iL}I_L + c_i) \\ - (a_i + b_{i1}\bar{I}_1 + b_{i2}\bar{I}_2 + \cdots + b_{iL}\bar{I}_L)]^2$$

Rearranging, and noticing that the a_i cancel, yields:

$$\sigma_i^2 = E[(b_{i1}(I_1 - \bar{I}_1) + b_{i2}(I_2 - \bar{I}_2) + \cdots + b_{iL}(I_L - \bar{I}_L) + c_i]^2$$

Next the terms in the brackets are squared. To proceed with this concentrate on the first index, and the rest of the terms involving the other indexes follow directly. The first index times itself and all other terms yields:

$$E[(b_{i1}{}^2(I_1 - \bar{I}_1)^2 + b_{i1}b_{i2}(I_1 - \bar{I}_1)(I_2 - \bar{I}_2) + \cdots + \\ b_{i1}b_{iL}(I_1 - \bar{I}_1)(I_L - \bar{I}_L) + b_{i1}(I_1 - \bar{I}_1)(c_i)]$$

Remembering that:

$$E[(I_i - \bar{I}_i)(I_j - \bar{I}_j)] = 0, \quad \text{and} \quad E[(I_i - \bar{I}_i) c_i] = 0$$

the only nonzero term involving index one is expressed:

$$b_{i1}^2 E(I_1 - \bar{I}_1)^2 = b_{i1}^2 \sigma_{I1}^2$$

Because all terms involving c_i are zero and $E(c_i)^2 = \sigma_{ci}^2$:

$$\sigma_i^2 = b_{i1}^2 \sigma_{I1}^2 + b_{i2}^2 \sigma_{I2}^2 + \cdots + b_{iL}^2 \sigma_{IL}^2 + \sigma_{ci}^2 \qquad \text{(10B.3)}$$

The covariance of the returns between security i and j utilizing the multiple-index model can be expressed:

$$\sigma_{ij} = E[(R_i - r_i)(R_j - r_j)]$$

Again, substituting for R_i, r_i, R_j, and r_j:

$$\sigma_{ij} = E[[(a_i + b_{i1}I_1 + b_{i2}I_2 + \cdots + b_{iL}I_L + c_i) \\ - (a_i + b_{i1}\bar{I}_1 + b_{i2}\bar{I}_2 + \cdots + b_{iL}\bar{I}_L)]* \\ [(a_j + b_{j1}I_1 + b_{j2}I_2 + \cdots + b_{jL}I_L + c_j) \\ - (a_j + b_{j1}\bar{I}_1 + b_{j2}\bar{I}_2 + \cdots + b_{jL}\bar{I}_L)]]$$

Again, noting that the a_i cancel and combining the terms involving the same b's:

$$\sigma_{ij} = E\{[b_{i1}(I_1 - \bar{I}_1) + b_{i2}(I_2 - \bar{I}_2) + \cdots + b_{iL}(I_L - \bar{I}_L) + c_i] \\ \times [b_{j1}(I_1 - \bar{I}_1) + b_{j2}(I_2 - \bar{I}_2) + \cdots + b_{jL}(I_L - \bar{I}_L) + c_j]\}$$

Next multiply out terms, again concentrating on the terms involving b_{i1}:

$$E[b_{i1}b_{j1}(I_1 - \bar{I}_1)^2 + b_{i1}b_{j2}(I_1 - \bar{I}_1)(I_2 - \bar{I}_2) + \cdots + b_{i1}b_{jL}(I_1 - \bar{I}_1)(I_L - \bar{I}_L) + b_{i1}(I_1 - \bar{I}_1)c_j]$$

Because the covariance between two indexes is zero, and the covariance between any residual and an index is zero:

$$b_{i1}b_{j1}E(I_1 - \bar{I}_1)^2 = b_{i1}b_{j1}\,\sigma_{I1}^2$$

To conclude, remember that the covariance of the residuals is equal to zero and therefore:

$$\sigma_{ij} = b_{i1}b_{j1}\sigma_{I1}^2 + b_{i2}b_{j2}\sigma_{I2}^2 + \cdots + b_{iL}b_{jL}\sigma_{IL}^2 \qquad \textbf{(10B.4)}$$

REFERENCES

Beaver, W., P. Kettler, and M. Scholes. "The Association Between Market Determined and Accounting Determined Risk Measures." *The Accounting Review,* v. 45 (October 1970), pp. 654–82.

Blume, M. "Betas and Their Regression Tendencies." *Journal of Finance,* v. 20 (June 1975), pp. 785–95.

Brenner, M. "On the Stability of the Distribution of the Market Component in Stock Price Changes." *Journal of Financial and Quantitative Analysis,* v. 9 (December 1974), pp. 945–61.

Elton, E. J., M. J. Gruber, and T. Urich. "Are Betas Best?" *Journal of Finance,* v. 23 (December 1978), pp. 1375–84.

Fouse, W., W. Jahnke, and B. Rosenberg. "Is Beta Phlogiston?" *Financial Analysts Journal,* v. 30, (January/February 1974), pp. 70–80.

Frankfurter, G., and H. Phillips. "Alpha-Beta Theory: A Word of Caution." *Journal of Financial Management,* v. 3 (Summer 1977), pp. 35–40.

_____, and J. Seagle. "Performance of the Sharpe Portfolio Selection Model: A Comparison." *Journal of Financial and Quantitative Analysis,* v. 11 (June 1976), pp. 195–204.

Gibbons, M. R. "Multivariate Tests of Financial Models, A New Approach." *Journal of Financial Economics,* v. 10 (March 1982), pp. 3–27.

Haugen, R., and D. Wichern. "The Intricate Relationship Between Financial Leverage and the Stability of Stock Prices." *Journal of Finance,* v. 20 (December 1975), pp. 1283–92.

Jacob, N. "A Limited-Diversification Portfolio Selection Model for the Small Investor." *Journal of Finance,* v. 19 (June 1974), pp. 847–56.

King, B. "Market and Industry Factors in Stock Price Behavior." *Journal of Business,* v. 39 (January 1966), pp. 139–40.

Latane, H., D. Tuttle, and A. Young. "How to Choose a Market Index." *Financial Analysts Journal,* v. 27 (September/October 1971), pp. 75–85.

Levy, R. "Beta Coefficients as Predictors of Return." *Financial Analysts Journal,* v. 30 (January/February 1974), pp. 61–69.

Markowitz, H. *Portfolio Selection.* Cowles Foundation Monograph 16. John Wiley & Sons, Inc., 1959.

Morgan, I. G. "Grouping Procedures for Portfolio Formation." *Journal of Finance.* v. 21 (December 1977), pp. 1759–65.

Roll, R. "Bias in Fitting the Sharpe Model to Time Series Data." *Journal of Financial and Quantitative Analysis,* v. 4 (September 1969), pp. 271–89.

Rosenberg, B., and J. Guy. "Prediction of Beta from Investment Fundamentals." *Financial Analysts Journal,* v. 32 (May/June 1976), pp. 60–72.

————. "Prediction of Beta from Investment Fundamentals, Part II." *Financial Analysts Journal,* v. 32 (July/August 1976), pp. 62–70.

————, and W. McKibben. "The Prediction of Systematic and Specific Risk in Common Stocks." *Journal of Financial and Quantitative Analysis,* v. 8 (March 1973), pp. 317–33.

————, and V. Marathe. "The Prediction of Investment Risk: Systematic and Residual Risk." Berkeley Working Paper Series, 1974.

Ross, S. A. "Arbitrage Theory of Capital-Asset Pricing." *Journal of Economic Theory,* v. 8 (December 1976), pp. 341–60.

————. "Return, Risk and Arbitrage." In *Risk and Return in Finance,* v. 1, ed. by I. Friend and J. L. Bicksler. Ballinger, 1977, pp. 187–208.

Sharpe, W. F. "A Linear Programming Algorithm for Mutual Fund Portfolio Selection." *Management Science,* v. 13 (1967), pp. 499–510.

————. *Portfolio Theory and Capital Markets.* McGraw-Hill Book Co., 1970.

Smith, K. V. "Stock Price and Economic Indexes for Generating Efficient Portfolios." *Journal of Business,* v. 42 (July 1969), pp. 326–35.

Stone, B. "A Linear Programming Formulation of the General Portfolio Selection Problem." *Journal of Financial and Quantitative Analysis,* v. 8 (September 1973), pp. 621–36.

11 Arbitrage Pricing Theory: Theory, Evidence, and Applications

From the viewpoint of a security analyst, knowledge of an equilibrium-market pricing model is important because it allows the analyst to determine the theoretical value of a firm and estimate its cost of capital. The importance of these valuation concepts is demonstrated by the abundance of efforts from theoretician and practitioner alike to formulate pricing models.

In finance a great deal of the theoretical and empirical work is based on the modern portfolio theory of Harry Markowitz (1952), out of which has evolved the **capital asset pricing model (CAPM).** Although the CAPM has contributed greatly to our knowledge of how asset prices are determined, there are some deficiencies in the CAPM approach. These deficiencies, contained in the CAPM's stringent assumptions, have been demonstrated by the results of empirical studies. As an alternative approach to explaining the pricing of assets, Ross (1976, 1977) has developed **arbitrage pricing theory (APT).**

APT offers many advantages over and above the traditional CAPM in terms of less stringent assumptions while retaining a higher degree of generality. Nevertheless, while theoretically APT seems to have opened up a whole new area in finance, its empirical testing still faces some problems that need to be resolved.

This chapter approaches APT by first extending the traditional CAPM to a multi-index model, thereby establishing a more congruent base from which to lead into APT. A discussion of multi-index models is followed by an examination of the specification of the arbitrage pricing model: its underlying arguments are developed and alternative model specifications are examined. The investigation then turns to the criteria of realism, and the methodologies, results, and problems are examined with empirical tests. The APT and CAPM are then compared and contrasted, and the original CAPM is shown to be a special case of the APT. The current and potential

applications of APT are discussed along with future directions for model improvement. The appendixes present an alternative specification of the APT as well as a method of identifying the APT model's common factors.

MULTI-INDEX MODELS

Chapter 9 developed and examined the tenets of the CAPM. The CAPM implies that an asset's return is determined strictly by its inherent degree of systematic or nondiversifiable risk. This type of risk, which can also be referred to as *market risk,* is essentially a normalized measure of the covariability of returns between the individual asset and the market portfolio. Remember that beta, the measure of systematic risk, is defined as Cov (R_i, R_m)/Var (R_m). Thus, the traditional CAPM suggests that only one independent variable, the market portfolio, is necessary for explaining asset expected returns. Nevertheless, both researchers and practitioners believe that there are influences beyond the market that cause stock prices to move. King (1966) presents evidence for the existence of industry influences. To handle additional influential factors for the explanation of asset returns and their movement over time, **multi-index models** have been proposed. Investment houses have organized their security analysis efforts along industry lines or sectors—for example, interest-sensitive stocks. Both practitioners and academics have begun to add additional factors to their models that are used to explain asset returns.

Simply adding these influences to the general return equation will, it is hoped, allow significant additional sources of covariance between securities to be taken into account. Hence, consider the following return-generating model:

$$R_i = a_i + b_{i1}I_1 + b_{i2}I_2 + \cdots + b_{iL}I_L + e_i \qquad \textbf{(11.1)}$$

where:

I_h = the actual level of some index h ($h = 1, \ldots, L$); and
b_{ih} = a measure of the responsiveness of the return on stock i to changes in index h or its sensitivity, to index h.

Essentially, then, b_{ih} may be interpreted in much the same light as βi for the single-index model. Finally, the portion of security i's return that is not accounted for by the indexes is apportioned into variables a_i and e_i. The a_i term represents the unique portion of the securities return that could be expected if it were to be unrelated to all of the explanatory indexes (that is, all $b_{ih} = 0$). The e_i term corresponds to the random component of the return, with a mean of zero and variance of e_i.

To simplify both the computation of risk and the selection of optimal portfolios in using the multi-index model, it is advantageous for the indexes to be uncorrelated (orthogonal). This poses no significant mathematical

problem, as was shown in Chapter 10; thus, for the remainder of this section it can be assumed that the indexes do exhibit the mathematical properties associated with being uncorrelated with one another [that is, they are independent, $\rho(I_h, I_k) = 0$].

Now, what do or should these explanatory indexes represent? While no precise answer exists for this question, theory, intuition, and empirical tests can jointly suggest a number of possibilities. As was previously mentioned, King found that in addition to an overall market factor, various factors related to industry-type indexes are significant in explaining the returns-generating process for a particular security. Other potential additional indexes could be related to interest-rate movements and firm capitalization size. Sharpe (1984) finds quite a wide array of these additional factors, which he classifies as either a *systematic influence* or a *sector influence*. Among those defined as systematic influences on security returns, Sharpe finds five.

1. Beta (the slope of the regression of excess return for the security against excess return on the S&P index)
2. Dividend yield
3. Size
4. Bond beta
5. Alpha

The significant sector influences includes eight factors.

1. Basic industries
2. Capital goods
3. Construction
4. Consumer goods
5. Energy
6. Finance
7. Transportation
8. Utilities

Another study by Fogler, John, and Tipton (1981) finds that the first three sources of variation in a study sample of 100 stocks are related to the market, the interest rate on U.S. government securities, and the interest rate on AA utility bonds.

Some of the other factors that have been considered include: (1) price/earnings ratio, (2) stock-issue size, (3) marketability and liquidity, (4) taxes, and (5) the time of year that the purchase or sale took place (the so-called January effect). There is no reason to believe that the number of important factors will stay constant over time or that the composition of the group of important factors will remain unchanged. Think of the OPEC oil crisis of the 1970s and its influence on pricing assets in financial markets during that period. Although during the 1980s OPEC's influence seems to have waned with respect to its influence on security pricing, perhaps in the

future some other energy-related factor will emerge as an important influence in security prices.

Although empirical research supports the significance of additional explanatory indexes in addition to some market influence, the real question to put forward is how well multi-index models perform in explaining the pricing of securities. Nevertheless, to effectively carry on any discussion concerning performance it is necessary to first reconsider the multi-index model's construction, the underlying assumptions, and the resultant implications.

By construction the equation

$$R_i = a_i + b_{i1}I_i + b_{i2}I_2 + \cdots + b_{iL}I_L + e_i \qquad (11.2)$$

has the following characteristics.

1. The mean of e_i and $E(e_i) = 0$ for all stocks, where $i = 1, \ldots, n$.
2. The covariance between indexes h and l equals $E[(I_h - \bar{I}_h)(I_l - \bar{I}_l)] = 0$ for all indexes where $h = 1, \ldots, L$ and $l = 1, \ldots, L$ $(h \neq l)$.
3. The covariance between the residual for stock i and index h equals Cov $(e_i, I_h) = 0$ for all stocks and indexes, where $i = 1, \ldots, n$ and $h = 1, \ldots, L$.
4. The covariance between e_i and e_j is zero. $[E(e_i, e_j) = 0]$ for all stocks, where $i = 1, \ldots, n$ and $j = 1, \ldots, n$ $(j \neq i)$.

If the multi-index model does sufficiently describe the return-generating process for common stocks, the expected return, variance, and covariance can then be computed between securities as follows (see Appendix 10B). The expected return for security i can be expressed:

$$\overline{R}_i = a_1 + b_{i1}\bar{I}_1 + b_{i2}\bar{I}_2 + \cdots + b_{iL}\bar{I}_L \qquad (11.3)$$

Its variance of return can be expressed:

$$\sigma_i^2 = b_{i1}^2\sigma_{I1}^2 + b_{i2}^2\sigma_{I2}^2 + \cdots + b_{iL}^2\sigma_{IL}^2 + \sigma_{ei}^2 \qquad (11.4)$$

The covariance between securities i and j can be expressed:

$$\sigma_{ij} = b_{i1}b_{j1}\sigma_{I1}^2 + b_{i2}b_{j2}\sigma_{I2}^2 + \cdots + b_{iL}b_{jL}\sigma_{IL}^2 \qquad (11.5)$$

It is necessary to examine the implication of the fourth model assumption, that $E[e_i, e_j] = 0$. This statistical requirement implies that the only reason stocks vary together is because of common comovement with the set of indexes that have been specified in the model. No other factors beyond these indexes should account for any of the comovement between two securities. However, there is nothing in the estimation of the model that requires this condition to be true. Rather, the model is more likely to be an approximation of reality. The model's performance is therefore dependent on how well the model approximates the true return-generating process for securities. Moreover, the accuracy of approximation will depend heavily upon how well the chosen indexes capture the actual pattern of comovement between securities and to what extent historical patterns of comovement persist into the future.

To judge the performance of multi-index models it is essential first to point out that all index models lead to the same estimates of expected returns and a stock's own variance (but not covariances), when estimated from historical returns and variances. Moreover, if the stock analyst uses a personal estimate for the stock's expected return and variance, then all that is left for the model to estimate are the covariances. Yet since the covariance is the product of standard deviations and security coefficients, any disparities in performance that exist must arise from differences in estimating the correlation structure of security returns. Consequently, then, the most direct test of alternative models is to evaluate how well they estimate the future correlation matrix of security returns. Upon measuring the difference between actual results and forecasts, it can be determined whether such forecasting deficiencies are statistically significant. Another mode of analysis for evaluating model performance is to test the economic significance of the difference in return or profit that results from basing forecasts on various models (for a prespecified level of risk).

The empirical results for testing the multi-index model on statistical and economic grounds do not offer a great deal of support. For instance, Elton and Gruber (1973) note that, in general, adding additional indexes to the single-index model leads to a decrease in performance on both statistical and economic grounds. These authors conclude that the addition of more indexes lead to a better explanation of the historical correlation matrix, yet it resulted in both a poorer prediction of the future correlation matrix and a selection of portfolios that at each risk level tended to have lower returns. Thus, the use of multiple indexes in the forecasting process results in the introduction of more random noise than real information.

In another test of the multi-index model, Cohen and Pogue (1967) formulate the additional explanatory indexes on the basis of standard industrial classifications. Comparing the forecasts of a single-index model to one including both a market and industry index, these authors conclude that the single-index model leads to lower expected risks and is much simpler to use.

As was previously mentioned, the performance of the multi-index model largely depends on which indexes are chosen and how they are formed. The study by Cohen and Pogue utilizes standard industrial classifications to devise their additional indexes. Nevertheless, this method has its problems. The increase in the number of multi-product firms and the prevalence of company diversification has made the classification by product difficult and sometimes arbitrary. Moreover, classification by product or service may be useful for some purposes, but falls far short of being a universal classification in all cases. For instance, although General Motors and Chrysler are in the same industry there is substantial divergence between their performance and the degree of risk to which they are subject.

To combat this problem, Farrell (1974) formulates homogeneous groups of firms (''pseudo-industries'') to form indexes as input to a multi-index model. Utilizing a procedure known as **principal-components analysis** Farrell finds that his large sample of stocks can be classified into four pseudo-

industries. Due to the nature of stocks in each group the author is able to associate characteristics with each of them and correspondingly labels the four groups:

1. Growth stocks
2. Cyclical stocks
3. Stable stocks
4. Oil stocks

While it is not surprising that his model does a superior job of accounting for the historical correlation matrix of returns, it is significant that this model performs somewhat better based on economic criteria than the models of Cohen and Pogue. *Economic criteria* test whether there is a better predictor of the correlation structure of returns. Thus, evidence arises that when the explanation indexes are correctly formed the multi-index model can potentially outperform the single-index model, perhaps yielding greater insight into the inherent return-generating processes among securities. This chapter can now focus on the arbitrage pricing theory, which devises a more generalized equilibrium framework than the multi-index model for describing and forecasting security returns. Indeed, one of the central issues in APT concerns the formation, interpretation, and correct number of "pseudo-indexes" to use.

MODEL SPECIFICATION OF ARBITRAGE PRICING THEORY

Suppose there are two riskless assets offering rates of return r and r', respectively. Assuming no transaction costs, one of the strongest statements that can be made in positive economics is that:

$$r = r' \qquad (11.6)$$

This is based on the law of one price, which says that the same good cannot sell at different prices. In terms of securities, the law of one price says that securities with identical risks must have the same expected return. Essentially, Equation (11.6) is an **arbitrage condition** that must be expected to hold in all but the most extreme circumstances. This is because if $r > r'$, the first riskless asset could be purchased with funds obtained from selling the second riskless asset. This arbitrage transaction would yield a return of $r - r'$ with no risk and no net wealth invested. If investors were to come across such a disequilibrium relationship, they would surely seize the opportunity to make a return of $r - r'$ without having to make any new investment of funds or take on any additional risk. In the process of buying the first asset and selling the second, investors would bid up the former's price and bid down the latter's price. This repricing mechanism would continue up to the point where these two assets' respective prices equalled each other, and thus $r = r'$.

FIGURE 11-1   Expected Returns and Factor Sensitivity

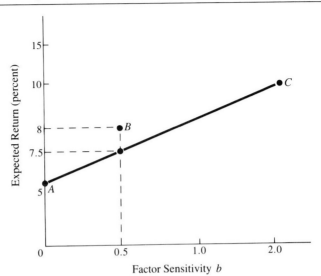

Security	Expected Return (percent)	Factor Sensitivity
A	5	0.0
B	8	0.5
C	15	2.0

Put in the context of securities that are traded in markets and held in portfolios, consider the following simple example. There exist three assets A, B, and C, all of which are related to the same basic underlying factor. The characteristics of these three assets are shown in Figure 11-1. Securities A and C are both correctly priced given the sensitivity they have to the factor.[1] However, security B appears to be mispriced; it offers a return of 8 percent, which exceeds the expected return of 7.5 percent for securities with a sensitivity of 0.5. To take advantage of this mispricing, an investor can perform an arbitrage among the three securities. By buying $1 worth of security B and short selling $0.75 of security A and $0.25 of security C, the investor can generate a risk-free return of 0.5 percent. This arbitrage is shown in Table 11-1. The arbitrage allows the investor to earn a return of 0.5 percent with no risk and no investment. There is only one factor in this example, but the arbitrage argument can be extended to include many factors. As long as there exists a mispricing of one of the securities on one of

---

[1] Strictly speaking, A, B, or C or some combination may be mispriced. However, the validity of the argument still holds.

TABLE 11-1   Arbitrage Results

	Expected Return	*Factor Sensitivity*
Buy $1 of B.	$(1 \times 8\%) = 8\%$	$(1 \times 0.5) = 0.5$
Sell $0.75 of A short.	$-(0.75 \times 5\%) = -3.75\%$	$-(0.75 \times 0) = 0$
Sell $0.25 of C short.	$-(0.25 \times 15\%) = -3.75\%$	$-(0.25 \times 2) = -0.5$
Total investment $= 0$	Total return $= +0.5\%$	Total sensitivity $= 0$

the factors, an arbitrage opportunity will exist until investors drive the market into equilibrium.

Arbitrage pricing theory (APT) utilizes this robust type of argument and extends its application to the pricing of risky assets. The net result of APT's development is a more generalized and less restrictive framework than the CAPM for the pricing of risky assets. More explicitly, to make its equilibrium statement for asset returns, APT does not require quadratic utility functions for investors or joint normality of returns between individual assets and the market portfolio. (APT does not require that market portfolio be mean-variance efficient or even that it exist at all!) Finally, APT is not limited to a single period, as is the original form of the CAPM.

Ross's Arbitrage Model Specification

This section focuses on two related forms of the arbitrage pricing model. The first of these is the model as originally proposed by Ross (1976).

The initial and probably the most prominent assumption made by APT concerns the return-generating process for assets. Specifically, individuals are assumed to believe (homogeneously) that the random returns on the set of assets being considered are governed by a k-factor generating model of the form:

$$\tilde{r}_i = E_i + b_{i1}\tilde{\delta}_1 + \cdots + b_{ik}\tilde{\delta}_k + \tilde{\epsilon}_i \qquad (i = 1, \ldots, n) \qquad \textbf{(11.7)}$$

where:

$\tilde{r}_i$ = random return on the ith asset;

E_i = expected return on the ith asset;

$\tilde{\delta}_j$ = jth factor common to the returns of all assets under consideration with a mean of zero, common factors that in essence capture the systematic component of risk in the model;

b_{ij} = a coefficient called a *factor loading* that quantifies the sensitivity of asset i's returns to the movements in the common factor $\tilde{\delta}_j$ (and is analogous to the beta in the CAPM); and

$\tilde{\epsilon}_i$ = an error term, or unsystematic risk component, idiosyncratic to the ith asset, with mean zero and variance equal to $\tilde{\sigma}_\epsilon^2$.

Moreover, it is assumed that the $\bar{\epsilon}_i$ reflects the random influence of information that is unrelated to other assets. Thus, the following condition is assumed to hold:

$$E\{\bar{\epsilon}_i|\bar{\epsilon}_j\} = 0 \tag{11.8}$$

as well as $\bar{\epsilon}_i$ and $\bar{\epsilon}_j$ independence for all $i \neq j$. Also, for any two securities i and j:

$$E\{\bar{\epsilon}_i, \bar{\epsilon}_j\} = 0 \tag{11.9}$$

for all i and j, where $i \neq j$. If this last condition did not hold—that is, if there was too strong a dependence between $\bar{\epsilon}_i$ and $\bar{\epsilon}_j$—it would be equivalent to saying that more than simply the k-hypothesized common factors existed. Finally, it is assumed for the set of n assets under consideration that n is much greater than the number of factors k.

Before developing Ross's riskless arbitrage argument, it is essential to examine Equation (11.7) more closely and draw some implications from its structure. First, consider the effect of omitting the unsystematic risk terms $\bar{e}_i$. Equation (11.7) would then imply that each asset i has returns $\bar{r}_i$ that are an exact linear combination of the returns on a riskless asset (with constant return) and the returns on k other factors or assets (or column vectors) $\bar{\delta}_i, \ldots, \bar{\delta}_k$. Moreover, the riskless return and each of the k factors can be expressed as a linear combination of $k + 1$ other returns—for example, r, through r_{k+1}—in this type of setting. Taking this logic one step further, since any other asset return is a linear combination of the factors, it must also be a linear combination of the returns of the first $k + 1$ assets. Hence, portfolios composed from the first $k + 1$ assets must be perfect substitutes for all other assets in the market. Consequently, there must be restrictions on the individual returns generated by the model, since perfect substitutes must be priced equivalently. This sequence of mathematical logic is the core of APT. That is, only a few systematic components of risk exist in the economy; and consequently many portfolios will be close substitutes, thereby demanding the same value.

To initiate Ross's arbitrage argument about APT it is best to start with the assumption of Equation (11.7). Next, presume an investor who is contemplating an alteration of the currently held portfolio. The difference between any new portfolio and the old portfolio will be quantified by changes in the investment porportions x_i ($i = 1, \ldots, n$). The x_i represents the dollar amount purchased or sold of asset i as a fraction of total invested wealth. This investor's portfolio investment is constrained to hold to the following condition:

$$\sum_{i=1}^{n} x_i = 0 \tag{11.10}$$

In words, Equation (11.10) says that additional purchases of assets must be financed by sales of others. Portfolios that require no net investment such as

$x \equiv (x_j, \ldots, x_n)$ are called *arbitrage portfolios*. Table 11–1 shows exactly this situation: the proceeds from the short sale of A and C were used to purchase B.

Now, consider an arbitrage portfolio chosen in the following manner. First the portfolio must be chosen to be well diversified by keeping each element, x_i of order $1/n$ in size. Second, the x of the portfolio must be selected in such a way as to eliminate all systematic risk (for each h):

$$xb_h \equiv \sum_{i=1}^{n} x_i b_{ih} = 0 \qquad (h = 1, \ldots, k) \tag{11.11}$$

The returns on any such arbitrage portfolios can be described:

$$
\begin{aligned}
x\tilde{r} &= (xE) + (xb_1)\,\tilde{\delta}_1 + \cdots + (xb_k)\,\tilde{\delta}_k + (x\tilde{\epsilon}) \\
&\approx xE + (xb_1)\,\tilde{\delta}_1 + \cdots + (xb_k)\,\tilde{\delta}_k \\
&= xE
\end{aligned}
\tag{11.12}
$$

where $x\tilde{r} = \sum_{i=1}^{n} x_i \tilde{r}_i$ and $xE = \sum_{i=1}^{n} x_i E_i$. Note that the term $(x\tilde{\epsilon})$ is (approximately) eliminated by the effect of holding a well-diversified portfolio of n assets where n is large. Using the law of large numbers, if σ^2 denotes the average variance of the $\tilde{\epsilon}_i$ terms, and assuming for simplicity that each x_i approximately equals $1/n$ and that the ϵ_i are mutually independent:

$$
\begin{aligned}
\mathrm{Var}\,(x\tilde{\epsilon}) &= \mathrm{Var}\left(\frac{1}{n}\sum_i \epsilon_i\right) \\
&= \frac{\mathrm{Var}\,(\tilde{\epsilon}_i)}{n^2} \\
&= \frac{\sigma^2}{n^2}
\end{aligned}
$$

Thus if n is large the variance of $x\tilde{\epsilon}$ will be negligible.

Reconsidering the steps up to this point, note that a portfolio has been created that has no systematic or unsystematic risk and using no wealth. Under **conditions of equilibrium** it can be stated unequivocally that *all portfolios of these n assets that satisfy the conditions of using no wealth and having no risk must also earn no return on average*. In other words, there are no free lunches in an efficient market, at least not for any extended period of time. Therefore the expected return on the arbitrage portfolio can be expressed:

$$x\tilde{r} = xE = \sum_{i=1}^{n} x_i E_i = 0 \tag{11.13}$$

Another way to state the preceding statements and results is through linear algebra. In general, any vector x with elements on the order of $1/n$ that is orthogonal to the constant vector and to each of the coefficient vectors b_h ($h = 1, \ldots, k$) must also be orthogonal to the vector of expected returns. A further algebraic consequence of this statement is that the expected return vector E must be a linear combination of the constant vector and the

b vectors. Using algebraic terminology, there exist $k + 1$ weights $(\lambda_0, \lambda_1, \ldots, \lambda_k)$ such that:

$$E_i = \lambda_0 + \lambda_1 b_{i1} + \cdots + \lambda_k b_{ik}, \qquad \text{for all } i \qquad \textbf{(11.14)}$$

In addition, if there exists a riskless asset with return E_0 which can be said to be the common return on all zero-beta assets—that is, $b_{ih} = 0$ (for all h)—then:

$$E_0 = \lambda_0$$

Utilizing this definition and rearranging:

$$E_i - E_0 = \lambda_1 b_{i1} + \cdots + \lambda_k b_{ik} \qquad \textbf{(11.15)}$$

The pricing relationship depicted in Equation (11.15) is the central conclusion of the APT. Before exploring the consequences of this pricing model through a simple numerical example, it is best to first give some interpretation to the λ_h, the factor risk premium. If portfolios are formed with a systematic risk of 1 relative to factor h and no risk on other factors, then each λ_h can be interpreted as:

$$\lambda_h = E^h - E_0 \qquad \textbf{(11.16)}$$

In words, each λ_h can be thought of as the excess return or market risk premium on portfolios with only systematic factor h risk. Hence, Equation (11.15) can be rewritten:

$$E_i - E_0 = (E^1 - E_0) b_{i1} + \cdots + (E^k - E_0) b_{ik} \qquad \textbf{(11.17)}$$

The implications that arise from the arguments concerning APT that have been constructed thus far can be summarized in the following statement: *APT yields a statement of relative pricing on subsets of the universe of assets.* Moreover, note that the arbitrage pricing model of Equations (11.15) or (11.17) can be tested by examining only subsets of the set of all returns. Consequently, the market portfolio plays no special role in APT, since any well-diversified portfolio could serve the same purpose. Hence, it can be empirically tested on any set of data, and the results should be generalizable to the entire market. The following three sample problems give further illustration.

Sample Problem 11.1

To reinforce the concepts and workings of the arbitrage mechanism, consider a simple example. Suppose that the returns on two well-diversified portfolios can be described by a linear function in the following arbitrage pricing model (APM) form:

$$(E_i - E_0) = (\lambda_1 b_{i1} + \lambda_2 b_{i2})$$

or,

$$= (E^1 - E_0)b_{i1} + (E^2 - E_0)b_{i2} + (E^3 - E_0)b_{i3}$$

in which E_0 is the constant return on the riskless asset.

Next, assume these portfolios have the following sensitivity coefficients (factor loadings) with the three identified factors (first table).

Portfolio	b_{i1}	b_{i2}	b_{i3}
1	0.6	1.0	0.8
2	0.3	0.7	0.5

Assuming the riskless rate is 7 percent (E_0), the expected returns and their relative returns per unit of risk as defined by the Treynor performance measure can be expressed as in the table at the top of page 328. In addition a

Expected Return and Factor Sensitivity

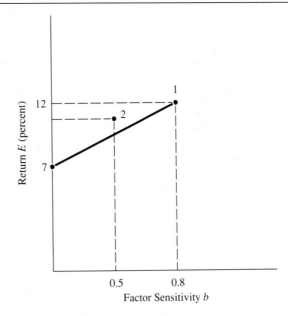

graph can be drawn of each portfolio's expected return versus the averaged value of its sensitivity coefficients, as indicated in the figure. This is somewhat analogous to the analysis in CAPM.

Portfolio	E_i (percent)	$\dfrac{(E_i - E_0)}{\left(\sum\limits_{i=1}^{3} b_{ih}/3\right)}$
1	12	6.25
2	8	2.00

As was demonstrated through the determination of each portfolio's expected return-per-risk measure, the graph again points out that the second portfolio is overpriced. That is, its expected return per unit of risk is lower than that of the first portfolio relative to the riskless rate of 7 percent.

	Investment	Systematic Risk (b_{ih})	Expected Return (percent)
For Portfolio 2, sell short.	$1,000,000	− 0.5	− 8.0
For Portfolio 1, buy.	($625,000)	(0.625 × 0.8) = 0.5	(0.625 × 12.0) = 7.5
Invest remainder in T-bills.	($375,000)	(0.375 × 0) = 0	(0.375 × 7.0) = 2.625
Net investment:	$0		
Net risk:		0.0	
Total excess return earned:			2.125%

The proper "arbitrage strategy" to follow in order to profit from this apparent mispricing is shown in the third table, above. However appealing the logic of the previous arbitrage argument, some specific assumptions are required for the APT.

1. Investors are return maximizers.
2. Borrowing and lending is done at the riskless rate.
3. There are no market restrictions such as transaction costs, taxes, or restrictions on short selling.
4. Investors agree on the number and identity of the factors that are priced.
5. Riskless profitable opportunities above the risk-free rate are immediately arbitraged away.

Hence, since any market equilibrium must be consistent with no arbitrage profits, every equilibrium will be characterized by a linear relationship

between each asset's expected return and its sensitivity to the common priced factors●

Sample Problem 11.2

Given the three portfolios in the table with expected return R_i and sensitivity factors b_{i1} and b_{i2}, what is the equation of the plane in R_i, b_{i1}, and b_{i2} space defined by these portfolios?

Solution

Portfolio	R_i	b_{i1}	b_{i2}
A	14.0	0.8	0.8
B	10.8	0.6	0.4
C	11.2	0.4	0.6

The information can be used to derive the equation for the risk–return plan of Equation (11.14) as follows. Substituting returns and sensitivity-factor information into Equation (11.14):

$$14 \ \ = \lambda_0 + 0.8\lambda_1 + 0.8\lambda_2 \qquad \text{(i)}$$
$$10.8 = \lambda_0 + 0.6\lambda_1 + 0.4\lambda_2 \qquad \text{(ii)}$$
$$11.2 = \lambda_0 + 0.4\lambda_1 + 0.6\lambda_2 \qquad \text{(iii)}$$

Subtract (ii) from (i):

$$3.2 = 0.2\lambda_1 + 0.4\lambda_2 \qquad \text{(iv)}$$

Subtract (ii) from (iii):

$$0.4 = -0.2\lambda_1 + 0.2\lambda_2 \qquad \text{(v)}$$

From Equations (iv) and (v) $\lambda_2 = 6$. From Equation (v) $\lambda_1 = 4$. Finally, from Equation (i), solving for λ_0:

$$\lambda_0 = 14 - 0.8\lambda_1 - 0.8\lambda_2$$
$$= 14 - 3.2 - 4.8$$
$$= 6$$

Hence the equation of the plane describing equilibrium risk–return space can be expressed:

$$E_i = 6 + 4b_{i1} + 6b_{i2} \qquad ●$$

Sample Problem 11.3

Using the portfolios in Sample Problem 11.2, determine how much arbitrage profit, if any, can be made by buying or selling (short) the following portfolios (individually).

Portfolio	R_i (percent)	b_{i1}	b_{i2}
D	14.0	0.5	0.7
E	15.2	0.8	1.0
F	9.0	0.6	0.5

Solution

From portfolios A, B, and C, the risk/return relationship is $r_i = 6 + 4b_{i1} + 6b_{i2}$.

For portfolio D, an equivalent portfolio can be composed from a linear combination of A, B, and C. Given sensitivity factors $b_{i1} = 0.5$ and $b_{i2} = 0.7$, the expected return would be:

$$r_0 = 6 + 4(0.5) + 6(0.7)$$
$$= 12.2\%$$

Since $12.2\% < 14\%$, portfolio D is undervalued. A riskless, costless arbitrage profit can be made by buying portfolio D and selling an equivalent amount of a portfolio composed of A, B, and C.

For portfolio E, an equivalent portfolio can be constructed with yield:

$$r_{equiv} = 6 + 4(0.8) + 6(1.0) = 15.2\%$$

This is exactly the yield of portfolio E; therefore, no arbitrage opportunities remain.

For portfolio F:

$$r_{equiv} = 6 + 4(0.6) + 6(0.5) = 11.4\%$$

Since $11.4\% > 9\%$, the F portfolio is overpriced. Therefore, portfolio F should be sold and the equivalent portfolio should be bought.

	Initial CF		Ending CF	Risk Factors	
				b_{i1}	b_{i2}
Portfolio D	−$10,000,000		+1,140,000	0.5	0.7
Equivalent portfolio	+$10,000,000		−1,122,000	−0.5	−0.7
	0	+	18,000	0	0

	Initial CF	Ending CF	Sens. Factors b_{i1}	b_{i2}
Portfolio F	+$10,000,000	−1,090,000	−0.8	−1.0
Equivalent portfolio	−$10,000,000	+1,114,000	+0.8	+1.0
	0 +	24,000	0	0

A riskless, costless arbitrage profit of $24,000 can be made by selling $10 million worth of portfolio F and by buying $10 million of an equivalent portfolio made up of A, B, and C●

Even though the APT is very general and based on few assumptions, it provides little guidance concerning the identification of the priced factors. Hence empirical research must achieve two goals.

1. Identify the number of factors.
2. Identify the various economics underlying each factor.

Empirical Test Methodology

Empirical tests of the APT are evolving at an increasing rate as academics attempt to verify its conclusions. In particular, recent empirical work in this area has sought to determine whether there exist multiple underlying factors for asset returns—and, if they exist, whether they are associated with risk premiums. It is hypothesized that there exist nonzero $\lambda_1, \ldots, \lambda_k$ such that

$$E_i - E_0 = \lambda_1 b_{i1} + \cdots + \lambda_k b_{ik} \qquad (11.18)$$

for all i. To empirically test this hypothesis, a two-step procedure is typically utilized. In the first step the statistical technique of factor analysis is used to estimate the expected returns and the factor loadings ($b_{i1}, \ldots, b_{ik}$) from time-series data of asset returns. In the second step these estimates are used in the basic cross-sectional pricing equation of the APT to estimate the risk premium (λ_h), thereby performing the hypothesis test.

While this two-step procedure is analogous to familiar CAPM empirical work, it is free of some major conceptual difficulties in CAPM tests. Most important of these is that the APT can be applied to subsets of the universe of assets, eliminating any need to specify as well as justify any particular choice of a proxy for the market portfolio.

It would be ideal to perform the factor analysis in the first step on all asset returns as a whole; nevertheless, the resulting huge covariance matrix would be beyond the normal processing capacity of computers. To compromise with this technical constraint several approaches have been taken in the empirical studies of APT. However, to date no one approach has yet been

proposed that is free of shortcomings. To better clarify the testing procedures required for APT along with the inherent problems, some of the major empirical studies are now offered, followed by an example of an empirical test of the APT.

The most comprehensive and widely recognized study of the APT is that of Roll and Ross (RR, 1980). These authors use daily returns for a sample of 1,260 selected securities from both the NYSE and AMEX over the period July 3, 1962, to December 31, 1972. Roll and Ross arrange the sample into 42 groups with 30 securities in each, on the basis of alphabetical order. Next, RR perform maximum-likelihood factor analysis on each of the 42 groups to estimate the respective factor loadings. The estimated factor loadings are then used as the explanatory variables in the **second-stage cross-sectional regression test.**

The dominant problem associated with this approach is that the return-generating process cannot be compared across groups. This results from the complexity that factors in different groups might not lie in the same dimensionality. More explicitly, the first factor in one group may not correspond to the first factor in the other group. Quite conceivably then, the first factor in one group might be equivalent to the third factor in the other group. Hence, after the cross-sectional distributions of the loading coefficients are tabulated, there could be a mixing of estimates which apply to different "true" factors. Moreover, there is no way to ascertain that the same three (or four) factors (the number RR found) generate the returns in every group.

A second approach in testing the APT, called the **small-sample approach,** is employed by Chen (1983), and Oldfield and Rogalski (1981). Using the small-sample approach, assets are divided into several groups as before. However, now for only a single group (as opposed to every group) is factor analysis applied and corresponding factor loadings estimated. The estimates of factor loadings for assets in the remaining groups are inferred from the covariance of their returns with the loading coefficients of the factor analyzed group.

The small-sample approach assures the comparability of factors across groups, a definite strength over the RR approach. However, because only a relatively small number of asset returns are used in the factor-estimation procedure, the statistical problem of inefficient estimation is encountered. Moreover, as other researchers have demonstrated, the estimation bias in the original estimation of factor loadings can be magnified further when the remaining loadings are derived. The central consequence of this estimation bias is that "spurious" explanatory factors may be extracted.

To surpass the hindrance of inefficient estimation, Reinganum (1981) applies a third approach, the **portfolio approach.** Here assets are grouped into portfolios, and factor analysis is performed on the covariance matrix among these portfolio returns instead of that of individual asset returns (as in the previous two approaches). The problem with this methodology is that as the number of assets in a portfolio increases, the portfolio returns tend to

reflect a single-factor model even when a multi-factor model is true. Thus, it is not surprising that the studies using the portfolio approach find but one significant factor.

Thus it has been shown that any efficient estimation procedure for testing the APT requires the utilization of all assets in the sample. Moreover, the portfolio approach stresses the importance of using the covariance matrix among individual assets in order to avoid the tendency toward a single-factor model. Yet the constraint of computer capacity makes the comparative analysis of the covariance matrix of the entire population of assets virtually impossible. Consequently, as Roll and Ross's study (1980) points out, dividing the population into a manageable number of smaller groups creates a problem in identifying what the explanatory factors are and determining whether their relative significance across groups is consistent.

ARBITRAGE PRICING THEORY: EMPIRICAL RESULTS AND IMPLICATIONS

Following the empirical tests of the APT it is important to examine some of the findings in relation to the following questions.

1. How many factors have been identified? How many should there be?
2. Has empirical research been able to verify APT?
3. If the theory is correct and significant factors have been identified, what do these factors represent?

In what has quickly become the classic article for testing the APT, Roll and Ross (1980) found that there are at least three, but probably no more than four, significant explanatory factors in the model structure. While the remaining empirical literature in this area is still somewhat scarce compared with that of the CAPM, most of the other studies settle on five as being the significant number of relevant factors [for example, see Hughes (1981) and Chen (1983)]. In a recent paper challenging the robustness of the APT, Cho et al. (1984) found at least five and as many as six explanatory factors while using the RR methodology.

Now consider whether four to six factors can constitute a correctly and significantly specified pricing model. While most of the previously mentioned researchers would say yes to the above, there remains a considerable amount of dissent in the finance corps. For instance, in their critical reexamination of the APT, Dhrymes, Friend, and Gultekin (1984) develop evidence indicating that the number of significant factors found tends to increase as the size of the sample groups is increased. This type of phenomenon is related to the factor-analysis methodology so widely used in tests of the APT.

Lee and Wei (1984) apply the Ramsey and Schmidt (1976) specification-error test to see whether a five-factor APT model may not be enough to explain the return-generating process of all securities. Using this type of F-test, these authors find specification error present in the five-factor model at the 5-percent level of significance. (However, this degree of specification error at the same significance level was not apparent when the same hypothesis was tested for a ten-factor model.) Their results are shown in Appendix 11B at the end of this chapter.

Thus, discrepancies in results among empirical tests may result from differing time periods of study, methodologies, and sample-group sizes. Moreover, the findings up to this point indicate that although relatively substantial evidence is accumulating that lends support to the APT's validity, its actual affirmation remains unsubstantiated. Part of this inability to develop conclusive proof of the APT relates to the potential inadequacy of factor analysis as a methodology for identifying common factors. Shanken (1982) exposes a previously unnoticed property of the factor-model representation of returns. By "repackaging" a given set of securities the factor model can be manipulated rather arbitrarily. More specifically, Shanken shows that a new set of returns and a corresponding factor model can be produced, with virtually any prespecified random variables as the factors. Hence, formulating the APT model in terms of factor analytic methods can be taken to imply the proposition that all securities have the same expected return.

To combat some of this criticism, Roll and Ross (1980) emphasize that if a more powerful test with factor analysis could be devised, as many factors as there are sets of assets would probably be found. Nevertheless, almost all of these additional factors would be diversifiable and thus irrelevant in terms of pricing.

Dybvig and Ross (1985) argue that the APT is a good approximation in theory. They counter Shanken's (1982) claim that the APT is untestable. They explain that empirical tests are performed using actual assets, not on arbitrage recombination as shown in Shanken's paper. Therefore Shanken's empirical version of the APT is unrelated to existing empirical work. They also show that the APT is testable.

Furthermore, Dybvig and Ross (1985) argue that Shanken's (1982) critique of the APT rests on two fallacies. First, the version of APT Shanken uses assumes that it can be applied to arbitrary portfolios, which is inconsistent with the theoretical and empirical work on the APT. Second, a good approximation that can be treated empirically as an equality can be manipulated arbitrarily as an equality. When Shanken creates the portfolios from the original assets, he finds all randomness, systematic factors, and idiosyncratic noise alike. That is, he treats all these factors as idiosyncratic noise. This is the opposite of diversification, and it is therefore not surprising that applying the APT to the transformed assets proves a paradox.

IDENTIFYING THE MODEL FACTORS

Although APT still lacks a wide base of empirical support, its intuitive content and formulation remain quite appealing. Still, more testing is needed before the APT pricing relationship can be seriously applied by security analysts and other practitioners concerned with the correct allocation of resources in our economy. Some of the testing that is going on now takes a more universal scope in testing and interpreting the APT. These studies have focused on identifying the specific macroeconomic forces which influence security returns.

Chen, Roll, and Ross (1986) develop a theoretical guide to help identify the economic-state variables that are likely to be important for asset pricing. The relevant affecting economic factors identified by these authors include:

1. Unanticipated inflation
2. Expected inflation
3. Unanticipated change in the term structure of interest rates
4. Monthly and yearly growth rates in industrial production
5. Unexpected changes in the yearly growth rate of industrial production
6. Change in the expected rate of yearly growth in industrial production
7. Unanticipated changes in the risk premiums embedded in interest rates
8. Percentage changes in real consumption
9. Growth rate in oil prices
10. Return on the equal-weighted NYSE index
11. Return on the value-weighted NYSE index
12. Treasury-bill (T-bill) rates

Chen, Roll, and Ross (CRR, 1986) then devise data series to represent these economic-state variables and proceed to test their influence on stock-market returns. The results show a good number of these economic variables to be important explanators of expected stock returns. These results gain additional credibility due to the insignificance of the NYSE index variables when used in conjunction with the other state variables. Hence, the CRR study adds support to the dimension of APT, which argues that expected returns can be explained by the sensitivities of stock returns to innovations in macroeconomic-state variables.

In a related but more recent study, Lee and Wei (1984) attempt to uncover the pricing influences of a similar set of macroeconomic-state variables on the returns of securities. They classify these state variables into five categories.

1. Money supply
2. Real production

3. Inflation
4. Interest rate
5. Market return

In addition to the types of state variables used by CRR, this study also includes variables for transaction volume, the absolute level and velocity of money supply (MS), the risk premium decomposed into maturity and default components, and real auto and home production. A complete list of the explanatory state variables and results appears in Appendix 11B.

Summarizing these results, Lee and Wei find that in addition to the market index, only the risk-free rate, expected inflation, and industrial production significantly influence stock-market returns. In terms of relating some of their explanatory state variables to the common factors of the APT model, nothing conclusive was obtained. However, evidence does arise that associates the first factor with some market index, the second factor with expected inflation and industrial production, and the fourth factor with the risk-free rate and industrial production. No other state variables show significant correlation with the other two factors usually identified in APT tests.

Up to this point, intuitive arguments about APT have been provided as well as empirical support for its use. As APT can be viewed as a potentially preferable competitor of the capital asset pricing model (CAPM), it seems appropriate at this time to relate, compare, and contrast these pricing theories.

ARBITRAGE PRICING THEORY VERSUS MODERN PORTFOLIO THEORY AND THE CAPITAL ASSET PRICING MODEL

For more than two decades **modern portfolio theory (MPT)** has been the most widely accepted investment theory among academicians and practitioners alike. The best-known outcome of MPT has been the capital asset pricing model (CAPM). Hence APT faces stiff competition in becoming a widely accepted and applied theory in the finance profession. A comparison and contrast of these two theories therefore seems appropriate at this point in order to understand the implications of the new versus the old.

First, recall the discussion of multi-index models at the beginning of this chapter. The focus was the return-generating process that utilized explanatory indexes or factors in addition to (or instead of) some market index. This model was of the type:

$$R_i = a_i + b_{i1}I_1 + b_{i2}I_2 + e_i \tag{11.19}$$

in which I_1 and I_2 were indexes representing industry influences or broader economic effects such as interest rates or inflation. Once again look at the simple CAPM as discussed in Chapter 9:

$$\overline{R}_i = R_f + \beta_i(\overline{R}_m - R_f) \tag{11.20}$$

If the return-generating function is more complex than this, then can the simple CAPM still hold? The answer is yes. Recall from earlier discussions that the simple CAPM does not assume the market is the only source of covariance between returns. Therefore, Equation (11.20) could be extended to Equation (11.21) within the context of CAPM, as long as it is assumed that the set of indexes used capture all the sources of covariance between securities [for example, $E(e_i, e_j) = 0$].

Within the framework of APT, the equilibrium model can be formulated for this same multifactor return-generating process, assuming some riskless asset, as follows:

$$\overline{R}_i = R_f + b_{i1}\lambda_1 + b_{i2}\lambda_2 \tag{11.21}$$

in which λ_1 and λ_2 represent the excess returns that occur for bearing the risk associated with that factor (or relatedly, the particular index of securities), and b_{i1} again is the sensitivity of security i to the explanatory factor λ_1.

If the CAPM is the equilibrium model for describing security returns, it must also hold for portfolios of securities. Suppose that the indexes in Equation (11.20) represent portfolios of securities. As has already been stated (and will be expanded upon later), the λ can be interpreted as the excess return for a portfolio with a b_{ih} equal to 1 for one index and a b_{ih} equal to zero for all other indexes:

$$\lambda_1 = \overline{R}_1 - R_f$$
$$\lambda_2 = \overline{R}_2 - R_f$$

Presuming that the CAPM holds, the λ_h can be rewritten in terms of their equilibrium return as defined by the CAPM:

$$\lambda_1 = c_1 (\overline{R}_m - R_f)$$
$$\lambda_2 = c_2 (\overline{R}_m - R_f) \tag{11.22}$$

in which c_1 and c_2 are adjustment factors. Then by substituting the equalities of (11.22) into the APT equation of (11.21):

$$\overline{R}_i = R_f + b_{i1} c_1 (\overline{R}_m - R_f) + b_{i2} c_2(\overline{R}_m - R_f)$$
$$\overline{R}_i = R_f + (b_{i1} c_1 + b_{i2}c_2) (\overline{R}_m - R_f)$$

Now β_i needs to be defined to be equal to $(b_{i1}c_1 + b_{i2}c_2)$ in order to have the pricing relationship for R_i expressed within the CAPM framework:

$$\overline{R}_i = R_f + \beta_i(\overline{R}_m - R_f)$$

From this exercise it has been shown that the APT with multiple factors appropriately priced is fully consistent with the Sharpe-Lintner-Mossin form of the CAPM.

The proponents of APT contend that their theory is superior to that of MPT with the CAPM. The primary reason for viewing APT in this light is a

result of its greater degree of generality, which is achieved utilizing fewer simplifying assumptions. In fact, the CAPM can be considered a special case of the APT. That case arises when only one explanatory factor exists for individual security returns, the market portfolio.

Among the ways that APT and MPT are similar is that both theories assume that investors prefer more wealth to less and that they are risk averse. These two assumptions together imply that investors have positive but diminishing marginal utility of wealth, and thus make investment decisions which will maximize their expected utility of wealth. This assumption on either theory's part is quite realistic.

Another assumption used by both theories is that capital markets are perfect. This condition is debatable in some financial arenas. Yet the resulting additional model complexity that generally arises if this assumption is not made is not worth the extra bit of market reality that the model is able to portray. However, the homogeneous-expectations assumption utilized in both APT and MPT is a weakness in each. Essentially, homogeneous expectations imply that all investors share the same risk and return perceptions for all assets in the market. By utilizing this assumption both models obviate the need to explain differences among investors' expectations.

The following assumptions are required for the CAPM but not the APT.

1. The CAPM is restricted to a single-period planning horizon.
2. The CAPM is restricted to rates of price change that conform to a normal (or log normal) empirical probability distribution of returns.
3. The CAPM depends on rather strong assumptions about investors' utility functions in order to generate a two-parameter model.
4. The CAPM requires the existence of a market portfolio that is a uniquely desirable investment medium.

From this rather extensive list of additional assumptions for the CAPM which the APT does not require, the greater generality of the APT is readily apparent. Thus, the APT provides a theoretically more robust and more testable alternative to the CAPM. Wei (1988) and Burmeister and McElroy (1988) have derived an asset pricing model unifying the CAPM and APT.

APPLICATIONS OF ARBITRAGE PRICING THEORY

Potential applications of the APT are similar to those for the CAPM. These include:

1. Security analysis
2. Portfolio management
3. Performance measurement
4. Capital budgeting
5. Cost of equity capital for public utilities and other types of companies

The CAPM is probably the most widely accepted method in all of these corporate applications. Recently, the Federal Energy Regulation Commission proposed that the CAPM be used as the principal measure of risk for the electric utilities it regulates. The CAPM beta (β) can be found to be the predominant measure of risk from a glance through the financial literature or a survey of the corporate world. However, the CAPM has been the target of a growing body of skeptics who have been finding significantly noticeable drawbacks in its empirical pricing framework.

Alternatively, the APT offers a more global framework for measuring a company's or a portfolio's sensitivity to various economic factors. However, at the current stage of the APT's development, it has seen little application in the domain of the practitioner. Nevertheless, empirical research has been emerging that not only points out differences in their estimates of company (portfolio) returns but, more importantly, suggests that the APT might be a preferable alternative to the CAPM in such uses.

The central application of APT is in estimating required rates of return, or equivalently the cost of equity capital. Recent work by Bower, Bower, and Logue (BBL, 1984) and Bubnys and Lee (1990) includes the use of the APT and the CAPM in a comparison of their respective abilities to effectively describe the return-generating process for stocks in terms of historical and forecasted results.

Utilizing a large sample of stocks from the NYSE and AMEX exchanges over the 1971–1979 period, these authors grouped their data into industry portfolios. Based on Roll and Ross's previous results, the BBL factor analyzed the portfolio returns' covariance matrix to produce monthly scores for four factors. For comparison, the CAPM was run on the data as well to devise estimates of the portfolio betas and required return. Using the average betas and sensitivity coefficients from the cross-sectional tests, BBL summarize the market model formulation results as shown in Table 11–2.

The results from these two models indicate conflicting information for regulators. The CAPM suggests that regulators should provide electric utilities the opportunity for a return of more than 1 percent above natural-gas distribution companies. Conversely, APT indicates that it is the gas distribution companies that require the higher rate of return and that the difference is close to 2 percent.

To discern which pricing model provides a better policy guide, BBL compared the CAPM and APT on the basis of two types of evidence. The first of these concerns what APT and CAPM can explain of the returns used in their estimation. To test the following equations:

$$E(R_i) = R_f + \beta_i (\overline{R}_m - R_f) \tag{11.23}$$

$$E(R_i) = R_0 + \lambda_1 b_{i1} + \lambda_2 b_{i2} + \lambda_3 b_{i3} + \lambda_4 b_{i4} \tag{11.24}$$

BBL use the CAPM β's and APT b_{ih}'s estimated for each portfolio in the time-series work just described. Cross-sectional regressions were run for each month with return as the dependent variable and the risk coefficients as independent variables. The mean values of the risk premiums for the 108

TABLE 11-2   Market-Model Formulation Results Using CAPM and APT

	CAPM	APT
Return–risk relationship	$E(R_J) = 0.0555 + 0.1085\beta$	$E(R_J) = 0.0621 - 1.8550\, b_{i1}$ $+ 1.4448\, b_{i2} + 0.1244\, b_{i3}$ $- 2.7240\, b_{i4}$
Systematic risk		
Electrics	$\beta_I = 0.71$	$b_{i1} = -0.0318$ $b_{i2} = -0.0114$ $b_{i3} = -0.0022$ $b_{i4} = -0.0017$
Gas distribution	$\beta_I = 0.58$	$b_{i1} = -0.0329$ $b_{i2} = -0.0065$ $b_{i3} = -0.0138$ $b_{i4} = -0.0093$
Required return $E(R_I)$		
Electrics	13.2%	10.9%
Gas distribution	11.8%	13.7%

Source: Bower et al., *Journal of Finance* (1984), p. 1044.

monthly CAPM and APT return/risk equations, the t-values (in paren-theses), and the average R^2 for the 108 monthly cross-sectional regressions are listed in Table 11–3. Using the average $\overline{R}^2$, these findings favor the APT in terms of explanatory ability. However, a second, more convincing test is carried out since conclusions from the preceding test are limited due to the origin of the APT factor scores in the return date.

By forming a holdout group of 127 utilities not included in the original coefficient estimation for CAPM and APT, these authors forecast expected monthly returns for each utility over the 108 months from 1971–1979. The results are summarized in Table 11–4. To assess the quality of each model's forecast BBL used U^2, the sum of squared differences of each stock's average return $\overline{R}_i$ for the 1971–1979 period from its CAPM or APT forecast

TABLE 11-3   Risk Premiums, t-Values, and Average R^2 for CAPM and APT

	b_0	b_1	b_2	b_3	b_4	$\overline{R}$
CAPM						
Equation (11.25)	0.00463	0.00904	—	—	—	0.274
	(4.53)	(1.72)				
APT						
Equation (11.26)	0.00517	−0.15458	0.12040	0.01037	−0.2270	0.425
		(−0.159)	(0.81)	(0.11)	(−2.52)	

Source: Bower et al. (1984), p. 1046.

TABLE 11-4 Required Return for Industries Represented in the Holdout Sample Using APT and CAPM Return/Risk Relationships Estimated from Monthly Data Without Utility Portfolios for 1971-1979

$$\text{APT: } \overline{R}_j = 0.005173 - 0.154584b_{i1} - 0.120404b_{i2} + 0.010366b_{i3} - 0.227002b_{i4}$$
$$\text{CAPM: } \overline{R}_i = 0.004629 + 0.009038\beta_1$$

Industry	APT Sensitivity Coefficients				CAPM β_1	Forecast Return		Actual Return R
	b_{i1}	b_{i2}	b_{i3}	b_{i4}		R_{APT}	R_{CAPM}	
4911	−0.03181	−0.01141	−0.00219	−0.00168	0.70873	0.00870	0.01103	0.00457
4931	−0.03121	−0.01051	−0.00737	−0.00260	0.64692	0.00925	0.01048	0.00492
4922	−0.04212	−0.00601	+0.01387	−0.01214	0.95347	0.01386	0.01325	0.01140
4923	−0.03271	−0.01008	+0.00944	−0.01465	0.73650	0.01244	0.01129	0.01270
4924	−0.03290	−0.00649	−0.01382	−0.00932	0.57709	0.01150	0.00984	0.00807
4811	−0.02573	−0.00830	+0.00506	−0.00409	0.54211	0.00825	0.00953	0.00402
9999	−0.06471	−0.00814	+0.00372	+0.00433	1.32504	0.01413	0.01660	0.01595

Source: Bower et al. (1984), p. 1047.

of return $\hat{R}_i$, and the sum of the squared differences of average return for each stock from the average return of all stocks $\overline{R}$. The ratio of these squared differences, U^2, for all stocks is used to evaluate the contribution of the model as a forecasting device. It follows then that the smaller the ratio, the better is the model forecast relative to the naive forecast. The results:

$$
U^2 = \frac{\sum_{i=1}^{127} (\overline{R}_i - \hat{R}_i)^2}{\sum_{i=1}^{127} (\overline{R}_i - \overline{R})^2}
$$
$$
= 0.822 \text{ (APT)}
$$
$$
= 1.115 \text{ (CAPM)}
$$

Thus, as a forecasting model of required or expected return, APT does better than CAPM. Moreover, when the holdout sample is included in the original estimation of the APT (it is essentially included in both cases for the CAPM), the results are even more in favor of the APT. The figure from APT falls to 0.505 while that for the CAPM improves only a little, falling to 1.018.

While no single study can be taken to be the final word on which pricing theory is superior, these empirical findings do provide strong evidence in favor of the APT. More important, they show that the APT should be considered usable by practitioners for determining required rates of return of individual firms.

SUMMARY

This chapter has pushed forward into the newer areas of finance theory. Arbitrage pricing theory (APT) embodies a good deal of the more robust efforts of academicians to formulate less restrictive and more applicable models for asset pricing. Much research on APT and associated testing methodologies lies ahead; nevertheless, its alluring intuitive arguments and generalized construction make APT a formidable competitor to the CAPM. But perhaps APT should be considered an evolutionary step from the realm of CAPM theory rather than a revolutionary one. (In fact, it has been shown that the original CAPM is actually a special case of the APT model.)

Flaws and deficiencies within the methodologies used to empirically test APT have drawn the attention of a good part of the APT literature. Nevertheless, empirical results do lend some concrete support to APT pricing tenets. Much of the direction of the current research is focused on identifying the correct factor structure—that is, the appropriate number—along with identifying what economic-state variables might be associated with these explanatory factors.

The APT has not been developed to the stage of being usable by security analysts in predicting security returns. Studies at this point indicate that the APT describes the long-term expected return on a security and therefore would not be as beneficial to those concerned with short-term deviations in equilibrium conditions. Nevertheless, APT's potential ability to efficiently describe the long-run expected return for a firm's equity has valuable application in the area of capital budgeting.

QUESTIONS AND PROBLEMS

1. What is an arbitrage opportunity? Carefully explain why arbitrage opportunities must not exist in an efficient market.
2. You are given the following information about two stocks, A and B, and the market.

$$E(R_M) = 10\%$$
$$R_f = 6\%$$
$$\beta_A = 1.5$$
$$\beta_B = 2.0$$

   (a) Plot the SML.
   (b) Calculate the expected returns for stocks A and B that are consistent with the capital asset pricing model (CAPM).
   (c) Now assume that stock A has an expected return of 14 percent while stock B has an expected return of 13 percent. Does an arbitrage opportunity exist? Carefully explain how you could exploit this opportunity.
3. Compare a one-factor arbitrage pricing theory (APT) model, where the factor is the expected return on the market with the CAPM.
4. What are the advantages of the APT over the CAPM? What are the disadvantages of the APT over the CAPM?
5. Assume that returns for XYZ Company's stock are related to three factors in the following way.

$$E(R_{XYZ}) = \lambda_0 + b_{1,XYZ}\,\lambda_1 + b_{2,XYZ}\,\lambda_2 + b_{3,XYZ}\,\lambda_3$$

   (a) Carefully explain what the b's measure.
   (b) Assume $b_{1,XYZ} = 0.4$, $b_{2,XYZ} = 1.4$, $b_{3,XYZ} = 0.9$, and that the risk-free rate is 4 percent, the λ_1 risk premium is 5 percent, λ_2 is 6 percent, and λ_3 is 2 percent. What is the expected return for XYZ Company's stock?
6. Describe some of the problems associated with empirically testing the APT.

7. Assume that the following single-index model describes returns:

$$R_i = a_i + b_i I + e_i$$

Also use the information given in the table.

Portfolio	E(R) (percent)	b_{i1}
A	9	0.2
B	12	1.2

(a) Find the equation of the line that describes equilibrium returns.
(b) Explain the arbitrage opportunity that would exist if a new portfolio C existed with the following properties:

$$E(R_C) = 5\%, \ b_C = 1.5$$

8. Suppose equilibrium returns are generated by the following two-index models.

$$R_j = a_j + b_{j1} I_1 + b_{j2} I_2 + e_j$$

And assume that we observe the portfolios in the table.

Portfolio	E(R) (percent)	b_{i1}	b_{i2}
G	8	1.0	0.3
H	12	1.5	0.4
K	17	1.7	-0.1

(a) Find the equation of the plane that describes equilibrium returns.
(b) Explain the arbitrage opportunity that would exist if a portfolio Z were observed with the following properties:

$$E(R_Z) = 20\%, \ b_{Z1} = 0.5, \ b_{Z2} = -0.4$$

9. Describe Lloyd and Lee's block recursive system asset pricing model. (See Appendix 11A.)

10. Describe how APT can be used to estimate cost of capital for an electric utility company.

APPENDIX 11A: ALTERNATIVE SPECIFICATIONS OF ARBITRAGE PRICING THEORY

By using the relationship between premium (excess) return and the factor scores, Jobson (1982) has derived a multivariate linear-regression model for testing the arbitrage pricing theory. Jobson concludes that individual company excess returns can be linearly related to all other returns in the market or some subset of returns. In relation to all other returns in the market we can define Jobson's regression model as:

$$r_{it} = \alpha_i + \sum_{j=1}^{n} \beta_j r_{jt} + \epsilon_{jt} \quad i \neq j \qquad (11A.1)$$

where:

r_{it} = excess return for company i at time t;
α_i = intercept term;
β_j = respective betas for excess return on company i and the excess returns on all other (N) companies;
r_{jt} = excess returns on all other (N) companies in the market at time t; and
ϵ_{jt} = error term at time t.

Even more significantly, Jobson has shown that his model can hold when the independent observations of r_{jt} are some subset k of the total set of returns, n. This testable form of the Jobson derivation can be defined:

$$r_{it} = \alpha_i + \sum_{j=1}^{k} \beta_j r_{jt} + \epsilon_{it} \quad (i \neq j) \qquad (11A.2)$$

where $i \neq j$ and $k < n$.

If all excess returns are assumed to be multivariate normally distributed, and if all the r_{jt} (either individual or portfolio excess returns) are linearly independent, then testing the APT with Equation (11A.2) becomes equivalent to a test of the intercept term. For the APT to hold, the intercept term α_i in (11A.2) should not be significantly different from zero. By construction, Equation (11A.2) is equivalent to Equation (11A.1), which includes all excess returns in the market; therefore, if β_j is significantly different from zero, it implies that there are additional determinants that affect a company's excess return besides all other excess returns in the market. APT rests on the concept of relative pricing in that each company is priced relative to all others with regard to each respective risk–return characteristic. A significant intercept term in (11A.2) would substantially weaken this argument.

Jobson's model is similar to that proposed by Lloyd and Lee (1976) and Lee and Lloyd (1978), who utilize an econometric model called a "block

recursive system'' to explain the covariability among company returns. Applying this equation system to the thirty stocks that constitute the Dow-Jones Industrial Average, these authors empirically determined that other companies' rates of return can be utilized in addition to some market index to explain the return-generating process for individual companies.

The block recursive system can be represented by the following series of equations:

$$R_1 = \beta_{11}X_{11} + \beta_{12}X_{12} + \cdots + \beta_{1k}X_{1k} + \epsilon_1$$
$$r_{21}R_1 + R_2 = \beta_{21}X_{21} + \beta_{22}X_{22} + \cdots + \beta_{2k}X_{2k} + \epsilon_2$$

$$\vdots$$

$$r_{L1}R_1 + r_{L2}R_2 + \cdots + \gamma_{LL}R_{L-1} + R_L = \beta_{L2}X_{L1} + \beta_{L2}X_{L2} + \cdots + \beta_{LK}X_{LK} + \epsilon_L$$

where:

$$L = \text{number of jointly determined (dependent) variables;}$$
$$K = \text{number of exogenous explanatory variables;}$$
$$\gamma_{LL-1} = \text{coefficients on the jointly determined variables;}$$
$$\beta_{LK} = \text{coefficients on the exogenous variables;}$$
$$X_{LK} = \text{general economic or firm-related variables;}$$
$$R_L = \text{returns on the } L\text{th security in the model; and}$$
$$\epsilon_L = \text{error term.}$$

Lloyd and Lee's application of this system uses only one exogenous variable (X) on the right side of the equations, which is a proxy for the market index (the S&P 500). After breaking up the Dow 30 into eight homogeneous clusters using factor analysis, the stocks within each cluster (sub or system) are ordered according to their independence. That is, the stock most independent of the system is placed first while the most dependent one is placed last. This type of ordering is a requirement of the equation system and is carried out by regressing each stock upon the other securities in the subsystem. The resulting $\overline{R}^2$ is then used as the measure of dependence.

The block recursive system is run as follows. For each subsystem the most independent security return is regressed on the market-index return. Consequently, the first run in each subsystem is equivalent to the traditional market-model formulation. Next, the second most independent variable is added to the left-hand side of the equation. This dependent variable is determined by the endogenous variables R_1 and ϵ_2. Since the random component of R_1 is ϵ_1, which is assumed to be independent of ϵ_2, R_1 may be regarded as predetermined with respect to R_2. This exact line of reasoning is continued for the rest of the equations in the subsystems.

As evidenced for the high explanatory potential of the block recursive system, Table 11A–1 shows the eight stock clusters or subsystems, the

TABLE 11A-1   Grouping of Companies Based on Correlation with a Common Factor

	$\overline{R}^2$ Sharpe	$\overline{R}^2$ Recursive		$\overline{R}^2$ Sharpe	$\overline{R}^2$ Recursive
Subsystem 1			Subsystem 6		
Owens Illinois	0.275	0.275	Eastman Kodak	0.311	0.311
General Foods	0.234	0.237	United Aircraft	0.221	0.213
Subsystem 2			Subsystem 7		
Anaconda	0.309	0.309	Texaco	0.373	0.373
Woolworth	0.278	0.282	Standard Oil of		
American Brands	0.243	0.293	California	0.347	0.612
American Can	0.210	0.224	Exxon	0.250	0.540
Subsystem 3			Subsystem 8		
Proctor & Gamble	0.235	0.235	ATT	0.380	0.380
Swift & Company	0.109	0.112	DuPont	0.251	0.243
			Chrysler	0.449	0.469
Subsystem 4			Johns-Manville	0.292	0.279
International Nickel	0.316	0.316	Alcoa	0.350	0.340
			International Harvester	0.195	0.220
Subsystem 5			Goodyear	0.321	0.345
Sears	0.311	0.311	International Paper	0.526	0.643
General Electric	0.416	0.411	Union Carbide	0.323	0.434
Westinghouse	0.243	0.302	General Motors	0.573	0.699
			Allied Chemical	0.357	0.493
			U.S. Steel	0.387	0.619
			Bethlehem Steel	0.390	0.793

Source: Lloyd and Lee (1976), p. 1107.

ordering of securities within the subsystem, and a comparison of the percentage of variation in the individual security's return explained by the Sharpe market model and the percentage explained by the block recursive model. Notice, as mentioned earlier, that the first equation in each subsystem is equivalent to the Sharpe market model; thus $\overline{R}^2$'s are the same. However, for many of the other equations there are large increases in the explanatory power, as evidenced by the $\overline{R}^2$. For example, the $\overline{R}^2$ for Bethlehem Steel increased from 0.390 in the Sharpe model to 0.793 in the block recursive model. These improvements in explanatory power are a result of the significant relationships among individual securities, which emerge in addition to each individual security's relationship with the stock-market index. All of these interrelationships violate a basic assumption of the Sharpe market model—that is, $E(\epsilon_1, \epsilon_2) = 0$.

APPENDIX 11B: LEE AND WEI'S EMPIRICAL RESULTS

The following two tables describe eleven economic-state variables used to identify common factors of the APT model and time-series regression factors from Ross's APT on indicators. Both result from extensive research by Lee and Wei (1984).

TABLE 11B-1   Lee and Wei's Eleven Economic-State Variables Used to Identify the APT Model's Common Factors

Variable	Definition
1. RM	*Return on the market portfolio:* the return on NYSE common stock composite index; equal weighted (RME), valued weighted (RMV).
2. VL	*Transaction volume:* the change rate in the transaction volume (shares) for all of the NYSE common stocks.
3. RF	*Real riskless rate:* the real interest rate on three-month Treasury bills.
4. MP	*Maturity risk premium:* the difference between the real interest rates on long-term Treasury bonds (ten or more years) and on three-month Treasury bills.
5. DP	*Default risk premium:* the difference between the real interest rates on new AA corporate bonds and three-month Treasury bills.
6. CPI	*Consumer price index inflation rate:* the change rate in urban consumer price index for all items.
7. M2	*Money supply:* the real change rate in money stock as measured by M2 (M1 + time deposits).
8. PI/M2	*Velocity of money supply:* the ratio of personal income to money supply M2. This is an alternative measure of money supply.
9. IP	*Real industrial production:* the change rate in real total industrial production.
10. IPA	*Real auto production:* the change in real automotive products.
11. IPH	*Real home production:* the change rate in real home goods.

Source: Lee and Wei (1984).

TABLE 11B-2 Time-Series Regression Factors from Ross's APT on Indicators

Part A: RMV and VL Included

Indicator	Factor 1	Factor 2	Factor 3	Factor 4	Factor 5
RMV	0.206**	0.075**	−0.025	0.016	−0.037**
	(32.646)	(4.712)	(−1.527)	(0.973)	(−2.185)
VL	0.291**	−0.831**	0.057	−0.530	0.668*
	(2.119)	(−2.398)	(0.161)	(−1.465)	(1.832)
RF	−0.153	−0.808**	0.960**	−0.631	−0.356
	(−0.964)	(−2.017)	(2.352)	(−1.509)	(−0.843)
MP	−0.418	−2.316	0.509	0.422	0.269
	(−0.601)	(−1.318)	(0.284)	(0.230)	(0.145)
DP	0.096	2.472**	2.242*	−0.820	−0.107
	(0.196)	(1.990)	(1.770)	(−0.632)	(−0.082)
CPI	−0.257	−0.737*	0.480	0.160	0.064
	(−1.637)	(−1.865)	(1.191)	(0.387)	(0.155)
M2	0.005	−0.290	−0.634**	0.251	0.004
	(0.050)	(−1.202)	(−2.582)	(0.998)	(0.017)
IP	0.0324	−0.194**	−0.044	−0.058	−0.053
	(1.138)	(−2.708)	(−0.600)	(−0.778)	(−0.706)
Constant	−0.054	0.292	−0.189	−0.079	0.019
	(−0.593)	(1.282)	(−0.813)	(−0.334)	(0.080)
$\bar{R}^2$	0.860	0.1103	0.076	0.030	0.012

Part B: RME and VL Included

Indicator	Factor 1	Factor 2	Factor 3	Factor 4	Factor 5
RME	0.174**	0.001	0.011	0.021*	−0.000
	(89.236)	(0.047)	(0.869)	(1.662)	(−0.025)
VL	0.038	−0.166	−0.298	−0.643*	0.344
	(0.699)	(−0.453)	(−0.834)	(−1.770)	(0.926)
RF	−0.325**	−0.630	0.858	−0.674	−0.443
	(−5.130)	(−1.499)	(2.090)	(−1.614)	(−1.036)
MP	−0.862**	−1.348	−0.117	0.248	−0.203
	(−3.105)	(−0.732)	(−0.007)	(0.136)	(−0.109)
DP	0.652**	2.084	2.476*	−0.704	0.082
	(3.319)	(1.598)	(1.944)	(−0.544)	(0.062)
CPI	−0.364**	−0.682	0.445	0.140	0.038
	(−5.831)	(−1.647)	(1.099)	(0.339)	(0.089)
M2	−0.068*	−0.254	−0.657**	0.238	−0.013
	(−1.799)	(−1.008)	(−2.664)	(0.948)	(−0.051)
IP	0.013	−0.194**	−0.045	−0.061	−0.053
	(1.138)	(−2.584)	(−0.617)	(−0.813)	(−0.700)
Constant	−0.051	0.305	−0.195	−0.081	0.013
	(−1.417)	(1.279)	(−0.838)	(−0.341)	(0.053)
$\bar{R}^2$	0.978	0.025	0.070	0.038	−0.008

TABLE 11B-2   *(concluded)*

Part C: Market Variables Excluded

Indicator	Factor 1	Factor 2	Factor 3	Factor 4	Factor 5
RF	0.405	−0.632	0.896	−0.603	−0.434
	(0.982)	(−1.521)	(2.202)	(−1.449)	(−1.035)
MP	2.855	−1.381	0.141	0.527	−0.116
	(1.582)	(−0.759)	(0.079)	(0.289)	(0.063)
DP	−1.143	2.090	2.384*	−0.877	0.061
	(−0.891)	(1.616)	(1.885)	(−0.677)	(0.046)
CPI	−0.024	−0.687*	0.455	0.157	0.050
	(−0.058)	(−1.668)	(1.129)	(0.382)	(0.118)
M2	0.069	−0.251	−0.643**	0.265	−0.019
	(0.275)	(−1.000)	(−2.618)	(1.054)	(−0.074)
IP	0.038	−0.194**	−0.044	−0.059	−0.053
	(0.515)	(−2.599)	(−0.606)	(−0.789)	(−0.691)
Constant	0.037	0.301	−0.197	−0.086	0.021
	(0.159)	(1.269)	(−0.850)	(−0.363)	(0.088)
$\bar{R}^2$	0.047	0.0322	0.074	0.029	−0.004

** and * indicate 10 percent and 5 percent significant level, respectively.

Source: Lee and Wei (1984).

REFERENCES

Arnott, Robert. "Cluster Analysis and Stock Price Comovement." *Financial Analysts Journal,* v. 36 (November/December 1980), pp. 56–62.

Black, Fisher. "Capital Market Equilibrium with Restricted Borrowing." *Journal of Business,* v. 45 (July 1972), pp. 444–54.

Bower, D., R. Bower, and D. Logue. "A Primer on APT." *Midland Corporate Finance Journal,* v. 2 (Fall 1984), pp. 31–40.

————. "Arbitrage Pricing and Utility Stock Returns." *Journal of Finance,* v. 39 (September 1984), pp. 1041–54.

Breeden, D. "An Intertemporal Asset Pricing Model with Stochastic Consumption and Investment Opportunities." *Journal of Financial Economics,* v. 7 (September 1979), pp. 265–96.

Bubnys, E. L., and C. F. Lee. "Simulating and Forecasting Utility Stock Returns." *Financial Review* (1990), forthcoming.

Burmeister, E., and M. B. McElroy. "Joint Estimation of Factor Sensitivities and Risk Premia for the Arbitrage Pricing Theory. *Journal of Finance,* v. 43 (July 1988), pp. 721–35.

Chamberlain, G., and M. Rothschild. "Arbitrage, Factor Structure, and Mean-Variance Analysis on Large Asset Markets." *Econometrica*, v. 51 (September 1983), pp. 1281–1304.

Chen, N. F. "Some Empirical Tests of the Theory of Arbitrage Pricing." *Journal of Finance*, v. 38 (December 1983), pp. 1393–1414.

Chen, N., R. Roll, and S. Ross. "Economic Forces and the Stock Market." *Journal of Business*, v. 59 (July 1986), pp. 383–403.

Cheng, P. L., and R. Grauer. "An Alternative Test of the Capital Asset Pricing Model." *The American Economic Review*, v. 70 (September 1980), pp. 660–71.

———. "An Alternative Test of the Capital Asset Pricing Model: Reply." *The American Economic Review*, v. 72 (December 1982), pp. 1201–07.

Cho, D., E. Elton, and M. Gruber. "On the Robustness of the Roll and Ross Arbitrage Pricing Theory." *Journal of Financial and Quantitative Analysis*, v. 19 (March 1984), pp. 1–10.

Cohen, K., and G. Pogue. "An Empirical Evaluation of Alternative Portfolio Models." *Journal of Business*, v. 40 (1967), pp. 166–93.

Connor, G. "A Unified Beta Pricing Theory." *Journal of Economic Theory*, v. 21 (October 1984), pp. 13–31.

Dhrymes, P. "Arbitrage Pricing Theory." *Journal of Portfolio Management*, v. 11 (Summer 1984), pp. 35–44.

———, I. Friend, and N. Gultekin. "A Critical Reexamination of the Empirical Evidence on the APT." *Journal of Finance*, v. 39 (June 1984), pp. 323–46.

Dybvig, P., and S. Ross. "Yes, the APT is Testable." *Journal of Finance*, v. 40 (September 1985), 1173–88.

Elton, E. J., and M. J. Gruber. "Estimating the Dependence Structure of Share Prices—Implications for Portfolio Selection." *Journal of Finance*, v. 27 (December 1973), pp. 1203–33.

———, and J. Rentzler. "The Arbitrage Pricing Model and Returns on Assets Under Uncertain Inflation." *Journal of Finance*, v. 38 (May 1983), pp. 525–38.

Farrell, J. L. "Analyzing Covariation of Returns to Determine Homogeneous Stock Grouping." *Journal of Business*, v. 47 (April 1974), pp. 186–207.

Fogler, H. "Common Sense on CAPM, APT and Correlated Residuals." *Journal of Portfolio Management*, v. 9 (Summer 1982), pp. 20–28.

———, K. John, and J. Tipton. "Three Factors, Interest Rate Differentials and Stock Groups." *Journal of Finance*, v. 36 (May 1981), pp. 323–36.

Gibbons, M. "Multivariate Tests of Financial Models: A New Approach." *Journal of Financial Economics*, v. 10 (March 1982), pp. 3–27.

Huberman, G. "A Simple Approach to Arbitrage Pricing Theory." *Journal of Economic Theory*, v. 19 (October 1982), pp. 183–91.

Hughes, P. "A Test of the Arbitrage Pricing Theory." Working Paper, University of British Columbia, 1981.

Ingersoll, J., Jr. "Some Results in the Theory of Arbitrage Pricing." *Journal of Finance,* v. 39 (September 1984), pp. 1021–54.

Jarrow, R., and A. Rudd. "A Comparison of the APT and CAPM." *Journal of Banking and Finance,* v. 17 (June 1983), pp. 295–303.

Jobson, J. "A Multivariate Linear Regression Test for the Arbitrage Pricing Theory." *Journal of Finance,* v. 37 (September 1982), pp. 1037–42.

King, B. J. "Market and Industry Factors in Stock Price Behavior." *Journal of Business,* v. 39 (January 1966), pp. 139–90.

Kryzanowski, L., and M. To. "General Factor Models and the Structure of Security Returns." *Journal of Financial and Quantitative Analysis,* v. 18 (March 1983), pp. 48–49.

Lee, Cheng F., and W. P. Lloyd. "Block Recursive Systems in Asset Pricing Models: An Extension." *Journal of Finance,* v. 32 (May 1978), pp. 640–44.

————, and John K. C. Wei. "Multi-Factor Multi-Indicator Approach to Asset Pricing Model: Theory and Empirical Evidence." BEBR, The University of Illinois, Urbana-Champaign, Working Paper #1062, 1984.

Lintner, John. "The Valuation of Risk Assets and the Selection of Risky Investments in Stock Portfolios and Capital Budgets." *Review of Economics and Statistics,* v. 47 (February 1965), pp. 13–37.

Lloyd, W. P., and Cheng F. Lee. "Block Recursive Systems in Asset Pricing Models." *Journal of Finance,* v. 30 (December 1976), pp. 1101–14.

Long, J., Jr. "Stock Prices, Inflation and the Term Structure of Interest Rates." *Journal of Financial Economics,* v. 2 (July 1974), pp. 131–70.

Markowitz, H. "Portfolio Selection." *Journal of Finance,* v. 6 (March 1952), pp. 77–91.

Merton, R. "An Inter-Temporal Capital Asset Pricing Model." *Econometrica,* v. 41 (September 1973), pp. 867–87.

Mossin, Jan. "Equilibrium in a Capital Asset Market." *Econometrica,* v. 34 (October 1966), pp. 768–873.

Oldfield, G. S., and R. J. Rogalski. "Treasury Bill Factors and Common Stock Returns." *Journal of Finance,* v. 35 (May 1981), pp. 337–49.

Ramsey, J. B., and P. Schmidt. "Some Further Results on the Use of OLS and BLUS Residuals in Specification Error Tests." *Journal of American Statistical Association,* v. 66 (1976), pp. 471–74.

Reinganum, M. "The Arbitrage Pricing Theory: Some Empirical Results." *Journal of Finance,* v. 36 (May 1981), pp. 313–21.

Roll, R. "A Critique of the Asset Pricing Theory's Tests." *Journal of Financial Economics,* v. 5 (May 1977), pp. 129–76.

————, and R. Ross. "An Empirical Investigation of the Arbitrage Pricing Theory." *Journal of Finance,* v. 5 (December 1980), pp. 1073–1103.

————. "The APT Approach to Strategic Portfolio Planning." *Financial Analysts Journal,* v. 40 (May/June 1984), pp. 14–26.

Ross, S. "The Arbitrage Theory of Capital Asset Pricing." *Journal of Economic Theory,* v. 13 (December 1976), pp. 341–60.

————. "Return, Risk and Arbitrage." In *Risk and Return in Finance,* v. I, Friend and Bicksler, eds. Ballinger, 1977.

————. "Mutual Fund Separation in Financial Theory—the Separating Distributions." *Journal of Economic Theory,* v. 15 (April 1978), pp. 254–86.

Schipper, K., and R. Thompson. "Common Stocks as Hedges Against Shifts in the Consumption on Investment Opportunity Set." *Journal of Business,* v. 54 (April 1981), pp. 305–28.

Shanken, Jay. "The Arbitrage Pricing Theory: Is It Testable?" *Journal of Finance,* v. 37 (December 1982), pp. 1129–40.

————. "Multi-Beta CAPM or Equilibrium-APT?: A Reply." *Journal of Finance,* v. 40 (September 1985), pp. 1189–90.

Sharpe, William. "Capital Asset Prices: A Theory of Market Equilibrium under Conditions of Risk." *Journal of Finance,* v. 19 (September 1964), pp. 425–42.

————. "Factor Models, CAPMs and the APT." *Journal of Portfolio Management,* v. 11 (Fall 1984), pp. 21–25.

————. "Factors in NYSE Security Returns." *Journal of Portfolio Management,* v. 18 (Summer 1982), pp. 5–19.

Solnick, B. "International Arbitrage Pricing Theory." *Journal of Finance,* v. 38 (May 1983), pp. 449–58.

Stambaugh, R. "On the Exclusion of Assets from Tests of the Two-Parameter Model: A Sensitivity Analysis." *Journal of Financial Economics,* v. 10 (November 1982), pp. 237–68.

Theil, H. *Principles of Econometrics.* John Wiley and Sons, Inc., 1971.

Varian, H. R. "The Arbitrage Principle in Financial Economics." *Journal of Economic Perspectives,* v. 1 (Fall 1987), pp. 55–72.

Wei, John K. C. "An Asset-Pricing Theory Unifying the CAPM and APT." *Journal of Finance,* v. 43 (September 1988), pp. 881–92.

12 Futures Valuation and Hedging

A basic assumption of finance theory is that investors are risk averse. If we equate risk with uncertainty, can we question the validity of this assumption? What evidence is there?

As living, functional proof of the appropriateness of the risk aversion assumption, there exist entire markets whose sole underlying purpose is to allow investors to display their uncertainties about the future. These particular markets, with primary focus on the future, are called just that, **futures markets.** These markets allow for the transfer of risk from hedgers (risk-averse individuals) to speculators (risk-seeking individuals), a key element necessary for the existence of futures markets is the balance between the number of hedgers and speculators who are willing to transfer and accept risk.

A **futures contract** is a standardized legal agreement between a buyer and a seller, who promise now to exchange a specified amount of money for goods or services at a future time. Of course, there is nothing really unusual about a contract made in advance of delivery. For instance, whenever something is ordered rather than purchased on the spot, a futures (or forward) contract is involved. Although the price is determined at the time of the order, the actual exchange of cash for the merchandise takes place later. For some items the lag is a few days, while for others (such as a car) it may be months. Moreover, a futures contract imparts a legal obligation to both parties of the contract to fulfill the specifications. To guarantee fulfillment of this obligation, a ''good-faith'' deposit, also called **margin,** may be required from the buyer (and the seller, if he or she does not already own the product).

To ensure consistency in the contracts and to help develop liquidity, futures exchanges have been established. These exchanges provide a central location and a standardized set of rules in order to enhance the credibility of these markets and thus generate an orderly, liquid arena for the price determination of individual commodities at distinct points in the future.

A substantial increase in the number of types of futures contracts offered by the exchanges has been occurring over the last decade. At the same time, the growth in futures trading volume has been phenomenal. Two explanations can be offered for this increase in futures activity. These increases can be intuitively correlated with the growing levels of uncertainty in many facets of the economic environment—for example, inflation and interest rates. A second view is based on the argument that even though the world has not become any more uncertain, the increased integration of financial and real markets has increased the risk exposure of any given individual. The tremendous growth in the home-mortgage and consumer-debt financial markets has allowed the purchase of more and more expensive and real assets. This increase in the rise of individual financial leverage has increased individual exposure to interest-rate fluctuations, thereby increasing the requirements for risk-sharing across markets or between individuals with varied portfolios. Futures markets have the potential to help people manage or transfer the uncertainties that plague the world today.

This chapter examines the basic types of futures contracts offered and the functioning of futures markets. In addition the uses of financial and index futures are illustrated, and the theoretical pricing concepts related to these financial instruments are discussed. The important terms associated with futures contracts and futures markets are defined and the futures market is compared to the forward market. An analysis of futures market follows. A theory of valuation is introduced, and the chapter closes with a discussion of various hedging strategies and concepts.

The following section analyzes the differences between **forward contracts** and futures contracts. Table 12A–1 at the end of this chapter briefly defines related terminology.

FUTURES VERSUS FORWARD MARKETS

While futures and forward contracts are similar in many respects, their differences are more important to fully understanding the nature and uses of these financial instruments. Both futures and forward contracts specify a transaction to take place at a future date and include precise requirements for the commodity to be delivered, its price, its quantity, the delivery date, and the delivery point. Nevertheless, these two types of contracts for future delivery of a commodity and the markets in which they are traded differ in a number of significant ways, some of which are included in Table 12–1.

Although most people are unlikely ever to become involved in the forward market, it is important to understand some of its attributes, particularly as a good deal of the literature on pricing futures contracts typically refers to these two contracts interchangeably. Specifically, it might be inferred from Table 12–1 that differences resulting from liquidity, credit risk, search, margin, taxes, and commissions could cause futures and forward contracts

TABLE 12-1   A Comparison of Futures and Forward Markets

Futures Market	*Forward Market*
1. Trading is conducted in a competitive arena by "open outcry" of bids, offers, and amounts.	1. Trading is done by telex or telephone, with participants generally dealing directly with broker-dealers.
2. Contract terms are standardized with all buyers and sellers negotiating only with respect to price.	2. All contract terms are negotiated privately by the parties.
3. Nonmember participants deal through brokers (exchange members) who represent them on the exchange floor.	3. Participants deal typically on a principal-to-principal basis.
4. Participants include banks, corporations, financial institutions, individual investors, and speculators.	4. Participants are primarily institutions dealing with one other and other interested parties dealing through one or more dealers.
5. The clearinghouse of the exchange becomes the opposite side to each cleared transaction; therefore, the credit risk for a futures-market participant is always the same and there is no need to analyze the credit of other market participants.	5. A participant must examine the credit risk and establish credit limits for each opposite party.
6. Margin deposits are to be required of all participants.	6. Typically, no money changes hands until delivery, although a small margin deposit might be required of nondealer customers on certain occasions.
7. Settlements are made daily through the exchange clearinghouse. Gains on open positions may be withdrawn, and losses are collected daily.	7. Settlement occurs on date agreed upon between the parties to each transaction.
8. Long and short positions are usually liquidated easily.	8. Forward positions are not as easily offset or transferred to other participants.
9. Settlements are normally made in cash, with only a small percentage of all contracts resulting in actual delivery.	9. Most transactions result in delivery.
10. A single, round-trip (in and out of the market) commission is charged. It is negotiated between broker and customer and is relatively small in relation to the value of the contract. Commissions range from $18 to over $100 per round-turn.	10. No commission is typically charged if the transaction is made directly with another dealer. A commission is charged to both buyer and seller, however, if transacted through a broker.
11. Trading is regulated by the exchange and by a federal agency, the Commodity Futures Trading Commission (CFTC).	11. Trading is mostly unregulated.
12. The delivery price is the spot price.	12. The delivery price is the forward price.

not to be priced identically. Some of the major users of forward contracts include:

1. *Public utilities:* Public utilities sometimes engage in fairly long-term perpetual forward contracts for the delivery of coal or natural gas.
2. *Savings-and-loan associations:* A typical thrift institution might contract to deliver a pool of mortgages to another thrift in ninety days.
3. *Apparel or toy manufacturers:* Stores often contract for the delivery of the "new fall line" in early spring.
4. *Import-export businesses:* A U.S. exporter may contract for the delivery of a foreign currency in sixty days, after it receives payment in the foreign currency for goods sold overseas.

FUTURES MARKETS: OVERVIEW

In the most general sense, the term **commodity futures** is taken to embrace all existing futures contracts. Nevertheless, for purposes of clarity and classification its meaning here is restricted to a limited segment of the total futures markets. Accordingly, futures contracts can be classified into three main types.

1. Commodity futures
2. Financial futures
3. Index futures

Within this classification commodity futures include all agriculturally related futures contracts with underlying assets, such as corn, wheat, rye, barley, rice, oats, sugar, coffee, soybeans, frozen orange juice, pork bellies, live cattle, hogs, and lumber. Also, within the commodity-futures framework are futures contracts written on precious metals, such as gold, silver, copper, platinum, and palladium, and contracts written on petroleum products, including gasoline, crude oil, and heating oil. Many of the futures contracts on metals and petroleum products have been introduced as recently as the early 1980s.

Producers, refineries, and distributors, to name only a few potential users, employ futures contracts to assure a particular price or supply—or both—for the underlying commodity at a future date.

Futures-market participants are divided into two broad classes: hedgers and speculators. **Hedging** refers to a futures-market transaction made as a temporary substitute for a cash-market transaction to be made at a later date. The purpose of hedging is to take advantage of current prices by using futures transactions. For example, banks and corporations can be hedgers when they use futures to fix future borrowing and lending rates.

Futures market **speculation** involves taking a short or long futures position solely to profit from price changes. If you think that interest rates will rise because of an increase in inflation, you can sell T-bill futures and make a profit if interest rates do rise and the value of T-bills falls. Sample Problem 12.1 provides further illustration.

Sample Problem 12.1

An investor has a portfolio of T-bills with a face value of $1 million, currently worth $950,000 in the cash market. A futures contract with a face value of $1,000,000 worth of T-bills is currently selling for $95\frac{16}{32}$ per hundred dollars. Interest rates rise and the value of the T-bills falls to $946,875, while the value of the T-bill futures contract falls to $95\frac{6}{32}$ per hundred dollars. If the investor were to hedge the T-bill position with T-bill futures, what would be the net result of this interest-rate change on the value of the hedged position? If the investor were to speculate that interest rates would fall, what is the next effect on the portfolio value?

Solution
See the two tabular worksheets that show the results of hedged and speculative positions, respectively●

Financial futures are a trading medium initiated with the introduction of contracts on foreign currencies at the International Monetary Market (IMM) in 1972. In addition to futures on foreign currencies, financial futures include contracts based on Treasury bonds (T-bonds), Treasury bills (T-bills), Treasury notes (T-notes), bank certificates of deposit, Eurodollars, and

Hedged Position for Sample Problem 12.1

Time	T-Bill Value in Cash Market	Time	Futures Value	
t	$950,000	t	Sell ten T-bill contracts at $95\frac{16}{32}$ (1,000,000 × 0.955).	$955,000
$t + 1$	$946,875	$t + 1$	Buy ten T-bill contracts at $95\frac{6}{32}$ (1,000,000 × 0.951875).	$951,875
Loss in cash market	− $3,125		Gain on short position in futures	+ $3,125
	Net change in value of hedged portfolio = $0			

GNMA mortgage securities. These latter types of financial futures contracts are also referred to as *interest-rate futures* since their underlying asset is an interest-bearing security. While foreign-currency futures arose with the abolition of the Bretton Woods fixed exchange-rate system during the early 1970s, interest-rate futures surged in popularity and number following the change in U.S. monetary policy in October, 1979. The effect of the Federal Open Market Committee's decision to deemphasize the traditional practice of "pegging" interest rates was to greatly increase the volatility of market interest rates. Thus, interest-rate changes have become a highly prominent risk to corporations, investors, and financial institutions. (Figures 12–1A and 12–1B exhibit the changing volatility of T-bill prices and rates of return from 1970 to 1988.)

Index futures represent the newest and boldest innovation in the futures market to date. An index-futures contract is one for which the underlying asset is actually a portfolio of assets—for example, the Major Market Index (MMI) includes twenty stocks traded on the NYSE and the S&P Index includes the five hundred stocks of the S&P Index. Contracts on more diverse types of indexes include a high-quality bond index, an interest-rate index composed of interest-bearing market securities, and the consumer price index.

The S&P 500 Index, requiring delivery of the five hundred stocks constituting the S&P 500 stock index, would certainly have dampened enthusiasm for this and similar index contracts. Because of this, an index-futures contract is settled on the basis of its cash value when the contract matures. The cash value of the contract is equal to the closing index value on its last trading day, times a dollar amount of $500.

Speculative Position for Sample Problem 12.1

Time	T-Bill Value in Cash Market	Time	Futures Value	
t	$950,000	t	Buy ten T-bill contracts at $95\frac{16}{32}$ $(1,000,000 \times 0.955)$.	$955,000
$t + 1$	$946,875	$t + 1$	Sell ten T-bill contracts at $95\frac{6}{32}$ $(1,000,000 \times 0.951875)$.	$951,875
Loss in cash market	$-$3,125		Loss on sale	$-$3,125

Net change in value of unhedged portfolio plus speculation loss = $6,250

FIGURE 12–1A   Monthly T-Bill Prices, 1970–1988

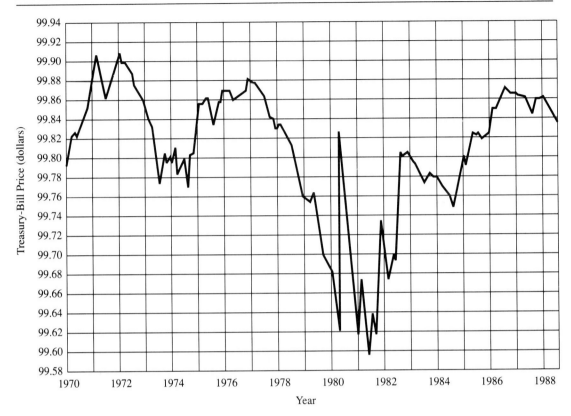

Many portfolio managers are taking advantage of index futures to alter their portfolios' risk–return distributions. Some applications that have arisen are discussed later in this chapter.

COMPONENTS AND MECHANICS OF FUTURES MARKETS

This section discusses components and mechanics of futures markets: the exchanges, the clearinghouse, margin, order execution, and T-bill futures transactions.

The Exchanges

A **futures exchange,** just like a stock exchange, is the arena for the actual daily trading of futures contracts. The exchange is a nonprofit organization whose members include those allowed to trade on its floor. Members include individual traders, brokerage firms, and other types of institutions. The

FIGURE 12-1B   Monthly T-Bill Returns, 1970–1988

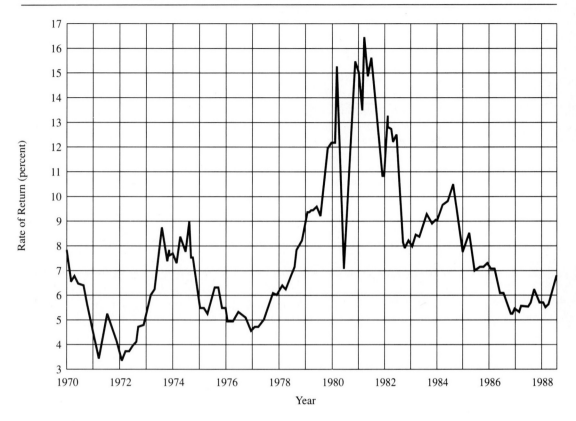

exchange's governing rules and procedures are determined by its members, who serve on various policy committees and elect the officers of the exchange.

The fees paid by an exchange's members support not only the daily operation of its trading venue but also other functions and services performed by staff members for the exchange, such as research, public relations, presentations and seminars for users, lobbying of government, and planning for the exchange's future.

Another term for an exchange membership is a **seat**. A prospective member may buy a full seat, allowing him or her to trade any of the offered futures contracts. To encourage volume on newer or less liquid contracts, most exchanges usually also offer a partial seat, permitting its owner to trade only a designated number of contracts. Usually, to get onto an exchange to trade, an investor needs to buy or lease a seat from a current owner. The value of an exchange seat can vary substantially; for example, the high and low prices for a full seat on the International Monetary Market (IMM) exchange range from $300,000 to $100,000, respectively. Such exchanges are

entrusted with clearinghouse responsibilities that are vital to the efficient operation of the futures market.

The Clearinghouse

Central to the operation of organized futures markets is the **clearinghouse** or clearing corporation for the exchange. Whenever someone enters a position in a futures contract on the long or short side, the clearinghouse always takes the opposite side of the contract. That is, it becomes a buyer to every seller and a seller to every buyer. The advantages of having a central organization providing this role are threefold.

1. The clearinghouse eliminates concern over the creditworthiness of the party on the other side of the transaction.
2. It frees the original trading partners from the obligation of delivery or offset with each other.
3. It provides greater flexibility in opening or closing a position.

For example, if an investor originally bought a T-bill futures contract in January that matures in March, but in February desired to liquidate his position by selling the same contract at the current market price, he would not have to find the original seller of the contract. Instead, he need only call up his broker with instructions to place an order to sell at the market price in the trading pit, allowing any other trader to buy the contract. On the other hand, if the investor decided to hold his T-bill futures contract to its March expiration and take delivery of the $1,000,000 of thirteen-week T-bills that the contract calls for, he would not need to locate the original seller of the contract. Rather, he would need only notify the exchange's clearinghouse of his intentions; upon the contract's expiration the clearinghouse would randomly select someone with an open short position in the same contract to make delivery.

The clearinghouse guarantees the integrity of such transactions by its guaranty fund, increased from $33 million to $36 million on July 1, 1989 for the Chicago Mercantile Exchange. The fund is made up of contributions from clearing member firms and is available to be drawn upon in the event of a clearing member's failure to discharge financial obligations to the exchange's clearinghouse. The clearinghouse also oversees the daily marking to market of required margin deposits for all open accounts.

Margin

Whenever someone enters into a contract position in the futures market, a security deposit, commonly called a **margin requirement,** must be paid. While the futures margin seems to be a partial payment for the security on which the futures contract is based, it only represents security to cover any losses that could result from adverse price movements.

The minimum margin requirements set by the exchange must be collected by the clearing member firms (members of the exchange involved in the clearinghouse operations) when their customers take positions in the market. In turn, the clearing member firms must deposit a fixed portion of these margins with the clearinghouse. At the end of each trading day, every futures-trading account is incremented or reduced by the corresponding increase or decrease in the value of all open futures positions. This daily adjustment procedure is applied to the margin deposit and is called **marking to market.** For example, if an investor is long on a T-bill futures contract, and by the end of a day its market value has fallen $1,000, he or she would be asked to add an additional $1,000 to the margin account. Why? Because the investor is responsible for its initial value. For example, if a futures contract is executed at $10,000 with initial margin of $1,000 and the value of the position goes down $1,000 to $9,000, the buyer would be required to put in additional margin of $1,000 because the investor is responsible for paying $10,000 for the contract. Otherwise, if the investor is unable to comply or refuses to do so, the clearing member firm that he or she trades through would automatically close out the position. On the other hand, if the contract's value was up $1,000 for the day, the investor might immediately withdraw the profit if he or she so desired. The procedure of marking to market implies that all potential profits and losses are immediately realized.

Due to the difficulty of calling all customers whose margin accounts have fallen in value for the day, a clearing member firm will usually require that a sum of money be deposited at the initiation of any futures position. This additional sum is called **maintenance margin.** In most situations the original margin requirement may be established with a risk-free, interest-bearing security such as a T-bill. However, the maintenance margin, which must be in cash, is adjusted for daily changes in the contract value.

Margin requirements may vary among brokerage houses and may certainly differ for the type of futures trading engaged in. The largest margin deposit is required of a speculator—that is, someone who has an outright long or short position in the futures, with no corresponding position in a related security or the actual underlying asset. This results from the fact that the speculator takes on the most risk and stands to lose the most. However, for someone who owns the asset underlying the futures contract and enters the market in order to hedge the spot position, margin requirements are significantly lower. That is, the hedger's spot position stands as collateral, and the overall position is subject to a much smaller degree of price risk. Lower margins are also required from *spreaders*—traders taking an opposite futures position in a distant contract month or a related contract, or who are taking a position in an option on the futures contract. For instance, if a spreader is long the September, 1988 T-bill futures, and short the same but more distant March, 1989 contract, the margin requirement would be lower than that required for an outright speculative position.

Although *margin calls* can be an inconvenience, are disruptive to cash flow, and involve an interest opportunity cost, the actual size of the required

margin deposit is very small compared to the value of the contract it controls. For a T-bill futures contract worth $1,000,000 the required margin might be as little as $2,700. This is a leverage factor of $37\times$. For the much more volatile stock-index futures, such as the contract on the S&P 500 index, a speculative position requiring $8,500 in total margin would typically control a position worth $75,000 to $85,000. This is still a leverage factor of roughly $10\times$, one reason that futures contracts are growing in popularity.

Order Execution

Each order to buy and sell futures contracts comes to the exchange floor either by telephone or by a computerized order-entry system. It is received by a member firm at its communications desk and is time-stamped. The person receiving the order is called a *phone clerk*.

The phone clerk then hands the order to a *runner,* who relays it to the appropriate trading area or *pit*. Futures contracts are traded in separate pits, which are divided into a number of sections designated for trading in specific contract months.

The runner gives the order to the firm's *floor broker,* who handles the firm's trades in a specific contract or delivery month and takes responsibility for executing the order. If the order is to buy, the floor broker sounds out a bid for the appropriate type and number of futures contracts at the requested price to the other brokers and traders in the pit. If the order is to sell, the floor broker sounds out an offer. Once someone calls back an acknowledgment to the broker's bid or offer, the order is executed.

When the order is executed, the floor broker endorses its time, price, and size while a specially trained employee of the exchange, the *pit observer,* records the price for immediate entry into the exchange's computerized price-reporting system. The system then instantaneously transmits information to market participants around the world.

Finally, the executed order is returned from the trading pit to the phone clerk again via the runner. Once more, at the firm's communications desk the phone clerk time-stamps the executed order and immediately confirms its execution to the customer who entered it. In all, the entire order-handling process on the exchange floor takes as little as two to three minutes.

As an aside, the time-stamping serves to indicate how long the firm took to execute or *fill* the order. Some orders—such as a market order, where the firm is instructed to buy or sell at the going market price—are typically allowed only three minutes for complete execution, and the firm can be penalized by the customer through the exchange if the order is not completed in the time allowed.

A Sample T-Bill Futures Transaction

Suppose that on October 2, 1990, a trader buys one December, 1990 T-bill futures contract at the opening index price of 94.83. Once the transaction is complete the trader is contractually obligated to buy a $1 million face-value

thirteen-week T-bill yielding $100 - 94.83 = 5.17$ percent on a discount basis on the contract delivery date, which is December 18, 1990. At the time of the initial transaction, however, the trader pays only a commission and deposits the required margin with the broker.

Suppose the futures price falls two basis points during the next day's trading session; this means that the discount rate on T-bills for future delivery has been increased. Each basis-point change in the T-bill index is worth $25. The trader in this case will lose $50 if he or she sells the contract at the closing price. The procedure of handling this loss is now the focus for discussion.

The practice of marking futures contracts to market at the end of each trading session means that the trader is forced to realize this loss even if the trader does not sell the contract, because $50 is subtracted from the trader's margin account. This money is then transferred to the seller's margin account. After the contract is marked to market, the trader is still obligated to buy a T-bill on December 18, 1990, but now at a discount yield of 5.19 percent. In effect the trader pays $50 less for the T-bill at delivery because he has paid $50 to the potential seller by marking to market. Every day the old futures contract is essentially cancelled and replaced by a new contract with a delivery price equal to the new futures price—that is, the settlement price at the end of the day.

If the trader chooses to hold the contract to maturity, the contract is marked to market one last time at the close of trading on December 18. All longs with open positions at that time must be prepared to buy the deliverable T-bill at a price determined by the closing futures price.

The final settlement price or purchase price for an International Money Market T-bill contract is determined as follows. First, the total discount is calculated from the face value of the T-bill:

$$\text{Discount} = \frac{\text{Days to maturity} \times [(100 - \text{Index}) \times 0.01] \times \$1,000,000}{360}$$

where $(100 - \text{Index}) \times 0.01$ is the futures discount yield expressed as a fraction. Second, the purchase price is computed by subtracting the old discount from the face value of the deliverable bill. For example, if the final index price is $94.81, the settlement price for the delivery is

$$\$986,880.83 = \$1,000,000 - \frac{91 \text{ days} \times 0.0519 \times \$1,000,000}{360}$$

where $0.0519 = [100 - \text{Index}] \times 0.01$.

Because buying a futures contract during the last trading session is essentially equivalent to buying a T-bill in the spot market, futures prices tend to converge to the spot price of the deliverable security on the final day of futures trading for a given contract. Otherwise, risk-free arbitrage results. Thus the settlement futures discount yield should equal the spot market discount yield at the end of the trading day. Sample Problem 12.2 provides further illustration.

Sample Problem 12.2

What is the settlement value for delivery for a IMM T-bill contract when the final index is 93?

Solution

$$\text{Discount} = \frac{\text{Days to maturity} \times [(100 - \text{Index}) \times 0.01] \times \$1,000,000}{360}$$

$$= \frac{91\,[(100 - 93) - 0.01] - \$1,000,000}{360}$$

$$= \$17,194.44$$

$$\begin{aligned}
\text{Settlement value} &= \$1,000,000 - \text{Discount} \\
&= \$1,000,000 - \$17,194.44 \\
&= \$982,305.56
\end{aligned}$$

The minimum yield change for T-bill futures contracts is one basis point (0.001), or a hundredth of 1 percent. To calculate the change in dollar value for a change of one basis point the discount relationship can be modified. For example, for a 90-day IMM T-bill contract each change of one basis point is equivalent to a change of $25.

$$\Delta(\$) = \frac{\text{Days to maturity} \times \Delta(\text{basis points}) \times \$1,000,000}{360}$$

$$= \frac{90 \times 0.001 \times \$1,000,000}{360}$$

$$= \$25$$

The two important variables in the above relationship are the days to maturity and the face value of the contract.

THE VALUATION OF FUTURES CONTRACTS

The discussions of each of the three classifications of futures contracts have pointed out pricing idiosyncrasies and have examined specific pricing models for particular types of contracts. Nevertheless, the underlying tenets of any particular pricing model have their roots in a more general theoretical framework of valuation. Consequently, the focus is now on the traditional concepts of futures contracts valuation as a prelude to more specific discussions in Chapter 13.

The Arbitrage Argument

An instant before the futures contract matures, its price must be equal to the spot (cash) price of the underlying commodity, or:

$$F_{t,T} = S_t \qquad (12.1)$$

where:

$F_{t,T}$ = the price of the futures contract at time t, which matures at time T, where $T > t$ and $T - t$ is a very small interval of time; and

S_t = the spot price of the underlying commodity at time t.

If Equation (12.1) did not hold, an arbitrage condition would prevail. More specifically, when $t = T$ at the maturity of the contract, all trading on the contract ceases and the futures price equals the spot price. If an instant before maturity $F_{t,T} < S_t$, one could realize a sure profit (an arbitrage profit) by simultaneously buying the futures contract (which is undervalued) and selling the spot commodity (which is overvalued). The arbitrage profit would equal:

$$S_t - F_{t,T} \qquad (12.2)$$

However, if $F_{t,T} > S_t$ is the market condition an instant before maturity, smart traders would recognize this arbitrage condition and sell futures contracts and buy the spot commodity until $t = T$ and $F_{t,T} = S_t$. In fact, the effect of selling the futures and buying the spot would bid their prices down and up, respectively. Thus, the arbitrage process would alleviate any such pricing disequilibrium between the futures contract and its underlying spot commodity.

Interest Costs

The previous simplified argument demonstrated that the futures and spot prices must be equal an instant before the contract's maturity. This development assumes no costs in holding the spot commodity or carrying it (storing it) across time. If such a market condition held, Equation (12.1) could be extended to apply to any point of time where $t < T$. However, by having to buy or sell the spot commodity to carry out the arbitrage process, the trader would incur certain costs. For instance, if the spot commodity were purchased because it is undervalued relative to the futures, the trader or *arbitrageur* would incur an opportunity or interest cost. Any funds he or she tied up in the purchase of the commodity could alternatively be earning some risk-free interest rate R_f through investment in an interest-bearing risk-free security. Therefore, the futures price should account for the interest cost of holding the spot commodity over time, and consequently Equation (12.1) can be modified to:

$$F_{t,T} = S_t (1 + R_{f,T-t}) \qquad (12.3)$$

where $R_{f,T-t}$ is the risk-free opportunity cost or interest income that is lost by tying up funds in the spot commodity over the interval $T - t$. Sample Problem 12.3 provides further illustration.

Sample Problem 12.3

On September 1 the spot price of a commodity is $100. The current risk-free rate is 12 percent. What is the value on September 1 of a futures contract that matures on October 1 with a price of $100?

Solution

$$F_{t,T} = S_t (1 + R_{f,T-t})$$

$$F_{t,T} = \$100 \left(1 + \frac{0.12}{12}\right)$$

$$F_{\text{Sept. 1, Oct. 1}} = \$101$$

Since the investment is for one month only, the annualized rate of 12 percent must be converted to a monthly rate of 1 percent; this is done for $R_{f,T-t}$ by dividing the annual rate by twelve●

Carrying Costs

Since theories on the pricing of futures contracts were developed long before the introduction of financial or index futures, the costs of storing and insuring the spot commodity were considered relevant factors in the price of a futures contract. That is, someone who purchased the spot commodity to hold from time t to a later period T, incurs the costs of actually housing the commodity and insuring it in case of fire or theft. In the case of livestock such as cattle or hogs, the majority of this cost would be in feeding. The holder of a futures contract avoids these costs borne by the spot holder, making the value of the contract relative to the spot commodity increase by the amount of these carrying costs. Therefore, Equation (12.3) can be extended:

$$F_{t,T} = S_t(1 + R_{f,T-t}) + C_{T-t} \tag{12.4}$$

where C_{T-t} is the carrying costs associated with the spot commodity for the interval $T - t$. Sample Problem 12.4 provides further illustration.

Sample Problem 12.4

Extending the problem in Sample Problem 12.3, if the carrying cost is $0.04 per dollar of value per month, what is the value of the futures contract on September 1?

Solution

$$F_{t,T} = S_t (1 + R_{f,T-t}) + C_{T-t}$$

$$F_{t,T} = \$100 \left(1 + \frac{0.12}{12}\right) + \$100 \, (\$0.04/\text{month})(1 \text{ month})$$

$$F_{\text{Sept. 1, Oct. 1}} = \$105$$

Supply and Demand Effects

As for other financial instruments or commodities, the price of a futures contract is affected by expectations of future supply and demand conditions. The effects of supply and demand for the current spot commodity (as well as for the future spot commodity) have not yet been considered in this analysis.

If the probability exists that future supplies of the spot commodity might significantly differ from current supplies, then this will affect the futures price. The discussion up to this point has assumed that the aggregate supply of the commodity was fixed over time and that demand remained constant; however, for agricultural, financial, and index futures this is a very unrealistic assumption. For instance, if it is expected that the future available supply of wheat for time T will decline because of poor weather, and demand is expected to remain unchanged, one would then expect the future spot price of wheat to be higher than the current spot price. Furthermore, a futures contract on wheat that matures at time T can also be considered to represent the expected spot price at time T and consequently should reflect the expected change in supply conditions. In a more extreme fashion, if it is assumed there is no current supply of wheat, then the futures price would reflect only future supply conditions and the expected future spot price at time T. This can be expressed as:

$$F_{t,T} = E_t(\tilde{S}_T) \tag{12.5}$$

where $E_t(\tilde{S}_T)$ is the spot price at a future point T expected at time t, where $t < T$. The tilde above S_T indicates that the future spot price is a random variable because future factors such as supply cannot presently be known with certainty.

Equation (12.5) is called the **unbiased-expectations hypothesis** because it postulates that the current price of a futures contract maturing at time T represents the market's expectation of the future spot price at time T. Which of these expressions for the price of a futures contract at time t will hold in the market—the arbitrage pricing relationship in Equation (12.4) or the unbiased-expectations hypothesis in Equation (12.5)? The answer is that, because the markets are assumed to be efficient, the market price of the futures contract will take on the minimum value of either of these two pricing relationships, or:

$$F_{t,T} = \text{Min}\,[E_t(\tilde{S}_T),\, S_t(1 + R_{f,T-t}) + C_{T-t}] \tag{12.6}$$

Sample Problem 12.5 provides further illustration.

Sample Problem 12.5

Continuing Sample Problems 12.3 and 12.4, suppose that the consensus expectation is that the price of the commodity at time T will be $103. What is the price that anyone would pay for a futures contract on September 1?

Solution

$$F_{t,T} = \text{Min } [E_t (\tilde{S}_T), S_t (1 + R_{f, T-t}) + C_{T-t}]$$

$$F_{t,T} = \text{Min } (\$103, \$105)$$

$$F_{\text{Sept. 1, Oct. 1}} = \$103$$

●

For any storable commodity on a given day t, the futures price $F_{t,T}$ will be higher than the spot price S_t on day t; $F_{t,T} > S_t$. The amount by which the futures price exceeds the spot price $(F_{t,T} - S_t)$ is called the **premium.** In most cases this premium is equal to the sum of financial costs $S_t R_{f,T-t}$ and carrying costs C_{T-t}. The condition of $F_{t,T} > S_t$ is associated with a commodity market called a **normal carrying-change market.**

In general, the difference between the futures price $F_{t,T}$ and the spot price S_t is called the **basis.**

$$\text{Basis} = F_{t,T} - S_t \qquad \textbf{(12.7)}$$

The Effect of Hedging Demand

John Maynard Keynes (1930), who studied the futures markets as a hobby, proposed that for some commodities there was a strong tendency for hedgers to be concentrated on the short side of the futures market. That is, to protect themselves against the risk of a price decline in the spot commodity, the spot holder or producer (such as a farmer) would hedge the risk by selling futures contracts on his or her particular commodity. This demand for hedging, producing an abundant supply of futures contracts, would force the market price below that of the expected spot price at maturity (time T). Moreover, the hedgers would be transferring their price risk to speculators. This difference between $E_t (\tilde{S}_T)$ and $F_{t,T}$, when $F_{t,T} < E_t(\tilde{S}_T)$, can be thought of as a risk premium paid to the speculators for holding the long futures position and bearing the price risk of the hedger. This risk premium can be formulated as:

$$E_t(R_p) = E_t(\tilde{S}_T) - F_{t,T} \qquad \textbf{(12.8)}$$

where $E_t(RP)$ is the expected risk premium paid to the speculator for bearing the hedger's price risk.

Keynes described this pricing phenomenon as **normal backwardation.** When the opposite conditions exist—hedgers are concentrated on the long side of the market and bid up the futures spot pricing $F_{t,T}$ over the expected future spot $E_t(\tilde{S}_T)$—the pricing relationship is called **contango** (that is, $E_t(R_p) = F_{t,T} - E_T(\tilde{S}_T)$). To reflect the effect of normal backwardation or contango on the current futures price, the $E_t(\tilde{S}_T)$ term in Equation (12.8) must be adjusted for the effects of hedging demand:

$$F_{t,T} = \text{Min } [E_t(\tilde{S}_T) + E(R_p), S_t(1 + R_{f,T-t}) + C_{T-t}] \qquad \textbf{(12.9)}$$

Equation (12.9) expresses a broad pricing framework for the value of a futures contract. Over the life of the futures contract the futures price must move toward the cash price, because at the maturity of the futures contract the futures price will be equal to the current cash price. If hedgers are in a net short position, then futures prices must lie below the expected future spot price and futures prices would be expected to rise over the life of the contract. However, if hedgers are net long, then the futures price must lie above the expected futures spot price and the price of the futures would be expected to fall. Either a falling futures price (normal backwardation) or a rising futures price (contango) determines the boundaries within which the actual futures price will be located. This region is shown in Figure 12–2.

However, numerous other factors can alter and distort the relationship shown by Equation (12.9). For instance, the analysis implicitly assumes that interest rates remain constant from time t to the contract's maturity date at time T. However, since market interest rates fluctuate, an increasing or decreasing term structure of interest rates would bias the price of the futures contract higher or lower. In fact, the more accurate one's forecast of future interest rates, the more accurate the current valuation of the futures contract.

Empirical research casts rather strong doubt on the size of the expected risk-premium component of futures prices, particularly for financial and

FIGURE 12–2   Bounds for Futures Prices

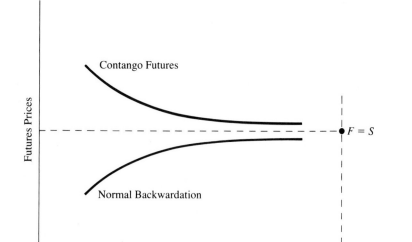

index futures. In fact, the expectations of speculators, along with actual futures contract supply and demand conditions in the pit, can combine to reverse the effect expected by Keynes. This results in part from the makeup of futures' users, a clear majority of whom are not hedgers as suggested by Keynes. Additionally, a futures contract for which an illiquid level of trading volume exists would put the bid and offer prices for the contract further apart. A seller of such a futures contract would require more than the theoretical fair price as compensation for the risk undertaken. The risk is of prices starting to rise in an illiquid market in which the position cannot be immediately closed out. It costs money to maintain the position; therefore, a premium is required to cover this cost.

HEDGING CONCEPTS AND STRATEGIES

The underlying motivation for the development of futures markets is to aid the holders of the spot commodity in hedging their price risk; consequently, the discussion now focuses on such an application of futures markets. Four methodologies based on various risk–return criteria are examined; moreover, to fully clarify the hedger's situation some of the common problems and risks that arise in the hedging process are analyzed.

Hedging Risks and Costs

As mentioned previously, hedging refers to a process designed to alleviate the uncertainty of future price changes for the spot commodity. Typically this is accomplished by taking an opposite position in a futures contract on the same commodity that is held. If an investor owns the spot commodity, as is usually the case (a long position), the appropriate action in the futures market would be to sell a contract (a short position). However, disregarding for the moment the correct number of futures contracts to enter into, a problem arises if the prices of the spot commodity and the futures contract on this commodity do not move in a perfectly correlated manner. This nonsynchronicity of spot and futures prices is related to the basis and is called the **basis risk.**

The basis has been defined as the difference between the futures and spot prices. Basis risk is the chance that this difference will not remain constant over time. Four types of risk contribute to basis risk; these are defined in Table 12–2. These four types of risks prevent the hedger from forming a perfect hedge (which would have zero risk). Even though the hedger is reducing the amount of risk, it has not been reduced to zero. It is often said that hedging replaces price risk with basis risk.

The potential causes of basis risk are not necessarily limited to those identified in Table 12–2. Hence, basis risk is the prominent source of uncertainty in the hedging process. Among other probable causes are: (1) supply–demand conditions, and (2) cross-hedging consequences.

TABLE 12-2   The Components of Basis Risk

Type of Risk	Components
Expiration-date risk	Futures contracts are not usually available for every month. If a hedger needed a futures contract for July and the only contracts that were available were for March, June, September, and December, the hedger would have to select either the June or September contract. Either of these contracts would have a different price series than a July contract (if one existed). Hence, the hedger cannot form a perfect hedge and is faced with the chance that the basis may change.
Location risk	The hedger requires delivery of the futures contract in location Y, but the only futures contracts available are for delivery in location X. Hence, the hedger cannot form a perfect hedge because of the transportation costs from X to Y; this may cause the basis to change.
Quality risk	The exact standard or grade of the commodity required by the hedger is not covered by the futures contract. Therefore, the price movement of commodity grade A may be different from the price movement of commodity grade B, which will cause the basis to change and prevent the hedger from forming a perfect hedge.
Quantity risk	The exact amount of the commodity needed by the hedger is not available by a single futures contract or any integer multiple thereof. Hence, the amount of the commodity is not hedged exactly; this prevents the hedger from forming a perfect hedge, and the underhedged or overhedged amount is subject to risk.

Even if the futures contract is written on the exact commodity that the hedger holds, differing supply and demand conditions in the spot market and futures market could cause the basis to vary over time. Occasionally, speculators in the futures market will bid the futures price above or below its equilibrium position, due perhaps to the excitement induced by an unexpected news release. Of course, the market forces of arbitrage will eventually bring the spot and futures prices back in line. The limiting case is at the expiration of the futures contract, when its price must converge to the spot price.

Consequently, the disequilibrating influence on the basis stemming from supply–demand forces can be alleviated by entering a futures contract that matures on the exact day that the hedger intends to sell the spot commodity. But although most futures contracts are quite flexible, it is unlikely that any contract would correlate so precisely with the hedger's needs. In some cases (such as for agricultural commodities, where futures contracts are offered that mature each month) the basis risk due to nonsimultaneous maturities is

not so great. However, for other commodities, particularly financial instruments, futures contracts maturing three months apart are more typically offered. Thus, at the time the hedger needs to sell the spot commodity in the market, any protection in price risk over the hedging period could conceivably be wiped out by a temporary adverse change in the basis.

Cross-hedging refers to hedging with a futures contract written on a nonidentical commodity (relative to the spot commodity). While not often necessary with agricultural futures, cross-hedging is frequently the best that can be done with financial and index futures. Changes in the basis risk induced by the cross-hedge are caused by less than perfect correlation of price movements between the spot and futures prices—even at maturity. That is, because the spot commodity and futures contract commodity are different their respective prices will tend to be affected (even though minutely at times) by differing market forces. While the futures price must equal the price of its underlying spot commodity at the contract's maturity date, this condition does not necessarily hold when the hedger's commodity is not the "true" underlying asset. Therefore, even when the liquidation of the spot commodity coincides with the maturity of the futures contract, there is no guarantee of obtaining the original price for the commodity that held at the initiation of the hedge.

Sample Problem 12.6

Basis risk is illustrated in Table 12–3. The spot price is $100 and the futures price is $105 on day t. The top half of the exhibit shows what can happen if the spot price falls at day $t+1$, and the bottom half shows what happens if the spot price rises. It is assumed that the hedger is trying to create a fully hedged position in each of the cases presented.

If the basis is unchanged, the hedged position will neither gain nor lose. As can be seen in Table 12–3, the gain or loss on the hedged position is related to the change in the basis. Hence, the asset position's exposure to price risk is zero and the only risk the hedger faces is a change in the basis●

The Classic Hedge Strategy

The implicit assumption of the classic hedge ratio equal to one is that the prices of the spot commodity (in this case, the stock portfolio) and the futures contract will remain perfectly correlated over the entire hedge period. Then if the stock market does turn down as expected, any losses in the portfolio due to price declines in its composite stocks will be exactly offset by the gain on the futures position. Conversely, if stock prices rise, the portfolio's gains will be offset by equal losses on the futures position. Therefore, the portfolio manager attempts to lock in current profits by taking

TABLE 12-3 Examples of Basis Risk

		Spot Market	Futures Market		Basis (F − S)
Drop in Cash Price					
t	buy	100	sell	105	5
t + 1	sell	95	buy	100	5
		− 5		+ 5	change = 0
		Net hedge = 0		No change in basis	
t	buy	100	sell	105	5
t + 1	sell	95	buy	101	6
		− 5		+ 4	change = +1
		Net hedge = −1		Basis increases	
t	buy	100	sell	105	5
t + 1	sell	95	buy	99	4
		− 5		+ 6	change = −1
		Net hedge = +1		Basis decreases	
Increase in Cash Price					
t	buy	100	sell	105	5
t + 1	sell	105	buy	110	5
		− 5		− 5	change = 0
		Net hedge = 0		No change in basis	
t	buy	100	sell	105	5
t + 1	sell	105	buy	111	6
		+ 5		− 6	change = +1
		Net hedge = −1		Basis increases	
t	buy	100	sell	105	5
t + 1	sell	105	buy	109	4
		+ 5		− 4	change = −1
		Net hedge = +1		Basis decreases	

on a hedge position. Such a strategy implies that the objective of the classic hedge is risk minimization or elimination.

To apply the **classic hedge strategy** to the hedging problem, an opposite and equal position is taken in the futures market for the underlying commodity. More specifically, if a cautious portfolio manager believed that the stock market was going to turn downward for the next month and she wanted to lock in previously unrealized capital gains on her $7.5 million stock portfolio, she would sell $7.5 million worth of stock-index futures

contracts. Furthermore, that portfolio manager would keep her initial futures position constant over the entire hedge period.

Sample Problem 12.7

In the example of the implementation of the classic hedge strategy shown in Table 12–4 the current scenario is extended and it is assumed that (1) there are no associated costs for entering or liquidating a futures position (for example, commission costs or margin costs) and (2) a perfect correlation exists between the spot and futures price movements (for example, there is no basis risk). The S&P 500 Index futures contract is used as the hedging instrument●

It is not difficult to imagine the consequences of this strategy if the spot

TABLE 12–4   The Classic Hedge Strategy

	Cash-Market Position	Futures-Market Position (index = 150)
July 1, 1989	$7,500,000 in well-diversified stock portfolio	Short (sell) 100 contracts, equal to 100 × ($500 × 150) = $7,500,000.
August 1, 1989	Scenario I: Stock prices fall (index = 145).	
	$7,250,000 value of portfolio	Buy 100 contracts, equal to 100 × ($500 × 145) = $7,250,000.
	Net Results from Hedging	
	Gain or (loss) ($250,000)	Gain or (loss) $250,000
	Net Gain = $0	
	Scenario II: Stock prices rise (index = 155).	
	$7,750,000 value of portfolio	Buy 100 contracts, equal to 100 × ($500 × 55) = $7,750,000.
	Net Results from Hedging	
	Gain or (loss) $250,000	Gain or (loss) ($250,000)
	Net Gain = $0	

and futures prices are not perfectly correlated. In fact, if the spot- and futures-contract commodities are not identical, or if the hedging horizon does not coincide with the maturity of the futures contract, perfectly correlated spot and futures prices will always be the exception and not the rule.

Hence, there are identifiable risks associated with hedging. Two such types are (1) the risk of margin calls and (2) liquidity. Hedgers, like all participants in futures markets, must mark to market each day. In the simplified example, the decline (increase) in the value of the futures position is offset by gains (decreases) from the cash position. Nevertheless, gains from the cash position are typically not realized immediately, while futures contracts are marked to market at the end of each trading session. This practice of marking to market causes an imbalance in the cash flow of the hedger, who must balance paper gains in the cash market against realized (cash) outflows in the futures market. And although futures contracts are usually more liquid than the underlying cash instrument, liquidity may be a problem for some contracts. Hence hedgers who find it impossible to execute orders for the purchase or sale of a futures contract may need to be able to satisfy the delivery requirements of their hedge.

Liquidity is most likely a problem for futures contracts with delivery dates more than a year away. Trading activity in futures contracts is heaviest in contracts for the nearby delivery months. Trading in the most distant contract is typically very thin, hence less liquid.

Because of these problems with hedging, researchers have tried to incorporate the risk of hedging into the way the relative futures position is determined.

The Working Hedge Strategy

The **Working hedge strategy,** formulated by Holbrook Working (1953), makes explicit the speculative aspect of hedging. That is, in any hedged position the basis will not be constant over time. Therefore, the hedger in a certain sense is speculating on the future course of the basis. Yet it is expected that the changes in the basis will involve a smaller degree of risk than the corresponding price risk of the unhedged position.

This speculative aspect to hedging is exploited in Working's model by simultaneously determining positions in the spot and futures markets in order to capture increased return arising from relative movements in spot and futures prices. By studying the year-to-year constancy of the relation between spot and futures prices in various markets, Working discerned that a large *positive basis* (spot price less than futures price) was likely to be followed by a large negative change in the basis (basis narrows), and, conversely, a large negative basis by a large positive change in the basis. Figure 12–3 graphs a hypothetical basis relationship over time and designates the points considered indicative of large positive or negative basis.

FIGURE 12–3 A Hypothetical Basis Relationship Over Time

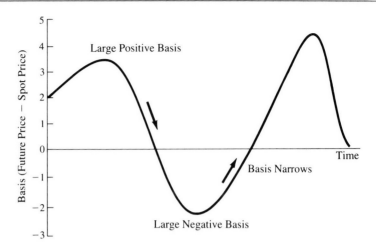

The implications of Working's 1953 model for the hedger are as follows. A short position in futures (of equal magnitude to the commodity held) is entered into only if the basis is sufficiently wide and positive. Thus, on the expectation that this large positive basis will narrow over time, the hedger will (it is hoped) profit from the combined spot and futures position.

Sample Problem 12.8

As an example of the implementation of this hedging rule, assume that the manager of the well-diversified portfolio of stocks worth $7.5 million sees a difference between the stock-index futures price for the S&P 500 near-term contract and the spot price of 2.85 (152.85 − 150.00) on July 1. Her portfolio is highly correlated with the S&P 500 index, and she sells ninety-eight contracts to achieve an approximately equally valued position in the futures. Table 12–5 summarizes the results of this hedge strategy one month later. As Table 12–5 shows for this simplified example, the hedger, by entering a short futures position when the basis was sufficiently positive, nearly triples the return on her portfolio. However, if the basis had widened over the hedging horizon, the net gain on the hedged position would have been reduced correspondingly●

For the most part, the Working strategy provides a relatively simple decision rule to facilitate speculation on the basis. Moreover, the hedger should create a hedged position with the futures only if the basis is sufficiently wide and positive at the beginning of the hedge period. Both the decision to hedge and the size of the hedging commitment are essentially predetermined and therefore relatively easy to implement. Finally, in order

TABLE 12-5   The Working Hedge Strategy

	Spot-Market Position *(spot price = $150)*	*Futures-Market Position* *(futures price = $152.88)*
July 1, 1989	$7,500,000 in well-diversified stock portfolio	Sell 98 contracts, equal to 98 × ($500 × 152.85) = $7,489,650. Basis = 2.85
August 1, 1989	$7,525,000 value of portfolio	Buy 98 contracts, equal to 98 × ($500 × 152.00) = $7,448,000. Basis = 1.50
Results from Hedging	Gain or (loss) $25,000	Gain or (loss) $41,650
	Gross Profit = $66,650	

to evaluate the Working strategy versus the classic one-to-one hedge, the following ex-post measure of hedging effectiveness has been suggested:

$$GP = (S_2 - S_1) - H(F_2 - F_1) \tag{12.10}$$

where:

GP = gross profit;
H = hedge ratio;
S_1, S_2 = beginning and end-of-period spot prices; and
F_1, F_2 = beginning and end-of-period futures prices.

In the example, gross profit is $66,650. This sum could then be compared to either the gross profit (or loss) from an unhedged position or to the gross profit generated from an alternative hedging strategy.

The Johnson Minimum-Variance Hedge Strategy

Developed within the framework of modern portfolio theory, the **Johnson hedge model** (1960) retains the traditional objective of risk minimization but defines risk as the variance of return on a two-asset hedge portfolio. As in the two-parameter world of Markowitz (1959), the hedger is assumed to be infinitely risk averse (that is, the investor desires zero variance). Moreover, with the risk-minimization objective defined as the variance of return on the combined spot and futures position, the Johnson hedge ratio is expressed in terms of expectations of variances and covariances for price changes in the spot and futures markets.

The Johnson hedge model can be expressed in regression form as:

$$\Delta S_t = a + H\Delta F_t + e_t \tag{12.11}$$

where:

ΔS_t = change in the spot price at time t;
ΔF_t = change in the futures price at time t;
a = constant;
H = hedge ratio; and
e_t = residual term at time t.

Furthermore, the hedge ratio measure can be better understood by defining it in terms of its components:

$$\frac{X_f^*}{X_s} = -\frac{\sigma_{\Delta S, \Delta F}}{\sigma_{\Delta F}^2} = H \qquad (12.12)$$

where:

X_f^* and X_s = the dollar amount invested in futures and spot;
$\sigma_{\Delta S, \Delta F}$ = the covariance of spot and futures price changes; and
$\sigma_{\Delta F}^2$ = the variance of futures price changes.

Thus H, the minimum-variance hedge ratio computed in variability, is also a measure of the relative dollar amount to be invested in futures per dollar of spot holdings. In a sense it is a localized beta coefficient similar in concept to the beta of a stock *a la* capital asset pricing theory.

As a measure of hedging effectiveness, Johnson utilizes the squared simple-correlation coefficient between spot and futures price changes, ρ^2. More formally, Johnson's hedging-effectiveness measure can be ascertained by first establishing the following expression:

$$HE = 1 - \frac{V_H}{V_u} \qquad (12.13)$$

where:

V_u = variance of the unhedged spot position = $X_s^2 \, \sigma_{\Delta S}^2$
$\sigma_{\Delta S}^2$ = *variance of spot price changes; and*
V_H = the variance of return for the hedged portfolio
   = $X_s^2 \, \sigma_{\Delta S}^2 \, (1 - \rho^2)$.

By substituting the minimum-variance hedge position in the futures, X_f^*:

$$HE = \left[1 - \frac{X_S^2 \, \sigma_{\Delta S}^2 (1 - \rho^2)}{X_S^2 \, \sigma_{\Delta S}^2} \right] = \rho^2 \qquad (12.14)$$

In simpler terms then, the Johnson measure of hedging effectiveness is the R^2 of a regression of spot-price changes on futures-price changes. To utilize this hedging method, it is necessary to regress historical data of spot-price changes on futures-price changes. The resulting beta coefficient from the regression would be the localized Johnson hedge ratio, and the regression R^2 would represent the expected degree of variance minimization using this hedge ratio over the hedging horizon. "Localized" and "expected" must be emphasized because, first of all, although the Johnson hedge ratio

can be re-estimated, it nonetheless is a static measure based on historical data. What held for the past may not hold precisely for the future. Moreover, large price moves may distort this hedge ratio considerably. Hence, R^2 is what can be expected based on the past in terms of variance reduction for the total hedge position. It should not be expected to hold exactly. (A sample computation of a hedge ratio using the Johnson model is presented in a later section.)

The Howard–D'Antonio Optimal Risk–Return Hedge Strategy

The classic one-to-one hedge is a naive strategy based upon a broadly defined objective of risk minimization. The strategy is naive in the sense that a hedging coefficient of one is used regardless of past or expected correlations of spot- and futures-price changes. Working's strategy brings out the speculative aspects of hedging by analyzing changes in the basis and, accordingly exercising discrete judgment about when to hedge and when not to hedge. The underlying objective of Working's decision rule for hedgers is one of profit maximization. Finally, Johnson (1960), in applying the mean-variance criteria of modern portfolio theory, emphasizes the risk-minimization objective but defines risk in terms of the variance of the hedged position. Although Johnson's method improves on the naive strategy of a one-to-one hedge, however, it essentially disregards the return component associated with a particular level of risk. Rutledge (1972) uses both mean and variance information to derive hedge ratio.

In a recent paper by Howard and D'Antonio (1984), a hedge ratio and measure of hedging effectiveness are derived in which the hedger's risk and return are both explicitly taken into account. Moreover, some of the variable relationships derived from their analysis help explain some of the idiosyncrasies of hedging that occur in practice.

Using a mean-variance framework, the **Howard–D'Antonio strategy** begins by assuming that the "agent" is out to maximize the expected return for a given level of portfolio risk. With a choice of putting money into three assets—a spot position, a futures contract, and a risk-free asset—the agent's optimal portfolio will depend on the relative risk–return characteristics of each asset. For a hedger, the optimal portfolio may contain a short futures position, a long futures position, or no futures position at all. In general, the precise futures position to be entered into will be determined by (1) the risk-free rate, (2) the expected returns and the standard deviations for the spot and futures positions, and (3) the correlation between the return on the spot position and the return on the futures.

Howard and D'Antonio arrive at the following expressions for the hedge ratio and the measure of hedging effectiveness:

$$\text{Hedge ratio } H = \frac{(\lambda - \rho)}{\gamma\pi(1 - \lambda\rho)} \tag{12.15}$$

and

$$\text{Hedging effectiveness } HE = \sqrt{\frac{1 - 2\lambda\rho + \lambda^2}{1 - \rho^2}} \qquad \textbf{(12.16)}$$

where:

$\pi = \sigma_f/\sigma_s$ = relative variability of futures and spot returns;

$\alpha = \bar{r}_f/(\bar{r}_s - i)$ = relative excess return on futures to that of spot;

$\gamma = P_f/P_s$ = current price ratio of futures to spot;

$\lambda = \alpha/\pi = (\bar{r}_f/\sigma_f)/[(\bar{r}_s - i)/\sigma_s]$ = risk-to-excess-return relative of futures versus the spot position;

P_s, P_f = the current price per unit for the spot and futures respectively;

ρ = simple correlation coefficient between the spot and futures returns;

σ_s = standard deviation of spot returns;

σ_f = standard deviation of futures returns;

$\bar{r}_s$ = mean return on the spot over some recent past interval;

$\bar{r}_f$ = mean return on the futures over some recent past interval; and

i = risk-free rate.

By analyzing the properties of λ these authors discern some important insights for the coordinated use of futures in a hedge portfolio. Numerically, λ expresses the relative attractiveness of investing in futures versus the spot position. When $\lambda < 1$, $\lambda = 1$, and $\lambda > 1$, the futures contract offers less, the same, and more excess return per unit of risk than the spot position, respectively. Since this analysis is being undertaken from a hedger's point of view, it is assumed $\lambda < 1$. An assumption that $\lambda > 1$ would inappropriately imply that theoretically it is possible to hedge the futures position with the spot asset.

First, consider the effect of the relationship of λ to ρ on the optional hedge ratio, H. Table 12–6 summarizes the hedging implications for different magnitudes of the ratio of the risk–return relative λ to the simple correlation coefficient of spot and futures returns ρ. Of particular note is the case when $\lambda = \rho$. Such a condition implies that no benefit exists for going short or long in futures. Furthermore, this result rather clearly demonstrates that the holding of futures as a hedge against price risk is not simply related to ρ but

TABLE 12–6   The Hedging Implications of Different Relative Magnitudes of λ and ρ

Relative Magnitude	Hedge Ratio	Implied Futures Position
$\lambda < \rho$	$H < 0$	short
$\lambda = \rho$	$H = 0$	none
$\lambda > \rho$	$H > 0$	long

is also dependent on the relative return–risk relationship between the futures and the spot asset.

Next, a careful examination of Howard and D'Antonio's hedging effectiveness measure in Equation (12.16) is warranted. It is important to note that this hedging effectiveness measure *HE* is different from the measures studied so far because it takes into account the risk–return relationship between futures and spot as well as the correlation of returns. The Howard–D'Antonio *HE* measure indicates the degree (in terms of return) to which the hedger (investor) could enhance the portfolio by entering into the appropriate futures position, as indicated by Equation (12.14). For instance, if $\lambda = 0.60$ and $\rho = 0.80$, then $HE = 1.054$, meaning that a hedger could expect to enhance the excess return of the portfolio of the risk-free and spot assets by 5.4 percent by going short ($\lambda < \rho$) the number of futures contracts indicated by Equation (12.15).

The relationship among ρ, λ, and *HE* is seen more clearly in Figure 12–4 and is summarized in Table 12–7; see page 384. As can be seen from Figure 12–4, *HE* is symmetrical about $\lambda = \rho$. Moreover, it is shown that as ρ approaches 1, *HE* increases. That is, the hedging properties of futures improve as ρ approaches 1. However, this effect is entirely contingent on $\lambda \neq \rho$. Even if $\rho \neq 1$ there will be no benefit to holding a futures contract if $\lambda = \rho$.

The last result is at odds with past studies on hedging, especially Johnson's (1960) work. Yet the implications from this result can help provide insight into the cross-hedging process. While past studies have indicated that the correlation of futures- and spot-price movements is the determinant of a hedge's effectiveness and would almost necessarily attribute superior hedging qualities to a futures contract on the true underlying asset (a straight hedge), these results indicate that the effectiveness of one's hedge—be it a cross-hedge or a straight hedge—depends on the relationship between λ and ρ.

From a practitioner's perspective it is also important to note that even when $\lambda \neq \rho$, a hedged position using the futures may not provide a real net improvement in the risk–return performance of a portfolio. Unless *HE* is significantly greater than 1, other factors such as transaction costs, taxes, the potential for margin calls, and liquidity may negate the overall benefit of hedging with futures. This point, along with the previous results about hedging, helps explain why certain futures contracts highly correlated with their underlying assets are not used extensively as hedging vehicles as might be expected.

SUMMARY

This chapter has focused on the basic concepts of futures markets. Important terms were defined and basic models to evaluate futures contracts were discussed. The differences between futures and forward markets also received treatment. Finally hedging concepts and strategies were analyzed and

FIGURE 12-4 Hedging Effectiveness *(HE)* versus the Risk–Return Relative for Various Correlations (ρ).

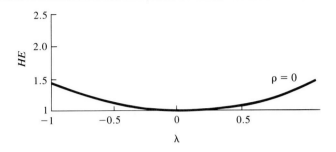

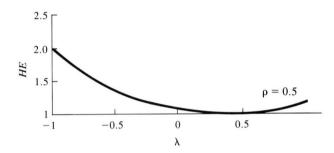

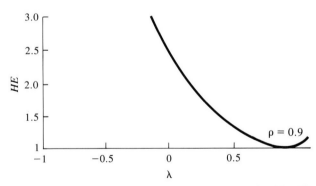

Source: C. T. Howard and L. J. D'Antonio, ''A Risk-Return Measure of Hedging Effectiveness.'' *Journal of Financial and Quantitative Analysis,* v. 19 (March 1984), p. 109. Reprinted with permission.

TABLE 12-7 The Relationship of λ, ρ, and *HE*

	Effect on the HE Measure	*Benefit of Hedging with Futures*
λ < ρ	*HE* > 1.0	positive
λ = ρ	*HE* = 1.0	none
λ > ρ	*HE* > 1.0	positive

alternative hedging ratios were investigated in detail. These concepts and valuation models can be used in security analysis and portfolio management related to futures and forward contracts. The next chapter investigates in depth commodity futures, financial futures, and index futures.

QUESTIONS AND PROBLEMS

1. Define the following terms:
   (a) basis   (b) backwardation
   (c) contango   (d) hedger
   (e) speculator   (f) arbitrager

2. Carefully explain the difference between a futures contract and a forward contract.

3. Explain the importance of futures markets.

4. Carefully discuss the importance of the clearinghouse in futures markets.

5. What is marking to market? How does marking to market affect the cash flows of a futures contract?

6. What is the relationship between the price of the futures contract and the spot price of the underlying commodity as the expiration of the futures contract is approached?

7. Carefully explain how the interest rate determines the relationship between future and spot prices.

8. Carefully explain how carrying costs determine the relationship between future and spot prices.

9. On February 1 the spot price of a commodity is $250 and the current risk-free rate is 9 percent. What is the value on February 1 of a futures contract that matures on March 1? on April 1?

10. Carefully explain the difference between hedging and speculation.

11. Suppose an investor has a portfolio of T-bills with a face value of $1 million, currently worth $960,000. Assume the T-bills in this portfolio mature in three months. A three-month T-bill futures contract is currently selling for $96\frac{24}{32}$. Assume that interest rates rise and the value of the T-bills falls to $950,125, while the value of the T-bills futures contract falls to $96\frac{8}{32}$.
    (a) Use the T-bill futures to hedge your T-bill position.
    (b) Is it possible to create a riskless hedge for this example?
    (c) If it is not possible to create a riskless hedge, what does this say about the market for T-bills and T-bill futures?
    (d) Calculate the net change in the value of the hedged portfolio.

12. Calculate the change in settlement for a T-bill contract for a 6-basis-point change in the yield. Assume the contract matures in 180 days.

13. What is the settlement value for an IMM T-bill contract when the final index is 94?

14. Suppose the spot price for hog bellies is 44 cents per pound on July 1. What is the value on July 1 of a futures contract that matures on September 1 with a price of 44 cents per pound? Assume that the risk-free rate is 8 percent.

15. Recalculate the value of the futures contract presented in Sample Problem 12.4 if the carrying cost changes to $0.02 per pound per month.

16. Explain the logic behind the following formula.

$$F_{t,T} = \text{Min } [E_t(\tilde{S}_T), S_t(1 + R_{f,T-t}) + C_{T-t}]$$

17. Explain the role of each of the following in the futures market.
    (a) hedger
    (b) speculator
    (c) arbitrager
    If any one of these groups is not participating in the futures market, what happens to the market? Answer this question for each group.

18. What are the various risk components of basis risk? What can be done about reducing or eliminating them?

19. What is the economic rationale for the existence of futures markets?

20. What is the difference between a forward market and a futures market?

21. An investor with $10 million in T-bills wishes to hedge his position. Given the following information, what is the gain or loss on the cash and futures positions?

at $t = 0$	T-bills sell at 98 percent of par.
	Futures contract ($1 million face) is $98\frac{1}{4}$.
at $t \leq t + 1$	Interest rates have fallen.
	T-bills sell at $98\frac{1}{2}$ percent of par.
	Futures contract ($1 million face) is $98\frac{3}{4}$.

22. Compare and contrast the uses of the word *margin* in the stock market and in the futures market.

23. What is the current futures price of commodity X if the spot price of X is $10 and the futures contract has two months to delivery? The current interest rate is 12 percent.

24. Given the information in question 23 and a carrying cost of $0.10 per dollar value per month, what is the current futures price?

25. Given the information in questions 23 and 24, if the spot price for X is expected to be $10, what is the futures price at $t = 0$? If the spot price of X is expected never to change, perhaps it is guaranteed by some sort of government program. Would you trade in futures contracts for X?

26. Given the following information, what is the basis at $t = 0$? What is the basis at $t \leq 1$? Why has the basis changed?

$$t = 0 \quad \text{Spot price} = \$10 \qquad t \le 1 \quad \text{Spot price} = \$9.75$$
$$\text{Futures price} = \$11.50 \qquad \text{Futures price} = \$10.75$$
$$\text{Basis} = \text{Future} - \text{Spot}$$
$$f = S(1 + r) + \text{Carrying costs}$$

27. Using the Howard–D'Antonio model, what is the hedge ratio if

$$\lambda = 0.5$$
$$\rho = 0.9$$
$$\gamma = 1.01$$
$$\pi = 1.2$$

What is the hedging effectiveness?

APPENDIX 12A: BASIC FUTURES TERMINOLOGY

Although related to other securities markets, such as those for stocks or bonds, the futures market is unique not only in nature but also with regard to some of its terminology. Table 12A–1 lists some commonly used terms for these markets.

TABLE 12A–1   Basic Futures Terminology

Term	Definition
Arbitrage	The simultaneous purchase and sale of similar financial instruments or commodity futures in order to benefit from an anticipated change (correction) in their price relationship.
Basis	The difference between futures price and the spot price. Basis is one kind of risk in investment; it is explored later in this chapter.
Bid	An offer to purchase at a specified price.
Car	A loose term sometimes used to describe the quantity of a contract—for example, "I am long *a car of bellies*." (Derived from the fact that quantities of the product specified in a contract used to correspond closely to the capacity of a railroad car.)
Cash commodity	The actual physical commodity, as distinguished from a futures commodity. A commodity delivered at the time of sale is a cash commodity while a commodity to be delivered at a specific future date is a future commodity.

TABLE 12A–1   (*continued*)

Term	Definition
Clearinghouse	The third party of every futures contract, which guarantees that every futures contract will be carried out even if one of the parties defaults. The clearinghouse also facilitates trading of futures contracts before they are due for delivery.
Contract amount	The number of units of the good or service to be delivered.
Contract month	The month in which a futures contract is scheduled to mature by making or accepting a delivery.
Contract specification	The precise definition of the good or service to be delivered in the futures contract.
Delivery	The tender and receipt of an actual commodity or financial instrument, or cash in settlement of a futures contract.
Delivery point	A point designated by a futures exchange at which the financial instrument or commodity covered by futures contract may be delivered in fulfillment of such contract.
Equity	The residual dollar value of a futures trading account (over and above margin requirements), assuming its liquidation at the going market price.
Floor broker	A licensed member of the exchange who is paid a fee for executing orders for clearing members or their customers.
Floor trader	An exchange member who generally trades only for his or her own account, or for an account controlled by him or her. (Also called "local.")
Forward contract	A prespecified contract similar to a futures contract except that it is tailored to suit the particular needs of the individual parties. Forward contracts are not generally traded on exchanges because they lack standardization, they do not have the daily mark-to-market requirement, and they typically require no transfers of money until delivery.
Futures contract	A legally binding, standardized agreement made within the confines of an exchange trading area, specifying the good or service involved, the quantity, and the future date and price at which the contract is to be fulfilled.
Hedger	A market participant who has or will have a position in the cash commodity and who attempts to eliminate or reduce risk exposure by taking an offsetting position in the futures or forward market.
Liquidation	Any transaction that offsets or closes out a long or short position. (Also called "evening up" or "offset.")

TABLE 12A-1   (*continued*)

Term	Definition
Long position	The purchase of a futures contract in anticipation of taking eventual delivery of the commodity (or financial instrument) or an expected increase in the underlying asset's price.
Margin	A cash amount of funds that must be deposited with the broker for each futures contract as a guarantee of its fulfillment.
Margin call	A demand for additional cash funds for each futures position held because of an adverse price movement.
Mark to market	The daily adjustment of a futures trading account to reflect profits or losses due to daily changes in the value of the futures contract.
Open contracts	Contracts that have been bought or sold without the transactions having been completed by subsequent sale or purchase, or by making or taking actual delivery of the financial instrument or physical commodity. Measured by "open interest," as reported in the press.
Settlement price	A figure determined by the closing-price range that is used to calculate daily gains and losses in futures-market accounts (and thus margin calls) and invoice prices for deliveries.
Short position	The sale of a futures contract in anticipation of a fall in the price of the underlying asset. Also obligates delivery of the commodity or financial instrument (and payment) if the position is left open to maturity.
Speculator	A market participant who is willing (for a price) to take on the risk the hedger wishes to eliminate. This trader goes long or short on a contract without having, or intending to take, an opposite position in the cash market.
Spot price	The current price of the commodity if purchased in the cash or "spot" market.
Spread	Refers to the simultaneous purchase and sale of futures contracts for (1) the same commodity or instrument with different maturity months or (2) commodities in different but related markets.
Tick	Refers to a change in price, either up or down. The amount varies with each contract.
Volume	The number of transactions in a futures contract made during a specified period of time.

REFERENCES

Black, F. "The Pricing of Commodity Contracts." *Journal of Financial Economics,* v. 3 (September 1976), pp. 167–79.

Castelino, Mark. "Basis Volatility: Implications for Hedging." *Journal of Financial Research,* Summer 1989.

———, and Jack Francis. "Basis Speculation in Commodity Futures: The Maturity Effect." *Journal of Futures Markets,* v. 2, no. 2 (1982), 195–207.

Cheng, E. "Returns of Speculators and the Theory of Normal Backwardation." *Journal of Finance,* v. 40 (March 1985), pp. 193–208.

Chicago Board of Trade. *GNMA Futures.* Chicago Board of Trade, 1987.

———. *Ten-Year Treasury Futures.* Chicago Board of Trade, 1987.

———. *U.S. Treasury Bond Futures.* Chicago Board of Trade, 1987.

Cornell, B., and K. French. "Taxes and the Pricing of Stock Index Futures." *Journal of Finance,* v. 38 (June 1983), pp. 675–94.

Cox, J., J. Ingersoll, and S. Ross. "The Relation Between Forward and Futures Prices." *Journal of Financial Economics,* v. 9 (December 1981), pp. 321–46.

Daigler, R. "Futures Bibliography." *Journal of Futures Markets,* v. 8 (Spring 1988), pp. 131–43.

Dusak, K. "Futures Trading and Investor Returns: An Investigation of Commodity Market Risk Premiums." *Journal of Political Economy,* v. 81 (November/December 1973), pp. 1306–13.

Ederington, L. H. "The Hedging Performance of the New Futures Markets." *Journal of Finance,* v. 34 (March 1979), pp. 157–70.

Elton, E., M. Gruber, and J. Rentzler. "Intraday Tests of the Efficiency of the T-Bill Futures Market." *Review of Economics and Statistics,* v. 66 (February 1984), pp. 129–37.

Fama, E. "Forward Rates as Predictors of Future Spot Rates." *Journal of Financial Economics,* v. 3 (October 1976), pp. 361–77.

Figlewski, S. *Hedging with Financial Futures for Institutional Investors.* Ballinger Publishing Co., 1986.

Howard, C. T., and L. J. D'Antonio. "A Risk-Return Measure of Hedging Effectiveness." *Journal of Financial and Quantitative Analysis,* v. 19 (March 1984), pp. 101–12.

International Monetary Market. *Opportunities in Interest Rates: T-Bill Futures.* IMM, 1988.

———. *Inside CD Futures.* IMM, 1988.

———. *Inside Eurodollar Futures.* IMM, 1988.

———. *Inside SP500 Stock Index Futures.* IMM, 1988.

———. "International Monetary Market. IMM, 1988.

———. "Understanding Futures in Foreign Exchange. IMM, 1988.

_____. *The S & P 100 Stock Index Futures Contract: Flexibility for Today's Investor*. IMM, 1988.

Jacob, N. L., and R. R. Petit. *Investments*. Richard D. Irwin, Inc., 1984.

Jarrow, R., and G. Oldfield. "Forward Contracts and Futures Contracts." *Journal of Financial Economics*, v. 8 (December 1981), pp. 373–82.

Johnson, L. L. "The Theory of Hedging and Speculation in Commodity Futures." *Review of Economic Studies*, v. 27 (March 1960), pp. 139–51.

Junkus, J. C., and C. F. Lee. "Use of Three Stock Index Futures in Hedging Decisions." *Journal of Futures Markets*, v. 5 (Summer 1985), pp. 201–22.

Kamara, A. "Issues in Futures Markets: A Survey." *Journal of Futures Markets*, v. 2 (Fall 1982), pp. 261–94.

Keynes, J. M. *A Treatise on Money*, v. 2. Macmillan & Co., 1930.

Khoury, S. J. *Investment Management: Theory and Application*. Macmillan Publishing Co., Inc., 1983.

Kolb, R. *Understanding Futures Markets*. Scott, Foresman and Co., 1984.

Loosigian, A. M. *Interest Rate Futures*. Dow Jones-Irwin Inc., 1980.

Markowitz, H. *Portfolio Selection*. John Wiley and Sons, Inc., 1959.

Modest, D. M., and M. Sundaresan. "The Relationship between Spot and Futures Prices in Stock Index Futures Markets: Some Preliminary Evidence." *The Journal of Futures Markets*, v. 3 (Spring 1983), pp. 15–42.

Poole, W. "Using T-Bill Futures to Gauge Interest Rate Expectations." *Federal Reserve Bank of San Francisco Economic Review* (Spring 1978), pp. 7–19.

Powers, M., and D. Vogel. *Inside the Financial Futures Markets*. John Wiley and Sons, Inc., 1981.

Rutledge, D. J. S. "Hedgers' Demand for Futures Contracts: A Theoretical Framework with Applications to the United States Soybean Complex." *Food Research Institute Studies*, v. 11 (March 1972), pp. 237–56.

Schwarz, E., J. Hill, and T. Schneeweis. *Financial Futures: Fundamentals Strategies, and Applications*. Richard D. Irwin, 1986.

Sharpe, W. F. *Investments*, 3rd ed. Prentice-Hall, Inc., 1987.

Telser, L. "Why There Are Organized Futures Markets." *Journal of Law and Economics*, v. 24 (April 1981), pp. 1–22.

_____. "Futures and Actual Markets: How They Are Related." *Journal of Business*, v. 59 (April 1986), pp. 5–20.

Toevs, A., and D. Jacob. "Futures and Alternative Hedge Ratio Methodologies." *Journal of Portfolio Management*, v. 12 (Spring 1986), pp. 60–70.

Weiner, N. S. "The Hedging Rationale for a Stock Index Futures Contract." *Journal of Futures Market*, v. 1 (Spring 1981), pp. 59–76.

_____. *Stock Index Futures*. John Wiley and Sons, Inc., 1984.

Working, H. "Hedging Reconsidered." *Journal of Farm Economics*, v. 35 (June 1953), pp. 544–61.

13 Commodity Futures, Financial Futures, and Stock-Index Futures

From the viewpoint of a security analyst and portfolio manager, knowledge of alternative futures instruments is important because these instruments allow the analyst and manager to invest for profit and/or to hedge for risk. (How to use futures as portfolio insurance is discussed in Chapter 21.)

Following the basic concepts, valuation, and hedging strategies of futures instruments and markets discussed in Chapter 12, Chapter 13 investigates commodity futures, financial futures, and index futures. The first topic for discussion is commodity futures, which is followed by a discussion of financial futures and a study of stock-index futures.

COMMODITY FUTURES

Futures trading in the United States originated in the early 1800s for agricultural commodities. With no organized trading exchanges at that time, these original **commodity futures** contracts were actually forward agreements. The use of forward contracts evolved from necessity as spot markets increasingly proved their inability to handle excess supply or demand for commodities. However, these forward contracts also proved to have their limitations in that they were not sufficiently liquid for hedgers.

Today, there are eleven commodity exchanges offering futures contracts on more than thirty different commodities. Why are futures contracts traded on some commodities and not others? Remember that price risk is the underlying reason for the existence of futures markets. Any good (or service) that has a volatile price, either due to macroeconomic or environmental factors that can affect future supply and demand conditions, is a prime candidate to be traded in a futures market. Think of agricultural crops for a moment. The annual supply of a particular crop can be devastatingly affected by adverse weather conditions. So, if heavy rains and unexpectedly cold weather damaged a large portion of the wheat crop, supply would be

reduced and prices that processors have to pay would rise. Conversely, if weather conditions turned out better than expected and the wheat harvest was very large, an overabundant supply of the crop would push prices down, hurting the farmer. Thus for good reason the agricultural industry was the first to utilize forward-pricing arrangements to aid in transferring the inherent price risks to those more willing to bear it.

Consider the alternatives open to the farmer for dealing with price uncertainty. Assume it is spring and crop planting is taking place. The farmer observes that although market prices are comfortably high, the wheat harvest may be large enough to force prices to become significantly lower. If prices drop, the farmer will lose money on the invested efforts and expenses. If the farmer does nothing and waits to see what happens to prices, the risk is substantial, especially if the odds increase that weather conditions will be better than expected. The farmer's other alternative would be to hedge the price risk in the futures market. To do this, the farmer would go into the futures market (through a commodities broker) and sell (go short) wheat futures contracts that expire at the same time that the crop would be brought to market. By taking such an action the farmer is indicating satisfaction with the current contracted price, as taking a position in the futures market essentially "locks in" the contracted futures price. Sample Problem 13.1 provides further illustration.

Sample Problem 13.1

Suppose that Farmer Smith is planting enough wheat to yield 50,000 bushels to bring to market in July. Furthermore, Farmer Smith observes that while

	Cash Market	*Futures Market*
Prices fall	March 1: Plants 50,000 bu (spot price = $5.00/bu).	Sells ten contracts at $5.00.
	July 15: Sells 50,000 bu at $4.50/bu.	Buys ten contracts at $4.50.
	Profit (loss) = ($0.50/bu) × 50,000 bu = ($25,000)	Profit (loss) = $0.50/bu × 10 × 5,000 bu = $25,000
	Net gain = 0	
Prices rise	March 1: Plants 50,000 bu (spot price = $5.00/bu).	Sells ten contracts at $5.00.
	July 15: Sells 50,000 bu at $5.50/bu.	Buys ten contracts at $5.50.
	Profit (loss) = $0.50/bu × 50,000 bu = $25,000	Profit (loss) = ($0.50/bu) × 10 × 5,000 bu = ($25,000)
	Net gain = 0	

current market prices are quite attractive at $5.00 per bushel, a record wheat crop is expected. So, Farmer Smith decides to hedge his price risk by going into the futures market and effectively selling his crop ahead of time through the sale of ten wheat futures contracts (a contract represents 5,000 bushels) at $5.00 per bushel, expiring in July. Assuming there is no basis risk, the outcomes of this transaction for falling and rising prices over the interim period are shown in the table on page 393●

While Sample Problem 13.1 is simplified, its purpose is to demonstrate how the futures market is used and how the locking in of a price is achieved through hedging. That is, the farmer received $5.00 per bushel at market time whether prices went lower or higher over the interim. Of course, it would be logical to wonder who would buy the futures contracts from the farmer if prices were expected to fall. As a matter of fact, it is the market participants known as the **speculators** who would do so. Contrary to the farmer, who as a hedger took a position in the futures market opposite to the actual commodity that he owned, the speculator has no offsetting position in the actual commodity. Instead, the speculator would buy the futures contracts from the farmer on the chance that prices would actually rise and not fall as expected. If prices rose, the speculator, who is long the contract, would profit handsomely because of the leverage involved. However, the large potential return is balanced by a large potential loss should prices fall.

The speculator's role in the futures market has been questioned throughout the history of futures markets. Essentially, what the speculator appears to be doing is gambling. Yet without the speculator the futures markets would cease to function efficiently, if at all. That is, the farmer (hedger) who goes into the market to hedge the price risk is actually transferring it to someone else, the speculator. When the hedger needs to liquidate a futures position by buying ten contracts (as in the example), the speculator is there to sell them. So the speculator contributes to the functioning of futures markets in two invaluable ways: (1) risk transference and (2) liquidity. Finally, remember that the speculator does not intend to provide such invaluable economic services for no return; the speculator takes on price risk and provides liquidity in return for potential profits.

For any futures contract there are a number of specifications and trading characteristics concerning the good to be delivered. Table 13A-1 at the end of this chapter lists these specifications and characteristics by contract and exchange. Figure 13-1 displays commodity-futures prices as they are printed daily in the press.

FUTURES QUOTATIONS

As indicated in Figure 13-1, *The Wall Street Journal* reports daily information on various types of futures contracts. There are a number of important terms and quotations related to futures contracts (and used in *The Wall Street Journal*) that are useful to know; these are shown in Table 13-1.

FIGURE 13-1 Commodity Futures Prices

COMMODITY FUTURES PRICES

Monday, April 10, 1989.
Open Interest Reflects Previous Trading Day.

(The figure reproduces a full page of commodity futures price quotations from The Wall Street Journal, organized into columns of markets — Grains and Oilseeds, Livestock & Meat, Food & Fiber, Metals & Petroleum, Wood, and Other Commodity Futures — each listing Open, High, Low, Settle, Change, Lifetime High, Lifetime Low, and Open Interest.)

EXCHANGE ABBREVIATIONS
(for commodity futures and futures options)

CBT-Chicago Board of Trade; CME-Chicago Mercantile Exchange; CMX-Commodity Exchange, New York; CRCE-Chicago Rice & Cotton Exchange; CTN-New York Cotton Exchange; CSCE-Coffee, Sugar & Cocoa Exchange, New York; IPE-International Petroleum Exchange; KC-Kansas City Board of Trade; MCE-MidAmerica Commodity Exchange; MPLS-Minneapolis Grain Exchange; NYM-New York Mercantile Exchange; PBOT-Philadelphia Board of Trade; WPG-Winnipeg Commodity Exchange.

Source: The Wall Street Journal, April 10, 1989, p. C-18.

TABLE 13–1   Futures Terms

Term	Definition
Open	The price for the day's first trade, registered during the period designated as the opening of the market.
High	Highest price at which the commodity sold during the day.
Low	Lowest price at which the commodity sold during the day.
Settle	Since each contract is marked to market each day, the settlement price or the marking-to-market price is very important to investors. The settlement price is a figure determined by formula from within the closing range or it may be the closing price.
Change	The amount the settlement price changed from the previous day.
Lifetime high or low	The highest and lowest prices recorded for each contract maturity from the first day it was traded to the present.
Open interest	The number represents the quantity of open long positions at the exchange's clearinghouse for each contract.
Volume	The number of contracts actually traded on the exchange for a given trading session.

Also of concern are *commodity, exchanges, contract size,* and *prices.* For example, the commodity traded is corn. The exchange refers to the place where the futures contracts are traded: CBT signifies the Chicago Board of Trade. The contract size refers to the amount of spot commodity that the contract represents—for example, 5,000 bushels of corn. The price is the manner in which the prices are quoted; for instance, corn at 162 means corn sells for $1.62 per bushel. Specifications for commodity futures are listed in Table 13A–1 at the end of this chapter.

FINANCIAL FUTURES

Financial futures take many forms. The following discussion focuses on foreign-currency futures, T-bill futures, and T-bond futures.

Financial futures are standardized futures contracts whose market prices are established through open outcry and hand signals in regulated commodity exchange. They represent a legally enforceable commitment to buy and sell a prespecified quantity and quality of a specific financial instrument during a predetermined future delivery month.

Foreign-Currency Futures

Foreign-currency futures and their valuation theory are discussed in this section. A foreign-currency futures contract is similar to other commodity-futures contracts. It promises future delivery of a standard amount of a foreign currency at a specified time, place, and price. This instrument can be used to hedge foreign-exchange risk for investors and firms involved in the import and export business.

Evolution.   The concept of financial futures on currencies emerged as an anticipatory reaction to the end of the Bretton Woods Agreement, which called for the elimination of fixed parities between major currencies. So on May 16, 1972, the International Monetary Market (IMM) division of the Chicago Mercantile Exchange (CME) opened and offered the first organized trading of standardized futures contracts on foreign currencies. The application of the futures market and its trading mechanics to financial products was supported by a number of economists at the time, including Milton Friedman.

The need for these exchange-rate hedging tools has intensified in the last decade. The change in U.S. monetary policy in October 1979, which went from essentially "pegging" interest rates to letting them float in accordance with market forces, resulted in a significant increase in the volatility of market interest rates. The effects of highly volatile U.S. interest rates were felt heavily in other countries as well. Consequently, the already volatile foreign-exchange-rate market became even more turbulent, as investors and governments moved their funds from one currency to another in search of higher returns.

As interest rates change in one country, so does the value of its currency relative to those of other countries. So a U.S. corporation that contracts to purchase materials from some foreign firm with payment to be made three months from now is exposing itself to foreign-exchange risk. If at the end of the three-month period the U.S. dollar's value falls against the home currency of the foreign firm, the U.S. company will actually end up paying more for the materials than originally intended.

Advantages.   Although forward markets have existed for some time to help alleviate exchange-rate or currency risk, they generally do not offer the liquidity or flexibility of the futures market. The establishment of foreign-currency futures has provided a means by which Interbank dealers can hedge their positions in spot or forward markets. Moreover, because each trade is guaranteed by the exchange's clearinghouse, participants need not analyze the credit risk of a large number of market counterparts, as might be necessary in establishing a forward contract. The funds of participants are protected by daily settlement of the change in position values; they are also safeguarded by the exchange's clearinghouse, whose members together guarantee all trades. Finally, futures markets allow dealers to trade anony-

mously and provide price insurance and arbitrage opportunities in the spot and forward markets.

The **International Monetary Market (IMM)** is one of the exchanges that offer futures contracts on foreign currencies. Presently, the foreign currencies for which futures contracts are traded include British pounds (ticker code BP); Canadian dollars (CD); West German Deutschmarks (DM); French francs (FF); Japanese yen (JY); and Swiss francs (SF). Trading volume is concentrated in the futures on pounds, marks, Swiss francs, yen, and the Canadian dollar. Contract specifications appear in Table 13A–1 (pages 433–440), and cash and futures prices are shown in Figure 13–2.

When dealing with foreign exchange, it is important to realize that the price of a currency is in terms of a second currency. Both the numerator and denominator of the price ratio are in terms of money. For example, in Figure 13–2 the French franc is worth $0.1574 (6.3520 French francs per dollar). All foreign-exchange rates are related as reciprocals. Looking again at Figure 13–2, some currencies have only one price quoted. For example, the Brazilian cruzado is worth $1.0101 in the spot market. For other currencies (usually the currencies of the major trading nations), not only are the spot rates quoted but also the forward rates. For example, the franc, in addition to the spot rate, has quotes for the forward rates of 30, 60, and 90 days. The 30-day forward rate of 0.1576 means that a trader could buy French francs for delivery in thirty days at this price. The actual forward transaction takes place in thirty days. As is typical of forward markets, there is no specific location where trading takes place. Instead bankers around the world are linked together electronically. It is over this communication linkage that currencies are bought and sold in the spot and forward markets.

Futures-market quotes for foreign exchange are also shown in Figure 13–2. The futures market is different from the forward market. In the futures market the maturity date of a given contract is fixed by the rules of the exchange. As each day passes, the futures contract gets closer to maturity. In the forward market, thirty-, sixty-, and ninety-day contracts (or any other number of days) are available. However, contracts in the futures market mature four times a year (June, September, December, and March). In the forward market they mature every day.

In the forward market the contract size is determined between the buyer and seller. In the futures market only contracts of standardized amounts are traded—for example, 12.5 million yen for the Japanese-yen futures contract traded on the International Money Market.

Pricing Foreign-Currency Futures.   The arbitrage argument used to establish the price of a currency futures contract relative to the spot price is called **interest-rate parity** (which will be addressed again shortly). In the case of the U.S. dollar/British pound:

$$F_{t,T} = S_t \frac{(1 + R_{t,T}^\$)}{(1 + R_{t,T}^\pounds)} \tag{13.1}$$

FIGURE 13-2   Foreign-Currency Futures, Spot and Forward Prices

EXCHANGE RATES

Monday, April 10, 1989

The New York foreign exchange selling rates below apply to trading among banks in amounts of $1 million and more, as quoted at 3 p.m. Eastern time by Bankers Trust Co. Retail transactions provide fewer units of foreign currency per dollar.

Country	U.S. $ equiv.		Currency per U.S. $	
	Mon	Fri	Mon	Fri
Argentina (Austral) ...	.020946	020395	47.74	49.03
Australia (Dollar)	8075	.8074	1.2383	1.2385
Austria (Schilling)	.07551	.07582	13.24	13.188
Bahrain (Dinar)	2.6525	2.6525	.37700	.37700
Belgium (Franc)				
Commercial rate	.02538	.02547	39.40	39.25
Financial rate	.02529	.02538	39.54	39.39
Brazil (Cruzado)	1.0101	1.0101	.99000	.99000
Britain (Pound)	1.6980	1.6960	.5889	.5896
30-Day Forward ...	1.6943	1.6922	.5902	.5909
90-Day Forward ...	1.6859	1.6840	.5931	.5938
180-Day Forward ...	1.6762	1.6737	.5965	.5974
Canada (Dollar)	.8406	.8385	1.1895	1.1925
30-Day Forward ...	.8392	.8371	1.1916	1.1946
90-Day Forward ...	.8364	.8341	1.1956	1.1988
180-Day Forward ...	.8329	.8304	1.2006	1.2041
Chile (Official rate) ...	.0040014	.0039706	249.91	251.85
China (Yuan)	268817	.268817	3.7200	3.7200
Colombia (Peso)	.002777	.002773	360.00	360.50
Denmark (Krone)	.1365	.1373	7.3225	7.2825
Ecuador (Sucre)				
Floating rate	.001960	.001953	510.00	512.00
Finland (Markka)	.2366	.2369	4.2250	4.2200
France (Franc)	.1574	.1578	6.3520	6.3360
30-Day Forward ...	.1576	.1580	6.3435	6.3275
90-Day Forward ...	.1586	.1584	6.3255	6.3095
180-Day Forward ...	.1587	.1591	6.2985	6.2835
Greece (Drachma) ...	.006250	.006281	160.00	159.20
Hong Kong (Dollar) ...	.128435	.128534	7.7860	7.7800
India (Rupee)	.0638977	.0640204	15.65	15.62
Indonesia (Rupiah)	.0005737	.0005737	1743.00	1743.00
Ireland (Punt)	1.4215	1.4110	.7034	.7087
Israel (Shekel)	.5662	.5526	1.7660	1.8095
Italy (Lira)	.0007243	.0007275	1380.50	1374.50
Japan (Yen)	.007532	.007541	132.75	132.60
30-Day Forward ...	.007568	.007576	132.13	131.98
90-Day Forward ...	.007640	.007648	130.89	130.70
180-Day Forward ...	.007747	.007756	129.08	128.93
Jordan (Dinar)	1.8968	1.8968	.5272	.5272
Kuwait (Dinar)	3.4482	3.4423	.2900	.2905
Lebanon (Pound)	.002409	.002409	415.00	415.00
Malaysia (Ringgit)	.36396	.36403	2.7475	2.7470
Malta (Lira)	2.9069	2.8860	.3440	.3465
Mexico (Peso)				
Floating rate	.0004229	.0004222	2368.00	2368.00
Netherland(Guilder) .	.4708	.4728	2.1240	2.1150
New Zealand (Dollar) ..	.6075	.6100	1.6460	1.6393
Norway (Krone)	.1464	.1467	6.8300	6.8150
Pakistan (Rupee)	.05089	.05102	19.65	19.60
Peru (Inti)	.0006906	.0007002	1448.00	1428.00
Philippines (Peso)	.048309	.048309	20.70	20.70
Portugal (Escudo)	.006451	.006416	155.00	155.85
Saudi Arabia (Riyal) ..	.2666	.2667	3.7500	3.7490
Singapore (Dollar)	.5115	.5136	1.9550	1.9470
South Africa (Rand)				
Commercial rate	.3912	.3920	2.5563	2.5508
Financial rate	.2415	.2410	4.1400	4.1500
South Korea (Won) ...	.0014918	.0014918	670.30	670.30
Spain (Peseta)	.008561	.008598	116.80	116.30
Sweden (Krona)	.1561	.1564	6.4050	6.3900
Switzerland (Franc) ..	.6025	.6064	1.6595	1.6490
30-Day Forward ...	.6046	.6086	1.6539	1.6431
90-Day Forward ...	.6088	.6128	1.6425	1.6316
180-Day Forward ...	.6151	.6128	1.6256	1.6145
Taiwan (Dollar)	.03705	.03663	26.99	27.30
Thailand (Baht)	.039215	.039215	25.50	25.50
Turkey (Lira)	.0004943	.0004987	2023.00	2005.00
United Arab(Dirham) .	.2722	.2722	3.6725	3.6725
Uruguay (New Peso)				
Financial	.001943	.001974	514.50	506.50
Venezuela (Bolivar)				
Floating rate	.02747	.02747	36.40	36.40
W. Germany (Mark) ..	.5310	.5330	1.8830	1.8760
30-Day Forward ...	.5327	.5347	1.8770	1.8699
90-Day Forward ...	.5361	.5382	1.8651	1.8580
180-Day Forward ...	.5411	.5431	1.8479	1.8410

SDR	1.29651	1.30060	0.771301	0.768875
ECU	1.10809	1.11268		

. Special Drawing Rights (SDR) are based on exchange rates for the U.S., West German, British, French and Japanese currencies. Source: International Monetary Fund.

European Currency Unit (ECU) is based on a basket of community currencies. Source: European Community Commission.

FUTURES

	Open	High	Low	Settle	Change	Lifetime High	Low	Open Interest
JAPANESE YEN (IMM) 12.5 million yen; $ per yen (.00)								
June	.7623	.7629	.7609	.7611	− .0007	.8485	.7500	49,342
Sept	.7725	.7731	.7714	.7717	− .0008	.8580	.7690	1,547
Dec				.7823	− .0009	.8635	.7735	326

Est vol 17,855; vol Fri 32,638; open int 51,298, +1,401.

W. GERMAN MARK (IMM) − 125,000 marks; $ per mark								
June	.5364	.5367	.5346	.5348	− .0019	.5975	.5317	43,886
Sept	.5411	.5416	.5393	.5396	− .0019	.5977	.5366	914
Dec	.5450	.5454	.5450	.5446	− .0020	.5895	.5430	207

Est vol 15,950; vol Fri 36,357; open int 45,007, +1,176.

CANADIAN DOLLAR (IMM) − 100,000 dlrs.; $ per Can $								
June	.8380	.8384	.8368	.8375	+ .0025	.8433	.7670	18,258
Sept	.8341	.8342	.8335	.8337	+ .0025	.8385	.7990	1,017
Dec				.8301	+ .0025	.8370	.7920	240

Est vol 2,559; vol Fri 4,687; open int 19,565, −1,879.

BRITISH POUND (IMM) − 62,500 pds.; $ per pound								
June	1.6854	1.6920	1.6846	1.6868	+ .0012	1.8370	1.6200	21,314
Sept	1.6752	1.6810	1.6750	1.6762	+ .0004	1.8030	1.6580	499
Dec				1.6704	− .0002	1.7450	1.6540	114

Est vol 5,375; vol Fri 8,954; open int 22,077, +501.

SWISS FRANC (IMM) − 125,000 francs-$ per franc								
June	.6084	.6097	.6065	.6068	− .0042	.7145	.6062	31,378
Sept	.6145	.6159	.6127	.6129	− .0045	.7210	.6127	543
Dec				.6200	− .0043	.6653	.6195	153

Est vol 14,193; vol Fri 25,957; open int 32,074, +122.

AUSTRALIAN DOLLAR (IMM) − 100,000 dlrs.; $ per A.$								
June	.7946	.7969	.7946	.7952	− .0018	.8725	.7800	1,740
Sept				.7825	− .0015	.8000	.7750	218

Est vol 152; vol Fri 326; open int 1,958, +65.

U.S. DOLLAR INDEX (FINEX) 500 times USDX								
June	97.49	97.74	97.35	97.72	+ .23	99.23	90.20	6,708
Sept	97.62	97.80	97.50	97.79	+ .23	98.80	90.40	1,677
Dec	97.90	97.90	97.90	97.87	+ .23	98.94	95.05	164

Est vol 3,800; vol Fri 2,371; open int 8,549, +320.
The index: High 97.70; Low 97.47; Close 97.70 +.18

—OTHER CURRENCY FUTURES—

Settlement prices of selected contracts. Volume and open interest of all contract months.

British Pound (MCE) 12,500 pounds; $ per pound
Jun 1.6868 +.0012; Est. vol. 30; Open· Int. 363
Japanese Yen (MCE) 6.25 million yen; $ per yen (.00)
Jun .7611 −.0007; Est. vol. 150; Open Int. 259
Swiss Franc (MCE) 62,500 francs; $ per franc
Jun .6068 −.0042; Est. vol. 200; Open Int. 243
West German Mark (MCE) 62,500 marks; $ per mark
Jun .5348 −.0019; Est. vol. 120; Open Int. 405
FINEX − Financial Instrument Exchange, a division of the New York Cotton Exchange. IMM − International Monetary Market at the Chicago Mercantile Exchange. MCE − MidAmerica Commodity Exchange.

Source: The Wall Street Journal, April 11, 1989, p. C-13.

where:

$F_{t,T}$ = equilibrium price at time t for a currency futures contract maturing at time T;

S_t = spot price at time t for the foreign currency (to which the futures contract applies);

$R^\$_{t,T}$ = U.S. interest rate on risk-free securities maturing at time T; and

$R^\pounds_{t,T}$ = British interest rate on risk-free securities maturing at time T.

Sample Problem 13.2 provides further illustration.

Sample Problem 13.2

As an example, suppose the U.S. dollar is currently quoted in the spot currency market for the British pound at \$1.80/£. Interest rates in the United States and Britain for three months are 3 percent and 4 percent, respectively. What is the price of a three-month deposit futures contract for pounds?

Solution
Substituting all information into Equation (13.1):

$$F_{t,3 \text{ mo}} = (\$1.80/\pounds)\left(\frac{1 + 0.03}{1 + 0.04}\right)$$

$$= \$1.78/\pounds$$

Empirical tests have shown that the pricing relationship described by interest-rate parity holds very closely in the foreign-currency markets. The following is offered for clarification.

In the previous section on pricing theory for futures prices, spot prices of foreign currency were described as following a random walk. Thus, money as a liquid financial instrument incorporates anticipations of its future value into its current value. This is analogous to the manner in which future stock prices and dividend estimates are reflected in today's stock price. Using this rational-expectations hypothesis and momentarily assuming no inventory costs:

$$S_t = E_t(S_T) \tag{13.2}$$

or, today's price reflects the expected price for the foreign currency at time T.

Equation (13.2) can be reversed:

$$E_t(S_T) = S_t \tag{13.3}$$

Hence, the best estimate for the spot price at some future point in time T is the current spot price of the currency. Since the currency-futures price at

time t for a contract maturing at time T reflects the expected spot price for the foreign currency at time T (assuming no carrying costs):

$$F_{t,T} = E_t(S_T) \qquad\qquad (13.4)$$

Consequently:

$$F_{t,T} = S_t \qquad\qquad (13.5)$$

So without carrying costs the current futures price equals the current spot price for any foreign currency. Sample Problem 13.3 provides further illustration.

Sample Problem 13.3

To see how the carrying cost (or relative opportunity cost) associated with interest has an effect on the valuation of foreign currency futures, assume that the spot and one-year futures prices for the British pound are $1.30 and $1.33, respectively. Suppose an American investor who bought $1,300,000 worth of pounds (£1,000,000) then invests £1,000,000 at the 10-percent riskless rate yielded by one-year British-government securities. Furthermore, in order to hedge himself against fluctuations in the dollar–pound exchange rate, the investor sells £1,000,000 worth of one-year futures contracts on pounds at 1.33 (equal to the value of forty contracts). Assuming the investor holds his futures position to its maturity and then delivers the initial £1,000,000 investment to close the position, here is a summary of the transactions and closing position value.

January 1, 1989
  Buy $1.3 million worth of pounds.
  Invest proceeds at 10-percent British rate.
  Sell £1,000,000 worth of futures at $1.33.

January 1, 1990

Proceeds from earned interest	$ 130,000
Deliver £1,000,000 against short futures position at $1.33/£1.00.	$1,330,000
Gross revenue	$1,460,000
Less initial investment	$1,300,000
Net profit	$ 160,000
Annual return	12.3 percent

From all these transactions the investor earns an annualized return of 12.3 percent on the original investment of $1,300,000. This return is composed of the interest earned on the riskless British-government security and the 0.03 difference in spot and one-year futures prices for the pound (that is, the investor sold the pound at $1.33 but only paid $1.30).

If the investor can borrow U.S. dollars at a rate less than 12.3 percent, then a riskless arbitrage opportunity is available. For instance, if the U.S. lending rate is 11.0 percent, the investor could borrow the initial capital of $1,300,000 and after one year repay the interest of 11 percent and clear a 1.3-percent risk-free return. However, this opportunity will not pass unnoticed. Arbitragers will buy pounds (bidding their price up), invest the pounds in one-year British-government securities yielding 10 percent (bidding their price up and yield down), and sell an equivalent number of futures contracts (forcing their price down). Finally, these arbitrage portfolios will be financed by borrowing U.S. dollars at the going 11.0-percent rate (forcing the rate to increase). All pressures discussed in this problem will continue until the arbitrage opportunity has dissipated. That point will be attained when:

$$S_t(1 + R_{t,T}^{\$}) = F_{t,T}(1 + R_{t,T}^{\pounds}) \tag{13.6}$$

where $R_{t,T}^{\$}$ and $R_{t,T}^{\pounds}$ interest rates on securities with the same maturity as the futures contract (one year, in this case).

Rearranging Equation (13.6) to solve for $F_{t,T}$, the futures price for a one-year contract on British pounds, we have:

$$F_{t,T} = S_t \frac{(1 + R_{t,T}^{\$})}{(1 + R_{t,T}^{\pounds})} \tag{13.7}$$

This is the interest-rate parity relationship from Equation (13.1). Thus the equilibrium one-year futures price for British pounds that would eliminate the arbitrage opportunity in the example can be computed

$$F_{t,T} = (\$1.30/\pounds) \frac{(1 + 0.11)}{(1 + 0.10)}$$
$$= \$1.3118/\pounds \qquad \bullet$$

The Traditional Theory of International Parity

The writings of Keynes, Cassel, and Irving Fisher implicitly require four conditions for international currency parity.

1. Financial markets are perfect. There are no controls, transaction costs, taxes, and so on.
2. Goods markets are perfect. Shipment of goods anywhere in the world is costless.
3. There is a single consumption good common to everyone.
4. The future is known with certainty.

Interest-Rate Parity.   For any two countries, the difference in their domestic interest rates must be equal to the forward exchange-rate differential:

$$\frac{1 + R_i^t}{1 + R_j^t} = \frac{F_{ij}^t}{S_{ij}^t}$$

where:

R_i^t and R_j^t = the interest rate for countries i and j, respectively, in time t;

F_{ij}^t = the forward exchange rate of currency i in units of currency j quoted at time t for delivery at $t + 1$; and

S_{ij}^t = the spot exchange rate of currency i in units of currency j at time t.

Keynes (1930) developed this relationship by using only the first assumption.

Purchasing-Power Parity.   Cassel (1916) derived a **purchasing-power parity** theorem based on the first and third assumptions. According to the laws of one price in perfect markets, identical goods must have the same real price everywhere. Since it is assumed that every country consumes the same good (or basket of goods), a given currency has the same purchasing power in every country:

$$\frac{P_i^t}{P_j^t} = S_{ij}^t$$

where:

S_{ij}^t = the spot rate between countries i and j at time t; and

P_i^t and P_j^t = price level in countries i and j at time t, respectively.

Fisherian Relation.   Using the first, third, and fourth assumptions Irving Fisher (1930) showed that the nominal interest rate in every country will be equal to the real rate of interest plus the expected future inflation rate (this is called the **Fisherian relation**):

$$(1 + R_j^t) = (1 + r_j^t)(1 + I_j^t)$$

where:

r_j^t = the real rate of interest in country j at time t;

R_j^t = the nominal rate of interest at time t; and

I_j^t = the inflation rate at time t.

The implication of this relationship is that if the real rate of interest is equal everywhere, then the inflation differential between countries is fully reflected in their nominal interest rates.

Forward Parity.   The forward exchange rate (F_{ij}^t) must be equal to the spot exchange rate at some future point in time (S_{ij}^{t+1}):

$$S_{ij}^{t+1} = F_{ij}^t$$

This relationship **(forward parity)** must be true given the first three relationships derived above; otherwise, arbitrage opportunities would exist. Sample Problem 13.4 provides further illustration.

Sample Problem 13.4

Note that $1 + I_j^t = P_j^{t+1}/P_j^t$. Then, assuming that $1 + r_j^t = 1 + r_i^t$, it follows that:

$$\frac{(1 + R_j^t)}{(1 + R_i^t)} = \frac{P_i^t}{P_j^t}\frac{P_j^{t+1}}{P_i^{t+1}} = \frac{S_{ij}^t}{S_{ij}^{t+1}}$$

which is equal to 1 plus the rate of currency appreciation (or depreciation)●

In order to understand the pricing of futures contracts, the four relationships above must be used as building blocks. The linkages among interest rates, price levels, expected inflation, and exchange rates are all relevant in pricing a foreign-currency futures contract.

Interest-Rate Futures

Financial futures-related, interest-rate-sensitive instruments such as the GNMA futures and U.S. Treasury debt futures are the focus of this section. Sample daily price quotations for interest-rate futures are shown in Figure 13–3.

The GNMA Futures Contract.   Introduced at the Chicago Board of Trade (CBT) on October 20, 1975, the GNMA futures contract was the first of the interest-rate futures. Although it is not being traded today, because it was the first contract it remains of historical importance. The underlying security to the GNMA contract was the mortgage-backed certificate guaranteed by the Government National Mortgage Association (also known as "Ginnie Mae" or just GNMA). Ginnie Mae was created by the government in 1968. One of its primary purposes is to buy up packages of government-backed mortgages from lenders, thus freeing up capital for additional home lending. Ginnie Mae then assembles the pooled mortgages, typically thirty-year single-family loans, and creates certificates that represent a prorated share in these pools. The GNMA certificate is then sold through dealers, such as an investment banker or government-securities dealer. Each certificate is a long-term debt obligation, entitling its owner to a monthly payment of interest and principal. These certificates are guaranteed by Ginnie Mae.

The GNMA futures contract called for the delivery (or receipt) of a $100,000 principal balance of GNMA certificates with an 8-percent yield and thirty-year maturity. However, equivalent GNMA certificates could be delivered as well, such as one with a $93,167.70 principal balance and a 9-percent stated yield.

Like the actual Ginnie Mae securities, contract prices were quoted as a percentage of par plus $\frac{1}{32}$ point. Ginnie Mae prices reported in the daily financial newspapers are abbreviated so that $66\frac{25}{32}$ (corresponding to a 13.891-percent yield) is shown as 66–25. Furthermore, since the $100,000

FIGURE 13-3 Daily Closing Prices of Interest-Rate Futures

FUTURES

	Open	High	Low	Settle	Chg	Yield Settle	Chg	Open Interest

TREASURY BONDS (CBT) – $100,000; pts. 32nds of 100%

	Open	High	Low	Settle	Chg	Settle	Chg	Interest
June	88-09	88-14	88-03	88-12 +	2	9.290	– .007	248,952
Sept	88-08	88-18	88-02	88-12 +	2	9.290	– .007	36,414
Dec	88-06	88-13	88-02	88-12 +	2	9.290	– .007	13,610
Mr90	88-13	88-13	88-13	88-13 +	2	9.286	– .008	5,129
June	88-04	88-13	88-04	88-13 +	2	9.286	– .008	3,037
Sept				88-11 +	2	9.294	– .007	303
Dec				88-09 +	2	9.301	– .008	281
Mr91				88-06 +	2	9.313	– .007	97
June				88-02 +	2	9.328	– .008	196

Est vol 165,000; vol Fri 310,652; op int 308,027, +11,685.

TREASURY BONDS (MCE) – $50,000; pts. 32nds of 100%

	Open	High	Low	Settle	Chg	Settle	Chg	Interest
June	88-02	88-14	88-02	88-10 +	2	9.297	– .008	9,544

Est vol 3,200; vol Fri 5,321; open int 9,629, +169.

T – BONDS (LIFFE) U.S. $100,000; pts of 100%

	Open	High	Low	Settle	Chg			
June	88-05	88-12	88-02	88-11	– 0-06	89-14	86-10	5,573

Est vol 1,257; vol Fri 3,275; open int 5,583. – 520.

TREASURY NOTES (CBT) – $100,000; pts. 32nds of 100%

	Open	High	Low	Settle	Chg	Settle	Chg	Interest
June	92-02	92-04	91-30	92-02	....	9.233	....	80,252
Sept	92-02	92-06	92-02	92-05	....	9.217	....	5,430
Dec	92-05	92-09	92-05	92-08	....	9.202	....	200

Est vol 2,500; vol Fri 26,671; open int 85,882, –1,983.

5 YR TREAS NOTES (CBT) $100,000; pts. 32 of 100%

	Open	High	Low	Settle	Chg	Settle	Chg	Interest
June	94-17	94-20	94-16	94-18	– 2.0	9.39	+ .02	45,097
Sept				94-225	– 2.0	9.35	+ .02	726

Est vol 2,929; vol Fri 3,515; open int 45,823, – 405.

5 YR TREAS NOTES (FINEX) $100,000; pts. 32 of 100%

	Open	High	Low	Settle	Chg	Settle	Chg	Interest
June	94-115	94-145	94-105	94-13	– 2.5	9.43	+ .02	16,187
Sept	94-16	94-195	94-16	94-18	– 2.5	9.39	+ .02	612

Est vol 1,100; vol Fri 2,839; open int 16,799, +1,072.

TREASURY BILLS (IMM) – $1 mil.; pts. of 100%

	Open	High	Low	Settle	Chg	Discount Settle	Chg	Open Interest
June	91.15	91.18	91.11	91.16	– .01	8.84	+ .01	14,661
Sept	91.03	91.04	90.98	91.02	– .04	8.98	+ .04	3,792
Dec	90.91	90.97	90.91	90.94	– .04	9.06	+ .04	1,295
Mr90	91.11	91.23	91.11	91.23	– .02	8.77	+ .02	332

Est vol 4,578; vol Fri 4,251; open int 20,104, +152.

MUNI BOND INDEX(CBT)$1,000; times Bond Buyer MBI

	Open	High	Low	Settle	Chg	High	Low	Open Interest
June	89-18	89-27	89-17	89-24 +	3	91-22	77-06	11,552
Sept	88-20	89-00	88-20	88-30 +	3	91-00	78-06	800
Dec	88-08	88-11	88-07	88-09 +	3	90-21	81-10	290
Mr90	87-22	87-25	87-21	87-23 +	3	90-14	85-19	166

Est vol 500; vol Fri 3,077; open int 12,805, – 279.
The index: Close 90-12; Yield 7.81.

EURODOLLAR (IMM) – $1 million; pts of 100%

	Open	High	Low	Settle	Chg	Yield Settle	Chg	Open Interest
June	89.46	89.50	89.43	89.50	– .02	10.50	+ .02	281,865
Sept	89.32	89.36	89.28	89.34	– .05	10.66	+ .05	158,824
Dec	89.26	89.31	89.24	89.30	– .05	10.70	+ .05	103,310
Mr90	89.61	89.67	89.58	89.66	– .02	10.34	+ .02	64,246
June	89.86	89.94	89.83	89.91	– .02	10.09	+ .02	32,701
Sept	90.01	90.09	89.99	90.07	– .02	9.93	+ .02	26,403
Dec	90.02	90.11	90.00	90.08	– .02	9.92	+ .02	24,438
Mr91	90.19	90.25	90.15	90.22	– .02	9.78	+ .02	13,010
June	90.26	90.32	90.22	90.30	– .01	9.70	+ .01	10,293
Sept	90.29	90.36	90.26	90.34	– .01	9.66	+ .01	20,988
Dec	90.29	90.38	90.29	90.35	– .01	9.65	+ .01	11,164
Mr92	90.35	90.43	90.34	90.40	– .01	9.60	+ .01	2,796

Est vol 105,369; vol Fri 246,568; open int 750,038, +17,931.

EURODOLLAR (LIFFE) – $1 million; pts of 100%

	Open	High	Low	Settle	Change	Lifetime High	Low	Open Interest
June	89.48	89.49	89.44	89.48	– .03	91.10	88.76	28,411
Sept	89.33	89.33	89.29	89.33	– .05	91.83	88.72	12,420
Dec	89.29	89.30	89.26	89.29	– .05	91.67	88.93	6,903
Mr90	89.62	89.62	89.60	89.63	– .05	91.37	88.88	1,813
June	89.89	89.89	89.86	89.88	– .06	90.63	89.31	350
Sept	90.02	90.02	90.02	90.04	– .06	90.64	89.89	474
Dec	90.02	90.02	90.02	90.04	– .06	90.36	90.02	116

Est vol 5,245; vol Fri 12,014; open int 50,491, +312.

STERLING (LIFFE) – £500,000; pts of 100%

	Open	High	Low	Settle	Change	High	Low	Open Interest
June	86.60	86.76	86.60	86.73 +	.02	90.95	86.60	35,551
Sept	87.23	87.28	87.17	87.25 –	.05	90.47	87.17	16,122
Dec	87.79	87.84	87.73	87.83 –	.04	90.32	87.07	5,940
Mr90	88.12	88.16	88.05	88.14 –	.06	90.15	88.05	2,952
June	88.20	88.35	88.20	88.35 +	.02	89.80	88.20	1,709
Sept	88.30	88.30	88.30	88.40 –	.03	89.65	88.30	828
Dec	88.33	88.34	88.33	88.45 +	.02	89.37	88.33	598

Est vol 21,647; vol Fri 31,453; open int 63,749, +33.

LONG GILT (LIFFE) – £50,000; 32nds of 100%

	Open	High	Low	Settle	Chg	High	Low	Open Interest
June	95-00	95-09	94-24	95-08 +	0-08	99-28	94-30	24,609
Sept				96-06 +	0-10	98-20	96-03	249

Est vol 15,872; vol Fri 20,507; open int 24,858, +772.

– OTHER INTEREST RATE FUTURES –

Settlement prices of selected contracts. Volume and open intrest of all contract months.

30 – Day Interest Rate (CBT) $5 million; pts. of 100%
May 89.92 – .03; Est. vol. 180; Open Int. 2,327
2 Yr. Treas. Notes (FINEX) $200,000; pts. 32nds of 100%
Jun 96-31¼ – .25; Est. vol. 600; Open Int. 3,476

CBT – Chicago Board of Trade. FINEX – Financial Instrument Exchange, a division of the New York Cotton Exchange. IMM – International Monetary Market at Chicago Mercantile Exchange. LIFFE – London International Financial Futures Exchange. MCE – MidAmerica Commodity Exchange.

Source: The Wall Street Journal, April 11, 1989, p. C-20.

contract amount is one-tenth the size of a regular cash-market trade, the dollar value of a $\frac{1}{32}$ price fluctuation in the futures contract is \$31.25 (\$100,000 $\times$ 0.01 $\times$ $\frac{1}{32}$). Thus, the dollar value of a contract quoted at 66–25 is \$66,781.25 (\$100,000 $\times$ 66$\frac{25}{32}$).

GNMA futures provided a mortgage-rate-related hedging tool for savings and loans, banks, mortgage bankers, and other types of long-term-equity lenders. To better understand their hedging potential, an example of hedging with GNMA futures is discussed in the following section. Note, however, that GNMA futures stopped trading in 1987.

Hedging with GNMA Futures.   Mortgage bankers are in the business of originating mortgage loans for resale to investors. Unlike savings-and-loan associations, which also provide funds to the mortgage market and normally retain the loans they originate in their own investment portfolios, mortgage-banking firms operate on a limited capital base and depend on the turnover of a highly leveraged inventory to maintain profitability. Consequently, even a minor price depreciation in inventory induced by a rise in interest rates can seriously impair a firm's capital and jeopardize its future.

While mortgage bankers are in the process of assembling a mortgage pool or "warehousing" it pending resale, a rise in mortgage interest rates could easily impose an inventory loss that exceeds the company's profits from origination and servicing fees. Here is an example of how a hedge can reduce this risk.

ABC Mortgage Co. originated VA/FHA mortgages for inclusion in a Ginnie Mae pool over a five-day period. To hedge themselves against a rise in interest rates before the pooled mortgages could be placed with a permanent investor, ABC Co. sold GNMA futures contracts expiring nearest to the current period. Using Johnson's hedge model the company determined that the appropriate hedge ratio was 0.8101, based on sixty recent days of observations from the cash and futures markets. Twenty days after they put on the short hedge, ABC Co. placed their pooled mortgages and closed out their hedge position. Over the interim period of twenty days interest rates rose slightly. Table 13–2 summarizes the transactions and results from the hedge. Note that the hedge was put on over five days so that it remained balanced with the accumulating cash position.

The results in Table 13–2 show that hedging works both ways. That is, if an unexpected yet advantageous event occurs (in this case, falling rates), then one's profit will be limited by the hedge, due to the corresponding loss in the futures market.

U.S. Treasury Debt Futures

The United States Treasury issues debt securities to finance government operations and the federal deficit. These securities are backed by the government and are considered to be free of default risk. All Treasury debt is virtually identical except for differing maturities and yields. Corporations,

TABLE 13–2   Short Hedge with GNMA Futures to Reduce Interest-Rate Risk

Item	Time to Maturity (years)
U.S. Treasury bills	1
U.S. Treasury notes	1 to 10
U.S. Treasury bonds	more than 10

Date	Spot Market Position (Cost)	Number of Contracts Sold	Price	Dollar Value of Futures-Market Position
7/16	$250,429	3	66–25	$200,343
7/17	83,594	1	66–28	66,875
7/18	167,345	2	66–30	133,876
7/19	83,281	1	66–20	66,625
7/20	82,891	1	66–10	66,313
Total	$667,540	8		$534,032
	(face value of $1,000,000)			(face value of $1,000,000)

Rates fall instead of rising as expected.

8/19	Sell pooled GNMA mortgages for $680,671.	Buy 8 GNMA futures contracts at a price of 68–15: (8 × 68) − (15 × $100,000) = $547,750.

Results

Net loss on futures position ($534,032 − $547,750)	$(13,718)
Net gain on sale of GNMA mortgage, benefited by the decline in interest rates ($680,671 − $667,540)	$ 13,131
Net loss on hedge	$ (587)

financial institutions, investment funds, and state and local governments all utilize short-term U.S. Treasury securities as a repository for temporary surpluses of cash. Individual, institutional, and foreign investors use longer-term U.S. Treasury securities to secure their capital and insure its return for more extended periods of time. U.S. Treasury debt can be classified into three types, depending on the time to maturity: (1) U.S. Treasury bills, with a time to maturity of one year, (2) U.S. Treasury notes, with a time to maturity of more than one year up to and including ten years, and (3) U.S. Treasury bonds, with a time to maturity of more than ten years.

One of the attractive features of U.S. Treasury securities is that they can easily be resold, because a strong secondary market exists for them. More

than thirty primary dealers in government securities around the country (approved by the Federal Reserve Board) maintain a large and very liquid market for the purchase and sale of outstanding government securities (mostly those of the Treasury).

Considering the existence of such a well-developed secondary market, it might be surprising that futures markets do exist for these cash securities. The reason is interest-rate risk. Moreover, the homogeneity, relative risklessness, and correlation with the rates on other risky-market debt securities make U.S. Treasury securities an ideal instrument on which to trade futures for hedging purposes.

Treasury bill (T-bill) futures are traded at the IMM, while T-note futures and T-bond futures are offered by the CBT. Potential users of these contracts include:

1. Banks
2. Government-securities dealers
3. Investment bankers
4. Bond-fund managers
5. Pension-fund managers
6. Trust-fund managers
7. Corporate treasurers
8. Insurance-company portfolio managers
9. Speculators
10. Arbitragers

The potential applications of T-bill, T-note, and T-bond futures include:

1. Locking in yields on future purchases of T-bills, T-notes, or T-bonds.
2. Protecting the value of a portfolio comprised of government securities.
3. Hedging participation in auctions for T-bills, T-notes, and T-bonds.
4. Hedging corporate debt issuance.
5. Cross-hedging other domestic and Eurodollar financial instruments.
6. Pursuing speculative opportunity with risk capital.
7. Profiting from price differentials (arbitrage).
8. Discovering current and forward price information.

Characteristics of T-Bill Futures.   A futures contract on ninety-day T-bills was initiated by the IMM on January 6, 1976. This futures contract calls for the delivery of a ninety-day T-bill with a face value of $1,000,000. Prices are quoted in terms of the IMM index (see Figure 13–3). T-bills (as well as T-notes and T-bonds) are traditionally quoted in terms of their yield to maturity. Since interest rates (or yields) and prices of debt securities move inversely, the common perception that a long position makes money as the quoted values increase does not apply to such instruments. That is, if

someone bought a ninety-day T-bill with a 10.00-percent yield and yields then rose, the investor would lose money on a long position.

The IMM quote system for its interest-rate securities is essentially an index based on the difference between the actual T-bill price and 100.00. Hence a T-bill yield of 10.00 percent would be quoted on the IMM at 90.00. This method fits the traditional quotation procedures in futures trading where the bid price is lower than the offer (to sell) price. Furthermore, each 0.01 move in the price of a T-bill futures contract is equal to one basis point, which is equal to $25.

When the IMM T-bill futures contract reaches the maturity date, the seller of the contract may have to make delivery of the underlying T-bill. Figure 13–4 illustrates the delivery process. The major function of the clearinghouse is to see that the transfer and payment (4B and 4S in Figure 13–4) take place in a timely fashion. Should either party default in any way, the clearinghouse will complete the transaction and then seek to recover from the defaulting party.

Pricing T-Bill Futures Contracts.   Studies by Poole (1978) and Rendleman and Carabini (1979) determined upper and lower bounds for the theoretical price of a T-bill futures contract. In following their derivation, which is based upon an arbitrage relationship between the spot and futures markets, first consider the situation of an investor faced with the following choice. (1) Invest in a 182-day T-bill, or (2) Invest in a 91-day T-bill and buy a futures

FIGURE 13–4   Delivery of an IMM T-Bill Futures Contract

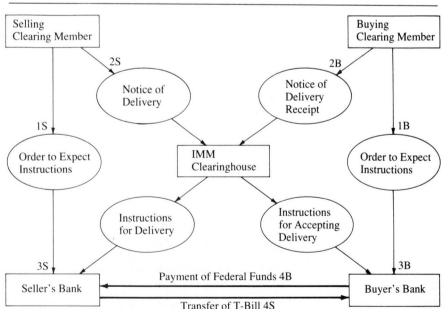

contract maturing 91 days hence. In a perfectly efficient market, the investor should be indifferent between these equivalent investments, since both offer the same return. Now let

$$Y_m = \text{yield on a 91-day T-bill, } m = 1;$$
$$Y_n = \text{yield on a 182-day T-bill, } m = 2;$$
$$Y_{Fu,m} = \text{yield on a futures contract maturing } m \text{ days from now; and}$$
$$Y_{Fw,n-m} = \text{implied forward rate on a T-bill with a life equal to } n - m.$$

If the market is to be in equilibrium, then:

$$[(1 + Y_m)(1 + Y_{Fu,m})]^{1/n} =$$
$$[(1 + Y_m)(1 + Y_{Fw,n-m})]^{1/n} = (1 + Y_n) \quad \textbf{(13.8)}$$

In other words, investing in a 91-day T-bill and then buying a futures contract maturing in 91 more days is equivalent to initially investing in an 182-day T-bill.

Arbitrage conditions will arise if:

$$Y_{Fu,m} < Y_{Fw,n-m}$$
$$Y_{Fu,m} > Y_{Fw,n-m} \quad \textbf{(13.9)}$$

To compute $Y_{Fw,n-m}$, the implied forward rate of a T-bill with a life of $n-m$, the following example is utilized. Assume that the 182-day T-bill rate is 11 percent and the three-month T-bill rate is 10 percent. The implied three-month forward rate is then:

$$Y_{Fw,3} = \frac{(1 + Y_n)^{n/m}}{(1 + Y_m)} - 1 = \frac{(1 + 0.11)^2}{(1 + 0.10)} - 1$$
$$= 12.01\% \quad \textbf{(13.10)}$$

If an arbitrager observed that the futures rate was above 12 percent (or had a price less than 88.00), he or she could profit from the following strategy.

1. Borrow money at 11 percent (assuming lending and borrowing rates are equal) by selling short a six-month T-bill.
2. Buy a three-month T-bill.
3. Simultaneously, buy one T-bill futures contract with a time to maturity of three months.

Combining the spot and futures T-bill positions results in a synthetic six-month T-bill with a yield exceeding that realized on the actual six-month T-bill. For instance, if the futures contract has a rate of 13 percent, the six-month annualized return on the synthetic position is:

$$\sqrt{(1 + 0.10)(1 + 0.13)} - 1 = 11.48\%$$

The **arbitrage profit** is equal to the realized yield on the synthetic position less the cost of establishing that position or 11.48% − 11.00% = 0.48%. On

a $1,000,000 position the arbitrager would have made $4,800 essentially risk-free.

Of course, this scenario could be reversed for the situation where the observed futures rate was less than 12 percent (or had a price greater than 88.00). Based on these examples, the theoretical price for a T-bill future can be derived from Equation (13.8). First, by taking its inverse:

$$\frac{1}{(1 + Y_m)} \cdot \frac{1}{(1 + Y_{Fu,m})} = \frac{1}{(1 + Y_n)^n} \tag{13.11}$$

or, equivalently:

$$P_m \cdot P_{Fu} = P_n \tag{13.12}$$

where P_n is the price of an n-day T-bill paying $1 at maturity. And, therefore:

$$P_{Fu} = \frac{P_n}{P_m} \tag{13.13}$$

where:

P_{Fu} = price of a T-bill futures contract, quoted as the difference between $100 and the annualized discount from par assuming 360 days in a year;
P_n = spot price of an n-day T-bill; and
P_m = spot price of an m-day T-bill ($n > m$).

Equation (13.13) can be altered to account for transaction costs such as commissions and a greater than zero bid–ask dealer spread (or bid–offer). In doing so the boundary conditions for the price of a T-bill futures contract are obtained:

$$100 \frac{P_n^A}{P_m^B} - CC \leq P_{Fu} \leq 100 \frac{P_n^A}{P_m^B} + CC$$

where:

CC = round-trip commission costs per $100 of face value;
P_n^A = the price at which a dealer will sell an n-day T-bill; and
P_m^B = the price at which a dealer will buy an m-day T-bill.

Sample Problem 13.5 provides further illustration.

Sample Problem 13.5

Using Equation (13.13), compute the theoretical futures price for the IMM December 1989 contract as of June 7, 1988. Assume that the deliverable bill (in period) against the futures contract is the T-bill maturing March 21, 1989,

with a bid price of 10.67 and ask price of 10.59. Also assume $0.004 per $100 of face value as the round-trip commission cost.

Solution

1. Determine the T-bill rate corresponding to the m period—the interval between June 7, 1989, and the third Thursday of December 1989, the delivery date of the contract (that is, $m = 188$ days).
2. Find the price of this T-bill maturing in (approximately) 188 days (December 27) from the U.S. T-bill data listed earlier. Its bid price is 10.47 and its ask price is 10.41.
3. Now calculate P_{Fu} without commission costs using Equation (13.13) and an average of the bid and ask prices for the m period and n period and n-period T-bills.

$$P_{Fu} = \frac{100 - [10.63 \times (279/360)]}{100 - [10.44 \times (188/360)]}$$

$$= \frac{100 - 8.238}{100 - 5.452} = \frac{91.762}{84.548} = 0.97053$$

Now, to get the quarterly yield (price) for the futures:

$$100 - 97.053 = 2.947$$

And the annualized yield:

$$2.947 \times \frac{360}{91} = 11.658$$

Finally, compute the theoretical futures price P_{Fu}:

$$P_{Fu} = 100 - 11.658 = 88.342$$

In comparing this price with the market price of 88.32 for the December 1989 T-bill futures contract it becomes clear that the calculated price is upwardly biased. This disparity could be due to neglect of transaction costs such as commissions. So the commission costs will be calculated on an annualized basis (like the futures price) and subtracted from the computed price.

$$0.004 \times \frac{360}{91} = 0.016$$

And:

$$P_{Fu} = 88.342 - 0.016 = 88.326$$

Characteristics of T-Note and T-Bond Futures. **T-bond futures** as on the CBT require the delivery of a U.S. Treasury bond with a face value of $100,000 and maturing at least fifteen years from maturity. Prices are quoted as a percentage of par in the same way as GNMA futures prices are quoted.

With daily trading volume in excess of 100,000 contracts on average, the T-bond futures contract is currently the most successful futures contract ever. The depth of trading in this contract is revealed by the existence of outstanding T-bond contracts with maturities nearly three years into the future.

Growing in popularity is the **T-note futures** contract, also offered by the CBT. One of the underlying stimuli for its success is the growing proportion of total Treasury debt, which is represented by T-note securities. The T-note futures contract specifies the delivery of a U.S. Treasury note with a face value of $100,000 and a maturity of no less than 6.5 years and no more than ten years from the date of delivery. Additional contract specifications for T-note and T-bond futures are listed in Table 13–3 on page 414.

Bank Certificate of Deposit Futures

Certificates of deposit, more commonly referred to as **large negotiable CDs** were created in the early 1960s by the larger U.S. banks. At the time, banks were hungry for cash to fund an unexpected surge in loan demand. CDs were meant to tap the short-term surplus funds of corporations—money that up to this point had largely been invested in low-yielding Treasury securities—by offering higher yields and more flexible terms.

Since its introduction, the CD instrument has been tremendously successful. Moreover, CDs have become a means of permanently increasing the size of the major money-center banks. The concept of managing the size of the bank with CDs has come to be known as **liability management.**

The success of CDs can be associated with their two primary attributes: (1) CDs allow major U.S. banks greater control over the size of their banks and over net earnings, and (2) CDs provide a higher return for the bank's corporate customers as well as allowing them specific maturities for investing their excess cash. However, using CDs to fund loans with different maturities subjects the bank to interest-rate risk. For instance, when short-term rates are lower than long-term rates (an upward-sloping yield curve), the bank will want to lend long and borrow short to maximize the spread between the rates at which they lend and borrow funds. This interest-rate spread is the bank's primary source of income. Yet to keep the long-term loan funded, the bank will have to roll over its short-term borrowings (liabilities) until the long-term loan (asset) matures. Should short-term rates rise over this interim period, the bank will be forced to fund its long-term loan at a higher and higher cost, thereby reducing its profitability.

Unlike the secondary markets for Treasury securities (which are liquid on both sides, making it easy to buy or sell), the secondary market for cash CDs is not particularly efficient. One reason is the lack of homogeneity of CDs, making them difficult to price. Moreover, because banks do not issue CDs at predictable times and with specific maturities, it is nearly impossible to short a CD. Hence, dealing or trading in cash CDs is a risky activity. This has spurred the introduction of CD futures to help accommodate the hedging needs of banks.

TABLE 13–3   T-Bond and T-Note Futures: CBOT Contract Specification Highlights

U.S. Treasury-Bond Futures		*U.S. Treasury-Note Futures*	
Basic trading unit	U.S. Treasury bonds with $100,000 face value	Basic trading unit	U.S. Treasury notes with $100,000 face value
Deliverable grade	U.S. Treasury bonds maturing at least 15 years from first day of delivery month if not callable, and if callable not so for at least 15 years from first day of delivery month	Deliverable grade	U.S. Treasury notes maturing at least $6\frac{1}{2}$ years but not more than 10 years from first day of delivery month. Coupon based on an 8-percent standard
Delivery method	Federal Reserve book entry wire transfer system	Delivery method	Federal Reserve book entry wire transfer system
Price quotation	Percentage of par in points of $1,000, e.g. 94–01 or $94\frac{1}{32}$	Price quotation	Percentage of par in points of $1,000, e.g., 65–01 or $65\frac{1}{32}$
Minimum fluctuation	$\frac{1}{32}$ of a point or $31.25 (one tick) per contract	Minimum fluctuation	$\frac{1}{32}$ of a point or $31.25 (one tick) per contract
Daily price limit	3 points ($3,000 per contract) above and below the previous day's settlement price	Daily price limit	3 points ($3,000 per contract) above or below the previous day's settlement price
Contract months	Mar/June/Sept/Dec	Contract months	Mar/June/Sept/Dec
Trading hours	7:20 a.m. to 2:00 p.m. (Chicago time), Monday through Friday 5:00 to 8:30 p.m. standard time or 6:00 to 9:30 p.m. daylight time, Sunday through Thursday	Trading hours	7:20 a.m. to 2:00 p.m. (Chicago time), Monday through Friday 5:00 to 8:30 p.m. standard time or 6:00 to 9:30 p.m. daylight time, Sunday through Thursday
Last trading day	7 business days prior to the last business day of the delivery month	Last trading day	7 business days prior to the last business day of the delivery month
Last delivery day	Last business day of the delivery month	Last delivery day	Last business day of the delivery month
Ticker symbol	US	Ticker symbol	TY

Source: Chicago Board of Trade, 1987 (T-Bonds) and 1986 (T-Notes).

CD futures have increasingly grown in use by banks to hedge interest-rate risk created by the asset–liability gap described earlier. As of early 1988 the IMM was the only exchange to offer CD futures contracts. The size of each contract is $1,000,000 and the delivery instrument is a CD with restrictions on its defining parameters. Contract prices are quoted in terms of the IMM index with a minimum price fluctuation of one basis point (which is 0.01 or $25). The rest of the details of CD futures contract specifications are

summarized in the table in Sample Problem 13.6, which concerns a short hedge with CD futures to minimize a bank's interest-rate risk.

Sample Problem 13.6

A Short Hedge with CD Futures. With current short-term rates lower than current long rates the ABC bank finds it more profitable to fund the six-month commercial loan made on June 12 with a three-month CD. To keep the loan funded, however, the bank will have to roll over or issue another three-month CD for roughly the same original amount. The bank's forecast of interest rates over the next three months indicates a flattening of the yield curve caused by an increase in short-term rates.

In order to reduce the interest-rate risk that their asset–liability gap has created, the bank decides to hedge with CD futures. Using futures, the bank is attempting to lock in the current (and lower) CD rate, and maximize the return on its asset (the loan). The transactions are summarized in the following table. Note that we assumed a one-to-one (dollar-per-dollar) hedge ratio for the calculations.

	Cash Transaction	*Futures-Market Transaction*
June 12	Lend $1,000,000 for 6 months at 14.00 percent (1 percent over prime). Issue a $1,000,000 3-month CD at 11.30 percent.	Sell one CD futures contract for September delivery at 88.60 (11.40 percent).
September 14: interest rates rise as expected.	Issue another $1,000,000 3-month CD at 13.30 percent (increase of 2.0 percent in the funding cost of the loan).	Buy one CD futures contract for September delivery at a price of 86.70 (13.30 percent).
Results	Sold futures contract at Bought futures contract at Profit on the contract (+ 190 basis points) Dollar value of profit (each basis point is worth $25): 190 × $25 × 1 contract Loss of return on loan due to higher refunding cost: $[(1.02)^{0.25} - 1] \times$ $1,000,000 Total net loss	88.60 (11.40%) 86.70 (13.30%) (1.90%) $4750 ($4963) ($ 213)

As the results from this hypothetical example indicate, CD futures offer a viable mechanism for hedging interest-rate risk. In this case, ABC bank nearly eliminated the higher funding cost for its loan by the profit on its futures position●

The Eurodollar Futures Market

A **Eurodollar** is any dollar on deposit outside the United States. Typically this refers to dollar balances on the books of the London branches of the U.S. and other major world-class banks. On occasion Eurodollars are also deposited in other locations, such as Nassau or the Grand Cayman Islands. An important aspect of these deposits is that, because of their location outside of the U.S. they do not fall under U.S. jurisdiction. Therefore, Eurodollars are not governed by the same regulations that apply to domestic deposits, set by the Federal Reserve.

Evolution.   The Eurodollar market evolved in the 1950s in response to Federal Reserve restrictions on the maximum allowable interest rate to be paid on a deposit. Foreign merchant banks were able to pay a larger rate on dollar deposits than was allowed by Regulation Q and still make an arbitrage profit by selling dollars in their own country on a forward basis for a return even higher than that offered the dollar depositors. To defend themselves against a loss of deposits, U.S. banks eventually reacted to this unconventional banking practice by allowing their London branches to enter this market and also take in dollar deposits.

By the mid 1960s the Eurodollar market had grown significantly and funds became available for dollar-denominated loans to be made by European banks to commercial lenders. Moreover, in 1966 Eurodollar CDs were issued by banks in the United Kingdom to increase the attractiveness of the Euro market to depositors and to meet the increased demand for funds from the United States. These securities were negotiable instruments among the investor and the (foreign) banking institution. As the Eurodollar markets developed and matured, formal lines of credit and sovereign risk limitations were formalized by participants.

A bank lending funds in the Eurodollar market is exposed to essentially three risks:

1. Interest-rate risk
2. Credit risk
3. Sovereign risk

The interest-rate risk involved with a Eurodollar loan is virtually identical to that in previous explanations and examples. Credit risk, while present to some extent in the U.S. cash CD market, is a larger concern in the Eurodollar market because of the difficulties that can arise when trying to analyze a foreign borrower's financial position. Finally, sovereign risk is

unique to the arena of international lending. **Sovereign risk** refers to the unfavorable consequences that can have impact on a bank's investment if a foreign government is overthrown, becomes economically unstable, or passes detrimental regulations affecting the movement of funds. Most banks will have sovereign-risk limitations restricting the total amount placed on deposit with (or loaned to) institutions in any one country.

The relationship between three-month rates offered on Eurodollar deposits (as measured by the LIBOR rate), U.S. CDs, and U.S. T-bills can be visualized for a two-year period in Figure 13–5. A number of aspects of the relationship between these three securities can be noted from this chart. Most prominent among the rate relationships is that Eurodollar rates are higher than CD rates, which are higher than T-bill rates—a ranking consistent with the level of risk inherent in these securities. Not so obvious is the variation in the spread (difference) between Eurodollar rates and CD rates, which do not simply rise together when rates rise and fall together when

FIGURE 13–5   Three-Month Rates on Eurodollar Deposits, U.S. CDs, and U.S. T-Bills, 1985–1988 (quarterly data)

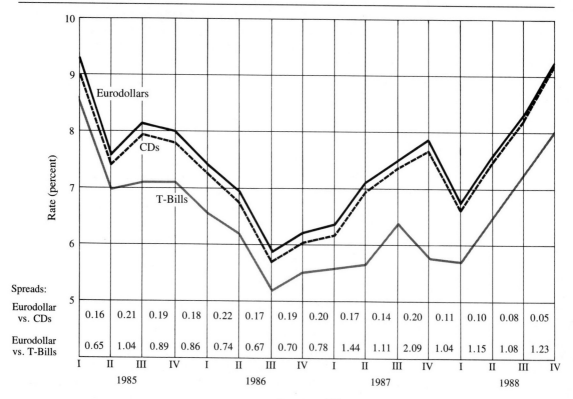

	I	II	III	IV	I	II	III	IV	I	II	III	IV	I	II	III	IV
Eurodollar vs. CDs	0.16	0.21	0.19	0.18	0.22	0.17	0.19	0.20	0.17	0.14	0.20	0.11	0.10	0.08	0.05	
Eurodollar vs. T-Bills	0.65	1.04	0.89	0.86	0.74	0.67	0.70	0.78	1.44	1.11	2.09	1.04	1.15	1.08	1.23	

Spreads:

Quarter and Year

Source: Federal Reserve Bulletin.

rates fall. Rather, changes in the interest-rate spread are affected by a variety of unpredictable market forces and decisions of U.S. and foreign governments. For example, increasing U.S. interest rates tend to strengthen the dollar, narrowing the spread between Eurodollars and domestic CD rates. Unlike the behavior of the spread between Eurodollar and CD rates, the Eurodollar rates and Treasury rates have a less predictable tendency to rise together as rates rise.

The rationale for briefly discussing the Eurodollar market and the relationship of its rates to domestic rates is to provide a basis for understanding exactly what Eurodollar futures are, as well as to make it easier to understand why Eurodollar futures exist and how they can be used. Hence, the focus now turns to the Eurodollar futures contract and market.

Eurodollar Futures.   **Eurodollar futures** are traded on the IMM and the London International Financial Exchange (LIFFE). (Due to similarities and a desire to keep the analysis as simple as possible, the sole focus here is on the IMM contract.) The Eurodollar futures contract has as its underlying instrument a three-month Eurodollar time deposit in the amount of $1,000,000. However, this contract, like those of the index futures, is settled in cash. As with CD and T-bill futures, the Eurodollar futures contract is quoted in terms of the IMM index. Thus a quote of 88.17 for the September 1984 contract is equivalent to a current contract value of $881,700.

The primary use of Eurodollar futures as a hedging vehicle is similar to that of other hedging vehicles; they are capable of protecting against detrimental changes in interest rates. Sample Problem 13.7 is offered to help clarify their application.

Sample Problem 13.7

A Long Hedge with Eurodollar Futures. Suppose that the London branch of a U.S. bank anticipates a decline in rates from September 16 to December 16. Furthermore, on June 12 the bank makes a three-month loan in the Eurodollar market and finances the loan with the funds from a six-month Eurodollar CD. When the three-month loan matures, the bank will relend the principal and interest received for another three months. Such a reverse liability–asset gap is partially the result of a downward-sloping yield curve where short-term rates are higher than longer-term rates.

Since the bank's profit is the spread between the higher rate at which they loan money and the lower rate at which they borrow money, a decline in the former without a corresponding decline in the latter will adversely affect profitability. In this scenario where declining rates are expected by the end of the first three-month loan, the bank is prone to reinvestment-rate risk.

To alleviate the problem, the bank chooses to fix the reinvestment rate for the latter three-month investment horizon through a long position in Eu-

rodollar Futures. On June 12 the Eurodollar contract for September delivery
was priced at an index of 86.53 (100 − 13.47 percent), the six-month
Eurodollar CD rate was 13.00 percent, and the initial three-month loan was
made at the LIBOR rate of 14.00 percent. The table summarizes the transactions results. Note that a dollar-per-dollar hedge ratio for this example is
assumed.

	Spot-Market Transaction	*Futures-Market Transaction*
June 12	Issue a $1,000,000 six-month Euro CD at 13.00 percent. Loan the $1,000,000 in the Euro market for three months at 14.00 percent.	Buy one Eurodollar futures contract for September delivery at 86.53 (13.47 percent).
September 14: interest rates fall as expected.	Return the $1,000,000 principal plus interest of $33,299 at the current LIBOR rate of 12.00 percent (a net reinvestment rate decline of 2.0 percent).	Sell one Eurodollar futures contract at 88.00 (12.00 percent).
Results	Bought futures contract at Sold futures contract at Profit on the contract (+ 147 basis points) Dollar value of profit from futures transaction (each basis point is worth $25): 147 × $25 × 1 contract Loss caused by decline in LIBOR lending rate: $[(1.02)^{0.25} − 1] ×$ $1,033,299 Total net loss	86.53 (13.47 percent) 88.00 _____ 1.47 (1.47 percent) $3,675 ($5,128) ($1,453)

As the table indicates, the use of the futures position to hedge the interest-
rate risk allows the bank to reduce its reinvestment rate loss by 71 percent.
Use of a more sophisticated hedge ratio such as Howard and D'Antonio's
might have resulted in an even stronger position in futures, further cutting
the bank's losses

STOCK-INDEX FUTURES

Stock-index futures offer the investor a medium for expressing an opinion on the general course of the market. In addition, these contracts can be used by portfolio managers in a variety of ways to alter the risk–return distribution of their stock portfolios. For instance, much of a sudden upward surge in the market could be missed by the institutional investor due to the time it takes to get money into the stock market. By purchasing stock-index futures contracts, the institutional investor can enter the market immediately and then gradually unwind the long futures position as he or she is able to get more funds invested in stocks. Conversely, after a run up in the value of the stock portfolio (assuming it is well diversified and correlates well with one of the major indexes) a portfolio manager might desire to lock in the profits until after being required to report the quarterly return on the portfolio. By selling an appropriate number of stock-index futures contracts, the institutional investor could offset any losses on the stock portfolio with corresponding gains on the futures position. Before presenting examples using stock-index futures, the origination of these contracts, the different types offered, and their theoretical pricing models are reviewed.

The first stock-index futures contract was offered by the Kansas City Board of Trade (KCBT) on the Value Line Composite Stock Index (VLCI) on February 24, 1982. Contracts on the S&P 500 stock index and NYSE composite stock index were soon offered by the IMM (a division of the Chicago Mercantile Exchange) and the NYSE, respectively. A futures contract on the S&P 100 stock index began trading on the IMM in January of 1983, and most recently the CBT initiated trading in a futures contract based on the AMEX Major Market Index (MMI). The MMI is a portfolio of twenty stocks from the Dow Jones Industrial Average and, not surprisingly, correlates very well with the highly visible DJIA index.

The calculation of the market value for a stock-index futures contract on any given day is simply a matter of multiplying the current index price for the contract by the appropriate dollar amount. Table 13–4 lists the multiplier that is used to determine the dollar value of the futures contract for each index future offered. Each of the U.S. stock-index futures is listed in order of market popularity. Each contract bought and sold on a particular day is included in the calculation of daily trading volume. Figure 13–6 shows prices, volume, and open interest for U.S. indexes. Open interest represents the number of open contract positions on a given day with only one side counted—that is, when the buyer and seller make their transaction, only one position is counted as being open, not two. S&P 500 futures are by far the most highly traded of the contracts, with daily volume typically in excess of 50,000 and open interest above 30,000. At the other extreme, the S&P 100 futures have daily trading volume of less than 500 contracts on average and open interest around 700. The NYSE composite futures and MMI futures are roughly equal in volume, with daily trading around 14,000 contracts and

TABLE 13–4   Multipliers of Stock-Index Futures Contracts

Futures Contract	Exchange	Multiplier
S&P 500 Index	IMM	× $500
NYSE Index	NYSE	× $500
Major Market Index	CBOT	× $100
VLCI	KCBT	× $500
S&P 100 Index	IMM	× $200
TSE 300	Toronto Stock Exchange	× $10 Canadian
FTSE 100	LIFFE	× 25
All Ordinary	Sydney Futures Exchange	× $100 Australian
Hong Seng	Hong Kong Futures Exchange	× $50 Hong Kong
Nikkei Dow Jones	Singapore Investment Monetary Exchange	× 1,000 yen

FIGURE 13–6   Daily Closing Prices of Stock-Index Futures

FUTURES

S&P 500 INDEX (CME) 500 times index

	Open	High	Low	Settle	Chg	High	Low	Open Interest
June	300.90	301.55	299.70	300.25	− .65	306.20	263.80	132,735
Sept	305.20	305.90	304.10	304.60	− .70	309.70	271.50	2,101
Dec	308.75	310.20	308.70	309.00	− .70	313.20	298.90	929

Est vol 27,361; vol Fri 32,230; open int 135,765, +189.
Indx prelim High 297.94; Low 296.85; Close 297.11 − .05

NYSE COMPOSITE INDEX (NYFE) 500 times index

	Open	High	Low	Settle	Chg	High	Low	Open Interest
June	168.85	169.35	168.35	168.60	− .35	171.60	149.60	6,359
Sept	171.00	171.50	170.70	170.85	− .40	173.40	153.90	990
Dec	173.35	173.35	173.35	173.20	− .35	175.10	161.10	434

Est vol 3,704; vol Fri 6,376; open int 7,812, +220.
The index: High 167.33; Low 166.78; Close 166.89 − .04

MAJOR MKT INDEX (CBT) $250 times index

	Open	High	Low	Settle	Chg	High	Low	Open Interest
Apr	455.70	456.60	454.25	454.75	− .70	468.50	440.50	5,396
May	456.50	457.40	455.20	455.75	− .95	469.30	443.00	801
June	458.50	459.40	457.20	457.78	− .90	471.40	442.50	189

Est vol 2,500; vol Fri 3,589; open int 6,386, +187.
The index: High 455.51; Low 453.21; Close 453.70 − .23

KC VALUE LINE INDEX (KC) 500 times index

	Open	High	Low	Settle	Chg	High	Low	Open Interest
June	268.10	268.80	267.20	268.00	....	271.20	245.65	1,148

Est vol 100; vol Fri 84; open int 1,194, −44.
The index: High 265.75; Low 265.21; Close 265.49 +.10

CRB INDEX (NYFE) 500 times index

	Open	High	Low	Settle	Chg	High	Low	Open Interest
May	238.10	240.50	237.85	240.45	+ 2.00	251.00	232.00	1,089
July	238.00	240.70	237.90	240.55	+ 2.25	250.50	233.00	750
Sept	238.15	240.35	238.15	241.05	+ 2.60	249.10	236.15	426
Dec	....	....	....	241.55	+ 2.85	244.70	241.50	107

Est vol 932; vol Fri342; open int 2,372, +6.
The index: High 239.71; Low 237.56; Close 239.71 +1.90

—OTHER INDEX FUTURE—

Settlement price of selected contract. Volume and open interest of all contract months.

KC Mini Value Line (KC) 100 times index
Jun 268.00 +.10; Est. vol. 25; Open Int. 113

CBT–Chicago Board of Trade. CME–Chicago Mercantile Exchange. KC–Kansas City Board of Trade. NYFE–New York Futures Exchange, a unit of the New York Stock Exchange.

Source: The Wall Street Journal, April 11, 1989, p. C-11.

open interest near 9,000. Finally, the original index-futures contract on the VLCI has relatively constant daily volume and open-interest statistics averaging about 4,000 and 3,000, respectively.

The importance of trading-volume data is that it represents the relative liquidity of the various index-futures contracts. This is important information for users (particularly hedgers) trying to decide which would best suit their purposes. The higher a contract's liquidity the easier to enter and exit positions and to trade in larger lots of contracts without overly impacting price. Of course, the extent to which an institutional investor's stock portfolio correlates with each of the underlying stock indexes will also influence the decision of which futures contract to hedge with. Table 13–5 summarizes additional contract specifications for each of the stock-index futures.

All index-futures contracts call for cash settlement or delivery. This means that on the expiration date of the contract, no security or portfolio of securities is delivered. Rather, the difference in the value of the contract between buying and selling is delivered in cash. For example, if the S&P 500 contract was purchased when the index was 300 and delivered when the index was 310, the purchaser would receive $5,000 from the seller (310 × $500 = $155,000 settlement value minus 300 × $500 = $150,000 purchase value).

Pricing Stock-Index Futures Contracts

Although the theoretical pricing of these contracts has not yet reached a conclusive level, an examination of the components of the models offered to date will further an understanding of the general pricing factors involved.

A paper by Modest and Sundaresan (1983) proposes theoretical pricing boundaries for a stock-index futures contract based on arbitrage conditions. First, for the case where no dividends are paid by the stocks in the underlying index, interest rates are nonstochastic, and there are no transaction costs, the price of a futures contract can be stated as:

$$F_{t,T} = S_t(1 + R_{f,T-t}) \qquad (13.14)$$

The argument for this relationship was presented earlier. Next, Modest and Sundaresan extend Equation (13.14) to a set of boundary conditions by taking into account transaction costs. To simplify, let the price of a discount bond $[1/(1 + R_{f,T-t})]$ be stated as $B_{t,T}$. So now:

$$\frac{S_t + C_{LS} + C_{SF}}{B_{t,T}} \geq F_{t,T} \geq \frac{S_t - C_{SS} - C_{LF}}{B_{t,T}} \qquad (13.15)$$

where:

S_t = market value of the underlying stock index at time t;

$F_{t,T}$ = theoretically bounded price for a stock-index futures contract at time t, that matures at time T, where $T > t$;

$B_{t,T}$ = price of a discount bond = $1/(1 + R_{f,T-t})$;

TABLE 13–5 Stock-Index Futures: Contract Specifications

	SP	SX	YX		MMI
	S&P 500 Stock-Index Futures (IMM)	S&P 100 Stock-Index Futures (IMM)	NYSE Stock-Index Futures (NYSE)	VLCI Stock-Index Futures (KCBT)	MMI Stock-Index Futures (CBOT)
Contract size	$500 × S&P 500 index	$200 × S&P 100 index	$500 × NYSE index	$500 × VLCI	$1000 × MMI
Approximate value (nearest contract, 8/15/84)	$82,325 ($500 × 164.65)	$32,910 ($200 × 164.55)	$47,500 ($500 × 95.00)	$90,875 ($500 × 181.75)	$23,525 ($100 × 235.25)
Minimum price change	0.05 = $25	0.05 = $10	0.05 = $25	0.05 = $25	$\frac{1}{8}$ = 0.125 = $12.50
Daily price limit	None	None	None	None	None
Trading hours (Central Time)	9:00am –3:15pm	9:00am –3:15pm	9:00am –3:15pm	9:00am –3:15pm	8:45am –3:15pm
Contract months	March, June, September, December	Monthly	March, June, September, December	March, June, September, December	Monthly
Last trading day	Third Thursday of delivery month	Third Thursday of delivery month	Second to last business day in delivery month		
Settlement day (cash)	Business day following last trading day	Business day following last trading day	Last business day in delivery month	Business day following last trading day	
Composition of underlying index	500 stocks value weighted	100 stocks value weighted	All NYSE listed stocks (1600) value weighted	1683 stocks, geometric average	20 stocks price weighted
Margin: Speculative	$6000 (I)/ $2500 (M)	3300 (I)/ $1200 (M)	$3500 (I)/ $1500 (M)	$6500 (I)/ $3250 (M)	
Hedge	3000/2500	1500/1200	1500/1200		
Spread	400/200	200/100	200/100		

$$C_{LS} = \text{cost of being long in the spot index (transactions costs);}$$
$$C_{SS} = \text{cost of being short in the spot index;}$$
$$C_{LF} = \text{cost of being long in the futures; and}$$
$$C_{SF} = \text{cost of being short in the futures.}$$

There are two steps to be taken to establish the validity of the arbitrage argument behind Equation (13.15). The first step is to show that $B_{t,T}F_{t,T} < (S_t + C_{LS} + C_{SF})$ [equivalent to $F_{t,T} \leq (S_t + C_{LS} + C_{SF})/B_{t,T}$]. To do so, suppose that the reverse is true. Then at time t the following transactions can be undertaken to guarantee riskless profits.

1. Buy the spot index by investing \$$(S_t + C_{LS})$.
2. Sell futures short by incurring \$$C_{SF}$.

At time T cover the short position in the futures by delivering the stock index (assuming this was allowed) and receive $F_{t,T}$ for certain. The present value at time t for the futures price received at time T is $B_{t,T}F_{t,T}$. Thus, if $B_{t,T} F_{t,T} > S_t + C_{LS} + C_{SF}$ then arbitrage profits would be available. Hence:

$$B_{t,T} F_{t,T} < S_t + C_{LS} + C_{SF}$$

The second step is to show that $B_{t,T}F_{t,T} \geq (S_t - C_{SS} - C_{LF})$, or equivalently that $F_{t,T} \geq (S_t - C_{SS} - C_{LF})/B_{t,T}$. Once again, assume that the reverse pricing condition is true and pursue the following transactions at time t to obtain riskless profits.

1. Sell the spot index short. This produces an inflow of \$$(S_t - C_{SS})$.
2. Buy futures (long position) incurring $-$ \$$C_{LF}$.

At time T collect the stock in the futures market by paying $F_{t,T}$ and covering the short position. The inflow at time t is $(S_t - C_{SS} - C_{LF})$, and its value at time T is simply the same amount compounded from t to T by $B_{t,T}$ (that is, divide the dollar sum by $B_{t,T}$, the price of a discount bond, which in the case of nonstochastic rates is the future-value interest factor). The outflow at time T is $F_{t,T}$, so, if $(S_t - C_{SS} - C_{LF})/B_{t,T} > F_{t,T}$, then arbitrage profits can be made. Therefore, efficient markets infer that the opposite condition is true.

To adjust the bounds for dividends paid out by the stocks in the spot index, simply subtract their discounted value from each side of the boundaries. Why? Since the holder of a stock-index futures contract does not receive the dividends paid out by the underlying stock index, its value must be diminished by their present value. Assuming that dividends d are nonstochastic and paid out at known futures periods, such that $t < \tau < T$, their value can be discounted back to the present by a discount factor of $B_{t,t+T}$. Summing the present value of all future dividends paid by the spot index between t and T, the pricing boundary conditions can be adjusted downward in Equation (13.15):

$$\frac{S_t + C_{LS} - \left(\sum_{\tau=1}^{T-t} B_{t,T} + \tau d\tau \right)}{B_{t,T}} \geq F_{t,T} \geq \frac{S_t - C_{SS} - C_{LF} - \left(\sum_{\tau=1}^{T-t} B_{t,T} + \tau d\tau \right)}{B_{t,T}}$$

$$\text{(13.16)}$$

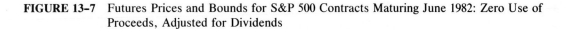

FIGURE 13-7   Futures Prices and Bounds for S&P 500 Contracts Maturing June 1982: Zero Use of Proceeds, Adjusted for Dividends

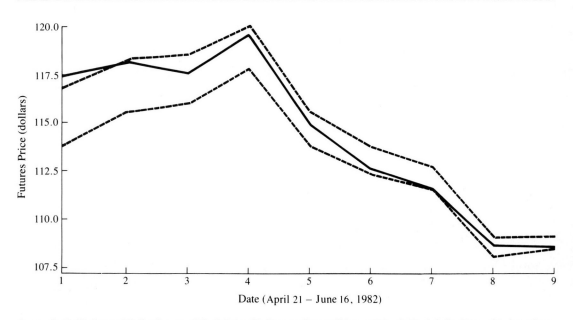

Source: D. M. Modest and M. Sundaresan, "The Relationship Between Spot and Futures Prices in Stock-Index Futures Markets: Some Preliminary Evidence." *Journal of Futures Markets*, v. 3 (Spring 1983), page 27. Copyright © 1983 by John Wiley and Sons, Inc. Reprinted by permission of John Wiley and Sons, Inc.

Figures 13–7 and 13–8 show how well the price for S&P 500 futures contracts maturing in June 1982 followed the boundary conditions in Equation (13.16). Figure 13–7 assumes that zero percent of any proceeds from a short sale of the spot index was available for use. Figure 13–8 assumes that 50 percent of such proceeds could be used by the investor for reinvestment. As can be seen, allowance for the use of 50 percent of short-sale proceeds increases the bounds and indicates that either they are upwardly biased or that the June 1982 futures contract was slightly undervalued during this period.

An analysis of the components in Equation (13.16) can help discern how the futures price should be affected by a change in any one of the variables.

$$\frac{\partial F_{t,T}}{\partial B_{t,T}} > 0 \qquad \text{As the price of a discount bond increases or equivalently, interest rate falls, the futures price will increase.} \qquad \textbf{(13.17A)}$$

$$\frac{\partial F_{t,T}}{\partial S_t} > 0 \qquad \text{As the underlying spot price increases so will the futures price.} \qquad \textbf{(13.17B)}$$

FIGURE 13–8 Futures Prices and Bounds for S&P 500 Contracts Maturing June 1982: Half Use of Proceeds, No Adjustment for Dividends

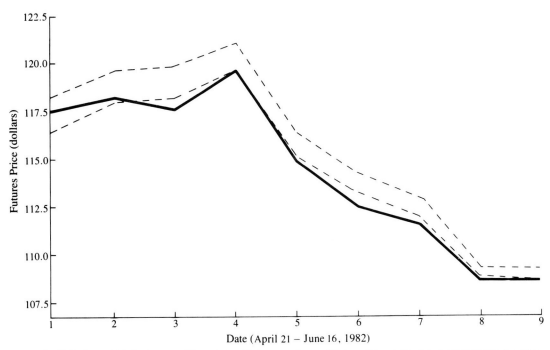

Source: D. M. Modest and M. Sundaresan, "The Relationship Between Spot and Futures Prices in Stock-Index Futures Markets: Some Preliminary Evidence." *Journal of Futures Markets*, v. 3 (Spring 1983), page 31. Copyright © 1983 by John Wiley and Sons, Inc. Reprinted by permission of John Wiley and Sons, Inc.

$$\frac{\partial F_{t,T}}{\partial d} < 0 \qquad \text{As future dividend payments are expected to increase the futures price declines.} \qquad \textbf{(13.17C)}$$

$$\frac{\partial F_{t,T}}{\partial C} < 0 \qquad \text{As relevant transaction costs rise, the futures price will fall.} \qquad \textbf{(13.17D)}$$

If more than one of the denominator variables changes at the same time, the expression cannot be generalized for the resulting effect on the futures price. The precise change in the futures price will depend on the relative size of the two or more changing parameters. Nevertheless, it can be concluded that a correct valuation for a stock-index futures contract requires accurate forecasts of future interest rates and dividends. Sample Problem 13.8 provides further illustration.

Sample Problem 13.8

Hedging with Stock-Index Futures. In this example an institutional investor is going to use S&P 500 stock-index futures contracts to hedge an expected

market decline over the coming month. Assume the following: (1) the S&P 500 stock index is an exact proxy of the composition of the investor's stock portfolio, (2) no transaction costs are involved in entering or exiting either market, and (3) that the investor uses the Howard–D'Antonio hedge ratio equation [Chapter 12, Equation (12.15)] to determine how many futures contracts to sell. The figures used to compute the hedge ratio are from daily data over a two-month period.

The first step is to calculate the hedge ratio and corresponding hedging effectiveness measure. So, using the following figures:

i = 0.10 (the risk-free rate on 13-week T-bills);
$\bar{r}_f$ = 0.2241 (average daily return, annualized, for the nearby futures);
$\bar{r}_s$ = 0.2025 (average daily return, annualized, for the S&P 500 index);
σ_f = 0.1851 (standard deviation of daily returns on the nearby futures);
σ_s = 0.0792 (standard deviation of daily returns on the S&P 500 index);
ρ = 0.9815 (correlation coefficient among the returns on the S&P 500 index and nearby S&P 500 futures contract);
$\pi = \sigma_f/\sigma_s$ = 2.3371;
$r = r_f/(r_s - i)$ = 2.1863;
$\lambda = \alpha/\pi$ = 0.9355 (risk–return relative);
P_f = 167.60 (current futures price for September contract);
P_s = 165.54 (current value of S&P 500 index); and
$\gamma = P_f/P_s$ = 1.0124.

The hedge ratio is:

$$HHD = \frac{(\lambda - \rho)}{\gamma \pi (1 - \lambda\rho)} = \frac{0.9355 - 0.9815}{1.0124(2.3371)[1 - (0.9355)(0.9815)]}$$
$$= -0.238$$

The hedging effectiveness measure [Chapter 12, Equation (12.16)] is:

$$HE = \sqrt{\frac{1 - 2\lambda\rho + \lambda^2}{1 - \rho^2}} = \sqrt{\frac{1 - 2(0.9355)(0.9815) + (0.92355)}{1 - (0.9815)^2}}$$
$$= 1.0284$$

Assuming the investor's stock portfolio is $100\times$ the value of the S&P 500 index, the investor should sell twenty-four futures contracts to hedge the portfolio. Based on the past risk–return relationship between the futures and the spot markets, the institutional investor can expect to enhance the excess return to risk on his or her portfolio by 2.8 percent over the hedging period [(1.0284 − 1) × 100%]. The table on page 428 summarizes the transactions and results from the hedge.

Utilizing the Howard and D'Antonio hedging strategy, the loss on the spot position was reduced by 38 percent●

	Spot-Market Transaction	Futures-Market Transaction
August 1	Holding a stock portfolio duplicating the S&P 500 index but 100 × its spot value or 100 × $500 × 165.54 = $8,277,000.	Sell 24 September-delivery S&P 500 futures contracts at a price of 167.60 (market value of 24 × $500 × 167.60 = $2,011,200).
September 1: stock-market prices fall as expected.	S&P 500 index falls to 163.04; value of portfolio is now 100 × $500 × 163.04 = $8,152,000.	Buy 24 September S&P 500 futures contracts at a price of 163.60 (market value = 24 × $500 × 163.60 = $1,963,200).
Results	Sell 24 contracts at	167.60
	Buy 24 contracts at	163.60
	Net profit on futures (+ 400 basis points)	4.00
	Dollar value of profit (each basis point worth $5): 400 × $5 × 24 contracts or $2,011,200 − $1,963,200	$48,000
	Net loss on stock portfolio ($8,152,000 − $8,277,000)	($125,000)
	Net loss on hedge	($ 77,000)
	Portfolio loss reduced by hedge (percent)	38

Stock-Index Futures: Does the Tail Wag the Dog?

The rise in program trading based on a comparatively narrow blue-chip stock-market barometer, the **Major Market Index (MMI),** is said to be fueling the volatile price swings in the stock market, a case of the tail wagging the dog. The MMI is a price-weighted index of twenty very actively traded stocks, sixteen of which are included in the Dow Jones 30 Industrials. Because of its relatively small size, the MMI is expected to be more easily arbitragible than other stock-index futures contracts. Basically, program trading is taking a position (long or short) in a portfolio of stocks comprising the index and simultaneously taking an opposite position in the index-futures contracts. The objective of the program trade is to create a risk-free position that earns a return in excess of the currently available risk-free return.

These so-called program trades may move both the futures and the spot market. The chain of causality may work as follows.

1. Investors believe the stock market will rise and they purchase futures contracts in expectation of higher equity values. The purchase of futures contracts is preferable because they entail no initial investment and lower transaction costs than a position in the stock market.
2. The rise in futures prices causes an imbalance between the prices of the futures and the underlying index; as this premium between the futures and the index increases, it may become more profitable to execute a program trade.
3. The simultaneous sale of the futures and purchase of the underlying index will cause the premium between the futures and the index to shrink.

Changes in other factors, such as interest rates, can also have an effect on the equilibrium relationship between the index price and the futures price, thereby changing the premium or discount between the two markets. Program traders can take advantage of any change in the spread between the markets. It does not matter what causes the change in spread, either internal factors like changes in investor expectations or external factors such as interest-rate changes. All program trading does is to bring cash and futures prices together. The program trade may be an essential mechanism insuring that futures prices and the underlying equity prices are efficiently determined. Chapter 21 discusses the relationship between portfolio insurance and program trading.

To date most of the literature on the impact of futures trading on the cash market has focused on the changes in spot-price volatility because of the initiation or cessation of futures trading. A common conclusion of these studies is that the futures market has a smoothing effect on the cash market by stabilizing the spot price. The recent uproar about the "triple witching hour" and the so-called crises at expiration caused by the expiration of stock-index futures and options at the close on the third Friday of March, June, September, and December brings to question the smoothing influence that futures contracts have on the underlying index.

If the market is efficient, prices adjust instantaneously to reflect all relevant information, and knowledge of such information cannot lead to excess risk-adjusted returns. The central concept in the efficient-market hypothesis is the fair-game model. A sequence of past returns over time is a fair game if today's price reflects the then-available information, making it impossible to earn excess risk-adjusted returns by trading on that information. If the information set today contains all of the information known and used by the market participants in the spot market in determining the spot price, one of the components of the information set is the previous change in the price of futures contracts.

Using intraday spot and futures prices of the CBT's MMI over the period August 1984 to August 1986, Finnerty and Park (1987) provide the following evidence (Table 13–6) on a positive linkage between futures-price changes and subsequent spot-price changes. A majority of the contracts studied showed a significant relationship between the change in the futures price and the subsequent change in the index. This supports the notion that the tail is

TABLE 13-6   Linkage Between Futures-Price Changes and Subsequent Spot-Price Changes

Maxi Major Market Index		Major Market Index	
Number of contracts studied	11		24
Number showing significance at the 10 percent level	7		16
Number showing significance if results were random	1		2
Number significant before December 1985/number of contracts	0/4	Number significant before April 1985/number of contracts	3/9
Number significant after December 1985/number of contracts	7/7	Number significant after April 1985/number of contracts	13/15

Source: Finnerty and Park (1987).

wagging the dog. This result was present for both the Maxi and the regular MMI contracts. Of interest is the fact that when each of the contracts was first traded, there existed a period of time when there was no relationship between the change in the futures price and subsequent change in the index. For the Maxi contract this was the first four months of trading, from September to December 1985. And for the MMI during the first nine months of trading, six out of nine contracts showed no relationship between futures- and subsequent spot-price changes. This could indicate either that arbitrage opportunities were not available during the initial trading of the contracts, or that program traders were unable immediately to take advantage of the opportunities if they were available.

However, after the initial start-up periods the results indicate that there exists a strong relationship between futures- and subsequent index-price changes in seven out of the last seven months for the Maxi and thirteen out of the last fifteen months for the MMI contracts. These results indicate that it is reasonable to answer in the affirmative: the tail is wagging the dog, at least in the case of the MMI and Maxi MMI.

SUMMARY

In one sense, uncertainty and risk are equivalent; thus the more uncertain something is the more risky it is. The futures markets evolved to alleviate one particular kind of risk, that associated with unexpected price changes. The purpose of this chapter has been to help explain what futures contracts are, how markets for them operate, and most important, how they can be applied to the hedging of price risk for securities.

Although futures contracts originated on agricultural commodities, the 1970s saw the introduction of futures for financial instruments. Deregulation of the domestic financial sector, the 1979 change in monetary policy, elimination of fixed foreign-exchange rates, the growing interrelatedness of the world economy, and bouts with high levels of inflation are some of the major reasons for the growing need for and popularity of financial futures.

The general methodology for using futures to reduce price risk (or equivalently, interest-rate risk) should seem quite straightforward. If long the spot commodity or instrument, then sell or short the related futures contract in order to lock in a price (or rate). Nevertheless, exactly how to determine the appropriate hedge ratio and evaluate the effectiveness of the hedge has no all-conclusive answer.

QUESTIONS AND PROBLEMS

1. Carefully explain why a market for foreign-currency futures emerged.

2. What is interest-rate parity? What is the relationship between the concept of interest-rate parity and the futures and spot prices for foreign currency?

3. Assume that the six-month interest rate in the United States is 5 percent while the rate is 7 percent in Japan. If the spot price of dollars in terms of yen is 124 yen/dollar, what is the price of a six-month futures contract for dollars?

4. Suppose IBM is planning to issue thirty-year bonds to finance a new plant. Assume that it plans to issue these bonds in three months. Is there any way IBM can protect itself from unexpected increases in interest rates?

5. Carefully explain the function speculators serve in the futures markets.

6. Assume that sixty-day spot Treasury bills sell for $97.75 while ninety-day spot Treasury bills sell for $96.50. If the price of a thirty-day Treasury-bill future that matures in thirty days is $98.50, are there any arbitrage opportunities? If so, create a strategy to exploit this opportunity.

7. I. M. Ritch has a stock portfolio worth $50,000. He plans to use it for a down payment on a house he will be purchasing in six months. Is there any way Mr. Ritch can protect himself from an adverse change in stock prices? Are there any conditions that must be met for this strategy to work?

8. Calculate the implied forward rate of a T-bill with a life of 182 days if the 91-day T-bill rate is 9 percent and the nine-month T-bill rate is 10.5 percent.

9. What are Eurodollars? Why do they exist?

10. Carefully explain why a bank might choose to have a long position in Eurodollar futures.

11. Carefully explain the difference between a long hedge and a short hedge. When would an investor wish to use a long hedge? a short hedge?

12. Juan Valdez is a coffee grower who is planning to harvest 112,500 pounds of coffee on June 1. The current price for coffee is $1.34 per pound. A futures contract on coffee that matures on June 1 also costs $1.34.
    (a) To hedge his position in coffee, should Mr. Valdez buy or sell futures contracts?
    (b) If a contract consists of 37,500 pounds of coffee, how many contracts does Mr. Valdez need to buy or sell to hedge his position perfectly?
    (c) Show the net gain or loss if the price of coffee rises to $1.50 per pound on July 1.
    (d) Show the net gain or loss if the price of coffee falls to $1.20 per pound.

13. The spot price for a T-bill that matures in 91 days is 98.875 while the spot price for a T-bill that matures in 273 days is 95.125.
    (a) Calculate the theoretical price of a futures contract for a 182-day T-bill with delivery in 91 days.
    (b) Recompute your answer in (a) assuming that there is a round-trip commission cost of $0.006 per $100 of face value.

14. Because the yield curve was upward sloping, Friendly Bank decided it would be more profitable to finance three-year car loans with a six-month CD. Since a car loan matures in three years and a CD in only six months, it will be necessary for the bank to roll over or issue additional CDs to keep the load funded.
    (a) If Friendly Bank forecasts an increase in future short-term interest rates, should it use a long or short hedge to maximize the return on its loan?
    (b) Assume that the bank has two hundred $10,000 car loans to finance. How many CD futures does it need to buy or sell?

15. Assume that Friendly Bank has financed a six-month commercial loan using the funds from a five-year CD. When the loan matures in six months, the bank will relend the money to another company for another six months.
    (a) If the yield curve is inverted (downward sloping), should Friendly Bank use a long or a short hedge?
    (b) Carefully explain how this will work.

APPENDIX 13A: FUTURES-CONTRACT SPECIFICATIONS

Futures-contract specifications vary by commodity and by exchange. Table 13A–1 on pages 433–440 lists contract specifications for most of the important commodities traded on the major North-American exchanges.

TABLE 13A–1 Contract Specifications for Commodity and Financial Futures

Exchange	Commodity	Trading Months	Trading Hours (Central Time)	Contract Size	Price Quoted In	Minimum Price Fluctuation	Daily Limit
Chicago Board of Trade	Iced broilers	Jan/Feb/Mar/Apr/ Sept/Oct/Nov	9:15–1:05	30,000 lbs	¢/lb	2.5/100¢/lb = $7.50	2¢ = $600
	Corn	Mar/May/July/Sept/Dec	9:30–1:15	5,000 bu	¢/bu	1/4¢/bu = $12.50	10¢ = $500
	GNMA	Mar/May/June/Sept/ Oct/Nov/Dec	8:00–2:00	$100,000 principal	32nds per point	1/32 point = $31.25	64/32 = $2,000
	Gold	All months	8:25–1:35	100 troy oz	$/oz	10¢/oz = $10.00	$25 = $2,500
	Oats	Mar/May/July/ Sept/Dec	9:30–1:15	5,000 bu	¢/bu	1/4¢/bu = $12.50	6¢ = $300
	Plywood	Jan/Mar/May/July/ Sept/Nov	9:00–1:00	76,032 sq ft	$/thousand sq ft	10¢/1000 sq ft = $7.60 (1 pt = 76¢)	$7 = $532 (700 pts)
	Silver	Feb/Apr/June/Aug/ Oct/Dec	8:40–1:25	5,000 troy oz	¢/oz	1/10¢/oz = $5	40¢ = $2000
	Soybeans	Jan/Mar/May/July/ Aug/Sept/Nov	9:30–1:15	5,000 bu	¢/bu	1/4¢/bu = $12.50	30¢ = $1,500
	Soybean meal	Jan/Mar/May/July/ Aug/Sept/Oct/Dec	9:30–1:15	100 tons (200,000 lbs)	$/ton	10¢/ton = $10	$10 = $1,000
	Soybean oil	Jan/Mar/May/July/ Aug/Sept/Oct/Dec	9:30–1:15	60,000 lbs	¢/lb	1/100¢/lb = $6	1¢ = $600 (100 pts)
	Long-term U.S. Treasury bonds	Mar/June/Sept/Dec	8:00–2:00	Bonds with face value at maturity of $100,000 and coupon rate of 8%	32nds per point	1/32nd of a point = $31.25	64/32 = $2,000
	Wheat	Mar/May/July/Sept/Dec	9:30–1:15	5,000 bu	¢/bu	1/4¢/bu = $12.50	20¢ = $1,000
	Silver	Feb/Apr/June/Aug/ Oct/Dec	8:40–1:25	1,000 troy oz	¢/oz	1/10¢/oz = $1	40¢ = $400

Source: Archer Commodities, Inc.

TABLE 13A–1 (continued)

Exchange	Commodity	Trading Months	Trading Hours (Central Time)	Contract Size	Price Quoted In	Minimum Price Fluctuation	Daily Limit
MidAmerica Commodity Exchange	Corn	Mar/May/July/Sept/Dec	9:30–1:30	1,000 bu	¢/bu	1/8¢/bu = $1.25	10¢ = $100
	Gold	Mar/June/Sept/Dec	8:25–1:40	33.2 (troy oz)	$/oz	2.5¢/troy oz = $0.83	50¢ = $1,660
	Hogs	Feb/Apr/June/July/Aug/Oct/Dec	9:15–1:05	15,000 lbs	¢/lb	2.5/100¢/lb = $3.75 (1 pt = $1.50)	1.5¢ = $225 (150 pts)
	Oats	Mar/May/July/Sept/Dec	9:30–1:30	5,000 bu	¢/bu	1/8¢/bu = $6.25	6¢ = $300
	Silver	Feb/Apr/June/Aug/Oct/Dec/Spot	8:40–1:40	1,000 troy oz	¢/oz	5/100¢/oz = $0.50	40¢ = $400
	Cattle	Jan/Feb/Apr/June/Aug/Oct/Dec	9:05–1:00	20,000 lbs	¢/lb	2.5/100¢/lb = $5 (1 pt = $2)	1.5¢ = $300 (150 pts)
	Soybeans	Jan/Mar/May/July/Aug/Sept/Nov	9:30–1:30	1,000 bu	¢/bu	1/8¢/bu = $1.25	30¢ = $300
	Wheat	Mar/May/July/Sept/Dec	9:30–1:30	1,000 bu	¢/bu	1/8¢/bu = $1.25	20¢ = $200
Chicago Mercantile Exchange	Boneless beef	Feb/Apr/June/Aug/Oct/Dec	9:05–12:45	38,000 lbs	$/cwt	2.5/100¢/lb = $9.50 (1 pt = $3.80)	1.5¢ = $570 (150 pts)
	Broilers, fresh	Feb/Apr/June/Jul/Aug/Oct/Dec	9:10–1:00	30,000 lbs	¢/lb	2.5/100¢/lb = $7.50 (1 pt = $3.00)	2¢ = $600 (200 pts)
	Butter	Mar/May/Oct/Nov/Dec	9:25–12:35	38,000 lbs	¢/lb	2.5/100¢/lb = $9.50 (1 pt = $3.80)	1.5¢ = $570 (150 pts)
	Cattle, feeder	Jan/Mar/Apr/May/Aug/Sept/Oct/Nov	9:05–12:45	42,000 lbs	¢/lb	2.5/100¢/lb = $10.50 (1 pt = $4.20)	1.5¢ = $630 (150 pts)
	Cattle, live	Jan/Feb/Apr/June/Aug/Oct/Dec	9:05–12:45	40,000 lbs	¢/lb	2.5/100¢/lb = $10 (1 pt = $4)	1.5¢ = $600 (150 pts)

TABLE 13A–1 *(continued)*

Exchange	Commodity	Trading Months	Trading Hours (Central Time)	Contract Size	Price Quoted In	Minimum Price Fluctuation	Daily Limit
Chicago Mercantile Exchange (continued)	Eggs, shell (fresh)	All months except Aug	9:20–1:00	22,500 doz	¢/doz	5/100¢/doz = $11.25 (1 pt = $2.25)	2¢ = $450 (200 pts)
	Eggs, frozen	Jan/Sept/Oct/Nov/Dec	9:20–1:00	36,000 lbs	¢/lb	2.5/100¢/lb = $9 (1 pt = $3.60)	1.5¢ = $540 (150 pts)
	Eggs, nest run	All months	9:20–1:00	22,500 doz	¢/doz	5/100¢/doz = $11.25 (1 pt = $2.25)	2¢ = $450 (200 pts)
	Hams, skinned	Mar/July/Nov	9:10–1:00	36,000 lbs	¢/lb	2.5/100¢/lb = $9 (1 pt = $3.60)	1.5¢ = $540 (150 pts)
	Hogs	Feb/Apr/June/July/Aug/Oct/Dec	9:10–1:00	30,000 lbs	¢/lb	2.5/100¢/lb = $7.50 (1 pt = $3)	1.5¢ = $450 (150 pts)
	Lumber	Jan/Mar/May/July/Sept/Nov	9:00–1:05	100,000 board feet	$/thousand board ft	10¢/1,000 bd ft = $10 (1 pt = $1)	$5 = $500 (500 pts)
	Stud lumber	Jan/Mar/May/July/Sept/Nov	9:00–1:05	100,000 board feet	$/thousand board ft	10¢/1,000 bd ft = $10 (1 pt = $1)	$5 = $500 (500 pts)
	Milo	Mar/May/July/Sept/Oct/Dec	9:30–1:15	400,000 lbs	$/cwt	2.5/100¢/cwt = $10 (1 pt = $4.00)	15¢ = $600 (15 pts)
	Pork bellies	Feb/Mar/May/July/Aug	9:10–1:00	38,000 lbs	¢/lb	2.5/100¢/lb = $9.50 (1 pt = $3.80)	2¢ = $760 (200 pts)
	Potatoes, russet Burbank	Jan/Mar/May/Nov	9:00–1:00	80,000 lbs	¢/cwt	1¢/cwt = $8 (1 pt = $8.00)	50¢ = $400** (50 pts)
	Turkeys	Jan/Mar/May/Aug/Oct	9:10–12:45	36,000 lbs	¢/lb	2.5/100¢/lb = $9 (1 pt = $3.60)	1.5¢ = $540 (150 pts)

435

TABLE 13A-1 (*continued*)

Exchange	Commodity	Trading Months	Trading Hours (Central Time)	Contract Size	Price Quoted In	Minimum Price Fluctuation	Daily Limit
International Monetary Market of the Chicago Mercantile Exchange	Copper	Jan/Mar/May/July/Sept/Nov	8:45–1:15	12,500 lbs	¢/lb	10/100¢/lb = $12.50 (1 pt = $1.25)	5¢ = $625 (500 pts)
	Currencies:						
	British pound	Jan/Mar/Apr/Jun/Jul/Sept/Oct/Dec & Spot	7:30–1:24	25,000 BP	¢/BP	.0005/lb = $12.50 (1 pt = $2.50)	5¢ = $1,250 (500 pts)
	Canadian dollar	Jan/Mar/Apr/Jun/Jul/Sept/Oct/Dec & Spot	7:30–1:22	100,000 CD	¢/CD	.0001/CD = $10 (1 pt = $10)	3/4¢ = $750 (75 pts)
	French franc	Jan/Mar/Apr/Jun/Jul/Sept/Oct/Dec & Spot	7:30–1:28	250,000 FF	¢/FF	5/1000¢/FF = $12.50 (1 pt = $2.50)	1/2¢ = $1,250 (500 pts)
	Deutschmark	Jan/Mar/Apr/Jun/Jul/Sept/Oct/Dec & Spot	7:30–1:20	125,000 DM	¢/DM	.0001/DM = $12.50 (1 pt = $12.50)	.0100 = $1,250 (100 pts)
	Japanese yen	Jan/Mar/Apr/Jun/Jul/Sept/Oct/Dec & Spot	7:30–1:26	12,500,000 Yen	¢/Yen	.000001/Y = $12.50 (1 pt = $12.50)	.0001 = $1,250 (100 pts)
	Mexican peso	Jan/Mar/Apr/Jun/Jul/Sept/Oct/Dec & Spot	7:30–1:18	1,000,000 Peso	¢/Peso	.00001/P = $10 (1 pt = $10)	3/20¢ = $1,500 (150 pts)
	Swiss franc	Jan/Mar/Apr/Jun/Jul/Sept/Oct/Dec & Spot	8:45–1:13	125,000 SF	¢/SF	1/100¢/SF = $12.50 (1 pt = $12.50)	3/5¢ = $1,875 (150 pts)
	Gold	Jan/Mar/Apr/Jun/Jul/Sept/Oct/Dec & Spot	8:25–1:30	100 troy oz	$/oz	10¢/oz = $10 (1 pt = $1)	$50 = $5,000 (5000 pts)
	U.S. silver coins	Mar/June/Sept/Dec	8:50–1:25	$5,000 (5 bags @ $1,000)	$/bag	$2/bag = $10 (1 pt = $1)	$150 = $750 (150 pts)

TABLE 13A–1 (continued)

Exchange	Commodity	Trading Months	Trading Hours (Central Time)	Contract Size	Price Quoted In	Minimum Price Fluctuation	Daily Limit
International Monetary Market of the Chicago Mercantile Exchange (continued)	Treasury bills, 13-week	Jan/Mar/Apr/Jun/Jul/Sept/Oct/Dec	8:00–1:40	$1,000,000	Basis point (IMM Index)	.01 (1 basis point = $25)	60 pts = $1,250 (60 pts)
	Treasury bills, 1-year	Mar/June/Sept/Oct	8:15–1:35	250,000	Basis point (IMM Index)	(1 basis point = $25)	50 pts = $1,250
	Treasury notes, 4-year	Feb/May/Aug/Nov	8:20–1:55	$100,000		.01 (in 64ths of 1%, 1 pt = $15.62)	48 = $750
Commodity Exchange (Comex)	Copper	Jan/Feb/Mar/May/July/Sept/Dec	8:50–1:00	25,000 lbs	¢/lb	$5/100¢/lb = 12.50 (1 pt = $2.50)	5¢ = $1,250 (500 pts)
	GNMA	Jan/Feb/Apr/July/Oct/Dec	8:00–2:30	$100,000	$\$/\frac{1}{64}$	$\frac{1}{64} = \$15.62$	$\frac{64}{64} = \$1,000$
	Gold	Jan/Feb/Apr/June/Aug/Oct/Dec	8:25–1:30	3 kilo (100 troy oz)	$/oz	10¢/oz = $10	$25 = $2,500
	Silver	Jan/Feb/Mar/May/July/Sept/Dec	8:40–1:15	5,000 troy oz	¢/oz	10/100¢/oz = $25.00	50¢ = $2,500
	Treasury bills	Feb/May/Aug/Nov	8:00–2:30	$1,000,000	Basis point (Comex Index)	.01 = $25	60 pts = $1,500
	Treasury notes, 2-year	Mar/June/Sept/Dec	8:00–2:30	$100,000	$\$/\frac{1}{64}$	$\frac{1}{64} = \$15.62$	$\frac{64}{64} = \$1,000$
	Zinc	Jan/Feb/Mar/May/July/Sept/Dec	9:15–11:45	60,000 lbs	¢/lb	$5/100¢/lb = 30 (1 pt = $6.00)	3¢ = $1,800 (300 pts)

TABLE 13A–1 (continued)

Exchange	Commodity	Trading Months	Trading Hours (Central Time)	Contract Size	Price Quoted In	Minimum Price Fluctuation	Daily Limit
New York Coffee Sugar & Cocoa Exchange	Cocoa	Mar/May/July/Sept/Dec	8:30–2:00	10 metric tons	¢/ton	$1.00/ton = $10.00 (1 pt = $10.00)	$88 = $880 (88 pts)
	Coffee "C"	Mar/May/July/Sept/Dec	8:45–1:30	37,500 lbs	¢/lb	1/100¢/lb = $3.75 (1 pt = $3.75)	4¢ = $1,500 (400 pts)
	Coffee "B"	Mar/May/July/Sept/Dec	8:45–1:30	32,500 lbs	¢/lb	1/100¢/lb = $3.25 (1 pt = $3.25)	4¢ = $1,300 (400 pts)
	Sugar No. 11 (world)	Jan/Mar/May/July/Sept/ Oct	9:00–1:45	112,000 lbs	¢/lb (1 pt = $11.20)	1/100¢/lb = $11.20 (100 pts)	½¢ = $560 (50 pts)
	Sugar No. 12 (domestic)	Jan/Mar/May/July/Sept/ Nov	9:00–1:45	112,000 lbs	¢/lb	1/100¢/lb = $11.20 (1 pt = $11.20)	½¢ = $560 (50 pts)
New York Cotton Exchange	Cotton No. 2	All months	9:30–2:00	50,000 lbs	¢/lb	1/100¢/lb = $5 (1 pt = $5)	2¢ = $1,000 (200 pts)
	Crude oil	Mar/June/Sept/Dec	8:50–1:20	5,000 barrels	¢/barrel	1/10¢/barrel = $5	25¢ = $1,250 (250 pts)
	Orange juice	Jan/Mar/May/July/Sept/ Nov	9:15–1:45	15,000 lbs	¢/lb	5/100¢/lb = $7.50 (1 pt = $1.50)	5¢ = $750 (500 pts)
	Propane, liquified	Jan/Mar/May/July/Sept/ Dec	8:45–1:35	100,000 gals	¢/gal	1/100¢/gal = $10 (1 pt = $10)	1¢ = $1,000 (100 pts)
New York Mercantile Exchange	Gold	Jan/Mar/May/July/Sept/ Dec	8:25–1:30	1 kilo (32 troy oz)	$/oz	20¢/oz = $6.40	$24 = $768
	Gold, 400 oz	Mar/June/Sept/Dec	8:25–1:30	400 oz bar (four 100 oz bars) (12 or 13 kilo bars)	$/oz	5¢/oz = $20	$25 = $10,000
	Imported boneless beef	Jan/Mar/May/July/Sept/ Nov	9:15–12:45	36,000 lbs	$/100 lbs (or ¢/lb)	2¢/100 lbs = $7.20 (1 pt = $3.60)	$1.50 = $540 (150 pts)

TABLE 13A–1 *(continued)*

Exchange	Commodity	Trading Months	Trading Hours (Central Time)	Contract Size	Price Quoted In	Minimum Price Fluctuation	Daily Limit
New York Mercantile Exchange (continued)	Oil, heating No. 2	Jan/Feb/Mar/May/July/Aug/Sept/Nov/Dec	9:30–1:45	42,000 gal	¢/gal	$.0001/gal = $4.20	.02/gal = $840
	Oil, industrial No. 6	Jan/Feb/Mar/May/July/Sept/Nov/Dec	9:35–1:43	42,000 gal	¢/gal	$.0001/gal = $4.20	.02/gal = $840
	Palladium	Jan/Apr/July/Oct	8:35–1:20	100 troy oz	$/oz	5¢/oz = $5	$6 = $360 (600 pts)
	Platinum	Jan/Apr/July/Oct	8:30–1:30	50 troy oz	$/oz	10¢/oz = $5	$20 = $1,000
	Potatoes, Maine and round white	Mar/Apr/May/Nov	9:00–1:00	50,000 lbs	$/100 lbs (or ¢/lb)	1¢/100 lbs = $5 (1 pt = $5)	50¢ = $250 (50 pts)
	U.S. silver coins	Jan/Apr/July/Oct	8:40–1:15	$10,000 (10 bags @ $1,000)	$/bag	$1/bag = $10	$150 = $3,000 ($300 per bag)
New York Futures Exchange NYFE	U.S. Treasury bond, 20-year	Feb/May/Aug/Nov	8:00–2:00	$100,000	32nds per pt	1/32 of a point = $31.25	96/32 (3 pts) = $3,000
	Treasury bills, 90-day	Jan/Apr/July/Oct	8:00–2:00	$1,000,000	.01 (1 Basis Point)	.01 = $25	1.00 (100 Basis Points)
	British pound	Feb/May/Aug/Nov	7:30–1:30	25,000 BP	¢/Pound	.0005 (5 pts) = $12.50	No Limit
	Canadian dollar	Feb/May/Aug/Nov	7:30–1:30	100,000 CD	¢/CD	.0001/CD = $10 (1 pt = $10)	No Limit
	Deutschmark	Feb/May/Aug/Nov	7:30–1:30	125,000 DM	¢/DM	.0001/DM = $10 (1 pt = $10)	No Limit
	Japanese yen	Feb/May/Aug/Nov	7:30–1:30	12,500,000	¢/Yen	.000001 (1 pt = $12.50)	No Limit
	Swiss franc	Feb/May/Aug/Nov	7:30–1:30	125,000	¢/SF	.0001 = $10 (1 pt = $12.50)	No Limit

TABLE 13A–1 (continued)

Exchange	Commodity	Trading Months	Trading Hours (Central Time)	Contract Size	Price Quoted In	Minimum Price Fluctuation	Daily Limit
Minneapolis Grain Exchange	Spring wheat	Mar/May/July/Sept/Dec	9:30–1:15	5,000 bu	¢/bu	1/8¢/bu = $6.25	20¢ = $1,000
	Sunflower seed	Jan/Mar/May/July/Nov	9:30–2:15	100,000 lbs	¢/lb	1¢/lb = $10	50¢ = $500
Kansas City Board of Trade	Milo	Mar/May/July/Sept/Dec	9:30–1:15	5,000 bu	¢/bu	1/4¢/bu = $12.50	10¢ = $500
	Wheat (hard red winter)	Mar/May/July/Sept/Dec	9:30–1:15	5,000 bu	¢/bu	1/4¢/bu = $12.50	25¢ = $1,250
Winnipeg Commodity Exchange	Barley	May/July/Oct/Dec	9:30–1:15	20 metric tons	$/ton	10¢/ton = $10	$5 = $1,000
	Flaxseed	May/July/Oct/Nov/Dec	9:30–1:15	20 metric tons	$/ton	10¢/ton = $10	$10 = $2,000
	Gold, centum	Feb/May/Aug/Nov	8:15–1:30	100 oz	$/oz	5¢/oz = $5	$10 = $1,000
	Gold, standard	Jan/Apr/July/Oct	8:15–1:30	400 oz	$/oz	5¢/oz = $20	$10 = $4,000
	Oats	May/July/Oct/Dec	9:30–1:15	20 metric tons	$/ton	10¢/ton = $10	$5 = $1,000
	Rapeseed (Vancouver)	Jan/Mar/June/Sept/Nov	9:30–1:15	20 metric tons	$/ton	10¢/ton = $10	$10 = $2,000
	Rye	May/July/Oct/Nov/Dec	9:30–1:15	20 metric tons	$/ton	10¢/ton = $10	$5 = $1,000
	Wheat	May/July/Oct/Dec	9:30–1:15	20 metric tons	$/ton	10¢/ton = $10	$5 = $1,000

REFERENCES

Anderson, R. W., and J. P. Danthine. "Cross-hedging." *Journal of Political Economy,* v. 89 (November/December 1981), pp. 1182–96.

Bacon, P. W., and R. Williams. "Interest Rate Futures: New Tools for the Financial Manager." *Financial Management,* v. 5 (Spring 1976), pp. 32–38.

Benninga, S., and M. Smirlock. "An Empirical Analysis of the Delivery Option, Marking to Market and the Pricing of T-Bond Futures." *Journal of Futures Markets,* v. 5 (Fall 1985), pp. 361–74.

Black, F. L. "The Pricing of Commodity Contracts." *Journal of Financial Economics,* v. 3 (June 1976), pp. 167–79.

Capozza, D., and B. Cornell. "Treasury Bill Pricing in the Spot and Futures Markets." *Review of Economics and Statistics,* v. 61 (November 1979), pp. 513–20.

Cassel, G. "The Present Situation of Foreign Exchange I." *Economic Journal,* v. 26 (March 1916), pp. 62–65.

———. "The Present Situation of Foreign Exchange II." *Economic Journal,* v. 26 (September 1916), pp. 319–23.

Cornell, B., and K. French. "The Pricing of Stock Index Futures." *Journal of Futures Markets,* v. 3 (March 1983), pp. 1–14.

———. "Taxes and the Pricing of Stock Index Futures." *Journal of Finance,* v. 38 (June 1983), pp. 675–94.

Cornell, B., and M. Reinganum. "Forward and Futures Prices: Evidence from the Foreign Exchange Markets." *Journal of Finance,* v. 36 (September 1981), pp. 1035–45.

Cox, J., J. Ingersoll, Jr., and S. Ross. "The Relation Between Forward and Futures Prices." *Journal of Financial Economics,* v. 9 (September 1981), pp. 321–46.

Duncan, W. H. "Treasury Bill Futures: Opportunities and Pitfalls." *Review,* Federal Reserve Bank of Dallas (July 1977), pp. 1–5.

Ederington, L. "The Hedging Performance of the New Futures Markets." *Journal of Finance,* v. 34 (March 1979), pp. 157–70.

Fabozzi, F., and G. Kipnis. *Stock Index Futures.* Dow Jones-Irwin, 1984.

Figlewski, S. "Hedging with Stock Index Futures: Theory and Application in a New Market." *Journal of Futures Markets,* v. 5 (Summer 1985), pp. 183–200.

Figlewski, S., and S. J. Kon. "Portfolio Management with Stock Index Futures." *Financial Analysts Journal,* v. 20 (January/February 1982), pp. 52–60.

Finnerty, J., and H. Park. "Does the Tail Wag the Dog?" *Financial Analysts Journal,* v. 43, (March/April 1987), pp. 57–60.

Fisher, I. *The Rate of Interest*. Macmillan, 1907.

Francis, J., and M. Castelino. "Basis Speculation in Commodity Futures: The Maturity Effect." *Journal of Futures Markets*, v. 2 (Summer 1982), pp. 195–206.

Gay, R., R. Kolb, and R. Chiang. "Interest Rate Hedging: An Empirical Test of Alternate Strategies." *Journal of Financial Research*, v. 6 (March 1983), pp. 187–97.

———, and D. J. S. Rutledge. "The Economics of Commodity Futures Markets: A Survey." *Review of Marketing and Agricultural Economics*, v. 34 (March 1971), pp. 57–108.

Hansen, L. P., and R. J. Hordrick. "Forward Exchange Rates as Optimal Predictors of Future Spot Rates: An Econometric Analysis." *Journal of Political Economy*, v. 88 (October 1980), pp. 829–53.

Hill, J., and T. Schneeweis. "Reducing Volatility with Financial Futures." *Financial Analysts Journal*, v. 40 (November/December 1984), pp. 34–40.

Hilliard, J. "Hedging Interest Rate Risk with Futures Portfolios under Term Structure Effects." *Journal of Finance*, v. 39 (December 1984), pp. 1547–70.

Junkus, J. C., and C. F. Lee. "Use of Three Stock Index Futures In Hedging Decisions." *J. Futures Markets*, v. 5 (Summer 1985), pp. 201–22.

Kamara, A. "Issues in Futures Markets: A Survey." *Journal of Futures Markets*, v. 2 (Fall 1982), pp. 261–94.

Keynes, J. M. *A Treatise on Money*. Macmillan, 1930.

Khoury, S. *Speculative Markets*. Macmillan, 1984.

Kolb, R. *Understanding Futures Markets*. Scott, Foresman and Co., 1985.

———, and R. Chiang. "Duration, Immunization, and Hedging with Interest Rate Futures." In *Interest Rate Futures Concepts and Issues*, ed. G. D. Gay and R. W. Kolb, pp. 353–64.

———. "Improving Performance Using Interest Rate Futures." *Financial Management*, v. 10 (Autumn 1981), pp. 77–85.

Laufman, P. *Handbook of Futures Markets: Commodity, Financial Stock Indices and Options*. John Wiley and Sons, 1986.

Loosigian, A. M. *Interest Rate Futures*. Dow Jones-Irwin, 1980.

Modest, D. M., and M. Sundaresan. "The Relationship Between Spot and Futures Prices in Stock-Index Futures Markets: Some Preliminary Evidence." *Journal of Futures Markets*, v. 3 (Spring 1983), pp. 15–42.

Nelson, R., and R. Collins. "A Measure of Hedging Performance." *Journal of Futures Markets*, v. 5, (Spring 1985), pp. 45–55.

Poole, W. "Using T-Bill Futures to Gauge Interest Rate Expectations." *Economic Review*, Federal Reserve Bank of San Francisco (Spring 1978), pp. 7–19.

Powers, M. *Inside the Financial Futures Markets*. John Wiley and Sons, 1984.

Rendleman, R., and C. Carabini. "The Efficiency of the T-Bill Futures." *Journal of Finance,* v. 34 (September 1979), pp. 895–914.

Rishard, S., and M. Sundaresan. "A Continuous Time Equilibrium Model of Forward Prices and Futures Prices in a Multigood Economy." *Journal of Financial Economics,* v. 9 (September 1981), pp. 347–72.

Rothstein, N., ed. *Handbook of Financial Futures*. McGraw-Hill, 1986.

Rutledge, D. J. S. "Hedgers' Demand for Futures Contracts: A Theoretical Framework with Applications to the United States Soybean Complex." *Food Research Institute Studies,* v. 11 (March 1972), pp. 237–56.

Schwarz, E., J. Hill, and T. Schneeweis. *Financial Futures: Fundamental Strategies and Applications*. Irwin, 1986.

Senchack, A., J., Jr., and J. C. Easterwood. "Cross Hedging CDs with Treasury Bill Futures." *Journal of Futures Markets,* v. 3 (Winter 1983), pp. 429–38.

Weiner, N. S. "The Hedging Rationale for a Stock Index Futures Contract." *Journal of Futures Market,* v. 1 (Spring 1981), pp. 59–76.

14 Options and Option Strategies

The use of stock options for risk reduction and return enhancement has expanded at an astounding pace over the last twenty years. Among the causes of this growth, two are most significant. First, the establishment of the Chicago Board Option Exchange (CBOE) in 1973 brought about the liquidity necessary for successful option trading, through public listing and standardization of option contracts. The second stimulus emanated from academia. In the same year that the CBOE was established, Professors Fischer Black and Myron Scholes published a paper in which they derived a revolutionary option-pricing model. The power of their model to predict an option's fair price has since made it the industry standard.

The development of option-valuation theory shed new light on the valuation process. Previous pricing models such as CAPM were based on very stringent assumptions, such as there being an identifiable and measurable market portfolio, as well as various imputed investor attributes, such as quadratic utility functions. Furthermore, previous theory priced only market risk since investors were assumed to hold well-diversified portfolios. The strength of the Black–Scholes and subsequent option-pricing models is that they rely on far fewer assumptions. In addition, the option-valuation models price total risk and do not require any assumptions concerning the direction of the underlying securities price. The growing popularity of the option concept is evidenced by its application to the valuation of a wide array of other financial instruments (such as common stock and bonds) as well as more abstract assets including leases and real estate agreements.

This chapter aims to establish a basic knowledge of options and the markets in which they are traded. It begins with the most common types of options, calls, and puts, explaining their general characteristics and discussing the institutions where they are traded. In addition, the concepts relevant to the new types of options on indexes and futures are introduced. The next focus is the basic pricing relationship between puts and calls, known as put–call parity. The final study concerns how options can be used as invest-

ment tools. The chapter on option valuation that follows utilizes all these essential concepts to afford a deeper conceptual understanding of valuation theory.

THE OPTION MARKET AND RELATED DEFINITIONS

This section discusses option-market and related definitions of options, which are needed to understand option valuations and option strategies.

What Is an Option?

An **option** is a contract conveying the right to buy or sell a designated security at a stipulated price. The contract normally expires at a predetermined time. The most important element of an option contract is that there is no obligation placed upon the purchaser: it is an "option." This attribute of an option contract distinguishes it from other financial contracts. For instance, while the holder of an option has the opportunity to let his or her claim expire unused if so desired, futures and forward contracts obligate their parties to fulfill certain conditions.

Types of Options and Their Characteristics

A **call option** gives its owner the right to buy the underlying asset, while a **put option** conveys to its holder the right to sell the underlying asset.

An option is specified by five essential parts.

1. The type (call or put)
2. The underlying asset
3. The exercise price
4. The expiration date
5. The option price

While the most common type of underlying asset for an option is an individual stock, other underlying assets for options exist as well. These include futures contracts, foreign currencies, stock indexes, and U.S. debt instruments. In the case of common stock options (on which this discussion is exclusively centered), the specified quantity to which the option buyer is entitled to buy or sell is one hundred shares of the stock per option.

The **exercise price** (also called the **striking price**) is the price stated in the option contract at which the call (put) owner can buy (sell) the underlying asset up to the **expiration date,** the final calendar date on which the option can be traded. Options on common stocks have expiration dates three months apart in one of three fixed cycles.

1. January/April/July/October
2. February/May/August/November
3. March/June/September/December

The normal expiration date is the third Saturday of the month. (The third Friday is the last trading date for the option.)

As an example, an option referred to as an ''ABC June 25 call'' is an option to buy one hundred shares of the underlying ABC stock at $25 per share, up to its expiration date in June. Option prices are quoted on a per-share basis. Thus, a stock option that is quoted at $5 would cost $500 ($5 × 100 shares), plus commission and a nominal SEC fee.

A common distinction among options pertains to when they can be exercised. **Exercising an option** is the process of carrying out the right to buy or sell the underlying asset at the stated price. American options allow the exercise of this right at any time from when the option is purchased up to the expiration date. On the other hand, European options allow their holder the right of exercise only on the expiration date itself. The distinction between an American and European option has nothing to do with the location at which they are traded. Both types are currently bought and sold in the United States. There are distinctions in their pricing and in the possibility of exercising them prior to expiration.

Finally, when discussing options, the two parties to the contract are characterized by whether they have bought or sold the contract. The party buying the option contract (call or put) is the **option buyer** (or **holder**), while the party selling the option is the **option seller** (or **writer**). If the writer of an option does not own the underlying asset, he or she is said to write a naked option.

Figure 14–1 shows a listing of publicly traded options from *The Wall Street Journal*.

Relationships Between the Option Price and the Underlying Asset Price

A call (put) option is said to be **in the money** if the underlying asset is selling above (below) the exercise price of the option. An **at-the-money call** (put) is one whose exercise price is equal to the current price of the underlying asset. A call (put) option is **out of the money** if the underlying asset is selling below (above) the exercise price of the option.

Suppose ABC stock is selling at $30 per share. An ABC June 25 call option is in the money ($30 − 25 > 0), while an ABC June 35 call option is out of the money ($30 − 35 < 0). Of course, the expiration dates could be any month without changing the option's standing as in, at, or out of the money.

The relationship between the price of an option and the price of the underlying asset indicates both the amount of **intrinsic value** and **time value** inherent in the option's price, as shown in Equation (14.1):

FIGURE 14–1 Listed Option Quotations

LISTED OPTIONS QUOTATIONS

Friday, January 20, 1989

Options closing prices. Sales unit usually is 100 shares. Stock close is New York or American exchange final price.

MOST ACTIVE OPTIONS

CHICAGO BOARD

CALLS		Sales	Last	Chg.	N.Y. Close
SP100	Jan270	22770	1 5/8	– 1	271.66
SP100	Feb270	12223	5 1/2	– 1/2	271.66
SP100	Jan275	9981	1-16	– 1/8	271.66
I B M	Jan125	7611	1-16	– 1/8	123 3/4
SP100	Mar280	7190	3 1/4	– 1/4	271.66

PUTS		Sales	Last	Chg.	N.Y. Close
SP100	Feb270	12279	3 3/8	......	271.66
SP100	Jan270	11685	1-16	– 3-16	271.66
SP100	Feb265	10176	1 15-16	......	271.66
SP100	Jan275	7985	3 3/8	+ 5/8	271.66
SP100	Feb255	6280	5/8	– 1/8	271.66

AMERICAN

CALLS		Sales	Last	Chg.	N.Y. Close
MMIdx	Jan440	8571	1-16	– 1 3-16	438.31
Texaco	Jan55	5497	5/8	+ 3/8	55 5/8
Texaco	Apr50	4833	6 1/2	+ 5/8	55 5/8
Dig Eq	Jan105	4691	2 1/2	+ 1 15-16	107 1/4
Texaco	Apr55	4354	3 1/4	+ 3/8	55 5/8

PUTS		Sales	Last	Chg.	N.Y. Close
MMIdx	Jan440	4392	1 3/4	– 1/4	438.31
MMIdx	Feb420	4154	1 5/8	......	438.31
MMIdx	Jan435	3781	1-16	– 3/8	438.31
MMIdx	Feb430	2427	3 5/8	+ 1/8	438.31
MMIdx	Feb410	2070	7/8	+ 1-16	438.31

PHILADELPHIA

CALLS		Sales	Last	Chg.	N.Y. Close
TexEst	Feb45	4303	3 1/2	+ 1 3/8	47 3/8
USShoe	Jan25	3963	3/4	– 1/4	26
USShoe	Feb25	3841	2 1/8	– 1-16	26
TexEst	Feb50	2951	15-16	+ 5/8	47 3/8
TexEst	Apr45	2520	4 3/8	+ 1 1/8	47 3/8

PUTS		Sales	Last	Chg.	N.Y. Close
TexEst	Feb40	2036	7-16	– 1-16	47 3/8
TexEst	Feb45	1085	1	– 5-16	47 3/8
LinB	Feb75	737	1 3/8	+ 1/4	80 7/8
LinB	Feb80	414	3 1/4	+ 1/2	80 7/8
TexEst	Apr45	323	2	– 1/2	47 3/8

PACIFIC

CALLS		Sales	Last	Chg.	N.Y. Close
Marion	Jan22 1/2	4506	1-16	– 1-16	22 7/8
SmkB	Jan50	2473	1 1-16	– 9-16	51 1/4
Unocal	Jan40	1840	1 5/8	+ 1/4	41 3/4
CircK	Jan12 1/2	1492	1/4	+ 1/8	12 7/8
Gentch	Jan17 1/2	1411	1 1/8	+ 1-16	18 5/8

PUTS		Sales	Last	Chg.	N.Y. Close
Gentch	Jan20	2043	1 3/8	– 3-16	18 5/8
Gentch	Feb20	1382	1 3/4	– 1/8	18 5/8
CircK	Feb12 1/2	682	7-16	– 3-16	12 7/8
HospCp	Feb40	625	3-16	......	46 3/8
GMills	Feb55	439	1 1/8	– 1/4	55 1/8

NEW YORK

CALLS		Sales	Last	Chg.	N.Y. Close
JRiver	Mar30	1901	3/4	+ 1/8	28 5/8
Maytag	Feb20	1197	7/8	+ 1-16	20 1/8
DigCom	Feb25	965	1 11-16	+ 5/8	24 1/2
Maytag	Feb22 1/2	790	5-16	+ 1-16	20 1/8
Maytag	Jan20	750	1-16	– 1-16	20 1/8

PUTS		Sales	Last	Chg.	N.Y. Close
Maytag	Jan20	328	1-16	– 1-16	20 1/8
DigCom	Feb22 1/2	160	7/8	– 7-16	24 1/2
Maytag	Feb20	104	1/2	– 3-16	20 1/8
Maytag	Jan22 1/2	99	2 1/2	– 1/8	20 1/8
DigCom	Feb25	85	2 1/8	– 1/8	24 1/2

54 1/8	55	1/8	1 3/8	r	1 1/16	2 1/4	r
54 1/8	60	r	s	1 7/16	r	s	r
Motrla	35	7 7/8	r	8 1/2	r	r	r
43	40	2 7/8	3 3/4	4 1/4	1/16	3/8	1 1/4
43	45	r	11/16	1 5/8	2 1/4	r	3 3/4
43	50	r	s	7/16	r	s	r
Mylan	7 1/2	1 3/8	r	r	r	r	1/4
8 5/8	10	r	1/16	1/4	1	r	r
NetwSy	7 1/2	2 1/8	2 1/2	r	r	r	r
9 3/4	10	1/8	r	15/16	3/8	r	7/8
9 3/4	12 1/2	r	r	1/4	r	r	r
Nordst	25	6 1/4	r	7	r	r	r
31 3/8	30	1 1/2	2 1/4	3 1/4	r	1/2	1 3/16
31 3/8	35	1/16	r	3/4	3 1/2	r	r
PacEnt	40	r	1/4	1	1 3/4	r	r
Penwlt	95	8	r	r	r	r	r
103	100	3	5 1/4	r	1/16	1 3/8	r
103	105	1/8	2 1/2	4 3/4	1 5/8	3 1/4	r
103	110	r	1	r	r	r	r
Pnwlt o	70	33 3/4	s	r	r	s	r
103	75	28 1/8	s	r	r	s	r
103	80	23	s	r	r	s	r
103	85	18	s	r	r	s	r
103	90	12 3/4	s	r	r	s	r
103	95	8	r	r	r	r	r
103	100	2 5/8	5 1/4	7 1/2	r	1 3/8	r
103	105	1/16	2 5/8	4 5/8	2 1/8	3 1/4	r
103	110	r	1 1/4	r	6 3/4	r	r
Phelps	40	18	s	19	r	s	r
58 1/2	45	13 1/2	r	14	r	r	3/8
58 1/2	50	8 1/4	8 5/8	9 1/2	r	1/4	7/8
58 1/2	55	3 3/4	4 1/4	6 3/8	r	3/4	2 3/8
58 1/2	60	s	1 9/16	3 3/8	s	3	4 1/2
Pitney	45	1/16	r	1 5/8	1 1/8	r	r
Proc G	75	r	s	r	r	s	3/16
52 5/8	60	r	r	1/2	r	r	r
PhilPt	15	s	6 3/4	r	s	r	1/16
21 3/4	17 1/2	4 1/4	4 1/4	4 1/2	r	1/16	1/4
21 3/4	20	1 11/16	1 3/4	2 7/16	r	3/16	13/16
21 3/4	22 1/2	r	7/16	1 1/4	r	1 3/8	1 7/8
Primca	23	s	r	1 3/16	s	r	r
Quantm	40	14	r	r	r	r	r
54 1/4	45	9	9 1/2	r	r	r	7/8
54 1/4	50	4 1/4	4 7/8	6 1/4	r	1/2	1 7/8
54 1/4	55	1/16	1 1/2	3 3/4	5/8	2 1/2	4
54 1/4	60	r	7/16	2	5 1/2	6 1/2	7 1/2
54 1/4	65	r	r	1 1/4	r	r	r
RoyDut	55	4 1/2	r	r	r	r	r
59 3/4	57 1/2	2 3/8	2 3/4	4 1/4	r	r	r
59 3/4	60	1/16	1	2 1/2	r	15/16	r
Tmplln	45	r	r	r	r	r	3/8
53 1/2	55	r	1	2 5/8	r	r	r
Tennco	45	r	4 3/8	r	r	r	r
49	50	r	7/16	1 3/8	3/4	1 5/8	r
49	55	r	1/8	r	r	r	r
Torchm	30	2 1/8	r	r	r	r	r
31 7/8	35	r	r	1/2	r	r	r
UniNV	60	r	2	3 1/4	r	r	1 7/8
Varian	25	r	4 1/8	r	r	r	r
28 1/2	30	r	1 1/16	2 1/8	r	r	r
Zenith	15	4 7/8	5 1/4	r	r	r	r
20	17 1/2	2 1/2	2 3/4	3 7/8	r	1/4	5/8
20	20	1/16	15/16	2 1/4	1/8	3/4	1 7/8
20	22 1/2	s	7/16	1 3/16	s	r	r
20	25	s	1/4	5/8	s	r	r
		Jan	**Apr**	**Jul**	**Jan**	**Apr**	**Jul**
Inco	15	14 3/8	r	r	r	r	r

Total call vol 225,221 **Call open int** 1,951,452
Total put vol 70,744 **Put open int** 605,297

OhMatt	15	4	4 1/8	4 3/4	r	r	r
19 1/4	17 1/2	1 7/8	2	2 3/4	r	r	13/16
19 1/4	20	1/16	3/4	1 7/16	7/8	1 1/4	r
19 1/4	22 1/2	s	1/4	1/2	s	r	r
P H M	10	7/8	r	r	r	r	r
Panhdl	25	1 1/4	1 1/2	r	r	r	r
26 1/8	30	r	1/4	3/8	r	r	r
QkrOat	45	10 1/4	r	r	r	r	r
55 1/8	50	5	6	6 1/2	r	r	r
55 1/8	55	1/16	1 3/8	3 1/4	1/16	1	1 5/8
55 1/8	60	r	s	1	r	s	r
55 1/8	65	r	s	3/8	r	s	r
RiteA	30	2 3/8	r	r	r	r	r
Salomn	20	6 1/2	s	r	r	s	r
26 3/8	22 1/2	3 5/8	r	4 3/8	r	r	r
26 3/8	25	1	1 3/4	2 1/4	r	5/16	r
26 3/8	30	1/16	1/8	1/2	3 7/8	r	r
ScotP	35	4 3/4	5 1/4	r	r	r	r
40	40	1/16	1 1/8	1 7/8	r	r	r
40	45	r	r	1/2	r	r	r
SvMrch	10	7 7/8	s	r	r	s	r
17 7/8	12 1/2	5 1/8	s	5 3/4	r	s	r
17 7/8	15	2 3/4	3 1/4	3 5/8	r	r	r
17 7/8	17 1/2	3/16	1 1/4	r	r	3/4	r
17 7/8	20	r	7/16	1	r	r	r
SupVal	20	4 3/4	r	r	r	r	r
24 7/8	22 1/2	2 1/8	2 3/4	r	r	r	r
24 7/8	25	1/16	3/4	1 3/8	3/8	r	r
TexEst	25	r	21 1/8	22 1/8	r	r	r
47 3/8	30	17 1/8	17 3/4	17	1/8	1/8	r
47 3/8	35	12 1/8	11 5/8	12 1/4	r	3/16	r
47 3/8	40	7	8	8 1/2	r	7/16	7/8
47 3/8	45	s	3 1/2	4 3/8	s	1	2
47 3/8	50	s	15/16	1 1/2	s	3 1/2	4
TycoLb	30	3 1/2	r	r	r	3/16	r
33 1/2	35	r	1/2	1 1/4	1 5/8	r	2 1/8
USF&G	25	r	r	5 3/8	r	r	r
30	30	1/16	1/2	11/16	1/8	r	r
30	35	r	r	r	5	r	r
USShoe	20	6	6 1/8	7	r	r	r
26	22 1/2	3 3/8	3 7/8	5 1/2	r	1/4	3/4
26	25	3/4	2 1/8	3 1/4	1/16	7/8	1 5/8
26	30	1/16	1/2	7/8	r	4	4 3/4
		Jan	**Feb**	**May**	**Jan**	**Feb**	**May**
Abbt L	45	1 1/2	2 3/8	r	r	r	1 1/8
46 3/4	50	r	1/4	1 1/16	r	r	3 7/8
A Hess	30	3 3/8	3 3/4	4 3/4	r	1/16	1/2
33 1/2	35	1/16	9/16	1 9/16	r	r	2 1/4
Armco	10	1	1	1 3/8	r	r	1/2
10 7/8	12 1/2	r	1/16	1/2	r	r	r
AutDt	35	4 1/4	r	r	r	r	r
39 1/2	40	1/16	13/16	2	1	3/4	r
39 1/2	45	r	1/16	r	r	r	r
BkBost	22 1/2	r	r	r	r	r	3/4
23 7/8	25	r	1/2	r	1	1 1/2	2
BurlRs	30	7 3/8	8 3/4	r	r	r	1/4
38 3/4	35	3 7/8	4 1/8	6 3/8	r	5/16	1
38 3/4	40	r	1 3/8	3 1/8	r	2	r
CinMil	20	r	3 3/8	r	r	r	r
23 3/8	25	s	1/4	r	s	2	r
Cmdrln	10	3 1/2	3 7/8	4 1/8	r	r	r
13 3/4	12 1/2	1 1/2	1 1/2	2 5/16	r	r	r
13 3/4	15	r	7/16	1 1/8	r	r	r
CntlCp	35	r	r	7/8	r	r	r
CoopTr	20	3 5/8	r	4 3/4	r	r	r
23 7/8	22 1/2	1 1/4	2	r	r	r	5/8
23 7/8	25	r	13/16	1 3/4	1 3/8	1 3/4	r
23 7/8	30	r	1/4	r	r	r	r
GSignl	50	1/4	r	r	1/4	r	r
GaGulf	65	17 7/8	r	r	r	r	r
83 7/8	70	13	r	r	r	1/8	r
83 7/8	75	9	9 3/4	10 1/4	r	1/4	2
83 7/8	80	4 1/4	5 1/4	8	1/16	1 3/8	r
83 7/8	85	s	2 1/2	5 3/4	s	2 3/4	r
GoldWF	35	1/8	7/8	r	r	r	r
Harnis	17 1/2	r	r	7/8	r	r	r
17 1/8	20	s	r	1/2	s	r	r
HomeD	30	1/8	1 1/8	2 3/4	1/16	7/8	r
30	35	1/8	r	r	r	r	r
Lehman	15	r	r	r	r	r	3 1/8
LinB	50	r	r	r	r	r	1/4
80 7/8	55	28	r	28 5/8	r	1/8	5/16
80 7/8	60	r	r	22 3/4	r	1/8	1/4
80 7/8	65	15 1/4	16 1/4	18 1/2	r	3/16	r
80 7/8	70	10 3/8	11 1/2	16 1/4	r	7/16	1 5/8
80 7/8	75	5 1/4	7 1/2	11 5/8	r	1 3/8	2 3/4
80 7/8	80	s	4 7/8	7 3/4	s	3 1/4	4 7/8
80 7/8	85	s	2 3/4	5 3/8	s	5 3/4	r
80 7/8	90	s	1 3/4	4 1/4	s	9	9 3/4
La Lnd	35	r	r	r	r	r	2 1/8
Lubriz	35	15/16	1 7/8	r	r	r	r
36	40	r	r	r	r	r	3 7/8
M C A	40	7 5/8	8	r	r	1/16	r
47 3/4	45	2 7/16	3 3/8	5 1/2	r	5/8	r
47 3/4	50	1/16	1 1/8	3 1/4	r	r	4 1/4
47 3/4	55	s	3/8	1 3/8	s	r	r
McDln	15	2	2	2 1/4	r	r	r
17	17 1/2	r	r	3/4	r	r	1 1/4
17	20	s	r	1/4	s	r	r
McGHll	60	10 1/2	9 3/4	12 1/4	r	5/16	r
64 3/8	70	r	5/8	2 1/8	5 7/8	r	7
Daisy	7 1/2	r	1/8	1/2	1 3/8	r	r
Datapd	10	3 3/8	r	4 1/8	r	r	r
13 3/4	12 1/2	1 1/4	2	2 3/8	r	3/8	r
13 3/4	15	r	11/16	1 3/8	1 1/8	1 7/8	r
DayHud	40	1	1 11/16	2 5/8	r	11/16	1
41 1/8	45	r	r	3/4	r	r	r
Deluxe	20	6	s	s	r	s	s
26 1/2	25	1 1/4	1 3/8	2	r	1/4	r
26 1/2	30	r	r	3/16	r	r	r
EchoB	12 1/2	2 5/8	r	r	r	r	1/8
15 1/4	15	3/16	7/8	1 3/8	1/16	r	7/8
15 1/4	17 1/2	r	s	3/8	2 1/2	s	r
15 1/4	20	r	s	1/8	r	s	5 1/8
Ethyl	20	2 1/2	2 3/4	r	r	r	r
22 5/8	22 1/2	1/16	9/16	1	1/8	r	1
22 5/8	25	r	r	1/4	r	r	r
FMogul	50	1/8	r	3 1/4	1/16	r	r
50 1/4	55	r	5/8	1 3/8	r	r	r
FedPap	20	r	1 7/8	r	r	r	r
FUnion	20	1	r	r	r	r	r
FostWh	12 1/2	2 3/8	r	r	r	r	r
14 7/8	15	1/16	3/8	r	1/8	r	r
Gannett	30	6 1/2	r	r	r	r	r
36 1/2	35	1 5/8	1 3/4	2 3/4	r	r	5/8
Gentch	12 1/2	r	s	6 1/4	r	s	1/8
18 5/8	15	3 5/8	3 5/8	4 1/8	r	r	5/16
18 5/8	17 1/2	1 1/8	1 1/2	2 3/8	r	3/8	13/16
18 5/8	20	1/16	7/16	1 1/8	1 3/8	1 3/4	2 1/8
18 5/8	22 1/2	r	s	1/2	3 7/8	s	4 1/8
18 5/8	25	r	s	3/16	6 3/8	s	r
GMills	50	5 1/4	5 1/2	6	r	r	5/8
55 1/8	55	1/16	1 3/8	2 1/2	1/8	1 1/8	2
55 1/8	60	r	1/4	1 1/8	r	5 1/4	5 3/8
Hasbro	15	2 1/8	r	2 7/8	r	r	r
17 3/8	17 1/2	1/16	9/16	1 1/8	1/4	r	r
17 3/8	20	s	r	1/2	s	r	r
Hilton	40	13	s	13 5/8	r	s	r
52 5/8	45	7 3/8	s	r	r	s	r
52 5/8	50	2 5/8	3 5/8	r	r	r	1 1/4
52 5/8	55	1/8	7/8	2 1/8	r	2	3 1/2
52 5/8	60	r	1/4	3/4	r	r	r
Hosp	35	11 3/8	s	r	r	s	r
46 3/8	40	6 1/8	6 7/8	7 3/4	r	3/16	1/2
46 3/8	45	1 1/4	2 5/16	3 1/4	r	9/16	1
46 3/8	50	1/16	r	5/16	r	r	3 5/8
Jerico	15	r	1/2	r	1/8	1/2	1
14 3/4	17 1/2	r	r	3/8	r	r	r
JiffyL	5	3/4	1	1 1/2	r	r	3/8
6	7 1/2	1/16	r	3/8	1 3/4	r	1 13/16
6	10	r	s	1/8	4 1/8	s	4 1/4
6	12 1/2	r	s	1/16	r	s	r
Kinder	7 1/2	r	r	7/16	r	r	r
7 3/8	10	r	r	1/16	r	r	r
MAPCO	50	r	r	6 5/8	r	1/8	r
55 1/4	55	1/4	r	r	r	r	r
55 1/4	60	r	r	1	r	r	r
Marion	17 1/2	5 1/4	s	5 3/4	r	s	1/4
22 7/8	20	2 11/16	2 7/8	3 3/8	r	1/8	7/16
22 7/8	22 1/2	1/16	15/16	1 7/8	s	s	s
22 7/8	22 1/2	s	s	s	1/16	5/8	1 1/4
22 7/8	25	s	3/16	13/16	s	2 1/8	s
MarshM	55	2	r	3 1/4	r	r	r
57	60	r	r	1	r	r	r
Maxtor	7 1/2	1 1/4	r	1 7/8	r	r	r
8 3/4	10	r	1/4	1/2	r	r	r
Maxus	5	2 1/4	r	2 1/2	r	r	r
7 3/8	7 1/2	r	1/4	1/2	r	r	r
7 3/8	10	r	s	r	2 3/4	s	r
Medco	12 1/2	1	r	r	r	r	r
Mentor	10	1/16	5/8	1 1/8	r	r	r
10 1/8	12 1/2	1/16	r	r	r	2 1/4	r
Micron	12 1/2	3 1/8	3 1/4	r	r	r	r
15 5/8	15	5/8	1 1/4	2 1/8	r	1/2	1 1/16
15 5/8	17 1/2	1/16	3/8	1	1 15/16	r	2 5/8
15 5/8	20	r	r	r	4 1/2	4 3/8	r
Micrsft	40	r	s	r	r	s	3/16
54 1/8	45	9	r	10 1/8	r	r	1/2
54 1/8	50	3 7/8	4 5/8	6	r	1/2	1 3/8
54 1/8	55	1/16	1 7/16	3	7/8	2 1/4	3 5/8
54 1/8	60	r	s	1 5/16	5 5/8	s	r
54 1/8	65	r	s	s	11 1/8	s	s
Mintnk	15	1/16	1/2	3/4	1/2	5/8	1
NYTimes	25	2 3/8	r	3 1/8	r	r	r
27 3/8	30	r	r	1/2	r	r	r
Nike	22 1/2	r	8	r	r	r	r
29 1/2	25	4 3/8	r	5 1/2	r	r	1/2
29 1/2	30	1/8	1	2	3/8	r	2
PacTel	30	2 1/4	r	2 5/8	r	r	r
32 1/4	35	r	r	1/4	2 7/8	r	r
PhilEl	20	5/16	r	r	r	r	r
PicNSv	12 1/2	5/16	r	r	r	r	1/2
PricCo	35	1 1/2	r	r	r	r	r
36 1/2	40	r	r	1 1/4	r	r	r
PrimMI	30	r	r	4	r	r	r
33	35	r	r	r	1 1/8	r	r
Raychm	30	1 9/16	2	r	r	7/8	1 3/8
31 5/8	35	r	r	1 1/4	3 7/8	r	s
31 5/8	35	s	s	s	s	s	4
Reebok	12 1/2	r	1/4	r	r	r	r

Source: The Wall Street Journal, January 23, 1989, p. C-11.

$$\text{Intrinsic value} = \text{Underlying asset price} - \text{Option exercise price} \quad \textbf{(14.1)}$$

For a call (put) option that is in the money (underlying asset price > exercise price), its intrinsic value is positive. And for at-the-money and out-of-the-money options the intrinsic value is zero. An option's time value is the amount by which the option's premium (or market price) exceeds its intrinsic value. For a call or put option:

$$\text{Time value} = \text{Option premium} - \text{Intrinsic value} \quad \textbf{(14.2)}$$

where intrinsic value is the maximum of zero or stock price minus exercise price. Thus an option premium or market price is composed of two components, intrinsic value and time value. In-the-money options are usually most expensive because of their large intrinsic-value component. An option with an at-the-money exercise price will have only time value inherent in its market price. Deep out-of-the-money options have zero intrinsic value and little time value and consequently are the least expensive. Deep in-the-money cases also have little time value, and time value is the greatest for at-the-money options. In addition, time value (as its name implies) is positively related to the amount of time the option has to expiration. The theoretical valuation of options focuses on determining the relevant variables that affect the time-value portion of an option premium and the derivation of their relationship in option pricing.

In general, the call price should be equal to or exceed the intrinsic value:

$$C \geq \text{Max}\,(S - E,\ 0)$$

where:

C = the value of the call option;
S = the current stock price; and
E = the exercise price.

Figure 14–2 illustrates the relationship between an option's time value and its exercise price. When the exercise price is zero, the time value of an option is zero. Although this relationship is described quite well in general by Figure 14–2, the exact relationship is somewhat ambiguous. Moreover, the identification of options with a mispriced time-value portion in their total premium motivates interest in a theoretical pricing model.

One more aspect of time value that is very important to discuss is the change in the amount of time value an option has as its duration shortens. As previously mentioned, options with a longer time to maturity and those near to the money have the largest time-value components. Assuming that a particular option remains near to the money as its time to maturity diminishes, the rate of decrease in its time value, or what is termed the effect of time decay, is of interest. How time decay affects an option's premium is an important question for the valuation of options and the application of option strategies. To best see an answer to this question refer to Figure 14–3.

FIGURE 14–2 The Relationship Between an Option's Exercise Price and Its Time Value

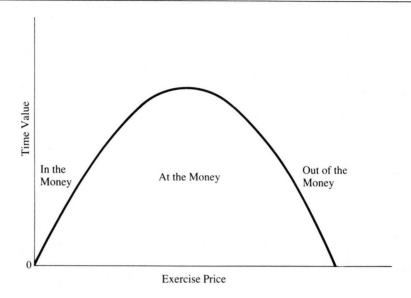

FIGURE 14–3 The Relationship Between Time Value and Time to Maturity for a Near-to-the-Money Option (Assuming a Constant Price for the Underlying Asset)

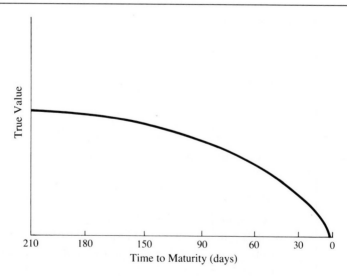

In general, the value of call options with the same exercise price increases as time to expiration increases: $C(S_1, E_1, T_1) \leq C(S_1, E_1, T_2)$ where $T_1 \leq T_2$ and T_1 and T_2 are the time to expiration.

Notice that for the simple case in Figure 14–3 the effect of time decay is smooth up until the last month before expiration, when the time value of an option begins to decay very rapidly. Why this effect occurs is made clearer in the next chapter, when the components of the option-pricing model are examined. Sample Problem 14.1 shows the effect of time decay.

Sample Problem 14.1

It is January 1, the price of the underlying ABC stock is $20 per share, and the time premiums are shown in the following table. What is the value for the various call options?

Exercise Price X	January	April	July
15	$0.50	$1.25	$3.50
20	1.00	2.00	5.00
25	0.50	1.25	3.50

Solution

$$\text{Call premium} = \text{Intrinsic value} + \text{Time premium}$$
$$C_{15,\text{Jan}} = \text{Max } (20 - 15, 0) + 0.50$$
$$= \$5.50 \text{ per share or } \$550 \text{ for 1 contract}$$

Exercise Price X	January	April	July
15	$5.50	Max $(20 - 15, 0) + 1.25$ $= \$6.25$	Max $(20 - 15, 0) + 3.50$ $= \$8.50$
20	Max $(20 - 20, 0) + 1.00$ $= \$1.00$	Max $(20 - 20, 0) + 2.00$ $= \$2.00$	Max $(20 - 20, 0) + 5.00$ $= \$5.00$
25	Max $(20 - 25, 0) + 5.0$ $= \$0.50$	Max $(20 - 25, 0) + 1.25$ $= \$1.25$	Max $(20 - 25, 0) + 3.50$ $= \$3.50$

Other values are shown in the table above ●

Additional Definitions and Distinguishing Features

Options may be specified in terms of their classes and series. A **class of options** refers to all call and put contracts on the same underlying asset. For example, all AT&T call and put options at various exercise prices and

expiration months form one class. A **series** is a subset of a class and consists of all contracts of the same class (such as AT&T) having the same expiration date and exercise price.

When an investor either buys or sells an option (that is, is long or short) as the initial transaction, the option exchange adds this opening transaction to what is termed the **open interest** for an option series. Essentially, open interest represents the number of contracts outstanding at a particular point in time. If the investor reverses the initial position with a closing transaction (that is, sells the option if he or she originally bought it or vice versa) then the open interest for the particular option series is reduced by one.

While open interest is more of a static variable, indicating the number of outstanding contracts at one point in time, **volume** represents a dynamic characteristic. More specifically, volume indicates the number of times a particular option is bought and sold during a particular trading day. Volume and open interest are measures of an option's liquidity, the ease with which the option can be bought and sold in large quantities. The larger the volume and/or open interest, the more liquid the option.

Again, an option holder who invokes the right to buy or sell is exercising the option. Whenever a holder exercises an option, a writer is assigned the obligation to fulfill the terms of the option contract by the exchange on which the option is traded. If a call holder exercises the right to buy, a **call writer** is assigned the obligation to sell. Similarly, when a put holder exercises the right to sell, a **put writer** is assigned the obligation to buy.

The seller or writer of a call option must deliver 100 shares of the underlying stock at the specified exercise price when the option is exercised. The writer of a put option must purchase 100 shares of the underlying stock when the put option is exercised. The writer of either option receives the premium or price of the option for this legal obligation. The maximum loss an option buyer can experience is limited to the price of the option. However, the maximum loss from writing a naked call is unlimited; the maximum loss possible from writing a naked put is the exercise price less the original price of that put. To guarantee that the option writer can meet these obligations, the exchange clearinghouse requires margin deposits.

The payment of cash dividends affects both the price of the underlying stock and the value of an option on the stock. Normally, no adjustment is made in the terms of the option when a cash dividend is paid. However, strike price or number of shares may be adjusted if the underlying stock realizes a stock dividend or stock split. For example, an option on XYZ Corporation with an exercise price of $100 would be adjusted if XYZ Corporation stock split two for one. The adjustment in this case would be a change in the exercise price from $100 to $50, and the number of contracts would be doubled. In the case of a noninteger split (such as three for two), the adjustment is made to the exercise price and the number of shares covered by the option contracts. For example, if XYZ Corporation had an

exercise price of $100 per share and had a three-for-two split, the option would have the exercise price adjusted to $66⅔, and the number of shares would be increased to 150. Notice that the old exercise value of the option, $10,000 ($100 × 100 shares), is maintained by the adjustment ($66⅔ × 150 shares).

Types of Underlying Asset

Although most people would identify common stocks as the underlying asset for an option, a variety of other assets and financial instruments can assume the same function. In fact, options on agricultural commodities were introduced by traders in the United States as early as the mid 1800s. After a number of scandals, agricultural commodity options were banned by the government. They were later reintroduced under tighter regulations and in a more standardized tradable form. Today, futures options on such agricultural commodities as corn, soybeans, wheat, cotton, sugar, live cattle, and live hogs are actively traded on a number of exchanges.

The biggest success for options has been realized for options on financial futures. Options on the S&P 500 index futures contracts, NYSE index futures, foreign-currency futures, thirty-year U.S. Treasury bond futures, and gold futures have all realized extraordinary growth since their initial offerings back in 1982. Options on futures are very similar to options on the actual asset, except that the futures options give their holders the right (not the obligation) to buy or sell predetermined quantities of specified futures contracts at a fixed price within a predetermined period.

Options on the actual asset have arisen in another form as well. While a number of options have existed for various stock-index futures contracts, options now also exist on the stock index itself. Because of the complexity of having to provide all the stocks in an index at the spot price should a call holder exercise his or her buy right, options on stock indexes are always settled in cash. That is, should a call holder exercise his or her right to buy because of a large increase in the underlying index, that holder would be accommodated by a cash amount equal to the profit on his contract, or the current value of the option's premium. Although the options on the S&P 100 stock index at the Chicago Board Options Exchange (CBOE) are the most popular among traders, numerous index options are now traded as well. These include options on the S&P 500 index, the S&P OTC 250 index, the NYSE composite and AMEX indexes (computer technology, oil and gas, and airline), the Philadelphia Exchange indexes (gold/silver), the Value Line index, and the NASDAQ 100 index.

It should be mentioned that options are traded on all major currencies, U.S. debt obligations, precious metals such as gold, and a growing number of other financial and nonfinancial commodities. Table 14A–1 at the end of this chapter lists all the major exchanges and the option contracts they offer.

Institutional Characteristics

Probably two of the most important underlying factors leading to the success of options have been the standardization of contracts through the establishment of option exchanges and the trading anonymity brought about by the Option Clearing Corporations and clearinghouses of the major futures exchanges.

An important element for option trading is the interchangeability of contracts. Exchange contracts are not matched between individuals. Instead, when an investor or trader enters into an option contract, the Option Clearing Corporation (or clearinghouse for the particular futures exchange) takes the opposite side of the transaction. So rather than having to contact a particular option writer to terminate an option position, a buyer can simply sell it back to the exchange at the current market clearing price. This type of anonymity among option-market participants is what permits an active secondary market to operate.

The sources of futures options traded on the various futures exchanges mentioned earlier are determined by the **open-auction bidding,** probably the purest form of laissez-faire price determination that can be seen today. With the open-auction-bidding price mechanism there are no market makers, only a large octagonal pit filled with traders bidding among themselves to buy and sell contracts. While some traders buy and sell only for themselves, many of the participants are brokers representing large investment firms. Different sides of the pit usually represent traders who are dealing in particular expiration months. As brokers and other pit participants make trades they mark down what they bought or sold, how much, at what price, and from whom. These cards are then collected by members of the exchange who record the trades and post the new prices. The prices are displayed on "scoreboards" surrounding the pit.

While stock options and options on commodities and indexes are traded in a similar fashion, one major difference prevails—the presence of **market makers.** Market makers are individuals who typically trade one type of option for their own account and are responsible for ensuring that a market always exists for their particular contract. In addition, some option exchanges utilize **board brokers** as well. These individuals are charged with the maintenance of the book of limit orders (orders from outside investors that are to be executed at particular prices or when the market goes up or down by a prespecified amount). Essentially, market makers and board brokers on the options exchanges share the duties performed by the specialists on the major stock exchanges.

Although stocks can be bought with as little as 50 percent margin, no margin is allowed for buying options—the cost of the contract must be fully paid. Because options offer a high degree of leverage on the underlying asset, additional leveraging through margins is considered by regulators to be excessive. However, if more than one option contract is entered into at

the same time—for instance, selling and buying two different calls—then, of course, a lower cost is incurred, since the cost of one is partially (or wholly) offset by the sale of the other.

INDEX AND FUTURES OPTIONS

When asked what the underlying asset of an option usually is, most people would say common stock. While this is correct, options currently exist and are soon to be introduced for a number of different types of financial instruments, some of which are highly innovative (see Figure 14–4). Two of the fastest growing types of options are those on futures contracts and indexes.

An option on a futures contract (or a **futures option,** as they are more commonly called) conveys to its owner the right to enter into a futures contract on either a long or short side (buy or sell the contract) at a prespecified price anytime up to the maturity date of the option. The advantage to buying a futures option instead of a futures contract is its limited risk. For either a call or put option, the most a purchaser can lose is the initial investment, the option premium. The premium on a futures option is usually multiplied by some fixed dollar amount to determine its cost. While this amount is substantial in an absolute sense, it is rather small relative to the dollar amount of the underlying commodity being controlled.

Index options are options on the index of an actual group of commodities. Presently options are available on nine different stock indexes, by far the most popular of which are the options offered on the S&P 100 stock index at the CBOE. Daily volume for S&P 100 index options typically exceeds 300,000 trades for each of the call and put options. Since the amount that one option controls is $200 times the index value (currently around 200), the volume for S&P 100 index options alone is equivalent to about $12 billion of transactions a day!

Due to the difficulty of trying to deliver a whole portfolio of stocks should a call buyer exercise his or her right, index options have a unique settlement feature: they are settled in cash. When an option is exercised the buyer pays the seller $200 times the exercise price of the option. The seller receives $200 times the current market price of the index (for call options on the S&P 100 index). Sample Problem 14.2 provides further illustration.

Sample Problem 14.2

On June 25, being rather bearish, you purchase one S&P 100 September 150 put option (expires in September with exercise price of 150) for $2\frac{1}{2}$ (actual cost = $200 × premium = $500), with the S&P 100 spot index at 152.85. On July 27 the spot index has dropped to 149.58 and you decide to take your profits and get out.

FIGURE 14–4   Daily Quotations for Options, Futures, and Options on Futures

INTEREST RATE INSTRUMENTS

OPTIONS

Friday, May 26, 1989

For Notes and Bonds, decimals in closing prices represent 32nds; 1.01 means 1 1/32. For Bills, decimals in closing prices represent basis points; $25 per .01.

Chicago Board Options Exchange

U.S. TREASURY BOND—$100,000 principal value
Total call vol. 0   Call open int. 8,221
Total put vol. 0   Put open int. 3,828
5-YEAR U.S. TREASURY NOTE—$100,000 principal value
Total call vol. 0   Call open int. 200
Total put vol. 0   Put open int. 1
  3 p.m. prices of underlying issues supplied by The Chicago Corp.: T-Bonds 7¼% 85.12; 8⅞% 102.24; 9% 103.26; 9⅛% 105.00. T-Notes 8⅞% 100.07; 9½% 102.26.

FUTURES OPTIONS

T-BONDS (CBT) $100,000; points and 64ths of 100%

Strike	Calls—Last			Puts—Last		
Price	Sep-c	Dec-c	Mar-c	Sep-p	Dec-p	Mar-p
88	5-08	5-30	....	0-24	0-57	....
90	3-31	4-05	....	0-45	1-27	....
92	2-11	2-56	....	1-22	2-12	....
94	1-12	1-59	....	2-22	3-08	....
96	0-38	1-14	....	3-47	....	....
98	0-19	0-49	....	5-26	....	....

Est. vol. 39,000, Thur. vol. 28,813 calls, 16,742 puts
Open interest Thur; 190,376 calls, 143,196 puts

T-NOTES (CBT) $100,000; points and 64ths of 100%

Strike	Calls—Last			Puts—Last		
Price	Sep-c	Dec-c	Mar-c	Sep-p	Dec-p	Mar-p
93	3-15	3-41	....	0-25	0-50	....
94	2-29	....	....	0-38	1-00	....
95	1-50	2-15	....	0-59	1-21	....
96	1-14	1-44	....	1-23	....	....
97	0-51	....	....	1-55	....	....
98	0-31	....	....	2-33	....	....

Est. vol. 1,200, Thur vol. 5,476 calls, 579 puts
Open interest Thur; 15,431 calls, 14,527 puts

MUNICIPAL BOND INDEX (CBT) $100,000; pts. & 64ths of 100%

Strike	Calls—Settle			Puts—Settle		
Price	Jun-c	Sep-c	Dec-c	Jun-p	Sep-p	Dec-p
90	3-14	....	....	0-02	....	....
92	1-24	1-55	....	0-10	....	....
94	0-19	....	....	....	....	....
96	0-02	....	....	....	....	....
98						
100						

Est. vol. 205, Thur vol. 30 calls, 135 puts
Open interest Thur; 2,850 calls, 3,633 puts

EURODOLLAR (CME) $ million; pts. of 100%

Strike	Calls—Settle			Puts—Settle		
Price	Jun-c	Sep-c	Dec-c	Jun-p	Sep-p	Dec-p
9070	0.53	0.99	1.06	0.02	0.13	0.22
9025	0.31	0.78	0.90	0.05	0.17	0.28
9050	0.14	0.63	0.74	0.13	0.25	0.34
9075	0.05	0.47	0.60	0.29	0.34	0.45
9100	0.02	0.34	0.48	0.51	0.46	0.58
9125	0.01	0.24	0.36	0.75	0.60	....

Est. vol. 23,320, Thur vol. 7,834 calls, 9,365 puts
Open interest Thur; 216,224 calls, 233,742 puts

EURODOLLAR (LIFFE) $1 million; pts. of 100%

Strike	Calls—Settle			Puts—Settle		
Price	Jun-c	Sep-c	Dec-c	Jun-p	Sep-p	Dec-p
9000	0.51	0.98	1.13	0.02	0.12	0.25
9025	0.29	0.79	0.94	0.05	0.18	0.31
9050	0.12	0.61	0.78	0.13	0.25	0.40
9075	0.04	0.46	0.63	0.30	0.35	0.50
9100	0.02	0.34	0.49	0.58	0.48	0.61
9125	0.01	0.23	0.38	0.77	0.62	0.75

Est. Vol. Fri, 63 Calls, 110 Puts.
Open Interest Thurs 5,041, Calls, 5,395 Puts.

LONG GILT (LIFFE)—b-£50,000; 64ths of 100%

Strike	Calls—Settle			Puts—Settle		
Price	Jun-c	Sep-c	Dec-c	Jun-p	Sep-p	Dec-p
92	3.53	3.60	....	0.11	0.34	....
93	2.60	3.13	....	0.18	0.51	....
94	2.09	2.34	....	0.31	1.08	....
96	1.30	1.62	....	0.52	1.36	....
97	0.60	1.31	....	1.18	2.05	....
98	0.39	1.06	....	1.61	2.44	....

Est. Vol. Fri, 701 Calls, 1,190 Puts.
Open Interest Thurs 3,425, Calls, 5,300 Puts.

—OTHER INTEREST RATE OPTION—

Final or settlement prices of selected contract. Volume and open interest are totals in all contract months.

Treasury Bills (IMM) $1 million; pts. of 100%

Strike	Sep-c	Dec-c	Mar-c	Sep-p	Dec-p	Mar-p
9225	0.34	0.56	....	0.34	0.43	....

Est. vol. 7. Thur vol. 31. Op. Int. 402.

CBT—Chicago Board of Trade. CME—Chicago Mercantile Exchange. FINEX—Financial Instrument Exchange, a division of the New York Cotton Exchange. IMM—International Monetary Market at Chicago Mercantile Exchange. LIFFE—London International Financial Futures Exchange.

CURRENCY TRADING

OPTIONS
PHILADELPHIA EXCHANGE

Option & Underlying	Strike Price	Calls—Last			Puts—Last		
		Jun	Jul	Sep	Jun	Jul	Sep
50,000 Australian Dollars-cents per unit.							
ADolr	...70	r	r	r	r	r	0.50
75.77	...71	r	r	r	0.30	r	0.72
75.77	...72	r	r	r	0.40	0.34	r
75.77	...73	r	r	r	0.65	0.53	r
75.77	...74	r	r	r	0.95	r	r
75.77	...75	0.45	r	r	1.60	1.23	2.35
75.77	...76	0.74	r	r	r	r	2.98
75.77	...77	0.41	r	r	r	r	r
75.77	...78	0.12	0.42	0.67	2.86	r	r
75.77	...79	0.14	r	r	5.05	r	r
75.77	...80	0.07	0.18	r	r	r	r
75.77	...81	0.04	r	r	r	r	6.92
75.77	...92	r	r	r	s	s	0.40
31,250 British Pounds-cents per unit.							
BPound	150	r	r	r	r	r	1.68
159.10	...155	r	r	r	r	r	2.60
159.10	157½	2.80	4.60	r	1.48	r	3.50
159.10	...160	1.50	2.75	3.20	2.70	r	5.65
159.10	162½	0.75	1.80	r	4.40	r	7.40
159.10	...165	r	1.60	r	r	r	8.10
159.10	167½	r	r	r	8.60	r	r
159.10	...175	r	r	r	15.00	r	r
31,250 British Pounds-European Style.							
159.10	...160	r	r	3.25	2.85	r	r
50,000 Canadian Dollars-cents per unit.							
CDolr	...82	r	r	r	r	r	0.75
83.15	...82½	r	0.85	r	0.20	r	r
83.15	...83	0.40	r	r	0.45	r	r
83.15	...83½	0.16	r	r	r	0.93	r
50,000 Canadian Dollars-European Style.							
CDolr	83½	0.18	r	r	r	r	r
83.15	...84	r	0.30	r	r	r	r

Option & Underlying	Strike Price	Calls—Last			Puts—Last		
62,500 West German Marks-cents per unit.							
DMark	...47	r	r	r	r	r	0.28
50.38	...48	r	r	r	r	0.18	0.46
50.38	...49	2.15	1.88	r	0.20	0.37	0.72
50.38	...50	0.83	1.17	1.71	0.52	0.71	1.00
50.38	...51	0.42	0.82	1.18	0.94	1.05	r
50.38	...52	0.15	0.44	0.84	1.74	1.51	r
50.38	...53	0.07	0.23	0.59	2.63	r	2.52
50.38	...54	0.02	0.16	0.36	r	3.60	r
50.38	...56	r	r	r	5.15	r	r
250,000 French Francs-10ths of a cent per unit.							
FFranc	...15	r	r	3.54	r	r	r
148.98	15½	r	r	r	6.20	r	7.40
6,250,000 Japanese Yen-100ths of a cent per unit.							
JYen	...67	r	r	r	r	0.17	r
70.93	...68	r	r	r	0.13	0.27	r
70.93	...69	r	r	r	0.18	0.35	0.64
70.93	...70	r	1.95	r	0.41	0.75	1.06
70.93	...71	1.00	1.28	2.07	r	r	1.52
70.93	...72	0.43	r	r	r	1.40	r
70.93	...73	0.18	0.70	r	2.13	1.86	r
70.93	...74	0.13	0.32	0.87	r	r	3.27
70.93	...75	0.04	0.22	r	r	r	r
70.93	...78	r	0.20	r	r	r	r
70.93	...80	r	r	r	8.63	r	r
62,500 Swiss Francs-cents per unit.							
SFranc	...54	r	r	r	0.03	0.11	r
57.70	...55	r	r	r	0.07	0.29	0.55
57.70	...56	r	r	2.65	0.23	0.46	0.63
57.70	...57	1.56	r	2.48	0.50	0.75	1.18
57.70	...58	0.68	1.04	1.77	r	0.92	1.52
57.70	...59	0.38	0.96	1.23	1.30	1.70	r
57.70	...60	0.10	0.44	0.82	r	r	2.72
57.70	...61	0.01	0.27	r	r	r	3.20
57.70	...62	0.04	r	r	r	r	r
57.70	...67	r	r	r	8.80	r	r

Total call vol.   37,597   Call open int.   599,060
Total put vol.   33,470   Put open int.   459,720
r—Not traded.   s—No option offered.
Last is premium (purchase price).

INDEX TRADING

Friday, May 26, 1989

OPTIONS

Chicago Board

S&P 100 INDEX

Strike Price	Calls—Last			Puts—Last		
	Jun	Jul	Aug	Jun	Jul	Aug
260	....	....	....	⅛	5/16	¾
265	....	....	....	⅛	½	⅞
270	30¼	....	....	⅛	11/16	1¾
275	26	....	....	5/16	15/16	1⅞
280	21⅜	24⅛	....	⅜	1¾	2¼
285	17	19½	....	⅝	2	3⅛
290	12⅜	15¾	16¼	1 1/16	2⅞	3⅞
295	7¾	11¾	13½	2 1/16	4⅛	5⅜
300	4⅞	8½	9⅞	3⅞	5⅞	7¼
305	2½	6	7¾	6¼	8½	9¾
310	1⅛	3⅞	5⅜	10¾	11⅞	13
315	7/16	2⅞	3⅞	15½	15½	....

Total call volume 47,392   Total call open int. 264,971
Total put volume 40,887   Total put open int. 315,266
The index: High 300.04; Low 297.68; Close 300.04, +2.31.

S&P 500 INDEX

Strike Price	Calls—Last			Puts—Last		
	Jun	Jul	Sep	Jun	Jul	Sep
175	146	....	....	1/16	....	....
225	....	....	....	1/16	....	⅛
250	71¾	....	....	1/16	....	....
255	66½	....	....	1/16	....	⅛
275	46½	....	....	1/16	....	1⅛
280	....	....	....	⅛	....	1⅛
285	37¼	....	....	⅛	....	1 7/16
290	31⅞	....	37	3/16	....	....
295	27¾	....	....	¼	....	....
300	....	....	....	7/16	....	2¾
305	....	....	....	⅝	1 9/16	....
310	13	16½	20½	¾	3⅛	5⅛
315	8¼	....	....	1 9/16	4¼	....
320	5¼	....	....	3⅛	....	....
325	2¾	6½	....	5½	....	....
330	1 3/16	4⅜	8	9	10⅞	....
335	9/16	....	....	13⅛	....	....
350	1/16	....	2⅞	28½	....	....

Total call volume 27,564   Total call open int. 196,603
Total put volume 25,344   Total put open int. 228,806
The index: High 321.59; Low 319.14; Close 321.59, +2.42.

American Exchange

MAJOR MARKET INDEX

Strike Price	Calls—Last			Puts—Last		
	Jun	Jul	Aug	Jun	Jul	Aug
440	....	....	....	¼	....	....
445	....	....	....	5/16	....	....
450	....	....	....	¾	1½	....
455	....	....	....	7/16	1 13/16	....
460	....	....	37¼	⅜	2 3/16	3⅜
465	....	....	....	⅞	r	....
470	22	....	....	1 5/16	3½	5⅛
475	....	....	....	1⅞	4⅜	....

480	13¾	19⅞	....	2 11/16	6	....
485	10	16¾	....	4⅛	7⅜	9⅞
490	6⅞	....	16½	6⅛	9⅛	11⅜
495	4⅞	....	....	8¾	....	....
500	3⅛	7⅞	....	12	....	....
505	1 13/16	6⅝	....	....	....	....
510	1	4½	....	....	....	....
515	½	3⅜	6⅛	....	....	....
520	....	2 9/16	....	....	....	....

Total call volume 7,565   Total call open int. 25,807
Total put volume 5,937   Total put open int. 27,765
The Index: High 489.85; Low 487.32; Close 489.71, +1.97.

COMPUTER TECHNOLOGY INDEX
Total call volume 20   Total call open int. 29
Total put volume 0   Total put open int. 72
The Index: High 105.89; Low 105.22; Close 105.89, +0.60.

OIL INDEX

Strike Price	Calls—Last			Puts—Last		
	Jun	Jul	Aug	Jun	Jul	Aug
200	....	....	....	....	⅜	1 1/16
205	5⅞	....	....	....	....	....
210	2¾	....	....	....	....	....

Total call volume 20   Total call open int. 346
Total put volume 8   Total put open int. 282
The Index: High 209.09; Low 208.21; Close 208.97, +0.48.

INSTITUTIONAL INDEX

Strike Price	Calls—Last			Puts—Last		
	Jun	Jul	Aug	Jun	Jul	Aug
275	....	....	....	1/16	....	....
285	34¾	....	....	⅛	....	....
300	....	....	....	7/16	....	....

Total call volume 121   Total call open int. 32,041
Total put volume 85   Total put open int. 26,511
The Index: High 319.44; Low 317.21; Close 319.44, +2.23.

Philadelphia Exchange

GOLD/SILVER INDEX

Strike Price	Calls—Last			Puts—Last		
	Jun	Jul	Aug	Jun	Jul	Aug
95	1¾	2¼	....	....	....	....

Total call volume 10   Total call open int. 329
Total put volume 14   Total put open int. 210
The Index: High 86.88; Low 85.75; Close 86.50, +0.75.

VALUE LINE INDEX OPTIONS

Strike Price	Calls—Last			Puts—Last		
	Jun	Jul	Aug	Jun	Jul	Aug
275	10	....	....	½	....	....

Total call volume 0   Total call open int. 1,673
Total put volume 8   Total put open int. 732
The Index: High 283.81; Low 282.06; Close 283.80, +1.75.

NATIONAL O-T-C INDEX
Total call volume 0   Total call open int. 327
Total put volume 0   Total put open int. 28
The Index: High 320.08; Low 317.34; Close 319.92, +2.38.

UTILITIES INDEX

Strike Price	Calls—Last			Puts—Last		
	Jun	Jul	Aug	Jun	Jul	Aug
200	....	....	....	....	....	1⅞

Total call volume 5   Total call open int. 3,122
Total put volume 20   Total put open int. 2,670
The Index: High 204.56; Low 203.17; Close 204.52, +1.42.

Source: The Wall Street Journal, May 30, 1989, p. C-11.

There are two ways you could do this. The easier and most common way is simply to resell the put at its going market price of $3\frac{1}{4}$ ($650) for a profit of $150 ($650 − 550). Alternatively, you could exercise your put's right to sell the index at the market price of $149.58 × $200. To do this you would notify the CBOE clearinghouse to act as a middleman and assign your exercise randomly to someone who sold an S&P 100 put with the same expiration month and exercise price (September 150). The assigned put seller would then be required to buy the index at the original exercise price of $150 × $200. The transaction flows are shown in the diagram.

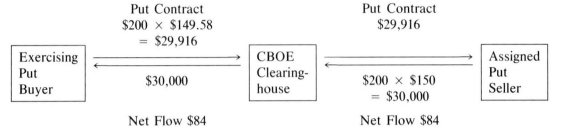

You may have noticed that (subtracting $29,916 from $30,000) the put buyer's profit is only $84 when exercising the option, while it was $150 when the put was simply resold in the market. Why the discrepancy? Time value! Since the put has nearly two months to expiration, it has a considerable amount of time value left in its premium (that is, the possibility still exists that the S&P 100 index may drop even further in the next two months). Because this time value is not part of the index's value, it is always more profitable to take your profits in the option itself. Consequently, actual exercise of index options is a rarity●

Along with index options and futures options there exists a hybrid of the two known as **index-futures options.** Futures options are currently offered on two stock-index futures (the S&P 500 index futures at the CME and the NYSE index futures at the NYSE). In addition, there are S&P 100 index options at the CBT, major market index options at the American Exchange, Value Line index options at the Philadelphia Exchange, and NYSE index options at the NYSE. Finally, there are T-bill futures options and T-note futures options at the CBT, and Eurodollar futures options at the CME and the LIFFE.

The popularity of the major index and index-futures options stems from their speculative and hedging applications. With relatively little money, an investor can express an opinion on the general movement of the stock market versus that of a single stock. Just as important, the manager of a large stock portfolio can use options to accentuate the portfolio's overall return (writing calls, for example) or truncate its downside risk exposure (buying puts). Options also allow one to hedge against adverse movements in interest rates or inflation.

Further discussions of the valuation and hedging uses of these options are taken up in the next chapter.

PUT–CALL PARITY

This section addresses a most important concept, called **put–call parity** (for option valuation). The discussion includes European options, American options, and future options.

European Options

As an initial step to examining the pricing formulas for options, it is essential to discuss the relationships between the prices of put and call options on the same underlying asset. Such relationships among put and call prices are referred to as the *put–call parity theorems*. Stoll (1969) was the first to introduce the concept of put–call parity. Dealing strictly with **European options** he showed that the value of a call option would equal the value of a portfolio composed of a long put option, its underlying stock, and a short discounted exercise price. Before stating the basic put–call parity theorem as originally devised by Stoll, it must be assumed that the markets for options, bonds, and stocks (or any other underlying asset we choose) are frictionless.

Theorem 1. *Put–Call Parity for European Options with No Dividends.*

$$C_{t,T} = P_{t,T} + S_t - EB_{t,T} \qquad (14.3)$$

where:

$C_{t,T}$ = value of a European call option at time t that matures at time T $(T > t)$;

$P_{t,T}$ = value of a European put option at time t, that matures at time T;

S_t = value of the underlying stock (asset) to both the call and put options at time t;

E = exercise price for both the call and put options;

$B_{t,T}$ = price at time t of a default-free bond that pays \$1 with certainty at time T (if it is assumed that this risk-free rate of interest is the same for all maturities and equal to r—in essence a flat-term structure—then $B_{t,T} = e^{-r(T-t)}$, under continuous compounding), or $B_{t,T} = 1/(1 + r)^{T-t}$ for discrete compounding.

Equation (14.3) uses the following principle. If the options are neither dominant nor dominated securities, and if the borrowing and lending rates are equal, then the return patterns of a European call and a portfolio composed of a European put, a pure discount bond with a face value equal to the options exercise price E, and the underlying stock (or asset) are the same.[1]

---

[1] Any security x is dominant over any security y if the rate of return on x is equal to or greater than that of y for all states of nature and is strictly greater for at least one state. For an expanded discussion of this subject, see Merton (1973) and Smith (1976).

In understanding why the put–call parity theorem holds, and to support the theorem, two additional properties of option pricing must be provided:

Property 1: At maturity (time T) the call option is worth the greater of $S_T - E$ dollars or zero dollars:

$$C_T = \text{Max } (0, S_T - E) \qquad (14.4)$$

As an example, suppose that the call option has an exercise price of $30. At maturity, if the stock's (asset's) price is $25, then the value of the call is the maximum of $(0, 25 - 30)$ or $(0, -5)$, which of course is zero. If an option sells for less than $(S_t - E)$, its intrinsic value, an arbitrage opportunity will exist. Investors would buy the option and short sell the stock, forcing the mispricing to correct itself. Consequently, this first property implies that a call option's value is always greater than zero. An equivalent property and argument exist for the value of a put option as well.

Property 2: At maturity, the value of a put option is the greater of $E - S_T$ dollars or zero dollars:

$$P_T = \text{Max } (0, E - S_T) \qquad (14.5)$$

Using the same line of reasoning and argument as for the call option, the second property also implies that the value of a put option is never less than zero. Table 14–1 provides proof of this first put–call parity theorem. Suppose at time t, two portfolios are formed: portfolio B is just a long call option on a stock with price S_t, an exercise price of E, and a maturity date at T. Portfolio A consists of purchasing one hundred shares of the underlying stock (since stock options represent one hundred shares), purchasing (going long) one put option on the same stock with exercise price E and maturity date T, and borrowing at the risk-free rate an amount equal to the present

TABLE 14–1   Put–Call Parity for a European Option with No Dividends

	Time T (Maturity)		
Time t Strategy	$S_T > E$	$S_T = E$	$S_T < E$
Portfolio A			
1. Buy 100 shares of the stock (S_t).	S_T	S_T	S_T
2. Buy a put $(P_t$, maturity at T with exercise price E).	0	0	$E - S_T$
3. Borrow $EB_{t,T}$ dollars.	$-E$	$-E$	$-E$
Portfolio A value at time T	$(S_T - E)$	0	0
Portfolio B			
1. Buy a call $(C_t$ maturing at T with exercise price E).	$(S_T - E)$	0	0

value of the exercise price or $EB_{t,T}$ with face value of E. (This portion of the portfolio finances the put, call, and stock position.)

At maturity date T, the call option (portfolio B) has value only if $S_T > E$, which is in accordance with Property 1. For portfolio A, under all these conditions the stock price and maturing loan values are the same, whereas the put option has value only if $E > S_T$. Under all three possible outcomes for the stock price S_T, it can be seen that the values of portfolios A and B are equal. Proof has been established for the first put–call parity theorem. Sample Problem 14.3 provides further illustration.

Sample Problem 14.3

A call option with one year to maturity and exercise price of $110 is selling for $5. Assuming discrete compounding, a risk-free rate of 10 percent, and a current stock price of $100, what is the value of a European put option with a strike price of $110 and one-year maturity?

Solution

$$P_{t,T} = C_{t,T} + EB_{t,T} - S_t$$
$$P_{0,1\,yr} = \$5 + \$110 \left(\frac{1}{(1.1)^1}\right) - \$100$$
$$P_{0,1\,yr} = \$5$$

American Options

Of course, this first put–call parity theorem holds only under the most basic conditions (that is, no early exercise and no dividends). Jarrow and Rudd (1983) give an extensive coverage of the effects of more complicated conditions on put–call parity. These authors demonstrate that the effect of known dividends is simply to reduce, by the discounted value (to time t) of the dividends, the amount of the underlying stock purchased. In considering stochastic dividends, the exactness of this pricing relationship breaks down and depends on the degree of certainty that can be maintained about the range of future dividends. Put–call parity for **American options** is also derived under various dividend conditions. Jarrow and Rudd demonstrate that as a result of the American option's early exercise feature, strict pricing relationships give way to boundary conditions dependent on the size and certainty of future dividends, as well as the level of interest rates and the size of the exercise price. To summarize, they state that for sufficiently high interest rates and/or exercise prices it may be optimal to exercise the put prior to maturity (with or without dividends). So the basic put–call parity for an American option with no dividends and constant interest rates is described by the following theorem.

Theorem 2.   *Put–Call Parity for an American Option with No Dividends.*

$$P_{t,T} + S_t - EB_{t,T} > C_{t,T} > P_{t,T} + S_t - E \qquad \text{(14.6)}$$

Increasing the generality of conditions results in increasing boundaries for the equilibrium relationship between put and call options. The beauty of these arguments stems from the fact that they require only that investors prefer more wealth to less. If more stringent assumptions are made, then the bounds can be made tighter. For an extensive derivation and explanation of these theorems see Jarrow and Rudd (1983). Sample Problem 14.4 provides further illustration.

Sample Problem 14.4

A put option with one year to maturity and an exercise price of $90 is selling for $15; the stock price is $100. Assuming discrete compounding and a risk-free rate of 10 percent, what are the boundaries for the price of an American call option?

Solution

$$P_{t,T} + S_t - EB_{t,T} > C_{t,T} > P_{t,T} + S_t - E$$

$$\$15 + \$100 - \$90 \left(\frac{1}{(1.1)^1}\right) > C_{t,T} > \$15 + \$100 - \$90$$

$$\$33.18 > C_{t,1\text{yr}} > \$25 \qquad \bullet$$

Futures Options

As a final demonstration of put–call parity the analysis is extended to the case where the underlying asset is a futures contract. The topic of futures contracts and their valuation will be more fully examined in the next chapter. Nevertheless, this chapter takes time to apply put–call parity when the options are on a futures contract because of the growing popularity and importance of such futures options. A futures contract as described in Chapter 12 is a contract in which the party entering into the contract is obligated to buy or sell the underlying asset at the maturity date for some stipulated price. While the difference between European and American options still remains, the complexity of dividends can be ignored since futures contracts do not pay dividends. Put–call parity for a European futures option (when interest rates are constant) is as follows:

Theorem 3.   *Put–Call Parity for a European Futures Option.*

$$C_{t,T} = P_{t,T} + B_{t,T} (F_{t,T} - E) \qquad \text{(14.7)}$$

where $F_{t,T}$ is the price at time t for a futures contract maturing at time T (which is the underlying asset to both the call and put options).

Option pricing Properties 1 and 2 for call and put options apply in an equivalent sense to futures options as well. However, to understand this relationship as stated in Equation (14.7) it must be assumed that the cost of a futures contract is zero. While a certain margin requirement is required, the majority of this assurance deposit can be in the form of interest-bearing securities. Hence as an approximation a zero cost for the futures contract is not unrealistic.

Again, the easiest way to prove this relationship is to follow the same path of analysis used in proving Theorem 1. Table 14–2 indicates that the argument for this theorem's proof is similar, with only a few notable exceptions. The value of the futures contract at time T (maturity) is equal to the difference between the price of the contract at time T and the price at which it was bought, or $F_{TT} - F_{t,T}$. This is an outcome of the fixed duration of a futures contract as opposed to the perpetual duration of common stock. Second, because no money is required to enter into the futures contract, the exercise price is reduced by the current futures price and the total is lent at the risk-free rate. (Actually this amount is either lent or borrowed depending on the relationship between $F_{t,T}$ and E at time t. If $F_{t,T} - E < 0$ then this amount will actually be borrowed at the risk-free rate.)

Why are there options on spot assets as well as options on futures contracts for the spot assets? After all, at expiration the basis of a futures contract goes to zero and futures prices equal spot prices; thus, options in the spot and options on the future are related to the same futures value, and their current values must be identical. Yet a look at the markets shows that options on spot assets and options on futures for the same assets sell at different prices. One explanation for this is that investors who purchase options on spot must pay a large sum of money when they exercise their options, whereas investors who exercise an option on a future need only pay

TABLE 14–2   Put–Call Parity for a European Futures Option

	Time T (Maturity)		
Time t Strategy	$F_{TT} > E$	$F_{TT} = E$	$F_{TT} < E$
Portfolio A			
1. Buy a futures contract ($F_{t,T}$).	$F_{TT} - F_{t,T}$	$F_{TT} - F_{t,T}$	$F_{TT} - F_{t,T}$
2. Buy a put ($P_{t,T}$ on $F_{t,T}$ with exercise price E and maturity T).	0	0	$E - F_{TT}$
3. Lend $B_{t,T}(F_{t-T} - E)$ dollars.	$F_{t,T} - E$	$F_{t,T} - E$	$F_{t,T} - E$
Portfolio A's value at time T	$F_{TT} - E$	0	0
Portfolio B			
1. Buy a call ($C_{t,T}$ on $F_{t,T}$, with exercise price E and maturity T).	$F_{TT} - E$	0	0

enough to meet the initial margin for the futures contract. Therefore, if the exercise of the option is important to an investor, that investor would prefer options on futures rather than options on spot and would be willing to pay a premium for the option on the future, whereas the investor who has no desire to exercise the option (remember, the investor can always sell it to somebody else to realize a profit) is not willing to pay for this advantage and so finds the option on spot more attractive.

Market Application

Put options were not listed on the CBOE until June 1977. Before that time, brokers satisfied their clients' demands for put option risk–return characteristics by a direct application of put–call parity. By combining call options and the underlying security, brokers could construct a **synthetic put.**

To illustrate, the put–call parity theorem is used when a futures contract is the underlying asset. Furthermore, to simulate the option broker's circumstances on July 1, 1984, the equation is merely rearranged to yield the put's "synthetic" value:

$$P_{t,T} = C_{t,T} - B_{t,T} F_{t,T} + B_{t,T} E \qquad \textbf{(14.8)}$$

So instead of a futures contract being purchased, it is sold. Assume the following values and use the S&P 500 index futures as the underlying asset.

$C_{t,T} = \$\ \ 3.35;$
$F_{t,T} = \ \ 154.85$ (September contract);
$E = \ \ 155.00;$ and
$B_{t,T} = 0.9770$ (current price of a risk-free bond that pays \$1 when the option and futures contract expire, average of bid and ask prices for T-bills from *The Wall Street Journal*).

According to Equation (14.8), the put's price should equal the theorem price: $P_{t,T} = \$3.497$. The actual put price on this day (July 1, 1984) with the same exercise price and expiration month was $P_{t,T} = \$3.50$. With repeated comparisons of the theorem using actual prices, it becomes clear that put–call parity is a powerful equilibrium mechanism in the market.

RISK–RETURN CHARACTERISTICS OF OPTIONS

One of the most attractive features of options is the myriad of ways in which they can be employed to achieve a particular combination of risk and return. Whether through a straight option position in combination with the underlying asset or some portfolio of securities, options offer an innovative and relatively low-cost mechanism for altering and enhancing the risk–return tradeoff. In order to better grasp these potential applications this section analyzes call and put options individually and in combination, relative to their potential profit and loss and the effects of time and market sentiment.

Long Call

The purchase of a call option is the simplest and most familiar type of option position. The allure of calls is that they provide the investor a great deal of leverage. Potentially, large percentage profits can be realized from only a modest price rise in the underlying asset. In fact, the potential profit from buying a call is unlimited. Moreover, the option purchaser has the right but no obligation to exercise the contract. Therefore, should the price of the underlying asset decline over the life of the call, the purchaser need only let the contract expire worthless. Consequently, the risk of a long call position is limited. Figure 14–5 illustrates the profit profile of a **long call** position. The following summarizes the basic risk–return features for a long-call position.

Profit potential: unlimited

Loss potential: limited (to cost of option)

Effect of time decay: negative (decreases option's value)

Market expectation: bullish

As the profit profile indicates, the time value of a long call declines over time. Consequently, an option is a wasting asset. If the underlying asset's price does not move above the exercise price of the option E by its expiration date T, the buyer of the call will lose the value of his initial investment (the option premium). Consequently, the longer an investor holds a call, the more time value the option loses, thereby reducing the price of the option. This leads to another important point—taking on an option position. As with any other investment vehicle, the purchase of a call expresses an opinion about the market for the underlying asset. Whereas an investor can essentially express one of three different sentiments (bullish, neutral, or bearish)

FIGURE 14–5   Profit Profile for a Long Call

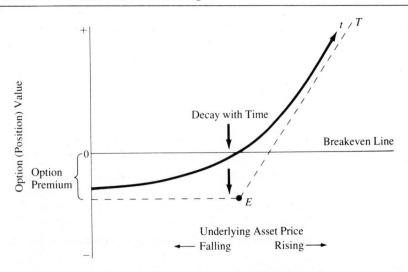

FIGURE 14-6   Profit Profile for a Short Call

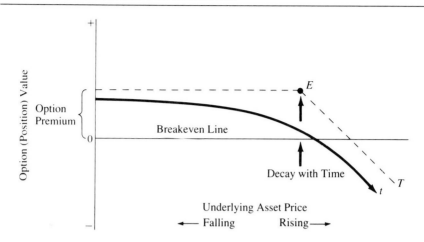

about future market conditions, the long call is strictly a bullish position. That is, the call buyer only wins if the underlying asset rises in price. However, depending on the exercise price of the call, the buyer can express differing degrees of bullishness. For instance, since out-of-the-money calls are the cheapest, a large price increase in the underlying asset will make these calls the biggest percentage gainers in value. So an investor who is extremely bullish would probably go with an out-of-the-money call, since its intrinsic value is small and its value will increase along with a large increase in the market.

Short Call

Selling a call (writing it) has risk–reward characteristics which are the inverse of the long call. However, one major distinction arises when writing calls (or puts) rather than buying them. That is, the writer can either own the underlying asset upon which he or she is selling the option (a **covered write**), or simply sell the option without owning the asset (a **naked write**). The difference between the two is of considerable consequence to the amount of risk and return taken on by the seller. Let us first examine the profit profile and related attributes of the naked **short call,** displayed in Figure 14–6.

When the writer of a call does not own the underlying asset, his or her potential loss is unlimited. Why? Because if the price of the underlying asset increases, the value of the call also increases for the buyer. The seller of a call is *obliged* to provide a designated quantity of the underlying asset at some prespecified price (the exercise price) at any time up to the maturity date of the option. So if the asset starts rising dramatically in price and the call buyer exercises his or her *right,* the naked-call writer must go into the market to buy the underlying asset at whatever the market price. The naked-

call writer suffers the loss of buying the asset at a price S and selling it at a price E when $S > E$ (less the original premium collected). When common stock is the underlying asset, there is no limit to how high its price could go. Thus, the naked-call writer's risk is unlimited as well. Of course, the naked-call writer could have reversed position by buying back the original option he sold—that is, zeroing out the position—however, this also done at a loss. The following summarizes the basic risk–return features for a naked short-call position.

Profit potential: limited (to option premium)

Loss potential: unlimited

Effect of time decay: positive (makes buyer's position less valuable)

Market expectation: bearish to neutral

The naked short-call position is obviously a bearish position. If the underlying asset's price moves down, the call writer keeps all of the premium received for selling this call, since the call buyer's position becomes worthless. Once again, the naked-call writer can express the degree of bearishness by the exercise price at which he or she sells the call. By selling an in-the-money call, the writer stands to collect a higher option premium. Conversely, selling an out-of-the-money call conveys only a mildly bearish to neutral expectation. If the underlying asset's price stays where it is, the value of the buyer's position, which is solely time value, will decay to zero; and the call writer will collect the entire premium (though a substantially smaller premium than for an in-the-money call).

While the passing of time has a negative effect on the value of a call option for the buyer, it has a positive effect for the seller. One aspect of an option's time value is that in the last month before the option expires its time value decays most rapidly. Why? Time value is related to the probability that the underlying asset's price will move up or down enough to make an option position increase in value. This probability declines at an accelerating (exponential) rate as the option approaches its maturity date. The consideration of time value, then, is a major element when investing in or hedging with options. Unless an investor is extremely bullish, it would probably be unwise to take a long position in a call in its last month before maturity. Conversely, the last month of an option's life is a preferred time to sell since its time value can more easily and quickly be collected.

Now consider the other type of short-call position, covered-call writing. Because the seller of the call owns the underlying asset in this case, the risk is truncated. The purpose of writing a call on the underlying asset when it is owned is twofold. First, by writing a call option, one always decreases the risk of owning the asset. Second, writing a call can increase the overall realized return on the asset. The profit profile for a covered short call (or a covered write) in Figure 14–7 provides further illustration. The following summarizes the basic risk–return features for the covered short-call position.

FIGURE 14-7   Profit Profile for a Covered Short Call

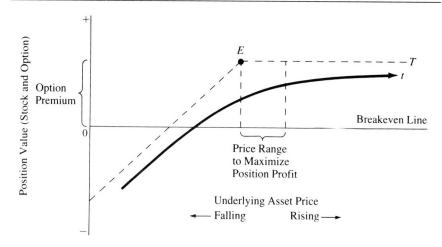

Profit potential: limited (exercise price − asset price + call premium)

Loss potential: limited (asset price − call premium)

Effect of time decay: positive

Market expectation: neutral to mildly bullish

By owning the underlying asset, the covered-call writer's loss on the asset for a price decline is decreased by the original amount of the premium collected for selling the option. The total loss on the position is limited to the extent that the asset is one of limited liability, such as a stock, and cannot fall below zero. The maximum profit on the combined asset and option position is higher than if the option was written alone, but lower than simply owning the asset with no short call written on it. Once the asset increases in price by a significant amount the call buyer will very likely exercise the right to purchase the asset at the prespecified exercise price. Thus, covered-call writing is a tool or strategy for enhancing an asset's realized return while lowering its risk in a sideways market.

Long Put

Again, the put option conveys to its purchasers the right to sell a given quantity of some asset at a prespecified price on or before its expiration date. Similar to a long call, a **long put** is also a highly leveraged position, but the purchaser of the put makes money on the investment only when the price of the underlying asset declines. While a call buyer has unlimited profit potential, a put buyer has limited profit potential since the price of the underlying asset can never drop below zero. Yet like the long-call position, the put buyer can never lose more than the initial investment (the option's

FIGURE 14-8 Profit Profile for a Long Put

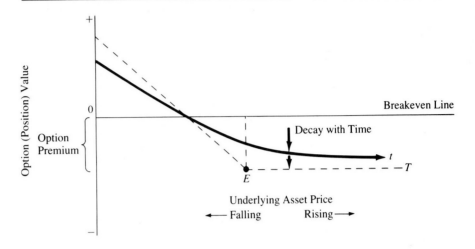

premium). The profit profile for a long put is seen in Figure 14-8. The following summarizes the basic risk–return features for the profit profile of a long-put position.

Profit potential: limited (asset price must be greater than zero)

Loss potential: limited (to cost of put)

Effect of time decay: negative or positive

Market expectation: bearish

An interesting pricing ambiguity for this bearish investment is how the put's price is affected by the time decay. With the long call there is a clearcut relation—that is, the effect of the time decay is to diminish the value of the call. The relationship is not so clear with the long put. Although at certain prices for the underlying asset the value of the long-put position decreases with time, there exist lower asset prices for which its value will increase with time. It is the put's ambiguous relationship with time that makes its correct price difficult to ascertain. (This topic will be further explored in Chapter 15.)

One uniquely attractive attribute of the long put is its negative relationship with the underlying asset. In terms of the capital asset pricing model, it has a negative beta (though usually numerically larger than that of the underlying asset, due to the leverage affect). Therefore, the long put is an ideal **hedging instrument** for the holder of the underlying asset who wants to protect against a price decline. If the investor is wrong and the price of the asset moves up instead, the profit from the asset's price increase is only moderately diminished by the cost of the put. More on hedging and related concepts is discussed in Chapter 15.

Short Put

As was true for the short-call position, put writing can be covered or uncovered (naked). The risk–return features of the uncovered (naked) **short put** are discussed first.

For taking on the obligation to buy the underlying asset at the exercise price, the put writer receives a premium. The maximum profit for the uncovered-put writer is this premium which is initially received. Figure 14–9 provides further illustration.

While the loss potential is limited for the uncovered-put writer, it is nonetheless still very large. Thus, someone neutral on the direction of the market would sell out-of-the-money (lower exercise price) puts. A more bullish sentiment would suggest that at-the-money options be sold. The investor who is convinced the market will go up should maximize return by selling a put with a larger premium. As with the long put, the time-decay effect is ambiguous and depends on the price of the underlying asset. The following summarizes the basic risk–return features for the profit profile of an uncovered short-put position.

Profit potential: limited (to put premium)

Loss potential: limited (asset price must be greater than zero)

Effect of time decay: positive or negative

Market expectation: neutral to bullish

Referring again to Figure 14–7 for the combined short-call and long-asset position, notice the striking resemblance of its profit profile at expiration to that for the uncovered short put. This relationship can be seen mathematically by using put–call parity. That is, the synthetic put price $P_T = E_c + C_T - S_T$, or at expiration the value of the put should equal the exercise price

FIGURE 14–9 Profit Profile for an Uncovered Short Put

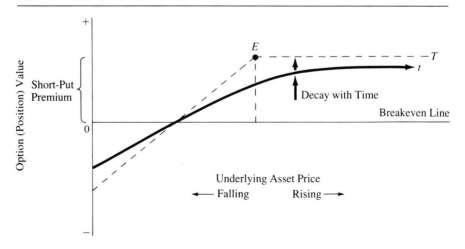

of the call option plus the call option's value minus the value at time T of the underlying asset. Buying (writing) a call and selling (buying) the underlying asset (or vice versa) allows an investor to achieve essentially the same risk–return combination as would be received from a long put (short put). This combination of two assets to equal the risk and return of a third is referred to as a synthetic asset (or synthetic option in this case). Synthesizing two financial instruments to resemble a third is an arbitrage process and is a central concept of finance theory.

Now a look at covered short puts is in order to round out the basics of option strategies. For margin purposes and in a theoretical sense, selling a put against a short-asset position would be the sale of a covered put. However, this sort of position has a limited profit potential that is obtained if the underlying asset is anywhere below the exercise price of the put at expiration. This position also has unlimited upside risk, since the short position in the asset will accrue losses while the profit from the put sale is limited. Essentially, this position is equivalent to the uncovered or naked short call, except that the latter has less expensive transaction costs. Moreover, because the time value for put options is generally less than that of calls, it will be advantageous to short the call.

Strictly speaking, a short put is covered only if the investor also owns a corresponding put with exercise price equal to or greater than that of the written put. Such a position, called a spread, is discussed later in this chapter.

Long Straddle

A straddle is a simultaneous position in both a call and a put on the same underlying asset. A **long straddle** involves purchasing both the call and the put. By combining these two seemingly opposing options an investor can get the best risk–return combination that each offers. The profit profile for a long straddle in Figure 14–10 illustrates the nature of this synthetic asset. The following summarizes the basic risk–return features for the profit profile of a long-straddle position.

Profit potential: unlimited on upside, limited on downside

Loss potential: limited (to cost of call and put premiums)

Effect of time decay: negative

Market sentiment: bullish or bearish

The long straddle's profit profile makes clear that its risk–reward picture is simply that of the long call overlapped by the long put, with each horizontal segment truncated (represented by the horizontal dashed lines on the bottom). An investor will profit on this type of position as long as the price of the underlying asset moves sufficiently up or down to more than cover the original cost of the option premiums. Thus, a long straddle is an effective strategy for someone expecting the volatility of the underlying asset to

FIGURE 14–10   Profit Profile for a Long Straddle

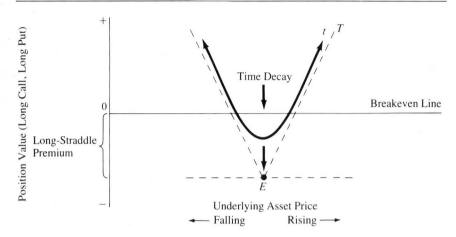

increase in the future. In the same light, the investor who buys a straddle expects the underlying asset's volatility of price to be greater than that imputed in the option price.

Since time decay is working against the value of this position, it might be unwise to purchase a straddle composed of a call and put in their last month to maturity when their time decay is greatest. It would be possible to reduce the cost of the straddle by purchasing a high-exercise-price call and a low-exercise put (out-of-the-money options); however, the necessary up or down movement in the asset's price in order to profit is larger. Sample Problem 14.5 provides further illustration.

Sample Problem 14.5

Situation: An investor feels the stock market is going to break sharply up or down but is not sure which way. However, the investor is confident that market volatility will increase in the near future. To express his position the investor puts on a long straddle using options on the S&P 500 index, buying both at-the-money call and put options on the September contract. The current September S&P 500 futures contract price is 155.00. Assume the position is held to expiration.

Transaction:

1. Buy 1 September 155 call at $2.00.   ($1,000)
2. Buy 1 September 155 put at $2.00.   ($1,000)
   Net initial investment (position value)   ($2,000)

Results:

1. If futures price = 150.00:
   (a) 1 September call expires at $0.   ($1,000)
   (b) 1 September put expires at $5.00. $2,500
   (c) Less initial cost of put   ($1,000)
   Ending position value (net profit) $ 500

2. If futures price = 155.00:
   (a) 1 September call expires at $0.   ($1,000)
   (b) 1 September put expires at $0.   ($1,000)
   Ending position value (net loss) $2,000

3. If futures price = 160.00:
   (a) 1 September call expires at $5.00. $2,500
   (b) 1 September call expires at $0.   ($1,000)
   (c) Less initial cost of put   ($1,000)
   Ending position value (net profit) $ 500

Summary:

Maximum profit potential: unlimited. If the market had contributed to move below 150.00 or above 160.00, the position would have continued to increase in value.

Maximum loss potential: $2,000, the initial investment.

Breakeven points: 151.00 and 159.00, for the September S&P 500 futures contract.[2]

Effect of time decay: negative, as evidenced by the loss incurred, with no change in futures price (result 2)●

Short Straddle

For the most part, the **short straddle** implies the opposite risk–return characteristics of the long straddle. A short straddle is a simultaneous position in both a short call and a short put on the same underlying asset. Contrary to the long-straddle position, selling a straddle can be an effective strategy when an investor expects little or no movement in the price of the underlying asset. A similar interpretation of its use would be that the investor expects the future volatility of the underlying asset's price that is currently im-

---

[2] Breakeven points for the straddle are calculated as follows.

		Upside BEP	=	Exercise price	+	Initial net investment (in points)
		159.00	=	155.00	+	4.00
		Downside BEP	=	Exercise price	−	Initial net investment (in points)
		151.00	=	155.00	−	4.00

FIGURE 14–11 Profit Profile for a Short Straddle

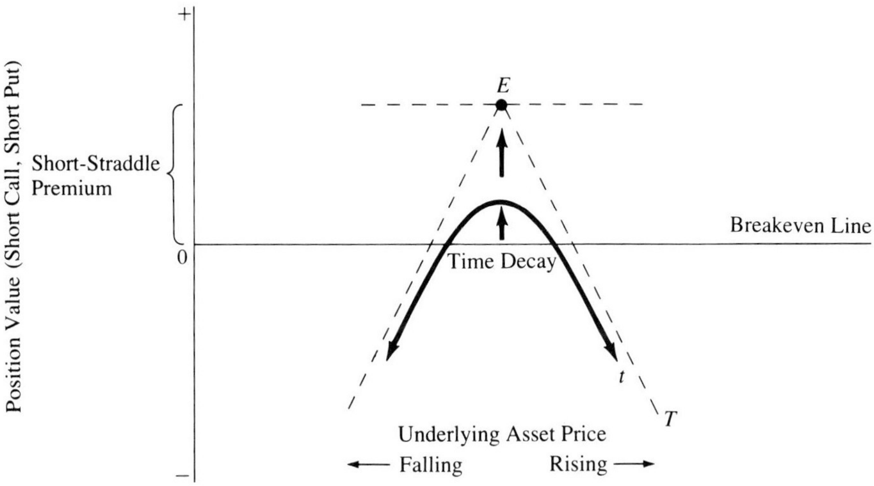

pounded in the option premiums to decline. Moreover, since the time decay is a positive effect for the value of this position, one appropriate time to set a short straddle might be in the last month to expiration for the combined call and put. Figure 14–11 shows the short straddle's profit profile, and Sample Problem 14.6 provides further illustration. The following summarizes the basic risk–return features for the profit profile of a short-straddle position.

Profit potential: limited (to call and put premiums)

Loss potential: unlimited on upside, limited on downside

Effect of time decay: positive

Market expectation: neutral

Sample Problem 14.6

Situation: An investor feels the market is overestimating price volatility at the moment and that prices are going to remain stable for some time. To express his opinion, the investor sells a straddle consisting of at-the-money call and put options on the September S&P 500 futures contract, for which the current price is 155.00. Assume the position is held to expiration.

Transaction:

1. Sell 1 September 155 call at $2.00 (× $500 per point).	$1,000
2. Sell 1 September 155 put at $2.00.	$1,000
Net initial inflow (position value)	$2,000

Results:

1. If futures price = 150.00:
    (a) 1 September 155 call expires at 0. $1,000
    (b) 1 September 155 put expires at $5.00.   ($2,500)
    (c) Plus initial inflow from sale of put $1,000
    Ending position value (net loss)   ($ 500)

2. If futures price = 155.00:
    (a) 1 September 155 call expires at 0. $1,000
    (b) 1 September 155 put expires at 0. $1,000
    Ending position value (net profit) $2,000

3. If futures price = 160.00:
    (a) 1 September 155 call expires at $5.00.   ($2,500)
    (b) 1 September put expires at 0. $1,000
    (c) Plus initial inflow from sale of call $1,000
    Ending position value (net loss)   ($ 500)

Summary:

Maximum profit potential: $2,000, result 2, where futures price does not move.

Maximum loss potential: unlimited. If futures price had continued up over 160.00 or down below 145.00, this position would have kept losing money.

Breakeven points: 151.00 and 159.00, an eight-point range for profitability of the position.[3]

Effect of time decay: positive, as evidenced by result 2●

Long Vertical (Bull) Spread

When dealing strictly in options, a **spread** is a combination of any two or more of the same type of options (two calls or two puts, for instance) on the same underlying asset. A **vertical spread** specifies that the options have the same maturity month. Finally, a **long vertical spread** designates a position for which one has bought a low-exercise-price call (or a low-exercise-price put) and sold a high-exercise-price call (or a high-exercise-price put) that both mature in the same month. A long vertical spread is also known as a **bull spread** because of the bullish market expectation of the investor who enters into it.

Actually, the long vertical spread (or bull spread) is not a strongly bullish position, because the investor limits the profit potential in selling the high-exercise-price call (or high-exercise-price put). Rather, this is a popular position when it is expected that the market will more likely go up than down. Therefore, the bull spread conveys a bit of uncertainty about future

---

[3] Breakeven points for the short straddle are calculated in the same manner as for the long straddle: exercise price plus initial prices of options.

FIGURE 14–12   Profit Profile for a Long Vertical Spread

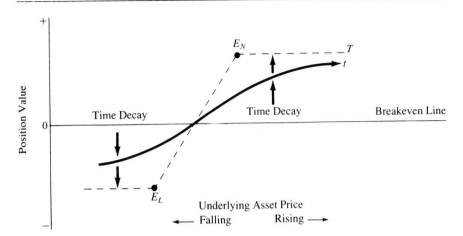

market conditions. Of course, the higher the exercise price at which the call is sold, the more bullish the position. An examination of the profit profile for the long vertical spread (see Figure 14–12) can tell more about its risk–return attributes. The following summarizes the basic risk–return features for the profit profile of a long-vertical-spread position.

Profit potential: limited (up to the higher exercise price)

Loss potential: limited (down to the lower exercise price)

Effect of time decay: mixed

Market expectation: cautiously bullish

Although profit is limited by the shorted call on the upside, the loss potential is also truncated at the lower exercise price by the same short call. There are other reasons for this being a mildly bullish strategy. The effect of time decay is ambiguous up to the expiration or liquidation of the position. That is, if the asset price—call it S_t— is near the exercise price of the higher-price option E_H, then the position acts more like a long call and time-decay effect is negative. Conversely, if S_t is near the exercise price of the lower-price option E_L, then the bull spread acts more like a short call and the time-decay effect is neutral.

Consequently, unless an investor is more than mildly bullish, it would probably be unwise to put on a bull spread with the low exercise price call near the current price of the asset while both options are in their last month to expiration. Sample Problem 14.7 provides further illustration.

Sample Problem 14.7

Situation: An investor is moderately bullish on the West German mark. He would like to be long but wants to reduce the cost and risk of this position in

case he is wrong. To express his opinion, the investor puts on a long vertical spread by buying a lower-exercise-price call and selling a higher-exercise-price call with the same month to expiration. Assume the position is held to expiration.

Transaction:

1. Buy 1 September 0.37 call at 0.0047 ($\times$ 125,000 per point). ($ 587.50)
2. Sell 1 September 0.38 call at 0.0013. $ 162.50
   Net initial investment (position value) ($ 425.00)

Results:

1. If futures price = 0.3700:
   (a) 1 September 0.37 call expires at 0. ($ 587.50)
   (b) 1 September 0.38 call expires at 0. $ 162.50
   Ending position value (net loss) ($ 425.00)

2. If futures price = 0.3800:
   (a) 1 September 0.37 call expires at 0.0100. $1,250.00
   (b) 1 September 0.38 call expires at 0. $ 162.50
   Less initial cost of 0.37 call ($ 587.50)
   Ending position value (net profit) $ 825.00

3. If futures price = 0.3900:
   (a) 1 September 0.38 call expires at 0.0200. $2,500.00
   (b) 1 September put expires at 0. ($1,250.00)
   Less initial premium of 0.37 call ($ 587.50)
   Plus initial premium of 0.38 call $ 162.50
   Ending position value (net profit) ($ 825.00)

Summary:

Maximum profit potential: $825.00, result 2.

Maximum loss potential: $425.00, result 1.

Breakeven point: 0.3734.[4]

Effect of time decay: mixed, positive if price is at high end of range and negative if at low end●

Short Vertical (Bear) Spread

The **short vertical spread** is simply the reverse of the corresponding long position. That is, an investor buys a high-exercise-price call (or put) and sells a low-exercise-price call (or put), both having the same time to expiration left. As the more common name for this type of option position is **bear spread,** it is easy to infer the type of market sentiment consistent with this position. The profit profile for the short vertical spread is seen in Figure 14–13.

---

[4] Breakeven point for the long vertical spread is computed as lower exercise price plus price of long call minus price of short call (0.3734 = 0.3700 + 0.0047 − 0.0013).

FIGURE 14-13   Profit Profile for a Short Vertical Spread

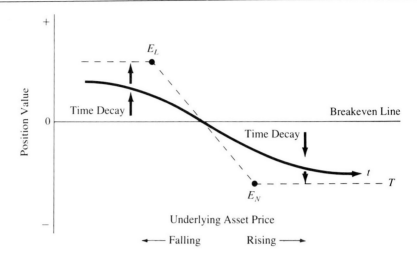

As the profit profile indicates, this strategy is profitable as long as the underlying asset moves down in price. Profit is limited to a price decline in the asset down to the lower exercise price, while risk is limited on the upside by the long-call position. From the time-decay effects shown, a mildly bearish investor might consider using options in the last month to expiration with the E_L option near the money. The following summarizes the basic risk–return features for the profit profile of a short-vertical-spread position.

Profit potential: limited (down to E_L)

Loss potential: limited (up to E_H)

Effect of time decay: mixed (opposite to that of long vertical spread)

Market sentiment: mildly bearish

Calendar (Time) Spreads

A **calendar spread** (also called a **time** or **horizontal spread**) consists of the sale of one option and the simultaneous purchase of another option with the same exercise price but a longer term to maturity. The objective of the calendar spread is to capture the faster erosion in the time-premium portion of the shorted nearer-term-to-maturity option. By taking a position in two of the same type options (two calls or two puts), both with the same exercise price, the investor utilizing this strategy expresses a neutral opinion on the market. In other words, the investor is interested in selling time rather than predicting the price direction of the underlying asset. Thus, a calendar spread might be considered appropriate for a sideways-moving or quiet market. However, if the underlying asset's price moves significantly up or down, the calendar spread will lose part of its original value. Figure 14–14 displays the calendar spread's profit profile and related risk–return attributes.

FIGURE 14–14   Profit Profile for a Neutral Calendar Spread

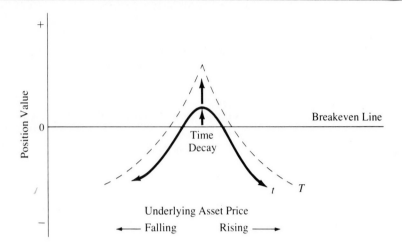

The profit profile shows that this strategy will make money for a rather narrow range of price movement in the underlying asset. While similar in nature to the short straddle (both are neutral strategies), the calendar spread is more conservative. The reason? It has both a lower profit potential and lower (limited) risk than the short straddle. The lower potential profit is the result of only benefiting from the time decay in one option premium instead of two (the call and the put) for the short straddle. Moreover, taking opposite positions in the same type of option at the same exercise price adds a loss limit on each side against adverse price moves. The following summarizes the basic risk–return features for the profit profile of a neutral calendar-spread position.

Profit potential: limited

Loss potential: limited (to original cost of position)

Effect of time decay: positive. (Option sold loses value faster than option bought.)

Market sentiment: neutral

The calendar spread does not have to be neutral in sentiment. By diagonalizing this spread it is possible to express an opinion on the market. For instance, by selling a near-term higher-exercise-price option and purchasing a longer-term lower-exercise-price option, the investor is being bullish in position. Such a position is thus referred to as a bullish calendar spread. Why is it bullish? Remember that with the neutral calendar spread we are concerned solely with benefiting from the faster time decay in the premium of the shorted near-term option. Any significant movement in price upwards, for instance, would have not been profitable because it would have slowed the time decay and increased the intrinsic value of the shorted near-term option. In fact we would eventually lose money, because the difference

in premiums between the near-term and the longer-term options (the spread) would narrow as the underlying asset's price increased. However, the bullish calendar spread is much like a long vertical (or bull) spread in that a modest increase in price for the asset up to the higher exercise price will be profitable. At the same time, though, the bullish calendar spread also reaps some of the benefits from the greater time decay in the nearer-term option's premium. While this strategy might sound superior to the straight bull spread, it really depends on market conditions. With a bullish calendar spread, its gain from time decay will probably not be as great as that from a neutral calendar spread, nor will its bullish nature be as profitable as a straight bull spread in the event of a modest price increase for the underlying asset.

SUMMARY

This chapter has introduced some of the essential differences between the two most basic kinds of option, calls and puts. A delineation was made of the relationship between the option's price or premium and that of the underlying asset. The option's value was shown to be composed of intrinsic value, or the underlying asset price less the exercise price, and time value. Moreover, it was demonstrated that the time value decays over time, particularly in the last month to maturity for an option.

Index and futures options were studied to introduce these important financial instruments. Put–call parity theorems were developed for European, American, and futures options in order to show the basic valuation relationship between the underlying asset and its call and put options. Finally, investment application of options and related combinations were discussed, along with relevant risk–return characteristics. A thorough understanding of this chapter is essential as a basic tool to successful study of option-valuation models in the next chapter.

QUESTIONS AND PROBLEMS

1. Define the following terms.
   (a) call option   (g) exercise price
   (b) put option   (h) put–call parity
   (c) striking price   (i) intrinsic value
   (d) straddle   (j) European option
   (e) option   (k) American option
   (f) spread   (l) time value

2. Compare the following pairs of investment strategies.
   (a) Which is riskier, buying or selling a call option?
   (b) Which is riskier, writing a naked call option or writing a covered call option?
   (c) Other things being equal, which option has greater value, an American call option or a European call option?
   (d) Other things being equal, which option should have greater value, the option written on a low-beta stock or the option written on a high-beta stock?

3. Plot profit versus the stock price for a call option with an exercise price of $100 and a premium of $3.

4. HHH, Inc. is a company doing medical research. It has decided to place all of its resources into finding a cure for AIDS. If HHH is successful, the value of its stock will increase tenfold. If the company is unsuccessful, it will be bankrupt in ten years.
   (a) If you believe that there is a 50-percent chance of success, is there an investment strategy you can devise using put and call options to exploit this situation?
   (b) How might your answer in (a) change if you believe that there is only a 33-percent chance of success?

5. Carefully explain the difference between a vertical bull spread and a vertical bear spread. When would you use the vertical bull spread? When would you use the vertical bear spread?

6. You would like to purchase a put option on XYZ Company's stock. If only call options exist on XYZ's stock, explain how you could create your own put option.

7. What is the benefit of purchasing a call option over purchasing the underlying stock? What are the disadvantages?

8. Carefully explain why the value of an option can never be negative.

9. Compare an option to a futures contract. How are they similar? How are they different?

10. What is a butterfly spread? When would an investor purchase a calendar spread?

11. Plot the profit opportunities for an investor who purchases a long straddle. Assume that the exercise price on the put and call options is $100.

12. Use the information given in the previous question to plot the profit opportunities for a short straddle. Compare these two positions.

13. Explain what is meant by an option that is:
    (a) in the money.
    (b) at the money.
    (c) out of the money.

14. Explain how the time value of an option behaves as the option moves closer to expiration.

15. Given a stock valued at $25 on February 1, 1989, and the following information about call-option premiums, what is the time value for each of the options?

Exercise Price	March	June	September
20	$5.75	$6.75	$7.50
25	1.00	2.00	3.00
30	0.25	0.50	0.75

16. What impact does the payment of cash dividends by XYZ Company have on the put options of XYZ? How does it affect the call options of XYZ?

17. Discuss the uses of an option on foreign currencies.

18. Why would you never exercise an index option before the exercise date?

19. Explain the logic behind the put–call parity relationship shown in Table 14–2.

20. A call option with six months to maturity and an exercise price of 20 is selling for $3. Assuming discrete compounding, a risk-free rate of interest of 8 percent, and a current stock price of $19, what is the value of a European put option with a strike price of 20 and one year to maturity?

21. For a stock with a price of $10, a put option with three months to maturity and an exercise price of $12 is selling for $3. Assuming discrete compounding and a risk-free rate of 8 percent, what are the boundaries of the price for an American call option?

22. What are the major advantages of an option on futures over an option on an underlying asset?

23. What is a synthetic put? Why would a synthetic put be useful if you have listed put options?

24. Compare the risk–return features of a long call with a short naked call. If these two types of call positions were to be continued indefinitely, what would be the result?

25. Compare the risk–return features for a short covered call with an uncovered short put. Be sure to discuss the time decay.

26. An investor wants to use a long straddle, the current market index being 150. He buys the three-month 150 call for $5.00 and the three-month 150 put at $4.50. If the market rises to 180 at the end of three months, what is the investor's profit or loss? If the market falls to 125 at the end of three months, what is the investor's profit or loss? If the market stays at 150 at the end of three months, what is the profit or loss?

27. Calculate the breakeven points (upside and downside) for the straddle described in the previous problem.
28. An investor wants to use a short straddle; the current market index is 100. He sells a one-month 100 call for $1.50 and a one-month 100 put for $1.75. At the end of one month the market index is: (a) 100, (b) 90, or (c) 80. What is the profit or loss for (a), (b), and (c)?
29. If an investor sells a high-exercise-price call and buys a low-exercise-price call of the same month to expiration, what does he hope for the price of the underlying asset?
30. How do you profit from a neutral calendar spread?

APPENDIX 14A: OPTIONS AND EXCHANGES

American exchanges trade in a wide variety of options. Table 14A–1 on pages 482–483 summarizes the more important options and option exchanges.

REFERENCES

Ball, C., and W. Torous. "Bond Prices Dynamics and Options." *Journal of Financial and Quantitative Analysis*, v. 18 (December 1983), pp. 517–32.

Bhattacharya, M. "Empirical Properties of the Black-Scholes Formula Under Ideal Conditions." *Journal of Financial and Quantitative Analysis*, v. 15 (December 1980), pp. 1081–1106.

Black, F. "Capital Market Equilibrium with Restricted Borrowing." *Journal of Business*, v. 45 (July 1972), pp. 444–45.

―――. "Fact and Fantasy in the Use of Options." *Financial Analysts Journal*, v. 31 (July/August 1985), pp. 36–72.

―――, and M. Scholes. "The Pricing of Options and Corporate Liabilities." *Journal of Political Economy*, v. 31 (May/June 1973), pp. 637–54.

Bodhurta, J., and G. Courtadon. "Efficiency Tests of the Foreign Currency Options Market." *Journal of Finance*, v. 41 (March 1986), pp. 151–62.

Bookstaber, R. M. *Option Pricing and Strategies in Investing*. Addison-Wesley Publishing Company, 1981.

―――, and R. Clarke. *Option Strategies for Institutional Investment Management*. Addison-Wesley Publishing Company, 1983.

TABLE 14A–1 Summary of the Types of Options Offered by Different Exchanges

Exchange Symbol	Stock Options	Commodity Options	Index Options	Interest-Rate Options	Currency Options	Futures Options
AMEX	More than 100 stocks		Major Market Index Amex Market Value Index Computer Technology Index Oil and Gas Index Airline Index	U.S. T-note		
CBOE	More than 140 stocks		S&P 100 Index S&P 500 Index S&P OTC 250 Index	U.S. 30-year T-bonds		
NASD			NASDAQ 100 Index			
NYSE	NYSE stocks		NYSE Index NYSE Double Index			
PHLX	More than 70 stocks		Gaming/Hotel Stock Index Gold/Silver Stock Index Value Line National OTC Index		British pound Swiss franc Canadian dollar Japanese yen West German mark French franc	
PSE	More than 60 stocks		Technology Index			
ACC						Gold futures (large contract)
CBT					British pound Swiss franc Canadian dollar	T-note futures Silver futures Soybean futures

TABLE 14A–1 *(continued)*

Exchange Symbol	Stock Options	Commodity Options	Index Options	Interest-Rate Options	Currency Options	Futures Options
CBT						Corn futures
CME and IMM					Japanese yen West German mark French franc	S&P 500 Index futures Eurodollar futures Swiss franc futures British pound futures Cattle futures Hog futures
COMEX						Gold futures (large contract) Index futures
CSCE						Sugar futures
CTN						Cotton futures
KC						Wheat futures
LIFFE						Sterling futures Eurodollar futures
MID-AM						Gold futures (small contract) Wheat futures Soybean futures
MPLS						Wheat futures
NYFE						NYSE Composite Index futures
NYME						No. 2 heating oil futures Crude oil futures

Brennan, M., and E. Schwartz. "The Valuation of American Put Options." *Journal of Finance,* v. 32 (May 1977), pp. 449–62.

Cox, J. C., and M. Rubinstein. *Option Markets.* Prentice-Hall, 1985.

———. "Option Pricing: A Simplified Approach." *Journal of Financial Economics,* v. 8 (September 1979), pp. 229–63.

Eckardt, W., and S. Williams. "The Complete Options Indexes." *Financial Analysts Journal,* v. 40 (July/August 1984), pp. 48–57.

Ervine, J., and A. Rudd. "Index Options: The Early Evidence." *Journal of Finance,* v. 40 (June 1985), pp. 743–56.

Finnerty, J. "The Chicago Board Options Exchange and Market Efficiency." *Journal of Financial and Quantitative Analysis,* v. 13 (March 1978), pp. 28–38.

Galai, D., and R. W. Masulis. "The Option Pricing Model and the Risk Factor of Stock." *Journal of Financial Economics,* v. 3 (March 1976), pp. 53–81.

———, R. Geske, and S. Givots. *Option Markets.* Addison-Wesley Publishing Company, 1988.

Gastineau, G. *The Stock Options Manual.* McGraw-Hill, 1979.

Geske, R., and K. Shastri. "Valuation by Approximation: A Comparison of Alternative Option Valuation Techniques." *Journal of Financial and Quantitative Analysis,* v. 20 (March 1985), pp. 45–72.

Jarrow, R. A., and A. Rudd. *Option Pricing.* Richard D. Irwin, 1983.

Macbeth, J., and L. Merville. "An Empirical Examination of the Black-Scholes Call Option Pricing Model." *Journal of Finance,* v. 34 (December 1979), pp. 1173–86.

Merton, R. "Theory of Rational Option Pricing." *Bell Journal of Economics and Management Science,* v. 4 (Spring 1973), pp. 141–83.

Rendleman, R. J. Jr., and B. J. Barter. "Two-State Option Pricing." *Journal of Finance,* v. 34 (September 1979), pp. 1093–1110.

Ritchken, P. *Options: Theory, Strategy, and Applications.* Scott, Foresman, 1987.

Rubinstein, M., and H. Leland. "Replicating Options with Positions in Stock and Cash." *Financial Analysts Journal,* v. 37 (July/August 1981).

———, and J. Cox. *Option Markets.* Prentice-Hall, 1985.

Sears, S., and G. Trennepohl. "Measuring Portfolio Risk in Options." *Journal of Financial and Quantitative Analysis,* v. 17 (September 1982), pp. 391–410.

Smith, C. "Option Pricing: A Review." *Journal of Financial Economics,* v. 3 (January 1976), pp. 3–51.

Stoll, H. "The Relationships Between Put and Call Option Prices." *Journal of Finance,* v. 24 (December 1969), pp. 801–24.

Trennepohl, G. "A Comparison of Listed Option Premium and Black-Scholes Model Prices: 1973-1979." *Journal of Financial Research,* v. 4 (Spring 1981), pp. 11-20.

Weinstein, M. "Bond Systematic Risk and the Options Pricing Model." *Journal of Finance,* v. 38 (December 1983), pp. 1415-30.

Welch, W. *Strategies for Put and Call Option Trading.* Winthrop, 1982.

Whaley, R. "Valuation of American Call Options on Dividend Paying Stocks: Empirical Tests." *Journal of Financial Economics,* v. 10 (March 1982), pp. 29-58.

15 Option Valuation and Hedging

The option-pricing model (OPM) stands out as a powerful tool in finance. This is a result not only of its unique construction, but of the wide applicability of its analytic method to nearly any financial security as well. Black and Scholes (1973) developed the original model using complicated mathematics; fortunately, one does not need extensive quantitative training to understand their model. Another approach to option valuation, the binomial option-pricing model, has been developed since Black and Scholes by Cox, Ross, and Rubenstein (1979). The binomial approach yields substantially the same outcome as the Black and Scholes model, and even falls into the original model's form as it becomes more generalized. Nevertheless, the binomial pricing model (BPM) offers a more intuitive understanding for the option-valuation process.

This chapter discusses and utilizes examples of both the OPM and BPM; it also examines modifications to the Black and Scholes model for dividends and the particular case of futures options. The sensitivity of the option price to the Black–Scholes inputs is shown along with other measures of risk for the option. The pricing of put options is analyzed, and the basic tenets of option-pricing theory are extended to valuation of other financial securities. The chapter concludes with a critique of the Black–Scholes model. A formal derivation of the binomial option-pricing model and an examination of its relation to the Black and Scholes model is undertaken in Appendix 15A at the end of this chapter.[1]

THE BINOMIAL OPTION-PRICING APPROACH

Before explaining the **binomial option-pricing model (BOPM),** its two major underlying assumptions must be defined. First, the binomial approach assumes that trading takes place in discrete time—that is, on a period-by-

---

[1] Other methods for deriving Black and Scholes's (1973) option-pricing model are explored in Chapter 22.

period basis. (Appendix 15A demonstrates that reducing the duration of each period causes the binomial model to eventually fall into the Black and Scholes construction: their model assumes continuous time trading.) Second, it is assumed that the stock price (underlying asset) can take on only two possible values each period—in essence, it can go up or go down. (This latter assumption is called a *binomial process* and should probably be familiar from some past mathematics or statistics course.) Finally, the binomial model and the Black and Scholes model are illustrated using options on common stock, since these options are the best known.

This chapter opens with a simple example in which a stock with current price S can advance or decline during the next period by either a factor of u (up) or d (down), respectively. Therefore, the value S in the next period is either uS or dS. Next, suppose that a call option exists on this stock with a current price C and an exercise price of X, and that it has one period left to maturity. At its expiration, this option's value, which is uniquely related to that of its underlying stock, will be either

$$C_u = \text{Max}\,(0,\, uS - X) \tag{15.1}$$

(if S changes by a fraction equal to $u - 1 \geq 0$, that is, increases or remains the same); or

$$C_d = \text{Max}\,(0,\, dS - X) \tag{15.2}$$

(if S changes by a fraction equal to $d - 1 < 0$, that is, decreases).

Also for the moment, assume that the riskless interest rate r for both borrowing and lending is equal to 7 percent over the one time period and that the exercise price of the option is equal to X.

To intuitively grasp the underlying concept of option pricing, a **riskless portfolio** must be set up—that is, a combination of assets that earns the riskless rate of interest over the chosen investment horizon. The investment horizon is assumed to be one period; the duration of this period can be any length of time—an hour, day, week, and so on. To do this h shares of the stock are sold and the call option is purchased at its current price of C. Moreover, the value of h is chosen such that the portfolio yields the same payoff whether the stock goes up or down.

$$C_u - h(uS) = C_d - h(dS) \tag{15.3}$$

By solving for h, the number of shares of stock to be sold short for each call option bought can be obtained:

$$h = \frac{C_u - C_d}{(u - d)S} \tag{15.4}$$

h is called the **hedge ratio.** Since the portfolio yields the same return under either of the two possible states for the stock, it is riskless and therefore should yield the riskless rate of return, r. It is important to remember that this must be true; otherwise arbitrage would result. Furthermore, because the ending portfolio value is equal to $(1 + r)$ times the beginning portfolio

value, the beginning portfolio value should equal its ending value discounted back to the present by a factor of $(1 + r)$, or:

$$C - hS = \frac{C_u - h(uS)}{1 + r} \tag{15.5}$$

Setting $R = 1 + r$, rearranging to solve for C and expanding h:

$$C = \frac{\dfrac{R - d}{u - d} C_u + \dfrac{u - R}{u - d} C_d}{R} \tag{15.6}$$

To simplify this equation:

$$p = \frac{R - d}{u - d} \quad \text{so} \quad 1 - p = \frac{u - R}{u - d} \tag{15.7}$$

Thus the option's value with one period to expiration is expressed:

$$C = \frac{pC_u + (1 - p)C_d}{R} \tag{15.8}$$

This is the binomial option-valuation equation in its most basic form.

To illustrate the model's functional qualities at this point, the following values are utilized while assuming the option has one period to expiration.

The same basic approach can be used to value put options. The put–call parity relationship derived in Chapter 14 can be used to derive the binomial option-pricing model. Starting with the put–call parity relationship from Equation (14.3):

$$C_{t,T} = P_{t,T} + S_t - X B_{t,T} \tag{14.3}$$

the value for C can be substituted from Equation (15.8) and P can be solved for, since this is a one-period model ($B = 1/R$) and the subscripts t and T can be dropped:

$$P = \frac{pCu + (1 - p)Cd + X}{R} - S \tag{15.8A}$$

which is the binomial solution of a put option.

For a put option with the following values the value of the put can be calculated using (15.8A):

$$
\begin{aligned}
X &= \$50 \\
S &= \$50 \\
u &= 1.10 \qquad uS = 55 \\
d &= 0.90 \qquad ud = 45 \\
R &= 1.05
\end{aligned}
$$

$$P = \frac{\dfrac{1.05 - 0.90}{1.10 - 0.90} 5 + \dfrac{1.10 - 1.05}{1.10 - 0.90} 0 + 50}{1.05} - 50$$

$$P = \$1.19$$

Summary of Binomial Option Pricing

At this stage, what is known about the binomial option-pricing relationship can be summarized.

1. The price does not depend on the preferences of investors: it works for all types of risk preferences.
2. The value of the option depends on u, d, R, X, and S. It requires no assumptions about stock prices S relative to any other securities or market index. Thus market factors and covariances with other securities are not needed.

Let

$X = \$100$
$S = \$100$
$u = (1.10)$, so $uS = \$110$
$d = (0.90)$, so $dS = \$ 90$; and
$R = 1.07$

First, the two possible option values at maturity need to be calculated as indicated in Figure 15–1, next page. Next, the value of p is calculated as indicated in Equation (15.7):

$$p = \frac{1.07 - 0.90}{1.10 - 0.90} = 0.85$$

and

$$1 - p = \frac{1.10 - 1.07}{1.10 - 0.90} = 0.15$$

Solving the binomial valuation equation as indicated in Equation (15.6):

$$C = \frac{0.85(10) + 0.15(0)}{1.07}$$
$$= \$7.94$$

The correct value for this particular call option today under the specified conditions is $7.94. The hedge ratio is computed as:

$$h = \frac{10 - 0}{(1.10 - 0.90)100} = 0.5$$

How can this information be useful in a market setting? Here are two examples. First, consider the situation where the actual current market price for this option is only $6.50. According to the calculations, this option is severely underpriced and should be purchased. Nevertheless, because assets are frequently mispriced relative to other assets—in this case the option relative to its underlying stock and a risk-free bond—any of the three can adjust to alleviate the mispricing. If the option were bought because it was thought to be undervalued and then the stock price dropped, the option's absolute dollar value would fall and any correction in its price relative to the

FIGURE 15-1   Possible Option Values at Maturity

Today		
Stock (S)	*Option (C)*	*Next Period (Maturity)*

$$uS = \$110$$

$$
\begin{aligned}
C_u &= \text{Max } (0, \ uS - X) \\
&= \text{Max } (0, \ 110 - 100) \\
&= \text{Max } (0, \ 10) \\
&= \$10
\end{aligned}
$$

$$\$100 \qquad C$$

$$dS = \$90$$

$$
\begin{aligned}
C_d &= \text{Max } (0, \ dS - X) \\
&= \text{Max } (0, \ 90 - 100) \\
&= \text{Max } (0, \ -10) \\
&= \$0
\end{aligned}
$$

stock's would be lost. Therefore, to eliminate such price risk, an offsetting position must be taken in the stock itself. The number of shares to sell (in this case) is given by h, the hedge ratio, which is equal to 0.5. Since an option controls one hundred shares of stock, this ratio implies that we would sell fifty shares of stock short. Furthermore, to make the portfolio entirely riskless and costless, the proceeds from the short sale of stock (less the cost of the option, $\$6.50 \times 100 = \$650$) are lent at the riskless rate of interest, 7 percent. A summary of this hedging strategy, and its resulting value under both possible outcomes for the stock, is shown in Table 15-1. For the sake of simplicity in presentation, it is assumed that there are neither transaction costs nor margin restrictions, and that the market is frictionless.

The results from Table 15-1 suggest an interesting phenomenon. The strategy earns the same amount of money whether the stock price goes up or down. Moreover, no money is invested at the outset of our position; thus, the riskless return can be obtained with no net investment. This type of

TABLE 15-1   Hedging Strategy for an Undervalued Option

Current Position Strategy		End-of-Period Position	
		S = 90	*S = 110*
Buy 1 call option.	($ 650)	0	$1000
Sell 50 shares of stock.	$5000	($4500)	($5500)
Lend at 7 percent.	($4350)	$4654	$4654
Value of position	0	$ 154	$ 154

portfolio is called an **arbitrage portfolio** and the resulting profit an **arbitrage profit.** In fact, whenever arbitrage profits are available, an investor has the opportunity to make unlimited profits simply by increasing his or her position by as large a factor as desired.

For instance, if the current market price for this option is $9.50, so that it is overpriced in the market, the reverse strategy could be implemented: sell one call option, buy fifty shares of stock, and borrow the residual cost of the position at the riskless rate of 7 percent. The outcome of this strategy is depicted in Table 15–2. Once again, the arbitrage portfolio has earned a riskless profit.

There is only one price at which this arbitrage profit will be eliminated: when the option premium equals $7.94. This, of course, is the theoretical price calculated earlier from the one-period binomial model. The impetus behind this example of the law of one price is that if a pricing disparity should occur, market participants would quickly discover and rectify the situation to their profit. If the option should be underpriced, buying the option would force its price up, selling the stock would push its price down, and lending at the risk-free rate would send this rate lower. These market forces would continue to operate until the option's price converged to its ''correct'' value.

The arbitrage argument discussed above is the foundation of option-pricing models in use today. An understanding of this argument provides a starting point for extensions and modifications of the basic option-pricing models to a more general model, which is discussed next.

The Generalized Binomial Model

This section focuses on the general binomial formula, its components, and its use. (Its strict derivation can be found in Appendix 15A of this chapter.) The general binomial pricing model with n periods to maturity is expressed:

$$C = \frac{1}{R^n} \sum_{k=0}^{n} \frac{n!}{k! \, (n - k)!} p^k (1 - p)^{n-k} \, \text{Max} \, (0, \, u^k d^{n-k} S - X) \qquad \textbf{(15.9)}$$

TABLE 15–2 Hedging Strategy for an Overvalued Option

		End-of-Period Position	
Current Position Strategy		*S = 90*	*S = 110*
Sell 1 call option.	$ 950	0	($1000)
Buy 50 shares of stock.	($5000)	$4500	$5500
Borrow remainder at 7 percent.	$4050	($4333)	($4333)
Ending value of position	0	$ 167	$ 167

in which n is the number of time periods, k represents the number of upward price movements, and all other terms are defined as before.

When compared to the one-period model, the general **binomial pricing model** may appear significantly more complicated; yet it is computationally simple. Note, however, that the variables u, d, and R are dependent on the length of the time period used. So if one-month periods are used (that is, each n is equal to one month), then R should be one plus the interest rate on a riskless bond maturing in one month, and u and d should correspond to the stock price's movement over a one-month period.

The factorial symbol $n!$ means to multiply all the whole numbers from 1 to n together. Thus:

$$n! = n(n-1)(n-2) \cdots 3 \times 2 \times 1 = n \times (n-1)!$$

For example:

    0! = 1
    1! = 1 × 0! = 1
    2! = 2 × 1! = 2
    3! = 3 × 2 × 1 = 3 × 2! = 6
    4! = 4 × 3 × 2 × 1 = 4 × 3! = 24
    5! = 5 × 4 × 3 × 2 × 1 = 5 × 4! = 120

The factorial symbol provides a useful notation for representing large numbers of the type encountered in the study of numerous outcomes, as shown in Equation (15.9).

It is useful to study Equation (15.9) in segments in order to more readily understand its construction. The first term of the summation is

$$\frac{n!}{k!(n-k)!} p^k(1-p)^{n-k} \tag{15.10}$$

This portion of the model is the binomial formula, interpreting p as the probability that a movement of u in the stock price will occur at each period k during the total n time periods. Looking at the second term from the summation:

$$\text{Max}(0, u^k d^{n-k}S - X) \tag{15.11}$$

The value of the option at expiration is available if there are k increases (out of a total of n) in the stock price of u percent within the total of n time periods. By summing all these terms the sum of the products can be obtained from multiplying the possible terminal option values by the probabilities that they will occur. Consequently, since the generalized binomial pricing formula (Equation 15.9) yields the expected value for the call option *at its maturity,* this value must be discounted back over the n periods at the riskless rate. Again, $R^n = (1 + r)^n$, as in the one-period model.

Efficiently illustrating the use of the binomial pricing model with multiple

time periods without using a computer requires limiting the number of time periods to three. First, the following values are assumed:

$S = \$100$
$X = \$100$
$R = 1.07$
$n = 3$ (the number of periods to expiration)
$u = 1.1$
$d = 0.90$

We can calculate the value of p from Equation (15.7) as 0.85 and $1 - p$ as 0.15. Next, it is necessary to calculate the four possible ending values for the call option after three periods:

$$C = \text{Max} [0, (1.1)^3 (0.90)^0 100 - 100] = 33.10$$
$$C = \text{Max} [0, (1.1)^2 (0.90)100 - 100] = 8.90$$
$$C = \text{Max} [0, (1.1) (0.90)^2 100 - 100] = 0$$
$$C = \text{Max} [0, (1.1)^0 (0.90)^3 100 - 100] = 0$$

Now these numbers are inserted into the model and the terms are summed:

$$
\begin{aligned}
C &= \frac{1}{(1.07)^3}\left[\frac{3!}{0!3!} (0.85)^0(0.15)^3 \times 0 + \frac{3!}{1!2!} (0.85)^1(0.15)^2 \times 0 \right.\\
&\quad \left. + \frac{3!}{2!1!} (0.85)^2(0.15)^1 \times 8.90 + \frac{3!}{3!0!} (0.85)^3(0.15)^0 \times 33.10\right]\\
&= \frac{1}{1.225}\left[0 + 0 + \frac{3\times2\times1}{2\times1\times1} (0.7225) (0.15) (8.90) + \frac{3\times2\times1}{3\times2\times1\times1}\right.\\
&\quad \left. \times (0.61413)(1)(33.10)\right]\\
&= \frac{1}{1.225}[(0.32513 \times 8.90) + (0.61413 \times 33.10)]\\
&= \$18.96
\end{aligned}
$$

As is easily seen from this example, working out a multiple-period problem by hand with this formula could become laborious as the number of periods increased. Fortunately, programming this model into a computer is not too difficult.

The Black–Scholes Option-Pricing Model (OPM)

In this section the option-pricing concept is extended to the continuous-time domain. While the binomial option-pricing model (BOPM) assumes discrete binomial changes in the underlying asset's price, the **Black–Scholes option-pricing model (OPM)** allows for continuous price changes. As the time period that is used becomes smaller and the number of periods to expiration increases, the BOPM approaches the Black–Scholes OPM as a limit. The

Black and Scholes model uses stochastic differential equations; their formula is actually the continuous-time equivalent of the generalized BOPM.[2]

This section displays the Black–Scholes model, interprets its components, and undertakes a simple example to demonstrate its use. The Black–Scholes option-pricing model is defined in Equation (15.12).

$$C_t = S_t N(d_1) - Xe^{-r\tau}N(d_2) \qquad (15.12)$$

where:

$$d_1 = \frac{\ln\frac{S_t}{X} + \left(r + \frac{\sigma_S^2}{2}\right)\tau}{\sigma_S\sqrt{\tau}}$$

$d_2 = d_1 - \sigma_S\sqrt{\tau}$

S_t = current stock price (or whatever the underlying asset may be);

X = options exercise price; and

τ = time to maturity in terms of a year, $(T - t)/365$, where $T-t$ is the number of days to maturity;

r = riskless rate for a security (usually a U.S. T-bill) that matures when the option does (assumed to be constant);

σ_S^2 = the instantaneous variance of the continuous returns on the stock (assumed to be constant over the life of the option);

$N(\ )$ = the normal cumulative distribution function;

e = the exponential (2.718282); and

$\ln$ = the natural logarithm.

Additionally, the Black–Scholes model assumes that:

1. Financial markets are frictionless.
2. The fractional change in the underlying security's price over any interval is distributed log normally.
3. The underlying security pays no dividends.
4. Taxes and transaction costs are zero.
5. The price determination mechanism (trading) takes place in a continuous-time domain.

From the Black–Scholes formula it can be seen that an option's price is a function of five variables:

$$C = f(S_t, X, \tau, r, \sigma_S^2) \qquad (15.13)$$

One of the strengths of this model (and the binomial model) is that no assumptions are made about the investor's assessment of the probabilities that the stock will go up or down. Rather, it is only required that investors

---

[2] Derivation of Black and Scholes's model in terms of stochastic differential equations is explored in Chapter 22.

agree on the *range* of possible prices for the underlying asset. This assessment of range is reflected in the σ_S^2 term within the Black–Scholes model. In fact, the other four determinants of the option's price (S, X, τ, r) are quite readily accessible in the financial press; it is therefore the estimate of σ_S^2 that remains as the crucial determinant of the option's price. Before becoming involved in an exploration of this important issue, however, it is necessary to examine the inherent structure of the Black–Scholes model.

Recall from the first option-pricing property mentioned earlier (Chapter 14) that the ending value of a call option is always

$$C_T = \text{Max} (0, S_T - X) \tag{15.14}$$

where C_T is the value at maturity. So to obtain the value of the call today at time t it is necessary to discount its ending value back to the present at some rate, or in continuous time by $e^{-r\tau}$. So:

$$C_t = e^{-r\tau} E[\text{Max} (0, S_T - X)] \tag{15.15}$$

Notice that an expectation operator $E[\ ]$ has been added in front of the term representing the option's maturity value. This is because the value of the stock S at time T is unknown. Suppose, however, that the stock is expected to earn some constant interest rate for the remainder of the option's life:

$$S_t = e^{-r\tau} S_T \tag{15.16}$$

where r is the constant interest rate, and τ is the time remaining in the option's life in terms of a year. Correspondingly, Equation (15.15) can be simplified into the following form:

$$C_t = \text{Max} [0, (e^{-r\tau} S_T - e^{-r\tau} X)] \tag{15.17}$$

Moreover, since the option has time remaining before it matures ($T - t$), it will have some time value (no matter how small that might be). That is, the probability exists that within the remaining time period $T - t$ the option may become worth more than when the investor originally bought it. Consequently, Equation (15.17) can be further simplified while for the moment assuming that $S_t > e^{-r\tau} X$. This ensures that the value of the option at expiration is greater than zero; hence the Max $[\ ]$ operator can be dropped from the equation, leaving:

$$C_t = e^{-r\tau} S_T - e^{-r\tau} X \tag{15.18}$$

The close resemblance of this expression to the construction of the Black–Scholes formula, Equation (15.12), is apparent. Equation (15.18) represents the current value for a call option when the probability that $S_T < X$ is zero. This is the perfect certainty condition: you are sure of making money on the option because the stock price will exceed the exercise price at maturity. To arrive at an expression that holds for the case of uncertainty consider the elements in Equation (15.18) separately.

First, what does $e^{-r\tau}X$, the discounted value of the exercise price, represent? Assuming that exercise can take place only at the option's maturity

date (a European-style option), $e^{-r\tau}X$ can be thought of as the cost of exercising the call at expiration, in present-value terms. Since the stock would be purchased only if $S_T > X$, then the probability that $S_T > X$ is of greatest interest. So for the moment:

$$p = \text{Prob } (S_T > X) \tag{15.19}$$

The present value of the cost of exercising the call times the probability that $S_T > X$ is represented by:

$$(e^{-r\tau}X) \, p \tag{15.20}$$

Next, look at the S_T term of Equation (15.18), the present value of the stock's price at expiration. Essentially, given that the call is exercised, $e^{-r\tau}S_T$ can be interpreted as the present value of what is received for paying $e^{-r\tau}X$. At expiration, when $S_T > X$, the value of the call will be positive because X dollars would have been paid and S_T dollars would have been received. Conversely, if $S_T < X$, the call would not be exercised, allowing it to expire worthless.

Moreover, in order to value the option, given that $S_T > X$, an investor would want to know by *how much* S_T exceeds X. Or similarly, how much would the investor receive in terms of $S_T - X$ by paying X dollars? Notationally:

$$X \, (S_T \mid S_T > X) \, p \tag{15.21}$$

So replacing S_T with Equation (15.21) yields:

$$C_t = e^{-r\tau}X \, (S_T \mid S_T > X) \, p - (e^{-r\tau}X) \, p \tag{15.22}$$

Before moving to the final step, interpretation of Equation (15.22) is in order. The equation says that the current value of a call option is the present value of the expected value of S_T, given that the stock ends up in the money $(S_T > X)$, times the probability that it will, minus the present value of what the option would cost to exercise times the probability of exercise, [Prob $(S_T > X)$].

Now to make matters a little simpler, define $q \equiv X(S_T \mid S_T > X)p$. Furthermore, if we evaluate q by rewriting it in terms of its integral and simplifying, and evaluate p by expanding S_T in terms of the assumed underlying stochastic process, the following values are obtained.[3]

$$q = e^{r\tau} \, S_t N(d_1) \tag{15.23}$$

$$p = N(d_1 - \sigma_S \sqrt{\tau}) = N(d_2) \tag{15.24}$$

Substituting these two expressions for q and p into Equation (15.22):

$$C_t = S_t N(d_1) - e^{-r\tau}XN(d_2)$$

which is the Black–Scholes option-pricing formula.

---

[3] These steps are bypassed in order not to overcomplicate the analysis. However, for a formal evaluation of these terms, see Jarrow and Rudd (1983).

The Hedge Ratio

One question remains unanswered from our exploration of the components of the Black–Scholes model. What is the appropriate interest rate (r)? Recall from the binomial approach that a hedge ratio was derived based on a portfolio of the call option and stock that yielded the same return whether the stock price went up or down. Furthermore, since the portfolio yielded the same return for each possible outcome of the call and stock prices (up or down), the portfolio was riskless and therefore should yield the riskless rate of interest (otherwise arbitrage profits would be available). For instance, if the riskless portfolio, composed of one call and an appropriate number of shares of stock, yielded less than the riskless rate of interest, we would profit (risklessly) by selling the overvalued portfolio and investing the proceeds in higher-yielding risk-free securities. Thus the arbitrage argument was utilized to demonstrate the relative pricing mechanism between three assets. Once the BOPM was developed based on these conditions, it became apparent that the appropriate interest rate to use in the model was the riskless rate. Moreover, the appropriate number of shares of stock to hold or sell was determined to be the hedge ratio.

The riskless hedging argument also prevails in the Black–Scholes model's derivation, and the appropriate hedge ratio between the call option and stock is formulated through a similar series of conditions. However, the derivation of the Black–Scholes OPM and corresponding hedge ratio uses the rather complex tools of stochastic calculus. Suffice it to say for now that their derivation and assumptions also suggest that the interest rate to be used in the model is the riskless rate.[4]

In addition, the Black–Scholes hedge ratio (delta) is

$$h_t = N(d_1) = \partial C_t / \partial S_t \qquad (15.25)$$

The Black–Scholes hedge ratio reports the resulting change in the option price from a $1 change in the stock price. Assuming an investor is long one option, h_t tells the investor the number of shares of stock that should be sold short in order to maintain a riskless combined position (or vice versa, if he or she is short one call option).

It is quite important to notice the t subscript on the hedge ratio. This t subscript designates a particular point in time and implies that the hedge ratio is only a *local measure*. That is, its ability to assure a riskless position between the option and its stock is confined to small increments of time and small changes in the stock's price. Therefore, the hedge ratio will vary over time—more precisely, it is time variant. A time-variant hedge ratio necessarily implies that hedging, in the sense of eliminating risk resulting from price changes, is a dynamic process. Such was Black and Scholes's underlying reason for necessarily assuming in their model's derivation that trading takes place in *continuous* time. Later works have shown, however, that the

---

[4] See Black and Scholes (1973) for their original argument and derivation.

model is still valid for the more realistic case of trading in *discrete* time.[5] Sample Problem 15.1 provides further illustration.

Sample Problem 15.1

Using the Black–Scholes OPM to compute the theoretical option price to implement the Black–Scholes formula, the following information is utilized for IBM and its October 100 call option.

$$
\begin{aligned}
S_t &= 108.375 \\
X &= 100.00 \\
T - t &= 81 \text{ days} \\
\tau &= 81/366 = 0.22131 \\
r &= 0.1065 \\
\sigma &= 0.22 \text{ (an historical measure)} \\
\sigma^2 &= 0.0484
\end{aligned}
$$

Solution
First, d_1 and d_2 are computed.

$$
d_1 = \frac{\ln \dfrac{108.375}{100} + \left(0.1065 + \dfrac{0.484}{2}\right) 0.22131}{0.22\sqrt{0.22131}}
$$

$$
= 1.056
$$

$$
d_2 = 1.05637 - (0.22 \times 0.22131) = 0.953
$$

Next $N(d_1)$ and $N(d_2)$ are determined. Turn to the cumulative normal distribution function N shown in Table V at the end of this book to evaluate d_1 and d_2. The row and column border numbers are the values for d_1 and d_2, while the inner numbers represent N. Interpolating:

$$
\begin{aligned}
N(d_1) &= 0.5 + 0.3545 = 0.8545 \\
N(d_2) &= 0.5 + 0.3297 = 0.8297
\end{aligned}
$$

Also:

$$
e^{-0.1065(0.22131)} = 0.9767
$$

Now the Black–Scholes formula can be solved for the theoretically correct option price on July 30:

$$
\begin{aligned}
C_t &= 108.375(0.8545) - (0.9767)100(0.8297) \\
&= \$11.57
\end{aligned}
$$

The actual market price for the IBM October 100 call in Sample Problem 15.1 was $11.00. Consequently, either this option was currently undervalued

---

[5] See for example Lee, Rao, and Auchmuty (1981).

by the market (by $0.57), or the historical estimate for the volatility parameter was inaccurate (in this case, too low). Nevertheless, if the volatility estimate was accurate and the option was undervalued by the market, the following steps could be taken to benefit from this disequilibrium condition.

1. Buy IBM Oct 100 call option at $11.00.	($1,100)
2. Sell 85 [hedge ratio − $N(d_1)$] shares of IBM short at 108.375.	$9,212
Net credit position	$8,112
3. Lend $8122 at 10.65 percent.	($8,112)
	0

Unfortunately, the proceeds from a short sale are typically not made available to be reinvested for all investors. So in a more realistic framework at least $1,100 would have to be invested to carry out this transaction and then deduct lost interest income and commission from this return once the mispricing corrected itself.

The Sensitivity of the Black–Scholes OPM to the Inputs

Another way to more clearly understand the Black–Scholes OPM is to examine the sensitivity of its price to a single-unit change in the value of either a state variable or a parameter. This type of sensitivity analysis is known as a **comparative statics analysis.**

The sensitivities, or first partial derivatives, of the formula with respect to each of its inputs, as discussed in Jarrow and Rudd (1983:119–20) and Cox and Rubinstein (1985:221) are:

$$\frac{\partial C}{\partial S} = N(d_1) > 0 \tag{15.26A}$$

$$\frac{\partial C}{\partial X} = e^{-r\tau}N(d_2) < 0 \tag{15.26B}$$

$$\frac{\partial C}{\partial \tau} = \frac{S\sigma}{2\sqrt{\tau}} N'(d_1) + rXe^{-r\tau} N(d_2) > 0 \tag{15.26C}$$

$$\frac{\partial C}{\partial \sigma} = S\sqrt{\tau} N'(d_1) > 0 \tag{15.26D}$$

$$\frac{\partial C}{\partial r} = \tau Xe^{-r\tau}N(d_2) > 0 \tag{15.26E}$$

and

$$\frac{\partial^2 C}{\partial S^2} = \frac{1}{S\sigma\sqrt{\tau}} N'(d_1) > 0 \tag{15.26F}$$

where:

$$N'(d_1) = \frac{1}{\sqrt{2\pi}} e^{-d_1^2/2} \tag{15.27}$$

The resulting change in the call option's price for an increase in the stock price, exercise price, or time to maturity is positive, negative, and positive, respectively. These relationships, discussed earlier, are also quite intuitive. The call's price is also positively related to the volatility of the underlying stock. Since a call option has no downside risk (except for its cost), increasing risk simply enlarges the probability that the option will end up in the money by expiration (hence, with a larger intrinsic value). In addition, the call price will increase with a rise in interest rates because increasing r also increases the size of the discount factor ($e^{-r\tau}$). Consequently, the present value of the exercise price, in the event that exercise occurs, is smaller.

Equation (15.26F), the second derivative of C with respect to S, represents the change in the hedge ratio for a unit change in the stock's price. In essence, it will indicate how much exposure (to price risk) an option and stock position will incur as the stock price rises or falls. This expression is sometimes referred to as **gamma** and is very important for investors hedging with options. Also, notice once again the natural decay in the option's value as its time to maturity diminishes; Equation (15.26C) expresses mathematically what was discussed earlier on a more intuitive level. In order to illustrate these interpretations, the relationships of Equations (15.26) parts A to F appear in Figure 15–2(a) to (f).

Option Elasticity and Beta

The concept of **option elasticity** can help establish a better understanding of the riskiness of a call option in relation to the stock. An elasticity measurement gives the percentage change in the call option's value for a one-percent change in the stock's value. Using the Greek letter eta (η) to designate this measure, the elasticity for the call option can be expressed:

$$\eta_t = N(d_1) \frac{S_t}{C_t} = \left(\frac{\partial C_t}{\partial S_t}\right)\left(\frac{S_t}{C_t}\right) \tag{15.28}$$

To understand why this relationship would represent the sensitivity of the call's rate of return to a particular rate of return on the stock, consider:

$$\frac{\frac{\Delta C}{C_t}}{\frac{\Delta S}{S_t}} = \left(\frac{\partial C_t}{\partial S_t}\right)\left(\frac{S_t}{C_t}\right) \tag{15.29}$$

The option's elasticity can also be used to relate the systematic risk of the stock to the systematic risk of the option. Using Merton's (1973) **intertemporal capital asset pricing model,** the stock's beta can be defined:

$$\beta_{S_t} = \frac{\text{Cov}\left(\frac{\Delta S}{S_t}, \frac{\Delta M}{M_t}\right)}{\text{Var}\left(\frac{\Delta M}{M_t}\right)} \tag{15.30}$$

FIGURE 15–2   Sensitivities of the Call-Option Price to the OPM Inputs

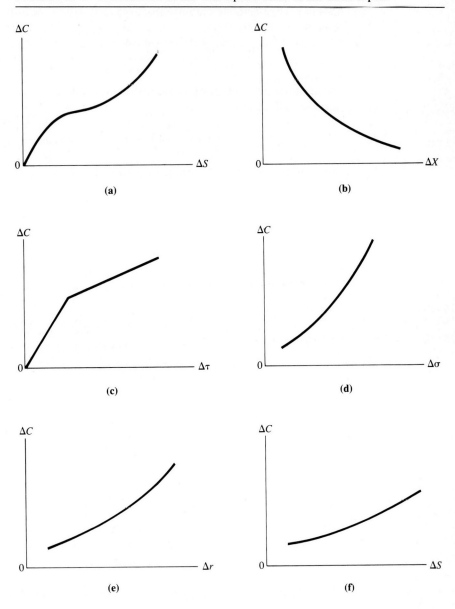

in which $\Delta M/M_t$ is the return on the market portfolio. The option's beta is:

$$\beta_{C_t} = \frac{\text{Cov}\left(\dfrac{\Delta C}{C_t}, \dfrac{\Delta M}{M_t}\right)}{\text{Var}\left(\dfrac{\Delta M}{M_t}\right)} \qquad \textbf{(15.31)}$$

To derive the relationship between the stock and call betas consider $\Delta C/C_t$ using a Taylor-series expansion:

$$\frac{\Delta C}{C_t} = \frac{\left(\frac{\partial C_t}{\partial t}\Delta t + \frac{\partial C_t}{\partial S_t}\Delta S + \frac{1}{2}\frac{\partial^2 C_t}{\partial S_t^2}S_t^2\,\Delta t\right)}{C_t} + 0(\Delta t) \qquad (15.32)$$

Then, taking the variance of both sides, calculate the variance of the return on the call options:

$$\text{Var}\left(\frac{\Delta C}{C_t}\right) = \text{Var}\left(\frac{N(d_1)\Delta S}{C_t}\right) + 0(\Delta t) = \eta^2\,\text{Var}\left(\frac{\Delta S}{S}\right) + 0(\Delta t) \quad (15.33)$$

Substituting $[N(d_1)\,S/C_t]$ from Equation (15.32) into Equation (15.31):

$$\beta_{C_t} = \frac{\text{Cov}\left(N(d_1)\frac{\Delta S}{C_t},\frac{\Delta M}{M_t}\right)}{\text{Var}\left(\frac{\Delta M}{M_t}\right)} + 0(\Delta t) \qquad (15.34)$$

Finally, multiplying the right side of Equation (15.34) by $S_t/S_t\,(=1)$:

$$\beta_{C_t} = N(d_1)\frac{S_t}{C_t}\frac{\text{Cov}\left(\frac{\Delta S}{S_t},\frac{\Delta M}{M_t}\right)}{\text{Var}\left(\frac{\Delta M}{M_t}\right)} + 0(\Delta t) \qquad (15.35)$$

The call option's beta can thus be defined as the option's elasticity times the stock's beta:

$$\beta_C = \eta\beta_r \qquad (15.36)$$

In general, the option's beta will be larger than the stock's beta because η is normally greater than one. More important, since the elasticity for an option is a function of both the stock price and time, the option's beta will change over its life even if the beta for the underlying stock remains constant. Another observation that can be discerned from Equation (15.36), when considered in conjunction with a pricing model such as the CAPM, is that the expected excess return on the call is greater than that for the stock.

Calculating and Interpreting the Option Sensitivity, Elasticity, and Beta

In order to determine more specifically how changes in the input variables affect the call option's model price, the example of Sample Problem 15.1, using IBM's October 100 call option and stock, is extended. First, using the same data presented earlier, the following computations for the six derivatives in Equations (15.26A) through (15.26F) are made:

1. $$\frac{\partial C}{\partial S} = 0.855$$

2. $$\frac{\partial C}{\partial X} = -0.810$$

3. $$\frac{\partial C}{\partial \tau} = 13.592 \times \frac{1}{365} = \$0.037$$

4. $$\frac{\partial C}{\partial \sigma} = 9.983 \times 0.01 = 0.0998$$

5. $$\frac{\partial C}{\partial r} = 17.934 \times 0.01 = 0.1793$$

6. $$\frac{\partial^2 C}{\partial S^2} = 0.017$$

These results can be interpreted as follows.

1. An increase of $1 in IBM's common stock price would cause the October 100 call option's price to go up by 85.5 cents.
2. Increasing the exercise price by $1 would reduce the call's price by 81.0 cents.
3. Over the course of a year, this option would lose $13.59 in its value; however, interpolating this value linearly to get a daily figure shows that on average this call will lose 3.7 cents of time value per day. This is only an average figure; as shown in the last chapter, the time-decay effect on an option's price accelerates in the last month before it expires.
4. The call's value will increase by 9.98 cents for a 0.01 increase in the standard deviation. Since this input is the most difficult to estimate, the higher model price in the previous example for this option versus what it actually was in the market could have been the result of using a standard deviation estimate that was too high.
5. For a 1-percent, or 0.01, change in the interest rate, the call price will increase by 17.93 cents, although a change in the volatility input is usually considered to have the most effect on an option's price (excluding a change in S). It is clear that this relationship is not necessarily true for deep-in-the-money options; instead, the interest-rate effect dominates.
6. The change in the hedge ratio for a $1 change in the stock's price is 0.017. So if IBM's stock price rose to $109.375, the model price for the option would be $12.43 and have a hedge ratio of 0.884.

Using Equation (15.28) the October 100 call option's elasticity measure is determined for July 30:

$$\eta = 0.8545(109.375/11.57) = 8.08$$

Thus, a 1-percent change in the value of IBM's stock will cause a corresponding 8.08-percent change in the value of this particular option. In general, there will be a leverage factor of slightly more than $8 \times$ for this call option. Finally, by employing an historical estimate of 0.76 for IBM's beta (using the NYSE index as the market proxy), the beta for this call option can be determined:

$$\beta_C = 8.08(0.76) = 6.14$$

Notice that even though a call option is being used in the IBM example, practically a market proxy in the option's beta is still larger than even the riskiest stock; this demonstrates, then, that an option held alone is very speculative.

ESTIMATING THE INPUTS

Overall the Black–Scholes formula is relatively easy to use. Moreover, most of the required inputs are readily available in the daily financial press. Nevertheless, some precautions and problems must be considered when gathering or estimating the input values. Remember ''GIGO''—garbage in, garbage out.

Stock Price

Obtaining the current stock price is a relatively easy task; nearly any daily paper lists stock prices. However, the press is not an unbiased source of data, so one must be aware of a number of deficiencies. First, there are occasional typographical errors in the paper. Second, is the reported price the closing bid, ask, or mid price? Which of the three is printed cannot readily be determined. Third, although the stock price used in the formula must be a traded price or realistic quote, some papers only print composite prices, which are either averages of the closing prices from several exchanges on which the stock is traded or the closing price on the exchange that closes latest in the evening. Newspapers such as *The Wall Street Journal* report that closing stock price from the NYSE (or AMEX) in the same table as the option prices.

Exercise Price

Since the exercise price is part of the contract specification, it does not change through the life of the option. Nevertheless, the effects of stock splits and stock dividends must be evaluated when they occur.

Time to Maturity

As with the exercise price, the expiration date for the option is specified in its contract. Therefore, counting the number of calendar days from the present up to and including the last trading day (the third Friday of the expiration month), then dividing by the number of days in the year, yields the option's remaining time to maturity in annual terms of a fraction of a year.

Interest Rate

According to the model's derivation the appropriate interest rate to use should be the riskless rate. Moreover, this rate should measure the risk-free borrowing and lending rates over the remaining life of the option. A well-accepted proxy for the riskless rate is the effective interest rate on Treasury bills (T-bills). Taking the bid and ask rates for a T-bill maturing as close to the option as possible (from *The Wall Street Journal,* for example), one can calculate the effective rate for a T-bill using the following formulas:

$$\text{TBP} = 10,000\left[1 - \left(\frac{i_a + i_b}{2}\right)\left(\frac{T - t}{365}\right)\right] \tag{15.37}$$

$$r = (10,000/\text{TBP})^{365/(T-t)} - 1 \tag{15.38}$$

where:

$\quad$ TBP = Treasury-bill price;
$\quad\quad i_a$ = asking discount rate;
$\quad\quad i_b$ = bidding discount rate;
$\quad T - t$ = number of calendar days to the option's maturity; and
$\quad\quad r$ = effective risk-free rate for a T-bill maturity near the option.

Although anyone can lend money at the riskless rate (by buying a T-bill), few can actually borrow money at this rate. Consequently, the T-bill rate will underestimate the applicable rate. Some have suggested that a better rate to use might be the certificate of deposit (CD) rate or the rate for top-quality commercial paper. It has also been argued that the riskless borrowing and lending rate available to the investor who uses a margin account would be more appropriate. A possible proxy for this rate might be the interest rate charged to investors for loans in margin accounts. Typically, the margin-account rate is set at a premium of 1 or 2 percent above the **call-loan money rate,** the rate charged by banks to brokers who deposit securities as collateral. The call-loan money rate and other money rates are printed in *The Wall Street Journal.*

Fortunately, in general the option price is not sensitive to a small change in the interest rate (except for deep-in-the-money options), as can be seen in the sensitivity graph, Figure 15–2(e). Usually a one-percent change or mis-estimation of the interest rate will change the option price by only a few cents.

Volatility

Among the inputs for the OPM, the volatility parameter is definitely the most difficult to estimate and interpret. One of the key estimation problems in determining the volatility for the underlying asset is that the volatility measure is not necessarily constant over time. This empirically documented

observation conflicts with the Black–Scholes model's original assumption that the volatility is constant. Thus measuring volatility for use in this model is essentially an exercise in forecasting the volatility of the underlying asset over the option's remaining life. There are three ways in which this is typically done.

Historical Variance.   The original method used to estimate volatility was to calculate the variance of continuous stock returns using past data. How far back and how often this data should be collected are difficult questions. The farther back data is checked, the less representative the variance estimate is likely to be of future price movements. Nevertheless, the greater the number of observations, the better the statistical properties of the estimate. One investment strategy sometimes used in practice is to match an investment horizon for the options with the time period between observations. For example, a day trader would use daily observations for the variance estimate, while someone interested in a longer position duration (more than a week) might use weekly observations. To demonstrate the computational procedures, daily observations over the last thirty trading days are used.

As a first step, the continuously compounded return is approximated and its mean calculated. (The arithmetic mean is used for simplicity.)

$$m = \frac{1}{30} \sum_{t=1}^{30} \ln \left(\frac{P_t}{P_{t-1}} \right) = \frac{1}{30} \ln \left(\frac{P_{30}}{P_0} \right) \tag{15.39}$$

where:

$$\ln ( ) = \text{natural log function;}$$
$$P_t \text{ and } P_{t-1} = \text{price per share on day } t \text{ and } t-1, \text{ respectively;}$$
$$\frac{P_t}{P_{t-1}} = R_t, \text{ or the daily holding period return on the stock; and}$$
$$m = \text{mean of the continuously compounded daily return on the stock.}$$

Next the annualized variance to be used in the OPM formula is computed:

$$\sigma^2 = 365 \times \left(\frac{1}{30-1} \right) \sum_{t=1}^{30} (\ln R_t - m)^2 \tag{15.40}$$

Since daily observations have been used, the resulting number (daily variance estimate) must be multiplied by 365 to arrive at an annualized term.

Another important consideration when choosing the sample size and interval period is the variability of historical variance. For a stock with a variance measure that has frequently or to a great extent fluctuated in the past, using a larger sample size and interval period may result in an estimate less representative of future price movements. Also, it is important always to use quotes that come from the same time of day, particularly when daily intervals are used. If the Wednesday and Friday quotes are from 4:00 but the Thursday quote is from 1:00, the intervals between observations will be inconsistent, making the estimated variance imprecise.

How good an estimate of future volatility is the historical variance? Not very good, according to past studies. One way to combat the forecasting bias from using historical variance is to use a moving average of variances computed over a shorter total interval of time, such as five, ten, or twenty days. Then using equal or exponential weighting, a weighted historical variance measure is computed and updated daily. For instance, a very volatile stock might justify a weighting approach that places more importance on recent variance estimates. Using ten-day periods and a five-day exponential moving average, the weighted variance measure could be computed and updated as follows:

$$\sigma^2(\text{EMA5}) = 0.5661\sigma^2_{t,t-10} + 0.3205\sigma^2_{t-1,t-11} + 0.1027\sigma^2_{t-2,t-12}$$
$$+ 0.0105\sigma^2_{t-3,t-13} + 0.0001\sigma^2_{t-4,t-14} \qquad \textbf{(15.41)}$$

where:

$\sigma^2_{t,t-10}$ = the historical daily variance computed for the most recent ten-day period in period t; and

$\sigma^2(\text{EMA5})$ = a five-day exponentially weighted average of the five most recent historical variance estimates.

Figure 15–3 illustrates the time-series relationship between actual and historical variance.

Time-Series Analysis.   A **time-series analysis** approach developed by **Box and Jenkins** (1970) can be a powerful tool for estimating the return-generating process for historical price movements. Also known as the *Box and Jenkins autoregressive integrated moving-average (ARIMA) technique,* this

FIGURE 15–3   The Forecast of Volatility Using Past Average Volatility

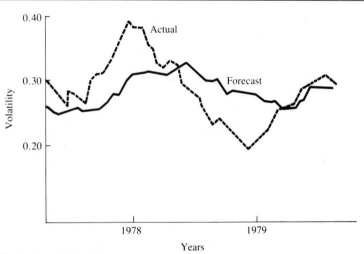

Source: Bookstaber (1982), p. 80.

modeling method enters past values of the stock price movement into a weighted-form equation. The weights in the equation reflect identifiable characteristics about the movement of the volatility. Whereas in the last section the weights for the five-day moving average of historical variances were subjectively selected in an ad hoc fashion, time-series analysis lets the data determine the weighting scheme (via maximum-likelihood estimation).

There are two ways of applying time-series analysis to the variance-estimation process. First, since there is usually an underlying mean for the historical variance series, if the current estimate was substantially above this mean value, it would eventually decrease towards the mean. Generally, when the stock's price rises its variance decreases, and when the price falls its variance increases. By applying time-series analysis to the price series itself (or the changes thereof) estimates could be generated of the future changes and the directions of change for the price series. This information could be used to forecast when the variance estimate will fall and by how much.

More straightforwardly, time-series analysis could be applied to a past series of historical variance estimates to forecast the future movement. An illustrated example appears in Figure 15–4.

Implicit Volatility. The state of the art method in the markets today for estimating the volatility is the **implied-variance estimate.** Implied variance can generally be regarded as the market's opinion about the future variance of the stock. Originally proposed by Latane and Rendleman (1976), the idea

FIGURE 15–4 The Forecast of Volatility from Time-Series Analysis of Historical Variance

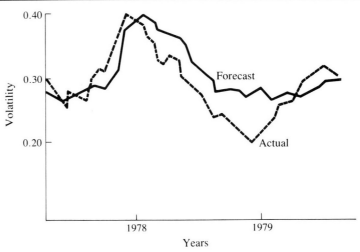

Source: Bookstaber (1982), p. 81.

behind the estimation of the implied variance is to equate the Black–Scholes model price to the current market price and solve iteratively for the remaining unknown variance. No closed-form solution is available to compute the implied variance, so a numerical search procedure such as the Newton–Raphson search or linear least-squares regression must be used. Appendix 15B of this chapter outlines the ordinary least-squares (OLS) method for calculating implied variance.

Issues abound concerning the use of implied variance; the first of them is the weighting issue. If the implied variance inherent in the market price for each outstanding option on a stock (underlying asset) were calculated, there would be as many estimates of the stock's implied variance as there are options. Disregarding the possibility of market mispricings for the moment, a number of other factors may also be able to help explain the observed discrepancies.

1. Exercise price (amount in or out of the money) differences
2. Time-to-maturity differences
3. Trading-volume differences among the individual options
4. Market conditions

While not conclusive, there is strong empirical evidence that supports at least three of these factors as being explanatory sources of the individual implied variance differences among a single stock's options. Although a more extensive interpretation of three factors will be saved for later sections, it is important to mention now that the volume effect is also inherent in the exercise price and time-to-maturity effects to some degree. For instance, deep-in-the-money options have lower trading volume than near-the-money options because of their higher cost and lower probability of going more into the money. Consequently, traders who write these options are exposed to a greater liquidity risk of not being able to get out of their position quickly, should prices start to rise. It is likely, then, that traders will ask a higher price when writing these options to compensate them for this risk. All other inputs being the same, a higher market price for the option must be reflected in a larger implied variance.

The weighting issue is concerned with whether the individual implied variances should be weighted among the available options on a given security—and, if so, how the weights should be determined. A considerable amount of common practice in the option markets is to weight all the implied variances together to achieve a single number for the market's estimate of the stock's future volatility. However, Park and Sears (1985) have found significant differences between using a single-weighted implied-variance measure and one that is weighted only for options of the same maturity. The time-to-maturity effect that these authors have found (implied variance generally declined over time) could add a bias to the Black–Scholes price, if one used the single-weighted measure.

Another recent study has found a similar bias for differences in exercise price.[6] But how can a stock's price have more than one volatility at a single point in time? The answer can be directed back to the Black–Scholes model, and a new question can be asked. Is the Black–Scholes OPM misspecified to some degree? While such an issue is a crucial one considering how much their model is used, the weighting issue remains unresolved at this time.

If one inputed the concurrently calculated implied variance into the Black–Scholes formula, there would be no such thing as a mispriced option. Yet the vast amount of trading that goes on in options is evidence enough that mispricings do occur. So from which past point in time should one compute the implied variance to price an option today? Again, no definite answer exists. Some practitioners simply use yesterday's estimate, while others formulate a weighting scheme of past implied variances measured daily or weekly. Keep in mind that an attempt is being made here to predict the future volatility for the underlying stock over the remaining life of the option. Time-series analysis can also be applied to the time series of implied variances for a stock or a single option, as was discussed earlier for historical variance. In fact, recent research has shown that these series can be successfully modeled with the ARIMA technique.[7]

This topic could easily be expanded into a separate book. Let it suffice for now, however, to stress that the volatility input for the Black–Scholes formula is the key variable to understanding and forecasting accurately in order to get the most out of the model's pricing capabilities.

Dividend Payments and Ex-Dividend Dates

Although the discussion of dividend corrections to the Black–Scholes model has been saved for a later portion of this chapter, it is relevant to mention now that future dividend payments for the stock over the remaining life of the option will decrease the option's price. Therefore, to correctly value an option on a stock expected to pay dividends sometime before the option expires, a forecast must be made of the size of the dividend payment and the ex-dividend date(s).

Fortunately, since most corporations attempt to maintain a relatively stable dividend policy, a fairly accurate prediction of cash dividends over the next nine months is generally not too difficult. One particularly good source of data is, again, *The Wall Street Journal*. Its column, "Corporate Dividend News," reports the payments of cash dividends and ex-dividend dates and announcements of future dividends and payment dates.

Finally, since the earlier evaluation of the IBM option did not account for dividends, this could have been the reason for the lower market price of the IBM call option.

---

[6] Hotopp, Maloney, and Lee (1985).
[7] See Hotopp, Maloney, and Lee (1985).

EXTENSIONS OF THE BLACK–SCHOLES OPM

Up to this point it has been assumed that no dividends (or other cash flows) are paid on the underlying asset over the remaining life of the option. Furthermore, the only underlying asset considered thus far is a common stock. Extensions of the Black–Scholes model that account for dividends are now examined as well as the use of a futures contract as the underlying asset.

The OPM Adjusted for Dividends

Although Black and Scholes originally derived their model assuming that no dividends or other payouts were made to stockholders during the option's life, dividends do occur and can have a significant effect on the option's price.[8] Dividend payments directly affect (and generally reduce) the stock's price and thus, indirectly, the option's price. While most stock options have an early exercise feature (American-style option), it has not been necessary to consider its effects because it is never optimal to exercise a call option early on a stock paying no dividend. Nevertheless, the consideration of dividend payments can significantly alter these conclusions and even cause the arbitrage argument of the pricing formula to break down.

Since dividend payments generally cause a reduction in the stock's price, the option price will most likely drop as well. In some cases the holder of the call option may find it advantageous to exercise her right just before the stock goes ex-dividend, in order to capture the full value of the stock before its decline. Of course, this valuation problem only applies to in-the-money options, as they alone face the risk of early exercise. The problem involves the pricing of these particular options under two contingencies—that the option is exercised early and that it is not. The greater of these two values at a defined point in time is then used in deriving the option's formula. Roll (1977) has derived an option-pricing model for the American call option with known dividends. Empirical tests have shown that it more accurately prices call options than the Black–Scholes model. Nevertheless, the example will sidestep an explanation of Roll's model and the consideration of early exercise to show instead two simpler adjustments to the Black–Scholes model that yield results reasonably close to those from using Roll's model.[9]

Stochastic Dividends.   In adjusting the Black–Scholes model for the case of stochastic dividends, assume a continuous payout over the life of the option. First assume that the stock's dividend yield will remain constant over the option's life:

---

[8] By assuming no dividends they could apply their model to American options. See Black and Scholes (1973), Merton (1973), Bookstaber (1982), and Jarrow and Rudd (1983).

[9] For example, see Whaley (1982).

$$D(S_t, t) \equiv D \qquad\qquad (15.42)$$

where D is a constant representing the continuous dividend yield, that is, the dollar dividend divided by the dollar price of the stock. The adjustment to the Black–Scholes model is to replace S_t, the current stock price, with $S_t e^{-D\tau}$, which represents the present value of the capital-gains portion of the stock price at time t. This adjustment term is equal to the current market price of the stock minus the present value of the (stochastic) dividends paid out over the option's life. Now the option's price is a function of six variables:

$$C_{SD,t} = F(S, D, \tau, r, \sigma, X) \qquad\qquad (15.43)$$

and the Black–Scholes model with the adjustment for stochastic dividends is

$$C_{SD,t} = S_t e^{-D\tau} N(d_1) - X e^{-r\tau} N(d_2) \qquad\qquad (15.44)$$

where:

$C_{SD,t}$ = call-option value with stock divided adjustment

$$d_1 = \frac{\ln \frac{S_t}{X} + \left(r - D + \frac{\sigma_S^2}{2}\right)\tau}{\sigma_S \sqrt{\tau}} \qquad\qquad (15.45)$$

$$d_2 = d_1 - \sigma_S \sqrt{\tau} \qquad\qquad (15.46)$$

In addition to the discounting adjustment made to S_t in Equation (15.44), notice in Equation (15.45) that the constant dividend yield D is subtracted from the riskless rate r. This is because dividends will reduce the expected return on the arbitrage portfolio. Once again, this approach does not provide an exact solution, only an approximate one.

Known Dividends.   Given that the maturities of all options are less than or equal to nine months, it is not unreasonable to assume that there are a finite number of dividend payments within the option's life. Moreover, since most corporations strive to maintain consistent dividend policies, it is also assumed here that the finite number of dividend payments are known (certain). For simplicity of presentation assume that only one dividend payment is to be made within the option's remaining maturity period, at time t_1, where $t < t_1 < T$. So at time t_1 a known dividend of D_1 occurs, with D_1 being constant.

Next decompose the stock price S_t into two parts: (1) a risky part G_t and (2) a riskless part $D_1 e^{-r\tau_1}$. The risky portion of the stock's price, G_t, represents its capital value, so that the capital gain on the stock over any holding period is the difference between the values of G at the beginning and end of the period. Hence G_t is the stock's price without any accrued dividends. The riskless portion of the stock's price, $D_1 e^{-r\tau_1}$, represents the present value of the certain dividend. So now S_t is the stock price with accrued dividends. Separating the stock price into its two components is similar to the pricing of many fixed-income instruments. However, the underlying purpose for doing

so is rather different and is related to the assumption concerning the specified stochastic process for the stock's return. S_t can be defined for different periods of time:

$$S_t = G_t + D_1 e^{-r\tau_1} \qquad \text{For } t < t_1$$
$$S_t = G_t \qquad\qquad\quad \text{For } t > t_1 \tag{15.47}$$

Only the risky portion of the stock price G_t is assumed to follow a log normal diffusion process. At expiration the call option's value will be

$$C_{\text{KD},t} = e^{-r\tau} E \operatorname{Max}(G_T - X, 0) \tag{15.48}$$

where the stochastic process for G_t (instead of S_t) must have an expected return of r. Additionally, the development of these conditions into a model formulation shows that the dividend portion of the stock price also earns r percent, an outcome of the arbitrage argument.

Bypassing the related derivations and proofs at this point, the Black–Scholes OPM is adjusted for one known and constant dividend of D_1 occurring at time t_1 (the ex-dividend date) where $t < t_1 < T$:

$$C_{\text{KD},t} = (S_t - D_1 e^{-r\tau_1})N(d_1) - Xe^{-r\tau} N(d_2) \tag{15.49}$$

$$d_1 = \frac{\ln \dfrac{G_t}{X} + \left(r + \dfrac{\sigma_G^2}{2}\right)\tau}{\sigma_G \sqrt{\tau}} \tag{15.50}$$

$$d_2 = d_1 - \sigma_G \sqrt{\tau} \tag{15.51}$$

where:

$\tau_1 = (t_1 - t)/365;$

$D_1 = $ the known and constant dividend to be paid at time t;

$G_t = S_t - D_1 e^{-r\tau_1}$, the current stock price diminished by the present value of the dividend D_1 to be paid at time t_1, discounted at the riskless rate r; and

$C_{\text{KD},t} = $ model value for a call option on the stock that pays one known dividend.

Though the situation of only one known dividend occurring over the option's life has been described, the formula is easily expanded to include additional known dividends in the same manner. Once again, note that this adjustment to the Black–Scholes model for known dividends gives only an approximate solution.

Black's OPM for Futures Options. Black (1976) has derived an option-pricing model that pertains to the case where the underlying instrument is a futures contract. With the introduction of options on stock-index futures, precious-metals futures, foreign-currency futures, and traditional commodity futures, and the increasing popularity of these contracts, Black's OPM is seeing widespread application.

Using essentially the same framework of assumptions as for the Black–Scholes model, Black derives the following formula:

$$C_{t,f} = e^{-r\tau}[F\,N(d_1) - X N(d_2)] \qquad \textbf{(15.52)}$$

$$d_1 = \frac{\ln\dfrac{F_t}{X} + \dfrac{\sigma_f^2\tau}{2}}{\sigma_f\sqrt{\tau}} \qquad \textbf{(15.53)}$$

$$d_2 = d_1 - \sigma_f\sqrt{\tau} \qquad \textbf{(15.54)}$$

where:

F_t = current price of the underlying futures contract;

σ_f^2 = instantaneous variance of the continuous returns on the futures contract; and

$C_{t,f}$ = model value for a call option on the futures at time t.

There are several differences between Black's model for futures options and the Black and Scholes model for stock options (call options in both cases).

1. In Equation (15.52), the current futures price is discounted from the option's maturity to the present at the riskless rate of interest. As discussed in Chapter 12, the cost of entering a futures position is only the deposit of a minimum amount of margin to secure the contract. Since the majority of margin can be held as interest-earning T-bills, the remaining cash portion required for maintenance margin is relatively small compared to the actual value of the contract. Therefore, the effective cost of a futures contract is theoretically considered to be zero and the specified price within the contract is solely related to the transaction to take place when the futures contract expires. Since it is a negotiated price to be transacted in the future, it must be discounted to the present to determine the call's current value. It is assumed in this model that both the futures contract and its option mature on the same date—a relatively realistic assumption.

2. The r term in the computation of d_1 and d_2 drops out in the derivation of the Black model.[10] This occurs because it is assumed that the value of a futures contract (with time remaining) is zero. As was just discussed, since theoretically nothing is invested when one enters a futures contract, its value must be zero. So, when establishing the hedge portfolio in the model's development, the equity in the position is the entire value of the option. This assumption implies that today's futures price reflects tomorrow's futures price, which is essentially equivalent to saying that futures prices follow a martingale over time. One of the properties of a martingale

---

[10] Compare Equations (15.53) and (15.54) with Equations (15.12A) and (15.12B).

distribution is that $E(f_{t+1}, T) = f_{t,T}$, that is, the expected futures price is equal to the current futures price.

One additional adjustment to make when using this model is in the computed hedge ratio. The hedge ratio for a call option on a futures contract is:

$$h_{t,f} = e^{r(T-t)} N(d_1) \tag{15.55}$$

which is the number of futures contracts to enter into for each call option position. That is, the hedge ratio from the model value of $N(d_1)$ must be discounted back to the present from the maturity at the riskless rate. The necessity for this can be seen by referring to Equation (15.52).

Put-Option Valuation

In a survey of the literature on option pricing a disproportionate amount of focus on call-option pricing would be noticed. This disparity exists for good reasons, of which the most important is that, unlike the case of the call option, there are no situations where the possibility of early exercise for the American put option can be ruled out *a priori*. Any attempt to model the American put pricing process is immediately confronted with the need to analyze the incremental value of the put's early-exercise provision. Consequently, to date there is no generally accepted analytical formula for pricing an American put. This section surveys three methods for approximating a put's price when the possibility of early exercise has been removed; bounds are also established for the American put's price.

Put–Call Parity Revisited.   Recall from Chapter 14 that when European options and no dividend payments are assumed, a very straightforward pricing relationship can be established between the security and both its call and put options. This pricing relationship is called **put–call parity** and can be used to estimate a theoretical value for the put. According to the put–call parity theorem, the price of a European put with no dividends is

$$P_t = C_t - S_t + Xe^{-r\tau} \tag{15.56}$$

When a known single-dividend payment on the stock is expected during the remaining life of the put, Equation (15.56) can be restated to account for the effect of this cash distribution on the put's price:

$$P_t = C_t - S_t + D_1 e^{-r\tau} + Xe^{-r\tau} \tag{15.57}$$

Notice that in Equation (15.57) dividends on a security will increase the put's value. Remember that the put gains value only if the underlying security's price falls. Since cash dividends generally cause the stock's price to adjust downward on the ex-dividend date, such payouts have positive effects on the put's price.

When the early-exercise provision is considered for this particular pricing relationship, the precision of the formula breaks down and what remains is a set of boundary conditions for the American put's price. For an American put with a single known dividend, the put–call parity boundaries are:

$$C_t - S_t + D_1 e^{-r\tau} + X e^{-r\tau} \leq P_t(C_t - S_t + D_1 e^{-r\tau} + X) \quad (15.58)$$

The Black–Scholes European-Put Pricing Model. Without the complexity introduced by allowing early exercise, the Black–Scholes option-pricing model can be easily derived for the put option. Since the development of the original has already been covered in considerable detail, the Black–Scholes model as applied to European put options with no dividends is presented as follows:

$$P_t = X e^{-r\tau} N(d_2) - S_t N(-d_1) \quad (15.59)$$

$$-d_1 = \frac{-\ln \dfrac{S}{X} - \left(r + \dfrac{\sigma_S^2}{2}\right)\tau}{\sigma_S \sqrt{\tau}} \quad (15.60)$$

$$d_2 = \sigma_S \sqrt{\tau} - d_1 \quad (15.61)$$

The hedge ratio for the put is:

$$h_{t,P} = \frac{\partial P_t}{\partial S_t} = \frac{\partial C_t}{\partial S_t} - 1 = N(-d_{1t}) \leq 0 \quad (15.62)$$

The put's hedge ratio is equal to the call's hedge ratio minus one. Furthermore, the put's hedge ratio is always negative or zero because the call's hedge ratio is always zero or positive.

As with the analysis of the call option, the put's elasticity and beta, and the sensitivity of its price to the model inputs, can be determined. First, the put option's elasticity is

$$\eta_{p,t} = \frac{S_t}{P_t} \frac{\partial P_t}{\partial S_t} = \frac{S_t}{P_t} h_{t,P} \quad (15.63)$$

As would be expected, the elasticity of the put is negative, since the hedge ratio is negative. Similarly, the beta of the put option is calculated as follows:

$$\beta_{p,t} = \eta_{p,t} \beta_{S,t} \quad (15.64)$$

An important observation here is that the put will always have a negative beta. Hence, the suitability of the put option as a hedging instrument for the underlying security can be seen in the context of modern portfolio theory.

One additional use of call and put elasticity measures is for determining the elasticity of a position composed of these two derivative assets. For example, the elasticity of a straddle (a combination of a call and a put with

the same underlying security exercise price and time to maturity) can be defined as:

$$\eta_{V,t} = \left(\frac{P_t}{V_t}\right)^n_{p,t} + \left(\frac{C_t}{V_t}\right)^n_{c,t} \tag{15.65}$$

in which V_t equals $P_t + C_t$, or the total current value of the position. It can therefore be seen that the portfolio elasticity for an option-combination position is the weighted sum of the component option elasticities, where the weights are the proportions of the total position's value that each component option currently represents.

Finally, the sensitivity of the put's price to the Black–Scholes model's inputs can be examined.

$$\frac{\partial P}{\partial S} = -N(-d_1) < 0 \tag{15.66A}$$

$$\frac{\partial P}{\partial X} = e^{-r\tau}N(d_2) > 0 \tag{15.66B}$$

$$\frac{\partial P}{\partial \tau} = \frac{S_t\,\sigma_S}{2\sqrt{\tau}}\,N'(d_1) - rXe^{-r\tau}N(d_2) \gtreqless 0 \tag{15.66C}$$

$$\frac{\partial P}{\partial \sigma_S} = S\sqrt{\tau}\,N'(d_1) > 0 \tag{15.66D}$$

$$\frac{\partial P}{\partial r} = -\tau Xe^{-r\tau}N(d_2) < 0 \tag{15.66E}$$

$$\frac{\partial^2 P}{\partial S^2} = \frac{N'(d_1)}{S\,\sigma_S\sqrt{\tau}} > 0 \tag{15.66F}$$

The majority of these sensitivity relationships should be clear if the same process of reasoning is applied that was used for the previous analysis involving the call. Still, Equation (15.66C) may not be so clear. The effect of a change in the remaining time to expiration on the put's price is ambiguous. This is a result of the conflicting influence of the time variable in the model. For instance, a decrease in time to maturity will simultaneously increase the present value of the exercise price to be received by the put holder and diminish the likelihood of a favorable outcome for the stock's price. While the first effect increases the put price, the second decreases it.

The Binomial Option-Pricing Model Applied to Puts.   To use the binomial option-pricing model approach for valuing put options, the boundary condition need only be reversed at maturity for a call to get that for a put:

$$P_t = \frac{1}{R^n} \sum_{k=0}^{n} \frac{n!}{k!(n-k)!}\,p^k(1-p)^{n-k}\,\text{Max}\,(0, u^k d^{n-k}X - S_t) \tag{15.67}$$

Notice that the only difference from Equation (15.9), the binomial model for call prices, is the reversal of the last term $S_t - X$ to $X - S_t$.

PRICING OTHER FINANCIAL SECURITIES USING OPTION-PRICING THEORY

A major stimulus underlying the growing popularity of option-pricing theory has been the natural carryover of its concepts to the pricing of other financial securities. A strong reason for **valuing claims** to assets with OPT is that it uses only observable variables (except perhaps σ). Moreover, the arbitrage argument, a basic tenet of OPT, complements the powerful insights of Modigliani and Miller (1958). They recognized that in the absence of market imperfections any claims contingent on other assets are simply financial tools for offering alternative modes of ownership for the same economic stream of returns. Consequently, the aggregate value of any claims against the returns of a firm should be independent of the types of claims issued. Hence, Black and Scholes's (1973) results extend this underlying theme of financial theory: in an intertemporal as well as in a static setting, two things that can be shown to be equivalent must sell for the same price.

Option-pricing theory is continually being adapted to additional types of financial claims. Among its uses, OPT has been applied to the pricing of the claims of a firm, such as common stock, preferred stock, regular debt, convertible bonds, and bonds with call provisions. Other applications include valuing loan commitments and real-estate investment trusts (REITs).

This section develops the reasoning behind the application of OPT to various financial claims on the firm and demonstrates the actual pricing process of such instruments using variations of the original model.

The Analogy Between Equity and a Call Option

Picture a firm with a simplified capital structure composed of only a common-stock issue and a debt issue. The outstanding debt is a discount bond that pays B dollars at its maturity. When the bond matures the firm is sold for its market value V, the proceeds being distributed to the equity holders and the bondholders. While the bondholders receive their promised sum of B dollars, the common stockholders receive the residual value, or $V - B$ dollars. Should the firm go bankrupt ($V < B$), the bondholders will receive the total remaining value of the firm V and the stockholders will receive nothing. Since common-stock ownership has limited liability, the shareholders are protected from any further claims by the bondholders.

Keeping the scenario simple for the moment, the market value of the firm's equity at the bond's maturity date can be stated to be the maximum of 0 or $V - B$. Or, to put this relationship into a familiar OPT format, at the end of the period the value of E (equity) will be Max $(0, V - B)$. Notice that

analogous relation to the option's terminal value; that is, the ending value of the underlying stock S is replaced by the terminal value of the firm V. The option's exercise price X is replaced by the size of the bond payment B, and the time-to-maturity component is now that of the debt.

The relationship between the equity of a firm and a call option should by now be much clearer. Just as the holder of a call option has the right to the value of the underlying stock in excess of the exercise price, $S - X$, the holder of common stock has the right to the value of the (underlying) firm in excess of the bondholder's claim, $V - B$. More explicitly, the equity of a firm is an option on the value of the firm. Since it is possible that the market value of the firm V will fall below the face value of the debt B by the maturing date for the debt, it is similarly possible that the firm's stock will be worthless at that point. Of course, the market value of a firm is usually significantly higher than its total outstanding debt. Thus the firm's stock will behave like a deep-in-the-money option and follow the value of the firm very closely.

However, when a firm is near bankruptcy the analysis through OPT is very revealing. Remember that an option's value is positively related to the total risk of the stock. For instance, an out-of-the-money option on a stable, low-volatility stock will be worth less than a similar option on a risky, highly volatile stock. The larger the volatility or riskiness of the underlying stock, the greater the probability that the out-of-the-money option will move into the money (establishing intrinsic value).

Now consider a situation of analogous dimensions for the stock. Suppose there exists a firm in a stable industry with debt obligations considerably higher than its equity value. If all the firm's debt matures a year from now, how much is its stock worth at the present time? Next, consider an identical scenario for a firm that operates in a very volatile or high-growth industry. What should be the value of this firm's equity? For the first firm, the stability of its industry creates a low probability that the firm can increase its market value by a significant amount within one year. Therefore, its stock should be worth approximately $0 right now. With such a large probability that the firm will go bankrupt in a year, most investors would be able to find a more desirable charity to donate their money to. However, because the second firm's business is so volatile, there exists a chance (from a speculator's point of view) that the firm could greatly increase its value within a year. As a result, this more volatile stock would be expected to have at least some amount of market value similar to the time value of the call option on common stock previously considered.

A perplexing issue arises for the management of the first firm operating in the stable industry. A basic doctrine of finance is for management to "maximize the wealth of the shareholders." Since management is hired by the shareholders, its loyalties should be to the firm's owners and not to its creditors. Which course of action should the management of this firm choose? By taking on risky ventures with large potential returns, management would be pursuing the interests of the owners. On the other hand, they

would be increasing the risk that the bondholders would have even less to collect when the debt issue matures in a year. So while the shareholders would favorably view the pursuing of high-risk ventures, the bondholders would be quite adverse to such a strategy. Most bond indenture agreements contain clauses to protect the bondholders against situations of this type. As can be seen, OPT highlights this area of finance (called **agency theory**) and helps explain the interrelationships among the financial securities of a firm as well as the sometimes conflicting priorities of the owners and creditors.

Pricing Common Stock with the OPM

Using an original M and M (1958) argument the return structure of a leveraged firm can be replicated by mixing the equity of an unleveraged firm with the riskless asset. By purchasing the stock and selling the riskless asset an investor could create such a homemade leverage position. Having identical risk–return characteristics, the leveraged firm and the combination of unleveraged firm and riskless asset should be valued equivalently. This arbitrage argument is analogous to the one employed in the derivation of the Black–Scholes OPM, between the combined riskless asset and option and the stock. Hence the Black–Scholes approach has been applied to the derivation of a pricing formula for a firm's common stock (assuming it has outstanding debt as well):

$$F_t = V_t N(X_1) - Be^{-r\tau} N(X_2) \tag{15.68}$$

where:

$$X_1 = \frac{\ln \dfrac{V_t}{B} + \left(r + \dfrac{\sigma_v^2}{2} \right)\tau}{\sigma_v \sqrt{\tau}}$$

$X_2 = X_1 - \sigma_v \sqrt{\tau};$

$F_t =$ the theoretical value for the firm's common stock at time t;

$V_t =$ market value of firm at time t;

$B =$ face value of all outstanding debt;

$r =$ riskless rate for a government security maturing at the same time as the debt;

$\sigma_v^2 =$ the instantaneous variance for the continuous returns on the returns on the firm's total value; and

$\tau =$ the remaining time to maturity for the outstanding debt in terms of a year (years).

There are several barriers to applying this formula.

1. The firm's current market value is generally rather difficult to observe and thus to determine. One suggestion is to use the market value of the firm's total assets from its most recent balance sheet.

2. A firm will generally have debt issues maturing at different points in the future, so calculating time to maturity can be quite ambiguous. A suggestion here is to use a weighted average time to maturity, weighting the remaining time to maturity of each outstanding debt issue by the percentage its face value represents of the firm's total debt.

3. Again, the variance term might not be constant. Yet it is very likely that the σ_v^2 for the entire firm's value will be more stable than that for its stock. Furthermore, since the time-to-maturity variable would probably be in years, the historical measure would probably be more representative of a longer future period.

Sample Problem 15.2 provides further illustration.

Sample Problem 15.2

A firm with a value V_t of $100 has $50 face value of debt which matures in one year. The riskless rate is 10 percent and the volatility of the firm's value is 0.5. What is the value of the firm's stock at time zero?

Solution

$$V_t = \$100, \quad B = \$50, \quad r = 0.1, \quad \sigma_v^2 = 0.5, \quad \tau \le 1 \text{ year}$$
$$F_0 = V_t N(X_1) - Be^{-r\tau} N(X_2)$$

$$X_1 \le \frac{\ln \dfrac{V_t}{B} + \left(r + \dfrac{\sigma_v^2}{2}\right)\tau}{\sigma_v \sqrt{\tau}}$$

$$X_2 \le X_1 - \sigma_v \sqrt{\tau}$$

$$X_1 = \frac{\ln \dfrac{100}{50} + \left(0.1 + \dfrac{0.5}{2}\right)1}{0.707\sqrt{1}}$$

$$= 0.7374$$
$$X_2 \le 0.7374 - 0.707 \sqrt{1}$$
$$= 0.0304$$
$$F_0 = 100N\,(0.7374) - 50e^{-0.1(1)}\,N(0.0304)$$
$$= 100\,(0.7696) - 45.25\,(0.5122)$$
$$F_0 = \$53.78$$

Pricing Discount Bonds with the OPM

The **terminal value** for the debt of a firm is $B = \text{Min}\,(V, B)$. If the firm's terminal value V is greater than the face value of debt B, the bondholders will simply receive the payment that they were originally promised, B. However, if the firm goes bankrupt by the end of the period $(V < B)$, then all that will be left to compensate the bondholders is V. So debt can be

considered a claim contingent on the end of period value of the firm, and the Black and Scholes framework can be applied to its valuation. The same arbitrage conditions hold—that is, by combining a firm's debt and the riskless asset, the value of a leveraged firm can be equated with the equity of an unleveraged firm.

Merton (1974) shows that the formula for the valuation of a firm's debt can be derived directly from the valuation formula for equity (Equation 15.68). This formula can be written:

$$D_t = Be^{-r\tau} [N(h_1) + \frac{1}{d_1}N(h_2)] \tag{15.69}$$

where:

$$d_1 = Be^{-r\tau}/V_t, \text{ the current debt ratio;} \tag{15.69A}$$

$$h_1 = -\frac{\frac{\sigma_v^2 \tau}{2} - \ln(d_1)}{\sigma_v\sqrt{\tau}}; \text{ and} \tag{15.69B}$$

$$h_2 = -\frac{\frac{\sigma_v^2 \tau}{2} - \ln(d_1)}{\sigma_v\sqrt{\tau}} \tag{15.69C}$$

with the other variables as defined before.

Equation (15.69) is equivalent to $V - F(V, \tau, B, r, \sigma_v^2)$, Equation (15.68), for, of course, the combined value of a firm's debt and equity must equal its total value, V. It is important to note that the valuation Equation (15.69) applies to debt paid off as one lump sum at a specified date. However, the same analysis can be adapted to more conventional debt that pays coupons over its life along with a balloon payment at the end. Sample Problem 15.3 provides further illustration.

Sample Problem 15.3

For the firm in Sample Problem 15.2, what is the value of the firm's bonds at time zero?

Solution

$$V_0 = F_0 + D_0$$
$$\$100 = \$53.78 + D_0$$
$$D_0 = \$46.22$$

or:

$$D_0 = Be^{-r\tau} \left[N(h_1) + \frac{1}{d_1} N(h_2)\right]$$
$$d_1 = \frac{Be^{-r\tau}}{V_0} = \frac{50e^{-0.1(1)}}{100} = 42.25$$

$$h_1 = - \frac{\frac{0.5(1)}{2} - \ln (0.4525)}{0.707 \sqrt{1}} = 1.475$$

$$h_2 = - \frac{\frac{0.5(1)}{2} + \ln (0.4525)}{0.707 \sqrt{1}} = 0.7680$$

$$D_0 = 50e^{(-0.1)(1)} \left[N(1.475) + \frac{1}{0.4525} N(0.7680) \right]$$

$$D_0 = \$46.22$$

Figure 15–5 graphs the value of debt and equity as a function of the value of the firm. Notice that the straight line representing the value of debt for different values of equity and the firm resembles that of a short put (Chapter 14). That is, the creditors, in lending the firm money, are betting that the value of the firm will not decline over the debt's time to maturity and that the coupon payments they receive will be equivalent to the premium one would receive for selling a put. Similarly, the amount of money that the creditors lend the firm can be considered the same as the margin required of put writers who do not own the underlying security (in case the asset's price drops). Furthermore, the short put and a firm's debt have the same loss potential, since the asset can never fall below zero in value.

Finally, the debt of a firm with market value substantially larger than the present value of B will behave much like a riskless asset (a low-exercise-price, or out-of-the-money put). On the other hand, if B is much larger than V, the debt of the firm will behave much like the equity of an unleveraged firm (a high-exercise-price, deep-in-the-money put). In the first case there is

FIGURE 15–5 The Value of Debt and Equity as a Function of the Firm's Value
(Profit Profile of Debt's Value at Maturity)

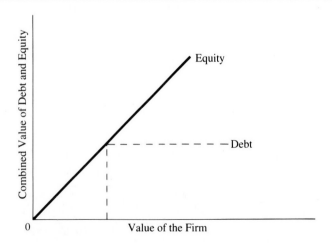

little to no risk of default (exercise); in the second case, with the firm nearing bankruptcy as the bonds come due, there is a high probability of default (exercise) by the owners (purchasers of the put). That is, it is very likely that the bondholders will become the equityholders.

Pricing Convertible Bonds with the OPM

The holder of a convertible bond is promised a specified payment, as is the holder of an ordinary bond. Nevertheless, the convertible bond may also be exchanged for a specified number of shares of the firm's stock at any time. To see how this convertible feature can be priced using OPM, examine the **profit profile** for a convertible bond at maturity in Figure 15–6.

First, notice that the convertible bond is a combination of a short put with exercise price B^* and a long call with exercise price V^*. The convertible feature has a cost (as a long call demands a premium) that reduces the expected receipts from the ordinary debt portion of the convertible bond (or in an analogous fashion, decreases the premium received for writing the put). A convertible can be thought of as a bullish position. The investor thinks the company has much upside potential, but does not want to take on a purely speculative position such as buying only the common stock of the company (or similarly a call option). So instead, this investor goes for a safer position that will assure a guaranteed return should the firm's value remain the same, yet will allow participation in the benefits of any eventual large upswing in the price of the firm's stock. The convertible is just such a position. Moreover, it should be discernable that this position is equivalent to writing an out-of-the-money put (low exercise price) and buying a far out-of-the-money call (high exercise price).

When the value of the firm surpasses V^*, the convertible bondholders will find it profitable to exercise their conversion right. In particular, if the firm has N total shares outstanding and the bondholders have a right to acquire n more shares, in the event the firm's value exceeds V^* there will be $(n + N)$ shares outstanding. Thus, should the firm's value be V_2 at the time of

FIGURE 15–6 Profit Profile for a Convertible Bond at Maturity

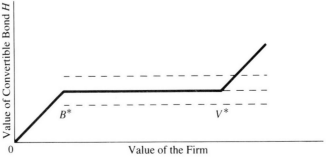

exercise, the total value of the convertible bonds will be $[n/(n + N)]V_2$, or the total proportion of the equity now owned by the former bondholders times the total value of the firm, V_2. The proportion $n/(n + N)$ is called the **dilution factor** and is designated by g. Using this notation the total value of the convertible bonds can be restated as gV_2.

To more clearly illustrate the possible values for this claim, consider the range of values it can take on at maturity:

$$
\begin{aligned}
H(V, T) &= V & \text{if} \quad 0 < V < B^* \\
&= B^* & \text{if} \quad B^* < V < V^* \\
&= gV_2 & \text{if} \quad V^* < V
\end{aligned}
\tag{15.70}
$$

Since the convertible bond is a combination of two option positions it can be expected that its valuation through the Black–Scholes approach will proceed in two steps. That is, first the bond (or short put) is valued and then the value computed for the convertible feature (long call) is added, so that:

$$
H(V, B, r, \sigma_v^2, \sigma_S^2) = D(V_t, B, \tau, r, \sigma_v^2) + C(gV_t, V^*, \tau, r, \sigma_S^2) \tag{15.71}
$$

As can be discerned from Equation (15.71), the conversion-option portion of the convertible bond will make it worth more than the ordinary debt by itself. Hence the convertible bond will be priced at a premium above a simple discount bond.

Pricing Convertible Bonds with Call Provisions

When a call feature is attached to the provisions for a convertible bond, the owners of the firm have the right to repurchase the bonds from their holders for some prespecified payment K at any time prior to their maturity. Adding a call feature to the analysis complicates the valuation process. Now the bondholders must consider in their conversion decisions whether the firm will call the bonds if they do not exercise them.

It has been shown that a call option on a stock paying no dividends should not be exercised prior to maturity. To simplify the analysis here assume the same characteristic for the firm at hand. Therefore, it will not be optimal for the convertible bondholder to exercise his or her right before maturity. However, the firm may be interested in calling the bonds before maturity if the value of equity becomes sufficiently high. Specifically, $V^* < K_t < V_2$, so if the stock's value exceeds K, the firm will be better off to call in the bonds and pay K dollars now instead of a potentially higher amount V_2 later on.

Ingersoll (1977) has shown that if the value of the firm (equity) reaches $V_2 = K_t/g$, the firm will be better off to call in the bonds. Such a constraint adds an upper boundary to the maximum value of the convertible bond. To modify Equation (15.71) to reflect the call-provision constraint, the functional relationship between K and time can be used as specified by Ingersoll, which is $K_t = Be^{-RT}$ (that is, that the current call price is equal to the face value of the bond discounted at some interest rate R). The larger R will be the diminishing effect of the call provision on the convertible bond's value.

Considering $R = r$, the riskless rate, as a limiting case, the price of a convertible bond with call provision can be defined as:

$$H(V, B, r, \sigma_v^2, \sigma_S^2) = D(V_t, B, \tau, r, \sigma_v^2) + C(gV_t, V^*/g, \tau, r, \sigma_S^2) \quad \textbf{(15.72)}$$

From Equation (15.72) it is clear that the effect of the call provision is to raise the exercise price for the conversion option V^* to V^*/g. Since the value of a call decreases as its exercise price increases, Equation (15.72) explicitly shows once again that the call provision reduces the value of the convertible by limiting the amount by which the conversion option can go into the money.

EVALUATING THE BLACK–SCHOLES OPTION-PRICING MODEL

On the basis of the applications of the Black–Scholes OPM that have been presented in this chapter it might seem that the uses of this model are limitless. The power of its underlying arbitrage argument and relative ease of use have made the Black–Scholes OPM very popular among the academic and investment communities. However, the Black–Scholes formula is only a model of the true valuation process for contingent claims. Its accuracy and reliability are bounded by how much reality violates its underlying assumptions. Effectively utilizing this model's strengths requires knowledge of its limitations and drawbacks. In critiquing the Black–Scholes OPM in this section two evaluative aspects are examined based on empirical and theoretical research. The criteria of interest are (1) the model's accuracy and reliability, and (2) the validity of its assumptions.

Tests of the Black–Scholes Model's Accuracy and Reliability

Overall empirical tests of the Black–Scholes model have found that it performs relatively well, especially for at-the-money options. Nevertheless, significant deviations from model prices are consistently observed for deep-in- and deep-out-of-the-money call options. The direction of pricing bias for these two options is ambiguous. More specifically, Black (1975) in a test of the model found that deep-in-the-money options were underpriced and deep-out-of-the-money options were overpriced by the formula. In a more recent study, MacBeth and Merville (1979) analyzed more than 12,000 stock-option prices and found completely reversed pricing biases, with deep-out-of-the-money options underpriced and deep-in-the-money options overpriced.

Explanations of the cause of these pricing biases and why they change over time are complicated by a number of factors. Most authors testing the Black–Scholes formula or developing an alternative model point to model misspecification as the source of pricing bias. In addition, the effects of changing market expectations can influence the change in direction of pricing bias. Discerning the "true" source of bias is complicated by two basic forces.

1. There is a problem of market synchronization. Since most studies use closing prices, a bias arises if the final stock and option prices did not occur at the same time of the day. Moreover, differences in trading volume are not accounted for.
2. Any test of the Black–Scholes model's validity is also a joint test of market efficiency. Deciphering whether the Black–Scholes model is significantly misspecified or whether the market is just inefficient is nearly impossible.

The Validity of the Black–Scholes Assumptions

The most blatant market violations of the Black–Scholes assumptions are the observed nonconstancy of interest rates and the various volatility measures. Since certain basic changes in the Federal Reserve's monetary policy were established in October 1979, interest rates have gyrated wildly in the financial markets. Thus, the assumption of a constant interest rate is a not very realistic one.

Merton (1973) derived a version of the Black–Scholes model that allows for stochastic interest rates. Yet, the advantage of using this model is only as good as the forecasts one makes of future interest rates. Fortunately, except for deep-in-the-money options, changes in interest rates do not have a particularly detrimental impact on the model's pricing accuracy.

The nonstationarity generally observed for the variance rate is a more pressing problem because of its generally large impact on the option's price. Recall from the earlier discussion on implied variance that when computed for each option on some underlying instrument, the individual implied variances (IV) differed significantly by exercise price and maturity. If the Black–Scholes model is specified correctly, the observed differences in individual IV should not exist. One can surmise, therefore, that the misspecifications of the Black–Scholes model are impounded by the market into the individual IV terms. Exactly how the model might be misspecified is not easy to discern.

A number of authors have developed option models based on alternative assumptions concerning the true underlying stochastic return-generating process and the distribution of the continuous returns. Some of the more distinguished efforts include the following. Merton (1976) developed an option-pricing model that allows for the possibility of jumps in an underlying asset's price, which Black and Scholes assumed to follow a diffusion process. Merton's model has much intuitive appeal, but the estimation of the "jump" adjustment to the variance term is rather ambiguous at this point. An earlier model developed by Cox (1975) allows for a changing volatility parameter. Called the **constant elasticity-of-variance** formula, this model allows the variance term to follow a diffusion process in which its elasticity is always constant. An attractive feature of this model is that it will allow the variance of the rate of return to vary inversely with stock price, which is observed in practice.

Geske (1979) presents another interesting perspective. He suggests that if a firm's stock can be valued and considered as a call option, then an actual call option on the stock is an option on an option, or a compound option. The argument for this model suggests that since the variance of the stock's rate of return is nonconstant over time, a modified formula would be expected for the value of the call that takes account of the influence of the capital structure of the firm on the stock-return distribution.

Lee, Rao, and Auchmuty (1981) offer a model assuming discrete trading in securities markets where the underlying asset and market returns are bivariate log normally distributed, and investors have increasing concave utility functions exhibiting skewness preference. Also challenging the distribution assumption, Jarrow and Rudd (1982) have developed a model that prices the differences in the second, third, and fourth moments when the "true" distribution of continuous returns is not log normal as Black–Scholes assume.

At this point in time no definitive tests exist to determine which of these models performs best and whether any do better than the Black–Scholes model. An additional hypothesis about the Black–Scholes misspecification question comes from Hotopp, Maloney, and Lee (1985), who use individual implied variances to help explain the sources of misspecification as well as to improve the actual valuation process. These authors suggest that the Black–Scholes model does not account for market imperfections and subjectivities, such as differences in trading volume for individual options and the type of intensity of market expectations (bull versus bear, for instance). Consequently, since the Black–Scholes model does not really account for these imperfections, they become a part of the implied variance, giving it a residual character considerably more diverse than a simple volatility measure.

For the moment it can be cautiously concluded that the Black–Scholes model offers the best combination of ease in use and accuracy in pricing. However, the real effectiveness of this model is limited to the accuracy of one's forecasts of the volatility parameter.

SUMMARY

This chapter has presented extensive coverage of option-pricing theory. Starting with the most basic approach, the binomial option-pricing model, the essential concepts of option pricing were discussed, including arbitrage portfolios and the hedge ratio. Using a basic knowledge of the binomial approach, the analysis was extended to the Black–Scholes option-pricing model. After interpreting and developing the components of Black–Scholes a study was made of the sensitivity of its price to changes in its input

parameters. The partial derivative of the call's price with respect to the stock price is the hedge ratio, delta. Also of importance is the fact that the call option's price is highly sensitive to changes in the volatility parameter.

To correctly utilize the Black–Scholes model it is necessary to employ accurate data; thus some of the potential pitfalls and barriers to collecting or estimating the input values were mentioned. The volatility estimate is certainly the hardest to observe. Accordingly, three estimation or forecasting techniques for volatility were discussed: (1) historical variance, (2) time-series analysis, and (3) implicit volatility. Of the three, the implicit volatility method is currently the state of the art in all options markets. However, problems with its interpretation and weighting still exist.

Two prominent adjustments for known and stochastic dividends to the Black–Scholes OPM were discussed, as well as Black's (1976) model for pricing options on futures. Put-option pricing for American options is still inconclusive because of the value of the early-exercise feature, even when the underlying security makes no payouts such as dividends. Therefore, three similar models for evaluating European put options were reviewed, including put–call parity, the Black–Scholes European-put pricing model, and the BOPM adjusted to evaluate puts. As with the call options, the put's price sensitivity to the model's inputs was examined, and its elasticity and beta were calculated. In the context of capital asset pricing theory the put is a desirable hedging instrument because of its inherent negative beta.

OPT was then taken a step further and applied to the interpretation and valuation of other financial securities, such as common stock, discount bonds, convertible bonds, and convertible bonds with a call provision. Finally, in evaluating the Black–Scholes model it was noted that no other simple model has yet proved itself superior in terms of accuracy and ease of use. However, its successful use depends on accurate input estimation.

The appendices relate the binomial and Black–Scholes models in a more explicit manner, and describe the ordinary least-squares approach of Whaley (1982) to estimate the implied standard deviation.

The last two chapters have focused on the characteristics, uses, and valuation of options. The material should have been challenging, and additional rereading of these chapters is recommended. Options will continue to see a growing number of applications for the student of finance.

QUESTIONS AND PROBLEMS

1. What is the hedge ratio? What is a riskless portfolio? What is the relationship between the hedge ratio and the riskless portfolio?
2. Calculate the hedge ratio for XYX Company given an exercise price of $75, a current stock price of $75, $u = 1.12$, and $d = 0.80$.

3. Assume that the rate of return on a risk-free asset is 5 percent. Use the information given in question 2 to calculate the value of the call option.

4. Now suppose the call option in questions 2 and 3 is not priced correctly. Carefully explain how you could profit from this mispriced option.

5. Carefully explain how the binomial option-pricing model can be modified to describe a continuous-time domain.

6. Use the Black–Scholes OPM to compute the theoretical price for a call option on ABC Company's stock given the following information.

$$S_t = \$48.75 \qquad r = 0.095$$
$$X = \$50.25 \qquad \sigma^2 = 0.35$$
$$T - t = 90 \text{ days}$$

7. Use the information and the price you calculated for the call option in question 6 to compute the minimum price of a put option written on the same stock with the same exercise price.

8. In using the Black–Scholes OPM, what parameter is the most difficult to estimate? List some of the ways to estimate this parameter.

9. What is the relationship between the interest rate and the value of a call option? What is the relationship between the interest rate and the value of a put option?

10. Why is it more difficult to value a put option than a call option?

11. Carefully explain why an option whose underlying stock pays no dividend will never be exercised early.

12. Define the following:
    (a) binomial process   (b) riskless portfolio
    (c) hedge ratio   (d) e^{-rT}
    (e) $N(d)$ (f) gamma
    (g) put–call parity

13. Using the binomial model, what is the value of a put option given the following information.

$$X = 55 \qquad d = 0.75$$
$$S = 60 \qquad R = 1.10$$
$$u = 1.25$$

Given the same information, what is the value of a call?

14. What are the important assumptions underlying the binomial option-pricing model?

15. What is the value of a call option for two-period binomial model?

$$S = 30 \qquad u = 1.15$$
$$X = 30 \qquad d = 0.85$$
$$n = 2 \qquad R = 1.1$$

16. What are the assumptions used to derive the Black–Scholes option-pricing model?

17. Given the following diagram, which shows the relationship between the value of a call option and stock price, what inferences can you make?

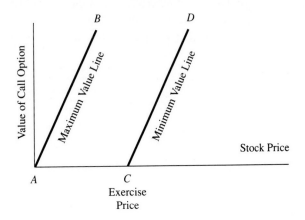

18. Using the Black–Scholes option-pricing model, what is the value of the following call option?

$$S = 73 \qquad T = 90 \text{ days}$$
$$X = 75 \qquad \sigma = 0.04$$
$$R = 1.10$$

If the estimate of σ is made with a 10-percent error (that is, it could be in the range of 0.36 to 0.44), what effect does this have on the price of the option? What is the range of option prices?

19. What is the relationship between the beta of a stock and the beta of an option on the stock?

20. Given the following information:

$$\partial C/\partial S = 0.65 \qquad \partial C/\partial \sigma = 11$$
$$\partial C/\partial E = -0.75 \qquad \partial C/\partial r = 21$$
$$\partial C/\partial T = 15 \qquad \partial^2 C/\partial S^2 = 0.02$$

What does this say about how the options will perform?

21. Given the information in question 20, what is the beta of an option on stock XYZ whose beta_{XYZ} is 1.1?

22. Which input to the Black–Scholes option-pricing model is hardest to estimate? Why is this so? What can be done about it?

23. What effect does the payment of a dividend have on the put and call options written on the dividend paying stock?

24. What is the value of a call option given the following information:

$$S = 50 \qquad T = 90 \text{ days}$$
$$X = 50 \qquad \sigma = 0.04$$
$$R = 1.1$$
$$d = \$0.20 \text{ per share to be paid in 15 days}$$

25. What input will a change in time to expiration have on the value of a put option?

26. Explain the existence of bond indentures limiting management actions in the context of option-pricing theory.

27. What is the value of JF Corporation stock given the following information:

$$V_0 = 500 \qquad \sigma_V^2 = 0.4$$
$$\beta = 300 \qquad \tau = 2 \text{ years}$$
$$r = 0.1$$

28. Compare the stock-valuation models of Gordon, Modigliani, and Miller with that derived from the option-pricing model. What are the key determinants of value for each model?

APPENDIX 15A: DERIVATION OF THE BINOMIAL FORMULA AND ITS RELATION TO THE BLACK–SCHOLES OPM

Early in this chapter, the binomial formula was derived for an option with one period to expiration. Moreover, the generalized binomial model for multiple periods to expiration was presented. This appendix demonstrates how the generalized model can be derived from the one-period binomial formula, and then, taking the generalized binomial model to its limiting case, how it becomes the Black–Scholes OPM.

Recall that by equating two portfolios involving the stock and a call option (one for the case of the stock rising and one if it were to fall) the hedge ratio h can be derived:

$$h = \frac{C_u - C_d}{(u - d)S} \tag{15.4}$$

Additionally, since a portfolio was created that earned the same return whether the stock price increased or decreased, it was reasoned that either portfolio was riskless and should earn the riskless rate. So combining the stock and option into a portfolio according to the hedge ratio should be equivalent to using either of the original one-period-ahead portfolios discounted to the present at the riskless rate. Solving this relationship for C and expanding h:

$$C = \frac{\left(\dfrac{R - d}{u - d}\right)C_u + \left(\dfrac{u - R}{u - d}\right)C_d}{R} \tag{15.6}$$

where R, the riskless rate actually equals $1 + r$. To simplify this equation:

$$P = \frac{R - d}{u - d} \quad \text{So:} \quad 1 - p = \frac{u - R}{u - d} \tag{15.7}$$

The result is the binomial option-pricing model for a call option with one period to expiration:

$$C = \frac{pC_u + (1 - p)C_d}{R} \qquad \textbf{(15.8)}$$

where C_u = Max $(0, uS - X)$, and C_d – Max $(0, dS - X)$.

From this point, it was demonstrated that the information provided by this model could be exploited in a market setting through the establishment of an arbitrage portfolio. That is, if the option price is lower than the formula states, the option should be bought, h shares of stock should be sold, and the difference should be lent at the riskless rate. This position, which had zero investment and zero risk, earned a return (which was called an arbitrage profit). It is exactly this process of creating arbitrage portfolios to profit from temporary pricing disequilibriums that forces the pricing mechanism of the market to work.

Now the one-period binomial model is extended to the consideration of two periods. Assuming that the stock follows a binomial process from one period to the next, it can only go up by a factor of u or down by a factor of d. After one period the stock's price is either uS or dS. Between the first and second periods the stock's price can once again go up by u or down by d; therefore, the possible prices for the stock two periods from now are uuS, udS, or ddS. Figure 15A–1 demonstrates this process in tree-diagram form. Notice that the option's price at expiration, two periods from now, is a function of the same relationship that determined its expiration price in the one-period model. More specifically, the call option's maturity value is always:

$$C_T = \text{Max } (0, S_T - X) \qquad \textbf{(15A.1)}$$

where T designates the maturity date of the option.

To derive the option's price with two periods to go, it is first helpful as an intermediate step to derive the value of C_u and C_d with one period to expiration when the stock price is uS and dS, respectively.

FIGURE 15A–1   Price Changes over Two Periods for a Stock and an Option

Two Periods to Expiration	*One Period to Expiration*	*Expiration Date*
Stock S	uS / dS	uuS / udS / ddS
Option C	C_u / C_d	C_{uu} = Max $(0, uuS - X)$ / C_{ud} = Max $(0, udS - X)$ / C_{dd} = Max $(0, ddS - X)$

$$C_u = \frac{pC_{uu} + (1 - p)C_{ud}}{R} \tag{15A.2}$$

$$C_d = \frac{pC_{du} + (1 - p)C_{dd}}{R} \tag{15A.3}$$

Equation (15A.2) shows that if the value of the option after one period is C_u, it will be worth either C_{uu} or C_{ud} after one more period at its expiration date. Similarly, Equation (15A.3) shows that if the value of the option is C_d after one period, it will be worth either C_{du} or C_{dd} at its expiration. By replacing C_u and C_d in Equation (15.8) with their expressions in (15A.2) and (15A.3) respectively, the resulting equation can be simplified to yield the two-period equivalent of the one-period binomial pricing formula:

$$C = \frac{pC_{uu} + 2p(1 - p)C_{ud} + (1 - p)C_{dd}}{R^2} \tag{15A.4}$$

The values of the parameters S and X are known. Assuming that R, u, and d will remain constant over time, the possible maturity values for the option can be determined exactly. Thus, deriving the option's fair value with two periods to maturity is a relatively simple process of working backwards from the possible maturity values.

Using this same procedure of going from a one-period model to a two-period model, the binomial approach can eventually be extended to its more generalized form, with n periods to maturity:

$$C = \frac{1}{R} \sum_{k=0}^{n} \frac{n!}{k!(n - k)!} p^k(1 - p)^{n-k} \text{Max} (0, u^k d^{n-k} S - X) \tag{15.9}$$

To actually obtain this form of the binomial model the two-period model could be extended to three periods, then from three periods to four periods, and so on. Equation (15.9) would be the result of these efforts. An interpretation of this model's components was presented earlier in the chapter; now we will illustrate the relationship between the binomial OPM and the Black–Scholes OPM. As a first step to see this, Equation (15.9) can be rewritten:

$$C = S\left[\sum_{k=m}^{n} \frac{n!}{k!(n - k)!} p^k(1 - p)^{n-k} \frac{u^k d^{n-k}}{R^n} \right] -$$
$$\frac{X}{R^n}\left[\sum_{k=m}^{n} \frac{n!}{k!(n - k)!} p^k(1 - p)^{n-k} \right] \tag{15A.5}$$

Furthermore, rewriting the Black–Scholes model underneath this one:

$$C = SN(d_1) - Xe^{-rT} N(d_2) \tag{15.12}$$

by expanding the d_1 and d_2 terms:

$$C = SN\left(\frac{\ln\frac{S}{X} + \left(r + \frac{\sigma_S^2}{2}\right)\tau}{\sigma_S\sqrt{\tau}}\right) - \frac{X}{e^{r\tau}}N\left(\frac{\ln\frac{S}{X} - \left(r + \frac{\sigma_S^2}{2}\right)\tau}{\sigma_S\sqrt{\tau}}\right) \quad \textbf{(15A.6)}$$

The terms within the brackets in Equation (15A.5) are from the complementary binomial-distribution function. Meanwhile the terms in parentheses in Equation (15A.6) are from the complementary cumulative normal probability-distribution function. The qualitative similarities between these two formulas can be easily observed, but some of the quantitative differences need to be examined to increase understanding of their interrelationship.

The Black and Scholes model takes place in continuous time; therefore it discounts the exercise price to the present at the continuous riskless rate, $e^{-r\tau}$. Since the binomial model assumes discrete time changes its discount factor is R^{-n}. If the size of the discrete time changes is made increasingly small, k approaches 0; then it follows that R^{-n} approaches $e^{-r\tau}$. It can be shown further that the cumulative normal probability function (or simply the normal distribution function) is the limiting case of the binomial distribution function as the duration of each discrete time change becomes increasingly small, k approaches 0 (or similarly, n approaches infinity).

Finally, to display the relationship among the variables within the brackets of each equation, the parameters u, d, and p are set in the binomial model equal to:[11]

$$p = 0.5$$

$$u = \frac{\left(r - \frac{\sigma_S^2}{2}\right)\tau}{n} + \frac{\sigma_S}{\sqrt{\frac{\tau}{n}}} \quad \textbf{(15A.7)}$$

$$d = \frac{\left(r - \frac{\sigma_S^2}{2}\right)\tau}{n} - \frac{\sigma_S}{\sqrt{\frac{\tau}{n}}}$$

Jarrow and Rudd (1983) show that as the number of periods to expiration becomes increasingly large, $n \to \infty$, choosing the binomial parameters in this way results in the binomial models converging with the Black–Scholes model. Using the parameters u, d, and p in this form and with n sufficiently large, both models will produce the same option price (common practice typically uses $n = 150$ to 200).

---

[11] For a detailed derivation and proof of the validity of Equation (15A.7), see Jarrow and Rudd (1983).

FIGURE 15A–2   The Binomial Option-Pricing Model for Various Time Periods (*N*) in a Six-Month Maturity

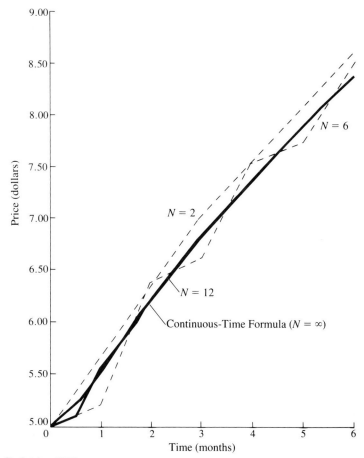

Source: Bookstaber (1982), p. 69.

As a final illustrative example of the relationship between the binomial and Black–Scholes models, see Figure 15A–2, which shows how the pricing differences between the two models diminish with larger values for *n*.

APPENDIX 15B: ESTIMATING THE IMPLIED STANDARD DEVIATION WITH OLS

This appendix explains the method for estimating implied standard deviation as first proposed by Whaley (1982). Although Whaley's original intent for this method was to improve upon the existing weighting techniques, his

ordinary least-squares (OLS) approach can also be used to derive the implied standard deviations (ISD) for single options.

To begin the development of his method, Whaley applies a Taylor-series expansion around some initial value of the standard deviation and omits higher-order terms. Mathematically, this is expressed as:

$$C_{j,t}^M = C_{j,t}^T(\sigma_0) + \left[\left(\frac{\partial C_{j,t}^T}{\partial \sigma}\right)/\sigma_0\right](\sigma - \sigma_S) + e_{j,t} \qquad \textbf{(15.B1)}$$

$$(j = 1, 2, \ldots, J)$$

where:

$C_{j,t}^M$ = market price for the option j at time t;

$C_{j,t}^T$ = theoretical model price for the option j at time t based on an estimated value for the ISD (σ_0);

σ_0 = the estimated ISD evaluated from some initialization value up to some minimum level of tolerance of error;

σ = true or actual ISD; and

$e_{j,t}$ = random disturbance term for option t.

Rearranging Equation (15.B1) yields:

$$[C_{j,t}^M - C_{j,t}^T(\sigma_0)] + \sigma_0\left[\left(\frac{\partial C_{j,t}^T}{\partial \sigma}\right)/\sigma_0\right] = \left[\left(\frac{\partial C_{j,t}^T}{\partial \sigma}\right)/\sigma_0\right] + e_{j,t} \qquad \textbf{(15B.2)}$$

$$(j = 1, 2, \ldots, J)$$

Furthermore, recall from Equation (15.26D) that the partial derivative of the option price with respect to the standard deviation of the log normally distributed continuous returns for the underlying asset can be expressed as:

$$\frac{\partial C}{\partial \sigma} = S\sqrt{\tau}N'(d_1) = \frac{S\sqrt{\tau}}{\sqrt{2\pi}}e^{-d_1^2/2} \qquad \textbf{(15.26D)}$$

Since $C_{j,t}^M$ is observable $(\partial C/\partial \sigma)_{j,t}/\sigma_0$ and $C_{j,t}^T(\sigma_0)$ can be evaluated at any given value using Equation (15.26B).

Whaley then applies OLS, which minimizes the sum of squared residuals, to achieve a single, weighted σ from the options on a particular security. The actual estimation procedures begin from a linearization of the option-pricing model around 0, and then OLS is applied to Equation (15.26B). The process thus proceeds in an iteration manner until the estimate (the estimated ISD) satisfies an acceptable tolerance of:

$$\left|\frac{\sigma_1 - \sigma_0}{\sigma_0}\right| < Q \qquad \textbf{(15.B3)}$$

where Q is a small positive number (Whaley uses 0.0001). Also, $\hat{\sigma}_1$ is the estimate for σ (the "true" ISD). If the tolerance criterion is not satisfied, σ_1 becomes the new initialization value and the OLS procedure is repeated.

REFERENCES

Becker, H. P., and W. H. Degler. "19 Option Strategies and When to Use Them." *Futures,* June 1984, pp. 46–51.

Beckers, S. "Standard Deviations Implied in Option Prices as Predictors of Futures Stock Price Variability." *Journal of Banking and Finance,* v. 5 (September 1981), pp. 363–82.

Black, F. "Fact and Fantasy in the Use of Options." *Financial Analysts Journal,* v. 3 (July/August 1975), pp. 36–72.

_____. "The Pricing of Commodity Contracts." *J. Financial Economics,* v. 3 (March 1976), pp. 167–79.

_____, and M. Scholes. "The Pricing of Options and Corporate Liabilities." *J. Political Economy,* v. 31 (May/June, 1973), pp. 637–59.

Bookstaber, R. M. *Option Pricing and Strategies in Investing.* Addison-Wesley, 1982.

Box, G. E. P., and G. M. Jenkins. *Time Series Analysis: Forecasting and Control.* Holden Day, Inc., 1970.

Boyle, P., and D. Emmanuel. "Discretely Adjusted Option Hedges." *Journal of Financial Economics,* v. 8 (September 1980), pp. 259–82.

Brenner, M. *Option Pricing: Theory and Applications.* Lexington Books, 1983.

Chu, C. C. "Alternative Methods for Determining the Expected Market Risk Premia: Theory and Evidence." Doctoral Dissertation, University of Illinois at Champaign-Urbana, 1984.

Cox, J. "Notes on Option Pricing I: Constant Elasticity of Diffusions." Working Paper, Stanford University, 1975.

_____, and M. Rubinstein. *Option Markets.* Prentice-Hall, 1985.

_____, and S. A. Ross. "The Valuation of Options for Alternative Stochastic Processes." *J. Financial Economics,* v. 3 (March 1976), pp. 145–66.

_____, _____, and M. Rubinstein. "Option Pricing: A Simplified Approach." *Journal of Financial Economics,* v. 7 (September 1979), pp. 229–63.

Finnerty, J. "The CBOE and Market Efficiency." *Journal of Financial and Quantitative Analysis,* v. 13 (March 1978), pp. 29–38.

Geske, R. "The Valuation of Compound Options." *Journal of Financial Economics,* v. 7 (March 1979), pp. 63–81.

_____, and R. Roll. "On Valuing American Call Options with the Black–Scholes Formula." *Journal of Finance,* v. 39 (June 1984), pp. 443–55.

Hotopp, S. M., W. S. Maloney, and C. F. Lee. "Improving the Estimation

of Volatility for SP500 Futures Options." Unpublished work, University of Illinois at Champaign-Urbana, 1985.

Ingersoll, J. "An Examination of Corporate Call Policies on Convertible Securities." *Journal of Finance,* v. 32 (May 1977), pp. 463–78.

Jarrow, R., and A. Rudd. "Approximate Option Valuation for Arbitrary Stochastic Processes." *J. Financial Economics,* v. 10 (September 1982), pp. 347–69.

————. *Option Pricing.* Richard D. Irwin, 1983.

Klemkosky, R., and B. Resnick. "Put Call Parity and Market Efficiency." *Journal of Finance,* v. 34 (December 1979), pp. 1141–55.

Latane, H., and R. Rendleman. "Standard Deviations of Stock Price Ratios Implied by Option Premia." *J. Finance,* v. 31 (May 1976), pp. 369–82.

Lee, W. Y., R. K. S. Rao, and J. F. G. Auchmuty. "Option Pricing in a Lognormal Securities Market with Discrete Trading." *J. Financial Economics,* v. 9 (March 1981), pp. 75–101.

Leland, H. "Option Pricing and Replication with Transaction Costs." *Journal of Finance,* v. 40 (December 1985), pp. 1283–1301.

MacBeth, J. D., and L. J. Merville. "An Empirical Examination of the Black–Scholes Call Option Pricing Model." *J. Finance,* v. 33 (September 1979), pp. 1173–86.

McMillan, L. G. *Options as a Strategic Investment.* New York Institute of Finance, 1980.

Mayer, T. S. *Commodity Options. A User's Guide to Speculating and Hedging.* New York Institute of Finance, 1983.

Merton, R. C. "Theory of Rational Option Pricing." *Bell Journal of Economics and Management Science,* v. 4 (Spring 1973), pp. 125–44.

————. "On the Pricing of Corporate Debt." *Journal of Finance,* v. 29 (May 1974), pp. 449–70.

————. "Option Pricing When Underlying Stock Returns Are Discontinuous." *J. Financial Economics,* v. 3 (March 1976), pp. 125–44.

Modigliani, F., and M. Miller. "The Cost of Capital, Corporation Finance and the Theory of Investment." *American Economic Review,* v. 47 (June 1958), pp. 261–97.

Park, H. Y., and R. S. Sears. "Changing Volatility and the Pricing of Options on Stock Index Futures." *Journal of Financial Research,* v. 8 (Winter 1985), pp. 265–96.

Roll, R. "An Analytic Valuation Formula for Unprotected American Call Option on Stocks with Known Dividends." *Journal of Financial Economics,* v. 5 (November 1977), pp. 251–58.

Sterk, W. "Tests of Two Models for Valuing Call Options on Stocks with Dividends." *Journal of Finance,* v. 37 (December 1982), pp. 1229–38.

Trennepohl, G. "A Comparison of Listed Option Premiums and Black–Scholes Model Prices: 1973–1979." *Journal of Financial Research,* v. 4 (Spring 1981), pp. 11–20.

Whaley, R. "Valuations of American Call Options on Dividend Paying Stocks: Empirical Test." *Journal of Financial Economics,* v. 10 (March 1982), pp. 29–58.

16 The Efficient-Market Hypothesis and Security Valuation

Previous chapters have discussed alternative theories and methods for evaluating stocks, bonds, futures, options, and options on futures and other securities. One of the assumptions used to discuss valuation theory and methods is that the capital market is efficient. In an *efficient capital market* security prices fully reflect all available information. Therefore, empirical investigation of whether the capital market is efficient is important for security analysis and portfolio management. In finance research, a statistical hypothesis used to test whether the capital market is efficient is called the **efficient-market hypothesis (EMH).**

This chapter focuses on the EMH and its relationship to security valuation. Valuation concepts and financial theories and models discussed in previous chapters are utilized to show the degree of efficiency with which both market-based and accounting information is reflected in current stock prices. Four major areas are discussed. The first is the relationship between market value and book value. Following this is an analysis of the market model and the capital asset pricing model (CAPM) used for testing the EMH. The EMH is then divided into three forms according to strength of efficiency, and the empirical evidence of market efficiency is presented. Last to be discussed are other recent issues related to the EMH.

MARKET VALUE VERSUS BOOK VALUE

One source of data used in security analysis is economic and market information. Another source—the primary source of information available to the security analyst—is accounting information from the financial statements of the firm, discussed earlier in Chapter 2. One of the key accounting items—assets—is the focus of the following section.

Assets

In general, the financial statements of the firm value the physical assets at historical cost less accumulated depreciation. This is known as **book value.** Unfortunately, the expired service of assets recorded as depreciation rarely reflects the change in the actual market value of the assets. For this reason, the book value of assets is often not relevant to the valuation of the firm.

The Securities and Exchange Commission (SEC) now requires the nation's large companies to disclose replacement-cost information for the firm's assets. This information allows investors to analyze the difference between the book value and the cost of replacing the firm's current productive capacity. The SEC also requires disclosure of replacement cost and depreciation charges estimated on the basis of replacement cost of productive capacity.

Conventional accounting procedures do not allow assets to be written up in value except when purchased. If one firm acquires another firm at a purchase price in excess of book value, some of the assets of the acquired firm may be written up if they are deemed undervalued.

Land is not depreciated in the financial statements of the firm; neither is any increase in the **market value** (value in terms of market price) of property recognized in the balance sheet, unless some "arm's length" transaction has taken place to objectively verify the value.

The firm's portfolio of marketable equity securities is usually recorded at the lower of initial cost or market value. Marketable debt securities are generally recorded at historical cost, although the lower of cost or market value may be used for debt investments as well. A decline in the market value of an equity-security portfolio below its cost is recorded in the valuation-allowance account. This loss on the valuation of marketable equity securities flows through to the income statement. Any subsequent increase in the market value of the portfolio is recognized as a recovery of loss on the valuation of marketable equity securities. However, the recovery of loss can never exceed the amount previously recorded in the valuation-allowance account. This means that securities are always valued at the lower of cost or market value.

Long-term bond investments are recorded at initial cost. Any difference between initial cost and the face value of the bond is amortized over the remaining life of the bond. The investment account is adjusted periodically to reflect the amortization of the discount or premium. Generally, the market value of the bond investment and its net carrying value differ substantially. Note that bonds in default must be marked to market.

Stock held as an investment in another corporation can be accounted for under one of two methods, (1) the equity method or (2) the lower-of-cost-or-market-value method. The equity method is used if the investing firm exercises significant control over the other corporation (investee). Under this method the investment is recorded at cost. Any net earnings of the investee are recorded in proportion to the investor's share of ownership as an in-

crease in the investment account of the investor. Dividends or net losses of the investee result in a decrease in the investing firm's investment account. The lower of the cost or market value is used if no evidence of significant control exists. These securities are handled in the same way as marketable equity securities.

Liabilities and Owner's Equity

Most current liabilities reflect their current values because they mature in less than one year. However, long-term debt in the form of bonds presents a more difficult problem.

Bond liabilities are recorded at the price at which they were sold when issued. If the bonds were not sold at par value, the discount or premium is amortized over the life of the issue. At the date of each interest payment, the amortization of a bond premium is deducted from the bonds-payable account while amortization of a discount is added to the bonds-payable account. Obviously, the market value of the bond issue will change radically with interest-rate fluctuations over time. However, the balance-sheet account will steadily change (due to the amortization) toward the par value on the maturity date of the issue.

The stockholders' equity account of the firm consists of contributed and earned capital. Contributed capital includes capital stock and additional paid-in capital. Earned capital is better known as retained earnings. When a firm issues common stock, the capital-stock account is increased by the par value of the issue. The par value is a nominal value per share. If stock is issued at a value greater than par, a premium results. This increases the additional paid-in capital of the firm. Stock issued at less than par results in a discount and decreases the additional paid-in-capital account. Again, the book value of the stockholders' equity can differ greatly from the actual market value of common stock.

The true market value of any firm is the sum of the market prices of all the firm's outstanding debt and equity issues. This value is often substantially different than the accounting value or book value of the firm.

Ratios and Market Information

Many ratios computed using accounting data can also be computed using market information (as discussed in Chapter 3). For example, the long-term debt-to-assets ratio might be computed using the market value of all outstanding debt. The return-on-equity ratio could be computed using accounting information for earnings and market information for the value of equity.

Ratios should be calculated using both kinds of information to determine whether there is a difference (relative to each other or to other firms in the industry) between the two methods. Large differences indicate a need for further analysis. The following section examines some market information-related ratios.

Market-to-Book Ratio

The ratio of market to book value for common equity is defined as

$$\frac{\text{Price per share of common stock}}{\text{Book value per share}} = \text{Market-to-book ratio} \quad \textbf{(16.1)}$$

in which the book value per share is computed by dividing the total of stockholders' equity from the balance sheet by the number of common shares outstanding. The **market-to-book ratio** is a measure of the management's ability to operate the company and to manage its financial affairs profitably. It also is an indication of the premium the market is willing to pay for the stock, given expectations about the future profitability of the firm. If this ratio is less than one, the market has taken a dim view of the future prospects for the company. Conversely, if it is greater than one, the market is favorably impressed with the firm. Sample Problem 16.1 provides further illustration.

Sample Problem 16.1

The XYZ Company's financial statements and certain market information are given in the table below. Calculate the market-to-book ratio and indicate what it implies about XYZ. The stock sells for $20 per share.

XYZ Company Year-End Balance Sheet ($ million)

Current assets	$10	Current liabilities	$10
Fixed assets	20	Long-term debt	25
Intangibles	10	Equity (in shares outstanding*)	5
Total assets	$40	Total liabilities and equity	$40

(*1 million shares are outstanding)

Solution

$$\frac{\text{Price per share}}{\text{Book value per share}} = \text{Market-to-book ratio}$$

$$\frac{\$20}{\dfrac{\$5,000,000}{1,000,000 \text{ shares}}} = 4/1$$

A market-to-book ratio greater than one indicates that the market likes the future prospects of XYZ. This may be due to the understatement of the value of XYZ's assets on the balance sheet (they are recorded at historic cost instead of future profitability potential), or because the market is placing value on something that doesn't appear on the balance sheet—for example, a new breakthrough or discovery, market leadership, expected increases in future earnings, and so on.

When attempting to estimate the weighted average cost of capital for a firm, only market values should be used in calculating the relative debt and equity weights as well as current interest costs and required returns. Book values reflect conditions at the date of issuance of the securities, whereas market values reflect the current situation facing the firm.

In addition to the market-to-book ratio given in Equation (16.1), the relationship between price per share and earnings per share (**P/E ratio**) as in Equation (16.2) is an important market-value-related ratio.

$$\text{P/E ratio} = \frac{\text{Price per share}}{\text{Earnings per share}} \qquad \textbf{(16.2)}$$

This ratio has been widely used by security analysts to determine whether the market price per share is reasonable. Sample Problem 16.2 provides further illustration.

Sample Problem 16.2

Given the data about XYZ Company from Sample Problem 16.1, and the income statement for the current period in the table below, calculate the P/E ratio for XYZ and indicate what it implies about the company. The market P/E ratio for the NYSE average is 15.

XYZ Company Year-End Income Statement ($ million)	
Revenues	$90
Expenses	− 86
Operating income	4
Interest	− 2
Taxable income	2
Tax	− 0.67
Profit	1.33/1,000,000 shares = $1.33/share

Solution

$$\text{Earnings per share} = \frac{\$1,330,000}{1,000,000} = \$1.33$$

$$\frac{\text{Price per share}}{\text{Earnings per share}} = \text{P/E ratio}$$

$$\frac{\$20}{\$1.33} = 15 \text{ times}$$

XYZ is selling at fifteen times current earnings—that is, it has a P/E ratio of 15. The current market P/E ratio for a broad-based average (NYSE) is 15. This implies that the market views XYZ's earnings as similar to the average firm listed on the NYSE.

A ratio called **Tobin's q ratio** [developed by Tobin (1969)] as defined in Equation (16.3) has recently been used by financial managers to determine a firm's investment behavior.

$$q = \frac{\text{Firm's market value}}{\text{Firm's replacement cost}} \tag{16.3}$$

where the firm's market value is taken to be the sum of the market value of common stock, the market value of preferred stock, the market value of the firm's debt. A firm's replacement cost can be found in its financial-accounting reports either in a supplementary statement or in the notes to the financial statement. Lindenberg and Ross (1981) have developed some theoretical and empirical implications associated with the Tobin q for economic and financial analysis. The q ratio might be useful to security analysts in determining the future market value of a firm (especially in light of the recent wave of takeovers). Sample Problem 16.3 provides further illustration.

Sample Problem 16.3

Again, this problem concerns XYZ Company. Information about its replacement value and the market value of its debt is given below. Calculate Tobin's q ratio for XYZ and indicate what information it conveys about the firm.

Replacement cost of total assets $50 million
Market value of XYZ's debt $30 million

Solution

$$\frac{\text{Firm's market value}}{\text{Firm's replacement cost}} = q$$

$$\frac{\$30 \text{ million} + \$20 \text{ million}}{\$50 \text{ million}} = 1$$

A q ratio of 1 indicates that the firm is fairly priced in terms of the current or replacement cost of its assets. A look at the q and P/E ratios for XYZ shows that they are fairly priced by the market. The high market-to-book ratio is caused by the understatement of the value of the firm's assets resulting from the use of historical costs for accounting purposes●

Overall, market/book ratio, P/E ratio, and Tobin's q ratio are calculated by dividing market information by some form of accounting information. These ratios are important for both security analysts and portfolio managers.

MARKET EFFICIENCY IN A MARKET-MODEL AND CAPM CONTEXT

The quality of market valuation methods depends heavily on the concept of **market efficiency.** An efficient capital market is an important part of the economy. This is an ideal capitalistic economy in which prices are accurate signals for capital allocation. If the capital market is to function properly in the allocation of economic and financial resources, prices of securities must be accurate indicators of intrinsic value.

A useful way to begin a discussion of efficient markets is to note the difference between *perfect* capital markets and *efficient* capital markets. A **perfect market** means an economy in continuous equilibrium—that is, a market which instantly and correctly responds to new information, providing signals for real economic decisions. The following are necessary conditions for perfect capital markets.

1. Markets are frictionless.
2. Production and securities markets are perfectly competitive.
3. Markets are informationally efficient.
4. All individuals are rational expected-utility maximizers.

Given these conditions, it follows that both product and securities markets will be both allocationally and operationally efficient. Markets are allocationally efficient when resources are directed to the best available opportunities, signalled correctly by relative prices; markets are operationally efficient when transaction costs are reduced to the minimum level possible.

The overall concept of **allocational efficiency** is one in which security prices are set in such a way that investment capital is directed to its optimal use. Because of the position of the United States in the world economy, the allocational responsibility of U.S. financial markets can be categorized into international and domestic efficiency. Also, since the overall concept of allocational efficiency is too general to test, operational efficiency must be focused upon as a testable concept.

The concept of capital-market efficiency is much less restrictive than the notion of perfect capital markets. In an efficient capital market prices fully and instantaneously reflect all available information; thus when assets are traded, prices are accurate signals for capital allocation.

The question that follows immediately is what is meant by the words *fully* and *instantaneously*. The issue reduces to the definition of information considered relevant and the speed of adjustment of prices to new information. Fama (1970) defines three "types" of efficiency, each of which is based on a different notion of exactly what type of information is understood to be relevant. They are:

1. **Weak-form efficiency:** No investor can earn excess returns by developing trading rules based on historical price or return information.
2. **Semi-strong-form efficiency:** No investor can earn excess returns from trading rules based on publicly available information.
3. **Strong-form efficiency:** No investor can earn excess returns using any information, whether or not publicly available.

The concept of capital-market efficiency can now be stated precisely. Fama (1976) defines efficient capital markets as those where the joint distribution of security prices (p_{jt}), given the set of information that the market uses (Φ_{t-1}^m) to determine security prices at time $t - 1$, is identical to the joint distribution of prices that would exist if all relevant information (Φ_{t-1}) at $t - 1$ were used. Formally:

$$f_m(p_{1t}, \ldots, p_{nt}|\Phi_{t-1}^m) = f(p_{1t}, \ldots, p_{nt}|\Phi_{t-1})$$

However, empirical testing of the efficient-market hypothesis needs still another input—namely, a theory about the time-series behavior of prices of capital assets. Three theories are considered.

1. The fair-game model. Based on average returns across a large number of observations, the expected return on an asset equals its actual return—that is

$$z_{j,t+1} = r_{j,t+1} - E(r_{j,t+1}|\Phi_t)$$

and

$$E(z_{j,t+1}) = E(r_{j,t+1} - E(r_{j,t+1}|\Phi_t)) = 0$$

in which $z_{j,t+1}$ is the error term between the jth stock's actual return $r_{j,t+1}$ at time $t + 1$ and its expected return $E(r_{j,t+1}|\Phi_t)$. The fair-game model is an expected return efficient-market model. In search of a fair game, investors can invest in securities at their current prices and can be confident that these prices fully reflect all available information and are consistent with the risks involved.

2. The submartingale model. A submartingale is a fair-game model where prices in the next period are expected to be greater than prices in the current period. Formally:

$$\frac{E(P_{j,t+1}|\Phi_t) - P_{j,t}}{P_{j,t}} = E(r_{j,t+1}|\Phi_t) \geq 0$$

When the equality holds, it is a *martingale* model. A submartingale model is appropriate for an expanding economy, one with real economic growth, or an inflationary economy, one with nominal price increases.

3. The random-walk model. In this case there is no difference between the distribution of returns conditional on a given information structure and the unconditional distribution of returns. The definition of capital-market efficiency is a random walk in prices. In returns form:

$$f(r_{1,t+1}, \ldots, r_{m,t+1}) = f(r_{1,t+1}, \ldots, r_{m,t+1}|\Phi_t)$$

It is immediately apparent that random walks are much stronger conditions than fair games or submartingales because they require that the joint distribution of returns remain stationary over time (all the parameters of the distribution should be the same with or without an information structure).

Some major empirical implications are outlined in Fama (1970). First, fair-game models rule out the possibility of profitable trading systems based only on historical information on Φ_t. Second, the submartingale model implies that trading rules based only on historical information on Φ_t cannot have greater expected profits than a policy of buying and holding the security. Finally, Fama thinks it best to consider the random-walk model an extension of the general expected-return or fair-game efficient-market model.

With this as background, the discussion now turns to the empirical testing of the efficient-market hypothesis. It is constructive, however, first to discuss the model used when this theory is tested. The determination of efficient security-market pricing can be usefully placed in the pricing framework of the market model and the capital asset pricing model as developed by Sharpe (1964), Lintner (1965), and Mossin (1966). These models express the required rate of return on any individual security as an additive function of the return required on a risk-free security and the return premium required to compensate investors for the assumption of risk.

Market Model

Following Chapters 3 and 9, the market model can be defined as

$$R_{j,t+1} = \alpha_j + \beta_j R_{m,t+1} + u_{j,t+1} \tag{16.4}$$

where:

$$R_{j,t+1} = \text{the rate of return on security } j \text{ for the period for } t \text{ to } t + 1;$$
$$R_{m,t+1} = \text{the corresponding return on a market index } m;$$
$$\alpha_j \text{ and } \beta_j = \text{parameters that vary from security to security; and}$$
$$u_{j,t+1} = \text{error term.}$$

Using the context of an efficient-market pricing model in which Φ_t is the set of relevant information available for determining security prices at time t, Equation (16.4) may be rewritten:

$$E(R_{j,t+1}|\Phi_t) = \alpha_j(\Phi_t) + \beta_j(\Phi_t) E(R_{m,t+1}|\Phi_t) \tag{16.5}$$

The application of this model for the EMH test is explored later in this chapter. Since the riskless rate of return, $R_{f,t+1}$, is part of the information set Φ_t:

$$\alpha_j(\Phi_t) = R_{f,t+1}[1 - \beta_j(\Phi_t)] \tag{16.6}$$

and:

$$\beta_j(\Phi_t) = \frac{\text{Cov}(R_{j,t+1}, R_{m,t+1}/\Phi_t)}{\sigma^2(R_{m,t+1}/\Phi_t)} \tag{16.7}$$

Sharpe-Lintner CAPM Model

Following Chapter 9, the CAPM can be defined as

$$E(R_{j,t+1}|\Phi_t) = R_{f,t+1} + \left[\frac{E(R_{m,t+1}|\Phi_{it}) - R_{f,t+1}}{\sigma(R_{m,t+1}|\Phi_t)} \right] \left[\frac{\text{Cov}(R_{j,t+1}, R_{m,t+1}|\Phi_t)}{\sigma(R_{m,t+1}|\Phi_t)} \right] \tag{16.8}$$

where:

$$R_{m,t+1} = \text{the return on the market portfolio, a market value weighted portfolio of all available investment assets;}$$

$$\sigma(R_{m,t+1}|\Phi_t) = \text{the standard deviation about } R_{m,t+1} \text{ given } \Phi_t; \text{ and}$$

$$\text{Cov}(R_{j,t+1}, R_{m,t+1}|\Phi_t) = \text{the covariance between } R_{jt} \text{ and } R_{mt}, \text{ given } \Phi_t.$$

In the CAPM model the second bracketed term in Equation (16.8) is referred to as the risk of an individual asset, and the bracketed term by which it is multiplied is called the **market price of risk.**

TESTS FOR MARKET EFFICIENCY

As discussed above, there are three general categories that have been used to define market efficiency—(1) the weak form, (2) the semi-strong form, and (3) the strong form. Moreover, market efficiency is analyzed in both its static and dynamic forms. In a static analysis efficiency is considered in terms of reflection boundaries, as discussed by Cootner (1962) and Shiller (1981), and in a dynamic analysis by Hillmer and Yu (1979). The speed of adjustment of information impounded into security prices is their focus.

Weak-Form Efficiency

The nature of the information set determines the distinctions of the three forms of efficiency. For the weak form, this set of information includes

historical prices, price changes, and any related volume information. Current prices reflect all of this stock-market information, so that the use of such data cannot be of any assistance in the prediction of future price changes.

Two basic types of tests have been used to evaluate the weak form: (1) those that test for statistical independence in sequences of process and price changes, and (2) those that use technical trading rules to devise a profit beyond random selection. Many authors, including Samuelson (1973) and Fama (1965), have demonstrated that the evidence is against any significant dependence in successive price changes. The only contrary evidence seems to be from studies of individual transaction-price data as they become immediately available on the stock exchanges—for example, Niederhoffer and Osborne (1966) and Summers (1986). Nevertheless, it is not at all likely that the significant serial correlation found in the sequence of individual transaction prices could be used to generate excess profits after transaction costs.

The weak-form test of technical trading rules is characterized by the filter tests of Alexander (1961) and Fama and Blume (1966). A typical filter rule works as follows: buy a stock if its daily closing price increases by at least z percent from a previous low and hold it until its price decreases by at least z percent from a previous high. Then simultaneously sell and go short. When the stock price again increases by at least z percent above a previous low, close the short position and go long. Ignore price changes of less than z percent. This process is repeated continually over a fixed time period, at which time the results are compared with those from a buy-and-hold strategy over the same period. The conclusions reached from such studies have shown that only by using small filters and not taking into account trading costs can one achieve above-average profits.

Still another type of weak-form testing involves examining the correlation of excess returns (actual return minus expected return) to see if any correlation exists. Fama and MacBeth (1973) examined return series using the capital asset pricing model (CAPM) to estimate expected return on a security. They then examined the correlation of excess returns and found virtually no correlation.

Both Galai (1977) and Roll (1970) used different models of expected returns and then examined the correlation of excess returns. In both cases, the market is shown to be weak-form efficient. Bernard and Thomas (1989) found that post-earnings-announcement drift is essentially due to delayed price response.

Semi-Strong-Form Efficiency

The information for semi-strong-form efficiency includes not only stock market data but *all publicly available* information. Current prices under this form already include any piece of information that might otherwise be expected to be useful in achieving above-average rates of return. Tests of

this form include examinations of the speed of adjustment of stock prices to new information and studies that consider whether investors can achieve above-average profits by trading on the basis of any publicly available information.

There are several problems with the filter tests discussed in the previous section. They test only the weak form of the efficient-market hypothesis (EMH). The filter-rule test also fails to take into account the differential risk of assets; nevertheless, through a joint test of the EMH and capital asset pricing model (CAPM) the various levels of risk across different securities can be taken into account. If capital markets are not efficient, the CAPM is invalid. The assumptions upon which the CAPM is based do not hold under conditions of market inefficiency; however, if capital markets are efficient and the CAPM is the right tool, the CAPM can be used simultaneously to test the efficiency of the capital market and the validity of the CAPM, as shown by Roll (1977).

The CAPM indicates that the only relevant risk is systematic risk. Based upon the CAPM the return of a security can be viewed as a fair-game model conditional on the security's systematic risk as measured by beta. A fair-game model says that the expected abnormal return for the security is zero.

Mathematically, the expected return on security j for time t can be written conditional upon the estimate of the firm's beta:

$$E\left(R_{jt}|\beta_{jt}\right) = R_{ft} + [E(R_{mt}) - R_{ft}]\,\beta_{jt} \tag{16.9}$$

where:

$$\beta_{jt} = \left[\frac{\mathrm{Cov}\,(R_{j,t+1},\,R_{m,t+1})}{\sigma^2\,(R_{m,t+1})}\right]$$

The difference between the expected return and the actual return is defined as the residual:

$$\epsilon_{jt} = R_{jt} - E(R_{jt}|\beta_{jt}) \tag{16.10}$$

The residual reflects the abnormal return of the security. If the CAPM is true and if markets are efficient:

$$E(\epsilon_{jt}) = 0 \tag{16.11}$$

The joint tests of the EMH and the CAPM are made by evaluating this residual term.

Several studies have used a similar method, the **cumulative average residual (CAR),** to perform the tests. As before, the residual is defined for the jth firm, in time period t:

$$\epsilon_{jt} = R_{jt} - E(R_{jt}|\beta_{jt}) \tag{16.12}$$

For a sample of N companies a cross-sectional average residual for each time period can be defined:

$$AR_t = \frac{1}{N} \sum_{j=1}^{N} \epsilon_{jt} \qquad (16.13)$$

By summing all the average residuals over time a cumulative average residual results:

$$CAR = \sum_{t=1}^{T} AR_t \qquad (16.14)$$

where:

T = the number of months being summed ($T = 1, 2, \ldots , M$); and
M = the total number of months in the sample.

Finding that the CAR is not significantly different from zero would mean that the CAPM and EMH do hold.

The CAR method has been found appropriate for testing the semi-strong form by focusing on some informational event—for example, a dividend or earnings announcement taken to occur at time $t = 0$. The residuals are studied for a number of periods prior to and after the announcement. Perhaps the best known of these studies is the Fisher, Fama, Jensen, and Roll (FFJR, 1969) analysis of the information impact of stock splits. It was hypothesized that any abnormal information to be derived from the split would show up in the residuals from a regression of individual stock returns on the returns in the market and would result in a permanently higher level of cash flows than would be expected by using only the CAPM. Their results indicate that those firms that also increased their cash dividend had slightly positive returns after the split, while those firms that did not increase their dividends had a negative return after the split. (The anomalies analysis related to these results is discussed later in this chapter.) It should be noted that in the FFJR study, the actual day of the stock split, rather than the announcement day, was used as the base period for their empirical study. This may have biased their results, but not to any significant degree.

Ball and Brown (1968), using methodology similar to FFJR, studied the effects of annual earnings announcements. From their study they conclude that no more than about 10–15 percent of the information in the annual earnings announcement had not been anticipated by the month of the announcement. This is viewed as further evidence consistent with the semi-strong theory of market efficiency.

The FFJR method has also been used by many scholars—including Gibbons and Hess (1981), Keim and Stambaugh (1984), and others—to investigate the phenomena known as the **weekend effect** in stock returns. The weekend effect refers to the fact that stock prices tend to rise all week long to a peak price level on Friday. The stock prices then tend to trade on Mondays at reduced prices. Recently, Cornell (1985) used a similar approach to show that a weekend effect exists in stock-index real return. However, he found that a weekend effect does not exist in real returns on stock-index futures.

Waud (1970) used the FFJR methodology to examine the effects of discount-rate changes by the Federal Reserve Bank. He finds evidence of a statistically significant **announcement effect** on stock returns for the first trading day following an announcement; the magnitude of the adjustment is small, however, never exceeding 0.5 percent.

The issue of an announcement effect for Federal Reserve policy changes was investigated by Lynge (1981), Urich and Ulachter (1981), and Cornell (1979, 1983A, 1983B). All of these studies find that only unanticipated money-supply changes affected the market rates. The anticipated component of the money-supply change was shown to have no significant impact on the market rate. This seems to indicate, on one hand, that the market is efficient while, on the other hand, it implies that the macro variables need to be analyzed by portfolio managers and security analysts.

In other studies, Sunder (1973, 1975) evaluates the effect of inventory methods, and Kaplan and Roll (1972) investigate the impact of accounting revisions that involve no changes in cash flow. These studies confirm that excess returns could be made with inside information, thus violating strong-form efficiency but not semi-strong-form efficiency.

Before leaving this discussion of the EMH with the conclusion that the semi-strong form holds all the time, it is necessary to consider several factors. All of these studies were made on widely held and heavily traded stocks. Research has shown that efficiency is at its best when the stock is heavily traded. Where there is thin or sporadic trading, efficiency may be impaired. Because the market mechanism does not function as well in thinly traded stocks, the new information cannot be impounded as easily in the stock's price. This implies that for thinly traded stocks the market may not be efficient and, therefore, the possibility for abnormal returns does exist.

Another problem related to the volume of trading is that of investors of differing ability. The theory assumes all investors have homogeneous expectations and abilities. However, as a result of greater skill or better resources, some investors are in a position to extract more valuable information from the historical data available. The information they can extract may be more valuable because they can figure it out sooner than the rest of the market and thus establish a position before the stock price has had a chance to react to the information. In heavily traded stocks, many talented investors compete against one another, ensuring the market's efficiency. However, in the thinly traded stocks the investor with a greater ability may be able to secure an advantage. Thus, while semi-strong efficiency holds for a large part of the market, caution must be emphasized.

This section has examined the issue of market efficiency. The use of joint tests of the EMH and CAPM has shown that the validity of both is supported by research. Moreover, the value of using the CAPM in tests of market efficiency has been demonstrated. Because the CAPM allows adjustment for the risk involved, it allows the testing of a higher form of market efficiency,

the semi-strong form, relative to using the filter tests to test the EMH. The filter tests generally only support the weak-form efficient market.

Strong-Form Efficiency

The mention of insider information leads naturally into a discussion of strong-form efficiency. The information set for the strong form includes not only all publicly available information but also insider information. It may seem that this form goes too far in its implication or impounding of "unavailable" information into stock prices. However, it really just shows that monopoly-type information such as that possessed by company insiders and stock exchange specialists is also reflected in stock prices as it becomes available. The distinction between this information set and that assumed for the weak and semi-strong forms is that the strong-form information set is not available to all participants in the market, only to those relatively small groups that monopolize its source. As a result, there is only a partial reflection of the information in the market price of the stock. If the size of the monopoly group represents only 0.10 percent of the overall set of market participants, only a negligible impact should be expected as compared to what it would otherwise have been.

Niederhoffer and Osborne (1966) have pointed out that specialists on the New York Stock Exchange apparently use their monopolistic access to information concerning unfilled limit orders to generate monopoly profits. Jaffe's (1974) and Finnerty's (1976) studies, using insider-trading information, found that excess returns could be obtained. Their results indicate that even after eight months excess returns still occurred. Unless these insiders just happened to possess superior analytical ability, their excess returns must have resulted from the illegal exploitation of insider information. The Levine and Boesky scandal of 1987, the Wong and Lee scandal of 1988, and the SEC crackdown on insiders trading indicate that insiders can and do exploit their access to information in order to outperform the market.

The strong form has been shown to hold in tests such as those that found that mutual-fund managers have been unable to outperform the market average consistently. In general, mutual funds performed worse than a naive strategy of random selection or mixing the market with the riskless asset. It should be noted that in examining the question of strong-form efficiency, it is relevant to look at performance after transaction costs involved with the purchase and sale of securities have been exceeded. Jensen (1968) found that mutual funds seem not to earn enough extra returns to cover the portion of the management fee that represents analysis costs. Thus, Jensen's evidence supports strong-form efficiency. Recent works by Merton (1981), Hendriksson and Merton (1981), and Hendriksson (1984) suggest that the poor performance of mutual funds may result from the methodology used to estimate the performance of the fund. (Mutual-fund performance is discussed in more detail in Chapter 17.)

OTHER METHODS OF TESTING THE EMH

This section discusses other methods and issues relating to testing the EMH. These include: (1) the random walk with reflecting barriers, (2) the variance-bound approach, (3) Hillmer and Yu's relative EMH test, and (4) market anomalies.

Random Walk with Reflecting Barriers

Cootner's (1962) analysis of stock-market behavior suggests that a random walk with reflecting barriers describes changes in stock prices over time. Cootner's model is a compromise model that allows both random and systematic changes in stock price to be taken into account.

Cootner's model has two types of investor, (1) the uninformed investor and (2) the informed investor. Uninformed investors engage in occupations in which they have comparative advantage and are compensated highly relative to other occupations. It is very costly, at least in terms of opportunity cost per unit of relevant information uncovered, for them to devote time to stock-market research. As a result they tend to accept present prices as roughly representing true differences in value, and they choose between stocks largely on the grounds of their attitudes toward risk. Therefore, for uninformed investors there exists a random walk of stock-market prices.

Informed investors, on the other hand, specialize in the stock market. As professionals their opportunity cost of research is much less than that of the uninformed. They do have an idea of what is going to happen in the future, but they cannot profit from it unless the current price deviates enough from the expected price to cover their opportunity costs. Their profits will come when prices have deviated enough from the expected price. Informed investors can expect future surprises to force prices toward their mean more often than not.

Another random-walk environment operates within the informed-investor class. There is no reason that changes in the price expectations of professionals should occur in other than a random manner. Therefore, the path of stock prices over any substantial period of time would be composed of a random number of trends, each of which is a random walk with reflecting barriers.

Some believe that common-stock prices tend to move in a deterministic, cyclical manner, where the term **cyclical** is taken in the mechanical sense of a movement perfectly predictable in timing and extent. These cycles may be quite complex, but diligent effort will eventually unravel the patterns: excess returns can be captured through trading based on these patterns. Those who adhere to this point of view are know as **chartists** and their work as **technical analysis.**

Except for a small fringe of opinion largely confined to stock-market professionals, this point of view has largely been refuted by efficient-market-hypothesis scholars. These academics believe that securities markets are efficient enough to make technical analysts unable to obtain unusual profit using only past security prices. However, Cootner (1962) revived this theory by producing a model of stock-market behavior that he felt was perfectly compatible with much of what he interpreted Wall Street chart reading to be all about. More recently, Treynor and Ferguson (1985) have come to the defense of technical analysis. They have shown that past prices, when combined with other valuable information, can indeed be helpful in achieving unusual profit. However, they also argue that nonprice information creates this opportunity and that past prices serve only to permit its efficient exploitation. (Such technical analysis is discussed in Chapter 17.)

In understanding Cootner's work, it is first necessary to understand what **kurtosis** and **skewness** mean. In considering the effects of nonnormality it is convenient to use the measure γ_1 of skewness and γ_2 of kurtosis of the distribution of a random variable x. If the mean and variance of the distribution are denoted by μ and σ^2, respectively, its skewness γ_1 is defined as:

$$\gamma_1 = \frac{E[(x - \mu)^3]}{\sigma^3}$$

and its kurtosis γ_2 as:

$$\gamma_2 = \frac{E[(x - \sigma)^4]}{\sigma^4} - 3$$

These measures do not depend on the location or scale of the distribution. For a symmetrical distribution γ_1 is zero. Positive values for γ_1 indicate that the distribution is skewed to the right, so that the right tail is in a certain sense heavier than the left compared to a symmetric distribution. Imagine deforming a normal probability-density curve, keeping it symmetric and unimodal: a deformation in which the tails are heavier and the central part is more sharply peaked would have $\gamma_2 > 0$, and one in which the tails are lighter and the central part is flatter, giving an effect of shoulders (a pattern identified in technical analysis), would have $\gamma_2 < 0$.

According to Cootner, if the random-walk hypothesis is correct, kurtosis of a price series should be near three at weekly intervals and get closer to three as time goes on. If the reflecting barrier or trend hypothesis is correct, kurtosis should be greater than three to begin with and should approach the kurtosis of the rectangular distribution in the limit if a single trend is involved. Cootner's result found the average kurtosis of the 45-price series used to be 4.90. If successive changes were independent, price changes over longer intervals would be expected to more closely approach the average kurtosis of a normal distribution. In fact, in Cootner's results the kurtosis decreases so rapidly that it very soon falls below that of a normal distribu-

tion. This tends to refute the efficient-market theory that stock prices are independent.

Monthly data from the Dow Jones 30 during January 1, 1980–December 31, 1984, have been tested for any indication of skewness or kurtosis. Table 16–1 indicates evidence of both skewness and kurtosis in the price series. The average skewness and kurtosis are 0.5137 and 0.6137, respectively. As can be seen, the question of skewness and kurtosis for security analysis and portfolio management is a nontrivial issue—one that will be taken up in later chapters.

Variance-Bound Approach Test

Shiller (1981A, 1982B), LeRoy and Porter (1981), and others have proposed a **variance-bound approach** to test the EMH. This kind of model, as defined in Equation (16.17), is based on the dividend-valuation model discussed in Chapter 4.

$$P_t = \sum_{k}^{\infty} \gamma^{k+1} E_t d_{t+k} = E_t P_t^*$$

where:

P_t = a price or yield;

$P_t^* = \sum_{k=0}^{\infty} \gamma^{k+1} d_{t+k}$ is an estimate based on perfect foresight of the ex-post rational price or yield not known at time t;

E_t = a mathematical expectation conditional on information at time t;

$\gamma = \dfrac{1}{1+r}$ = a discount factor; and

r = a discount rate.

By using S&P 500 index data and yield-to-maturity data on long-term bonds, Shiller (1981) showed that the movements in P_t appear to be too large to be justified by subsequent changes in dividends. Overall, Shiller concluded that the use of a random-walk model for dividends to test the efficient-market hypothesis does not appear to be promising. Other possibilities are that ex-ante real interest rates show very large movements or, alternatively, that markets are irrational or subject to fads. This issue will be discussed in detail in the next chapter.

The use of volatility measures to assess market efficiency is conceptually similar to Cootner's random walk with reflecting barriers approach. Although the method used to perform the precise statistical testing is relatively complicated, it is conceptually easy to understand and useful for security analysis. Chapter 17 explores this topic in more detail.

Hillmer and Yu's Relative EMH Test

Hillmer and Yu (1979) propose a relative method for testing the EMH. Instead of dichotomizing the market into an efficient or nonefficient class, they emphasize that there are various degrees of efficiency based on the

TABLE 16-1 Statistical Estimates of Monthly Returns for the Dow Jones Average (January 1980–December 1984)

			Mean	Standard	Skewness	Kurtosis	Coefficient of Variation
1	ALD	Allied Corporation	0.0084	0.0810	-0.0726	-0.0875	9.643
2	AA	Aluminum Company of America	0.0127	0.0880	0.7539	-0.0432	6.929
3	AC	American Can Company	0.0217	0.0955	1.9404	5.6991	4.401
4	AXP	American Express	0.0229	0.0872	0.3994	-0.3353	3.808
5	T	American Telephone & Telegraph	0.0146	0.0487	0.7756	0.5276	3.336
6	BS	Bethlehem Steel	0.0060	0.0991	0.2220	-0.4793	16.517
7	CHV	Chevron Corporation	0.0113	0.0990	0.8511	1.7590	8.761
8	DD	E. I. Du Pont de Nemours	0.0107	0.0656	0.1448	-0.2358	6.131
9	EK	Eastman Kodak	0.0125	0.0578	-0.0703	-0.0081	4.624
10	XON	Exxon	0.0174	0.0602	0.4545	-0.2266	3.46
11	GE	General Electric	0.0189	0.0576	0.3195	-0.4114	3.048
12	GM	General Motors	0.0147	0.0673	0.2331	0.9265	4.578
13	GT	Goodyear Tire & Rubber	0.0201	0.0786	0.4684	-0.3129	3.91
14	N	Inco Limited	-0.0023	0.1158	0.3691	-0.1981	-50.34
15	IBM	International Business Machines	0.0163	0.0553	0.2598	-0.2662	3.393
16	HR	International Harvester	-0.0113	0.1698	1.1670	1.6490	-15.027
17	IP	International Paper	0.0142	0.0849	0.3347	-0.1259	5.979
18	MCD	McDonalds	0.0195	0.0579	0.2241	-0.8820	2.969
19	MRK	Merck & Company	0.0087	0.0544	-0.1290	-0.8728	6.253
20	MMM	Minnesota Mining & Manufacturing	0.0129	0.0523	0.8002	0.5231	4.054
21	OI	Owens Illinois	0.0196	0.0861	0.5446	0.3821	4.393
22	MO	Philip Morris	0.0187	0.0567	0.2050	-0.4283	3.032
23	PG	Procter & Gamble	0.0125	0.0519	-0.0382	-0.4600	4.152
24	S	Sears Roebuck	0.0178	0.0781	1.1050	1.3520	4.388
25	TX	Texaco	0.0133	0.0880	1.3790	4.9840	6.617
26	UK	Union Carbide	0.0056	0.0709	-0.2174	1.6710	14.107
27	X	United States Steel	0.0153	0.0843	0.5456	0.6774	5.51
28	UTX	United Technologies	0.0153	0.0750	0.5598	0.3280	4.902
29	WX	Westinghouse Electric	0.0239	0.0855	0.6889	0.9027	3.917
30	Z	F. W. Woolworth	0.0156	0.0827	1.1920	2.4040	5.301
	Mean		0.0136	0.0778	0.5137	0.6137	4.7896

particular market variable and particular type of information. Consequently, Hillmer and Yu argue that the security analyst's efforts can be directed to discovering how various types of information affect different types of stocks. Hillmer and Yu's model for testing EMH is called a **relative** (instead of absolute) **EMH test.** Patell and Wolfson (1984) use this definition of EMH to study the intraday speed of adjustment of stock price to earnings and dividend announcements. They find that the speed of adjustment is generally less than an hour. The findings of Bernard and Thomas (1989) differ, however.

This section has discussed three alternative viewpoints to Fama's EMH test. These different hypotheses on EMH give some justification for active instead of passive approaches for security analysis and portfolio management. Despite the general applicability of EMH, there exist anomalies in the finance literature in which the efficient-market theory does not hold. These anomalies, dealing with the P/E ratio, size effect, and January effect, are discussed in the next section.

MARKET ANOMALIES

The idea of an efficient market is very important to the study of security analysis and portfolio management. If information is fully reflected in security prices, the market is efficient and it is not worthwhile to pay for information that is already impounded in security prices. The evidence seems to indicate that markets are efficient with respect to most types of information. However, there appear to be certain types of information associated with irregularities in the financial markets. Such irregularities are called **market anomalies.** Three of the most heavily researched anomalies are the P/E effect, the size effect, and the January effect.

The P/E Effect

The **price-earnings (P/E) effect** has been used to study whether the market is efficient.

Some security analysts have followed the strategy of buying stocks with below-average P/E ratios in order to earn above-average risk-adjusted returns. Basu (1977) found that high E/P or low P/E stocks produced excess returns for a sample of 750 NYSE stocks for the period September 1956 to August 1971. Ranking the stocks by their year and P/Es, he compared the yearly risk-adjusted returns for portfolios composed of 150 stocks with the highest P/E, 150 stocks with the next highest P/E, down to the final portfolio of 150 stocks with the lowest P/E. The results of this study show that the annual rate of return on a risk-adjusted basis was 9 percent for the high-P/E stocks and 16 percent for the low-P/E stocks. Additionally, the low-P/E stock portfolio had lower risk than the high-P/E portfolio.

The Size Effect

In a follow-up on the earlier study Basu (1983) found that these results were continuing over time. The results indicate that with respect to certain types of publicly available information—that is, P/E ratios—the market may not be semi-strong-form efficient. Reinganum (1981) presents the argument that in actuality, the P/E-ratio effect found by Basu is a proxy for the small-firm or **size effect.** Basu (1983) claims that the size effect is in reality more related to the P/E effect. In either case, evidence is available that the market may not be semi-strong-form efficient.

Banz (1981) ranks all NYSE firms by the total market value of the firm. Reinganum (1981) ranks all stocks on both the NYSE and the ASE in a similar fashion. They both divide their samples into five equal portfolios based on the market-value ranking. Their results indicate that the portfolios of the firms with the smallest market value experienced returns that were, both economically and statistically, significantly greater than the portfolios of the firms with large market value.

Much effort has been expended in trying to explain the size anomaly. Roll (1981, 1983) identifies statistical problems with measuring the riskiness of small, less frequently traded firms as being a probable explanation of the size-effect results. However, even after adjusting the methodology to account for Roll's criticism, the return pattern of the size effect still persists. Arbel, Carvell, and Strebel (1983) suggest that the size effect may be related to the disproportionate amount of institutional interest in the larger firms. Stoll and Whaley (1983) provide information on the trading costs of high-priced versus low-priced stocks and show that after the appropriate adjustment for size-related transaction costs, the small-firm effect is reduced. The size anomaly has not been adequately explained to date and still exists as evidence that refutes the semi-strong form of the efficient-market hypothesis.

The January Effect

The final anomaly of interest is called the **January effect** (or the **year-end effect**). Branch (1977) provides evidence that investors tend to sell stocks in which they have experienced capital losses at the end of the year in order to take advantage of the U.S. tax laws. This selling pressure depresses stock prices during the month of December. During January, the selling is reversed as investors return to the market and buying pressure is evident. The returns calculated for the month of January are above average because the ending prices in December are lower than they should be and the ending prices in January are higher than they should be.

Keim (1983) presents evidence that supports the tax-loss explanation. However, Roll (1982) plays down the tax-loss selling argument and presents evidence that the January effect is size related. Reinganum (1983) dismisses the tax-selling effect because of evidence indicating that firms with both

gains and losses during the previous year experience abnormal returns in January.

Haugen and Lakonishok (1988) offer a thorough review of the January effect with an explanation for its existence based on the trading behavior and patterns of institutional investors. As with the other anomalies, the January effect has not yet been completely explained in the context of an efficient market.

SUMMARY

This chapter has examined the basic tenets and empirical support for the efficient-market hypothesis and has outlined some of its implications for security valuation and portfolio management.

The relationship between market value and book value and its development into the concept of a q ratio was found to be very useful to security analysts in their estimates of the future value of a firm's financial securities. The efficient-market hypothesis (EMH) was categorized into three forms: weak, semi-strong, and strong. The main distinguishing feature among these forms was pointed out to be the information set assumed to be impounded into the market price of a firm's securities. For the weak form, the information set was shown to include historical prices, price changes, and related volume data; for the semi-strong form it was shown to include all publicly available information; and for the strong form it was shown to include all information, whether or not publicly available.

While empirical testing has provided good support for the weak and semi-strong forms of the EMH, the strong form has been upheld only in cases where, for example, mutual-fund managers have been unable to consistently outperform market averages. Tests involving corporate insiders and stock-exchange specialists have in general indicated that these groups do possess monopoly information and are able to use it to generate above-average returns.

Besides Fama's (1970) EMH, the discussion briefly included the random walk with reflecting barriers, the variance-bound test of EMH, and the market anomalies that refute EMH. This implies that the security-analysis and portfolio-management theory and methods discussed in this text are worthwhile tools for security analysts and portfolio managers. The next chapter discusses timing and selectivity of stocks and mutual funds.

QUESTIONS AND PROBLEMS

1. Define or explain the following:
   (a) weak form
   (b) semi-strong form
   (c) strong form
   (d) P/E ratio

   (e) Tobin's q (f) fair game

   (g) random walk   (h) market anomalies

2. What is the difference between a firm's market value and its book value? Which is a more meaningful measure?

3. What does the existence of market anomalies—that is, size, weekend, January effects, and so on—do to acceptance or rejection of the EMH?

4. ABC Bank's balance sheet is presented in the table. Calculate the market-to-book ratio for ABC and indicate what it implies about ABC. ABC stock trades at $8 per share.

ABC Bank's Balance Sheet ($ billions)

Cash	$ 10	Short-term deposits	$ 80
Investment	50	Long-term deposits	30
Loans	50	Equity (1 billion	
Fixed assets	10	shares outstanding)	10
	$120		$120

5. ABC Bank has a P/E ratio of 4. Given the income statement for ABC, what does that ratio say about the bank? The current average P/E ratio for similar banks is 10.

ABC Bank's Income Statement ($ billions)

Revenues	$10.20
Interest per year	6.00
Operating earnings	4.20
Provision for loan losses	2.00
Taxed income	2.20
Tax (10 percent)	0.20
Earnings	$ 2.00

6. What is Tobin's q ratio for MNO Corp. given the following information? What does this value of q say about MNO?

Replacement cost of total assets	$100
Market value of debt	$ 50
Market value of equity	$ 40

7. What is meant by a perfect market? Compare a perfect market to an efficient market.

8. How can the market model and the CAPM be used to test whether the market is efficient?

9. If the market is not efficient, what does this indicate about the validity of the CAPM?

10. How is volume of trading related to market efficiency?

11. Does the SEC crackdown on insider trading (in such cases as Levine and Boesky, Lee and Wong, and so on) imply that the market is becoming more strong-form efficient?

12. What do the results of Cootner's research imply about technical analysis?

13. What are the alternative viewpoints to Fama's EMH?

14. Explain an investment strategy or strategies that may be useful in taking advantage of the known market anomalies. If these strategies work, what will happen to the market anomalies?

REFERENCES

Alexander, S. S. "Price Movements in Speculative Markets: Trends or Random Walks." *Industrial Management Review,* v. 2 (May 1961), pp. 7–26.

Arbel, A., S. Carvell, and P. Strebel. "Giraffes, Institutions and Neglected Firms." *Financial Analysts Journal,* v. 39 (May/June 1983), pp. 2–8.

Ball, R., and P. Brown. "An Empirical Evaluation of Accounting Income Numbers." *Journal of Accounting Research,* v. 16 (Autumn 1968), pp. 159–78.

Banz, R. W. "The Relationship Between Return and Market Value of Common Stocks." *Journal of Financial Economics,* v. 9 (March 1981), pp. 3–18.

Barry, C., and S. Brown. "Anomalies in Security Returns and the Specification of the Market Model." *Journal of Finance,* v. 39 (July 1984), pp. 807–18.

Basu, S. "The Relationship Between Earnings Yield, Market Value, and the Return for NYSE Stocks: Further Evidence." *Journal of Financial Economics,* v. 12 (March 1983), pp. 129–56.

———. "Investment Performance of Common Stocks in Relation to Their Price-Earnings Ratios: A Test of the Efficient Market Hypothesis." *Journal of Finance,* v. 32 (June 1977), pp. 663–82.

Bernard, V. L., and J. K. Thomas. "Post-Earnings Announcement Drift: Delayed Price Response or Risk Premium." *Journal of Accounting Research* (1989), forthcoming.

Bjerring, J., L. Lakonishok, and T. Vermaelen. "Stock Prices and Financial Analysts' Recommendations." *Journal of Finance,* v. 38 (March 1983), pp. 187–204.

Branch, B. "A Tax Loss Trading Rule." *Journal of Business,* v. 50 (April 1977), pp. 198–207.

Brealey, R. *An Introduction to Risk and Return from Common Stocks*. MIT Press, 1983.

Brown, L., and M. Rozeff. "The Superiority of Analysts' Forecasts as Measures of Expectations: Evidence from Earnings." *Journal of Finance,* v. 33 (March 1978), pp. 1–16.

Brown, S., and J. Warner. "Using Daily Stock Returns: The Case of Event Studies." *Journal of Financial Economics,* v. 14 (March 1985), pp. 3–32.

————, and W. Nichols. "Assimilating Earnings and Split Information: Is the Capital Market Becoming More Efficient?" *Journal of Financial Economics,* v. 10 (September 1981), pp. 309–14.

Constantinades, G. "Optimal Stock Trading with Personal Taxes: Implications for Prices and the Abnormal January Returns." *Journal of Financial Economics,* v. 13 (March 1984), pp. 65–90.

Cootner, Paul. "Stock Prices: Random vs. Systematic Changes." *Industrial Management Review,* v. 3 (Spring 1962), pp. 24–25.

Cornell, Bradford. "Do Money Supply Announcements Affect Short-Term Interest Rates?" *Journal of Money Credit and Banking,* v. 11 (February 1979), pp. 80–86.

————. "The Money Supply Announcements Puzzle: Review and Interpretation." *American Economic Review,* v. 73 (September 1983), pp. 644–57.

————. "Money Supply Announcements and Interest Rates: Another View." *Journal of Business,* v. 56 (January 1983), pp. 1–24.

Dimson, E., and P. Marsh. "An Analysis of Brokers' and Analysts' Unpublished Forecasts of UK Stock Returns." *Journal of Finance,* v. 39 (December 1984), pp. 1257–92.

Emery, J. "The Information Content of Daily Market Indicators." *Journal of Financial and Quantitative Analysis,* v. 8 (March 1973), pp. 183–90.

Epps, T. "Security Price Changes and Transaction Volumes: Theory and Evidence." *American Economic Review,* v. 65 (September 1975), pp. 586–97.

Fama, E. F. "The Behavior of Stock Market Prices." *Journal of Business,* v. 38 (January 1965), pp. 34–105.

————. "A Note on the Market Model and the Two-Parameter Model." *Journal of Finance,* v. 28 (December 1973), pp. 1181–85.

————. *Foundation of Finance*. Basic Books, Inc., 1976.

————. "Efficient Capital Markets: A Review of Theory and Empirical Work." *Journal of Finance,* v. 25 (May 1970), pp. 383–417.

————. "Reply." *Journal of Finance,* v. 31 (March 1976), pp. 143–47.

————, and M. Blume. "Filter Rules and Stock Market Trading Profits." *Journal of Business,* v. 39 (Special Supplement, January 1966), pp. 226–41.

————, and J. MacBeth. "Risk, Return and Equilibrium: Empirical Tests." *Journal of Political Economy,* v. 31 (May/June 1973), pp. 607–36.

————, L. Fisher, M. Jensen, and R. Roll. "The Adjustment of Stock Prices to New Information." *International Economic Review,* v. 10 (February 1969), pp. 1–21.

Finnerty, J. "Insiders' Activity and Inside Information: A Multivariate Analysis." *Journal of Financial and Quantitative Analysis,* v. 11 (June 1976), pp. 205–15.

————. "The CBOE and Market Efficiency." *Journal of Financial and Quantitative Analysis,* v. 13 (March 1978), pp. 29–38.

————. "Insiders and Market Efficiency." *Journal of Finance,* v. 31 (September 1976), pp. 1141–48.

Francis, J. "Intertemporal Differences in Systematic Stock Price Movements." *Journal of Financial and Quantitative Analysis,* v. 10 (June 1975), pp. 205–19.

French, K. "Stock Returns and the Weekend Effect." *Journal of Financial Economics,* v. 9 (March 1980), pp. 55–70.

Galai, Dan. "Tests of Market Efficiency of the Chicago Board Options Exchange." *Journal of Business,* v. 50 (April 1977), pp. 421–42.

Gibbons, M., and P. Hess. "Day of the Week Effects and Asset Returns." *Journal of Business,* v. 54 (October 1981), pp. 579–96.

Gonedes, N. "Evidence of the Information Content of Accounting Numbers: Accounting Based and Market Based Estimates of Systematic Risk." *Journal of Financial and Quantitative Analysis,* v. 8 (June 1973), pp. 407–43.

Haugen, R., and J. Lakonishok. *The Incredible January Effect: The Stock Market's Unsolved Mystery.* Dow Jones-Irwin, 1988.

Hawawini, G. *European Equity Markets: Price Behavior and Efficiency.* Monograph, 1984-4, Salomon Brothers Center, New York University, 1984.

Henriksson, R. D. "Mutual Fund Timing and Mutual Fund Performance: An Empirical Investigation." *Journal of Business,* v. 57 (January 1984), pp. 73–96.

————, and R. C. Merton. "On Market Timing and Investment Performance, II. Statistical Procedures for Evaluating Forecasting Skills." *Journal of Business,* v. 54 (October 1981), pp. 513–33.

Hillmer, S. C., and P. L. Yu. "The Market Speed of Adjustment to New Information." *Journal of Financial Economics,* v. 7 (September 1979), pp. 321–45.

Ibbotson, R., and J. Jaffe. "Hot Issues Market." *Journal of Finance,* v. 30 (September 1975), pp. 1027–42.

Jaffe, J. "The Effect of Regulation Changes on Insider Trading." *The Bell Journal of Economics and Management Science,* v. 5 (Spring 1974), pp. 93–121.

_____, and R. Westerfield. "The Weekend Effect in Common Stock Returns: The International Evidence." *Journal of Finance*, v. 40 (June 1985), pp. 433–54.

Joy, M., R. Litzenberger, and R. McEnally. "The Adjustment of Stock Prices to Announcements of Unanticipated Changes in Quarterly Earnings." *Journal of Accounting Research*, v. 25 (Autumn 1977), pp. 207–25.

Kaplan, R. S., and R. Roll. "Investor Evaluation of Accounting Information: Some Empirical Evidence." *Journal of Business*, v. 45 (April 1972), pp. 225–57.

Keim, D. B. "Size-Related Anomalies and Stock Return Seasonality: Further Empirical Evidence." *Journal of Financial Economics*, v. 11 (June 1983), pp. 13–32.

Keim, Donald B., and Robert F. Stambaugh. "A Further Investigation of the Weekend Effect in Stock Returns." *Journal of Finance*, v. 39 (July 1984), pp. 819–35.

LeRoy, S. F., and R. Potter. "The Present Value Relation: Tests Based on Implied Variance Bounds." *Econometrica*, v. 49 (May 1981), pp. 555–74.

Lindenberg, E. B., and S. A. Ross. "Tobin's q Ratio and Industrial Organization." *Journal of Business*, v. 54 (January 1981), pp. 1–32.

Lintner, J. "The Valuation of Risk Assets and the Selection of Risky Investments in Stock Portfolios and Capital Budgets." *The Review of Economics and Statistics*, v. 47 (February 1965), pp. 13–37.

Merton, R. C. "On Market Timing and Investment Performance I. An Equilibrium Theory of Valuation for Market Forecasts." *Journal of Business*, v. 54 (July 1981), pp. 363–406.

Morgan, I. "Stock Prices and Heteroscedasticity." *Journal of Business*, v. 49 (October 1976), pp. 496–508.

Mossin, J. "Equilibrium in a Capital Asset Market." *Econometrica*, v. 34 (October 1966), pp. 768–83.

Niederhoffer, V., and M. F. M. Osborne. "Market Making and Reversal on the Stock Exchange." *Journal of the American Statistical Association*, v. 61 (December 1966), pp. 897–917.

Ohlson, J., and S. Penman. "Volatility Increases Subsequent to Stock Splits: An Empirical Observation." *Journal of Financial Economics*, v. 14 (June 1985), pp. 251–66.

Oppenheimer, H., and G. Schlarbaum. "Investing with Ben Graham: An ExAnte Test of the EMH." *Journal of Financial and Quantitative Analysis*, v. 16 (September 1981), pp. 341–508.

Patell, J. M., and M. A. Wolfson. "The Intraday Speed of Adjustment of Stock Prices to Earnings and Dividend Announcements." *Journal of Financial Economics*, v. 13 (June 1984), pp. 223–52.

Penman, S. "Insider Trading and the Dissemination of Firm's Forecast Information." *Journal of Business*, v. 55 (October 1982), pp. 92–116.

Reinganum, M. R. "Misspecification of Capital Asset Pricing: Empirical

Anomalies Based on Earnings Yields and Market Values.'' *Journal of Financial Economics,* v. 8 (March 1981), pp. 13–32.

_____. ''The Anomalies Stock Market Behavior of Small Firms in January: Empirical Tests for Tax-Loss Selling Effect.'' *Journal of Financial Economics,* v. 12 (March 1983), pp. 89–104.

_____. ''Abnormal Returns in Small Firms' Portfolios.'' *Financial Analysts Journal,* v. 37 (March/April 1981), pp. 52–57.

Roll, R. *The Behavior of Interest Rates: An Application of the Efficient Market Model to U. S. Treasury Bills.* Basic Books, 1970.

Roll, R. ''The Turn of the Year Effect and the Return Premium on Small Firms.'' *Journal of Portfolio Management,* v. 7 (1982), pp. 18–28.

_____. ''On Computing Mean Returns and the Small Firm Premium.'' *Journal of Financial Economics,* v. 12 (November 1983), pp. 371–86.

_____. ''A Possible Explanation of the Small Firm Effect.'' *Journal of Finance,* v. 36 (September 1981), pp. 879–88.

_____. ''A Critique of the Asset Pricing Theory's Tests.'' *Journal of Financial Economics,* v. 4 (March 1977), pp. 129–76.

Samuelson, P. ''Proof that Properly Discounted Present Values of Assets Vibrate Randomly.'' *Bell Journal of Economics and Management Science,* v. 4 (Autumn 1973), pp. 369–74.

Schwart, W. ''Stock Exchange Seats as Capital Assets.'' *Journal of Financial Economics,* v. 5 (January 1977), pp. 51–78.

Schwartz, R., and D. Whitcomb. ''Evidence on the Presence and Causes of Serial Correlation in the Market Model Residuals.'' *Journal of Financial and Quantitative Analysis,* v. 12 (June 1977), pp. 291–315.

Sharpe, W. F. ''Capital Asset Prices: A Theory of Market Equilibrium Under Conditions of Risk.'' *Journal of Finance,* v. 19 (September 1964), pp. 425–42.

Shiller, R. J. ''The Use of Volatility Measures in Assuming Market Efficiency.'' *Journal of Finance,* v. 36 (May 1981), pp. 291–304.

_____. ''Do Stock Prices Move Too Much to Be Justified by Subsequent Changes in Dividends?'' *American Economic Review,* v. 71 (June 1981), pp. 421–36.

Stevenson, R., and R. Bear. ''Commodity Fixtures: Trends or Random Walks?'' *Journal of Finance,* v. 25 (March 1970), pp. 65–81.

Stoll, H., and W. Whaley. ''Transaction Costs and the Small Firm Effect.'' *Journal of Financial Economics,* v. 12 (June 1983), pp. 57–80.

Summers, L. H. ''Do We Really Know that Financial Markets Are Efficient?'' Harvard University Discussion Paper No. 1237, May 1986.

Sunder, S. ''Stock Price and Risk Related to Accounting Changes in Inventory Valuation.'' *Accounting Review,* v. 50 (April 1975), pp. 305–15.

———. "Relationship Between Accounting Changes and Stock Prices: Problems of Measurement and Some Empirical Evidence." *Empirical Research in Accounting: Selected Studies,* 1973, pp. 1–45.

Taylor, S. "Tests of the Random Walk Hypothesis Against a Price Trend Hypothesis." *Journal of Financial and Quantitative Analysis,* v. 17 (March 1982), pp. 37–62.

Tobin, J. "A General Equilibrium Approach to Monetary Theory." *Journal of Money, Credit and Banking,* v. 1 (February 1969), pp. 15–29.

Treynor, J. L., and R. Ferguson. "In Defense of Technical Analysis." *Journal of Finance,* v. 40 (July 1985), pp. 757–75.

Waud, Roger N. "Public Interpretation of Federal Reserve Discount Rate Change: Evidence on the "Announcement Effect." *Econometrica,* v. 38 (March 1970), pp. 231–50.

West, R. "On the Difference Between Internal and External Market Efficiency." *Financial Analysts Journal,* v. 31 (November/December 1975), pp. 30–34.

Westerfield, R. "The Distribution of Common Stock Price Changes: An Application of Transaction Time and Subordinate Stochastic Models." *Journal of Financial and Quantitative Analysis,* v. 12 (December 1977), pp. 743–66.

17 Timing and Selectivity of Stocks and Mutual Funds

The role of security analysts and portfolio managers is to select the right stocks at the right time. They can generally use theory and methods (as discussed in most of the previous chapters) to determine which stock (or stocks) they should buy or sell at the appropriate point. Security-analysis and portfolio-management methodologies can be classified into fundamental analysis and technical analysis.

This chapter discusses methods and applications of fundamental analysis and technical analysis. In addition, it investigates the ranking performance of the Value Line and the timing and selectivity of mutual funds. A detailed investigation of technical versus fundamental analysis is first presented. This is followed by an analysis of regression time-series and composite methods for forecasting security rates of return. Value Line ranking methods and their performance then are discussed, leading finally into a study of the classification of mutual funds and the mutual-fund managers' timing and selectivity ability. All of these topics can help improve performance in security analysis and portfolio management.

FUNDAMENTAL VERSUS TECHNICAL ANALYSIS

This section explores the relationship between two components of security analysis and portfolio management: fundamental analysis and technical analysis.

Fundamental Analysis

The job of a security analyst is to estimate the value of securities. If a security's estimated value is above its market price, the security analyst will recommend buying the stock; if the value is below the market price, the security should be sold before its price drops. Underpriced stocks are

purchased until their price is bid up to equal their value; overpriced stocks are sold, driving their price down until it equals their value.

There are two schools of thought as to how one determines an overpriced or underpriced security. **Fundamental analysis** (the fundamentalist school) studies the fundamental facts affecting a stock's value. Fundamental analysts delve into companies' earnings, their management, earnings forecasts, the firm's competition, market conditions, and many other business and economic factors. The second school of thought determines an overpriced or underpriced security by studying the way security prices behave over time. **Technical analysis** concentrates almost totally on charts of security-market prices and related summary statistics of security trading.

The macro approach to fundamental analysis emphasizes first the analysis of the aggregate economy and market, then industry analysis, and finally the examination of specific companies within the industry. Changes in the national economy and credit conditions are associated with changes in interest rates, capitalization rates, and multipliers. Therefore, an aggregate economic and market analysis must be done in conjunction with determining the security's appropriate multiplier. A multiplier of ten may be appropriate for normal economic conditions, whereas a multiple of fifteen may be more realistic in an environment of rapid economic growth and prosperity.

All of the fundamentalist's research is based upon some valuation model. The analyst prepares his or her estimate of the intrinsic value per share at time 0, P_{i0}, by multiplying the ith stock's normalized earnings per share at time 0, E_{i0}, times the share's earnings multiplier, m_{it}:

$$P_{i0} = E_{i0}m_{it} \qquad t = 0 \tag{17.1}$$

where:

$$m_{it} = \frac{P_{i0}}{E_{i0}} = \frac{\dfrac{d_{i1}}{E_{i0}}}{k_i - g_i}$$

The earnings multiplier P_{i0}/E_{i0} is called the **price–earnings ratio.** The ratio d_{i1}/E_{i0} is called the **dividend-payout ratio.** k_i and g_i are the **required rate of return** and **growth rate,** respectively. This model was explored in detail in Chapter 4.

Much of the fundamental analyst's work centers on determining the appropriate capitalization rate, or equivalently the appropriate multiplier to use in valuing a particular security's income. This encompasses the micro approach to estimating future values for the stock market. It involves using a two-step approach: (1) estimating the expected earnings for some market-indicator series (Dow Jones Industrial Average or Standard & Poor's Industrial Index) or some stock, and (2) estimating the expected earnings multiplier for the market series or stock. The main factors that must be considered in determining the correct multiplier are (1) the risk of the security, (2) the growth rate of the dividend stream, (3) the duration of any expected growth, and (4) the dividend-payout ratio.

In determining the price–earnings ratio to use in valuing a firm's securities, three factors must be estimated: (1) the capitalization rate, (2) the dividend growth rate, and, (3) the dividend-payout ratio. Algebraically:

$$\frac{P_0}{E} = \frac{\frac{d_1}{E}}{k - g} \quad \text{or} \quad P_0 = \frac{d_1}{k - g} = \frac{d_0(1 + g)}{k - g} \tag{17.2}$$

where:

d_1/E = the dividend-payout ratio;
k = the capitalization rate; and
g = the expected growth of dividends.

Given this equation, a positive relationship is expected between the earnings multiplier and the dividend payout, and with the growth rate of dividends, all things being equal. Alternatively, there should be a negative relationship between the earnings multiplier and the capitalization rate. Sample Problems 17.1 and 17.2 provide further illustration.

Sample Problem 17.1

The stock of XYZ Corporation is currently paying a dividend of $1.00 per share. The firm's dividend growth rate is expected to be 10 percent. For firms in the same risk class as XYZ, market analysts agree that the capitalization rate is approximately 15 percent. Current earnings for XYZ are $2.00 per share and they are expected to grow at 10 percent. What are the P/E ratio and the price of XYZ shares given this information?

Solution

$$P/E = \frac{d_1/E}{k - g}$$

$$= \frac{\$1.00 \, (1 + 0.1)/2.00(1 + 0.1)}{15 - 10}$$

$$= 10$$

$$P = \frac{d_0(1 + g)}{k - g}$$

$$= \frac{1.00 \, (1 + 0.1)}{0.15 - 0.10}$$

$$= \$22/\text{share}$$

Sample Problem 17.2

XYZ in Sample Problem 17.1 is expected to experience an increase in growth rate from 10 percent to 12 percent. What is the impact on XYZ's P/E ratio and price?

Solution

$$P/E = \frac{d_1/E}{k - g}$$

$$= \frac{\$1.00 \ (1.12)/2.00(1.12)}{0.15 - 0.12}$$

$$= 16.67$$

$$P = \frac{d_0(1 + g)}{k - g}$$

$$= \frac{\$1.00(1.12)}{0.15 - 0.12}$$

$$= \$37.33$$

As can be seen from comparing Sample Problems 17.1 and 17.2, a 20-percent increase in growth has led to a 67-percent increase in P/E ratio and a 69-percent increase in price. It is clear, therefore, that the accuracy of the analyst's growth estimate is very important.

The capitalization rate varies with a firm's risk class and the prevailing market conditions (therefore the necessity of the macro approach). Since future expectations are influenced by past experience, one way to estimate a firm's risk class is to examine historical data. The capitalization rate is determined by (1) the economy's risk-free rate, (2) the expected rate of price increase (annual rate of inflation), and (3) a risk premium for common stocks that reflects investor uncertainty regarding future returns.

The capital asset pricing model (CAPM) discussed in Chapter 9 suggests using the systematic risk for common stocks to determine the size of the risk premium. In theory, this measure of risk should be the beta for common stocks relative to the market portfolio for all risky assets. Since a portfolio of all risky assets does not exist, an alternative is to examine fundamental factors. These factors examine the relationship between the systematic risk (beta) for a security and various proxies for business risk and financial risk. A generally accepted measure of a firm's business risk is the coefficient of variation of the firm's operating income.

Financial risk is determined by the financing decisions of the firm, or, more specifically, by the extent of financial leverage employed. The most

common measures of financial risk are the debt/equity ratio and the fixed-charge coverage ratio.

Studies of securities listed on the New York Stock Exchange have shown that their historical average-earnings capitalization rate varies directly with the security's volatility coefficient. The fundamental analyst can measure the risk of the company in recent periods, adjust these historical risk statistics for any expected changes, and then use these forecasted risk statistics to obtain capitalization rates. (Chapters 8 and 9 explain how to measure a stock's risk in more detail.)

The growth of dividends is a function of the growth of earnings and changes in the dividend-payout ratio. It is usually fairly simple to estimate the growth rate in cash dividends or earnings per share. (Measuring these growth rates is discussed in Chapter 3.) The growth rate is as important as the capitalization rate in estimating multipliers. The effects of the dividend-payout ratio are more direct than the effect of the growth rate. If other things remain constant, reducing a corporation's dividend payout cuts its multiplier and thus its intrinsic value proportionately. For companies whose payout ratio fluctuates widely, it is necessary to estimate the corporation's normalized earnings per share averaged over a complete business cycle. After a share's normal earnings are estimated, all that need be done is to divide normalized earnings per share into the corporation's regular cash dividend per share to find the payout ratio for use in the determination of an earnings multiplier.

Reilly, Griggs, and Wong (1983) find that the fundamental factors such as the payout ratio, growth, risk-free rate, earnings variability, the debt/equity ratio, and the failure rate of firms going bankrupt combine to form the determinants of the aggregate stock-market earnings multiple. Using these fundamental factors as independent variables in an ordinary least-squares (OLS) regression and multiple discriminate analysis, predictions are made for the multiplier.

They then use the OLS model to simulate investment strategies. If the model predicted a decline in the multiple, an investment in T-bills was indicated; if the model predicted an increase in the multiple, an investment in common stock was indicated. Their results strongly support the multiple-prediction model compared to buying and holding common stocks. Not only is the rate of return substantially higher, but risk as measured by the standard deviation is lower for the model stock portfolio than for the buy-and-hold portfolio. Their results indicate that on the basis of analyzing macro variables, it is possible to estimate the likely future direction of the market-earnings multiple, which in turn is a major indicator of total stock-market movements over time. For those portfolio managers who invest in stocks, using this model is superior to a buy-and-hold strategy.

Technical analysts study charts of aggregate stock movements in an attempt to determine trends in the stock market that influence movements in individual stocks. It is the fundamental analysts, however, who have delved into the driving forces behind these movements. Shiller (1984) presents a

demand-side theory explaining the market movement. He considers the supply of corporate stock to be fixed, at least in the short run, while investment demand for stocks fluctuates according to economic states. The decline in the demand for shares may not be accompanied by a decline in supply. Therefore, when many investors wish to sell their shares, for whatever reason, the price of those shares must fall. Shiller proposes that the demand side accounts for the majority of stock-market movements.

A competing story that is equally attractive is the supply-side story. By this explanation, the main reason for the decline in stock prices is the decline in the expected future supply of dividends. However, in its extreme form the theory implies that stock prices move only because of new information about future dividends. The theory is generally expressed today in conjunction with the assumption of efficient markets. Therefore, stock prices equal the present value of optimally forecasted future dividends.

The third theory of stock market fluctuations rests on a "market fads" theory. According to this theory, stock prices move because people tend to be vulnerable to waves of optimism or pessimism, not because of any economically identifiable shocks either to demand or supply. Highly publicized events or statements by influential figures have impact on the market far beyond their true importance. The great crash of October 19, 1987, might well be thought of in this light.

Shiller (1984) uses the following model to test the supply-side theory:

$$P_t = \sum_{k=1}^{\infty} \frac{E_t(D_{t+k})}{(1 + r)^k} \tag{17.3}$$

where:

P_t = the real ex-dividend price of a share at time t;

$E_t(D_{t+k})$ = the mathematical expectation conditional on information at time t of the real dividend accruing to a share at time $t + k$; and

r = the real discount rate.

Since dividends are not known out to infinity, but there is roughly a century of dividends on Standard and Poor's stock, Shiller evaluates the model over historical data using:

$$P_t = E_t(P_t^*) \tag{17.4A}$$

$$P_t^* = \sum_{k=1}^{1981-t} \frac{D_{t+k}}{(1 + r)^k} + \frac{P_{1981}^*}{(1 + r)^{1981-t}} \qquad t \le 1981 \tag{17.4B}$$

The variable P_t^* is the "perfect foresight" or "ex-post rational" stock price.

By replacing P_t^* with P_{1981} Shiller is able to obtain an approximation P_{st}^* (the subscript s refers to the supply-side theory) to the ex-post rational price:

$$P_{st}^* = \sum_{k=1}^{1981-t} \frac{D_{t+k}}{(1 + r)^k} + \frac{P_{1981}^*}{(1 + r)^{1981-t}} \qquad t \le 1981 \tag{17.5}$$

FIGURE 17-1   Real Stock-Price Index P_t^* and Ex-Post Rational Counterpart P_{st}^* Based on Real Dividends, 1889–1981

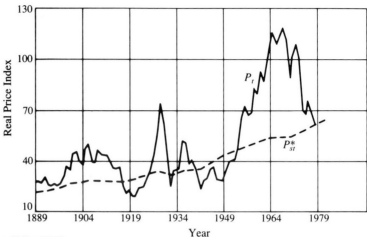

Source: Shiller (1984).

By plotting P_{st}^* along with the real Standard and Poor's price index P_t (Figure 17-1), Shiller finds that the two series are quite divergent. It appears that P_{st}^* behaves much like a simple growth trend, while P_t oscillates wildly around it. P_{st}^* is smooth increasing because it is a weighted moving average of dividends, and moving averages serve to smooth the series averaged. Moreover, real dividends are themselves a fairly stable and upward trending series.

Using a basic economic theory of the two-period consumption with marginal rate of substitution s_t to derive a consumption beta similar to Breeden [1979], Shiller constructs a demand-side model to explain aggregate stock-price movements. Shiller shows that if i_t is the return on stock (found by dividing the sum of capital gain and dividend by price) between t and $t + 1$ and if $E_t(1 + i_t)s_t = 1$ at all times, then the price is the expected value of P_t^* where P_t^* is the present value of dividends discounted by marginal rates of substitution:

$$P_t = E_t(P_t^*) \tag{17.4A}$$

$$P_t^* = \sum_{k=1}^{\infty} s_t^{(k)} D_{t+k} \tag{17.6}$$

and $s_t^{(k)}$ is the marginal rate of substitution between C_t and C_{t+k}. The function for the marginal rate of substitution is $s_t^{(k)} = \delta^k (C_t/C_{t+k})^4$; that is, $s_t^{(k)}$ is proportional to the consumption ratio to the fourth power. This functional form embodies the concavity we expect in indifference curves—that is, the marginal rate of substitution declines as C_{t+k} rises relative to C_t.

The fourth power was chosen because it makes P^* roughly fit the data. The δ^k represents impatience, so that (if $\delta < 1$) at a zero interest rate the person would consume more this period than in future periods.

Substituting Equation (17.6) for the marginal rate of substitution and assuming that dividends are expected to follow the trend $D_t = D_0 (1 + g)^t$ with certainty:

$$P^*_{dt} = C^4_t \left[D_0(1 + g)^t \sum_{k=1}^{\infty} \delta(1 + g)^k C^{-4}_{t+k} \right] \qquad \textbf{(17.7)}$$

This expression and the assumption that $P_t = E_t(P^*_{dt})$ means essentially that stock prices should be high when aggregate consumption is high and low when consumption is low. The subscript d for P^*_{dt} means "according to the demand-side theory."

By plotting P^*_{dt} along with real price per share P_t (Figure 17–2), Shiller finds that P^*_{dt} moves a great deal more than P^*_{st}. P^*_{dt} and P_t resemble each other much more than P^*_{st} and P_t. Unfortunately, Shiller finds that the theory seems to break down after 1950. Shiller concludes that movements over the last century in aggregate real dividends just fail to explain the movements in aggregate stock prices. Therefore, the supply-side efficient-market theory does not look promising. On the other hand, the demand-side theory looks more promising than the supply-side theory. It predicts a business-cycle correlation for stock prices that was, until 1950, actually observed. How-

FIGURE 17–2   Real Stock-Price Index P_t and Ex-Post Rational Counterpart P^*_{dt} Based on Real Consumption, 1889–1981

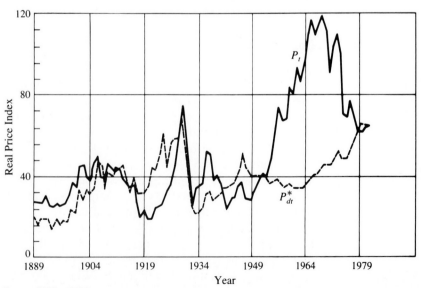

Source: Shiller (1984).

ever, since 1950 the demand-side theory has failed to explain the dramatic increase of real stock prices.

Regardless of the reasons fundamentalists will find for aggregate stock movements, technicians will continue to ignore the driving forces, whatever they may be, and will make their stock predictions based upon shapes seen in the plotting aggregate stock movements.

Technical Analysis

Technical analysts, rather than working through the large amount of fundamental information about an investment such as company earnings, competitive products, and forthcoming legislation, searched for a summary of all facts by studying the way security prices behave historically. Over the past decades technical analysts have focused their attention almost totally on charts of security market prices and related summary statistics.

Technical analysis is based on the widely accepted premise that security prices are determined by the supply of and the demand for securities. Typically technical analysts record historical financial data on charts, study these charts in an effort to find meaningful patterns, and use these patterns to predict future prices. Technical analysts believe that past patterns of market action will recur in the future and that past patterns can be used for predictive purposes.

Rather than try to evaluate the intrinsic value of a security, the technical analysts seek to estimate security prices; that is, they try to forecast short-run shifts in supply and demand that will affect the market price of one or more securities. Some of the tools used by chartists to measure supply and demand and to forecast security prices are the Dow theory charts, odd-lot theory, confidence index, breadth-of-market indicators, relative-strength analysis, and trading-volume data.

Dow Theory

One of the tools used by technical analysts to measure supply and demand and forecast security prices is the **Dow theory.** The Dow theory is used to indicate reversals and trends in the market as a whole or in individual securities. According to the theory, there are three movements going on in the markets at all times. These movements are (1) daily fluctuations (the narrow movement from day to day), (2) secondary movements (short-run movements over two weeks to a month or more), and (3) primary trends, major movements covering at least four years in duration. The theory asserts that daily fluctuations are meaningless. However, daily asset prices or the market average must be plotted in order to outline the primary and secondary trends. In plotting the asset prices, the Dow theorists search for price patterns indicating market tops and bottoms.

Technical analysts use three basic types of charts: (1) line charts, (2) bar charts, and (3) point-and-figure charts. Bar charts have vertical bars repre-

senting each day's price movement. Each bar spans the distance from the day's highest price to the day's lowest price with a small cross on the bar marking the closing price. Lines are used to connect successive day's prices. Patterns indicating market tops or bottoms are then searched for in these line charts by technical analysis. *The Wall Street Journal* uses the bar charts to show daily fluctuations in the Dow Jones Average.

Point-and-figure charts are more complex than line or bar charts. These charts draw the percentage change directly. They are not only used to detect reversals in a trend but are also employed to set actual price forecasts.

The construction of a point-and-figure chart varies with the price level of the stock being charted. Only significant changes are posted to a point-and-figure chart. As a result there are one-point, two-point, three-point, and five-point point-and-figure charts.

To set the price target (forecasted stock price) which a stock is expected to attain, point-and-figure chartists begin by finding a congestion area. A congestion area is a horizontal band created by a series of reversals around a given price level. Congestion areas are supposed to result when supply and demand are equal. A breakout is said to have occurred when a column of price increase rises above the top of a congestion area. Breakout refers to a price rise or fall in which the price rises above or falls below the horizontal band which contained the congestion area. A penetration of the top of a congestion area is a signal for continued price rise. Penetration of the bottom of a congestion area by a column of price declines is a bearish signal.

To establish estimates of the new prices that a security should attain, point-and-figure chartists measure the horizontal width of a congestion area as they watch for a breakout. When a breakout occurs, the chartist projects the horizontal count upward or downward in the same direction as the breakout to establish the new price target.

The Odd-Lot Theory

The **odd-lot theory** is one of several theories of contrary opinion. In essence, the theory assumes that the common man is usually wrong and it is therefore advantageous to pursue strategies opposite to his thinking. In order to find out what the common man is doing, statistics on odd-lot trading are gathered. Most odd-lot purchases are made by amateur investors with limited resources—that is, by the common man, who is a small, unsophisticated investor.

Odd-lot trading volume is reported daily. The odd-lot statistics are broken down into the number of shares purchased, sold, and sold short. The index of odd-lot purchases less odd-lot sales is typically plotted concurrently with some market index. The odd-lotter's net purchases are used by chartists as a leading indicator of market prices. That is, positive net purchases are presumed to forecast falls in market prices, and net selling by odd-lotters is presumed to occur at the end of a bear market.

The Confidence Index

The **confidence index** is designed to measure how willing investors are to take a chance in the market. It is the ratio of high-grade bond yields to low-grade bond yields. This ratio is started below one. When bond investors grow more confident about the economy, they shift their holdings from high-grade to lower-grade bonds, lowering their yield relative to high-grade bonds and increasing the confidence index. In other words, the confidence ratio moves close to one.

Confidence-index technicians believe that the confidence index leads the stock market by two to eleven months. An upturn in the confidence index is supposed to foretell of rising optimism and rising prices in the stock market. A fall in the confidence index represents the fact that low-grade bond yields are rising faster or falling more slowly than high-grade yields. This is supposed to reflect increasing risk aversion by institutional money managers who foresee an economic downturn and rising bankruptcies and defaults. Analysts who have examined the confidence index conclude that it conveys some information for security analysis.

Trading Volume

Many technical analysts believe that it is possible to detect whether the market in general and/or certain security issues are bullish or bearish by studying the volume of trading. Volume is supposed to be a measure of the intensity of investors' emotions. If high volume occurs on days when prices move up, the overall nature of the market is considered to be bullish. If the high volume occurs on days when prices are falling, this is a bearish sign.

Moving Average

Moving-average (or rate-of-change) technicians focus on prices and/or moving averages of prices. The moving average is used to provide a smoothed stable reference point against which the daily fluctuations can be gauged. When the daily prices penetrate above the moving-average line, technicians interpret this penetration as a bearish signal. When the daily prices move downward through the moving average, they frequently fail to rise again for many months.

Moving-average analysts recommend buying a stock when: (1) the 200-day moving average flattens out and the stock's price rises through the moving average, (2) the price of a stock falls below a moving-average line that is rising, and (3) the price of a stock that is above the moving-average line falls but turns around and begins to rise again before it ever reaches the moving-average line.

Moving-average chartists recommend selling a stock when: (1) the moving-average line flattens out and the stock's price drops downward through the moving-average line, (2) a stock's price rises above a moving-average

line that is declining, and (3) a stock's price falls downward through the moving-average line and turns around to rise but then falls again before getting above the moving-average line.

There are many tools for technical analysts. All the technical-analysis tools have one thing in common—they attempt to measure the supply and demand for some group of investors. Shifts in supply and demand are presumed to be gradual, not instantaneous. When changes in prices are detected, they are presumed to be the result of gradual shifts in supply and demand rather than a series of instantaneous shifts. Since these shifts are expected to continue as the price gradually reacts to news or other factors, they are used to predict further price changes.

There has been a lack of published research on technical analysis. Most of the work that has been done is held privately and forms the basis of trading recommendations. Academic studies in this area have concentrated on the random-walk model, which implies that daily price changes are uncorrelated. A paper by Irwin and Uhrig (1984) combined trading-system optimization and efficient-market tests to investigate the validity of technical analysis for the future market. Irwin and Uhrig's specific objectives were (1) to test whether the random-walk model is a reasonable description of daily future-price behavior, (2) to simulate the trading of four technical systems, and (3) to deduce the market-efficiency implications of both sets of results.

If the futures market is either weak-form efficient or the random-walk model describes price generation, the implication is that the expected profit of a technical trading system will be no greater than zero. Two approaches have been adopted to test futures-market efficiency. The first, statistical analysis of the random-walk model, by Taylor (1982), has been rejected as a description of price behavior for futures markets in the United States, United Kingdom, and Australia. The second approach is to simulate the trading of a technical system and examine the resulting profits or losses. These two applications have been confined almost exclusively to examining **Alexander's** (1961) **filter rule,** which results in the existence of trading profits. However, the significance and importance of filter-rule research are difficult to assess objectively. See Sweeny (1988).

Irwin and Uhrig (1984) try to improve upon earlier efforts by: (1) testing both the random-walk model and the trading-system tests over the same data, (2) optimizing the trading systems and then simulating the optimized system over out-of-sample data, (3) deducting for both commission and transaction costs, and (4) examining trading systems actively used by trading advisors. Their data consist of eight series of daily future-price closes.

The authors examine four technical trading systems selected as representative of the three main types of trading systems: price channels, moving averages, and momentum oscillators. The four systems examined are the Donchian system (DONCH), and the moving-average with a percentage price band system (MAPB), the dual moving-average crossover system (DMAC), and the directional indicator system (DI).

The **DONCH system** is part of a family of technical systems known as price channels. The system generates a buy signal any time the daily high price is outside (greater than) the highest price in the specified time interval. A sell signal is generated any time the daily high breaks outside (lower than) the lowest price in the same interval. The system always generates a signal for the trader to take a position, long or short, in the futures market.

The **MAPB system** belongs to a technical family derived from moving averages. Moving averages come in many forms—that is, simple moving averages, exponentially weighted, linearly weighted, and so on. The MAPB system employs a simple moving average with a band based on a percentage of price centered around it. A signal to initiate a position occurs whenever the closing price breaks outside the band. A signal to exit a position occurs when the price recrosses the moving average. The band creates a neutral zone in which the trader is neither long nor short.

The **DMAC system** employs logic similar to the MAPB system by seeking to find when the short-term trend rises above or below the long-term trend. The MAPB represents the short-term trend by the daily price and the long-term trend by the moving average. The DMAC uses a short-term moving average and long-term moving average to represent the short- and long-term trend. A change in the price trend is signaled when these two moving averages cross. Specifically, a buy signal is generated when the shorter moving average is greater than (above) the longer moving average, and a sell signal when the shorter moving average is less than (below) the longer moving average. The trader always maintains a long or short position in the futures market.

The **DI system** is from a technical family known as momentum oscillators. Whereas the previous systems outlined deal with the futures-price level, oscillators deal with price changes. The logic employed by the directional-indicator system is that any trending period can be characterized as having a significant excess of either positive or negative price movements. Periods when prices are quickly moving upwards will have more upwards price change than downward price change, and vice versa. It is this relative price change that the DI estimates.

Irwin and Uhrig (1984), using the Lyung–Box test on the autocorrelation analysis for nonrandomness, find their results indicated that the random-walk model could be rejected for futures on corn, soybeans, sugar, wheat, cocoa, and live cattle. However, the random-walk model could not be rejected for futures on copper and live hogs.

The data are divided into three sample periods (1960–1981, 1960–1972, and 1973–1981) to account for the structural and policy changes that occurred in the early 1970s. Each trading system is optimized; that is, the highest profit parameter is found. The optimum parameters are used as the basis for trading in a time period after their development. Substantial trading-system profits are evident over the 1960–1981 period for all commodities. However, these are almost exclusively concentrated in the years 1973 to 1981. As a result futures-market efficiency cannot be rejected for the

1960–1972 period and was rejected for the 1973–1981 period. It is felt that structural and policy changes during 1973–1981 prevented futures prices from adjusting instantaneously to new information, resulting in significant profits from technical trading systems utilizing significant price trends.

Technical analysis seems to have some merit when the market involved is not efficient. By studying price trends the analyst is able to realize excess profits.

ANOMALIES AND THEIR IMPLICATIONS

Chapter 16 briefly introduced the anomalies in the efficient-market literature. Four authors—Basu, Banz, Reinganum, and Keim—deal with the anomalies centered around the P/E ratio, size effect, and January effect. This section looks at these anomalies in the context of technical and fundamental analysis.

Basu's Findings

Basu (1977) tries to determine empirically whether the investment performance of common stocks is related to their P/E ratios. The primary data for this study come from a data base that includes the Compustat file of NYSE industrial firms, the investment-return file from the CRSP tape, and a delisted file containing selected accounting data and investment returns for securities delisted from the NYSE. The data base represents 1,400 industrial firms, all of which actually traded on the NYSE between September 1956 and August 1971.

For any given year under consideration, three criteria are used in selecting sample firms: (1) the fiscal year ends on December 31, (2) the firm actually traded on the NYSE as of the beginning of the portfolio-holding period and is included in the merged tape, and (3) the relevant investment-return and financial-statement data are not missing.

Beginning with 1956, the P/E ratio of every sample security is computed. The numerator of the ratio is defined as the market value of common stock as of December 31, and the denominator as reported annual earnings available for common stockholders. These ratios are ranked and five portfolios are formed.

This procedure, repeated annually on each April 1, gives fourteen years (April 1967–March 1971) of return data for each of the P/E portfolios.

Basu uses the performance-evaluation measures of Jensen, Sharpe, and Treynor. His results indicate that during the period April 1957–March 1971 low-P/E portfolios seem to have (on average) earned higher absolute and risk-adjusted rates of return than the high-P/E portfolios. Even after accounting for a bias in the performance measure resulting from the effect of risk, above-normal returns are found.

The results are consistent with the view that P/E-ratio information is not fully reflected in security prices in as rapid a manner as postulated by the semi-strong form of the efficient-market hypothesis. To the extent that low-P/E portfolios did earn superior returns on a risk-adjusted basis, the proposition of the price-ratio hypothesis (on the relationship between investment performance of equity securities and their P/E ratios) seems to be valid. There appear to be lags and frictions in the process of adjusting security prices to publicly available information. Therefore, publicly available P/E ratios may possess information content and may warrant an investor's attention at the time of portfolio formation or revision.

Reinganum's Findings

Reinganum's (1981) study documents an empirical anomaly that suggests that either the simple one-period capital asset pricing model is misspecified or that capital markets are inefficient. He forms portfolios based upon firm size or earnings/price ratios. The data, collected primarily from *The Wall Street Journal*, consists of corporate quarterly earnings and announcement dates from the fourth quarter of 1975 and the subsequent eight quarters. The sample consists of 566 NYSE and AMEX stocks with fiscal-year ends in December.

The sample is divided into portfolios based upon standardized unexpected earnings (SUE). The high-SUE portfolio contains the twenty securities with the highest SUE, while the low-SUE portfolio consist of twenty firms with the lowest SUE. Each twenty-security portfolio is subdivided into two equal-weighted portfolios of ten securities. One portfolio contains the ten securities with the highest estimated betas, and the other consists of the ten firms with the lowest estimated betas. Weights are selected for the two ten-security portfolios so that the overall twenty-security portfolio has an estimated beta equal to one.

Reinganum's results indicate that abnormal returns cannot be earned over the period studied by constructing portfolios on the basis of a firm's standardized unexpected earnings. These results offer support for the assumption of market efficiency.

Reinganum uses the same data source computed earnings/price ratios for the firms in his sample. Earnings/price ratios are computed as the quarterly net income divided by the value of the common stock. The value of the common stock is calculated with both pre-earnings and post-earnings announcement prices. If capital markets rapidly incorporate information into prices, then rankings based upon post-announcement prices should reflect only the equilibrium effect between E/P ratios and asset pricing.

Results indicate that during 1976 and 1977 an abnormal return of about 0.1 percent per day on the average can be earned by forming portfolios based on E/P ratios. That is, the mean return of a high-E/P portfolio exceeds the mean return of a low-E/P portfolio by about 0.1 percent per day, even after adjusting for beta risk. Ignoring transaction costs, this mean spread is

greater than six percent per quarter, and it persists for at least two quarters. Reinganum suggests that the evidence indicates a misspecification in CAPM rather than any informational inefficiencies.

The evidence in this study suggests that the simple one-period CAPM is misspecified. The set of factors omitted from the equilibrium pricing mechanism seems to be more closely related to firm size than E/P ratios. According to Reinganum, the misspecification does not appear to be a market inefficiency in the sense that abnormal returns arise because of transaction costs or informational lags. Rather, the source of the misspecification seems to be risk factors that are omitted from the CAPM as is evidenced by the persistence of abnormal returns for at least two years.

Banz's Findings

Banz (1981) examines the empirical relationship between the return and the total market value of NYSE common stocks. His sample includes all common stocks quoted on the NYSE for at least five years between 1926 and 1975. The securities are assigned to one of twenty-five portfolios containing similar numbers of securities, first from one to five on the basis of the market value of the stock, then the securities in each of those five are in turn assigned to one of five portfolios on the basis of their beta. Five years of data are used for the estimation of the security beta; the next five years' data are used for the reestimation of the portfolio betas. Stock price and number of shares outstanding at the end of the five-year periods are used for the calculation of the market proportions. The portfolios are updated every year.

The results indicate that shares of firms with large market values have had smaller risk-adjusted returns, on average, than similar small firms over a forty-year period. This size effect is not linear in proportion to market value, but is most pronounced for the smallest firms in the sample. In addition, the effect is not very stable through time. Banz argues that the P/E ratio serves as a proxy for the size of a firm and not vice versa. He cites a study by Reinganum (1981) where the results show that the P/E effect disappears for both NYSE and AMEX stocks when Reinganum controls for size, but that there is a significant size effect even when he controls for the P/E ratio.

To summarize, the size effect exists, but it is not clear why it exists. Although it has been conjectured that the effect may be due to restricted distribution of information about small firms, it has not been established that size is not just a proxy for yet another effect.

Keim's Findings

Keim (1983) examines, month by month, the empirical relation between abnormal returns and the market value of NYSE and AMEX common stocks. Evidence is provided that daily abnormal return distributions in January have large means relative to the remaining eleven months, and that

the relation between abnormal returns and size is always negative and more pronounced in January than in any other months. In particular, nearly 50 percent of the average magnitude of the size effect over the period 1963–1979 is due to January abnormal returns. Further, more than 50 percent of the January premium is attributable to large abnormal returns during the first week of trading in the year, particularly on the first trading day.

The data for this study are drawn from the CRSP daily stock files for a seventeen-year period, 1963–1979. The sample consists of firms listed on the NYSE and AMEX that had returns on the CRSP files during the entire calendar year under consideration.

Additional Findings

Although several hypotheses regarding the January effect have been suggested, the more prominent are a tax-loss selling hypothesis by Branch (1977) and an information hypothesis. However, neither has been theoretically or empirically linked to the seasonal return.

Since February 1984 (and prior to February 1980), each Thursday, following the close of financial markets, the Federal Reserve has released an estimate of the seasonally adjusted average M-1 money supplies prevailing over the week ending Wednesday eight days earlier. (Between February 1980 and February 1984 the weekly money-supply announcement was moved from Thursday to Friday afternoon.) Therefore the announcement effect cannot occur until the markets open on Monday. Other events over the weekend may have camouflaged the money-supply announcement effect during this period.

Cornell (1983) examines the money-supply announcement effect upon various assets, including three-month Treasury bills, thirty-year Treasury bonds, German marks, and the Standard & Poor's 500 stock index. Notationally his model can be described as follows:

$$DA_t = A_0 + a_1 UM_t + a_2 EM_t + U_t \qquad (17.8)$$

where:

DA_t = the change in asset return;
UM_t = the unexpected monetary announcement;
EM_t = the expected monetary announcement; and
U_t = the random disturbance.

Cornell summarizes four major hypotheses that explain why money-supply announcements affect asset prices. First, the expected-inflation hypothesis states that the announcements alter analysts' inflation forecasts. Second, the Keynesian hypothesis predicts that in response to an announced innovation in the money stock, analysts expect the Fed to take offsetting action. Third, the real-activity hypothesis alleges that money-supply announcements provide the market with information about future output, and thereby future money demand. Finally, the risk-premium hypothesis states that money-

supply announcements alter the required real return on financial assets by providing the market with information about aggregate risk preferences and beliefs. None of the hypotheses explained the reaction of all four assets. Therefore, at best, the market is responding to money-supply announcements in an eclectic manner.

Using data from January 5, 1978, to December 18, 1981, divided into two intervals to take account of the Federal Reserve's stated change in operating procedure on October 6, 1979, Cornell finds that the market was only responsive to monetary announcements after October 6, 1979. Others, notably Urich and Wachtel (1981) have found some evidence that the announcement effect did exist prior to the change in Fed policy. In addition, Cornell finds that only the unanticipated portion of the announcement is significant, and that a definite relationship exists between the asset-price change and the unanticipated money-supply change. In summary, the existence of anomalies tends to indicate that the market is not perfectly efficient. Due to this inefficiency, technical analysts have hope for some success in capturing excess profits.

Treynor and Ferguson (1985) further defends the use of technical analysis by using a Bayesian probability estimate to assess whether, in using past price data, the market has already incorporated some firm-specific information available to the investor. If the market has not discovered this information and past price data confirms this, the informed investor may be able to realize excess returns. Their results show that past prices, combined with other valuable information, can be used to achieve excess returns. However, they note that it is the firm-specific information that creates the opportunity while past prices serve to permit its exploitation.

SECURITY RATE-OF-RETURN FORECASTING

This section discusses alternative methods to forecast security rate of return in security analysis. In order to do security-return forecasting, regression analysis, time-series analysis, and a composite approach are often utilized. In forecasting security rates of return both the fundamental and the technical analyst may use the regression approach. The time-series approach is more often associated with the technical school.

Regression Approach

A **regression approach** captures the relationship between independent variable(s) X_{it} and a dependent variable R_{jt} in a linear format. One can choose either a linear or log linear model as defined below:

1.
$$R_{jt} = a + bX_t + \epsilon_t \tag{17.9A}$$

2.
$$\log R_{jt} = a' + b' \log X_t + \epsilon_t' \tag{17.9B}$$

in which ϵ_t and ϵ_t' are error terms. The choice between Equations (17.9A) and (17.9B) depends on whether the related variables, X_t and R_{jt}, are normally or log normally distributed.

In order to obtain the best linear model to predict R_{jt} given X_t, it is necessary to find the equation that minimizes the squared error term. The error term (ϵ_t) represents the difference between the actual value of R_{jt} and the predicted value of R_{jt}. The estimated value of R_{jt}, $\hat{R}_{jt}$, can be defined as

$$\hat{R}_{jt} = \hat{a} + \hat{b}X_t$$

In general, if X_t is the series to be forecasted and y_{it} is the possible explanatory series, then a further example of an explanatory model is

$$X_t = a + b_1 y_{1t} + b_2 y_{2t} + \cdots + b_n y_{nt} + e_t$$

To forecast one step ahead, write this as

$$X_{t+1} = a + b_1 y_{1t+1} + b_2 y_{2t+1} + \cdots + b_n y_{nt+1} + e_{t+1}$$

Another model is therefore required to provide a forecast for y_{it+1} so that a forecast for X_{t+1} can be constructed. The regression model can be classified into fixed-coefficient and time-varying-coefficient versions. These two versions are now discussed using the market model of Chapters 9 and 10.

Fixed-Coefficient Market Model.   A common model found in finance literature used to estimate the return on security j is the **fixed-coefficient market model.**

$$R_{jt} = \alpha_j + \beta_j R_{mt} + \epsilon_{jt} \qquad (17.10)$$

where:

R_{jt} = return on security j in period t;
α_j = regression intercept term in period t;
R_{mt} = return on the market portfolio in period t;
β_j = estimated parametric coefficient in period t; and
ϵ_{jt} = error term in period t.

Using the estimated coefficient α_j and β_j from period t and forecasting the return on the market for time period $t + 1$, $R_{m,t+1}$, the return on security j can be forecasted for period $t + 1$:

$$R_{j,t+1} = \alpha + \beta_j R_{m,t+1} + \epsilon_{j,t+1} \qquad (17.11)$$

Time-Varying-Coefficient Market Model.   A variation of the fixed-coefficient market model, the **time-varying-coefficient market model** allows the coefficient to vary with time. Algebraically:

1. $$R_{jt} = \alpha_j + \beta_{jt} R_{mt} + \epsilon_{jt} \qquad (17.12A)$$

2. $$\beta_{jt} = \beta_j + \gamma_1 X_1 + \gamma_2 X_2 + \cdots + \gamma_n X_n + \tau_{jt} \qquad (17.12B)$$

Rosenberg and McKibben (1973) use this format to predict stock returns. In

their analysis they use historical accounting variables (X) to predict the time-varying beta.

Substituting Equation (17.12B) into (17.12A) leads to a multiple-regression format where:

$$R_{jt} = \alpha_j + \beta R_{mt} + \gamma_1(X_1 R_{mt}) + \gamma_2(X_2 R_{mt}) + \cdots$$
$$+ \gamma_n(X_n R_{mt}) + (\epsilon_{jt} + \tau_{jt} R_{mt}) \tag{17.13}$$

In order to use this format to forecast $R_{j,t+1}$, not only must R_{mt+1} be forecasted but also $\beta_{j,t+1}$, which indicates that a forecast of variable X_j must be available. As one can see this is a much more complex situation than forecasting using a constant beta.

Time-Series Approach

A **time series** is a set of observations generated sequentially in time. If the set is continuous the time series is said to be *continuous*. If the set is discrete, the time series is said to be *discrete*.

The use at time t of available observations from a time series to forecast its value at some future time $t + 1$ can provide a base for economic and business planning, production planning, inventory and production control, and optimization of industrial processes. To calculate the best forecasts it is also necessary to specify their accuracy, so that the risks associated with decisions based upon the forecasts may be calculated.

Two major approaches to time-series analysis are component analysis and sample-function analysis. **Component analysis** regards the time series as being composed of several influences or components that are generally taken to be trend-cycle, seasonal, and random movements. In component analysis the seasonal and trend movements are modeled in a deterministic manner. The trend might be fitted by a polynomial of a given degree and the seasonal component by a Fourier series (a trigonometric function with a given period and amplitude).

Sample-function analysis regards a time series as an observed sample function representing a realization of an underlying stochastic process. Complicated parametric statistical-estimation procedures are used to determine the properties of time-series data. Since empirical results obtained from component analysis are easier to understand and interpret, henceforth this chapter concerns only component analysis.

Component Analysis.   Component analysis is based on the premise that seasonal fluctuations can be measured in an original series of economic data and separated from trend, cyclical, trading-day, and random fluctuation. The seasonal component reflects a long-term pattern of variation which is repeated constantly or in an evolving fashion from year to year. The trend-cycle component includes the long-term trend and the business cycle. The trading-day component consists of variations which are attributed to the composition of the calendar. The random component is composed of re-

sidual variations that reflect the effect of random or unexplained events in the time series.

Decomposing past time series and discovering the relative percentage contribution of the trend, seasonal, and random components to changes in the series provide insight to financial analysts. The trend-cycle component reflects permanent information in both a short- and long-run economic time series. The seasonal component is considered to represent a permanent pattern underlying the short-run time series. The random component contains the randomness that exists in the time series for both short- and long-run analysis. The higher the relative percentage contribution of the random component in a time series, the greater the uncertainty and thus the greater the probability of forecasting errors.

Gentry and Lee (1987) use the decomposition method known as the X-II to measure the relative percentage contribution of trend-cycle, seasonal, and random components to changes in the original series of income-statement variables. Their results indicate that the relative percentage contribution of the trend-cycle, seasonal, and random components were directly affected by the length of the time period of data. The shorter the time period of data, the greater is the relative percentage contribution of the irregular component. The longer the time period, the greater is the relative contribution of the trend-cycle component and the smaller the seasonal component. In addition, the relative percentage contribution of the components varied widely among companies for all of the income-statement variables tested. These results have serious implications both for internal management and external analysis. An industry index of the percentage contribution of the random components for each income statement variable would provide a useful benchmark to measure the reliability of an analyst's forecast.

ARIMA Models. This section examines a class of models used in forecasting time-series data. It is best to begin by examining the simplest of all possible time series, a purely random series. A series that is purely random is sometimes referred to as a white-noise or **random-walk** model. Mathematically such a series can be described by the following equation:

$$y_t = a_t \tag{17.14}$$

in which the series a_t is assumed to have a mean of zero, to be unrelated to its past values, and to have a constant variance over time. Mathematically, these assumptions can be summarized:

$$E(a_t) = 0$$
$$E(a_t, a_{t-i}) = 0 \qquad \text{for all } t \text{ and } i \neq 0$$
$$\text{Var} (a_t) = \sigma_a^2 \qquad \text{for all } t$$

Modifying Equation (17.14) to allow the series to be concentrated around a nonzero mean δ, the series could now be described:

$$y_t = \delta + a_t \tag{17.15}$$

Equation (17.15) is a model that can be used to represent many different time series in economics and finance. For example, in an efficient market a series of stock prices might be expected to randomly fluctuate around a constant mean. So the actual stock price observed in time period t would be equal to its average price plus some random shock in time period t.

The question now is how to model a purely random series. Fortunately, a theorem known as **Wold's decomposition** provides the answer. Wold's decomposition proves that any stationary time series (a series is stationary if it is centered around a constant mean) can be considered as a sum of self-deterministic components. This theorem states that a time series can be generated from a weighted average of past random shocks of infinite order. A model such as this is known as a **moving average of infinite order** and can be expressed by the following equation:

$$y_t = \delta + \Theta_1 a_{t-1} + \Theta_2 a_{t-2} + \cdots + \Theta_\infty a_{t-\infty} + a_t \tag{17.16}$$

where:

δ = mean of the process;
$a_{t-\infty}$ = random shock that occurred ∞ periods earlier; and
Θ_∞ = parameter that relates the random shock ∞ periods earlier to the current value of y.

The moving-average model just discussed should not be confused with the moving-average concept previously discussed in this chapter. Previously, the term *moving average* was used to refer to an arithmetic average of stock prices over a specified number of days. The term *moving average* was used because the average was continually updated to include the most recent series of data. In time-series analysis, a moving-average process refers to a series generated by a weighted average of past random shocks.

Because it would be impossible to estimate a model of infinite order, in practice it is best to specify a model of finite order. A moving-average process of order q with zero mean would be expressed:

$$y_t = \Theta_1 a_{t-1} + \cdots + \Theta_q a_{t-q} + a_t \tag{17.17}$$

A moving-average process is not the only way to model a stationary time series. Again, consider a moving-average process of infinite order:

$$y_t = \Theta_1 a_{t-1} + \Theta_2 a_{t-2} + \cdots + a_t \tag{17.18}$$

Equation (17.18) can be rewritten in terms of the error term a_t:

$$a_t = y_t - \Theta_1 a_{t-1} - \Theta_2 a_{t-2} - \cdots \tag{17.19}$$

Because Equation (17.19) is recursive in nature it is easy to generate an expression for a_{t-1}:

$$a_{t-1} = y_{t-1} - \Theta_1 a_{t-2} - \Theta_2 a_{t-3} - \cdots \qquad (17.20)$$

By substituting the expression for a_{t-1} into Equation (17.19):

$$\begin{aligned} a_t &= y_t - \Theta_1 (y_{t-1} - \Theta_1 a_{t-2} - \Theta_2 a_{t-3} - \cdots) \\ &\quad - \Theta_2 a_{t-2} - \Theta_3 a_{t-3} - \cdots \\ &= y_t - \Theta_1 y_{t-1} + (\Theta_1^2 - \Theta_2) a_{t-2} + (\Theta_1 \Theta_2 - \Theta_3) a_{t-3} + \cdots \end{aligned}$$

$$(17.21)$$

By generating expressions for a_{t-2}, a_{t-3}, ... and substituting them into Equation (17.21) a_t can be expressed in terms of past values of y_t:

$$a_t = y_t + \phi_1 y_{t-1} + \phi_2 y_{t-2} + \cdots \qquad (17.22)$$

Rearranging Equation (17.22) in terms of y_t:

$$y_t = -\phi_1 y_{t-1} - \phi_2 y_{t-2} - \cdots + a_t \qquad (17.23)$$

where $\phi_1 = \phi_1$ and $\phi_2 = \Theta_1^2 - \Theta_2$.

Equation (17.23) is known as an **autoregressive process of infinite order.** The term *autoregressive* refers to the fact that y_t is expressed in terms of its own past values $y_{t-1}, y_{t-2}, \ldots$.

Again, because it is impossible to estimate a model of infinite order an approximate model of finite order is specified. An autoregressive process of order p can be expressed:

$$y_t = -\phi_1 y_{t-1} - \cdots - \phi_p y_{t-p} + a_t \qquad (17.24)$$

Thus a stationary time series can be expressed in two ways: (1) as a moving-average process in which the series can be represented as a weighted average of past random shocks, or (2) as an autoregressive process in which the series can be represented as a weighted average of its past values. A third possibility is that a series may involve some combination of the two processes. This process is referred to as a mixed **autoregressive moving-average (ARMA) process.**

An ARMA process of infinite order can be expressed:

$$y_t = \Theta_1 a_{t-1} + \Theta_2 a_{t-2} + \cdots - \phi_1 y_{t-1} - \phi_2 y_{t-2} - \cdots + a_t$$

$$(17.25)$$

Again, an ARMA process of finite order must be specified in order to make estimation possible. An ARMA (p, q) process can be expressed:

$$y_t = \Theta_1 a_{t-1} + \cdots + \Theta_q a_{t-q} - \phi_1 y_{t-1} - \cdots - \phi_p y_{t-p} + a_t$$

$$(17.26)$$

So far the discussion has focused on the estimation of stationary time series. Suppose the process of interest is not stationary. Fortunately, a nonstationary series can usually be made stationary by transforming the data in an appropriate manner. The most popular method of transforming a nonstationary series to a stationary one is by differencing the series. For example, suppose the series $y_1, y_2, \ldots, y_t$ is nonstationary. By differencing

the series a new series, $Z_1, Z_2, \ldots, Z_{t-1}$, is created. The new series can be defined:

$$Z_1 = y_2 - y_1$$
$$Z_2 = y_3 - y_2$$
$$\cdot$$
$$\cdot$$
$$\cdot$$
$$Z_{t-1} = y_t - y_{t-1}$$

If the series Z_t is not stationary, it may be necessary to difference the series Z_t.

The modeling of a series that has been differenced is referred to as an **autoregressive integrated moving-average (ARIMA) process.** A detailed discussion of ARIMA modeling is beyond the scope of this book; nevertheless a brief outline of the ARIMA modeling procedure is in order. [See Nelson (1973) or Nazem (1988) for details of the ARIMA procedure.]

The ARIMA process uses the following three steps.

1. Identification
2. Estimation
3. Forecasting

The first step is to identify the appropriate model. Identification involves determining the degree of differencing necessary to make the series stationary and to determine the form (ARMA or ARIMA) and order of the process.

After a suitable model is identified, the parameters $\phi_1, \ldots, \phi_p, \Theta_1, \ldots, \Theta_q$ need to be estimated. The final step in the ARIMA process is to use the model for forecasting. Oftentimes the adequacy of the model is checked by using the model to forecast within the sample. This allows a comparison of the forecasted values to the actual values. If the model is determined to be adequate, the model can be used to forecast future values of the series.

Composite Forecasting

Numerous approaches running from sophisticated multiple-equation regression techniques to rather naive extrapolations or intuitive estimates are being utilized to produce forecasts. Bessler and Brandt (1979) examine three alternative procedures for forecasting time-dependent quarterly observations on hog, cattle, and broiler prices along with composite forecasts based on various linear combinations of these three procedures. The alternative methods for forecasting these prices are econometric models, time series (ARIMA), and expert opinion.

The results obtained by Bessler and Brandt for selected performance measures (mean-squared error and turning points) applied to the forecasts of each method over the period 1976 quarter I through 1979 quarter II suggest that no method consistently outperformed or was outperformed by the other

two methods. In terms of mean-squared error performance forecasts based on the ARIMA processes are lowest for hog and cattle prices while the econometric model gives lowest mean-squared error forecasts for broiler prices.

The mean forecast error is determined by taking the average of the difference between the summation of the overpredictions and the summation of the underpredictions. A negative sign would indicate that the average forecast series is above the mean of the actual series; a positive sign suggests an average forecast which is low. The mean absolute forecast error is simply the average of the absolute values of the forecast errors.

Composite forecasts based on the forecasts of the individual methods are formed using three procedures: minimum variance, adaptive weighting, and simple average composites. The empirical results from all three composite forecasting schemes generate performance levels that are at least as good as any of the individual forecasts and usually much better. In particular, the mean-squared error of the best individual forecasting method is compared with that of the best composite for each of the three commodities. The composite forecast errors of the three commodities average 14 percent lower than the errors of the best individual forecasts.

The **econometric model** is essentially based on representations of the underlying economic behavioral system for a particular commodity. These representations attempt to identify and model the relevant supply-and-demand factors that together determine market price and quantity.

As an alternative to statistical models for forecasting, forecasts based upon expert opinions are available. These forecasts represent an accumulation of knowledge about the particular industry, commodity, or stock in question. In many respects, the forecasts of experts are like those of econometric- or ARIMA-model forecasting in that they incorporate much of the same information from the same data sources. Expert opinions, however, are less restrictive or structured, in that the expert can change the weights assigned to different bits of information, or can select with relative ease the sources from which to draw the data. In addition, these expert forecasts are able to incorporate information that cannot, perhaps, be included in a more quantitative model in the form of data.

Recognizing that most forecasts contain some information that is not used in other forecasts, it seems possible that a combination of forecasts will quite often outperform any of the individual forecasts. Bessler and Brandt (1979) construct composite forecasts based upon composite weighting schemes. Bessler and Brandt use various tests or measures of performance to evaluate the price forecasts of econometric, ARIMA, expert-opinion, and composite methods. Of the single-variable measures, they use the mean-squared error, the mean forecast error, and the mean absolute forecast error. The mean-squared error is a non-parametric statistic that provides a measure of the size of individual forecast errors from the actual values. Because the error is squared, large errors detract significantly from the performance of the method.

Performance indicators that track the movements of actual and forecast price series are called tracking measures. Examples of tracking measures are the number of turning points missed or falsely predicted compared with those correctly forecasted. Although these measures will not indicate which forecasting method most closely approximates the actual series, they are particularly useful when the forecaster is interested in knowing when a series is likely to turn upward or downward from its current pattern.

Bessler's and Brandt's study does not find any specific forecasting method to be universally superior in terms of the performance measures. Although the ARIMA model performs best for two of three commodities, its performance is poorest for the third commodity in terms of the mean-squared error criterion. The composite forecasting method's mean-squared errors are lower than or nearly as low as the best of the individual methods. More important, in no case does a composite method of forecast generate errors that are as large as the worst of the individual methods.

The results of the performance evaluation suggest that forecasters should seriously consider using composite forecasting techniques. The idea that alternative forecasting methods use a variety of different information sources and means for assimilating the information and generating forecasts, a variety that can be captured by a composite forecast, is not only theoretically appealing but, in Bessler's and Brandt's study, somewhat empirically substantiated. Appendix 17A presents the composite forecasting method.

VALUE LINE RANKING

The **Value Line Investment Survey** is an independent weekly investment-advisory service registered with the U. S. Securities and Exchange Commission. The weekly Value Line survey comes in three sections:

1. *Rating and Reports* contains full-page reports on each of 1700 stocks. The stocks are classified into 92 industry groups. A report on the industry precedes reports on the stocks in it. Every week, about 130 stocks in seven or eight industries are covered on a preset sequential schedule.
2. The *Summary and Indexes* is a weekly alphabetical catalog of all 1700 stocks at their most recent prices, with their current ranking for timeliness and safety.
3. *Selection and Opinion* gives Value Line's opinion of business prospects, the stock-market outlook, and the advisable investment strategy.

Criteria of Ranking

By means of the two rankings, timeliness and safety, Value Line relays its expectations about the performance of individual stocks and industries. The timeliness rank runs on a scale from 1 (highest) down to 5 (lowest). The

safety rank is a measure of risk avoidance. It is based mainly on the company's relative financial strength and the stock's price stability. The safety rank changes infrequently and may be taken as a forecast of risk avoidance. Safety ranks run on a scale of 1 (safest) to 5 (riskiest).

The rankings are drawn almost completely from published information about the earnings and price history of the companies that are followed, and are based on ten years of history on earnings and prices. The rankings are produced primarily by a computer using as input the earnings and price history. The system tends to assign high ranks to stocks with low price-earnings ratios relative to historic norms and to the current price-earnings ratio of the market. The system also tends to assign high ranks to stocks whose quarterly earnings reports show an upward momentum, relative to the quarterly earnings on the market as a whole, and to stocks that have upward price momentum. These factors are weighted by the program. The weights used on the different factors are chosen by doing a cross-sectional regression on past data. The set of weights that seems to give the best predictive ability is then chosen. In sum, the one-year rankings are based on growth in earnings, price momentum, and the price-earnings ratio of each stock relative to the market and to historical standards for the stock.

The evaluation of a single stock involves:

1. Choosing stocks that are acceptable in terms of timeliness rankings;
2. Among the stocks chosen for timeliness, picking those that are in industries also shown to be timely;
3. Among the most timely stocks in the most timely industries, picking those that conform to the investor's safety constraints;
4. Among those stocks that meet the investor's timeliness and safety constraints, choosing those that meet the investor's current yield requirement.

Performance Evaluation

In studies to determine the profitability of the investment advice given by various brokerages and investment advisors, Value Line recommendations yield a portfolio that earns a few percentage points more return per year than could be earned by picking a large portfolio randomly. Fischer Black (1972), advocate of the buy-and-hold strategy, using monthly data over a given year commencing with April 1965, tested for the investment performance of the Value Line rankings. He used Jensen's time-series test of consistency of performance, calculating the return on the market at frequent intervals. A time-series regression of the excess return on the portfolio against the excess on the market was run; the intercept of that regression shows the extra returns the portfolio is able to achieve adjusted for risk. The intercept is then tested for significance.

Black constructed portfolios of all the stocks in each ranking and weighted each stock equally each month. Purchases were assumed to occur

at the close of the markets on Friday, which is when most subscribers receive their reports. The results of Black's tests show that the success of the rankings are very consistent over time, and thus very significant in a statistical sense. The extra return of rank 1 stocks is about 10 percent per year; it is about minus 10 percent per year for the rank 5 stocks. Black notes that if weekly returns and associated portfolio revisions had been used, rank 1 would have earned an extra 20 percent per year rather than an extra 10 percent per year.

In sum, the use of Jensen's CAPM time-series test tends to indicate that rankings clearly provide a profitable portfolio strategy for investors who can execute orders at low transaction costs. Even in reducing the turnover activity involved, significant excess returns were achieved.

Similar studies were performed by Holloway (1981) and Copeland and Mayers (1982). Holloway (1981) found significant performance for rank 1 firms over the 1974–1977 period. Copeland and Mayers (1982) noted that rank 1 firms outperformed rank 5 firms by 6.8 percent per year on a risk-adjusted basis over the 1965–1978 period for portfolios updated semi-annually. A later work by Chen, Copeland, and Mayers (1986) using an APT framework has results that are similar to the Copeland and Mayers (1982) results.

Stickel (1985), using an event-study methodology, examines evidence on (1) the differential impact of the various types of rank change and (2) the speed of adjustment of individual security prices to new information. His results indicate that although Value Line rank changes have information content, the effect varies by the type of rank change. Changes from rank 2 to rank 1 have the most dramatic effect on prices. A cross-sectional analysis finds that smaller firms have a greater reaction to a rank change than larger firms. Finally, a speed-of-adjustment test suggests that individual securities with significant abnormal performance on event day 0 or +1 adjust to the information in rank change over a multiple-day period.

Lee and Park (1987), using a specification-analysis approach, investigated the effect of Value Line ranking changes for the beta coefficients. Following Equation (17.12), they generalized the additional market model:

(A)
$$R_{jt} = \alpha_j + \beta_{jt}R_{mt} + \epsilon_{jt}$$

(B)
$$\beta_{jt} = \beta_j + CV_{jt}$$

(17.27)

where:

R_{jt} = rate of return for the jth firm in period t;
R_{mt} = market rate of return in period t;
β_{jt} = beta coefficient for the jth firm in period t; and
V_{jt} = Value Line ranking for the firm in period t.

Substituting Equation (17.27B) into (17.27A):

$$R_{jt} = \alpha_j + \beta_j R_{mt} + C(V_{jt}R_{mt}) + E_{jt}$$

(17.28)

In Equation (17.28) the interaction variable $V_{jt}R_{mt}$ can be used to test whether the Value Line ranking exhibits some market-timing ability on the jth firm's rate-of-return determination. Their empirical results using monthly stock-return data and Value Line weekly rankings over the period July 1978 to February 1983 suggest that firm's betas are affected by the change of a Value Line ranking more than 40 percent of the time. Most of the estimated Cs are negative; hence it can be concluded that an increase in rank will reduce the beta coefficient and rate of return of the firm.

These studies suggest that Value Line's recommendations are better than picking stocks randomly. Such favorable studies have never been published for other investment-advisory services by unbiased outside researchers.

MUTUAL FUNDS

Mutual funds are one of the most important investments for individual investors. In this section mutual-fund classification and mutual-fund managers' timing and selectivity abilities are discussed.

Mutual-Fund Classification

According to the Investment Company Act of 1940 mutual funds must publish a written statement of their investment objectives and make it available to their shareholders. This objective can be changed only if the majority of the shareholders consent in advance to the new objective. The investment objectives of mutual funds can be classified into the following four categories.

1. Growth
2. Income and growth
3. Income
4. Income, growth, and stability (balanced fund)

These objectives are listed in descending order of the aggressiveness with which the fund's management implies it will seek a high average rate of return and assume the corresponding risks.

The **balanced funds** offer a complete investment program to their clients, so far as marketable securities are concerned. Their portfolios are presumably structured to include bonds and stocks in a ratio considered appropriate for an average individual investor given the return outlook for each sector and possibly a risk and volatility constraint.

By and large, however, these funds have been much less popular with investors than growth funds. **Growth funds** are structured to include a well diversified combination of common stocks. Basically, three reasons may be cited. First, empirical studies of common stocks have almost invariably

shown their long-term total returns to exceed those on bonds. Second, stock is generally conceded to be a better hedge against inflation risk than bonds. Third, many small investors may prefer to hold obligations of financial institutions as their major fixed-income securities because of their convenience and safety resulting from government insurance programs.

Income funds are composed of well diversified selections of bonds. Empirical studies of long-term bond returns have indicated a widely diversified list of medium-quality bonds that have been superior to high-quality bonds. In order to obtain appropriate representation in this sector of the bond universe, which includes both corporates and municipals, a large pool of funds is required to obtain the desired degree of diversification. One should be alert to the possibility that in order to show highly attractive yields on a competitive basis, an income fund may acquire a heavy proportion of speculative bonds on which the default risk is high.

Income-and-growth funds are composed of a combination of common stock and bonds. Whether the emphasis is on income or growth determines what percentage of bonds or common stock is in the portfolio.

Mutual-Fund Manager's Timing and Selectivity

When faced with the problem of deriving a performance measure, there are two considerations: (1) the collective performance of the security portfolio and (2) the relative performance of the security portfolio. Evidence about the collective performance is relevant to the efficient-market hypothesis, and thereby to an understanding of the process of security-price determination. Evidence about the relative performance of individual mutual funds or portfolios is of obvious interest to entities with investment funds to allocate. In examining relative performance, market-timing activities as well as careful selection of individual securities are of concern.

Performance evaluations originally employed a one-parameter risk–return benchmark like that developed by Jensen (1968, 1969) and refined by Black, Jensen, and Scholes (1972) and Blume and Friend (1973). Such investigations have effectively focused on the fund manager's security-selection skills, since the examined portfolios' risk levels have been assumed to be stationary through time. Fama (1972) and Jensen (1972) point out the empirical measurement problems involved in evaluating properly the constituents of investment performance when portfolio risk levels are non-stationary as indicated by Chang and Lewellen (1984).

Fama (1972), rather than follow previous research on performance measurement by Sharpe (1966), Treynor (1965), and Jensen (1968) (where performance was evaluated in a two-dimensional framework of risk and return), looked for a finer breakdown of performance. Up to that time the notion underlying performance measurement was a comparison of the returns on a managed portfolio relative to an annually selected portfolio with similar risk. The Sharpe-Lintner-Mossin version of the capital asset pricing model

(CAPM) was used to obtain the benchmark portfolio return of the naively selected portfolio.

To obtain the benchmark portfolio Fama (1972) uses Sharpe's (1964) method to derive the efficient portfolio and ex-ante security-market line. The efficient portfolios are formed according to:

$$R_x = x \, R_f + (1 - x)R_m \qquad x \le 1 \tag{17.29}$$

so that:

$$E(R_x) = x \, R_f + (1 - x) \, E(R_m) \tag{17.30}$$

$$\sigma(R_x) = (1 - x) \, \sigma(R_m) \tag{17.31}$$

in which R_m, $E(R_m)$ and $\sigma(R_m)$ are one-period return, expected return, and standard deviation of return for the market portfolio m, respectively, and x is the weight associated with the risk-free asset.

Following Appendix 9A, the ex-ante security-market line can be defined:

$$E(R_j) = R_f + \left[\frac{E(R_m) - R_f}{\sigma(R_m)}\right] \frac{\text{Cov}\,(R_j, R_m)}{\sigma(R_m)} \tag{17.32}$$

in which Cov (R_j, R_m) is the covariance between the return on asset j and the return on the market portfolio.

The benchmark or naively selected portfolios are just the combination of the riskless asset R_f and the market portfolio R_m obtained with different values of x (where x is a weight). Given the ex-post or realized return R_m for the market portfolio, for the naively selected portfolio ex-post return is

$$R_x = x \, R_f + (1 - x) \, R_m \qquad x \le 1 \tag{17.33}$$

Moreover:

$$\beta_x = \frac{\text{Cov}\,(R_x, R_m)}{\sigma(R_m)} = \frac{\text{Cov}\,[(1 - x)\,R_m, R_m]}{\sigma(R_m)}$$

$$= (1 - x)\sigma(R_m) = \sigma(R_x). \tag{17.34}$$

That is, for the benchmark portfolio risk and standard deviation of return are equal.

For the naively selected portfolios, Equations (17.33) and (17.34) imply the following relationship between risk of an asset β_x and ex-post return R_x:

$$R_x = R_f + \left(\frac{R_m - R_f}{\sigma(R_m)}\right)\beta_x \tag{17.35}$$

That is, for the naively selected portfolios there is a linear relationship between risk and return. In performance-evaluation models using this methodology a benchmark is provided against which the returns on managed portfolios are judged.

To use Equation (17.35) as a benchmark for evaluating ex-post portfolio returns requires estimates of risk β_p and dispersion $\sigma(R_p)$ of the managed

portfolios, as well as an estimate of $\sigma(R_m)$, the dispersion of the return on the market portfolio. In order for the performance evaluation to be objective, it must be possible to obtain reliable estimates of these parameters from historical data. Evidence suggests that, at least for portfolios of ten or more securities, β_p and $\sigma(R_p)$ seem to be fairly stationary over long periods of time and likewise for $\sigma(R_m)$. However, if market timing is to be a consideration the problem of nonstationary β_p, $\sigma(R_p)$, and $\sigma(R_m)$ must be considered.

In addition, an assumption of normal return distributions is held, even though evidence suggests that actual return distributions conform more closely to nonnormal, two-parameter stable distributions. Finally, the available empirical evidence indicates that the average returns over time on securities portfolios deviate systematically from the predictions of the standard CAPM model. In short, the evidence suggests that CAPM does not provide the best benchmark for the average return–risk tradeoffs available in the market from naively selected portfolios.

Fama (1972) first introduced the concept of **selectivity,** defined as how well a chosen portfolio does relative to a naive portfolio with the same level of risk. Algebraically, this measure of performance of the chosen portfolio a is

$$\text{Selectivity} = R_a - R_x(\beta_a) \tag{17.36}$$

where:

$$R_a = \frac{V_{a,t+1} - V_{a,t}}{V_{a,t}};$$

$V_{a,t}, V_{a,t+1} = $ the total market values at t and $t + 1$ of the actual portfolio chosen at time t; and

$R_x(\beta_a) = $ the return on the combination of the riskless asset f and the market portfolio m that makes risk β_x equal to β_a, the risk of the chosen portfolio a.

Selectivity is the sole measure of performance in the work of Sharpe, Treynor, and Jensen, as discussed in chapters 7 and 9. Fama introduced the concept of overall performance. Overall performance is the difference between the return on the chosen portfolio and the return on the riskless asset. Overall performance is in turn split into two parts, (1) selectivity and (2) risk. Algebraically:

$$\underset{\substack{\text{Overall} \\ \text{performance}}}{[R_a - R_f]} = \underset{\text{Selectivity}}{[R_a - R_x(\beta_a)]} + \underset{\text{Risk}}{[R_x(\beta_a) - R_f]} \tag{17.37}$$

Figure 17–3 graphically presents the components related to mutual-fund performance of Equation (17.37). Jensen's measure of performance, is, of course, the height of the line $A'A$. Fama refers to this distance as the return due to selectivity. In addition, Figure 17–3 indicates overall performance $R_a - R_f$ and risk $R_x(\beta_a) - R_f$. The risk measures the return for the decision to take one positive amount of risk. It will be determined by the level of risk

FIGURE 17-3   Overall Components of Mutual-Fund Performance

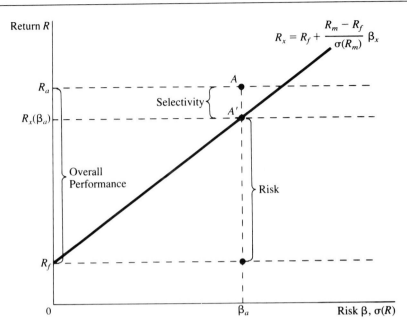

chosen (the value of β_a) and the security-market line defined in Equation (17.35).

It does not matter whether this portfolio is a small part of the holdings of an investor, because diversifiable risk will be diversified away when looking at the investor's total holdings. If, on the other hand, the portfolio represents their entire holdings, it does matter. The question that now arises is whether beta or the standard deviation is the appropriate measure of risk for evaluating portfolio management. If total risk is the appropriate measure, then a Sharpe measure is the appropriate measurement tool.

Fama (1972) further decomposes Equation (17.37) by breaking up risk into two parts, (1) total portfolio risk $\sigma(R_a)$ and (2) market risk β_a. Fama then goes on to show that the portfolio risk $\sigma(R_a)$ will be greater than the market risk β_a as long as the portfolio's returns are not perfectly correlated with the returns on the market. This can be seen by looking at the correlation coefficient $\rho_{a,m}$ between R_a and R_m:

$$\rho_{a,m} = \frac{\text{Cov}(R_a, R_m)}{\sigma(R_a)\,\sigma(R_m)}$$

Multiplying both sides by $\sigma(R_a)$ yields:

$$\rho_{a,m}\,\sigma(R_a) = \frac{\text{Cov}(R_a, R_m)}{\sigma(R_m)}$$

Notice that the right-hand side of the equation is just the measure of market risk β_a. So β_a can be written:

$$\rho_{a,m}\, \sigma(R_a) = \beta_a$$

So:

$$\beta_a \leq \sigma(R_a) \quad \text{when} \quad \rho_{a,m} \leq 1$$

Because total risk $\sigma(R_a)$ is greater than market risk β_a, Fama is now able to decompose selectivity into two parts, net selectivity and diversification. In Figure 17–4 the quantity $R_x\,[\sigma(R_a)] - R_a$ is a measure of the extra return earned on portfolio a compared to a naive portfolio with the same total risk. Fama calls $R_x[\sigma(R_a)] - R_a$ net selectivity. He calls the distance $R_x[\sigma(R_a)] - R_x(\beta_a)$ diversification, decomposing $R_x[\sigma(R_a)] - R_x(\beta_a)$ into $R_a - R_x(\beta_a)$, selectivity, and $R_x[\sigma(R_a)] - R_a$, net selectivity.

The decomposition of selectivity can be seen algebraically:

$$\overset{\text{Selectivity}}{[R_a - R_x(\beta_a)]} = \text{Net Selectivity} + \overset{\text{Diversification}}{[R_x(\sigma(R_a)) - R_x(\beta_a)]} \quad \textbf{(17.38A)}$$

$$\text{Net selectivity} = \overset{\text{Selectivity}}{[R_a - R_x(\beta_a)]} - \overset{\text{Diversification}}{\{R_x(\sigma(R_a)) - R_x(\beta_a)]} \quad \textbf{(17.38B)}$$
$$= R_a - R_x\,[\sigma(R_a)]$$

FIGURE 17–4   Detailed Components of Mutual-Fund Performance

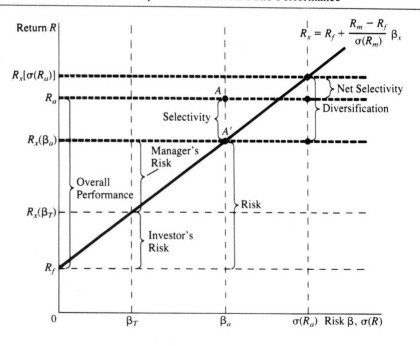

Diversification measures the extra portfolio return that a less than optimally diversified portfolio must earn to justify itself. When the return on the market is greater than the return on the risk-free asset, diversification measures the additional return that would just compensate the investor for the diversifiable dispersion $[\sigma(R_a) - \beta_a]$. However, when the return on the market is less than the return on the risk-free asset, diversification measures the return lost from taking on diversifiable dispersion rather than choosing the naively selected portfolio with market risk and standard deviation both equal to β_a, the market risk of the portfolio actually chosen.

Net selectivity may be negative if a manager's selectivity was not sufficient to make up for the avoidable risk taken. In Fama's example shown in Figure 17–4 related to $\sigma(R_a)$, you can see that the area measured by the diversification is larger than the area measured by selectivity. Therefore, net selectivity must be negative, according to Equation (17.38B).

If the investor has a target risk level β_T, the part of the overall performance due to risk can be allocated to the investor and to the portfolio manager as follows:

$$\underset{\text{Risk}}{[R_x(\beta_a) - R_f]} = \underset{\text{Manager's risk}}{[R_x(\beta_a) - R_x(\beta_T)]} + \underset{\text{Investor's risk}}{[R_x(\beta_T) - R_f]} \qquad \textbf{(17.39)}$$

in which $R_x(\beta_T)$ is the return on the investor's newly selected portfolio with the target level of market risk the investor has chosen. The manager's risk is composed of the risk assumed by the manager by taking on a level of risk β_a different from the investor's target level β_T. This decomposition is indicated in Figure 17–4 related to β_T.

Manager's risk might in part result from a timing decision. That is, the manager might have chosen a portfolio with a higher or lower level of risk than desired by the investor due to his evaluation of economic or industry trends. Using an ex-ante CAPM market line, risk can be subdivided as follows:

$$\underset{\text{Risk}}{\{R_x(\beta_a) - R_f\}} = \overset{\text{Manager's timing}}{\underset{\text{Total timing}}{\{R_x(\beta_a) - E[R_x(\beta_a)]\}}} - \overset{}{\underset{\text{Market conditions}}{\{R_x(\beta_T) - E[R_x(\beta_T)]\}}} \qquad \textbf{(17.40)}$$
$$+ \overset{\text{Manager's expected risk}}{\{E[R_x(\beta_a)] - E[R_x(\beta_T)]\}} + \overset{\text{Investor's risk}}{\{R_x(\beta_T) - R_f\}}$$

The manager's risk of Equation (17.39) is the sum of the first three terms. The manager's expected risk is the incremental expected return from the manager's decision to take on a nontarget level of risk. The expression for market conditions measures how much the market deviated from expectations at the target level of risk. Total timing is the difference between the ex-post return on the naively selected portfolio with risk β_a and the ex-ante expected return. When the return on the market is greater than the expected return on the market, total timing is positive (and more positive the larger the value of β_a). When the return on the market is less than expected return,

total timing is negative (and more negative the larger the value of β_a). Manager's timing is the difference between total timing and market conditions. The manager's timing is only positive (negative) when the chosen level of market risk is above (below) the target level and return on the market is above (below) the expected return on the market. It is, therefore, a more sensitive indicator of the manager's timing ability than total timing.

At times, a target level of risk may not be relevant; if this is the case, the market portfolio may be treated as the target portfolio. That is

$$
\underset{\text{Risk}}{\{R_x(\beta_a) - R_f\}} = \underset{\text{Total timing}}{\{R_x - E[R_x(\beta_a)]\}} - \underset{\text{Market conditions}}{\{R_m - E(R_m)\}}
$$

$$
+ \underset{\substack{\text{Expected deviation} \\ \text{from the market}}}{\{E[R_x(\beta_a)] - E(R_m)\}} + \underset{\substack{\text{Market} \\ \text{risk}}}{\{R_m - R_f\}}
$$

$$(17.41)$$

Fama was, therefore, one of the first to suggest that the return on a portfolio could be subdivided into two parts: the return from security selection and the return from the bearing of risk in attempting to predict general market-price movements. Therefore, a manager's performance can be attributed either to skill in selecting an underpriced security or in market-timing ability. However, Fama noted his concerns about current benchmark portfolios. They included the fact that β_p, $\sigma(R_p)$, and $\sigma(R_m)$ are stable for long periods of time (for example, ten years); but in order to capture market timing, the relevant period for evaluation must be considerably shorter. Although the observed return–risk relationships seem to be linear, the tradeoff of risk for return is in general less than predicted by the standard CAPM. In short, evidence suggests that standard CAPM framework may not provide the best benchmarks for the average return–risk tradeoffs available in the market from naively selected portfolios.

One of the principal applications of modern capital-market theory has been to propose a structural specification within which to measure investment performance and thereby to identify superior performers if they exist. In this structure it is usually assumed that forecasting skills can be partitioned into two distinct components: (1) forecasts of price movements of selected individual stocks (**microforecasting**), and (2) forecasts of price movements of the general stock market as a whole (**macroforecasting**). Usually microforecasting involves the identification of individual stocks that are undervalued or overvalued relative to an index for equities. Using the CAPM as a framework, a microforecaster attempts to identify individual stocks whose expected returns lie significantly above or below the security-market line. The microforecaster, in essence, forecasts the nonsystematic or nonmarket-explained component of the return on individual stocks. Using the CAPM framework, the random variable return per dollar $Z_j(t)$ on security j at time t can be algebraically shown as:

$$
Z_j(t) = R(t) + \beta_j[Z_m(t) - R(t)] + \epsilon_j(t)
$$

$$(17.42)$$

In Equation (17.42), $Z_m(t)$ is the return on the market, $R(t)$ is the return on the riskless asset, and $\epsilon_j(t)$ is the error term with the property that its expectation is conditional on knowing that the outcome of $Z_m(t)$ is equal to its unconditional expectation [$\epsilon_j(t)$ follows a martingale process]. Given such a model, a microforecaster would be interested in forecasting based on the properties of $\epsilon_j(t)$.

A macroforecaster, on the other hand, attempts to identify when equities in general are undervalued or overvalued relative to other types of security, such as fixed-income securities. Macroforecasters try to forecast when stocks will outperform bonds using bonds as a proxy for other types of securities—that is, $Z_m(t) > R(t)$—and when bonds will outperform stocks—that is, $Z_m(t) < R(t)$. Therefore, a microforecaster forecasts only the statistical properties of $Z_m(t)$ and a macroforecaster tries to forecast $Z_m(t) - R(t)$. As a result, macroforecasters' forecasts can only be used to predict differential performance among individual stocks arising from the systematic or market-explained components of their returns, $\{\beta_j[Z_m(t) - R(t)] + R(t)\}$.

Jensen (1972) developed a theoretical structure for the evaluation of the micro- and macroforecasting performance of investment managers where the basis for the evaluation is a comparison of ex-post performance of the manager's fund with the returns on the market. In the Jensen analysis, the market timer is assumed to forecast the actual return on the market portfolio, and the forecasted return and the actual return on the market are assumed to have a joint normal distribution. Under these assumptions a market timer's forecasting ability can be measured by the correlation between the market timer's forecast and the realized return on the market. Jensen points out that the separate contributions of micro- and macroforecasting cannot be identified using the structure of the CAPM framework unless for each period the market-timing forecast, the portfolio adjustment corresponding to that forecast, and the expected return on the market are known.

Grant (1977) shows that market-timing actions will affect the results of empirical tests that focus only on microforecasting skills. That is, using the following CAPM framework:

$$Z_j(t) - R(t) = \alpha_j + \beta_j[Z_m(t) - R(t)] + \epsilon_j(t) \qquad \textbf{(17.43)}$$

where $Z_j(t)$ is the return on security j, $R(t)$ is the return on the risk-free asset, and α_j is the expected excess return from microforecasting. Market-timing ability will cause the regression estimate α_j to be downward-biased due to microforecasting ability.

Treynor and Mazuy (1966) add a quadratic term to the previous CAPM framework to test for market-timing ability. They argue that the performance measure should not be a linear function. They contend that the investment manager who can forecast market returns will hold a greater proportion of the market portfolio when the return on the market is high and a lower proportion when the market return is low. Therefore, the portfolio return will be a nonlinear function of the market return.

Kon and Jen (1979) use the Quandt (1972) switching regression technique in a CAPM framework to examine the possibility of changing levels of market-related risk over time for mutual-fund portfolios. Using a maximum likelihood test, they find evidence that many mutual funds do have discrete changes in the level of market-related risk they choose.

Merton (1981) developed a model that is not based on the CAPM framework; from it he is able to analyze market timing through the theoretical structure of the pattern of future returns based upon a posterior distribution of returns. Merton is able to show that up to an additive noise term, the pattern of returns from an investment strategy based upon market timing will be the same as the pattern of returns from a partial protective put-option investment strategy. If this noise (which is caused by forecast error) is diversifiable then, independent of investor's preferences, endowments, or probability beliefs, the equilibrium management fee is proportional to the price of a put option on the market portfolio. These results are obtained with no specific assumptions about the distribution of returns on the market or the way in which the option prices are determined.

Henriksson and Merton's (1981) forecast model, which assumes that a manager's forecasts are observable, is as follows. Let $\gamma(t)$ be the market timer's forecast variable where $\gamma(t) = 1$ if the forecast, made at time $t - 1$ for the time period t, is that $Z_m(t) > R(t)$ and $\gamma(t) = 0$ if the forecast is that $Z_m(t) \leq R(t)$. The probabilities for $\gamma(t)$ conditional upon the realized return on the market are defined by:

$$P_1(t) = \text{Prob}\left[\gamma(t) = 0 \big| Z_m(t) \leq R(t)\right]$$
$$1 - P_1(t) = \text{Prob}\left[\gamma(t) = 1 \big| Z_m(t) \geq R(t)\right]$$

and:

$$P_2(t) = \text{Prob}\left[\gamma(t) = 1 \big| Z_m(t) > R(t)\right]$$
$$1 - P_2(t) = \text{Prob}\left[\gamma(t) = 0 \big| Z_m(t) < R(t)\right]$$

Therefore, $P_1(t)$ is the conditional probability of a correct forecast given that $Z_m(t) \leq R(t)$, and $P_2(t)$ is the conditional probability of a correct forecast given that $Z_m(t) > R(t)$. Assuming that $P_1(t)$ and $P_2(t)$ do not depend upon the magnitude of $|Z_m(t) \leq R(t)|$, the sum of the conditional probabilities of a correct forecast, $P_1(t) + P_2(t)$ is a sufficient statistic for the evaluation of forecasting ability.

However, if a manager's forecasts are not observable, Henriksson and Merton consider a parametric test for the joint hypothesis of no market-timing ability and an assumed generating process for the returns or securities. They assume a pattern of equilibrium security returns that is consistent with the security-market line of the CAPM. They further assume that as a function of a manager's forecast there are discretely different systematic-risk levels that depend on whether or not the return on the market portfolio is forecasted to exceed the return on riskless securities for those portfolios chosen by the portfolio manager. That is, the manager is assumed to have one target beta when predicting that $Z_m(t) > R(t)$ and another target beta

when predicting that $Z_m(t) \leqq R(t)$: their parametric tests are open to the same criticisms that any performance measure is when based upon a CAPM structure.

Using the parametric and nonparametric techniques presented in Henriksson and Merton (1981), Henriksson (1984) evaluated the market-timing performance of 116 open-end mutual funds using monthly data from February 1968 to June 1980. Using a weighted least-squares regression analysis with a correction for heteroscedasticity, the separate contribution from forecasting and market timing were obtained. Results show little evidence of market-timing ability. In fact, 62 percent of the funds had negative estimates of market-timing. Further examination of the estimates for the individual funds shows the existence of a strong negative correlation between microforecasting (selectivity) and macroforecasting (market timing). This negative correlation seems to imply that funds that earn superior returns from stock selection also seem to have negative market-timing ability and performance.

These results tend to be somewhat disturbing, and the possibility of misspecification of the return-generating process must be considered. One potential source of error is the misspecification of the market portfolio. This results from the fact that the proxy used for the market portfolio does not include all risk assets. Another potential source of error is omission of relevant factors in addition to the return on the market portfolio from the return-generating process. If the omitted factor can be identified, then the return-generating process can be modified to take into account the omitted factor.

Chang and Lewellen (1984) compare the performance estimates derived from Henriksson and Merton's (1981) model and the single-factor market model. In order to test Henriksson and Merton's model, first they divide data into two subsets based on the sign of $X(t) = Z_m(t) - R(t)$, the market risk premium. Secondly, they estimate the least-squares lines in each of the two market conditions for every mutual fund, pursuant to the requirement that the lines share a common intercept for each fund. And finally they test whether the coefficient estimates for the two lines β_1^* and β_2^* differ significantly.

Chang and Lewellen's results indicate that the fit of the single-factor market model is little different from Henriksson and Merton's model for the mutual-fund return data examined. Out of the sixty-seven mutual funds studied only four funds indicate any statistical evidence of market timing. Approximately this number might be expected to emerge by chance alone. A similar conclusion applies to the evaluation of the fund manager's security-selection abilities. Only five funds indicate any statistical evidence of selectivity ability. Again, chance alone could produce virtually the same findings.

Their findings show that not much, if any, systematic market-timing activity was undertaken by portfolio managers in the 1970s—and to the extent that it was undertaken, it was often in the wrong direction. This may explain why the fit of the single-factor market model is not very different from the Henriksson and Merton model. Lee and Rahman (1989) update and

improve Chang and Lewellen's results by using better econometric techniques. In addition they estimate the risk-aversion parameter empirically. They find that mutual-fund managers indeed have some timing and selectivity abilities.

Nevertheless, if the individual fund level is considered, it can be seen that Henriksson and Merton's approach has the clear potential to provide a much richer insight into the nature and sources of managed-portfolio performance differentials. For example, of the seven funds that indicate excess-return intercepts from the single-factor market model, only one of the cases coincides with those for which the Henriksson–Merton regression specification gives rise to a significant intercept. Of the other six funds, four have negative and two have positive estimate intercepts according to the single-factor market model; but the Henriksson–Merton model suggests that these differentials can be imputed to market-timing behavior rather than to security-selection activities. In addition, the Henriksson–Merton-model estimates indicate for several additional funds that a combination of significant timing and selectivity phenomena is present—but in opposite directions, resulting in statistically insignificant intercepts.

In short, Chang and Lewellen's results show that although Henriksson and Merton's model is an enhancement of the CAPM that provides a more complete appraisal of the constituents of that model and can eliminate certain biases in the estimates provided by it, neither skillful market timing nor clever security selections are evident in observed mutual-fund return data—nor does their model address the general critique of the CAPM as a benchmark.

Kon and Jen (1979) point out that Jensen's assumption of stationarity of risk through time may be in direct conflict with a managed portfolio. If in a managed portfolio the level systematic risk is adjusted substantially in either direction, a violation of the specifications of the ordinary least-squares (OLS) model occurs. The effect is that the loss of the known distributional properties of the OLS parameter is made conditional on these estimates. One possible problem could be heteroscedastic disturbances, which increase sampling variances of the OLS estimates and reduce their t-values.

Kon and Jen's model assumes a sequence of discrete risk-level decisions; thereby each observation of excess return (total returns on a portfolio minus the risk-free rate) over the measurement interval of n observation was generated by one of N distinct regression equations. In the Jensen model's estimating equation:

$$R'_{jt} = \alpha_j + \beta_j R'_{mt} + \epsilon_{jt}$$

where:

$$R'_{jt} = R_j - R_{ft};$$
$$R'_{mt} = R_{mt} - R_{ft};$$

ϵ_{jt} = normally distributed with a mean of zero and a constant variance;
α_j = the performance measure; and
β_j = assumed stationary.

The stationary assumption is only valid if the fund manager never engages in market timing and if the expected excess return on the market, the variance of the market given information at time $t - 1$, and the percentage change of the variance of the excess return of the portfolio with respect to the expected excess return of the portfolio remain constant. However, if the observations can be indexed according to risk, the Jensen performance measure conditional on the risk level chosen by the fund manager in period t can be applied.

Kon and Jen's model is the performance of the portfolio over the measurement interval relative to a naively selected portfolio with risk level β_i. Total overall selectivity investment performance is the summation of the weighted αs of each subset. Their model is a Jensen model over N distinct risk levels. The actual number (N) of distinct risk levels chosen during the measurement interval is an empirical issue; the actual number of regression regimes must be determined for each mutual fund by statistical inference.

The change in β_t may be merely a change in the target level rather than an active timing decision. Therefore, even if the target risk-level evidence indicates $N > 1$, the timing performance measure may not be meaningful without additional procedure to estimate $R_{ft} - E_t(R_{ft})$ and $R_{mt} - E_t(R_{mt})$. Nevertheless, the empirical methodology used implies that selectivity performance can still be estimated if changes in risk level are the result of a changing investment-opportunity set.

Kon and Jen's methodology utilizes the N regime-switching regression model proposed by Quandt (1972), with a new identifiability condition. In order to ensure that the parameters are identified, the identifiability condition $\beta_N > \beta_{N-1} > \cdots > \beta_1$ is imposed. The strict ordering of risk levels is a result of the ordering of fund managers' forecasts of the unanticipated returns on the market portfolio, $E_t(R_{mt}) - E_t(R_{mt}|\phi_{t-1})$. It is this additional prior information that identifies the model.

Because Kon and Jen's maximum-likelihood estimation procedure presented here assumes an unknown probability that the fund manager will choose regime i for generating observations, the estimation procedure is only applicable to analyzing selectivity performance given the timing decision. In addition, it faces the problem of nonstationarity of market-level parameters. The third problem is a proxy for the fund's target risk level.

The Kon–Jen data consist of mutual funds with complete monthly return data from January 1960 to December 1971. The market proxy is the equal-weighted market-index-form CRSP with a thrity-day Treasury bill rate as a proxy for the risk-free rate. Their simulated results provide confidence in their methodology. Tests of the model specification on a sample of forty-nine mutual funds indicate that for many individual funds it is more likely that the data were generated by a mixture of two or three regression equations rather than by that of a standard linear model. The null hypothesis of risk-level stationarity was rejected by many individual funds, giving a specification for each fund determined by the likelihood-ratio test. This could

explain Jensen's (1968) finding of so few significant t-values in his evidence on selectivity performance. By neglecting this phenomenon and utilizing OLS, the resulting heteroscedastic disturbances increase the sampling variance and reduce the t statistics.

In addition, Jensen's (1968) frequency distribution of $\hat{\alpha}$ was negatively skewed, whereas Kon and Jen found their frequency distribution of $\hat{\alpha}$s to be approximately symmetric about zero. Moreover, if management expenses were added to the mutual fund's rate of return as in the Jensen study, there would certainly be many more significantly positive performance measures. This evidence is clearly inconsistent with the efficient-market hypothesis.

It can be argued that one could expect managers to be successful in forecasting from time to time, whether by uncovering special information or by keener insight into the implications of publicly available information. However, in an efficient market they cannot do this consistently over time. There is very little evidence that any individual fund was able to consistently generate significantly superior performance. In addition, the evidence for the EMH is based on the bias in favor of low-risk securities using the SML benchmark. Therefore, Kon and Jen's evidence is not inconsistent with the hypothesis that mutual-fund managers individually and on average are unable to forecast the future prices on individual securities consistently enough to recover their research expenses, management fees, and commission expenses.

Much of the empirical evidence [Henriksson (1984), Chang and Lewellen (1984), and Kon (1983)] indicates that timing ability is rare. In addition, if timing ability is present, it is often negative, and those funds that do exhibit significant timing performance show negative performance more often than positive performance. Henriksson (1984) found a negative correlation between the measure of security selection and market timing. A number of potential explanations for these results has been suggested, including errors-in-variables bias, misspecification of the market portfolio, and use of a single-factor rather than a multifactor asset-pricing model. Jagannathan and Korajczk (1986) suggest another explanation for the empirical results, which relies on the nonlinear payoff structure of options and option-like securities as well as the specification of the proxy for the market portfolio. They show that the portfolio strategy of buying call options exhibits positive timing performance and negative security selection even though no market forecasting or security-specific forecast is done. If market-timing ability can be viewed as a call option, evidence of positive market timing occurs but the return is reduced by the premium paid for the option, thereby leading to negative security-selection evidence.

The **market proxy** is a portfolio of stocks that are, to a greater or lesser extent, options. The sign of market-timing performance of a given mutual fund may depend on whether the average stock held by the mutual fund has more or less of an option effect than the average stock in the index. The average negative timing performance found in Kon (1983), Chang and

Lewellen (1984), and Henriksson (1984) may be due to the fact that the mutual funds in the sample tend to invest in firms that are larger, better established, and less leveraged than the average firm on the NYSE.

Jagannathan and Korajczyk (1986), using the option-pricing model, found that when the proxy for the market portfolio contains optionlike securities, portfolios with greater (lower) concentration in optionlike securities will show positive (negative) timing performance and negative (positive) selectivity. This provides a possible explanation of previous empirical findings indicating that mutual funds have negative timing ability on average, and that selectivity and timing performance are negatively correlated. If mutual funds tend to invest in higher-quality securities, then average timing performance would be expected to be negative. Also, negative correlation would be expected between selectivity and timing performance if investments were in securities that are less like options. However, Lehman and Modest (1987) and Lee and Rahman (1990) have found that mutual-fund managers have positive timing ability.

A possible explanation for the lack of evidence of timing ability on the aggregate is the possible use of an immunization strategy by the funds. Although timing may be an important aspect within the fund, where assets are bought and sold to maintain a fund's duration, the fund in the aggregate may not display any timing influences. If, indeed, mutual funds do follow an immunization strategy, this could aid in explaining the empirical results, revealing timing activity within funds but not at the aggregate level.

SUMMARY

This chapter has employed the concepts and theory of technical and fundamental analysis to show that security analysts and portfolio managers might utilize theory, methodology, and data information to outperform the market. Both Value Line ranking performance and mutual-fund managers' performance are used to support this conclusion. Overall, this chapter has culled information discussed in previous chapters to explore how security analysis and portfolio management can more effectively be executed.

The next chapter integrates concepts and formulae of performance measures with optimal portfolio-selection models to simplify the procedures and methods for choosing optimal portfolios discussed in Chapters 8 and 10.

QUESTIONS AND PROBLEMS

1. Define or explain the following terms.
    (a) technical analysis
    (b) fundamental analysis
    (c) price–earnings ratio
    (d) Dow theory
    (e) market anomalies
    (f) selectivity
    (g) time series
    (h) ARIMA

2. ABC Corporation is currently paying $2.00 per share in dividends with a payout ratio of 50 percent. Its growth rate is expected to be 10 percent for both earnings and dividends. The firm's cost of capital is 16 percent. What is the current price per share and the P/E ratio for ABC?

3. For ABC Corporation in Question 2 the growth rate is expected to fall to 5 percent for both dividends and earnings. What will happen to the price and P/E ratio if this occurs?

4. If you were interested in testing the relationship between dividends and share value, how would you design a research project to investigate the relationship?

5. Compare technical analysis and fundamental analysis. Which approach makes more sense from an economic viewpoint?

6. Discuss Basu's findings on the relationship between P/E ratios and investment performance. What does this mean in the context of the efficient-market hypothesis?

7. Discuss the two major approaches to time-series analysis.

8. Discuss the procedure Value Line uses in its ranking. What does the success of Value Line's ranking mean in the context of the efficient-market hypothesis?

9. Given the various investment objectives for mutual funds—growth; income and growth; income; and income, growth, and stability—what sort of strategies or investment policies do mutual-fund managers follow in order to achieve these objectives?

10. Compare and contrast Fama's overall performance measure with the performance measures of Sharpe, Treynor, and Jensen.

11. Compare the approaches of a macroforecaster and a microforecaster.

12. Suppose a portfolio manager's performance has been evaluated as superior when compared to the Dow Jones, the S&P, and the NYSE composite index. Does this evaluation make you feel comfortable about this manager's true ability?

13. What is the January effect? Offer some explanations for this anomaly.

14. Discuss how the timing and selectivity of a mutual fund's performance can be tested empirically.

APPENDIX 17A: COMPOSITE FORECASTING METHOD

Most forecasts contain some information that is independent of that contained in other forecasts; thus a combination of the forecasts will, quite often, outperform any of the individual forecasts.

Nelson (1973) has shown that a composite forecast of unbiased forecasts is unbiased. For n individual unbiased forecasts X_i ($i = 1, 2, \ldots, n$) with n

weights a_i, each greater than or equal to zero and all weights summing to one, and a composite forecast X, the value of X is then given as:

$$X = \sum_{i=1}^{n} a_i X_i \qquad \sum_{i=1}^{n} a_i = 1, \, a_i \geq 0$$

The expected value of X is

$$E(X) = E\left(\sum_{i=1}^{n} a_i X_i\right) = \sum_{i=1}^{n} a_i \, E(X_i) = \sum_{i=1}^{n} a_i(\mu_x) = \mu_x$$

in which μ_x is the expected value of X_i. Therefore, the expected value of a combination of n unbiased forecasts is itself unbiased.

If, however, a combination of n forecasts is formed, m of which are biased, the result is generally a biased composite forecast. By letting the expected value of the ith biased forecast be represented as $E(X_i) = \mu_x + \epsilon_i$, the composite bias can be represented as follows:

$$
\begin{aligned}
E(X) &= \sum_{i=1}^{n} a_i \, E(X_i) \\
&= \sum_{i=1}^{m} a_i(\mu + \epsilon_i) + \sum_{i=m+1}^{n} a_i \, (\mu_x) \\
&= \mu_x + \sum_{i=1}^{m} a_i \, \epsilon_i
\end{aligned}
$$

The composite of m biased forecasts has a bias given by a combination of the individual forecast biases. This suggests that the composite of a biased forecast can be unbiased only if $\sum_{i=1}^{m} a_i \, \epsilon_i = 0$. In particular, combining two forecasts, one with a positive bias and one with a negative bias, can, for proper choices of weights, result in an unbiased composite. However, for biased forecasts that do not balance each other, and assuming the assignment of zero weights to biased forecasts is not desired, numerous combinations of weights can be selected, each of which gives a composite that is unbiased.

The choice of weights can follow numerous approaches. These range from the somewhat naive rule of thumb to more involved additive rules. One rule of thumb is that when several alternative forecasts are available but a history of performance on each is not, the user can combine all forecasts by finding their simple average.

Some additive rules may combine the econometric and ARIMA forecasts into a linear composite prediction of the form:

$$A_t = B_1 \, (\text{Econometric})_t + B_2(\text{ARIMA})_t + \epsilon_t \qquad \textbf{(17A.1)}$$

where:

$$
\begin{aligned}
A_t &= \text{actual value for period } t; \\
B_1 \text{ and } B_2 &= \text{fixed coefficients; and} \\
\epsilon_t &= \text{composite prediction error.}
\end{aligned}
$$

Least-squares fitting of (17A.1) requires minimization of the sum of errors over values of B_1 and B_2 and, therefore, provides the minimum mean-square-error linear composite prediction for the sample period. In the case that both the econometric model and ARIMA predictions are individually unbiased, then (17A.1) can be rewritten:

$$A_t = B(\text{Econometric}) + (1 - B)(\text{ARIMA})_t + \epsilon_t \qquad \textbf{(17A.2)}$$

The least-squares estimate of B in (17A.2) is then given by:

$$\hat{B} = \frac{\sum_{t=1}^{N} [(\text{ECM})_t - (\text{ARIMA})_t][A_t - (\text{ARIMA})_t]}{\sum_{t=1}^{N} [(\text{ECM})_t - (\text{ARIMA})_t]^2} \qquad \textbf{(17A.3)}$$

in which $(\text{ECM})_t$ and $(\text{ARIMA})_t$ represent forecasted values from econometric model and ARIMA model, respectively. Equation (17A.3) is seen to be the coefficient of the regression of ARIMA prediction errors $[A_t - (\text{ARIMA})_t]$ on the difference between the two predictions. As would seem quite reasonable, the greater the ability of the difference between the two predictions to account for error committed by $(\text{ARIMA})_t$, the larger will be the weight given to $(\text{Econometric})_t$.

Composite predictions may be viewed as portfolios of predictions. If the econometric model's and ARIMA's errors are denoted by u_{1t} and u_{2t}, respectively, then from (17A.2) the composite prediction error is seen to be

$$\epsilon_t = B(u_{1t}) + (1 - B)(u_{2t}) \qquad \textbf{(17A.4)}$$

The composite error is the weighted average of individual errors. The objective is to minimize the variance of the weighted average, given its expected value. In the case of prediction portfolios the weighted average always has expectation zero if individual predictions are unbiased; or it may be given expectation zero by addition of an appropriate constant.

Minimizing composite error variance over a finite sample of observations leads to the estimate of B given by

$$\hat{B} = \frac{s_2^2 - s_{12}}{s_1^2 + s_2^2 - 2s_{12}} \qquad \textbf{(17A.5)}$$

where s_1^2, s_2^2, and s_{12} are the sample variance of u_{1t}, the sample variance of u_{2t}, and the sample covariance of u_{1t} and u_{2t}, respectively. For large samples, or in the case that the variances Var (u_{1t}) and Var (u_{2t}) and the covariance Cov $(u_{1t}u_{2t})$ are known, Equation (17A.5) becomes

$$B = \frac{\text{Var } (u_{2t}) - \text{Cov } (u_{1t}, u_{2t})}{\text{Var } (u_{1t}) + \text{Var } (u_{2t}) - 2 \text{ Cov } (u_{1t}, u_{2t})} \qquad \textbf{(17A.6)}$$

The minimum variance weight is seen to depend on the covariance between individual errors as well as on their respective variances. Holding the covariance constant, the larger the variance of the ARIMA error relative to

that of the econometric error, the larger the weight given to the econometric prediction.

REFERENCES

Alexander, S. "Price Movements in Speculative Markets: Trends or Random Walks." *Industrial Management Review,* v. 2 (May 1961), pp. 7–26.

Banz, R. W. "The Relationship Between Return and Market Value of Common Stocks." *Journal of Financial Economics,* v. 9 (March 1981), pp. 3–18.

Basu, S. "Investment Performance of Common Stocks in Relation to Their Price-Earnings Ratios: A Test of the Efficient Markets Hypothesis." *Journal of Finance,* v. 32 (June 1977), pp. 663–82.

Bessler, David A., and Jon A. Brandt. "Composite Forecasting of Livestock Prices: An Analysis of Combining Alternative Forecasting Methods." Department of Agricultural Economics Agricultural Experiment Station, Station Bulletin No. 265 (December 1979). Purdue University, West LaFayette, Indiana.

Black, F. "Active and Passive Monetary Policy in a Neoclassical Model." *Journal of Finance,* v. 27 (September 1972), pp. 801–14.

_____, Michael C. Jensen, and Myron Scholes. "The Capital Asset Pricing Model: Some Empirical Tests." In *Studies in the Theory of Capital Markets,* ed. Michael C. Jensen. Praeger, 1972.

Blume, Marshall E., and Irwin Friend. "A New Look at the Capital Asset Pricing Model." *Journal of Finance,* v. 28 (March 1973), pp. 19–34.

Bower, Dorothy H., Richard S. Bower, and Dennis F. Logue. "Arbitrage Pricing Theory and Utility Stock Returns." *Journal of Finance,* v. 39 (September 1984), pp. 1041–54.

Box, George P., and Gwilym M. Jenkins. *Time Series Analysis: Forecasting and Control.* Holden-Day, 1976.

Branch, B. "A Tax Loss Trading Rule." *Journal of Business,* v. 50 (April 1977), pp. 198–207.

Chang, Eric C., and Wilbur G. Lewellen. "Market Timing and Mutual Fund Investment Performance." *Journal of Business,* v. 57 (January 1984), pp. 57–72.

Chen, Nai-Fu, Richard Roll, and Stephen A. Ross. "Economic Forces and the Stock Market: Testing the APT and Alternative Asset Pricing Theories." *Journal of Business,* v. 59 (July 1986), pp. 383–404.

Chen, N., T. E. Copeland, and D. Mayers. "A Comparison of Single and Multifactor Portfolio Performance Methodologies." *Journal of Financial and Quantitative Analysis,* v. 22 (December 1987), pp. 401–17.

Chen S., and C. F. Lee. "Bayesian and Mixed Estimators of Time Varying Betas." *Journal of Economics and Business,* v. 34 (November 1982), pp. 291–301.

Cho, Chinhyung, Edwin J. Elton, and Martin J. Gruber. "On the Robustness of the Roll and Ross Arbitrage Theory." *Journal of Financial and Quantitative Analysis,* v. 19 (March 1984), pp. 1–10.

Copeland, T. E., and D. Mayers. "The Value Line Enigma (1965–1978): A Case Study of Performance Evaluation Issues." *Journal of Financial Economics,* v. 10 (November 1982), pp. 289–322.

Cornell, Bradford. "The Money Supply Announcements Puzzle: Review and Interpretation." *American Economic Review,* v. 73 (June 1983), pp. 644–57.

_____. "Asymmetric Information and Portfolio Performance Measurement." *Journal of Financial Economics,* v. 7 (December 1979), pp. 381–90.

Dhrymes, Phoebus, J., Irwin Friend, and N. Bulent Gultekin. "A Critical Re-examination of the Empirical Evidence on the Arbitrage Pricing Theory." *Journal of Finance,* v. 39 (June 1984), pp. 323–46.

Dybvig, Phillip H., and Stephen A. Ross. "Differential Information and Performance Measurement Using a Security Market Line." *Journal of Finance,* v. 40 (June 1985B), pp. 383–99.

_____. "Yes, the APT Is Testable." *Journal of Finance,* v. 40 (September 1985C), pp. 1173–88.

_____. "The Analytics of Performance Measurement Using a Security Market Line." *Journal of Finance,* v. 40 (June 1985A), pp. 401–16.

Fabbozzi, F. J., C. F. Lee, and S. Rahman. "Errors-in-Variables, Functional Form and Mutual Fund Returns." Mimeo, 1989.

Fama, Eugene F. "Components of Investment Performance." *Journal of Finance,* v. 27 (June 1972), pp. 551–67.

Gehr, Adam, Jr. "Some Tests of the Arbitrage Pricing Theory." *Journal of the Midwest Finance Association,* v. 7 (March 1976), pp. 91–105.

Gentry, James A., and Cheng F. Lee. "Financial Forecasting and the X-11 Model: Preliminary Evidence." In *Advances in Planning and Forecasting,* ed. Cheng F. Lee. JAI Press, 1987.

Grant, D. "Portfolio Performance and the 'Cost' of Timing Decisions." *Journal of Finance,* v. 32 (June 1977), pp. 837–46.

Henriksson, Roy D. "Market Timing and Mutual Fund Performance: An Empirical Investigation." *Journal of Business,* v. 57 (January 1984), pp. 73–96.

_____, and Robert C. Merton. "On Market Timing and Investment Performance II, Statistical Procedures for Evaluating Forecasting Skills." *Journal of Business,* v. 54 (October 1981), pp. 513–33.

Holloway, C. "A Note on Testing and Aggressive Investment Strategy

Using Value Line Ranks." *Journal of Finance,* v. 36 (June 1981), pp. 711–19.

Irwin, Scott H., and J. W. Uhrig. "Do Technical Analysts Have Holes in Their Shoes?" *Review of Research and Future Markets,* v. IV (Winter 1984), pp. 264–77.

Jagannathan, Ravi, and Robert A. Korajczyk. "Assessing the Market Timing Performance of Managed Portfolios." *Journal of Business,* v. 59 (April 1986), pp. 217–235.

Jensen, Michael C. "Optimal Utilization of Market Forecasts and the Evaluation of Investment Performance." In *Mathematical Methods in Investment and Finance,* ed. G. P. Szego and K. Shell. North-Holland, 1972.

———. "Risk, the Pricing of Capital Assets and the Evaluation of Investment Portfolios." *Journal of Business,* v. 42 (April 1969), pp. 167–247.

———. "The Performance of Mutual Funds in the Period 1945–1964." *Journal of Finance,* v. 39 (May 1968), pp. 389–416.

Keim, D. B. "Size-Related Anomalies and Stock Return Seasonality: Further Empirical Evidence." *Journal of Financial Economics,* v. 11 (June 1983), pp. 13–32.

Kon, Stanley J. "The Market-Timing Performance of Mutual Fund Managers." *Journal of Business,* v. 56 (July 1983), pp. 323–47.

———, and Jen, F. C. "The Investment Performance of Mutual Funds: An Empirical Investigation of Timing, Selectivity, and Market Efficiency." *Journal of Business,* v. 52 (July 1979), pp. 363–89.

Lee, C. F., and S. Rahman. "Market Timing, Selectivity and Mutual Fund Performance: An Empirical Investigation." *Journal of Business* (1990), forthcoming.

Lee, C. F., and E. Bubnys. "The Stability of Return, Risk and the Cost of Capital for the Electric Utility Industry." In *Proceedings of the Fifth NARUC Biennial Regulating Information Conference.* Ed. by R. E. Burns. 1986.

Lee, C. F., and H. Park. "Value Line Investment Survey Rank Changes and Beta Coefficients." *Financial Analysts Journal,* v. 43 (November/December 1987), pp. 70–72.

Lee, C. F., and Kuo C. John Wei. "Multi-Factor Multi Indicator Approach to Asset Pricing: Methods and Empirical Evidence." Working Paper, University of Illinois, 1984.

Lintner, John. "The Valuation of Risk Assets and the Selection of Risky Investments in Stock Portfolios and Capital Budgets." *Review of Economics and Statistics,* v. 47 (February 1965), pp. 13–37.

Litzenberger, Robert H., and Krishna Ramaswamy. "The Effect of the Personal Taxes and Dividends on Capital Asset Prices." *Journal of Financial Economics,* v. 76 (June 1979), pp. 163–95.

Mayers, David, and Edward M. Rice. "Measuring Portfolio Performance and the Empirical Content of Asset Pricing Models." *Journal of Financial Economics,* v. 7 (March 1979), pp. 3–28.

Merton, Robert C. "On Market Timing and Investment Performance. I, An Equilibrium Theory of Value for Market Forecasts." *Journal of Business,* v. 54 (July 1981), pp. 363–406.

Mossin, Jan. "Equilibrium in a Capital Asset Market." *Econometrica,* v. 34 (October 1966), pp. 768–83.

Nazer, S. M. *Applied Time Series Analysis for Business and Economic Forecasting.* Marcel Dekker, 1988.

Nelson, Charles R. *Applied Time Series Analysis for Managerial Forecasting.* Holden-Day, 1973.

Quandt, R. E. "A New Approach to Estimating Switching Regressions." *Journal of the American Statistical Association,* v. 67 (June 1972), pp. 306–10.

Reilly, Frank K., Frank T. Griggs, and Wenchi Wong. "Determinants of the Aggregate Stock Market Earnings Multiple." *Journal of Portfolio Management,* v. 10 (Fall 1983), pp. 36–45.

Reinganum, M. R. "Misspecification of Capital Asset Pricing: Empirical Anomalies Based on Earnings Yields and Market Values." *Journal of Financial Economics,* v. 8 (March 1981), pp. 19–46.

Roll, Richard. "A Reply to Mayers and Rice (1979)." *Journal of Financial Economics,* v. 7 (September 1979), pp. 391–400.

––––––. "A Critique of the Asset Pricing Theory's Test Part I: On Past and Potential Testability of the Theory." *Journal of Financial Economics,* v. 4 (March 1977), pp. 129–76.

––––––. "Ambiguity When Performance Is Measured by the Securities Market Line." *Journal of Finance,* v. 33 (September 1978), pp. 1051–69.

––––––, and Stephen A. Ross. "An Empirical Investigation of the Arbitrage Pricing Theory." *Journal of Finance,* v. 35 (December 1980), pp. 1073–1103.

Rosenberg, Barr, and Walt McKibben. "The Prediction of Systematic and Specific Risk in Common Stocks." *Journal of Financial and Quantitative Analysis,* v. 8 (March 1973), pp. 317–33.

Ross, Stephen A. "Return, Risk, and Arbitrage." In *Risk and Return in Finance,* ed. I. Friend and J. L. Bicksler. Ballinger, 1977.

––––––. "The Arbitrage Theory of Capital Asset Pricing." *Journal of Economic Theory,* v. 13 (December 1976), pp. 341–60.

Shanken, Jay. "The Arbitrage Pricing Theory: Is It Testable?" *Journal of Finance,* v. 37 (December 1982), pp. 1129–40.

Sharpe, William F. "Capital Asset Prices: A Theory of Market Equilibrium Under Condition of Risk." *Journal of Finance,* v. 19 (September 1964), pp. 425–42.

————. "Mutual Fund Performance." *Journal of Finance,* v. 39 (January 1966), pp. 119–38.

Shiller, Robert J. "Theories of Aggregate Stock Price Movements." *Journal of Portfolio Management,* v. 10 (Winter 1984), pp. 28–37.

Stickel, S. E. "The Effect of Value Line Investment Survey Rank Changes on Common Stock Prices." *Journal of Financial Economics,* v. 14 (March 1985), pp. 121–43.

Sweeny, R. J. "Some New Filter Rule Tests: Methods and Results." *Journal of Financial and Quantitative Analysis,* v. 23 (September 1988), pp. 285–300.

Taylor, S. J. "Tests of the Random Walk Hypothesis Against a Price-Trend Hypothesis." *Journal of Financial and Quantitative Analysis,* v. 17 (March 1982).

Treynor, Jack L. "How to Rate Management of Investment Funds." *Harvard Business Review,* v. 43 (January/February 1965), pp. 63–75.

————, and R. Ferguson. "In Defense of Technical Analysis." *Journal of Finance,* v. 40 (July 1985), pp. 757–75.

————, and F. Mazuy. "Can Mutual Funds Outguess the Market?" *Harvard Business Review,* v. 44 (July/August 1966), pp. 131–36.

Ulrich, Thomas, and Paul Wachtel. "Market Response of the Weekly Money Supply Announcements in the 1970s." *Journal of Finance,* v. 36 (December 1981), pp. 1063–71.

18 Performance-Measure Approaches for Selecting Optimum Portfolios

Chapter 8 discussed Markowitz's (1952, 1959) full variance-covariance approach to determine optimal weights of a portfolio. Chapter 10 utilized Sharpe's index-model approach to simplify Markowitz's optimal portfolio-selection process. This chapter assumes the existence of a risk-free borrowing and lending rate and advances one step further to simplify the calculation of the optimal weights of a portfolio and the efficient frontier. First discussed are Lintner's (1965) and Elton et al.'s (1976) Sharpe performance-measure approaches for determining the efficient frontier with **short sales allowed.** This is followed by a discussion of the Treynor performance-measure approach for determining the efficient frontier with short sales allowed. The Treynor measure approach is then analyzed for determining the efficient frontier with **short sales not allowed.** And finally, Dow Jones 30 data from January 1980 through December 1984 are employed to demonstrate how the Treynor method can be applied in the real world. Overall, this chapter relates the performance-measure concepts and methods discussed in Chapters 7, 9, and 17 to the portfolio-selection models discussed in Chapters 8 and 10 to make more accessible the insights of optimal portfolio selection.

SHARPE PERFORMANCE-MEASURE APPROACH WITH SHORT SALES ALLOWED

In deriving the capital asset pricing model (CAPM) discussed in Chapter 9, Lintner (1965) suggests a performance-measure approach for determining the efficient frontier discussed in Chapters 8 and 10. Lintner arrived at this approach through a sequence of logical steps.

Following Chapter 8, the objective function for portfolio selection can be expressed:

$$\text{Max } L = \sum_{i=1}^{n} W_i \overline{R}_i + \lambda_1 \left\{ \left[\sum_{j=1}^{n} \sum_{i=1}^{n} W_i W_j \text{ Cov } (R_i, R_j) \right]^{1/2} - \sigma_p \right\}$$
$$+ \lambda_2 \left(\sum_{i=1}^{n} W_i - 1 \right) \quad \textbf{(18.1)}$$

where:

$$\overline{R}_i = \text{average rates of return for security } i;$$
$$W_i \text{ (or } W_j) = \text{the optimal weight for } i\text{th (or } j\text{th) security};$$
$$\text{Cov } (R_i, R_j) = \text{the covariance between } R_i \text{ and } R_j;$$
$$\sigma_p = \text{the standard deviation of a portfolio; and}$$
$$\lambda_1, \lambda_2 = \text{Lagrangian multipliers.}$$

Chapter 8 minimized the variance given the targeted expected rate of return. Equation (18.1) maximizes the expected rates of return given targeted standard deviation.

If a constant risk-free borrowing and lending rate R_f is subtracted from Equation (18.1):

$$\text{Max } L' = \sum_{i=1}^{n} (W_i \overline{R}_i - R_f) + \lambda_1 \left\{ \left[\sum_{i=1}^{n} \sum_{j=1}^{n} W_i W_j \text{ Cov } (R_i, R_j) \right]^{1/2} - \sigma_p \right\} + \lambda_2 \left(\sum_{i=1}^{n} W_i - 1 \right)$$
$$\textbf{(18.2)}$$

Equations (18.1) and (18.2), both formulated as a constrained maximization problem, can be used to obtain optimum portfolio weights W_i ($i = 1, 2, \ldots, n$). Since R_f is a constant, the optimum weights obtained from Equation (18.1) will be equal to those obtained for Equation (18.2). Chapter 8 used the methodology of **Lagrangian multipliers**; it can be shown that Equation (18.2) can be replaced by a nonconstrained maximization method as follows. Incorporating the constant $\sum_{i=1}^{n} W_i = 1$ into the objective function by substituting

$$R_f = (1)R_f = \left(\sum_{i=1}^{n} W_i \right) R_f = \sum_{i=1}^{n} W_i R_f$$

into Equation (18.2):

$$\text{Max } L' = \sum_{i=1}^{n} W_i (\overline{R}_i - R_f) + \lambda_1 \left[\left(\sum_{i=1}^{n} \sum_{j=1}^{n} W_i W_j \text{ Cov } (R_i, R_j) \right)^{1/2} - \sigma_p \right]$$
$$\textbf{(18.2A)}$$

A two-Lagrangian multiplier problem has been reduced to a one-Lagrangian problem as indicated in Equation (18.2A). By using a special property of the relationship between $\sum_{i=j}^{n} (\overline{R}_i - R_j)$ and $\left(\sum_{i=1}^{n} \sum_{j=1}^{n} W_i W_j \text{ Cov } (R_i, R_j) \right)^{1/2}$ the constrained optimization of Equation (18.2A) can be reduced to an unconstrained optimization problem, as indicated in Equation (18.3).[1]

---

[1] Since the ratio of Equation (18.3) is homogeneous of degree zero with respect to W_i. In other words, the ratio L is unchanged by any proportionate change in the weight of W_i.

$$\text{Max } L = \frac{\sum_{i=1}^{n} W_i \, (\overline{R}_i - R_f)}{\left(\sum_{i=1}^{n} W_i^2 \sigma_i^2 + \sum_{i=1}^{n} \sum_{j=1}^{n} W_i W_j \, \sigma_{ij}\right)^{1/2}} \qquad i \neq j \qquad \textbf{(18.3)}$$

where $\sigma_{ij} = \text{Cov }(R_i, R_j)$. Alternatively, the objective function of Equation (18.3) can be developed as follows. This ratio L is equal to excess average rates of return for the ith portfolio divided by the standard deviation of the ith portfolio. This is a **Sharpe performance measure,** as discussed in Chapters 7 and 17.

Following Sharpe (1964) and Lintner (1965), if there is a risk-free lending and borrowing rate (R_f) and short sales are allowed, then the efficient frontier (efficient set) will be linear, as discussed in Chapter 9. In terms of return (R_p) standard-deviation (σ_p) space, this linear efficient frontier is indicated as line $R_f E$ in Figure 18–1. AEC represents a feasible investment opportunity in terms of existing securities to be included in the portfolio when there is no risk-free lending and borrowing rate. If there is a risk-free lending and borrowing rate, then the efficient frontier becomes $R_f E$. An infinite number of linear lines represent the combination of a riskless asset and risky portfolio, such as $R_f A$, $R_f B$, and $R_f E$. It is obvious that line $R_f E$ has the highest slope, as represented by:

$$\Theta = \frac{\overline{R}_p - R_f}{\sigma_p} \qquad \textbf{(18.4)}$$

in which $\overline{R}_p = \sum_{i=1}^{n} W_i \overline{R}_i$, R_f, and σ_p are defined as in Equation (18.2). Thus the efficient set is obtained by maximizing Θ. By imposing the constraint $\sum_{i=1}^{n} W_i = 1$, Equation (18.4) is expressed:

FIGURE 18–1 Linear Efficient Frontier

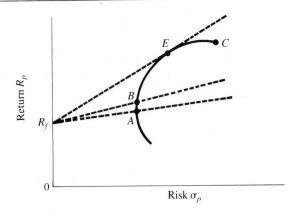

$$\Theta' = \frac{\overline{R}_p - R_f}{\sigma_p} + \lambda \left(\sum_{i=1}^{n} W_i - 1 \right) \tag{18.5}$$

By using the procedure of deriving Equation (18.2A), Equation (18.5) becomes

$$\Theta' = \frac{\sum\limits_{i=1}^{n} W_i (\overline{R}_i - R_f)}{\left(\sum\limits_{i=1}^{n} W_i^2 \sigma_i^2 + \sum\limits_{i=1}^{n} \sum\limits_{j=1}^{n} \sigma_{ij} \right)} \qquad i \neq j \tag{18.5A}$$

This equation is equivalent to Equation (18.3). This approach is used by Elton and Gruber (1987) to derive their objective function for optimal portfolio selection.[2]

Following the maximization procedure discussed earlier in Chapters 8 and 10, it is clear that there are n unknowns to be solved in either Equation (18.3) or Equation (18.5A). Therefore, calculus must be employed to compute n **first-order conditions** to formulate a system of n simultaneous equations:

$$1 \qquad \frac{dL}{dW_1} = 0$$

$$2 \qquad \frac{dL}{dW_2} = 0$$

$$\vdots \qquad \vdots$$

$$n \qquad \frac{dL}{dW_n} = 0$$

From Appendix 18A, the n simultaneous equations used to solve H_i are

$$\begin{aligned}
\overline{R}_1 - R_f &= H_1 \sigma_1^2 + H_2 \sigma_{12} + H_3 \sigma_{13} + \cdots + H_n \sigma_{1n} \\
\overline{R}_2 - R_f &= H_1 \sigma_{12} + H_2 \sigma_2^2 + H_3 \sigma_{23} + \cdots + H_n \sigma_{2n} \\
&\vdots \\
\overline{R}_m - R_f &= H_1 \sigma_{1n} + H_2 \sigma_{2n} + H_3 \sigma_{3n} + \cdots + H_n \sigma_n^2
\end{aligned} \tag{18.6}$$

where:

$H_i = kW_i \ (i = 1, 2, \ldots, n)$; and

$k = -\dfrac{\overline{R}_p - R_f}{\sigma_p^2}$.

The Hs are proportional to the optimum portfolio weight $W_i \ (i = 1, 2, \ldots, n)$ by a constant factor K. To determine the optimum weight W_i, H_i is first

---

solved from the set of equations indicated in Equation (18.6). Having done so the H_i must be called to calculate W_i, as indicated in Equation (18.7).

$$W_i = \frac{H_i}{\sum\limits_{i=1}^{n} H_i} \tag{18.7}$$

If there are only three securities, then Equation (18.6) reduces to:

$$\begin{aligned}
\overline{R}_1 - R_f &= H_1\sigma_1^2 + H_2\sigma_{12} + H_3\sigma_{13} \\
\overline{R}_2 - R_f &= H_1\sigma_{12} + H_2\sigma_2^2 + H_3\sigma_{23} \\
\overline{R}_3 - R_f &= H_1\sigma_{13} + H_2\sigma_{23} + H_3\sigma_3^2
\end{aligned} \tag{18.6A}$$

Sample Problem 18.1 provides further illustration.

Sample Problem 18.1

Let

$$\begin{array}{lll}
\overline{R}_1 = 15\% & \overline{R}_2 = 12\% & \overline{R}_3 = 20\% \\
\sigma_1 = 8\% & \sigma_2 = 7\% & \sigma_3 = 9\% \\
r_{12} = 0.5 & r_{13} = 0.4 & r_{23} = 0.2 \\
R_f = 8\% & &
\end{array}$$

Substituting this information into Equation (18.6A):

$$\begin{aligned}
15 - 8 &= 64H_1 + (0.5)(8)(7)H_2 + (0.4)(8)(9)H_3 \\
12 - 8 &= 0.5(8)(7)H_1 + 49H_2 + (0.2)(7)(9)H_3 \\
20 - 8 &= 0.4(8)(9)H_1 + (0.2)(7)(9)H_2 + 81H_3
\end{aligned}$$

Simplifying:

$$\begin{aligned}
7 &= 64H_1 + 28H_2 + 28.8H_3 \\
4 &= 28H_1 + 49H_2 + 12.6H_3 \\
12 &= 28.8H_1 + 12.6H_2 + 81H_3
\end{aligned} \tag{18.6B}$$

Using Cramer's rule, H_1, H_2, and H_3 can be solved for as follows:

$$H_1 = \frac{\begin{vmatrix} 7 & 28 & 28.8 \\ 4 & 49 & 12.6 \\ 12 & 12.6 & 81 \end{vmatrix}}{\begin{vmatrix} 64 & 28 & 28.8 \\ 28 & 49 & 12.6 \\ 28.8 & 12.6 & 81 \end{vmatrix}}$$

$$= \frac{(4233.6 + 1451.5 + 27783) - (1111.3 + 9072 + 16934.4)}{(10160.6 + 10160.6 + 254016) - (10160.6 + 63504 + 40642.6)}$$

$$= \frac{33468.1 - 27.1177}{160030} = \frac{6350.4}{160030} = 3.97\%$$

$$H_2 = \frac{\begin{vmatrix} 64 & 7 & 28.8 \\ 28 & 4 & 12.6 \\ 28.8 & 12 & 81 \end{vmatrix}}{\begin{vmatrix} 64 & 28 & 28.8 \\ 28 & 49 & 12.6 \\ 28.8 & 12.6 & 81 \end{vmatrix}}$$

$$= \frac{(2540.2 + 9676.6 + 20736) - (9676.8 + 15876 + 3317.8)}{160030}$$

$$= \frac{32952.8 - 28870.6}{160030}$$

$$= 2.55\%$$

$$H_3 = \frac{\begin{vmatrix} 64 & 28 & 7 \\ 28 & 49 & 4 \\ 28.8 & 12.6 & 12 \end{vmatrix}}{\begin{vmatrix} 64 & 28 & 28.8 \\ 28 & 49 & 12.6 \\ 28.8 & 12.6 & 81 \end{vmatrix}}$$

$$= \frac{(3225.6 + 2469.6 + 37632) - (3225.6 + 9408 + 9878.4)}{160030}$$

$$= \frac{20815.2}{160030}$$

$$= 13.01\%$$

Using Equation (18.7), W_1, W_2, and W_3 are obtained:

$$W_1 = \frac{H_1}{\sum\limits_{i=1}^{3} H_i} = \frac{3.97}{3.97 + 2.55 + 13.01} = \frac{3.97}{18.53}$$

$$= 20.33\%$$

$$W_2 = \frac{H_2}{\sum\limits_{i=1}^{3} H_i} = \frac{2.55}{19.53}$$

$$= 13.06\%$$

$$W_3 = \frac{H_3}{\sum\limits_{i=1}^{3} H_i} = \frac{13.01}{19.53}$$

$$= 66.61\%$$

$\overline{R}_p$ and σ_p^2 can be calculated by employing these weights:

Efficient Frontier for Sample Problem 18.1

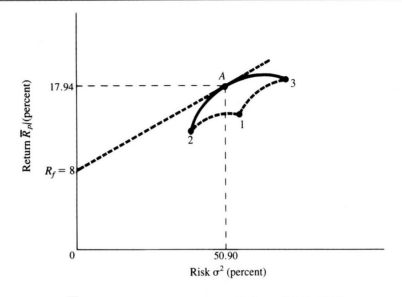

$$\overline{R}_p = (15)(0.2033) + (12)(0.1306) + (20)(0.6661)$$
$$= 3.049 + 1.5672 + 13.322$$
$$= 17.9382\%$$

$$\sigma_p^2 = \sum_{i=1}^{3} W_i^2 \sigma_i^2 + \sum_{i=1}^{3} \sum_{j=1}^{3} W_i W_j r_{ij} \sigma_i \sigma_j \quad i \neq j$$

$$= (0.2033)^2(64) + (0.1306)^2(49) + (0.6661)^2(81)$$
$$+ 2(0.2033)(0.1306)(0.5)(8)(7)$$
$$+ 2(0.2033)(0.6661)(0.4)(8)(9)$$
$$+ 2(0.2)(0.1306)(0.6661)(7)(9)$$
$$= 2.645 + 0.836 + 35.939 + 1.487 + 7.8 + 2.192$$
$$= 50.899\%$$

The efficient frontier for this example is shown in the figure. A represents an efficient portfolio with $\overline{R}_p = 17.94$ percent and $\sigma_p^2 = 50.90$ percent●

TREYNOR-MEASURE APPROACH WITH SHORT SALES ALLOWED

Using the single-index market model discussed in Chapter 10, Elton et al. (1976) define:

$$\sigma_p = \left(\sum_{i=1}^{n} W_i^2 \beta_i^2 \sigma_m^2 + \sum_{\substack{i=1 \\ j \neq i}}^{n} \sum_{j=1}^{n} W_i W_j \beta_i \beta_j \sigma_m^2 + \sum_{i=1}^{n} W_i^2 \sigma_{\epsilon i}^2 \right)^{1/2}$$

Substituting of this value of σ_p into Equation (18.3):

$$L = \frac{\sum\limits_{i=1}^{n} W_i\,(\overline{R}_i - R_f)}{\left(\sum\limits_{i=1}^{n} W_i^2\beta_i^2\sigma_m^2 + \sum\limits_{i=1}^{n}\sum\limits_{j=1}^{n} W_iW_j\beta_i\beta_j\sigma_m^2 + \sum\limits_{i=1}^{n} W_i^2\sigma_{\epsilon i}^2\right)^{1/2}} \tag{18.8}$$

$$j \neq i$$

In order to find the set of W_is that maximizes L, take the derivative of the above equation with respect to each W_i. Let

$$H_i = \left(\frac{R_p - R_f}{\sigma_p^2}\right) W_i$$

since $(\overline{R}_p - R_f)/\sigma_p^2$ is a constant factor for each security to be included in the portfolio. Hence, it can be cancelled by using a standard scaling method:

$$W_i = \frac{H_i}{\sum\limits_{i=1}^{n} H_i} \tag{18.9}$$

From Appendix 18B H_i can be obtained as follows:

$$H_i = \frac{(\overline{R}_i - R_f)}{\sigma_{\epsilon i}^2} - \left(\frac{\sigma_m^2 \sum\limits_{j=1}^{n} \dfrac{(\overline{R}_j - R_f)\,\beta_j}{\sigma_{\epsilon j}^2}}{1 + \sigma_m^2 \sum\limits_{j=1}^{i} \dfrac{\beta_j^2}{\sigma_{ej}^2}}\right)\left(\frac{\beta_i^2}{\sigma_{\epsilon i}^2}\right) \tag{18.10}$$

Equation (18.10) can be modified to:

$$H_i = \frac{\beta_i}{\sigma_{\epsilon i}^2}\left(\frac{\overline{R}_i - R_f}{\beta_i} - C^*\right) \tag{18.11}$$

in which $(\overline{R}_i - R_f)/\beta_i$ is the **Treynor performance measure** as discussed in Chapters 7 and 17. C^* can be defined as:

$$C^* = \frac{\sigma_m^2 \sum\limits_{j=1}^{n} \dfrac{(\overline{R}_j - R_f)\beta_j}{\sigma_{\epsilon j}^2}}{1 + \sigma_m^2 \sum\limits_{j=1}^{i} \dfrac{\beta_j^2}{\sigma_{\epsilon j}^2}} \tag{18.12}$$

The H_is must be calculated for all of the stocks in the portfolio. If H_i is a positive value, this indicates the stock will be held long, whereas a negative value indicates that the stock should be sold short. This method is called the Treynor measure approach. The argument will be clearer when the case of portfolio selection with short sales not allowed is discussed.

To determine the **optimum portfolio** from the H_is (such that 100 percent of funds are invested) the weights must be scaled. One method follows the

standard definition of short sales, which presumes that a short sale of a stock is a source of funds to the investor; it is called the **standard method of short sales.** This standard scaling method is indicated in Equation (18.9). In Equation (18.9), H_i can be positive or negative. This scaling factor includes a definition of short sales and the constraint:

$$\sum_{i=1}^{n} |W_i| = 1$$

A second method (**Lintner's** [1965] **method of short sales**) assumes that the proceeds of short sales are not available to the investor and that the investor must put up an amount of funds equal to the proceeds of the short sale. The additional amount of funds serves as collateral to protect against adverse price movements. Under these assumptions, the constraints on the W_is can be expressed:

$$\sum_{i=1}^{n} |W_i| = 1$$

and the scaling factor is expressed as:

$$W_i = \frac{H_i}{\sum_{i=1}^{n} |H_i|} \qquad \textbf{(18.13)}$$

Sample Problem 18.2 provides further illustration.

Sample Problem 18.2

The following example shows the differences in security weights in the optimal portfolio due to the differing short-sale assumptions. Data associated with regressions of the single-index model are presented in the table. The mean return, $\overline{R}_i$, the excess return $\overline{R}_i - R_f$, the beta coefficient β_i, and the variance of the error term $\sigma_{\epsilon i}^2$ are presented in columns 2 through 5.

(1) Security Number	(2) $\overline{R}_i$	(3) $\overline{R}_i - R_f$	(4) β_i	(5) $\sigma_{\epsilon i}^2$
1	15	10	1	30
2	13	8	2	50
3	10	5	1.43	20
4	9	4	1.33	10
5	7	2	1	30

From the information in the table, using Equations (18.10) and (18.11), H_i ($i = 1, 2, \ldots, 5$) can be calculated:

$$H_1 = \left(\frac{1}{30}\right)\left(\frac{15 - 5}{1}\right) - 3.067 = 0.2311$$

$$H_2 = \left(\frac{2}{50}\right)\left(\frac{13 - 5}{2}\right) - 3.067 = 0.0373$$

$$H_3 = \left(\frac{1.43}{20}\right)\left(\frac{10 - 5}{1.43}\right) - 3.067 = 0.0307$$

$$H_4 = \left(\frac{1.33}{10}\right)\left(\frac{9 - 5}{1.33}\right) - 3.067 = -0.0079$$

$$H_5 = \left(\frac{1}{30}\right)\left(\frac{7 - 5}{1}\right) - 3.067 = -0.0356$$

According to Lintner's method:

$$\sum_{i=1}^{5} |H_i| = 0.3426$$

Now to scale the H_i values into an optimum portfolio, apply Equation (18.13):

$$W_1 = \frac{0.2311}{0.3426} = 0.6745$$

$$W_2 = \frac{0.0373}{0.3426} = 0.1089$$

$$W_3 = \frac{0.0307}{0.3426} = 0.0896$$

$$W_4 = \frac{-0.0079}{0.3426} = -0.0231$$

$$W_5 = \frac{-0.0356}{0.3426} = -0.1039$$

Thus the Lintner model states that an investor should invest 67.45 percent in security 1, 10.89 percent in security 2, and 8.96 percent in security 3. The investor should then sell short 2.31 percent and 10.39 percent of securities 4 and 5, respectively.

If this same example is scaled using the standard definition of short sales $\left(\sum_{i=1}^{5} H_i\right)$, which provides funds to the investor:

$$\sum_{i=1}^{5} H_i = 0.2556$$

$$W_1 = \frac{0.2311}{0.2556} = 0.9041$$

$$W_2 = \frac{0.0373}{0.2556} = 0.1459$$

$$W_3 = \frac{0.0307}{0.2556} = 0.1201$$

$$W_4 = \frac{-0.0079}{0.2556} = -0.0309$$

$$W_5 = \frac{-0.0356}{0.2556} = -0.1393$$

Using this definition of short sales provides that the investor should invest 90.41 percent of his or her money in security 1, and so on. If all W_is are added together, they equal 100 percent. This is true because the definition says that the funds received from selling short a security should be used to purchase more of the other securities●

The difference between Lintner's method and the standard method arc due to the different definitions of short selling discussed earlier. The standard method assumes that the investor has the proceeds of the short sale, while Lintner's method assumes that the short seller does not receive the proceeds and must provide funds as collateral.

The method discussed in this section does not require the inputs of covariance among individual securities. Hence, it is a simpler method than that of the Sharpe performance-measure method discussed in the previous section.

The relative advantage of the Sharpe performance method over the Treynor performance method is exactly identical to the relative advantage of the Markowitz model, discussed in Chapter 8, over the Sharpe single-index model, discussed in Chapter 10. In sum, the Treynor performance method for portfolio selection requires the information of both the risk-free rate and the market rates of return.

TREYNOR-MEASURE APPROACH WITH SHORT SALES NOT ALLOWED

Elton et al. (1976) also derive a Treynor-measure approach with short sales not allowed. From Appendix 18C, Equation (18.11) should be modified to:

$$H_i = \frac{\beta_i}{\sigma_{\epsilon i}} \left(\frac{\overline{R}_i - R_f}{\beta_i} - C_i^* \right) + \mu_i \qquad \textbf{(18.15)}$$

where:

$$C_i^* = \frac{\sigma_m^2 \sum_{j=1}^{i} \frac{\overline{R}_j - R_f}{\sigma_{\epsilon j}^2} \beta_j}{1 + \sigma_m^2 \sum_{j=1}^{i} \frac{\beta_j^2}{\sigma_{\epsilon j}^2}} \qquad \textbf{(18.16)}$$

If all securities have positive β_is, the following three-step procedure from Elton et al. can be used to choose securities to be included in the optimum portfolio.[3]

1. Use the Treynor performance measure $(\overline{R}_i - R_f)/\beta_i$ to rank the securities in descending order.
2. Use Equation (18.16) to calculate C_i^* for all securities.
3. Include in the portfolio all securities for which $(\overline{R}_i - R_f)/\beta_i$ is larger than C_i^*.

Sample Problem 18.3 provides further illustration.

Sample Problem 18.3

The Center for Research in Security Prices tape was the source of five years of monthly return data, from January 1980 through December 1984, for the thirty stocks in the Dow Jones Industrial Averages. The value-weighted average of the NYSE index was used as the market while three-month Treasury-bill rates were used as the risk-free rate.

The single-index model was used with an ordinary least-squares regression procedure to determine each stock's beta. The following data were compiled for each stock.

1. The mean monthly return $\overline{R}_i$
2. The mean excess return $\overline{R}_i - R_f$
3. The beta coefficient
4. The variance of the residual errors
5. The Treynor performance measure $(\overline{R}_i - R_f)/\beta_i$

All data are listed in the worksheet on page 633, which lists the companies in descending order of Treynor performance measure.[4]

To calculate the C_i^* as defined in Equation (18.16), calculate $(\overline{R}_j - R_f)\beta_j/\sigma_{\epsilon j}^2$, $\sum_{j=1}^{i} [(\overline{R}_j - R_f)\beta_j/\sigma_{\epsilon j}^2]$, and $\beta_j^2/\sigma_{\epsilon j}^2$. $\sum_{j=1}^{i} (\beta_j^2/\sigma_{\epsilon j}^2)$ is calculated and presented in the worksheet. Substituting $\sigma_m^2 = 0.00207$, $\sum_{j=1}^{i} [(\overline{R}_j - R_f) \beta_j/\sigma_{\epsilon j}^2$, and $\sum_{j=1}^{i} (\beta_j^2/\sigma_{\epsilon j}^2)$ into Equation (18.16) produces C_i^* for every firm as listed in the last column in the worksheet.

Using company 13 as an example:

---

[3] If the beta coefficient β_i for ith security is positive, then the size of H_i depends on the sign of the term in parentheses. Therefore, if a security with a particular $(\overline{R}_i - R_f)/\beta_i$ is included in the optimum portfolio, all securities with a positive beta that have higher values of $(\overline{R}_i - R_f)/\beta_i$ must be included in the optimum portfolio.

[4] This set of data has been analyzed in Chapter 16. The names of these thirty firms can be found in Table 16–1.

Worksheet for Dow Jones Industrial Averages

Security Number	Mean ($\bar{R}_i$)	Standard Deviation (σ_i)	(1) $\bar{R}_i - R_f$	(2) Beta (β_i)	(3) σ_{ei}^2	(4) $\dfrac{(\bar{R}_i - R_f)}{\beta_i}$	(5) $\dfrac{(\bar{R}_i - R_f)\beta_i}{\sigma_{ei}^2}$	(6) Cumulative Sum (5)	(7) $\dfrac{\beta_i^2}{\sigma_{ei}^2}$	(8) Cumulative Sum (7)	(9) C_i^*
5	0.0146	0.0487	0.0056	0.3052	0.00219	0.0183	0.7804	0.7804	42.53	42.53	0.001484
22	0.0187	0.0567	0.0097	0.5440	0.00264	0.0178	1.9988	2.7792	112.10	154.63	0.004358
3	0.0217	0.0955	0.0127	0.7164	0.00812	0.0177	1.1205	3.8997	63.21	217.84	0.005563
30	0.0156	0.0827	0.0065	0.4512	0.00644	0.0144	0.4554	4.3551	31.61	249.45	0.005945
18	0.0152	0.0579	0.0062	0.4348	0.00275	0.0143	0.9803	5.3354	68.75	318.19	0.006658
4	0.0229	0.0872	0.0139	1.0480	0.00545	0.0133	2.6729	8.0082	201.52	519.72	0.007985
11	0.0189	0.0576	0.0099	0.8900	0.00177	0.0111	4.9780	12.9862	447.51	967.23	0.008954
29	0.0239	0.0855	0.0149	1.3677	0.00364	0.0109	5.5986	13.5848	513.90	1481.13	0.009461
13	0.0201	0.0786	0.0111	1.0605	0.00398	0.0105	2.9577	21.5424	282.58	1763.71	0.009588
15	0.0163	0.0553	0.0072	0.7214	0.00204	0.0100	2.5461	24.0886	255.11	2018.82	0.009628
24	0.0178	0.0781	0.0087	0.9286	0.00441	0.0094	1.8319	25.9205	195.53	2214.35	0.009609
10	0.0174	0.0602	0.0083	0.8890	0.00207	0.0093	3.5646	29.4851	381.80	2596.15	0.009575
12	0.0147	0.0673	0.0057	0.6414	0.00372	0.0089	0.9828	30.4679	110.59	2706.74	0.009551
21	0.0196	0.0861	0.0106	1.1991	0.00459	0.0088	2.7692	33.2370	313.26	3019.99	0.009487
9	0.0125	0.0578	0.0034	0.4033	0.00302	0.0084	0.4540	33.6911	53.86	3073.85	0.009471
23	0.0125	0.0519	0.0035	0.5368	0.00213	0.0065	0.8821	34.5731	135.28	3209.13	0.009363
27	0.0153	0.0843	0.0062	1.0035	0.00513	0.0062	1.2128	35.7860	196.30	3405.43	0.009202
20	0.0129	0.0523	0.0038	0.7361	0.00168	0.0052	1.6650	37.4509	322.53	3727.96	0.008893
28	0.0153	0.0750	0.0062	1.2668	0.00248	0.0049	3.1670	40.6179	647.09	4375.05	0.008360
2	0.0127	0.0880	0.0037	0.9167	0.00609	0.0040	0.5569	41.1749	137.99	4513.03	0.008241
25	0.0133	0.0880	0.0043	1.0770	0.00548	0.0040	0.8451	42.0200	211.67	4724.70	0.008068
17	0.0142	0.0849	0.0052	1.4099	0.00331	0.0037	2.2149	44.2349	600.55	5325.25	0.007615
7	0.0113	0.0990	0.0023	1.3117	0.00643	0.0018	0.4692	44.7041	267.58	5592.83	0.007357
8	0.0107	0.0656	0.0017	0.9693	0.00247	0.0018	0.6671	45.3712	380.38	5973.21	0.007027
1	0.0084	0.0810	-0.0006	1.1621	0.00392	-0.0005	-0.1779	45.1934	344.51	6317.72	0.006645
19	0.0087	0.0544	-0.0004	0.4489	0.00256	-0.0009	-0.0710	45.1232	78.72	6396.44	0.006559
6	0.0060	0.0991	-0.0031	1.4217	0.00586	-0.0022	-0.7521	44.3711	344.92	6741.36	0.006141
26	0.0056	0.0709	-0.0034	0.8519	0.00360	-0.0040	-0.8046	43.5666	201.59	6942.95	0.005866
14	-0.0023	0.1158	-0.0114	1.4883	0.00908	-0.0077	-1.8686	41.6980	243.95	7186.90	0.005436
16	-0.0113	0.1698	-0.0203	1.2886	0.02561	-0.0158	-1.0214	40.6766	64.84	7251.74	0.005258

$R_m = 0.0125$
$R_f = 0.0090$
$Var(R_m) = 0.00207$

Positive Optimum Weights for Ten Securities

Security Number	H_i	$\beta_i/\sigma^2_{\epsilon i}$	$\dfrac{(\bar{R}_i - R_f)}{\beta_i}$	(A) Optimum Percentage	(B) Mean $\bar{R}_i$	(A) × (B)
5	1.2093	139.45	0.0183	0.1736	0.0146	0.0025
22	1.6833	205.98	0.0178	0.2416	0.0187	0.0045
3	0.7206	88.18	0.0178	0.1034	0.0218	0.0023
30	0.3416	70.11	0.0145	0.0490	0.0156	0.0008
18	0.7232	158.18	0.0142	0.1038	0.0152	0.0016
4	0.7056	192.16	0.0133	0.1013	0.0229	0.0023
11	0.7408	503.28	0.0111	0.1063	0.0189	0.0020
29	0.4778	375.61	0.0109	0.0686	0.0239	0.0016
13	0.2325	266.66	0.0105	0.0334	0.0201	0.0007
15	0.1314	353.19	0.0100	0.0189	0.0163	0.0003
Total =	6.9661			1.0000	$\bar{R}_p$ =	0.0186

$C^* = 0.009628$

$$C^*_{13} = \frac{(0.00207)(21.5424)}{1 + (0.00207)(1763.71)} = 0.009588$$

From C^*_i of the worksheet it is clear that there are ten securities that should be included in the portfolio. The estimated $\beta_i/\sigma^2_{\epsilon i}$, $(\bar{R}_i - R_f)/\beta_i$, and C^*_i of these ten securities are listed in the table at the top of this page. Substituting this information into Equation (18.15) produces H_i for all ten securities. Using security 5 as an example:

$$H_5 = (139.45)(0.0183 - 0.009628) = 1.2093$$

Using Equation (18.12) the optimum weights can be estimated for all ten securities, as indicated in the table. In other words, 17.36 percent of our fund should be invested in security 5, 24.16 percent in security 22, 10.34 percent in security 3, 4.90 percent in security 30, 10.38 percent in security 18, 10.13 percent in security 4, 10.63 percent in security 11, 6.86 percent in security 29, 3.34 percent in security 13, and 1.63 percent in security 15. Based upon the optimal weights, the average rate for the portfolio $\bar{R}_p$ is calculated as 1.86 percent, as presented in the last column of the table above●

IMPACT OF SHORT SALES ON OPTIMAL-WEIGHT DETERMINATION

Chapter 8 discussed the Markowitz model of portfolio analysis. The Markowitz model requires a large number of inputs, as it is necessary to estimate the covariance between each pair of securities. In Chapter 10 the analysis was simplified by the assumption that security returns were related through

a common response to some market index. This model, known as Sharpe's single-index model, greatly reduces the number of inputs necessary to analyze the risk and return characteristics of portfolios. In both the Markowitz and Sharpe models, the analysis is facilitated by the presence of short selling.

This chapter discusses a method proposed by Elton and Gruber for the selection of optimal portfolios. Their method involves ranking securities based on their excess return to beta ratio, and choosing all securities with a ratio greater than some particular cutoff level C^*. It is interesting to note that while the presence of short selling facilitated the selection of the optimum portfolio in both the Markowitz and Sharpe models, it complicates the analysis when we use the Elton and Gruber approach. From Sample Problem 18.3, using the Dow Jones Industrial Average (DJIA), absence of short selling allowed formation of the optimal portfolio using only ten stocks. When short selling was allowed, the number of securities needed to hold or sell short included all thirty securities on the DJIA, as presented in Table 18–1. Table 18–1 indicates that all securities should be included in the optimal portfolio, which includes eighteen securities buying long and twelve securities selling short. In this case, the average rate of return for the optimal portfolio $\overline{R}_p$ is 3.69 percent.

ECONOMIC RATIONALE OF THE TREYNOR PERFORMANCE-MEASURE METHOD

Cheung and Kwan (1988) have derived an alternative simple rate of optimal portfolio selection in terms of the single-index model. First, Cheung and Kwan relate C_i^* as defined in Equation (18.12) to the correlation coefficient between the portfolio rates of return with i securities R_i and market rates of return $R_m(\rho_i)$:

$$\rho_i = \frac{C_i^*}{\sigma_m \Theta_i} \tag{18.17}$$

where:

$$\rho_i = \sigma_{im}/\sigma_i\sigma_m;$$
$$\sigma_{im} = \text{covariance between } R_i \text{ and } R_m;$$
$$\Theta_i = (\overline{R}_i - R_f)/\sigma_i, \text{ the Sharpe performance measure associated}$$
with the ith portfolio; and
$$\sigma_i \text{ and } \sigma_m = \text{standard deviation for } i\text{th portfolio and market portfolio,}$$
respectively.

Cheung and Kwan show that ρ_i and C_i^* display the same functional behavior for optimal portfolio selection. In other words, if portfolios are formed by adding securities successively from the highest rank to the lowest rank, the optimal portfolio is reached when the correlation of the portfolio returns and

TABLE 18-1   Optimal Weights for Dow Jones 30 Securities (Short Sales Allowed)

	Z_i	$\beta_i/\sigma_{\epsilon i}^2$	$(\overline{R}_i - R_f)/\beta_i$	(A) Optimum Percentage	(B) Mean $(\overline{R}_i)$	(A) × (B)
6	1.8290	139.45	0.0183	0.1934	0.0146	0.0028
3	2.5906	205.98	0.0178	0.2740	0.0187	0.0051
4	1.1084	88.18	0.0178	0.1172	0.0218	0.0026
30	0.6493	70.11	0.0145	0.0687	0.0156	0.0011
13	1.4187	158.18	0.0142	0.1500	0.0152	0.0023
5	1.5476	192.16	0.0133	0.1637	0.0229	0.0038
12	2.9869	503.28	0.0111	0.3159	0.0189	0.0060
29	2.1333	375.61	0.0109	0.2256	0.0239	0.0054
15	1.4092	266.66	0.0105	0.1490	0.0201	0.0030
17	1.7034	353.19	0.0100	0.1802	0.0163	0.0029
24	0.8856	210.78	0.0094	0.0937	0.0178	0.0017
11	1.7870	429.67	0.0094	0.1890	0.0174	0.0033
14	0.6351	172.23	0.0089	0.0672	0.0147	0.0010
22	0.9535	261.35	0.0088	0.1008	0.0196	0.0020
10	0.4414	134.24	0.0085	0.0467	0.0125	0.0006
23	0.3382	252.57	0.0065	0.0358	0.0125	0.0004
27	0.1973	195.71	0.0062	0.0209	0.0153	0.0003
21	0.0015	439.05	0.0052	0.0002	0.0129	.0000
28	− 0.1443	511.50	0.0049	− 0.0153	0.0153	− 0.0002
2	− 0.1783	150.42	0.0040	− 0.0189	0.0127	− 0.0002
25	− 0.2411	196.68	0.0040	− 0.0255	0.0133	− 0.0003
19	− 0.6427	425.71	0.0037	− 0.0680	0.0142	− 0.0010
8	− 0.7106	203.91	0.0017	− 0.0752	0.0113	− 0.0008
9	− 1.3697	392.78	0.0017	− 0.1449	0.0107	− 0.0015
1	− 1.6984	296.67	− 0.0005	− 0.1796	0.0084	− 0.0015
20	− 1.0584	175.05	− 0.0008	− 0.1119	0.0087	− 0.0010
7	− 1.7824	242.55	− 0.0021	− 0.1885	0.0060	− 0.0011
26	− 2.1752	236.37	− 0.0040	− 0.2301	0.0056	− 0.0013
16	− 2.1036	163.96	− 0.0076	− 0.2225	− 0.0023	0.0005
18	− 1.0559	50.32	− 0.0158	− 0.1117	− 0.0113	0.0013
Total	9.4551			1.0000		$\overline{R}_p = 0.0369$

$Z_i = [\beta_i/\sigma_{\epsilon i}^2]\{[(\overline{R}_i - R_f)/\beta_i] - C^*\};\ C^* = 0.0052.$

the index is at its maximum. Since the expected return on the index must be positive if the investor is to invest in stocks, an objective of the investor's using the single-index model to establish the risk-return tradeoff is to pick securities that benefit the most from a market upswing. Hence, the role of index in the selection of securities for an optimum portfolio is demonstrated explicitly.

Based upon the single-index model and the risk decomposition discussed in Chapter 7, the following relationships can be defined:

1.
$$\rho_i = \frac{\sigma_{im}}{\sigma_i \sigma_m}$$

2.
$$\sigma_{im} = \beta_i \sigma_m^2 \qquad \textbf{(18.18)}$$

3.
$$\sigma_i^2 = \beta_i^2 \sigma_m^2 + \sigma_{\epsilon i}^2$$

From Equation (18.18), Cheung and Kwan define ρ_i in terms of β_i, σ_m^2, and σ_i as

$$\rho_i = \sqrt{\beta_i^2 \sigma_m^2 / \sigma_i^2} = \sqrt{1 - \frac{\sigma_{\epsilon i}^2}{\sigma_i^2}}$$

in which $\sigma_{\epsilon i}^2$ is the nonsystematic risk for the ith portfolio. They use both ρ_i and Θ_i to select securities for an optimum portfolio, and they conclude that ρ_i can be used to replace Θ_i in selecting securities for an optimum portfolio. Nevertheless, Θ_i information is still needed to calculate the weights for each security. Hence, Cheung and Kwan's ρ_i criteria is good only for understanding Elton and Gruber's performance-measure method for portfolio selection.

SUMMARY

Following Elton et al. (1976) and Elton and Gruber (1987) we have discussed the performance-measure approaches to selecting optimal portfolios. We have shown that the performance-measure approaches for optimal portfolio selection are complementary to the Markowitz full variance-covariance method discussed in Chapter 8 and the Sharpe index-model method discussed in Chapter 10. These performance-measure approaches are thus worthwhile for students of finance to study following an investigation of the Markowitz variance-covariance method and Sharpe's index approach.

QUESTIONS AND PROBLEMS

1. Define or explain the following terms.
   (a) short selling   (b) single-index model
   (c) Treynor measure   (d) Sharpe measure
2. A portfolio earns an annual rate of return of 15 percent with a standard deviation of 10 percent. The risk-free rate is 7 percent and the return on the market is 12 percent. The portfolio beta is 0.8.
   (a) Calculate Sharpe's performance index.
   (b) Calculate Treynor's performance index.
   (c) Which measure is most useful in assessing performance?
3. Given the information in the table at the top of page 638, calculate each security's weight in the optimal portfolio using (a) Lintner's method and (b) the standard method. Why are the weights different?

Security	$\overline{R}_i$	$\overline{R}_i - R_f$	β_i	σ_i^2
A	10	6	1.3	30
B	9	5	1.2	20
C	8	4	1.7	50
D	7	3	0.6	10

4. Given the following information, use the Sharpe performance-measure approach with short sales allowed to calculate the return and risk of the optimum portfolio. Draw a graph of the efficient frontier.

Security	$\overline{R}_i$	σ_i	r_{AB}	r_{AC}	r_{BC}	R_f
A	10%	10%	0.5			6%
B	8%	6%		0.3		
C	7%	5%			0.8	

5. Review and compare the alternative portfolio-selection methods discussed in Chapters 8, 10, and 18. Which method do you like most? Why?

APPENDIX 18A: DERIVATION OF EQUATION (18.6)

The objective function L as defined in Equation (18.3) can be rewritten:

$$\text{Max } L = \left[\sum_{i=1}^{n} W_i(\overline{R}_i - R_f) \right] \left[\sum_{i=1}^{n} W_i^2 \sigma_i^2 + \sum_{i=1}^{n} \sum_{j=1}^{n} W_i W_j \sigma_{ij} \right]^{-1/2} \qquad i \neq j$$

Then, following the product and chain rule, we have:

$$\frac{dL}{dW_i} = \frac{d}{dW_i} \left[\sum_{i=1}^{n} W_i(\overline{R}_i - R_f) \right] \left[\sum_{i=1}^{n} W_i \sigma_i^2 + \sum_{i=1}^{n} \sum_{j=1}^{n} W_j \sigma_{ij} \right]^{-1/2} \qquad i \neq j$$

$$= \left[\sum_{i=1}^{n} W_i^2 \sigma_i^2 + \sum_{i=1}^{n} \sum_{j=1}^{n} W_i W_j \sigma_{ij} \right]^{-1/2} \times \frac{d}{dw_i} \left[\sum_{i=1}^{n} W_i(\overline{R}_i - R_f) \right]$$

$$+ \left[\sum_{i=1}^{n} W_i(\overline{R}_i - R_f) \right] \frac{d}{dw_i} \left[\sum_{i=1}^{n} W_i^2 \sigma_i^2 + \sum_{i=1}^{n} \sum_{j=1}^{n} W_i W_j \sigma_{ij} \right]^{-1/2}$$

$$= \left[\sum_{i=1}^{n} W_i^2 \sigma_i^2 + \sum_{i=1}^{n} \sum_{j=1}^{n} W_i W_j \sigma_{ij} \right]^{-1/2} [\overline{R}_i - R_f] \qquad \text{(18A.1)}$$

$$- \tfrac{1}{2} \left[\sum_{i=1}^{n} W_i(\overline{R}_i - R_f) \right] \left[\sum_{i=1}^{n} W_i^2 \sigma_i^2 + \sum_{i=1}^{n} \sum_{j=1}^{n} W_i W_j \sigma_{ij} \right]^{-3/2}$$

$$\times \left[2W_i\sigma_i^2 + 2\sum_{j=1}^{n} W_j\sigma_{ij} \right]$$
$$= 0 \quad (i = 1, 2, \ldots, n)$$

Multiplying Equation (18A.1) by $\left[\sum_{i=1}^{n} W_i^2\sigma_i^2 + \sum_{i=1}^{n}\sum_{j=1}^{n} W_iW_j\sigma_{ij} \right]^{1/2}$, $i \neq j$, and rearranging yields:

$$\bar{R}_i - R_f = \left(\frac{\sum_{i=1}^{n} W_i(\bar{R}_i - R_f)}{\sum_{i=1}^{n} W_i^2\sigma_i^2 + \sum_{j=1}^{n}\sum_{j=1}^{n} W_iW_j\sigma_{ij}}{i \neq j} \right)(W_i\sigma_i^2 + \sum_{j=1}^{n} W_j\sigma_{ij}) \textbf{(18A.2)}$$

Defining

$$k = \frac{\sum_{i=1}^{n} W_i(\bar{R}_i - R_f)}{\sum_{i=1}^{n} W_i^2\sigma_i^2 + \sum_{i=1}^{n}\sum_{j=1}^{n} W_iW_j\sigma_{ij}} \quad i \neq j$$

yields

$$-k\left(W_i\sigma_i^2 + \sum_{i=1}^{n} W_i\sigma_{ij}\right) + (\bar{R}_i - R_f) = 0 \quad j \neq i$$

Therefore:

$$\frac{dL}{dW_i} = -(kW_1\sigma_{1i} + kW_2\sigma_{2i} + \cdots + kW_i\sigma_i^2 + \cdots$$
$$+ kW_n\sigma_{ni}) + (R_i - R_f)$$
$$= 0$$

Define $H_i = kW_i$, where the W_i are the fractions to invest in each security and the H_i are proportional to this fraction. Substituting H_i for kW_i:

$$\bar{R}_i - R_f = H_i\sigma_{1i} + H_2\sigma_{2i} + \cdots + H_i\sigma_i^2 + \cdots + H_n\sigma_{ni}$$

There is one equation like this for each value of i.

$$\bar{R}_1 - R_f = H_1\sigma_1^2 + H_2\sigma_{12} + \cdots + H_n\sigma_{1n}$$
$$\bar{R}_2 - R_f = H_1\sigma_{21} + H_2\sigma_2^2 + \cdots + H_n\sigma_{2n}$$
$$\vdots$$
$$\bar{R}_n - R_f = H_1\sigma_{n1} + H_2\sigma_{n2} + \cdots + H_n\sigma_n^2$$

This is Equation (18.6) in the text.

APPENDIX 18B: DERIVATION OF EQUATION (18.10)

Following the optimization procedure for deriving Equation (18A.2) in Appendix 18A:

$$\frac{dL}{dW_i} = (\overline{R}_i - R_f) - \frac{\sum\limits_{i=1}^{n} W_i(\overline{R}_i - R_f)}{\sigma_p^2} (W_i\beta_i^2\sigma_m^2 + \beta_i \sum\limits_{j=1}^{n} W_j\beta_j\sigma_m^2 + W_i\sigma_{\epsilon i}^2)$$
$$= 0 \quad j \neq i$$

Let $H_i = [(\overline{R}_P - R_f)/\sigma_p^2] W_i$ and, solving for any H_i,

$$H_i = \frac{\overline{R}_i - R_f}{\sigma_{\epsilon i}^2} - \frac{\beta_i\sigma_m^2 \sum\limits_{j=1}^{n} H_j\beta_j}{\sigma_{\epsilon i}^2} \tag{18B.1}$$

Multiplying both sides of the equation by β_i:

$$H_i\beta_i = \frac{(\overline{R}_i - R_f)\beta_i}{\sigma_{\epsilon i}^2} - \frac{\beta_i\sigma_m^2 \sum\limits_{j=1}^{n} H_j\beta_j^2}{\sigma_{\epsilon i}^2} \tag{18B.2}$$

Adding together the n equations of this form yields:

$$\sum\limits_{j=1}^{n} H_j\beta_j = \frac{\sum\limits_{j=1}^{n} \dfrac{(\overline{R}_j - R_f)\beta_j}{\sigma_{\epsilon j}^2}}{1 + \sigma_m^2 \sum\limits_{j=1}^{n} \dfrac{\beta_j^2}{\sigma_{\epsilon j}^2}} \tag{18B.3}$$

By substituting Equation (18B.3) into Equation (18B.1), Equation (18.10) is obtained.

APPENDIX 18C: DERIVATION OF EQUATION (18.16)

This appendix discusses the use of performance measures to examine the optimal portfolio with short sales not allowed. Therefore, Equation (18B.1) from Appendix 18.B must be modified:

$$H_i = \frac{\overline{R}_i - R_f}{\sigma_{\epsilon i}^2} - \frac{\beta_i\sigma_m^2}{\sigma_{\epsilon i}^2} \sum\limits_{j=1}^{n} \beta_j H_j + \mu_i \tag{18C.1}$$

where $H_i \geq 0$, $\mu_i \geq 0$, and $\mu_i H_i = 0$ for all i.

The justification of this equation can be found in Elton et al. (1976). Assuming all stocks that would be in an optimal portfolio (called d) can be

found, and then arranging these stocks as $i = 1, 2, \ldots, d$, for the subpopulation of stocks that make up the optimal portfolio:

$$H_i = \frac{\overline{R}_i - R_f}{\sigma_{\epsilon i}^2} - \frac{\beta_i \sigma_m^2}{\sigma_{\epsilon i}^2} \sum_{j=1}^{d} H_j \beta_j \quad \text{and} \quad \mu_i = 0 \qquad \text{(18C.2)}$$

Multiplying both sides by β_j, summing over all stocks in d, and rearranging yields:

$$\sum_{j=1}^{d} H_j \beta_j = \frac{\displaystyle\sum_{j=1}^{d} \left(\frac{\overline{R}_j - R_f}{\sigma_{\epsilon j}^2} \beta_j \right)}{1 + \sigma_m^2 \displaystyle\sum_{j=1}^{d} \frac{\beta_j}{\sigma_{\epsilon j}^2}} \qquad \text{(18C.3)}$$

Notice since the set d contains all stocks with positive H_i:

$$\sum_{j=1}^{n} H_j \beta_j = \sum_{j=1}^{d} H_j \beta_j$$

and let:

$$C = \sigma_m^2 \frac{\displaystyle\sum_{j=1}^{d} \frac{R_j - \overline{R}_f}{\sigma_{\epsilon j}^2} \beta_j}{1 + \sigma_m^2 \displaystyle\sum_{j=1}^{n} \frac{\beta_j^2}{\sigma_{\epsilon j}^2}} \qquad \text{(18C.4)}$$

Using (18C.4), the following equation for H_i is obtained after substitution and rearranging from Equation (18C.1):

$$H_i = \frac{\beta_i}{\sigma_{\epsilon i}^2} \left(\frac{\overline{R}_i - R_f}{\beta_i} - C \right) + \mu_i \qquad \text{(18C.5)}$$

Since $\mu_i \geq 0$, the inclusion of μ_i can only increase the value of H_i. Therefore, if H_i is positive with $\mu_i = 0$, μ_i can never make it zero and the security should be included. If $H_i < 0$ when $\mu_i = 0$, positive values of μ_i can increase H_i. However, because the product of μ_i and H_i must equal zero, as indicated in Equation (18C.1), positive values of μ_i imply $H_i = 0$. Therefore, any security $H_i < 0$ when $\mu_i = 0$ must be rejected. Therefore, Equation (18.16) in the text can be used to estimate the optimal weight of a portfolio.

REFERENCES

Alexander, G. J., and B. J. Resnick. "More on Estimation Risk and Single Rules for Optimal Portfolio Selection." *Journal of Finance*, v. 40 (March 1985), pp. 125–34.

Chen, S. N., and S. J. Brown. "Estimation Risk and Simple Rules for Optimal Portfolio Selection." *Journal of Finance,* v. 38 (September 1983), pp. 1087–93.

Cheung, C. S., and C. C. Y. Kwan. "A Note on Simple Criteria for Optimal Portfolio Selection." *Journal of Finance,* v. 43 (March 1988), pp. 241–45.

Elton, E. J., and M. J. Gruber. *Modern Portfolio Theory and Investment Analysis,* 3d ed. John Wiley and Sons, 1987.

_____, and M. W. Padberg. "Simple Criteria for Optimal Portfolio Selection." *Journal of Finance,* v. 31 (December 1976), pp. 1341–57.

Kwan, C. C. Y. "Portfolio Analysis Using Single Index, Multi-Index, and Constant Correlation Models: A Unified Treatment." *Journal of Finance,* v. 39 (December 1984), pp. 1469–83.

Lintner, J. "The Valuation of Risk Asset on the Selection of Risky Investments in Stock Portfolio and Capital Budgets." *The Review of Economics and Statistics,* v. 57 (February 1965), pp. 13–37.

Markowitz, H. "Portfolio Selection." *Journal of Finance,* v. 7 (March 1952), pp. 77–91.

_____. *Portfolio Selection: Efficient Diversification of Investments.* John Wiley and Sons, 1959.

Sharpe, W. F. "A Simplified Model for Portfolio Analysis." *Management Science,* v. 9 (January 1963), pp. 277–93.

_____. "Capital Asset Prices: A Theory of Market Equilibrium Under Conditions of Risk." *Journal of Finance,* v. 19 (September 1964), pp. 425–42.

19 International Diversification

A large number of investors, both sophisticated money managers and individual portfolio holders, routinely restrict their investment activities to only a few of the available world investment opportunities. This chapter explores the broad topic of international diversification, with emphasis on providing an understandable overview of the theoretical issues involved as well as a review of the mechanics and risks of international investing.

The first topics for discussion are foreign-currency markets and exchange-rate risk. The foreign-exchange market adds a significant additional variable to investing that is not a factor in domestic investment. Next are the theoretical effects of international diversification and the international investment markets. This chapter examines whether the world markets are integrated or segmented; also examined are the implications of extending the capital asset pricing (CAPM) and arbitrage pricing (APT) security-valuation models to the international markets, developed using data collected on U.S. securities. Other issues, notably the impact of differential inflation rates and empirical evidence on international diversification, are examined as well. An analysis of applied international diversification is then presented that summarizes the various investment vehicles available and discusses their relative advantages and disadvantages.

Investing in the world market and buying foreign securities have become very popular. Hence, the impact of international investments on the diversification of a portfolio is important for both security analysts and portfolio managers. The major difference between international diversification and domestic diversification is the existence of foreign exchange in international investment; therefore, a discussion of the issues of foreign-exchange risk follows.

EXCHANGE-RATE RISK

Securities denominated in a currency other than the currency used by the purchaser have an additional element of risk, **exchange-rate** (or **currency**) **risk.** That is, the total return an investor receives will equal the stock return

643

times the change in the currency the security is denominated in relative to the investor's domestic currency, or:

$$\text{Total return} = \frac{\text{Security}}{\text{return}} \times \frac{\text{Change in relative}}{\text{exchange rate}} \qquad \textbf{(19.1)}$$

In this chapter the primary investment vehicle is assumed to be the foreign security; the use of the foreign-exchange markets as an investment tool in their own right is a separate subject.

Equation (19.1) can be rewritten in a modified security-return format:

$$R_1^f = \left(\frac{D_1^f + P_1^f}{P_0^f}\right)\left(\frac{S_1^{d/f}}{S_0^{d/f}}\right) - 1 \qquad \textbf{(19.2)}$$

where:

R_1^f = total return on the foreign investment;

P_0^f and P_1^f = prices of the foreign security at the time of purchase and the time of sale;

D_1^f = total dividends paid during the holding period; and

$S_0^{d/f}$ and $S_1^{d/f}$ = the prices of the foreign currency in units of domestic currency in time periods 0 and 1, respectively.

It can be seen from Equation (19.2) that the foreign-security yield R_1^f can be modified by the change in the exchange rate $S_1^{d/f}/S_0^{d/f}$.

Table 19–1 illustrates this principle, from the U.S. perspective, for the period November 1986 through November 1987 for nineteen stock markets. As is clear, the currency return can affect the total return both negatively and positively. Investing in the French stock market, for example, would have yielded a return of about -0.7 percent in the local currency. Because of the weakness of the U.S. dollar, however, from the perspective of a U.S. investor the return would have been 1.6 percent during this period. On the other hand, investing in the Canadian stock market would have yielded a 3.2-percent return offset by a 0.9-percent foreign-exchange loss, for a net return of 2.3 percent. The impression that the effect of the currency return, on average over time and country, is largely positive is erroneous. It depends on the movement of the dollar vis à vis the other currencies. Sometimes the dollar strengthens (foreign returns are lowered) and sometimes the dollar weakens (foreign returns are enhanced). Most of the time period covered by Table 19–1 is one in which the dollar was declining relative to most foreign currencies, resulting, on average, in improved yields for non-dollar-denominated investments.

The above discussion leads to the following pertinent questions.

1. Is currency risk related in any systematic way to security risk, or is it random?
2. If there is a correlation between security risk and currency risk, is it positive, tending to exaggerate swings, or is it negative, tending to dampen swings?

TABLE 19-1 Global Stock Markets

	In Local Currencies			In U.S. Dollars[1]		
Index	Change (percent)	11/5/87	52-Week Range	Change (percent)	11/5/87	52-Week Range
The World	+2.0	318.5	410.2– 295.9	+3.6	399.6	495.9– 334.1
E.A.F.E.[2]	+1.2	447.3	574.5– 412.5	+3.7	720.5	876.1– 550.0
Australia	–0.8	240.1	433.2– 235.2	–0.1	144.6	285.3– 135.0
Austria	–2.4	211.8	270.2– 208.8	+0.3	465.9	532.2– 421.6
Belgium	+0.0	267.1	395.0– 267.1	+2.6	377.8	514.1– 339.6
Canada	+3.2	333.6	460.4– 316.3	+2.3	271.4	374.5– 252.2
Denmark	+1.4	342.9	417.5– 338.3	+3.9	396.1	463.5– 345.2
France	–0.7	309.5	467.6– 295.6	+1.6	301.5	427.4– 279.2
Germany	–2.8	169.7	264.0– 169.7	–0.3	369.2	505.4– 369.2
Hong Kong	–9.0	1415.0	2803.4–1415.0	–9.0	1006.6	1994.1–1006.6
Italy	–2.8	392.9	598.9– 392.9	–0.8	198.0	290.0– 198.0
Japan	+3.4	1097.4	1360.1– 835.0	+6.1	2921.4	3439.2–1831.5
Mexico	–21.0	34114.7	78086.7–7592.2	–21.9	257.7	618.2– 115.2
Netherlands	–3.4	219.2	332.5– 216.5	–1.1	418.4	567.3– 394.3
Norway	–4.2	443.9	728.5– 443.9	–1.3	497.4	784.3– 420.2
Singapore/Malaya	+2.8	462.9	848.3– 450.2	+3.8	694.7	1236.4– 669.2
Spain	+12.1	205.3	284.6– 163.0	+15.3	127.4	163.7– 84.2
Sweden	–2.9	724.5	1058.3– 698.4	–0.5	619.0	857.3– 563.0
Switzerland	–4.3	151.1	220.7– 151.1	–1.0	469.7	619.6– 464.9
U.K.	–2.8	491.9	736.2– 475.5	–0.1	363.6	500.7– 280.8
U.S.A.	+3.8	238.0	313.9– 210.5	+3.8	238.0	313.9– 210.5

Base: Jan. 1, 1970 = 100
[1] Adjusted for foreign exchange fluctuations relative to the U.S. $.
[2] Europe, Australia, Far East Index.

Source: Morgan Stanley Capital International Perspective, Geneva, 1988.

3. Are currency-return changes systematic across a portfolio of foreign securities, or are they random and thus diversifiable?

4. Do the added risks and transaction costs of going from dollars to foreign currency to foreign security to foreign currency and back to dollars make foreign investing unattractive?

5. If the investment goal is primarily foreign-security diversification, is there any way that currency effects can be eliminated?

The first two questions have been the subject of several studies but have not been conclusively answered. Grubel (1968) and Levy and Sarnat (1970) showed that the optimum portfolios were entirely different with and without incorporating foreign-exchange-rate risk. Grubel found that accounting for foreign-exchange risk did not have a significant impact on the variance of returns. Other studies have attempted to show that since investors evaluate

their investment opportunities in real terms only, and since changes in currency rates are caused only by inflationary expectations, the exchange-rate risk is irrelevant to investors.

Solnik (1974C) explored the implications of financial markets in a world where individuals in different countries consume different baskets of goods. His conclusion is that "exchange risk," less the effects of differential inflation, is really just "business" risk. The following example, from Solnik's (1974C) paper, illustrates this point.

> We consider an idealized situation in which there is no inflation and only two countries are considered, Japan and France. Additionally, at time zero (superscript 0) the conversion rate is one yen to one franc and the price of one unit of wine is the same as one unit of sake. There are only two goods in each country's baskets, sake (s), produced in Japan, and wine (w), produced in France. The French consumption basket is $9w_F^0 + 1s_F^0 = 10$, and the Japanese consumption basket is $9s_J^0 + 1w_J^0 = 10$. Suppose a "shock" occurs (say, significant damage to the French wine crop). The new relative price (at time 1) is $w_F^1 = 1.5s_F^1$ and $w_J^1 = 1.5s_J^1$. The new consumption baskets are $8w_F^1 + 1.5s_F^1 = 12s_F^1 + 1.5s_F^1 = 13.5s_F^1$ for France, and $9.5s_J^1 + 0.33w_J^1 = 9.5s_J^1 + 0.5s_J^1 = 10s_J^1$ for Japan.

Because there is no inflation and because of the law of one price, the price of sake must be the same in both countries. Therefore, after the shock the new exchange rate is $10/13.5 = 0.741$. Thus, those in France who have invested in Japan when the exchange rate was 1 F = 1 yen get only 0.741 of what they expected to get in francs without exchange-rate effect. Because the "risk was caused by a change in the relative price of goods," it is an exchange-rate risk; however, it is essentially no different than a business risk.

The bad harvest caused the exchange rate to change. An event like a bad harvest is the type of risk faced by any agricultural business. The answer to the first question is that, since currency risk is a business-type risk, it is not systematically related to stock-price movements in general and therefore can be diversified away. The correlation between security risk and currency risk is probably very close to zero.

The third question concerns the correlation, or lack of correlation, of different foreign currencies with the domestic currency and with each other. Table 19–2 shows the correlation of returns for seven local bond markets and currency (1971–1985). Generalizing on these and other results:

1. Some reduction in currency risk can be obtained through diversification into several countries' securities.
2. Nevertheless, a substantial portion of the risk will still remain for U.S. investors because of the tendency of the foreign currencies' movements to be correlated positively with each other.
3. If the domestic currency were not the U.S. dollar, diversification benefits could be greater due to the negative correlation with the dollar.

These results are consistent, to a great extent, with the dollar's position as the world currency. Thus currency variations consist of two components:

TABLE 19–2 Correlations of Returns from Local Bond Markets and Currency (1971–1985)

U.S.	1					
Japan	0.20	1				
Germany	0.37	0.37	1			
U.K.	0.23	0.19	0.21	1		
Yen	0.13	0.34	0.15	0.14	1	
DM	0.11	0.23	0.25	0.01	0.54	1
Sterling	0.16	0.14	0.20	0.25	0.46	0.54	1

Source: From Carl Beidelman, ed., *Handbook of International Investing* (1987), page 622. Reprinted by permission of Probus Publishing Company. Data from J. P. Morgan Investment, 1986.

the random fluctuations of all currencies with each other due to specific local conditions and general changes in tastes, and the general fluctuation of all nondollar currencies with the world (dollar) standard. For the U.S. investor the first risk can be diversified completely, and the second risk can be modified only by adjusting the total portion of the portfolio in nondollar investments in relation to the total in dollar investments.

The fourth of the questions posed earlier is that, since domestic investors in each country do not face currency risks and currency-exchange transaction costs, and since each of the domestic markets should be priced efficiently, wouldn't investors be worse off by adding the risks and transaction costs of foreign diversification? The answer is that the diversification benefits (that is, the reduction in the market-portfolio risk premium due to the expanded market portfolio) have to outweigh the increased risk and transaction costs. (This diversification benefit is the subject of much of the rest of this chapter.) Some of the increased currency risk can be diversified, as discussed above. The additional transaction costs are comparatively small, at least for all major world currencies, as a result of the immense volume, easy divisibility, and consequent liquidity of the currency markets. Additionally, there are ways to hedge this risk and ways to diversify internationally in dollar-denominated investments.

Foreign-exchange risk can be minimized by covering all transactions in the foreign-exchange forward or futures markets. Two markets are available: the Interbank Foreign Exchange Market and the International Monetary Market. The first is made up of both a spot and a forward market, while the second, a subsidiary of the Chicago Mercantile Exchange, is a futures market only. By purchasing futures contracts for an amount equal to the expected net proceeds of the future dividends and sales price, Equation (19.2) becomes

$$R_1 = \left(\frac{D_1^f + P_1^f}{P_0^f}\right)\left(\frac{F_{0,1}^{d/f}}{S_0^{d/f}}\right) - 1 \tag{19.3}$$

Note that the second term does not reduce to one because $F_{0,1}^{d/f}$, the future exchange rate (period 1) at time zero of the foreign currency, does not equal

the current exchange rate. Thus the currency effect has not been eliminated, but the unknown price, or the price risk, has. Nevertheless, the total risk still has not been eliminated, because it has been necessary to use an estimate of the future net receipts in the foreign currency. The risk will still remain in proportion to the difference in actual receipts from forecast receipts. Also, this procedure adds two more transaction costs, on the purchase and on the sale of the futures contract.

The question of interest to most investors is what happens when the securities of several countries are included in a portfolio. According to the information discussed so far, the potential exists for higher return, lower risk, or both. Portfolio theory indicates that as we diversify internationally, as long as all of the economies of the world are not perfectly positively correlated with each other we should expect gains from diversification. It is a fact that, given any particular group of assets, various optimal weightings of those assets exist that create portfolios with the maximum possible return for a given level of risk. These are the so-called **efficient-frontier portfolios.**

The efficient frontier for an internationally diversified portfolio lies above the efficient frontier for portfolios limited to their own domestic market, because the range of potential returns is wider internationally and because the correlations of return are typically lower. As a result, the internationally diversified investor has the potential to achieve a higher level of return than the domestic investor for any given level of risk, or, viewed from a different perspective, to expect a lower variability of return than a domestic investor for any given level of return. These relationships are shown in Figure 19–1.

THEORETICAL EFFECTS OF INTERNATIONAL DIVERSIFICATION

This section analyzes theoretical issues related to international diversification. Empirical evidence of international diversification is discussed in the next section.

Segmented versus Integrated World Markets

This section presents the results of research for the past decade with the objective of discovering whether international markets are segmented or integrated, and how this will affect the risk–return tradeoff available to the investor.

The question of whether the international market is integrated or segmented appears particularly elusive. The difficulty surrounding this important issue was made clear by Solnik (1974B). The segmented market theory states that capital assets are priced in terms of their "domestic systematic risk." The capital asset pricing model (CAPM) can be extended to account

FIGURE 19-1   International versus Domestic Efficient Frontiers

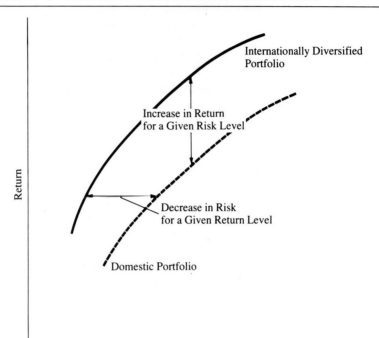

for the correlation between national securities markets in determination of securities on a given international market:

$$E(R_i^j) = R_f + \beta_{di}^j[E(R_m) - R_f] \tag{19.4}$$

where:

$E(R_i^j)$ = expected rate of return on ith security (or portfolio) in jth country;

$E(R_m)$ = expected market rates of return in jth country;

β_{di}^j = the beta coefficient for jth country in terms of domestic country's market rate of return; and

R_f = the risk-free rate in the domestic country.

Equation (19.4) is a nationalistic model that postulates that security rates of return on each marketplace have in common a national factor, R_m. This national factor R_m is in turn dependent on a single common world factor, R_w (return for the world market portfolio), defined:

$$E(R_m) = R_f + \beta_w^j [E(R_w) - R_f] \tag{19.5}$$

where β_w^j is the **international systematic risk** of country j.

From Equation (19.5), it can be concluded that the lower the correlation between the two markets the lower the β_w^j, the lower the expected return,

and the higher the value of international diversification. So it can be inferred that an investor who holds a portfolio of domestic securities would hold an underdiversified portfolio with respect to world diversification. Therefore, by holding an international portfolio (or security), the investor can reduce the systematic risk of his portfolio. Solnik, using his **international asset pricing model (IAPM)** to test whether assets are best regarded as being traded in segmented (national) or integrated (international) markets, found some evidence that markets are integrated. Furthermore, in his international mean-variance (MV) analysis, Solnik (1977) showed that as long as expected excess returns are positive and covariances low, MV analysis will produce optimal internationally diversified portfolios to reduce risk. Solnik's work was recently tested by Cho, Eun, and Senbet (1987). The result of the test "lends tentative support" that only "mild segmentation" exists and that this segmentation does not affect required returns on "eligible securities."

Suppose for a moment that the world is one big economy and that markets are fully integrated. Then the risk- (world beta-) adjusted average return across national markets should be similar to those of U.S. markets. The integrated-market theory stipulates that all securities in the world are priced in terms of their global systematic risk. This can be stated as:

$$E(R_i^j) = R_f + \beta_{wi}^j [E(R_w) - R_f] \qquad (19.6)$$

where:

$E(R_i^j)$ = expected rate of return on ith security (or portfolio) in country j;
R_f = the risk-free rate of interest;
$E(R_w)$ = expected rate of return on the world market portfolio;
β_{wi}^j = $(\rho_{i,w}\sigma_i\sigma_w)/\sigma_w^2$, or the correlation coefficient between the rate of return on security i in country j and the world market, times the standard deviation of security i, times the standard deviation of the world market, divided by the variance of the world market portfolio.

Solnik (1974A) shows that the relationship between β_d^j, β_w^j, and β_{wi}^j can be defined:

$$\beta_{wi}^j = \beta_w^j \beta_{di}^j \qquad (19.7)$$

Equation (19.7) indicates that the international systematic risk of a security i in country j (β_{wi}^j) is equal to the product of the national systematic risk of that security (β_{di}^j) and the international systematic risk (β_w^j).

From the formula it can be inferred that the riskiness of a portfolio results from the covariance of a portfolio rate of return with a national stock-market index. Nevertheless, that index is not the only way to determine the price of a portfolio since the national market now has a relationship with the world market and has a certain influence on the world portfolio. That influence depends on the weight that the nation's financial market index has on the world market index. Grubel and Fadner (1971) measured the strength of relationship between the U.S. portfolio and foreign portfolios. Specifically,

TABLE 19-3   Industries' Foreign Trade and Levels of Correlation Quarterly Holding Periods

| | U.S. 1958 (Import and Export) | | Correlation of U.S. Industry with | | | |
| | | | West Germany | | United Kingdom | |
Industry	Output	Rank	R	Rank	R	Rank
Shipping	0.107	1	0.43	7	0.39	12
Machinery	0.107	2	0.44	5	0.68	2
Paper	0.106	3	0.49	2	0.45	11
Chemicals	0.082	4	0.52	1	0.77	1
Tobacco	0.075	5	0.37	11	0.12	18
Rubber	0.069	6	−0.06	18	0.28	15
Electrical equipment	0.065	7	0.38	10	0.68	3
Automobile	0.062	8	0.45	4	0.55	9
Food	0.061	9	0.39	8	0.65	5
Aircraft	0.048	10	0.31	13	0.24	17
Household goods	0.046	11	0.46	3	0.63	6
Steel	0.039	12	0.44	6	0.37	13
Electronics	0.037	13	0.29	14	0.57	8
Textiles	0.034	14	0.38	9	0.67	4
Retail store	0.015	15	0.36	12	0.51	10
Oil	0.013	16	0.27	16	0.28	16
Publishing	0.010	17	0.29	15	0.36	14
Finance company	0.005	18	0.25	17	0.63	7

Source: Trade data, U.S. 1958 Input-Output Table, *Survey of Current Business,* September 1965, pp. 33–39.
Note: In some cases rank was determined by digits computed but not reproduced here.

Source: Grubel and Fadner, "The Interdependence of International Equity Markets." *Journal of Finance,* v. 26 (March 1971), p. 93.

they were measuring the correlation among pairs of identical industries. Their results are summarized in Table 19-3. From this table it can be concluded that the correlation is greater the larger the ratio of an industry's exports plus imports over output, which means that international diversification pays off.

The following conclusions can be drawn from the available knowledge on the subject of world market integration:

1. The world market lies in an area of being "mildly segmented"—that is, the economy of each country is its own world, to a significant degree of integration (the economy of each country has a substantial impact on the world economy, depending on the role that the particular country plays in the world markets as a whole).

2. International diversification can substantially reduce the risk and increase the wealth of the portfolio holders of any country, provided that the portfolio is properly constructed to accommodate the utility function of the portfolio holder.

The argument for segmented markets relies on the existence of barriers that prevent the free flow of capital around the world. These barriers include (1) legal restrictions, (2) transaction costs, (3) lack of information, and (4) discrimination against foreign investors either by taxation or outright exclusion. Whether the world markets are segmented or integrated seems to ebb and flow as world conditions change. Presently the trend appears to be toward a greater degree of integration as the barriers mentioned are reduced or eliminated.

The CAPM and the APT Applied Internationally

The capital asset pricing model (CAPM) assumes that each investor faces the same efficient frontier of potential portfolios. In general, the efficient frontier will differ among investors because of differences in expectations. In a portfolio context, the concern of the investor with the characteristics of individual securities is justified in terms of the effect that each security has on the distribution of the rate of return of the portfolio. Specifically, the CAPM states that the relevant risk of a single security is the nondiversifiable risk, beta, the covariance of the security with the market divided by the variance of the market. The issue in an international context, therefore, is how international diversification affects the riskiness of the portfolio and its rate of return. Asset-pricing models similar in form to the CAPM have been derived for international financial assets in a manner parallel to the CAPM. Solnik (1974) developed an **international asset pricing model (IAPM)** and tested it. In his empirical tests Solnik used daily data on stocks of eight European countries and the United States. The results were weakly consistent with his IAPM. However, Solnik generated some empirical estimates for the risk of an internationally diversified portfolio compared to a purely domestic portfolio. Using weekly data on stocks in eight major European countries and the United States, Solnik found that an internationally diversified portfolio would be one tenth as risky as a typical security and one half as risky as a well diversified U.S. portfolio.

A new development in the field of IAPM parallels an advance in the **domestic asset pricing theory.** Breeden (1979) developed an asset-pricing model which explicitly noted that individuals derive their utility from consumption. Maximizing lifetime utility from consumption, Breeden developed a more complete model for asset pricing, wherein pricing of an asset depended on covariances with aggregate consumption rather than any market index or portfolio. Application of the Breeden model to various economies of the world may give some insight into how financial assets are priced.

The **arbitrage pricing theory (APT),** formulated by Ross in 1976, offers a feasible alternative to the CAPM. It is worthwhile in the context of this chapter to examine the implications of extending the APT to include the world market. The APT assumes that the rate of return on any security is a linear function of k factors, or:

$$\tilde{R}_i = E(\tilde{R}_i) + b_{i1}\tilde{F}_1 + \cdots + b_{ik}\tilde{F}_k + \tilde{e}_i \qquad (19.8)$$

where:

$\tilde{R}_i$ = the random rate of return on the ith asset;
$E(\tilde{R}_i)$ = the expected rate of return on the ith asset;
b_{ik} = the sensitivity of the ith assets returns to the kth factor;
$\tilde{F}_k$ = the kth factor common to all assets; and
$\tilde{e}_i$ = a random mean noise term for the ith asset.

The most important feature of the APT is that in equilibrium all portfolios that can be selected from among the set of assets under consideration and that satisfy the two conditions of (1) using no wealth and (2) having no risk must earn no return on average.

Solnik (1983) extended the APT to the international capital markets, leading to the **international arbitrage pricing theory (IAPT).** In this article Solnik shows that IAPT overcomes the problem of aggregation when asset demands are summed in the universe of investors who use different numeration to measure returns. This is because the portfolios in the IAPT context represent weighted averages of individual assets. Further, Solnik shows that even in foreign terms the domestic arbitrage portfolio bears no risk and hence should earn zero return in equilibrium.

Cho, Eun, and Senbet (1987) empirically tested the IAPT and rejected the first hypothesis, that the international capital market is integrated and that the APT is valid internationally. However, their study used international common factors. Abbeyekra and Mahojocar (1985) utilized domestic common factors and directly tested Solnik's (1983) claim on the IAPT. The results of their study ''strongly support the hypothesis that the IAPT accurately predicts the risk-free rate.''

Inflation and Exchange-Rate Risks

It is appropriate to question how, from a theoretical point of view, two significant potential differences between one-country investing and world investing affect the risk and return potential for an investor. These two variables are (1) exchange-rate differences and (2) differences in the rates of inflation. Domestic investors do not face exchange-rate risk, so it is a substantive theoretical difference with models developed purely for domestic purposes. This issue was discussed in the previous section; it is enough to restate here that much of the risk can be either diversified away or hedged against. Additionally, as pointed out by Solnik (1974), exchange-rate risk is essentially just another form of business risk.

Inflation differential risk is the second added dimension of international diversification. Suppose an investor in the United States has a security in England whose return is fixed in terms of the pound. Assuming that there is no inflation in the United States but that the inflation rate in England is

uncertain, the dollar value of the investment at the end of the period is uncertain and hence risky. The position has an **exchange risk,** which in this case is an inflation risk. This connection between exchange risk and inflation risk is not coincidental. There is an explicit set of connections between any country's exchange rate and its inflation rate. The Fisher effect, used to take into account inflation, can be expanded internationally:

$$(1 + R_m^d) = (1 + R_{\text{real}}^d)(1 + I^d) \tag{19.9}$$

$$(1 + R_m^f) = (1 + R_{\text{real}}^f)(1 + I^f) \tag{19.10}$$

where R_{real} is the real rate of interest, R_m is the nominal interest rate, and I is the inflation rate. The superscript d and f indicate domestic and foreign rates, respectively. Equations (19.9) and (19.10) can be combined to solve for the relative nominal rates:

$$\frac{1 + R_m^f}{1 + R_m^d} = \left(\frac{1 + R_{\text{real}}^f}{1 + R_{\text{real}}^d}\right)\left(\frac{1 + I^f}{1 + I^d}\right) \tag{19.11}$$

This equation can be interpreted to state that, for every country, the nominal interest rate is connected to its own real rate and inflation and the real rate and the inflation of the other country.

As a first-order approximation, the nominal interest-rate differential between two countries can be shown to be

$$R_m^f - R_m^d = R_{\text{real}}^f - R_{\text{real}}^d + I^f - I^d \tag{19.11A}$$

That is, the difference in the nominal rates is approximately equal to the difference in the real rates and the rates of inflation between the two countries. Sample Problem 19.1 provides further illustration.

Sample Problem 19.1

The real rate of interest in the United States and Germany is 4 percent, the inflation rate in the United States is expected to be 5 percent, and the inflation rate in Germany is expected to be 1 percent. What is the difference in the nominal rates between the two countries?

Solution
Using Equation (19.11A) as an approximation:

$$\begin{aligned}
R_m^{\text{US}} - R_m^{\text{Ger}} &= R_{\text{real}}^{\text{US}} - R_{\text{real}}^{\text{Ger}} + I^{\text{US}} - I^{\text{Ger}} \\
&= 0.05 - 0.05 + 0.05 - 0.01 \\
&= 0.04
\end{aligned}$$

The nominal rate in the United States should be 4 percent higher than the nominal rate in Germany. If Equation (19.11) were used to solve this problem, the exact difference in the nominal interest rates would be 3.9604 percent. This is approximately equal to the 4 percent found using Equation (19.11A)●

Recall for a moment the example with the United States and England. Suppose that the inflation in England is known precisely and that inflation in the United States is somewhat less than in England. The inflation rate in each country will have an impact on the value of the currency in that particular country. The amount of the impact can be determined relatively precisely since the parity between currencies must be observed by the law of price equilibrium. This relationship can be expressed in the following formula:

$$\frac{E(S_1^{d/f}) - S_0^{d/f}}{S_0^{d/f}} = \frac{E(I^d) - E(I^f)}{1 + E(I^d)} \tag{19.12}$$

where $E(S_1^{d/F})$ is the expected future exchange rate between the foreign and the domestic currency and $S_0^{d/F}$ is the current spot exchange rate.

Equation (19.12) states that the difference between current and future exchange rates is equal to the differences in inflation rates. Thus, it appears inflation is fixed into exchange rates in the marketplace. The exposure of a business firm to exchange risk is defined by its cash-flow and asset-stock position. These in turn depend on expected future receipts and payments on the firm's net monetary position—that is, on the relationship between current assets and current liabilities. So unless payments and receipts in relation to the future net monetary position of the firm exactly balance, the firm is exposed to declines or increases in the value of foreign currencies. This exposure to risk can be eliminated in the world of inflation by appropriate indexation of contracts in real terms. Sample Problem 19.2 provides further illustration.

Sample Problem 19.2

The current spot exchange rate between the U.S. dollar and the British pound is $2.00/£, the expected inflation in the United States is 5 percent, and the expected inflation in England is 10 percent. What is the expected future spot rate ($/£)?

Solution
Using Equation (19.12):

$$\frac{E(S^d/£^1) - \$2.00/£}{\$2.00/£} = \frac{0.05 - 0.10}{1.05}$$

$$E(S_1^{d/£}) = \$2.00/£ + \$2.00/£ - \left(\frac{0.05}{1.05}\right)$$

$$= \$1.9048/£$$

The higher inflation rate in England will cause the pound to devalue relative to the dollar, so that instead of $2.00/£, it will only cost $1.9048 to buy £1.00 in the future

This discussion on inflation and exchange-rate risk can be concluded by stating that there are two types of exchange-rate risk to consider: the risk of inflation and **relative price risk.** Since the risk of inflation is nominal, this risk can be eliminated by appropriate indexing of contracts in real terms. The relative price risk is due to changes in supply-and-demand conditions in various countries. Eliminating inflation risk results in an exchange risk that is a form of business risk resulting from changes in relative prices, which reflect changes in supply-and-demand conditions. This aspect of exchange risk is much more difficult to hedge or eliminate.

Are World Markets Efficient?

A final issue of importance in the theoretical discussion of international diversification is whether the world market is efficient. Domestic theoretical models such as the CAPM and the APT are dependent to a considerable extent on the assumption of market efficiency. The validity of extending these models to world markets will be seriously threatened if the international market is not as efficient as the U.S. market.

An efficient market, again, is a market where any new information would be immediately and fully reflected in prices, and the adjustment in price would be very rapid. Therefore, investors using publicly available information will not be able to earn above-average returns.

The issue of **world market efficiency** has been tested by Roll (1979). He set the expected return on international speculation conditional on information at the beginning of the period equal to zero, using **purchasing-power parity (PPP),** which means that people will value currencies for what they will buy. He concludes that the deviations from PPP attributable to relative price fluctuations are dominated by the effects of inflation on the exchange rate. Hence relative inflation is an important determinant of exchange rates.

One requirement of market efficiency is that arbitrage profits are zero. Frankel and Levich (1975) tested whether deviations of interest-rate parity outside of the countries of transactions can exist. They concluded that if arbitrage assets are comparable, arbitrage opportunities do not exist.

Simple tests of market efficiency have implied that the forward exchange rate should be an unbiased predictor of the spot rate. However, Stockman's (1980) theoretical development states that a bias should exist, since a premium is associated with the risk investors face in forward exchange markets. Nevertheless, Stockman and Cornell (1977) have found evidence of a bias for only a few countries and then only when the risk premium changes erratically.

There have been many studies on the efficiency of national stock markets around the world. Hawawini (1984), Kato and Schallheim (1985), Jaffe and Westerfield (1985), and Ang and Pohlman (1978), to name a few, all conclude that the national stock markets they studied are at least semi-strong-form efficient. Given the increasing interest in financial analysis and portfolio management in these markets, these findings are not too suprising.

One issue remains unresolved at present: the efficiency of the world market. In other words, is it possible for portfolio managers to allocate funds to certain national markets and thereby generate performance that is better than a world market index? To date there is little empirical evidence to resolve this issue. What is required is a simultaneous evaluation of financial markets, currency markets, and real markets to ascertain whether they are efficient from a world perspective.

Empirical Evidence Supporting International Diversification

As early as 1968 evidence was being accumulated in empirical studies regarding the potential advantages of international diversification. Grubel (1968) found that international diversification can pay off, if portfolios are properly selected. More recently, Stehle (1977) showed that low-beta securities of internationally diversified portfolios outperformed high-beta securities of domestically diversified portfolios, on a beta-adjusted basis. Adler and Dumas (1983) stated in their study that "the potential of international diversification to reduce the risk seems unquestionable."

The growth of international financial markets coincided with the increasing integration of national financial institutions through international firms. Integration of financial institutions as well as portfolio investment was a major phenomenon of the 1970s and 1980s. The effect of market integration has important implications in many sectors of the economy. It is important, therefore, when studying effects of international financial integration, to realize the benefits that could be used as a reference for policy making.

Studies by Senchack and Beedle (1980) and Jacquillat and Solnick (1978) suggest that U.S. investors who hold portfolios of U.S. multinational firms do not receive the same risk reduction as investors who hold portfolios of U.S. and foreign securities. This probably results from the restrictions imposed on the multinational management by the various governments of the countries in which they operate.

APPLIED INTERNATIONAL DIVERSIFICATION

Once the investor or portfolio manager has decided to diversify internationally, how does he or she go about doing so? There are several different vehicles: (1) direct purchase of foreign securities, (2) purchase of securities of American-listed firms with large foreign operations, (3) American depository receipts, (4) Eurobonds, and (5) international mutual funds. Along with deciding which vehicle to use, the investor must consider how to obtain information, what will be the impact of market imperfections such as local taxes and restrictions on capital flow, and whether to hedge against currency risk.

Direct Foreign Investment

The manager of a large portfolio would probably consider the direct foreign-investment option first. The costs of gathering information and the additional currency-transaction cost would be a much smaller proportion of the total portfolio return and therefore a worthwhile tradeoff to achieve a higher degree of choice in the selection of securities and countries, as well as greater flexibility in the timing of transactions. The following are brief discussions of some of the most easily available foreign-investment opportunities.

Canada.   The Canadian stock market has had a correlation with the U.S. market (S&P 500) ranging from 0.83 to 0.91 over the last twenty years. Thus, diversification benefits (beyond those due only to the increased number of available securities) are minimal. This makes sense in light of the economic and geographic proximity of the two countries. Additionally, Canada imposes a 15-percent withholding tax on returns earned by U.S. investors.

Canada has three major stock exchanges, in Toronto, Montreal, and Vancouver. The Toronto Stock Exchange is the most important.

West Germany.   West Germany is the third-largest Western industrial nation. The correlation of the West German stock market with the U.S. stock market has ranged from -0.58 to $+0.56$ over the last twenty years. Diversification benefits should therefore be substantial.

West Germany has eight stock exchanges; the two most important are the Frankfurt and Düsseldorf exchanges. Trading is thin by U.S. standards. The debt market has always been of interest to U.S. investors due to the stability of the mark. There is a 15-percent withholding tax on dividends but none on interest.

Japan.   The Japanese stock market correlation with the U.S. market has ranged from 0.07 to 0.84. Japan has had one of the healthiest economies in the world and has been increasing its market share in many high-growth industries.

Japan imposes a 10-percent withholding tax on interest and dividends. There are eight stock exchanges, of which the Tokyo Exchange is the most important.

Other Pacific-Basin Countries.   The Pacific basin is considered the best growth area in the world for the next decade or longer. Hong Kong has been a leader as a result of its inexpensive labor, its location on key Asian trade routes, and its position as a financial center for Asia. The uncertainty of Hong Kong's outlook after the U.K. lease expires in 1997 has been somewhat resolved and remains less of a risk than in prior years.

Taiwan, South Korea, and Singapore are also growth economies as a result of inexpensive labor and the general attitude of both the governments

and the labor forces. All three areas are benefiting from the trend to manufacture electronics and other goods outside the higher-cost, more developed countries. Additionally, Singapore is well situated geographically and is a major regional center for finance, commerce, and oil refining.

Australia and Malaysia are both resource-rich countries. They are favorably located for growth with the expanding Pacific-basin manufacturing economies.

United Kingdom.   The United Kingdom's stock market has an historical correlation coefficient range of 0.17 to 0.79 with the U.S. market. The British economy has been plagued with negative growth, high inflation, and heavy government interference. The large North Sea oil discoveries and the reform programs of the Thatcher government have given some hope of a remedy for these economic ills. However, large transaction costs and taxes are incurred when trading on the London exchange.

On the positive side, the current weakness may provide more potential for growth. The United Kingdom is still the world's most important financial center. The London Stock Exchange is organized in a fashion similar to the U.S. exchanges, and trading volume is heavier than on other European exchanges.

Indirect Foreign Investment

The purchase of U.S. securities with large foreign operations can be a lower-cost, lower-risk way to diversify internationally. Foreign-exchange risks are not incurred directly, information is more easily available, and the markets and regulations are the ones that are familiar to the investor.

Unfortunately, as discussed earlier, statistical studies have found that U.S. multinational firms seem to track the U.S. stock market very closely. One study (Jacquillat and Solnik, 1978) found that when the returns of twenty-three U.S.-based multinationals were regressed on various countries' market indexes, the only significant explanatory variable was the U.S. market. It seems that this low-cost, low-risk alternative does not result in significant international diversification benefits.

American Depository Receipts (ADRs).   American depository receipts (ADRs) were introduced in 1927 by the Morgan Guaranty Trust Company. They are financial instruments issued by U.S. banks (called depositories) against shares deposited with the bank's overseas branch or a custodian. The ADRs allow U.S. investors to buy, sell, and own foreign securities without ever taking physical possession of them. They are ordinarily issued on a one-to-one basis, one ADR for every share, and they can be traded in exactly the same way as shares of U.S. corporations. The issuing bank acts as the intermediary in all transactions; it notifies the ADR holder of dividends and distributes these dividends in dollars; it deducts foreign taxes; and

it furnishes information on stock rights, stockholders' meetings, new issues, and tender offers. For these services the bank charges a fee.

Although ADRs are dollar-denominated, they include the full effect of changes in both the underlying security and the exchange rate. Investors who do not want to incur exchange-rate risk must still hedge in the foreign-exchange markets exactly as if they were purchasing securities on a foreign market. On the other hand, investors who feel that changes in foreign-exchange rates may work in their favor can use ADRs without having to incur the added transaction costs and complications of investing directly in foreign markets.

Other advantages of utilizing ADRs rather than direct foreign investment include (1) avoidance of some foreign taxes; (2) improved and more easily obtained information, which is also from one source (the bank) and in English; (3) avoidance of foreign regulations; (4) improved security (an ADR is registered with a major U.S. bank whereas many foreign securities are bearer securities and their value will be gone if the security is lost or stolen); and (5) improved liquidity. There is an active domestic ADR market, and transactions can be performed by a broker over the phone. Foreign securities, on the other hand, must often be mailed overseas; and it is sometimes necessary to wait long periods for the proceeds of the sale.

Eurobonds.   A **Eurobond** is an international bond denominated in a currency other than that of the country of the issuer. The forming of the Association of International Bond Dealers (AIBD) in 1968 brought about an efficient, uniform exchange system for Eurobonds and marks the beginning of their rapid growth. By 1987, $50 billion in new Eurobonds were being offered annually. While Europe is the center of Eurobond activity, there is also significant activity in the U.S. and in Japan. About 68 percent of Eurobonds are denominated in U.S. dollars. Another 19 percent are denominated in German marks. Another form is the **European Currency Unit (ECU)**, comprised of the currencies of the members of the European Economic Community (EEC). One EUA is valued at 0.88867 grams of gold. Two other forms of denomination are the **European Monetary Unit,** consisting of the currencies of the six original EEC members, and the **special drawing rights (SDRs).** SDRs are a form of currency created by the IMF in the 1970s to increase world liquidity. SDRs are a weighted average of the U.S. dollar, the German mark, the Japanese yen, the French franc, and the British pound.

Eurobonds are extremely flexible financial instruments. In addition to issues in the major currencies—dollar, yen, mark, pound, and Swiss franc—**currency cocktails** (combinations of currencies) are also used. It is very common for Eurobonds to be convertible or to have warranties attached so that bondholders can participate in the profits and growth of the firm's equity. Both fixed- and floating-rate bonds are issued.

Despite the broad variety, some features are common to almost all Eurobonds. Generally Eurobonds (1) have low default risk, as they are high-quality issues; (2) have intermediate maturities, usually about seven years;

(3) are thinly traded issues with very small secondary markets; (4) have extremely complex trading; (5) give higher yields than comparable U.S. bonds; (6) are bearer bonds, with all of the accompanying risk; (7) pay interest not subject to foreign taxes; and (8) provide (mostly) for a sinking fund or a repurchase fund. Given these characteristics it seems obvious that while Eurobonds can be very attractive for the skilled professional with adequate resources, they should be avoided by individual investors. However, individuals can participate through mutual funds.

International Mutual Funds.   Investors, both small and large, may want the advantages of international diversification without having to be experts on the subject themselves. In this case, they may delegate the management of the international portion of their investments to a mutual fund. Many funds are available to choose from. The Dean Witter Worldwide Investment Trust Fund is a typical one. Appendix 19A gives excerpts from the 1984 prospectus for this fund, which has typical objectives and policies.

At present, about fifty international mutual funds are available to U.S. investors. They are classified into three types: country, international, and global funds. A country fund only invests in the securities of a particular country—for example, the Korea Fund only invests in Korean securities. The Korean market is at present closed to foreign investors, so the Korea Fund offers one of the only means by which investors can hold Korean securities. The distinction between global funds and international funds is based on the degree of investment outside of the U.S. A global fund has at least 25 percent of its assets in foreign investments; an international fund has at least 50 percent of its assets invested overseas.

Proffitt and Seitz (1983) evaluated the performance of U.S. international funds over the period 1974–1982. Using both the Sharpe and Treynor performance measures discussed in Chapter 17, they find that ten international mutual funds outperformed the S&P 500 index for both measures. They conclude, at least for the time period of their study, that U.S. investors were better off investing internationally than investing in the U.S. market.

The Morgan Guaranty Trust Company (1979) presents the empirical evidence which is necessary for evaluating international portfolio investment. The return, variance of return, and correlation coefficients between the United States and foreign markets are presented. Figure 19–2 shows the rates of return for the United States and five major foreign stock markets. The average annual compounded rate of return is calculated in two ways, with the assets valued in the local currency and with the assets valued in U.S. dollars. The U.S. returns fall in the middle of the six markets studied over the period.

As has been noted, the variability of return on any portfolio depends both on the standard deviation of returns of the individual assets and on the correlation of returns among them. If the standard deviations of foreign markets are very high, this will tend to make international portfolios more variable than domestic portfolios. However, if the correlations among re-

FIGURE 19-2   Historical Compound Annual Rates of Return (Price Only—Twenty
Years, 1959–1978, percent)

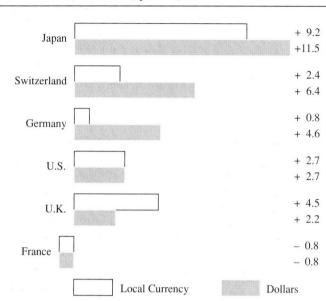

Japan	+ 9.2
	+11.5
Switzerland	+ 2.4
	+ 6.4
Germany	+ 0.8
	+ 4.6
U.S.	+ 2.7
	+ 2.7
U.K.	+ 4.5
	+ 2.2
France	− 0.8
	− 0.8

Local Currency   Dollars

Source: Morgan Guaranty Trust Company. *Investing Internationally.* 1978.

turns are very low, this will tend to make international portfolios less volatile
than domestic portfolios. Which of these two effects is stronger, the high
standard deviations or the low correlations?

Unlike rates of return, which can be substantially different when measured in dollars rather than in local currency units, the variability of return is
not significantly different whether measured in local currencies or in dollars.
This is evident in Figure 19–3. Typically, the variability in dollars is slightly
more than the variability measured in local currency units; thus, the focus of
concentration can be the variability measured in dollars. The U.S. market
has been one of the least variable markets over the time period studied.
Table 19–4 shows correlation coefficients of foreign equity markets.

The basic conclusions to be drawn from the correlation coefficients
shown in Table 19–4 are these.

1. The correlations of returns have not been constant but have tended to
   increase somewhat as world markets have become more integrated.
2. Very substantial variations exist in the degree to which other equity
   markets tend to move with the U.S. market.
3. The size of the correlations tends to be low, which indicates that there
   can be substantial risk reductions through international diversification.

FIGURE 19-3 Historical Standard Deviations of Returns (Price Only—Twenty Years, 1959–1978, percent)

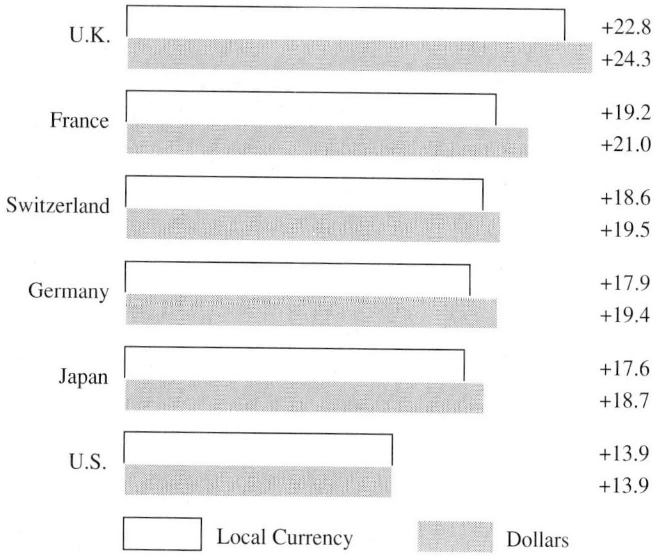

U.K.	+22.8 / +24.3
France	+19.2 / +21.0
Switzerland	+18.6 / +19.5
Germany	+17.9 / +19.4
Japan	+17.6 / +18.7
U.S.	+13.9 / +13.9

Local Currency   Dollars

Source: Morgan Guaranty Trust Company. *Investing Internationally.* 1978.

Following Eun and Resnick (1987), summary statistics of monthly returns for fifteen major stock markets (1973–1982) are presented in Table 19-5. In this table correlation coefficients, mean and standard deviation (SD) of monthly returns, beta coefficient, and Sharpe performance measure (SHP) are presented. The beta coefficient is the β_{jw}^j defined in Equation (19.5); the Sharpe measure is as defined in Chapter 7.

Based on the available evidence, it would appear that investors can improve returns and lower risk by investing internationally.

As the caveats in the Dean Witter prospectus point out (see Appendix 19A), foreign investing involves many risks and problems not normally encountered by U.S. investors. Nevertheless, the research, while not conclusive, appears substantial enough to indicate that the benefits outweigh the risks. Care must be taken to choose the countries and the investment vehicles that are appropriate to the investor's individual utility function, portfolio size, and the time the investor can afford to personally spend on the foreign portion of the portfolio.

The correlation coefficients of foreign markets with the U.S. market indicate that the world markets lie somewhere between the theoretical extremes of totally segmented individual-country markets and the integrated one-world market. This lack of complete integration is one of the attractions of international diversification.

TABLE 19-4   Correlation Coefficients of Foreign Equity Markets with the United States (Monthly Data)

	1959–1978	*1959–1963*	*1964–1968*	*1969–1973*	*1974–1978*
Local currencies					
Australia	0.40	−0.01	0.29	0.34	0.61
Austria	0.13	0.33	0.09	−0.06	0.29
Belgium	0.49	0.50	0.51	0.37	0.58
Canada	0.75	0.79	0.83	0.77	0.70
Denmark	0.15	−0.02	0.03	0.15	0.30
France	0.34	0.45	0.01	0.25	0.46
Germany	0.31	0.48	0.12	0.37	0.24
Italy	0.22	0.34	0.05	0.04	0.33
Japan	0.20	0.02	0.06	0.42	0.27
Netherlands	0.56	0.67	0.60	0.50	0.53
Norway	0.32	0.38	0.05	0.06	0.62
Spain	0.11	0.05	0.01	0.12	0.17
Sweden	0.34	0.34	0.34	0.33	0.35
Switzerland	0.49	0.52	0.34	0.53	0.54
United Kingdom	0.41	0.29	0.20	0.39	0.52
Average of 15	0.35	0.34	0.22	0.30	0.43
U.S. dollars					
Australia	0.41	−0.01	0.29	0.35	0.60
Austria	0.16	0.33	−0.09	0.01	0.24
Belgium	0.46	0.50	0.52	0.33	0.55
Canada	0.75	0.81	0.84	0.76	0.69
Denmark	0.19	−0.03	0.05	0.19	0.34
France	0.33	0.46	0.01	0.20	0.47
Germany	0.33	0.48	0.12	0.38	0.29
Italy	0.21	0.34	0.04	0.09	0.26
Japan	0.21	0.02	0.06	0.44	0.27
Netherlands	0.57	0.67	0.61	0.53	0.54
Norway	0.34	0.38	0.04	0.06	0.68
Spain	0.12	0.11	0.02	0.10	0.16
Sweden	0.36	0.33	0.34	0.34	0.38
Switzerland	0.48	0.52	0.34	0.49	0.51
United Kingdom	0.39	0.29	0.19	0.38	0.48
Average of 15	0.35	0.35	0.23	0.31	0.43

Source: Morgan Guaranty Trust Company. *Investing Internationally.* 1978.

TABLE 19–5 Summary Statistics of the Monthly Returns for Fifteen Major Stock Markets, 1973–1982 (all returns converted to U.S. dollars)

	Correlation Coefficient																	
Stock Market	*AU*	*BE*	*CA*	*FR*	*GE*	*HK*	*IT*	*JA*	*NE*	*SG*	*SP*	*SD*	*SW*	*UK*	*Mean (percent)*	*SD (percent)*	β	*SHP*
Australia (AU)															0.63	7.97	1.25	0.027
Belgium (BE)	0.36														0.80	5.92	0.84	0.065
Canada (CA)	0.62	0.36													0.78	6.52	1.16	0.056
France (FR)	0.46	0.61	0.46												0.67	8.04	1.16	0.032
Germany (GE)	0.33	0.65	0.31	0.52											0.83	5.44	0.73	0.076
Hong Kong (HK)	0.34	0.36	0.27	0.30	0.33										1.10	14.54	1.52	0.047
Italy (IT)	0.29	0.36	0.28	0.39	0.28	0.21									0.27	8.47	0.74	0.017
Japan (JA)	0.34	0.43	0.29	0.40	0.49	0.45	0.37								0.85	5.77	0.78	0.075
Netherlands (NE)	0.43	0.69	0.53	0.59	0.70	0.45	0.30	0.44							1.01	5.80	1.06	0.102
Singapore (SG)	0.46	0.40	0.41	0.38	0.38	0.48	0.23	0.43	0.54						1.08	10.20	1.54	0.065
Spain (SP)	0.28	0.28	0.24	0.26	0.28	0.20	0.25	0.32	0.31	0.15					−0.46	6.12	0.45	−0.143
Sweden (SD)	0.30	0.44	0.28	0.29	0.42	0.24	0.16	0.35	0.46	0.34	0.23				1.18	5.89	0.66	0.130
Switzerland (SW)	0.48	0.72	0.46	0.60	0.75	0.38	0.38	0.46	0.78	0.53	0.25	0.52			0.77	6.01	1.00	0.059
United Kingdom (UK)	0.46	0.50	0.48	0.53	0.40	0.36	0.38	0.32	0.63	0.58	0.22	0.32	0.54		1.02	9.27	1.47	0.065
United States (US)	0.53	0.37	0.68	0.41	0.32	0.24	0.16	0.27	0.58	0.48	0.15	0.36	0.49	0.46	0.57	4.84	1.03	0.032

Source: C. Eun and B. Resnick, "International Diversification under Estimation Risk: Actual vs. Potential Gains." Reprinted by permission of the publisher from *Recent Developments in International Banking and Finance*, Vol. 1, edited by Sarkis J. Khoury and Alo Ghosh, Lexington, Mass.: Lexington Books, D.C. Heath & Co. Copyright 1987, D.C. Heath.

SUMMARY

This chapter has explored international diversification from both theoretical and empirical viewpoints. It was demonstrated that the exchange risk and inflation risk will affect the return of international investment, and, therefore, should be a major factor for analyzing international diversification.

Theoretically, the question of whether the world market is segmented or integrated has been shown to be important in investigating the effectiveness of international diversification. Both international CAPM and APT were used to discuss these related issues.

Both direct and indirect investment in foreign securities were used to show the benefit of international diversification. Finally, international mutual funds were employed to illustrate the usefulness of international diversification.

QUESTIONS AND PROBLEMS

1. Define the following terms.
   (a) exchange-rate risk   (b) segmented market
   (c) integrated market   (d) the Fisher effect
   (e) spot rate   (f) forward rate
   (g) direct foreign investment   (h) international portfolio investment
   (i) ADR

2. What are the returns to a U.S. investor for the investments shown in the table?

	Foreign Return (percent)	Currency Change (percent)
A	12	2
B	10	−5
C	7	0
D	10	−20

3. Can currency risk be diversified away for the U.S. investor?

4. Show the efficient frontiers for domestic portfolios and international diversified portfolios. Give some reasons why this relationship should exist.

5. Why would world capital markets be segmented?

6. The nominal interest rate in the U.S. is 10 percent; the nominal rate in Germany is 5 percent. What impact will this difference have on the exchange rate? On what factors does it depend?

7. The spot rate for the French franc is $1 = 6 FF. The inflation rate is 5 percent in the U.S. and 10 percent in France. What is the expected future spot rate for the franc in dollars?

8. Are world capital markets efficient? What factors need to be considered in answering this question?

9. What are the advantages of an ADR for the U.S. investor?

10. What is a Eurobond? Why would a U.S. investor want to own such a security?

APPENDIX 19A: OBJECTIVES AND POLICIES
OF AN INTERNATIONAL MUTUAL FUND

The investment objective of the Fund is to seek to obtain total return on its assets primarily through long-term capital growth and to a lesser extent from income . . . . The Fund will seek to achieve such objective through investment in all types of common stocks and equivalents, preferred stocks and bonds, and other debt obligations of domestic and foreign companies and governments and international organizations. There is no limitation on the percent or amount of the Fund's assets which may be invested for growth or income.[1]

. . . The percentage of the Fund's assets invested in particular geographic sectors will shift from time to time in accordance with the judgment of the Investment Advisers. . . .

Notwithstanding the Fund's investment objective of seeking total return, the fund may, for defensive purposes, with limitation, invest in: obligations of the United States Government, its agencies or instrumentalities, cash and cash equivalents in major currencies, repurchase agreements, money market instruments, and high quality commercial paper.

The Fund may also invest in securities of foreign issuers in the form of American Depository Receipts, European Depository Receipts or similar securities convertible into securities of foreign issuers . . . .

The Fund may enter into forward foreign currency exchange contracts as a hedge against fluctuations in future foreign exchange rates.

Since investments in foreign companies will usually involve currencies of foreign countries, and since the Fund may temporarily hold funds in bank deposits in foreign currencies during the course of investment programs, the

---

[1] Reproduced by courtesy of Dean Witter Worldwide Investment Trust Fund.

value of the assets of the Fund as measured in United States dollars may be affected by changes in foreign currency exchange rates, exchange control regulations, and the Fund may incur costs in connection with conversion between various currencies.

. . . when management of the Fund believes that the currency of a particular foreign country may suffer a substantial decline against the U.S. dollar, it may enter into a forward contract to sell, for a fixed amount of dollars, the amount of foreign currency approximating the value of some or all of the Fund's portfolio securities denominated in such foreign currency. The precise matching of the forward contract amounts and the value of the securities involved will not generally be possible since the future value of such securities in foreign currencies will change as a consequence of market movements in the value of those securities between the date the forward contract is entered into and the date it matures.

. . . In making the allocation of assets among the various markets, the Investment Advisers will consider such factors as recent developments in the various countries, the condition and growth potential of various economies and securities markets, currency and tax considerations and other pertinent financial social, national and political factors. . . .

. . . there may be the possibility of expropriations or confiscatory taxation, political, economic or social instability or diplomatic developments which could affect assets of the Fund held in foreign countries.

There may be less publicly available information about foreign companies comparable to reports and ratings published about United States companies. Foreign stock markets have substantially less volume than the New York Stock Exchange and securities of some foreign companies are less liquid and more volatile than securities of comparable United States companies. Brokerage commissions and other transactions costs on foreign securities exchanges are generally higher than in the United States.

REFERENCES

Abbeyekra, S. P. "The International Arbitrage Pricing Theory: An Empirical Investigation." Working paper, presented June 1985, Western Finance Association Annual Meeting.

Adler, M., and B. Dumas. "International Portfolio Choice and Corporate Finance: A Synthesis." *Journal of Finance,* v. 38 (June 1983), pp. 925–84.

Adler, M., and D. Simon. "Exchange Risk Surprises in International Portfolios." *Journal of Portfolio Management,* v. 12 (Winter 1986), pp. 44–53.

Ang, J., and R. Pohlman. "A Note on the Price Behavior of Far Eastern Stocks." *Journal of International Business Studies,* v. 9 (Spring 1978), pp. 103–07.

Black, F. "International Capital Market Equilibrium with Investment Barriers." *Journal of Financial Economics,* v. 1 (December 1974), pp. 337–52.

————. "The Ins and Outs of Foreign Investment." *Financial Analysts Journal,* v. 34 (May/June 1978), pp. 25–32.

Bomberger, W. A., and W. J. Frazer. "Interest Rates, Uncertainty, and the Livingston Data." *Journal of Finance,* v. 36 (June 1981), pp. 661–79.

Breeden, D. T. "An Intertemporal Asset Pricing Model with Stochastic Consumption and Investment Opportunities." *Journal of Financial Economics,* v. 7 (September 1979), pp. 265–96.

Cho, D. C., C. S. Eun, and L. W. Senbet. "International Arbitrage Pricing Theory: An Empirical Investigation." *Journal of Finance,* v. 41 (June 1986), pp. 313–29.

Cohn, R. A., and J. J. Pringle. "Imperfection in International Financial Markets: Implications for Risk Premium and the Cost of Capital to Firms." *Journal of Finance,* v. 28 (March 1973), pp. 59–66.

Cornell, B. "Spot Rates, Forward Rates, and Exchange Market Efficiency." *Journal of Financial Economics,* v. 5 (August 1977), pp. 55–65.

————. "Inflation, Relative Price Changes, and Exchange Risk." *Financial Management,* v. 9 (Autumn 1980), pp. 30–34.

Dean Witter. "Dean Witter World Wide Investment Trust." Prospectus, June 1984.

Errunza, V. R., and L. Senbet. "The Effects of International Operations on the Market Value of the Firm: Theory and Evidence." *Journal of Finance,* v. 36 (May 1981), pp. 401–17.

Eun, C. S. "International Portfolio Diversification." In D. K. Eiteman and A. I. Stonehill, *Multinational Business Finance.* Addison–Wesley, 1989.

————, and B. Resnick. "Estimating the Correlation Structure of International Share Prices." *Journal of Finance,* v. 39 (December 1984), pp. 1311–24.

————, and B. Resnick. "Estimating the Dependence Structure of Share Prices: A Comparative Study of the U.S. and Japan." *The Financial Review,* v. 23 (November 1988), pp. 387–401.

————. "International Diversification Under Estimation Risk: Actual vs. Potential Gains." In S. Khoury and A. Gosh, eds., *Recent Developments in International Banking and Finance.* Lexington Books, 1987, pp. 135–147.

Fama, E. F., and A. Farber. "Money Bonds and Foreign Exchange." *American Economic Review,* v. 69 (September 1979), pp. 639–50.

Frankel, J., and R. Levich. "Covered Interest Arbitrage: Unexploited Profits?" *Journal of Political Economy,* v. 83 (April 1975), pp. 325–38.

Grauer, F., R. Litzenberger, and R. Stehle. "Sharing Rules and Equilibrium in an International Capital Market under Uncertainty." *Journal of Financial Economics,* v. 3 (June 1976), pp. 233–56.

Grubel, H. G. "Internationally Diversified Portfolios: Welfare Gains and Capital Flows." *American Economic Review,* v. 58 (December 1968), pp. 1299–1314.

_____, and K. Fadner. "The Interdependence of International Equity Markets." *Journal of Finance*, v. 26 (March 1971), pp. 89–94.

Hawawini, G. *European Equity Markets: Price Behavior and Efficiency.* Salomon Brothers Center, New York University, Monograph 1984-9.

Ibbotson, R., L. Siegel, and K. Love. "World Wealth: Market Values and Returns." *Journal of Portfolio Management*, v. 11 (Fall 1985), pp. 4–23.

Jacob, N. L., and R. R. Pettit. *Investments.* Richard D. Irwin, Inc., 1984.

Jacquillat, B., and Solnik. "Multinationals Are Poor Tools for Diversification." *Journal of Portfolio Management*, v. 4 (Winter 1978), pp. 8–12.

Jaffe, J., and R. Westerfield. "Patterns in Japanese Common Stock Returns: Day of the Week and Turn of the Year Effects." *Journal of Financial and Quantitative Analysis*, v. 20 (June 1985), pp. 261–72.

Jorion, R. "International Portfolio Diversification with Estimation Risk." *Journal of Business*, v. 58 (July 1985), pp. 259–78.

Kato, K., and J. S. Schallheim. "Seasonal and Size Anomalies in the Japanese Stock Market." *Journal of Financial and Quantitative Analysis*, v. 20 (June 1985), pp. 243–60.

Lee, W. Y., and K. Sachdeva. "The Role of Multinational Firm in the Integration of Segmented Capital Markets." *Journal of Finance*, v. 32 (May 1977), pp. 479–92.

Lessard, D. R. "International Portfolio Diversification: A Multivariate Analysis for a Group of Latin American Countries." *Journal of Finance*, v. 28 (June 1973), pp. 619–33.

_____. "World, Country, and Industry Relationships in Equity Returns: Implications for Risk Reduction Through International Diversification." *Financial Analysts Journal*, v. 32 (January/February 1976), pp. 32–38.

Levy, H., and M. Sarnat. "International Diversification of Investment Portfolios." *American Economic Review*, v. 60 (September 1970), pp. 668–75.

Maldonado, R., and A. Saunders. "International Portfolio Diversification and the Intertemporal Stability of International Stock Market Relationships." *Financial Management*, v. 10 (Autumn 1981), pp. 54–63.

Morgan Guaranty Trust Company. *Investing Internationally.* 1978.

Proffitt, D., and N. Seitz. "The Performance of Internationally Diversified Mutual Funds." *Journal of the Midwest Finance Association*, v. 12 (March 1983), pp. 39–53.

Robichek, A. A., and M. R. Eaker. "Foreign Exchange Hedging and Capital Asset Pricing Model." *Journal of Finance*, v. 33 (June 1978), pp. 1011–18.

Roll, R. "A Critique of Asset Pricing Theories Tests. Part I: On Past and Potential Testability of the Theory." *Journal of Financial Economics*, v. 4 (March 1977), pp. 129–76.

_____. "Violations of Purchasing Power Parity and Their Implications for Efficient International Commodity Markets." In *International Finance and Trade*, ed. M. Sarnat and G. Szego. Bollinger, 1979.

_____, and B. Solnik. "A Pure Foreign Exchange Asset Pricing Model." *Journal of International Economics*, v. 13 (May 1977), pp. 161–79.

Senchack, A., and W. Beedles. "Is Indirect International Diversification Desirable?" *Journal of Portfolio Management*, v. 6 (Winter 1980), pp. 49–57.

Solnik, B. *International Investments*. Addison-Wesley, 1988.

_____. "The International Pricing of Risk: An Empirical Investigation of the World Capital Market Structure." *Journal of Finance*, v. 29 (May 1974 (A)), pp. 365–78.

_____. "Why Not Diversity Internationally Rather than Domestically?" *Financial Analysis Journal*, v. 29 (July/August 1974 (B)), pp. 48–54.

_____. "An Equilibrium Model of the International Capital Market." *Journal of Economic Theory*, v. 8 (August 1974 (C)), pp. 500–25.

_____. "An International Model of Security Price Behavior." *Journal of Financial and Quantitative Analysis*, v. 9 (September 1974 (D)), pp. 537–54.

_____. "Testing International Asset Pricing: Some Pessimistic Views." *Journal of Finance*, v. 32 (May 1977), pp. 503–12.

Stehle, R. "An Empirical Test of the Alternate Hypothesis of National and International Pricing of Risky Assets." *Journal of Finance*, v. 32 (May 1977), pp. 493–507.

Stockman, A. "A Theory of Exchange Rate Determination." *Journal of Political Economy*, v. 88 (August 1980), pp. 673–99.

Stulz, R. "On the Effects of Barriers to International Investment." *Journal of Finance*, v. 36 (September 1981), pp. 923–34.

_____. "A Model of International Asset Pricing." *Journal of Financial Economics*, v. 9 (December 1981), pp. 383–406.

Subrashmanyam, M. "On the Optimality of International Capital Market Integration." *Journal of Financial Economics*, v. 2 (August 1975), pp. 3–28.

20 Bond Portfolios: Management and Strategy

Portfolio theory has had a limited impact on the management of fixed-income portfolios. For the most part the techniques and strategies used in managing a bond portfolio are unique. This chapter presents techniques that are commonly used in bond-portfolio management and discusses the impact that portfolio theory has had on bond-portfolio management.

This chapter first focuses on the bond strategies of riding the yield curve and structuring the maturity of the bond portfolio in order to generate additional return. This is followed by a discussion of swapping. Next is an analysis of duration or the measure of the portfolio sensitivity to changes in interest rates, after which immunization is the focus. Finally, a case study is presented of bond-portfolio management in the context of portfolio theory.

BOND STRATEGIES

How are yield curves useful for investors and analysts? The primary ways in which they are used in the market include: (1) to improve the forecasting of interest rates, (2) as a measure to help identify mispriced debt securities, (3) to "ride the yield curve," and (4) to help investors manage their portfolio-maturity structures. This section concerns the third and fourth uses of yield curves.

Riding the Yield Curve

Riding the yield curve is an investment strategy designed to take advantage of yield-curve shapes that are expected to be maintained for a period of time. Given the yield-curve shape, an investor then decides whether to purchase a debt security that matures at the end of his or her time horizon or to purchase a longer-term debt security which can be sold at time T. (The investor may also purchase securities that mature before T and reinvest out

to T.) If the yield curve is upward sloping and is expected to remain stable over the investor's horizon period, purchasing a longer-term security and holding on to it as the end of the horizon period approaches would lead to an increasing selling price (bond value) as the yield declines. Even though reinvestment rates for coupons would also be declining, the total realized yield would be higher than the direct investment in a shorter-term security that matures at the end of the holding period. Similar strategies could be illustrated for other yield-curve shapes. The problem with successfully using such strategies is that yield curves do not remain unchanged for long periods of time; they can and do change abruptly and seemingly without warning. The best advice to those with a specific horizon period but little forecasting skill would likely be to invest in short-maturity bonds to maintain reinvestment flexibility.

Maturity-Structure Strategies

A common practice among bond-portfolio managers is to evenly space the maturity of their securities. Under the **staggered-maturity plan** bonds are held to maturity, at which time the principal is reinvested in another long-term maturity instrument. Little managerial expertise is required to maintain the portfolio, and the maturing bonds and regular interest payments provide some liquidity.

An alternative to a staggered portfolio is the **dumbbell strategy.** Dumbbell portfolios are characterized by the inclusion of some proportion of short and intermediate term bonds that provide a liquidity buffer to protect a substantial investment in long-term securities. In Figure 20–1 it is apparent why this is called the dumbbell strategy—the resulting graph looks like a weight lifter's dumbbell.

The dumbbell portfolio divides its funds between two components. The shortest maturity is usually less than three years, and the longest maturities are more than ten years. The portfolio is weighted at both ends of the

FIGURE 20–1   Dumbbell Maturity Strategy

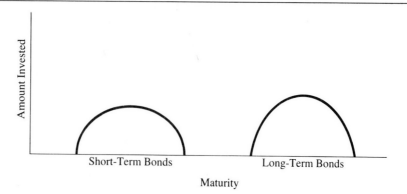

maturity spectrum (again like a dumbbell). The logic and mechanics of the dumbbell strategy are straightforward: the short-term Treasury notes (T-notes) provide the least risk and highest liquidity, while long-term bonds provide the highest return. The best risk/return portfolio combination may very well be a combination of these extremes. Assuming an upward-sloping yield curve, no intermediate bonds will be held since they have (1) less return than the longest-maturity bonds, and (2) less liquidity and safety than the shortest T-note.

The performance of staggered and dumbbell strategies differs with respect to price fluctuations and return. During periods when interest rates are expected to increase, the return will most likely be lower for a dumbbell portfolio than for a staggered portfolio. When rates are constant or cyclical and the yield curve is upward sloping, the dumbbell is superior to the staggered portfolio in yield; nevertheless, the price fluctuation will be greater for a dumbbell than for a staggered-maturity structure.

Swapping

When a market is in turmoil, great distortions take place. Some bonds drop further than they should, others less. A bond swapper can improve yield and pick up a substantial capital gain. In swapping, timing is all-important.

Swapping strategies generally concentrate on highly specialized trading relationships. A commonly accepted method for classifying such swaps is Homer and Leibowitz's four types: (1) pure yield-pickup swap, (2) interest-rate anticipations, (3) intermarket swap, and (4) substitution swap. The expected return from any swap is usually based upon several motives, not just one—thus, these "types" of swaps are really just sources of return.

Substitution Swap.   The substitution swap is the simplest of all. The swap attempts to profit from a change in yield spread between two nearly identical bonds. The trade is based upon a forecasted change in the yield spread between the two nearly identical bonds. The forecast is generally based upon the past history of the yield-spread relationship between the two bonds, with the assumption that any aberration from the past relationship is temporary, thereby allowing profit by buying the bond with the lower (higher) yield if the spread will become wider (or narrower). This trade is later reversed, leaving the investor in the original position, but with a trading profit from the relative changes in prices.

The substitution swap is simple in concept. Both the H-bond (the bond now held) and the P-bond (the proposed purchase) are equivalent in quality, coupon, and maturity. The swap is executed at a time when the bonds are mispriced relative to each other. This mispricing is expected to be corrected by the end of the workout period. Sample Problem 20.1 provides further illustration.

Sample Problem 20.1

Substitution Swap. Suppose the investor holds a thirty-year Aa utility 7-percent coupon bond (the H-bond), currently priced at par. He is offered to swap another thirty-year Aa utility 7-percent coupon bond (the P-bond) at a yield to maturity of 7.10 percent. Assume the workout period is one year. During this period, the prevailing reinvestment rate for coupon remains unchanged at 7 percent. At the end of the workout period both the H-bond and the P-bond are priced at par to yield 7.00 percent. See the evaluation worksheet that follows.

Evaluation Worksheet for a Sample Substitution Swap

	H-Bond *30-year 7s @ 7.00%*	*P-Bond* *30-year 7s @ 7.10%*
	Workout time: 1 year Reinvestment rate: 7%	
Original investment per bond	$1,000.00	$ 987.70
Two coupons during year	70.00	70.00
Interest on one coupon @ 7% for one-half year	1.23	1.23
Principal value at end of year @ 7.00 yield to maturity	1,000.00	1,000.00
Total accrued	1,071.23	1,071.23
Total gain	71.23	83.53
Gain per invested dollar	0.07123	0.08458
Realized compound yield (percent)	7.00	8.29
Value of swap	129 basis points in one year	

Source: Homer, S., and M. L. Leibowitz, *Inside the Yield Book*. Prentice-Hall and New York Institute of Finance, 1972, p. 84.

The worksheet gain of 129 basis points in realized compound yield is achieved only during the single year of the workout period. To obtain such a realized compound yield over the extended thirty-year period, the investor must continue to swap an average of once a year, picking up ten basis points with each swap, or at least averaging such a pickup on balance.

At the very worst, the workout period may take the entire thirty years, at which time the realized compound-yield gain would be 4.3 basis points. This is less than the initial ten-basis-point gain in yield to maturity because the same reinvestment rate will prevail for reinvesting the coupons of both the H-bond and the P-bond. This reinvestment rate benefits the bond with the lower starting yield relative to the bond with the higher starting yield. Thus, it pulls the total returns together. The relative benefit of the reinvest-

ment rate to the lower-yield issue will be greater at low future reinvestment rates and less at high future rates.

Effect of Workout Time on Substitution Swap: 30-Year 7s Swapped from 7% YTM to 7.10% YTM

Workout Time	Realized Compound Yield Gain
30 years	4.3 basis points/year
20	6.4
10	12.9
5	25.7
2	64.4
1	129.0
6 months	258.8
3 months	527.2

Source: Homer and Leibowitz, 1972, p. 85.

As the workout time is reduced, the relative gain in realized compound yield over the workout period rises dramatically, as seen in the second table, above. The substitution swap may not work out exactly as anticipated due to: (1) a slower workout time than anticipated, (2) adverse interim spreads,

Effect of Major Rate Changes on the Substitution Swap: 30-Year 7s Swapped from 7% to 7.1%, Realized Compound Yields—Principal Plus Interest

Reinvestment Rate and Yield to Maturity (percent)	1-Year Workout			30-Year Workout		
	H-Bond	P-Bond	Gain (Basis Points)	H-Bond	P-Bond	Gain (Basis Points)
5	34.551	36.013	146.2	5.922	5.965	4.3
6	19.791	21.161	137.0	6.445	6.448	4.3
7	7.00	8.29	129.0	7.000	7.043	4.3
8	(4.117)	(2.896)	122.1	7.584	7.627	4.3
9	(13.811)	(12.651)	116.0	8.196	8.239	4.3

Source: Homer and Leibowitz, 1972, p. 87.

(3) adverse changes in overall rates, and (4) the P-bond's not being a true substitute. In the substitution swap, major changes in overall market yields affect the price and reinvestment components of both the H- and P-bond. However, as these effects tend to run parallel for both the H- and P-bond,

the relative gain from the swap is insensitive even to major rate changes, as seen in the third table●

Intermarket-Spread Swap.   The intermarket spread swap works on trading between sector-quality-coupon categories, based upon a forecasted change in yield spread between two different categories. The most common forecasting method is to observe historical yield spreads at various points in the interest-rate cycle, and then to adjust for current supply-and-demand effects. However, this is most difficult, as shown by the 1977–78 period of extremely narrow spreads between AA's and U.S. government issues. Many managers bought government issues early in 1977, expecting the spread to widen, only to have to sit on their position through the next eighteen months as both inflation and government spending continued unabated.

In the intermarket-spread swap the offered P-bond is essentially a different bond from the investor's H-bond, and the yield spread between the two bonds is largely determined by the yield spread between two segments of the bond market itself. The investor believes the "intermarket" yield spread is temporarily out of line, and the swap is executed in the hope of profiting when the discrepancy in this spread is resolved.

The intermarket-spread swap can be executed in two directions. The swap can be made into a P-bond having a greater yield to maturity than the H-bond. This is done either for the extra yield (in belief that the spread will not widen), or in the belief that the intermarket spread will narrow, resulting in a lower relative yield to maturity for the P-bond, thus a higher relative price for the P-bond. The investor is always assured of a gain of the initial basis-point spread, less any adjustment to the YTM of the swapped bond due to reinvestments at a higher coupon rate by maturity. Sample Problem 20.2 provides further illustration.

Sample Problem 20.2

Intermarket-Spread Swap.   Suppose an investor holds the thirty-year 4s priced at 67.18 to yield 6.50 percent and views the thirty-year 7s at par as appropriate for an intermarket-spread swap. This investor feels that the fifty-basis-point spread is excessive and anticipates a shrinkage of ten basis points over the coming year. The price of the H-bond (4s) is kept constant for ease in computation. The evaluation worksheet on page 678 illustrates this situation.

The 24.5-basis-point gain over thirty years (see table of spread realizations on page 678) is less than the initial fifty-basis-point gain due to the fact that the same reinvestment rate benefits the bond with lower starting yield relative to the bond with the higher starting yield. Thus, it pulls the total returns together.

Evaluation Worksheet for a Sample Intermarket-Spread Swap in a Yield-Pickup Direction

	H-Bond *30-year 4s @ 6.50%*	P-Bond *30-year 7s @ 7.00%*
Initial yield to maturity (percent)	6.50	7.00
Yield to maturity at workout	6.50	6.90
Spread narrows 10 basis points from 50 basis points to 40 basis points.		
	Workout time: 1 year Reinvestment rate: 7%	
Original investment per bond	$671.82	$1,000.00
Two coupons during year	40.00	70.00
Interest on one coupon @ 7% for 6 months	0.70	1.23
Principal value at end of year	675.55	1,012.46
Total accrued	716.25	1,083.69
Total gained	44.43	83.69
Gain per invested dollar	0.0661	0.0837
Realized compound yield (percent)	6.508	8.200
Value of swap	169.2 basis points in one year	

Source: Homer and Leibowitz, 1972, p. 90.

Effect of Various Spread Realignments and Workout Times on the Sample Yield-Pickup Intermarket Swap: Basis-Point Gain (Loss) in Realized Compound Yields (Annual Rate)

Spread Shrinkage	*Workout Time*				
	6 Months	*1 Year*	*2 Years*	*5 Years*	*30 Years*
40	1083.4	539.9	273.0	114.3	24.5
30	817.0	414.6	215.8	96.4	24.5
20	556.2	291.1	159.1	78.8	24.5
10	300.4	169.2	103.1	61.3	24.5
0	49.8	49.3	47.8	44.0	24.5
(10)	(196.0)	(69.3)	(6.9)	26.8	24.5
(20)	(437.0)	(186.0)	(61.0)	9.9	24.5
(30)	(673.0)	(301.2)	(114.5)	(6.9)	24.5
(40)	(904.6)	(414.8)	(167.4)	(23.4)	24.5

Source: Homer and Leibowitz, 1972, p. 91.

The **yield-giveup** version of the intermarket-spread swap works against the investor over time. Therefore, when a swap involves a loss in yield, there is a high premium to be placed on achieving a favorable spread change within a relatively short workout period. Here the investor trades the higher yield-to-maturity H-bond for a lower yield-to-maturity bond (P-bond). The

investor will profit only if the yield spread widens, leading to relatively lower P-bond yields and consequently relatively higher P-bond prices, which would more than offset the yield loss.

As an example, assume the H-bond is the thirty-year 7s priced at par, and the P-bond is the thirty-year 4s priced at 67.18 to yield 6.50 percent. The investor believes that the present fifty-basis-point spread is too narrow and will widen, as shown in the second evaluation worksheet.

Evaluation Worksheet for a Sample Intermarket-Spread Swap with Yield Giveup

	H-Bond *30-year 7s @ 7%*	*P-Bond* *30-year 4s @ 6.50%*
Initial yield to maturity (percent)	7	6.5
Yield to maturity at workout (percent)	7	6.4
	Spread growth: 10 basis points Workout time: 1 year Reinvestment rate: 7%	
Original investment per bond	$1,000.00	$671.82
Two coupons during year	70.00	40.00
Interest on one coupon @ 7% for 6 months	1.23	0.70
Principal value at end of year	1,000.00	685.34
Total accrued	1,071.23	726.04
Total gain	71.23	54.22
Gain per invested dollar	0.0712	0.0807
Realized compound yield (percent)	7	7.914
Value of swap	91.4 basis points in one year	

Source: Homer and Leibowitz, 1972, p. 88.

Effect on Various Spread Realignments and Workout Times on the Sample Yield-Giveup Intermarket Swap: Basis-Point Gain (Loss) in Realized Compound Yields (Annual Rate)

Spread Growth	Workout Time				
	6 Months	*1 Year*	*2 Years*	*5 Years*	*30 Years*
40	1,157.6	525.9	218.8	41.9	(24.5)
30	845.7	378.9	150.9	20.1	(24.5)
20	540.5	234.0	83.9	(1.5)	(24.5)
10	241.9	91.4	17.6	(22.9)	(24.5)
0	(49.8)	(49.3)	(47.8)	(44.0)	(24.5)
(10)	(335.3)	(187.7)	(112.6)	(64.9)	(24.5)
(20)	(614.9)	(324.1)	(176.4)	(85.6)	(24.5)
(30)	(888.2)	(458.4)	(239.1)	(106.0)	(24.5)
(40)	(1,155.5)	(590.8)	(302.1)	(126.3)	(24.5)

Source: Homer and Leibowitz, 1972, p. 89.

General market moves over the short term would have little effect on the swap's value provided the spread changes as originally anticipated. The potential risk of this swap must be viewed in the context of changes in overall rate levels and the realignment of spread relationships among the many market components. As can be seen from the last table, there is a high premium to be placed on achieving a favorable spread change within a relatively short workout period●

Interest-Rate Anticipation Swap. The investor who feels that the overall level of interest rates is going to change will want to effect a swap that will net a relative gain if this happens. Most commonly these swaps consist of shortening maturities if higher long-term yields are expected, and lengthening maturities if lower long-term yields are expected.

The decisive factor is the expected long rate: the change in the long rate will almost always be the chief determinant of the value of the swap. Maturity swaps are highly speculative. If yields do not rise or fall as expected in a short period of time, often a large penalty due to the immediate loss in yield will occur. If the yield curve is positive, as one moves from long to short a large yield loss occurs. Conversely, if the curve is negative, moving from short to long involves little or no yield pickup and sometimes a yield loss. Time works heavily against the swapper. Nevertheless, these periods of maximum yield loss are usually the best times to make maturity swaps in both directions.

In evaluating maturity swaps, capital gains or losses will be critical over the first year or so. As time goes on, coupon income and compounded interest become more important. The concept of duration easily explains this fact, for as time increases the present-value factor declines. Therefore, capital gains or losses are valued at the lower present-value factor. Sample Problem 20.3 provides further illustration.

Sample Problem 20.3

Interest-Rate-Anticipation Swap. Suppose an investor holds a 7-percent thirty-year bond selling at par. He expects rates to rise from 7 to 9 percent within the year. Therefore, a trade is made into a 5-percent Treasury note maturing in one year and selling at par, as in the worksheet on page 681.

The portfolio manager who shortens maturities drastically at a large loss in yield within the long range must expect a substantial increase in yields within the short range—otherwise his long-range yield loss will exceed his short-term gain. The swapper into longs at a big yield increase has time in his favor, but over the near term he can fare badly if long yields rise further. Finally, the swapper from short to long at a yield loss also has time against him●

Evaluation Worksheet for a Sample Interest-Rate-Anticipation Swap

	H-Bond 30-year 7s @ 100	P-Note 1-year 5s @ 100
	Anticipated rate change: 9% Workout time: 1 year	
Original investment per bond	$1,000	$1,000
Two coupons during year	70	50
Interest on one coupon @ 7%	1.23	—
Principal value at end of year	748.37	1,000
Total accrued	819.60	1,050
Total gain	(180.4)	50
Gain per invested dollar	(0.1804)	0.05
Realized compound yield (percent)	(13.85)	5.00
Value of swap	1,885 basis points in one year	

Source: Homer and Leibowitz, 1972, p. 94.

Pure Yield-Pickup Swap.   In a pure yield-pickup swap there is no expectation of market changes, but a simple attempt to increase yield. Basically, two bonds are examined to establish their difference in yield to maturity, with a further adjustment to consider the impact of interim reinvestment of coupons at an assumed rate or return between now and the maturity date. Sample Problem 20.4 provides further illustration.

Sample Problem 20.4

Pure Yield-Pickup Swap.   Suppose an investor swaps from the thirty-year 4s at 671.82 to yield 6.50 percent into thirty-year 7s at 100 to yield 7.00 percent for the sole purpose of picking up the additional 105 basis points in current income or the fifty basis points in the yield to maturity. The investor is not motivated by a judgment that the intermarket spread will shrink or that yields will rise or fall. He has no explicit concept of a workout period—he intends to hold the 7s to maturity.

To evaluate a swap of this sort, which is based on holding the P-bond to maturity, three factors must be taken into account: (1) the coupon income, (2) the interest on interest, and (3) the amortization to par. Interim market-price changes may be ignored. A simple addition of the three money flows just listed, divided by the dollars invested, will give a total return in dollars which, with the aid of a compound-interest table, will give the total realized compound yield as a percent of each dollar invested, as shown in the worksheet, next page.

Evaluation Worksheet for a Sample Pure Yield-Pickup Swap

	H-Bond *30-year 4s @ 6.50%*	*P-Bond* *30-year 7s @ 7.00%*
	(one bond)	(0.67182 of one bond)
Coupon income over thirty years	$1,200.00	$1,410.82
Interest on interest at 7%	2,730.34	3,210.02
Amortization	328.18	0
Total return	$4,258.52	$4,620.84
Realized compound yield (percent)	6.76	7.00
Value of swap	24 basis points per annum at 7% reinvestment rate	

Source: Homer and Leibowitz, 1972, p. 99.

Although the principal invested in both issues is only $671.82 per bond, over a period of thirty years the switch results in a gain of $210.82 per bond in coupon income, a gain of $479.68 per bond in interest on interest, and a loss of $328.18 per bond in capital gain. These three factors add up to a net gain of $362.32 per bond, or a net gain of twenty-four basis points per year●

DURATION

The traditional role of bonds as an asset category has changed over the past fifteen years due to surging interest rates and the resultant price volatility. The use of bond maturity to reduce interest-rate risk in bond portfolios through maturity matching has become increasingly inadequate. By the 1970s several researchers had recognized that maturity is an incomplete measure of the life and risk of a coupon bond.

In 1971 Fisher and Weil recommended a practical measurement tool that could help immunize bond portfolios against interest-rate risk, and in 1973 Hopewell and Kaufman demonstrated that it could also be used as a measure of price risk for bonds. This concept is **duration,** which has emerged as an important tool for the measurement and management of interest-rate risk. Bierwag, Kaufman, and Toevs (BKT) noted in 1983 that only the introduction of beta in the 1960s has generated as much interest in the investment community as has duration.

The purpose of this section is to review briefly the historical development of duration and to examine its potential use by investors in alternative bond-portfolio immunization strategies, as well as to look at certain reservations that should be considered when using duration to immunize bond portfolios.

In 1938 Frederick Macaulay developed the concept of duration as part of an overall analysis of interest rates and bond prices. He was attempting to develop a more meaningful summary measure of the life of a bond that would correlate well with changes in bond price; he arrived at a weighted average of the time to each bond payment, with the weights being the present values of each payment relative to the total present value of all the flows:

$$D = \frac{\sum_{t=0}^{n} t\left[\frac{C_t}{(1 + k_d)^t}\right]}{\sum_{t=0}^{n} \frac{C_t}{(1 + k_d)^t}} \tag{20.1}$$

where:

C_t = the coupon-interest payment in periods 1 through $n - 1$;
C_n = the sum of the coupon-interest payment and the face value of the bond in period n;
k_d = the YTM or required rate of return of the bondholders in the market; and
t = the time period in years.

Thus, for the first semi-annual payment in the series between 0 and n, t would equal 0.5. The denominator of this equation is equal to the current price of the bond as estimated by the present value of all future cash flows.

The duration of a bond with a fixed maturity date declines just as maturity with the passage of time. The duration of a coupon bond, however, is always shorter than its maturity. Only for pure discount (zero-coupon) bonds will duration equal maturity. Duration is also affected by the size of the coupon and its YTM, decreasing as either increases.

It is useful to place the concept of duration in the perspective of other summary measures of the timing of an asset's cash flow. Because the cash flows from bonds are specific, both as to timing and amount, analysts have derived a precise measure of the timing for bonds. The most commonly used timing measure is term to maturity (TM), the number of years prior to the final payment on the bond. The advantage of TM is that it is easily identified and measured. However, the disadvantage is that TM ignores interim cash flows. Moreover, TM ignores the substantial difference in coupon rates and the difference in sinking funds.

Weighted-Average Term to Maturity (WATM)

In an attempt to rectify the deficiency of TM, a measure that considered the interest payments and the final principal payment was constructed. The **weighted-average term to maturity (WATM)** computes the proportion of each individual payment as a percentage of all payments and makes this proportion the weight for the year the payment is made:

$$\text{WATM} = \frac{\text{CF}_1}{\text{TCF}}(1) + \frac{\text{CF}_2}{\text{TCF}}(2) + \ldots + \frac{\text{CF}_n}{\text{TCF}}(n) \qquad \textbf{(20.2)}$$

where:

CF_t = the cash flow in year t;
t = the year when cash flow is received;
n = maturity; and
TCF = the total cash flow from the bond.

Sample Problem 20.5 provides further illustration.

Sample Problem 20.5

Suppose a ten-year, 4-percent bond will have total cash-flow payments of $1400. Thus, the $40 payment in CF_1 will have a weight of 0.0287 ($40/$1400), each subsequent interest payment will have the same weight, and the principal payment in year 10 will have a weight of 0.74286 ($1040/1400). Therefore:

$$\text{WATM} = \frac{\$40}{\$1400}(1) + \frac{\$40}{\$1400}(2) + \frac{\$40}{\$1400}(3) +$$
$$\ldots + \frac{\$40}{\$1400}(9) + \frac{\$1040}{\$1400}(10) = 8.71 \text{ years}$$

The WATM is definitely less than the term to maturity, because it takes account of all interim cash flows in addition to the final payment. In addition, a bond with a larger coupon has a shorter weighted-average term to maturity because a larger proportion of its total cash flows is derived from the coupon payments prior to maturity—that is, the coupon-weighted average of the larger coupon is larger than the smaller coupon bond. The weighted-average term can be utilized to take into account sinking-fund payments, thus lowering the weighted-average term to maturity●

Weighted-Average Term to Maturity versus Duration Measure

A major advantage of WATM is that it considers the timing of all cash flows from the bond, including interim and final payments. One disadvantage is that it does not consider the time value of the flows. The interest payment of the first period is valued the same as the last period.

The **duration measure** is simply a weighted-average maturity, where the weights are stated in present value terms. In the same format as the weighted-average term to maturity, duration is

$$D = \frac{\text{PVCF}_1}{\text{PVTCF}}(1) + \frac{\text{PVCF}_2}{\text{PVTCF}}(2) + \ldots + \frac{\text{PVCF}_n}{\text{PVTCF}}(n) \qquad \textbf{(20.3)}$$

where:

PVCF_t = the present value of the cash flow in year t discounted at current yield to maturity;

t = the year when cash flow is received;

n = maturity; and

PVTCF = the present value of total cash flow from the bond discounted at current yield to maturity.

The time in the future when a cash flow is received is weighted by the proportion that the present value of that cash flow contributes to the total present value or price of the bond. Similar to the weighted-average term to maturity, the duration of a bond is shorter than its term to maturity because of the interim interest payment. Duration is inversely related to the coupon of the bond. The one variable that does not influence the average term to maturity but can affect duration is the prevailing market yield. Market yield does not affect WATM because this measure does not consider the present value of flows. Nevertheless, market yield affects both the numerator and denominator of the duration computation, and it affects the numerator more. As a result, there is an inverse relation between a change in the market yield and a bond's duration.

Tables 20-1 and 20-2, taken from Frank K. Reilly and Rupinder S. Sidhu's (1980) article, "The Many Uses of Bond Duration," illustrate the

TABLE 20-1 Weighted-Average Term to Maturity (Assuming Annual Interest Payments)

	Bond A $1,000, 10 years, 4%				Bond B $1,000, 10 years, 8%		
(1) *Year*	*(2)* *Cash Flow*	*(3)* *Cash Flow/TCF*	*(4)* *(1) × (3)*	*(5)* *Year*	*(6)* *Cash Flow*	*(7)* *Cash Flow/TCF*	*(8)* *(5) × (7)*
1	$ 40	0.02857	0.02857	1	$ 80	0.04444	0.04444
2	40	0.02857	0.05714	2	80	0.04444	0.08888
3	40	0.02857	0.08571	3	80	0.04444	0.13332
4	40	0.02857	0.11428	4	80	0.04444	0.17776
5	40	0.02857	0.14285	5	80	0.04444	0.22220
6	40	0.02857	0.17142	6	80	0.04444	0.26664
7	40	0.02857	0.19999	7	80	0.04444	0.31108
8	40	0.02857	0.22856	8	80	0.04444	0.35552
9	40	0.02857	0.25713	9	80	0.04444	0.39996
10	1,040	0.74286	7.42860	10	1,080	0.60000	6.00000
Sum	$1,400	1.00000	8.71425	Sum	$1,800	1.00000	7.99980
Weighted-average term to maturity = 8.71 years				Weighted-average term to maturity = 8.00 years			

Source: Reilly and Sidhu, "The Many Uses of Bond Duration," *Financial Analysts Journal* (July/August 1980), p. 60.

TABLE 20-2 Duration (Assuming 8-Percent Market Yield)

(1) Year	(2) Cash Flow	(3) PV at 8%	(4) PV of Flow	(5) PV as % of Price	(6) (1) × (5)
Bond A					
1	$ 40	0.9259	$ 37.04	0.0506	0.0506
2	40	0.8573	34.29	0.0469	0.0938
3	40	0.7938	31.75	0.0434	0.1302
4	40	0.7350	29.40	0.0402	0.1608
5	40	0.6806	27.22	0.0372	0.1860
6	40	0.6302	25.21	0.0345	0.2070
7	40	0.5835	23.34	0.0319	0.2233
8	40	0.5403	21.61	0.0295	0.2360
9	40	0.5002	20.01	0.0274	0.2466
10	1,040	0.4632	481.73	0.6585	6.5850
Sum			$ 731.58	1.0000	8.1193

Duration = 8.12 years

Bond B					
1	$ 80	0.9259	$ 74.07	0.0741	0.0741
2	80	0.8573	68.59	0.0686	0.1372
3	80	0.7938	63.50	0.0635	0.1906
4	80	0.7350	58.80	0.0588	0.1906
5	80	0.6806	54.44	0.0544	0.2720
6	80	0.6302	50.42	0.0504	0.3024
7	80	0.5835	46.68	0.0467	0.3269
8	80	0.5403	43.22	0.0432	0.3456
9	80	0.5002	40.02	0.0400	0.3600
10	1,080	0.4632	500.26	0.5003	5.0030
Sum			$1000.00	1.0000	7.2470

Duration = 7.25 years

Source: Reilly and Sidhu, 1980, p. 61.

difference between the timing measures. These two tables respectively show the weighted-average term to maturity and the duration. Due to the consideration of the time value of money in the duration measurement, duration is the superior measuring technique.

Weighted-average term to maturity is always longer than the duration of a bond, and the difference increases with the market rate used in the duration formula. This is consistent with the duration property of an inverse relation between duration and the market rate.

Yield to Maturity

Yield to maturity is an average maturity measurement in its own way because it is calculated using the same rate to discount all payments to the bondholder—thus it is an average of spot rates over time. For example, if

the spot rate for period two, r_2, is greater than that for period one, r_1, the YTM on a two-year coupon bond would be between r_1 and r_2—an underestimate of the two-year spot rate. Likewise, the opposite condition would overestimate the two-year spot rate. With the high volatility of interest rates that has existed in recent years, the difference can be dramatic. For example, in Britain during 1977 the twenty-year spot rate of interest was approximately 20 percent, while the YTM on twenty-year coupon bonds was only 13 percent. The reason for the large discrepancy was that YTM was calculated as an average of the relatively low short-term spot rates and the relatively high long-term spot rates.

Until the 1970s, when interest-rate and bond-price volatility increased dramatically, the significance of the superiority of duration over average-maturity measurements remained largely unnoticed. More precision in the measurement of bond-portfolio risk was required for immunization against interest-rate risk. Studies comparing the success of portfolios immunized with a duration strategy and a maturity strategy have shown that duration outperforms maturity 75 percent of the time for a variety of planning periods. Duration also produces lower variances between realized and promised returns than either the maturity strategy or the naive strategy of annually rolling over twenty-year bonds.

The motivation for bond investment is to secure a fixed cash flow over a particular investment horizon. Asset and liability portfolios of financial institutions often generate future cash-flow patterns that must conform to certain solvency and profitability restrictions. For example, insurance companies and pension funds, with definite future commitments of funds, invest now so that their future cash-flow stream will match well with their future commitment stream. Bond-immunization strategies are designed to guarantee the investor in default-free and option-free bonds a rate of return that approximates the promised rate (or YTM) computed at the outset of the investment. Nevertheless, the YTM will be equal to the realized yield (RY) only if the interim coupon payments are reinvestable at the YTM. If interest rates change, the RY will be lower or higher than YTM, depending upon the relationship between the bond's measured duration D and the investor's expected holding period H. Babcock (1975) devised a simple formula in which realized yield is computed as a weighted average of the YTM and the average reinvestment rate (RR) available for coupon payments:

$$\text{RY} = \left(\frac{D}{H}\right)(\text{YTM}) + \left(1 - \frac{D}{H}\right)(\text{RR}) \tag{20.4}$$

Therefore, the realized yield (RY) would equal the YTM only if the duration on the bond were kept equal to the time horizon of the investor. An increase in the reinvestment rate would increase the return from reinvested coupons, but would at the same time decrease the bond value. Only holding the bond to maturity would prevent this value reduction from affecting the realized yield. Therefore, the overall impact of reinvestment-rate increases depends upon the extent to which the income effect offsets the value reduction. On the other hand, a decrease in the reinvestment rate will decrease the return

from reinvested coupons, but it will increase the bond values in the market. As shown in Equation (20.4), these opposite impacts on RY will exactly offset each other only when D equals H.

If a more complete time spectrum of zero-coupon bonds of all types were readily available, bond-portfolio immunization would be a relatively simple process. Simply by choosing bonds with maturities equal to the length of an investor's investment horizon, the rate of return would always be as promised by the YTM, regardless of interest-rate changes. Beginning with Treasury-bond sales of February 15, 1985, the U.S. Treasury has been cooperating with Wall Street firms in the stripping of coupon payments from new Treasury issues through separate registration of coupon and maturity payments, thus manufacturing a series of zero-coupon issues. However, since this applies only to Treasury issues, it is still necessary for investors to use duration models to immunize portfolios of non-Treasury bonds.

To immunize a bond portfolio, investors must match the duration of the portfolio with the length of their investment horizons. This must be accomplished within their assumed stochastic process of interest-rate movements and changes in the yield curve. If the yield curve changes during the holding period, the immunization process will break down and the RY will not equal the YTM as promised.

Since the hoped-for results of the passive duration-immunization method can be upset by interest-rate shifts, some investors may prefer to try to predict interest-rate changes and undertake an active immunization strategy. This would involve the formation of bond portfolios with durations intentionally longer or shorter than the investment-planning period. Since it is usually assumed that the market consensus about future interest rates is the most likely possibility, investors should pursue active strategies only if their forecasts of rates differ from those of the market. The investor who expects interest rates to be higher than the market forecast, should form a bond portfolio with a duration shorter than the length of the investment horizon. If successful, the income gains from reinvestment of coupons and maturing bonds will exceed the value loss on unmatured bonds: RY will exceed the YTM promised. If unsuccessful, the reinvestment return will not be enough to offset the value loss and RY will be less than YTM.

If the investor expects interest rates to be lower than the market forecast, the procedure would be the reverse of that described above—that is, to purchase a bond portfolio with a duration longer than the investment horizon. If successful, the lower reinvestment returns will be more than offset by the bond-value gains. Thus the active immunization strategy relies solely upon the ability of the investor to predict the direction of future interest-rate changes and to take full advantage of market opportunities for realized returns greater than market rates. While this provides the investor with an opportunity for substantial returns, it can also result in substantial losses. Because of this, Leibowitz and Weinberger (LW, 1981) derived a "stop loss" active immunization strategy which they called contingent immunization. In this method, the portfolio manager pursues higher returns through active management unless the value of the portfolio declines to a level that

threatens a minimum target return. At this point, the portfolio is switched into a pure immunization mode designed to provide the minimum target specified at the outset. Other researchers have developed similar strategies that rely on two portfolios—one actively and the other passively immunized. Interest changes could take place that would virtually wipe out the active portfolio, but they would not greatly affect the minimum target return of the two-portfolio combination.

The Macaulay Model

The duration model that is still most widely used because of its simplicity is the **Macaulay model.** However, basic limitations affect the use of this model. First, the current and forward spot rates are assumed to be equal over a specific planning horizon—that is, the yield curve is assumed to be flat. This is also one of the basic weaknesses of the YTM measurement. Second, this model provides an accurate measure of interest-rate risk only when there is a single parallel shift in the term of structure of interest rates—that is, there is only one shift within the holding period and it does not involve a change in yield-curve shape.

Most studies surveyed seem to indicate that the Macaulay model assumptions are unrealistic and too restrictive. Cox, Ingersoll, and Ross (1979) noted that it does not take into account the dynamic nature of the term structure observed in the real world, in which yield curves can and do change in shape as well as location. As a result, a number of more complex duration models have been developed to measure risk when multiple term-structure shifts can affect the shape and location of the yield curve. Because the actual underlying stochastic process governing interest-rate changes is not known, only empirical analysis can determine whether the extra complexity of these models justifies their usage. Bierwag, Kaufman, and Toevs (1983) extensively tested the Macaulay model along with four more complex duration models and found that duration-matching strategies generated realized returns consistently closer to promised yields than a maturity-matching strategy. Even more interesting, the Macaulay measure appeared to perform as well as the more complex models. Their findings suggest that single-factor duration matching is a feasible immunization strategy that works reasonably well, even with the less complex (and thus less costly) Macaulay model.

Duration appears a better measure of a bond's life than maturity because it provides a more meaningful relationship with interest-rate changes. This relationship has been expressed by Hopewell and Kaufman (1973) as:

$$\frac{\Delta P}{P} = D \, \Delta i \qquad\qquad (20.5)$$

where:

Δ = "change in";
P = bond price;
D = duration; and
i = market interest rate.

For example, a bond with five years' duration will decline in price by approximately ten percent when market yield increases by two percent. Note that $\Delta P/P$ on the left side of Equation (20.5) is the percentage change in price, and Δi is the absolute change in yield level, not percentage change.

Other useful generalizations can be made concerning the relationships of duration to various bond characteristics, as follows.

1. The higher the coupon, the shorter the duration, because the face-value payment at maturity will represent a smaller proportional present-value contribution to the makeup of the current bond value. In other words, bonds with small coupon rates will experience larger capital gains or losses as interest rates change. Additionally, for all bonds except zero-coupon-rate bonds, as the maturity of the bond lengthens the duration at the limit will approach $(1 + YTM)/YTM$. Table 20–3 shows the relationship between duration, maturity, and coupon rates for a bond with a yield to maturity of 6 percent. At the limit (maturity goes to infinity), the duration will approach 17.667 [that is; $(1 + 0.06)/0.06$].

As can be seen in Table 20–3, the limit is independent of the coupon rate: it is always 17.667. However, when the coupon rate is the same as or greater than the yield rate (the bond is selling at a premium), duration approaches the limit directly. Conversely, for discount-priced bonds (coupon rate is less than yield to maturity), duration can increase beyond the limit and then recede to the limit. In the case of the bond with the 2-percent coupon at a maturity of fifty years, the duration is 19.452—and this approaches the limit as maturity keeps increasing. These relationships are shown in Figure 20–2.

Regardless of coupon size, it is nearly impossible to find bonds with durations in excess of twenty years; most bonds have a limit of about fifteen years.

2. The higher the YTM, the shorter the duration, because YTM is used as the discount rate for the bond's cash flows and higher discount rates diminish the proportional present-value contribution of more distant payments.

TABLE 20–3   Duration, Maturity, and Coupon Rate

Maturity (years)	Coupon Rates			
	0.02	*0.04*	*0.06*	*0.08*
1	0.995	0.990	0.985	0.981
5	4.756	4.558	4.393	4.254
10	8.891	8.169	7.662	7.286
20	14.981	12.98	11.904	11.232
50	19.452	17.129	16.273	15.829
100	17.567	17.232	17.12	17.064
∞	17.667	17.667	17.667	17.667

FIGURE 20–2   Duration and Maturity for Premium and Discount Bonds

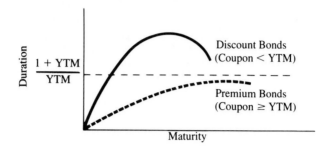

As has been shown, at the limit duration is equal to (1 + YTM)/YTM; in Table 20–4 the relationship between duration and YTM is shown.

3. A typical sinking fund (one in which the bond principal is gradually retired over time) will reduce duration. Duration can be reduced by the sinking-fund or call provision. A large proportion of current bond issues do have sinking funds, and these can definitely affect a bond's duration. An example will illustrate this fact. A ten-year 4-percent bond with a sinking fund of 10 percent of face value per year starting at the end of the fifth year has a duration of 7.10 years as compared to the duration of 8.12 years of a similar bond without a sinking fund. Table 20–5 provides further illustration.

The effect of a sinking fund on the time structure of cash flows for a bond is certain to the issuer of the bond, since the firm must make the payments: they represent a legal cash-flow requirement that will affect the firm's cash flow. However, the sinking fund may not affect the investor since the money put into the sinking fund may not necessarily be used to retire outstanding bonds. Even if it is, it is not certain that a given investor's bonds will be called for retirement.

TABLE 20–4   Duration and Yield to Maturity

YTM	Duration at Limit (maturity → ∞)
0.02	51
0.04	26
0.08	13.5
0.10	11
0.20	6
0.30	4.33
0.50	3

TABLE 20-5   Duration With and Without Sinking Funds (Assuming 8-Percent Market Yield)

	Cash Flow	Present-Value Factor	Present Value of Cash Flow	Weight	Duration
Bond A—No Sinking Fund					
1	$ 40	0.9259	$ 37.04	0.0506	0.0506
2	40	0.8573	34.29	0.0469	0.0938
3	40	0.7938	31.75	0.0434	0.1302
4	40	0.7350	29.40	0.0402	0.1608
5	40	0.6806	27.22	0.0372	0.1860
6	40	0.6302	25.21	0.0345	0.2070
7	40	0.5835	23.34	0.0319	0.2233
8	40	0.5403	21.61	0.0295	0.2360
9	40	0.5002	20.01	0.0274	0.2466
10	1,040	0.4632	481.73	0.6585	6.5850
Sum			$731.58	1.0000	8.1193
Duration = 8.12 years					
Bond A—Sinking Fund (10% per year from fifth year)					
1	$ 40	0.9259	$ 37.04	0.04668	0.04668
2	40	0.8573	34.29	0.04321	0.08642
3	40	0.7938	31.75	0.04001	0.12003
4	40	0.7350	29.40	0.03705	0.14820
5	140	0.6806	95.28	0.12010	0.60050
6	140	0.6302	88.23	0.11119	0.66714
7	140	0.5835	81.69	0.10295	0.72065
8	140	0.5403	75.64	0.09533	0.76264
9	140	0.5002	70.03	0.08826	0.79434
10	540	0.4632	250.13	0.31523	3.15230
Sum			$793.48	1.00000	7.09890
Duration = 7.10 years					

Source: Reilly and Sidhu, 1980, pp. 61–62.

4. For bonds of less than five years to maturity, the magnitudes of duration changes are about the same as those for maturity changes. For bonds of five to fifteen years' maturity, changes in the magnitude of duration are considerably less than those of maturity. For bonds with more than twenty years to maturity, changes in the magnitude of duration are very small relative to changes in maturity. As can be seen in Figure 20-3, in the range of zero to five years the relationship between duration and maturity is shown approximately by a straight line with a slope of 45 degrees. In the range of five to ten years the slope of the line is less, indicating a smaller change in duration for a given change in maturity. And for more than twenty

FIGURE 20–3   Duration versus Maturity

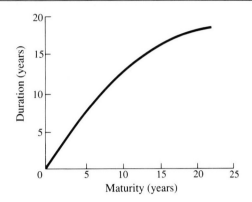

years the line is almost horizontal, showing a smaller change in duration for a given change in maturity.

5. In contrast to a sinking fund, all bondholders will be affected if a bond is called. The duration of a callable bond will be shorter than a noncallable bond.

When a bond is callable, the cash flow implicit in the yield-to-maturity figure is subject to possible early alteration. Most corporate bonds issued today are callable, but with a period of call protection before the call option can be exercised. At the expiration of this period the bond may be called at a specified call price, which usually involves some premium over par.

To provide some measure of the return in the event that the issuer exercises the call option at some future point, the yield to call is calculated instead of the yield to maturity. This computation is based on the assumption that the bond's cash flow is terminated at the "first call date" with redemption of principal at the specified call price. The crossover yield is defined as that yield where the yield to maturity is equal to the yield to call. When the price of the bond rises to some value above the call price, and the market yield declines to a value below the crossover yield, the yield to call becomes the minimum yield. At this price and yield, the firm will probably exercise a call option when it is available. When prices go below the call price, the yield to maturity is the minimum yield. Sample Problem 20.6 provides further illustration.

Sample Problem 20.6

To calculate the crossover yield for a 8-percent, thirty-year bond selling at par with ten-year call protection, the annual return flow divided by the

average investment can be used as an approximation for the yield. The implied crossover yield is 8.46 percent:

$$\text{Crossover yield:} \quad \frac{80 + \dfrac{1080 - 1000}{10}}{\dfrac{1080 + 1000}{2}} = 8.46\%$$

In one year's time the bond's maturity will be twenty-nine years with nine years to call. If the market rate has declined to the point where the yield to maturity of the bond is 7 percent, which is below the crossover yield of 8.46 percent, the bond's yield to call will be 6 percent.

$$\text{Yield to call} = \frac{80 + \dfrac{1000 - 1123.43}{9}}{\dfrac{1080 + 1123.43}{2}} = 6\%$$

If a bond-portfolio manager ignored the call option and computed the duration of this bond to maturity at a market yield of 7 percent, the duration would be 12.49 years. If duration was computed recognizing the call option at a price of $1,080 and using the yield to call of 6 percent, it would be 6.83 years●

Since a majority of corporate bonds have a call option, the effect of the call option upon a bond's duration could have an effect on the bond manager's investment decision. Therefore, the bond's duration, both disregarding the call option and regarding the call option, must be considered in an investment decision. That is, if interest rates stabilize or continue to rise, the call-option duration is of less importance than the bond's duration disregarding the call option. If interest rates fall, the call-option duration is of more importance.

CONTINGENT IMMUNIZATION

Contingent immunization allows a bond-portfolio manager to pursue the highest yields available through active strategies while relying on the techniques of bond immunization to assure that the portfolio will achieve a given minimal return over the investment horizon. Using this strategy, the portfolio manager attempts to earn returns in excess of the immunized return, but at the same time attempts to constrain or control losses that may result from poor forecasts of interest-rate movements.

Risk control is the major objective of contingent immunization. At the inception of the strategy, the manager determines the degree of risk he is willing to accept. If a sequence of interest-rate movements causes the portfolio to approach the predetermined risk level, the manager alters the

portfolio's duration to completely immunize it from any further risk. On the other hand, if the interest-rate movements provide additional returns, the portfolio manager does nothing.

The difference between the minimal, or floor, rate of return and the rate of return on the market is called the cushion spread. Equation (20.6) shows the relationship between the market rate of return R_m and the cushion C to be the floor rate of return, R_{FL}.

$$R_{FL} = R_m - C \qquad\qquad (20.6)$$

Interest-rate movement favorable to the bond-portfolio manager's position will enlarge the spread—that is, R_m goes up and the portfolio is long bonds, thereby increasing the realized return. Adverse interest-rate movements will reduce the cushion spread $R_m - C$ up to the point that $R_{FL} = R_m$. At this point the portfolio manager will immunize the portfolio, which will ensure that the realized return will equal R_{FL}.

Figure 20–4 is a graphical presentation of contingent immunization. The realized change in the market rate of return is shown on the horizontal axis, and the potential rate of return for the portfolio is shown on the vertical axis. The potential return is a function of the market return, the floor return, and the cushion. If the interest-rate change is $+2$ percent, the portfolio manager shifts to an immunization strategy that locks in the R_{FL} at 10 percent for the planning horizon. Regardless of interest-rate movements thereafter, the portfolio will realize a return of 10 percent. If interest rates were to go down, the portfolio would earn a return in excess of the R_{FL} because of the

FIGURE 20–4   Contingent Immunization

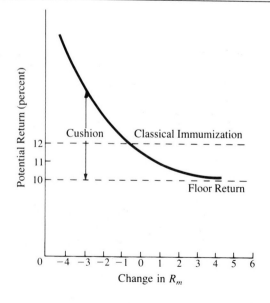

manager's ability to have a portfolio with a duration larger than the investment horizon.

The contingent-immunization approach allows the portfolio manager the ability to follow the active investment strategies discussed earlier in this chapter. At the same time the manager is able to protect a minimum return by using a duration-based immunization strategy. There is an old saying in the market: "Let your winners run and cut your losses." This is exactly the philosophy behind the contingent-immunization strategy.

BOND PORTFOLIOS: A CASE STUDY

Ron Allen is the President of Merchant's Bank and Trust Co.[1] Mr. Allen has been the CEO of the $80-million community bank for less than a year. The bank has always been successful and, in years past, provided its stockholders with a slightly better return than its peers. However, the return on the bank's investment portfolio had suffered somewhat in the early 1980s because of its inability to cope with the dramatic rise and continued fluctuation of interest rates. Now Allen wants the bank to become more of an investment manager than simply a buyer and seller of bonds. It is Allen's belief that by using duration theory he can achieve a bond portfolio that is not as sensitive to changes in rates and yet will still produce a better-than-average return.

Duration is the weighted-average number of years until an initial cash investment is recovered, with the weight expressed as the relative present value of each payment of interest and principal. For example, suppose a bank bought a five-year, $1,000 bond with a 10-percent coupon at par. If the going rate of interest remains at 10 percent, what would be the duration of the bond? The bond would produce a cash income in the amount of $100.00 per year for five years before maturing. To calculate the weighted present value, it is necessary to find the present value of each payment and multiply it by the number of periods until the payment is received. The first year the bank will receive $100.00 in coupon income. Discounted at 10 percent, the present value of the payment is $90.01 (see Table 20–6). Column 3, the present-value interest factor (PVIF), is obtained by using the formula $1/(1 + i)^n$, in which n is the number of compounding periods and i is the interest rate.

The present value of the second year's coupon income of $100.00 will be $82.64. The value is multiplied by two—that is, the number of years until receipt; the weighted present value of $165.28 is obtained. The present value of the third-year cash flow is $75.13; the weighted present value is $225.39. For the fourth year the present value is $68.30 and the weighted present

---

[1] This case study is based on Altmix (1984). Raymond A. Altmix is currently vice-president, First of America Bank–Kankakee.

TABLE 20-6 Weighted Present Value

(1)	(2)	(3) $\dfrac{1}{(1 + i)^n}$	(4) (2) × (3)	(5) (1) × (4)
Year	Coupons	Unweighted PV	Weighted P	
1	100.00	0.9091	90.91	90.91
2	100.00	0.8264	82.64	165.28
3	100.00	0.7513	75.13	225.39
4	100.00	0.6830	68.30	273.20
5	1,100.00	0.6211	683.01	3,415.05
	1,500.00		1,000.00	4,169.83

4,169.83 ÷ 1,000.00 = 4.17 years duration

value is $273.20. For the last year it is necessary to calculate both the present value of the $100.00 coupon and that of the maturing $1,000.00 bond. This sum is equal to $683.01, which when multiplied by five equals $3,415.05. As presented in the yield-giveup evaluation worksheet in Sample Problem 20.2, the cumulative weighted present values total $4,169.83. When this total is divided by the unweighted present value of the bond, $1,000.00, we have the duration of the bond, 4.1698 years. Thus, the initial duration of a five-year, 10-percent bond selling at par is 4.17 years. (This example assumes that no costs are incurred in buying and selling of bonds and in reinvesting the funds received as bond coupons are paid.)

The basic problem that faces Mr. Allen, as with any bond portfolio manager, is obtaining a given rate of return to satisfy the yield requirements of a specific date—that is, the investment horizon. If the market rates never changed between the purchase and the maturity of a bond, it would be possible to acquire a bond that would guarantee return over all of a portfolio manager's investment horizon. However, the term structure of interest rates is dynamic and the market rates are constantly changing. Because of the changes in the term structure, bond-portfolio managers are faced with interest-rate risk. Interest-rate risk is the combination of two risks, price risk and coupon-reinvestment risk.

Price-risk occurs if interest rates change before the target date and the bond is sold prior to maturity. At that time the market price will differ from the value at the time of purchase. If rates increase after the purchase date, the price the bond would be sold at would be below what had been anticipated. If the rates decline, the realized price would be above what had been expected.

Increases in interest rates will reduce the market value of a bond below its par value. But it will increase the return from the reinvestment of the coupon interest payments. Conversely, decreases in interest will increase the market value of a bond above its par value but decrease the return on the reinvestment of the coupons. In order for a bond to be protected from the

changes in interest rates after purchase, the price risk and coupon reinvestment must offset each other.

Of equal importance is **coupon-reinvestment risk.** It is the expected yield calculated by assuming that all coupon cash flows would be reinvested at the same yield that exists at the time of purchase. If rates began to fall, it would be impossible to reinvest the coupon at a rate high enough to produce the anticipated yield. Obviously, if rates increase, the coupon cash flow will be reinvested at higher rates and produce a return above expectations. Duration is the time period at which the price risk and coupon-reinvestment risk of a bond are of equal magnitude but opposite in direction. The result is that the expected yield is realized.

The duration strategy may protect the bank's bond portfolio from these unexpected changes in the yield. Merchant's Bank set its desired holding period at four years in order to protect the portfolio. This means that the duration of the bond portfolio should equal four years. In order to give the portfolio a four-year duration, the weighted-average duration is set at the desired length and the bank invests all future cash flows with duration equal to the remaining expected value.

An example of the effect of attempting to protect a portfolio by matching the investment horizon and the duration of a bond portfolio is contained in Table 20–7 using a single bond. Merchant's Bank has an investment horizon of four years. The current yield to maturity for a four-year bond is 10.50 percent. Therefore, the ending wealth ratio should be 1.4909 [$1/(1.105)^4$]. This assumes a completely protected portfolio. Two investment strategies are computed in Table 20–7. The first is the maturity strategy, where the term to maturity is set at four years. The second is the duration strategy, where the duration is four years. In this case, the bank would acquire a five-year, 10.5-percent bond that has a duration of 4.13 years, assuming a 10.5-percent yield to maturity. For this example, it is assumed that there is a single interest-rate change at the end of year two and the market yield goes from 10.5 percent to 8 percent through the fourth year.

As Table 20–7 shows, the wealth ratio for the maturity strategy fell short of the desired ending wealth ratio on this particular bond. This is due to the interest-rate change in year two, which results in a lower reinvestment rate. In the maturity strategy the price risk of the bond itself is eliminated because the bond matures in the fourth year. However, the duration strategy actually created a wealth ratio above what was expected. This is because the return that was lost in the reinvestment was offset by the increase in the value of the bond in its fourth year. In this case, a premium would be paid for a bond with a coupon $2\frac{1}{2}$ percent over the market rate by the purchaser in a secondary market.

The fact that a premium would be paid for this five-year bond at the end of four years is an important factor in the effectiveness of the duration concept. There is a direct relationship between the duration of a bond and the price

TABLE 20–7 Comparison of the Maturity Strategy and Duration Strategy for a Five-Year Bond

Year	Cash Flow	Reinvestment Rate (percent)	Value
Maturity Strategy			
1	105.00	10.5	105.00
2	105.00	10.5	221.03
3	105.00	8.0	343.71
4	105.00	8.0	1,476.01
			2,145.75
Duration Strategy			
1	105.00	10.5	105.00
2	105.00	10.5	221.03
3	105.00	8.0	343.71
4	1,125.10*	8.0	1,496.31
			2,166.05

Expected wealth ratio is 1,491.00.

* The bond could be sold at its market value of $1,125.12, which is the value for a 10.5-percent bond with one year to maturity priced to yield 8 percent.

volatility for the bond assuming given changes in the market rates of interest. This relationship can be expressed in the formula:

$$BPC = -D^*(r)$$

where:

BPC = the percent of change in price for the bond;
D^* = the adjusted duration of the bond in years, equal to $D/(1 + r)$; and
r = the change in the market yield in basis points divided by 100 (for example, a fifty-basis-point decline would be -0.5).

Using the values from Table 20–7 the percentage of change in the price of the five-year bond can be calculated. The duration is 4.13 years and interest-rate range from 8.00 percent to 10.5 percent.

$$D^* = 3.738$$
$$BPC = -3.738(100/100)$$
$$= -3.738(1)$$
$$= -3.738$$

In this example the price of the bond should decline by about 3.7 percent for every 100-basis-point increase in market rates. The accuracy of the formulas may vary depending on the length of duration. However, the

important point is in the relationship between duration and interest-rate risk. The longer the duration of a bond, the greater the price volatility of the bond for changes in interest rates.

Developing an interest-rate forecast is essential in any bond-portfolio manager's program. To aid them in the development of this forecast Merchant's Bank has secured the services of two well-known investment firms. Both firms publish monthly forecasts that will be used along with forecasts provided by Mr. Allen's staff. Investment Firm A predicts that short-term interest rates, over 0–6 months, will average between $9\frac{1}{2}$ and 11 percent, and long-term rates will fluctuate between 11 and 12 percent. Firm B has a similar forecast for short-term rates, but Firm B predicts a downward-sloping yield curve with long-term interest rates in the 9- to 10-percent range. Mr. Allen's problem here is that the firms' forecasts of long-term interest rates move in opposite directions. If interest rates increase, the bank's bond portfolio will not perform well unless it is protected using duration. However, if interest rates fall, the return provided by using duration will not be as great as the maturity strategy would provide. In this case, Mr. Allen may miss an opportunity to earn above-average returns.

Mr. Allen now must develop an interest-rate forecast for his Board of Directors. At the same time he will attempt to show them that duration can be an effective management tool. Merchant's Bank and Trust Co. has $750,000 in bonds maturing from the existing portfolio. Table 20–8 is a list of bonds Mr. Allen is considering for purchase. His decisions, based on the future of interest rates, will be closely monitored by the Board of Directors. It is important that Mr. Allen consider the advantages and disadvantages of using duration as a bond-portfolio management tool.

TABLE 20–8   Bonds Being Considered for Purchase by Merchant's Bank and Trust Co.

Amount*	Name	Rate (percent)	Maturity
$150,000	Agency A	10.90	3
$200,000	Government 1	10.85	3
$100,000	Government 2	11.00	4
$100,000	Agency B	11.10	4
$150,000	Agency C	11.25	4
$100,000	Government 3	11.25	5
$200,000	Agency D	11.35	5
$250,000	Agency E	11.40	5
$100,000	Agency F	11.30	5
$200,000	Government 4	11.25	6
$150,000	Agency G	11.70	6
$200,000	Government 5	12.50	10

* All bonds are purchased at par and are assumed to have an annual coupon.

SUMMARY

The management of a fixed-income portfolio involves techniques and strategies that are unique to the specific area of bonds. This chapter has discussed riding the yield curve, swaps, and duration as three techniques that are familiar to all managers of fixed-income portfolios. A comparison of these techniques was presented in the previous section in the context of a case situation.

Overall, this chapter has related bond-valuation theory to bond-portfolio theory and has developed bond-portfolio management strategies. The next chapter discusses portfolio insurance, using not only valuation concepts and valuation theory for stocks and bonds, but also valuation concepts and theory for futures and options, discussed in Chapters 12–15.

QUESTIONS AND PROBLEMS

1. Define the following terms.
   (a) riding the yield curve   (b) swapping
   (c) workout period   (d) duration
   (e) immunization   (f) crossover yield

2. What is the duration of bond A if it has the following characteristics?

$$PV = \$1,000 \qquad principal = \$1,000$$
$$coupon\ rate = 15\% \qquad YTM = 15\%$$
$$n = 3\ years$$

3. What kinds of risks does duration involve?

4. What is the value of a substitution swap for the following two bonds?

H- (Hold) Bond	P- (Purchaser) Bond
20-year 10% purchased at par	20-year 10% priced at $950
Workout time: 1 year	
Reinvestment rate: 10%	

5. What is the value of an intermarket swap for the following two bonds?

H- (Hold) Bond	P- (Purchaser) Bond
Price of bond: 5% @ beginning $680	Price of bond: 10% @ beginning $1,000
YTM: 10%	YTM: 11%
YTM at workout: 10%	YTM: 10½%
Workout time: 1 year	
Reinvestment rate: 10%	
Price of bond in one year: $685	Price of bond in one year: $1,015

6. What impact does a longer workout period have on the value of swaps?

7. Explain an interest-rate-anticipation swap. What are the tradeoffs that the bond investor is relying on?

8. What is the relationship between maturity and duration for a zero-coupon bond? What is the relationship between maturity and duration for a coupon bond selling at par? What is the relationship between maturity and duration for a coupon bond selling at a discount? What is the relationship between maturity and duration for a coupon bond selling at a premium?

9. What is the relationship between weighted-average term to maturity and duration?

10. Calculate the duration and weighted-average term to maturity for the following bonds. What impact do changing market interest rates have on duration and weighted-average term to maturity?

Bond A	Bond B	Bond C
Principal $1000	Principal $1000	Principal $1000
Maturity 5 years	Maturity 5 years	Maturity 5 years
Coupon 5%	Coupon 5%	Coupon 5%
PV $957.60	PV $1044.65	PV $1000

11. If you expect interest rates to fall, how should you structure your bond portfolio with respect to duration and holding period?

12. For a given maturity, how does coupon rate affect the duration of a bond?

13. How is the duration of a callable bond related to the duration of a noncallable bond?

14. What is the crossover yield of a bond with a 10-percent coupon selling at $1,100 with a call protection of 10 years?

15. What is the duration of a 20-year 10-percent bond selling at par that is callable in 5 years at $1,050?

REFERENCES

Altmix, Raymond A. "Duration, Bond Portfolio Protection: Case Study." Unpublished manuscript, 1984.

Bierwag, G. O. *Duration Analysis: Managing Interest Rate Risk*. Ballinger Publishing Co., 1987.

_____, G. Kaufman, and C. Khang. "Duration and Bond Portfolio Analysis: An Overview." *Journal of Financial and Quantitative Analysis*, v. 13 (November 1978), pp. 671–81.

————, G. Kaufman, and A. Toevs. "Single-Factor Duration Models in a Discrete General Equilibrium Framework." *Journal of Finance*, v. 37 (May 1982), pp. 325–38.

————. "Immunization Strategies for Funding Multiple Liabilities." *Journal of Financial and Quantitative Analysis*, v. 18 (March 1983), pp. 113–23.

Bookstaber, R. *The Complete Investment Book*. Scott, Foresman and Co., 1985.

Boquist, John A., George Racette, and Gary G. Schlarbaum. "Duration and Risk Assessment for Bonds and Common Stocks." *Journal of Finance*, v. 30 (December 1975), pp. 1360–65.

Chua, J. "A Closed Form Formula for Calculating Bond Duration." *Financial Analysts Journal*, v. 40 (May/June 1984), pp. 76–78.

Cox, John, Jonathan E. Ingersoll, and Stephen A. Ross. "Duration and Measurement of Basis Risk." *Journal of Business*, v. 52 (January 1979), pp. 51–61.

Fisher, L., and R. Weil. "Coping with the Risk of Interest Rate Fluctuations: Returns to Bondholders from Naive and Optimal Strategies." *Journal of Business*, v. 44 (October 1971), pp. 408–31.

Fong, H., and F. Fabozzi. *Fixed Income Portfolio Management*. Dow Jones-Irwin, 1985.

Hawawini, G., Ed. *Bond Duration and Immunization: Early Developments and Recent Contributions*. Garland Publishing, 1982.

Hessel, C., and L. Huffman. "The Effect of Taxation on Immunization Rules and Duration Estimation." *Journal of Finance*, v. 36 (December 1981), pp. 1127–42.

Homer, Sidney, and Martin L. Leibowitz. *Inside the Yield Book*. Prentice-Hall, and New York Institute of Finance, 1972.

Hopewell, M., and G. Kaufman. "Bond Price Volatility and Terms to Maturity: A Generalized Respecification." *American Economic Review*, v. 63 (September 1973), pp. 749–53.

Ingersoll, J., J. Skelton, and R. Weil. "Duration: Forty Years Later." *Journal of Financial and Quantitative Analysis*, v. 13 (November 1978), pp. 627–50.

Lanstein, R., and W. Sharpe. "Duration and Security Risk." *Journal of Financial and Quantitative Analysis*, v. 13 (November 1978), pp. 653–68.

Leibowitz, Martin L., and Alfred Weinberger. "The Uses of Contingent Immunization." *Journal of Portfolio Management*, v. 8 (Fall 1981), pp. 51–55.

————. "Contingent Immunization, Part I: Risk Control Procedures." *Financial Analysts Journal*, v. 38 (November/December 1982), pp. 17–32.

————. "Contingent Immunization, Part II: Problem Cases." *Financial Analysts Journal*, v. 39 (January/February 1983), pp. 35–50.

Macaulay, F. *Some Theoretical Problems Suggested by the Movements of Interest Rates, Bond Yields, and Stock Prices in the U.S. Since 1865.* National Bureau of Economic Research, 1938.

McEnally, R. "Duration as a Practical Tool in Bond Management." *Journal of Portfolio Management,* v. 3 (Summer 1977), pp. 53–57.

Reilly, F. K., and R. S. Sidhu. "Many Uses of Bond Duration." *Financial Analysts Journal,* v. 36 (July/August 1980), pp. 58–72.

Weil, R. "Macaulay's Duration: An Appreciation." *Journal of Business,* v. 46 (October 1973), pp. 589–92.

Yawitz, J. "The Relative Importance of Duration and Yield Volatility on Bond Price Volatility." *Journal of Money Credit and Banking,* v. 9 (February 1977), pp. 97–102.

CHAPTER

21 Portfolio Insurance and Synthetic Options

Previous chapters of this book have discussed concepts, valuation models, and theory to evaluate stocks, bonds, futures, options, and futures options. In addition, portfolio diversification concepts and the selection method have been developed for domestic equity portfolios, international equity portfolios, and bond portfolios. This chapter discusses how futures, options, and futures options can be used in portfolio insurance (dynamic hedging). In addition, the techniques of combining stocks and futures to derive synthetic options are explored.

Portfolio insurance is a strategy that may allow portfolio managers and investors to limit downside risk while maintaining upside potential. In this context the word *insurance* is somewhat misleading: portfolio insurance is not a true form of insurance, where the insured pays a premium to someone who accepts the risk of some adverse event. Rather, portfolio insurance is an asset-allocation or hedging strategy that allows the investor to alter the amount of risk he or she is willing to accept by giving up some return. This chapter looks at the basic concept of portfolio insurance, the various alternative methods available to the portfolio manager to hedge the portfolio, the impact of portfolio insurance on the stock market and the pricing of equity securities and market regulation, and finally, empirical studies of portfolio insurance.

BASIC CONCEPTS OF PORTFOLIO INSURANCE

Portfolio insurance refers to any strategy that protects the value of a portfolio of assets. It can be used for stock, bonds, or real assets. If the value of the asset declines, the insurance or hedge will increase in value to help offset the decline in price of hedged assets. If the price of the asset increases, the increase of the insured portfolio will be less than the increase in the asset but will nevertheless still increase.

TABLE 21-1   Mechanics of Portfolio Insurance: An Example

Initial investment	$100
Cost of portfolio insurance	$-$ 5$
Amount of investment going toward securities	$ 95
Amount invested $= \$100$	

Value of Portfolio at Year End (dollars)	Return on Uninsured Portfolio (percent)	Value of Insured Portfolio (dollars)	Net Return on Insured Portfolio (percent)
75	-25	95	-5
80	-20	95	-5
85	-15	95	-5
90	-10	95	-5
95	-5	95	-5
100	0	95	-5
105	5	100	0
110	10	105	5
115	15	110	11
120	20	115	15
125	25	120	20
130	30	125	25

Table 21-1 illustrates how portfolio insurance works. In this example, the underlying asset is purchased for $95 and $5 is spent on portfolio insurance. The minimum amount that the insured investor can realize is $95, but the uninsured portfolio can fall in value to a low of $75 if the market falls. If the value of the asset increases, the value of the insured portfolio will increase, but at a smaller rate. Figure 21-1 illustrates the profit and loss of the insured and uninsured portfolio.

Rubinstein (1985) states that the portfolio shown in Figure 21-1 has the three properties of an insured portfolio.

1. The loss is limited to a prescribed level.

2. The rate of return on the insured portfolio will be a predictable percentage of the rate of return on the uninsured portfolio.

3. The investments of the portfolio are restricted to a market index and cash. The expected return on the market index is above the expected return from holding cash, and the insurance is fairly priced. This guarantees that the insured portfolio has a higher expected return than the uninsured portfolio.

Portfolio insurance allows market participants to alter the return distribution to fit investors' needs and preferences for risk. Figure 21-2 shows the effect of insurance on the expected returns of a portfolio. Notice that the expected return of the insured portfolio is greater than the expected return of

FIGURE 21-1   Gains and Losses of Insured and Uninsured Portfolios: An Example

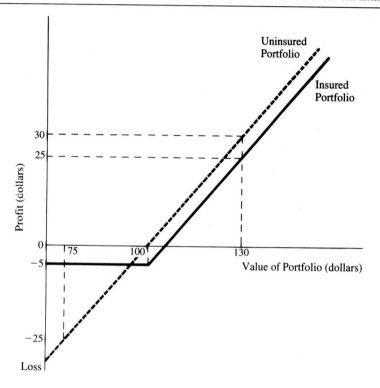

FIGURE 21-2   Expected Returns on Insured and Uninsured Portfolios

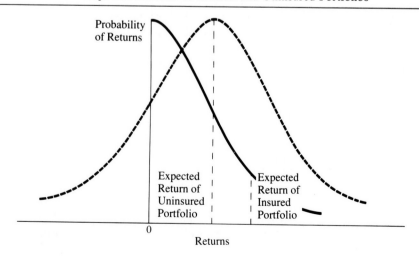

the uninsured portfolio, according to the third property listed above. It should be noted that in an efficient market at a fair price the insurance will be used until the expected return on insured and uninsured portfolios are the same.

The uninsured portfolio has greater upside potential as well as greater downside risk, whereas the insured portfolio limits the downside loss to the cost of the hedge. The upside potential of the insured portfolio is always below that of the uninsured portfolio. The cost of the insurance is the lower return for the insured portfolio should prices increase. While some investors would prefer the greater upside potential that the uninsured portfolio offers, risk-averse investors would prefer the limited-risk characteristics that the hedged portfolio offers.

In general, portfolio insurance can be thought of as holding two portfolios. The first portfolio can be viewed as the safe or riskless portfolio with value equal to the level of protection desired. This level is called the **floor** and is the lowest value the portfolio can have. For certain strategies this can be held constant or allowed to change over time as market conditions or needs change. The second portfolio consists of the difference between the total value of the portfolio and the floor, commonly called the **portfolio cushion.** These assets consist of a leveraged position in risky assets. To insure the portfolio, the cushion should be managed so as never to fall below zero in value because of the limited-liability property of common stock. Figure 21–3 shows the relationship between the total value of the portfolio, the cushion, and the floor. The actual investment or allocation of the portfolio funds between risky and risk-free assets is determined by changing market conditions or the changing requirements of the portfolio manager.

A simple example of changing the mix between risky and risk-free assets in response to market changes offers the opportunity to demonstrate the dynamic nature of portfolio insurance. As shown in Figure 21–3, half the current portfolio is invested in risky assets and half in risk-free assets. The exposure at this point is $500. The cushion is $200. If this is a reasonable relationship that the portfolio manager wishes to maintain, the relationship between these two, defined as the **multiple,** can be calculated:

$$\text{Multiple} = \frac{\text{Exposure}}{\text{Cushion}} \qquad \textbf{(21.1)}$$

$$m = \frac{e}{c}$$
$$= \frac{500}{200} = 2.5 \qquad \textbf{(21.2)}$$

As the market for the risky assets changes, the exposure and the cushion value change, causing a change in the multiple. Given a predetermined trigger or change in multiple, the portfolio manager can trade to restore the balance between the cushion and the exposure. If, for example, the market value of the risky asset rises 20 percent, the value of the cushion increases to

FIGURE 21-3   Components of an Insured Portfolio Valued at $1000

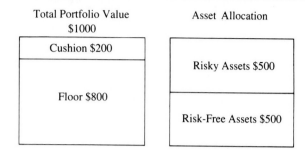

$300 and the value of the risky assets rises to $600. The total value of the portfolio is the value of the risky assets plus the value of the risk-free assets ($500 + $600, or $1,100). The value of the floor remains at $800 so that the cushion goes to $300 ($1,100 − $800). The multiple has fallen to:

$$m = \frac{e}{c} = \frac{600}{300} = 2 \tag{21.3}$$

If the target multiple is 2.5, an adjustment must be made by the portfolio manager, who must sell some of the risk-free assets and purchase risky assets until the multiple is 2.5. Hence, the manager needs to rebalance the portfolio so that $750 is invested in risky assets and $350 is invested in risk-free assets. This mix will restore the multiple to the desired level of 2.5:

$$m = \frac{e}{c} = \frac{750}{300} = 2.5 \tag{21.4}$$

Figure 21-4 shows the portfolio after rebalancing.

Increasing the portfolio's risky assets as the market rises allows the manager to participate in the bull market. As long as the market continues its rise, the manager continues to shift assets to the risky-asset portfolio to

FIGURE 21-4   Components of an Insured Portfolio Rebalanced after a Market Rise

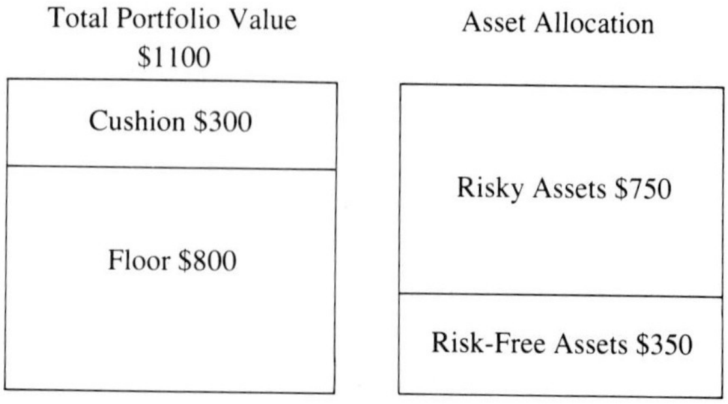

Total Portfolio Value
$1100

Asset Allocation

| Cushion $300 |
| Floor $800 |

| Risky Assets $750 |
| Risk-Free Assets $350 |

participate in the market gain. However, when the market turns bearish and begins to go down, the manager needs to sell off risky assets and invest in risk-free assets. For example, if the market declined by $16\frac{2}{3}$ percent back to its original level at the beginning of this example, the value of the risky assets would be \$625 (\$750 × 0.8333). At this new level the multiple would be

$$m = \frac{e}{c} = \frac{625}{175} = 3.56 \tag{21.5}$$

The target multiple of 2.5 is below the actual multiple of 3.56, so the portfolio manager must sell some of the risky assets and place the proceeds into risk-free assets. The total value of the portfolio has fallen to \$975 (\$625 + \$350). The value of the cushion has fallen to \$175 (\$975 − \$800). In order to have a multiple of 2.5 the risky assets have to be reduced to:

$$m = \frac{e}{175} = 2.5$$
$$e = \$437.50 \tag{21.6}$$

Hence \$187.50 of the risky assets must be sold and this amount must be invested in the risk-free assets. The position of the insured portfolio after this rebalancing is shown in Figure 21–5.

As the market falls, the portfolio manager sells off risky assets and invests the proceeds in risk-free assets, thereby reducing exposure to a falling market. In general this strategy can best be described as "run with your winners and cut your losses." *Underlying this discussion are the assumptions that the rise and fall of the market takes place over a time interval long enough for the portfolio manager to rebalance the position, and that the market has sufficient liquidity to absorb the value of the risky assets.* This may not always be the case, however. October 19, 1987, commonly called Black Monday, and October 26, 1987, commonly called Blue Monday, as well as October 13, 1989, are examples of a rapid fall in prices in a very illiquid market for risky assets.

This general discussion of portfolio insurance is based on an article by Perold (1986). The simplicity of this approach makes it an ideal way to

FIGURE 21–5 Components of an Insured Portfolio Rebalanced after a Market Fall

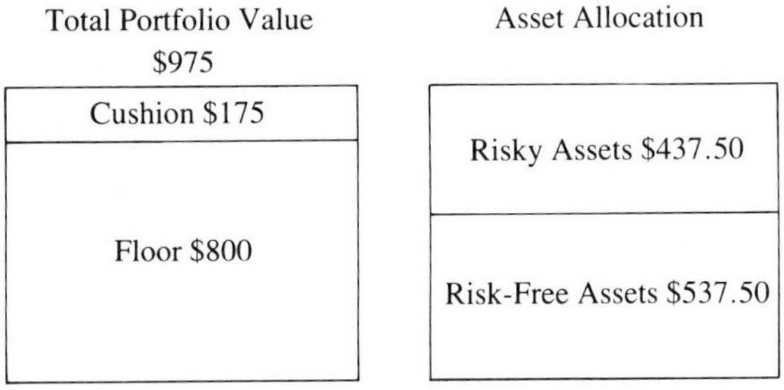

Total Portfolio Value $975		Asset Allocation
Cushion $175		Risky Assets $437.50
Floor $800		Risk-Free Assets $537.50

explain the general way of accomplishing portfolio insurance or portfolio hedging. Perold has called this **constant-proportion portfolio insurance (CPPI).** As has been seen, it involves holding the risk-free asset in an amount equal to the level of protection desired (floor), plus holding the remainder of the portfolio in a risky asset. The multiple of the risky asset to the cushion is then held in a constant proportion.

As will be seen, there are a number of ways of insuring or hedging a portfolio to keep the multiple constant. These are discussed in the next section.

STRATEGIES AND IMPLEMENTATION OF PORTFOLIO INSURANCE

Portfolio insurance allows the investor to participate in the appreciation of value of a risky portfolio while limiting the potential losses of the portfolio. This is very similar to the features available from an investment in options. There are four basic strategies to implementing a portfolio-insurance program: (1) the use of stop-loss orders, (2) the purchase of exchange-traded put options, (3) the creation of synthetic put options, and (4) dynamic hedging using futures contracts. All of these strategies are detailed below.

Stop-Loss Orders

A **stop-loss order** is a conditional market order to sell portfolio stock if the value of the stock drops to a given level. For example, if you held an index portfolio when the market index is at $100 and you expected the market to rise, you could limit your downside risk by placing a stop-loss order at $95. If the market fell to $95, your stop-loss order would become a market sell order, and the portfolio would be sold at the prevailing market price. The use of a stop-loss order does not guarantee that you would get exactly $95; you could get more or less. Still, you would begin to liquidate your position at a predetermined level. As you can see, the placement of stop-loss orders is a kind of crude portfolio insurance in that it allows you to make money if the market goes up and cuts your losses (approximately) to a predetermined level should the market fall.

As pointed out by Rubinstein (1985), the major problem of using stop-loss orders to approximate portfolio insurance is the path dependence of this technique—that is, if the market falls, the stop-loss order is executed, and the portfolio is sold, the portfolio manager needs to make a decision about when to get back into the market. The worst thing that could happen would be for the market to rebound immediately after the execution of the stop-loss order and sale of the portfolio. In such a case, the portfolio would consist of 100 percent cash. Because of this cash position, the portfolio would not benefit from the increase in stock price as the market rises. On the other

hand, if the market were to continue to fall after the execution of the stop-loss order, the portfolio manager with 100 percent cash would be in a position enhanced by the portfolio insurance—that is, 100 percent cash in a falling market. Hence, the success of the portfolio-insurance strategy is dependent on the subsequent market movement. Ideally, portfolio insurance should work regardless of the subsequent movement of the market; thus it should be **path independent.** Clearly, in the case of stop-loss orders it is path dependent, and this strategy is not a very useful form of portfolio insurance.

Portfolio Insurance with Listed Put Options

Put options can be purchased on a stock index on various exchanges and used for creating an insured portfolio. Table 21-2 lists the indexes and exchanges on which options are available. If the market falls, the drop in the value of the portfolio will be offset by the gain in value of the put option. On the other hand, if the market increases in value, the portfolio will increase in value but the premium paid for the put option will be lost. For example, a portfolio manager with a $100-million portfolio purchases four thousand Major Market Index (MMI) options with an exercise price of $250 with the cost of each option at $500. If the market value of the portfolio declines by $10 million by the expiration date of the option and the MMI index drops to $225, the portfolio manager can exercise the puts to offset the losses on the stock portfolio. The portfolio manager delivers the four thousand put options and receives $10 million. Since the puts cost $2 million, the net gain on the puts is $8 million. The $8-million gain on the puts offsets some of the $10-million loss on the portfolio, for a net loss of $2 million. If the portfolio increases in value by $20 million and the MMI index closes above $250, the net gain on the portfolio will be $20 million from the increase in equity value

TABLE 21-2 Listed Options on Market Indexes

Chicago Mercantile Exchange	Chicago Board Options Exchange	American Stock Exchange
S&P 500 Index	S&P 100 Index S&P 500 Index	Major Market Index Computer Technology Index Oil Index Institutional Index
Philadelphia Stock Exchange	*New York Stock Exchange*	*Pacific Exchange*
Utilities Index Value Line Index National OTC Index	NYSE Composite Index NYSE Beta Index	Financial News Composite Index

FIGURE 21-6 Gains and Losses of Insured and Uninsured Portfolios

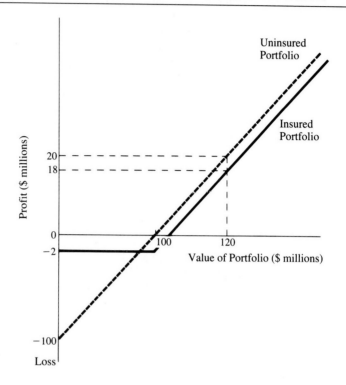

minus the $2-million premium paid for the options—a net gain of $18 million. The portfolio returns for this example are depicted in Figure 21-6.

A perfect hedge is usually not possible because the correlation between the market index and the portfolio may not be perfect. This is called the **tracking problem.** The greater the correlation between the portfolio and the index, the more effective the hedge. The lower the correlation, the less effective the hedge as a portfolio insurance strategy.

In the example it was assumed that the beta coefficient between the portfolio and the MMI was equal to one. If the beta in reality were not equal to one, more or less put contracts would be needed to insure the portfolio. For a beta less than one fewer puts would be needed, and for a beta greater than one more puts would be needed. For example, if the portfolio had a beta of 1.20, 20 percent more put options would be needed to hedge the portfolio.

The price change of the market inde· and the value of the portfolio, as well as the movement of the price of the option on the index, are all related. The success of a portfolio-insurance strategy depends on correct determination of the hedge ratio. The hedge ratio is the ratio of the value of the portfolio to the value of the options contracts used to hedge the portfolio:

$$\text{Hedge ratio} = \frac{\text{Number of contracts} \times \text{Face value of contracts}}{\text{Face value of portfolio}}$$

In discussing the use of put options for portfolio insurance two characteristics were assumed about the nature of the options used.

1. They are available with long maturities or with maturities that match the portfolio manager's investment horizon.
2. They are exercisable only at maturity—that is, they are European-type options.

Unfortunately, all the index options listed in Table 21–2 are American options. American options can be exercised at any time before expiration, hence have a higher value to certain investors. This is so because American options have all the advantages of European options plus the privilege of early exercise. The portfolio manager who uses American options for portfolio insurance finds that he is paying for the early-exercise privilege when in fact he doesn't really need it. Second, listed options are not protected against normal cash-dividend payments. When a firm's stock goes ex-dividend, the price of the stock is expected to fall by the amount of the dividend payment. This expected fall in the price of the stock is not offset by any changes in the option contract; hence the market price of the option will be affected by the ex-dividend behavior of the stock's price. As a result, options can be used to insure the capital-appreciation component of the stock return, but not the dividend component. Third, all listed options have a maximum maturity of nine months, with most of the trading taking place in the near contracts with maturities of three months or less. Given these problems, the usefulness of index put options for portfolio insurance is somewhat questionable.

Portfolio Insurance with Synthetic Options

Rubinstein and Leland (1981) suggest a strategy that replicates the returns on a call option by continuously adjusting a portfolio consisting of stock and a risk-free asset (T-bill, cash). This is called a **synthetic call-option strategy;** it involves increasing the investment in stock by borrowing when the value of stocks is increasing, and selling stock and paying off borrowing or investing in the risk-free asset when market values are falling.

The key variable in this strategy is the **delta value,** which measures the change in the price of a call option with respect to the change in the value of the portfolio of risky stocks (see also Chapter 14). For deep-in-the-money options, the delta value will be close to one because a $1 change in the stock value will result in approximately a $1 change in the option value. Thus to replicate the option with cash and stock, almost one share must be purchased and the amount borrowed will be approximately equal to the exercise price. For deep out-of-the-money options, the value of the delta will be close to zero, and the replicating portfolio will contain very few shares and little or

no borrowing. Hence in its simplest form the delta value largely depends on the relationship between the exercise price and the stock price. As the market moves to new levels, the value of the delta will change; hence the synthetic option portfolio must be rebalanced periodically to maintain the proper mix between equity and borrowing or cash.

In a similar manner, a portfolio manager can create replicated put options through a combination of selling short the asset and lending. The amount of stock sold short is equal to the delta value minus one. As the market decreases in value, more of the equity is sold (the short position increases), with the proceeds invested at the risk-free rate. If the market increases in value, money is borrowed to buy the stock and reduce the short position.

The logic behind a call-replicating strategy is shown in Figure 21–7, when the exercise price of the option and current share price are $100. The straight line starting from the origin and labeled "1 Stock + 0 Borrowing" is the value of an unleveraged long position in the stock. When the stock is worth zero, the option is worth zero; and for every $1 increase in the value of the

FIGURE 21–7   Synthetic Call Option

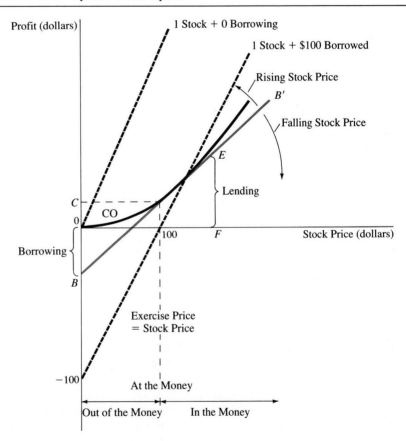

stock, the value of the position increases by $1. The straight line that starts from −100 on the profit axis (labeled "1 Stock + $100 Borrowed") is the leveraged position in which one share of stock is owned and the exercise price of the call ($100) is borrowed. The curved line labeled CO is the value of the call option and is an increasing function of the stock price. When the option is deep out of the money, changes in the stock price do not have much effect on the value of the call option (delta is small); hence the line is almost horizontal. However, as the stock price increases, the rate of change in the call price (the slope of CO) increases until it approaches one for an in-the-money call. The slope of CO is the number of shares to be held in the replicating portfolio. At low stock prices, few shares are held; at higher share prices, more shares are held.

The amount of borrowing needed to replicate the portfolio is represented by the dotted line BB'. The intercept of BB' and the stock-price axis repre-sents the amount of borrowing, and the line segment EF represents the amount of paying off borrowing or holding a risk-free asset. As the stock price rises, the dashed line BB' pivots counterclockwise, taking on increas-ing slope and an intercept farther from zero along the vertical axis. As the stock price falls, the BB' line pivots clockwise, with decreasing slope and an intercept closer to zero. The value C of the call option is shown on the profit axis. Thus at any stock price, the value of the portfolio invested in stock is the value of the call C plus the amount of borrowing B minus the amount borrowed B or C. The line CO shows how the value of the insured portfolio reacts to changes in the stock price. As the stock price increases (de-creases), the slope of the curved line becomes steeper (flatter) and the amount of borrowing increases (decreases).

If the call is in the money at the expiration date, the investor will own one share in the replicating portfolio and owe an amount equal to the exercise price. If the call finishes out of the money, no stock will be owned and the borrowing will be fully repaid. This is equivalent to the position of the call buyer at expiration. Hence a purchased call position can be replicated by a strategy of buying shares plus borrowing, where shares are bought (sold) and the borrowing is increased (decreased) as the stock price rises (falls).

The accuracy of the replicating strategy depends on four considerations. First, since the strategy may involve frequent trading, it is necessary that transaction costs be low. Second, it must be possible to borrow whatever amount is required. Third, trading in the stock may not provide continuous prices; there may be jumps or gaps. In this case, the strategy will not be able to exactly replicate the price movement of a traded call. Fourth, there may be uncertainty surrounding future interest rates, stock volatility, or divi-dends. This may affect the price of a traded call with an accompanying change in stock price. Hence, the value of the replicated option would not change, while the traded option price would change.

Figure 21–8 shows a synthetic put position in which the stock and exer-cise prices are $100. As the stock value increases (decreases), the slope of a line tangent to the put-value curve becomes flatter (steeper) and the number

FIGURE 21-8   Synthetic Put Option

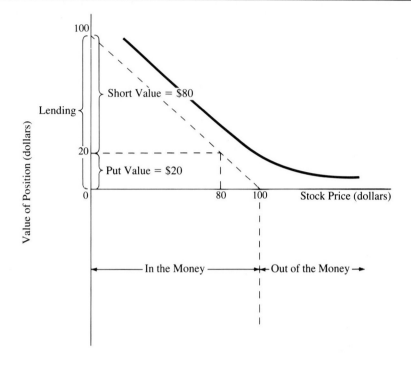

of shares sold short in the synthetic put decreases (increases). The intersection of the value axis gives the lending amount. The lending position increases as the stock declines in value because more proceeds are available from the short sale of the stock. If the put is in the money at expiration, the investor will be short one share of the stock (for example, $80) and will simultaneously lend the amount equal to the exercise price, $100. The total value of this position will equal the value of the listed put, $20.

Portfolio Insurance with Dynamic Hedging

As a practical matter, rather than buying, selling, or short selling stocks, a portfolio manager may trade (buy or sell) stock-index futures to adjust the exposure of a portfolio. If the stock market is declining, futures contracts are sold to effectively reduce the position in the portfolio. The selling of stock-index futures has the same effect on the portfolio as the sale of stocks and the investment in a risk-free asset. As the market turns around and begins to go up in value, the portfolio manager purchases futures contracts to cover the short position by liquidating the investment in the risk-free asset. This procedure is called **dynamic hedging.** Whether it works depends upon a high degree of correlation between the value of index-futures contracts and the value of the underlying index. For most time periods there is a very high

degree of co-movement between the index and the futures contract. However, this may not always be the case.

Suppose that a portfolio manager wishes to insure a portfolio of well-diversified stocks with a value of $1 million, and the portfolio beta is 1.1 when measured relative to the S&P 500. (This means that if the S&P 500 goes up or down by 1 percent, the change in the value of the portfolio will be 1.1 percent.) If the portfolio manager is worried about a market decline, he can insure his portfolio by selling S&P 500 index futures contracts. By selling futures contracts, the fall in value of the portfolio would be offset by gains in the futures market. If the strategy for portfolio insurance incorporates the beta, the following relationship is necessary to determine the number of contracts required to insure the portfolio:

$$\text{Number of contracts} = \frac{\text{Value of portfolio}}{\text{Value of futures contracts}} \times \beta \qquad \textbf{(21.7)}$$

Assume the S&P 500 index is selling at $110, and the portfolio is worth $1,000,000 on day 1. If the market falls by 10 percent, the value of the portfolio falls 11 percent to $890,000, the value of the S&P 500 futures contract falls to $99, and the scenario is as follows.

1. The portfolio has lost $110,000.
2. Each S&P 500 futures contract sold can be repurchased for $99 × 500 or $49,500, for a gain of $5500 ($55,000 − $49,500).

In order to have a perfect hedge, the portfolio manager would need $110,000/5500 = 20 contracts. Using Equation (21.7) we see that adjusting the number of contracts for the volatility or beta of the portfolio yields:

$$\text{Number of contracts} = \frac{\$1,000,000}{\$110 \times 500} \times 1.1 = 20 \text{ contracts}$$

This result of a perfect hedge is dependent upon two critical assumptions.

1. The relationship of the volatility of the portfolio to the volatility of the index remains the same or the beta does not change; and
2. The movement of the price of the futures contract is in lock step with the movement of the index; they are perfectly correlated.

In spite of the problems for portfolio insurance associated with the validity of these critical assumptions, the use of futures contracts for portfolio hedging is widespread. The main reason why futures have been accepted as a trading vehicle for portfolio insurance is the low trading costs. This and the reasons below have led to rapid growth in the use of futures contracts for insuring portfolios during the early part of the 1980s.

1. Low trading costs allow for rapid and frequent adjustments in implementing the portfolio strategy.
2. Futures markets are liquid enough for insurance programs for large institutional portfolios.

3. The use of futures allows for independence between management of the risky assets in the portfolio and the portfolio insurance.

COMPARISON OF ALTERNATIVE PORTFOLIO-INSURANCE STRATEGIES

This section compares alternative portfolio-insurance strategies—that is, synthetic options, listed put options, and dynamic hedging.

Synthetic Options

As previously discussed, **synthetic options** are not options but a strategy for allocating assets that replicates the return on a call option. There are four advantages to using a dynamic-hedging strategy instead of synthetic-option approach. First, the futures contracts have lower transaction costs than stocks. Kidder, Peabody reports that index funds pay one-way transaction costs of $125 for $100,000 of stock, or 0.125 percent (they assume a commission of $0.05 per share at an average price of $40), and institutional clients pay approximately $0.06 per share.[1] In contrast, one-way futures transaction costs for institutional investors are $15 per $100,000, or 0.015 percent. Thus the transaction costs for futures are one eighth to one tenth of the cost of trading stocks, thereby reducing the cost of dynamic hedging compared with synthetic options. Second, liquidity is much greater in the futures market than in options or stock markets. For example, during the large downside movement in the stock market on September 11–12, 1986, the consulting firm of Leland O'Brien Rubinstein Associates sold more than $500 million of stock-index futures.[2] Such large transactions could not be made in options markets.

The third advantage is that futures contracts are highly levered and less cash is necessary to carry out a dynamic-hedging strategy. As little as $2000 can control each futures contract. The fourth advantage is that because stocks are not sold, the management of the stock portfolio is independent of the portfolio insurance. In contrast, managers must be active when implementing a synthetic option because the underlying stock is bought or sold to replicate the returns on an option.

The main disadvantage of dynamic hedging with respect to synthetic options is the tracking error that might occur because the futures are not perfectly correlated with the stock. This is not a problem with synthetic options because the stock itself is purchased or sold.

---

[1] Joanne M. Hill. *Portfolio Insurance: Volatility Risk and Futures Mispricing.* Kidder, Peabody Financial Futures Department, 1987.

[2] George Anders. "Investors Rush for Portfolio Insurance." *The Wall Street Journal,* October 14, 1986, p. 6.

Another disadvantage of implementing either a dynamic-hedging or synthetic-option strategy is that they require continuous monitoring to insure that the delta of the replicated put equals the delta of a theoretical option. The replicated put must be rebalanced at certain intervals to maintain a proper mix of stock and futures. Here a tradeoff results: the more frequent the rebalancing, the better the replication of the theoretical put; however, more frequent rebalancing also results in higher transaction costs. Thus determining when to rebalance the portfolio is a major decision when implementing a synthetic-option or dynamic-hedging strategy in the presence of transaction costs.

There might be a price advantage or disadvantage to a dynamic-hedging strategy due to futures mispricing. When shorting futures for hedging purposes, the manager hopes that the futures sell at a premium and the basis (the cash price minus the futures price) widens. By selling futures when they are expensive and buying them back at a lower price, a profit results on the hedge. On the other hand, losses on the hedge will probably result if "cheap" futures are sold for hedging purposes. The following example illustrates these concepts. Suppose that a manager holds a portfolio worth $250 and shorts futures on the same portfolio that are worth $260. The basis is $250 − $260 = −$10. Because the basis is equal to zero at expiration, the negative basis will have to increase.

Value of Stock at Expiration of Futures	Value of Futures at Expiration	Profit or Loss on Stock	Profit or Loss on Futures	Profit or Loss
270	270	+20	−10	+10
230	230	−20	+30	+10

In this example the investor makes a profit of ten dollars on the hedge, regardless of how the portfolio performs. The profit is a result of selling "expensive" futures and waiting for the basis to increase. In contrast, suppose that an investor with a portfolio worth $250 shorts futures worth $245. In this example the investor will lose money if he waits until expiration, because the basis will decrease.

Value of Stock at Expiration of Futures	Value of Futures at Expiration	Profit or Loss on Stock	Profit or Loss on Futures	Profit or Loss
270	270	+20	−25	−5
230	230	−20	+15	−5

Here, the basis decreases and losses result for the hedger. Cheap futures will increase the costs of implementing a dynamic-hedging strategy and expensive futures will reduce the costs. The dynamic hedger hopes to sell futures selling at a premium and buy the futures at a discount.

The synthetic-call approach is usually used when implementing a portfolio-insurance strategy without futures. Thus, more of the risky asset is purchased when performance is favorable and the stock is sold when the asset declines. When implementing a dynamic-hedging strategy, the underlying stocks are not bought or sold, but rather stock-index futures are shorted to create a put option on the portfolio. In both cases, insurance is created for the portfolio, but the methods are different. In the synthetic-option case, the underlying portfolio behaves like a call option. For the dynamic-hedging case, the portfolio is not altered, only the futures position is changed to create a put option. A further discussion of the synthetic-call approach can be found in Becker (1988).

Listed Put Options

Portfolio insurance with **listed put options** does not require continuous monitoring because the delta of the listed option is automatically changed when the price of the underlying asset changes. Because of the automatic adjustment of the delta value, a listed-put strategy requires less monitoring and lower trading frequency than a synthetic-option or dynamic-hedging strategy.

There are a number of problems with using stock-index puts for portfolio insurance. First, because index options have at most a nine-month life, an investor may have to buy these short-term options even though the planning horizon might be much longer. These cumulative purchases of puts would result in a much greater cost than a longer-term option. This is due to the fact that for the long-term one-year put to be in the money, the market price must be below the exercise price after one year. In contrast, the value of the short-term options will have a positive value if the market price finished below the exercise price after nine months.

Second, the purchaser of portfolio insurance is not interested in exercising the option early, because this would leave the portfolio uninsured. The purchaser of insurance would prefer European options over American options because European options are cheaper. (However, the most popular index option, the OEX S&P 100, is American.) This early-exercise feature is of no value to the purchaser of portfolio insurance and adds to the cost of the insurance.

The third problem is that large-portfolio managers cannot purchase put options for insurance purposes because options markets do not provide the liquidity necessary to purchase large amounts of put options. Low liquidity might be even more of a problem for deep in- or out-of-the-money options or options that expire in the six- to nine-month range of maturities.

Like futures, there might be a tracking problem between the underlying stock or stocks and the instrument underlying the portfolio.

A replicated-option approach requires more management than a listed put-option strategy. The dynamic-hedging approach uses the highly liquid futures market to rebalance the portfolio. On the other hand, portfolio managers of large portfolios cannot purchase listed puts for portfolio insurance because of lack of liquidity in the options market. Futures mispricing will increase or decrease the cost of dynamic hedging; if the short hedger shorts expensive futures, profits will result from the hedges. If expensive futures are shorted, losses will be incurred.

Dynamic Hedging and Listed Put Options

The first difference between dynamic hedging and listed put options for portfolio insurance is that the delta value of a put option changes automatically while it must be adjusted continuously in a dynamic-hedging framework. Thus, dynamic hedging requires continuous monitoring and more frequent trading than listed puts.

Second, insurance costs (the premium paid for the option) for a listed-put strategy are known and paid up front. After the put is purchased, no more adjustments or monitoring are necessary. In contrast, insurance costs are unknown at the beginning of the period and are realized as the dynamic-hedging strategy is implemented. The cost of a dynamic-hedging strategy is the forgone profits that result from shorting futures. For example, suppose that a portfolio consists of $100,000 of stock and that $50,000 of futures contracts are shorted to replicate a put option (assume that this is one futures contract).

	Portfolio Value	Futures Value	Profit on Portfolio	Loss on Futures	Profit on Insured Portfolio
Period 1	100,000	50,000			
Period 2	120,000	60,000	20,000	−10,000	10,000

In the second period the value of the portfolio increased to $120,000 while the value of the futures contract appreciated to $60,000. If no futures were held, profit on the portfolio would be $20,000; however, the dynamic hedger lost $10,000 on the futures. Thus the cost of the dynamic-hedging strategy is the gain on the insured portfolio minus the gain on the uninsured portfolio ($10,000 − $20,000 = −$10,000).

Another difference is that a listed-option strategy is confined to fixed-interval exercise prices. In contrast, a dynamic-hedging strategy can be implemented around any exercise price.

Changing volatility can affect the cost of a portfolio-insurance strategy. For options, the cost of put protection is higher if the volatility declines. This is because the purchaser of the put locks in the volatility at the time of purchase. Thus, if the volatility declines, the put value declines. In contrast, an increase in volatility lowers the cost of put protection because the price of the put increase.

With a dynamic-hedging strategy, costs are lowered if volatility declines because the delta value will be reduced and not as many futures will be sold.

A replicated-option approach can be used for any asset—portfolios of stocks, various types of bonds, agricultural commodities, currencies, or metals. Since options markets are limited, replicated options must be created to simulate the returns of these investments.

IMPACT OF PORTFOLIO INSURANCE ON THE STOCK MARKET AND PRICING OF EQUITIES

Portfolio insurance is not formal insurance in the sense of a guarantee against loss. Rather, it is a method of hedging a portfolio either by selling a certain portion of the risky assets themselves, or futures contracts on stock indexes, when the market falls. Both techniques ultimately have the same affect, but index futures tend to be more popular because they entail smaller transaction costs.

When the stock market rises as it did almost uninterruptedly from December 1986 to August 1987, the hedge was hardly used as investors participated in the bull market. But when stocks began to fall in autumn 1987, investors started selling futures, usually contracts tied to the S&P 500 index, thereby making up any losses from falling prices by the gain on the futures contracts. The portfolio insurer sells futures contracts at index levels that, in a falling market, are higher than they will be later. The money from the sale of the futures is then invested in money-market instruments until it is needed to buy back the futures contracts at lower prices in the future when the market has bottomed out.

Consider the following sequence of events involving the linkages between the sale of futures contracts for portfolio insurance and the market index.

1. Your portfolio, valued at $100, is equally divided between the risk-free asset and risky assets. The market index is 1000, and there is no futures discount from the index level.

2. The market declines to an index of 900, and futures give a discount from the index of 10. As the market declines, portfolio insurance requires reducing your investment in the risky asset. This can be done by selling stock directly or by selling futures on the index. You increase your investment in the risk-free asset to $55, leaving your investment in the risky asset long stocks 45, short index 5.

3. Market arbitrageurs can now take advantage of mispricing between the index level and the price of futures because the investor has sold futures contracts, thereby increasing the discount between the futures price and the market index level. The discount has gone from zero to minus ten. These so-called program traders begin to sell stocks and buy index futures to lock in a risk-free return. This causes the market index to fall; and in a falling market the investor will want to reduce his exposure to the risky asset by selling futures and investing the funds in the risk-free asset. This action will increase the discount between the index and the futures value and again encourage program traders to execute arbitrage trades. Once the cycle starts, it may be difficult to stop.

Could the scenario described in the last few paragraphs ever really take place? Unfortunately, the answer is yes. On Monday, October 19, 1987—ever after to be known as Black Monday—this is precisely what happened on the New York Stock Exchange. Figures 21–9, 21–10, and 21–11 show the precipitous drop of 508 points on the Dow Jones index that took place on Black Monday. Figure 21–10 shows that for most of the day futures were selling at a discount to the index. What is more revealing is that every time the discount got wider, the index started to fall faster. The bottom panels in Figures 21–10 and 21–11 show the percentages of trading volume for futures

FIGURE 21–9   Daily Movement of the Dow Jones Industrial Average, October 19–22, 1987

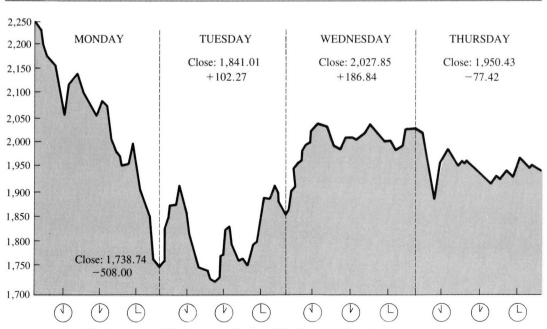

Source: Knight-Ridder Tradecenter, 1988. Courtesy of Knight-Ridder Financial Information.

FIGURE 21–10   S&P Index and Futures Contracts, Monday, October 19, 1987

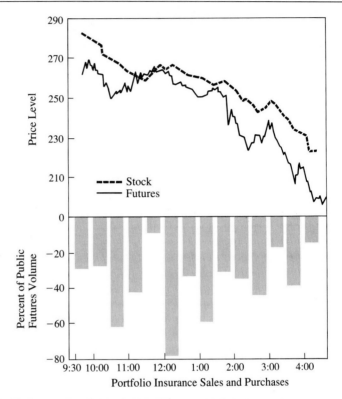

Source: *The Washington Post,* October 9, 1988. Copyright © 1988 by *The Washington Post.*

and the NYSE. It is apparent that a substantial amount of the record trading was being done by institutions trying to implement their portfolio-insurance strategies. What is especially unfortunate about Black Monday is that no one foresaw what would happen if every institution implemented a similar portfolio strategy simultaneously. Even the generally liquid NYSE could not handle the crushing volume of orders to sell as a result of portfolio-insurance strategies. Most recently, Blume et al. (1989) have shown the breakdown in the linkage between futures prices and the spot index on October 19 and October 20, 1987. In addition they have found breakdowns in the linkage among NYSE stocks.

Regulation and the Brady Report

In the aftermath of the October 1987 crash, the role of regulation in both the futures and the stock markets was hotly debated. Figure 21–12 shows the relationships of the Congress, Federal agencies, and the Federal Reserve

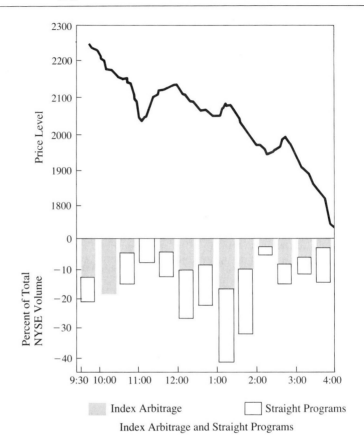

FIGURE 21-11   Dow Jones Industrial One-Minute Chart, Monday, October 19, 1987

Source: The Washington Post, October 9, 1988. Copyright © 1988 by *The Washington Post*.

with the two leading futures and stock exchanges. Some have argued that the separate regulation of futures and stocks contributed to the severity of the October 1987 crash. The role of portfolio insurance and index arbitrage in linking the futures and stock markets has brought into question the separation of regulatory authority. At the present time, what form the future regulatory structure will take is a matter of conjecture. One reasoned answer has been presented by the Brady Commission report. This report is likely to provide the framework for the debate of how to regulate U.S. security markets.

The Brady report makes five primary recommendations.

1. Information systems should be established to monitor transactions and conditions in related markets.

FIGURE 21–12   Regulating the Markets

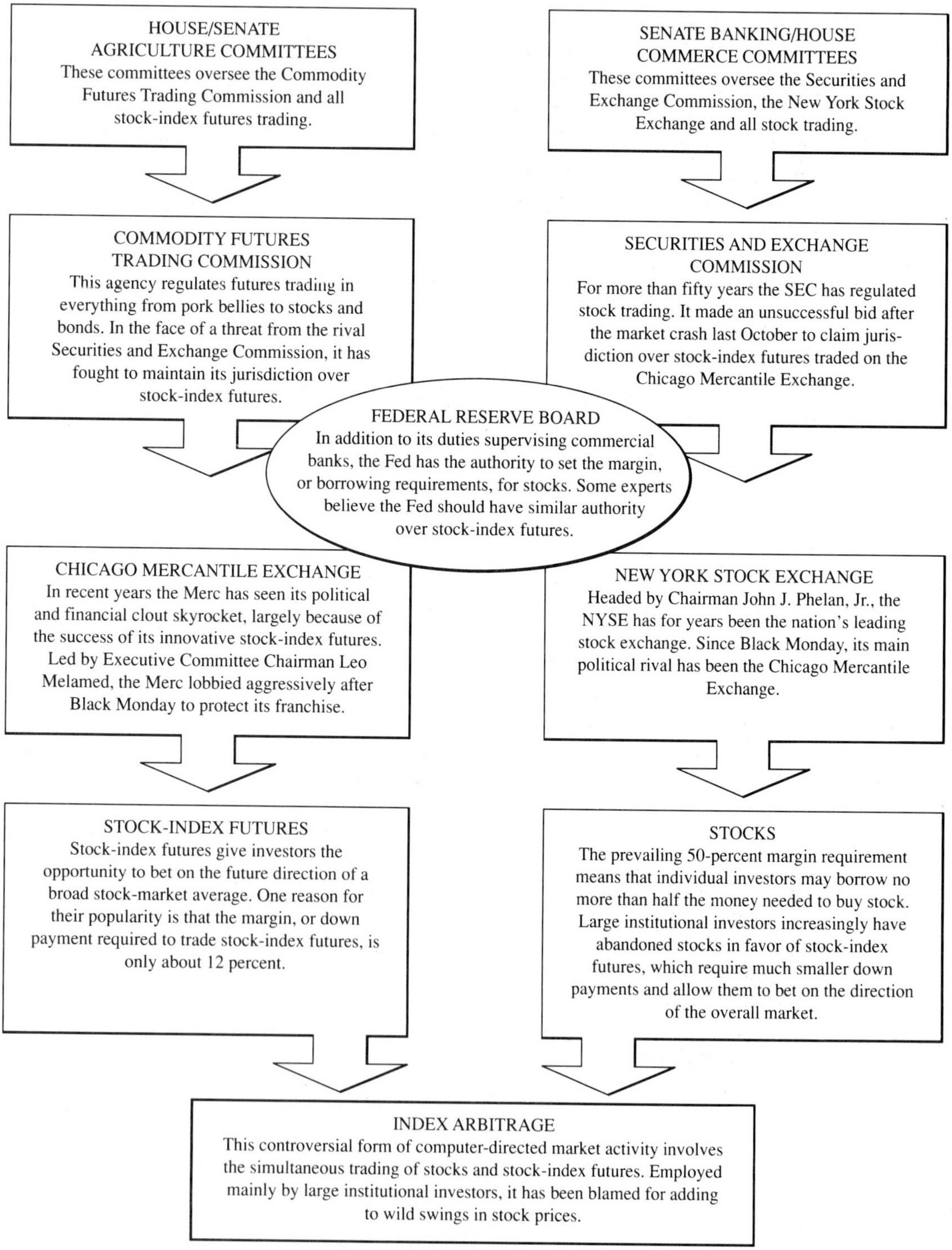

HOUSE/SENATE AGRICULTURE COMMITTEES
These committees oversee the Commodity Futures Trading Commission and all stock-index futures trading.

SENATE BANKING/HOUSE COMMERCE COMMITTEES
These committees oversee the Securities and Exchange Commission, the New York Stock Exchange and all stock trading.

COMMODITY FUTURES TRADING COMMISSION
This agency regulates futures trading in everything from pork bellies to stocks and bonds. In the face of a threat from the rival Securities and Exchange Commission, it has fought to maintain its jurisdiction over stock-index futures.

SECURITIES AND EXCHANGE COMMISSION
For more than fifty years the SEC has regulated stock trading. It made an unsuccessful bid after the market crash last October to claim jurisdiction over stock-index futures traded on the Chicago Mercantile Exchange.

FEDERAL RESERVE BOARD
In addition to its duties supervising commercial banks, the Fed has the authority to set the margin, or borrowing requirements, for stocks. Some experts believe the Fed should have similar authority over stock-index futures.

CHICAGO MERCANTILE EXCHANGE
In recent years the Merc has seen its political and financial clout skyrocket, largely because of the success of its innovative stock-index futures. Led by Executive Committee Chairman Leo Melamed, the Merc lobbied aggressively after Black Monday to protect its franchise.

NEW YORK STOCK EXCHANGE
Headed by Chairman John J. Phelan, Jr., the NYSE has for years been the nation's leading stock exchange. Since Black Monday, its main political rival has been the Chicago Mercantile Exchange.

STOCK-INDEX FUTURES
Stock-index futures give investors the opportunity to bet on the future direction of a broad stock-market average. One reason for their popularity is that the margin, or down payment required to trade stock-index futures, is only about 12 percent.

STOCKS
The prevailing 50-percent margin requirement means that individual investors may borrow no more than half the money needed to buy stock. Large institutional investors increasingly have abandoned stocks in favor of stock-index futures, which require much smaller down payments and allow them to bet on the direction of the overall market.

INDEX ARBITRAGE
This controversial form of computer-directed market activity involves the simultaneous trading of stocks and stock-index futures. Employed mainly by large institutional investors, it has been blamed for adding to wild swings in stock prices.

Source: The Washington Post, October 9, 1988. Copyright © 1988 by *The Washington Post.*

2. Clearing methods should be unified across marketplaces to reduce financial risk.

3. Margins should be made consistent across marketplaces to control speculation and financial leverage.

4. One agency should coordinate the few but critical regulatory issues that have an impact across the related market segments and throughout the financial system. The Federal Reserve is considered a reasonable candidate for this role.

5. Circuit-breaker mechanisms such as price limits and coordinated trading halts should be formulated and implemented to protect the market system.

How many of these recommendations are acted upon in restructuring the futures and stock markets remains to be seen. However, it is clear that practices such as portfolio insurance that link different markets together have forced study of the problems of a segmented regulatory system.

EMPIRICAL STUDIES OF PORTFOLIO INSURANCE

Much of the early research on portfolio insurance focused on simulation models to see whether synthetic-option strategies could successfully limit losses on portfolios of risky assets. In the early to mid 1980s, most of the empirical research on portfolio insurance was conducted by financial institutions such as Drexel, Burnham, Lambert and Salomon Brothers. However, more articles on the subject have appeared recently in journals such as *The Financial Analyst's Journal* and *Journal of Portfolio Management*.

Leland (1985)

Leland (1985) develops a replication strategy in the presence of transaction costs and tests this approach by using a simulation. As Leland points out, because transaction costs increase without limit as the revision period becomes shorter, it may be very costly to assure a given level of accuracy in the synthetic option. In addition, "transaction costs associated with replicating strategies are path-dependent: they depend not only on the initial and final stock prices, but also on the entire sequence of stock prices in between." Another problem with trying to create portfolio insurance in the presence of transaction costs is that transaction costs are correlated with the market. Leland poses the question, "In the presence of transaction costs, is there an alternative to the Black–Scholes replicating strategy which will overcome these problems?"

Leland proposes a procedure that adjusts upward the volatility estimate to the replicating procedure. The modification is a positive function of transaction costs and the replication period. This increase in the volatility

estimate is due to the fact that each time a transaction occurs, the associated trading costs cause the purchase cost to be higher and the selling proceeds to be lower than without these costs. With transaction costs, the cost of purchasing stock is higher than without these costs; similarly, the price of selling the stock is lower, inclusive of these costs. "This accentuation of up or down movements of the stock price can be modelled as if the volatility of the actual stock price was higher." The adjustment to volatility is

$$\sigma_A^2 = \sigma^2 \left(1 + \frac{\sqrt{2/\pi}\, k}{\sigma \sqrt{t}}\right) \qquad\qquad (21.8)$$

where:

σ_A^2 = the transaction-cost adjusted volatility;

σ = the annualized standard deviation of the natural logarithm of the price;

k = round-trip transaction costs as a proportion of the volume of transaction; and

t = the revision interval as a proportion of a year.

The modification to the volatility estimate has the following characteristics.

1. Transaction costs remain bounded as the revision period becomes short.
2. The strategy replicates the option return inclusive of transaction costs, with an error that is uncorrelated with the market and approaches zero as the revision period becomes short.
3. Expected turnover and associated transaction costs of the modified replicating strategy can easily be calculated, given the revision interval. Since the error inclusive of transaction costs is uncorrelated with the market, these transaction costs put bounds on the option prices.

The delta value of this strategy takes into account transaction costs and will be higher than without transaction costs. As can be seen from Equation (21.8), the volatility estimate increases as the revision period and transaction costs increase. Leland believes that the modified replication strategy is superior to following the Black–Scholes strategy and paying transaction costs that result from the strategy because the expected error is negative, "reflecting the fact that transaction costs are not 'covered' by the initial option price." He assumes that the Black–Scholes strategy will result in higher turnover than the modified strategy because the latter "is based on a higher volatility which tends to 'smooth' the required trading."

Leland uses a simulation to determine the effectiveness of this strategy. The risk-free rate in the simulation is 10 percent; the expected return for the stock is 16 percent, with a standard deviation of 20 percent. Leland uses rebalancing periods of one week, four weeks, and eight weeks to replicate options expiring in three months, six months, and twelve months. H is the difference between the listed call and the synthetic option after the revision period, Δt.

$$\Delta H = \Delta C - [C_s S + r(C - C_s S)] \qquad (21.9)$$

ΔC is the change in the listed call option over the revision period, C_s is the delta value and is the number of shares in the replicated portfolio, and r is the interest rate over the revision period. If the replicated option perfectly matches the changes in the listed option, ΔH will equal zero. For each of the revision periods, the mean and standard deviation of the errors is calculated.

Using simulated data with no transaction costs, the Black–Scholes strategy replicates the option with mean errors equal to zero for a revision period of one week. The standard deviation increases as the time until expiration decreases. As expected, the mean error increases as the revision period increases, with the greatest error occurring for the eight-week rebalancing period.

Leland uses his modification to the volatility estimate to calculate the accuracy of option replication with transaction costs. He compares the errors from the modified strategy with a Black–Scholes replicating scheme in which delta values and borrowing amounts are derived from the Black–Scholes model and then transaction costs are added on. In every case, the preciseness of the modified strategy exceeds the accuracy of the Black–Scholes design when round-trip transaction costs of 1 percent are used.

Asay and Edelsburg (1986)

Asay and Edelsburg use Monte Carlo simulations to determine how closely a synthetic-option strategy can match the returns on options on Treasury-bill futures. They state that there are three objections to a synthetic-option plan. First, changing delta values mean that positions must be continuously adjusted for the returns to be similar. However, rebalancing may not be possible if prices change overnight. If the position changes, too few or too many shares will be held in the underlying asset and the returns will not be the same as in the option position. The second problem with a synthetic strategy is that transaction costs may be significant, particularly if the rebalancing period is short.

The third problem is that the position could be whipsawed. **Whipsawing** occurs when the underlying asset increases enough to trigger rebalancing. After more shares are added, the underlying asset decreases in value and the additional shares are sold at a lower price than what was paid for them. A common remedy for this problem is to use a larger adjustment gap or filter rule; however, the wrong number of shares could be held if the filter rule were increased, particularly if the stock moved in a linear manner. Whipsawed positions commonly occur when the asset fluctuates around a constant level.

Asay and Edelsburg use a Monte Carlo simulation of an option on a Treasury-bill future to determine if these and other problems would cause a divergence between the theoretical and synthetic positions. Profits and losses on the synthetic option are compared with those that would be earned

through the purchase and sale of the option at the theoretical price if it were held to maturity. The profit on the replicated option is equal to the value of the option at maturity minus the price paid for option. They use adjustment gaps of 5–50 basis points in the simulated one-year interest-rate futures to trigger rebalancing.

Fifty simulations on six-month options were run. The option prices generated by the synthetic approach were very close to the options purchased at their theoretical values. Larger adjustment gaps proved more accurate when the futures traded in a narrow range, but the larger gaps were "disastrous" when the futures moved in one direction. Thus, they were unable to recommend a best adjustment gap. Asay and Edelsburg found the transaction cost of the replicating strategy to be insignificant.

To determine the amount of mispricing due to using an incorrect volatility estimate, they use a "correct" volatility measure for the listed option and an "incorrect" measure for the synthetic option. They find that inputting a wrong estimate into the option-pricing model seems "to have only a minimal effect through the resulting incorrect hedge ratio." The authors conclude that problems such as transaction costs, whipsawing, and frequent rebalancing do not negate the effectiveness of the synthetic option on Treasury-bill futures.[3]

Eizman (1986)

The purpose of Eizman's paper is to determine which rebalancing strategy is the most effective in a dynamic-hedging portfolio-insurance framework. He considers three rebalancing disciplines: (1) to fully rebalance the required stock/cash mix at discrete time intervals, (2) to fully rebalance every time the market changes by a specified percentage, and (3) to rebalance only when the actual mix lags the required mix by more than a specified lag factor in either direction, "and then rebalance only to the extent of bringing the actual mix up to a lag factor away from the required mix . . . ."

Log normal returns to generate one-year puts are obtained using a multi-year Monte Carlo simulation. Eizman assumes a standard deviation of 13 percent, an interest rate of 8 percent, futures transaction costs of 0.15 percent, and a dividend yield of 4 percent. Put premiums and delta values for the synthetic put were generated by the Black–Scholes model. Then average annual transaction costs and average annual replication errors are calculated. In all three strategies there is a tradeoff between transaction costs and accuracy; the liberal adjustment strategies had lower transaction costs and higher replication errors.

For the discrete-time adjustment strategy, he rebalances monthly, weekly, semi-weekly, daily, and hourly. The transaction costs increased and replication errors decreased as the rebalance periods shortened. He uses a

---

[3] M. Asay and C. Edelsburg, "Can a Dynamic Strategy Replicate the Returns of an Option?" *Journal of Futures Markets,* v. 6 (Spring 1986), pp. 63–70. Copyright © 1986 by John Wiley and Sons, Inc. Reprinted by permission of John Wiley and Sons, Inc.

utility function of Min $(X + Y)$, where X is average annual transaction costs and Y is average annual replication error, to determine the most effective rebalance period. Using this criterion, the best method is the weekly method, with the semi-weekly strategy coming in second.

For the second strategy, market moves of 5 to 0 percent are used to trigger rebalancing. Again, larger percentage rebalance periods lead to lower transaction costs and larger errors. The third discipline, in which the portfolio is rebalanced only if the actual futures/stock mix lags the required mix by more than a prescribed percentage, works the best, according to Eizman. Under this method, the adjustment is made so that the actual mix is brought up to the three-percent boundary and not up to the required mix. The lag that provided the best cost/error tradeoff was three percent.

Rendleman and McEnally (1987)

This study addresses the issue of portfolio-insurance cost. It tries to answer the following questions.

1. What is the probability that the portfolio will earn no more than its insured floor return?
2. What are the expected returns and utilities of return of the insured portfolio versus those of a reasonable alternative strategy?
3. What are the probabilities that the insured portfolio or the alternative will have the higher return?
4. Over the long run, how will the accumulation of value from the insured portfolio stack up against the alternative?

They use a Monte Carlo simulation with a 16-percent expected return and a 10-percent interest rate. The Black–Scholes model is used to derive delta values for the put option. In addition, a logarithmic utility function is specified to measure the utility of a portfolio-insurance strategy. Rendleman and McEnally simulate one- and three-year put options using minimum returns of 5 percent, 0 percent, and -5 percent, stock volatility of 20 percent and 18 percent, and interest rates of 10 percent and 6 percent. Various simulations are run and the costs of the put positions are calculated along with expected utility for the insured portfolio and an uninsured portfolio.

Probability distributions are generated to determine the probability that the insured and uninsured portfolios have a return greater than the minimum floor. They conclude that the "insured portfolio is . . . more likely than the optimal portfolio to achieve only the guaranteed minimum return." In addition, they find that portfolio insurance strategies " . . . suffer in comparison with an 'optimal' portfolio designed to maximize the rate of growth of portfolio value over time." Using the various inputs on the simulations, they determine that the insured portfolio can expect to have a lower return than a similar optimal portfolio. They conclude that portfolio-insurance strategies are optimal only when investors are highly risk averse.

Garcia and Gould (1987)

The main goal of this article is to compute the costs of a synthetic-call portfolio-insurance strategy. They do not deal with dynamic hedging because " . . . sufficient historical experience is not yet available to simulate meaningfully the results from long equities/short futures implementations." They use closing prices of the S&P 500 index from January 1, 1963, to December 31, 1983. They generate returns for 240 overlapping years by taking twenty January to January returns, then twenty February to February returns, and so on. This is the first published portfolio-insurance study to use real data as opposed to simulated data.

The returns for hedged and unhedged portfolios were calculated. Over the period of study, the arithmetic mean of the unhedged S&P 500 returns was 9.63 percent with a standard deviation of 16.22 percent; the mean return for a portfolio insurance strategy with a zero percent floor and 0.5 percent transaction costs was 7.08 with a lower standard deviation of 9.33 percent. The mean return for the strategy with a −5-percent floor was 8.18 percent with a standard deviation of 11.80 percent.

Opportunity costs of the portfolio insurance were calculated. If the return on the unhedged portfolio was 10 percent and the return on the hedged portfolio was 5 percent, the opportunity cost is 5 percent. They conclude that with a zero floor insurance investors gain 10.27 percent in a down year. When the market is up, hedged portfolios forgo 7.21 percent.

They conclude that the cost of portfolio insurance is 170 basis points for zero-floor insurance and 83 basis points for a −5-percent strategy, and that a dynamically balanced portfolio will not outperform a buy-and-hold portfolio.

SUMMARY

This chapter has discussed basic concepts and methods of portfolio insurance for stocks. Strategies and implementation of portfolio insurance have also been explored in detail. Other issues related to portfolio insurance and dynamic hedging have also been studied.

Portfolio insurance was described not as an insurance technique but rather as an asset-allocation or hedging technique. The general methods of portfolio insurance—(1) stop-loss orders, (2) market-traded index options, (3) synthetic options, and (4) futures trading—were discussed. One of the major issues facing investors and regulators during the later 1980s was introduced—the effect of portfolio insurance on the stock market.

Overall, this chapter has integrated most of the material discussed in previous chapters. It can be regarded as a synthesis of the whole book although another chapter follows. Chapter 22 shows how high-power mathematical and statistical tools can be used to derive the Black–Scholes option-pricing model more precisely.

QUESTIONS AND PROBLEMS

1. What is portfolio insurance? Identify and explain the various strategies that can be used to insure a portfolio.

2. What is the difference between hedging and portfolio insurance?

3. A manager is running a $10-million portfolio. She has decided to allocate $5 million to risky assets and $5 million to risk-free assets. She has set the floor of the portfolio at $7 million.
   (a) What is the cushion for this portfolio?
   (b) What is the exposure for this portfolio?
   (c) What is the multiple for this portfolio?

4. Given the information in question 3, if the market for risky assets increases by 30 percent:
   (a) What is the value of the total portfolio?
   (b) What is the new multiple?
   (c) What should the portfolio manager do to restore the portfolio to its target multiple?

5. Given the information in question 3, if the market for risky assets decreases by 10 percent:
   (a) What is the value of the total portfolio?
   (b) What is the new multiple?
   (c) What should the portfolio manager do to restore the portfolio to its target level?

6. What does the term *path dependence* mean? Why is it important for portfolio-insurance strategies to be path independent?

7. Define a synthetic option. Explain how the option position is adjusted in a rising or falling market.

8. What is a delta value? Why is it important?

9. A portfolio manager has $10 million invested in a well-diversified portfolio of common stock with a portfolio beta of 0.9 measured relative to the S&P 500. How many S&P 500 futures contracts are needed to insure the portfolio if the futures are currently selling for $105?

10. How could the strategy of hedging with futures contracts not provide a perfect hedge?

11. Compare and contrast portfolio insurance with options to portfolio insurance with futures.

12. Identify and discuss the linkage between trading futures contracts for portfolio insurance and market volatility. Does the tail wag the dog?

13. What is the difference between margin on equities and margin on futures?

REFERENCES

Anders, G. "Investors Risk for Portfolio Insurance." *The Wall Street Journal,* October 14, 1986, p. 6.

Asay, M., and C. Edelsburg. "Can a Dynamic Strategy Replicate the Returns of An Option?" *The Journal of Futures Markets,* v. 6 (Spring 1986), pp. 63–70.

Becker, K. "Rebalancing Strategies for Synthetic Call Options." Doctoral dissertation, University of Illinois, 1988.

Benninga, S., and M. Blume. "On the Optimality of Portfolio Insurance." *The Journal of Finance,* v. 40 (December 1985), pp. 1341–52.

Black, F., and R. Jones. *Simplifying Portfolio Insurance.* Goldman Sachs, 1986.

Blume, M. E., A. C. Mackinlay, and B. Terker. "Order Imbalances and Stock Price Movements on October 19 and 20, 1987." *Journal of Finance,* v. 44 (September 1989), pp. 827–48.

Brennan, M. J., and R. Solanki. "Optimal Portfolio Insurance." *Journal of Financial and Quantitative Analysis,* v. 16 (September 1981), pp. 279–300.

Dreher, W. "Does Portfolio Insurance Ever Make Sense?" *Journal of Portfolio Management,* v. 14 (Summer 1988), pp. 25–32.

Eizman, E. S. "Rebalance Disciplines for Portfolio Insurance." *Journal of Portfolio Management,* v. 13 (Fall 1986), pp. 59–62.

Finnerty, J., and H. Park. "How to Profit From Program Trading." *Journal of Portfolio Management,* v. 14 (Winter 1988), pp. 40–46.

———. "Stock Index Futures: Does the Tail Wag the Dog?" *Financial Analysts Journal,* v. 43 (March/April 1987), pp. 57–61.

Garcia, C. B., and F. J. Gould. "An Empirical Study of Portfolio Insurance." *Financial Analysts Journal,* v. 43 (July/August 1987), pp. 44–54.

Grossman, S. "Insurance Seen and Unseen: The Impact on Markets." *Journal of Portfolio Management,* v. 14 (Summer 1988), pp. 5–8.

———. "An Analysis of the Implications for Stock and Futures Price Volatility of Program Trading and Dynamic Hedging Strategies." *Journal of Business,* v. 61 (July 1988), pp. 275–98.

Hill, J. *Portfolio Insurance: Volatility Risk and Futures Mispricing.* Kidder, Peabody, and Co., 1987.

Kritzman, M. "What's Wrong with Portfolio Insurance?" *The Journal of Portfolio Management,* v. 13 (Fall 1986), pp. 13–16.

Leland, H. E. "Option Pricing and Replication with Transaction Costs." *Journal of Finance,* v. 40 (December 1985), pp. 1283–1307.

———. "Who Should Buy Portfolio Insurance?" *Journal of Finance,* v. 35 (May 1980), pp. 581–94.

Malkiel, B. "The Brady Commission Report: A Critique." *Journal of Portfolio Management,* v. 14 (Summer 1988), pp. 9–13.

O'Brien, T. "The Mechanics of Portfolio Insurance." *Journal of Portfolio Management,* v. 14 (Spring 1988), pp. 40–47.

Perold, A. F. "Constant Proportion Portfolio Insurance." Working Paper, Harvard Business School, 1986.

Presidential Task Force on Market Mechanisms. *The Brady Report.* U.S. Government Printing Office, 1988.

Rendleman, R. J., and R. W. McEnally. "Assessing the Cost of Portfolio Insurance." *Financial Analysts Journal,* v. 43 (May/June 1987), pp. 27–37.

Rubinstein, M. "Alternative Paths to Portfolio Insurance." *Financial Analysts Journal,* v. 41 (July/August 1985), pp. 42–52.

_____, and H. Leland. "Replicating Options with Positions in Stock and Cash." *Financial Analysts Journal,* v. 37 (July/August 1981), pp. 63–72.

Singleton, C., and R. Grieves. "Synthetic Puts and Portfolio Insurance Strategies." *Journal of Portfolio Management,* v. 10 (Spring 1984), pp. 63–69.

Tilley, J. A., and G. O. Latainer. "A Synthetic Option Framework for Asset Allocation." *Financial Analysts Journal,* v. 41 (May/June 1985), pp. 32–41.

22 Itô's Calculus: Derivation of the Black–Scholes Option-Pricing Model

The purpose of this chapter is to develop certain relatively recent mathematical discoveries known generally as **stochastic calculus** (or more specifically as **Itô's calculus**) and to illustrate their application in the pricing of options.[1] The topic is motivated by a desire to provide an *intuitive* understanding of certain probabilistic methods that have found significant use in financial economics. A rigorous presentation of the same ideas is presented briefly in Malliaris (1983) and extensively in Malliaris and Brock (1982).

Itô's calculus was prompted by purely mathematical questions originating in N. Wiener's work in 1923 on stochastic integrals and was developed by the Japanese probabilist Kiyosi Itô during 1944–1951. Two decades later economists such as Merton (1973) and Black and Scholes (1973) started using Itô's stochastic differential equation to describe the behavior of asset prices. Because stochastic calculus is now used regularly by financial economists, some attention must be given to its mathematical meaning, its appropriateness in economic modeling, and its applications to finance.

THE ITÔ PROCESS AND FINANCIAL MODELING

Stochastic calculus is the mathematics of random change in continuous time, unlike ordinary calculus, which deals with deterministic change. A key notion in stochastic calculus is the equation:

$$dS(t,w) = \mu[t,S(t,w)]\,dt + \sigma[t,S(t,w)]\,dZ(t,w) \tag{22.1}$$

---

[1] The main text of this chapter was written by Professor A. G. Malliaris, Loyola University of Chicago.

which is analogous to the ordinary differential equation $dS(t)/dt = \mu[t,S(t)]$. This section defines intuitively the Itô equation in Equation (22.1) and discusses its appropriateness to financial modeling.

A stochastic process is an Itô process if the random variable $dS(t,w)$ can be represented by Equation (22.1). The first term, $\mu[t,S(t,w)]\ dt$, is the expected change in $S(t,w)$ at time t. The second term, $\sigma[t,S(t,w)]\ dZ(t,w)$, reflects the uncertain term.

The Itô equation is a **random equation.** The domain of the equation is $[0,\ \infty) \times \Omega$, with the first argument t denoting time and taking values continuously in the interval $[0,\ \infty)$, and the second argument w denoting a random element taking values from a random set Ω. The range of the equation is the real numbers or real vectors. For simplicity only the real numbers, denoted by R, are considered as the range of Equation (22.1). Because time takes values continuously in $[0,\ \infty)$, the Itô equation is a **continuous-time random equation.**

Although at first a real random variable $S(t,w):[0,\infty) \times \Omega \to R$ is used—that is, a function having as domain $[0,\ \infty) \times \Omega$ and as range real numbers—Equation (22.1) expresses not the values of $S(t,w)$ but its infinitesimal differences $dS(t,w)$ as a function of two terms. For example, in finance $S(t,w)$ denotes the price of a stock at time t affected by the state of the economy described by the random element w; and (22.1) expresses the small changes in the stock price, $dS(t,w)$, at time t affected by the random element w. The mathematical meaning of this small difference can be explained as follows: $dS(t,w)$ may be viewed as the limit of larger finite differences $\Delta S(t,w)$ as Δt approaches zero. Note that $\Delta S(t,w) = S(t + \Delta t,w) - S(t,w)$, where Δt denotes the difference in the change in time. Thus, the Itô equation expresses random changes in the values of a variable taking place continuously in time.

Moreover, these random changes are given as the sum of two terms. The first term, $\mu[t,S(t,w)]$, is called the **drift component** of the Itô equation, and in finance it is used to compute the instantaneous expected value of the change in the random variable $S(t,w)$. Observe that $\mu[t,S(t,w)]$, as a function used in the computation of a statistical mean, is affected by both time and randomness. If at a given time t the expected change in $dS(t,w)$, expressed as $E[dS(t,w)]$, is desired, this can be answered by computing $E\{\mu[t,S(t,w)]dt\}$.

The second term $\sigma[t,S(t,w)]\ dZ(t,w)$ is itself the product of two factors. Each factor is important and needs special attention. The first factor, $\sigma[t,S(t,w)]$, is used in the calculation of the instantaneous standard deviation of the change in the random variable $S(t,w)$; it is a function of both time t and the range of values taken by $S(t,w)$. When $\sigma[t,S(t,w)]$ is squared to compute the instantaneous variance, it is usually called the **diffusion coefficient;** it measures the variability of $dS(t,w)$ at a given instance in time.

The second factor, $dZ(t,w)$, is called **white noise;** it models financial uncertainty in continuous time. Actually, $dZ(t,w)$ denotes an infinitesimal change in the **Wiener process,** $Z(t,w):[0,\infty) \times \Omega \to R$, a process with increments that are statistically independent and normally distributed with mean

zero and variance equal to the increment in time. In other words, for every pair of disjoint time intervals $[t_1, t_2]$, $[t_3, t_4]$ with, say, $t_1 < t_2 \le t_3 < t_4$, the increments $Z(t_4,w) - Z(t_3,w)$ and $Z(t_2,w) - Z(t_1,w)$ are independent and normally distributed random variables with means:

$$E[Z(t_4,w) - Z(t_3,w)] = E[Z(t_2,w) - Z(t_1,w)] = 0$$

and respective variances:

$$\text{Var } [Z(t_4,w) - Z(t_3,w)] = t_4 - t_3$$
$$\text{Var } [Z(t_2,w) - Z(t_1,w)] = t_2 - t_1$$

By convention it is assumed that at time $t = 0$, the Wiener process is zero—that is, $Z(0,w) = 0$.

The two factors have been described separately; an intuitive explanation of the product of $\sigma[t,S(t,w)]$ and $dZ(t,w)$ is now presented. Because $\sigma[t,S(t,w)]$ measures the instantaneous standard deviation or volatility of $dS(t,w)$ and because $dZ(t,w)$ is an infinitesimal increment (which is, by definition, purely random with mean zero and variance dt), the expression $\sigma[t,S(t,w)] \, dZ(t,w)$ is the product of two independent random variables, with:

$$E\{\sigma[t,S(t,w)] \, dZ(t,w)\} = 0 \tag{22.2}$$

$$\text{Var } \{\sigma[t,S(t,w)] \, dZ(t,w)\} = E\{\sigma[t,S(t,w)] \, dZ(t,w)\}^2$$
$$= E\{\sigma^2[t,S(t,w)] \, dt\} \tag{22.3}$$

Therefore, the product $\sigma[t,S(t,w)] \, dZ(t,w)$ is a random variable with mean and variances given by Equations (22.2) and (22.3), which, for a given time t and state of nature w, yields a real number. This number may be either positive or negative depending on the value of $dZ(t,w)$ since $\sigma[t,S(t,w)]$ represents a measure of standard deviation and is always positive. Furthermore, the magnitude of the product $\sigma[t,S(t,w)] \, dZ(t,w)$ depends on the magnitude of each of the two terms. Indeed, the methodological foundation of the Itô model is that the uncertainty magnitude $dZ(t,w)$ is multiplied by $\sigma[t,S(t,w)]$ to produce the **total contribution of uncertainty.** Therefore, $\sigma[t,S(t,w)] \, dZ(t,w)$ describes the total fluctuation produced by volatility as this volatility is aggrandized or reduced by pure randomness.

This analysis explains why uncertainty given by $dZ(t,w)$ is being modeled as a multiplicative factor in the product $\sigma[t,S(t,w)] \, dZ(t,w)$: to repeat once again, the multiplicative modeling of uncertainty allows the generation of values for $dS(t,w)$ that are above or below the instantaneous expected value, depending on whether uncertainty is positive or negative, respectively. In other words, the product $\sigma[t,S(t,w)] \, dZ(t,w)$ can be viewed as the total contribution of uncertainty to $dS(t,w)$, with such uncertainty being the product of two factors: the instantaneous standard deviation of changes and the purely random white noise.

The conceptual components of the Itô process can now be collected to offer a more general interpretation of its meaning in finance. If at a given

time t the possible future change in the price of an asset during the next trading interval is being evaluated, this change can be decomposed into two nonoverlapping components: the *expected* change and the *unexpected* change. The expected change, $E[dS(t,w)]$, is described by $E\{\mu[t,S(t,w)]\,dt\}$ and the unexpected change is given by $E\{\sigma[t,S(t,w)]\,dZ(t,w)\}$. As already noted, this unexpected change depends on the asset's volatility and pure randomness; and because uncertainty cannot be anticipated, the unexpected change is zero. This holds because $\sigma[t,S(t,w)]$ and $dZ(t,w)$ are independent random variables; and therefore, from Equation (22.2):

$$E\{\sigma[t,S(t,w)]\,dZ(t,w)\} = E\{\sigma[t,S(t,w)]\}E[dZ(t,w)] = 0$$

because by definition $E[dZ(t,w)] = 0$. Thus, Equation (22.1), which was developed by mathematicians, captures the spirit of financial modeling admirably because it is an equation that involves three important concepts in finance: *mean, standard deviation,* and *randomness.*

However, Equation (22.1) captures the spirit of finance not only because it involves means, standard deviations, and randomness but, more important, because it also expresses key methodological elements of modern financial theory. In an elegant paper, Merton (1982) identifies several foundational notions of the appropriateness of the Itô equation in modern finance.

1. Itô's equation allows uncertainty not to disappear even as trading intervals become extremely short. In the real world of financial markets uncertainty evolves continuously, and $dZ(t,w)$ captures this uncertainty because the value of $dZ(\Delta t,w)$ is not zero even as Δt becomes small. On the other hand, as trading intervals increase uncertainty increases because by definition

$$\text{Var}\,[Z(t + \Delta t,w) - Z(t,w)] = \Delta t.$$

2. Itô's equation incorporates uncertainty for all times. This means that uncertainty is present at all trading periods.

3. The rate of change described by $\mu[t,S(t,w)]\,dt$ is finite, and uncertainty does not cause the term $\sigma[t,S(t,w)]\,dZ(t,w)$ to become unbounded. These notions of the Itô equation are consistent with real-world observations of finite means, finite variances, and uncertainty (which evolves nicely by obtaining continuously finite values).

4. Finally, all that counts in an Itô equation is the present time t. In other words, the past and future are independent. This notion expresses mathematically the concept of economic market efficiency. That is, knowledge of past price behavior does not allow for above-average returns in the future.

Sample Problem 22.1 provides further illustration.

Sample Problem 22.1

Consider the following example of an Itô process describing the price of a given stock.

$$dS(t,w) = 0.001 \ S(t,w) \ dt + 0.025 \ S(t,w) \ dZ(t,w)$$

If both sides are divided by $S(t,w)$:

$$\frac{dS(t,w)}{S(t,w)} = 0.001 \ dt + 0.025 \ dZ(t,w) \qquad \textbf{(22.4)}$$

which gives the proportional change in the price of the stock. Assume that dt equals one trading period, such as one day. Using appropriate coefficients in Equation (22.4), dt could be denoted as one second. In Equation (22.4) the expected daily proportional change is given by:

$$E\left[\frac{dS(t,w)}{S(t,w)}\right] = E[0.001 \ dt + 0.025 \ dZ(t,w)] = 0.001 \qquad \textbf{(22.5)}$$

which means that at any given trading day, the price of the stock is expected to change by 0.1 percent. The standard deviation of the proportional change is $\sigma = 0.025$ or 2.5 percent.

What actually occurs at a given trading period depends on the evolution of the uncertainty as modeled by the normally distributed random variable $dZ(t,w)$, with zero mean and variance 1. From the properties of the normal distribution it can be deduced that although Equation (22.5) says that the expected daily proportional change is 0.001, there is a 68.26-percent probability that the daily proportional change will be between 0.001 ± (1) (0.025), or a 95.46-percent probability that it will be between 0.001 ± (2) (0.025), or a 99.74-percent probability that it will be between 0.001 ± (3) (0.025).

This example shows how the Itô equation combines the notion of a trading interval dt, the expected change in the price of a stock μ, the volatility of the stock σ, and pure uncertainty $dZ(t,w)$ to describe changes in the price of an asset. The same example will be used later to show the behavior of the price of the stock $S(t,w)$. Equation (22.5) illustrates only approximately the infinitesimal proportional change in the price of the stock, and its solution in Equation (22.5) will give the exact evolution of the stock price●

ITÔ'S LEMMA

The preceding two sections dealt with the Itô process, both its intuitive mathematical meaning and its financial interpretation. This section presents briefly Itô's lemma of stochastic differentiation. By formally integrating Equation (22.1):

$$S(t,w) = S(0,w) + \int_0^t \mu(u,w)\,du + \int_0^t \sigma(u,w)\,dZ(u,w) \qquad (22.6)$$

This last equation describes Itô's process in terms of the original random variable $S(t,w)$ rather than infinitesimal differences (differential form), as in Equation (22.1). Mathematically, Equations (22.1) and (22.6) are equivalent and (22.1) obtains clear meaning through (22.6). The analysis of Equation (22.6) is the topic of stochastic integration, which is not developed here because of its complexity. Nevertheless, note that it is the second integral, $\int_0^t \sigma(u,w)\,dZ(u,w)$, that presents the difficulties. The problem arises because uncertainty given by $dZ(u,w)$ in its limit does not have a precise meaning, and therefore the second integral cannot be treated like an ordinary Riemann integral. Itô's great accomplishment was to define the second integral as a random variable, that is, the limit in probability of a certain sequence of integrals of step functions multiplied by the uncertainty $dZ(u,w)$.

Suppose that a stochastic process is given by Equation (22.6) and that a new process $Y(t,w)$ is formed by letting $Y(t,w) = u[t,S(t,w)]$. Because stochastic calculus studies random changes in continuous time, the question arises: what is $dY(t,w)$? This question is important for both mathematical analysis and finance. The answer is given in Itô's lemma.

Itô's Lemma. Consider the nonrandom continuous function $u(t,S):[0,\infty) \times R \to R$ and suppose that it has continuous partial derivatives u_t, u_S, and u_{SS}. Let:

$$Y(t,w) = u[t,S(t,w)] \qquad (22.7)$$

with:

$$dS(t,w) = \mu[t,S(t,w)]\,dt + \sigma[t,S(t,w)]\,dZ(t,w) \qquad (22.8)$$

Then the process $Y(t,w)$ has a differential given by:

$$\begin{aligned} dY(t,w) = \{ &u_t[t,S(t,w)] + u_S[t,S(t,w)]\mu[t,S(t,w)] \\ &+ \tfrac{1}{2}u_{SS}[t,S(t,w)]\,\sigma^2[t,S(t,w)] \}\,dt \\ &+ u_S[t,S(t,w)]\,\sigma[t,S(t,w)]\,dZ(t,w) \end{aligned} \qquad (22.9)$$

The proof is presented in Gikhman and Skorokhod (1969: 387–89), and extensions of this lemma may be found in Arnold (1974: 90–99). Here the analysis is limited to three remarks.

1. Itô's lemma is a useful result because it allows the computation of stochastic differentials of arbitrary functions having as an argument a stochastic process that itself is assumed to possess a stochastic differential. In this respect, Itô's formula is as useful as the chain rule of ordinary calculus.

2. Given an Itô stochastic process $S(t,w)$ with respect to a given Wiener process $Z(t,w)$, and letting $Y(t,w) = u[t,S(t,w)]$ be a new process, Itô's

formula gives the stochastic differential of $Y(t,w)$, where $dY(t,w)$ is given with respect to the same Wiener process—that is, both processes have the same source of uncertainty.

3. An inspection of the proof of Itô's lemma reveals that it consists of an application of Taylor's theorem of advanced calculus and several probabilistic arguments to establish the convergence of certain quantities to appropriate integrals. Therefore, Itô's formula may be obtained by applying Taylor's theorem instead of remembering the specific result in Equation (22.6). More specifically, the differential of $Y(t,w) = u[t,S(t,w)]$, where $S(t,w)$ is a stochastic process with differential given by Equation (22.1), may be computed by using Taylor's theorem and the following multiplication rules:

$$dt \times dt = 0 \qquad dZ \times dZ = dt \qquad dt \times dZ = 0 \qquad \textbf{(22.10)}$$

as:

$$dY = u_t dt + u_S dS + \tfrac{1}{2}(dS)^2 = u_t dt +$$
$$u_S(\mu dt + \sigma dZ) + \tfrac{1}{2}u_{SS}(\mu dt + \sigma dZ)^2$$

By carrying out these multiplications and using the rules in Equation (22.10), Equation (22.9) is obtained.

STOCHASTIC DIFFERENTIAL-EQUATION APPROACH
TO STOCK-PRICE BEHAVIOR

This section demonstrates how a stochastic equation can be used to describe a stochastic price behavior.

As a special case of Equation (22.1) consider:

$$dS(t,w) = \mu S(t,w)\, dt + \sigma S(t,w)\, dZ(t,w) \qquad \textbf{(22.11)}$$

in which μ and σ are constants as in Sample Problem 22.1. Assume that Equation (22.11) describes the price behavior of a certain stock with $S(0,w)$ given. The solution $S(t,w)$ of Equation (22.11) is given by:

$$S(t,w) = S(0,w)\exp[(\mu - \tfrac{1}{2}\sigma^2)t + \sigma Z(t,w)] \qquad \textbf{(22.12)}$$

To show that the behavior of Equation (22.12) is the solution of Equation (22.11) use Itô's lemma as follows. First, start with Equation (22.12), which corresponds to the function $Y(t,w)$. In this case Equation (22.12) is a function of t and $Z(t,w)$, and instead of Equation (22.8):

$$dZ(t,w) = 0 \cdot dt + 1 \cdot dZ(t,w)$$

Next, compute the first- and second-order partials denoted by S_t, S_Z, and S_{ZZ}:

$$S_t(t,w) = \left(\mu - \frac{\sigma^2}{2}\right) S(t,w)$$

$$S_Z(t,w) = \sigma S(t,w)$$

$$S_{ZZ}(t,w) = \sigma^2 S(t,w)$$

Collect these results and use Equation (22.9) to conclude that Equation (22.11) holds:

$$dS(t,w) = \left[\left(\mu - \frac{\sigma^2}{2}\right) S(t,w) + \sigma S(t,w) \cdot 0 + \frac{\sigma^2}{2} S(t,w) \cdot 1\right] dt$$
$$+ \sigma S(t,w) \cdot 1 \cdot dZ(t,w)$$
$$= \mu S(t,w)dt + \sigma S(t,w)dZ(t,w)$$

This result is not only mathematically interesting; in finance it means that, assuming stock prices are given by an Itô process as in Equation (22.11), then Equation (22.12) holds as well. To see if Equation (22.12) accurately describes stock prices in the real world, rewrite it as:

$$\ln \frac{S(t,w)}{S(0,w)} = \left(\mu - \frac{\sigma^2}{2}\right)t + \sigma Z(t,w) \qquad \textbf{(22.13)}$$

which is a random variable normally distributed with mean $(\mu - \sigma^2/2)t$ and variance $\sigma^2 t$. This means that if the stock price follows an Itô process, it has a log normal probability distribution. Such a distribution for stock prices is reasonable because it is consistent with reality, where negative stock prices are not possible; the worst that can happen is that the stock price reaches zero. For a detailed analysis of the properties of a log normal random distribution see Cox and Rubinstein (1985: 201–04); for a list of bibliographical references on the empirical distribution of stock-price changes see Cox and Rubinstein (1985: 485–88). Sample Problem 22.2 provides further illustration.

Sample Problem 22.2

The analysis of this problem applies the results of the last two sections to the example in Sample Problem 22.1. Suppose that instead of Equation (22.11) Equation (22.14) is given. Then Equation (22.12) describes the solution of Equation (22.14):

$$S(t,w) = S(0,w) \exp\left[\left(0.001 - \frac{0.025^2}{2}\right)t + 0.025Z(t,w)\right] \qquad \textbf{(22.14)}$$

From Equation (22.14) the exact evolution of the price of the stock as influenced by a mean, a variance, time, and uncertainty is obtained. Using Equation (22.14) for $t = 1$ to compute:

$$E\left[\ln \frac{S(t,w)}{S(0,w)}\right] = \left(\mu - \frac{\sigma^2}{2}\right)t = \left[0.001 - \frac{(0.025)^2}{2}\right](0.1) = 0.0006875$$
$$\textbf{(22.15)}$$

$$\text{Var}\left[\ln\frac{S(t,w)}{S(0,w)}\right] = \sigma^2 t = (0.025)^2 (0.1) = 0.000625 \qquad \textbf{(22.16)}$$

which means that for a given trading day, the price of the stock is expected to experience a continuous change of 0.068 percent with a standard deviation of 0.025 percent. Computing Equations (22.15) and (22.16) for any t can be done easily; the same computations cannot be performed readily in Equation (22.4)●

THE PRICING OF AN OPTION

An **option** is a contract giving the right to buy or sell an asset within a specified period of time subject to certain conditions. The simplest kind of option is the **European call option,** which is a contract to buy a share of a certain stock at a given date for a specified price. The date the option expires is called the **expiration date (maturity date)** and the price that is paid for the stock when the option is exercised is called the **exercise price (striking price).**

In terms of economic analysis, several propositions about call-option pricing seem clear. The value of an option increases as the price of the stock increases. If the stock price is much greater than the exercise price, it is almost certain that the option will be exercised; and, analogously, if the price of the stock is much less than the exercise price, the value of the option will be near zero and the option will expire without being exercised. If the expiration date is very far in the future, the value of the option will be approximately equal to the price of the stock. If the expiration date is very near, the value of the option will be approximately equal to the stock price minus the exercise price, or zero if the stock price is less than the exercise price. In general, the value of the option is more volatile than the price of the stock, and the relative volatility of the option depends on both the stock price and maturity.

The first rigorous formulation and solution of the problem of option pricing was achieved by Black and Scholes (1973) and Merton (1973). Consider a stock option denoted by C whose price at time t can be written:

$$C(t,w) = C[t,S(t,w)] \qquad \textbf{(22.17)}$$

in which C is a twice continuously differentiable function. Here $S(t,w)$ is the price of some stock upon which the option is written. The price of this stock is assumed to follow Itô's stochastic differential equation:

$$dS(t,w) = \mu[t,S(t,w)]\,dt + \sigma[t,S(t,w)]\,dZ(t,w) \qquad \textbf{(22.18)}$$

Assume, as a simplifying case, that $\mu[t,S(t,w)] = \mu S(t,w)$ and $\sigma[t,S(t,w)] = \sigma S(t,w)$. For notational convenience w is suppressed from the various expressions, and sometimes t as well. Therefore Equation (22.18) becomes

$$dS(t) = \mu S(t)\,dt + \sigma S(t)\,dZ(t) \qquad \textbf{(22.19)}$$

Consider an investor who builds up a portfolio of stocks, options on the stocks, and a riskless asset (for example, government bonds) yielding a riskless rate r. The nominal value of the portfolio, denoted by $P(t)$, is

$$P(t) = N_1(t)S(t) + N_2C(t) + Q(t) \qquad (22.20)$$

where:

N_1 = the number of shares of the stock;
N_2 = the number of call options; and
Q = the value of dollars invested in riskless bonds.

Assume that the stock pays no dividends or other distributions. By Itô's lemma the differential of the call price using Equations (22.17) and (22.19) is

$$\begin{aligned} dC &= C_t\, dt + C_S\, dS + \tfrac{1}{2}C_{SS}\, dS^2 \\ &= (C_t + C_S\mu S + \tfrac{1}{2}C_{SS}\, \sigma^2 S^2)\, dt + C_S\sigma S\, dZ \qquad (22.21) \\ &= \mu_C C\, dt + \sigma_C C\, dZ \end{aligned}$$

Observe that in Equation (22.21):

$$\mu_C C = C_t + C_S\mu S + \tfrac{1}{2}C_{SS}\, \sigma^2 S^2 \qquad (22.22)$$

$$\sigma_C C = C_S\sigma S \qquad (22.23)$$

In other words, $\mu_C C$ is the expected change in the call-option price and $\sigma_C^2 C^2$ is the variance of such a change per unit of time. Itô's lemma simply indicates that if the call-option price is a function of a spot stock price that follows an Itô process, then the call-option price also follows an Itô process with mean and standard deviation parameters that are more complex than those of the stock price. The Itô process for a call is given by Equations (22.22) and (22.23).

The change in the nominal value of the portfolio dP results from the change in the prices of the assets because at a point in time the quantities of option and stock are given—that is, $dN_1 = dN_2 = 0$. More precisely:

$$\begin{aligned} dP &= N_1\, (dS) + N_2\, (dC) + dQ \\ &= (\mu\, dt + \sigma\, dZ)N_1 S + (\mu_C\, dt + \sigma_C\, dZ)N_2 C + rQ\, dt \end{aligned} \qquad (22.24)$$

Let w_1 be the fraction of the portfolio invested in stock, w_2 be the fraction invested in options, and w_3 be the fraction invested in the riskless asset. As before, $w_1 + w_2 + w_3 = 1$, that is, all of the funds available are invested in some type of asset. Set $w_1 = N_1 S/P$, $w_2 = N_2 C/P$, $w_3 = Q/P = 1 - w_1 - w_2$. Then Equation (22.24) becomes

$$\frac{dP}{P} = (\mu\, dt + \sigma\, dZ)w_1 + (\mu_C\, dt + \sigma_C\, dZ)w_2 + (r\, dt)w_3 \quad (22.25)$$

At this point the notion of **economic equilibrium** (also called **risk-neutral** or **preference-free pricing**) is introduced in the analysis. This notion plays an important role in modeling financial behavior, and its appropriate formulation is considered to be a major breakthrough in financial analysis.

More specifically, design the proportions w_1, w_2 so that the position is *riskless* for all $t \geq 0$—that is, let w_1 and w_2 be such that:

$$\text{Var}_t \left(\frac{dP}{P} \right) = \text{Var}_t \, (w_1 \, \sigma \, dZ + w_2 \, \sigma_C \, dZ) = 0 \qquad (22.26)$$

In the last equation, Var_t denotes variance conditioned on $S(t)$, $C(t)$, and $Q(t)$. In other words, choose $(w_1, w_2) = (\overline{w}_1, \overline{w}_2)$ so that:

$$\overline{w}_1 \sigma + \overline{w}_2 \sigma_C = 0 \qquad (22.27)$$

Then from Equation (22.25), because the portfolio is riskless it follows that the portfolio must be expected to earn the riskless rate of return, or:

$$E_t \left(\frac{dP}{P} \right) = [\mu \overline{w}_1 + \mu_C \overline{w}_2 + r(1 - \overline{w}_1 - \overline{w}_2)] \, dt = r(t) \, dt \qquad (22.28)$$

Equations (22.27) and (22.28) yield the Black–Scholes–Merton equations:

$$\frac{\overline{w}_1}{\overline{w}_2} = -\frac{\sigma_C}{\sigma} \qquad (22.29)$$

and:

$$r = \mu \overline{w}_1 + \mu_C \overline{w}_2 - r\overline{w}_1 - r\overline{w}_2 + r \qquad (22.30)$$

which simplify to

$$\frac{\mu - r}{\sigma} = \frac{\mu_C - r}{\sigma_C} \qquad (22.31)$$

Because the law of one price, Equation (22.31) says that the net rate of return per unit of risk must be the same for the two assets and describes an appropriate concept of economic equilibrium in this problem. If this were not the case, there would exist an arbitrage opportunity and investors would take advantage of the opportunity until this equality held. Using Equation (22.31) and making the necessary substitutions from Equations (22.22) and (22.23), the partial differential equation of the pricing of an option is obtained:

$$\tfrac{1}{2}\sigma^2 S^2 C_{SS}(t,S) + rSC_S(t, S) - rC(t, S) + C_t(t, S) = 0 \qquad (22.32)$$

The equation along with the boundary conditions for call options fully characterize the call price: $C(S, T) = \text{Max}\,(0, S - X)$, $S \geq 0$, $0 \geq E \geq T$. The solution to the differential equation (22.32) given these boundary conditions, is the Black–Scholes formula.

A REEXAMINATION OF OPTION PRICING

To illustrate the notion of economic equilibrium once again, consider the nominal value of a portfolio consisting of a stock and a call option on this stock and write:

$$P(t) = N_1(t) \, S(t) + N_2(t) \, C(t) \qquad (22.33)$$

using the same notation as in the previous section. Equation (22.33) differs from Equation (22.20) because the term $Q(t)$ has been deleted. Now concentrating on the two assets of the portfolio—that is, the stock and the call option—and using Equations (22.33) and (22.21), the change in the value of the portfolio is given by:

$$dP = N_1 dS + N_2 dC = N_1 dS + N_2[(C_t + \tfrac{1}{2}C_{SS} \, \sigma^2 S^2) \, dt + C_S \, dS]$$
$$(22.34)$$

Note that $dN_1 = dN_2 = 0$, since at any given point in time the quantities of stock and option are given. For arbitrary quantities of stock and option, Equation (22.34) shows that the change in the nominal value of the portfolio dP is stochastic because dS is a random variable. Suppose the quantities of stock and call option are chosen so that:

$$\frac{N_1}{N_2} = -C_S \qquad (22.35)$$

Note that C_S in Equation (22.35) denotes a hedge ratio and is called **delta**. Then, $N_1 dS + N_2 C_S dS = 0$, and inserting Equation (22.35) into Equation (22.34) yields:

$$dP = -N_2 C_S dS + N_2[(C_t + \tfrac{1}{2}C_{SS} \, \sigma^2 S^2) \, dt + C_S \, dS]$$
$$= N_2(C_t + \tfrac{1}{2}C_{SS} \, \sigma^2 S^2) \, dt \qquad (22.36)$$

Let $N_2 = 1$ in Equation (22.36) and observe that in equilibrium the rate of return of the riskless portfolio must be the same as the riskless rate $r(t)$. Therefore:

$$\frac{dP}{P} = r \, dt \qquad (22.37)$$

Equation (22.37) can be used to derive the partial differential equation for the value of the option. Making the necessary substitutions in Equation (22.36):

$$\frac{(C_t + \tfrac{1}{2}C_{SS} \, \sigma^2 S^2) \, dt}{-C_S S + C} = r \, dt$$

which upon rearrangement gives Equation (22.32). Note that the option-pricing equation is a second-order linear partial differential equation of the parabolic type. The boundary conditions of Equation (22.32) are determined by the specification of the asset. For the case of an option that can be exercised only at the expiration date t^* with an exercise price X, the boundary conditions are

$$C(t, S = 0) = 0, \qquad (22.38)$$

$$C(t = t^*, S) = \text{Max} \, (0, S - X). \qquad (22.39)$$

Observe that Equation (22.38) says that the call-option price is zero if the stock price is zero at any date t; Equation (22.39) says that the call-option price at the expiration date $t = t^*$ must equal the maximum of either zero or the difference between the stock price and the exercise price.

The solution of the option-pricing equation subject to the boundary conditions is given, for $T = t^* - t$, as:

$$C(T, S, \sigma^2, X, r) = SN(d_1) - \frac{X}{e^{rT}} N(d_2) \tag{22.40}$$

where N denotes the cumulative normal distribution, namely:

$$N(y) = -\frac{1}{\sqrt{2\pi}} \int_{-\infty}^{y} e^{-x^2/2} \, dx$$

In Equation (22.40), T is time to expiration (measured in years) and d_1 and d_2 are given by:

$$d_1 = \frac{\ln (S/X) + (r + \frac{1}{2}\sigma^2)T}{\sigma\sqrt{T}} \tag{22.41}$$

$$d_2 = \frac{\ln (S/X) + (r - \frac{1}{2}\sigma^2)T}{\sigma\sqrt{T}} \tag{22.42}$$

$$= d_1 - \sigma\sqrt{T}$$

It can be shown that:

$$\frac{\partial C}{\partial T} > 0, \quad \frac{\partial C}{\partial S} > 0, \quad \frac{\partial C}{\partial \sigma^2} > 0, \quad \frac{\partial C}{\partial X} < 0, \quad \frac{\partial C}{\partial r} > 0 \tag{22.43}$$

These partial derivatives justify the intuitive behavior of the price of an option, as was indicated in the beginning of the previous section. More specifically, these partials show the following:

1. As the stock price rises, so does the option price.
2. As the variance rate of the underlying stock rises, so does the option price.
3. With a higher exercise price, the expected payoff decreases.
4. The value of the option increases as the interest rate rises.
5. With a longer time to maturity, the price of the option is greater.

Before giving an example it is appropriate to sketch the solution of Equation (22.32) subject to the boundary conditions of Equations (22.38) and (22.39). Let t denote the current trading period that is prior to the expiration date t^*. At time t, two outcomes can be expected to occur at t^*. (1) $S(t^*) > X$—that is, the price of the stock at the time of the expiration of the call option is greater than the exercise price, or (2) $S(t^*) \leq X$. Note that the first outcome occurs with probability $p_0 \equiv p[S(t^*) > X]$ and the second occurs with probability $1 - p$. Obviously, the only interesting possibility is the first case when $S(t^*) > X$, because this is when the price of the call has positive

value. If $S(t^*) \leq X$, then $C(t^*) = 0$ from Equation (22.39). Again from Equation (22.39), if $S(t^*) > X$, then the price of the call option at expiration $C(t^*)$ can be computed from the expectation of Equation (22.39):

$$C(t^*) = E\{\text{Max } [0, S(t^*) - X]\} = E[S(t^*) - X] \qquad \textbf{(22.44)}$$

What is the price of a call option if the first outcome materializes at t instead of t^*? This can be answered immediately by appropriate continuous discounting. Using Equation (22.44):

$$C(t) = e^{-r(t^* - t)}E[S(t^*) - X] \qquad \textbf{(22.45)}$$

Recall, however, that $C(t)$ in Equation (22.45) holds only with probability p. Combine both possibilities to write:

$$\begin{aligned} C(t) &= p \cdot e^{-r(t^* - t)}E[S(t^*) - X] + (1 - p) \cdot 0 \\ &= p \cdot e^{-r(t^* - t)}E[S(t^*)|S(t^*) > X] - p \cdot e^{-r(t^* - t)}X \end{aligned} \qquad \textbf{(22.46)}$$

Detailed calculations in Jarrow and Rudd (1983: 92–94) show that because the price of the underlying stock is distributed log normally, it follows that:

$$p = P[S(t^*) > X] = N\left[\frac{\ln\dfrac{S(t)}{X} + (r + \frac{1}{2}\sigma^2)(t^* - t)}{\sigma\sqrt{t^* - t}}\right] \qquad \textbf{(22.47)}$$

$$p \cdot E[S(t^*)\,|S^* > X] = S(t)e^{r(t^* - t)}N\left[\frac{\ln\dfrac{S(t)}{X} + (r + \frac{1}{2}\sigma^2)(t^* - t)}{\sigma\sqrt{t^* - t}}\right] \qquad \textbf{(22.48)}$$

Combining Equations (22.47) and (22.48) with $T = t^* - t$ into Equation (22.46) yields Equation (22.40).

It is worth observing that the two terms of Equation (22.40) have economic meaning. The first term, $SN(d_1)$, denotes the present value of receiving the stock provided that $S(t^*) > X$. The second term gives the present value of paying the striking price provided that $S(t^*) > X$. In the special case when there is no uncertainty and $\sigma = 0$, observe that:

$$\begin{aligned} N(d_1) &= N(d_2) = N(\infty) = 1; \quad \text{and} \\ C &= S(t) - e^{-r(t^* - t)}X \end{aligned} \qquad \textbf{(22.49)}$$

that is, a call is worth the difference between the current value of the stock and the discounted value of the striking price provided $S(t^*) > X$; otherwise the call price would be zero. When $\sigma \neq 0$—that is, when uncertainty exists and the stock price is volatile—the two terms in Equation (22.49) are multiplied by $N(d_1)$ and $N(d_2)$, respectively, to adjust the call price for the prevailing uncertainties. These two probabilities can also be given an economic interpretation. As mentioned earlier, $N(d_1)$ is called delta; it is the partial derivative of the call price with respect to the stock price. $N(d_2)$ gives the probability that the call option will be in the money, as Equation 22.47 shows.

Assuming that investors in the economy have risk-neutral preferences, it will be possible to derive the Black–Scholes formula without using stochastic differential equations. Garven (1986) has shown that to derive Equation (22.40) knowledge is required of normal and log normal distributions and basic calculus, as presented in Appendix 22A. Sample Problem 22.3 provides further illustration.

Sample Problem 22.3

Equation (22.40) indicates that the Black–Scholes option-pricing model is a function of only five variables: T, the time to expiration, S, the stock price, σ^2, the instantaneous variance rate on the stock price, X, the exercise price, and r, the riskless interest rate. Of these five variables, only the variance rate must be estimated; the other four variables are directly observable. A simple example is presented to illustrate the use of Equation (22.40). The values of the observable variables are taken from *The Wall Street Journal*.

On Friday, September 12, 1986, the IBM closed at \$137.25. To estimate the price of a call option expiring on the third Friday in January 1987 with an exercise price \$135, the riskless rate and the instantaneous variance need to be estimated. The riskless rate is estimated by using the average of the bid and ask quotes on U.S. Treasury bills of approximately the same maturity as the option. The results of the Monday, September 8, 1986, auction show a riskless rate of 5.24 percent for U.S. Treasury bills maturing in thirteen weeks. The only missing piece of information is the instantaneous variance of the stock price.

Several different techniques have been suggested for estimating the instantaneous variance. In this regard the work of Latané and Rendleman (1976) must be mentioned; they derive standard deviations of continuous price-relative returns that are implied in actual call-option prices on the assumption that investors behave as if they price options according to the Black–Scholes model. In the example the implicit variance is calculated by using the actual January 1987 call price of an IBM option with an exercise price of \$130 to solve for an estimate of the instantaneous variance. More specifically, a numerical search is used to approximate the standard deviation implied by the Black–Scholes formula with these parameters: stock price $S = 137.25$, exercise price $X = 130$, time to expiration $T = 126/365 = 0.345$, riskless rate $r = 0.0524$, and call-option price $C = 12.50$. The approximated implicit standard deviation is found to be $\sigma = 0.21$. A program written in BASIC that runs on a personal computer and computes the implicit standard deviation can be found in Bookstaber (1985: 361–63). (The same book contains option-pricing programs written in BASIC, among many other programs for investment analysis.)

After the clarifications are made, the example is this: given $S = 137.25$, $X = 135$, $T = 0.345$, $r = 0.0524$, and $\sigma = 0.21$, use Equation (22.40) to compute C. Using Equations (22.41) and (22.42) calculate:

$$d_1 = \frac{\ln(137.25/135) + [0.0524 + \frac{1}{2}(0.21)^2](0.345)}{0.21 \sqrt{0.345}} = 0.342242$$

$$d_2 = \frac{\ln(137.25/135) + [0.0524 - \frac{1}{2}(0.21)^2](0.345)}{0.21 \sqrt{0.345}} = 0.218895$$

From Appendix 15C, giving the area of a standard normal distribution, $N(0.342242) = 0.633930$ and $N(0.218895) = 0.586665$. Finally,

$$C = (137.25)(0.633930) - \frac{135}{e^{(0.0524)(0.345)}}(0.586665) = 9.23$$

The calculated call-option price of $9.23 is very close to the actual call price of $9.25 reported in *The Wall Street Journal* on Monday, September 15, 1986.

This simple example shows how to use the Black–Scholes model to price a call option under the assumptions of the model. The example is presented for illustrative purposes only, and it relies heavily on the implicit estimate of the variance, its constancy over time, and all the remaining assumptions of the model. The appropriateness of estimating the implicit instantaneous variance is ultimately an empirical question, as is the entire Black–Scholes pricing formula. Boyle and Ananthanarayanan (1977) studied the implications of using an estimate of the variance in option-valuation models and showed that this procedure produces biased option values. However, the magnitude of this bias is not large.

One additional remark must be made. The closeness in this example of the calculated call option price to the actual call price is not necessarily evidence of the validity of the Black–Scholes model. Extensive empirical work has taken place to investigate how market prices of call options compare with price predicted by Black–Scholes; see MacBeth and Merville (1979) and Bhattacharya (1980)●

REMARKS ON OPTION PRICING

For a review on the literature on option pricing, see the two papers by Smith (1976, 1979). It is appropriate here to make a few remarks on the Black–Scholes option-pricing model to clarify its significance and its limitation.

First, the Black-Scholes model for a European call as originally derived, and as reported here, is based on several simplifying assumptions.

1. The stock price follows an Itô equation.
2. The market operates continuously.
3. There are no transaction costs in buying or selling the option or the underlying stock.
4. There are no taxes.

5. The riskless rate is known and constant.

6. There are no restrictions on short sales.

Several researchers have extended the original Black–Scholes model by modifying these assumptions. Merton (1973) generalizes the model to include dividend payments, exercise-price changes, and the case of a stochastic interest rate. Roll (1977) has solved the problem of valuing a call option that can be exercised prior to its expiration date when the underlying stock is assumed to make known dividend payments before the option matures. Ingersoll (1976) studies the effect of differential taxes on capital gains and income while Scholes (1976) determines the effects of the tax treatment of options on the pricing model. Furthermore, Merton (1976) and Cox and Ross (1976) show that if the stock-price movements are discontinuous, under certain assumptions the valuation model still holds. These and other modifications of the original Black–Scholes analysis indicate the model is quite robust about the relaxation of its fundamental assumptions.

Second, it is worth repeating that the use of Itô's calculus and the important insight concerning the appropriate concept of an equilibrium by creating a riskless hedge portfolio have let Black and Scholes obtain a closed-form solution for option pricing. In this closed-form solution several variables do not appear, such as (1) the expected rate of return of the stock, (2) the expected rate of return of the option, (3) a measure of investor's risk preference, (4) investor expectations, and (5) equilibrium conditions for the entire capital market.

Third, the Black–Scholes pricing model has found numerous applications. Among these are: (1) pricing the debt and equity of a firm; (2) the effects of corporate policy and, specifically, the effects of mergers, acquisitions, and scale expansions on the relative values of the debt and equity of the firm; (3) the pricing of convertible bonds; (4) the pricing of underwriting contracts; (5) the pricing of leases; and (6) the pricing of insurance. Smith (1976, 1979) summarizes most applications and indicates the original reference. See also Brealey and Myers (1988).

Fourth, Black (1976) shows that the original call-option formula for stocks can be easily modified to be used in pricing call options on futures. The formula is

$$C(T, F, \sigma^2, X, r) = e^{-rT}[FN(d_1) - XN(d_2)] \qquad \textbf{(22.50)}$$

$$d_1 = \frac{\ln (F/X) + \frac{1}{2}\sigma^2 T}{\sigma\sqrt{T}} \qquad \textbf{(22.51)}$$

$$d_2 = \frac{\ln (F/X) - \frac{1}{2}\sigma^2 T}{\sigma\sqrt{T}} \qquad \textbf{(22.52)}$$

In Equation (22.50) F now denotes the current futures price. The other four variables are as before—time to maturity, volatility of the underlying futures price, exercise price, and risk-free rate. Note that Equation (22.50) differs

from Equation (22.40) only in one respect: by substituting $e^{-rT}F$ for S in the original Equation (22.40) Equation (22.50) is obtained. This holds because the investment in a futures contract is zero, which causes the interest rate in Equations (22.51) and (22.52) to drop out.

Fifth, three important papers by Harrison and Kreps (1979) and Kreps (1981, 1982) consider some foundational issues that arise in conjunction with the arbitrage theory of option pricing. The important point to consider is this: the ability to trade securities frequently can enable a few multiperiod securities to span many states of nature. In the Black–Scholes theory there are two securities and uncountably many states of nature, but because there are infinitely many trading opportunities and because uncertainty resolves nicely, markets are effectively complete. Thus, even though there are far fewer securities than states of nature, markets are complete and risk is allocated efficiently. An interesting result of Harrison and Kreps (1979) is that certain self-trading strategies can create something out of nothing when there are infinitely many trading opportunities. The **doubling strategies** are the well-known illustrations of this phenomenon. Harrison and Kreps introduce the concept of a **simple strategy** to eliminate free lunches and conjecture that a nonnegative wealth constraint could rule out the doubling strategies. Duffie and Huang (1985) give an interpretation of admissible strategy as the limit of a sequence of simple strategies and use an integrability condition on the trading strategies. Dybvig and Huang (1986) show that under certain conditions the integrability condition and the nonnegative wealth constraint are functionally equivalent.

Finally, for an intensive survey of numerous empirical tests, see Galai (1983).

SUMMARY

This chapter has discussed the basic concepts and equations of stochastic calculus (Itô's calculus), which has become a very useful tool in understanding finance theory and practice. By using these concepts and equations, the manner by which Black and Scholes derived their famous option-pricing model was also illustrated. Although this chapter is not required to understand the basic ingredients of security analysis and portfolio management discussed in Chapters 1–21, it is useful for those with training in advanced mathematics to realize how advanced mathematics can be used in finance.

APPENDIX 22A: AN ALTERNATIVE METHOD TO DERIVE THE BLACK–SCHOLES OPTION-PRICING MODEL

Perhaps it is unclear why it is assumed that investors have risk-neutral preferences when the usual assumption in finance courses is that investors are risk averse. It is feasible to make this simplistic assumption because

investors are able to create riskless portfolios by combining call options with their underlying securities. Since the creation of a riskless hedge places no restrictions on investor preferences other than nonsatiation, the valuation of the option and its underlying asset will be independent of investor risk preferences. Therefore, a call option will trade at the same price in risk-neutral economy as it will in a risk-averse or risk-preferent economy.

Assumptions and the Present Value of the Expected Terminal Option Price

To derive the Black–Scholes formula it is assumed that there are no transaction costs, no margin requirements, and no taxes; that all shares are infinitely divisible; and that continuous trading can be accomplished. It is also assumed that the economy is risk neutral.

In the risk-neutral assumptions of Cox and Ross (1976) and Rubinstein (1976), today's option price can be determined by discounting the expected value of the terminal option price by the riskless rate of interest. As was seen earlier, the terminal call-option price can take on only two values: $S_t - X$ if the call option expires in the money, or 0 if the call expires out of the money. So today's call option price is

$$C = \exp{(-rt)} \, \text{Max} \, (S_t - X, 0) \tag{22A.1}$$

where:

C = the market value of the call option;
r = riskless rate of interest;
t = time to expiration;
S_t = the market value of the underlying stock at time t; and
X = exercise or striking price.

Equation (22A.1) says that the value of the call option today will be either $S_t - X$ or 0, whichever is greater. If the price of the stock at time t is greater than the exercise price, the call option will expire in the money. This simply means that an investor who owns the call option will exercise it. The option will be exercised regardless of whether the option holder would like to take physical possession of the stock. If the investor would like to own the stock, the cheapest way to obtain the stock is by exercising the option. If the investor would not like to own the stock, he or she will still exercise the option and immediately sell the stock in the market. Since the price the investor paid (X) is lower than the price he or she can sell the stock for (S_t), the investor realizes an immediate profit of $S_t - X$. If the price of the stock (S_t) is less than the exercise price (X), the option expires out of the money. This occurs because in purchasing shares of the stock the investor will find it cheaper to purchase the stock in the market than to exercise the option.

Assuming that the call option expires in the money, then the present value of the expected terminal option price is equal to the present value of the

difference between the expected terminal stock price and the exercise price, as indicated in Equation (22A.2):

$$C = \exp(-rt)\, E[\text{Max}\,(S_t - X, 0)]$$
$$= \exp(-rt)\int_x^\infty (S_t - X)\, h(S_t)\, dS_t \qquad \textbf{(22A.2)}$$

where $h(S_t)$ is the log normal density function of S_t. To evaluate the integral in (22A.2) rewrite it as the difference between two integrals:

$$C = \exp(-rt)\left[\int_x^\infty S_t h(S_t)\, dS_t - X\int_x^\infty h(S_t)\, dS_t\right]$$
$$= E_x(S_t)\cdot \exp(-rt) - X\cdot \exp(-rt)\cdot[1 - H(X)] \qquad \textbf{(22A.3)}$$

where:

$E_x(S_t)$ = the partial expectation of S_t, truncated from below at x; and
$H(X)$ = the probability that $S_t \leq X$.

Equation (22A.3) says that the value of the call option is the present value of the partial expected stock price (assuming the call expires in the money) minus the present value of the exercise price (adjusted by the probability that the stock's price will be less than the exercise price at the expiration of the option). The terminal stock price S_t can be rewritten as the product of the current price (S) and the t-period log normally distributed price ratio S_t/S, so $S_t = S(S_t/S)$. Equation (22A.3) can also be rewritten:

$$C = \exp(-rt)\left[S\int_{x/s}^\infty \frac{S_t}{S}\, g\!\left(\frac{S_t}{S}\right)\frac{dS_t}{S} - X\int_{x/s}^\infty g\!\left(\frac{S_t}{S}\right)\frac{dS_t}{S}\right]$$
$$= S\exp(-rt)\, E_{x/s}\!\left(\frac{S_t}{S}\right) - X\exp(-rt)\left[1 - G\!\left(\frac{X}{S}\right)\right] \qquad \textbf{(22A.4)}$$

where:

$$g\!\left(\frac{S_t}{S}\right) = \text{log normal density function of } S_t/S;$$

$$E_{x/s}\!\left(\frac{S_t}{S}\right) = \text{the partial expectation of } S_t/S, \text{ truncated from below at } x/S;$$
and

$$G\!\left(\frac{X}{S}\right) = \text{the probability that } S_t/S \leq X/S.$$

Present Value of the Partial Expectation of the Terminal Stock Price

The right-hand side of Equation (22A.4) is evaluated by considering the two integrals separately. The first integral, $S\exp(-rt)\,E_{x/s}\,(S_t/S)$, can be solved by assuming the return on the underlying stock follows a stationary random walk. That is

$$\frac{S_t}{S} = \exp{(Kt)} \tag{22A.5}$$

where K is the rate of return on the underlying stock per unit of time. Taking the natural logarithm of both sides of Equation (22A.5) yields:

$$\ln\left(\frac{S_t}{S}\right) = Kt$$

Since the ratio S_t/S is log normally distributed, it follows that Kt is log normally distributed with density $f(Kt)$, mean $\mu_K t$, and variance $\sigma_K^2 t$. Because $S_t/S = \exp{(Kt)}$, the differential can be rewritten, $dS_t/S = \exp{(Kt)t} \, dK$. $g(S_t/S)$ is a density function of a log normally distributed variable S_t/S; so following Garren (1986), it can be transformed into a density function of a normally distributed variable Kt according to the relationship $S_t/S = \exp{(Kt)}$ as:

$$g\left(\frac{S_t}{S}\right) = f(Kt)\left(\frac{S}{S_t}\right) \tag{22A.6}$$

These transformations allow the first integral in Equation (22A.4) to be rewritten:

$$S \exp{(-rt)} \, E_{x/S}\left(\frac{S_t}{S}\right) = S \exp{(-rt)} \int_{\ln(x/S)}^{\infty} f(Kt) \exp{(Kt)} \, t \, dK$$

Because Kt is normally distributed, the density $f(Kt)$ with mean $\mu_K t$ and variance $\sigma_K^2 t$ is

$$f(Kt) = (2\pi\sigma_K^2 t)^{-1/2} \exp{[-\tfrac{1}{2}(Kt - \mu_K t)^2/\sigma_K^2]}$$

Substitution yields:

$$\begin{aligned} S \exp{(-rt)} \, E_{x/S}\left(\frac{S_t}{S}\right) = {} & S \exp{(-rt)}(2\pi\sigma_K^2 t)^{-1/2} \\ & \times \int_{\ln(x/S)}^{\infty} \exp{[Kt]} \exp{[-\tfrac{1}{2}(Kt - \mu_K t)^2/\sigma_K^2 t]} \, t \, dK \end{aligned} \tag{22A.7}$$

Equation (22A.7)'s integrand can be simplified by adding the terms in the two exponents, multiplying and dividing the result by $\exp{(-\tfrac{1}{2}\sigma_K^2 t)}$. First, expand the term $(Kt - \mu_K t)^2$ and factor out t so that:

$$\exp{[Kt]} \exp{[-\tfrac{1}{2}(Kt - \mu_K t)^2/\sigma_K^2 t]}$$

Next, factor out t so:

$$\exp{(Kt)} \exp{\{-\tfrac{1}{2}t[(K^2 - 2\mu_K K + \mu_K^2)/\sigma_K^2]\}}$$

Now combine the two exponents:

$$\exp{\{-\tfrac{1}{2}t[K^2 - 2\mu_K K + \mu_K^2 - 2\sigma_K^2 K)/\sigma_K^2]\}}$$

Now, multiply and divide this result by $\exp{(-\tfrac{1}{2}\sigma_K^2 t)}$ to get:

$$\exp\{-\tfrac{1}{2}t[K^2 - 2\mu_K K + \mu_K^2 - 2\sigma_K^2 K + \sigma_K^4 - \sigma_K^4)/\sigma_K^2]\}$$

Next, rearrange and combine terms to get:

$$\exp\{(-\tfrac{1}{2}t)[(K - \mu_K - \sigma_K^2)^2 - \sigma_K^4 - 2\mu_K\sigma_K^2]/\sigma_K^2\} =$$
$$\exp[(\mu_K + \tfrac{1}{2}\sigma_K^2)t]\exp\{-\tfrac{1}{2}[Kt - (\mu_K + \sigma_K^2)t]^2/\sigma_K^2 t\} \quad \textbf{(22A.8)}$$

In Equation (22A.8), $\exp[(\mu_K + \tfrac{1}{2}\sigma_K^2)t] = E(S_t/S)$, the mean of the t-period log normally distributed price ratio S_t/S. So, Equation (22A.7) becomes:

$$S\exp(-rt)\,E_{x/S}\left(\frac{S_t}{S}\right) = S\,E\left(\frac{S_t}{S}\right)\exp(-rt)(2\pi\sigma_K^2 t)^{-1/2}$$
$$\qquad\qquad \textbf{(22A.9)}$$
$$\times \int_{\ln(x/S)}^{\infty} \exp(Kt)\exp\{-\tfrac{1}{2}[Kt - (\mu_K + \sigma_K^2)t]^2/\sigma_K^2 t\}$$

Since the equilibrium rate of return in a risk-neutral economy is the riskless rate, $E(S_t/S)$ may be rewritten as $\exp(rt)$:

$$S\,E\left(\frac{S_t}{S}\right)\exp(-rt) = S\exp(rt)\exp(-rt)$$
$$= S$$

So Equation (22A.9) becomes

$$S\exp(-rt)\,E_{x/S}\left(\frac{S_t}{S}\right) = S\,(2\pi\sigma_K^2 t)^{-1/2}$$
$$\qquad\qquad \textbf{(22A.10)}$$
$$\times \int_{\ln(x/S)}^{\infty} \exp\{-\tfrac{1}{2}[(Kt - (\mu_K + \sigma_K^2)t]^2/\sigma_K^2 t\}\,t\,dK$$

To complete the simplification of this part of the Black–Scholes formula, define a standard normal random variable y:

$$y = [Kt - (\mu_K + \sigma_K^2)t]/\sigma_K^2 t^{1/2}$$

Solving for Kt yields:

$$Kt = (\mu_K + \sigma_K^2)t + \sigma_K t^{1/2}\,y$$

and therefore:

$$t\,dK = \sigma_K t^{1/2}\,dy$$

By making the transformation from Kt to y the lower limit of integration becomes

$$[\ln(x/S) - (\mu_K + \sigma_K^2)t]/\sigma_K t^{1/2}$$

Further simplify the integrand by noting that the assumption of a risk neutral economy implies:

$$\exp[(\mu_K + \tfrac{1}{2}\sigma_K^2)t] = \exp(rt)$$

Taking the natural logarithm of both sides yields:

$$(\mu_K + \tfrac{1}{2}\sigma_K^2)\,t = rt$$

Hence, $(\mu_K + \sigma_K^2) t = (r + \frac{1}{2}\sigma_K^2) t$.

The lower limit of integration is now:

$$- [\ln (S/x) + (r + \frac{1}{2}\sigma_K^2)t]/\sigma_K t^{1/2} = -d_1$$

Substituting this into Equation (22A.10) and making the transformation to y yields:

$$S \exp (-rt) E_{x/S}\left(\frac{S_t}{S}\right) = S \int_{-d_1}^{\infty} \exp (-\tfrac{1}{2}y^2)/(2\pi)^{1/2} \, dy$$

Since y is a standard normal random variable (distribution is symmetric around zero) the limits of integration can be exchanged:

$$S \exp (-rt) E_{x/S}\left(\frac{S_t}{S}\right) = S \int_{\infty}^{-d_1} \exp (-\tfrac{1}{2}y^2)/(2\pi)^{1/2} \, dy$$

$$= S \, N(d_1) \qquad \text{(22A.11)}$$

where $N(d_1)$ is the standard normal cumulative distribution function evaluated at $y = d_1$.

Present Value of the Exercise Price under Uncertainty

To complete the derivation, the integral that corresponds to the term $X \exp (-rt)[1 - G(X/S)]$ must be evaluated. Start by making the logarithmic transformation:

$$\ln \left(\frac{S_t}{S}\right) = Kt$$

This transformation allows the rewriting of $g(S_t/S)$ to $(S/S_t) \, f(Kt)$ as mentioned previously. The differential can be written:

$$d \frac{S_t}{S} = \exp (Kt) \, t \, dK$$

Therefore:

$$X \exp (-rt)[1 - G(X/S)] = X \exp (-rt) \int_{\ln(X/S)}^{\infty} f(Kt) \, t \, dK =$$

$$X \exp (-rt)(2\pi\sigma_K^2 t)^{-1/2} \int_{\ln(X/S)}^{\infty} \exp [-\tfrac{1}{2}(Kt - \mu_K t)^2/\sigma_K^2 t] \, t \, dK \quad \text{(22A.12)}$$

The integrand is now simplified by following the same procedure used in simplifying the previous integral. Define a standard normal random variable Z:

$$Z = \frac{Kt - \mu_K t}{\sigma_K t^{1/2}}$$

Solving for Kt yields:

$$Kt = \mu_K t + \sigma_K t^{1/2} Z$$

and $t\, dK = \sigma_K t^{1/2}\, dZ$. Making the transformation from Kt to Z means the lower limit of integration becomes

$$\frac{\ln(X/S) - \mu_K t}{\sigma_K t^{1/2}}$$

Again, note that the assumption of a risk-neutral economy implies:

$$\exp\left(\mu_K + \tfrac{1}{2}\sigma_K^2 t\right) = \exp\left(rt\right)$$

Taking the natural logarithm of both sides yields:

$$\left(\mu_K + \tfrac{1}{2}\sigma_K^2\right) t = rt$$

or:

$$\mu_K t = \left(r - \tfrac{1}{2}\sigma_K^2\right) t$$

Therefore, the lower limit of integration becomes:

$$\frac{-[\ln (S/x) + (r - \tfrac{1}{2}\sigma_K^2)t]}{\sigma_K t^{1/2}} = -(d_1 - \sigma_K t^{1/2})$$
$$= -d_2$$

Substitution yields:

$$x \exp\left(-rt\right)[1 - G(X/S)] = x \exp\left(-rt\right)\int_{-d_2}^{\infty} \exp\left[-\tfrac{1}{2}Z^2/(2\pi)^{1/2}\right] dZ$$
$$= x \cdot \exp\left(-rt\right)\int_{-\infty}^{d_2} \exp\left[-\tfrac{1}{2}Z^2/(2\pi)^{1/2}\right] dZ$$
$$= x \cdot \exp\left(-rt\right) N(d_2) \qquad \textbf{(22A.13)}$$

where $N(d_2)$ is the standard normal cumulative distribution function evaluated at $Z = d_2$.

Substituting Equations (22A.11) and (22A.13) into Equation (22A.4) completes the derivation of the Black–Scholes formula:

$$C = S\, N(d_1) - X \exp\left(-rt\right) N(d_2) \qquad \textbf{(22A.14)}$$

This appendix provides a simple derivation of the Black–Scholes call-option pricing formula. Under an assumption of risk neutrality the Black–Scholes formula was derived using only differential and integral calculus and a basic knowledge of normal and log normal distributions.

REFERENCES

Arnold, L. *Stochastic Differential Equations: Theory and Applications.* John Wiley & Sons, 1974.

Bhattacharya, M. "Empirical Properties of the Black–Scholes Formula Under Ideal Conditions." *Journal of Financial Quantitative Analysis*, v. 15, (December 1980), pp. 1081–1105.

Black, F. "The Pricing of Commodity Contracts." *Journal of Financial Economics,* v. 3 (January–March 1976), pp. 167–78.

_____, and M. Scholes. "The Pricing of Options and Corporate Liabilities." *Journal of Political Economy,* v. 81 (May/June 1973), pp. 637–54.

Bookstaber, R. *The Complete Investment Book: Trading Stocks, Bonds and Options With Computer Applications.* Scott, Foresman and Company, 1985.

Boyle, P. P., and A. L. Ananthanarayanan. "The Impact of Variance Estimation in Option Valuation Models." *Journal of Financial Economics,* v. 5 (September 1977), pp. 375–87.

Brealey, R., and S. Myers. *Principles of Corporate Finance,* 3rd ed., McGraw-Hill, 1988.

Brennan, M., and E. Schwartz. "A Continuous Time Approach to the Pricing of Bonds." *Journal of Banking and Finance,* v. 3 (July 1979), pp. 133–55.

_____. "Finite Difference Method and Jump Processes Arising in the Pricing of Contingent Claims: A Synthesis." *Journal of Financial and Quantitative Analysis,* v. 13 (September 1978), pp. 461–74.

Courtadon, G. "A More Accurate Finite Difference Approximation for the Valuation of Options." *Journal of Financial and Quantitative Analysis,* v. 17 (December 1982), pp. 697–705.

Cox, J. C., and S. A. Ross. "The Valuation of Options for Alternative Stochastic Processes." *Journal of Financial Economics,* v. 3 (March 1976), pp. 145–226.

Duffie, D., and C. Huang. "Implementing Arrow-Debreu Equilibria by Continuous Trading of Few Long-Lived Securities." *Econometrica,* v. 53 (December 1985), pp. 1337–56.

Dybvig, P., and C. Huang. "Optimal Portfolios and a Positive Wealth Constraint." Yale University School of Management working paper, 1986.

Galai, D. "A Survey of Empirical Tests of Option-Pricing Models." In *Option Pricing,* ed. M. Brenner. Lexington Books, 1983. Pp. 45–80.

Garven, J. R. "A Pedagogic Note on the Derivation of the Black–Scholes Option Pricing Formula." *The Financial Review,* v. 21 (November 1986), pp. 337–44.

Geske, R., and K. Shostri. "Valuation by Approximation: A Comparison of Alternative Option Valuation Techniques." *Journal of Financial and Quantitative Analysis,* v. 20 (March 1985), pp. 45–71.

Gikhman, I., and A. V. Skorokhod. *Introduction to the Theory of Random Processes.* Saunders, 1969.

Harrison, J. M., and D. M. Kreps. "Martingales and Arbitrage in Multiperiod Securities Markets." *Journal of Economic Theory,* v. 20 (1979), pp. 381–408.

Harrison, J., and S. Pliska. "Martingales and Stochastic Integrals in the Theory of Continuous Trading." *Stochastic Processes and Their Application,* v. 2 (1981), pp. 261–71.

Ingersoll, J. E. "A Theoretical and Empirical Investigation of the Dual Purpose Funds: An Application of Contingent Claims and Analysis." *Journal of Financial Economics,* v. 3 (March 1976), pp. 83–123.

Itô, K., and H. McKean. *Diffusion Processes and Their Simple Paths.* Academic Press, 1964.

Jarrow, R., and A. Rudd. *Option Pricing,* R. D. Irwin, 1983.

————. "Approximate Option Valuation for Arbitrary Stochastic Processes." *Journal of Financial Economics,* v. 10, (November 1982), pp. 347–70.

Kreps, D. M. "Arbitrage and Equilibrium in Economics with Infinitely Many Commodities." *Journal of Mathematical Economics,* v. 8 (March 1981), pp. 15–35.

————. "Multiperiod Securities and the Efficient Allocation of Risk: A Comment on the Black–Scholes Option Pricing Model." In *The Economics of Information and Uncertainty,* ed. J. J. McCall. University of Chicago Press, 1982.

Latané, H. A., and R. J. Rendleman, Jr. "Standard Deviations of Stock Price Ratios Implied in Option Prices." *Journal of Finance,* v. 31 (May 1976), pp. 369–81.

MacBeth, J. D., and L. J. Merville, "An Empirical Examination of the Black–Scholes Call Option Pricing Model." *Journal of Finance,* v. 34 (December 1979), pp. 1173–86.

Malliaris, A. G. "Itô's Calculus in Financial Decision Making." *Society of Industrial and Applied Mathematics Review,* v. 25 (1983), pp. 482–96.

————, and W. A. Brock. *Stochastic Methods in Economics and Finance.* North-Holland, 1982.

Merton, R. C. "The Theory of Rational Option Pricing." *Bell Journal of Economics and Management Science,* v. 4 (Spring 1973), pp. 141–83.

————. "Theory of Finance from the Perspective of Continuous Time." *Journal of Financial and Quantitative Analysis,* v. 10 (December 1975), pp. 659–74.

————. "Option Pricing When Underlying Stock Returns are Discontinuous." *Journal of Financial Economics,* v. 3 (January–March 1976), pp. 125–44.

————. "On the Mathematics and Economics Assumption of Continuous-Time Models." In *Financial Economics: Essays in Honor of Paul Cootner,* ed. W. F. Sharpe and C. M. Cootner. Prentice-Hall, 1982. pp. 19–51.

Roll, R. "An Analytic Valuation Formula for Unprotected American Call Options on Stocks with Known Dividends." *Journal of Financial Economics,* v. 5 (March 1977), pp. 251–58.

Rubinstein, M. "The Valuation of Uncertain Income Streams and the Pricing of Options." *Bell Journal of Economics,* v. 7 (Fall 1976), pp. 407–25.

Scholes, M. "Taxes and the Pricing of Options." *Journal of Finance,* v. 31 (May 1976), pp. 319–32.

Smith, C. W., Jr. "Option Pricing: A Review." *Journal of Financial Economics,* v. 3 (January–March 1976), pp. 3–51.

——. "Applications of Option Pricing Analysis." In *Handbook of Financial Economics,* ed. J. L. Bicksler. North-Holland, 1979.

Appendix Tables

TABLE I Compound Sum of $1: $S_n = P(1 + r)^n$

Year	1%	2%	3%	4%	5%	6%	7%	8%	9%	10%	11%	12%	13%	14%	15%	16%
1	1.010	1.020	1.030	1.040	1.050	1.060	1.070	1.080	1.090	1.100	1.110	1.120	1.130	1.140	1.150	1.160
2	1.020	1.040	1.061	1.082	1.102	1.124	1.145	1.166	1.188	1.210	1.232	1.254	1.277	1.300	1.322	1.346
3	1.030	1.061	1.093	1.125	1.158	1.191	1.225	1.260	1.295	1.331	1.368	1.405	1.443	1.482	1.521	1.561
4	1.041	1.082	1.126	1.170	1.216	1.262	1.311	1.360	1.412	1.464	1.518	1.574	1.631	1.689	1.749	1.811
5	1.051	1.104	1.159	1.217	1.276	1.338	1.403	1.469	1.539	1.611	1.685	1.762	1.842	1.925	2.011	2.100
6	1.062	1.126	1.194	1.265	1.340	1.419	1.501	1.587	1.677	1.772	1.870	1.974	2.082	2.195	2.313	2.436
7	1.072	1.149	1.230	1.316	1.407	1.504	1.606	1.714	1.828	1.949	2.076	2.211	2.353	2.502	2.660	2.826
8	1.083	1.172	1.267	1.369	1.477	1.594	1.718	1.851	1.993	2.144	2.305	2.476	2.658	2.853	3.059	3.278
9	1.094	1.195	1.305	1.423	1.551	1.689	1.838	1.999	2.172	2.358	2.558	2.773	3.004	3.252	3.518	3.803
10	1.105	1.219	1.344	1.480	1.629	1.791	1.967	2.159	2.367	2.594	2.839	3.106	3.395	3.707	4.046	4.411
11	1.116	1.243	1.384	1.539	1.710	1.898	2.105	2.332	2.580	2.853	3.152	3.479	3.836	4.226	4.652	5.117
12	1.127	1.268	1.426	1.601	1.796	2.012	2.252	2.518	2.813	3.138	3.499	3.896	4.335	4.818	5.350	5.936
13	1.138	1.294	1.469	1.665	1.886	2.133	2.410	2.720	3.066	3.452	3.883	4.363	4.898	5.492	6.153	6.886
14	1.149	1.319	1.513	1.732	1.980	2.261	2.579	2.937	3.342	3.797	4.310	4.887	5.535	6.261	7.076	7.988
15	1.161	1.346	1.558	1.801	2.079	2.397	2.759	3.172	3.642	4.177	4.785	5.474	6.254	7.138	8.137	9.266
16	1.173	1.373	1.605	1.873	2.183	2.540	2.952	3.426	3.970	4.595	5.311	6.130	7.067	8.137	9.358	10.748
17	1.184	1.400	1.653	1.948	2.292	2.693	3.159	3.700	4.328	5.054	5.895	6.866	7.986	9.276	10.761	12.468
18	1.196	1.428	1.702	2.026	2.407	2.854	3.380	3.996	4.717	5.560	6.544	7.690	9.024	10.575	12.375	14.463
19	1.208	1.457	1.754	2.107	2.527	3.026	3.617	4.316	5.142	6.116	7.263	8.613	10.197	12.056	14.232	16.777
20	1.220	1.486	1.806	2.191	2.653	3.207	3.870	4.661	5.604	6.728	8.062	9.646	11.523	13.743	16.367	19.461

Source: Adapted from Jerome Bracken and Charles J. Christenson, *Tables for Use in Analyzing Business Decisions* (Homewood, Ill.: Richard D. Irwin, Inc., 1965).

TABLE II Present Value of $1: $P = S_n(1 + r)^{-n}$

Years Hence	1%	2%	4%	6%	8%	10%	12%	14%	15%	16%	18%	20%	22%	24%	25%	26%	28%	30%	35%	40%	45%	50%
1	0.990	0.980	0.962	0.943	0.926	0.909	0.893	0.877	0.870	0.862	0.847	0.833	0.820	0.806	0.800	0.794	0.781	0.769	0.741	0.714	0.690	0.667
2	0.980	0.961	0.925	0.890	0.857	0.826	0.797	0.769	0.756	0.743	0.718	0.694	0.672	0.650	0.640	0.630	0.610	0.592	0.549	0.510	0.476	0.444
3	0.971	0.942	0.889	0.840	0.794	0.751	0.712	0.675	0.658	0.641	0.609	0.579	0.551	0.524	0.512	0.500	0.477	0.455	0.406	0.364	0.328	0.296
4	0.961	0.924	0.855	0.792	0.735	0.683	0.636	0.592	0.572	0.552	0.516	0.482	0.451	0.423	0.410	0.397	0.373	0.350	0.301	0.260	0.226	0.198
5	0.951	0.906	0.822	0.747	0.681	0.621	0.567	0.519	0.497	0.476	0.437	0.402	0.370	0.341	0.328	0.315	0.291	0.269	0.223	0.186	0.156	0.132
6	0.942	0.888	0.790	0.705	0.630	0.564	0.507	0.456	0.432	0.410	0.370	0.335	0.303	0.275	0.262	0.250	0.227	0.207	0.165	0.133	0.108	0.088
7	0.933	0.871	0.760	0.665	0.583	0.513	0.452	0.400	0.376	0.354	0.314	0.279	0.249	0.222	0.210	0.198	0.178	0.159	0.122	0.095	0.074	0.059
8	0.923	0.853	0.731	0.627	0.540	0.467	0.404	0.351	0.327	0.305	0.266	0.233	0.204	0.179	0.168	0.157	0.139	0.123	0.091	0.068	0.051	0.039
9	0.914	0.837	0.703	0.592	0.500	0.424	0.361	0.308	0.284	0.263	0.225	0.194	0.167	0.144	0.134	0.125	0.108	0.094	0.067	0.048	0.035	0.026
10	0.905	0.820	0.676	0.558	0.463	0.386	0.322	0.270	0.247	0.227	0.191	0.162	0.137	0.116	0.107	0.099	0.085	0.073	0.050	0.035	0.024	0.017
11	0.896	0.804	0.650	0.527	0.429	0.350	0.287	0.237	0.215	0.195	0.162	0.135	0.112	0.094	0.086	0.079	0.066	0.056	0.037	0.025	0.017	0.012
12	0.887	0.788	0.625	0.497	0.397	0.319	0.257	0.208	0.187	0.168	0.137	0.112	0.092	0.076	0.069	0.062	0.052	0.043	0.027	0.018	0.012	0.008
13	0.879	0.773	0.601	0.469	0.368	0.290	0.229	0.182	0.163	0.145	0.116	0.093	0.075	0.061	0.055	0.050	0.040	0.033	0.020	0.013	0.008	0.005
14	0.870	0.758	0.577	0.442	0.340	0.263	0.205	0.160	0.141	0.125	0.099	0.078	0.062	0.049	0.044	0.039	0.032	0.025	0.015	0.009	0.006	0.003
15	0.861	0.743	0.555	0.417	0.315	0.239	0.183	0.140	0.123	0.108	0.084	0.065	0.051	0.040	0.035	0.031	0.025	0.020	0.011	0.006	0.004	0.002
16	0.853	0.728	0.534	0.394	0.292	0.218	0.163	0.123	0.107	0.093	0.071	0.054	0.042	0.032	0.028	0.025	0.019	0.015	0.008	0.005	0.003	0.002
17	0.844	0.714	0.513	0.371	0.270	0.198	0.146	0.108	0.093	0.080	0.060	0.045	0.034	0.026	0.023	0.020	0.015	0.012	0.006	0.003	0.002	0.001
18	0.836	0.700	0.494	0.350	0.250	0.180	0.130	0.095	0.081	0.069	0.051	0.038	0.028	0.021	0.018	0.016	0.012	0.009	0.005	0.002	0.001	0.001
19	0.828	0.686	0.475	0.331	0.232	0.164	0.116	0.083	0.070	0.060	0.043	0.031	0.023	0.017	0.014	0.012	0.009	0.007	0.003	0.002	0.001	
20	0.820	0.673	0.456	0.312	0.215	0.149	0.104	0.073	0.061	0.051	0.037	0.026	0.019	0.014	0.012	0.010	0.007	0.005	0.002	0.001	0.001	
21	0.811	0.660	0.439	0.294	0.199	0.135	0.093	0.064	0.053	0.044	0.031	0.022	0.015	0.011	0.009	0.008	0.006	0.004	0.002	0.001		
22	0.803	0.647	0.422	0.278	0.184	0.123	0.083	0.056	0.046	0.038	0.026	0.018	0.013	0.009	0.007	0.006	0.004	0.003	0.001	0.001		
23	0.795	0.634	0.406	0.262	0.170	0.112	0.074	0.049	0.040	0.033	0.022	0.015	0.010	0.007	0.006	0.005	0.003	0.002	0.001			
24	0.788	0.622	0.390	0.247	0.158	0.102	0.066	0.043	0.035	0.028	0.019	0.013	0.008	0.006	0.005	0.004	0.003	0.002	0.001			
25	0.780	0.610	0.375	0.233	0.146	0.092	0.059	0.038	0.030	0.024	0.016	0.010	0.007	0.005	0.004	0.003	0.002	0.001	0.001			
26	0.772	0.598	0.361	0.220	0.135	0.084	0.053	0.033	0.026	0.021	0.014	0.009	0.006	0.004	0.003	0.002	0.002	0.001				
27	0.764	0.586	0.347	0.207	0.125	0.076	0.047	0.029	0.023	0.018	0.011	0.007	0.005	0.003	0.002	0.002	0.001	0.001				
28	0.757	0.574	0.333	0.196	0.116	0.069	0.042	0.026	0.020	0.016	0.010	0.006	0.004	0.002	0.002	0.002	0.001	0.001				
29	0.749	0.563	0.321	0.185	0.107	0.063	0.037	0.022	0.017	0.014	0.008	0.005	0.003	0.002	0.002	0.001	0.001	0.001				
30	0.742	0.552	0.308	0.174	0.099	0.057	0.033	0.020	0.015	0.012	0.007	0.004	0.003	0.002	0.001	0.001	0.001					
40	0.672	0.453	0.208	0.097	0.046	0.022	0.011	0.005	0.004	0.003	0.001	0.001										
50	0.608	0.372	0.141	0.054	0.021	0.009	0.003	0.001	0.001	0.001												

Source: Adapted from Jerome Bracken and Charles J. Christenson, *Tables for Use in Analyzing Business Decisions* (Homewood, Ill.: Richard D. Irwin, Inc., 1965).

TABLE III Sum of an Annuity for $1 for n Years: $S_{n,r} = \$1 \left[\dfrac{(1+r)^n - 1}{r} \right] = \$1C_{n,r}$

Year	1%	2%	3%	4%	5%	6%	7%	8%	9%	10%	11%	12%	13%	14%	15%	16%
1	1.000	1.000	1.000	1.000	1.000	1.000	1.000	1.000	1.000	1.000	1.000	1.000	1.000	1.000	1.000	1.000
2	2.010	2.020	2.030	2.040	2.050	2.060	2.070	2.080	2.090	2.100	2.110	2.120	2.130	2.140	2.150	2.160
3	3.030	3.060	3.091	3.122	3.152	3.184	3.215	3.246	3.278	3.310	3.342	3.374	3.407	3.440	3.473	3.506
4	4.060	4.122	4.184	4.246	4.310	4.375	4.440	4.506	4.573	4.641	4.710	4.779	4.850	4.921	4.993	5.066
5	5.101	5.204	5.309	5.416	5.526	5.637	5.751	5.867	5.985	6.105	6.228	6.353	6.480	6.610	6.742	6.877
6	6.152	6.308	6.468	6.633	6.802	6.975	7.153	7.336	7.523	7.716	7.913	8.115	8.323	8.536	8.754	8.977
7	7.214	7.434	7.662	7.898	8.142	8.394	8.654	8.923	9.200	9.487	9.783	10.089	10.405	10.730	11.067	11.414
8	8.286	8.583	8.892	9.214	9.549	9.897	10.260	10.637	11.028	11.436	11.859	12.300	12.757	13.233	13.727	14.240
9	9.369	9.755	10.159	10.583	11.027	11.491	11.978	12.488	13.021	13.579	14.164	14.776	15.416	16.085	16.786	17.518
10	10.462	10.950	11.464	12.006	12.578	13.181	13.816	14.487	15.193	15.937	16.722	17.549	18.420	19.337	20.304	21.321
11	11.567	12.169	12.808	13.486	14.207	14.972	15.784	16.645	17.560	18.531	19.561	20.655	21.814	23.044	24.349	25.733
12	12.683	13.412	14.192	15.026	15.917	16.870	17.888	18.977	20.141	21.384	22.713	24.133	25.650	27.271	29.002	30.850
13	13.809	14.680	15.618	16.627	17.713	18.882	20.141	21.495	22.953	24.523	26.212	28.029	29.985	32.089	34.352	36.786
14	14.947	15.974	17.086	18.292	19.599	21.051	22.550	24.215	26.019	27.975	30.095	32.393	34.883	37.581	40.505	43.672
15	16.097	17.293	18.599	20.024	21.579	23.276	25.129	27.152	29.361	31.772	34.405	37.280	40.417	43.842	47.580	51.659

Source: Adapted from Jerome Bracken and Charles J. Christenson, *Tables for Use in Analyzing Business Decisions* (Homewood, Ill.: Richard D. Irwin, Inc., 1965).

TABLE IV Present Value of $1 Received Annually: $A_{n,r} = \$1\left[\dfrac{1 - (1 + r)^{-n}}{r}\right] = \$1P_{n,r}$

Year (n)	1%	2%	4%	6%	8%	10%	12%	14%	15%	16%	18%	20%	22%	24%	25%	26%	28%	30%	35%	40%	45%	50%
1	0.990	0.980	0.962	0.943	0.926	0.909	0.893	0.877	0.870	0.862	0.847	0.833	0.820	0.806	0.800	0.794	0.781	0.769	0.741	0.714	0.690	0.667
2	1.970	1.942	1.886	1.833	1.783	1.736	1.690	1.647	1.626	1.605	1.566	1.528	1.492	1.457	1.440	1.424	1.392	1.361	1.289	1.224	1.165	1.111
3	2.941	2.884	2.775	2.673	2.577	2.487	2.402	2.322	2.283	2.246	2.174	2.106	2.042	1.981	1.952	1.923	1.868	1.816	1.696	1.589	1.493	1.407
4	3.902	3.808	3.630	3.465	3.312	3.170	3.037	2.914	2.855	2.798	2.690	2.589	2.494	2.404	2.362	2.320	2.241	2.166	1.997	1.849	1.720	1.605
5	4.853	4.713	4.452	4.212	3.993	3.791	3.605	3.433	3.352	3.274	3.127	2.991	2.864	2.745	2.689	2.635	2.532	2.436	2.220	2.035	1.876	1.737
6	5.795	5.601	5.242	4.917	4.623	4.355	4.111	3.889	3.784	3.685	3.498	3.326	3.167	3.020	2.951	2.885	2.759	2.643	2.385	2.168	1.983	1.824
7	6.728	6.472	6.002	5.582	5.206	4.868	4.564	4.288	4.160	4.039	3.812	3.605	3.416	3.242	3.161	3.083	2.937	2.802	2.508	2.263	2.057	1.883
8	7.652	7.325	6.733	6.210	5.747	5.335	4.968	4.639	4.487	4.344	4.078	3.837	3.619	3.421	3.329	3.241	3.076	2.925	2.598	2.331	2.108	1.922
9	8.566	8.162	7.435	6.802	6.247	5.759	5.328	4.946	4.772	4.607	4.303	4.031	3.786	3.566	3.463	3.366	3.184	3.019	2.665	2.379	2.144	1.948
10	9.471	8.983	8.111	7.360	6.710	6.145	5.650	5.216	5.019	4.833	4.494	4.192	3.923	3.682	3.571	3.465	3.269	3.092	2.715	2.414	2.168	1.965
11	10.368	9.787	8.760	7.887	7.139	6.495	5.937	5.453	5.234	5.029	4.656	4.327	4.035	3.776	3.656	3.544	3.335	3.147	2.752	2.438	2.185	1.977
12	11.255	10.575	9.385	8.384	7.536	6.814	6.194	5.660	5.421	5.197	4.793	4.439	4.127	3.851	3.725	3.606	3.387	3.190	2.779	2.456	2.196	1.985
13	12.134	11.343	9.986	8.853	7.904	7.103	6.424	5.842	5.583	5.342	4.910	4.533	4.203	3.912	3.780	3.656	3.427	3.223	2.799	2.468	2.204	1.990
14	13.004	12.106	10.563	9.295	8.244	7.367	6.628	6.002	5.724	5.468	5.008	4.611	4.265	3.962	3.824	3.695	3.459	3.249	2.814	2.477	2.210	1.993
15	13.865	12.849	11.118	9.712	8.559	7.606	6.811	6.142	5.847	5.575	5.092	4.675	4.315	4.001	3.859	3.726	3.483	3.268	2.825	2.484	2.214	1.995
16	14.718	13.578	11.652	10.106	8.851	7.824	6.974	6.265	5.954	5.669	5.162	4.730	4.357	4.033	3.887	3.751	3.503	3.283	2.834	2.489	2.216	1.997
17	15.562	14.292	12.166	10.477	9.122	8.022	7.120	6.373	6.047	5.749	5.222	4.775	4.391	4.059	3.910	3.771	3.518	3.295	2.840	2.492	2.218	1.998
18	16.398	14.992	12.659	10.828	9.372	8.201	7.250	6.467	6.128	5.818	5.273	4.812	4.419	4.080	3.928	3.786	3.529	3.304	2.844	2.494	2.219	1.999
19	17.226	15.678	13.134	11.158	9.604	8.365	7.366	6.550	6.198	5.877	5.316	4.844	4.442	4.097	3.942	3.799	3.539	3.311	2.848	2.496	2.220	1.999
20	18.046	16.351	13.590	11.470	9.818	8.514	7.469	6.623	6.259	5.929	5.353	4.870	4.460	4.110	3.954	3.808	3.546	3.316	2.850	2.497	2.221	1.999
21	18.857	17.011	14.029	11.764	10.017	8.649	7.562	6.687	6.312	5.973	5.384	4.891	4.476	4.121	3.963	3.816	3.551	3.320	2.852	2.498	2.221	2.000
22	19.660	17.658	14.451	12.042	10.201	8.772	7.645	6.743	6.359	6.011	5.410	4.909	4.488	4.130	3.970	3.822	3.556	3.323	2.853	2.498	2.222	2.000
23	20.456	18.292	14.857	12.303	10.371	8.883	7.718	6.792	6.399	6.044	5.432	4.925	4.499	4.137	3.976	3.827	3.559	3.325	2.854	2.499	2.222	2.000
24	21.243	18.914	15.247	12.550	10.529	8.985	7.784	6.835	6.434	6.073	5.451	4.937	4.507	4.143	3.981	3.831	3.562	3.327	2.855	2.499	2.222	2.000
25	22.023	19.523	15.622	12.783	10.675	9.077	7.843	6.873	6.464	6.097	5.467	4.948	4.514	4.147	3.985	3.834	3.564	3.329	2.856	2.499	2.222	2.000
26	22.795	20.121	15.983	13.003	10.810	9.161	7.896	6.906	6.491	6.118	5.480	4.956	4.520	4.151	3.988	3.837	3.566	3.330	2.856	2.500	2.222	2.000
27	23.560	20.707	16.330	13.221	10.935	9.237	7.943	6.935	6.514	6.136	5.492	4.964	4.524	4.154	3.990	3.839	3.567	3.331	2.856	2.500	2.222	2.000
28	24.316	21.281	16.663	13.406	11.051	9.307	7.984	6.961	6.534	6.152	5.502	4.970	4.528	4.157	3.992	3.840	3.568	3.331	2.857	2.500	2.222	2.000
29	25.066	21.844	16.984	13.591	11.158	9.370	8.022	6.983	6.551	6.166	5.510	4.975	4.531	4.159	3.994	3.841	3.569	3.332	2.857	2.500	2.222	2.000
30	25.808	22.396	17.292	13.765	11.258	9.427	8.055	7.003	6.566	6.177	5.517	4.979	4.534	4.160	3.995	3.842	3.569	3.332	2.857	2.500	2.222	2.000
40	32.835	27.355	19.793	15.046	11.925	9.779	8.244	7.105	6.642	6.234	5.548	4.997	4.544	4.166	3.999	3.846	3.571	3.333	2.857	2.500	2.222	2.000
50	39.196	31.424	21.482	15.762	12.234	9.915	8.304	7.133	6.661	6.246	5.554	4.999	4.545	4.167	4.000	3.846	3.571	3.333	2.857	2.500	2.222	2.000

Source: Adapted from Jerome Bracken and Charles J. Christenson, *Tables for Use in Analyzing Business Decisions* (Homewood, Ill.: Richard D. Irwin, Inc., 1965).

TABLE V   Areas Under the Standard Normal Distribution

z	0.00	0.01	0.02	0.03	0.04	0.05	0.06	0.07	0.08	0.09
0.0	0.0000	0.0040	0.0080	0.0120	0.0160	0.0199	0.0239	0.0279	0.0319	0.0359
0.1	0.0398	0.0438	0.0478	0.0517	0.0557	0.0596	0.0636	0.0675	0.0714	0.0753
0.2	0.0793	0.0832	0.0871	0.0910	0.0948	0.0987	0.1026	0.1064	0.1103	0.1141
0.3	0.1179	0.1217	0.1255	0.1293	0.1331	0.1368	0.1406	0.1443	0.1480	0.1517
0.4	0.1554	0.1591	0.1628	0.1664	0.1700	0.1736	0.1772	0.1808	0.1844	0.1879
0.5	0.1915	0.1950	0.1985	0.2019	0.2054	0.2088	0.2123	0.2157	0.2190	0.2224
0.6	0.2257	0.2291	0.2324	0.2357	0.2389	0.2422	0.2454	0.2486	0.2517	0.2549
0.7	0.2580	0.2611	0.2642	0.2673	0.2704	0.2734	0.2764	0.2794	0.2823	0.2852
0.8	0.2881	0.2910	0.2939	0.2967	0.2995	0.3023	0.3051	0.3078	0.3106	0.3133
0.9	0.3159	0.3186	0.3212	0.3238	0.3264	0.3289	0.3315	0.3340	0.3365	0.3389
1.0	0.3413	0.3438	0.3461	0.3485	0.3508	0.3531	0.3554	0.3577	0.3599	0.3621
1.1	0.3643	0.3665	0.3686	0.3708	0.3729	0.3749	0.3770	0.3790	0.3810	0.3830
1.2	0.3849	0.3869	0.3888	0.3907	0.3925	0.3944	0.3962	0.3980	0.3997	0.4015
1.3	0.4032	0.4049	0.4066	0.4082	0.4099	0.4115	0.4131	0.4147	0.4162	0.4177
1.4	0.4192	0.4207	0.4222	0.4236	0.4251	0.4265	0.4279	0.4292	0.4306	0.4319
1.5	0.4332	0.4345	0.4357	0.4370	0.4382	0.4394	0.4406	0.4418	0.4429	0.4441
1.6	0.4452	0.4463	0.4474	0.4484	0.4495	0.4505	0.4515	0.4525	0.4535	0.4545
1.7	0.4554	0.4564	0.4573	0.4582	0.4591	0.4599	0.4608	0.4616	0.4625	0.4633
1.8	0.4641	0.4649	0.4656	0.4664	0.4671	0.4678	0.4686	0.4693	0.4699	0.4706
1.9	0.4713	0.4719	0.4726	0.4732	0.4738	0.4744	0.4750	0.4756	0.4761	0.4767
2.0	0.4772	0.4778	0.4783	0.4788	0.4793	0.4798	0.4803	0.4808	0.4812	0.4817
2.1	0.4821	0.4826	0.4830	0.4834	0.4838	0.4842	0.4846	0.4850	0.4854	0.4857
2.2	0.4861	0.4864	0.4868	0.4871	0.4875	0.4878	0.4881	0.4884	0.4887	0.4890
2.3	0.4893	0.4896	0.4898	0.4901	0.4904	0.4906	0.4909	0.4911	0.4913	0.4916
2.4	0.4918	0.4920	0.4922	0.4925	0.4927	0.4929	0.4931	0.4932	0.4934	0.4936
2.5	0.4938	0.4940	0.4941	0.4943	0.4945	0.4946	0.4948	0.4949	0.4951	0.4952
2.6	0.4953	0.4955	0.4956	0.4957	0.4959	0.4960	0.4961	0.4962	0.4963	0.4964
2.7	0.4965	0.4966	0.4967	0.4968	0.4969	0.4970	0.4971	0.4972	0.4973	0.4974
2.8	0.4974	0.4975	0.4976	0.4977	0.4977	0.4978	0.4979	0.4979	0.4980	0.4981
2.9	0.4981	0.4982	0.4982	0.4983	0.4984	0.4984	0.4985	0.4985	0.4986	0.4986
3.0	0.4987	0.4987	0.4987	0.4988	0.4988	0.4989	0.4989	0.4989	0.4990	0.4990

Acknowledgments

Page 4: Table 1–2 from D. Eiteman and A. Stonehill, *Multinational Business Finance,* copyright © 1989 by Addison-Wesley Publishing Co., Inc., Reading, Massachusetts. Reprinted with permission of the publisher. Pages 27–28: Excerpt from *Corporate Finance: Theory, Methods, and Applications* by Cheng F. Lee and Joseph E. Finnerty, copyright © 1990 by Harcourt Brace Jovanovich, Inc., reprinted by permission of the publisher. Excerpt from Baruch Lev, "Industry Averages as Targets for Financial Ratios," *Journal of Accounting Research* (Autumn 1969), pp. 290–299, adapted by permission.

Page 105: Figure 5–1 reprinted by permission of *The Wall Street Journal,* copyright © 1989 by Dow Jones & Company, Inc. All Rights Reserved Worldwide. Page 120 (Table 5–2): Moody's bond definitions adapted courtesy Moody's Investors Service. S&P definitions adapted from Standard & Poor's *Bond Guide,* October 1989 edition. Reprinted by permission. Page 152: Reprinted by permission of the author and publisher from Lawrence Fisher, "Some New Stock Market Indexes," *Journal of Business,* v. 39 (1966), pp. 191–225, copyright 1966 by the University of Chicago. Page 161: Reprinted by permission of *The Wall Street Journal,* copyright © 1989 by Dow Jones & Company, Inc. All Rights Reserved Worldwide.

Page 197: Reprinted by permission of the author and publisher from William F. Sharpe, "Mutual-Fund Performance," *Journal of Business,* v. 39 (1966), pp. 119–138, copyright 1966 by the University of Chicago. Page 199: Reprinted by permission of the author and publisher from Michael C. Jensen, "Risk, The Pricing of Assets, and the Evaluation of Investment Portfolios," *Journal of Business,* v. 42 (1969), pp. 167–185, copyright 1969 by the University of Chicago. Page 215: Excerpt from J. C. F. Mao, *Quantitative Analysis of Financial Decisions,* copyright © 1968 by J. C. F. Mao, reprinted by permission of Macmillan Publishing Company.

Pages 273–274: Reprinted by permission from J. Mincer and V. Zarnowitz, "The Evaluation of Economic Forecasts," in J. Mincer, ed., *Economic Forecasts and Expectations,* copyright © 1969 by National Bureau of

Economic Research, Inc., Cambridge, Massachusetts. Page 282: Reprinted by permission of Harcourt Brace Jovanovich from Fischer Black, Michael C. Jensen, and Myron Scholes, "The Capital Asset Pricing Model: Some Empirical Tests," in Michael C. Jensen, ed., *Studies in the Theory of Capital Markets,* Praeger Publishers Inc., 1972, copyright © 1972 by Harcourt Brace Jovanovich, Inc. Page 282: Reprinted by permission of the authors and publisher from Eugene F. Fama and J. MacBeth, "Risk, Return and Equilibrium Empirical Tests," *Journal of Political Economy,* v. 31 (1973), pp. 607–636, copyright © 1973 by the University of Chicago. Page 283: Reprinted by permission of the author and Elsevier Science Publishers B.V. from Robert C. Merton, "On Estimating the Expected Return on the Market, An Exploratory Investigation," *Journal of Financial Economics,* v. 8 (1980), pp. 323–361. Pages 283–284: Reprinted by permission of the author and Elsevier Science Publishers B.V. from Richard Roll, "A Critique of the Asset Pricing Theory's Tests—Part I: On Past and Potential Testability of the Theory," *Journal of Financial Economics,* v. 4 (1977), pp. 13–37.

Pages 323–326: Adapted by permission of Academic Press from S. Ross, "The Arbitrage Theory of Capital Asset Pricing," *Journal of Economic Theory,* v. 13 (1976), pp. 341–360. Page 335: Reprinted by permission of the authors and publisher from N. Chen, R. Roll, and S. Ross, "Economic Forces and the Stock Market," *Journal of Business,* v. 59 (1986), pp. 383–403, copyright © 1986 by The University of Chicago. Pages 348–350: Reprinted by permission from C. F. Lee and John K. C. Wei, "Multifactor Multi-Indicator Approach to Asset Pricing Model: Theory and Empirical Evidence," BEBR, The University of Illinois at Urbana-Champaign; Working Paper #1062, 1984. Pages 379–380: Reprinted by permission of the publisher from L. L. Johnson, "The Theory of Hedging and Speculation in Commodity Futures," *Review of Economic Studies,* v. 27 (1960), pp. 139–151.

Pages 395, 399, 405, 421, 447, and 455: Figures reprinted by permission of *The Wall Street Journal,* copyright © 1989 by Dow Jones & Company, Inc. All Rights Reserved Worldwide.

Pages 493–498: Adapted by permission of the authors and publisher from F. Black and M. Scholes, "The Pricing of Options and Corporate Liabilities," *Journal of Political Economy,* v. 31 (1973), pp. 637–659, copyright © 1973 by the University of Chicago. Page 499: From John C. Cox and Mark Rubinstein, *Options Markets,* page 221, copyright © 1985 by Prentice-Hall, Inc. Adapted by permission of Prentice-Hall, Inc., Englewood Cliffs, New Jersey. Pages 507–508 and 536: From Bookstaber and Clark, *Option Pricing and Strategies in Investing,* copyright © 1981 by Addison-Wesley Publishing Co., Inc., Reading, Massachusetts. Reprinted by permission of the publisher. Pages 513–514: Reprinted by permission of the author and Elsevier Science Publishers B.V. from F. Black, "The Pricing of Commodity Conracts," *Journal of Financial Economics,* v. 3 (1976), pp. 167–179. Pages 532–534: Reprinted by permission of the authors and Elsevier Science Publishers B.V. from J. Cox, S. A. Ross, and M. Rubinstein, "Option Pricing: A

Simplified Approach," *Journal of Financial Economics,* v. 7 (1979), pp. 229–263. Pages 536–537: Reprinted by permission of the author and Elsevier Science Publishers B.V. from R. Whaley, "Valuation of American Call Options on Dividend Paying Stocks: Empirical Test," *Journal of Financial Economics,* v. 10 (1982), pp. 29–58.

Page 546: Reprinted by permission of Ohio State University Press from J. Tobin, "A General Equilibrium Approach to Monetary Theory," *Journal of Money, Credit, and Banking,* v. 1 (1969), pp. 15–29. Page 548: Adapted by permission from E. F. Fama, *Foundations of Finance,* Basic Books, 1976, pp. 134–137. Pages 556–557: Adapted from Paul Cootner, "Stock Prices: Random vs. Systematic Changes," *Industrial Management Review,* v. 3. (1962), pp. 24–25. Copyright © 1962 by the Sloan Management Review Association. All rights reserved.

Pages 584–585: Reprinted by permission of the author and Elsevier Science Publishers B.V. from M. Reinganum, "Misspecification of Capital Asset Pricing: Empirical Anomalies Based on Earnings Yields and Market Values," *Journal of Financial Economics,* v. 8 (1981), pp. 19–46. Page 585: Reprinted by permission of the author and Elsevier Science Publishers B.V. from R. W. Banz, "The Relationship Between Return and Market Value of Common Stocks," *Journal of Financial Economics,* v. 9 (1981), pp. 3–18. Pages 593–595: Adapted by permission of the School of Agriculture, Purdue University, from David A. Bessler and Jon A. Brandt, *Composite Forecasting of Livestock Prices: An Analysis of Combining Alternative Forecasting Methods,* Station Bulletin No. 265, Department of Agricultural Economics, Agricultural Experiment Station, Purdue University. Pages 607–608: Reprinted by permission of the authors and publisher from Roy D. Henriksson and Robert C. Merton, "On Marketing Timing and Investment Performance II, Statistical Procedures for Evaluating Forecasting Skills," *Journal of Business,* v. 54 (1981), pp. 513–533, copyright © 1981 by The University of Chicago. Pages 609–610: Reprinted by permission of the authors and publisher from Stanley J. Kon and Frank C. Jen, "The Investment Performance of Mutual Funds: An Empirical Investigation of Timing, Selectivity, and Market Efficiency," *Journal of Business,* v. 52 (1979), pp. 363–389, copyright © 1979 by The University of Chicago.

Pages 621–629: Adapted by permission of Elsevier Science Publishers B.V. from J. Lintner, "The Valuation of Risk Assets on the Selection of Risky Investments in Stock Portfolio and Capital Budgets," *Review of Economics and Statistics,* v. 57 (1965), pp. 13–37. Pages 674–682: Reprinted from Sidney Homer and Martin L. Leibowitz, *Inside the Yield Book,* copyright © 1972 by Prentice-Hall, Inc. Used by permission of the publisher, Prentice-Hall, Inc., Englewood Cliffs, New Jersey. Page 683: Reprinted by permission from F. Macaulay, *Some Theoretical Problems Suggested by the Movements of Interest Rates, Bond Yields, and Stock Prices in the United States Since 1865,* copyright © 1938 by National Bureau of Economic Research, Inc., and Cambridge, Massachusetts.

Pages 737–745: Adapted by permission from K. Itô and H. P. McKean,

Author Index

Subject Index

A

accelerated cost recovery system (ACRS), 90
accounting beta, 269
accounting-based beta forecasting, 272–273
activity ratios, 22–24
ADRs, 659–660
agency bond, 107
agency theory, 184, 520
Alexander's filter rule, 581
allocational efficiency, 547
American depository receipts, 659–660
American option, 459–460
American Stock Exchange (AMEX)
   trading volume of, 3
   Major Market Index. *See* MMI
analysis, fundamental vs. technical, 570–583
announcement effect, 554
anomalies, implications of, 583–587
arbitrage, 387
   and futures contracts, 366–367
   index, 727
arbitrage condition, 321
arbitrage portfolio, 324–325, 491
arbitrage pricing theory (APT), 316–317
   advantages over CAPM, 316, 317, 323, 336–338
   alternative specifications of, 345–347
   applications of, 338–342
   empirical tests of, 331–334
   international, 652–653
   model specification of, 321–333
   MPT vs., 336–337
   structure of, 333–336
arbitrage profit, 410–411, 491

arbitrageurs, 724–725
ARIMA, 507–508
   forecasting models based on, 590–593
arithmetic mean, 42–43
ARMA, 592
ask price, 106, 185
Association of International Bond Dealers (AIBD), 660
at-the-money option, 446
Australia, stock market in, 659
autoregressive integrated moving-average process (ARIMA), 507–508, 590–593
autoregressive moving-average process, (ARMA), 592
autoregressive process of infinite order, 592
average collection period, 22

B

backwardation, normal, 370
balanced funds, 598
basis, 387
   in dynamic hedging, 720
   of futures contract, 370
basis risk, 372
Bayesian adjustment, 274–276
bear spread, 475–476
beta, 10, 93, 255
   accounting, 269
   Bayesian adjusted, 274–276
   bond, 116–119
   estimation of, 64, 300
   importance of, 264–265
   market model and, 299–301
   option, 503–504

J

January effect, 561–562, 585–586
Japan, stock market in, 658
Jensen's measure, 199, 201
Johnson hedge model, 379–381, 406

K

Kansas City Board of Trade (KCBT), 420, 440
Korea, South, stock market in, 658–659
kurtosis, 557

L

Lagrangian multiplier, 230–231, 622
large negotiable CDs, 413
Laspeyres price index, 151, 154
least-squares method, 10, 273
Lehman Brothers–Kuhn, Loeb, bond trading and, 115, 116
leverage
    homemade vs. corporate, 84
    operating, 270
leverage ratios, 21–22
Levine and Boesky scandal, 555
liability management, 413
lifetime high and low, 396
LIFFE, 418
linear-optimization model, 11–12
linear programming, 310–312
Lintner's method of short sales, 629–631
liquidation, 388
liquidity, 185
liquidity ratios, 20
liquidity risk, 184–185
listed put option, 721–723
location risk, 373
log normal distribution, 232–234
logarithms, 68–70
London International Financial Exchange (LIFFE), 418
London Stock Exchange, 659
long call, 463
long position, 389
long put, 466–467
long straddle, 469–470
long vertical spread, 473–474
long-term bond, 109

low, 396
lower-of-cost-or-market-value method, 542

M

M and M Proposition I, 84–85
M and M valuation theory, 80–88. *See also* Modigliani, F.; Miller, M.
Macaulay model, 689–693
macroforecasting, 605, 606
maintenance margin, 363
Major Market Index, 159, 420, 428–430
Malaysia, stock market in, 659
management risk, 182, 184
MAPB system, 581, 582
margin, 354, 356, 389
    maintenance, 363
    requirement in futures market, 362–364
margin calls, 363, 389
market
    efficiency of, 656–657
    portfolio insurance and, 723–728
    regulation of, 727
    world, 648–652, 656–657
market anomalies, 560–562
market-based beta forecasts, 272
market efficiency, 547
market index. *See* indexes
market maker, 453
market model, 262–267, 299–301, 549–550
    of risk, 63–65
    risk-premium version of, 263
market portfolio, 255
market price of risk, 550
market proxy, 611–612
market rate of return, 204–206
market risk, 60–61, 255, 265
market risk premium, 257
market-to-book ratio, 544–545
market value, 542
    of firm, 543
marketability, 184–185
marketability risk, 182, 184–185
marking to market, 363, 389
Markowitz model, 210, 211–249 passim
maturity, bond, 109
maturity date, 745
maximization, 11–12
maximum-return portfolio, 229
MDA model, 119–121